Frommer's®
Italy 2012

by Darwin Porter & Danforth Prince

WILEY

John Wiley & Sons, Inc.

Published by:
John Wiley & Sons, Inc.
111 River St.
Hoboken, NJ 07030-5774

ISBN 978-1-118-01728-9 (paper); ISBN 978-1-118-07689-7 (paper); ISBN 978-1-118-09431-0 (ebk); ISBN 978-1-118-09432-7 (ebk); ISBN 978-1-118-09433-4 (ebk)

Editor: Ian Skinnari
Production Editor: Jana M. Stefanciosa
Cartographer: Guy Ruggiero
Photo Editor: Richard Fox, Alden Gewirtz
Design and Layout by Vertigo Design
Graphics and Prepress by Wiley Indianapolis Composition Services

Front cover photo: ©Douglas Pearson / Getty Images; Sunrise over iconic Tuscan farmhouse, Val D'Orcia
Back cover photos: *Left:* ©Martin Strmiska / Alamy Images; sunset in Riomaggiore, Cinque Terre, Italy.
Middle: ©Nagelestock.com / Alamy Images; view of San Gimignano, grapes hanging off vine in foreground. *Right:* ©Riccardo De Luca; Pompeii: Villa of the Mysteries fresco

For information on our other products and services or to obtain technical support, please contact our Customer Care Department within the U.S. at 877/762-2974, outside the U.S. at 317/572-3993 or fax 317/572-4002.

Wiley also publishes its books in a variety of electronic formats. Some content that appears in print may not be available in electronic formats.

Manufactured in China

5 4 3 2 1

CONTENTS

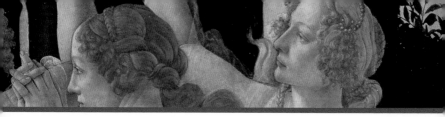

13 GENOA & THE ITALIAN RIVIERA 654

14 CAMPANIA: NAPLES, POMPEII & THE AMALFI COAST 693

15 APULIA 783

16 SICILY 807

LIST OF MAPS

ABOUT THE AUTHORS

As a team of veteran travel writers, **Darwin Porter** and **Danforth Prince** have produced numerous titles for Frommer's which have included France, Italy, the Caribbean, Spain, and Germany.

Porter wrote the first ever Frommer's guide to Paris and the first ever Frommer's guide to a single European country—back then it was called *England on $5 a Day*. He has lived, on occasion, in London and has traveled England extensively since he left college.

In 1982, he was joined by Danforth Prince, who was previously employed by the Paris bureau of the *New York Times*. Today he is the president of Blood Moon Productions and other media-related firms. Porter is also a film critic, columnist, broadcaster, and Hollywood biographer.

HOW TO CONTACT US

In researching this book, we discovered many wonderful places—hotels, restaurants, shops, and more. We're sure you'll find others. Please tell us about them, so we can share the information with your fellow travelers in upcoming editions. If you were disappointed with a recommendation, we'd love to know that, too. Please write to:

Frommer's Italy 2012
John Wiley & Sons, Inc. • 111 River St. • Hoboken, NJ 07030-5774
frommersfeedback@wiley.com

FROMMER'S STAR RATINGS, ICONS & ABBREVIATIONS

Every hotel, restaurant, and attraction listing in this guide has been ranked for quality, value, service, amenities, and special features using a **star-rating system.** In country, state, and regional guides, we also rate towns and regions to help you narrow down your choices and budget your time accordingly. Hotels and restaurants are rated on a scale of zero (recommended) to three stars (exceptional). Attractions, shopping, nightlife, towns, and regions are rated according to the following scale: zero stars (recommended), one star (highly recommended), two stars (very highly recommended), and three stars (must-see).

In addition to the star-rating system, we also use **seven feature icons** that point you to the great deals, in-the-know advice, and unique experiences that separate travelers from tourists. Throughout the book, look for:

special finds—those places only insiders know about

fun facts—details that make travelers more informed and their trips more fun

kids—best bets for kids and advice for the whole family

special moments—those experiences that memories are made of

overrated—places or experiences not worth your time or money

insider tips—great ways to save time and money

great values—where to get the best deals

The following abbreviations are used for credit cards:

AE	American Express	**DISC**	Discover	**V**	Visa
DC	Diners Club	**MC**	MasterCard		

TRAVEL RESOURCES AT FROMMERS.COM

Frommer's travel resources don't end with this guide. Frommer's website, **www.frommers. com**, has travel information on more than 4,000 destinations. We update features regularly, giving you access to the most current trip-planning information and the best airfare, lodging, and car-rental bargains. You can also listen to podcasts, connect with other Frommers.com members through our active-reader forums, share your travel photos, read blogs from guidebook editors and fellow travelers, and much more.

THE BEST OF ITALY

1

taly is so packed with attractions that it's hard to know where to start. But that's where we can help. In this chapter is our personal, opinionated list of what we consider to be Italy's top highlights. It will get you started and point you toward some of the possibilities for designing your own vacation. Whether this is your 1st trip or your 10th, you're bound to come away with your own favorites to add to the list.

THE best TRAVEL EXPERIENCES

o **Visiting the Art Cities:** When Italy consisted of dozens of principalities, art treasures were concentrated in many small capitals, each one blessed with the patronage of a papal representative or ducal family. Consequently, these cities became treasure-troves of exquisite paintings, statues, and frescoes displayed in churches, monasteries, and palaces, whose architects are now world acclaimed. Although Rome, Florence, and Venice are the best known, you'll find stunning collections in Assisi, Cremona, Genoa, Mantua, Padua, Palermo, Parma, Pisa, Siena, Taormina, Tivoli, Turin, Verona, and Vicenza.

o **Dining Italian Style:** One of the most cherished pastimes of the Italians is eating out. Regardless of how much pizza and lasagna you've had in your life,

One of Rome's many markets. PREVIOUS PAGE: Venice's Rialto Bridge.

Shopping in Milan.   Frescoes of St. Francis in Assisi.

you'll never taste any better than the real thing in Italy. Each region has its own specialties, some handed down for centuries. If the weather is fine and you're dining outdoors, perhaps with a view of a medieval church or piazza, you'll find your experience the closest thing to heaven in Italy. *Buon appetito!*

o **Attending Mass in St. Peter's Basilica:** With the exception of some sites in Jerusalem, St. Peter's in the Vatican is Christendom's most visible and important building. The huge size of the church is daunting. For many, attending Mass here is a spiritual highlight of their lives. In addition, many Catholic visitors to Rome await papal audiences every Wednesday morning, when the pope addresses the general public. (Confirm that the Wed audience will take place as scheduled by calling ahead or visiting the Vatican website prior to your visit.) There is a regularly updated list of ceremonies the pope will preside over, including celebrations of Mass, on the Vatican website. If the day is fair, these audiences are sometimes held in St. Peter's Square. Your fellow faithful are likely to come from every corner of the world. See "St. Peter's & the Vatican," in chapter 5.

o **Riding Venice's Grand Canal:** The S-shaped Canal Grande, curving for 3.3km (2 miles) along historic buildings and under ornate bridges, is the most romantic waterway in the world. Most first-timers are stunned by the variety of Gothic and Renaissance buildings, the elaborate styles of which could fill a book on architecture. A ride on the canal will give you ever-changing glimpses of the city's poignant beauty. Your ride doesn't have to be on a gondola; any public *vaporetto* (motorboat) sailing between Venice's rail station and Piazza San Marco will provide a heart-stopping view. See chapter 9.

St. Peter's Basilica in Rome.

o **Getting Lost in Venice:** The most obvious means of transport in Venice is by boat; but an even more appealing method is on foot, traversing hundreds of canals, large and small, and crossing over the arches of medieval bridges. Getting from one point to another can be like walking through a maze—but you won't be hassled by traffic, and the sense of the city's beauty, timelessness, and slow decay is almost mystical. See chapter 9.

o **Spending a Night at the Opera:** More than 2,000 new operas were staged in Italy during the 18th century, and since then, Italian opera fans have earned a reputation as the most demanding in the world. Venice was the site of Italy's first opera house, the Teatro di San Cassiano (1637), but it eventually gave way to the fabled La Fenice, which burned down in 1996 and was later rebuilt. Milan's **La Scala** is historically the world's most prestigious opera house, especially for *bel canto,* and has been restored to its former glory. There's also a wide assortment of outdoor settings, such as Verona's Arena, one of the largest surviving amphitheaters. Suitable for up to 20,000 spectators and known for its fine acoustics, the Arena presents operas in July and August, when moonlight and the perfumed air of the Veneto add to the charm.

o **Shopping Milan:** Milan is one of the world's hottest fashion capitals. You'll find a range of shoes, clothing, and accessories unequaled almost anywhere else. Even if you weren't born to shop, stroll along the streets bordering Via Montenapoleone and check out the elegant offerings from Europe's most famous designers. See "Milan" in chapter 11.

○ **Experiencing the Glories of the Empire:** Even after centuries of looting, much remains of the legendary Roman Empire. Of course, Rome boasts the greatest share (the popes didn't tear down everything to recycle into churches)—you'll find everything from the Roman Forum and the Pantheon to the Colosseum and the Baths of Caracalla. And on the outskirts, the long-buried city of Ostia Antica, the port of ancient Rome, has been unearthed and is remarkable. Other treasures are scattered throughout Italy, especially in Sicily. Hordes of sightseers also descend on Pompeii, the city buried by volcanic ash from Mount Vesuvius in A.D. 79, and Herculaneum, buried by lava on that same day. Our favorite spot is Paestum, along Campania's coast; its ruins, especially the Temple of Neptune, are alone worth the trip to Italy. See chapters 5, 14, and 16.

THE most romantic GETAWAYS

○ **Todi:** For the ultimate escape, the hilltop of Todi, 203km (126 miles) south of Florence, will transport you back to the Middle Ages. You can lose yourself in its tangle of ancient streets and wine-dark alleys. Let the sun shine on you at its central square, where you might seriously contemplate moving and living in a gentler time. See "A Side Trip to Todi" in chapter 7.

Bellagio, on Lake Como.

- **Spoleto:** Spoleto is as ancient as the Roman Empire and as timeless as the music presented there every summer during its world-renowned arts festival. The architecture of this quintessential Umbrian hill town is centered on a core of religious buildings from the 13th century. It's even more romantic during the off season, when the crowds are less dense. See "Spoleto" in chapter 7.

- **Bellagio:** Often called "the prettiest town in Europe," Bellagio is perhaps the loveliest town in Italy's beautiful Lake District. Its lakeside promenade, which follows the shores of Lake Como, is fragrant with flowers in bloom. Couples can spend their days exploring the arcaded streets and little shops, visiting lush gardens, and relaxing in the sun. See "Lake Como" in chapter 11.

- **Capri:** Floating amid azure seas south of Naples, Capri is called the "Island of Dreams." Everywhere, you'll find the aroma of lemon trees in bloom. Roman emperors Augustus and Tiberius both went there for R & R, and since the late 1800s celebrities have flocked to Capri for an escape. A boat ride around the island's rugged coastline is one of our favorite things to do. See "Capri" in chapter 14.

- **Ravello:** It's small, sunny, and loaded with notable buildings (such as its 1086 cathedral). Despite its choice position on the Amalfi coast, Ravello manages to retain the aura of an old-fashioned village. Famous residents have included writers Gore Vidal and John Ruskin and artist Joan Miró. See "Ravello" in chapter 14.

- **Taormina:** This resort, the loveliest place in Sicily, is brimming with regional charm, chiseled stonework, and a sense of the ages. Favored by wealthy Europeans and dedicated artists, especially in midwinter, when the climate is delightful, Taormina is a fertile oasis of olive groves, grapevines, and orchards. Visitors will relish the delights of the sun, the sea, and the medieval setting. See "Taormina" in chapter 16.

Spoleto.

Taormina.

THE best MUSEUMS

○ **The Vatican Museums** (Rome): Rambling, disorganized, and poorly labeled they might be, but these buildings are packed with treasures accumulated over the centuries by the popes. There's the incomparable Sistine Chapel, such priceless ancient Greek and Roman sculptures as *Laocoön* and the *Belvedere Apollo,* buildings whose walls were almost completely executed by Raphael (including his majestic *School of Athens*), and endless collections of art ranging from (very pagan) Greco-Roman antiquities to Christian art by famous European masters. See p. 141.

○ **Galleria Borghese** (Rome): One of the world's great small museums is set against the frescoes and decor of a 1613 palace. That's merely the backdrop for the collections, which include masterpieces of baroque sculpture by a young Bernini and paintings by Caravaggio and Raphael. See p. 167.

○ **National Etruscan Museum** (Rome): The mysterious Etruscans were the ancestors of the Romans. They left a legacy of bronze and marble sculpture, sarcophagi, jewelry, and representations of mythical heroes, some of which were excavated at Cerveteri, a stronghold north of Rome. Most startling about the artifacts is their sophisticated, almost mystical sense of design. The Etruscan collection is housed in a papal villa dating from the 1500s. See p. 168.

○ **Uffizi Gallery** (Florence): This 16th-century Renaissance palace was the administrative headquarters, or *uffizi* (offices), for the Duchy of Tuscany when the Medicis controlled Florence. It's estimated that up to 90% of Italy's artistic patrimony is stored in this building, the crown jewel of Italy's museums. This is the world's greatest collection of Renaissance paintings. See p. 246.

o **Bargello Museum** (Florence): Originally built as a fortress palace in 1255, this imposing structure is now a vast repository of some of Italy's most important Renaissance sculpture. Donatello's bronze *David* is a remarkable contrast to the world-famous Michelangelo icon. See p. 239.

o **National Gallery of Umbria** (Perugia): Italian Renaissance art has its roots in Tuscan and Umbrian painting from the 1200s. This collection, on the top floor of the Palazzo dei Priori (parts of which date from the 1400s), contains a world-class collection of paintings, most executed in Tuscany or Umbria between the 13th and 18th centuries. Included are works by Fra Angelico, Piero della Francesca, Perugino, Duccio, and Gozzoli, among others. See p. 346.

o **Accademia** (Venice): One of Europe's great museums, this is an incomparable collection of Venetian painting, exhibited chronologically from the 13th to the 18th century. It's one of the most richly stocked art museums in Italy, boasting hundreds of works by Bellini, Carpaccio, Giorgione, Titian, and Tintoretto. See p. 480.

o **Peggy Guggenheim Collection** (Venice): A comprehensive, brilliant modern art collection assembled by legendary arts patron Peggy Guggenheim is housed in an unfinished *palazzo* along the Grand Canal. The collection is a cavalcade of 20th-century art, including works by Max Ernst (one of Ms.

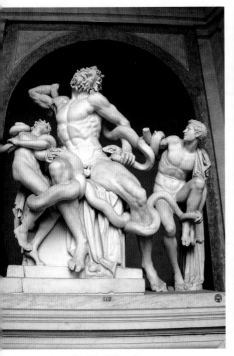

Laocoön at the Vatican Museum.

Detail from Carpaccio's St. Ursula cycle at the Accademia in Venice.

Guggenheim's former husbands), Picasso, Braque, Magritte, Giacometti, and Moore. See p. 485.

o **Brera Picture Gallery** (Milan): Milan is usually associated with wealth and corporate power, and those two things can buy a city its fair share of art and culture. The foremost place to see Milan's artistic treasures is the Brera Picture Gallery, whose collection—shown in a 17th-century palace—is especially rich in paintings from the schools of Lombardy and Venice. Three of the most important prizes are Mantegna's *Dead Christ,* Giovanni Bellini's *La Pietà,* and Carpaccio's *St. Stephen Debating.* See p. 583.

o **National Archaeological Museum** (Naples): Naples and the region around it have yielded a wealth of sculptural treasures from the Roman Empire. Many of these riches have been accumulated in a rambling building designed as a barracks for the Neapolitan cavalry in the 1500s. Much of the loot excavated from Pompeii and Herculaneum, as well as the Renaissance collections of the Farnese family, is in this museum, which boasts a trove of Greco-Roman antiquities. See p. 702.

THE best CATHEDRALS

o **St. Peter's Basilica** (Rome): Its roots began with the first Christian emperor, Constantine, in A.D. 324. By 1400, the Roman basilica was in danger of collapsing, prompting the Renaissance popes to commission plans for the largest, most impressive, most jaw-dropping cathedral the world had ever seen. Amid the rich decor of gilt, marble, and mosaics are countless artworks, including Michelangelo's *Pietà.* Other sights here are a small museum of Vatican treasures and the underground grottoes containing the tombs of former popes, including the most recently interred, John Paul II. An elevator ride (or a rigorous climb) up the tower to Michelangelo's glorious dome provides panoramic views of Rome. See p. 137.

o **The Duomo of Florence:** Begun in the late 1200s and consecrated 140 years later, the pink, green, and white marble Duomo was a symbol of Florence's prestige and wealth. It's loaded with world-class art and is one of Italy's largest and most distinctive religious buildings. A view of its red-tiled dome, erected over a 14-year period in what was at the time a radical new design by Brunelleschi, is worth the trip to Florence. Other elements of the Duomo are Giotto's campanile

Michelangelo's *Pietà,* St. Peter's Basilica.

(bell tower) and the octagonal Baptistery (a Romanesque building with bronze doors). See p. 249.

o **The Duomo of Siena:** Begun in 1196, this cathedral is one of the most beautiful and ambitious Gothic churches in Italy, with extravagant zebra-striped bands of marble. Masterpieces here include a priceless pavement of masterful mosaics, an octagonal pulpit carved by master sculptor Nicola Pisano, and the lavishly frescoed Piccolomini Library. See p. 315.

o **Basilica of St. Francis** (Assisi): St. Francis, protector of small animals and birds, was long dead when construction began on this double-tiered showcase of the Franciscan brotherhood. Giotto's celebrated frescoes reached a new kind of figurative realism in Italian art around 1300, long before the masters of the Renaissance carried the technique even further. Consecrated in 1253, the cathedral is one of the highlights of Umbria and the site of many pilgrimages. It took a direct hit from the 1997 earthquakes but has miraculously made a recovery. See p. 354.

o **The Duomo of Modena:** Begun in 1099, this cathedral in Emilia-Romagna is one of the crowning glories of Romanesque architecture in Italy. Divided into three parts, the facade is crowned by the Angel of Death carrying a fleur-de-lis, and the inside is filled with masterpieces of sculpture, including a rood screen that is supported by Lombard lions. See p. 416.

o **The Duomo of Orvieto:** A well-designed transition between the Romanesque and Gothic styles, this cathedral was begun in 1290 and completed in 1600. It sheltered an Italian pope (Clement VII) when French soldiers sacked

The Duomo of Florence.

The Duomo of Modena.   The Duomo of Siena.

Rome in 1527. Part of the building's mystery derives from Orvieto's role as an Etruscan stronghold long before Italy's recorded history. The cathedral is known for its great fresco cycles by Fra Angelico and Luca Signorelli. See p. 366.

- **St. Mark's Basilica** (Venice): Surely the most exotic and Eastern of the Western world's churches, the onion-domed and mosaic-covered San Marco took much of its inspiration from Constantinople. Somewhere inside the mysterious candlelit cavern of the 1,000-year-old church, which began as the private chapel of the doges, are the remains of St. Mark, patron saint of Venice's ancient maritime republic. See p. 475.

- **The Duomo of Milan:** It took 5 centuries to build this magnificent and ornate Gothic cathedral, the third-largest church in the world. It's marked by 135 marble spires, a stunning triangular facade, and thousands of statues flanking the massive but airy, almost fanciful exterior. See p. 584.

THE best RUINS

- **The Roman Forum** (Rome): Two thousand years ago, most of the known world was directly affected by decisions made in the Roman Forum. Today, classicists and archaeologists wander among its ruins, conjuring up the glory that was Rome. What you'll see today is a pale, rubble-strewn version of the site's original majesty—it's now surrounded by modern boulevards packed with whizzing cars. See p. 153.

- **Palatine Hill** (Il Palatino; Rome): According to legend, the Palatine Hill was the site where Romulus and Remus (the orphaned infant twins who survived by being suckled by a she-wolf) eventually founded the city. Although Il Palatino is one of the seven hills of ancient Rome, you'll find it hard to distinguish it as such because of the urban congestion rising all around. The site is enhanced by the Farnese Gardens (Orti Farnesiani), laid out in the 1500s on the site of Tiberius's palace. See p. 153.

- **The Colosseum** (Rome): Rome boasts only a handful of other ancient monuments that survive in such well-preserved condition. A massive amphitheater set incongruously amid a maze of modern traffic, the Colosseum was once the setting for gladiator combat, lion-feeding frenzies, and public entertainment whose cruelty was a noted characteristic of the Empire. All three of the ancient world's classical styles (Doric, Ionic, and Corinthian) are represented, superimposed in tiers one above the other. See p. 150.

- **Hadrian's Villa** (Villa Adriana; near Tivoli): Hadrian's Villa slumbered in rural obscurity until the 1500s, when Renaissance popes ordered its excavation. Only then was the scale of this enormous and beautiful villa, built between A.D. 118 and 134, appreciated. Its builder, Hadrian, who had visited almost every part of his empire, wanted to incorporate the wonders of the world into one building site—and he succeeded. See p. 189.

- **Ostia Antica** (near Rome): During the height of the Roman Empire, Ostia ("door" in Latin) was the harbor town set at the point where the Tiber flowed into the sea. As Rome declined, so did Ostia; by the early Middle Ages, the town had almost disappeared, its population decimated by malaria. In the early 1900s, archaeologists excavated the ruins of hundreds of buildings, many of which you can view. See p. 193.

- **Herculaneum** (Campania): Legend says that Herculaneum was founded by Hercules. The historical facts tell us that it was buried under rivers of volcanic mud one fateful day in A.D. 79 after the eruption of Mount Vesuvius. Seeping into the cracks of virtually every building, the scalding mud preserved the timbers of hundreds of structures that would otherwise have rotted during the normal course of time. Devote at least 2 hours to seeing some of the best-preserved houses from the ancient world. See "The Phlegrean Fields & Herculaneum," in chapter 14.

- **Pompeii** (Campania): Once it was an opulent resort filled with 25,000 wealthy Romans. In A.D.

The ruins at Segesta, in Sicily.

Pompeii's Villa of Mysteries.

79, the eruption that devastated Herculaneum (see above) buried Pompeii under at least 6m (20 ft.) of volcanic ash and pumice stone. Beginning around 1750, Charles of Bourbon ordered the systematic excavation of the ruins—the treasures hauled out sparked a wave of interest in the classical era throughout northern Europe. See "Pompeii" in chapter 14.

o **Paestum** (Campania): Paestum was discovered by accident around 1750 when local bureaucrats tried to build a road across the heart of what had been a thriving ancient city. Paestum originated as a Greek colony around 600 B.C., fell to the Romans in 273 B.C., and declined into obscurity in the final days of the Empire. Today amateur archaeologists can follow a well-marked walking tour through the excavations. See "Paestum & Its Glorious Greek Temples" in chapter 14.

o **The Valley of the Temples** (Sicily): Although most of the Valley of the Temples in Agrigento lies in ruins, it is one of Europe's most beautiful classical sites, especially in February and March when the almond trees surrounding it burst into pink blossoms. One of the site's five temples dates from as early as 520 B.C.; another (never completed) ranks as one of the largest temples in the ancient world. See "Agrigento & the Valley of the Temples" in chapter 16.

o **Segesta** (Sicily): Even its site is impressive: a rocky outcropping surrounded on most sides by a jagged ravine. Built around 430 B.C. by the Greeks, Segesta's Doric colonnade is one of the most graceful in the ancient world. The site is stark and mysterious. The temple was probably destroyed by the Saracens (Muslim raiders) in the 11th century. See "Palermo" in chapter 16.

o **Selinunte** (Sicily): The massive columns of Selinunte lie scattered on the ground, as if an earthquake had punished its builders, yet this is one of our favorite ancient ruins in Italy. Around 600 B.C., immigrants from Syracuse built Selinunte into an important trading port. The city was a bitter rival of neighboring Segesta (see above) and was destroyed around 400 B.C., and then again in 250 B.C. by the Carthaginians. See "Selinunte" in chapter 16.

THE best WINEGROWING REGIONS

- **Latium** (Lazio, outside Rome): The region around Rome is predominantly known for white wines that include Marino; Est! Est!! Est!!!; Colli Albani; and the famous Frascati ("the wine of the popes and the people"). All these are derived almost exclusively from Malvasia and Trebbiano grapes, or from combinations of the two. The region's most famous producers of Frascati are **Fontana Candida,** Via di Fontana Candida 11, 00040 Monte Porzio Catone, Roma (© **06-9401881;** www.fontanacandida.it), whose winery, 23km (14 miles) southwest of Rome, was built around 1900; and **Gotto D'Oro—Cantina Sociale di Marino,** Via del Divino Amore 115, 00040 Frattocchie, Roma (© **06-93022211;** www.gottodoro.it). To arrange visits, contact the **Gruppo Italiano Vini,** Villa Belvedere, 37010 Calmasino, Verona (© **045-6269600;** www.gruppoitalianovini.com). See "Reserving Winery Tours" in chapter 5.

- **Tuscany & Umbria:** Some of Italy's most scenic vineyards lie nestled among the verdant rolling hills of these two stately regions. In fact, the most famous kind of wine in Italy (Chianti) is indelibly associated with Tuscany, whereas the (usually white) Orvieto and the (usually red) Torgiano are closely associated with Umbria. One of Tuscany's largest vintners is **Banfi,** Castello Banfi, Sant'Angelo Scalo, Montalcino, 53024 Siena (© **0577-840111;** www.castellobanfi.com). Near Siena are two other good choices: **Biondi-Santi,** Loc. Greppo 183, 53024 Montalcino (© **0577-848087;** www.biondisanti.it), and **Casa Vinicola L. Cecchi,** Loc. Casina dei Ponti 56, 53011 Castellina in Chianti (© **0577-54311;** www.cecchi.net). See "The Chianti Road" in chapter 7.

- **Emilia-Romagna:** Composed of two distinct areas (Emilia, to the west of Bologna, around the upriver Po Valley; and Romagna, to the east, centered on the delta of the Po), the region is known to gastronomes as the producer of some of Italy's best food, with wines worthy of its legendary cuisine. Emilia's most famous wine is Lambrusco, 50 million bottles of which are produced every year near Modena and Reggio Emilia. Less well known but also highly rated are the Colli Piacentini wines, of which **Cantine Romagnoli,** Via Genova 20, Villò di Vigolzone

Grapes on the vine.

29020 (℡ **0523-870129;** www.cantineromagnoli.it), is a rising star. Wines from Romagna are made from Sangiovese, Trebbiano, and Albana grapes and are well respected, cropping up on wine lists throughout the country. See chapter 8.

○ **The Veneto:** The humid flatlands of the eastern Po Valley produce memorable reds and whites in abundance, including everything from soft-white Soaves and Pinot Grigios to red Valpolicellas and merlots. Important vineyards in the region are **Azienda Vinicola Fratelli Fabiano,** Via Verona 6, 37060 Sona, near Verona (℡ **045-6081111;** www.fabiano.it), and **Fratelli Bolla,** Piazza Cittadella 3, 37122 Verona (℡ **045-8090911;** www.bolla.it). Smaller, but well respected because of recent improvements to its vintages, is **Nino Franco** (known for its sparkling prosecco), in the hamlet of Valdobbiadene, Via Garibaldi 147, 31049 Treviso (℡ **0423-972051;** www.nino franco.it). For information on these and the dozens of other producers in the Veneto, contact the **Azienda di Promozione Turistica,** Via Degli Alpini no. 9, Piazza Bra, 37121 Verona (℡ **045-8068680;** www.tourism.verona.it). See chapter 10.

○ **Trentino–Alto Adige:** The two most important wine-producing regions of northwestern Italy are the Alto Adige (also known as the Bolzano or Sudtirol region) and Trento. The loftier of the two, the Alto Adige, was once part of the Austro-Hungarian province of the South Tirol. More Germanic than Italian, it clings to its Austrian traditions and folklore and grows an Italian version of the Gewürztraminers (a fruity white) that would more often be found in Germany, Austria, and the Alsace Region of France. Venerable winegrowers include **Alois Lageder** (founded in 1855), Tenuta Loüwengang, Vicolo dei Conti 9, 39040 in the hamlet of Magré (℡ **0471-809500;** www.lageder. com), and **Schloss Turmhof,** Via Castello 4, Niclara, 39040 Kurtatsch (℡ **0471-880122;** www.tiefenbrunner.com). The Trentino area, a short distance to the south, is one of the leading producers of chardonnay and sparkling wines fermented using methods developed centuries ago. A winery worth a visit is **Cavit Cantina Viticoltori,** Via del Ponte di Ravina 31, 38100 Trento (℡ **0461-381711;** www.cavit.it).

○ **Friuli–Venezia Giulia:** This region in the Alpine foothills of northeastern Italy produces a light, fruity vintage that's especially appealing when young. One of the largest and best-respected wineries is **Marco Felluga,** Via Gorizia 121, Gradisca d'Isonzo, 34072 Gorizia (℡ **0481-99164;** www.marcofelluga.it). Another producer known for its high-quality wines is **Eugenio Collavini Vini & Spumanti,** Loc. Gramogliano, Via della Ribolla Gialla 2, 33040 Corno di Rosazzo, Udine (℡ **0432-753222;** www.collavini.it).

○ **Lombardy:** The Po Valley has always been known for its flat vistas, midsummer humidity, fertile soil, and excellent wines. The region produces everything from dry, still reds to sparkling whites with a champagnelike zest. **Guido Berlucchi,** Piazza Duranti 4, Borgonato di Cortefranca, 25040 Brescia (℡ **030-984381;** www.berlucchi.it), one of Italy's largest wineries, is especially welcoming to visitors. See chapter 10.

○ **The Piedmont:** Reds with rich, complex flavors make up most of the wine output of this high-altitude region near Italy's border with France. One of the most interesting vineyards is in a 15th-century abbey near the hamlet of Alba:

The vineyard at Renato Rattie Cantina.

Renato Ratti Cantina, Abbazia dell'Annunziata, La Morra, 12064 Cuneo (✆ **0173-50185;** www.renatoratti.com). See chapter 11.

o **Campania:** The wines produced in the harsh, hot landscapes of Campania, around Naples in southern Italy, seem stronger, rougher, and, in many cases, more powerful than those grown in gentler climes. Among the most famous are the Lacryma Christi (Tears of Christ), a white that grows in the volcanic soil near Naples, Herculaneum, and Pompeii; Taurasi, a potent red; and Greco di Tufo, a pungent white laden with the odors of apricots and apples. One of the most frequently visited vineyards is **Mastroberardino,** Via Manfredi 75–81, Atripalda, 83042 Avellino (✆ **0825-614111;** www.mastro.it). See chapter 14.

o **Sicily:** Because of its hot climate and volcanic soil, Sicily is home to countless vineyards, many of which produce only simple table wines. Of the better vintages, the best-known wine is Marsala, a dessert wine produced in both amber and ruby tones. Its production was given a great boost by the British, whose fleet paid frequent calls in Sicily throughout England's Age of Empire. Lord Nelson was an avid connoisseur, encouraging its production and spurring local vintners to produce large quantities. Some of the best wineries producing Marsala include: **Cantina Pellegrino,** Via del Fante 37–39, 91025 Marsala (✆ **0923-719911;** www.carlopellegrino.it); **Rallo,** Via Florio 3, 91025 Marsala (✆ **0923-721633;** www.cantinerallo.net); and **Cantine Florio,** Via Florio 1, 91025 Marsala (✆ **0923-781111;** www.cantineflorio. it). See chapter 16.

THE best LUXURY HOTELS

o **St. Regis Grand** (Rome; www.starwoodhotels.com; ℭ **06-47091**): This is the grand dame of all Rome's hotels, lying near Stazione Termini and a goal of luxe travelers since the 1890s. See p. 93.

o **Hotel de Russie** (Rome; www.roccofortehotels.com; ℭ **800/323-7500** in North America, or 06-328881): Opulently furnished, this chic boutique hotel enjoys a spectacular location in a setting of terraced gardens near Rome's Piazza del Popolo. About three-quarters of the guest rooms are done in a stark, striking contemporary minimalist style. All are incredibly comfortable and offer lots of high-tech gadgets and thoughtful touches. See p. 106.

o **The Inn at the Spanish Steps** (Rome; www.atspanishsteps.com; ℭ **06-69925657**): This intimate, upscale inn is a real find. The former Roman residence of Hans Christian Andersen has been transformed into a small inn of charm and grace, with each bedroom boasting authentic period decor and furnished with modern comforts. See p. 106.

o **Four Seasons Hotel Florence** (Florence; www.fourseasons.com; ℭ **800/819-5053** in the U.S. and Canada, or 055-26261): The grandest hotel in Tuscany is really a city resort, though fairly close to the historic core with its Renaissance treasures. The capital of Tuscany has never seen the likes of such opulent living with an array of dazzling facilities. All the other deluxe properties are jealous of this new kid on the block. See p. 207.

o **Villa San Michele** (Fiesole, near Florence; www.villasanmichele.com; ℭ **800/237-1236** in the U.S., or 055-5678200): This former 15th-century monastery is set behind a facade reputedly designed by Michelangelo. Brigitte Bardot chose it for one of her honeymoons (no one remembers with which husband). With a decor no set designer could duplicate, it evokes the charm of an aristocratic villa. See p. 274.

o **Certosa di Maggiano** (Siena; www.certosadimaggiano.com; ℭ **0577-288180**): This early-13th-century Certosinian monastery has been impeccably restored and converted into an upscale Relais & Châteaux inn. The individually decorated guest rooms are spacious, with antiques, art objects, and sumptuous beds; one has a private walled garden. See p. 318.

o **Cipriani** (Venice; www.hotelcipriani.com; ℭ **041-5207744**): This exclusive, elegant hotel is situated in a 1.2-hectare (3-acre) garden on the isolated Isola della Giudecca, removed from the tourist bustle of Venice. It offers chic, contemporary surroundings; sumptuous guest rooms; and a wealth of recreational facilities, including an Olympic-size pool, a first-rate health club, and Venice's only tennis court. Service is the best in town, with two employees for every room. See p. 456.

o **Gritti Palace** (Venice; www.gritti.hotelinvenice.com; ℭ **800/325-3535** in the U.S., or 041-794611): The Gritti, in a stately, central Grand Canal setting, is the renovated *palazzo* of 15th-century doge Andrea Gritti. It's quite formal, and it simply oozes glamour and history. Expect superb service, and elegant rooms with nice touches such as hypoallergenic pillows, bottled water, two-line phones, and marble bathrooms with deep soaking tubs. See p. 442.

The entrance to the Gritti Palace in Venice.

- **Four Seasons Hotel Milano** (Milan; www.fourseasons.com; ✆ **02-77088**): The building was first a 15th-century monastery, then the residence of the Habsburg-appointed governor of northern Italy in the 1850s. The Four Seasons chain has created one of Italy's finest hotels, incorporating the medieval facade, many of the frescoes and columns, and the original monastic details into a modern edifice accented with stone floors, pearwood cabinetry, Murano chandeliers, and acres of Fortuny fabrics. The guest rooms are cool, sleek, and spacious, with a sense of understated luxury and state-of-the-art bathrooms. Service is impeccable. See p. 568.

- **Grand Hotel Villa d'Este** (Cernobbio; www.villadeste.it; ✆ **031-3481**): Built in 1568, this palace in the Lake District is one of Europe's finest resort hotels. Step inside, and you're surrounded by frescoed ceilings, gorgeous antiques, and other exquisite details. Four magnificently landscaped hectares (10 acres), parts of which have been nurtured since the 1500s, surround the hotel. Guests enjoy dining on outdoor terraces, swimming in the gorgeous pools, using the health club, reveling in spa treatments, and much more. Cool breezes are provided by nearby Lake Como. See p. 619.

- **Hotel Splendido and Splendido Mare** (Portofino; www.hotelsplendido. com; ✆ **800/223-6800** in the U.S., or 0185-267801): Built as a monastery in the 14th century and abandoned because of attacks by North African pirates, this monument was rescued during the 19th century by an Italian baron, who converted it into a summer home for his family. The posh hillside retreat on the Italian Riviera now accommodates a sophisticated crowd, including many film stars. The views over the sea are stunning; you can enjoy the hotel's own lovely pool, or the staff will take you by boat to a private cove with changing cabins and lounge chairs. See p. 684.

o **Capri Palace Hotel & Spa** (Capri; www.capripalace.com; ℂ **081-9780111**): Luxury living along the southern coast of Italy doesn't get more elegant than this escapist retreat for well-heeled hedonists. Evoking a Mediterranean palace from the 18th century, this deluxe enclave is a pocket of posh, offering panoramic views of the bay, landscaped gardens, and grand living, especially in the Marilyn Monroe suite. See p. 750.

o **Hotel di San Pietro** (near Positano; www.ilsanpietro.it; ℂ **089-875455**): The only marker identifying this cliff-side hotel is a 15th-century chapel set beside the winding road. The hotel doesn't advertise and offers a quiet place to escape from it all, but this Relais & Châteaux property, with its gorgeous views, is the most luxurious retreat in the south of Italy. Strands of bougainvillea twine around the dramatically terraced white exterior walls; the spacious rooms are super-glamorous. An elevator takes you down the cliff ledges to a private beach. See p. 762.

o **Palazzo San Domenico** (Taormina; http://sandomenicopalace.hotelsinsicily. it; ℂ **0942-613111**): This is the grande dame of all of Sicily's hotels and one of the greatest in Italy. It's a virtual museum, a national monument, and one of the most elegant, comfortable, and tasteful hotels in the south of Italy. It originated in the 14th century as a monastery. See p. 819.

The gardens at Grand Hotel Villa d'Este.

THE best MODERATELY PRICED HOTELS

- **Fontanella Borghese** (Rome; http://fontanellaborghese.com; ☏ **06-68809-504**): Near the Spanish Steps, this charmer occupies two floors of a *palazzo* from the 1700s. You sleep in chambers once occupied by the princes of the Borghese family. Modern amenities have been installed, of course. See p. 109.

- **Hotel Bellettini** (Florence; www.hotelbellettini.com; ☏ **055-213561**): If you're looking for a place with *A Room with a View* atmosphere, head for this Renaissance *palazzo* midway between the Duomo and the rail station. It's a family-run affair with an old-time atmosphere evoked by terra-cotta floors and stained-glass windows. The rooms are a bit plain but very comfortable. See p. 217.

- **Palazzo Ravizza** (Siena; www.palazzoravizza.it; ☏ **0577-280462**): Right in the heart of Siena, a short walk from Piazza del Campo, this elegant building was converted from a 19th-century palace. Every guest room has a few antiques along with ceiling frescoes. See p. 319.

- **La Residenza** (Venice; www.venicelaresidenza.com; ☏ **041-5285315**): Set on a residential square, this hotel is housed in a 14th-century building that looks like a miniature Doge's Palace. You enter through an enormous salon filled with antiques, 300-year-old paintings, and some of the most marvelously preserved walls in Venice. The guest rooms aren't as grand, but they're comfortable and offer remarkably good value for pricey Venice. See p. 448.

- **Hotel Menardi** (Cortina d'Ampezzo; www.hotelmenardi.it; ☏ **0436-2400**): Built a century ago, this family-run Alpine inn is adorable, with wooden balconies and shutters and blazing fireplaces. Its rear windows open onto a flowery meadow and a view of the Dolomite peaks. The Menardi is a great buy in a high-priced resort town. See p. 557.

- **Victoria Hotel** (Turin; www.hotelvictoria-torino.com; ☏ **011-5611909**): One of Turin's best hotel buys, the Victoria has the distinct flavor of a British manor. You get touches of luxury, and even a private garden. See p. 639.

- **Hotel La Villarosa** (Ischia; www.dicohotels.it; ☏ **081-991316**;): In a semi-tropical garden setting, this is the island's finest *pensione*. It's like a Mediterranean-style country villa with antiques and tiles adorning bright, airy rooms. See p. 735.

THE best RESTAURANTS

- **La Terrazza** (Rome; ☏ **06-478121**): You get two winning elements here: some of the finest cuisine in Rome and a panoramic view toward Michelangelo's dome of St. Peter's. The constantly changing menu takes advantage of the best seasonal ingredients, and the chef constantly dazzles discerning palates with new taste sensations. This prestigious restaurant is located in the Hotel Eden. See p. 120.

- **La Giostra** (Florence; ☏ **055-241341**): A prince, with a title left over from the Austro-Hungarian Empire, and his twin sons invite you to enjoy their regionally based repertoire of imaginative, exquisite dishes. Many of their dishes, especially those made with truffles, are worthy of not only a prince but also a king. The chefs make great use of the bounty of the Tuscan countryside. See p. 234.

o **Gran Gotto** (Genoa; ℐ **010-583644**): You may—just may—get your best seafood dinner along the Italian Riviera at this longtime family-run favorite, which opened back in 1937. It was good then (so we hear), and possibly is even better today. The chefs shop for the finest catches of the day, which they fashion into dishes of robust freshness and flavor. See p. 671.

o **San Domenico** (Imola, outside Bologna; ℐ **0542-29000**): Foodies from all over Europe flock to the town of Imola to visit this, our pick as Italy's best restaurant. Convenient to Bologna and Ravenna, San Domenico features a cuisine that seems to feature modern French influences. But owner Gian Luigi Morini claims that his heavenly offerings are nothing more than adaptations of festive regional dishes—they're just lighter, more subtle, and served in manageable portions. Enjoy a vintage from one of Italy's finest wine cellars to accompany your memorable meal here. Simply marvelous! See p. 398.

o **Antico Martini** (Venice; ℐ **041-5224121**): Founded in 1720 as a spot to enjoy the new trend of drinking coffee, this restaurant is one of the best in Venice. Replete with paneled walls and glittering chandeliers, the Martini specializes in Venetian cuisine. See p. 459.

o **Ristorante Il Desco** (Verona; ℐ **045-595358**): Set in a former *palazzo,* this restaurant is the best in the Veneto region of northeastern Italy. Its culinary repertoire emphasizes a *nuova cucina* (nouvelle cuisine) that makes use of the freshest ingredients. The wine selections are excellent. See p. 536.

o **Joia** (Milan; ℐ **02-29522124**): The vegetarian dishes here are among the best in Italy, but Swiss chef Pietro Leemann also excels in seafood. This is a hot dining ticket in Italy's city of fashion. See p. 578.

Antico Martini.

○ **La Cantinella** (Naples; ✆ **081-7648684**): The only Michelin-starred restaurant in Naples, La Cantinella serves some of the best and most refined seafood in Campania. Opening onto the bay of Santa Lucia, this will be the highlight of your culinary tour of the area. Time-tested Neapolitan classics are served, along with an array of more imaginative dishes. Grilled fish can be prepared as you like it—and chances are, you'll like it a lot. See p. 716.

THE best BUYS

○ **Ceramics:** The town of Faenza, in Emilia-Romagna, has been the center of pottery making, especially majolica, since the Renaissance. Majolica, also known as faience, is a type of hand-painted, glazed, and heavily ornamented earthenware. Of course, you don't have to go to Faenza to buy it because shops throughout the country carry it. Tuscany and Umbria are also known for their earthenware pottery, carried by many shops in Rome and Florence.

○ **Fashion:** Italian fashion is world-renowned. Pucci and Valentino led the parade, to be followed by Armani, Missoni, Gucci, Versace, and Ferrè. Following World War II, Italian design began to compete seriously against the French fashion monopoly. Today Italian designers such as Krizia are among the arbiters of the world fashion scene. Milan dominates with the largest selection of boutiques, followed by Rome and Florence. Ironically, a lot of "French" fashion is now designed and manufactured in Italy, in spite of what the label says.

○ **Glass:** Venetian glass, ranging from the delicate to the grotesque, is world famous. In Venice, you'll find literally hundreds of stores peddling Venetian glass in a wide range of prices. Here's the surprise: A great deal of Venetian glass today is manufactured not on Murano (an island in the Venetian lagoon) but in the Czech Republic. But that doesn't mean that the glass is unworthy. Many factories outside Italy turn out high-quality glass products that are then shipped to Murano, where many so-called glass factories aren't factories at all, but storefronts selling this imported "Venetian" glass. See "Shopping" in chapter 9.

○ **Gold:** The tradition of shaping jewelry out of gold dates from the time of the Etruscans, and this ancient tradition is going strong today, with artisans still toiling in tiny studios and workshops. Many of the designs are based on ancient Roman originals. Of course, dozens of jewelers don't follow tradition at all but design original and often daring pieces. Many shops will even melt down your old gold jewelry and refashion it into something more modern.

○ **Lace:** For centuries, Italy has been known for its exquisite and delicate lace, fashioned into everything from women's undergarments to heirloom

Murano glass being made in Venice.

tablecloths. Florence long ago distinguished itself for the *punto Firenze* (Florentine stitch) made by cloistered nuns, although this tradition has waned. Venetian lace is even more famous, including some of the finest products in the world, especially *tombolo* (pillow lace), macramé, and an expensive form of lace known as *chiacchierino*. Of course, the market is also flooded with cheap machine-made stuff, which a trained eye can quickly spot. Although some pieces, such as a bridal veil, might cost hundreds of euros, you'll often find reasonably priced collars, handkerchiefs, and doilies in Venice and Florence boutiques. See "Shopping" in chapters 6 and 9.

o **Leather:** The Italians craft the finest leather in the world. From boots to luggage, from leather clothing to purses (or wallets), Italian cities—especially Rome, Florence, Venice, and Milan—abound in leather shops selling quality goods. This is one of Italy's best values, in spite of the substandard work that's now appearing. If you shop carefully, you can find lots of quality handcrafted leather products.

o **Prints & Engravings:** Wood engravings, woodcuts, mezzotints, copper engravings—you name it and you'll find it, especially in Rome and Florence. Of course, you have to be a careful shopper. Some prints are genuine antiques and works of rare art, but others are rushed off the assembly line and into the shops.

Leather goods for sale in Florence.

o **Religious Objects & Vestments:** The religious objects industry in Italy is big and bustling, centered mostly in the Vatican area in Rome. The biggest concentration of shops is near the Church of Santa Maria Sopra Minerva. These shops have it all, from cardinals' birettas and rosaries to religious art and vestments.

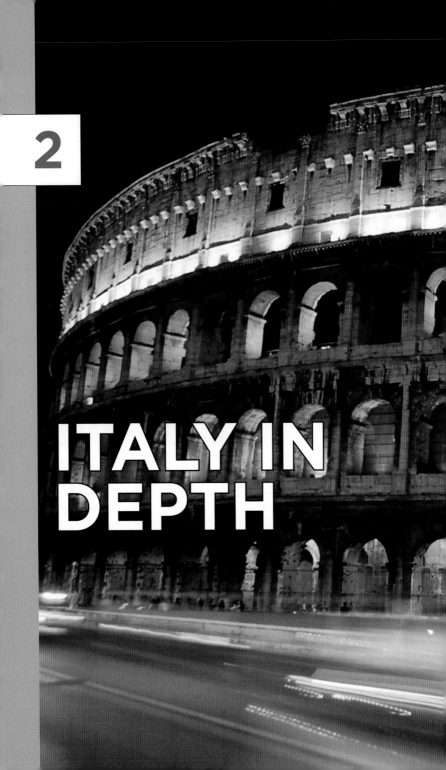

2

ITALY IN DEPTH

T he best way to begin your Italian adventure is with a little prep work. The more you know about Italy, with its vast and varied history, the better you can understand and appreciate its charms.

ITALY TODAY

As in most other countries of the world, the global crisis has had a disastrous effect on Italy's economy, causing the worst recession since World War II. Once one of the world's strongest economies and a European Union powerhouse, Italy may be on the verge of a financial meltdown. Beginning in 2009, Italy began to deal with unemployment through social subsidies, but with a dwindling bank account it's debatable how long that measure can be in force. Currently Italy has the third biggest public debt in the world.

On another front, Italy's population is declining, with a birthrate of 8.7 per 1,000 people. That rate is matched with a death rate of 10.4 per 1,000 people. In all, the population stands roughly at 60 million.

The vacuum is being filled by immigrants, especially those from eastern Europe, notably Romania and Albania. It's estimated, for example, that there may be one million Romanians living in Italy today.

Italian security forces valiantly struggle to turn back massive illegal immigration, not only from the East but also from impoverished parts of North Africa. Sadly, undocumented migrants still pour into southern Italy, especially Sicily, on anything that floats. Many are arrested and sent back, but thousands escape detection. Once in Sicily, they can make their way to the Italian mainland, where they hope to find jobs and a better life.

Inevitably, conflicts arise between these undocumented workers and the local citizens. Polls have shown that a majority of Italians associate immigrants with sex workers and drug trafficking. In spite of that view, in taking a job, the average immigrant replenishes the rapidly shrinking Italian workforce.

Like most countries of western Europe, Italy suffers from overdevelopment, especially along its coastlines and in its northern cities. The only major area left for development is the south, including Calabria. However, Italian authorities, seeing the mistakes made in their past development, are putting the brakes on uncontrolled growth in what is left of their virgin south.

Even though the government wants to develop the south and improve the living standards of its people, it is also controlling real estate expansion with an array of new laws. For example, development has been forbidden within 300m (984 ft.) of any beach. Other stringent building codes and antipollution measures are in force as well.

With all its changes and all its problems, Italy remains on that coveted list of the four or five countries that most people want to visit at least once in their lifetime. All roads in Italy still lead to Rome, but there is so much to see along the way there.

PREVIOUS PAGE: **Rome's Colosseum.**

A Roman deli.

As film director Fellini once said, "A man should visit Italy at least twice in his life—once when he's young and can enjoy so many 'forbidden' fruits, and again when he's old and can sit in our timeless sun and enjoy *il dolce far niente,* or the sweetness of doing nothing."

LOOKING BACK AT ITALY

The Etruscans

Of all the early inhabitants of Italy, the most significant were the Etruscans. But who were they? No one knows, and the many inscriptions that they left behind (mostly on graves) are of little help because the Etruscan language has never been fully deciphered by modern scholars. It's thought they arrived on the eastern coast of Umbria several centuries before Rome was built, around 800 B.C. Their religious rites and architecture show an obvious contact with Mesopotamia; the Etruscans might have been refugees from Asia Minor who traveled west about 1200 to 1000 B.C. Within 2 centuries, they had subjugated Tuscany and Campania and the Villanova tribes that lived there.

While the Etruscans were building temples at Tarquinia and Caere (present-day Cerveteri), the few nervous Latin tribes that remained outside their sway were gravitating to Rome, then little more than a village of sheepherders. As Rome's power grew, however, it increasingly profited from the strategically important Tiber crossing, where the ancient salt road (Via Salaria) turned northeastward toward the central Apennines.

From their base at Rome, the Latins remained free of the Etruscans until about 600 B.C. But the Etruscan advance was inexorable, and although the Latin tribes concentrated their forces at Rome for a last stand, they were swept away by the sophisticated conquerors. The new overlords introduced gold tableware and jewelry, bronze urns and terra-cotta statuary, and the best art and culture of Greece and Asia Minor. They also made Rome the governmental seat of all Latium. Roma is an Etruscan name, and the kings of Rome had Etruscan names: Numa, Ancus, Tarquinius, and even Romulus.

The Etruscans ruled until the Roman revolt around 510 B.C., and by 250 B.C., the Romans and their Campania allies had vanquished the Etruscans, wiping out their language and religion. However, many of the former rulers' manners and beliefs remained and were assimilated into the culture. Even today, certain Etruscan customs and bloodlines are believed to exist in Italy, especially in Tuscany.

The best places to see the legacy left by these mysterious people are in Cerveteri and Tarquinia, outside Rome. Especially interesting is the **Etruscan Necropolis,** just 6.4km (4 miles) southeast of Tarquinia, where thousands of tombs have been discovered. To learn more about the Etruscans, visit the **National Etruscan Museum** (p. 168) in Rome.

The Roman Republic

After the Roman Republic was established in 510 B.C., the Romans continued to increase their power by conquering neighboring communities in the highlands and forming alliances with other Latins in the lowlands. They gave to their Latin allies, and then to conquered peoples, partial or complete Roman citizenship, with the obligation of military service. Citizen colonies were set up as settlements of Roman farmers, and many of the famous cities of Italy originated as colonies. For the most part, these colonies were fortified and linked to Rome by military roads.

The stern Roman Republic was characterized by a belief in the gods, the necessity of learning from the past, the strength of the family, education through reading books and performing public service, and, most important, obedience. The all-powerful Senate presided as Rome defeated rival powers one after the other and grew to rule the Mediterranean. The Punic Wars with Carthage in the 3rd century B.C. cleared away a major obstacle, although people said later that Rome's breaking of its treaty with Carthage (which led to that city's total destruction) put a curse on Rome.

No figure was more towering during the republic than Julius Caesar, the charismatic conqueror of Gaul—"the wife of every husband and the husband of every wife." After defeating the last resistance of the Pompeians in 45 B.C., he came to Rome and was made dictator and consul for 10 years. By then he was almost a king. Conspirators, led by Marcus Junius Brutus, stabbed him to death in the Senate on March 15, 44 B.C. Beware the ides of March.

Marc Antony, a Roman general, assumed control by seizing Caesar's papers and wealth. Intent on expanding the republic, Antony met with the Egyptian queen, Cleopatra, at Tarsus in 41 B.C. She seduced him, and he stayed in Egypt for a year. When Antony eventually returned to Rome, still smitten with Cleopatra, he made peace with Caesar's willed successor, Octavius, and, through the pacts of Brundisium, soon found himself married to Octavius's sister, Octavia. This marriage, however, didn't prevent him from marrying Cleopatra in 36 B.C. The furious Octavius gathered western legions and defeated Antony at the Battle of Actium on September 2, 31 B.C. Cleopatra fled to Egypt, followed by Antony, who committed suicide in disgrace a year later. Cleopatra, unable to seduce his successor and thus retain her rule of Egypt, followed suit with the help of an asp.

The Roman Empire

By 49 B.C., Rome ruled the entire Mediterranean world, either directly or indirectly, because all political, commercial, and cultural pathways led straight to Rome, the sprawling city set on seven hills. The potential for wealth and glory to be found in Rome lured many people, draining other Italiac communities of human resources. Foreign imports, especially agricultural imports, hurt local farmers and landowners. Municipal governments faltered, and civil wars ensued. Public order was restored by the Caesars (planned by Julius but brought to fruition under Augustus). On the eve of the birth of Christ, Rome was a mighty empire whose generals had brought the Western world under the sway of Roman law and civilization.

Born Gaius Octavius in 63 B.C., Augustus, the first Roman emperor, reigned from 27 B.C. to A.D. 14. His reign, called "the golden age of Rome," led to the Pax Romana, 2 centuries of peace. He had been adopted by, and eventually became the heir of, his great-uncle Julius Caesar. In Rome you can still visit the remains of the **Forum of Augustus,** built before the birth of Christ.

The emperors, whose succession started with Augustus's principate after the death of Julius Caesar, brought Rome to new, almost giddy, heights. Augustus transformed the city from brick to marble, much the way Napoleon III transformed Paris many centuries later. But success led to corruption. The emperors wielded autocratic power, and the centuries witnessed a steady decay in the ideals and traditions on which the Empire had been founded. The army became a fifth column of barbarian mercenaries, the tax collector became the scourge of the countryside, and for every good emperor (Augustus, Claudius, Trajan, Vespasian, and Hadrian, to name a few), there were three or four debased heads of state (Caligula, Nero, Domitian, Caracalla, and others).

After Augustus died (by poison, perhaps), his widow, Livia—a crafty social climber who had divorced her first husband to marry Augustus—set up her son, Tiberius, as ruler through a number of intrigues and poisonings. A long series of murders ensued, and Tiberius, who ruled during Pontius Pilate's trial and crucifixion of Christ, was eventually murdered in an uprising of landowners. In fact, murder was so common that a short time later, Domitian (A.D. 81–96) became so obsessed with the possibility of assassination that he had the walls of his palace

The view from Rome's Capitoline Hill.

Roman bust.

covered in mica so that he could see behind him at all times. (He was killed anyway.)

Excesses and scandal ruled the day: Caligula (a bit overfond of his sister, Drusilla) appointed his horse a lifetime member of the Senate, lavished money on foolish projects, and proclaimed himself a god. Caligula's successor, his uncle Claudius, was deceived and publicly humiliated by one of his wives, the lascivious Messalina (he had her killed for her trouble); he was then poisoned by his final wife, his niece Agrippina, to secure the succession of Nero, her son by a previous marriage. Nero's thanks were later to murder not only his mother but also his wife, Claudius's daughter, and his rival, Claudius's son. The disgraceful Nero was removed as emperor while visiting Greece; he committed suicide with the cry, "What an artist I destroy!"

By the 3rd century A.D., corruption had become so prevalent there were 23 emperors in 73 years. How bad were things? So bad that Caracalla, to secure control of the Empire, had his brother Geta slashed to pieces while Geta was lying in his mother's arms. Rule of the Empire changed hands so frequently that news of the election of a new emperor commonly reached the provinces together with a report of that emperor's assassination.

The 4th-century reforms of Diocletian held the Empire together, but at the expense of its inhabitants, who were reduced to tax units. Diocletian reinforced imperial power while paradoxically weakening Roman dominance and prestige by dividing the Empire into east and west halves and establishing administrative capitals at outposts such as Milan and Trier, Germany. He instituted not only heavy taxes but also a socioeconomic system that made professions hereditary. This edict was so strictly enforced that the son of a silversmith could be tried as a criminal if he attempted to become a sculptor instead.

Constantine became emperor in A.D. 306, and in 330, he made Constantinople (or Byzantium) the new capital of the Empire, moving the administrative functions away from Rome altogether, partly because the menace of possible barbarian attacks in the west had increased greatly. Constantine took the best Roman artisans, politicians, and public figures with him, creating a city renowned for its splendor, intrigue, jealousies, and passion. Constantine was the first Christian emperor, allegedly converting after he saw the True Cross in the heavens, accompanied by the legend "IN THIS SIGN SHALL YOU CONQUER." He then defeated the pagan Maxentius and his followers in battle.

The Empire Falls

The eastern and western sections of the Roman Empire split in A.D. 395, leaving the Italian peninsula without the support it had once received from east of the Adriatic. When the Goths moved toward Rome in the early 5th century, citizens in the provinces, who had grown to hate and fear the cruel bureaucracy set up by Diocletian and followed by succeeding emperors, welcomed the invaders. And then the pillage began.

Rome was first sacked by Alaric, king of the Visigoths, in August 410. The populace made no attempt to defend the city (other than trying vainly to buy him off, a tactic that had worked 3 years earlier); most people simply fled into the hills or headed to their country estates if they were rich. The feeble Western emperor Honorius hid out in Ravenna the entire time.

More than 40 troubled years passed. Then Attila the Hun invaded Italy to besiege Rome. Attila was dissuaded from attacking, thanks largely to a peace mission headed by Pope Leo I in 452. Yet relief was short-lived: In 455, Gaiseric the Vandal carried out a 2-week sack that was unparalleled in its pure savagery. The empire of the West lasted for only another 20 years; finally, in 476, the sacks and chaos ended the once-mighty city, and Rome was left to the popes, under the nominal auspices of an exarch from Byzantium (Constantinople).

The last would-be Caesars to walk the streets of Rome were both

A plaster cast, meant to show what one of the victims at Pompeii may have looked like.

barbarians: The first was Theodoric, who established an Ostrogoth kingdom at Ravenna from 493 to 526; the second was Totilla, who held the last chariot races in the Circus Maximus in 549. Totilla was engaged in an ongoing battle with Belisarius, the general of the Eastern emperor Justinian, who sought to regain Rome for the Eastern empire. The city changed hands several times, recovering some of its ancient pride by bravely resisting Totilla's forces, but eventually it was entirely depopulated by the continuing battles.

Christianity, a new religion that created a new society, was probably founded in Rome about a decade after the death of Jesus. Gradually gaining strength despite early persecution, it was finally accepted as the official religion. The best way today to relive the early Christian era is to visit Rome's Appian Way and its Catacombs, along **Via Appia Antica,** built in 312 b.c. According to Christian tradition, it was here that an escaping Peter encountered the vision of Christ. The **Catacombs of St. Callixtus** form the first cemetery of the Christian community of Rome.

The Middle Ages

A ravaged Rome entered the Middle Ages, its once-proud population scattered and unrecognizable in rustic exile. A modest population started life again in the swamps of the Campus Martius, while the seven hills, now without water because the aqueducts were cut, stood abandoned and crumbling.

After the fall of the Western empire, the pope took on more imperial powers, yet there was no political unity. Decades of rule by barbarians and then by Goths were followed by takeovers in different parts of the country by various strong warriors, such as the Lombards. The former empire became divided into several spheres of control. In 731, Pope Gregory II renounced Rome's dependence on Constantinople and thus ended the twilight era of the Greek exarch who had nominally ruled Rome.

Papal Rome turned toward Europe, where the papacy found a powerful ally in Charlemagne, a king of the barbarian Franks. In 800, he was crowned emperor by Pope Leo III. The capital that he established at Aachen (*Aix-la-Chapelle* in French) lay deep within territory known to the Romans a half-millennium before as the heart of the barbarian world. Although Charlemagne pledged allegiance to the church and looked to Rome and its pope as the final arbiter in most religious and cultural affairs, he launched northwestern Europe on a course toward bitter political opposition to the meddling of the papacy in temporal affairs.

The successor to Charlemagne's empire was a political entity known as the Holy Roman Empire (962–1806). The new Empire defined the end of the Dark Ages but ushered in a period of long, bloody warfare. The Lombard leaders battled Franks. Magyars from Hungary invaded northeastern Lombardy and, in turn, were defeated by the increasingly powerful Venetians. Normans gained military control of Sicily in the 11th century, divided it from the rest of Italy, and altered forever the island's racial and ethnic makeup and its architecture. As Italy dissolved into a fragmented collection of city-states, the papacy fell under the power of Rome's feudal landowners. Eventually, even the process for choosing popes came into the hands of the increasingly Germanic Holy Roman emperors, although this balance of power would very soon shift.

Rome during the Middle Ages was a quaint, rural town. Narrow lanes with overhanging buildings filled many areas, such as the Campus Martius, that had once been showcases of imperial power. Great basilicas were built and embellished with golden-hued mosaics. The forums, mercantile exchanges, temples, and theaters of the Imperial Era slowly disintegrated and collapsed. The decay of ancient Rome was assisted by periodic earthquakes, centuries of neglect, and in particular, the growing need for building materials. Rome receded into a dusty provincialism. As the seat of the Roman Catholic church, the state was almost completely controlled by priests, who had an insatiable need for new churches and convents.

By the end of the 11th century, the popes shook off control of the Roman aristocracy, rid themselves of what they considered the excessive influence of the emperors at Aachen, and began an aggressive expansion of church influence and acquisitions. The deliberate organization of the church into a format modeled on the hierarchies of the ancient Roman Empire put it on a collision course with the Empire and the other temporal leaders of Europe. The result was an endless series of power struggles.

The southern half of the country took a different road when, in the 11th century, the Normans invaded southern Italy, wresting control from the local strongmen and, in Sicily, from the Muslim Saracens who had occupied the region throughout the Dark Ages. To the south, the Normans introduced feudalism, a repressive social system that discouraged individual economic initiative, and whose legacy accounts for the social and economic differences between north and south that persist to this day.

In the mid–14th century, the Black Plague ravaged Europe, killing a third of Italy's population. Despite such setbacks, the northern Italian city-states grew wealthy from Crusade booty, trade with one another and with the Middle East, and banking. These wealthy principalities and pseudorepublics ruled by the merchant elite flexed their muscles in the absence of a strong central authority.

The Renaissance

The story of Italy from the dawn of the Renaissance in the 15th century to the Age of Enlightenment in the 17th and 18th centuries is as varied and fascinating as that of the rise and fall of the Empire. The papacy soon became essentially a feudal state, and the pope was a medieval (later Renaissance) prince engaged in many of the worldly activities that brought criticism on the church in later centuries. The 1065 fall of the Holy Land to the Turks catapulted the papacy into the forefront of world politics, primarily because of the Crusades, many of which the popes directly caused or encouraged (but most of which were judged military and economic disasters). During the 12th and 13th centuries, the bitter rivalries that rocked Europe's secular and spiritual bastions took their toll on the Holy Roman Empire, which grew weaker as city-states, buttressed by mercantile and trade-related prosperity, grew stronger and as France emerged as a potent nation in its own right. Each investiture of a new bishop to any influential post resulted in endless jockeying for power among many factions.

These conflicts reached their most visible impasse in 1303 during the Great Schism, when the papacy was moved to the French city of Avignon. For more than 70 years, until 1377, viciously competing popes (one in Rome, another under the protection of the French kings in Avignon) made simultaneous claims to the legacy of St. Peter, underscoring the degree to which the church was both a victim and a victimizer in the temporal world of European politics.

The seat of the papacy was eventually returned to Rome, where successive popes were every bit as interesting as the Roman emperors they had replaced.

A close-up of Michelangelo's marble statue of *David*, in Florence.

The great families (Barberini, Medici, Borgia) enhanced their status and fortunes impressively when one of their sons was elected pope. For a look at life during this tumultuous period, you can visit Rome's **Castel Sant'Angelo** (p. 146), which became a papal residence in the 14th century.

Despite the centuries that had passed since the collapse of the Roman Empire, the age of siege wasn't yet over. In 1527, Charles V, King of Spain, carried out the worst sack of Rome ever. To the horror of Pope Clement VII (a Medici), the entire city was brutally pillaged by the man who was to be crowned Holy Roman Emperor the next year.

During the years of the Renaissance, the Reformation, and the Counter-Reformation, Rome underwent major physical changes. The old centers of culture reverted to pastures and fields, and great churches and palaces were built with the stones of ancient Rome. This construction boom, in fact, did far more damage to the temples of the Caesars than any barbarian sack had done. Rare marbles were stripped from the imperial baths and used as altarpieces or sent to limekilns. So enthusiastic was the papal destruction of Imperial Rome that it's a miracle anything is left.

This era is best remembered because of its art. The great ruling families—especially the Medicis in Florence, the Gonzagas in Mantua, and the Estes in Ferrara—not only reformed law and commerce but also sparked a renaissance in art. Out of this period arose such towering figures as **Leonardo da Vinci** and **Michelangelo.** Many visitors come to Italy to view what's left of the art and glory of that era—everything from Michelangelo's **Sistine Chapel** at the Vatican to his statue of *David* in Florence, from Leonardo's *Last Supper* in Milan to **Il Duomo (Cattedrale di Santa Maria del Fiore)** in Florence, graced by Brunelleschi's dome.

A United Italy

The 19th century witnessed the final collapse of the Renaissance city-states. These units, eventually coming under the control of a *signore* (lord), were essentially regional states, with mercenary soldiers, civil rights, and assistance for their friendly neighbors. Some had attained formidable power under such *signori* as the Estes in Ferrara, the Medicis in Florence, and the Viscontis and Sforzas in Milan.

During the 17th, 18th, and 19th centuries, turmoil continued through a succession of many European dynasties. Napoleon made a bid for power in Italy beginning in 1796, fueling his war machines with what was considered a

Leonardo da Vinci's *Adoration of the Magi,* which can be seen at the Uffizi Gallery in Florence.

relatively easy victory. During the Congress of Vienna (1814–15), which followed Napoleon's defeat, Italy was once again divided among many factions: Austria was given Lombardy and Venetia, and the Papal States were returned to the pope. Some duchies were put back into the hands of their hereditary rulers, and southern Italy and Sicily went to a Bourbon dynasty. One historic move, which eventually contributed to the unification of Italy, was the assignment of the former republic of Genoa to Sardinia (which, at the time, was governed by the House of Savoy).

Political unrest became a fact of Italian life, at least some of it encouraged by the rapid industrialization of the north and the lack of industrialization in the south. Despite those barriers, in 1861, thanks to the brilliant efforts of patriots Camillo Cavour (1810–61) and Giuseppe Garibaldi (1807–82), the Kingdom of Italy was proclaimed and Victor Emmanuel (Vittorio Emanuele) II of the House of Savoy, king of Sardinia, became the head of the new monarchy.

Although the hope, promoted by Europe's theocrats and some of its devout Catholics, of attaining one empire ruled by the pope and the church had long faded, there was still a fight, followed by generations of hard feelings, when the Papal States—a strategically and historically important principality under the pope's temporal jurisdiction—were confiscated by the new Kingdom of Italy.

The establishment of the kingdom, however, didn't signal a complete unification of Italy because Rome was still under papal control and Venetia was still held by Austria. This was partially resolved in 1866, when Venetia joined the rest of Italy after the Seven Weeks' War between Austria and Prussia; in 1871, Rome became the capital of the newly formed country. The Vatican, however, didn't yield its territory to the new order, despite guarantees of nonintervention proffered by the government, and relations between the pope and the country of Italy remained rocky.

The Rise of Il Duce & World War II

In 1915, Italy entered World War I on the side of the Allies, joining Britain and France to help defeat Germany. Although Italians seemed to have little enthusiasm for this war, they were "bribed" in a secret treaty in London. If an Allied victory could be achieved, Italy would be ceded the Trentino, the south Tyrol (which belonged to Austria), Trieste, and some Dalmatian Islands. These territories, which belonged to other countries, came at a high price for Italy, which suffered heavy casualties on the northern front. At the end of the war, Italians suffered from rising unemployment and horrendous inflation. As in Germany, this political crisis led to the emergence of a dictator.

On October 28, 1922, Benito Mussolini, who had started his Fascist Party in 1919, knew the time was ripe for change. He gathered 50,000 supporters for a march on Rome. Inflation was soaring and workers had just called a general strike, so rather than recognizing a state under siege, King Victor Emmanuel II recognized Mussolini as the new government leader. In 1929, Il Duce defined the divisions between the Italian government and the Vatican by signing a concordat granting political and fiscal autonomy to Vatican City. The agreement also made Roman Catholicism the official state religion—but that designation was removed in 1978 by a revision of the concordat.

Wine bottles featuring former dictator Benito Mussolini on their labels.

During the Spanish Civil War (1936–39), Mussolini's support of Franco's Fascist party, whose members had staged a coup against the democratically elected government of Spain, helped encourage the formation of the Axis alliance between Italy and Nazi Germany. Despite having outdated military equipment, Italy added to the general horror of the era by invading Abyssinia (Ethiopia) in 1935. In 1940, Italy invaded Greece through Albania; and, in 1942, it sent thousands of Italian troops to assist Hitler in his disastrous campaign along the Russian front. In 1943, Allied forces, under the command of U.S. Gen. George Patton and British Gen. Bernard Montgomery, landed in Sicily and quickly secured the island and prepared to move north toward Rome.

In the face of likely defeat and humiliation, Mussolini was overthrown by his cabinet (Grand Council). The Allies made a separate deal with Victor Emmanuel III, who had collaborated with the Fascists and easily shifted allegiances. A politically divided Italy watched as battalions of fanatical German Nazis released Mussolini from his Italian jail cell to establish the short-lived Republic of Salò, headquartered on the edge of Lake Garda. Mussolini had hoped for a groundswell of popular opinion in favor of Italian Fascism, but events quickly proved this to be a futile dream.

In April 1945, with almost a half-million Italians rising in a mass demonstration against him and the German war machine, Mussolini was captured by Italian partisans as he fled to Switzerland. Along with his mistress, Claretta Petacci, and several others, he was shot and strung upside-down from the roof of a Milan gas station.

The Postwar Years

Italy's citizens voiced dissatisfaction with the monarchy and its identification with the fallen Fascist dictatorship. In 1946, they voted for the establishment of a republic. The major political party that emerged following World War II was the Christian Democratic Party, a right-of-center group whose leader, Alcide De Gasperi (1881–1954), served as premier until 1953. The second-largest party was the Communist Party; however, by the mid-1970s, it had abandoned its revolutionary program in favor of a democratic form of "Eurocommunism." (In 1991, the Communists even changed their name to the Democratic Party of the Left.)

Even though after the war Italy had been stripped of all its overseas colonies, it quickly succeeded in rebuilding its economy, in part because of U.S. aid under the Marshall Plan (1948–52). By the 1960s, as a member of the European Community (founded in Rome in 1957), Italy had become one of the world's leading industrialized nations, prominent in the manufacture of automobiles and office equipment.

But the country continued to be plagued by economic inequities between the industrially prosperous north and the economically depressed south. It suffered an unprecedented flight of capital (frequently aided by Swiss banks only too willing to accept discreet deposits from wealthy Italians) and an increase in bankruptcies, inflation (almost 20% during much of the 1970s), and unemployment.

During the late 1970s and early 1980s, Italy was rocked by the rise of terrorism, instigated both by neo-Fascists and by left-wing intellectuals from the Socialist-controlled universities of the north.

Into the New Millennium

In the early 1990s, the Italians reeled as many leading politicians were accused of wholesale corruption. As a result, a newly formed right-wing group, led by media magnate Silvio Berlusconi, swept to victory in 1994's general elections. Berlusconi became prime minister at the head of a coalition government. However, in December 1994, he resigned as prime minister after the federalist Northern League Party defected from his coalition and he lost his parliamentary majority. Treasury Minister Lamberto Dini, a nonpolitical banker with international financial credentials, was named to replace Berlusconi.

Dini signed on merely as a transitional player in the topsy-turvy political game. His austere measures enacted to balance Italy's budget, including cuts in pensions and healthcare, weren't popular among the mostly blue-collar workers or the influential labor unions. Aware of a predicted defeat in a no-confidence vote, Dini stepped down. His resignation in January 1996 left beleaguered Italians shouting *"Basta!"* (Enough!) This reshuffling in Italy's political deck prompted President Oscar Scalfaro to dissolve both houses of Parliament.

Once again the Italians were faced with forming a new government. The April 1996 elections proved a shocker, not only for the defeated politicians but also for the victors. The center-left coalition known as the Olive Tree, led by Romano Prodi, swept both the Senate and the Chamber of Deputies. The Olive Tree, whose roots stem from the old Communist Party, achieved victory by shifting toward the center and focusing its campaign on a strong platform protecting social benefits and supporting Italy's bid to become a solid member of the European Union.

Prodi carried through on his commitment when he announced a stringent budget for 1997, in a bid to be among the first countries to enter the monetary union. That year saw further upheavals in the Prodi government as he continued to push ahead with cuts to the country's generous social-security system. By autumn, though, Prodi was forced to submit his resignation when he lost critical support in Parliament from the Communist Refounding Party, which balked at pension and welfare cuts in the 1998 budget. The party eventually backed off with its demands, and Prodi was returned to office, where he pledged to see legislation for a 35-hour workweek passed by 2001.

In September 1997, twin earthquakes (5.7 and 5.6 on the Richter scale) struck within hours of each other. Umbria sustained considerable damage, especially in Acciano and Assisi, where 11 people were killed and another 13,000 were forced to take refuge in tents.

On the political front, Massimo D'Alema became the first former Communist to lead a western European government in October 1998, when he formed Italy's 56th postwar government. He replaced departing prime minister Romano Prodi.

As 1999 neared its end, the big financial news was Italy's entrance under the euro umbrella.

Italy spent all of 2000 welcoming Jubilee Year visitors from around the world, but everything wasn't a celebration. At the time, there was popular disillusionment with the costs of E.U. membership, and the predicted weakness of the euro against the U.S. dollar and the British pound.

In 2002, Italians officially abandoned their long-beloved lire and began trading in euros along with their neighbors to the north, including France and

Germany. As the new currency went into effect, counterfeiters and swindlers had a field day. But in general, especially among businesses, the transition went relatively smoothly.

On other fronts, during 2003, the Italian Parliament sent troops to Iraq after Baghdad was occupied by American forces, an event ending in tragedy when 18 service personnel were killed, Italy's highest number of military deaths since World War II.

Right before Christmas in 2004, Prime Minister Silvio Berlusconi received a present from judges in Milan. In a corruption trial that had dragged on for 4 years, he was absolved of all alleged crimes, including such serious charges as buying off judges. Berlusconi blamed the charges on "vindictive left-wing prosecutors." Judges ruled that there was "some substance" to one of the allegations—that is, funneling $434,404 into the private bank account of a judge—but noted that the statute of limitations had run out.

As much of the world watched and prayed, Pope John Paul II died in April 2005, at the age of 84, ending a reign of 26 years as pope. Worldwide mourning was proclaimed among Catholics. Later in the month, a new pope, Cardinal Joseph Ratzinger, was elected by his fellow cardinals. The Vatican's hard-liner on church doctrine took the papal throne as Benedict XVI.

Through 2006, Italy continued to make headlines around the world, beginning in January when the country announced that it was withdrawing nearly 3,000 troops from Iraq, a defeat for President George Bush. Italy's defense minister, Antonio Martino, disliked calling it a "retreat," preferring to use the word "return."

The year 2006 also saw the brief return of Romano Prodi, who took the office of prime minister after narrowly defeating the controversial Silvio Berlusconi.

During much of 2007, Prodi was called a solid, competent, but boring prime minister, not exactly known for either charisma or accomplishment. His political enemies called him *Mortadella,* named after the famous but rather bland sausage of Bologna. But following a scandal in the Ministry of Justice, Prodi lost a vote of confidence in the Senate and resigned as prime minister in January 2008.

In April 2008, Berlusconi won a third term as Italy's prime minister, with a strong mandate to deal with deep economic and social problems. The new PM swept into office with a vow to cut taxes and rein in the country's monstrous debt, all this in the midst of numerous sex scandals and charges of corruption. With the return of Berlusconi, Italians elected their 62nd government since World War II.

Italy's growth rate has been slowing down for a decade, and by 2010 it suffered massive losses of its market share of world trade with the global financial crisis. The meltdown has revealed structural weaknesses in the Italian economy, underscoring the urgency of structural reform. The authorities are working to gradually reduce the deficit to below 3% of GDP by 2012.

ART & ARCHITECTURE

The mysterious Etruscans, whose origins lay probably somewhere in Mesopotamia, brought the first truly impressive art and architecture to mainland Italy, although the Greeks had left behind great monuments, especially in Sicily.

Art 101

ETRUSCANS & ROMANS   Etruscan remains are mostly found in museums (the best in the Tuscan towns **Volterra, Cortona,** and **Chiusi,** and at Rome in the **Villa Giulia** and **Vatican museums**). Notable works include the bronze Chimera at Florence's archaeology museum, carved alabaster urns and the elongated bronze statuette *Shade of the Evening* in Volterra's Guarnacci museum, and terra-cotta sarcophagi covers of reclining figures in museums across Tuscany and in Rome's Villa Giulia.

As Rome asserted its own identity and overpowered its Etruscan masters, it borrowed heavily from themes established by Etruscan artists and architects. In time, however, the Romans discovered Greek art and fell in love with that country's Hellenistic tradition, which the Romans continued in a somewhat altered—some say corrupted—form in the West.

The greatest Greek or Hellenistic statues are to be seen today in the Vatican Museums in Rome.

Along with an army of also-ran statues and busts gracing most archaeological collections in Italy, you'll find a few standouts. In Rome, look for the marble **bas-reliefs** (sculptures that project slightly from a flat surface) on the Arch of Constantine, the sculpture and mosaic collections at the Museo Nazionale Romano, and the gilded equestrian statue of Marcus Aurelius at the Capitoline Museums.

BYZANTINE & ROMANESQUE   Art and architecture in the centuries that followed the collapse of Rome (5th–13th c.) became known as Byzantine and Romanesque art.

The **Byzantine** style of painting and mosaic was very stylized and static. Faces (and eyes) were almond shaped with pointy little chins; noses were long, with a spoonlike depression at the top; and folds in robes (always blue over red) were represented by stylized crosshatching in gold leaf.

The best examples of Byzantine art are found in the churches of Ravenna with their stylized mosaics, especially at San Vitale. Of course, the greatest example of a late Byzantine church is the Basilica di San Marco in Venice.

Romanesque sculpture was more fluid but still far from naturalistic. Often wonderfully childlike in its narrative simplicity, the work frequently mixes biblical scenes with the myths and motifs of local pagan traditions that were being slowly incorporated into early medieval Christianity.

The 48 relief panels of the bronze doors of the Basilica San Zeno Maggiore in Verona are one of the greatest remaining examples of Romanesque sculpture in Italy, dating from the 9th to the 11th centuries. The exterior of the baptistery at Parma sports a series of Romanesque allegorical friezes, masterpieces by **Benedetto Antelami.**

GOTHIC   As the appeal of Romanesque and the Byzantine faded, a Gothic or late-medieval style flourished from the 13th to the 15th centuries. Although the Gothic age continued to be religious, many secular buildings arose, including an array of *palazzos* showing off the prestige and wealth of the ruling families. Artists such as **Cimabue** (1251–1302), the Florentine painter, and **Giotto** (1266–1337), the greatest Gothic artist, lifted painting from its Byzantine funk and set it on the road to realism. Giotto's best works are fresco cycles in Assisi's Basilica di San Francesco. He was a harbinger of the oncoming Renaissance, which would forever change art and architecture.

THE FLOWERING OF THE RENAISSANCE   The Italian Renaissance was born in Florence during the 15th century and flourished until the mid–17th century. The powerful Medici family emerged as Italy's greatest art patrons. Innovative young painters, sculptors, and architects broke with static medieval traditions in pursuit of a greater degree of expressiveness and naturalism. Sculptors such as **Donatello** (1386–1466) cast the first free-standing nude since antiquity (see Donatello's *David* in Florence's Bargello Museum), along with others of his masterpieces.

Ghiberti (1378–1455) labored for 50 years to complete the doors now known as the "Gates of Paradise," for Florence Baptistery. **Raphael** (1483–1520) produced a body of work in 37 short years that ignited European painters for generations to come. See his Madonnas and papal portraits in Florence's Uffizi and Palazzo Pitti.

But the world's greatest artist in sculpture, painting, and architecture was **Michelangelo** (1475–1564), whose career marked the apogee of the Renaissance. His *David* at the Galleria dell'Accademia in Florence is the world's most famous statue, and his Sistine Chapel frescoes have lured millions to the Vatican Museums in Rome.

The epitome of the Renaissance man, **Leonardo da Vinci** (1452–1519), gave the world his fresco *The Last Supper,* now in Milan's Santa Maria delle Grazie, and the *Annunciation* (1481) in Florence's Uffizi, but his masterpiece, the *Mona Lisa,* rests in the Louvre in Paris.

Titian's *Man with the Gray Eyes,* which hangs in the Uffizi in Florence.

Piazza Maggiore, with the Basilica di San Petronio, Bologna.

A detail of God giving life to Adam, from Michelangelo's ceiling of the Sistine Chapel in Rome.

The period known as the **High Renaissance** was said to last for only about 25 years, beginning in the early 16th century. The father of the Venetian High Renaissance was **Titian** (1485–1576), known for his devotion to color and tonality. His masterpieces rest in such galleries as Florence's Uffizi or its Palazzo Pitti, and in the galleries of Venice. In time, the High Renaissance stagnated, producing vapid works of technical perfection but with little substance. Several artists sought ways out of this downward artistic spiral.

BAROQUE & ROCOCO In the late 16th and early 17th centuries, lasting into the 18th century, **baroque** art and architecture swept Europe, including Italy.

The baroque, a more theatrical and decorative take on the Renaissance, mixes a kind of superrealism based on using peasants as models and an exaggerated use of light and dark, called chiaroscuro, with compositional complexity and explosions of dynamic fury, movement, color, and figures. The even more dramatic **rococo** is this later baroque art gone awry, frothy and chaotic.

The baroque period produced many fine artists, but only a few true geniuses, including **Caravaggio** (1571–1610), who added his chiaroscuro technique of playing areas of harsh light off deep, black shadows. Among his masterpieces are the *St. Matthew* (1599) cycle in Rome's San Luigi dei Francesi, a series of paintings in Rome's Galleria Borghese, the *Deposition* (1604) in the Vatican Museums, and several more in Florence's Uffizi Gallery and Palazzo Pitti.

Bernini (1598–1680) was the greatest baroque sculptor, a fantastic architect, and no mean painter. His finest sculptures are in Rome. In the Galleria Borghese are his *Aeneas and Anchises* (1613), *Apollo and Daphne* (1624), and *David* (1623–24)—his version recalls a baroque man of action rather than a Renaissance man of contemplation like Michelangelo's *David.*

Tiepolo (1696–1770), arguably the best of the rococo artists, specialized in ceiling frescoes and canvases meant to be placed in a ceiling with frothy, cloud-filled heavens of light, angels, and pale, early morning colors. He painted many works for villas of the Veneto.

LATE 18TH CENTURY TO TODAY   After carrying the banner of artistic innovation for more than a millennium, Italy began to run out of steam with the baroque, leaving countries such as France to develop the heights of **neoclassicism** (although Italy produced a few fine neoclassical sculptures) and the late-19th-century Impressionism (Italy had its own version, called the **Macchiaioli,** in Tuscany).

Prior to that, during the late 18th century, it produced a few great artists. Among the more notable is **Antonio Canova** (1757–1822), Italy's major neoclassical sculptor, who became notorious for painting both Napoleon and his sister Pauline as nudes. His works are in Venice's Correr Civic Museum, Rome's Galleria Borghese, and Florence's Palazzi Pitti.

In the early 20th century, the largely Italian Futurist movement flourished. In simplistic terms, it rejected everything old, favoring the technology of the future and extolling the glories of the industrial age. Painting and sculpture were heavily influenced by this movement.

Among the artists emerging from this period was **Giorgio de Chirico** (1888–1978). He was hailed for his oneiric cityscapes, but after 1918 he became a classicist, claiming he was the heir to Titian.

Amedeo Modigliani (1884–1920) bridged the gap between Toulouse-Lautrec and the 1920s Art Deco painters. The victim of a tragic life, he excelled in both painting and sculpture and was not really part of any movement, but he was highly individualistic in his vast output before his early death.

Umberto Boccioni (1882–1916), a painter and sculptor, was a purer Futurist, capturing speed, technology, and dynamism in his output. Boccioni's scene of railroad station farewells, launched in 1911, immortalized him.

Architecture 101

In Italy, very few buildings (especially churches) were constructed in only one particular style. Massive, expensive structures often took centuries to complete, during which time tastes changed and plans were altered.

CLASSICAL: GREEKS & ROMANS   The **Greeks** from the 6th century B.C. to the 4th century A.D. settled Sicily and southern Italy, and left behind some of the best-preserved ancient temples in the world.

Even so, it was Rome that flourished magnificently in architecture, advancing in size and majesty far beyond the examples set by the Greeks. Much of this development was because of the discovery of a primitive form of concrete and the fine-tuning of the arch, which was used with a logic, rhythm, and ease never before seen.

Monumental buildings were erected, each an embodiment of the strength, power, and organization of the empire itself. Some of the best examples still stand today in Rome, notably Trajan's Forum, Caracalla's Baths, the Colosseum, and Hadrian's Pantheon.

Classical orders were simplified into types of column capitals, with the least ornate used on a building's ground level and the most ornate used on the top: Doric (a plain capital), Ionic (a capital with a scroll), and Corinthian (a capital with flowering acanthus leaves).

Three **Roman cities** have been preserved, with street plans and, in some cases, even buildings remaining intact: doomed **Pompeii** and its neighbor **Herculaneum** (both buried by Vesuvius's A.D. 79 eruption), and Rome's ancient seaport **Ostia Antica.**

ROMANESQUE   Flourishing from A.D. 800 to 1300, Romanesque architecture took its inspiration and rounded arches from ancient Rome. Its architects concentrated on building large churches with wide aisles to accommodate the masses.

Modena's Duomo (12th c.) marks one of the earliest appearances of rounded arches, and its facade is covered with great Romanesque reliefs. **Milan's Basilica di San Ambrogio** (11th–12th c.) is festooned with the tiered loggias and arcades that became hallmarks of the Lombard Romanesque.

Pisa's cathedral group (1153–1360s) is typical of the Pisan-Romanesque style, with stacked arcades of mismatched columns in the cathedral's facade (and wrapping around the famous Leaning Tower of Pisa) and blind arcading set with lozenges. **Lucca's Cattedrale di San Martino** and **San Michele in Foro** (11th–14th c.) are two more prime examples of the style.

GOTHIC   By the late 12th century, engineering developments freed architecture from the heavy, thick walls of the Romanesque and allowed ceilings to soar, walls to thin, and windows to proliferate.

The Gothic style was characterized by cross vaults, flying buttresses, pointed arches, and stained-glass windows.

The only truly French-style Gothic church in Italy is Milan's massive Duomo and Baptistery (begun ca. 1386), a lacy festival of pinnacles, buttresses, and pointy arches. Siena's Duomo (1136–1382), though started in the late Romanesque, has enough Giovanni Pisano sculptures and pointy arches to be considered Gothic.

RENAISSANCE   As in painting, Renaissance architectural rules from the 15th to the 17th centuries stressed proportion, order, classical inspiration, and mathematical precision to create unified, balanced structures.

An architect, **Filippo Brunelleschi** (1377–1476), in the early 1400s, grasped the concept of "perspective" and provided artists with ground rules for creating the illusion of three dimensions on a flat surface. Among his masterpieces in **Florence** are the Basilica di Santa Croce's **Pazzi Chapel** (1442–46), decorated with Donatello roundels; the interior of the **Basilica di San Lorenzo** (1425–46); and, most famous, the ingenious **dome** capping **Il Duomo** (1420–46). Brunelleschi traveled to Rome and studied the Pantheon up close to unlock the engineering secrets of its vast dome to build his own.

Michelangelo (1475–1564) took up architecture late in life, designing **Florence's Medici Laurentian Library** (1524) and **New Sacristy** (1524–34), which houses the Medici Tombs at Basilica di San Lorenzo. In **Rome,** you can see his crowning glory, the soaring **dome of St. Peter's Basilica,** among other structures.

The third great High Renaissance architect was **Andrea Palladio** (1508–80), who worked in a classical mode of columns, porticoes, pediments, and other ancient temple–inspired features. His masterpieces include **Villa Foscari** and the great **Villa Rotonda,** both in the **Veneto** countryside around Vicenza.

BAROQUE & ROCOCO   More than any other movement, the **baroque** (17th–18th c.) aimed toward a seamless meshing of architecture and art. The stuccoes, sculptures, and paintings were all carefully designed to complement each other—and the space itself—to create a unified whole. Excessively complex and dripping with decorative tidbits, **rococo** is kind of a twisted version of the baroque.

The baroque flourished across Italy. Though relatively sedate, Carlo Maderno's facade and Bernini's sweeping elliptical colonnade for Rome's **St. Peter's Square** make one of Italy's most famous baroque assemblages. One of the quirkiest and most felicitous baroque styles flourished in the churches of the Apulian city **Lecce.** For the rococo—more a decorative than architectural movement—look no further than Rome's **Spanish Steps** (1726), by architect de Sanctis, or the **Trevi Fountain** (1762), by Salvi.

NEOCLASSICAL TO MODERN   As a backlash against the excesses of the baroque and rococo, architects began turning to the austere simplicity and grandeur of the classical age and inaugurated the **neoclassical** style by the middle of the 18th century. Their work was inspired by the rediscovery of Pompeii and other ancient sites.

The **Industrial Age** of the 19th century brought with it the first genteel shopping malls of glass and steel. The country's take on the early-20th-century Art Nouveau movement was called **Liberty style.** Mussolini made a spirited attempt to bring back ancient Rome in what can only be called **Fascist architecture.** Since then, Italy has built mostly concrete-and-glass **skyscrapers,** like the rest of the world, although a few architects in the medium have stood out.

Of the **neoclassical, Caserta's Royal Palace** (1752–74), outside Naples, was a conscious attempt to create a Versailles for the Bourbon monarchs. The unbelievably huge (and almost universally derided) **Vittorio Emanuele Monument** (1884–1927) in Rome has been compared to a wedding cake or a Victorian typewriter.

Fascist architecture still infests corners of Italy. You can see it at its best in Rome's planned satellite community called **EUR,** which includes a multistory "square Colosseum" so funky that it has been featured in many a film and music video. The **mid–20th century** was dominated by **Pier Luigi Nervi** (1891–1979) and his reinforced concrete buildings, Florence's **Giovanni Berta Stadium** (1932), Rome's **Palazzeto dello Sport stadium** (1960), and Turin's **Exposition Hall** (1949).

ITALY IN POPULAR CULTURE: BOOKS, FILMS & MUSIC

Recommended Reading

GENERAL & HISTORY   Luigi Barzini's *The Italians* (Macmillan) should almost be required reading for anyone contemplating a trip to Italy. It's hailed as the liveliest analysis yet of the Italian character.

Edward Gibbon's 1776 *The History of the Decline and Fall of the Roman Empire* is published in six volumes, but Penguin issues a manageable abridgement. It has been noted as one of the greatest histories ever written.

ART & ARCHITECTURE   One of the best accounts of the Renaissance is Peter Murray's *The Architecture of the Italian Renaissance* (Schocken). The same subject is covered by Frederick N. Hartt in his *History of Italian Renaissance Painting* (Abrams).

Giorgio Vasari's *The Lives of the Most Eminent Italian Architects, Painters, and Sculptors* was published in 1550, and it remains the definitive work on Renaissance artists—by one who knew many of them personally—from Cimabue to Michelangelo. Penguin Classics issues a paperback abridged version called *Lives of the Artists*.

FICTION & BIOGRAPHY   Writers have tried to capture the peculiar nature of Italy in such notable works as Thomas Mann's *Death in Venice* (Random House) and E. M. Forster's *A Room with a View* (Random House). Fred M. Stewart spins a lively tale in *Century* (NAL), tracing the saga of several generations of an Italian family.

Umberto Eco is popular worldwide, and his first blockbuster murder mystery *The Name of the Rose* (Harcourt Brace) can be an entertaining primer on the political and monastic world of medieval Italy.

The novels of Alberto Moravia (1907–90) are classified as neorealism. Moravia is one of the best-known Italian writers read in English. Notable works include *Roman Tales* (Farrar, Straus & Giroux), *The Woman of Rome* (Penguin), and *The Conformist* (Greenwood Press).

Michelangelo's life was novelized (and later made into a movie) by Irving Stone in *The Agony and the Ecstasy* (Doubleday), which also offers an insight into the Florentine politics of the day.

Recommended Viewing

Although Italy continues to produce talented new actors, writers, and directors, the Italian film industry has, on the whole, never regained the glory enjoyed in the postwar era. The golden oldies are still the best.

Roberto Rossellini's *Rome, Open City* (1946) influenced Hollywood's films noir of the late 1940s. Set in a poor section of occupied Rome, the film tells the story of a partisan priest and a Communist who aid the Resistance.

The Leopard (1963), set in Sicily, gained a world audience for Luchino Visconti and was the first major Italian film made in color.

Federico Fellini burst into Italian cinema with his highly individual style, beginning with *La Strada* (1954) and going on to such classics as *Juliet of the Spirits* (1965), *Amarcord* (1974), and *The City of Women* (1980). *La Dolce Vita* (1961) helped to define an era.

Federico Fellini's *La Dolce Vita*.

Marxist, homosexual, and practicing Catholic, Pier Paolo Pasolini was the most controversial of Italian filmmakers until his mysterious murder in 1975. Explicit sex scenes in *Decameron* (1971) made it a world box-office hit.

Bernardo Bertolucci, once an assistant to Pasolini, achieved fame with such films as *The Conformist* (1970), based on the novel by Moravia. One of his biggest international films was *Last Tango in Paris* (1971), starring Marlon Brando.

Ralph Fiennes starred in director Anthony Minghella's *The English Patient* (1996), which used many small towns in Tuscany for its setting. Minghella also directed *The Talented Mr. Ripley* (1999), with its wonderful scenes of Italy. Cher, impersonating Peggy Guggenheim, appeared in *Tea with Mussolini* (1999), a semiautobiographical tale from the early life of director Franco Zeffirelli. Frances Mayes's *Under the Tuscan Sun* (2003), directed by Audrey Wells, was as light as a gentle glass of wine and just as enjoyable.

Russell Crowe won an Oscar for his appearance in Ridley Scott's *Gladiator* (2000). Matera, Italy, served as the backdrop for the Crucifixion in Mel Gibson's controversial *The Passion of the Christ* (2004).

Recommended Listening

MEDIEVAL & RENAISSANCE MUSIC A recording that might expose you to the fruit of the labors of medieval Guido Monaco of Arezzo is *Sunday Vespers/ Vespers of the Madonna,* recorded by S. Giorgio Maggiore Schola Choir, G. Ernetti, conductor (Cetra Records LPU 0046). Religious music was greatly enhanced several centuries later by the compositions of Palestrina, whose work is admirably recorded in *Missa de Beata Virgine (Three Motets),* sung by the Spandauer Kantorei (Turnabout TV 34-309).

One well-received interpretation of Monteverdi's famous choral work *L'Incoronazione di Poppea* was recorded by the Concentus Musicus Wien (Telefunken 6.35-247 HB). By the same composer, but in a different genre, is Monteverdi's *Seventh Book of Madrigals,* sung by an Italian vocal quartet known as the Ensemble Concerto (Tactus TAC 560 31103).

An excellent collection of the late Renaissance's sonatas, canzonettas, and madrigals is titled *Music from the Time of Guido Reni,* recorded by the Aurora Ensemble (Tactus TAC 56012001).

ORCHESTRAL & OPERATIC WORKS One excellent (and exhaustive) overview of the work of Corelli is his *Complete Works,* recorded by the Academia Byzantina, conducted by Carlo Chiarappa (Europa Musica Eur 350-202).

Bottesini's *Virtuoso Works for Double-Bass and Strings,* performed by I Solisti Agilani and conducted by Vittorio Antonelli (Nuova Era NUO 6810), might be one of the finest showcases ever for the double bass. Cherubini's *Harpsichord Sonatas Nos. 1–6* provides a highly genteel and attractively restrained insight into the work of a conservative Italian classicist.

A good assemblage of great opera from the most evocative and dramatic singer who ever hit a high C on the operatic stage is Maria Callas's *La Voce: Historic Recordings of the Great Diva* (Suite SUI 5002). This recording brings together Callas's spectacular arias.

CURRENT MUSIC STARS Worthy of the "electric" in his name, **Filippo Voltaggio** is a high-voltage singer and songwriter who records songs Italians and would-be Italians love to listen to. **Paolo Conte** writes and performs his own material in his grainy, resonant voice redolent of Francophone singers such as Jacques Brel. His albums selling in the millions, Italian singer and composer **Lucio Dalla** tours the world, finding new fans in places like South America.

Laura Pausini, an Italian pop singer from Ravenna, has sold more than 26 million records and has more than 160 platinum albums.

Finally, there is **Andrea Bocelli,** one of our favorites. One critic wrote that a voice like Bocelli's only comes along every generation or so. Bocelli has wonderful opera skills and is a powerful pop singer as well. His language of love is universal.

A TASTE OF ITALY

Italians are among the world's greatest cooks. Just ask any one of them. Despite the unification of Italy, regional tradition still dominates the various kitchens, from Rome to Lombardy, from the Valle d'Aosta to Sicily. The term "Italian cuisine" has little meaning unless it's more clearly defined as Neapolitan, Roman, Sardinian, Sicilian, Venetian, Piedmontese, Tuscan, or whatever. Each region has a flavor and a taste of its own, as well as a detailed repertoire of local dishes.

Food has always been one of life's great pleasures for the Italians. This has been true even from the earliest days: To judge from the lifelike banquet scenes found in Etruscan tombs, the Etruscans loved food and took delight in enjoying it. The Romans became famous for their never-ending banquets and for their love of exotic treats, such as flamingo tongues.

Although culinary styles vary, Italy abounds in *trattorie* specializing in local dishes—some of which are a delight for carnivores, such as the renowned *bistecca alla fiorentina* (cut from flavorful Chianina beef and then chargrilled and served with a fruity olive oil). Other dishes, especially those found at the antipasti buffet, would appeal to every vegetarian's heart: peppers, greens, onions, pastas, beans, tomatoes, and fennel.

Fresh tomatoes, for sale at a Roman market, are a staple of Italian cuisine.

Incidentally, except in the south, Italians don't use as much garlic in their food as many foreigners seem to believe. Many Italian dishes, especially those in the north, are butter-based. And spaghetti and meatballs isn't an Italian dish, although certain restaurants throughout the country have taken to serving it "for homesick Americans."

Cuisines Around the Country

Rome is the best place to introduce yourself to Italian cuisine because it boasts specialty restaurants representing every region. Throughout your Roman holiday, you'll encounter such specialties as *zuppa di pesce* (a soup or stew of various fish, cooked in white wine and flavored with herbs), cannelloni (tube-shaped pasta baked with any number of stuffings), *riso con i gamberi* (rice with shrimp, peas, and mushrooms, flavored with white wine and garlic), *scampi alla griglia* (grilled prawns), *quaglie col risotto e tartufi* (quail with rice and truffles), *lepre alla cacciatora* (hare flavored with tomato sauce and herbs), zabaglione (a creamy dessert made with sugar, egg yolks, and Marsala), *gnocchi alla romana* (potato-flour dumplings with a meat sauce, covered with grated cheese), *abbacchio* (baby spring lamb, often roasted over an open fire), *saltimbocca alla romana* (literally "jump-in-your-mouth"—thin slices of veal with sage, ham, and cheese), *fritto alla romana* (a mixed fry likely to include everything from brains to artichokes), *carciofi alla romana* (tender artichokes cooked with herbs such as mint and garlic, flavored with white wine), *fettuccine all'uovo* (egg noodles with butter and cheese), *zuppa di cozze* (a hearty bowl of mussels cooked in broth), *fritto di scampi e calamaretti* (baby squid and prawns, fast-fried), *fragoline* (wild strawberries, in this case from the Alban Hills), and finocchio (fennel, a celery-like raw vegetable with the flavor of anisette, often eaten as a dessert or in a salad).

From Rome, it's on to **Tuscany,** where you'll encounter the hearty cuisine of the Tuscan hills. The main ingredient for almost any meal is the superb local olive oil, adored for its low acidity and lovely flavor. In Italy's south, the olives are gathered only after they've fallen off the trees, but here they're handpicked off the trees so that they won't get bruised (ensuring lower acidity and milder aroma). Typical Tuscan pastas are pappardelle and penne mingled with a variety of sauces, many of which are tomato based. Tuscans are extremely fond of strong cheeses such as Gorgonzola, fontina, and parmigiano. Meat and fish are prepared simply and might seem undercooked; locals would argue that it's better to let the inherent flavor of the ingredients survive the cooking process.

Long ago, flavors from the **Venezia** district were called "tasty, straightforward, and homely" by one food critic, and we concur. Two of the most typical dishes are *fegato alla veneziana* (liver and onions) and *risi e bisi* (rice and fresh peas). Seafood figures heavily in the Venetian diet, and grilled fish is often served with the bitter red radicchio, a lettuce that comes from Treviso.

In **Lombardy,** the cooking is more refined and flavorful. No dish here is more famous than *cotoletta alla milanese* (cutlets of tender veal dipped in egg and bread crumbs and fried in olive oil until they're a golden brown)—the Viennese call it Wiener schnitzel. *Osso buco* is the other great dish of Lombardy; this is cooked with the shin bone of veal in a ragout sauce and served on rice and peas. *Risotto alla milanese* is also a classic—rice that can be dressed in almost any way, depending on the chef's imagination. It's often flavored with saffron, butter, and chicken giblets; it's seemingly always served with heaps of Parmigiano-Reggiano cheese. Polenta, a cornmeal mush that's "more than mush," replaces pasta in some parts of northeastern Italy.

Cheese for sale in Pienza.

The cooking in the **Piedmont** and the **Aosta Valley** is different from that in the rest of Italy. Cuisine here is said to appeal to strong-hearted men returning from a hard day's work in the mountains. You get such dishes as *bagna cauda,* a sauce made with olive oil, garlic, butter, and anchovies, in which you dip uncooked fresh vegetables. *Fonduta* is also celebrated—made with melted fontina cheese, butter, milk, egg yolks, and, for an elegant touch, white truffles.

In the **Trentino–Alto Adige** area, the cooking is naturally influenced by the traditions of the Austrian and Germanic kitchens. South Tirol, of course, used to belong to Austria, and here you get tasty strudel pastries.

Liguria turns to the sea for a great deal of its cuisine, as reflected by its version of bouillabaisse, a *burrida* flavored with spices. But its most famous food item is pesto, a sauce made with fresh basil, garlic, cheese, and walnuts, which is used to dress pasta, fish, and many other dishes.

Emilia-Romagna is one of the country's great gastronomic centers. Rich in produce, its school of cooking produces many notable pastas now common around Italy: *tagliatelle,* tortellini, and cappelletti (larger than tortellini and made in the form of "little hats"). *Tagliatelle,* of course, are long strips of macaroni, and tortellini are little squares of dough stuffed with chopped pork, veal, or whatever. Equally popular is lasagna, which by now everybody has heard of. In Bologna, it's often made by adding finely shredded spinach to the dough. The best-known sausage of the area is mortadella, and equally famous is a *cotoletta alla bolognese* (veal cutlet fried with a slice of ham or bacon). The distinctive and famous cheese Parmigiano-Reggiano is a product of Parma and also Reggio Emilia. *Zampone* (stuffed pig's foot) is a specialty of Modena. Parma is also known for its ham, which is fashioned into air-cured *prosciutto di Parma.* Served in paper-thin slices, it's deliciously sweet and hailed by gourmets as the finest in the world.

Much of the cookery of **Campania** (spaghetti with clam sauce, pizzas, and so forth) is already familiar to North Americans because so many Neapolitans moved to the New World and opened restaurants. Mozzarella is the classic cheese of this area. Mixed fish fries, done a golden brown, are a staple of nearly every table.

Sicily has a distinctive cuisine, with good, strong flavors and aromatic sauces. A staple of the diet is *maccheroni con le sarde* (spaghetti with pine nuts, fennel, spices, chopped sardines, and olive oil). Fish is good and fresh in Sicily (try swordfish). Among meat dishes, you'll see *involtini siciliani* (rolled meat with a stuffing of egg, ham, and cheese cooked in bread crumbs) on the menu. A *caponata* is a flavorful way of cooking eggplant in tomato sauce. The desserts and homemade pastries are excellent, including cannoli, cylindrical pastry cases stuffed with ricotta and candied fruit (or chocolate). Their ice creams, called gelati, are among the best in Italy.

And Some Vino to Wash It All Down . . .

Italy is the largest wine-producing country in the world; as far back as 800 B.C. the Etruscans were vintners. It's said that more soil is used in Italy for the cultivation of grapes than for the growing of food. Many Italian farmers produce wine just for their own consumption or for their relatives in "the big city." However, it wasn't until 1965 that laws were enacted to guarantee regular consistency in winemaking. Wines regulated by the government are labeled "DOC" (*Denominazione di Origine Controllata*). If you see "DOCG" on a label (the "G" means *garantita*), that means even better quality control.

THE VINEYARDS OF ITALY

Following traditions established by the ancient Greeks, Italy produces more wine than any other nation. More than 1.6 million hectares (4 million acres) of soil are cultivated as vineyards, and recently there has been an increased emphasis on recognizing vintages from lesser known growers who might or might not be designated as working within a zone of controlled origin and name. (It's considered an honor, and usually a source of profit, to own vines within a DOC. Vintners who are presently limited to marketing their products as unpretentious table wines—*vino di tavola*—often expend great efforts lobbying for an elevated status as a DOC.)

Italy's wine producers range from among the most automated and techno-logically sophisticated in Europe to low-tech, labor-intensive family plots that turn out just a few hundred bottles per year. You can sometimes save money by buying directly from a producer (the signs beside the highway of any wine-pro-ducing district will advertise VENDITA DIRETTA). Not only will you avoid paying the retailer's markup, but you also might get a glimpse of the vines that produced the vintage you carry home with you.

Useful vocabulary words for such endeavors are *bottiglieria* (a simple wine shop) and *enoteca* (a more upscale shop where many vintages, from several grow-ers, are displayed and sold like magazines in a bookstore). In some cases, you can buy a glass of the product before you buy the bottle, and platters of cold cuts or cheeses are sometimes available to offset the tang (and alcoholic effects) of the wine.

REGIONAL WINES

Here we've cited only a few popular wines. Rest assured that there are hundreds more, and you'll have a great time sampling them to find your own favorites.

Latium: In this major wine-producing region, many of the local wines come from the Castelli Romani, the hill towns around Rome. Horace and Juve-nal sang the praises of Latium wines even in imperial times. These wines, experts agree, are best drunk when young, and they're most often white, mellow, and dry (or "demi-sec"). There are seven types, including **Falerno** (straw yellow in color) and **Cecubo** (often served with roast meat). Try also **Colli Albani** (straw yellow with amber tints, served with both fish and meat). The golden yellow wines of **Frascati** are famous, produced in both a demi-sec and a sweet variety, the latter served with dessert.

Tuscany: Tuscan wines rank with some of the finest reds in France. **Chi-anti** is the best known, and it comes in several varieties. The most highly regarded is **Chianti Classico,** a lively ruby-red wine mellow in flavor with a bouquet of violets. A good label is Antinori. A lesser known but remarkably fine Tuscan wine is **Brunello di Montalcino,** a brilliant garnet red served with roasts and game. The ruby-red, almost purple **Vino Nobile di Montepulciano** has a rich, rugged body; it's a noble wine that's aged for 4 years. The area around San Gimignano produces a light, sweet white wine called **Vernaccia.** While you're in Tuscany, order the wonderful dessert wine called **Vin Santo,** which tastes almost like sherry and is usually accompanied by biscotti that you dunk into your glass.

Emilia-Romagna: The sparkling **Lambrusco** of this region is by now best known outside of Italy, but this wine can be of widely varying quality. Most of it is a brilliant ruby red. Be more experimental and try such wines as the dark ruby-red **Sangiovese** (with a delicate bouquet) and the golden yellow **Albana,** somewhat sweet. **Trebbiano,** generally dry, is best served with fish.

The Veneto: From this rich breadbasket in northeastern Italy come such world-famous wines as **Bardolino** (a light ruby red often served with poultry), **Valpolicella** (produced in "ordinary quality" and "superior dry," best served with meats), and **Soave** (beloved by W. Somerset Maugham), which has a pale amber color with a light aroma and a velvety flavor. Also try one of the **cabernets,** either the ruby-red **Cabernet di Treviso** (ideal with roasts and game) or the even deeper ruby-red **Cabernet Franc,** which has a marked herbal bouquet and is served with roasts.

Trentino–Alto Adige: This area produces wine influenced by Austria. Known for its vineyards, the region has some 20 varieties of wine. The straw-yellow, slightly pale-green **Riesling** is served with fish, as is the pale greenish-yellow **Terlano. Santa Maddalena,** a cross between garnet and ruby, is served with wild fowl and red meats, and **Traminer,** straw yellow, has a distinctive aroma and is served with fish. A **pinot bianco,** straw yellow with greenish glints, has a light bouquet and a noble history, and is also served with fish.

Friuli–Venezia Giulia: This area attracts those who enjoy a "brut" wine with a trace of flint. From classic grapes come **merlot,** deep ruby in color, and several varieties of **pinot,** including **pinot grigio,** whose color ranges from straw yellow to gray-pink (good with fish). Also served with fish, the **sauvignon** has a straw-yellow color and a delicate bouquet.

Lombardy: These wines are justly renowned—and, if you don't believe us, would you instead take the advice of Leonardo da Vinci, Pliny, and Virgil? These great men have sung the praises of this wine-rich region bordered by the Alps to the north and the Po River to the south. To go with the tasty, refined cuisine of the Lombard kitchen are such wines as **Frecciarossa** (a pale straw-yellow color with a delicate bouquet—order it with fish), **Sassella** (bright ruby red—order it with game, red meat, and roasts), and the amusingly named **Inferno** (a deep ruby red with a penetrating bouquet; order it with meats).

The Piedmont: The finest wines in Italy, mostly red, are said to be produced on the vine-clad slopes of the Piedmont. Of course, **Asti Spumante,** the color of straw with an abundant champagnelike foam, is the prototype of Italian sparkling wines. While traveling through this area of northwestern Italy, you'll want to sample **Barbaresco** (brilliant ruby red with a delicate flavor—order it with red meats), **Barolo** (also brilliant ruby red, best when it mellows into a velvety old age), **Cortese** (pale straw yellow with green glints—order it with fish), and **Gattinara** (an intense ruby-red beauty in youth that changes with age). Piedmont is also the home of **vermouth,** a white wine to which aromatic herbs and spices, among other ingredients, have been added; it's served as an aperitif.

Liguria: This area doesn't have as many wine-producing regions as other parts of Italy, yet it grows dozens of different grapes. These are made into such wines as **Dolceacqua** (lightish ruby red, served with hearty food) and **Vermentino Ligure** (pale yellow with a good bouquet, often served with fish).

Campania: From the volcanic soil of Vesuvius, the wines of Campania have been extolled for 2,000 years. Homer praised the glory of **Falerno,** straw yellow in color. Neapolitans are fond of ordering a wine known as **Lacrima Christi (Tears of Christ)** to accompany many seafood dishes. It comes in amber, red, and pink. With meat dishes, try the dark mulberry-color **Gragnano,**

which has a faint bouquet of faded violets. The reds and whites of Ischia and Capri are also justly renowned.

Apulia: The heel of the Italian boot, Apulia, produces more wine than any other part of Italy. Try **Castel del Monte,** which comes in shades of pink, white, and red. Other wines of the region are the dull-red **Aleatico di Puglia,** with a mellow taste so sweet and aromatic that it's almost a liqueur; **Barletta,** a highly alcoholic wine made from grapes grown around Troia; the notably pleasant and fragrant **Mistella,** a really fleshy wine usually offered with desserts; the brilliant amber **Moscato della Murge,** aromatic and sweet; **Moscato di Trani,** which is velvety and tastes of a bouquet of faded roses; and **Primitivo di Gioia,** a full-bodied acid wine that, when dry, appears with roasts and, when sweet, appears with desserts. One of the region's best wines to drink with fish is **Torre Giulia,** which is dark yellow tending toward amber—a "brut" wine with a distinctive bouquet.

Sicily: The wines of Sicily, called a "paradise of the grape," were extolled by the ancient poets, including Martial. Caesar himself lavished praise on **Mamertine** when it was served at a banquet honoring his third consulship. **Marsala,** an amber wine served with desserts, is the most famous wine of Sicily; it's velvety and fruity and sometimes used in cooking, as in veal Marsala. The wines made from grapes grown in the volcanic soil of Etna come in both red and white varieties. Also try the **Corvo Bianco di Casteldaccia** (straw yellow, with a distinctive bouquet) and the **Corvo Rosso di Casteldaccia** (ruby red, almost garnet, full-bodied and fruity).

Other Drinks

Italians drink other libations as well. The most famous drink is **Campari,** bright red in color and flavored with herbs; it has a quinine bitterness to it. It's customary to serve it with ice cubes and soda.

Limoncello, a bright yellow drink made by infusing pure alcohol with lemon zest, has become Italy's second-most popular drink. It has long been a staple in the lemon-producing region along the Amalfi Coast in Capri and Sorrento, and recipes for the sweetly potent concoction have been passed down by families there for generations. About a decade ago, restaurants in Sorrento, Naples, and Rome started making their own versions. Visitors to those restaurants as well as the Sorrento peninsula began singing limoncello's praises and requesting

Lemons, used in making limoncello.

bottles to go. Now it's one of the most up-and-coming liqueurs in the world, thanks to heavy advertising promotions.

Beer, once treated as a libation of little interest, is still far inferior to wines produced domestically, but foreign beers, especially those of Ireland and England, are gaining great popularity with Italian youth, especially in Rome. This popularity is mainly because of atmospheric pubs, which now number more than 300 in Rome alone, where young people linger over a pint and a conversation. Most pubs are in the Roman center, and many are licensed by Guinness and its Guinness Italia operations. In a city with 5,000 watering holes, 300 pubs might seem like a drop, but because the clientele is young, the wine industry is trying to devise a plan to keep that drop from becoming a steady stream of Italians who prefer grain to grapes.

High-proof **grappa** is made from the "leftovers" after the grapes have been pressed. Many Italians drink this before or after dinner (some put it into their coffee). It's an acquired taste—to an untrained foreign palate, it often seems rough and harsh.

3

SUGGESTED ITALY ITINERARIES

t would be a delight to get "lost" in Italy, wandering about at your leisure, discovering unspoiled villages off the beaten path. But few of us have such a generous amount of time, and a lean-and-mean schedule is called for if you want to experience the best of a country in a ridiculously short amount of time.

If you're a time-pressed traveler, as most of us are, with only 1 or 2 weeks for the country, you may want to take our "Italy in 1 Week" or "Italy in 2 Weeks" trips. If you've been to Italy before, especially Rome and Florence, you may want to cut short your time in those cities and, say, spend a week touring increasingly chic Tuscany. Families might want to consider the family-fun tour, with more focus on sights that appeal to kids.

Italy is so vast and treasure-filled that it's hard to resist the temptation to pack in too much in too short a time. It's a challenging, daunting destination, and you can't even skim the surface in 1 or 2 weeks—so relax, don't even try. If you're a first-time visitor, we recommend you go just for the nuggets, such as Rome, Siena, Florence, and Venice.

Italy ranks with Germany and France in offering Europe's best-maintained superhighways (called autostrade), and it also boasts one of the fastest and most efficient public transportation systems in the world, especially its national rail line. Rome or Milan stands at the hub of a vast transportation empire with many once-remote cities or towns now within easy reach of either metropolis—for example, from Rome, Florence can be reached in only 2 hours, and Naples in 2½ hours.

The itineraries that follow take you to some major attractions and some charming towns. The pace may be a bit breathless for some visitors, so skip a town or sight occasionally to have some chill-out time—after all, you're on vacation. Of course, you can use any of these itineraries as a jumping-off point to develop your own custom-made trip that more closely matches your interests—review chapter 1 to see what experiences or sights have special appeal to you.

THE REGIONS IN BRIEF

Italy isn't enormous, but the peninsula's shape gives you the impression of a much larger area; the ever-changing seacoast contributes to this feeling, as do the large islands of Sicily and Sardinia. Bordered on the northwest by France, on the north by Switzerland and Austria, and on the east by Slovenia, Italy is a land largely surrounded by the sea.

Two areas within Italy's boundaries aren't under the control of the Italian government: the **State of Vatican City** and the **Republic of San Marino.** Vatican City's 44 hectares (109 acres) were established in 1929 by a concordat between Pope Pius XI and Benito Mussolini, acting as head of the Italian government; the agreement also gave Roman Catholicism special status in Italy. The pope is the sovereign of the State of Vatican City, which has its own legal system and post office. The Republic of San Marino, with a capital of the same name,

PREVIOUS PAGE: **Gondola, Venice.**

The Regions of Italy

Enjoying an evening stroll near the Pantheon in Rome.

sits astride the slopes of Mount Titano, 23km (14 miles) from Rimini. It's small and completely surrounded by Italy, so it still exists only by the grace of Italy.

Here's a brief rundown of the cities and regions covered in this guide:

Rome & Latium

The region of **Latium** is dominated by **Rome,** capital of the ancient empire and the modern nation of Italy, and **Vatican City,** the independent papal state. Much of the civilized world was once ruled from here, from the days when Romulus and Remus are said to have founded Rome in 753 B.C. For generations, Rome was referred to as *caput mundi* (capital of the world). Its fortunes have fallen, of course, but it remains a timeless city, ranking with Paris and London as one of the top European destinations. There's no place with more artistic monuments—not even Venice or Florence. How much time should you budget for the capital? Italian writer Silvio Negro said, "A lifetime is not enough."

Florence, Tuscany & Umbria

Tuscany is one of the most culturally and politically influential provinces—the development of Italy without Tuscany is simply unthinkable. Tuscany, with its sun-warmed vineyards and towering cypresses, inspired the artists of the Renaissance. Nowhere in the world is the impact of the Renaissance still felt more fully than in its birthplace, **Florence,** the repository of artistic works left by Leonardo da Vinci, Michelangelo, and others. Since the 19th century, travelers have been flocking to Florence to see the Donatello bronzes, the Botticelli smiles, and all the other preeminent treasures. Alas, it's now an invasion, so you run the risk of being trampled underfoot as you explore the historic heart of the city. To escape, head for the nearby Tuscan hill towns, former stamping ground of the Guelphs and Ghibellines. The main cities to visit are **Lucca, Pisa,** and especially **Siena,** Florence's great historical rival with an inner core that appears to be caught in a time warp. As a final treat, visit **San Gimignano,** northwest of Siena, celebrated for its medieval "skyscrapers."

Pastoral, hilly, and fertile, **Umbria** is similar to Tuscany, but with fewer tourists. Its once-fortified network of hill towns is among the most charming in Italy. Crafted from millions of tons of gray-brown rocks, each town is a testament to the masonry and architectural skills of generations of craftsmen. Cities particularly worth a visit are **Perugia, Gubbio, Assisi, Spoleto** (site of the world-renowned annual arts festival), and **Orvieto,** a mysterious citadel once used as a stronghold by the Etruscans. Called the land of shadows, Umbria is often covered in a bluish haze that evokes an ethereal painted look. Many local artists have tried to capture the province's glow, with its sun-dappled hills, terraced vineyards, and miles of olive trees. If you're short on time, visit Assisi to check out Giotto's frescoes at the Basilica di San Francesco (they've been repaired since the 1997 earthquakes), and Perugia, the largest and richest of the province's cities.

Bologna & Emilia-Romagna

Italians seem to agree on only one thing: The food in **Emilia-Romagna** is the best in Italy. The region's capital, **Bologna,** boasts a stunning Renaissance core

with plenty of churches and arcades, a fine university with roots in the Middle Ages, and a populace with a reputation for leftist leanings. The region has one of the highest standards of living in Italy. When not dining in Bologna, you can take time to explore its artistic heritage. Other art cities abound—none more noble than Byzantine **Ravenna,** still living off its past glory as the one-time capital of the declining Roman Empire.

If you can visit only one more city in the region, make it **Parma,** to see the city center with its Duomo and baptistery and to view its National Gallery. This is the home of Parmigiano-Reggiano cheese and prosciutto. Also noteworthy is the home-town of the late opera star Luciano Pavarotti, **Modena,** known for its cuisine, its cathedral, and its Este Gallery. The Adriatic resort of **Rimini** and the medieval stronghold of **San Marino** are at the periphery of Emilia-Romagna.

The narrow streets of Bologna.

The Piazza San Marco in Venice, with a view of St. Mark's Cathedral.

Venice, the Veneto & the Dolomites

Northeastern Italy is one of Europe's treasure-troves, encompassing **Venice** (arguably the world's most beautiful city), the surrounding **Veneto** region, and the mighty **Dolomites** (including the **South Tyrol,** which Italy annexed from Austria after World War I). The Veneto, dotted with rich museums and some of the best architecture in Italy, sprawls across the verdant hills and flat plains between the Adriatic, the Dolomites, Verona, and the edges of Lake Garda. For many generations, the fortunes of the Veneto revolved around Venice, with its sumptuous palaces, romantic waterways, Palazzo Ducale, and Basilica di San Marco. Aging, decaying, and sinking into the sea, Venice is so alluring we almost want to say, visit it even if you have to skip Rome and Florence. Also recommended are three fabled art cities in the "Venetian Arc": **Verona,** of Romeo and Juliet fame; **Vicenza,** where 16th-century aristocrats lived in the villas of Andrea Palladio; and **Padua,** with its Giotto frescoes.

The region of **Trentino–Alto Adige** is far richer in culture, artistic treasures, and activities than the Valle d'Aosta (see "Piedmont & Valle d'Aosta," below), and its ski resort, **Cortina d'Ampezzo,** is far more fashionable than Courmayeur in the northwestern corridor. Its most interesting base (especially if you want to see the Austrian version of Italy) is **Trent (Trento),** the capital of Trentino. In the northeastern corner of Italy, the region of **Friuli-Venezia Giulia** is, in its own way, one of the most cosmopolitan and culturally sophisticated in Italy. Its capital is the port of **Trieste.** The area is filled with art from the Roman, Byzantine, and Romanesque-Gothic eras, and many of the public buildings (especially in Trieste) might remind you of Vienna.

Milan, Lombardy & the Lake District

Flat, fertile, prosperous, and politically conservative, **Lombardy** is dominated by **Milan** just as Latium is dominated by Rome. Lombardy is one of the world's leading commercial and cultural centers, and it has been ever since Milan developed into Italy's gateway to northern German-speaking Europe in the early Middle Ages. Although some people belittle Milan as an industrial city with a snobbish contempt for the poorer regions to the south, its fans compare it to New York. Milan's cathedral is Europe's third largest, its La Scala opera house is world renowned, and its museums and churches are a treasure-trove, with one containing Leonardo's *Last Supper*. However, Milan still doesn't have the sights and tourist interest of Rome, Florence, or Venice. Visit Milan if you have the time, though you'll find more charm in the neighboring art cities of **Bergamo, Brescia, Pavia, Cremona,** and **Mantua.** Also competing for your time will be the gorgeous lakes of **Como, Garda,** and **Maggiore,** which lie near Lombardy's eastern edge.

Piedmont & Valle d'Aosta

At Italy's extreme northwestern edge, sharing a set of Alpine peaks with France (which in some ways it resembles), **Piedmont** was the district from which Italy's dreams of unification spread in 1861. Long under the domination of the Austro-Hungarian Empire, Piedmont enjoys a cuisine laced with Alpine cheeses and dairy products. It's proud of its largest city, **Turin,** called the "Detroit of Italy" because it's the home of the Fiat empire, vermouth, Asti Spumante, and the Borsalino hat. Even though Turin is a great cosmopolitan center, it doesn't have the antique charm of Genoa or the sophistication, world-class dining, and chic shopping of Milan. Turin's most controversial sight is the Sacra Sindone (Holy Shroud), which many Catholics believe is the cloth in which Christ's body was wrapped when lowered from the cross.

Italy's window on Switzerland and France, the **Valle d'Aosta** (the smallest region) often serves as an introduction to the country, especially for those journeying from France through the Mont Blanc tunnel. The introduction is misleading, however, because Valle d'Aosta stands apart from the rest of Italy, a semiautonomous region of towering peaks and valleys in the northwestern corridor. It's more closely linked to France (especially the region of Savoy) than to Italy, and its residents speak an ancient French-derived dialect. The most important city in this region is the old Roman city of **Aosta,** which, except for some ruins, is rather dull. More intriguing are two of Italy's major ski resorts, **Courmayeur** and **Breuil-Cervinia,** which are topped only by Cortina d'Ampezzo in the Dolomites (see "Venice, the Veneto & the Dolomites," above). Many of the region's villages are crafted from gray rocks culled from the mountains that rise on all sides. The best time to visit is in summer or the deep of winter. Late spring and fall get rather sleepy in this part of the world.

Genoa & the Italian Riviera

Comprising most of the **Italian Riviera,** the region of **Liguria** incorporates the steeply sloping capital city of **Genoa,** charming medieval ports (**Portofino, Ventimiglia,** and **San Remo**), a huge naval base (**La Spezia**), and five

The Regions in Brief

Portofino.

traditional coastal communities **(Cinque Terre).** There's also a series of beach resorts **(Rapallo** and **Santa Margherita Ligure**) that resemble the French Riviera. Although overbuilt and overrun, the Italian Riviera is still a land of great beauty. It's actually two Rivieras: the **Riviera di Ponente** to the west, running from the French border to Genoa, and the **Riviera di Levante** to the east. Faced with a choice, we always gravitate toward the more glamorous and cosmopolitan Riviera di Levante. Italy's largest port, Genoa, also merits a visit for its rich culture and history.

Naples, the Amalfi Coast & Capri

More than any other region, **Campania** reverberates with the memories of the ancient Romans, who favored its strong sunlight, fertile soil, and bubbling sulfurous springs. It encompasses both the anarchy of **Naples** and the elegant beauty of **Capri** and the **Amalfi Coast.** The region also contains many sites specifically identified in ancient mythology (lakes defined as the entrance to the Kingdom of the Dead, for example) and some of the world's most renowned ancient ruins (including **Pompeii, Herculaneum,** and **Paestum**). Campania is overrun, overcrowded, and over-everything, but it still lures visitors. Allow at least a day for Naples, which has amazing museums and the world's worst traffic outside Cairo. Pompeii, Herculaneum, and Paestum are for the ruins collectors, while those seeking fun in the sun head for Capri or Portofino. The leading resorts along the Amalfi Drive (even though they're not exactly undiscovered) are **Ravello** (not on the sea) and **Positano** (on the sea). **Amalfi** and **Sorrento** also have beautiful seaside settings. However, their more affordable hotels tend to make them that much more crowded.

Apulia

Sun-drenched and poor, **Apulia** (depending on the dialect, Le Puglie or Puglia) forms the heel of the Italian boot. It's the most frequently visited province of

Italy's far south; part of its allure lies in its string of coastal resorts. The *trulli* houses of **Alberobello** are known for their unique cylindrical shapes and conical flagstone-sheathed roofs. Among the region's largest cities are **Bari** (the capital), **Foggia,** and **Brindisi** (gateway to Greece, with which the town shares many characteristics). Each of these is a modern disaster, filled with tawdry buildings, heavy traffic, and rising crime rates (tourists are often the victims). Most visitors pass through Bari (though it's a favorite with backpackers), and the only reason to spend a night in Brindisi is to catch the ferry to Greece the next morning.

Sicily

The largest Mediterranean island, **Sicily,** is a land of beauty, mystery, and world-class monuments. It's a bizarre mix of bloodlines and architecture from medieval Normandy, Aragónese Spain, Moorish North Africa, ancient Greece, Phoenicia, and Rome. Since the advent of modern times, part of the island's primitiveness has faded, as thousands of cars clog the narrow lanes of its biggest city, **Palermo.** Poverty remains widespread, yet the age-old stranglehold of the Mafia seems less certain because of the increasingly vocal protests of an outraged Italian public. On the eastern edge of the island is Mount Etna, the tallest active volcano in Europe. Many of Sicily's larger cities (**Trapani, Catania,** and **Messina**) are relatively unattractive, but areas of ravishing beauty and eerie historical interest include **Syracuse, Taormina, Agrigento,** and **Selinunte.** Sicily's ancient ruins are rivaled only by those of Rome itself. The Valley of the Temples is worth the trip here.

Sardinia

Sardinia (Sardegna) is called Italy's best kept secret. It's part of Italy, of course, but seems almost an island nation unto itself, with its own unique landscape, culture, and cuisine. Standing isolated in the Mediterranean, it is filled with dusty olive groves, dramatic coastlines, and volcanic mountain landscapes. For centuries it was fought over by major sea powers, ranging from the Romans and Phoenicians right up to the Genovese and the Aragonese. Sardinia is rich in folklore, crafts, traditions, and festivals.

The island lies some 116 miles west of the Italian mainland, and about the same distance from North Africa. Costa Smeralda (Emerald Coast) is perhaps the most desirable place to be in August, when the rich and famous descend on its posh resorts. But Sardinia is a year-round destination for those who want to explore its culture while based in such cities and towns as Cagliari, Sardinia's main port of entry by both sea and air. The other major town of interest is Alghero, capital of the "Coral Riviera," with its great ramparts by the sea.

Pasta with seafood.

TRAVEL LOCALLY—vespa style

Auto Europe is debuting scooter-rental service in France and Italy that will enable visitors to do their exploring like the locals do. Italian Vespas are available for rent in Rome, Venice, Milan, and Florence, while Yamaha YP 125 Majesty scooters are available in Paris, Marseille, Nice, and Cannes. The company is touting the benefits of sidewalk parking and ease of maneuvering in high-traffic locations, along with saving money on gas. To book, see www.autoeurope.com/scooters.cfm.

ITALY IN 1 WEEK

The very title of this tour is a misnomer. There is no way you can see Italy in 1 week. But you can have a memorable vacation in Rome and see some of the highlights of Siena, Florence, and Venice if you budget your time carefully.

You can use the following itinerary to make the most out of a week in Italy, but feel free to drop a place or two to save a day to relax. One week provides enough time, although barely, to introduce yourself to the attractions of Rome, such as the Colosseum, the Roman Forum, and the Vatican (with a stop at St. Peter's).

After 2 days you can head north to the great Tuscan city of Siena, which still carries the aura of the Middle Ages. With time remaining you can budget 2 nights for Florence, taking in its Pitti Palace, the Duomo, and the masterpiece-loaded Uffizi galleries.

After that, you can end your trip in Venice, sailing along the Grand Canal to such attractions as the Basilica di San Marco, the Doge's Palace, and the Galleria dell'Accademia.

DAYS 1 & 2: Arrive in Rome ★★★

Take a flight that arrives in Rome as early as possible on **Day 1.** Check into your hotel and hit the nearest cafe for a pick-me-up cappuccino before sightseeing.

Two days in Rome is just too brief—after all, Rome wasn't built in a day. But you can make the most of your limited time. There are two major areas to focus on in a 2-day trip: the legacy of Imperial Rome, such as the Forum and the Colosseum, plus St. Peter's Basilica and the Vatican Museums (unlike any other in the world).

On **DAY 1,** those who have come to see ancient Rome and the glory of the Caesars can start their tour at **Michelangelo's Campidoglio** (p. 147), or Capitoline Hill. From here you can look out over the Roman Forum area before venturing forth to discover Rome. After the overview, walk east along Vie dei Fori Imperiali, taking in a view of the remains of the **Imperial Forums** (p. 151), which can be seen from the street. This route leads you to the ruins of the **Colosseum** (p. 150). After a visit to this amphitheater, cross over to spend the rest of the day exploring the ruins of the **Roman Forum** (p. 153) and **Palatine Hill** (p. 153) to the west of the Colosseum.

For a change of pace, stop in at the **Church of San Pietro in Vincoli** (p. 157), which is near ancient Rome. Here you can gaze upon Michelangelo's celebrated statue *Moses*.

You can spend **DAY 2** exploring St. Peter's and the Vatican Museums, which will be one very busy time indeed. The tiny walled "city-state" of the Vatican, the capital of the Catholic world, contains such a wealth of splendor that you could spend more than a week trying to see it all, but most people are content to hit the highlights in 1 busy day.

After exploring **St. Peter's Basilica** (p. 137), including a climb to Michelangelo's panoramic dome, take a lunch break before strolling over to the **Vatican Museums** (p. 141). This array of galleries contains one of the

St. Peter's Basilica, Rome.

most jaw-dropping collections of art and antiquities in the world, all of it culminating in the gloriously restored **Sistine Chapel** (p. 144). By now, you'll probably be exhausted, but, if you can keep going, take in a final attraction, the **Castel Sant'Angelo** (p. 146).

Have dinner your final night in Rome at a restaurant in Trastevere.

DAY 3: North to Siena ★★★

On **DAY 3,** drive north from Rome for 230km (143 miles), following the signs into Siena, the second-greatest city of Tuscany (after Florence, of course). After checking into a hotel, set out to visit the **Piazza del Campo** (p. 311), the main square, including its attractions such as the **Museo Civico** (p. 327) in the **Palazzo Pubblico.** You can also visit the *palazzo* itself, climbing the **Torre del Mangia** (p. 314) for a panoramic view of the city and the surrounding countryside. Afterward, head for the **Duomo** (p. 315), where you can spend at least 2 hours taking in other adjoining attractions, including **Museo dell'Opera Metropolitana** (p. 315) and the **Battistero** (p. 300). If time remains, return to the Piazza del Campo for some cafe sitting and people-watching.

DAYS 4 & 5: Florence: City of the Renaissance ★★★

On the morning of **DAY 4,** leave as early as you can and drive north from Siena to Florence, a distance of only 34km (21 miles). Spend the rest of the morning exploring the masterpieces of the **Uffizi** (p. 246), followed by a light lunch at a cafe opening onto **Piazza della Signoria** (p. 253). After lunch, see some of the sculpture in the **Museo dell'Opera del Duomo** (p. 252) before visiting the **Duomo** (p. 249) itself (best seen from the outside). Climb to the top for one of the great panoramas of Europe. Follow up with a visit to the adjoining **Battistero San Giovanni** (p. 251) and the **Campanile di Giotto** (p. 250) before walking down to the **Galleria dell'Accademia** (p. 242) for a look at Michelangelo's monumental *David.* End the afternoon with a sunset stroll along **Ponte Vecchio** (p. 255).

On **DAY 5,** spend the morning on the "left bank" of the Arno, taking in the masterpieces of the **Palazzo Pitti** (p. 243). Afterward, wind down in the adjacent **Giardini di Boboli** (p. 243). After lunch, cross over to the right side of the river to view a grand array of Renaissance treasures, including the **Cappelle Medicee** (p. 256) with Michelangelo's grand sculptures. A nearby visit is in order to explore the **Basilica di San Lorenzo** (p. 255), climaxed by a late-afternoon visit to the art-filled **Palazzo Vecchio** (p. 254).

DAYS 6 & 7: Venice: La Serenissima ★★★

Leave Florence early in the morning on **DAY 6** and drive 267km (166 miles) northeast to Italy's most spectacular city. You'll ride into the heart of Venice on a *vaporetto* (water bus), taking in the **Grand Canal,** perhaps the world's greatest thoroughfare. After checking into a hotel, head for the **Piazza San Marco** for a coffee and a long look before striking out on a sightseeing expedition.

The **Basilica di San Marco** (p. 475) is right in front of you. After exploring it, visit the nearby **Palazzo Ducale (Doge's Palace)** before walking over the **Bridge of Sighs** (p. 474). Climb the **Campanile,** also nearby, for the grandest view of Venice and its lagoon. Have dinner in a typical Venetian tavern along the lagoon.

On **DAY 7,** take in two of Venice's grandest art collections, each very different: the **Gallerie dell'Accademia** (p. 480), and for those with more modern taste, the **Peggy Guggenheim Collection** (p. 485). Walk the **Ponte di Rialto (Rialto Bridge)** and explore some of the small shops in the area. Before the afternoon fades, try to take in one of the churches of Venice, perhaps **San Rocco** (p. 489) for its great art. If it's summer, head for a dinner on the **Lido.** The boat ride alone is worth the trip.

ITALY IN 2 WEEKS

In this tour, we can take in all the same sights covered in "Italy in 1 Week" (see above), but we can also include a lot more of Naples (with its great archaeological treasures); Pompeii (with Italy's most spectacular ruins); the stunning Amalfi Drive (the most thrilling but hair-raising road in the country); Bologna (gourmet citadel); Padua (with its Giotto frescoes); and even Verona of *Romeo and Juliet* fame; as well as the industrial city of Milan with its great cathedral and art museums.

DAYS 1 & 2: Arrive in Rome ★★★

Follow sightseeing suggestions as outlined in **DAYS 1 AND 2** under "Italy in 1 Week," above.

DAY 3: South to Naples ★★

On **DAY 3,** drive south to Naples, a distance of 219km (136 miles) southeast of Rome. Leave as early in the morning as you can in order to take in the major attractions of Naples: **Museo Archeologico Nazionale** (p. 702); **Museo e Gallerie Nazionale di Capodimonte** (p. 703); and, if time remains, **Certosa di San Martino** and **Museo Nazionale di San Martino** (p. 701). Perhaps head for a pizzeria that night—Neapolitans claim they invented the pie. Stay overnight in Naples to end Day 3.

DAY 4: Pompeii: Europe's Best-Preserved Ruins

On **DAY 4,** drive 24km (15 miles) south of Naples to spend a day wandering the archaeological garden of Pompeii. The city was buried for 2,000 years, having suffered devastation when nearby Vesuvius erupted. Some of the great treasures of southern Italy—including the remarkable patrician villa Casa dei Vettii—are found here. Return to Naples for overnighting.

DAY 5: Death-Defying Amalfi Drive ★★★

On the morning of **DAY 5,** drive 49km (30 miles) south of Naples along A3 until you see the turnoff for Sorrento. At Sorrento, you can head east along the curvy Amalfi Drive, of which Andre Gide said "[there is] nothing more beautiful on this earth." The drive winds around the twisting, steep coastline.

Follow it to the southern resorts of Positano or Amalfi, either of which would make an idyllic stopover. Allow at least 3 hours for this drive because it is slow moving—not only because of heavy traffic, but also from all the rubbernecking of fellow motorists. Positano lies 16km (10 miles) east of Sorrento, with Amalfi reached after going 18km (11 miles) east of Positano.

DAY 6: North to Siena ★★★

It's a long day and a long drive, but you can head north along the autostrada to Rome, bypassing it and continuing north to the cutoff for Siena. You'll arrive in Siena in the afternoon, time enough to see the Duomo complex and the Piazza del Campo. For more sight details, follow the suggestions given in **DAY 3** under "Italy in 1 Week," above.

DAYS 7 & 8: Florence: Birthplace of the Renaissance

Follow the touring suggestions given in **DAYS 4 AND 5,** listed under "Italy in 1 Week" (see above).

DAY 9: Bologna: Gastronomic Capital of Italy

Leave Florence on the morning of **DAY 9,** driving 105km (65 miles) northeast to Bologna. The major sights lie in the immediate center. The best of them are the **Basilica di San Petronio** (p. 388); **Pinacoteca Nazionale di Bologna** (p. 388); and **Tower of the Garisenda** (p. 391), all of which can be seen in one afternoon. One of the pleasures of Bologna is merely wandering its arcaded streets; even getting lost is fun. Stay overnight in the city to end Day 9.

DAYS 10 & 11: Venice: City That Defies the Sea

Leave Bologna on the morning of **DAY 10** and drive northeast to Venice, a distance of 151km (94 miles). Once in Venice, follow the sightseeing suggestions as outlined under Days 6 and 7 (see "Italy in 1 Week," above).

Italy in 2 Weeks

CROATIA

0   100 mi
0   100 km

BOSNIA &
HERZEGOVINA

1 & **2** Rome
3 Naples
4 Pompeii
5 *The Amalfi Drive*
5A Sorrento
5B Positano
5C Amalfi
6 Siena
7 & **8** Florence
9 Bologna
10 & **11** Venice
12 Padua
13 Verona
14 Milan

DAY 12: Padua & Its Giotto Frescoes

While still based in Venice, you can explore Padua, lying only 40km (25 miles) to the west. In one fairly easy day, you can visit the **Basilica di Sant'Antonio** with its Donatello bronzes and tomb of St. Anthony of Padua (p. 516) and the **Cappella degli Scrovegni** with its Giotto frescoes (p. 517). If time remains, explore **Chiesa degli Eremitani** (p. 518) as well. Return to Venice for the night.

DAY 13: Verona of Romeo & Juliet Fame

Leave Venice on the morning of **DAY 13,** heading west for 114km (71 miles) to Verona, where Shakespeare set the world's most famous love story, *Romeo* *and Juliet.* Wander **Piazza dei Signori** (p. 528) and take in another square, **Piazza delle Erbe** (p. 530), before descending on the **Arena di Verona** (p. 530), evoking Rome's Colosseum, and the Romanesque church, **Basilica San Zeno Maggiore** (p. 531). Spend a night in Verona.

DAY 14: Milan: Italy's Most Dynamic City

Leave Verona in the morning, driving west for 157km (98 miles) until you reach the most bustling city of Italy, Milan. It's not all industry and commerce. Milan possesses one of the great cathedrals of Italy, **Il Duomo** (p. 584), and its **Biblioteca-Pinacoteca Ambrosiana** (p. 583), with its cartoons by Raphael, is one of the great galleries of Italy. Its **Pinacoteca di Brera** (p. 583) is a fabulous treasure-trove of art, laden with masterpieces from Lombard and Venetian masters. If it can be arranged, at least make an attempt to see Leonardo's fading but still magnificent *The Last Supper* (p. 585). Stay overnight in Milan, a city that is one of the major transportation hubs of Europe, ideal for departures for your next destination.

ITALY FOR FAMILIES

Italy offers hundreds of attractions that kids enjoy. It is, in fact, the friendliest family vacation destination in all of Europe.

Most families that plan to tour Italy in a week focus on its three major cities: Rome, Florence, and Venice. Of the big three, Rome and Venice have far more activities for children to enjoy, because the true glory of Florence, the city of the Renaissance, is its art and architectural monuments.

Perhaps the main concern in traveling with children, other than safety issues, is pacing your museum visits so that you get a chance to see some of the world's greatest masterpieces without having young kids suffer a meltdown after too many paintings of saints and bambini.

Our suggestion for this tour is to spend 2 days in Rome, followed by a night in Tuscany (Siena), then 2 days in Florence (regardless of what the kids say), ending your trip in Venice, which most children think was created by Disney anyway.

DAYS 1 & 2: Arrive in Rome ★★★

Arrive in Rome as early as you can to get a running start on the attractions. With your brood in tow, have a good breakfast to prepare for a long day of walking. Wear comfortable shoes.

The ruins of the **Imperial Forums** (p. 151) do not depend on opening hours but can be viewed at any time. These ruins can be seen from the street along Via dei Fori Imperiali. Walk east along this broad avenue until you arrive at the ruins of the **Colosseum** (p. 150), which should then be open. Spend at least an hour and a half wandering its ruins. Kids can let off a lot of steam here as they make their way over this monument.

It takes a good 3 hours to wander the **Roman Forum** (p. 153) and the **Palatine Hill** (p. 153), so you might want to break these attractions into two parts, a prelunch jaunt followed by an afternoon visit after you've fortified your gang with bowls of Roman pasta. By 3pm, you should have climbed every hill and inspected every classical ruin.

Italy for Families

1 & 2 Rome
3 Siena
4 & 5 Florence
6 & 7 Venice

Cap the afternoon by exploring the **Villa Borghese** (p. 167), a monumental park in the heart of Rome. Cold drinks are available here, and if your child is old enough, you can rent bikes for rides in the park. There is also a small zoo in the northeast of the park grounds.

After rest and showers back at your hotel, wander into the **Piazza Navona** (p. 161), where there is always entertainment. Pick one of our restaurants in the area. After dinner, let your kid sample some of Rome's legendary gelato (ice cream) before calling it a night.

On **DAY 2,** head for **St. Peter's Basilica** (p. 137). Kids are generally in awe of this grand monument and the supreme church for the Catholic order. They find it spooky wandering the Vatican grottoes, and few can resist climbing up to Michelangelo's dome at 114m (375 ft.).

After time out for lunch, begin your descent on the **Vatican Museums** and the **Sistine Chapel** (p. 141). Even if your kids don't like art museums, they will probably gawk at the grandeur of this place, as they look up at Michelangelo's Sistine Chapel and thrill at such art as the *Laocoön,* depicting a father and his two sons locked in mortal combat with serpents.

Later in the day head for the **Spanish Steps** (p. 162) before wandering over to the **Trevi Fountain** (p. 164). Here, give the kids coins to toss into the fountain, which is said to ensure their return to Rome—perhaps when they are older and can better appreciate the artistic attractions.

DAY 3: Siena, a Medieval City ★★★

Leave Rome early on the morning of **DAY 3,** driving north into Tuscany, arriving for a day at Siena, a distance of 230km (143 miles) northwest of Rome.

Count yourself lucky if you're here in July or August for the famous 4-day **Palio** celebration. The whole family can enjoy the colorful parades with medieval costumes and banners and the horse races around **Piazza del Campo** (p. 313). Even if you can't come at those times, Siena remains a year-round attraction.

In the center of town, the whole family can climb **Torre del Mangia** (p. 314), the bell tower of the **Palazzo Pubblico,** for a dramatic view of the city and the enveloping countryside. Even kids are fascinated by the Lorenzetti frescoes in the Palazzo Pubblico's Sala della Pace—this art is called "one big, long picture show."

The **Duomo** (p. 293) is jazzy enough to interest those children who are normally bored with cathedrals—its black-and-white floors remind them of zebra stripes. Even the art here, including *The Last Judgment,* showing people squirming in the jaws of hell, holds a morbid fascination.

Spend the rest of the day wandering at leisure along the medieval streets, very evocative. One kid thought that all of Siena had been designed as the setting for some movie about the Middle Ages. Settle in overnight in Siena.

DAYS 4 & 5: Florence, City of Stone ★★★

Leave Siena in the morning, driving north for 34km (21 miles) to Florence. Check into a hotel for a 2-night stay. As mentioned, Florence is more of an adult attraction, but there's nothing wrong with exposing your children to some culture early in life. Begin the day on the monumental main square of Florence, **Piazza della Signoria** (p. 202), with its remarkable open-air museum of statues. The **Palazzo Vecchio** (p. 254) dominates one end of this square, another formed by the 14th-century **Loggia della Signoria** (p. 253). It will all look like a stage set to kids.

Begin your descent onto the **Uffizi** (p. 246). One of the world's great museums, this gallery has so much to dazzle the eye that only the most bored of children will find little of interest here. We've observed kids staring in fascination at a painting (especially the gruesome ones) when parents are eager to press on. Allow at least 2 hours for a visit.

After lunch at a Florentine *trattoria,* wander down to the stunning red-tiled **Duomo** (p. 249). Kids will delight in climbing to the top of the dome for a classic panorama. Afterward, you, along with your children, can climb

Sunset at Piazzale Michelagniolo, Florence.

the 414 steps up to the **Campanile di Giotto** (p. 250) for another remarkable view. After you descend, spend some time looking at the doors to the **Battistero San Giovanni** (p. 251).

As the afternoon wanes, stroll along the **Ponte Vecchio** (p. 255), the city's oldest bridge, which is lined with fascinating shops vending mostly jewelry. To cap the day, head to the **Piazzale Michelangiolo** (p. 260) at sunset for a panoramic sweep over all of Florence.

On **DAY 5,** cross over the Arno to the left side where you can view some of the treasures of the **Palazzo Pitti** (p. 243), the second great art museum of Florence. There is much to interest visitors of all ages here, including a museum of costumes and the elegant private apartments once occupied by the Medici. Afterward, head to the nearby **Giardini di Boboli** (p. 243) for an hour or two of wandering around the gardens. Stop in a deli before your visit and pick up the makings of a picnic lunch for all the family to enjoy.

After your meal, visit the **Cappelle Medicee** (p. 256) to see the famous statues by Michelangelo. Afterward spend an hour or two of discovery, just wandering Florence's medieval streets—which for many kids is more pleasurable than any museum. As the afternoon fades, walk over to the **Galleria dell'Accademia** (p. 242) to see Michelangelo's colossal giant, *David.* No visit to Florence would be complete without it. Take your entire family to one of the typical *buche* (cellar restaurants) for a real Florentine experience before turning in for the night.

DAYS 6 & 7: Venice, City on the Lagoon ★★★

Leave Florence on the morning of **DAY 6** for the long 267km (166-mile) drive northeast into Venice. Venice is the great kid pleaser of Italy, the fun beginning the moment you arrive and take a boat ride along the Grand Canal to the hotel of your choice.

After checking in, head for **Piazza San Marco** (p. 471), where children delight in feeding the pigeons. Wander into the **Basilica di San Marco** (p. 475), which dominates the square. After leaving the cathedral, you can take an elevator to the top of the **Campanile di San Marco** (p. 472), the bell tower, for a panoramic vista of Venice. After lunch, visit the **Palazzo Ducale** (p. 474) and take your kids for a walk over the infamous **Bridge of Sighs** (p. 474). Afterward, spend the rest of the time wandering with your brood through the narrow streets of Italy's most fascinating city.

On **DAY 7,** visit the **Gallerie dell'Accademia** (p. 480) in the morning, saving some time for **San Rocco** (p. 489), where kids view the episodic Tintoretto paintings like a picture book. After lunch go for a boat ride in the lagoon to the island of **Murano** (p. 505), where you can see glass being blown. If it's summer spend time on the beach at the **Venetian Lido** (p. 492).

If you're leaving the following day, Venice has both rail and air connections to Rome and Milan, where chances are you'll be flying out of Italy.

TUSCANY FOR ART & ARCHITECTURE LOVERS

The true devotee of art will want to spend the most time in Florence or Siena. Frankly, those two cities, especially Florence, have grabbed up the greatest art in all of Tuscany, not to mention the world. The city of Siena, its rival, contains collections of great art from the Sienese School of the Middle Ages.

In the Middle Ages and during the Renaissance, artists who wanted to make a living went to Florence or Siena because they depended on wealthy patrons, especially powerful churches or, in the case of Florence, the art-loving Medici rulers. The art stayed where it was created.

That doesn't mean you won't find great art off the beaten trail. You will, as in the case of Arezzo and Sansepolcro (see below), where devotees of Piero della Francesco trek to study his rare masterpieces.

In contrast, even small towns such as Lucignano and Pienza have architecture that will attract aficionados from all over the world.

DAY 1: Lucca: Walled City ★★★

Leave Florence early in the morning and drive 72km (45 miles) west of Florence on the A11.

Inside its thick swath of Renaissance walls, bordered by gardens, Lucca still follows its medieval street plan. For the devotee of architecture, the city is one of the most richly rewarding cities of Tuscany. Best appreciated for their facades, its Romanesque churches are in the Lombard-Pisan style, richly embroidered with polychrome marble insets and relief carvings. Most of the carvings were by visiting Lombard and Pisan sculptors.

Lucca's main attractions are detailed in chapter 7. They include the **Duomo,** or **Cattedrale di San Martino,** with its green-and-white marble

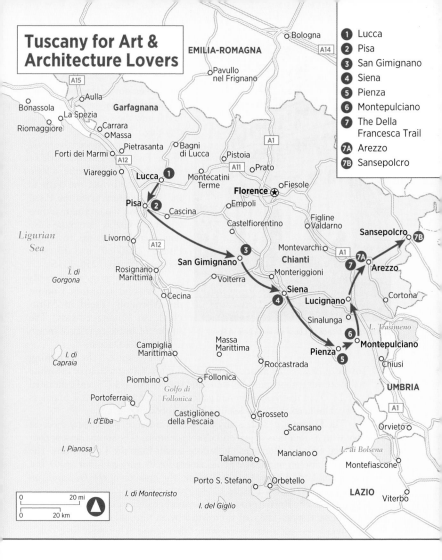

Tuscany for Art &
Architecture Lovers

1	Lucca
2	Pisa
3	San Gimignano
4	Siena
5	Pienza
6	Montepulciano
7	The Della Francesca Trail
7A	Arezzo
7B	Sansepolcro

facade designed by the architect Guidetto da Como. The exceptionally tall facade of **San Michele in Foro** is another stellar example of the Luccan-Pisan style. This is one of the most beautiful church facades in all of Tuscany, with its delicately twisted columns and arcades. Dare we suggest it's a poetic confection?

Before the Pisan style of architecture swept Lucca, there was the church of **San Frediano** in the Lucca-Romanesque style. Its facade is graced with white marble from the ancient Roman amphitheater. The rest of the day is yours as you wander **Città Vecchia,** the streets of the old town, which are full of Gothic and Renaissance *palazzi* and other delights, finishing up over a nice dinner.

The towering facade of Lucca's San Michele in Foro.

DAY 2: Pisa & Its Leaning Tower ★★★

Lucca lies only 21km (13 miles) northeast of Pisa. Take A12 south and follow the signs to Pisa in the morning.

This city introduced the world to the Pisan Romanesque style of architecture and sculpture, a style that flourished from the 11th to the 13th century when the Pisan Republic was a powerful maritime city-state. Gothic sculpture also flourished here thanks to Nicola Pisano (1220–80) and his son, Giovanni Pisano (1250–1315).

Pisa's foremost monuments center around its historic **Campo dei Miracoli (Field of Miracles),** so touring is easy. The square of miracles is also known as Piazza del Duomo.

Of course, the **Leaning Tower** (p. 302) is the most compelling structure. Construction of the white marble tower with its pure Romanesque style began in 1173 and continued until 1350. Six floors of columned galleries wind around the spiral. Stainless steel cables keep the tower leaning instead of falling.

The **Duomo** (p. 302) is an even greater treasure, particularly the west front with its four tiers of graceful marble columns. The south transept door is graced with fine Romanesque bronze panels from the 12th century. The interior is also an impressive achievement for its nave and four aisles, but mainly for its stunningly beautiful pulpit, the creation of son Giovanni, on which he labored from 1302 to 1311.

The nearby **Battistero** (p. 313) is another stellar example of the Pisan Romanesque style. The roof is crowned by an unusual Gothic dome with four doorways, each decorated with fine carving. The impressive pulpit inside is from papa Pisano. If time remains, check out the **Museo dell'Opera del Duomo** (p. 301), with sculptures removed from the monuments in the Piazza del Duomo for safekeeping. Some from the Romanesque period are masterpieces by unknown artists.

Enjoy an overnight at a hotel in Pisa. For a complete description of what to see and do in Pisa, see chapter 7.

DAY 3: San Gimignano & Its Medieval Towers ★★★

This city lies 92km (57 miles) southeast of Pisa. To reach San Gimignano from Pisa, head east along the Pisa/Livorno/Firenze autostrada (called the FI.PI.LI) until you near the town of Empoli. Then leave the autostrada and head south along S429 until you come to the turnoff heading southwest near the town of Poggibonsi. San Gimignano is signposted at this point. Cut west on S324 to San Gimignano.

For the architectural enthusiast, wandering into San Gimignano is a journey back to the Middle Ages. This is Italy's best-preserved medieval town, and some one dozen towers remain. These well-preserved towers were more than just defensive strongholds; they were symbols of a family's prestige and worth—the taller they were, the more powerful the ruling dynasty.

Although San Gimignano is unique in appearance today, in the Middle Ages, towns throughout central Italy looked like San Gimignano. Amazingly, in the heyday of San Gimignano, there were nearly 70 such towers. In some prescient way, it might have looked like a diminutive version of a skyscraper city of the future.

Today's visitors who wander through this medieval landscape follow in the footsteps of Dante, Savonarola, and Machiavelli. The "time capsule" streets are beautiful, as are the public buildings—and those towers are truly awesome.

For a complete rundown on the attractions, along with hotels and restaurants for overnighting, coverage begins on p. 305.

DAY 4: Siena: Homage to the Middle Ages ★★★

Our next stopover, the biggest attraction yet, lies 42km (26 miles) southeast of San Gimignano. Head east on S324 to Poggibonsi and take the Firenze/Siena autostrada south to the signposted exits.

Of all the cities of Tuscany, except for Florence, **Siena** (p. 311) caters more than all others to the lover of both art and architecture—and does so in great abundance. Although our hurried tour calls for only 1 day here, 2 days is preferable if your schedule can accommodate it.

San Gimignano.

The Museo dell'Opera in Siena.

One of the greatest art cities in all of Italy, Siena once rivaled Florence as an artistic center. But when Sienese artists hung on to Greek and Byzantine formulas longer than Florence, Siena was left behind by the Renaissance.

Duccio and Simone Martini were pioneers in bringing greater realism to the more static Byzantine art. Flowing lines and expressive features were introduced. Gothic arrived in Siena when Giovanni Pisano overhauled the Duomo (cathedral), and Jacopo della Quercia became a towering figure in Gothic sculpture in Siena. The Black Death of 1348 brought a crippling blow to Sienese artistic aspirations.

The great repository of Sienese art, an extensive collection, is housed in the **Pinacoteca Nazionale** (p. 316). It's not the Uffizi, but it is a showcase of Sienese masterpieces created between the 13th and 16th centuries. Here you'll see works by all the famous artists associated with Siena, including Duccio and the great Simone Martini. Numerous paintings by the Lorenzetti brothers and the works of many other masters, notably Beccafumi and Il Sodoma, are also on parade.

Some of the city's greatest sculpture is exhibited in the **Museo dell'Opera Metropolitana** (p. 315), especially sculpture by Duccio and Jacopo della Quercia. The **Duomo** itself (p. 315) is a great treasure-trove of Tuscan and Sienese art, with Nicola Pisano's masterpiece, a 13th-century pulpit.

After a hard day's sightseeing, unwind over a meal and a good night's rest in Siena.

DAY 5: Pienza, the Ideal Renaissance City ★

The village of Pienza lies 55km (33 miles) southeast of Siena. From Siena, take the S2 south to the S146 and follow the signs.

This village owes its overall look to its homegrown son, Pope Pius II, born here in 1405. He set out to transform Pienza into a model Renaissance village—and succeeded admirably. Bernardo Rossellino, a protégé of the great Renaissance theorist Leon Battista Alberti, carried out the mandate of the pope, creating a **Cattedrale** with a Renaissance facade, the **Palazzo**

Piccolomini (Rossellino's masterpiece), and a main square, **Piazza Pio II,** which remains a Renaissance jewel.

Critics of the Vatican denounced all the money spent on Pienza, calling it "the pope's folly." Sure, it was a bit costly, but this grand achievement remains today, luring all devotees of architecture to Tuscany. Regrettably, the pope died before his dream could be fully achieved.

End **DAY 5** with an overnight in Pienza.

DAY 6: Montepulciano & Its Noble Wine ★

On the morning of the following day, drive a mere 13km (8 miles) east to Montepulciano following S146.

The trouble with visiting this idyllic town is that you may never want to leave and will decide to retire here. One of the region's highest hill towns, it opens onto panoramic views of the countryside and is graced with quaint medieval streets and harmonious architecture. Spend a day wandering and discovering its treasures, beginning with the parade of Renaissance *palazzi* flanking its main street, "Corso."

The chief attractions for the devotee of Tuscan architecture are the **Duomo, Palazzo Neri-Orselli, Palazzo Nobili-Tarugi,** and **Tempio di San Biagio** (a masterpiece of High Renaissance architecture), everything centering around the monumental **Piazza Grande.**

After taking in the attractions and having lunch, you will still have time to explore nearby **Lucignano** in the afternoon. From Montepulciano, drive east to the autostrada, taking it north toward Florence but exiting at the signs for Lucignano, which lies to the immediate west of the autostrada.

The little town of Lucignano, unique in the annals of Italian hill towns for its street plan, will have you going around in circles. Like a maze, it's laid out in four concentric ellipses, centering around four colorful squares. Visit its **Collegiata** and its **Palazzo Comunale.**

Montepulciano makes the best place for overnighting in the area, and it's just a quick drive back.

DAY 7: Arezzo/Sansepolcro: The Della Francesca Trail ★★

On the morning of your final day of discovery, leave Montepulciano and drive east to the autostrada, taking it north to the turnoff for Arezzo in the east. The distance is 53km (33 miles).

Arezzo marks the beginning of the "Piero della Francesca Trail." Piero della Francesca was a visionary early Renaissance artist, one of the towering figures of the Italian *quattrocento*. A native of Sansepolcro, he created a dramatic style and explored the geometry of perspective. Born sometime in the early 15th century, he spent his life painting and writing books on geometry and perspective until he went blind at the age of 60.

In the morning at Arezzo you can visit della Francesca's masterpiece, the frescoes depicting *Legend of the True Cross* (1452–66) on the walls of the apse at the **Basilica di San Francesco** (p. 332). Treated with great realism, these frescoes evoke the Renaissance ideals of serenity and, in their subtle lighting, a sense of timelessness.

In the afternoon, head east along S73 for 39km (64 miles), following the signs to Sansepolcro, the birthplace of Piero della Francesca.

We like to spend a lazy afternoon here, wandering at leisure through the town's **Museo Civico,** Via Aggiunti 65 (© **0575-732218**), returning time and time again to admire the paintings by della Francesca, including *Resurrection* and his lovely polyptych of the *Virgin of Mercy.* Art lovers will also find much to admire in other paintings here, including works by Signorelli and Bassano.

Plan to end your week of Tuscan art with an overnight in either Sansepolcro or Arezzo, both of which have suitable if not always admirable accommodations.

4

SETTLING INTO ROME

Rome is a city of images and sounds, all vivid and all unforgettable. You can see one of the most striking images at dawn—ideally from Janiculum Hill (Gianicolo)—when the Roman skyline, with its bell towers and cupolas, gradually comes into focus. As the sun rises, the Roman symphony begins. First come the peals of church bells calling the faithful to Mass. Then the streets fill with cars, taxis, tour buses, and Vespas, the drivers gunning their engines and blaring their horns. Next the sidewalks are overrun with office workers, chattering as they rush off to their desks, but not before ducking into a cafe for their first cappuccino. Shop owners loudly throw up the metal grilles protecting their stores; the fruit-and-vegetable stands are crowded with Romans out to buy the day's supply of fresh produce, haggling over prices and caviling over quality.

Around 10am, the visitors—you included, with your guidebook in hand—take to the streets, battling the crowds and traffic as they wend from Renaissance palaces and baroque buildings to ancient ruins like the Colosseum and the Forum. After you've spent a long day in the sun, marveling at the sights you've seen millions of times in photos and movies, you can pause to experience the charm of Rome at dusk.

Find a cafe at summer twilight, and watch the shades of pink and rose turn to gold and copper as night falls. That's when a new Rome awakens. The cafes and restaurants grow more animated, especially if you've found one in an ancient piazza or along a narrow alley deep in Trastevere. After dinner, you can stroll by the lighted fountains and monuments (Trevi Fountain and the Colosseum look magical at night) or through Piazza Navona and have a gelato. The night is yours.

ESSENTIALS
Arriving

BY PLANE Chances are, you'll arrive at Rome's **Leonardo da Vinci International Airport** (© **06-65951;** www.adr.it), popularly known as **Fiumicino,** 30km (19 miles) from the city center. (If you're flying by charter, you might land at Ciampino Airport, discussed below.) There is a tourist information office at the airport's Terminal B, International arrival, open daily 9am to 6:30pm.

A *cambio* (money exchange) operates daily from 7:30am to 11pm, offering surprisingly good rates, and there are ATM machines in the airport.

PREVIOUS PAGE: **Fountain of the Four Rivers, Rome.**

There's a **train station** in the airport. To get into the city, follow the signs marked TRENI for the 30-minute shuttle to Rome's main station, **Stazione Termini.** The shuttle (the Leonardo Express) runs from 5:52am to 11:36pm for 14€ one-way. On the way, you'll pass a machine dispensing tickets, or you can buy them in person near the tracks if you don't have small bills on you. When you arrive at Termini, get out of the train quickly and grab a baggage cart. (It's a long schlep from the track to the exit or to the other train connections, and baggage carts can be scarce.)

A **taxi** from da Vinci airport to the city costs 45€ and up for the 1-hour trip, depending on traffic. The expense might be worth it if you have a lot of luggage. Call *©* **06-6645,** 06-3570, or 06-4994 for information.

If you arrive on a charter flight at **Ciampino Airport** (*©* **06-65951;** www.adr.it), you can take a Terravision bus (*©* **06-4880086**) to Stazione Termini. Trip time is about 45 minutes and costs 4€. A **taxi** from here to Rome costs the same as the one from the da Vinci airport (see above), but the trip is shorter (about 40 min.).

BY TRAIN OR BUS Trains and buses (including trains from the airport) arrive in the center of old Rome at the silver **Stazione Termini,** Piazza dei Cinquecento (*©* **892021**). This is the train, bus, and subway transportation hub for all Rome, and it is surrounded by many hotels (especially cheaper ones).

If you're taking the **Metropolitana** (subway), follow the illuminated red-and-white M signs. To catch a bus, go straight through the outer hall and enter the sprawling bus lot of **Piazza dei Cinquecento.** You'll also find **taxis** there.

The station is filled with services. At a branch of the Banca San Paolo IMI (at tracks 1 and 24), you can exchange money. **Informazioni Ferroviarie** (in the outer hall) dispenses information on rail travel to other parts of Italy. There are also a **tourist information booth,** baggage services, newsstands, and snack bars.

BY CAR From the north, the main access route is the **Autostrada del Sole (A1).** Called "Motorway of the Sun," the highway links Milan with Naples via Bologna, Florence, and Rome. At 754km (469 miles), it is the longest Italian autostrada and is the "spinal cord" of Italy's road network. All the autostrade join with the **Grande Raccordo Anulare,** a ring road encircling Rome, channeling traffic into the congested city. Long before you reach this road, you should study a map carefully to see what part of Rome you plan to enter and mark your route accordingly. Route markings along the ring road tend to be confusing.

Warning: Return your rental car immediately, or at least get yourself to a hotel, park your car, and leave it there until you leave Rome. Don't even think about driving in Rome—the traffic is just too nightmarish.

Visitor Information

Information is available at **Azienda Provinciale di Turismo** (APT; *©* **06-421381;** www.aptprovroma.it), Via XX Settembre 26. The headquarters is open Monday to Friday 9am to 1pm. On Monday and Thursday it also is open 2 to 4pm.

More helpful, and stocking maps and brochures, are the offices maintained by the **Comune di Roma** at various sites around the city. They're staffed daily from 9:30am to 7pm, except the one at Termini (daily 8am–8:30pm). Here are the addresses of others in Stazione Termini: at Piazza Pia near the Castel Sant'Angelo; on Via Nazionale 183, near the Palazzo delle Esposizioni; on Piazza Sonnino, in Trastevere; on Piazza Cinque Lune, near Piazza Navona; and on Via dell'Olmata, near Piazza Santa Maria Maggiore. All phone calls for Comune di Roma are directed through a centralized number: © **06-0608**; www.turismo roma.it. Call daily 9am to 9pm.

Enjoy Rome, Via Marghera 8A (© **06-4451843**; www.enjoyrome.com), was begun by an English-speaking couple, Fulvia and Pierluigi. They dispense information about almost everything in Rome and are far more pleasant and organized than the Board of Tourism. They'll also help you find a hotel room, with no service charge (in anything from a hostel to a three-star hotel). Hours are Monday to Friday 8:30am to 5pm, and Saturday 8:30am to 2pm.

City Layout

Arm yourself with a detailed street map, not the general overview handed out free at tourist offices. Most hotels hand out a pretty good version at their front desks.

The bulk of ancient, Renaissance, and baroque Rome (as well as the train station) lies on the east side of the **Tiber River (Fiume Tevere),** which meanders through town. However, several important landmarks are on the other side: **St. Peter's Basilica** and the **Vatican,** the **Castel Sant'Angelo,** and the colorful **Trastevere** neighborhood.

The city's various quarters are linked by large boulevards (large, at least, in some places) that have mostly been laid out since the late 19th century. Starting from the **Vittorio Emanuele Monument,** a controversial pile of snow-white Brescian marble that's often compared to a wedding cake, there's a street running practically due north to **Piazza del Popolo** and the city wall. This is **Via del Corso,** one of the main streets of Rome—noisy, congested, crowded with buses and shoppers, and called simply "Il Corso." To its left (west) lie the Pantheon, Piazza Navona, Campo de' Fiori, and the Tiber. To its right (east) you'll find the Spanish Steps, the Trevi Fountain, the Borghese Gardens, and Via Veneto.

Back at the Vittorio Emanuele Monument, the major artery going west (and ultimately across the Tiber to St. Peter's) is **Corso Vittorio Emanuele.** Behind you to your right, heading toward the Colosseum, is **Via dei Fori Imperiali,** laid out in the 1930s by Mussolini to show off the ruins of the Imperial Forums he had excavated, which line it on either side. Yet another central conduit is **Via Nazionale,** running from **Piazza Venezia** (just in front of the Vittorio Emanuele Monument) east to **Piazza della Repubblica** (near Stazione Termini). The final lap of Via Nazionale is called **Via Quattro Novembre.**

The Neighborhoods in Brief

This section will give you some idea of where you might want to stay and where the major attractions are. It might be hard to find a specific address, because of the narrow streets of old Rome and the little, sometimes hidden, *piazze* (squares). Numbers usually run consecutively, with odd numbers on one side of the street and evens on the other. However, in the old districts the numbers sometimes run up one side and then run back in the opposite direction on the other side. Therefore, no. 50 could be opposite no. 308.

NEAR STAZIONE TERMINI   The main train station, **Stazione Termini,** adjoins **Piazza della Repubblica,** and most likely this will be your introduction to Rome. Much of the area is seedy and filled with gas fumes from all the buses and cars, but it has been improving. If you stay here, you might not get a lot of atmosphere, but you'll have a lot of affordable options and a convenient location, near the transportation hub of the city and not far from ancient Rome. There's a lot to see here, including the **Basilica di Santa Maria Maggiore** and the **Baths of Diocletian.** Some high-class hotels are sprinkled in the area, including the **Grand,** but many are long past their heyday.

The neighborhoods on either side of Termini have been improving greatly, and some streets are now attractive. The best-looking area is ahead and to your right as you exit the station on the Via Marsala side. Most budget hotels here occupy a floor or more of a *palazzo* (palace); many of their entryways are drab, although upstairs they're often charming or at least clean and livable. In the area to the left of the station as you exit, the streets are wider, the traffic is heavier, and the noise level is higher. This area off Via Giolitti is being redeveloped, and now most streets are in good condition. A few still need improvement; take caution at night.

VIA VENETO & PIAZZA BARBERINI   In the 1950s and early 1960s, **Via Veneto** was the swinging place to be, as the likes of King Farouk, Frank Sinatra, and Swedish actress Anita Ekberg paraded up and down the boulevard to the delight of the paparazzi. The street is still here and is still the site of luxury hotels and elegant cafes and restaurants, though it's no longer the happening place to be. It's lined with restaurants catering to those visitors who've heard of this boulevard from decades past, but the restaurants are mostly overpriced and overcrowded tourist traps. Rome city authorities would like to restore this street to some of its former glory by banning vehicular traffic on the top half. It still makes for a pleasant stroll.

To the south, Via Veneto comes to an end at **Piazza Barberini,** dominated by the 1642 **Triton Fountain (Fontana del Tritone),** a baroque celebration with four dolphins holding up an open scallop shell in which a triton sits blowing into a conch. Overlooking the square is the **Palazzo Barberini.** In 1623, when Cardinal Maffeo Barberini became Pope Urban VIII, he ordered Carlo Maderno to build a palace here; it was later completed by Bernini and Borromini.

ANCIENT ROME   Most visitors explore this area first, taking in the **Colosseum, Palatine Hill, Roman Forum, Imperial Forums,** and **Circus Maximus.** The area forms part of the *centro storico* (historic district)—along with **Campo de' Fiori** and **Piazza Navona** and the **Pantheon,** which are described below (we've considered them separately for the purposes of helping you locate hotels and restaurants). Because of its ancient streets, airy squares, classical atmosphere, and heartland location, this is a good place to stay. If you base yourself here, you can walk to the monuments and avoid Rome's inadequate public transportation.

This area offers only a few hotels—most of them inexpensive to moderate in price—and not a lot of great restaurants. Many restaurant owners have their eyes on the cash register and the tour-bus crowd, whose passengers are often hustled in and out of these restaurants so fast that they don't know whether the food is any good.

CAMPO DE' FIORI & THE JEWISH GHETTO   South of Corso Vittorio Emanuele and centered on **Piazza Farnese** and the market square of **Campo de' Fiori,** many buildings in this area were constructed in Renaissance times as private homes. Stroll along **Via Giulia**—Rome's most fashionable street in the 16th century—with its antiques stores, hotels, and modern art galleries.

West of Via Arenula lies one of the city's most intriguing districts, the old Jewish **Ghetto,** where the dining options far outnumber the hotel options. In 1556, Pope Paul IV ordered the Jews, about 8,000 at the time, to move here. The walls weren't torn down until 1849. Although ancient and medieval Rome has more atmosphere, this working-class area is close to many attractions. You're more likely to dine here than stay here.

PIAZZA NAVONA & THE PANTHEON   One of the most desirable areas of Rome, this district is a maze of narrow streets and alleys dating from the Middle Ages. It is filled with churches and palaces built during the Renaissance and baroque eras, often with rare marble and other materials stripped from ancient Rome. The only way to explore it is on foot. Its heart is **Piazza Navona,** built over Emperor Domitian's stadium and bustling with side-walk cafes, *palazzi,* street artists, musicians, and pickpockets. There are several hotels in the area and plenty of *trattorie.*

Rivaling Piazza Navona—in general activity, the cafe scene, and night-life—is the area around the **Pantheon,** which remains from ancient Roman times and is surrounded by a district built much later. (This "pagan" temple was turned into a church and rescued, but the buildings that once surrounded it are long gone.)

PIAZZA DEL POPOLO & THE SPANISH STEPS   **Piazza del Popolo** was laid out by Giuseppe Valadier and is one of Rome's largest squares. It's characterized by an obelisk brought from Heliopolis in lower Egypt during the reign of Augustus. At the end of the square is the **Porta del Popolo,** the gateway in the 3rd-century Aurelian wall. In the mid–16th century, this was one of the major gateways into the old city. If you enter the piazza along Via del Corso from the south, you'll see twin churches, **Santa Maria dei Miracoli** and **Santa Maria in Montesanto,** flanking the street. But the square's major church is **Santa Maria del Popolo** (1442–47), one of the best examples of a Renaissance church in Rome.

Since the 17th century, the **Spanish Steps** (the former site of the Spanish ambassador's residence) have been a meeting place for visitors. Some of Rome's most upscale shopping streets fan out from it, including **Via Condotti.** The elegant **Hassler,** one of Rome's grandest hotels, lies at the top of the steps. This is the most upscale part of Rome, full of expensive hotels, designer boutiques, and chic restaurants.

AROUND VATICAN CITY   Across the Tiber, **Vatican City** is a small city-state, but its influence extends around the world. The **Vatican Museums, St. Peter's,** and the **Vatican Gardens** take up most of the land area, and the popes have lived here for 6 centuries. The neighborhood around the Vatican—called the "Borgo"—contains some good hotels (and several bad ones), but it's removed from the more happening scene of ancient and Renaissance Rome and getting to and from it can be time consuming. The area is rather dull at night and contains few, if any, of Rome's finest restaurants. For the average visitor, Vatican City and its surrounding area are best

SETTLING INTO ROME | Essentials

for exploring during the day. Nonetheless, the area is popular for those whose sightseeing or business interests center around the Vatican.

TRASTEVERE In Roman dialect, Trastevere means "across the Tiber." For visitors arriving in Rome decades ago, it might as well have meant Siberia. All that has changed. This once medieval working-class district has been gentrified and overrun with visitors from all over the world. It started to change in the 1970s when expats and others discovered its rough charm. Since then Trastevere has been filling up with tour buses, dance clubs, offbeat shops, sidewalk vendors, pubs, and little *trattorie* with menus printed in English. There are even places to stay, but as of yet it hasn't burgeoned into a major hotel district. There are some excellent restaurants here as well.

The original people of the district—and there are still some of them left—are of mixed ancestry, mainly Jewish, Roman, and Greek. For decades they were known for speaking their own dialect in a language rougher than that spoken in central Rome. Even their cuisine was spicier.

The area centers on the ancient churches of **Santa Cecilia** and **Santa Maria.** It remains one of Rome's most colorful quarters, even if a bit overrun. Known as a "city within a city," it is at least a village within a city.

TESTACCIO & THE AVENTINE In A.D. 55, Nero ordered that Rome's thousands of broken amphorae and terra-cotta roof tiles be stacked in a carefully designated pile to the east of the Tiber, just west of Pyramide and today's Ostia Railway Station. Over the centuries, the mound grew to a height of around 61m (200 ft.) and then was compacted to form the centerpiece for one of the city's most unusual working-class neighborhoods, **Testaccio.** Eventually, houses were built on the terra-cotta mound and caves were dug into its mass to store wine and foodstuffs. Once home to the slaughterhouses of Rome and its former port on the Tiber, Testaccio means "ugly head" in Roman dialect. Bordered by the Protestant cemetery, Testaccio is known for its authentic Roman restaurants. Chefs here still cook as they always did, satisfying local—not tourist—palates. Change is on the way, however, and this is a neighborhood on the rise. Nightclubs have sprung up in the old warehouses, although they come and go rather quickly.

Another offbeat section of Rome is **Avantine Hill,** south of the Palatine and close to the Tiber. According to records, in 186 B.C., thousands of residents of the area were executed for joining in "midnight rituals of Dionysos and Bacchus." These bloody orgies are a thing of the past, and the Aventine area is now a leafy and rather posh residential quarter.

THE APPIAN WAY **Via Appia Antica** is a 2,300-year-old road that has witnessed much of the history of the ancient world. By 190 B.C., it extended from Rome to Brindisi on the southeast coast. Its most famous sights are the **Catacombs,** the graveyards of patrician families (despite what it says in *Quo Vadis?* they weren't used as a place for Christians to hide while fleeing persecution). This is one of the most historically rich areas of Rome, but it's not a good place to stay. It does contain some restaurants where you can have lunch after your visit to the Catacombs.

PRATI The little-known **Prati** district is a middle-class suburb north of the Vatican. It has been discovered by budget travelers because of its affordable hotels, although it's not conveniently located for sightseeing. The **Trionfale flower-and-food market** is worth the trip. The area abounds in shopping streets less expensive than in central Rome, and street crime isn't much of a problem.

PARIOLI   Rome's most elegant residential section, Parioli is framed by the green spaces of the **Villa Borghese** to the south and the **Villa Glori** and **Villa Ada** to the north. It's a setting for some of the city's finest restaurants, hotels, and nightclubs. It's not exactly central, however, and it can be a hassle if you're dependent on public transportation. Parioli lies adjacent to Prati but across the Tiber to the east; this is one of the safer districts. We'd call Parioli an area for connoisseurs, attracting those who shun the Spanish Steps and the overly commercialized Via Veneto, and those who'd never admit to having been in the Termini area.

MONTE MARIO   On the northwestern precincts of Rome, **Monte Mario** is the site of the deluxe **Cavalieri Hilton,** an excellent stop to enjoy a drink and the panorama of Rome. If you plan to spend a lot of time shopping and sightseeing in the heart of Rome, it's a difficult and often expensive commute. The area is north of Prati, away from the bustle of central Rome. Bus no. 913 runs from Piazza Augusto Imperator near Piazza del Popolo to Monte Mario.

GETTING AROUND

Rome is excellent for walking, with sites of interest often clustered together. Much of the inner core is traffic-free, so you'll need to walk whether you like it or not. However, in many parts of the city it's hazardous and uncomfortable because of the crowds, heavy traffic, and narrow sidewalks. Sometimes sidewalks don't exist at all, and it becomes a sort of free-for-all with pedestrians competing for space against vehicular traffic (the traffic always seems to win). Always be on your guard. The hectic crush of urban Rome is considerably less during August, when many Romans leave town for vacation.

By Subway

The **Metropolitana,** or **Metro,** for short, is the fastest means of transportation, operating daily 5:30am to 11:30pm Sunday to Thursday, and until 1:30am on Friday and Saturday. A big red м indicates the entrance to the subway.

Tickets are 1€ and are available from *tabacchi* (tobacco shops), many news-stands, and vending machines at all stations. Some stations have managers, but they won't make change. Booklets of tickets are available at *tabacchi* and in some terminals. You can also buy a **tourist pass** on either a daily or a weekly basis (see "By Bus & Tram," below).

Building a subway system for Rome hasn't been easy because every time workers start digging, they discover an old temple or other archaeological treasure, and heavy earth moving has to cease for a while.

By Bus & Tram

Roman buses and trams are operated by an organization known as **ATAC** (Agenzia del Trasporto Autoferrotranviario del Comune di Roma; ☎ **06-57003;** www.atac.roma.it), Piazzale degli Archivi 40, in the Eur suburb of Rome.

For 1€ you can ride to most parts of Rome, although it can be slow going in all that traffic, and the buses are often very crowded. Your ticket is valid for 75

Rome Metropolitana

minutes, and you can get on many buses and trams during that time by using the same ticket. Ask where to buy bus tickets, or buy them in *tabacchi* or bus terminals. You must have your ticket before boarding because there are no ticket-issuing machines on the vehicles.

At Stazione Termini, you can buy a special **tourist pass,** which costs 4€ for a day or 16€ for a week. This pass allows you to ride on the ATAC network without bothering to buy individual tickets. The tourist pass is also valid on the subway—but never ride the trains when the Romans are going to or from work, or you'll be smashed flatter than fettuccine. On the first bus you board, you place your ticket in a small machine, which prints the day and hour you boarded, and then you withdraw it. You do the same on the last bus you take during the valid period of the ticket. One-day and weekly tickets are also available at *tabacchi*, many newsstands, and at vending machines at all stations.

Buses and trams stop at areas marked FERMATA. At most of these, a yellow sign will display the numbers of the buses that stop there and a list of all the stops along each bus's route in order so you can easily search out your destination. In general, they're in service daily from 5am to midnight. After that and until dawn, you can ride on special night buses (they have an N in front of their bus number), which run only on main routes. It's best to take a taxi in the wee hours—if you can find one.

Two Bus Warnings

Any map of the Roman bus system will likely be outdated before it's printed. Many buses listed on the "latest" map no longer exist; others are enjoying a much-needed rest, and new buses suddenly appear without warning. There's also talk of completely renumbering the whole system soon, so be aware that the route numbers we've listed might have changed by the time you travel.

Take extreme caution when riding Rome's overcrowded buses—pickpockets abound! This is particularly true on bus no. 64, a favorite of visitors because of its route through the historic districts and thus also a favorite of Rome's pickpocketing community. This bus has earned various nicknames, including the "Pickpocket Express" and "Wallet Eater."

At the **bus information booth** at Piazza dei Cinquecento, in front of the Stazione Termini, you can purchase a directory with maps of the routes.

Although routes change often, a few old reliable routes have remained valid for years, such as **no. 75** from Stazione Termini to the Colosseum, **H** from Stazione Termini to Trastevere, and **no. 40** from Stazione Termini to the Vatican. But if you're going somewhere and are dependent on the bus, be sure to carefully check where the bus stop is and exactly which bus goes there—don't assume that it'll be the same bus the next day.

By Taxi

If you're accustomed to hopping a cab in New York or London, then do so in Rome. But don't count on hailing a taxi on the street or even getting one at a stand. If you're going out, have your hotel call one. At a restaurant, ask the waiter or cashier to dial for you. If you want to phone for yourself, try one of these numbers: ☏ 06-6645, 06-3570, or 06-4994.

The meter begins at 2.80€ for the first 3km (1¾ miles) and then rises .92€ per kilometer. The first suitcase is free. Every additional luggage costs 1€. There's another 5.80€ supplement from 10pm to 7am. Avoid paying your fare with large bills; invariably, taxi drivers claim that they don't have change, hoping for a bigger tip (stick to your guns and give only about 15%).

By Car

All roads might lead to Rome, but you don't want to drive once you get here. Because the reception desks of most Roman hotels have at least one English-speaking person, call ahead to find out the best route into Rome from wherever you're starting out. You're usually allowed to park in front of the hotel long enough to unload your luggage. You'll want to get rid of your rental car as soon as possible, or park in a garage.

You might want to rent a car to explore the countryside around Rome or drive to another city. You'll save the most money if you reserve before leaving home. But if you want to book a car here, know that **Hertz** is at Via Giovanni Giolitti 34 (☏ **06-4740389;** www.hertz.com; Metro: Termini), and **Avis** is at Stazione Termini (☏ **06-4814373;** www.avis.com; Metro: Termini). **Maggiore,** an Italian company, has an office at Stazione Termini (☏ **06-4880049;** www.maggiore.it; Metro: Termini). There are also branches of the major rental agencies at the airport.

By Bike

Other than walking, the best way to get through the medieval alleys and small piazzas of Rome is perched on the seat of a bicycle. The heart of ancient Rome is riddled with bicycle lanes to get you through the murderous traffic. The most convenient place to rent bikes is **Bici & Baci,** Via del Viminale 5 (✆ **06-4828443;** www.bicibaci.com), lying 2 blocks west of Stazione Termini, the main rail station. Prices start at 4€ per hour or 11€ per day.

[FastFACTS] ROME

American Express The Rome offices are at Piazza di Spagna 38 (✆ **06-67641;** Metro: Piazza di Spagna). The travel service is open Monday to Friday 9am to 5:30pm, Saturday 9am to 12:30pm. Hours for the financial and mail services are Monday to Friday 9am to 5pm. The tour desk is open all year-round Monday to Friday 9am to 5:30pm, Saturday 9am to 12:30pm.

Banks In general, banks are open Monday to Friday 8:30am to 1:30pm and 3 to 4pm. Some banks keep afternoon hours from 2:45 to 3:45pm. The bank office is open Monday to Friday 8:30am to 1:30pm.

Currency Exchange There are exchange offices throughout the city. They're also at all major rail and air terminals, including Stazione Termini, where the *cambio* beside the rail information booth is open daily 8am to 8pm. At some *cambio,* you'll have to pay commissions, often 1½%. Likewise, banks often charge commissions. ATM machines, with multilingual prompts, are commonplace throughout Rome.

Dentists For dental work, go to **American Dental Arts Rome,** Via del Governo Vecchio 73 (✆ **06-6832613;** www.adadentistsrome.com; bus: 41, 44, or 46B), which uses all the latest technology, including laser dentist techniques. There is also a 24-hour **G. Eastman Dental Hospital** at Viale Regina Elena 287B (✆ **06-844831;** Metro: Policlinico).

Doctors Call the U.S. Embassy at ✆ **06-46741** for a list of doctors who speak English. All big hospitals have a 24-hour first-aid service (go to the emergency room, *pronto soccorso*). You'll find English-speaking doctors at the privately run **Salvator Mundi International Hospital,** Viale delle Mura Gianicolensi 67 (✆ **06-588961;** bus: 75). For medical assistance, the **International Medical Center** is on 24-hour duty at Via Firenze 47 (✆ **06-4882371;** www.imc84.com;

Metro: Piazza Repubblica). You could also contact the **Rome American Hospital,** Via Emilio Longoni 69 (✆ **06-22551;** www.rah.it), with English-speaking doctors on duty 24 hours. A more personalized service is provided 24 hours by **MEDI-CALL,** Studio Medico, Via Cremera 8 (✆ **06-8840113;** www.medi-call.it; bus: 86). It can arrange for a qualified doctor to make a house call at your hotel or anywhere in Rome. In most cases, the doctor will be a general practitioner who can refer you to a specialist if needed. Fees begin at around 100€ per visit and can go higher if a specialist or specialized treatments are necessary.

Drugstores A reliable pharmacy is **Farmacia Internazionale,** Piazza Barberini 49 (✆ **06-4825456;** Metro: Barberini), open day and night. Most pharmacies are open from 8:30am to 1pm and 4 to 7:30pm. In general, pharmacies follow a rotation system, so several are always open on Sunday.

Embassies & Consulates See chapter 18.

Emergencies To call the police, dial ☎ **113;** an ambulance ☎ **118;** a fire ☎ **115.**

Internet Access You can log onto the Web in central Rome at **Internet Train,** Via dei Marrucini 12 (☎ **06-4454953;** www. internetcafe.it; bus: 3, 71, or 492). It is open Monday to Friday 9:30am to 1am, Saturday 10am to 1am, and Sunday 2pm to midnight. A 30-minute visit costs 1.50€.

Mail It's easiest to buy stamps and mail letters and postcards at your hotel's front desk. Stamps *(francobolli)* can also be bought at *tabacchi.* You can buy special stamps at the **Vatican City Post Office,** adjacent to the information office in St. Peter's Square; it's open Monday to Friday 8:30am to 7pm and Saturday 8:30am to 6pm. Letters mailed from Vatican City often arrive far more quickly than mail sent from Rome for the same cost.

Newspapers & Magazines You can buy major publications including the *International Herald Tribune,* the *New York Times,* and the London *Times* at most newsstands. The expat magazine (in English), *Wanted in Rome,* comes out monthly and lists current events and shows. If you want to try your hand at reading Italian, *Time Out* now has a Rome edition.

Police Dial ☎ **113.**

Safety Pickpocketing is the most common problem. Men should keep their wallets in their front pocket or inside jacket pocket. Purse snatching is also commonplace, with young men on Vespas who ride past you and grab your purse. To avoid trouble, stay away from the curb and keep your purse on the wall side of your body and place the strap across your chest. Don't lay anything valuable on tables or chairs, where it can be grabbed up. Gypsy children have long been a particular menace, although the problem isn't as severe as in years past. If they completely surround you, you'll often literally have to fight them off. They might approach you with pieces of cardboard hiding their stealing hands. Just keep repeating a firm *no!*

Telephone The **country code** for Italy is **39.** The **city code** for Rome is **06;** use this code when calling from *anywhere* outside or inside Italy—you must add it within Rome itself (and you must include the 0 every time, even when calling from abroad). See "Staying Connected" in chapter 18 for complete details on how to call Italy, how to place calls within Italy, and how to call home once you're in Italy.

Toilets Facilities are found near many of the major sights and often have attendants, as do those at bars, clubs, restaurants, cafes, and hotels, plus the airports and the rail station. (There are public restrooms near the Spanish Steps, or you can stop at the McDonald's there—it's one of the nicest branches of the Golden Arches you'll ever see!) The price for most public toilets is 1€. It's not a bad idea to carry some tissues in your pocket when you're out and about as well.

WHERE TO STAY

See the section "The Neighborhoods in Brief," earlier in this chapter, to get an idea of where you might want to base yourself.

If you like to gamble and arrive without a reservation, head quickly to the **airport information desk** or, once you get into town, to the offices of **Enjoy Rome** (see "Visitor Information," earlier in this chapter), where the staff can help you reserve a room, if any are available.

All the hotels listed serve breakfast (often a buffet with coffee, fruit, rolls, and cheese), but it's not always included in the rate, so check the listing carefully.

Nearly all hotels are heated in the cooler months, but not all are air-conditioned in summer, which can be vitally important during a stifling July or August. The deluxe and first-class ones are, but after that, it's a tossup. Be sure to check the listing carefully before you book a stay in the dog days of summer!

Near Stazione Termini

Despite a handful of pricey choices, this area is most notable for its concentration of cheap hotels. It's not the most picturesque location and parts of the neighborhood are still transitional, but it's certainly convenient in terms of transportation and easy access to many of Rome's top sights.

VERY EXPENSIVE

Exedra ★★   This neoclassical palace overlooking the Piazza della Repubblica at the rail terminal also fronts the Baths of Diocletian and Michelangelo's Basilica degli Angeli. The Exedra is a study in modern elegance combined with the romance of the past. It's luxury living on a grand scale, from the spacious standard double rooms to a variety of suites. Our favorite rooms are the top-floor accommodations in the Clementino Wing, each with bare brick walls and the original ceiling beams. Rooms feature such decorative notes as printed leather headboards and whorled silk wall coverings. You can take morning coffee on the rooftop garden terrace overlooking the Fountain of the Naiads. The spa is linked to the rooftop swimming pool by a glass elevator.

Piazza della Repubblica 47, 00185 Roma. ✆ **06-489381.** Fax 06-48938000. www.boscolo hotels.com. 240 units. 260€–700€ double; from 506€ junior suite; from 1,100€ suite. AE, DC, MC, V. Parking 35€. Metro: Repubblica. **Amenities:** 3 restaurants; 2 bars; babysitting; concierge; rooftop pool; room service; spa, Wi-Fi (20€ per 24 hr.). *In room:* A/C, TV, hair dryer, minibar.

St. Regis Grand ★★★   This restored landmark is more plush and upscale than any hotel in the area; for comparable digs, you'll have to cross town to check into the Excelsior or Eden. And for sheer opulence, not even those hotels equal it. Its drawback is its location at the dreary Stazione Termini, but once you're inside its splendid shell, all thoughts of railway stations vanish.

When César Ritz founded this outrageously expensive hotel in 1894, it was the first to offer a private bathroom and two electric lights in every room. Restored to its former glory, it is a magnificent Roman *palazzo* combining Italian and French styles in decoration and furnishings. Guest rooms, most of which are exceedingly spacious, are luxuriously furnished. Hand-painted frescoes are installed above each headboard. For the best rooms and the finest service, ask to be booked on the St. Regis floor.

Via Vittorio Emanuele Orlando 3, 00185 Roma. ✆ **06-47091.** Fax 06-4747307. www.stregis.com/ grandrome. 161 units. 337€–1,030€ double; from 1,260€ junior suite; from 2,500€ suite. AE, DC, MC, V. Parking 20€–30€. Metro: Repubblica. **Amenities:** Restaurant; bar; babysitting; concierge; exercise room; room service; spa. *In room:* A/C, TV, hair dryer, minibar, Wi-Fi (15€ per 24 hr.).

EXPENSIVE

Radisson Blu ES ★★   If you want a hypermodern atmosphere, this hotel is for you. This hotel is so dramatic, innovative, and high-tech that its opening sparked a bit of recovery in the old but decaying Esquilino quarter on the fringe of the Termini. A government-rated five-star luxe hotel, it is posh yet comfortably modern. It has everything from a Turkish bath to a business center. Don't judge

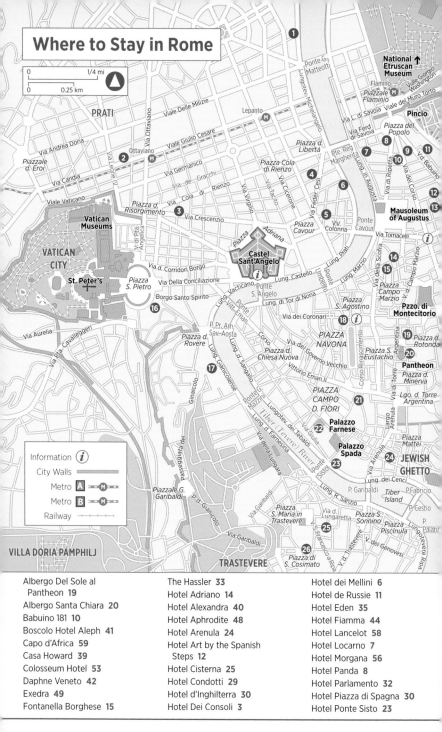

Where to Stay in Rome

0	1/4 mi
0	0.25 km

PRATI

Lepanto

National Etruscan Museum

Flaminio

Piazzale Flaminio

Pincio

Piazza del Popolo

VATICAN CITY

Vatican Museums

St. Peter's

Piazza S. Pietro

Castel Sant'Angelo

PIAZZA NAVONA

PIAZZA CAMPO D. FIORI

Palazzo Farnese

Palazzo Spada

Pantheon

Pzzo. di Montecitorio

Mausoleum of Augustus

JEWISH GHETTO

Tiber Island

VILLA DORIA PAMPHILJ

TRASTEVERE

Piazza di S. Cosimato

Piazza S. Maria in Trastevere

Information (i)

City Walls

Metro A

Metro B

Railway

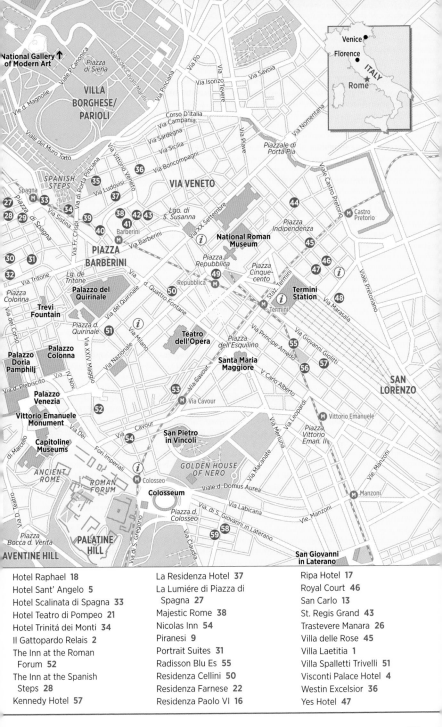

National Gallery of Modern Art

Piazza di Siena

VILLA BORGHESE/ PARIOLI

Viale del Muro Torto

SPANISH STEPS

Spagna

VIA VENETO

Lgo. di S. Susanna

National Roman Museum

Piazza Indipendenza

Castro Pretorio

PIAZZA BARBERINI

Barberini

Piazza Repubblica

Piazza Cinque-cento

Termini Station

Piazza Colonna

Lg. de Tritone

Palazzo del Quirinale

Repubblica

Trevi Fountain

Piazza d. Quirinale

Teatro dell'Opera

Piazza dell'Esquilino

Santa Maria Maggiore

SAN LORENZO

Palazzo Doria Pamphilj

Palazzo Colonna

Palazzo Venezia

Vittorio Emanuele Monument

Capitoline Museums

San Pietro in Vincoli

Piazza Vittorio Eman. II

Vittorio Emanuele

ANCIENT ROME

ROMAN FORUM

Colosseo

GOLDEN HOUSE OF NERO

Manzoni

Colosseum

Piazza d. Colosseo

Piazza Bocca d. Verità

PALATINE HILL

AVENTINE HILL

San Giovanni in Laterano

ITALY

Venice
Florence
Rome

the hotel by its rather dull seven-story exterior, which resembles an office building. Inside, the lobby showcases the ruins of a 2nd-century-A.D. Roman road. The midsize to spacious bedrooms emphasize minimalist Japanese designs, with wool rugs, glass desks, and plastic chairs in orange or pea green. Rooms are soundproof; some open onto balconies with city views.

Via Turati 171, 00185 Roma. © **06-444841.** Fax 06-44341396. www.eshotel.it. 235 units. 199€–330€ double; from 299€ junior suite; from 349€ suite. AE, DC, MC, V. Parking 15€. Metro: Vittorio Emanuele. **Amenities:** 2 restaurants; bar; babysitting; exercise room; rooftop outdoor pool; room service; spa. *In room:* A/C, TV, hair dryer, minibar, Wi-Fi (free).

Residenza Cellini ★ 📖 This undiscovered small hotel from the '30s is run by the English-speaking De Paolis family, which welcome you with warm hospitality. Gaetano, Donato, and Barbara have only a few rooms and they lavished attention on them, making them comfortable and stylish. Bedrooms are spacious and traditionally furnished, with polished wood pieces and Oriental carpets on the hardwood floors. The king-size beds have hypoallergenic orthopedic mattresses, and the bathrooms come with hydrojet shower or Jacuzzi.

Via Modena 5, 00184 Roma. © **06-47825204.** Fax 06-47881806. www.residenzacellini.it. 6 units. 145€–240€ double; 165€–280€ junior suite. Rates include buffet breakfast. AE, DC, MC, V. Parking 35€. Metro: Repubblica. **Amenities:** Bar; concierge; airport transfer (55€); room service. *In room:* A/C, TV, hair dryer, minibar, Wi-Fi (free).

MODERATE

Hotel Morgana Between Santa Maria Maggiore and Stazione Termini, the completely up-to-date Morgana is a hotel of style and substance. Bedrooms are most comfortable and furnished in a sleek modern styling based on traditional designs. The rooms have all the modern amenities and a vaguely English-style decor. The English-speaking staff is pleasant and will help guide you to some of the city's most important attractions, many of which lie only a short walk from the hotel. Since this hotel lies in a noisy section of Rome, all of the bedrooms are soundproof.

Via F. Turati 33–37, 00185 Roma. © **06-4467230.** Fax 06-4469142. www.hotelmorgana.com. 106 units. 100€–235€ double; 165€–250€ suite. Rates include buffet breakfast. AE, DC, MC, V. Parking 15€. Metro: Termini. **Amenities:** Bar; airport transfer (58€); babysitting; concierge; room service. *In room:* A/C, TV, hair dryer, minibar, Wi-Fi (10€ per 24 hr.).

Kennedy Hotel A 5-minute walk from the Termini Station, this completely restored hotel is one of the best bets for those who want to stay in the rail station area. The hotel, launched in 1963 when President Kennedy died, was named to honor his memory. The building itself is from the late 19th century, although it has been much restored and modernized over the years. The hotel is within an easy walk of many of the historical monuments of Rome, including the Basilica of S. Maria Maggiore, the Opera House, the Colosseum, and the Roman Forum. Bedrooms are renovated, with tasteful furnishings and double-glass soundproofing. Many rooms open to views of the antique Roman wall of Servio Tullio.

Via Filippo Turati 62–64, 00185 Roma. © **06-4465373.** Fax 06-4465417. www.hotelkennedy.net. 52 units. 69€–149€ double; 129€–240€ suite. Rates include buffet breakfast. AE, DC, MC, V. Metro: Termini. Parking 15€. **Amenities:** Bar; exercise room; room service. *In room:* A/C, TV, hair dryer, Wi-Fi (18€ per 24 hr.).

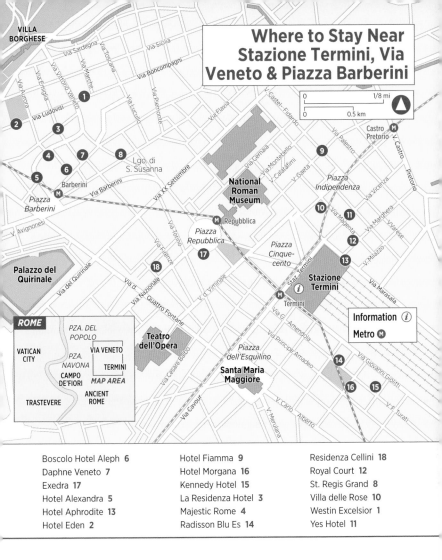

Where to Stay Near Stazione Termini, Via Veneto & Piazza Barberini

Boscolo Hotel Aleph 6
Daphne Veneto 7
Exedra 17
Hotel Alexandra 5
Hotel Aphrodite 13
Hotel Eden 2

Hotel Fiamma 9
Hotel Morgana 16
Kennedy Hotel 15
La Residenza Hotel 3
Majestic Rome 4
Radisson Blu Es 14

Residenza Cellini 18
Royal Court 12
St. Regis Grand 8
Villa delle Rose 10
Westin Excelsior 1
Yes Hotel 11

Royal Court ★ 📖 This winner lies in a restored Liberty-style palace a short walk from the Termini. The hotel evokes a tranquil, elegantly decorated private town house. Some of the superior rooms offer Jacuzzis in their bathrooms, but all units feature well-maintained and -designed bathrooms with tub/shower combinations. The superior rooms also come with small balconies opening onto cityscapes. Even the standard doubles are comfortable, but if you're willing to pay the price, you can stay in the deluxe doubles, which are like junior suites in most Rome hotels. Some of the bedrooms are large enough to sleep three or four guests comfortably.

Via Marghera 51, 00185 Roma. ℭ **06-44340364.** Fax 06-4469121. www.morganaroyalcourt. com. 24 units. 130€–250€ double. Rates include buffet breakfast. AE, DC, MC, V. Parking 25€.

Metro: Termini. **Amenities:** Bar; airport transfers (55€); babysitting; room service. *In room:* A/C, TV, hair dryer, minibar, Wi-Fi (10€ per 24 hr.).

Villa delle Rose ☺ Located less than 2 blocks north of the rail station, this hotel is an acceptable, if not exciting, choice. In the late 1800s, it was a villa with a dignified cut-stone facade inspired by the Renaissance. Despite many renovations, the ornate trappings of the original are still visible, including the lobby's Corinthian-capped marble columns and the flagstone-covered terrace that is part of the verdant back garden. The look is still one of faded grandeur. Much of the interior has been redecorated and upgraded with traditional wall coverings, carpets, and tiled bathrooms. Breakfasts in the garden do a lot to add country flavor to an otherwise very urban setting. Families often book here, asking for one of the three rooms with lofts that can sleep up to five.

Via Vicenza 5, 00185 Roma. ✆ **06-4451788.** Fax 06-4451639. www.villadellerose.it. 38 units (some with shower only). 72€–160€ double. Rates include buffet breakfast. AE, DC, MC, V. Free parking (only 4 cars). Metro: Termini or Castro Pretorio. **Amenities:** Bar; room service; free Wi-Fi (lobby). *In room:* A/C (in 30 rooms), TV, hair dryer, minibar (in some).

INEXPENSIVE

Hotel Aphrodite ⚓ Completely renovated, this government-rated three-star hotel in the heart of Rome is a four-story hotel offering good value. Directly next to Stazione Termini, it is a reliable and well-run choice, although the surrounding area is a little seedy at night. For rail passengers who want quick check-ins and fast getaways, it's the most convenient choice. Bedrooms are attractively and comfortably furnished with modern pieces and parquet floors, along with marble bathrooms with shower and mosaic tiles. A special feature here is the sunny rooftop terrace. Ask at the desk about the possibility of taking walking tours through the historic districts.

Via Marsala 90, 00185 Roma. ✆ **06-491096.** Fax 06-491579. www.accommodationinrome.com. 50 units. 90€–120€ double; 110€–150€ triple. Rates include continental breakfast. AE, DC, MC, V. Parking 15€. Metro: Termini. *In room:* A/C, TV, hair dryer, minibar, Wi-Fi (in some; free).

Hotel Fiamma Near the Baths of Diocletian, the Fiamma is in a renovated building, with four floors of bedrooms and a ground floor faced with marble and plate-glass windows. It's an old favorite, if a bit past its prime. The lobby is long and bright, filled with a varied collection of furnishings, including overstuffed chairs and blue enamel railings. On the same floor is an austere marble breakfast room. The comfortably furnished guest rooms range from small to medium in size, and the small bathrooms are tiled, with adequate shelf space.

Via Gaeta 61, 00185 Roma. ✆ **06-4818436.** Fax 06-4883511. www.leonardihotels.com. 79 units (shower only). 72€–135€ double; 110€–180€ triple. Rates include buffet breakfast. AE, DC, MC, V. Parking 20€. Metro: Termini. **Amenities:** Room service. *In room:* A/C, TV, hair dryer, minibar, Wi-Fi (5€ per 2 hr.).

Yes Hotel ⚓ We'd definitely say yes to this hotel, which lies only 100m (328 ft.) from Stazione Termini. Opened in 2007, it was quickly discovered by frugally minded travelers who want a good bed and comfortable surroundings for the night. It's a two-story hotel housed in a restored 19th-century building with simple, well-chosen furnishings resting on tiled floors. There is a sleek, modern look to both the bedrooms and public areas, and the staff is helpful but not effusive.

Via Magenta 15, 00185 Roma. ✆ **06-44363836.** Fax 06-44363829. www.yeshotelrome.com. 29 units. 94€–219€ double. DC, MC, V. Parking 17€. Metro: Termini. **Amenities:** Bar; babysitting; room service. *In room:* A/C, TV, hair dryer, Wi-Fi (5€ per 24 hr.).

Near Via Veneto & Piazza Barberini

If you stay in this area, you definitely won't be on the wrong side of the tracks. Unlike the area near the dreary rail station, this is a beautiful and upscale commercial neighborhood, near some of Rome's best shopping.

VERY EXPENSIVE

Hotel Eden ★★★   It's not as grand architecturally as the Westin Excelsior, nor does it have the views of the Hassler, and it's certainly not a summer resort like the Hilton. But the Eden is Rome's top choice for discerning travelers who like grand comfort but without all the ostentation.

For several generations after its 1889 opening, this hotel, about a 10-minute walk east of the Spanish Steps, reigned over one of the world's most stylish shopping neighborhoods. Recent guests have included Pierce Brosnan, Tom Cruise, Emma Thompson, and Nicole Kidman. The Eden's hilltop position guarantees a panoramic city view from most guest rooms; all are spacious and elegantly appointed with a decor harking back to the late 19th century, plus marble-sheathed bathrooms. Try to get one of the front rooms with a balcony boasting views over Rome.

Via Ludovisi 49, 00187 Roma. ✆ **06-478121.** Fax 06-4821584. www.edenroma.com. 121 units. 328€–840€ double; from 1,340€ suite. AE, DC, DISC, MC, V. Parking 60€. Metro: Piazza Barberini. **Amenities:** Restaurant (La Terrazza; p. 120); bar; airport transfers (85€); babysitting; concierge; exercise room; room service; sauna. *In room:* A/C, TV/DVD, CD player, hair dryer, minibar, Wi-Fi (19€ per 24 hr.).

Majestic Rome ★★   Built in 1889 in the center of Rome, this government-rated five-star hotel is completely modernized and up to date, and one of the grandest addresses of Rome, standing on the street that enjoyed its *La Dolce Vita* heyday in the 1950s. The Majestic was the center of high society life in Rome in the 1920s, when movie stars and royalty paraded through its lobby. It's still a home for many celebrities and political figures, and much of the past splendor has been regained in a sensitive restoration. The spacious rooms are beautifully appointed—often filled with antiques, including tapestries and frescoes—and many accommodations open onto private balconies. The on-site restaurant Filippo La Mantia specializes in discovering ancient Roman recipes.

Via Vittorio Veneto 50, 00187 Roma. ✆ **06-421441.** Fax 06-4880984. www.rome-hotels-majestic.com. 98 units. 335€–720€ double; from 1,200€ suite. AE, DC, MC, V. Parking 70€. Metro: Piazza Barberini. **Amenities:** Restaurant; bar; airport transfers (82€); babysitting; concierge; exercise room; room service. *In room:* A/C, TV/DVD, CD player, hair dryer, minibar, Wi-Fi (free).

Westin Excelsior ★   If money is no object, this is a good place to spend it. Architecturally more grandiose than either the Eden or the Hassler, the Excelsior is not as up-to-date or as beautifully renovated as either the Eden or the St. Regis Grand. The Excelsior has never moved into the 21st century the way some other grand hotels have. For our money today, we prefer the Hotel de Russie, and we've always gotten better service at the Hassler (see reviews for both later), but the Excelsior remains a favorite, especially among older visitors who remember it from decades past. The guest rooms come in two varieties: new (the result of a major renovation) and traditional. The older ones are a bit worn, while the newer ones have more imaginative color schemes and plush carpeting. All are spacious and elegantly furnished, always with antiques and silk curtains.

Via Vittorio Veneto 125, 00187 Roma. ✆ **800/325-3589** in the U.S., or 06-47081. Fax 06-4826205. www.westin.com/excelsiorrome. 316 units. 347€–550€ double; from 1,770€ suite. AE, DC, DISC, MC, V. Parking 43€–70€. Metro: Piazza Barberini. **Amenities:** Restaurant; bar; airport transfers (85€); babysitting; children's programs; concierge; exercise room; indoor heated pool; room service; spa. *In room:* A/C, TV, hair dryer, minibar, Wi-Fi (15€ per 24 hr.).

EXPENSIVE

Boscolo Hotel Aleph ★★ Called sexy and decadent by some hotel critics when it opened, this winning choice leads the pack among "new wave" Italian hotels. A luxury hotel in the center of Rome, Aleph was designed by Adam Tihany, who said he wanted to "humanize the rooms with indulgent details." Only a minute's walk from the Via Veneto, the hotel offers spacious guest rooms adorned with elegant Italian fabrics, a tasteful decor, and all the latest technology. Murano chandeliers, window blinds made of strings of metal beads, a dramatic roof terrace overlooking the heart of Rome, and an indoor swimming pool are just some of the features of this hotel. Tihany wanted something eccentric and intriguing, exclusive yet provocative—and his creation is all that and vastly comfortable as well, with a 1930s and 1940s-inspired style.

Via San Basilio 15, 00187 Roma. ✆ **06-422901.** Fax 06-42290000. www.boscolohotels.com. 96 units. 204€–380€ double; from 506€ junior suite; from 880€ suite. AE, DC, MC, V. Parking 35€. Metro: Barberini. **Amenities:** 2 restaurants; 2 bars; airport transfers (60€); babysitting; concierge; exercise room; indoor heated pool; room service; sauna; spa. *In room:* A/C, TV, hair dryer, minibar, Wi-Fi (20€ per 24 hr.).

Hotel Alexandra ★ 🎁 This is one of your few chances to stay on Via Veneto without going broke (although it's not exactly cheap). Set behind the stone facade of what was a 19th-century mansion, the Alexandra offers immaculate and soundproof guest rooms. The rooms range from cramped to midsize, but each has been redecorated, filled with antiques or tasteful contemporary pieces. They have extras such as swing-mirror vanities and brass or wooden bedsteads. The breakfast room is appealing: Inspired by an Italian garden, it was designed by noted architect Paolo Portoghesi.

Via Vittorio Veneto 18, 00187 Roma. ✆ **06-4881943.** Fax 06-4871804. www.hotelalexandra roma.com. 60 units (some with shower only). 280€ double; 390€ junior suite. Rates include buffet breakfast. AE, DC, MC, V. Parking 26€–36€. Metro: Piazza Barberini. **Amenities:** Babysitting; room service; Wi-Fi (4€ per hr.). *In room:* A/C, TV, hair dryer, minibar.

MODERATE

Daphne Veneto ★ 🎁 In a restored building from the 19th century deep in the heart of Rome, this is a top-notch B&B, just minutes on foot from the Trevi Fountain. The midsize guest rooms have an understated elegance with crisp linens and fluffy comforters on the beds. The public rooms contain sitting areas, cozy reading sections, a lending library, and high-speed Internet access. Floors are reached by elevator, and two of the units are two-bedroom, two-bathroom suites. Fresh fruit and freshly baked pastries are served with your morning coffee.

Via di San Basilio 55, 00187 Roma. ✆ **06-87450086.** Fax 06-233240967. www.daphne-rome.com. 8 units. 140€–220€ double; 320€–460€ suite. Rates include buffet breakfast. AE, MC, V. Nearby parking 30€. Metro: Piazza Barberini. **Amenities:** Airport transfers (55€). *In room:* A/C, hair dryer, Wi-Fi (free).

La Residenza Hotel ★★ In a superb but congested location, this little hotel successfully combines intimacy and elegance. A bit old-fashioned and homey, the converted villa has an ivy-covered courtyard and a series of public rooms with Empire divans, oil portraits, and rattan chairs. Terraces are scattered throughout. The guest rooms are generally spacious, containing bentwood chairs and built-in furniture, including beds. The dozen or so junior suites boast balconies. The bathrooms have robes, and rooms even come equipped with ice machines.

Via Emilia 22–24, 00187 Roma. ✆ **06-4880789.** Fax 06-485721. www.hotel-la-residenza.com. 29 units. 160€–280€ double; 230€–380€ suite. Rates include buffet breakfast. AE, MC, V. Parking (limited) 20€. Metro: Piazza Barberini. **Amenities:** Bar; babysitting; room service. *In room:* A/C, TV, hair dryer, minibar.

Near Ancient Rome

EXPENSIVE

Capo d'Africa ★ 🏨 Installed in a beautiful 19th-century building and boasting a strong colonial look, this hotel lies in the heart of Imperial Rome between the Forum and the Domus Aurea in the Celio district of Rome, a few steps from the Colosseum. Endowed with a "contemporary classic" look, it attracts visitors with its sophisticated interior design, works of art, high-tech facilities, and impeccable service. Best of all is a splendid rooftop terrace with a panoramic view over some of the dusty ruins of the world's most famous monuments. Rooms are midsize and furnished with good taste; they are spread across three floors.

Via Capo d'Africa 54, 00184 Roma. ✆ **06-772801.** Fax 06-77280801. www.hotelcapodafrica.com. 65 units. 380€–400€ double; 480€–540€ suite. Rates include buffet breakfast. AE, DC, MC, V. Parking 45€. Metro: Colosseo. **Amenities:** Restaurant; bar; babysitting; exercise room; room service. *In room:* A/C, TV, hair dryer, minibar.

The Inn at the Roman Forum ★ 🏨 This is one of the secret discoveries of Rome, with the Roman Forum itself as a neighbor. A restored 15th-century building dripping with antiquity, the inn even has a small section of Trajan's Market-place on-site. You enter the front doorway like a resident Roman, greeting your host in the living room. Sleek, classically styled bedrooms are spread across three upper floors, opening onto views of the heart of Rome. Three back bedrooms open onto a walled-in garden complete with fig and palm trees. The most elegant and expensive double has a private patio with a designer bathroom.

Via degli Ibernesi 30, 00184 Roma. ✆ **06-69190970.** Fax 06-45438802. www.theinnattheromanforum.com. 12 units. 210€–960€ double; from 1,040€ suite. Rates include buffet breakfast. AE, DC, MC, V. Parking 30€. Bus: 64 or 117. **Amenities:** Bar; airport transfers (55€); babysitting; concierge; room service. *In room:* A/C, TV/DVD, hair dryer, minibar, MP3 docking station, Wi-Fi (10€ per day).

MODERATE

Hotel Adriano This hotel is housed within the original walls of a 15th-century *palazzo,* and it's been converted into a well-run and government-rated three-star hotel to welcome guests and house them comfortably. The location is close to some of the major landmarks, including Piazza di Spagna, Piazza Navona, and the Pantheon, as well as lying a few steps from the Parliament. You can find a well-upholstered armchair waiting for you under the vaulted ceilings of the public rooms, perhaps facing a reproduction of a Titian nude. Rooms are decorated in shades of gray, taupe, and white. You can enjoy breakfast on the hotel's roof terrace.

Via di Pallacorda 2, 00186 Roma. ℭ **06-68802451.** Fax 06-68803926. www.hoteladriano.com. 80 units. 142€–297€ double; 337€–500€ suite. Rates include buffet breakfast. AE, DC, MC, V. Parking 30€. Bus: 95 or 175. **Amenities:** Bar; airport transfers (55€); babysitting; concierge; room service; Wi-Fi (5€ per 24 hr., in lobby). *In room:* A/C, TV, minibar.

INEXPENSIVE

Colosseum Hotel   Two short blocks southwest of Santa Maria Maggiore, this hotel offers affordable and small but comfortable rooms. Someone with flair and lots of money designed the public areas and upper halls, which hint at baronial grandeur. The drawing room, with its long refectory table, white walls, red tiles, and armchairs, invites lingering. The guest rooms are furnished with well-chosen antique reproductions (beds of heavy carved wood, dark-paneled wardrobes, and leatherwood chairs); all have stark white walls, and some have old-fashioned plumbing in the bathrooms.

Via Sforza 10, 00184 Roma. ℭ **06-4827228.** Fax 06-4827285. www.hotelcolosseum.com. 50 units. 85€–230€ double; 105€–285€ triple. Rates include buffet breakfast. AE, DC, MC, V. Parking 30€. Metro: Cavour. **Amenities:** Bar; babysitting; bikes; room service. *In room:* A/C, TV, hair dryer, Wi-Fi (10€ per 24 hr.).

Hotel Arenula ★ 🍴   At last a hotel has opened in Rome's old Jewish ghetto, and it's a winner and quite affordable. It takes its name from Via Arenula, that timeworn street linking Largo Argentina to Ponte Garibaldi and the Trastevere area. The restored building is from the 19th century, and the Patta family turned it into this undiscovered and comfortable inn. Close at hand are such attractions as the Pantheon, the Colosseum, and the Piazza Navona. Rooms are furnished in a tasteful, traditional way. They are most inviting and comfortable, with pale-wood pieces and immaculate bathrooms. There's no elevator, so be prepared to climb some stairs.

Via Santa Maria de Calderari 47, 00186 Roma. ℭ **06-6879454.** Fax 06-6896188. www.hotel arenula.com. 50 units. 100€–133€ double. Rates include buffet breakfast. AE, DC, MC, V. Metro: Colosseo. Bus: 40. **Amenities:** Room service. *In room:* A/C, TV, hair dryer.

Hotel Lancelot ★ 🍴   Close to the Colosseum, this hotel opened in 1953 but has been much renovated and altered ever since. Run by the Khan family, the hotel has been accurately hailed by *National Geographic Traveler* as one of Rome's best hotel values. Rooms range from midsize to spacious; all doubles have showers, and the lone suite comes with a bathtub. Bedrooms are comfortable and individually decorated, and some open onto private terraces. All the rooms at this hotel are soundproof. A charming on-site restaurant serves Roman specialties.

Via Capo d'Africa 47, 00184 Roma. ℭ **06-70450615.** Fax 06-70450640. www.lancelothotel. com. 60 units. 175€–210€ double; 300€ suite. Rates include buffet breakfast. AE, DC, MC, V. Parking 10€. Metro: Colosseo. **Amenities:** Bar; babysitting. *In room:* A/C, TV, hair dryer, Wi-Fi (free).

Nicolas Inn   Only 4 blocks from the Colosseum, this small B&B is also convenient for exploring the Roman Forum. In a warm, cozy atmosphere, a few guests are housed on the second floor of an early-20th-century building. Rich fabrics and cherry-colored wood make this hotel a winner, that and its comfortably furnished midsize to spacious bedrooms. A major asset of the inn is the personal attention provided for each guest. Guests find a complimentary map of Rome in their bedrooms.

Via Cavour 295, 00184 Roma. 📞 **06-97618483.** www.nicolasinn.com. 4 units. 100€–180€ double. Rates include continental breakfast. No credit cards. Parking 30€. Metro: Cavour. **Amenities:** Airport transfers (50€). *In room:* A/C, TV, fridge, hair dryer, Wi-Fi (free).

Near Campo De' Fiori

EXPENSIVE

Residenza Farnese ★ 🔥 Among the boutique hotels springing up around Campo de' Fiori, the new Farnese in a 15th-century mansion emerges near the top. Opt for one of the front rooms overlooking Palazzo Farnese, with Michelangelo's Renaissance cornice bathed in sunlight. Bedrooms are fresh and modernized, ranging in size from small to spacious, each with a freshly restored private bathroom with a shower. The location in the heart of ancient Rome puts you within walking distance of many of the major sights, particularly the Roman Forum or even St. Peter's. The owner, Signora Zema, is a gracious host who can provide much helpful advice. She has placed contemporary art throughout as a grace note, and she believes in a generous breakfast to fortify you for the day.

Via del Mascherone 59, 00186 Roma. 📞 **06-68210980.** Fax 06-80321049. www.residenzafarnese roma.it. 31 units. 145€–300€ double; 230€–500€ junior suite. Rates include buffet breakfast. MC, V. Bus: 64. **Amenities:** Bar; room service. *In room:* A/C, TV, hair dryer, minibar, Wi-Fi (.50€ per hr.).

MODERATE

Hotel Teatro di Pompeo ★★ 🎁 Built atop the ruins of the Theater of Pompey, this small charmer lies near the spot where Julius Caesar met his end on the Ides of March. Intimate and refined, it's on a quiet piazza near the Palazzo Farnese and Campo de' Fiori. The rooms are decorated in an old-fashioned Italian style with hand-painted tiles, and the beamed ceilings date from the days of Michelangelo. The guest rooms range from small to medium in size, each with a tidy but cramped bathroom.

Largo del Pallaro 8, 00186 Roma. 📞 **06-68300170.** Fax 06-68805531. www.hotelteatrodi pompeo.it. 13 units (shower only). 180€–210€ double; 240€–270€ triple. Rates include buffet breakfast. AE, DC, MC, V. Bus: 46, 62, or 64. **Amenities:** Bar; babysitting; room service; Wi-Fi (3€ per hr., in lobby). *In room:* A/C, TV, hair dryer, minibar.

Near Piazza Navona & the Pantheon

Travelers who want to immerse themselves in the atmosphere of ancient Rome, or those looking for romance, will prefer staying in this area over the more commercial Via Veneto area. Transportation isn't the greatest and you'll do a lot of walking, but that's the reason many visitors come here in the first place—to wander and discover the glory that was Rome. You're also within walking distance of the Vatican and the ruins of classical Rome. Many bars and cafes are within an easy walk of all the hotels located here.

VERY EXPENSIVE

Hotel Raphael ★★ With a glorious location adjacent to Piazza Navona, the Raphael is within easy walking distance of many sights. The ivy-covered facade invites you to enter the lobby, which is decorated with antiques that rival the cache in local museums (there's even a Picasso ceramics collection). The guest rooms (some quite small) were refurbished with a Florentine touch. Some of the suites have private terraces. The deluxe rooms, the executive units, and the junior suites were conceived by Richard Meier, the famous architect who has designed buildings all over the world. Each of them is lined with oak and equipped in a modern high-tech style that includes a digital sound system. The Raphael is often the top choice of Italian politicos in town for the opening of Parliament. We love its rooftop restaurant with views of all of the city's prominent landmarks.

Largo Febo 2, 00186 Roma. ✆ **06-682831.** Fax 06-6878993. www.raphaelhotel.com. 65 units. 272€–600€ double; 442€–900€ suite. AE, DC, MC, V. Parking 40€. Bus: 70, 81, 87, or 115. **Amenities:** Restaurant; bar; babysitting; concierge; exercise room; room service; sauna; Wi-Fi (free, in lobby). *In room:* A/C, TV/DVD, hair dryer, minibar.

EXPENSIVE

Albergo Del Sole al Pantheon ★   You're obviously paying for the million-dollar view, but you might find that it's worth it to be across from the Pantheon. This building was constructed in 1450 as a home, and the first records of it as a hostelry appeared in 1467, making it one of the world's oldest hotels. The layout is amazingly eccentric—prepare to walk up and down a lot of three- or four-step staircases. The guest rooms vary greatly in decor, much of it hit-or-miss, with compact, tiled full bathrooms. The rooms opening onto the piazza still tend to be noisy at all hours. The quieter rooms overlook the courtyard, but we always prefer to put up with the noise just to enjoy one of the world's greatest views. For the grandest view of the Pantheon, ask for room no. 106 or 108.

Piazza della Rotonda 63, 00186 Roma. ✆ **06-6780441.** Fax 06-69940689. www.hotelsole alpantheon.com. 30 units. Summer 380€–500€ double; 530€–800€ suite. Off season 230€–276€ double, from 372€ suite. Rates include buffet breakfast. AE, DC, MC, V. Bus: 64. **Amenities:** Bar; babysitting; Jacuzzi; room service. *In room:* A/C, TV, hair dryer, minibar.

MODERATE

Albergo Santa Chiara   This is a family run hotel near the Pantheon in the very inner core of historic Rome. Since 1838, the Corteggiani family has been welcoming sightseers to classic Rome. The white walls and marble columns here speak of former elegance, although the rooms today are simply furnished, functional, yet comfortable. The size? They range from the size of a broom closet to a suite large enough to be classified as a small Roman apartment. We go for those units facing the Piazza della Minerva, although you'll often have to listen to late-night revelers who don't know when to go home.

Via Santa Chiara 21, 00186 Roma. ✆ **06-6872979.** Fax 06-6873144. www.albergosantachiara. com. 98 units (half with shower only). 225€–280€ double; 460€–550€ suite. Rates include buffet breakfast. AE, DC, MC, V. Metro: Piazza di Spagna. **Amenities:** Bar; babysitting; room service. *In room:* A/C, TV, hair dryer, minibar.

Near Piazza Del Popolo & the Spanish Steps

This is a great place to stay if you're a serious shopper, but expect to part with a lot of extra euros for the privilege. This is a more elegant area than the Via Veneto—think Fifth Avenue all the way.

Where to Stay Near Piazza del Popolo & the Spanish Steps

VERY EXPENSIVE

The Hassler ★★   The Westin Excelsior is a grander palace, and the Eden and the de Russie are more up-to-date, but the Hassler has something that no other hotel can boast—a coveted location at the top of the Spanish Steps. The Hassler, rebuilt in 1944 to replace the 1885 original, is not quite what it used to be. But because it's such a classic, and because of that incredible location, it gets away with charging astronomical rates. The lounges and the guest rooms, with their "Italian Park Avenue" trappings, strike a faded, if still glamorous, 1930s note. The guest rooms range from small singles to some of the most spacious suites in town. High ceilings make them appear larger than they are, and many of them open onto private balconies or terraces. The front rooms, dramatically overlooking the Spanish Steps, are often noisy at night, but the views are worth it.

Piazza Trinità dei Monti 6, 00187 Roma. ✆ **800/223-6800** in the U.S., or 06-699340. Fax 06-6789991. www.hotelhassler.com. 100 units. 350€–760€ double; from 1,100€ suite. AE, DC, MC, V. Parking 30€. Metro: Piazza di Spagna. **Amenities:** 2 restaurants; bar; airport transfers (100€); babysitting; bikes; concierge; exercise room; room service; spa. *In room:* A/C, TV/DVD, hair dryer, minibar, Wi-Fi (20€ per 24 hr.).

Hotel Art by the Spanish Steps ★★ 🎁   This discovery lies near the Spanish Steps on "the street of artists," as Via Margutta is called. A former college has been turned into a hotel in a modern, minimalist style. Of particular interest is the Hall. The lobby, once a chapel, sits under a frescoed vaulted ceiling, where works of contemporary artists abound. The corridors of the four floors housing the rooms are decorated in blue, orange, yellow, and green. Forming a border for the corridors are stretches of milky glass with verses from poets such as Federico García Lorca. High-tech furnishings and bright colors adorn the bedrooms, which make good use of wood and Florentine leather. The rooms also feature glass, metal, and mosaic tiles that pick up the colors of the corridor.

Via Margutta 56, 00187 Roma. ✆ **06-328711.** Fax 06-36003995. www.hotelart.it. 46 units. 250€–350€ double; from 500€ suite. AE, DC, MC, V. Parking 25€. Metro: Piazza di Spagna. **Amenities:** Bar; babysitting; bikes; exercise room; room service; sauna. *In room:* A/C, TV, minibar.

Hotel de Russie ★★★ ☺   This government-rated five-star hotel has raised the bar for every other hotel in the city. For service, style, and modern luxuries, it beats out the Eden, the Westin Excelsior, and the St. Regis Grand. Just off the Piazza del Popolo, it reopened in 2000 to media acclaim for its opulent furnishings and choice location. Public areas are glossy and contemporary. About 30% of the bedrooms are conservative, with traditional furniture, while the remaining 70% are more minimalist, with a stark and striking style.

Via del Babuino 9, 00187 Roma. ✆ **800/323-7500** in North America, or 06-328881. Fax 06-3288888. www.roccofortehotels.com. 125 units. 680€–960€ double; from 1,430€ suite. AE, DC, MC, V. Parking 55€. Metro: Flaminia. **Amenities:** Restaurant; bar; airport transfers (85€); babysitting; children's programs; concierge; exercise room; room service; spa. *In room:* A/C, TV, fax, hair dryer, minibar, Wi-Fi (20€ per 24 hr.).

Hotel d'Inghilterra ★★   The Inghilterra holds on to its traditions and heritage, even though it has been renovated. Situated between Via Condotti and Via Borgogna, this hotel was the guesthouse of the 17th-century Torlonia princes. If you're willing to spend a king's ransom, Rome's most fashionable small hotel is comparable to the Hassler and the InterContinental. The rooms have mostly old pieces (gilt and lots of marble, mahogany chests, and glittery mirrors) complemented by modern conveniences. The preferred rooms are higher up, opening onto a tile terrace, with a balustrade and a railing covered with flowering vines and plants.

Via Bocca di Leone 14, 00187 Roma. ✆ **06-699811.** Fax 06-69922243. www.royaldemeure.com. 98 units. Summer 320€–580€ double; from 945€ suite. Off season 225€–348€ double; from 630€ suite. AE, DC, MC, V. Parking 25€. Metro: Piazza di Spagna. **Amenities:** Restaurant; bar; babysitting; room service. *In room:* A/C, TV/DVD, hair dryer, minibar.

The Inn at the Spanish Steps ★★★ 🎁   This intimate, upscale inn was the first new hotel to open in this location in years. The people who run Rome's most famous cafe, Caffè Greco, created it where Hans Christian Andersen once lived.

Andersen praised the balcony roses and violets, and so can you. Every room is furnished in an authentic period decor, featuring antiques, elegant draperies, and parquet floors. The superior units come with fireplace, a frescoed or beamed ceiling, and a balcony. The hotel is completely modern, from its hypoallergenic mattresses to its generous wardrobe space.

Via dei Condotti 85, 00187 Roma. ✆ **06-69925657.** Fax 06-6786470. www.atspanishsteps.com. 24 units. 230€–720€ double; from 680€ suite. Rates include buffet breakfast. AE, DC, MC, V. Metro: Piazza di Spagna. **Amenities:** Bar; babysitting; airport transfers (55€); concierge; room service. *In room:* A/C, TV, hair dryer, kitchenette (in some), minibar, MP3 docking station (in some).

Portrait Suites ★★ For those who don't want to stay at the Hassler but prefer the luxury of an intimate and deluxe boutique hotel, this all-suite inn is the answer. This six-story historic building is decorated in an elegant contemporary style, including walls lined with photographs and drawings by Salvatore Ferragamo. All accommodations are spacious, with such features as large marble bathrooms. On top of the building is a terrace opening onto a panoramic sweep of Rome.

Via Bocca di Leone 23, 00187 Roma. ✆ **06-69380742.** Fax 06-69190625. www.lungarnohotels. com. 14 units. 390€–780€ double; 680€–2,300€ suite. Rates include buffet breakfast. AE, DC, MC, V. Parking 25€. Metro: Piazza di Spagna. **Amenities:** Bar; babysitting; room service. *In room:* A/C, TV, hair dryer, kitchenette, minibar, Wi-Fi (free).

Villa Spalletti Trivelli ★★★ 🏛 On a side street on patrician Quirina Hill, this gem of a hotel offers a rare opportunity to experience home life as lived by a Roman nobleman and his family a century ago, in this case the Spalletti-Trivelli family, titled since 1667. A $4-million renovation has turned the early-20th-century neoclassical villa into a sumptuous address furnished with antiques, tapestries, and Italian art. Just steps from the Piazza del Quirinale and only a 5-minute walk from the Trevi Fountain, the villa opens onto a splendid Italian garden. The spacious bedrooms range from romantically decorated units to grand deluxe suites fit for a visiting president.

Via Piacenza 4, 00184 Roma. ✆ **06-48907934.** Fax 06-4871409. www.villaspalletti.it. 12 units. 360€–627€ double; from 759€ suite. AE, DC, MC, V. Metro: Barberini. **Amenities:** Restaurant; bar; exercise room; room service; sauna. *In room:* A/C, TV, minibar, Wi-Fi (free).

EXPENSIVE

Babuino 181 ★★ 🏛 Rome's newest boutique hotel is a welcome addition, especially to those who want to avoid cramped accommodations. The location is bull's-eye in the historic center a short stroll to the Piazza del Popolo, the Spanish Steps, art galleries, and smart cafes. Though Via Del Babuino positively vibrates during the day, it settles down in the evening. The owners, the little hotel group Alberto Moncada di Paternò, specializes in transforming historical residences by filling them inside with modern art and design. Special touches include Frette linens and bathrobes, a Nespresso machine, and a wall-mounted flatscreen TV. Bathrooms are clad in yellow marble, with toilets and a bidet in a separate little room. Bedrooms are spacious and furnished in a sleek contemporary style with muted gray and beiges.

Via del Babuino 181, 00187 Roma. ✆ **06/3229-5295.** 14 units. www.romeluxurysuites.com/ babuino. 305€–435€ double, 430€–550€ suite. AE, DC, MC, V. Metro: Flaminio. **Amenities:** Bar; airport transfers (65€); babysitting; concierge; room service. *In room:* A/C, TV, MP3 docking station, hair dryer, minibar, Wi-Fi (free).

Hotel Locarno   If you'd like to experience Rome as visitors such as Mary Pickford and Douglas Fairbanks found in the 1920s, head for this monument to Art Deco. In the heart of Rome, near Piazza del Popolo, this hotel opened its doors in 1925 and it's been receiving visitors ever since, even through a world war. In fair weather, breakfast is served in the garden or on the roof garden; this is an experience worth savoring. Bedrooms in the older section are a bit chintzy, but the newer wing has fresher accommodations. All of the original floors, doors, and bathroom fixtures in this newer section were recently refurbished. Rooms are reached by taking a bird-cage elevator.

Via della Penna 25, 00186 Roma. ✆ **06-3610841.** Fax 06-3215249. www.hotellocarno.com. 66 units. 270€–465€ double; 395€–1,200€ suite. Rates include buffet breakfast. AE, DC, MC, V. Parking 25€. Metro: Flaminio. Bus: 116 or 117. **Amenities:** Bar; airport transfers (55€); bikes; room service. *In room:* A/C, TV, minibar, Wi-Fi (free).

Hotel Scalinata di Spagna ★★★   This is Rome's most famous boutique hotel. The deluxe Hassler is across the street but far removed in price and grandeur from this intimate, upscale B&B at the top of the Spanish Steps. Its delightful little building—only two floors are visible from the outside—is nestled between much larger structures, with four relief columns across the facade and window boxes with bright blossoms. The recently redecorated interior features small public rooms with bright print slipcovers, old clocks, and low ceilings. The decor varies radically from one guest room to the next. Some have low beamed ceilings and ancient-looking wood furniture; others have loftier ceilings and more run-of-the-mill furniture.

Piazza Trinità dei Monti 17, 00187 Roma. ✆ **06-69940896.** Fax 06-69940598. www.hotel scalinata.com. 16 units (tubs only). 130€–290€ double; 230€–350€ junior suite. Rates include buffet breakfast. AE, MC, V. Parking 40€. Metro: Piazza di Spagna. **Amenities:** Bar; airport transfers (75€); babysitting; room service. *In room:* A/C, TV, hair dryer, minibar, Wi-Fi (free).

La Lumière di Piazza di Spagna ★ 👜   We never thought another little inn would open near the Spanish Steps because real estate was no longer available. Wrong. Along comes this charmer in a five-story 18th-century building of great character (with an elevator). Rooms are spacious and exquisitely furnished in a classic style, with a panoramic view of the Spanish Steps. All of them have adjoining bathrooms with Jacuzzi spa showers. When you're served a breakfast buffet on the panoramic terrace, the city of Rome is at your feet. Outside your door you'll find the best and most exclusive shops in Rome.

Via Belsiana 72, 00187 Roma. ✆ **06-69380806.** Fax 06-69294231. www.lalumieredipiazzadi spagna.com. 10 units. 120€–350€ double; 150€–410€ triple. Rates include buffet breakfast. AE, DC, MC, V. Parking 30€. **Amenities:** Airport transfers (65€); room service. *In room:* A/C, TV, hair dryer, minibar, Wi-Fi (free).

Piranesi ★★ 👜   Right off the Piazza del Popolo sits one of Rome's most select boutique hotels, boasting more affordable prices than you'll find at the Hotel de Russie, which fronts it. If you lodge here, you'll be staying in one of the most historic areas of Rome. Bedrooms are tranquil and decorated in a style evocative of the 18th-century Directoire. Bare pinewood floors and cherrywood furniture are grace notes, as are the immaculate bathrooms. The most dramatic aspect of the Piranesi is its panoramic rooftop terrace.

Via del Babuino 196, 00187 Roma. ✆ **06-328041.** Fax 06-3610597. www.hotelpiranesi.com. 32 units. 220€–350€ double; 298€–420€ suite. Rates include buffet breakfast. AE, MC, V. Parking

40€. Metro: Flaminio. Bus: 117. **Amenities:** Bar; exercise room; room service; sauna; Wi-Fi (12€ per 24 hr.). *In room:* A/C, TV, hair dryer, minibar.

MODERATE

Casa Howard ★ 🎁   It's rare to make a discovery in the tourist-trodden Piazza di Spagna area. That's why Casa Howard comes as a pleasant surprise. The B&B occupies about two-thirds of the second floor of a historic structure. The welcoming family owners maintain beautifully furnished guest rooms, each with its own private bathroom (although some bathrooms lie outside the bedrooms in the hallway). The Green Room is the most spacious, with its own en suite bathroom.

Via Capo le Case 18, 00187 Roma. ✆ **06-69924555.** Fax 06-6794644. www.casahoward.com. 5 units. 170€–250€ double. MC, V. Parking 25€. Metro: Piazza di Spagna. **Amenities:** Babysitting; room service; sauna. *In room:* A/C, TV, hair dryer, Wi-Fi (free).

Fontanella Borghese ★ 🎁   Close to the Spanish Steps in the exact heart of Rome, this hotel surprisingly remains relatively undiscovered. Much renovated and improved, it has been installed on the third and fourth floors of a palace dating from the end of the 18th century. The building once belonged to the princes of the Borghese family, and the little hotel looks out onto the Borghese Palace. It lies within walking distance of the Trevi Fountain, the Pantheon, and the Piazza Navona. The location is also close to Piazza Augusto and the Ara Pacis. In the midsize bedrooms, plain wooden furniture rests on parquet floors, and everything is in a classical tradition comfortably modernized for today's travelers. Half of the bathrooms come with tubs, the rest with showers. The staff of the front desk is one of the most helpful in central Rome.

Largo Fontanella Borghese 84, 00186 Roma. ✆ **06-68809-504.** Fax 06-6861295. www.fontanella borghese.com. 29 units. 160€–230€ double; 180€–280€ triple. AE, DC, MC, V. Nearby parking 25€. Metro: Piazza di Spagna. **Amenities:** Room service. *In room:* A/C, TV, hair dryer, minibar.

Hotel Condotti   The Condotti is small, choice, and terrific for shoppers intent on being near the tony boutiques. The born-to-shop crowd often thinks that the hotel is on Via Condotti because of its name—actually, it's 2 blocks to the north. The staff, nearly all of whom speak English, is cooperative and hardworking. The mostly modern rooms might not have much historical charm (they're furnished like nice motel units), but they're comfortable and soothing. Each room is decorated with traditional furnishings, including excellent beds (usually twins). Room no. 414 has a geranium-filled terrace.

Via Mario de' Fiori 37, 00187 Roma. ✆ **06-6794661.** Fax 06-6790457. www.hotelcondotti.com. 26 units (shower only). 94€–360€ double; 124€–390€ triple. Rates include buffet breakfast. AE, DC, MC, V. Parking 20€. Metro: Piazza di Spagna. **Amenities:** Airport transfers (60€); babysitting; bikes; room service. *In room:* A/C, TV, hair dryer, minibar, Wi-Fi (free).

Hotel Piazza di Spagna   About a block from the downhill side of the Spanish Steps, this hotel is small but classic, with an inviting atmosphere made more gracious by the helpful manager, Elisabetta Giocondi. The guest rooms boast a functional streamlined decor; some even have Jacuzzis in the tiled bathrooms. Accommodations are spread across three floors, with very tidy bedrooms with high ceilings and cool terrazzo floors.

Via Mario de' Fiori 61, 00187 Roma. ✆ **06-6796412.** Fax 06-6790654. www.hotelpiazzadispagna. it. 17 units (some with shower only). 120€–250€ double; 160€–350€ triple. Rates include buffet breakfast. AE, DC, MC, V. Nearby parking 20€. Metro: Piazza di Spagna. Bus: 117. **Amenities:** Bar;

airport transfers (65€); Internet (10€ per 24 hr., in lobby); room service. *In room:* A/C, TV, hair dryer, minibar.

Hotel Trinità dei Monti Between two of the most bustling piazzas in Rome (Barberini and Spagna), this is a friendly and well-maintained place. The hotel occupies the second and third floors of an antique building. Its guest rooms come with herringbone-pattern parquet floors and big windows, and are comfortable, if not flashy. Each has a tidy tiled bathroom. The hotel's social center is a simple coffee bar near the reception desk. Don't expect anything terribly fancy, but the welcome is warm and the location is ultraconvenient.

Via Sistina 91, 00187 Roma. ℂ **06-6797206.** Fax 06-6990111. www.hoteltrinitadeimonti.com. 25 units. 114€–220€ double; 150€–250€ triple. Rates include buffet breakfast. AE, DC, MC, V. Parking 35€. Metro: Barberini or Piazza di Spagna. **Amenities:** Bar; babysitting; room service. *In room:* A/C, TV, hair dryer, minibar, Wi-Fi (10€ per 24 hr.).

INEXPENSIVE

Hotel Panda This small hotel occupies two floors of a restored 19th-century building only 50m (160 ft.) from the Spanish Steps. Bedrooms are simply but adequately furnished, resting (for the most part) under vaulted wood-beamed ceilings on stone tiled floors. Some of the accommodations have 19th-century frescoes; others have hand-painted tiles in the bathrooms. This is one of the oldest hotels in the historical center of Rome, attracting patrons with its economical prices and its family-like atmosphere. Air-conditioning carries a daily supplement of 6€.

Via della Croce 35, 00187 Roma. ℂ **06-6780179.** Fax 06-69942151. www.hotelpanda.it. 20 units (8 with bathroom). 78€ double without bathroom; 108€ double with bathroom; 140€ triple with bathroom. AE, MC, V. Parking 30€. Metro: Piazza di Spagna. *In room:* A/C, Wi-Fi (free).

Hotel Parlamento The hard-to-find Parlamento has a two-star government rating and moderate prices. Expect a friendly *pensione*-style reception. The furnishings are antiques or reproductions, and carved wood or wrought-iron headboards back the firm beds. The bathrooms were recently redone with heated towel racks, phones, and (in a few) even marble sinks. Rooms are different in style; the best are no. 82, with its original 1800s furniture, and nos. 104, 106, and 107, which open onto the roof garden. You can enjoy the chandeliered and *trompe l'oeil* breakfast room, or carry your cappuccino up to the small roof terrace with its view of San Silvestro's bell tower.

Via delle Convertite 5 (at the intersection with Via del Corso), 00187 Roma. ℂ/fax **06-69921000.** www.hotelparlamento.it. 23 units. 90€–195€ double; 110€–205€ triple. Rates include buffet breakfast. AE, DC, MC, V. Parking 30€. Metro: Piazza di Spagna. **Amenities:** Bar; concierge; room service. *In room:* A/C, TV, hair dryer.

San Carlo Prices are surprisingly low for a building only 5 minutes on foot from the Spanish Steps and adjacent to the via Condotti with some of the best luxury shops and boutiques in Rome. The structure itself was meticulously renovated from a 19th-century mansion. Accommodations are spread across four floors. Equally desirable rooms lie in an annex with beamed ceilings, terra-cotta floors, and the occasional fresco. Accommodations are available as a single, double, triple, or quad. Superior rooms open onto a private terrace covered with an awning and containing outdoor furniture. Many of the bathrooms are clad in marble.

Via delle Carrozze 92/93, 00187 Roma. ✆ **06-6784548.** Fax 06-69941197. www.hotelsancarlo roma.com. 50 units. 125€–210€ double. Rates include buffet breakfast. AE, DC, MC, V. Parking 30€. Metro: Piazza di Spagna. **Amenities:** Bar; babysitting; concierge; room service. *In room:* A/C, TV, minibar, Wi-Fi (in some; free).

Near Vatican City

For most visitors, this is a rather dull area to base yourself—it's well removed from the ancient sites, and not a great restaurant neighborhood. But if the main purpose of your visit centers on the Vatican, you'll be fine here, and you'll be joined by thousands of other pilgrims, nuns, and priests.

VERY EXPENSIVE

Visconti Palace Hotel ★★   Completely restructured and redesigned, this palatial hotel is graced with one of the most avant-garde contemporary designs in town. Stunningly modern, it uses color perhaps with more sophistication than any other hotel. The location is idyllic, lying in the Prati district between Piazza di Spagna and St. Peter's. The rooms and corridors are decorated with modern art; the bathrooms are in marble; and there are many floor-to-ceiling windows and private terraces. Taste and an understated elegance prevail in this bright, welcoming, and functional atmosphere.

Via Federico Cesi 37, 00193 Roma. ✆ **06-3684.** Fax 06-3200551. www.viscontipalace.com. 242 units. 350€–380€ double; 450€ junior suite; 650€ suite. AE, DC, MC, V. Parking 35€. Metro: Ottaviano. Bus: 30, 70, or 913. **Amenities:** Bar; exercise room; room service; Wi-Fi (7€ per hr.). *In room:* A/C, TV, hair dryer, minibar.

EXPENSIVE

Hotel dei Consoli ★ 🏛   This rather elegant hotel in the Prati district is just a short stroll from the Vatican Museums. The hotel occupies three floors in a building restored in the imperial style, with cornices and columns. Stained glass and fine art create an inviting ambience. All of the bedrooms are handsomely furnished and decorated, but deluxe units have whirlpool tubs, as do the junior suites. Draperies and bedding are in elegant silks, and the bathrooms adorned with the finest porcelain. A roof terrace with a panoramic view crowns the building.

Via Varrone 2 D, 00193 Roma. ✆ **06-68892972.** Fax 06-68212274. www.hoteldeiconsoli.com. 28 units. 280€–320€ double; from 360€ triple. Rates include buffet breakfast. AE, DC, MC, V. Parking 28€–33€. Metro: Ottaviano–San Pietro. **Amenities:** Bar; room service. *In room:* A/C, TV, minibar, Wi-Fi (15€ per 24 hr.).

Hotel dei Mellini ★   On the right bank of the Tiber, this government-rated four-star hotel lies between St. Peter's Basilica and the Spanish Steps. There is much refined elegance here, and the public rooms evoke the setting of a privately owned manor house yet in the heart of Rome. Guest rooms are spacious and have a classic Art Deco styling in their choice of furnishings and fixtures. The roof terrace opens onto panoramic views.

Via Muzio Clementi 81, 00193 Roma. ✆ **06-324771.** Fax 06-32477801. www.hotelmellini.com. 80 units. 180€–295€ double; from 250€ suite. Rates include buffet breakfast. AE, DC, MC, V. Parking 30€. Metro: Lepanto. **Amenities:** Restaurant; bar; room service; Wi-Fi (25€ per 24 hr., in lobby). *In room:* A/C, TV, hair dryer, minibar.

Residenza Paolo VI ★★ 🛍 On the premises of a former monastery, this hotel opened in 2000. With its marvelous panorama of St. Peter's Square, it offers one of the great views in Rome. One reader wrote, "I felt I was at the gates of heaven sitting on the most beautiful square in the Western world." The hotel is filled with beautifully decorated and comfortable bedrooms, with modern bathrooms with tubs and showers in the junior suites, and showers only in the regular doubles. In spite of its reasonable prices, the inn is like a small luxury hotel.

Via Paolo VI 29, 00193 Roma. ✆ **06-684870.** Fax 06-6867428. www.residenzapaolovi.com. 29 units. 149€–367€ double; from 479€ junior suite. Rates include American buffet breakfast. AE, DC, MC, V. Metro: Ottaviano. Bus: 64, 91, or 916. **Amenities:** Bar; babysitting; room service. *In room:* A/C, TV, hair dryer, minibar, Wi-Fi (free).

MODERATE/INEXPENSIVE

Hotel Sant'Angelo This hotel, off Piazza Cavour (northeast of the Castel Sant'Angelo) and a 10-minute walk from St. Peter's, is in a relatively untouristy area. Operated by the Torre family, it occupies the second and third floors of an imposing 200-year-old building. The rooms are simple, modern, and clean, with wooden furniture and views of the street or a bleak but quiet courtyard. Rooms are small but not cramped, each with a comfortable bed, plus a tiled bathroom.

Via Mariana Dionigi 16, 00193 Roma. ✆ **06-3242000.** Fax 06-3204451. www.hotelsa.it. 31 units (shower only). 90€–200€ double; 120€–230€ triple. Rates include buffet breakfast. AE, DC, MC, V. Parking 25€–30€. Metro: Piazza di Spagna. **Amenities:** Bar; airport transfers (54€); babysitting; room service. *In room:* A/C, TV, hair dryer.

Il Gattopardo Relais 🌊 Close to St. Peter's and the Vatican Museums, this family run *pensione* is located in an elegantly restored building from the 19th century. In the historic Prati district, the Art Nouveau building is decorated in a romantic style with individually designed and soundproof rooms. Locals refer to it as a *hotel de charme*. A collection of antiques, tapestries, and Italian art is scattered throughout.

Viale Giulio Cesare 94, 00192 Roma. ✆ **06-37358480.** Fax 06-37501019. www.ilgattopardorelais. it. 6 units. 110€–220€ double; 150€–250€ triple; 130€–250€ junior suite. Rates include buffet breakfast. AE, DC, MC, V. Metro: Ottaviano. **Amenities:** Bar. *In room:* A/C, TV.

Villa Laetitia ★★★ Anna Fendi, of the fashion dynasty, has opened this stylish and superchic haven of elegance along the Tiber. With its private gardens, this Art Nouveau mansion lies between the Piazza del Popolo and the Prati quarter. The bedrooms are virtual works of art and are decorated with antique tiles gathered by Fendi on her world travels along with other objets d'art. For the smart, trendy, and well-heeled traveler, this is a choice address. Many of the rooms contain well-equipped kitchenettes. Accommodations are like small studios with terraces or gardens. Each rental unit has a different design and personality. Artists and designers in particular are attracted to this intimate, personalized hotel.

Lungotevere delle Armi 22-23, 00195 Roma. ✆ **06-3226776.** Fax 06-3232720. www.villalaetitia. com. 15 units. 190€–220€ double; 270€–350€ suite. AE, DC, MC, V. Metro: Lepanto. **Amenities:** Bar; airport transfers (55€); babysitting; room service; spa; Wi-Fi (free, in lobby). *In room:* A/C, TV/DVD, hair dryer, minibar.

In Trastevere

EXPENSIVE

Hotel Ponte Sisto ★ 👜 Steps from the River Tiber, this hotel lies on the most exclusive residential street in historic Rome at the gateway to Trastevere. The hotel is imbued with a bright, fresh look that contrasts with some of the timeworn buildings surrounding it. Windows look out on the core of Renaissance and baroque Rome. This 18th-century structure has been totally renovated with class and elegance. If you can live in the small bedrooms (the singles are really cramped), you'll enjoy this choice address with its cherrywood furnishings. Try for one of the upper-floor rooms for a better view; some come with their own terrace.

Via dei Pettinari 64, 00186 Roma. © **06-6863100.** Fax 06-68301712. www.hotelpontesisto.it. 103 units. 200€–320€ double; 450€–550€ suite. Rates include buffet breakfast. AE, DC, MC, V. Parking 26€. Tram: 8. **Amenities:** Airport transfers (55€); concierge; room service. *In room:* A/C, TV, hair dryer, minibar.

Ripa Hotel ★ 👜 This government-rated four-star hotel provides an unusual opportunity to stay across the Tiber in Trastevere, one of the oldest districts of Rome. The neighborhood may be historic, but the structure itself dates from 1973, although it's been completely restored since that time. The building is in concrete and glass, with a lobby of wooden and marble floors, filled with 1970s-style armchairs. The midsize to large bedrooms are furnished in minimalist modern. The Roscioli family, the owners, imbues both the public and private rooms of the hotel with a very contemporary look.

Via degli Orti di Trastevere 3, 00153 Roma. © **06-58611.** Fax 06-5882523. www.ripahotel.com. 170 units. 130€–240€ double; 260€–440€ suite. Rates include buffet breakfast. AE, DC, MC, V. Parking 18€. Bus: H. **Amenities:** Restaurant; bar; babysitting; concierge; exercise room; room service. *In room:* A/C, TV, hair dryer, minibar, Wi-Fi (15€ per 24 hr.).

INEXPENSIVE

Hotel Cisterna Well into its second decade, this hotel is just being discovered. It lies in a restored 18th-century palace in the colorful and evocative neighborhood of Trastevere. The prices and the very aura of the district are untouristy, which is what an increasing number of discerning visitors are seeking. It's a well-run little hotel with decent prices. Most bedrooms are midsize; they are not overly decorated but are comfortably furnished. The furnishings, though simple, are classic in style.

Via della Cisterna 8, 00153 Roma. © **06-5817212.** Fax 06-5810091. www.cisternahotel.it. 20 units. 140€ double; 165€ triple. Rates include buffet breakfast. AE, DC, MC, V. Bus: H. Closed Aug. **Amenities:** Room service. *In room:* A/C, TV, minibar, Wi-Fi (free).

Trastevere Manara ★ 🥄 Manara opened its restored doors in 1998 to meet the demand for accommodations in Trastevere. This little gem has fresh, bright bedrooms with immaculate tiles. All of the bathrooms, which also have been renovated and contain showers, are small. The price is hard to beat for those who want to stay in one of the most atmospheric sections of Rome. Most of the rooms open onto the lively Piazza San Cosimato, and all of them have comfortable, albeit functional, furnishings. Breakfast is the only meal served, but many good restaurants lie just minutes away.

Via L. Manara 24–25, 00153 Roma. ☎ **06-5814713.** Fax 06-5881016. www.hoteltrastevere.net. 18 units. 103€–105€ double. Rates include buffet breakfast. AE, DC, MC, V. Bus: H. Tram: 8. **Amenities:** Airport transfers 52€. *In room:* A/C, TV, hair dryer.

In Parioli

VERY EXPENSIVE

The Duke Hotel Roma ★★   This boutique hotel has burst into a renewed life, as celebrities are once again staying here. The Duke is nestled between the parks of Villa Borghese and Villa Glori. A free limo service links the hotel to the Via Veneto. The elegant bedrooms and superior suites are distributed across six floors, with many opening onto private balconies. All the accommodations are different in size and shape. The interior design combines a classical Italian bourgeois style with the warmth of an English gentleman's club.

Via Archimede 69, 00197 Roma. ☎ **06-367221.** Fax 06-36004104. www.thedukehotel.com. 78 units. 410€–515€ double; 920€–1,385€ suite. Rates include buffet breakfast. AE, DC, MC, V. Parking 25€. Metro: Piazza Euclide. **Amenities:** Restaurant; bar; airport transfers (65€); room service. *In room:* A/C, TV, hair dryer, minibar, Wi-Fi (6.50€ per hr.).

In Monte Mario

VERY EXPENSIVE

Cavalieri Hilton ★★ ☺   If you want resort-style accommodations and don't mind staying a 15-minute drive from the center of Rome (the hotel offers frequent, free shuttle service), consider the Hilton. With its pools and array of facilities, Cavalieri Hilton overlooks Rome and the Alban Hills from atop Monte Mario. It's set among 6 hectares (15 acres) of trees, flowering shrubs, and stonework. The guest rooms and suites, many with panoramic views, are contemporary and stylish. Soft furnishings in pastels are paired with Italian furniture in warmtoned woods, including beds with deluxe linen. Each unit has a spacious balcony.

Via Cadlolo 101, 00136 Roma. ☎ **800/445-8667** in the U.S. and Canada, or 06-35091. Fax 06-35092241. www.romecavalieri.com. 372 units. 310€–800€ double; from 650€ suite. AE, DC, DISC, MC, V. Parking 30€. **Amenities:** 2 restaurants; 3 bars; airport transfers 85€–336€; babysitting; children's playground; concierge; exercise room; 2 pools (including 1 heated indoor pool); room service; spa; 2 outdoor tennis courts (lit). *In room:* A/C, TV, DVD/CD player in suites, hair dryer, minibar, Wi-Fi (12€ per hr.).

At the Airport

Cancelli Rossi   If you're nervous about making your flight, you could book into this very simple motel-style place, located 2.5km (1½ miles) from the airport. Two floors are served by an elevator, and the decor is minimal. Rooms range from small to medium and are functionally furnished but reasonably comfortable, with good beds and tiled bathrooms. The atmosphere is a bit antiseptic, but this place is geared more for business travelers than vacationers. A restaurant in an annex nearby serves Italian and international food.

Via Portuense 2443, 00054 Fiumicino. ☎ **06-6507221.** Fax 06-65049168. www.cancellirossi.it. 50 units. 113€–150€ double. Rates include buffet breakfast. AE, DC, DISC, MC, V. Free parking. Airport shuttle to da Vinci Airport Mon–Sat 7–9:45am and 5:15–8:55pm every 20 min. 6€. **Amenities:** Restaurant; bar; babysitting; exercise room; room service. *In room:* A/C, TV, hair dryer, minibar.

Hilton Rome Airport   Only 200m (656 ft.) from the air terminal, this first-class hotel is the closest to FCO. The Hilton doesn't pretend to be more than it is—a bedroom factory at the airport. Follow the broad hallways to one of the midsize to spacious "crash pads," each with deep carpeting, generous storage space, and large, full bathrooms. The best units are the executive suites with extra amenities such as separate check-in, trouser press, and voice mail.

Via Arturo Ferrarin 2, 00050 Fiumicino. (*€*) **800/445-8667** in the U.S. and Canada, or 06-65258. Fax 06-65256525. www.hilton.com. 517 units. 170€–380€ double; 330€–455€ suite. AE, DC, MC, V. Parking 25€. Metro: Fiumicino Aeroporto. **Amenities:** 2 restaurants; bar; babysitting; children's center; exercise room; indoor pool (heated in winter); room service; sauna. *In room:* A/C, TV, hair dryer, minibar, Wi-Fi (27€ per 24 hr.).

WHERE TO DINE

Rome remains one of the world's great capitals for dining, with even more diversity today than ever. Most of its *trattorie* haven't changed their menus in a quarter of a century (except to raise the prices, of course), but there's an increasing number of chic, upscale spots with chefs willing to experiment, as well as a growing handful of Chinese, Indian, and other ethnic spots for those days when you just can't face another plate of pasta. The great thing about Rome is that you don't have to spend a fortune to eat really well.

Rome's cooking isn't subtle, but its kitchens rival anything the chefs of Florence or Venice can turn out. The city's chefs borrow—and even improve on—the cuisine of other regions. One of its oldest neighborhoods, Trastevere, is a gold mine of colorful streets and restaurants with time-tested recipes.

See "A Taste of Italy," in chapter 2, to learn about Roman wines. Most of the wines on the Roman table are from the Castelli Romani, the little hill towns surrounding Rome.

Restaurants generally serve lunch between 1 and 3pm, and dinner between about 8 and 10:30pm; at all other times, restaurants are closed. Dinner is taken late in Rome, so although a restaurant might open at 7:30pm, even if you get there at 8pm, you'll often be the only one in the place. A heavier meal is typically eaten at midday, and a lighter one is eaten in the evening.

What if you're hungry outside those hours? Well, if you don't take continental breakfast at your hotel, you can have coffee and a pastry at any **bar** (really a cafe, although there will be liquor bottles behind the counter) or a **tavola calda** (hot table). These are stand-up snack bar–type arrangements, open all day long and found all over the city.

A **servizio** (tip) of 10% to 15% is often added to your bill or included in the price, although patrons often leave an extra .50€ to 3€ as a token.

Near Stazione Termini

EXPENSIVE

Agata e Romeo ★★ NEW ROMAN   One of the most charming places near the Vittorio Emanuele Monument is this striking duplex restaurant done up in turn-of-the-20th-century Liberty style. You'll enjoy the creative cuisine of Romeo Caraccio (who manages the dining room) and his wife, Agata Parisella (who prepares her own version of sophisticated Roman food). The pasta specialty is *paccheri all'amatriciana* (large macaroni tubes with pancetta and a savory tomato sauce topped with pecorino cheese). The chef is equally adept at fish or meat

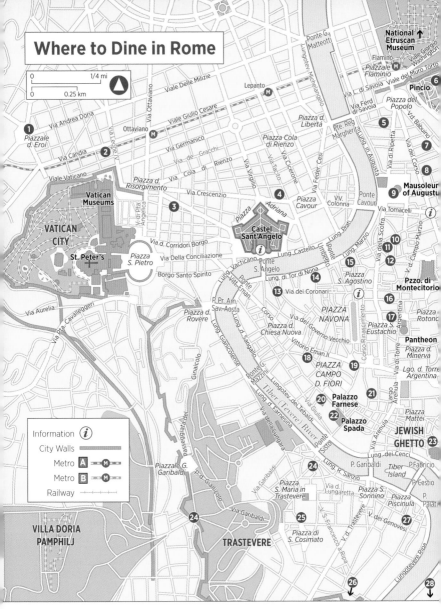

Where to Dine in Rome

dishes, including braised beef cheeks laid on chestnut purée or swordfish rolls scented with orange and fennel cream. The starters are a feast for the eye and palate, especially wild salmon with sour cream, chives, and salmon eggs, or else scallops wrapped in a crispy pancetta with leek sauce. The most luscious dessert is Agata's *millefoglie,* puff pastry stuffed with almonds. The wine cellar offers a wide choice of international and domestic wines.

Via Carlo Alberto 45. ⓒ **06-4466115.** www.agataeromeo.it. Reservations recommended. All pastas 30€; meat and fish 45€; fixed-price menus 110€–130€. AE, DC, MC, V. Tues–Fri 12:30-2:30pm; Mon–Fri 8-10:30pm. Closed Aug 8–30. Metro: Vittorio Emanuele.

MODERATE

Il Quadrifoglio NEAPOLITAN Situated in a grandiose palace, this well-managed restaurant lets you sample the flavors and herbs of Naples and southern Italy. You'll find a tempting selection of antipasti, such as anchovies, peppers, capers, onions, and breaded and fried eggplant, all garnished with fresh herbs and virgin olive oil. The pastas are made daily, and the linguine with small squids is especially delectable, as is the spaghetti with sea urchins. Try a zesty rice dish (one of the best is *sartù di riso,* studded with vegetables, herbs, and meats), followed by anchovy pie. Dessert anyone? A longtime favorite is *torta caprese,* with hazelnuts and chocolate.

Via del Boschetto 19. ⓒ **06-4826096.** Reservations recommended. Main courses 12€–20€. AE, DC, MC, V. Tues–Sat 7pm–midnight. Closed Aug 5-25. Metro: Cavour.

INEXPENSIVE

Arancia Blu ★★ 🍴 VEGETARIAN/ITALIAN This rustic, out-of-the-way charmer offers Rome's best vegetarian cuisine. Under soft lighting and wood ceilings, surrounded by wine racks and university intellectuals, the friendly waiters will help you compile a menu to fit any dietary need. The dishes at this trendy spot are inspired by peasant cuisines from across Italy and beyond. The appetizers range from hummus and tabbouleh to zucchini-and-saffron quiche or salad with apples, Gorgonzola, and balsamic vinegar. The main courses change seasonally and may be lasagna with red onions, mushrooms, zucchini, and ginger; couscous *con verdure* (vegetable couscous); or *ravioli ripieni di patate e menta* (ravioli stuffed with potatoes and mint served under fresh tomatoes and Sardinian sheep's cheese). They offer 600 wines and inventive desserts, such as dark-chocolate cake with warm orange sauce.

Via Prenestina 396E ⓒ **06-4454105.** www.aranciabluroma.com. Reservations highly recommended. Main courses 10€–13€; fixed-price menu 37€. No credit cards. Sat–Sun noon–3pm and 8pm–midnight; Mon–Fri 8pm–midnight. Bus: 5, 14, or 19.

Monte Arci ROMAN/SARDINIAN On a cobblestone street near Piazza Indipendenza, this restaurant is set behind a sienna-colored facade. It features Roman and Sardinian specialties such as *nialoreddus* (a regional form of *gnocchetti*); pasta with clams, lobster, or the musky-earthy notes of porcini mushrooms; and lamb sausage flavored with herbs and pecorino cheese. The best pasta dish we've sampled is *paglia e fieno al Monte Arci* (homemade pasta with pancetta, spinach, cream, and Parmesan). It's all home cooking, hearty but not that creative.

Via Castelfirdardo 33. ⓒ **06-4941220.** www.ristorantemontearci.com. Reservations recommended. Main courses 10€–18€. AE, MC, V. Mon–Fri 12:30–3pm; Mon–Sat 7-11:30pm. Closed Aug. Metro: Stazione Termini or Repubblica.

Where to Dine Near Stazione Termini, Via Veneto & Piazza Barberini

Information *ⓘ*
Metro Ⓜ

Trimani Wine Bar ★ CONTINENTAL Opened as a tasting center for French and Italian wines, spumantes, and liqueurs, this is an elegant wine bar with a stylish but informal decor and comfortable seating. More than 30 wines are available by the glass. To accompany them, you can choose from a bistro-style menu, with dishes such as salade niçoise, vegetarian pastas, herb-laden bean soups *(fagioli),* and quiche. Also available is a wider menu, including meat and fish courses. The specialty is the large range of little *bruschette* with cheese and radicchio—the chef orders every kind of prosciutto and cheese from all over Italy. The dishes are matched with the appropriate wines. The dessert specialty is cinnamon cake with apples and a flavor of fresh rosemary.

Trimani maintains a shop about 37m (120 ft.) from its wine bar, at V. Goito 20 (© **06-4469661**), where you can purchase an astonishing array of Italian wines.

Via Cernaia 37B. © **06-4469630.** www.trimani.com. Reservations recommended. Main courses 10€–18€; glass of wine (depending on vintage) 3€–29€. AE, DC, MC, V. Daily 11:30am–3pm and 5:30pm–12:30am. Closed 2 weeks in Aug. Metro: Repubblica or Castro Pretorio.

Near Via Veneto & Piazza Barberini

VERY EXPENSIVE

La Terrazza ★★★ ITALIAN/INTERNATIONAL   La Terrazza serves some of the city's finest cuisine; you get the added bonus of a sweeping view over St. Peter's. The service is formal and flawless, yet not intimidating. The chef prepares a seasonally changing menu that's among the most polished in Rome. You might start with braised artichokes with scallops, salted cod purée, and a basil-scented mousse, or else delectable zucchini blossoms stuffed with ricotta and Taleggio cheese, black olives, and cherry tomatoes. The pasta specialty is penne filled with ricotta cheese, plus mortadella, walnuts, and pecorino cheese, which might be followed by such dishes as grilled swordfish with sweet-and-sour spinach and a tomato fondue, oven-baked whole baby chicken with wild mushrooms, or grilled filet of beef with smoked pancetta and fresh thyme.

In the Hotel Eden, Via Ludovisi 49. © **06-478121.** Reservations recommended. Main courses 48€–60€; 6-course fixed-price menu 110€. AE, DC, MC, V. Daily 12:30–2:30pm and 7:30–10:30pm. Metro: Barberini.

MODERATE

Cesarina ☺ EMILIANA-ROMAGNOLA/ROMAN   Specializing in the cuisines of Rome and the region around Bologna, this place is named for Cesarina Masi, who opened it in 1960 (many old-timers fondly remember her strict supervision of the kitchen and how she lectured regulars who didn't finish their *tagliatelle*). Although Cesarina died in the 1980s, her traditions are kept by her family. This place has long been a favorite of Roman families. The polite staff rolls a cart from table to table laden with an excellent *bollito misto* (an array of well-seasoned boiled meats) and often follows with *misto Cesarina*—four kinds of creamy, handmade pasta, each with a different sauce. Equally appealing are the saltimbocca (veal with ham) and the *cotoletta alla Bolognese* (tender veal cutlet baked with ham and cheese). A dessert specialty is *semifreddo Cesarina* (ice cream with whipped cream) with hot chocolate, so meltingly good that it's worth the 5 pounds you'll gain.

Via Piemonte 109. © **06-4880828.** www.ristorantecesarinaroma.it. Reservations recommended. Main courses 13€–25€. Degustation menu 40€. AE, DC, MC, V. Mon–Sat 12:30–3pm and 7:30–11pm. Metro: Barberini. Bus: 53 or 910.

Colline Emiliane ★★ 👔 EMILIANA-ROMAGNOLA   Serving the *classica cucina Bolognese,* Colline Emiliane is a small, family-run place—the owner is the cook and his wife makes the pasta (about the best you'll find in Rome). The house specialty is an inspired *tortellini alla panna* (with cream sauce and truffles), but the less-expensive pastas, including *maccheroni al funghetto* (with mushrooms) and *tagliatelle alla Bolognese* (in meat sauce), are excellent, too. As an opener, we suggest *culatello di Zibello,* a delicacy from a small town near Parma that's known for having the world's finest prosciutto. Main courses include *braciola di maiale* (boneless rolled pork cutlets stuffed with ham and cheese, breaded, and sautéed) and an impressive *giambonnetto* (roast veal Emilian-style with roast potatoes).

Via degli Avignonesi 22 (off Piazza Barberini). ✆ **06-4817538.** Reservations highly recommended. Main courses 12€–22€. MC, V. Tues–Sun 12:45–2:45pm; Tues–Sat 7:45–10:45pm. Closed Aug. Metro: Barberini.

Tuna ★ SEAFOOD   This seafood emporium in the center of Rome, overlooking the via Veneto, is dedicated to serving some of the freshest fish in the capital. Not only is the fish fresh, but the chef also requires it to be of optimal quality. From crayfish to sea truffles, from oysters to sea urchins, the fish is turned into platters of delight with perfect seasonings and preparation. Start with the midget mussels or the octopus salad or else calamari and artichoke tempura. For a main course, the catch of the day is in general the best choice, or else you may order sliced sea bass with chives and fresh thyme.

11 via Veneto. ✆ **06-4201-6531.** www.tunaroma.it. Reservations required. Main courses 15€–30€. AE, MC, V. Mon–Fri 12:30–3pm; daily 7:30pm–midnight. Closed 2 weeks in Aug. Metro: Barberini.

Near Ancient Rome
EXPENSIVE

Crab ★ SEAFOOD   For Rome, this is an unusual name. Launched at the dawn of the 21st century, this *trattoria* is ideal after a visit to the nearby Basilica of San Giovanni. As you enter, you are greeted with a display of freshly harvested crustaceans and mollusks, which are what you can expect to headline the menu. The signature dish is king crab legs (hardly from the Mediterranean). Fish is shipped in "from everywhere," including oysters from France, lobster from the Mediterranean and the Atlantic, and some catches from the Adriatic. The antipasti is practically a meal in itself, including a savory sauté of mussels and clams, an octopus salad, and scallops gratin, which might be followed by a succulent lobster ravioli in *salsa vergine* (a lobster-based sauce). You can also order fresh sea urchins. For dessert, we recommend an arrangement of sliced tropical fruit that evokes the campy hat worn by Carmen Miranda in all those late-night movies. Most of the main courses, except for some very expensive shellfish and lobster platters, are closer to the lower end of the price scale.

Via Capo d'Africa 2. ✆ **06-7720-3636.** Reservations required. Main courses 15€–30€. AE, DC, MC, V. Mon 7:45–11:30pm; Tues–Sat 1–3:30pm and 8–11:30pm. Closed Aug. Metro: Colosseo. Tram: 3.

Trattoria San Teodoro ★ ☺ 🍴 ROMAN   At last there's a good place to eat in the former gastronomic wasteland near the Roman Forum and Palatine Hill. The helpful staff welcomes you to a shady terrace or a dimly lit dining room resting under a vaulted brick ceiling and arched alcoves. The chef handles seafood exceedingly well (try the mini baby squid sautéed with Roman artichokes). His signature dish is seafood carpaccio made with tuna, turbot, or sea bass. Succulent meats, such as medallions of veal in a nutmeg-enhanced cream sauce, round out the menu at this family friendly place. All the pastas are homemade, including black *tagliolini* pasta with anchovy jus and crispy cuttlefish.

Via dei Fienili 49–51. ✆ **06-6780933.** www.st-teodoro.it. Reservations recommended. Main courses 23€–29€. MC, V. Mon–Sat 12:30–3:30pm and 7:30pm–midnight. Closed 2 weeks at Christmas. Metro: Circo Massimo.

MODERATE

Scoglio di Frisio NEAPOLITAN/PIZZA   This *trattoria,* a longtime favorite, offers a great introduction to the Neapolitan kitchen. Here you can taste a genuine plate-size Neapolitan pizza (crunchy, oozy, and excellent) with clams and mussels. Or, you can start with a medley of savory stuffed vegetables and antipasti before moving on to chicken cacciatore or well-flavored tender veal scaloppini. Scoglio di Frisio also makes for an inexpensive night of hokey but still charming entertainment, as cornball "O Sole Mio" renditions and other Neapolitan songs issue forth from a guitar, mandolin, and strolling tenor. The nautical decor (in honor of the top-notch fish dishes) is complete with a high-ceiling grotto of fishing nets, crustaceans, and a miniature three-masted schooner.

Via Merulana 256. ☏ **06-4872765.** www.scogliodifrisio.com. Reservations recommended. Main courses 13€–22€; set menu 30€. AE, DC, MC, V. Daily noon–11:30pm. Metro: Vittorio Emanuele. Bus: 16 or 714.

INEXPENSIVE

Hostaria Nerone ★ ROMAN/ITALIAN   Built atop the ruins of the Golden House of Nero, this *trattoria* is run by the energetic de Santis family, which cooks, serves, and handles the crowds of hungry locals and visitors. Opened in 1929 at the edge of Colle Oppio Park, it contains two compact dining rooms and a flowering-shrub-lined terrace that offers a view over the Colosseum and the Bath of Trajan. The copious antipasti buffet offers the bounty of Italy's fields and seas. The pastas include savory spaghetti with clams and our favorite, *pasta e fagioli* (with beans). There are also grilled crayfish and swordfish, and Italian sausages with polenta. Roman-style tripe is a favorite, but maybe you'll skip it for the *osso buco* (veal shank) with mashed potatoes and seasonal mushrooms. The list of some of the best Italian wines is reasonably priced.

Via Terme di Tito 96. ☏ **06-4817952.** Reservations recommended. Main courses 12€–15€. AE, DC, MC, V. Mon–Sat noon–3pm and 7–11pm. Metro: Colosseo. Bus: 75, 85, 87, 117, or 175.

Near Campo De' Fiori & the Jewish Ghetto

Vegetarians looking for monstrous salads (or anyone who just wants a break from all those heavy meats and starches) can find great food at the neighborhood branch of **Insalata Ricca,** Largo dei Chiavari 85 (☏ **06-68803656;** www.linsalataricca.it). From Monday to Saturday there is a fixed-price lunch menu at 10€. It's open Monday to Saturday noon to 4pm and 7pm to midnight, and Sunday noon to midnight.

EXPENSIVE

Camponeschi ★ SEAFOOD/ROMAN   The fish dishes served here are legendary, and so is the front-row view of the Piazza Farnese. The restaurant is elegance itself, with a two-to-one staff/diner ratio. The cuisine is creative, refined, and prepared with only the freshest of ingredients, with a superb wine list. The chefs work hard to make their reputation anew every night, and they succeed admirably with such dishes as lobster with black truffles and raspberry vinegar for an appetizer, and foie gras with port and sultana. We love their generous use of truffles, particularly in a masterpiece of a dish, *tagliolini* soufflé flavored with white truffles. Among the more succulent pastas is one made with a roe deer sauce. If the pope ever dined here, he would assuredly bestow papal blessings on

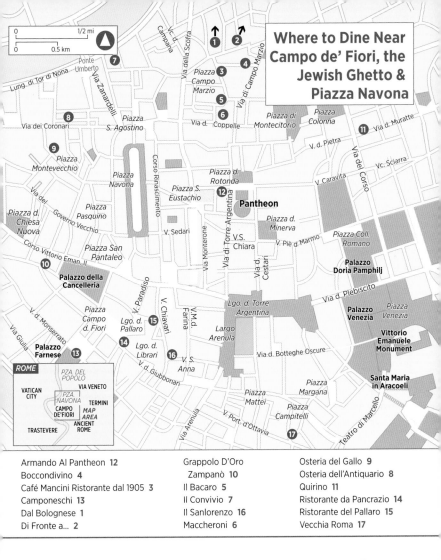

Where to Dine Near Campo de' Fiori, the Jewish Ghetto & Piazza Navona

such main courses as the rack of venison marinated with blueberries or a heavenly partridge in a brandy sauce with fresh mushrooms.

Piazza Farnese. © **06-6874927.** www.ristorantecamponeschi.it. Reservations required. Main courses 18€–37€. MC, V. Mon–Sat 8pm–midnight. Closed 2 weeks in Aug. Metro: Piazza Argentina.

MODERATE

Ristorante da Pancrazio ROMAN   This place is popular as much for its archaeological interest as for its good food. One of its two dining rooms is decorated in the style of an 18th-century tavern; the other occupies the premises of Pompey's ancient theater and is lined with carved capitals and bas-reliefs. In this historic setting, you can enjoy time-tested Roman food. Two particular classics are prepared with skill: saltimbocca and tender roast lamb with potatoes. Some superb main courses include beef rolls stuffed with ham, carrots, and celery in a tomato sauce; baby lamb's ribs fried with artichokes, and grouper in a zucchini flower sauce.

Piazza del Biscione 92. ✆ **06-6861246.** www.dapancrazio.it. Reservations recommended. Main courses 13€–25€. AE, DC, MC, V. Thurs–Tues noon–3pm and 7:30–11:15pm. Closed 3 weeks in Aug (dates vary). Bus: 46, 62, or 64.

Ristorante del Pallaro ★ ★ 🎁 ROMAN   The cheerful woman in white who emerges with clouds of steam from the bustling kitchen is owner Paola Fazi, who runs two dining rooms where value-conscious Romans go for good food at bargain prices. (She also claims—though others dispute it—that Julius Caesar was assassinated on this site.) The fixed-price menu is the only choice and has made the place famous. Ms. Fazi prepares everything with love, as if she were feeding her extended family. As you sit down, your antipasto, the first of eight courses, appears. Then comes the pasta of the day, followed by such main dishes as roast veal with broad beans and homemade potato chips, or roast pork cutlets, tender and flavorful. For your final courses, you're served mozzarella, cake with custard, and fruit in season.

Largo del Pallaro 15. ✆ **06-68801488.** Reservations recommended. Fixed-price menu 25€. No credit cards. Tues–Sun noon–3:30pm and 7pm–12:30am. Closed Aug 12–25. Bus: 40, 46, 60, 62, or 64.

Vecchia Roma ROMAN/ITALIAN   Vecchia Roma is a charming, moderately priced *trattoria* in the heart of the ghetto. Movie stars have frequented the place, sitting at the crowded tables in one of the four small dining rooms (the back room is the most popular). The owners are known for their *frutti di mare* (fruits of the sea), a selection of briny fresh seafood. A savory selection of antipasti, including salmon or vegetables, is always available. The pastas and risottos are savory, including spaghetti with baby octopus and black squid ink. The chef's specialties are lamb and *spigola* (a type of whitefish). Other signature dishes include veal kidneys in a sweet mustard sauce.

Piazza di Campitelli 18. ✆ **06-6864604.** www.ristorantevecchiaroma.com. Reservations recommended. Main courses 16€–22€. AE, DC, MC, V. Thurs–Tues 1–3:30pm and 8–11pm. Closed 10 days in Aug. Bus: 46, 64, 84, or 916. Metro: Colosseo.

Near Piazza Navona & the Pantheon
EXPENSIVE

Il Convivio ★ ROMAN/INTERNATIONAL   This is one of the most acclaimed restaurants in Rome, and one of the few to be granted a coveted Michelin star. Its 16th-century building is a classic setting in pristine white with accents of wood. The Troiani brothers turn out an inspired cuisine based on the best and freshest ingredients at the market. Their menu is seasonally adjusted to take advantage of what's good during any month. Start with a tantalizing fish and shellfish soup with green tomatoes and sweet peppers, and follow with such pastas as homemade lasagna with red prawns, coconut milk, pine nuts, artichokes, and mozzarella. More imaginative is the homemade duck ravioli in a red chicory sauce. A main dish might be oxtail served with spicy "smashed" potatoes and black truffles.

Vicolo dei Soldati 31. ℂ **06-6869432.** www.ilconviviotroiani.com. Reservations required. All main courses 28€–44€; fixed-price menu 98€. AE, DC, MC, V. Mon–Sat 8–11pm. Bus: C3, 30, 70, or 81. Metro: Piazza di Spagna.

MODERATE

Cafè Mancini Ristorante dal 1905 ITALIAN/SEAFOOD   Near the Pantheon and Piazza Navona, this restaurant was originally established in Naples in 1905—hence its name. Five generations of the Mancini family have since turned out a sublime cuisine based on regional fare and fish dishes from their native Campania. The chefs pay special attention to the products of the season. And somehow the family combines high-quality ingredients with moderate prices. We can make a meal out of the delectable appetizers, especially the *delizie di mare* with a tuna tartare and a skewer of prawns in a *tagliolini* pasta. It comes with a very soft sea bass carpaccio. Or else you might prefer *sfizi di cicci bacco,* with mozzarella, Parma ham, beef tartare, and zucchini flowers. All the pastas are homemade, including *tagliatelle* with prawns and almond pesto sauce. In-the-know locals favor such dishes as grilled squid with potatoes, zucchini, and a black-olive sauce. The setting is elegant and formal, the service top-notch.

Via Metastasio 21. ℂ **06-6872051.** www.cafemancini.com. Reservations recommended. Main courses 7€–25€. AE, DC, MC, V. Mon–Sat noon–3pm and 7–11:30pm. Metro: Piazza Navona.

Il Sanlorenzo MEDITERRANEAN/SEAFOOD   Right off the Piazza Navona and all its tourist trap restaurants is a bastion of good food and service, all at a moderate price. The decor is both sophisticated and contemporary, with antique wood furniture, plus modern art adorning the walls. Inspired by the bounty of the fields and streams of Latium, the chefs adroitly prepare a cuisine of both simplicity and elegance. Try the spaghetti with sea urchins, a real delicacy, or else the risotto with tiger prawns and black truffles. Paccheri is another homemade pasta dish, this one served with swordfish, eggplant, and smoked Provola cheese. You might start with a savory seafood fish soup. Small calamari appear in a delectable fry, or else you can order grilled dentice (a white fish) with a seafood sauce. For dessert, why not the chocolate soup with vanilla ice cream and a raspberry meringue?

Via dei Chiavari 4–5. ℂ **06-686-5097.** www.ilsanlorenzo.it. Reservations required. Main courses 18€–37€; 7-course degustation menu 75€. AE, DC, MC, V. Tues–Fri 12:45–2:45pm and 7:30–11:45pm; Sat–Mon 7:30–11:45pm. Closed 3 weeks in Aug. Bus: 60, or 64.

Osteria dell'Antiquario ★ 📷 INTERNATIONAL/ROMAN   This virtually undiscovered *osteria* enjoys a location a few blocks down the Via dei Coronari as you leave the Piazza Navona and head toward St. Peter's. In a stone-built stable from the 1500s, this restaurant has three dining rooms used in winter. In nice weather, try to get an outdoor table on the terrace; shaded by umbrellas, they face a view of the Palazzo Lancillotti. Begin with a delectable appetizer of sautéed shellfish (usually mussels and clams). Some of the more savory offerings include potato gnocchi with clams and wild mushrooms, stewed scorpion fish with tomato sauce, swordfish steak with a parsley-laced white-wine sauce, or veal escalope with ham and sage.

Piazzetta di S. Simeone 26–27, Via dei Coronari. ℂ **06-6879694.** www.osteriadellantiquario.it. Reservations recommended. Main courses 12€–30€. AE, DC, MC, V. Thurs–Tues 7–11pm. Closed 15 days in mid-Aug, Christmas, and Jan 6–30. Bus: 70, 81, or 90.

INEXPENSIVE

Armando al Pantheon ★ ROMAN In business for half a century, this incredibly inviting oasis lies near the Pantheon and off one of the most trafficked squares in historic Rome. The aura is romantic and classic, with paintings adorning the walls. Claudio and Fabrizio invite you into their little joint for a special dinner. If you want the tried and true, there are plenty of traditional recipes. But if you want fancier fare such as duck with prunes, you'll find that too. The most delightful dish is *tagliolini al tartufo,* a bowl of steaming hot pasta topped with rich black truffles uprooted in Umbria. Less grand is the spaghetti with fresh mushrooms and saffron. Spelt balls come in a truffle sauce, and guinea fowl is cooked in dark beer and served with fat porcini mushrooms.

Salita dei Crescenzi 31. ☎ **06/688-03-034.** Reservations recommended. Main courses 10€–24€. AE, DC, MC, V. Mon–Fri 12:30–3pm and 7–11pm; Sat 12:30–3pm.

Grappolo d'Oro Zampanò 🍴 ROMAN There's no need to pay a lot of money to eat very well near the tourist-clogged Piazza Navona. This *trattoria* offers good and filling Roman cuisine with most dishes given an inventive twist. The decor is simple, with walls adorned with modern art, but the food is not, and it's also market fresh. Appetizers are savory, especially the tart with anchovies and endive or the octopus salad in an olive sauce. A favorite of locals is the pecorino cheese flan with crispy bacon or a selection of antipasti. At least eight succulent pastas are served nightly, a specialty being pumpkin-filled fagottoni with Gorgonzola sauce and fresh rosemary. A classic Roman dish main course is salt cod with raisins, pine nuts, and fresh tomatoes, or else you may prefer the tangy grilled lamb ribs.

Piazza Della Cancelleria 80-84. ☎ **06/689-7080.** Reservations recommended. Main courses 7.50€–20€. MC, V. Sat–Mon 12:30–2pm and 7–11pm. Closed 2 weeks in Aug. Bus: 64.

Osteria del Gallo ★ 🍴 ROMAN You can escape the tourist traps of the Piazza Navona, such as Tre Scalini, by finding this place in a tiny little alley off the west-northwest side of the fabled square. It's very small, with a lovely area for outdoor seating, and is definitely off the beaten track. The chef/owner comes out to take your order personally. He is justly proud of his homemade pastas such as gnocchi with mussels and arugula, linguine with seafood, and a typical Roman recipe for *tagliolini cacio e pepe* (with cheese and pepper). Menu items include a variety of fresh fish dishes roasted in a salt crust to retain their juice and flavor. Other favorites include filet of beef cooked with green pepper. All desserts are homemade, including one of the best tiramisu turned out in the area.

Vicolo di Montevecchio 27. ☎ **06-6873781.** www.osteriadelgalloroma.it. Reservations highly recommended. Main courses 8€–14€. AE, DC, MC, V. Wed–Mon 11:30am–3pm and 6–11:30pm. Metro: Piazza Navona.

Quirino ROMAN/ITALIAN/SICILIAN Quirino is a good place to dine after you've tossed your coin into the Trevi. The atmosphere is typical Italian, with hanging Chianti bottles, a beamed ceiling, and muraled walls. We're fond of the mixed fry of tiny shrimp and squid rings, and the vegetarian pastas are prepared with only the freshest ingredients. The regular pasta dishes are fabulous, especially our favorite: *paccheri* (large pasta tubes) with swordfish, *bottarga* (tuna eggs), and cherry tomatoes. A variety of fresh and tasty fish is always available and always grilled to perfection. For dessert, try the yummy chestnut ice cream with hot chocolate sauce or the homemade cannoli.

Where to Dine

SETTLING INTO ROME

Via delle Muratte 84. ☏ **06-6794108.** Reservations recommended. Main courses 8€–18€; fish dishes 15€–20€. AE, MC, V. Mon–Sat noon–11:30pm. Closed 3 weeks in Aug. Metro: Barberini, Piazza di Spagna, or Colosseo.

Near Piazza Del Popolo & the Spanish Steps

VERY EXPENSIVE

Imàgo ★★★ INTERNATIONAL/ITALIAN   Great food and a sweeping panorama of ancient Rome lure patrons to the sixth floor of this deluxe hotel on the Spanish Steps. There's so much talk of the view that it is easy to overlook the superb traditional Italian cuisine. Chefs frequent the Roman markets early in the morning, securing the freshest products for their menu, which changes daily. The brilliant chef, Francesco Apreda, a Neapolitan, serves Italian food, but it's influenced by the rest of the world—for example, sea bass with a ginger sauce evocative of Thailand. The Kennedys and Princess Di used to dine here; now you are likely to see Silvio Berlusconi, feasting on pheasant ravioli with truffles. Apreda delights other guests with such delectable dishes as grilled veal shoulder with hazelnut oil, wild mushrooms, and persimmons, or roasted pigeon with black tea, artichokes, and a grape sauce.

In the Hotel Hassler, Piazza della Trinità dei Monti 6. ☏ **06-69934726.** www.imagorestaurant. com. Reservations required. Jacket and tie for men at dinner. Main courses 38€–45€; 7-course degustation menu 130€. AE, DC, MC, V. Daily 7:30–10:30pm. Metro: Piazza di Spagna.

EXPENSIVE

Brunello Ristorante ★★ ITALIAN   This chicly modern bar, lounge, and restaurant is helping bring back the Via Veneto as an elegant rendezvous place. The days of *La Dolce Vita* live on here. Your martini will arrive with a few drops of Chanel No. 5 rubbed along its glass stalk. Earthy tones such as brown dominate among the wall coverings and the upholstered seating in autumnal shades, along with gilt sculptures. The menu is impressively innovative, with fresh ingredients that explode in your mouth. The chef likes to experiment. Starters might include black fried king prawns, shrimp, and artichokes in a creamy sweet pepper sauce, or else crispy radicchio pie with cream cheese. Among the more tempting mains are vodka- and honey-marinated salmon with a sea terrine and citrus petals or else turbot escalopes with fresh herbs and vanilla-scented fennel. The wine cellar boasts 500 labels from every region of Italy.

In the Regina Hotel Baglioni, Via Vittorio Veneto 72. ☏ **06-48902867.** www.brunellorestaurant. com. Reservations recommended. Main courses 21€–34€ fixed-price 3-course lunch menu 37€. AE, DC, MC, V. Restaurant Mon–Sat 12:30-3pm and 7:30–11pm. Lounge Mon–Sat 6pm–1am. Metro: Piazza di Spagna.

Rhome ★★ ITALIAN   The name of the restaurant is a fusion of the words "Rome" and "home." The restaurant and its cuisine are modern and innovative, with a stunning interior design. A traditional Italian cuisine is based on the best of market-fresh ingredients obtained by shopping that morning. The chef cleverly selects appropriate herbs, spices, and fresh vegetables, which he transforms into classic dishes, such as fettuccine with artichokes and saffron; tonnarelli with goat cheese and sweet red peppers; or, simple but tasty, the veal meatballs with creamy mashed potatoes. The bean soup with field chicory is some of the best we've had, and in season you might delight in the deer medallions with chestnut honey. Later in the evening, diners enjoy music selected by a DJ, or, on occasion, live entertainment from international musicians.

Piazza Augusto Imperatore 42–48. ℮ **06-68301430.** www.ristoranterhome.com. Reservations required. Main courses 10€–22€. AE, DC, MC, V. Mon–Fri noon–3pm and 8pm–12:30am; Sat 8pm–12:30am. Closed 2 weeks in Aug. Metro: Piazza di Spagna.

MODERATE

Boccondivino ★ ITALIAN   Part of the fun of this restaurant involves wandering through historic Rome to reach it. Inside, you'll find delicious food and an engaging mix of the Italian Renaissance with imperial and ancient Rome, thanks to columns salvaged from ancient monuments by 16th-century builders. Modern art and a hip staff dressed in black and white serve as a tip-off, though, that the menu is completely up-to-date. Dishes vary with the seasons, but you might find linguine with lemon and cinnamon; carpaccio of beef; various risottos, including a version with black truffles; and grilled steaks and veal. Especially intriguing is duck breast with a fig sauce, red rice, and potato pie. If you're a seafood lover, look for either the marinated and grilled salmon or a particularly subtle blend of roasted turbot stuffed with foie gras. Desserts feature the fresh fruit of the season, perhaps marinated pineapple or fruit-studded house-made ice creams. The restaurant's name, incidentally, translates as "divine mouthful."

Piazza Campo di Marzio 6. ℮ **06-68308626.** www.boccondivino.it. Reservations required. Main courses 12€–28€. AE, DC, MC, V. Mon–Fri 12:30–3pm; Mon–Sat 7:30–11pm. Bus: 87 or 175.

Café Romano ★ INTERNATIONAL   On the most exclusive "fashion street" of Rome, this stylish venue is neither restaurant nor brasserie. Annexed to the landmark Hotel d'Inghilterra, the cafe can serve you throughout the day, beginning with a late breakfast or concluding with a post-theater dinner well after midnight. Two salons are divided by an arch resting on two columns under a barrel-vaulted ceiling with padded settees. The atmosphere is cosmopolitan, with an eclectic, well-chosen menu. You can taste dishes from around the world: from moussaka to fish couscous, from the Lebanese *mezze* (appetizers) to Chicago rib-eye steak, from the Thai-like green chicken curry to the Japanese-inspired salmon teriyaki. Flavors are beautifully blended in such starters as smoked goose breast with candied peaches or beef tartare with thyme-flavored mushrooms. Among the more appealing mains are homemade fusilli pasta with wild mushrooms, smoked bacon, and Parmesan, or sautéed roast tuna served with sweet peppers, olives, and capers. Everything is served on fine bone china with silver cutlery and crystal glassware.

In the Hotel d'Inghilterra, Via Borgognona 4. ℮ **06-69981500.** www.royaldemeure.com. Main courses 18€–35€. AE, DC, MC, V. Daily noon–10:30pm. Metro: Piazza di Spagna.

Caffetteria Canova Tadolini ROMAN   *La roma bene* (the upper class) flock to this cafe at the museum dedicated to the famous neoclassical sculptor Antonio Canova and his talented pupil Adamo Tadolini. Museum cafes can be trite, but this one is literally in the museum, with its period-piece *ottocento*-style tables and chairs stationed beneath statues and plaster fragments. The cafe/museum has been a great hit since it opened with its 400-bottle all-Italian wine list and 25 varieties of tea. The bar and cafeteria are located on the ground floor; the more formal restaurant is one flight up. The chef's special dishes begin with such appetizers as salmon and Roman lettuce salad with *crostini* served with a yogurt-and-ginger sauce, and follow with sautéed tuna steak or spaghetti with shrimp, zucchini, and cherry tomatoes. The location is in the very heart of Rome.

Via del Babuino 150 A–B. ℂ **06-32110702.** www.museoateliercanovatadolini.it. Reservations recommended. Main courses 16€–24€. AE, DC, MC, V. Mon–Sat 1–9pm. Metro: Piazza di Spagna.

Dal Bolognese ★ BOLOGNESE   This is one of those rare dining spots that's chic but actually lives up to the hype with noteworthy food. Young actors, models, artists from nearby Via Margutta, and even corporate types on expense accounts show up, trying to land one of the few sidewalk tables. To begin, we suggest *misto di pasta:* four pastas, each with a different sauce, arranged on the same plate. Another good choice is thin slices of savory Parma ham or the delectable prosciutto and vine-ripened melon. For your main course, specialties that win hearts year after year are *lasagne verdi* and *tagliatelle alla Bolognese.* The chefs also turn out the town's most recommendable veal cutlets Bolognese topped with cheese. They're not inventive, but they're simply superb.

You might want to cap your evening by dropping into the **Rosati** cafe next door (or the **Canova,** across the street) to enjoy one of the tempting pastries.

Piazza del Popolo 1–2. ℂ **06-3611426.** Reservations required. Main courses 19€–30€. AE, DC, MC, V. Tues–Sun 12:30–3pm and 7:30–11:30pm. Closed 3 weeks in Aug. Metro: Flaminio.

Di Fronte a . . . ITALIAN   After a hard morning's shopping in the Piazza di Spagna area, this is an ideal spot for a lunch break. Its name (which translates as "in front of . . .") comes from the fact that the restaurant lies right in front of a stationery shop (owned by the father of the restaurant's proprietor). We prefer the dining room in the rear, with its changing exhibitions of pictures. You'll be seated at a marble table on wrought-iron benches with leather cushions. The chef prepares a tasty cuisine that is simple but good—nothing creative, but a good boost of energy to hit the stores again. Salads are very large, as are the juicy half-pound burgers. You can also order more substantial food such as succulent pastas and tender steaks. The pizza isn't bad, either. For dessert, try the *pizza bianca,* which is a pizza crust topped with chocolate cream or seasonal fruit.

Via della Croce 38. ℂ **06-6780355.** Reservations recommended for dinner. Main courses 10€–19€. AE, DC, MC, V. Daily noon–3:30pm and 7–11pm. Metro: Piazza di Spagna.

Il Bacaro ★ ITALIAN   Unpretentious and accommodating to foreigners, this restaurant contains about a half-dozen tables and operates from an ivy-edged hideaway alley near Piazza di Spagna. The restaurant is known for its fresh and tasty cheese. This was a *palazzo* in the 1600s, and some vestiges of the building's former grandeur remain, despite an impossibly cramped kitchen where the efforts of the staff to keep the show moving are nothing short of heroic. The offerings are time tested and flavorful: spaghetti with tuna roe and crispy artichokes; grilled beef steak with cheese fondue; warm beef carpaccio with radicchio, chicory, and truffles; swordfish roulades with shrimp and zucchini; and a savory pasta, *trofie,* with a white meat ragout, porcini mushrooms, and sun-dried tomatoes.

Via degli Spagnoli 27, near Piazza delle Coppelle. ℂ **06-6872554.** www.ilbacaro.com. Reservations recommended. Main courses 13€–22€. MC, V. Mon–Sat 12:30–2:30pm and 8–11:30pm. Metro: Piazza di Spagna.

INEXPENSIVE

Maccheroni ROMAN   In a rustic tavern in the heart of Rome, you can savor food that you usually have to go to the countryside to enjoy. The decor is informal, with wood-paneled walls and pop art; and on a good night the place can seat

160 satisfied diners, both visitors and locals. The chef shops wisely for his bevy of regional dishes and backs up his menu with a well-chosen wine list that includes the house Chianti. Pasta is the house specialty, and it's never better than in the spaghetti flavored with bacon and onion. You can also order fettuccine with black-truffle sauce or ravioli with pumpkin flowers. The menu features a traditional Roman cuisine, and everything is well prepared, including *maccheroni all'amatriciana* (either the red version with tomatoes and bacon along with pecorino cheese, or the white version without tomatoes). Tender, juicy beefsteaks are also served.

Piazza della Copelle 44. (✆) **06-68307895.** www.ristorantemaccheroni.com. Reservations recommended. Main courses 8€–21€. AE, MC, V. Daily 1–3pm and 8pm–midnight. Metro: Piazza di Spagna. Bus: 64, 70, 87, or 116.

Otello alla Concordia ☺ ROMAN   On a side street amid the glamorous boutiques near the northern edge of the Spanish Steps, this is one of Rome's most reliable restaurants. A stone corridor from the street leads into the dignified Palazzo Povero. Choose a table in the arbor-covered courtyard or the cramped but convivial dining rooms. Displays of Italian bounty decorate the interior, where you're likely to rub elbows with the shopkeepers from the fashion district. The *spaghetti alle vongole veraci* (with clams) is excellent, as are Roman-style saltimbocca (veal with ham), *abbacchio arrosto* (roast lamb), eggplant parmigiana, a selection of grilled or sautéed fish dishes (including swordfish), and several preparations of veal.

Via della Croce 81. (✆) **06-6791178.** www.otello-alla-concordia.com. Reservations recommended. Main courses 8€–20€. AE, DC, MC, V. Mon–Sat 12:30–3pm and 6–11pm. Closed 2 weeks in Jan. Metro: Piazza di Spagna.

Near Vatican City

The no. 6 branch of **Insalata Ricca,** a salad-and-light-meals chain, is across from the Vatican walls at Piazza del Risorgimento 5 ((✆) **06-39730387;** www. linsalataricca.it).

MODERATE

Cesare ROMAN/TUSCAN   The area around the Vatican is not the place to look for great restaurants. But Cesare is a fine old-world dining room known for its deft handling of fresh ingredients. You can select your fresh fish from the refrigerated glass case at the entrance. We come here for the fresh and tender seafood salad, brimming with cuttlefish, shrimp, squid, mussels, and octopus, and dressed with olive oil, fresh parsley, and lemon. Our table was blessed with an order of *spaghetti all'amatriciana* in a spicy tomato sauce flavored with hot peppers and bits of salt pork. The *saltimbocca alla romana,* that classic Roman dish, is a masterpiece as served here—butter-tender veal slices topped with prosciutto and fresh sage and sautéed in white wine. Another specialty is smoked swordfish; you can order fresh sardines and fresh anchovies if you want to go truly Roman. The cooks also keep the wood-fired pizza ovens hot.

Via Crescenzio 13, near Piazza Cavour. (✆) **06-6861227.** www.ristorantecesare.com. Reservations recommended. Main courses 10€–28€; fixed-price Tuscan menu 38€. AE, DC, MC, V. Daily 12:30–3pm; Mon–Sat 7:30pm–midnight. Closed in Aug. Bus: 23, 34, or 49. Metro: Lepanto or Ottaviano.

INEXPENSIVE

Hostaria dei Bastioni ⚓ ROMAN/SEAFOOD   This simple but well-managed restaurant is about a minute's walk from the entrance to the Vatican Museums and has been open since the 1960s. Although a warm-weather terrace doubles the size during summer, many diners prefer the inside room as an escape from the roaring traffic. The menu features the staples of Rome's culinary repertoire, including fisherman's risotto (a broth-simmered rice dish with fresh fish, usually shellfish), a vegetarian *fettuccine alla bastione* with orange-flavored creamy tomato sauce, and an array of grilled fresh fish. The food is first rate—and a bargain at these prices.

Via Leone IV 29. ✆ **06-39723034.** Reservations recommended Fri–Sat. Main courses 8€–19€; fixed-price menus 10€–13€. AE, DC, MC, V. Mon–Sat noon–3pm and 7–11:30pm. Closed July 15–Aug 1. Metro: Ottaviano.

Siciliainbocca ★ 🍴 SICILIAN   The best Sicilian restaurant in Rome lies close to the Vatican, ideal for a lunch when visiting either St. Peter's or the papal museums. Natives of Sicily own and operate this place, and their specialties taste virtually the same as those encountered in Sicily itself. The menu features a large variety of delectable smoked fish, including salmon, swordfish, and tuna. The homemade pastas here are the best Sicilian versions in town, especially the classic *maccheroni alla Norma,* with ricotta, a savory tomato sauce, and sautéed eggplant. You might also opt for such dishes as linguine with sautéed scampi and cherry tomatoes; or a typical Palermitan pasta with sardines, wild fennel, and pine nuts. Other good-tasting and typical dishes include swordfish with capers, olives, tomatoes, and Parmesan cheese.

Via E. Faà di Bruno 26. ✆ **06-37358400.** www.siciliainboccaweb.com. Main courses 11€–25€. AE, DC, MC, V. Mon–Sat 1:30–3pm and 8–11:30pm. Closed 3 weeks in Aug. Metro: Ottaviano San Pietro.

Taverna Angelica SOUTHERN ITALIAN   This tavern is not luxurious in any way, but it serves good affordable food in a position only 200m (656 ft.) from the Vatican. Even priests from St. Peter's come here to dine on such well-prepared dishes as potato ravioli with *guanciale,* an Italian specialty made from dry pig cheeks. One of the most imaginative pastas is spelt spaghetti with a pesto made with pistachios and walnuts, or else the fettuccine with clams and porcini mushrooms served with an arugula pesto. All the dishes are based on fresh regional produce, including breast of guinea fowl stuffed with dried tomatoes and mozzarella.

Piazza A. Capponi 6. ✆ **06-6874514.** www.tavernaangelica.it. Reservations required. Main courses 10€–23€; 2-course fixed-price lunch menu 20€, 3-course 25€. AE, MC, V. Daily 6pm–midnight; Sun noon–3pm. Closed 10 days in Aug. Metro: Ottaviano San Pietro.

In Trastevere

MODERATE

Antico Arco ★ 🍴 ITALIAN   Named after one of the gates of early medieval Rome (Arco di San Pancrazio), which rises nearby, Antico Arco is on Janiculum Hill not far from Trastevere and the American Academy. It's a hip restaurant with a young, stylish clientele. Carefully crafted dishes with fresh ingredients include ravioli stuffed with beans in a seafood soup or green homemade *tagliolini* with red mullet and a saffron sauce. Other palate-pleasing dishes include crispy suckling pig in a sweet-and-sour sauce, with fennel and a citrus soufflé, or else crunchy shrimp with artichoke purée and an anise sauce. A white chocolate tiramisu is a heavenly concoction.

Piazzale Aurelio 7. ✆ **06-5815274.** www.anticoarco.it. Reservations recommended. Main courses 15€–32€; fixed-price menu 75€. AE, DC, MC, V. Daily 6pm–midnight. Bus: 115 or 870.

Asinocotto ITALIAN   Within a pair of cramped dining rooms (one on street level, the other upstairs), you'll be served by a cheerful staff that's well practiced in hauling steaming platters of food up the steep flight of stairs. The simple white-painted walls accented by dark timbers and panels are a nice background to the flavorful dishes that stream from the busy kitchens of Giuliano Brenna. The menu is fairly sophisticated, thanks to the owner's stint as a chef at the Hotel Eden, one of Rome's more upscale hotels. Look for elaborate antipasti such as quail and watercress in a "Parmesan basket," or smoked sturgeon on a salad of Belgian endive with black olives. You might follow with handmade ravioli filled with sea bass, lettuce, and a sauvignon sauce, or a zesty oxtail soup with artichoke hearts au gratin. Other imaginative dishes include *orecchiette* pasta with eggplant, bacon, and smoked ricotta, or guinea fowl breast with a flavoring of orange and green tea. The restaurant's name, incidentally, translates as "cooked donkey meat," but don't look for that on the menu anytime soon.

Via dei Vascellari 48. ✆ **06-5898985.** www.asinocotto.com. Reservations recommended. Main courses 13€–23€. AE, DC, MC, V. Mon–Fri noon–2:30pm; Tues–Sun 7:30–11pm. Tram: 8.

Glass ★ ★ 💼 ROMAN   When this chic restaurant and wine bar opened, management claimed it was an "attempt to give Trastevere back to the Romans." Pretend you're a native and you should have a good time here on one of its two floors. Theatrical lighting and lots of glass (including the floors) give the place a modernist aura, rather rare for the district. Glass doubles as a wine bar. The cuisine is both innovative and traditional. Some of our favorite dishes are gnocchi with pancetta, chanterelle mushrooms, and almonds; and risotto with almond milk, zucchini flowers, and king crab. Other innovative dishes are a filet of tuna under a coffee-flavored crust and pistachio-crusted scallops, fresh pork belly, and baby asparagus. One dessert is about as good as it gets: a caramelized banana tart with strawberry gelatin and peanut-butter ice cream.

Vicolo del Cinque 58. ✆ **06-58335903.** www.glass-hostaria.com. Reservations recommended. Main courses 18€–26€; fixed-price menus 60€–75€. AE, DC, MC, V. Restaurant daily 8–11:30pm. Wine bar daily 8pm–2am. Bus: 23 or 125.

Villa Borghese

EXPENSIVE

Casina Valadier ★ ROMAN   Once one of the hottest dining tickets in Rome, this chic restaurant closed its doors seemingly forever. But, once again the glitterati of Rome are flocking here for the to-die-for cocktails, the superb cuisine, and the panoramic views of Rome itself. In the heart of Villa Borghese, the terrace of the restaurant is the most evocative in the city. Placed on the site of the ancient Collis Hortulorum, the highest point of the Pincio district, the original building dates from 1816 and was the creation of the famous architect Giuseppe Valadier. In its heyday, this restaurant was the most fashionable place in Rome, attracting people such as King Farouk of Egypt and Gandhi.

Our favorite place for a picnic in all of Rome is in the Borghese Gardens, followed by a reserved visit to the Galleria Borghese. **Gina,** Via San Sebastianello 7A (☏ **06-6780251;** www.ginaroma.com), has come up with a marvelous idea. This deli will provide you with a picnic basket complete with thermos, glasses, and linen for a picnic to be enjoyed in the fabled gardens. For 40€, two persons can enjoy panini (tomato, eggplant, and mozzarella on focaccia) along with a fresh fruit salad, dessert, and coffee.

The best of the menu is a regionally based repertoire of savory dishes with imaginative, intelligent associations of flavors. Diners take delight in jazzed-up Roman classics such as rigatoni with bacon, onions, peppers, and pecorino, or a cherry- and sesame-encrusted pork filet. Start, perhaps, with a duck-breast carpaccio or a warm ricotta cheese round with an olive and pistachio pesto. For dessert, dare you try the fried zucchini flowers stuffed with rice and served with cinnamon ice cream?

Villa Borghese, Piazza Bucarest. ☏ **06-69922090.** www.casinavaladier.it. Reservations required. Main courses 15€–35€. AE, DC, MC, V. Tues–Sat 12:30–3pm and 8–11pm; Sun 12:30–3pm. Bus: 53.

In Testaccio

MODERATE

Checchino dal 1887 ★ ROMAN   During the 1800s, a wine shop flourished here, selling drinks to the butchers working in the nearby slaughterhouses. In 1887, the ancestors of the restaurant's present owners began serving food, too. Slaughterhouse workers in those days were paid part of their meager salaries with the *quinto quarto* (fifth quarter) of each day's slaughter (the tail, feet, intestines, and other parts not for the squeamish). Following centuries of Roman tradition, Ferminia, the wine shop's cook, transformed these products into the tripe and oxtail dishes that form an integral part of the menu. Many Italian diners come here to relish the *rigatoni con pajata* (pasta with small intestines), *coda alla vaccinara* (oxtail stew), *fagioli e cotiche* (beans with intestinal fat), and other examples of *la cucina povera* (food of the poor). In winter, a succulent wild boar with dried prunes and red wine is served. Safer and possibly more appetizing is the array of salads, soups, pastas, steaks, cutlets, grills, and ice creams. The English-speaking staff is helpful, tactfully proposing alternatives if you're not ready for Roman soul food.

Via di Monte Testaccio 30. ☏ **06-5743816.** www.checchino-dal-1887.com. Reservations recommended. Main courses 10€–25€; fixed-price menu 46€–63€. AE, MC, V. Tues–Sat 12:30–3pm and 8pm–midnight (June–Sept closed Sun–Mon). Closed Aug and 1 week in Dec (dates vary). Metro: Piramide. Bus: 75 from Termini Station.

Ketumbar ★ JAPANESE/ITALIAN   How chic can Roma get? Ketumbar (Malay for coriander) has brought sophistication to Testaccio, once known as a *paisano* sector of Roma. Featured in several magazines devoted to the high life in Italy, the decor is sleek and minimalist, or, as one critic dubbed it, "Gothic-cum-Asia-fantasia." A young and hip crowd heads out of the center of Rome to this neighborhood to sample the truly excellent food, but also to see and be seen on the circuit. The decorator obviously went to Indonesia for much of the furnishings. But the potsherds (pieces of broken Roman amphora) remind us that we're still in an ancient part of Rome. Everything we've sampled here has been a delight.

Via Galvani 24. ✆ **06-57305338.** www.ketumbar.it. Reservations required. Main courses 10€–18€. AE, DC, MC, V. Daily 8pm–midnight. Closed Aug. Metro: Piramide. Bus: 3, 23, or 75.

In Parioli

MODERATE

Al Ceppo ★★ ROMAN   Because the place is somewhat hidden (only 2 blocks from the Villa Borghese, near Piazza Ungheria), you're likely to rub elbows with more Romans than tourists. It's a longtime favorite, and the cuisine is as good as ever. "The Log" features an open wood-stoked fireplace on which the chef roasts lamb chops, liver, and bacon to perfection. The beefsteak, which comes from Tuscany, is succulent. Other dishes that we continue to delight in are *tagliatelle* with porcini mushrooms and roast sausage; cod ravioli with sautéed shrimp; braised beef with lemon meatballs; and baked scampi with cherry tomatoes and green olives.

Via Panama 2. ✆ **06-8419696.** www.ristorantealceppo.it. Reservations recommended. Main courses 17€–30€. AE, DC, MC, V. Tues–Sun 12:30–3pm and 8–11pm. Closed last 2 weeks of Aug. Bus: 56 or 310.

5

EXPLORING ROME

R ome's ancient monuments, whether time-blackened or gleaming white in the wake of a recent restoration, are a constant reminder that Rome was one of the greatest centers of Western civilization. In the heyday of the empire, all roads led to Rome, with good reason. It was one of the first cosmopolitan cities, importing slaves, gladiators, great art, and even citizens from the far corners of the world. Despite its carnage and corruption, Rome left a legacy of law, a heritage of great art, architecture, and engineering, and an uncanny lesson in how to conquer enemies by absorbing their cultures.

But ancient Rome is only part of the spectacle. The Vatican has had a tremendous influence on making the city a tourism center. Although Vatican architects stripped down much of the city's glory, looting ancient ruins for their precious marble, they created great Renaissance treasures and even occasionally incorporated the old into the new—as Michelangelo did when turning the Baths of Diocletian into a church. And in the years that followed, Bernini adorned the city with the wonders of the Baroque, especially his glorious fountains.

ST. PETER'S & THE VATICAN

If you want to know more about the Vatican, check out its website at **www. vatican.va**. There's also a detailed map of the area in the color insert at the front of this book.

In Vatican City

In 1929, the Lateran Treaty between Pope Pius XI and the Italian government created the **Vatican,** the world's smallest sovereign state. It has only a few hundred citizens and is protected (theoretically) by its own militia, the curiously uniformed (some say by Michelangelo) Swiss guards (a tradition dating from the days when the Swiss, known as brave soldiers, were often hired out as mercenaries for foreign armies).

The only entrance to the Vatican for the casual visitor is through one of the glories of the Western world: Bernini's **St. Peter's Square (Piazza San Pietro).** As you stand in the huge piazza, you'll be in the arms of an ellipse partly enclosed by a majestic **Doric-pillared colonnade.** Atop it stands a gesticulating crowd of some 140 saints. Straight ahead is the facade of **St. Peter's Basilica ★★★** (Sts. Peter and Paul are represented by statues in front, with Peter carrying the keys to the kingdom), and, to the right, above the colonnade, are the dark brown buildings of the **papal apartments** and the **Vatican Museums ★★★**. In the

PREVIOUS PAGE: **Detail from the ceiling of the Sistine Chapel, painted by Michelangelo.**

The Vatican's famed spiral ramp.

center of the square is an **Egyptian obelisk,** brought from the ancient city of Heliopolis on the Nile delta. Flanking the obelisk are two 17th-century **fountains.** The one on the right (facing the basilica), by Carlo Maderno, who designed the facade of St. Peter's, was placed here by Bernini himself; the other is by Carlo Fontana.

On the left side of Piazza San Pietro is the **Vatican Tourist Office** (*☏* **06-69882019;** Mon–Sat 8:30am–6:30pm). It sells maps and guides that'll help you make more sense of the riches you'll be seeing in the museums. It also accepts reservations for tours of the Vatican Gardens and tries to answer questions.

St. Peter's Basilica ★★★ In ancient times, the Circus of Nero, where St. Peter is said to have been crucified, was slightly to the left of where the basilica is now located. Peter was allegedly buried here in A.D. 64 near the site of his execution, and in 324 Constantine commissioned a basilica to be built over Peter's tomb.

That structure stood for more than 1,000 years, until it verged on collapse. The present basilica, mostly completed in the 1500s and 1600s, is predominantly High Renaissance and baroque. Inside, the massive scale is almost too much to absorb, showcasing some of Italy's greatest artists: Bramante, Raphael, Michelangelo, and Maderno. In a church of such grandeur—overwhelming in its detail of gilt, marble, and mosaic—you can't expect much subtlety. It's meant to be overpowering.

In the nave on the right (the first chapel) stands one of the Vatican's greatest treasures: Michelangelo's exquisite *Pietà* **★★★**, created while the master was still in his 20s but clearly showing his genius for capturing the human form. (The sculpture has been kept behind reinforced glass since a madman's act of

---

📎 A St. Peter's Warning

St. Peter's has a strict dress code: no shorts, no skirts above the knee, and no bare shoulders and arms. *Note: You will not be let in if you come dressed inappropriately.* In a pinch, men and women alike can buy a big, cheap scarf from a nearby souvenir stand and wrap it around their legs as a long skirt or throw it over their shoulders as a shawl. If you're still showing too much skin, a guard hands out blue paper capes similar to what you wear in a doctor's office. Only limited photography is permitted inside.

What to See & Do in Rome

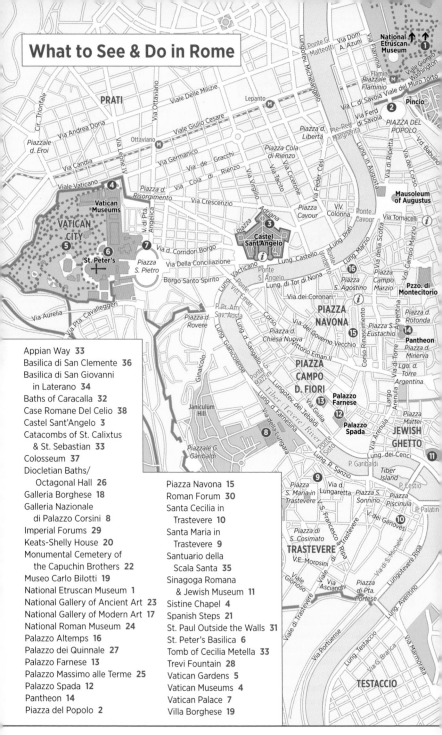

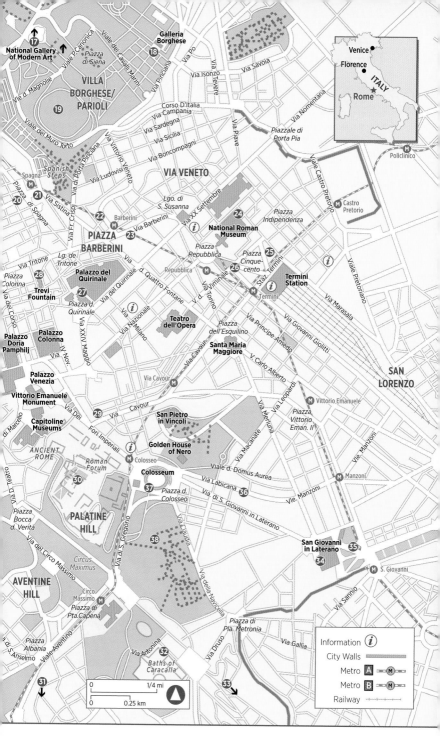

THE ETERNAL drinking water CITY

There's no excuse for being dehydrated in Rome.

At the height of the Roman Empire, 11 aqueducts brought the city 25 million gallons of water a day for its baths, ornamental fountains, and basic utilities. That tradition of hydroabundance continues in modern Rome: There are monumental fountains everywhere you look, and one of the city's most generous gifts to tourists and citizens alike is its free, perfectly drinkable spring water, in the form of *nasoni*.

In almost every piazza in town, on countless side streets, and in archaeological sites, you'll see these cast-iron hydrants marked SPQR, whose curved pipes emit a continuous stream of water into a drain below. These hydrants are properly called *fontanelle* ("little fountains") but in Roman slang, they're *nasoni* ("big noses"), for the shape of the spigots.

Naturally, many newcomers' first question is: Is it really safe to drink this water? The answer is an emphatic yes. *Fontanelle* draw on spring water in the hills outside the city—the same sources the ancients tapped for their aqueducts, minus the lead pipes—that tastes better and is cleaner than Rome's tap water, which is also potable. (Only a handful of fountains around town, mostly in the parks, are not potable, in which case they're clearly marked *acqua non potabile*.) What's more, the water issuing from the *fontanelle* is always ice-cold, even in the height of summer.

Once you have a plastic water bottle, you can just keep refilling it at *nasoni* all over town—for free. If you don't have a bottle handy, here's how the pros do it: Simply block up the bottom of the spigot with your finger, and the stream of water will come out a small hole in the top of the curved pipe, like a drinking fountain. Be careful with this method, though, as some *nasoni* are quite powerful and will shoot water all over you if you completely block up the bottom of the pipe.

Of course, in July or August, this might feel very refreshing.

When you master drinking from a *nasone*, it's time to move onto the big, ornamental fountains of Rome. No, we're not recommending you drink from their dirty basins, but from the side jets of water that feed fountains such as the Trevi and the Barcaccia at Piazza di Spagna. These jets are the same as *nasone* water, fresh and clean. Tradition even holds that the water supply for the Barcaccia guarantees eternal youth for all who drink it.

—Sylvie Hogg, *Frommer's Italy Day by Day*

vandalism in the 1970s.) Note the lifelike folds of Mary's robes and her youthful features; although she would've been middle-aged at the time of the Crucifixion, Michelangelo portrayed her as a young woman to convey her purity.

Much farther on, in the right wing of the transept near the Chapel of St. Michael, rests Canova's neoclassical **sculpture of Pope Clement XIII ★★**. The truly devout stop to kiss the feet of the 13th-century **bronze of St. Peter ★**, attributed to Arnolfo di Cambio (at the far reaches of the nave, against a corner pillar on the right). Under Michelangelo's dome is the celebrated twisty-columned **baldacchino ★★** (1524), by Bernini, resting over the papal altar. The 29m-high (96-ft.) ultrafancy canopy was created in part, so it's said, from bronze stripped from the Pantheon, although that's up for debate.

In addition, you can visit the **treasury ★**, which is filled with jewel-studded chalices, reliquaries, and copes. One robe worn by Pius XII strikes a simple note in these halls of elegance. The sacristy contains a **Historical Museum (Museo Storico) ★** displaying Vatican treasures, including the large 1400s bronze tomb of Pope Sixtus V by Antonio Pollaiuolo and several antique chalices.

You can head downstairs to the **Vatican grottoes ★★**, with their tombs of the popes, both ancient and modern (Pope John XXIII got the most adulation until the recent interment of Pope John Paul II). Behind a wall of glass is what's assumed to be the tomb of St. Peter himself.

To go even farther down, to the **Necropolis Vaticana ★★**, the area around St. Peter's tomb, you must send a fax or e-mail 3 weeks beforehand, or apply in advance in person at the Ufficio Scavi (✆/fax **06-69873017;** e-mail: scavi@fsp.va), through the arch to the left of the stairs up the basilica. You specify your name, the number in your party, your language, and dates you'd like to visit. When you apply at the Ufficio Scavi by fax or e-mail you also need to specify how you would like to be contacted (by e-mail, fax, or postal address). For details, check **www.vatican.va**. Children 14 and under are not admitted to the Necropolis Vaticana.

After you leave the grottoes, you'll find yourself in a courtyard and ticket line for the grandest sight: the climb to **Michelangelo's dome ★★★**, about 114m (375 ft.) high. You can walk up all the steps or take the elevator as far as it goes. The elevator saves you 171 steps, and you'll *still* have 320 to go after getting off. After you've made it to the top, you'll have an astounding view over the rooftops of Rome and even the Vatican Gardens and papal apartments—a photo op, if ever there was one.

Piazza San Pietro. ✆ **06-69881662.** Basilica (including grottoes) free admission. Guided tour of excavations around St. Peter's tomb 12€; children 14 and younger are not admitted. Stairs to the dome 5€; elevator to the dome 7€; sacristy (with Historical Museum) free. Basilica (including the sacristy and treasury) daily 9am–6pm. Grottoes daily 8am–5pm. Dome Oct–Mar daily 7am–6:30pm; Apr–Sept daily 7am–7pm. Bus: 49. Metro: Ottaviano/San Pietro, then a long stroll.

Vatican Museums (Musei Vaticani) & the Sistine Chapel (Cappella Sistina) ★★★ The Vatican Museums boast one of the world's greatest art collections. It's a gigantic repository of treasures from antiquity and the Renaissance, housed in a labyrinthine series of lavishly adorned palaces, apartments, and galleries leading you to the real gem: the Sistine Chapel. The Vatican Museums occupy a part of the papal palaces built from the 1200s on. From the former papal private apartments, the museums were created over a period of time to display the vast treasure-trove of art acquired by the Vatican.

You'll climb a magnificent spiral ramp to get to the ticket windows. After you're admitted, you can choose your route through the museum from **four color-coded itineraries** (A, B, C, D) according to the time you have (1½–5 hr.) and your interests. You determine your choice by consulting panels on the wall and then following the letter/color of your choice. All four itineraries culminate in the Sistine Chapel. Obviously, 1, 2, or even 20 trips will not be enough to see the wealth of the Vatican, much less to digest it. With that in mind, we've previewed only a representative sampling of the masterpieces on display (in alphabetical order).

Borgia Apartments ★: Frescoed with biblical scenes by Pinturicchio of Umbria and his assistants, these rooms were designed for Pope Alexander VI (the infamous Borgia pope). They may be badly lit, but they boast great splendor and style. At the end of the Raphael Rooms (see below) is the Chapel of Nicholas V, an intimate room frescoed by the Dominican monk Fra Angelico, the most saintly of all Italian painters.

Chiaramonti Museum: Founded by Pope Pius VII, also known as Chiaramonti, the museum includes the Corridoio (Corridor), the Galleria Lapidaria, and the Braccio Nuovo (New Side). The Corridor hosts an exposition of more than 800 Greek-Roman works, including statues, reliefs, and sarcophagi. In the Galleria Lapidaria are about 5,000 Christian and pagan inscriptions. You'll find a dazzling array of Roman sculpture and copies of Greek originals in these galleries. In the Braccio Nuovo, built as an extension of the Chiaramonti, you can admire the *Nile* ★, a magnificent reproduction of a long-lost Hellenistic original and one of the most remarkable pieces of sculpture from antiquity. The imposing statue of Augustus of Prima Porta presents him as a regal commander.

Collection of Modern Religious Art: This museum, opened in 1973, represents American artists' first invasion of the Vatican. Of the 55 rooms, at least 12 are devoted to American artists. All the works chosen were judged on their "spiritual and religious values." Among the American works is Leonard Baskin's 1.5m (5-ft.) bronze sculpture of *Isaac.* Modern Italian artists such as de Chirico and Manzù are also displayed, and there's a special room for the paintings of the Frenchman Georges Rouault. You'll also see works by Picasso, Gauguin, Guttuso, Chagall, Henry Moore, Kandinsky, and others.

Egyptian-Gregorian Museum: Experience the grandeur of the pharaohs by studying sarcophagi, mummies, statues of goddesses, vases, jewelry, sculptured pink-granite statues, and hieroglyphics.

Etruscan-Gregorian Museum ★: This was founded by Gregory XIV in 1837 and then enriched year after year, becoming one of the most important and complete collections of Etruscan art. With sarcophagi, a chariot, bronzes, urns, jewelry, and terra-cotta vases, this gallery affords remarkable insights into an ancient civilization. One of the most acclaimed exhibits is the Regolini-Galassi tomb, unearthed in the 19th century at Cerveteri. It shares top honors with the *Mars of Todi,* a bronze sculpture probably dating from the 5th century B.C.

Ethnological Museum: This is an assemblage of works of art and objects of cultural significance from all over the world. The principal route is a 1km (½-mile) walk through 25 geographical sections, displaying thousands of objects covering 3,000 years of world history. The section devoted to China is especially interesting.

Historical Museum: This museum tells the history of the Vatican. It exhibits arms, uniforms, and armor, some dating from the early Renaissance. The carriages displayed are those used by the popes and cardinals in religious processions.

Pinacoteca (Picture Gallery) ★★★: The Pinacoteca houses paintings and tapestries from the 11th to the 19th centuries. As you pass through room 1, note the oldest picture at the Vatican, a keyhole-shaped wood panel of the *Last Judgment* from the 11th century. In room 2 is one of the finest pieces—the *Stefaneschi Triptych* (six panels) by Giotto and his assistants. Bernardo Daddi's masterpiece of early Italian Renaissance art, *Madonna del Magnificat,* is also here. And you'll see works by Fra Angelico, the 15th-century Dominican monk who distinguished himself as a miniaturist (his *Virgin with Child* is justly praised—check out the Madonna's microscopic eyes).

In the **Raphael salon ★★★** (room 8), you can view three paintings by the Renaissance giant himself: the *Coronation of the Virgin,* the *Virgin of Foligno,* and the massive *Transfiguration* (completed shortly before his death). There are also eight tapestries made by Flemish weavers from cartoons by Raphael. In room 9, seek out Leonardo da Vinci's masterful but uncompleted **St. Jerome with the Lion ★★**, as well as Giovanni Bellini's *Pietà* and one of Titian's greatest works, the *Virgin of Frari.* Finally, in room 10, feast your eyes on one of the masterpieces of the baroque, Caravaggio's **Deposition from the Cross ★★**.

Pio Clementino Museum ★★★: Here you'll find Greek and Roman sculptures, many of which are immediately recognizable. The rippling muscles of the **Belvedere Torso ★★★**, a partially preserved Greek statue (1st c. B.C.) much admired by the artists of the Renaissance, especially Michelangelo, reveal an intricate knowledge of the human body. In the rotunda is a large gilded bronze of *Hercules* from the late 2nd century B.C. Other major sculptures are under porticoes opening onto the Belvedere courtyard. From the 1st century B.C., one sculpture shows **Laocoön ★★★** and his two sons locked in an eternal struggle with the serpents. The incomparable **Apollo Belvedere ★★★** (a late Roman reproduction of an authentic Greek work from the 4th c. B.C.) has become the symbol of classic male beauty, rivaling Michelangelo's *David.*

Raphael Rooms ★★: While still a young man, Raphael was given one of the greatest assignments of his short life: to decorate a series of rooms in the apartments of Pope Julius II. The decoration was carried out by Raphael and his workshop from 1508 to 1524. In these works, Raphael achieves the Renaissance aim of blending classic beauty with realism. In the first chamber, the Stanza dell'Incendio, you'll see much of the work of Raphael's pupils but little of the master—except in the fresco across from the window. The figure of the partially draped Aeneas rescuing his father (to the left of the fresco) is sometimes attributed to Raphael, as is the woman with a jug on her head to the right.

Raphael reigns supreme in the next and most important salon, the Stanza della Segnatura, the first room decorated by the artist, where you'll find the majestic **School of Athens ★★★**, one of his best-known works, depicting philosophers from the ages such as Aristotle, Plato, and Socrates. Many of the figures are actually portraits of some of the greatest artists of the Renaissance, including Bramante (on the right as Euclid, bent over and balding as he draws on a chalkboard), Leonardo da Vinci (as Plato, the bearded man in the center pointing heavenward), and even Raphael himself (looking out at you from the lower-right corner). While he was painting this masterpiece, Raphael stopped work to walk down the hall for the unveiling of Michelangelo's newly finished Sistine Chapel ceiling. He was so impressed that he returned to his *School of Athens* and added to his design a sulking Michelangelo sitting on the steps. Another well-known masterpiece here is the *Disputa del Sacramento.*

Detail from Raphael's *School of Athens.*

The *Stanza d'Eliodoro,* also by the master, manages to flatter Raphael's papal patrons (Julius II and Leo X) without compromising his art (although one rather fanciful fresco depicts the pope driving Attila from Rome). Finally, there's the *Sala di Constantino,* which was completed by his students after Raphael's death. The loggia, frescoed with more than 50 scenes from the Bible, was designed by Raphael, but the actual work was done by his loyal students.

Sistine Chapel ★★★: Michelangelo considered himself a sculptor, not a painter. While in his 30s, he was commanded by Julius II to stop work on the pope's tomb and to devote his considerable talents to painting ceiling frescoes (an art form of which the Florentine master was contemptuous). Michelangelo labored for 4 years (1508–12) over this epic project, which was so physically taxing that it permanently damaged his eyesight. All during the task, he had to contend with the pope's urging him to hurry up; at one point, Julius threatened to topple Michelangelo from the scaffolding—or so Vasari relates in his *Lives of the Artists.*

It's ironic that a project undertaken against the artist's wishes would form his most enduring legend. Glorifying the human body as only a sculptor could, Michelangelo painted nine panels, taken from the pages of Genesis, and surrounded them with prophets and sibyls. The most notable panels detail the expulsion of Adam and Eve from the Garden of Eden and the creation of man; you'll recognize the image of God's outstretched hand as it imbues Adam with spirit. (You might want to bring along binoculars so you can see the details.)

The Florentine master was in his 60s when he began the masterly *Last Judgment* ★★★ on the altar wall. Again working against his wishes, Michelangelo presented a more jaundiced view of people and their fate; God sits in judgment and sinners are plunged into the mouth of hell. A master of ceremonies under Paul III, Monsignor Biagio da Cesena, protested to the pope about the

papal AUDIENCES

When the pope is in Rome, he gives a public audience every Wednesday beginning at 10:30am (sometimes at 10am in summer). It takes place in the Paul VI Hall of Audiences, although sometimes St. Peter's Basilica and St. Peter's Square are used to accommodate a large attendance. With the ascension of Benedict XVI to the Throne of Peter, this tradition continues. You can check on the pope's appearances and ceremonies he presides over (including celebrations of Mass) on the Vatican website (www.vatican.va). Anyone is welcome, but you must first obtain a **free ticket** from the office of the Prefecture of the Papal Household, accessible from St. Peter's Square by the Bronze Door, where the colonnade on the right (as you face the basilica) begins. The office is open Monday through Saturday from 9am to 1pm. Tickets are available on Monday and Tuesday; sometimes you won't be able to get into the office on Wednesday morning.

Occasionally, if there's enough room, you can attend without a ticket.

You can also write ahead to the **Prefecture of the Papal Household,** 00120 Città del Vaticano (✆ **06-69885863**), indicating your language, the dates of your visit, and the number of people in your party. Tickets can be picked up at the office located just inside the Bronze Door (by the right colonnade of St. Peter's Sq.) at the following times: for general audiences from 3 to 7:30pm on the preceding day or on the morning of the audience from 8 to 10:30am.

At noon on Sunday, the pope speaks briefly from his study window and gives his blessing to the visitors and pilgrims gathered in St. Peter's Square. From about mid-July to mid-September, the Angelus and blessing take place at the summer residence at Castelgandolfo, some 26km (16 miles) out of Rome and accessible by Metro and bus.

"shameless nudes." Michelangelo showed that he wasn't above petty revenge by painting the prudish monsignor, with the ears of a jackass, in hell. When Biagio complained to the pope, Paul III maintained that he had no jurisdiction in hell. However, Daniele da Volterra was summoned to drape clothing over some of the bare figures, thus earning for himself a dubious distinction as a haberdasher.

On the side walls are frescoes by other Renaissance masters, such as Botticelli, Perugino, Signorelli, Pinturicchio, Roselli, and Ghirlandaio, but because they must compete unfairly with the artistry of Michelangelo, they're virtually ignored by most visitors.

The restoration of the Sistine Chapel in the 1990s touched off a worldwide debate among art historians. The chapel was on the verge of collapse, from both its age and the weather, and restoration took years, as restorers used advanced computer analyses in their painstaking and controversial work. They reattached the fresco and repaired the ceiling, ridding the frescoes of their dark and shadowy look. Critics claim that in addition to removing centuries of dirt and grime—and several of the added "modesty" drapes—the restorers removed a vital second layer of paint as well. Purists argue that many of the restored figures seem flat compared with the originals, which had more shadow and detail. Others have hailed the project for saving Michelangelo's masterpiece for future generations to appreciate and for revealing the vibrancy of his color palette.

Vatican City, Viale Vaticano (a long walk around the Vatican walls from St. Peter's Sq.). ℂ **06-69883332.** Admission 15€ adults, 8€ children 6–13, free for children 5 and under. Mon–Sat 9am–4pm. Closed Jan 1 and 6, Feb 11, Mar 19, Easter, May 1, June 29, Aug 14–15, Nov 1, and Dec 8 and 25–26. Reservations for guided tours 31€ per person through Vatican website at www. vatican.va. Metro: Cipro–Musei Vaticani.

Vatican Gardens ★ Separating the Vatican from the secular world on the north and west are 23 hectares (58 acres) of lush gardens filled with winding paths, brilliantly colored flowers, groves of massive oaks, and ancient fountains and pools. In the midst of this pastoral setting is a small summer house, Villa Pia, built for Pope Pius IV in 1560 by Pirro Ligorio. The gardens contain medi-

A priest in Vatican City.

eval fortifications from the 9th century to the present. Water spouts from a variety of fountains.

To make a reservation to visit the Vatican Gardens, you must book through the Vatican website at www.vatican.va. Once the reservation is accepted, you must go to the Vatican information office (at Piazza San Pietro, on the left side looking at the facade of St. Peter's) and pick up the tickets 2 or 3 days before your visit.

North and west of the Vatican. Tours of the gardens Mon–Tues and Thurs–Sun 10am (2 hr.; first half-hour by bus). Tour 31€. For further information, contact the Vatican Tourism Office (ℂ **06-69882019**).

Near Vatican City

Castel Sant'Angelo ★ This overpowering castle on the Tiber was built in the 2nd century as a tomb for Emperor Hadrian; it continued as an imperial mausoleum until the time of Caracalla. If it looks like a fortress, it should—that was its function in the Middle Ages. It was built over the Roman walls and linked to the Vatican by an underground passage that was used by the fleeing Pope Clement VII, who escaped from unwanted visitors such as Charles V during his 1527 sack of the city. In the 14th century, it became a papal residence, enjoying various connections with Boniface IX, Nicholas V, and Julius II, patron of Michelangelo and Raphael.

But its legend rests largely on its link with Pope Alexander VI, whose mistress bore him two children (those darlings of debauchery, Cesare and Lucrezia Borgia). Even those on a rushed visit might want to budget time for a stopover here because it's most intriguing sight, an imposing fortress that has seen more blood, treachery, and turmoil than any other left in Rome. An audio guide is available to help you understand what you're seeing.

The highlight here is a trip through the Renaissance apartments with their coffered ceilings and lush decoration. Their walls have witnessed some of the most diabolical plots and intrigues of the High Renaissance. Later, you can go through the dank cells that once echoed with the screams of Cesare's victims of torture. The most famous figure imprisoned here was Benvenuto Cellini, the eminent sculptor/goldsmith, remembered chiefly for his *Autobiography.* Now an art museum, the castle halls display the history of the Roman mausoleum, along with a wide-ranging selection of ancient arms and armor. You can climb to the top terrace for another one of those dazzling views of the Eternal City.

The bumper-to-bumper cars and buses that once roared around Castel Sant'Angelo are now gone. The area around the castle has been turned into a pedestrian zone. Visitors can walk in peace through the landscaped section with a tree-lined avenue above the Tiber and a formal garden. In 2000, the moat under the ramparts was opened to the public for the first time. You can wander the footpaths and enjoy the beeches providing shade in the sweltering summer.

Lungotevere Castello 50. ✆ **06-6819111.** www.castelsantangelo.com. Admission 5€. Tues–Sun 9am–7pm. Bus: 23, 40, 46, 49, 62, 80, 87, 280, 492, or 910. Metro: Ottaviano, then a long stroll.

THE COLOSSEUM, THE ROMAN FORUM & HIGHLIGHTS OF ANCIENT ROME

The Top Sights in Ancient Rome

Baths of Caracalla (Terme di Caracalla) ★   Named for the emperor Caracalla, the baths were completed in the early 3rd century. The richness of decoration has faded, and the lushness can be judged only from the shell of brick ruins that remain. In their heyday, they sprawled across 11 hectares (27 acres) and could handle 1,600 bathers at one time. A circular room, the ruined caldarium for very hot baths, is the traditional setting for operatic performances in Rome.

Via delle Terme di Caracalla 52. ✆ **06-39967700.** Admission 6€. Oct daily 9am–6:30pm; Nov–Feb 15 daily 9am–4:30pm; Feb 16–Mar 15 daily 9am–5pm; Mar 16–24 daily 9am–5:30pm; Mar 25–Aug daily 9am–7:15pm; Sept daily 9am–7pm. Last admission 1 hr. before closing. Closed holidays. Bus: 118, 160, or 628.

Capitoline Museum (Museo Capitolino) and Palazzo dei Conservatori ★★   Of Rome's seven hills, the Capitoline (Campidoglio) is the most sacred: Its origins stretch from antiquity; an Etruscan temple to Jupiter once stood on this spot. The approach is dramatic as you climb the long, sloping steps by Michelangelo. At the top is a perfectly proportioned square, **Piazza del Campidoglio** ★★, also laid out by the Florentine artist. Michelangelo positioned the bronze equestrian statue of Marcus Aurelius in the center, but it has now been moved inside for protection from pollution (a copy is on the pedestal). The other steps adjoining Michelangelo's approach will take you to Santa Maria d'Aracoeli (p. 157).

One side of the piazza is open; the others are bounded by the **Senatorium (Town Council),** the statuary-filled **Palace of the Conservatori (Curators),** and the **Capitoline Museum.** These museums house some of the greatest pieces of classical sculpture in the world.

The **Capitoline Museum,** built in the 17th century, was based on an architectural sketch by Michelangelo. In the first room is *The Dying Gaul* ★★, a work of majestic skill that's a copy of a Greek original dating from the 3rd century B.C. In a special gallery all her own is the *Capitoline Venus* ★★, who demurely covers herself. This statue was the symbol of feminine beauty and charm down through the centuries (it's a Roman copy of a 3rd-c.-B.C. Greek original). *Amore* (Cupid) and *Psyche* are up to their old tricks near the window.

The **equestrian statue of Marcus Aurelius** ★★, whose years in the piazza made it a victim of pollution, has been restored and is now kept in the museum for protection. This is the only such equestrian statue to have survived from ancient Rome, mainly because it was thought for centuries that the statue was that of Constantine the Great, and papal Rome respected the memory of the first Christian emperor. It's beautiful, although the perspective is rather odd. The statue is housed in a glassed-in room on the street level, the Cortile di Marforio; it's a kind of Renaissance greenhouse, surrounded by windows.

A **bronze horse** ★★★, possibly the work of a Parthenon sculptor, has gone on display after a decades-long restoration. Leaning on its hind legs with its head held back as if preparing to break into a wild dash, the horse is one of the few surviving bronze equestrian statues from Greek times—and it could be the most ancient. Some experts date it to the 5th century B.C. and attribute it to Phidias, who carved the frieze and the statue of the goddess Athene on the Parthenon in Athens. The life-size bronze once carried a figure on its back, perhaps a statue of Alexander the Great.

Palace of the Conservatori ★★, across the way, was also based on a Michelangelo architectural plan and is rich in classical sculpture and paintings. One of the most notable bronzes, a Greek work of incomparable beauty dating from the 1st century B.C., is *Lo Spinario* ★★★ (a little boy picking a thorn from his foot). In addition, you'll find *Capitoline Wolf (Lupa Capitolina)* ★★★, a rare Etruscan bronze that may date from the 5th century B.C. (Romulus and Remus, the legendary twins who were suckled by the wolf, were added at a later date.) The palace also contains a Pinacoteca (Picture Gallery)—mostly works from the 16th and 17th centuries. Notable canvases are Caravaggio's *Fortune-Teller* and his curious *John the Baptist;* the *Holy Family,* by Dosso Dossi; *Romulus and Remus,* by Rubens; and Titian's *Baptism of Christ.* The entrance courtyard is lined with the remains (head, hands, a foot, and a kneecap) of an ancient colossal statue of Constantine the Great.

Piazza del Campidoglio 1. ℂ **06-82059127.** www.museicapitolini.org. Admission 7.50€. Tues-Sun 9am–8pm. Bus: 44, 81, 95, 160, 170, 715, or 780.

Circus Maximus (Circo Massimo)   The Circus Maximus, with its elongated oval proportions and ruined tiers of benches, still evokes the setting for *Ben-Hur* on the late show. Today a formless ruin, the once-grand circus was pilfered repeatedly by medieval and Renaissance builders in search of marble and stone. At one time, 250,000 Romans could assemble on the marble seats while the emperor observed the games from his box high on the Palatine Hill. What the Romans called a "circus" was a large arena enclosed by tiers of seats on three or four sides, used especially for sports or spectacles.

The circus lies in a valley formed by the Palatine on the left and the Aventine on the right. Next to the Colosseum, it was the most impressive structure in ancient Rome, in one of the most exclusive neighborhoods. For centuries, the pomp and ceremony of chariot races filled it with the cheers of thousands.

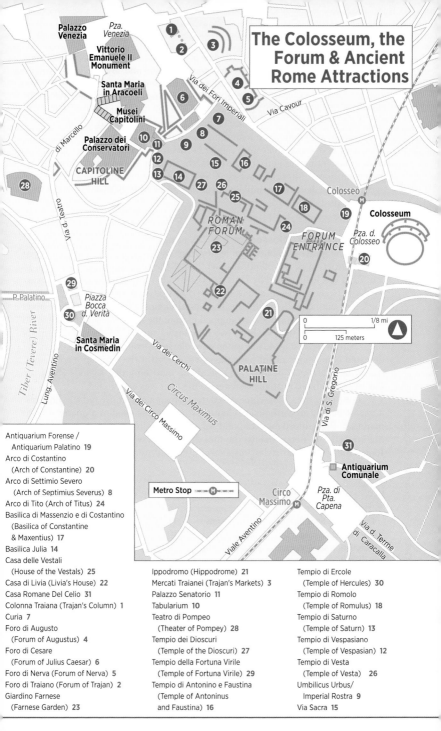

The Colosseum, the Forum & Ancient Rome Attractions

Palazzo Venezia
Pza. Venezia
Vittorio Emanuele II Monument
Santa Maria in Aracoeli
Musei Capitolini
Palazzo dei Conservatori
CAPITOLINE HILL
di Marcello
Via dei Fori Imperiali
Via Cavour
Colosseo
Colosseum
Pza. d. Colosseo
ROMAN FORUM
FORUM ENTRANCE
Via d. Teatro
Via di S. Gregorio
P. Palatino
Piazza Bocca d. Verità
Santa Maria in Cosmedin
Tiber (Tevere) River
Lung. Aventino
Via dei Cerchi
PALATINE HILL
Circus Maximus
Via dei Circo Massimo
0   1/8 mi
0   125 meters
Metro Stop ⊶Ⓜ⊷
Circo Massimo Ⓜ
Pza. di Pta. Capena
Antiquarium Comunale
Casa Romane Del Celio
Viale Aventino
Via d. Terme di Caracalla

When the dark days of the 5th and 6th centuries fell, the Circus Maximus seemed a symbol of the ruination of Rome. The last games were held in A.D. 549 on the orders of Totilla the Goth, who seized Rome in 547 and established himself as emperor. He lived in the still-glittering ruins on the Palatine and apparently thought the chariot races in the Circus Maximus would lend credibility to his charade of an empire. It must've been a miserable show because the decimated population numbered something like 500 when Totilla recaptured the city. The Romans of these times were caught between Belisarius, the imperial general from Constantinople, and Totilla the Goth, both of whom fought bloodily for control of Rome. After the travesty of 549, the Circus Maximus was never used again, and the demand for building materials reduced it, like so much of Rome, to a great dusty field.

Btw. Via dei Cerchi and Via del Circo Massimo. Metro: Circo Massimo.

The Colosseum (Colosseo) ★★★   Now a mere shell, the Colosseum still remains the greatest architectural legacy from ancient Rome. Vespasian ordered the construction of the elliptical bowl, called the Amphitheatrum Flavium, in A.D. 72; it was inaugurated by Titus in A.D. 80 with a bloody combat, lasting many weeks, between gladiators and wild beasts. At its peak, under the cruel Domitian, the Colosseum could seat 50,000. The Vestal Virgins from the temple screamed for blood, as exotic animals were shipped in from the far corners of the empire to satisfy jaded tastes (lion vs. bear, two humans vs. hippopotamus). Not-so-mock naval battles were staged (the canopied Colosseum could be flooded), and the defeated combatants might have their lives spared if they put up a good fight. Many historians now believe that one of the most enduring legends about the Colosseum—that Christians were fed to the lions—is unfounded.

Long after the Colosseum ceased to be an arena to amuse sadistic Romans, it was struck by an earthquake. Centuries later it was used as a quarry, its rich marble facing stripped away to build palaces and churches. On one side, part of the original four tiers remains; the first three levels were constructed in Doric, Ionic, and Corinthian styles, respectively, to lend variety. Inside, the seats are gone, as is the wooden floor.

No More Lines

The endless lines outside Italian museums and attractions are a fact of life. But new reservation services can help you avoid the wait, at least for some of the major museums.

Select Italy allows you to reserve your tickets for the Colosseum, the Roman Forum, Palatine Hill, the Galleria Borghese, and more, plus many other museums in Florence and Venice. The cost varies from 18€ to 35€, depending on the museum, and several combination passes are available. Contact Select Italy at ℂ **800/877-1755** in the U.S., or buy your tickets online at www.selectitaly.com.

Arch of Constantine ★★, the highly photogenic memorial next to the Colosseum, was erected by the Senate in A.D. 315 to honor Constantine's defeat of the pagan Maxentius (A.D. 306). Many of the reliefs have nothing whatsoever to do with Constantine or his works, but they tell of the victories of earlier Antonine rulers (apparently lifted from other, long-forgotten memorials).

Historically, the arch marks a period of great change in the history of Rome and thus the history of the world. Converted to Christianity by a vision on the battlefield, Constantine ended the

Detail of the Siege of Verona from the Arch of Constantine.

centuries-long persecution of the Christians (during which many devout follow-ers of the new religion had often been put to death in a most gruesome manner). While Constantine didn't ban paganism (which survived officially until the clos-ing of the temples more than half a century later), he espoused Christianity him-self and began the inevitable development that culminated in the conquest of Rome by the Christian religion. The same ticket that you buy for the Colosseum includes the visit to the Palatine Hill and the Palatine Museum.

Piazzale del Colosseo, Via dei Fori Imperiali. ⓒ **06-39967700.** Admission 12€ all levels. Nov–Feb 15 daily 8:30am–4:30pm; Feb 16–Mar 15 daily 8:30am–5pm; Mar 16–27 daily 8:30am–5:30pm; Mar 28–Aug daily 8:30am–7:15pm; Sept daily 9am–7pm; Oct daily 8:30am–7pm. Guided tours in English year-round daily at 10:15, 11:15am, 12:30, 3, 4:15, and 5:15pm. Tours 4€. Admission to Colos-seo includes visit to Palatine Hill.

Imperial Forums (Fori Imperiali) and Trajan's Market ★★ Mussolini issued the controversial orders to cut through centuries of debris and junky buildings to carve out Via dei Fori Imperiali, thereby linking the Colosseum to the grand 19th-century monuments of Piazza Venezia. Excavations under his Fascist regime began at once, and many archaeological treasures were revealed.

Begun by Julius Caesar as an answer to the overcrowding of Rome's older forums, the Imperial Forums were, at the time of their construction, flashier, bolder, and more impressive than the buildings in the Roman Forum. This site conveyed the unquestioned authority of the emperors at the height of their abso-lute power. On the street's north side, you'll come to a large outdoor restaurant, where Via Cavour joins the boulevard. Just beyond the small park across Via Cavour are the remains of the **Forum of Nerva,** built by the emperor whose 2-year reign (A.D. 96–98) followed that of the paranoid Domitian. You'll be struck by how much the ground level has risen in 19 centuries. The only really recogniz-able remnant is a wall of the Temple of Minerva with two fine Corinthian columns. This forum was once flanked by that of Vespasian, which is now gone. It's possible to enter the Forum of Nerva from the other side, but you can see it just as well from the railing.

The next forum you approach is the **Forum of Augustus ★★**, built before the birth of Christ to commemorate the emperor's victory over the assassins Cassius and Brutus in the Battle of Philippi (42 B.C.). Like the Forum of Nerva, you can enter this forum from the other side (cut across the wee footbridge).

Continuing along the railing, you'll see the vast semicircle of **Trajan's Market ★★**, whose teeming arcades stocked with merchandise from the far corners of the Roman world collapsed long ago, leaving only a few cats to watch after things. The shops once covered a multitude of levels. The historic market has reopened in Rome after years of restoration and now boasts the new Imperial Forums Museum.

Over two floors and more than 2,000 sq. m (21, 528 sq. ft.), visitors can roam through the Grande Aula and Corpo Centrale buildings. The buildings are home to 172 original marble fragments from the Fori Imperiali and here are also original remnants from the Foro di Augusto and the Foro di Nerva.

The museum occupies the ruins of boutiques, food stores, and workshops that formed Emperor Trajan's Market (nicknamed The World's First Shopping Mall). Across the street from the Roman Forum, the installation occupies the Great Hall and part of the central body of the market (built A.D. 100–110), and is designed to illustrate the history of ancient Rome's public meeting areas. Having fallen into total ruin, this once-bustling market was built over in the Middle Ages and then extensively excavated under Mussolini, who created Via dei Fori Imperiali to connect the Colosseum with Piazza Venezia.

Today it is one of Rome's main thoroughfares, cutting right through the heart of the classical remains. As a consequence, the Imperial Forums, many of which are still being excavated, are hard for ordinary visitors to understand, so the new Imperial Forums Museum uses replicas to help visitors orientate themselves, and has different galleries dedicated to forums and temples. It also houses a giant head of Constantine, found in 2005 in an old sewer, and 172 large marble fragments from the Imperial Forums, most of which had been in storage for years. They are also shown with drawings to illustrate where they fitted into the overall scheme. Also on view are 15 plaster models and 12 life-size re-creations of parts of Augustus's and Nerva's Forums next door. The models are painted in brilliant colors, which was typical in ancient Roman.

Admission to both Trajan's Market and the Imperial Forums Museum costs 9€, and the site is open Tuesday to Sunday 9am to 7pm. The website is www. mercatiditraiano.it.

Before you head down through the labyrinthine passages, you might like to climb the **Tower of the Milizie ★**, a 12th-century structure that was part of the medieval headquarters of the Knights of Rhodes. The view from the top (if it's open) is well worth the climb.

You can enter the **Forum of Trajan ★★** on Via Quattro Novembre near the steps of Via Magnanapoli. Once through the tunnel, you'll emerge into the newest and most beautiful of the Imperial Forums, built between A.D. 107 and 113, and designed by Greek architect Apollodorus of Damascus (who laid out the adjoining market). There are many statue fragments and pedestals bearing still-legible inscriptions, but more interesting is the great Basilica Ulpia, whose gray marble columns rise roofless into the sky. This forum was once regarded as one of the architectural wonders of the world.

Beyond the Basilica Ulpia is **Trajan's Column ★★★**, in magnificent condition, with an intricate bas-relief sculpture depicting Trajan's victorious campaign (though, from your vantage point, you'll be able to see only the earliest stages). The next stop is the **Forum of Julius Caesar ★★**, the first of the Imperial Forums. It lies on the opposite side of Via dei Fori Imperiali. This was the site of the Roman stock exchange, as well as the Temple of Venus.

After you've seen the wonders of ancient Rome, you might continue up Via dei Fori Imperiali to **Piazza Venezia ★★**, where the white Brescian marble **Vittorio Emanuele Monument** dominates the scene. (You can't miss it.) Italy's most flamboyant landmark, it was built in the late 1800s to honor the first king of Italy. It has been compared to everything from a wedding cake to a Victorian typewriter and has been ridiculed because of its harsh white color in a city of honey-gold tones. An eternal flame burns at the Tomb of the Unknown Soldier. The interior of the monument has been closed for years, but you'll come to use it as a landmark as you figure your way around the city.

> ### A View to Remember for a Lifetime
>
> Standing on Piazza del Campidoglio, walk around the right side of the Palazzo Senatorio to a terrace overlooking the city's best panorama of the Roman Forum, with the Palatine Hill and the Colosseum as a backdrop. At night, the Forum is dramatically floodlit and the ruins look even more impressive and haunting.

Via IV Novembre 94. ☎ **06-0608.** www.mercatiditraiano.it. Admission 11€. Tues–Sun 9am–7pm. Closed Dec 25, Jan 1, May 1. Metro: Colosseo. Keep to the right side of the street.

Roman Forum (Foro Romano), Palatine Hill (Palatino) & Palatine Museum (Museo Palatino) ★★★   When it came to cremating Caesar, purchasing a harlot for the night, sacrificing a naked victim, or just discussing the day's events, the Roman Forum was the place to be. Traversed by the **Via Sacra (Sacred Way) ★**, the main thoroughfare of ancient Rome, the Forum was built in the marshy land between the Palatine and Capitoline hills, and flourished as the center of Roman life in the days of the republic, before it gradually lost prestige to the Imperial Forums.

You'll see only ruins and fragments, an arch or two, and lots of overturned boulders, but with some imagination you can feel the rush of history here. That any semblance of the Forum remains today is miraculous because it was used for years as a quarry (as was the Colosseum). Eventually it reverted to what the Italians call a *campo vaccino* (cow pasture). But excavations in the 19th century began to bring to light one of the world's most historic spots.

By day, the columns of now-vanished temples and the stones from which long-forgotten orators spoke are mere shells. Bits of grass and weeds grow where a triumphant Caesar was once lionized. But at night, when the Forum is silent in the moonlight, it isn't difficult to imagine Vestal Virgins still guarding the sacred temple fire. The best view of the Roman Forum at night is from Campidoglio or Capitoline Hill, Michelangelo's piazza from the Renaissance, which overlooks the Forum.

You can spend at least a morning wandering through the ruins of the Forum. If you're content with just looking, you can do so at your leisure. But if you want the stones to have some meaning, buy a detailed plan at the gate (the temples are hard to locate otherwise).

Turn right at the bottom of the entrance slope to walk west along the old Via Sacra toward the arch. Just before it on your right is the large brick **Curia ★★**, the main seat of the Roman Senate, built by Julius Caesar. Pop inside to see the 3rd-century marble inlay floor.

The triumphal **Arch of Septimius Severus ★★** (A.D. 203) displays time-bitten reliefs of the emperor's victories in what are today Iran and Iraq. During the Middle Ages, Rome became a provincial backwater, and frequent flooding of the nearby river helped bury most of the Forum. This former center of the empire became a cow pasture. Some bits did still stick out aboveground, including the top half of this arch, which was used to shelter a barbershop! It wasn't until the 19th century that people really became interested in excavating these ancient ruins to see what Rome in its glory must have been like.

Just to the left of the arch, you can make out the remains of a cylindrical lump of rock with some marble steps curving off it. That round stone was the **Umbilicus Urbus,** considered the center of Rome and of the entire Roman Empire; and the curving steps are those of the **Imperial Rostra ★**, where great orators and legislators stood to speak and the people gathered to listen. Nearby, the much-photographed trio of fluted columns with Corinthian capitals supporting a bit of architrave form the corner of the **Temple of Vespasian and Titus ★★** (emperors were routinely turned into gods upon dying).

Start heading to your left toward the eight Ionic columns marking the front of the **Temple of Saturn ★★** (rebuilt in 42 B.C.), which housed the first treasury of republican Rome. It was also the site of one of the Roman year's biggest annual blowout festivals, the December 17 feast of Saturnalia, which, after a bit of tweaking, Christians now celebrate as Christmas. Turn left to start heading back east, past the worn steps and stumps of brick pillars outlining the enormous

Taking in the view of the Roman Forum from the Capitoline.

Basilica Julia ★★, built by Julius Caesar. Past it are the three Corinthian columns of the **Temple of the Dioscuri** ★★★, dedicated to the Gemini twins, Castor and Pollux. Forming one of the most celebrated sights of the Roman Forum, a trio of columns supports an architrave fragment. The founding of this temple dates from the 5th century B.C.

Beyond the bit of curving wall that marks the site of the little round **Temple of Vesta** (rebuilt several times after fires started by the sacred flame within), you'll find the partially reconstructed **House of the Vestal Virgins** ★★ (3rd–4th c. A.D.) against the south side of the grounds. This was the home of the consecrated young women who tended the sacred flame in the Temple of Vesta. Vestals were girls chosen from patrician families to serve a 30-year-long priesthood. During their tenure, they were among Rome's most venerated citizens, with unique powers such as the ability to pardon condemned criminals. The cult was quite serious about the "virgin" part of the job description—if one of Vesta's earthly servants was found to have "misplaced" her virginity, the miscreant Vestal was buried alive. (Her amorous accomplice was merely flogged to death.) The overgrown rectangle of their gardens is lined with broken, heavily worn statues of senior Vestals on pedestals.

The path dovetails back to join Via Sacra at the entrance. Turn right and then left to enter the massive brick remains and coffered ceilings of the 4th-century **Basilica of Constantine and Maxentius** ★★. These were Rome's public law courts, and their architectural style was adopted by early Christians for their houses of worship (the reason so many ancient churches are called "basilicas").

Return to the path and continue toward the Colosseum. Veer right to the second great surviving triumphal arch, the **Arch of Titus** ★★ (A.D. 81), on which one relief depicts the carrying off of treasures from Jerusalem's temple. Look closely and you'll see a menorah among the booty. The war that this arch glorifies ended with the expulsion of Jews from the colonized Judea, signaling the beginning of the Jewish Diaspora throughout Europe. From here you can enter and climb the only part of the Forum's archaeological zone that still charges admission, the **Palatine Hill** ★ (with the same hours as the Forum).

The Palatine, tradition tells us, was the spot on which the first settlers built their huts under the direction of Romulus. In later years, the hill became a patrician residential district that attracted such citizens as Cicero. In time, however, the area was gobbled up by imperial palaces and drew a famous and infamous roster of tenants, such as Livia (some of the frescoes in the House of Livia are in miraculous condition), Tiberius, Caligula (murdered here by members of his Praetorian Guard), Nero, and Domitian.

Only the ruins of its former grandeur remain today. You really need to be an archaeologist to make sense of them; they're more difficult to understand than those in the Forum. But even if you're not interested in the past, it's worth the climb for the panoramic view of both the Roman and the Imperial Forums, as well as the Capitoline Hill and the Colosseum.

The **Palatine Museum (Museo Palatino)** ★ displays a good collection of Roman sculpture from the digs in the Palatine villas. In summer you can take guided tours in English daily at 11 and 11:45am, and 4:15pm for 4€; call in winter to see if they're still available. If you ask the custodian, he might take you to one of the nearby locked villas and let you in for a peek at surviving frescoes and stuccoes. The same ticket that you buy for the Palatine Hill and the Palatine Museum includes the visit to the Colosseum.

Largo Romolo e Remo. *©* **06-39967700.** Forum and Palatine Hill 12€. Oct 30–Dec and Jan 2–Feb 15 daily 8:30am–4:30pm; Feb 16–Mar 15 daily 8:30am–5pm; Mar 16–24 daily 8:30am–5:30pm; Mar 25–Aug daily 8:30am–7:15pm; Sept daily 8:30am–7pm; Oct 1–29 daily 8:30am–6:30pm. Last admission 1 hr. before closing. Guided tours are given daily at 11am, lasting 1 hr., costing 4€. Closed holidays. Metro: Colosseo. Bus: 75 or 84.

Other Attractions near Ancient Rome

Basilica di San Clemente ★　From the Colosseum, head up Via San Giovanni in Laterano to this basilica. It isn't just another Roman church—far from it. In this church-upon-a-church, centuries of history peel away. In the 4th century A.D., a church was built over a secular house from the 1st century, beside which stood a pagan temple dedicated to Mithras (god of the sun). Down in the eerie grottoes (which you can explore on your own), you'll discover well-preserved frescoes from the 9th to the 11th centuries. The Normans destroyed the lower church, and a new one was built in the 12th century. Its chief attraction is the bronze-orange mosaic from that period adorning the apse, as well as a chapel honoring St. Catherine of Alexandria with frescoes by Masolino.

Via San Giovanni in Laterano at Piazza San Clemente. *©* **06-7740021.** www.basilicasanclemente.com. Basilica free admission; excavations 5€. Mon–Sat 9am–12:30pm and 3–6pm; Sun noon–6pm. Metro: Colosseo. Bus: 85, 87, or 850.

Basilica di San Giovanni in Laterano ★　This church (not St. Peter's) is the cathedral of the diocese of Rome, where the pope comes to celebrate Mass on certain holidays. Built in A.D. 314 by Constantine, it has suffered the vicissitudes of Rome, forcing it to be rebuilt many times. Only fragmented parts of the baptistery remain from the original.

The present building is characterized by its 18th-century facade by Alessandro Galilei (statues of Christ and the Apostles ring the top). A 1993 terrorist bomb caused severe damage, especially to the facade. Borromini gets the credit (some say blame) for the interior, built for Innocent X. It's said that, in the misguided attempt to redecorate, frescoes by Giotto were destroyed (remains believed to have been painted by Giotto were discovered in 1952 and are now on display against a column near the entrance on the right inner pier). In addition, look for the unusual ceiling and the sumptuous transept, and explore the 13th-century cloisters with twisted double columns. Next door, **Palazzo Laterano** (no admission) was the original home of the popes before they became voluntary "Babylonian captives" in Avignon, France, in 1309.

Across the street is the **Palace of the Holy Steps (Santuario della Scala Santa),** Piazza San Giovanni in Laterano (*©* **06-7726641**). Allegedly, the 28 marble steps here (now covered with wood for preservation) were originally at Pontius Pilate's villa in Jerusalem, and Christ climbed them the day he was brought before Pilate. According to a medieval tradition, the steps were brought from Jerusalem to Rome by Constantine's mother, Helen, in 326, and they've been in this location since 1589. Today pilgrims from all over come here to climb the steps on their knees. This is one of the holiest sites in Christendom, although some historians say the stairs might date only from the 4th century.

Piazza San Giovanni in Laterano 4. *©* **06-69886452.** Basilica free admission; cloisters 2€. Summer daily 9am–6:45pm (off season to 6pm). Metro: San Giovanni. Bus: 16, 81, 85, 87, 186, 218, or 650.

Case Romane del Celio ★ 🎁 The 5th-century Basilica of SS. Giovanni e Paolo stands over a residential complex consisting of several Roman houses of different periods. According to tradition, this was the dwelling of two Roman officers, John and Paul (not the apostles), who were beheaded during the reign of Julian the Apostate (361–362), when they refused to serve in a military campaign. They were later made saints, and their bones were said to have been buried at this site. A visit here will provide you with a unique picture of how several generations of Romans lived. Preserved at the site is a residence from the 2nd century A.D., a single home of a wealthy family, and a 3rd-century-A.D. apartment building for artisans. A religious sect, the Passionists, excavated the site in 1887, discovering naked genii figures painted on the walls. Scandalized at such a realistic depiction of male genitalia, they blurred some of the most obvious anatomical details. The two-story construction, with some 20 rooms, also contains a labyrinth of well-preserved pagan and Christian paintings.

Piazza Santi Giovanni e Paolo 13 (entrance on Clivo di Scauro). 𝒞 **06-70454544.** www.case romane.it. Admission 6€ adults, 4€ ages 12–18, free 11 and under. Thurs–Mon 10am–1pm and 3–6pm. Metro: Colosseo or Circo Massimo.

National Museum of Palazzo Venezia (Museo Nazionale di Palazzo di Venezia) ★ The Palazzo Venezia, in the geographic heart of Rome near Piazza Venezia, served as the seat of the Austrian Embassy until the end of World War I. During the Fascist regime (1928–43), it was the seat of the Italian government. The balcony from which Mussolini used to speak to the people was built in the 15th century. You can now visit the rooms and halls containing oil paintings, porcelain, tapestries, ivories, and ceramics. No one particular exhibit stands out—it's the sum total that adds up to a major attraction. The State Rooms occasionally open to host temporary exhibits.

Via del Plebiscito 118. 𝒞 **06-6780131.** Admission 5€. Tues–Sun 8:30am–7:30pm. Bus: 40, 63, 70, 75, or 81.

St. Peter in Chains (San Pietro in Vincoli) ★ This church, which has undergone recent renovations, was founded in the 5th century to house the chains that bound St. Peter in Palestine (they're preserved under glass). But the drawing card is the tomb of Pope Julius II, which features one of the world's most famous sculptures: **Michelangelo's *Moses* ★★★**. Michelangelo was to have carved 44 magnificent figures for the tomb. That didn't happen, of course, but the pope was given a great consolation prize—a figure intended to be "minor" that's now numbered among Michelangelo's masterpieces. In the *Lives of the Artists,* Vasari wrote about the stern father symbol of Michelangelo's *Moses:* "No modern work will ever equal it in beauty, no, nor ancient either."

Piazza San Pietro in Vincoli 4A (off Via degli Annibaldi). 𝒞 **06-4882865.** Free admission. Spring–summer daily 7am–12:30pm and 3:30–7pm (autumn–winter to 6pm). Metro: Colosseo or Cavour, then cross the blvd. and walk up the flight of stairs. Turn right, and you'll head into the piazza; the church will be on your left.

Santa Maria d'Aracoeli ★ On the Capitoline Hill, this landmark church was built for the Franciscans in the 13th century. According to legend, Augustus once ordered a temple erected on this spot, where a prophetic sibyl forecast the coming of Christ. In the interior are a coffered Renaissance ceiling and a mosaic of the Virgin over the altar in the Byzantine style. If you're enough of a sleuth, you'll find a tombstone carved by the great Renaissance sculptor Donatello. The church is known for its **Bufalini Chapel,** a masterpiece by Pinturicchio, who frescoed it with scenes illustrating the life and death of St. Bernardino of Siena. He also depicted St. Francis receiving the stigmata. These frescoes are a high point in early Renaissance Roman painting. You have to climb a long flight of steep steps to reach the church, unless you're already on neighboring Piazza del Campidoglio, in which case you can cross the piazza and climb the steps on the far side of the Museo Capitolino (earlier in this chapter).

Scala dell'Arce Capitolina 12. ✆ **06-6798155.** Free admission. Daily 9am–12:30pm and 2:30–5:30pm. Bus: 44, 46, 60, or 75.

Santa Maria in Cosmedin This little church was begun in the 6th century but was subsequently rebuilt. A Romanesque campanile (bell tower) was added at the end of the 11th century, although its origins go back to the 3rd century. The church was destroyed several times by earthquakes or by foreign invasions, but it has always been rebuilt.

People come not for great art treasures, but to see the **"Mouth of Truth,"** a large disk under the portico. As Gregory Peck demonstrated to Audrey Hepburn in the film *Roman Holiday,* the mouth is supposed to chomp down on the hands of liars who insert their paws. (According to local legend, a former priest used to keep a scorpion in back to bite the fingers of anyone he felt was lying.) The purpose of this disk (which is not of particular artistic interest) is unclear. One hypothesis says that it was used to collect the faithful's donations to God, which were introduced through the open mouth.

Piazza della Bocca della Verità 18. ✆ **06-6781419.** Free admission. Summer daily 9am–8pm; winter daily 9am–5pm. Metro: Circo Massimo. Bus: 30 or 170.

THE PANTHEON & ATTRACTIONS NEAR PIAZZA NAVONA & CAMPO DE' FIORI

The Pantheon & Nearby Attractions

The Pantheon stands on **Piazza della Rotonda,** a lively square with cafes, vendors, and great people-watching.

The Pantheon ★★★ Of all ancient Rome's great buildings, only the Pantheon ("All the Gods") remains intact. It was built in 27 B.C. by Marcus Agrippa and was reconstructed by Hadrian in the early 2nd century A.D. This remarkable building, 43m (142 ft.) wide and 43m (142 ft.) high (a perfect sphere resting in a cylinder) and once ringed with white marble statues of Roman gods in its niches, is among the architectural wonders of the world because of its dome and its concept of space. Hadrian himself is credited with the basic plan, an architectural design that was unique for the time. The once-gilded dome is merely show. A real dome, a perfect, massive hemisphere of cast concrete, is supported by a solid ring wall. Before the 20th century, the dome was the biggest pile of concrete ever constructed. The ribbed dome outside is a series of almost weightless cantilevered bricks. Animals were sacrificed and burned in the center, and the smoke escaped through the only means of light, the oculus, an opening at the top 5.5m (18 ft.) in diameter.

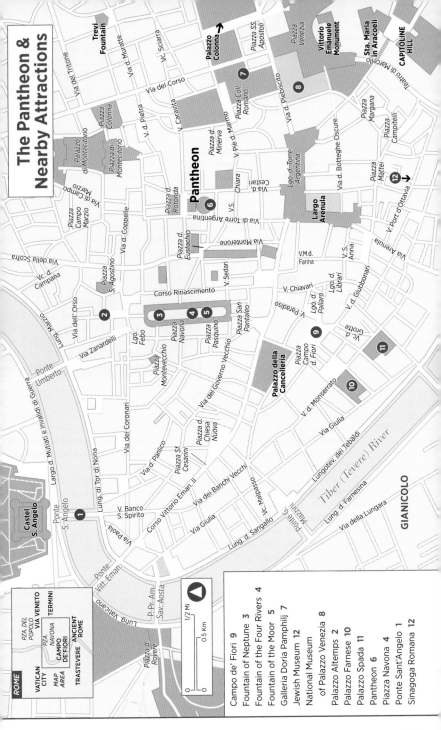

The Pantheon & Nearby Attractions

Pantheon

Trevi Fountain

Palazzo Colonna

Piazza SS. Apostoli

Piazza Venezia

Vittorio Emanuele Monument

Sta. Maria in Aracoeli

CAPITOLINE HILL

Piazza Colonna

Palazzo di Montecitorio

Piazza di Montecitorio

Piazza Campo Marzio

Piazza d. Minerva

Piazza Coll. Romano

Piazza Margana

Piazza Campitelli

Piazza d. Rotonda

Piazza S. Agostino

Piazza d. Eustachio

Via di Torre Argentina

Largo Arenula

Piazza Mattei

Piazza San Pantaleo

Piazza Navona

Piazza Pasquino

Piazza Montevecchio

Piazza di Chiesa Nuova

Palazzo della Cancelleria

Piazza Campo d. Fiori

Piazza St. Cesarini

Castel S. Angelo

Tiber (Tevere) River

GIANICOLO

ROME

VATICAN CITY

MAP AREA

TRASTEVERE   ANCIENT ROME

PZA. DEL POPOLO

VIA VENETO

TERMINI

PZA. NAVONA

CAMPO DE'FIORI

1/2 Mi

0.5 Km

Campo de' Fiori 9
Fountain of Neptune 3
Fountain of the Four Rivers 4
Fountain of the Moor 5
Galleria Doria Pamphilj 7
Jewish Museum 12
National Museum
  of Palazzo Venezia 8
Palazzo Altemps 2
Palazzo Farnese 10
Palazzo Spada 11
Pantheon 6
Piazza Navona 4
Ponte Sant'Angelo 1
Sinagoga Romana 12

159

Michelangelo came here to study the dome before designing the cupola of St. Peter's (whose dome is .5m/2 ft. smaller than the Pantheon's). The walls are 7.5m (25 ft.) thick, and the bronze doors leading into the building weigh 20 tons each. About 125 years ago, Raphael's tomb was discovered here (fans still bring him flowers). Vittorio Emanuele II, king of Italy, and his successor, Umberto I, are interred here as well. Today it is a Catholic church (Chiesa di Santa Maria ad Martyres). Until the 5th century, it was a temple dedicated to all the Roman gods. In 609, Emperor Phocas gave it to Pope Boniface IV, who consecrated it, dedicated it to St. Mary and all the Christian martyrs, and renamed it Santa Maria ad Martyres.

Piazza della Rotonda. ℂ **06-68300230.** Free admission. Mon–Sat 9am–7:30pm; Sun 9am–1pm. Bus: 30, 40, 62, 64, 81, or 492 to Largo di Torre.

Sunlight streams through the dome of the Pantheon.

Galleria Doria Pamphilj ★ This museum offers a look at what it was like to live in an 18th-century palace. It has been restored to its former splendor and expanded to include four rooms long closed to the public. It's partly leased to tenants (on the upper levels), and there are shops on the street level—but you'll overlook all this after entering the grand apartments of the Doria Pamphilj family, which traces its lineage to before the great 15th-century Genoese admiral Andrea Doria. The apartments surround the central court and gallery. The **ballroom, drawing rooms, dining rooms,** and **family chapel** are full of gilded furniture, crystal chandeliers, Renaissance tapestries, and family portraits. The **Green Room** is especially rich, with a 15th-century Tournay tapestry, paintings by Memling and Filippo Lippi, and a seminude portrait of Andrea Doria by Sebastiano del Piombo. The **Andrea Doria Room,** dedicated to the admiral and to the ship of the same name, contains a glass case with mementos of the great 1950s maritime disaster.

Skirting the central court is a **picture gallery** with a memorable collection of frescoes, paintings, and sculpture. Most important are the portrait of Innocent X, by Velázquez; *Salome,* by Titian; works by Rubens and Caravaggio; the *Bay of Naples,* by Pieter Bruegel the Elder; and a copy—not the original—of Raphael's portrait of Principessa Giovanna d'Arágona de Colonna (who looks remarkably like Leonardo's *Mona Lisa*). Most of the sculpture came from the Doria country estates: marble busts of Roman emperors, bucolic nymphs, and satyrs.

Piazza del Collegio Romano 2 (off Via del Corso). ℂ **06-6797323.** www.doriapamphilj.it. Admission 10€ adults, 7€ students/seniors. Daily 10am–5pm. Closed holidays. Private visits can be arranged. Metro: Barberini or Colosseo.

Piazza Navona & Nearby Attractions

Piazza Navona ★★★, one of the most beautifully baroque sites in all Rome, is an ocher-colored gem, unspoiled by new buildings or traffic. Its shape results from the ruins of the Stadium of Domitian that lie beneath it. Chariot races were once held here (some rather unusual, such as the one in which the head of the winning horse was lopped off as it crossed the finish line and was then carried by runners to be offered as a sacrifice by the Vestal Virgins atop the Capitoline). In medieval times, the popes used to flood the piazza to stage mock naval encounters. Today the piazza is packed with vendors and street performers, and lined with pricey cafes where you can enjoy a cappuccino or gelato and indulge in unparalleled people-watching.

Besides the twin-towered facade of 17th-century Santa Agnes, the piazza boasts several baroque masterpieces. The best known, in the center, is Bernini's **Fountain of the Four Rivers (Fontana dei Quattro Fiumi)** ★★★, whose four stone personifications symbolize the world's greatest rivers: the Ganges, Danube, della Plata, and Nile. It's fun to try to figure out which is which. (**Hint:** The figure with the shroud on its head is the Nile, so represented because the river's source was unknown at the time.) At the south end is the **Fountain of the Moor (Fontana del Moro),** also by Bernini. The **Fountain of Neptune (Fontana di Nettuno),** which balances that of the Moor, is a 19th-century addition.

Palazzo Altemps ★   This branch of the National Roman Museum is housed in a 15th-century palace that was restored and opened to the public in 1997. It is home to the fabled Ludovisi Collection of Greek and Roman sculpture. Among the masterpieces of the Roman Renaissance, you'll find the *Ares Ludovisi,* a Roman copy of the original dated 330 B.C. and restored by Bernini during the 17th century. In the Sala delle Storie di Mosè is *Ludovisi's Throne,* representing the birth of Venus. The Sala delle Feste (the Celebrations' Hall) is dominated by a sarcophagus depicting the Romans fighting against the Ostrogoth barbarians; this masterpiece, carved from a single block, dates back to the 2nd century A.D. and nowadays is called *Grande Ludovisi (Great Ludovisi).* Other outstanding art from the collection includes a copy of Phidias's celebrated *Athena,* which once stood in the Parthenon in Athens. (The Roman copy here is from the 1st c. B.C. because the original *Athena* is lost to history.) The huge *Dionysus with Satyr* is from the 2nd century A.D.

Piazza San Apollinare 48, near the Piazza Navona. (𝄞 **06-39967700.** Admission 10€. Tues–Sun 9am–7:45pm. Last admission 1 hr. before closing. Bus: 70, 81, 87, or 116.

Campo de' Fiori & the Jewish Ghetto

During the 1500s, **Campo de' Fiori** ★ was the geographic and cultural center of secular Rome, site of dozens of inns. From its center rises a statue of the severe-looking monk Giordano Bruno, whose presence is a reminder that heretics were occasionally burned at the stake here. Today, circled by venerable houses, the campo is the site of an **open-air food market** held Monday through Saturday from early in the morning until around noon (or whenever the food runs out).

Built from 1514 to 1589, the **Palazzo Farnese** ★, on Piazza Farnese, was designed by Sangallo and Michelangelo, among others, and was an astronomically expensive project for the time. Its famous residents have included a 16th-century member of the Farnese family, plus Pope Paul III, Cardinal Richelieu, and the former Queen Christina of Sweden, who moved to Rome after abdicating. During the 1630s, when the heirs couldn't afford to maintain the *palazzo,* it became the site of the French Embassy, as it still is (it's closed to the public). For the best view of it, cut west from Via Giulia along any of the narrow streets (we recommend Via Mascherone or Via dei Farnesi).

Palazzo Spada ★, Piazza Capo di Ferro 13 (*☎* **06-6861158**), was built around 1550 for Cardinal Gerolamo Capo di Ferro and later inhabited by the descendants of several other cardinals. It was sold to the Italian government in the 1920s. Its richly ornate facade, covered in high-relief stucco decorations in the Mannerist style, is the finest of any building from 16th-century Rome. The State Rooms are closed, but the richly decorated courtyard and a handful of galleries of paintings are open. Admission is 5€

A Roman deli in the former Ghetto.

Tuesday through Sunday from 8:30am to 7:30pm. To get there, take bus no. 46, 56, 62, 64, 70, 87, or 492.

Also in this neighborhood stands the **Sinagoga Romana Lungotevere Cenci** (*☎* **06-6840061**), open only for services. Trying to avoid all resemblance to a Christian church, the building (1874–1904) evokes Babylonian and Persian details. The synagogue was attacked by terrorists in 1982 and since then has been heavily guarded by *carabinieri* (a division of the Italian army) armed with machine guns. On the premises is the **Jewish Museum of Rome** (**Museo Ebraico di Roma;** www.museoebraico.roma.it), Via Catalana (same phone), which displays the collections of the Jews of Rome, including the works of 17th- and 18th-century Roman silversmiths, precious textiles from all over Europe, parchments, and marble carvings saved when the ghetto synagogues were demolished. The restored museum now has six permanent exhibition rooms. Admission (including guided tour of the synagogue) is 7.50€ for adults, 4€ for students, with children 10 and under admitted free. From June 15 to September 15, hours are Sunday to Thursday 10am to 7pm, Friday 10am to 4pm. At other times, hours are Sunday to Thursday 10am to 5pm, Friday 9am to 2pm (bus: 30, 40, 46, 63, 271, 280, 630, or 780).

THE SPANISH STEPS, THE TREVI FOUNTAIN & ATTRACTIONS NEARBY

On or Around Piazza di Spagna

The **Spanish Steps ★★** (**Scalinata di Spagna;** Metro: Piazza di Spagna) are alive with azaleas and other flowers in spring, and bustling with flower vendors, jewelry dealers, and photographers snapping pictures of visitors year-round. The steps and the square (Piazza di Spagna) take their names from the Spanish Embassy, which used to be headquartered here. Designed by Italian architect Francesco de Sanctis and built from 1723 to 1725, they were funded almost entirely by the French as a preface to Trinità dei Monti at the top.

The steps and the piazza below are always packed with a crowd: strolling, reading in the sun, browsing the vendors' carts, and people-watching. Near the steps, you'll also find an American Express office, public restrooms (near the Metro stop), and the most sumptuous McDonald's we've ever seen (cause for uproar among the Romans when it first opened).

Keats-Shelley House   At the foot of the Spanish Steps is this 18th-century house where John Keats died of consumption on February 23, 1821, at age 25. Since 1909, when it was bought by well-intentioned English and American literary types, it has been a working library established in honor of Keats and Percy Bysshe Shelley, who drowned off the coast of Viareggio with a copy of Keats in his pocket. Mementos range from kitsch to the immortal. The apartment where Keats spent his last months, tended by his close friend Joseph Severn, shelters a death mask of Keats as well as the "deadly sweat" drawing by Severn.

Piazza di Spagna 26. © **06-6784235.** www.keats-shelley-house.org. Admission 4€. Mon–Fri 10am–1pm and 2–6pm; Sat 11am–2pm and 3–6pm. Guided tours by appointment. Metro: Piazza di Spagna.

Palazzo del Quirinale ★★   Until the end of World War II, this palace was the home of the king of Italy; before the crown resided here, it was the residence of the pope. Despite its Renaissance origins (nearly every important architect in Italy worked on some aspect of its sprawling premises), this *palazzo* is rich in associations with ancient emperors and deities. The colossal statues of the Dioscuri Castor and Pollux, which now form part of the fountain in the piazza, were found in the nearby great Baths of Constantine; in 1793 Pius VI had the

The crowds at the Spanish Steps.

ancient Egyptian obelisk moved here from the Mausoleum of Augustus. The sweeping view of Rome from the piazza, which crowns the highest of the seven ancient hills of Rome, is itself worth the trip. This palace houses the president of the republic.

Piazza del Quirinale. No phone for visitor information. www.quirinale.it. Admission 5€. Sun 8:30am–noon. Closed late June to early Sept. Metro: Barberini.

Trevi Fountain (Fontana di Trevi) ★★   As you elbow your way through the summertime crowds around the Trevi Fountain, you'll find it hard to believe that this little piazza was nearly always deserted before the 1954 film *Three Coins in the Fountain* brought renewed interest to this lovely spot.

Supplied by water from the Acqua Vergine aqueduct and a triumph of the baroque style, it was based on the design of Nicola Salvi (who's said to have died of illness contracted during his supervision of the project) and was completed in

The Trevi Fountain at night.

1762. The design centers on the triumphant figure of Neptunus Rex, standing on a shell chariot drawn by winged steeds and led by a pair of tritons. Two allegorical figures in the side niches represent good health and fertility.

On the southwestern corner of the piazza is a somber, not particularly spectacular-looking church, **SS. Vincenzo e Anastasio,** with a strange claim to fame. Within it survive the hearts and intestines of several centuries of popes. According to legend, the church was built on the site of a spring that burst from the earth after the beheading of St. Paul; the spring is one of the three sites where his head is said to have bounced off the ground.

Piazza di Trevi. Metro: Barberini.

Around Via Veneto & Piazza Barberini

Piazza Barberini lies at the foot of several Roman streets, among them Via Barberini, Via Sistina, and Via Vittorio Veneto. It would be a far more pleasant spot were it not for the heavy traffic swarming around its principal feature, Bernini's **Fountain of the Triton (Fontana del Tritone)** ★. For more than 3 centuries, the strange figure sitting in a vast open clam has been blowing water from his triton. Off to one side of the piazza is the aristocratic side facade of the **Palazzo Barberini,** named for one of Rome's powerful families; inside is the **Galleria Nazionale d'Arte Antica** (see below). The Renaissance Barberini reached their peak when a son was elected pope as Urban VIII; he encouraged Bernini and gave him great patronage.

As you go up Via Vittorio Veneto, look for the small fountain on the right corner of Piazza Barberini—it's another Bernini, the **Fountain of the Bees (Fontana delle Api).** At first they look more like flies, but they're the bees of the Barberini, the crest of that powerful family complete with the crossed keys of St. Peter above them (the keys were always added to a family crest when a son was elected pope).

Monumental Cemetery of the Capuchin Brothers (Cimitero Monumentale dei Padri Cappuccini) One of the most mesmerizingly macabre sights in all Christendom, this is a series of chapels with thousands of skulls and bones woven into mosaic "works of art." To make this allegorical dance of death, the bones of more than 4,000 Capuchin brothers were used. Some of the skeletons are intact, draped with Franciscan habits. The creator of this chamber of horrors? The tradition of the friars is that it was the work of a French Capuchin. Their literature suggests that you should visit the cemetery while keeping in mind the historical moment of its origins, when Christians had a rich and creative cult for their dead and great spiritual masters meditated and preached with a skull in hand. Those who've lived through

Bone art at the Capuchin crypt.

the days of crematoriums and other such massacres might view the graveyard differently, but to many who pause to think, this site has a message. The entrance is halfway up the first staircase on the right of the church.

Beside the Church of the Immaculate Conception, Via Vittorio Veneto 27. ✆ **06-4871185.** www. cappucciniviaveneto.it. Donation required. Fri–Wed 9am–1pm and 3–6pm. Metro: Barberini.

National Gallery of Ancient Art (Galleria Nazionale d'Arte Antica) ★★ **Palazzo Barberini,** right off Piazza Barberini, is one of the most magnificent baroque palaces in Rome. It was begun by Carlo Maderno in 1627 and completed in 1633 by Bernini, whose lavishly decorated rococo apartments, the **Gallery of Decorative Art (Galleria d'Arte Decorativa),** are on view. This gallery is part of the **National Gallery of Ancient Art.**

The bedroom of Princess Cornelia Costanza Barberini and Prince Giulio Cesare Colonna di Sciarra stands just as it was on their wedding night, and many household objects are displayed in the decorative art gallery. In the chambers, which boast frescoes and hand-painted silk linings, you can see porcelain from Japan and Bavaria, canopied beds, and a wooden baby carriage.

On the first floor is a splendid array of paintings from the 13th to the 16th centuries, most notably *Mother and Child,* by Simone Martini, and works by Filippo Lippi, Andrea Solario, and Francesco Francia. Il Sodoma has some brilliant pictures here, including the *Rape of the Sabines* and the *Marriage of St. Catherine.* One of the best known is Raphael's *La Fornarina,* the baker's daughter who was his mistress and who posed for his Madonna portraits. Titian is represented by his *Venus and Adonis.* Also here are Tintorettos and El Grecos. Many visitors come just to see the magnificent Caravaggios, including *Narcissus.*

Via delle Quattro Fontane 13. ✆ **06-4824184.** www.galleriaborghese.it. Admission 6€. Tues–Sun 8:30am–6:30pm. Metro: Barberini.

Piazza del Popolo

The restored **Piazza del Popolo** ★★ is haunted with memories. According to legend, the ashes of Nero were enshrined here, until 11th-century residents began complaining to the pope about his imperial ghost. The **Egyptian obelisk** dates from the 13th century B.C.; it was removed from Heliopolis to Rome during Augustus's reign (it stood at the Circus Maximus). The piazza was designed in the early 19th century by Valadier, Napoleon's architect. The **Santa Maria del Popolo** ★★, with two Caravaggios, is at its northern curve, and opposite are almost-twin baroque churches, overseeing the never-ending traffic.

MAXXI (National Museum of the XXI Century Arts) ★ The city of Michelangelo has gone modern with the opening of this stunning building constructed on the site of former army barracks. The complex, costing 60 million euros, was the creation of an Iraqi-born architect, Zaha Hadid, who is known for her daring architecture. MAXXI (the first two letters stand for the Museum of Art), with the Roman numerals denoting the 21st century, houses Italy's growing national collection of contemporary art. In addition to its permanent collection, MAXXI will also host the most avant-garde exhibitions of modern art in Italy. The museum is divided into two sections—MAXXI art and MAXXI architecture. The museum lies north of piazza del Popolo.

Via Guido Reni 10, Flaminio. ✆ **06-321-01829.** www.maxxi.beniculturali.it. Admission 11€, free 13 and under. Tues, Wed, Fri, Sun 11am–7pm; Thurs and Sat 11am–10pm. Closed Mon. Metro to Flaminio stop, then tram 2.

IN THE VILLA BORGHESE

Villa Borghese ★★, in the heart of Rome, is 6km (3¾ miles) in circumference. One of Europe's most elegant parks, it was created by Cardinal Scipione Borghese in the 1600s. Umberto I, king of Italy, acquired it in 1902 and presented it to the city of Rome. With lovely landscaped vistas, the greenbelt is crisscrossed by roads, but you can escape from the traffic and seek a shaded area under a tree to enjoy a picnic or relax. On a sunny weekend, it's a pleasure to stroll here and see Romans at play, relaxing or in-line skating. There are a few casual cafes and some food vendors; you can also rent bikes here. In the northeast of the park is a small zoo; the park is also home to a few outstanding museums.

Galleria Borghese ★★★   This legendary art gallery includes such masterpieces as Bernini's *Apollo and Daphne,* Titian's *Sacred and Profane Love,* Raphael's *Deposition,* and Caravaggio's *Jerome.* The collection began with the gallery's founder, Scipione Borghese, who, by the time of his death in 1633, had accumulated some of the greatest art of all time, even managing to acquire Bernini's early sculptures. Some paintings were spirited out of Vatican museums and even confiscated when their rightful owners were hauled off to prison until they became "reasonable" about turning over their art. The collection suffered at the hands of Napoleon's sister, Pauline, who married Prince Camillo Borghese in 1807 and sold most of the collection (many works are now in the Louvre in Paris). One of the most popular pieces of sculpture in the gallery, ironically, is Canova's sculpture of Pauline as *Venus Victorious.* (When Pauline was asked whether she felt uncomfortable posing in the nude, she replied, "Why should I? The studio was heated.")

   Important information: No more than 360 visitors at a time are allowed on the ground floor, and no more than 90 are allowed on the upper floor. Reservations are essential, so call ✆ **06-32810** (Mon–Fri 9am–6pm; Sat 9am–1pm). However, the number always seems to be busy. If you'll be in Rome for a few

The Villa Borghese.

days, try stopping by in person on your first day to reserve tickets for a later day. Better yet, before you leave home, contact **Select Italy** (📞 **800/877-1755;** www.selectitaly.com).

Piazzale del Museo Borghese 5 (off Via Pinciana). 📞 **06-32810.** www.galleriaborghese.it. Admission 8.50€. Tues–Sun 8:30am–7:30pm. Bus: 5, 19, 52, 116, 204, 490, or 910.

Museo Carlo Bilotti ★ Who was this Carlo Bilotti, you ask? He was a retired Italian-American perfume executive from Palm Beach, Florida. He spent his life, when not hawking Old Spice, collecting one of the world's finest private collections of modern art. From Salvador Dalí to Andy Warhol, he knew all the "household names" in the art world—and was often their patron. At the end of his life in 2006, he donated his treasure-trove to the city of Rome, which restored a 16th-century palace in the Villa Borghese to house his collection. Bilotti was a friend of Giorgio de Chirico, and the permanent collection includes 22 canvasses by that surrealist artist. De Chirico spent most of his life in Rome, dying here in 1978. Other works are by Larry Rivers, Dubuffet, and Giacomo Manzù, who is represented here by a large cardinal in bronze.

Villa Borghese. 📞 **06-820-59-127.** www.museocarlobilotti.it. Admission 4.50€ adults, 3.50€ children. Tues–Sun 9am–7pm. Metro: Flaminio.

National Etruscan Museum (Museo Nazionale di Villa Giulia) ★★★ This 16th-century papal palace shelters a priceless collection of art and artifacts from the mysterious Etruscans, who predated the Romans. Known for their sophisticated art and design, they left a legacy of sarcophagi, bronze sculptures, terra-cotta vases, and jewelry, among other items. If you have time for only the masterpieces, head for room 7, with a remarkable 6th-century-B.C. *Apollo from Veio* (clothed, for a change). The other two widely acclaimed statues here are *Dea con Bambino (Goddess with a Baby)* and a greatly mutilated but still powerful *Hercules* with a stag. In room 8, you'll see the lions' sarcophagus from the mid–6th century B.C., which was excavated at Cerveteri, north of Rome.

Finally, one of the world's most important Etruscan art treasures is the bride-and-bridegroom coffin from the 6th century B.C., also dug out of the tombs of Cerveteri (in room 9). Near the end of your tour, another masterpiece of Etruscan art awaits you in room 33: the *Cista Ficoroni,* a bronze urn with paw feet, mounted by three figures, dating from the 4th century B.C.

Piazzale di Villa Giulia 9. 📞 **06-32810.** Admission 8€. Tues–Sun 8:30am–7:30pm. Metro: Flaminio.

National Gallery of Modern Art (Galleria Nazionale d'Arte Moderna) ★ This gallery of modern art is a short walk from the Etruscan Museum (see above). With its neoclassical and Romantic paintings and sculpture, it makes a dramatic change from the glories of the Renaissance and ancient Rome. Its 75 rooms also house the largest collection in Italy of 19th- and 20th-century works by Balla, Boccioni, de Chirico, Morandi, Manzù, Burri, Capogrossi, and Fontana. Look for Modigliani's *La Signora dal Collaretto* and large *Nudo.* There are also many works of Italian optical and pop art and a good representation of foreign artists, including Degas, Cézanne, Monet, and van Gogh. Surrealism and expressionism are well represented by Klee, Ernst, Braque, Mirò, Kandinsky, Mondrian, and Pollock. You'll also find sculpture by Rodin. Several other important sculptures, including one by Canova, are on display in the museum's gardens.

Viale delle Belle Arti 131. 📞 **06-322981.** www.gnam.beniculturali.it. Admission 8€, free for children and seniors. Tues–Sun 8:30am–7:30pm. Bus: 19, 95, or 490.

THE APPIAN WAY & THE CATACOMBS

Of all the roads that led to Rome, **Via Appia Antica** (built in 312 B.C.) was the most famous. It eventually stretched all the way from Rome to the seaport of Brindisi, through which trade with the colonies in Greece and the East was funneled. (According to Christian tradition, it was along the Appian Way that an escaping Peter encountered the vision of Christ, causing him to go back into the city to face subsequent martyrdom.) The road's initial stretch in Rome is lined with the great monuments and ancient tombs of patrician Roman families—burials were forbidden within the city walls as early as the 5th century B.C.—and, beneath the surface, miles of tunnels hewn out of the soft tufa stone.

These tunnels, or catacombs, were where early Christians buried their dead and, during the worst times of persecution, held church services discreetly out of the public eye. A few of them are open to the public, so you can wander through mile after mile of musty-smelling tunnels whose soft walls are gouged out with tens of thousands of burial niches (long shelves made for two to three bodies each). In some dank, dark grottoes (never stray too far from your party or one of the exposed light bulbs), you can still discover the remains of early Christian art. The requisite guided tours, hosted by priests and monks, feature a smidgen of extremely biased history and a large helping of sermonizing.

The Appia Antica has been a popular Sunday lunch picnic site for Roman families (following the half-forgotten pagan tradition of dining in the presence of one's ancestors on holy days). The Via Appia Antica is closed to cars on Sundays, open for the picnickers and bicyclists—along with in-line skaters and a Sunday-only bus route to get out here.

You can take bus no. 218 from the San Giovanni Metro stop, which follows the Appia Antica for a bit and then veers right on Via Ardeatina at Domine Quo Vadis Church. After another long block, the no. 218 stops at the square Largo M.F. Ardeatine, near the gate to the San Callisto Catacombs. From here, you can walk right on Via delle Sette Chiese to the San Domitilla Catacombs or walk left down Via d. Sette Chiese to the San Sebastiano Catacombs.

An alternative is to ride the Metro to the Colli Albani stop and catch bus no. 660, which wraps up the Appia Antica from the south, veering off it at the San Sebastiano Catacombs (if you're visiting all three, you can take bus 218 to the first two, walk to San Sebastiano, and then catch bus 660 back to the Metro).

Of the monuments on the Appian Way, the most impressive is the **Tomb of Cecilia Metella ★**, within walking distance of the Catacombs. The cylindrical tomb honors the wife of one of Julius Caesar's military commanders from the republican era. Why such an elaborate tomb for such an unimportant person in history? Cecilia Metella was singled out for enduring fame simply because her tomb has remained and the others have decayed.

Catacombs of St. Callixtus (Catacombe di San Callisto) ★★ "The most venerable and most renowned of Rome," said Pope John XXIII of these funerary tunnels. The founder of Christian archaeology, Giovanni Battista de Rossi (1822–94), called them "catacombs par excellence." These catacombs are often packed with tour-bus groups, and they have perhaps the cheesiest tour, but the tunnels are simply phenomenal. They're the first cemetery of the Christian community of Rome, burial place of 16 popes in the 3rd century. They bear the name of St. Callixtus, the deacon whom Pope St. Zephyrinus put in charge of them and who was later elected pope (A.D. 217–22) in his own right. The complex is a network of galleries stretching for nearly 19km (12 miles), structured in five levels and reaching a depth of about 20m (65 ft.). There are many sepulchral chambers and almost half a million tombs of early Christians. Paintings, sculptures, and epigraphs (with symbols such as the fish, anchor, and dove) provide invaluable material for the study of the life and customs of the ancient Christians and the story of their persecutions.

Entering the catacombs, you see at once the most important crypt, that of nine popes. Some of the original marble tablets of their tombs are still preserved. The next crypt is that of St. Cecilia, the patron of sacred music. This early Christian martyr received three ax strokes on her neck, the maximum allowed by Roman law, which, unfortunately for her, failed to kill her outright. Farther on, you'll find the famous Cubicula of the Sacraments with its 3rd-century frescoes.

Via Appia Antica 110–126. ✆ **06-5130151.** www.catacombe.roma.it. Admission 8€ adults, 5€ children 6–15, free for children 5 and under. Thurs–Tues 9am–noon and 2–5pm. Bus: 118.

Catacombs of St. Domitilla (Catacombe di San Domitilla) ★★★ This oldest of the catacombs is the hands-down winner for most enjoyable catacombs experience. Groups are small, most guides are genuinely entertaining and personable, and, depending on the mood of the group and your guide, the visit may last anywhere from 20 minutes to over an hour. You enter through a sunken 4th-century church. There are fewer "sights" than in the other catacombs—although the 2nd-century fresco of the Last Supper is impressive—but some of the guides actually hand you a few bones out of a tomb niche. (Incidentally, this is the only catacomb where you'll still see bones; the rest have emptied their tombs to rebury the remains in ossuaries on the inaccessible lower levels.)

Via d. Sette Chiese 280. ✆ **06-5110342.** www.catacombe.roma.it. Admission 8€ adults, 5€ children 6–14. Wed–Mon 9am–noon and 2–5pm. Closed Jan.

Catacombs of St. Sebastian (Catacombe di San Sebastiano) Today the tomb of St. Sebastian is in the basilica, but his original resting place was in the catacombs underneath it. From the reign of Valerian to the reign of Constantine, the bodies of Sts. Peter and Paul were hidden in the catacombs, which were dug from tufa, a soft volcanic rock. The big church was built in the 4th century. The tunnels here, if stretched out, would reach a length of 11km (6¾ miles). In the tunnels and mausoleums are mosaics and graffiti, along with many other pagan and Christian objects from centuries even before the time of Constantine. Unfortunately, though the catacombs are spectacular, the tour here is very restricted, one of the shortest and least satisfying of all the Catacombs visits.

Via Appia Antica 136. ✆ **06-7850350.** www.catacombe.org. Admission 8€ adults, 5€ children 6–15, free for children 5 and under. Mon–Sat 9am–noon and 2–5pm. Closed Nov 22–Dec 20.

MORE ATTRACTIONS
Around Stazione Termini

Basilica di Santa Maria Maggiore ★ This great church, one of Rome's four major basilicas, was built by Pope Liberius in A.D. 358 and rebuilt by Pope Sixtus III from 432 to 440. Its 14th-century **campanile** is the city's loftiest. Much doctored in the 18th century, the church's facade isn't an accurate reflection of the

Rome street scene.

treasures inside. The basilica is noted for the 5th-century Roman mosaics in its nave, and for its coffered ceiling, said to have been gilded with gold brought from the New World. In the 16th century, Domenico Fontana built a now-restored "Sistine Chapel." In the following century, Flaminio Ponzo designed the **Pauline (Borghese) Chapel** in the baroque style. The church also contains the **tomb of Bernini,** Italy's most important baroque sculptor/architect. Ironically, the man who changed the face of Rome with his elaborate fountains is buried in a tomb so simple that it takes a sleuth to track it down (to the right, near the altar).

Piazza di Santa Maria Maggiore. ℭ **06-4465836.** Free admission. Daily 7am–7pm. Metro: Termini.

MUSEO NAZIONALE ROMANO

This museum is divided into four different sections: Palazzo Massimo alle Terme; the Diocletian Baths (Terme di Diocleziano), with the annex Octagonal Hall; and Palazzo Altemps (which is near Piazza Navona; see p. 161 for a complete listing).

Diocletian Baths (Terme di Diocleziano) and the Octagonal Hall (Aula Ottagona) ★   Near Piazza dei Cinquecento, which fronts the rail station, this museum occupies part of the 3rd-century-A.D. Baths of Diocletian and part of a convent that may have been designed by Michelangelo. The Diocletian Baths were the biggest thermal baths in the world. Nowadays they host a marvelous collection of funereal artworks, such as sarcophagi, and decorations dating from the Aurelian period. The baths also have a section reserved for temporary exhibitions.

The **Octagonal Hall** occupies the southwest corner of the central building of the Diocletian Baths. Here you can see the *Lyceum Apollo,* a copy of the 2nd-century-A.D. work inspired by the Prassitele. Also worthy of a note is the *Aphrodite of Cyrene,* a copy dating from the second half of the 2nd century A.D. and discovered in Cyrene, Libya.

Viale E. di Nicola 79. ☎ **06-39967700.** Admission 7€. Tues–Sun 9am–7:45pm. Last admission 1 hr. before closing. Metro: Termini.

Palazzo Massimo alle Terme ★   If you'd like to go wandering in a virtual garden of classical statues, head for this *palazzo,* built from 1883 to 1887 and opened as a museum in 1998. Much of the art here, including the frescoes, stuccoes, and mosaics, was discovered in excavations in the 1800s but has never been put on display before.

If you ever wanted to know what all those emperors from your history books looked like, this museum will make them live again, togas and all. In the central hall are works representing the political and social life of Rome at the time of Augustus. Note the statue of the emperor with a toga covering his head, symbolizing his role as the head priest of state. Other works include an altar from Ostia Antica, the ancient port of Rome, plus a statue of a wounded Niobid from 440 B.C. that is a masterwork of expression and character. Upstairs, stand in awe at all the traditional art from the 1st century B.C. to the Imperial Age. The most celebrated mosaic is of the *Four Charioteers.* In the basement are a rare numismatic collection and an extensive collection of Roman jewelry.

Largo di Villa Peretti. ☎ **06-39967700.** Admission 7€. Tues–Sun 9am–7:45pm. Last admission 1 hr. before closing. Admission includes entrance to Terme di Diocleziano (see above). Metro: Termini.

In the Testaccio Area & South

St. Paul Outside the Walls (Basilica di San Paolo Fuori le Mura) ★   The Basilica of St. Paul, whose origins date from the time of Constantine, is Rome's fourth great patriarchal church. It was erected over the tomb of St. Paul, which was definitively identified in 2005 and can be visited. The basilica fell victim to fire in 1823 and was subsequently rebuilt. It is the second-largest church in Rome after St. Peter's. From the inside, its windows may appear to be stained glass, but they're actually translucent alabaster. With its forest of single-file columns and mosaic medallions (portraits of the various popes), this is one of the most streamlined and elegantly decorated churches in Rome. Its most important treasure is a 12th-century candelabrum by Vassalletto, who's also responsible for the remarkable cloisters containing twisted pairs of columns enclosing a rose garden. Of particular interest is the baldacchino (richly embroidered fabric of silk and gold, usually fixed or carried over an important person or sacred object) of Arnolf di Cambio, dated 1285, that miraculously wasn't damaged in the fire. The Benedictine monks and students sell a fine collection of souvenirs, rosaries, and bottles of Benedictine (a liqueur made by the monks) every day except Sunday and religious holidays.

Piazzale San Paolo 1. ☎ **06-69880800.** www.basilicasanpaolo.org. Free admission. Basilica daily 7am–6:30pm; cloisters daily 9am–1pm and 3–6pm. Metro: Basilica di San Paolo.

In Trastevere

From many vantage points in the Eternal City, the views are panoramic, but one of the best spots for a memorable vista is the **Janiculum Hill (Gianicolo) ★★**, across the Tiber. It's not one of the seven hills, but it's certainly one of the most visited (and a stop on many bus tours). The Janiculum was the site of a battle between Giuseppe Garibaldi and the forces of Pope Pius IX in 1870—an event commemorated with statuary. Take bus no. 41 from Ponte Sant'Angelo.

Galleria Nazionale di Palazzo Corsini ★   This palace was once the home
of Napoleon's brother and, later, Christina, the exiled queen of Sweden. Today it
houses one of Rome's greatest collections of Renaissance and baroque art. The
palace from the 1400s houses the original half of Rome's National Gallery of
paintings; the other half is in the Palazzo Barberini. Most of the paintings are
from the European school of the 17th and 18th centuries. The collection, formed
in the 18th century—often from possessions in the Corsini family—is unique in
that it is still intact today. Search out such notable works as Murillo's *Madonna
and Child,* Caravaggio's *St. John the Baptist,* a **triptych** by Fra Angelico, and
Guido Reni's *Salome with the Head of St. John the Baptist.* Also be on the lookout
for fine works by Andrea del Sarto, Rubens, van Dyck, Joos van Cleve, Guercino,
and Luca Giordano.

Via della Lungara 10. ☎ **06-68802323.** Admission 4€, free for children 14 and under. Tues–Sun
8:30am–7:30pm. Bus: 23, 65, or 280.

Santa Cecilia in Trastevere ★   A cloistered and still-functioning convent
with a fine garden, Santa Cecilia contains the *Last Judgment,* by Pietro Cavallini
(ca. 1293), a masterpiece of Roman medieval painting. Another treasure is a late-
13th-century baldacchino by Arnolfo di Cambio over the altar. The church is
built on the reputed site of Cecilia's long-ago palace, and for a small fee you can
descend under the church to inspect the ruins of some Roman houses, as well as
peer through a gate at the stucco grotto beneath the altar.

Piazza Santa Cecilia 22. ☎ **06-5899289.** Church free admission; Cavallini frescoes 2.50€; excavations 3€. Main church and excavations daily 9:30am–noon and 4-6:30pm; frescoes Tues and
Thurs 10am–noon, Sun 11:30am–noon. Bus: 8, 44, 75, 170, or 181.

Santa Maria in Trastevere ★   This Romanesque church at the colorful center of Trastevere was built around A.D. 350 and is one of the oldest in Rome. The
body was added around 1100, and the portico was added in the early 1700s. The

Mosaics in St. Cecilia in Trastevere.

restored mosaics on the apse date from around 1140, and below them are the 1293 mosaic scenes depicting the life of Mary done by Pietro Cavallini. The faded mosaics on the facade are from the 12th or 13th century, and the octagonal fountain in the piazza is an ancient Roman original that was restored and added to in the 17th century by Carlo Fontana.

Piazza Santa Maria in Trastevere. *Ⓒ* **06-5814802.** www.santamariaintrastevere.org. Free admission. Daily 7:30am–8pm. Bus: 23, 280, or 780.

ORGANIZED TOURS

Because of the sheer number of sights to see, some first-time visitors like to start out with an organized tour. While few things can really be covered in any depth on these overview tours, they're sometimes useful for getting your bearings.

One of the leading tour operators is **American Express,** Piazza di Spagna 38 (*Ⓒ* **06-67641;** Metro: Piazza di Spagna). One popular tour is a 4-hour orientation to Rome and the Vatican, which departs most mornings at 9:30am or afternoons at 2:20pm and costs 75€ per person. Another 4-hour tour, which focuses on the Rome of antiquity (including visits to the Colosseum, the Roman Forum, the ruins of the Imperial Palace, and St. Peter in Chains), costs 75€. From April to October, a popular excursion outside Rome is a 5-hour bus tour to Tivoli, where tours are conducted of the Villa d'Este and its spectacular gardens and the ruins of the Villa Adriana, all for 65€ per person. The American Express Travel Office is open Monday to Friday 9am to 5:30pm and Saturday 9am to 12:30pm.

Context Rome, Via Baccina (*Ⓒ* **800/691-6036** in the U.S., or 06-97625204; www.contexttravel.com), is a collaborative of scholars. Guides offer small-group tours, including visits to monuments, museums, and historic piazzas, as well as to neighborhood *trattorie.* Custom-designed tours are also available. Prices of the regular tours begin at 30€. There is also a special kids' program, including treasure hunts and other experiences that feature visits to museums of appeal to the younger set.

SHOPPING

Rome offers temptations of every kind. In our limited space below we've summarized certain streets known throughout Italy for their shops. The monthly rent on these famous streets is very high, and those costs are passed on to you. Nonetheless, a stroll down some of these streets presents a cross section of the most desirable wares in Italy.

The Top Shopping Streets

VIA BORGOGNONA   This street begins near Piazza di Spagna, and both the rents and the merchandise are chic and ultraexpensive. Like its neighbor, Via Condotti, Via Borgognona is a mecca for wealthy, well-dressed women and men from around the world. Its storefronts have retained their baroque or neoclassical facades.

VIA COLA DI RIENZO   Bordering the Vatican, this long, straight street runs from the Tiber to Piazza Risorgimento. Because the street is wide and clogged with traffic, it's best to walk down one side and then up the other. Via Cola di Rienzo is known for stores selling a wide variety of merchandise at reasonable prices—from jewelry to fashionable clothes and shoes.

VIA CONDOTTI Easy to find because it begins at the base of the Spanish Steps, this is Rome's poshest shopping street. A few down-to-earth stores have opened recently, but it's largely a playground for the superrich. For us mere mortals, it's a great place for window-shopping and people-watching.

VIA DEL CORSO Not attempting the stratospheric image or prices of Via Condotti or Via Borgognona, Via del Corso boasts styles aimed at younger consumers. Some gems are scattered amid the shops selling jeans and sporting equipment. The most interesting are nearest the cafes of Piazza del Popolo.

VIA FRANCESCO CRISPI Most shoppers reach this street by following Via Sistina (see below) 1 long block from the top of the Spanish Steps. Near the intersection of these streets are several shops well suited for unusual and less expensive gifts.

VIA FRATTINA Running parallel to Via Condotti, it begins, like its more famous sibling, at Piazza di Spagna. Part of its length is closed to traffic. Here the concentration of shops is denser, although some aficionados claim that its image is less chic and prices are slightly lower than at its counterparts on Via Condotti. It's usually thronged with shoppers who appreciate the lack of motor traffic.

VIA NAZIONALE The layout recalls 19th-century grandeur, but the traffic is horrendous. It begins at Piazza della Repubblica and runs down almost to the 19th-century monuments of Piazza Venezia. You'll find an abundance of leather stores (more reasonable in price than those in many other parts of Rome) and a welcome handful of stylish boutiques.

VIA SISTINA Beginning at the top of the Spanish Steps, Via Sistina runs to Piazza Barberini. The shops are small, stylish, and based on the tastes of their owners. The pedestrian traffic is less dense than on other major streets.

VIA VITTORIO VENETO Via Veneto is filled these days with expensive hotels and cafes and an array of relatively expensive stores selling shoes, gloves, and leather goods.

Shopping A to Z

ANTIQUES Prices have risen to alarming levels as wealthy Europeans increasingly outbid one another in a frenzy. Any antiques dealer who risks the high rents of central Rome is acutely aware of valuations, so although you might find gorgeous pieces, you're not likely to find any bargains.

Beware of fakes, remember to insure anything that you have shipped home, and, for larger purchases—anything more than 156€ at any one store—keep your paperwork in order to obtain your tax refund (see chapter 18).

Via dei Coronari, in a colorful section of the Campus Martius, is lined with stores offering magnificent vases, urns, chandeliers, chaises, refectory tables, and candelabra. To find the street's entrance, turn left out of the north end of Piazza Navona and pass the ruins of Domitian's

Stadium—it will be just ahead. There are more than 40 antiques stores in the next 4 blocks (most are closed 1–4pm).

A few minutes south of Piazza del Popolo, **Via Laurina** lies midway between Via del Corso and Via del Babuino. It is filled with beautiful stores where you can find anything from an antique print to a 17th-century chandelier.

BOOKSTORE The **Lion Bookshop,** Via dei Greci 36 (© **06-32654007;** www.thelionbookshop.it; Metro: Piazza di Spagna; bus: 116 or 117), is the oldest English-language bookshop in town, specializing in literature, both American and English. It also sells children's books and photographic volumes on both Rome and Italy. A vast choice of English-language videos is for sale or rent. It's closed in August.

COSMETICS & PERFUMES Since the 18th century, **Antica Erboristeria Romana,** Via di Torre Argentina 15 (© **06-6879493;** www.antica erboristeriaromana.it; Metro: Colosseo; bus: 40, 46, 62, or 64), has dispensed "wonders" from its tiny wooden drawers, some of which are labeled with skulls and crossbones. You'll find scented paper, licorice, and herbal remedies.

DEPARTMENT STORES In Piazza Colonna, **La Rinascente,** Via del Corso 189 (© **06-6784209;** www.rinascente.it; Metro: Piazza Barberini, Piazza di Spagna, or Colosseo; bus: 117), is an upscale store offering clothing, hosiery, perfume, cosmetics, housewares, and furniture. It also has attractively priced clothing for men, women, and children. This is the largest of the Italian department-store chains, with another branch at Piazza Fiume.

FABRICS **Bassetti Tessuti** ★★, Corso Vittorio Emanuele II 73 (© **06-6892326;** www.fratellibassetti.com; bus: 30, 40, 62, or 64), Rome's largest fabric store and a tradition since 1954, lies in a nondescript *palazzo* where many of Italy's top designers go for everything from lush silk from Lake Como to feather-soft wool from Piedmont. Seemingly endless aisles of fabric await you, and you are likely to rub elbows with some representatives from Italy's famed fashion houses, including such lines as Giorgio Armani. In all, there are some 200,000 fabrics sold here in every hue.

FASHION **Battistoni,** Via Condotti 61A (© **06-6976111;** www.battistoni. com; Metro: Piazza di Spagna), is known for the world's finest men's shirts. It also hawks a cologne, Marte (Mars), for the "man who likes to conquer."

Emporio Armani ★★, Via del Babuino 140 (© **06-36002197;** www.emporioarmanicom; Metro: Piazza di Spagna), stocks relatively affordable menswear crafted by the designer who has dressed perhaps more stage and screen stars than any other in Italy. If these prices aren't high enough for you, try the more expensive line a short walk away at **Giorgio Armani,** Via Condotti 77 (© **06-6991460;** www.giorgioarmani.com; Metro: Piazza di Spagna). The merchandise here is sold at sometimes staggering prices that are still often 30% less than what you'd pay elsewhere.

Blunauta, Piazza di Spagna 35 (© **06-6789806;** www.blunauta.it; Metro: Piazza di Spagna), has made a name for itself with its easy-to-wear men's and women's clothing made in natural fibers. We made off with a man's zip cardigan in gray heather wool. Women will be drawn to the likes of a velvet-trimmed watermelon-pink cashmere twin set.

Dating to 1870, **Schostal,** Via del Corso 158 (© **06-6791240;** www. schostalroma.com; bus: 117), is for men who like their garments (from underwear to cashmere overcoats) conservative and well crafted. The prices are more reasonable than you might think, and the staff is courteous and attentive.

Behind all the chrome mirrors is swank **Valentino** ★★, Via Condotti 13 (© **06-6790479;** www.valentino.it; Metro: Piazza di Spagna), where you can become the most fashionable woman in town—if you can afford to be. Valentino's men's haute couture is sold nearby at Via Bocca di Leone 15 (© **06-6787585;** Metro: Piazza di Spagna).

The prices at **Sisley,** Via Giolitti 9 (© **06-47825258;** www.sisley. com; Metro: Termini), are more down to earth. It's famous for sweaters, tennis wear, blazers, and sportswear.

One of the hottest, hippest designer boutiques in Rome is **L'Anatra all'Arancia** ★★, Via Tiburtina 105–9 (© **06-4456293;** Metro: Piazza Vittorio). In addition to some big and up-and-coming names, the owner, Donatella Baroni, stocks her own labels.

Max Mara, Via Frattina 28 (© **06-6793638;** www.maxmara.com; Metro: Piazza di Spagna), is one of the best outlets in Rome for chic women's wear. The fabrics are appealing and the alterations are free.

Rapidly approaching the stratospheric upper levels of Italian fashion is **Renato Balestra,** Via Abruzzi 3 (© **06-4821723;** www.renatobalestra.it; Metro: Piazza di Spagna or Barberini), whose women's clothing attains standards of lighthearted elegance at its best. This branch carries a complete line of the latest ready-to-wear.

FLEA MARKETS On Sundays from 7am to 1pm, every peddler from Trastevere and the surrounding Castelli Romani sets up a temporary shop at the sprawling **Porta Portese open-air flea market,** near the end of Viale Trastevere (catch bus 75 to Porta Portese, then a short walk to Via Portuense). The vendors are likely to sell everything from secondhand paintings of Madonnas and bushels of rosaries to 1947 TVs and books printed in 1835. Serious shoppers can often ferret out a good buy. If you've ever been impressed with the bargaining power of the Spaniard, you haven't seen anything until you've bartered with an Italian. By 10:30am, the market is full of people. As at any street market, beware of pickpockets.

FOOD & FOOD MARKETS At old-fashioned **Castroni** ★★, Via Cola di Rienzo 196 (© **06-6874383;** www.castronicoladirienzo.it; bus: 70 or 81), you'll find an array of unusual foodstuffs from around the Mediterranean. If you want herbs from Apulia, pepperoncino oil, cheese from the Valle d'Aosta, or an obscure brand of balsamic vinegar, Castroni will have it. It also carries foods that are exotic in Italy but commonplace in North America, like taco shells and peanut butter.

Near Santa Maria Maggiore, Rome's largest market takes place Monday through Saturday from 7am to noon at **Piazza Vittorio Emanuele** (Metro: Vittorio Emanuele). Most of the vendors at the gigantic market sell fresh fruit, vegetables, and other foodstuff, although some stalls are devoted to cutlery, clothing, and the like. There's probably little to tempt the serious shopper, but it's a fun glimpse into Roman life.

FROM LEFT: Fresh produce for sale at Castroni; Antico Forno Campo de' Fiori.

There's also a market Monday to Saturday 6am to noon at **Campo de' Fiori** (bus: 46, 62, or 64). It's Rome's most picturesque food market—but it's also the priciest. Things start bustling in the predawn as the florists arrange bouquets and fruit and vegetable vendors set up their stalls. After admiring the figs and peaches at the food market, stop for a delectable panino or *pizza Bianca* at **Antico Forno Campo de' Fiori,** Piazza Campo de' Fiori 22 (✆ **06-68806662;** www.fornocampodefiori.com), and then make your way to **Marco Roscioli Salumeria,** Via del Giubbonari 21 (✆ **06-6864045**), right down the street. Here you can inhale the intoxicating, though expensive, aroma of truffles and some of Rome's best prosciutto.

GLOVES A real little discovery, **Sergio di Cori,** Piazza di Spagna 53 (✆ **06-6784439;** www.dicorigloves.it; Metro: Piazza di Spagna), sells the most exquisite assortment of couture leather gloves in Rome. But the prices are reasonable, especially if you order the unlined gloves. Even if you don't, there are many bargains even in the silk-lined gloves.

HOUSEWARES **Spazio Sette,** hidden at Via d. Barberi 7, off Largo di Torre Argentina (✆ **06-6869747;** www.spaziosette.it; Metro: Colosseo), is far and away Rome's best housewares emporium, a design boutique of department-store proportions. It goes way beyond Alessi teakettles to fill three huge floors with the greatest names, and latest word, in Italian and international design.

Another good bet is **Bagagli,** Via Campo Marzio 42 (✆ **06-6871406;** www.bagaglivittorio.com; Metro: Piazza di Spagna), offering a good selection of Alessi, Rose and Tulipani, and Villeroy & Boch china in a pleasantly kitschy old Rome setting that comes complete with cobblestone floors.

If the big names don't do it for you, you may prefer **c.u.c.i.n.a.,** Via Mario de'Fiori 65 (✆ **06-6791275;** www.cucinastore.com; bus: 80, 81, 117, or 119), a stainless-steel shrine to everything you need for a proper

Italian kitchen, sporting designs that are as beautiful in their simplicity as they are utilitarian.

JEWELRY Rome's most prestigious jeweler for more than a century, **Bulgari** ★★★, Via Condotti 10 (✆ **06-6793876**; www.bulgari.com; Metro: Piazza di Spagna), boasts a shop window that's a visual attraction in its own right. Bulgari designs combine classical Greek aesthetics with Italian taste, changing in style with the years yet clinging to tradition.

The fantastical gold and silver pieces made at **Fausto Maria Franchi** ★★, Via del Clementino 98 (✆ **06-687-1558**; www.fmfranchi. com; bus: 115 or 913), fall somewhere between jewelry and sculpture. Franchi's designs have been hailed around the world. His artisan goldsmith and silversmith *bottega* lies in the heart of Rome on an ancient street commissioned by Sisto V. The art gallery displaying Franchi's wares stands alongside the vaulted workshop. Most of the jewelry designs incorporate precious stones; some of the jewelry is organic, even baroque.

One of the city's best gold- and silversmiths, **Federico Buccellati** ★★★, Via Condotti 31 (✆ **06-6790329**; www.federico buccellati.it; Metro: Piazza di Spagna), specializes in neo-Renaissance creations. The designs of the handmade jewelry and hollowware recall those of Renaissance gold master Benvenuto Cellini.

Luogo Myriam B, Via dei Volsci 75 (✆ **06-44361305**; www. myriamb.it; Metro: Termini), turns out a stunning array of extravagant bracelets and necklaces. Check out his earrings with latex, shells, tulle, rock crystal, and even industrial wire mesh.

LEATHER Italian leather is among the very best in the world; it can attain butter-soft textures more pliable than cloth. You'll find hundreds of leather stores in Rome, many of them excellent.

Window-shopping at famed jeweler Bulgari.

At **Alfieri,** Via del Corso 1–2 (✆ **06-3611976**; Metro: Piazza di Spagna; bus: 117), you'll find virtually any garment you can think of fashioned in leather. Opened in the 1960s with a funky counterculture slant, it prides itself on leather jackets, boots, bags, belts, shirts, hats, pants for men and women, short shorts, and skirts that come in at least 10 (sometimes neon) colors. Although everything is made in Italy, the emphasis is on reasonable prices rather than ultrahigh quality, so check the stitching and workmanship before you invest.

If famous names in leather wear appeal to you, you'll find most of the biggies at **Casagrande,** Via Cola di Rienzo 206

(© **06-6874610;** Metro: Lepanto; bus: 32 or 81), such as Fendi and its youth-conscious offspring, Fendissime, plus Cerruti, Mosquino, and Valentino. This well-managed store has developed an impressive reputation for quality and authenticity since the 1930s. The prices are more reasonable than those for equivalent merchandise in other parts of town.

Fendi ★★★, Largo Goldoni (© **06-334501;** www.fendi.com; Metro: Piazza di Spagna), is well known for its avant-garde leather goods, but it also has furs, stylish purses, ready-to-wear clothing, and a new line of men's clothing and accessories. Fendi also carries gift items, home furnishings, and sports accessories.

Of course, **Gucci ★★★**, Via Condotti 8 (© **06-6790405;**

Gucci, just one of the many Italian luxury brands with shops in Rome.

www.gucci.com; Metro: Piazza di Spagna), has been a legend since 1900. Its merchandise consists of high-class leather goods, such as suitcases, handbags, wallets, shoes, and desk accessories. It also has elegant menswear and women's wear, including beautiful shirts, blouses, and dresses, as well as ties and neck scarves. Prices have never been higher.

MOSAICS   Mosaics are an art form as old as the Roman Empire. **Maffettone Design,** Via di Panico 26 (© **06-6832754;** www.maioliche-maffettone.it; Metro: Piazza Paoli), is the best place in Rome to go for decorative tiles and mosaics inspired by ancient Roman designs. The tables and furniture are handmade in little workshops spread in the countryside around Rome—real quality craftsmanship. Take bus no. 40, 46, 62, or 64.

Many of the objects displayed at **Savelli ★**, Via Paolo VI 27 (© **06-68307017;** www.savellireligious.com; Metro: Ottaviano), were inspired by ancient originals discovered in thousands of excavations, including those at Pompeii and Ostia. Others, especially the floral designs, depend on the whim and creativity of the artist. Objects include tabletops, boxes, and vases. The cheapest mosaic objects are unsigned products crafted by students at an art school partially funded by the Vatican. Objects made in the Savelli workshops that are signed by the individual artists tend to be larger and more elaborate. The outlet also contains a collection of small souvenir items such as key chains and carved statues.

PAPER   The best selection of paper in Rome, really beautiful stationery, is found at **Fabriano,** Via del Babuino 173 (© **06-3260-0361;** www.fabriano boutique.com; Metro: Piazza di Spagna), a charming store found in the heart of Rome. Its motto is, "We sell everything you need to write on and with." The store also stocks photo albums and children's paper toys, and there are many lovely gift items to take home with you.

PRINTS & ENGRAVINGS At **Alberto di Castro,** Via del Babuino 71 (✆ **06-3613752;** www.dicastro.com; Metro: Piazza di Spagna), you'll find Rome's largest collection of antique prints and engravings. In rack after rack are depictions of everything from the Colosseum to the Pantheon.

Alinari, Via Alibert 16A (✆ **06-6792923;** www.alinari.com; Metro: Piazza di Spagna), takes its name from the famed 19th-century Florentine photographer. Original prints and photos of Alinari are almost as prized as paintings in national galleries, and you can pick up your own here.

Giovanni B. Panatta Fine Art Shop, Via Francesco Crispi 117 (✆ **06-6795948;** Metro: Piazza di Spagna, Barberini), sells excellent color and black-and-white prints covering a variety of subjects, from 18th-century Roman street scenes to astrological charts. There's also a selection of reproductions of medieval and Renaissance art that's attractive and reasonably priced.

SHOES **Ferragamo** ★★★, Via Condotti 66–73 (✆ **06-6781130;** www.salvatoreferragamo.it; Metro: Piazza di Spagna), sells elegant footwear, plus women's clothing and accessories and ties, in an atmosphere full of Italian style. There are always many customers waiting to enter the shop; management allows them to enter in small groups. Figure on a 30-minute wait.

WINE & LIQUOR At historic **Buccone,** Via Ripetta 19 (✆ **06-3612154;** www.enotecabuccone.com; Metro: Piazzale Flaminio), the selection of wines is among the finest in Rome.

Opened in 1821, **Trimani,** Via Goito 20 (✆ **06-4469661;** www.trimani.com; Metro: Castel Pretorio, Repubblica; bus: 86, 92, or 360), sells wines and spirits from Italy, among other offerings. Purchases can be shipped to your home.

Ai Monasteri, Corso Rinascimento 72 (✆ **06-68802783;** www.monasteri.it; Metro: Piazza di Spagna; bus: 30, 64, or 116), is a treasure-trove of liquors (including liqueurs and wines), honey, and herbal teas made in Italian monasteries and convents. You can buy excellent chocolates and other candies as well. You make your selections in a quiet atmosphere reminiscent of a monastery, 2 blocks from Bernini's Fountain of the Four Rivers in Piazza Navona. The shop will ship some items for you.

ROME AFTER DARK

When the sun goes down, Rome's palaces, ruins, fountains, and monuments are bathed in a theatrical white light. Few evening occupations are quite as pleasurable as a stroll past the solemn pillars of old temples or the cascading torrents of Renaissance fountains glowing under the blue-black sky.

The Fountain of the Naiads (Fontana delle Naiadi) on Piazza della Repubblica, the Fountain of the Tortoises (Fontana delle Tartarughe) on Piazza Mattei, and the Trevi Fountain are particularly beautiful at night. The Capitoline Hill (or Campidoglio) is magnificently lit after dark, with its measured Renaissance facades glowing like jewel boxes. The view of the Roman Forum seen from the rear of the trapezoidal Piazza del Campidoglio is the grandest in Rome, more so than even the Colosseum. Bus no. 84, 85, 87, 117, 175, 186, 271, 571, or 850 takes you here at night, or you can ask for a taxi. If you're across the Tiber, Piazza San Pietro (in front of St. Peter's) is impressive at night without the tour buses and crowds. And a combination of illuminated architecture, Renaissance fountains, and sidewalk shows and art expos enlivens Piazza Navona.

Even if you don't speak Italian, you can generally follow the listings of special events and evening entertainment featured in *La Repubblica,* a leading Italian newspaper. *Wanted in Rome* has listings of jazz, rock, and such and gives an interesting look at expatriate Rome. And *Un Ospite a Roma,* available free from the concierge desks of top hotels, is full of details on what's happening.

During the peak of summer, usually in August, all nightclub proprietors seem to lock their doors and head for the seashore, where they operate alternate clubs. Some close at different times each year, so it's hard to keep up-to-date. Always have your hotel check to see if a club is operating before you make a trek to it. (Dance clubs, in particular, open and close with freewheeling abandon.)

Be aware that there are no inexpensive nightclubs in Rome. Many of the legitimate nightclubs, besides being expensive, are frequented by prostitutes.

The Performing Arts

CLASSICAL MUSIC **Parco della Musica** ★, Viale de Coubertin (℄ 06-80241281; www.auditorium.com), is the largest concert facility in Europe, an ultramodern, almost sci-fi building constructed in 2002 by Renzo Piano, a world-famous architect. It offers 40,000 sq. m (430,600 sq. ft.) of gardens and three separate concert halls, plus one massive open-air theater. The best time to attend is summer, when concerts are often staged outside, and you can listen to the strains of Brahms or Schumann under a star-studded sky. Tickets and prices depend on the event. The auditorium can be reached by taking bus no. 53, 217, 231, or 910.

Teatro Olimpico, Piazza Gentile da Fabriano 17 (℄ **06-3265991;** www.teatroolimpico.it; Metro: Flaminio), hosts a wide range of performances, from pop to chamber music to foreign orchestras. *Note:* The theater box office is open daily 10am to 7pm.

Opera at the Baths of Caracalla

After a 10-year slumber, opera returned in 2003 to the ancient **Baths of Caracalla** ★★★, Via della Terme di Caracalla. Productions were shut down when it was feared that audiences of 5,000 were damaging the open-air ruins. Conservation-minded officials ordered that once-grandiose sets be scaled down and the stage moved to 39m (130 ft.) from the actual ruins, which are now a backdrop and not part of the scenery as before. Only 2,000 spots on the bleachers are now available. The season is a short one, lasting from July 1 to August 9, so tickets should be reserved as far in advance as possible. For tickets and information, call or go to the ticket office at Piazza Beniamino Gigli 1 (℄ **06-48160255;** www.operaroma.it), open Tuesday to Saturday 9am to 5pm and Sunday 9am to 1:30pm. Ticket prices range from 25€ to 110€.

The Teatro dell'Opera.

Check the daily papers for **free church concerts** given around town, especially near Easter and Christmas.

OPERA If you're in the capital for the opera season, usually from late December to June, you might want to attend the historic **Teatro dell'Opera,** Piazza Beniamino Gigli 1, off Via Nazionale (𝄞 **06-48160255;** www.operaroma.it; Metro: Repubblica). Nothing is presented in July and August; in summer, the venue usually switches elsewhere. Call ahead or ask your concierge before you go. Tickets are 11€ to 130€.

DANCE Performances of the Rome Opera Ballet are given at the **Teatro dell'Opera** (see above). The regular repertoire of classical ballet is supplemented by performances of internationally acclaimed guest artists, and Rome is on the major agenda for troupes from around the world. Watch for announcements in the weekly entertainment guides about other venues, including the Teatro Olimpico, or even open-air ballet performances.

Bars & Cafes

Unless you're dead set on making the Roman nightclub circuit, try what might be a far livelier and less expensive scene—sitting late at night on **Via Veneto, Piazza della Rotonda, Piazza del Popolo,** or one of Rome's other piazzas, all for the cost of an espresso, a cappuccino, or a Campari.

If you're looking for some scrumptious **ice cream,** see the entries for Café Rosati and Giolitti, below.

ON VIA VENETO Back in the 1950s (a decade that *Time* magazine gave to Rome, in the same way it conceded the 1960s and later the 1990s to London), **Via Vittorio Veneto** was the chic heart of Rome, crowded with aspiring and actual movie stars, their directors, and a group of card-carrying members of the jet set. Today the beautiful people wouldn't be caught dead on Via Veneto—it has become touristy. But visitors flock here by the thousands every night for cafe sitting and people-watching.

Sophisticated **Harry's Bar ★**, Via Vittorio Veneto 150 (𝄞 **06-4742103;** www.harrysbar.it; Metro: Piazza di Spagna or Barberini), is a perennial favorite for out-of-towners. Every Italian town seems to have a Harry's Bar, a name that seems tattooed into the collective memory of life in Italy during the *La Dolce Vita* era, but each is independent, and not part of a chain. In summer, tables are placed outside. For those who want to dine outdoors but want to avoid the scorching sun, there's an air-conditioned sidewalk cafe open from May to November. Meals inside cost about double what you'd pay outside. In back is a small dining room serving some of the finest (and priciest) food in central Rome. A piano bar features live music starting at 11pm.

NEAR THE TERMINI A century-old bar, **Bar Marani,** Via dei Volsci 57 (✆ **06-490016**; Metro: Termini), has been compared to an old Fellini movie set. By the marketplace, this is a coffee bar that attracts students, visitors, Japanese tourists, shopkeepers, artists, pickpockets, contessas, and rock stars, who come for espresso or delicious ice cream. Try to grab a table on the vine-covered terrace. It's closed on Monday and in August.

Treat yourself to a bellini at Harry's Bar.

Rive Gauche, Via dei Sabelli 43 (✆ **06-4456722**; www.rive-gauche.it; Metro: Termini), is a sleek bar that attracts Roman yuppies, who are deserting their traditional glass of wine to sample the dozens of whiskey- or rum-laced concoctions.

Tazio Wine Bar, Boscolo Hotel Exedra, Piazza della Repubblica 47 (✆ **06-489381**; www.boscolohotels.com; Metro: Repubblica), lies near the rail terminal fronting the Baths of Diocletian and Michelangelo's Basilica degli Angeli. A trendy gathering spot at night, it serves reasonably priced Italian wines along with champagnes and tasty meat or fish platters. In summer, the Tazio bar moves to the terrace overlooking the square.

NEAR CAMPO DE' FIORI In the center of Rome, a block from the Tiber, **Roof Top Lounge Bar** at the St. George Hotel, via Giulia 62 (✆ **06-686611**; www.stgeorgehotel.it; bus: 46, 62, or 64), is a summer rendezvous, attracting a young crowd who likes to enjoy a panoramic sweep over the rooftops and domes of Rome at night. Waiters from the wine bar serve at least 120 vintages by the glass along with snacks.

ON PIAZZA DEL POPOLO Café Rosati ★, Piazza del Popolo 5A (✆ **06-3225859**; www.rosatibar.it; Metro: Piazzale Flaminio; bus: 117), has been around since 1923 and attracts a crowd of all persuasions, both foreign and domestic, who drive up in Maseratis and Porsches. It's really a sidewalk cafe/ice-cream parlor/candy store/confectionery/restaurant that has been swept up in the fickle world of fashion. The later you go, the more interesting the action will be. It serves lunch and dinner daily from noon to 11pm.

The management of **Canova Café,** Piazza del Popolo 16 (✆ **06-3612231**; www.canovapiazzadelpopolo.it; bus: 117), has filled this place with boutiques selling expensive gift items, such as luggage and cigarette lighters, yet many Romans still consider the Canova to be *the* place on the piazza. It has a sidewalk terrace for people-watching, plus a snack bar, a restaurant, and a wine shop. In summer, you can sit in a courtyard with ivy-covered walls and flowers growing in terra-cotta planters. Food is served daily from noon to 3:30pm and 7 to 11pm, but the bar is open from 8am to midnight or 1am, depending on the crowd. Main courses cost 5.50€-12.50€.

NEAR THE PANTHEON The **Piazza della Rotonda,** across from the Pantheon, is the hopping place to be after dark, especially in summer. Although it's one of the most touristy places in Rome, locals come here, too, because it's a dramatic place to be at night when the Pantheon is lit up. Most cafes here are open until midnight or 2am.

Di Rienzo, Piazza della Rotonda 8–9 (✆ **06-6869097;** www. ristorantedirienzo.com; Metro: Piazza di Spagna; bus: 62 or 116), is the top cafe on this piazza. In fair weather, you can sit at one of the sidewalk tables (if you can find one free). There's a full menu, or you can just nurse a drink.

Salotto 42, Piazza di Pietra 2 (✆ **06-6785804;** www.salotto42.it; bus: 175), stands close to the Pantheon. This is the creation of a Swedish model, who runs a coffee shop by day and a chic cocktail bar after dark. Big books line the walls. At night patrons sip cocktails while sitting in stylish armchairs, enjoying Scandinavian snacks.

Tazza d'Oro, Piazza della Rotonda, Via degli Orfani 84 (✆ **06-6789792;** www.tazzadorocoffeeshop.com; Metro: Barberini; bus: 46, 62, or 116), is known for serving its own brand of espresso. Another specialty, ideal on a hot summer night, is *granita di caffè* (coffee that has been frozen, crushed into a velvety, slushlike ice, and placed in a glass btw. layers of whipped cream). Also tantalizing are chocolate-coated coffee beans and an aromatic coffee liqueur, Aroma di Roma.

Strongly brewed coffee is liquid fuel to Italians, and many Romans will walk blocks and blocks for what they consider a superior brew. **Caffè Sant'Eustachio ★**, Piazza Sant'Eustachio 82 (✆ **06-68802048;** www. santeustachioilcaffe.it; bus: 116), is one of Rome's most celebrated espresso shops, where the water supply is funneled into the city by an aqueduct built in 19 B.C. Rome's most experienced espresso judges claim the water plays an important part in the coffee's flavor, although steam forced through ground Brazilian coffee roasted on the premises has a significant effect as well.

Riccioli Cafe, Piazza delle Coppelle 13 (✆ **06-68210313;** www. ricciolicafe.com; Metro: Piazza di Spagna; bus: 70), is the best oyster and champagne bar in Rome. In elegant yet informal surroundings, you can order drinks and oysters on the half shell (or more substantial meals). Many come here to see and be seen. The loftlike wine cellar has an excellent selection.

NEAR THE SPANISH STEPS Since 1760, the **Antico Caffè Greco ★★**, Via Condotti 86 (✆ **06-6791700;** www.anticocaffegreco.eu; Metro: Piazza di Spagna), has been Rome's poshest coffee bar. Stendhal, Goethe, Keats, and D'Annunzio have sipped coffee here before you. Today you're more likely to see Japanese tourists and ladies who lunch, but there's plenty of atmosphere. In front is a wooden bar, and beyond is a series of small salons. You sit at marble-topped tables of Napoleonic design, against a backdrop of gold or red damask, romantic paintings, and antique mirrors. The house specialty is Paradise, made with lemon and orange.

One of the best places to taste Italian wines, brandies, and grappa is at **Antica Enoteca,** Via della Croce 76B (*℃* **06/6790896;** www.antica enoteca.com; Metro: Piazza di Spagna). A stand-up drink in its darkly antique confines is the perfect ending to a visit to the nearby Spanish Steps. You can opt for a postage-stamp table in back or stay at the bar.

Rome's chicest cafe continues to be **Caffetteria Canova Tadolini,** Via del Babuino, 150 A/B (*℃* **06-3211-0702;** www.museoateliercanova tadolini.it), part of a museum dedicated to Antonio Canova, the neoclassical sculptor, and his student Adamo Tadolini. Unlike most cafes at museums, the establishment here *is* the museum. You sit at *ottocentro*-style tables beneath statues and plaster fragments. The museum-cum-cafe serves drinks as well as full meals, including succulent pastas.

NEAR THE TREVI FOUNTAIN   At night we'd recommend a stroll by the Trevi Fountain, beautifully lit, followed by a stopover at an elegant ice-cream shop, **San Crispino,** Via della Panetteria 42 (*℃* **06-6793924;** www. ilgelatodisancrispino.it; Metro: Barberini). White-jacketed scoopers will dish out freshly made ice creams and sorbets in such flavors as ginger and cinnamon, fresh walnut and dried fig, chestnut and rum, whiskey, and even "ricotta soft." Sorbets are especially delectable, ranging from melon to pear, from Seville orange to fresh strawberry. Prices go from 1.70€ to 8€, and the place is closed on Tuesdays.

NEAR PIAZZA COLONNA   For gelato fans, **Giolitti,** Via Uffici del Vicario 40 (*℃* **06-6991243;** www.giolitti.it; Metro: Barberini; bus: 116), is one of the city's most popular nighttime gathering spots and the oldest ice-cream shop. Some of the sundaes look like Vesuvius about to erupt. Many people take gelato out to eat on the streets; others enjoy it in the postempire splendor of the salon inside.

NEAR PIAZZA NAVONA   Head for the **Antico Caffè della Pace,** Via della Pace 3–5 (*℃* **06-6861216;** www.caffedellapace.it; bus: 30, 40, or 46),

Desserts on display at Antico Caffè Greco.

A few of the many flavors of gelato available at Giolitti.

right off the heartbeat of Piazza Navona. In existence for more than a century, it attracts painters, musicians, writers, antique collectors, fashionistas, and politicians during the day. It's a wild scene on Saturday night, when it's packed with a gorgeous young crowd that comes to see and be seen.

Fluid, Via del Governo Vecchio 46–47 (**℃ 06-6832361;** www.fluid eventi.com; bus: 64) lies only a short walk from the Piazza Navona. This super-modern bar has a liquid theme. Some of the seating is on plastic cubes evoking ice. Walls and ceiling are sculpted to give the impression of a waterway grotto. Mostly it attracts patrons in the age range of 25 to 40, who enjoy an *aperitivo* buffet and a respectable wine *carte.*

IN TRASTEVERE   Fans of *Fellini's Roma* know what **Piazza Santa Maria** in Trastevere looks like at night. The square, filled with milling throngs in summer, is graced with an octagonal fountain and a 12th-century church. Children run and play on the piazza, and occasional spontaneous guitar fests break out when the weather is good.

Birreria La Scala, Piazza della Scala 60 (**℃ 06-5803763;** bus: 23 or 125), lies only 100m (328 ft.) from Piazza di Santa Maria in Trastevere, the heart of the district. Its selection of beer is the best in the area. There's live music Tuesday, Thursday, and Sunday nights, and the bar is open until 1am.

NEAR TESTACCIO   **Il Barone Rosso,** Via Libetta 13 (**℃ 06-57288961;** www. baronerosso.com), is the biggest and best German beer garden in Rome, and on a summer night this "Red Baron" can be a lot of fun. Opened in 1996, this 380-seat club is the largest in Rome, with a summer garden that always overflows in fair weather. The staff serves lots of beer and other drinks, along with Italian pizzas and German snacks, salads, and sandwiches. Hours are daily 7pm to 3am (Metro: Garbatella).

Live-Music Clubs

At **Alexanderplatz,** Via Ostia 9 (**℃ 06-58335781;** www.alexanderplatz.it; Metro: Ottaviano), you can hear jazz Monday through Saturday from 9pm to 2am, with live music beginning at 10pm. The good restaurant here serves everything from *gnocchi alla romana* to Japanese fare. There's no cover; instead you pay a 1-month membership fee of 10€.

Big Mama, Vicolo San Francesco a Ripa 18 (**℃ 06-5812551;** www.big mama.it; Metro: Piramide; bus: H or 780), is a hangout for jazz and blues musicians where you're likely to meet the up-and-coming stars of tomorrow, and sometimes even the big names. For big acts, the cover is 12€ to 30€, plus 14€ for a seasonal membership fee.

Fonclea, Via Crescenzio 82A (**℃ 06-6896302;** www.fonclea.it; bus: 49, 492, or 982), offers live music every night: Dixieland, rock, and R&B. This is basically a cellar jazz place and crowded pub that attracts folks from all walks of Roman life. The music starts at 7pm and usually lasts until 2am. There's also a restaurant featuring grilled meats, salads, and crepes. A meal starts at 20€, but if you want dinner, it's best to reserve a table.

Arciliuto, Piazza Monte Vecchio 5 (**℃ 06-6879419;** www.arciliuto.it; bus: 46, 62, or 64), is a romantic candlelit spot that was reputedly once the studio of Raphael. Monday through Saturday from 10pm to 1:30am, you can enjoy a music-salon ambience, with a pianist, guitarist, and violinist. The presentation also includes live Neapolitan songs, new Italian madrigals, and even current hits from Broadway or London's West End. This place is hard to find, but it's within walking distance of Piazza Navona. There is no cover, but there's a one-drink minimum with beverages starting at 10€. It's closed from July 15 to September 5.

Nightclubs & Dance Clubs

In a high-tech, futuristic setting, **Boheme,** Via Velletri 13–19 (☎ **06-8412212;** www.boeme.it; bus: 63, 86, or 92), provides two dance floors. The type of music played is house and pop music from the '80s, '90s, and today. It's open Friday to Sunday 11pm to 3:30am. Admission is 10€. It is closed in July and August.

> **A Nightlife Note**
>
> A neighborhood with an edge, **Testaccio** is radical chic—in other words, don't wander around alone at night. Although the area has its charms, its still has a long way to go before it can be called regentrified.

Piper, Via Tagliamento 9 (☎ 06-8555398; www.piper club.it; bus: 63), opened in 1965 in a former cinema and became the first modern disco of its kind in Italy. Many dances such as "the shake" were first introduced to Italy at this club. No longer what it was in those *La Dolce Vita* years, the Piper is still going strong. Today it lures with fashion shows, screenings, some of the hottest parties in town, and various gigs, drawing a casual and mixed-age crowd. The pickup scene here is hot and heavy. The kind of music you'll hear depends on the night. It's open Tuesday to Sunday 11pm to 5am, charging a cover of 20€ to 26€, including one drink.

Gilda, Via Mario de' Fiori 97 (☎ **06-6797396;** www.midra.it; Metro: Piazza di Spagna), is an adventurous nightclub/disco/restaurant that attracts a post-35 set, most often couples. In the past, it has hosted Diana Ross and splashy Paris-type revues. Expect first-class shows, and disco music played between the live acts. The disco (midnight–4am) presents music of the 1960s plus more current tunes. The attractive piano bar, Swing, features Italian and Latin music. The cover ranges from 15€ to 30€ and includes the first drink. It's closed on Monday.

Don't be put off by the facade of **Locanda Atlantide,** Via dei Lucani 22B (☎ **06-44704540;** www.locandatlantide.it; Metro: Porta Maggiore; bus: 71), thinking that you've arrived at a bunker for a Gestapo interrogation. This former warehouse in San Lorenzo is the setting of a nightclub, bar, concert hall, and theater. Every day there's something different—perhaps jazz on Tuesday, a play on Wednesday, or a concert on Thursday, giving way to dance-club action on Friday and Saturday with DJ music. The cover ranges from 3€ to 15€, depending on the evening; hours are Tuesday to Sunday from 8pm to 2am. It's closed June 15 to September 15.

Gay & Lesbian Clubs

L'Alibi, Via Monte Testaccio 44 (☎ **06-5743448;** www.lalibi.it; bus: 95), in Testaccio, is a year-round stop on many gay men's agenda. The crowd, however, tends to be mixed, both Roman and international, straight and gay, male and female. One room is devoted to dancing. It's open Wednesday through Sunday from 11pm to 4am, and the cover is 10€ to 15€.

Skyline, Via Pontremoli 36 (*©* **06-7009431;** www.skylineclub.it; Metro: San Giovanni), has moved to the San Giovanni district of Rome. It attracts a large number of gay men with a scattering of lesbians. It's amusing, fun, and often rowdy. Porn movies are shown every night. Conceived as an American bar on two levels, it offers two backrooms where the action is hot, hot, hot. Shows are presented weekly. It's open daily 10:30pm to 4am.

SIDE TRIPS FROM ROME: TIVOLI, OSTIA ANTICA & MORE

Tivoli & the Villas

Tivoli, known as Tibur to the ancient Romans, is 32km (20 miles) east of Rome on Via Tiburtina, about an hour's drive with traffic. If you don't have a car, take Metro Line B to the end of the line, the Rebibbia station. After exiting the station, board a COTRAL bus for the trip the rest of the way to Tivoli. Cotral buses to Tivoli depart from Ponte Mammolo metro station (line B). Generally, buses depart about every 20 minutes during the day.

EXPLORING THE VILLAS

Hadrian's Villa (Villa Adriana) ★★★   In the 2nd century A.D., the globe-trotting Hadrian spent the last 3 years of his life in the grandest style. Less than 6km (3¾ miles) from Tivoli, he built one of the greatest estates ever erected, and he filled acre after acre with some of the architectural wonders he'd seen on his

The grounds at Hadrian's Villa.

many travels. Perhaps as a preview of what he envisioned in store for himself, the emperor even created a representation of Hades. Hadrian was a patron of the arts, a lover of beauty, and even something of an architect. He directed the staggering feat of building much more than a villa: It was a self-contained world for a vast royal entourage and the hundreds of servants and guards they required to protect them, feed them, bathe them, and satisfy their libidos.

Hadrian erected theaters, baths, temples, fountains, gardens, and canals bordered with statuary throughout his estate. He filled the palaces and temples with sculpture, some of which now rests in the museums of Rome. In later centuries, barbarians, popes, and cardinals, as well as anyone who needed a slab of marble, carted off much that made the villa so spectacular. But enough of the fragmented ruins remain for us to piece together the story. For a glimpse of what the villa used to be, see the plastic reconstruction at the entrance.

After all the centuries of plundering, there's still a bit left. The most outstanding remnant is the **Canopo,** or Canopus, a re-creation of the town of Canope with its famous Temple of the Serapis. The ruins of a rectangular area, **Piazza d'Oro,** are still surrounded by a double portico. Likewise, the **Doric Pillared Hall** (or *sala dei pilastri dorici*) remains to delight, with its pilasters with Doric bases and capitals holding up a Doric architrave. The ruins of the **Baths** remain, revealing rectangular rooms with concave walls. The apse and the ruins of some magnificent vaulting are found at the Great Baths. Only the north wall remains of the **Pecile,** otherwise known as the Stoa Poikile or "Painted Porch," which Hadrian discovered in Athens and had reproduced here. The best is saved for last—the **Teatro Marittimo,** a circular maritime theater in ruins with its central building enveloped by a canal spanned by small swing bridges. For a closer look at some of the items excavated, you can visit the museum on the premises and a visitor center near the villa parking area.

Via di Villa Adriana. (✆ **0774-530203.** www.villa-adriana.net. Admission 6.50€. Daily 9am–sunset (about 7:30pm in summer, 5:30pm Nov–Mar). Closed New Year's Day and Christmas. Bus: 4 from Tivoli.

Villa d'Este ★★ Like Hadrian centuries before, Cardinal Ippolito d'Este of Ferrara believed in heaven on earth, and in the mid–16th century he ordered this villa built on a hillside. The dank Renaissance structure, with its second-rate paintings, is not that noteworthy; the big draw for visitors is the **spectacular gardens** below (designed by Pirro Ligorio).

You descend the cypress-studded slope to the bottom; on the way you're rewarded with everything from lilies to gargoyles spouting water, torrential streams, and waterfalls. The loveliest fountain is the Ovato Fountain (Fontana dell Ovato), by Ligorio. But nearby is the most spectacular achievement: the **Fountain of the Hydraulic Organ (Fontana dell'Organo Idraulico),** dazzling with its water jets in front of a baroque chapel, with four maidens who look tipsy. The work represents the genius of Frenchman Claude Veanard. The moss-covered **Fountain of the Dragons (Fontana dei Draghi),** also by Ligorio, and the so-called **Fountain of Glass (Fontana di Vetro),** by Bernini, are the most intriguing. The best walk is along the promenade, with 100 spraying fountains. The garden is worth hours of exploration, but it's a lot of walking, with some steep climbs.

Piazza Trento. (✆ **0774-312070.** www.villadestetivoli.info. Admission 10€. The bus from Rome stops near the entrance. Tues–Sun 8:30am to 1 hr. before sunset. Bus: Roma-Tivoli.

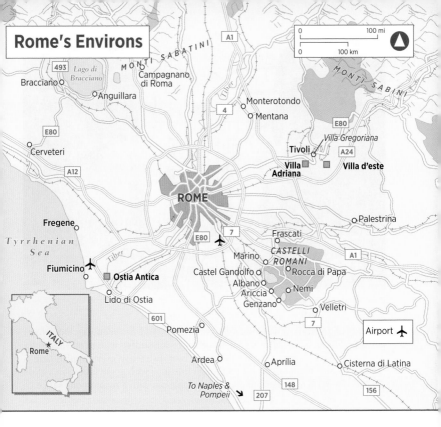

Rome's Environs

Villa Gregoriana ★   Villa d'Este dazzles with artificial glamour, but the Villa Gregoriana relies more on nature. The gardens were built by Pope Gregory XVI in the 19th century. At one point on the circuitous walk carved along a slope, you can stand and look out onto the most panoramic waterfall (Aniene) at Tivoli. The trek to the bottom on the banks of the Anio is studded with grottoes and balconies that open onto the chasm. The only problem is that if you do make the full descent, you might need a helicopter to pull you up again (the climb back up is fierce). From one of the belvederes, there's a panoramic view of the Temple of Vesta on the hill. Following a $5.5-million restoration, the property has been much improved, and hikers can now explore the on-site grottoes. However, wear rubber-soled shoes, and remember to duck your head. A former school has been converted into a visitor center designed by architect Gae Aulenti.

Largo Sant'Angelo. ⓒ **06-39967701.** www.villagregoriana.it. Admission 5€. Apr–Oct 15 Tues–Sun 10am–6:30pm; Mar and Oct 16–Nov Tues–Sat 10am–2:30pm, Sun 10am–4pm. The bus from Rome stops near the entrance.

WHERE TO DINE

Albergo Ristorante Adriano ITALIAN   In a stucco-sided villa a few steps from the ticket office sits an idyllic stop for either before or after you visit Hadrian's Villa. It offers terrace dining under plane trees or indoor dining in a high-ceilinged room with terra-cotta walls, neoclassical moldings, and white

The gardens at Villa d'Este.

Corinthian pilasters. The cooking is home style, and the menu includes roast lamb, grilled suckling pig with wild fennel, or ravioli stuffed with ricotta and spinach in a raw basil-laced tomato sauce. The best dish we've ever sampled here is the risotto with pumpkin flowers, although the quail with grape sauce ran a close second. Desserts include such delights as apple pie with a mascarpone sauce.

Via di Villa Adriana 222. ✆ **0774-382235.** www.hoteladriano.it. Reservations recommended. Main courses 10€–30€. AE, DC, MC, V. Mon–Sat 2:30–4pm and 8–10pm; Sun 12:30–2:30pm and 8–10:30pm.

Antica Trattoria del Falcone ROMAN   One of the town's more dependable choices lies in the historic core on the main artery leading off Largo Garibaldi. Because of its location, it attracts a lot of visitors, but that doesn't mean that it's a tourist trap. Far from it. The food is regionally inspired by a kitchen that specializes in market-fresh ingredients. Specialties include perfectly grilled fish as well as *saltimbocca alla romana* (a veal and ham dish). Mixed roast meats, done over the coals, are our favorites. Another dish we like is homemade *crespella,* which is like a rolled pancake. It's stuffed with ricotta, nuts, and fresh spinach.

Via del Trevio 34. ✆ **0774-312358.** www.anticatrattoriadelfalcone.it. Reservations recommended. Main courses 6€–10€; fixed-price menus 13€–18€. AE, DC, MC, V. Daily 11:30am–4pm and 6:30–11:30pm.

Ostia Antica: Rome's Ancient Seaport

Ostia Antica is one of the area's major attractions, particularly interesting to those who can't make it to Pompeii. If you want to see both ancient and modern Rome, grab your swimsuit, towel, and sunblock and take the Metro Line B from Stazione Termini to the Magliana stop. Change here for the Lido train to Ostia Antica, about 26km (16 miles) from Rome. Departures are about every half-hour, and the trip takes only 20 minutes. The Metro lets you off across the highway that connects Rome with the coast. It's just a short walk to the excavations.

Later, board the Metro again to visit the **Lido di Ostia,** the beach. Italy might be a Catholic country, but you won't detect any religious conservatism in the skimpy bikinis on the beach here. There's a carnival atmosphere, with dance halls, cinemas, and pizzerias. The Lido is set off best at Castelfusano, against a backdrop of pine woods. This stretch of shore is referred to as the Roman Riviera.

Ostia Antica's Ruins ★★   Ostia, at the mouth of the Tiber, was the port of ancient Rome, serving as the gateway for all the riches from the far corners of the empire. It was founded in the 4th century B.C. and became a major port and naval base primarily under two later emperors, Claudius and Trajan.

A prosperous city developed, full of temples, baths, theaters, and patrician homes. Ostia flourished for about 8 centuries before it began to wither away. Gradually it became little more than a malaria bed, a buried ghost city that faded into history. A papal-sponsored commission launched a series of digs in the 19th century; however, the major work of unearthing was carried out under Mussolini's orders from 1938 to 1942 (the work had to stop because of the war). The city is only partially dug out today, but it's believed that all the chief monuments have been uncovered. There are quite a few visible ruins unearthed, so this is no dusty field like the Circus Maximus.

These principal monuments are clearly labeled. The most important spot is **Piazzale delle Corporazioni,** an early version of Wall Street. Near the theater, this square contained nearly 75 corporations, the nature of their businesses identified by the patterns of preserved mosaics. Greek dramas were performed at the **ancient theater,** built in the early days of the empire. The classics are still aired here in summer (check with the tourist office for specific listings), but the theater as it looks today is the result of much rebuilding. Every town the size of Ostia had a forum, and during the excavations a number of pillars of the ancient **Ostia Forum** were uncovered. At one end is a 2nd-century-B.C. temple honoring a trio of gods, Minerva, Jupiter, and Juno (little more than the basic foundation remains). In addition, in the enclave is a well-lit **museum** displaying Roman statuary along with some Pompeii-like frescoes. Also of special interest are the ruins of **Thermopolium,** which was a bar; its name means "sale of hot drinks." The ruins of **Capitolium and Forum** remain; this was once the largest temple in Ostia, dating from the 2nd century A.D. A lot of the original brick remains, including a partial reconstruction of the altar. Of an *insula,* a block of apartments, **Casa Diana** remains, with its rooms arranged around an inner courtyard. There are perfect picnic spots beside fallen columns or near old temple walls.

Via dei Romagnoli 717. ℂ **06-56352830.** www.ostiaantica.net. Admission 6.50€. Nov-Feb Tues-Sun 8:30am-4pm; Mar Tues-Sun 8:30am-5pm; Apr-Oct Tues-Sun 8:30am-6pm. Metro: Ostia Antica Line Roma-Ostia-Lido.

The Roman Castles

For the Roman emperor and the wealthy cardinal in the heyday of the Renaissance, the Roman Castles (Castelli Romani) exerted a powerful lure, and they still do. The Castelli aren't castles, but hill towns—many of them with an ancient history. Several produce wines that are well regarded.

The ideal way to explore the hill towns is by car. But you can get a limited review by taking one of the buses that leaves every 20 minutes from Rome's Anagnina stop on Metro Line A.

NEMI

The Romans flock to Nemi in droves, particularly from April to June, for the succulent **strawberries** grown there, acclaimed by some gourmets as Europe's finest. In May, there's a strawberry festival. There are no direct buses from Rome to Nemi. To get to Nemi from Rome take the Cotral bus to Genzano from the Anagnina metro stop in Rome. From Genzano take another bus to Nemi. The trip lasts 1 hour and 15 minutes.

Nemi was also known to the ancients. A temple to the hunter Diana was erected on **Lake Nemi,** which was said to be her "looking glass." In A.D. 37, Caligula built luxurious barges to float on the lake. Mussolini drained Nemi to find the barges, but it was a dangerous time to excavate them from the bottom. They were senselessly destroyed by the Nazis during the infamous retreat.

At the **Roman Ship Museum (Museo delle Navi)** ★, Via di Diana 13 (℃ **06-39967900**), you can see two scale models of the ships destroyed by the Nazis. The major artifacts on display are mainly copies because the originals now rest in world-class museums. Opening hours are all year-round Monday to Saturday 9am to 7pm, Sunday 9am to 1pm. Admission is 3€. To reach the museum, head from the center of Nemi toward the lake.

The 15th-century **Palazzo Ruspoli,** a private baronial estate, is the focal point of Nemi, but the town itself invites exploration—particularly the alleyways that the locals call streets and the houses with balconies jutting out over the slopes.

Where to Dine

Ristorante Il Castagnone ROMAN/SEAFOOD This well-managed dining room of the town's best hotel takes pride in its menu, with Roman-based cuisine that emphasizes seafood above meat. The attentive formal service is usually delivered with gentle humor. Amid neoclassical accessories and marble, you can order fine veal, chicken, beef, and fish dishes such as fried calamari, spaghetti with shellfish in garlicky tomato-based sauce, and roasted lamb with potatoes and Mediterranean herbs. The agricultural treasures of the region are on display in such dishes as *pappardelle* with cuttlefish and artichokes, sea bass crepes in orange sauce, *tagliolini* in green sauce with porcini mushrooms, and salmon carpaccio with ricotta. There's a sweeping lake view from the restaurant's windows.

In the Diana Park Hotel, Via Nemorense 56. ℃ **06-9364041.** www.hoteldiana.com. Reservations recommended. Main courses 10€–22€. AE, DC, MC, V. Tues–Sun noon–3pm and 8–11pm. Closed Nov.

FRASCATI ★

About 21km (13 miles) from Rome on Via Tuscolana and 482m (1,581 ft.) above sea level, Frascati is one of the most beautiful hill towns. It's known for the wine to which it lends its name, as well as for its villas,

A few of Nemi's famed strawberries.

which were restored after the severe destruction caused by World War II bombers. To get there, take one of the COTRAL buses leaving from the Anagina stop of Metro Line A. From there, take the blue COTRAL bus to Frascati. Again, the transportation situation in Italy is constantly in a state of flux, so check your route at the station.

Although Frascati wine is exported and served in many of Rome's restaurants and *trattorie,* tradition holds that it's best near the vineyards from which it came. Romans drive up on Sunday just to drink it.

Stand in the heart of Frascati, at Piazza Marconi, to see the most important of the estates: **Villa Aldobrandini ★**, Via Massaia. The finishing touches to this 16th-century villa were added by Maderno, who designed the facade of St. Peter's in Rome. While you can't visit the interior, the gardens, with grottoes, yew hedges, statuary, and fountains, make for a nice outing. It is necessary to book the visit by phone at 📞 **06-6833785.** The gardens are open Monday to Friday 9am to 1pm and 3 to 5pm (to 6pm in summer).

You also might want to visit the bombed-out **Villa Torlonia,** adjacent to Piazza Marconi. Its grounds have been converted into a public park whose chief treasure is the Theater of the Fountains, designed by Maderno.

Cacciani Ristorante ROMAN   Cacciani is the top restaurant in Frascati, where the competition has always been tough. It boasts a terrace commanding a view of the valley, and the kitchen is exposed to the public. To start, we recommend the pasta specialties, such as pasta *cacio e pepe* (pasta with *caciocavallo* cheese and black pepper), or the original spaghetti with seafood and lentils. For a main course, the grilled baby lamb with chicory is always fine. Of course, there is a large choice of wine.

Via Armando Diaz 13. 📞 **06-9401991.** www.cacciani.it. Reservations required. Main courses 14€–17€. Fixed-price menus 25€–50€. AE, DC, MC, V. Tues–Sun 12:30–3pm and 7:30–10:30pm.

Etruscan Historical Sights

CERVETERI (CAERE)

As you walk through Rome's Etruscan Museum (Villa Giulia), you'll often see CAERE written under a figure vase or sarcophagus. This is a reference to the nearby town known today as Cerveteri, one of Italy's great Etruscan cities, whose origins could date from as far back as the 9th century B.C.

Of course, the Etruscan town has long since faded, but not the **Necropolis of Cerveteri ★★** (📞 **06-39967150**). Cerveteri is often called a "city of the dead," and the effect is eerie. When you go beneath some of the mounds, you'll discover the most striking feature: The tombs are like rooms in Etruscan homes.

The main burial ground is the Necropolis of Banditaccia. Of the graves thus far uncovered, none is finer than the **Reliefs' Tomb (Tomba Bella),** the burial ground of the Matuna family. Articles such as utensils and even house pets were painted in stucco relief. Presumably these paintings were representations of items that the dead family would need in the world beyond. The necropolis is open Tuesday to Sunday from 8:30am to 1 hour before sunset. Admission is 6€ for adults, 3€ for children.

Relics from the necropolis are displayed at the **Museo Nazionale Cerite,** Piazza Santa Maria Maggiore (☏ **06-9941354**). The museum, housed within the ancient walls and crenellations of Ruspoldi Castle, is open Tuesday through Sunday from 8:30am to 7:30pm. Free admission.

You can reach Cerveteri by bus or car. If you're driving, head out Via Aurelia, northwest of Rome, for 45km (28 miles). By public transport, take Metro Line A in Rome to the Cornelia stop; from here you can catch a COTRAL bus to Cerveteri. The trip takes about an hour and costs 3.50€. There is no number to call for information, but you can visit the COTRAL website at **www.cotralspa.it**. Once you're at Cerveteri, it's a 2km (1¼-mile) walk to the necropolis; follow the signs pointing the way.

TARQUINIA ★

If you want to see tombs even more striking and more recently excavated than those at Cerveteri, go to Tarquinia, a town with medieval turrets and fortifications atop rocky cliffs overlooking the sea. It would seem unusual for a medieval town to have an Etruscan name, but actually, Tarquinia is the adopted name of the old medieval community of Corneto, in honor of the major Etruscan city that once stood nearby.

The main attraction in the town is the **Tarquinia National Museum ★**, Piazza Cavour (☏ **06-39967150**), devoted to Etruscan exhibits and sarcophagi excavated from the necropolis a few miles away. The museum is housed in the Palazzo Vitelleschi, a Gothic palace from the mid–15th century. Among the exhibits are gold jewelry, black vases with carved and painted bucolic scenes, and sarcophagi decorated with carvings of animals and relief figures of priests and military leaders. But the biggest attraction is in itself worth the ride from Rome: the almost life-size pair of **winged horses ★★** from the pediment of a Tarquinian temple. The finish is worn here and there, and the terra-cotta color shows through; but the relief stands as one of the greatest Etruscan masterpieces ever discovered. The museum is open Tuesday to Sunday 8:30am to 7:30pm, and charges 6€ admission adults, 3€ for those 18 to 25 years old. A combination ticket for the Tarquinia National Museum and the Etruscan Necropolis costs 8€. It's closed Christmas, January 1, and May 1.

A 6€ fee for adults, 3€ for those age 18 to 25, admits you to the **Etruscan Necropolis ★★** (☏ **06-39967150**), covering more than 4.5km (2¾ miles) of rough terrain near where the ancient Etruscan city once stood. Thousands of tombs have been discovered, some of which haven't been explored even today.

Frescoes from the Etruscan Necropolis.

Others, of course, were discovered by looters, but many treasures remain even though countless pieces were removed to museums and private collections. The **paintings** on the walls of the tombs have helped historians reconstruct the life of the Etruscans—a heretofore impossible feat without a written history. The paintings depict feasting couples in vivid colors mixed from iron oxide, lapis lazuli dust, and charcoal. One of the oldest tombs (from the 6th c. B.C.) depicts young men fishing while dolphins play and colorful birds fly high above. Many of the paintings convey an earthy, vigorous, sex-oriented life among the wealthy Etruscans. The tombs are generally open Tuesday through Sunday from 8:30am to 1 hour before sunset. You can reach the gravesites by taking a bus from the Barriera San Giusto to the Cimitero stop. Or try the 20-minute walk from the museum. Inquire at the museum for directions.

To reach Tarquinia by car, take Via Aurelia outside Rome and continue on the autostrada toward Civitavecchia. Bypass Civitavecchia and continue another 21km (13 miles) north until you see the exit signs for Tarquinia. As for public transport, a *diretto* train from Roma Trastevere station takes 1 hour.

6

FLORENCE

With the exception of Venice, no other European city lives off its past like Florence (Firenze). After all, it was the birthplace of the Renaissance, an amazing outburst of activity from the 14th to the 16th century that completely changed this Tuscan town and the world. Under the benevolent eye (and purse) of the Medicis, Florence blossomed into an unrivaled repository of art and architectural treasures, with masterpieces by geniuses such as Botticelli, Brunelleschi, Cellini, Donatello, Fra Angelico, Ghiberti, Giotto, Leonardo, Michelangelo, and Raphael. Since the 19th century, it has been visited by millions wanting to see Michelangelo's *David,* Botticelli's *Birth of Venus,* Brunelleschi's dome on the Duomo, and Giotto's campanile (bell tower).

Florence might seem a bit foreboding at first glance. Architecturally, it's not a Gothic fantasy of lace like Venice. Many of its *palazzi* (palaces) look like severe fortresses, a characteristic of the Medici style—they were built to keep foreign enemies at bay. But these facades, however uninviting, mask treasures within, drawing thousands of visitors who overrun the narrow streets. The locals bemoan the tourist crush but welcome the business it brings. "The visitors have crowded our city and strained our facilities," a local merchant told us, "but they make it possible for me to own a villa in Fiesole and take my children on vacation to San Remo every year."

The city officials have been wise to keep the inner Renaissance core relatively free of modern architecture and polluting industry. Florence has industry, but it has been relegated to the suburbs. The city proper is relatively clean and safe, as Italian cities go. You can generally walk the narrow cobblestone streets at night safely, although caution is always advised.

May and September are the ideal times to visit. The worst times are the week before and including Easter, and from June until the first week of September—Florence is literally overrun during these times, and the streets weren't designed for mass tourism. Temperatures in July and August hover in the 30s Celsius (70s and 80s Fahrenheit), dropping to a low of 7°C (45°F) in December and January.

Biking the streets of Florence. PREVIOUS PAGE: Michelangelo's statue of *David* at Academia.

199

ESSENTIALS

Arriving

BY PLANE From Rome, you can catch a short domestic flight to **Galileo Galilei Airport** at Pisa (*©* **050-849111;** www.pisa-airport.com), 93km (58 miles) west of Florence. **Alitalia** (*©* **06-2222;** www.alitalia.it) offers four flights a day from New York to Pisa with one stop in Rome. You can take an express train for the hour-long trip to Florence. There's also a small domestic airport, **Amerigo Vespucci,** on Via del Termine, near A11 (*©* **055-3061300;** www.aeroporto.firenze.it), 5.5km (3½ miles) northwest of Florence, a 15-minute drive. From the airport, you can reach Florence by the "Vola in Bus" airport shuttle bus service operated by ATAF, which stops at the main Santa Maria Novella rail terminal. The airport shuttle bus costs 5€ one-way.

BY TRAIN If you're coming from Rome, count on a 2- to 3-hour trip, depending on your connection. **Santa Maria Novella rail station,** in Piazza della Stazione, adjoins Piazza Santa Maria Novella. For railway information, call *©* **892021.** Some trains stop at the **Stazione Campo di Marte,** on the eastern side of Florence. There is a train that runs between the two stations every 15 minutes from 5am to 11:10pm.

BY CAR Florence enjoys good autostrada connections with the rest of Italy, especially Rome and Bologna. A1 connects Florence with both the north and the south. Florence lies 277km (172 miles) north of Rome, 105km (65 miles) west of Bologna, and 298km (185 miles) south of Milan. Bologna is about an hour's drive away, and Rome is 3 hours away. The Tyrrhenian coast is only an hour from Florence on A11 heading west.

Use a car only to get *to* Florence, not to get around once you're there. Most of central Florence is closed to all vehicles except those of locals. If your hotel doesn't have parking, head for one of the city-run garages. Although you'll find a garage under the train station, a better deal is the **Parterre** parking lot under Piazza Libertà, north of Fortezza del Basso.

Visitor Information

Contact the **Azienda per il Turismo di Firenze (Florence Tourist Board),** which has several branches, including Via A. Manzoni 16 (*©* **055-23320;** www.firenzeturismo.it), open Monday through Friday from 9am to 1pm; and Via Cavour 1R (*©* **055-290832**), open year-round Monday to Saturday 8:30am to 6:30pm and Sunday 8:30am to 1:30pm. There are also information offices maintained by the **Comune di Firenze.** One is in Borgo Santa Croce 29R just south of Piazza Santa Croce (*©* **055-2340444**), open from March to October Monday to Saturday 9am to 7pm and Sunday 9am to 2pm. From November to February it's open Monday to Saturday 9am to 5pm and Sunday 9am to 2pm. A small **Ufficio Informazioni Turistiche** (also maintained by the Comune di Firenze) is outside the main train terminal, Piazza Stazione 4A (*©* **055-212245**); it's open Monday to Saturday 8:30am to 7pm and Sunday 8:30am to 2pm.

City Layout

Florence is a city designed for walking, with all the major sights in a compact area. The only problem is that the sidewalks are unbearably crowded in summer.

The Red & the Black

Florence has two street-numbering systems—red *(rosso)* numbers and black *(nero)* numbers. Red numbers identify commercial enterprises, such as shops and restaurants. Black numbers identify office buildings, private homes, apartment houses, and hotels. Renumbering without the color system is on the horizon, although no one seems exactly certain when it will be implemented. In this chapter, red-numbered addresses are indicated by an "R" following the building number, as in "39R."

Because street numbers are chaotic, it's better to get a cross street or some landmark if you're looking for an address along a long boulevard.

The *centro storico* (**historic center**) is split by the **Arno River,** which usually is serene but can at times turn ferocious with floodwaters. The major part of Florence, certainly its historic core with most of the monuments, lies on the north (right) side of the river. But the "left" side isn't devoid of attractions, including some wonderful *trattorie* and some great shopping finds, not to mention the Pitti Palace and the Giardini di Boboli, a series of impressive formal gardens. In addition, you'll want to cross over to check out the views of the city from Piazzale Michelangiolo—especially breathtaking at sunset.

The Arno is spanned by eight bridges, of which the **Ponte Vecchio (Old Bridge),** lined with overhanging jewelry stores, is the most celebrated and most central. Many of these bridges were ancient structures until the Nazis, in a hopeless last-ditch effort, senselessly destroyed them in their "defense" of Florence in 1944. With tenacity, Florence rebuilt its bridges, using pieces from the destroyed structures whenever possible. The **Ponte Santa Trínita** is the second-most important bridge. It leads to **Via dei Tornabuoni,** the right bank's most important shopping street (don't look for bargains, however). At the Ponte Vecchio you can walk, again on the right bank of the Arno, along **Via per Santa Maria,** which becomes **Via Calimala.** This leads you into **Piazza della Repubblica,** a commercial district known for its cafes.

From here, you can take **Via Roma,** which leads directly into **Piazza di San Giovanni,** where you'll find the baptistery and its neighboring sibling, the larger **Piazza del Duomo,** with the world-famous cathedral and Giotto bell tower. From the far western edge of Piazza del Duomo you can take **Via del Proconsolo** south to **Piazza della**

The Ponte Vecchio, which spans the Arno.

Signoria, to see the landmark Palazzo Vecchio and its sculpture-filled Loggia della Signoria.

High in the olive-planted hills overlooking Florence is the ancient town of **Fiesole,** with Etruscan and Roman ruins and a splendid cathedral.

At the very least, arm yourself with a map from the tourist office (see "Visitor Information," above). Ask for the one *con un stradario* (with a street index), which shows all the roads and is better for navigation than their more generalized orientation version. But if you'd like to see Florence in any depth—particularly those little side streets—buy a map, available at all bookstores and at most newsstands.

The Neighborhoods in Brief

Florence isn't divided into neighborhoods the way many cities are. Most locals refer to either the left bank or the right bank of the Arno, and that's about it, unless they head out of town for the immediate environs, such as Fiesole. The following "neighborhoods"—really just areas centering on a palace, church, or square—are rather arbitrary. This section will give you some idea of where you might want to stay and where the major attractions are.

CENTRO **Centro** could include all the historic heart of Florence, but mostly the term is used to describe the area southwest of the Duomo. This district isn't as important as it used to be because Piazza della Signoria (see below) now attracts more visitors. Centro's heyday was in the 1800s, when it was filled with narrow medieval streets that were torn down to make a grander city center. Lost forever were great homes of the Medicis and the Sacchettis, among others. **Piazza della Repubblica,** though faded, is still lively day and night with its celebrated cafes. Centro's **Via dei Tournabuoni** is the city's most elegant shopping street.

PIAZZA DEL DUOMO In the heart of Florence, **Piazza del Duomo** and its surrounding area are dominated by the tricolored **Duomo,** site of the former grain and hay markets. It's one of the largest buildings in the Christian world, and you come on it unexpectedly because the surrounding buildings weren't torn down to give it breathing room. Capped by Brunelleschi's dome, the structure now dominates the skyline. Every visitor flocks here to see not only the Duomo but also the neighboring **campanile (bell tower),** one of Italy's most beautiful, and the **baptistery** across the way (its doors are among the jewels of Renaissance sculpture). Also in this neighborhood is the **Museo dell'Opera del Duomo,** which includes some of the most important works of Donatello.

The Duomo is a central location that's loaded with hotels in all price categories. The streets north of the Duomo are long and often full of traffic, but those to the south make up a wonderful medieval tangle of alleys and tiny squares heading toward Piazza della Signoria.

PIAZZA DELLA SIGNORIA The core of pre-Renaissance Florence, this heavily visited square is home to the **Loggia dei Lanzi,** with Cellini's *Perseus* holding up a beheaded Medusa, Florence's most photographed statue, as well as Michelangelo's *David* (a copy—the original was moved inside to protect it from the elements). To the south are the **Galleria degli Uffizi** and the **Palazzo Vecchio.** This is the city's civic heart and perhaps the best bet for museum hounds. It's a well-polished part of the tourist zone, yet it still

Cellini's *Perseus* in the Piazza della Signoria.

retains the narrow medieval streets where Dante grew up—back alleys where tour-bus crowds rarely set foot. The few blocks just north of the Ponte Vecchio have good shopping, but unappealing modern buildings were planted here to replace the district that was destroyed in World War II. The whole neighborhood can be stiflingly crowded in summer, but in those moments when you catch it empty of tour groups, it remains the most romantic part of Florence.

Southwest of Piazza della Signoria is the **Ponte Vecchio** area. The oldest of Florence's bridges, it's flanked by jewelry stores and will carry you to the Oltrarno. This has always been a strategic crossing place, even when it was a stone bridge. In the Middle Ages, it was the center for leather craftsmen, fishmongers, and butchers, but over the years jewelers' shops have moved in. The **Vasari Corridor (Corridoio Vasariano)** runs the length of the bridge above the shops—built by Vasari in 5 months. One of the most congested parts of Florence, this area is on every visitor's itinerary.

PIAZZA SANTA MARIA NOVELLA & THE TRAIN STATION On the northwestern edge of central Florence is the large Piazza Santa Maria Novella, with its church of the same name. This area isn't all art and culture, however. Northwest of Santa Maria Novella is the city's busiest section, centered at **Piazza della Stazione,** where the **Stazione di Santa Maria Novella** is located. Like all rail stations in Italy, it's surrounded by budget hotels. Leading off **Piazza dell'Unitá Italiana,** Via del Melarancio goes a short distance east to **San Lorenzo,** the first cathedral of Florence. Beyond San Lorenzo is **Piazza Madonna degli Aldobrandini,** the entrance to the **Medici Chapels.** Thousands flock here to see Michelangelo's tombs, whose allegorical figures of *Day* and *Night* are among the most famous sculptures of all time. Southwest of Piazza Santa Maria Novella, toward the Arno, is **Piazza Ognissanti,** a fashionable (albeit congested) Renaissance square opening onto the river. On this square are two of the city's most legendary hotels: the **Grand** and the **Westin Excelsior.**

PIAZZA SAN MARCO Although Piazza San Marco has none of the grandeur of the square of the same name in Venice, the piazza and its surroundings on the northern fringe of Centro are nevertheless one of the most important in Florence—centered around its church, which houses the **Museo di San Marco.** Located in a former Dominican monastery, the museum is home to a collection of some of the greatest works by Fra Angelico, who decorated the walls of the monks' cells with edifying scenes.

In general, this area is overrun by visitors, most rushing to the **Galleria dell'Accademia** on Via Ricasoli to see the monumental figure of *David* (1501–04) by Michelangelo. Other area highlights include Piazza della Santissima Annunziata, Florence's most beautiful, graced by an equestrian statue of Ferdinand I de' Medici by Bologna.

The quiet back streets of the Oltrarno.

PIAZZA SANTA CROCE This section and its Piazza Santa Croce are in the southeastern part of the old town, near the Arno, dominated by the Gothic church of Santa Croce (Holy Cross), completed in 1442. The piazza served as the headquarters of the Franciscans, who established a firm base there in 1218. With the departure of the Franciscans, the piazza was used as a playing field for **calico** (soccer), jousts, and festivals. The area is always full of visitors but isn't as congested as the neighborhoods previously mentioned. The church contains the tombs of Michelangelo, Galileo and Machiavelli, among others. A little distance to the north of Santa Croce is the **Casa Buonarroti,** on Via Ghibellina, which Michelangelo acquired for his nephew. Today it's a museum with a collection of Michelangelo's works, mainly drawings, gathered by his nephew. From here you can follow Via Buonarroti to Piazza dei Ciompi, a lively square that's off the beaten track, filled with stalls peddling secondhand goods. Look for old coins, books, and even antique Italian military uniforms.

ACROSS THE ARNO The "left bank" of the Arno River, known as the **Oltrarno,** is home to the Palazzo Pitti, with its picture gallery and Giardini di Boboli; Masaccio's frescoes in the church of Santa Maria del Carmine; artisans' workshops; some good restaurants; and the postcard panorama of Florence and its dome from Piazzale Michelangiolo. At the top of the gardens is an elegant fortress known as the Forte Belvedere (1590–95), with a view of Florence that's well worth the climb. The center of this district is Piazza Santo Spirito, a lovely, shady square.

GETTING AROUND

Because Florence is so compact, walking is the ideal way to get around—and, at times, the only way because of numerous pedestrian zones. In theory, at least, pedestrians have the right of way at uncontrolled zebra crossings, but don't count on that if you meet up with a speeding Vespa.

By Bus

If you plan to use public buses, buy your ticket before boarding. For 1.20€, you can ride on any public bus for a total of 90 minutes. A 24-hour ticket costs 5€. You can buy bus tickets at *tabacchi* (tobacconists) and newsstands. Once on board, you must validate your ticket in the box near the rear door, or you stand to be fined 40€—no excuses accepted. The local **bus station** (which serves as the terminal for ATAF city buses) is at Piazza della Stazione (© **055-56501**), behind the train station.

Bus routes are posted at bus stops, but the numbers of routes can change overnight because of sudden repair work going on at one of the ancient streets—perhaps a water main broke overnight and caused flooding. We once found that a bus route map printed only 1 week beforehand was already outdated. Therefore, if you're dependent on bus transport, you'll need to inquire that day for the exact number of the vehicle you want to board.

By Taxi

You can find taxis at stands at nearly all the major squares. The charge is .90€ per kilometer, with a 3.30€ minimum, 6.60€ between 10pm and 6am. If you need a **radio taxi,** call © **055-4390** or 055-4242.

By Bicycle & Motor Scooter

Bicycles and motor scooters, if you avoid the whizzing traffic, are two other practical ways of getting around. **Alinari,** near the rail station at Via S. Zanobi 38R (© **055-280500;** www.alinarirental.com), rents bikes for 2.50€ per hour, or 12€ to 18€ per day, depending on the model. Also available are small-engined, rather loud motor scooters. Rentals cost from 10€ to 15€ per hour or 30€ to 55€ per day. Renters must be 18 or over and must leave a passport, a driver's license, and the number of a valid credit card. Alinari is open year-round Monday to Saturday 9am to 1pm and 3 to 6pm, and also Sunday April to October 10am to 1pm and 3 to 7pm.

By Car

Just forget it. Driving in Florence is hopeless—not only because of the snarled traffic and the maze of one-way streets, but also because much of what you've come to see is in a pedestrian-only zone. If you arrive by car, look for prominently posted blue signs with the letter P that will lead you to the nearest garage. Garage fees average 18€ to 25€ daily depending on the size of your car, although vans or luxury cars might cost as much as 35€.

The most centrally located garages are the **International Garage,** Via Palazzuolo 29 (© **055-282386;** www.internationalgarage.com); **Garage La Stazione,** Via Alamanni Luigi 3A (© **055-284768**); **Autoparking,** Via Fiesolana 19 (© **055-2477871**); and **Garage Anglo-Americano,** Via dei Barbadori 5 (© **055-214418**). If these are full, you can almost always find a space at the **Garage Porte Nuove,** Via delle Portenuove 21 (© **055-333355**).

You will, however, need a car to explore the surrounding countryside. Car-rental agencies include **Avis,** Borgo Ognissanti 128R (© **800/331-1212** in the U.S. and Canada, or 055-213629; www.avis.com); **Italy by Car,** Borgo Ognissanti 100R (© **055-213333;** www.italybycar.it); and **Hertz,** Via Maso Finiguerra 33 (© **800/654-3131** in the U.S. and Canada, or 055-2398205; www.hertz.com).

[FastFACTS] FLORENCE

Consulates The **U.S. Consulate** is at Lungarno Amerigo Vespucci 38 (℡ **055-266951**), open Monday to Friday from 9am to 12:30pm. The **U.K. Consulate** is at Lungarno Corsini 2 (℡ **055-284133**), near Piazza Santa Trinità, open Monday to Friday 9:30am to 12:30pm and 2:30 to 4:30pm. Citizens of other English-speaking countries, including **Canada, Australia,** and **New Zealand,** should contact their diplomatic representatives in Rome (see chapter 18).

Currency Exchange Local banks have the best rates, and most are open Monday through Friday from 8:30am to 1:30pm and 2:45 to 3:45pm. ATMs are found throughout the city.

Dentists & Doctors For a list of English-speaking doctors or dentists, consult your consulate (see above) or contact **Tourist Medical Service,** Via Lorenzo il Magnifico 59 (℡ **055-475411;** www. medicalservice.firenze.it). Visits without an appointment are possible only Monday to Friday 11am to noon and 5 to 6pm, and Saturday 11am to noon. After hours, an answering service gives names and phone numbers of dentists and doctors who are on duty.

Emergencies For fire, call ℡ **115;** for an ambulance, call ℡ **118;** for the police, call ℡ **113;** and for road service, call ℡ **803116.**

Hospitals Call the **General Hospital** of Santa Maria Nuova, Piazza Santa Maria Nuova 1 (℡ **055-27581**).

Internet Access You can check your messages or send e-mail at **Internet Train,** Via dell'Oriuolo 40R (℡ **055-2638968;** www. internettrain.it). Internet Train is open from Monday to Saturday 10am to 10pm, and Sunday 3 to 9pm.

Pharmacies The **Farmacia Molteni,** Via Calzaiuoli 7R (℡ **055-215472**), is open 24 hours.

Police Dial ℡ **113** in an emergency. English-speaking foreigners who want to see and talk to the police should go to the **Ufficio Immigrazione,** Via Della Fortezza 17 (℡ **055-4977602**), open Monday to Thursday 8:15 to 10am.

Post Office The **Central Post Office,** at Via Pellicceria 3, off Piazza della Repubblica (℡ **055-2736481;** www.poste.it), is open Monday to Friday 8:15am to 7pm, and Saturday 8:15am to 1:30pm. You can buy stamps and telephone cards at windows 21 and 22. A foreign exchange office is open during the same hours.

Safety Violent crimes are rare in Florence; crime consists mainly of pickpockets who frequent crowded tourist centers,

such as corridors in the Uffizi Galleries. Members of group tours who cluster together are often singled out as victims. Car thefts are relatively common: Don't leave your luggage in an unguarded car, even if it's locked in the trunk. Women should be especially careful in avoiding purse snatchers, some of whom grab a purse while whizzing by on a Vespa, often knocking the woman down. Documents such as passports and extra money are better stored in safes at your hotel, if available.

Telephone The **country code** for Italy is **39.** The **city code** for Florence is **055;** use this code when calling from *anywhere* outside or inside Italy— even within Florence (and you must now include the 0 every time, even when calling from abroad). See "Staying Connected" in chapter 18 for complete details on how to call Italy, how to place calls within Italy, and how to call home once you're in Italy.

Toilets Public toilets are found in most galleries, museums, bars and cafes, and restaurants, as well as bus, train, and air terminals. Usually they're designated as WC (water closet) or DONNE (women) or UOMINI (men). The most confusing designation is SIGNORI (gentlemen) and SIGNORE (ladies), so watch that final "i" and "e"!

WHERE TO STAY

For sheer charm and luxury, Florence's accommodations are among the finest in Europe; many grand old villas and palaces have been converted into hotels. There aren't too many cities where you can find a 15th- or 16th-century palace—tastefully decorated and most comfortable—rated a second-class *pensione* (guesthouse). Florence is equipped with hotels in all price ranges and with widely varying standards, comfort, service, and efficiency.

During summer, there simply aren't enough rooms to meet the demand, so **reserve well in advance.**

The most desirable place to stay in terms of shopping, nightlife, sightseeing, and restaurants is the historic heart on the Arno's right bank, especially in Centro and around the Duomo and Piazza della Signoria. Yes, this area is touristy and often expensive, but staying here is a lot better than staying on the outskirts—inadequate public transport makes commuting difficult. Driving into the center is impossible because of the heavy traffic and because major districts are pedestrian-only zones.

The cheapest lodgings in Centro are around the rail station; these are also the least desirable, with a few notable exceptions. The area directly around the Termini and Santa Maria Novella, though generally safe during the day, is the center of major drug dealing late at night and should be avoided then. This area isn't all budget lodgings, however; also here is Piazza Ognissanti (south of Piazza Santa Maria Novella toward the Arno), one of Florence's most fashionable squares and the home of the city's two most famous hotels. Also in the historic center, but less tourist-trodden and a bit more tranquil, is the area around Piazza San Marco and the university quarter.

Once you cross the Arno, lodgings are much scarcer, although there are places to stay, including some *pensioni.* In general, prices are lower across the Arno, and you'll be near one of the major attractions, the Pitti Palace. Many luxury hotels exist on the outskirts of Florence, as do cheaper boardinghouses. Again, these are acceptable alternatives if you don't mind the commute. As a final option, consider lodging in Fiesole, where it's cooler and much more tranquil. Bus no. 7 runs back and forth between Fiesole and Centro.

Near Giardino Della Gherardesca

VERY EXPENSIVE

Four Seasons Hotel Florence ★★★   The management calls this swank hotel, perhaps the grandest in Tuscany, "Italy's first city resort, with a park, a spa, and a pool." In spite of these features, it lies only a short walk from the historic center of Florence. Installed in the massively restored Palazzo della Gherardesca and a former convent, the hotel offers spectacular frescoes, museum-worthy sculptures, and Florentine artisanal works, with its oldest wing dating from the late 1440s. Its grounds are one of the largest private gardens in Florence.

Damask draperies, regal appointments in all the bedrooms, fabric-trimmed walls, majestic trees, an elegant spa, ceramic floors, rich marble bathrooms, luxurious beds and furnishings, pools equipped with phones, and wireless Internet access are just some of the features that make this perhaps the finest Four Seasons in Europe. The cuisine is reason enough to stay here. It's best summed up by a chef who said, "Our job is to exalt ingredients." If the Medicis should miraculously return to Florence, surely the clan would move in here.

Where to Stay in Florence

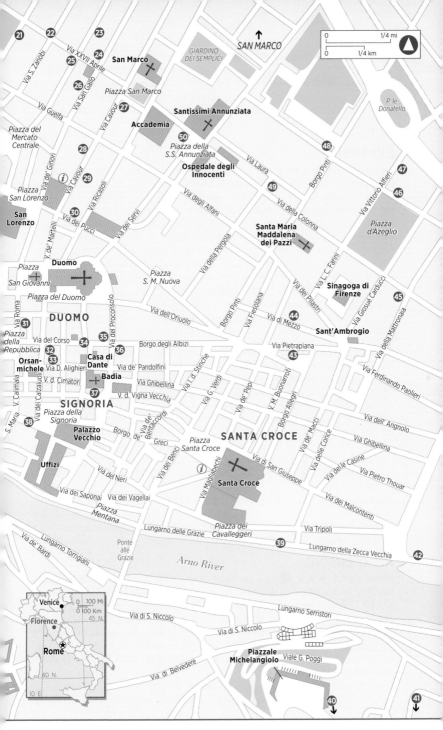

Borgo Pinti 99, 50121 Firenze. ✆ **800/819-5053** in the U.S. and Canada, or 055-26261. Fax 055-2626500. www.fourseasons.com. 116 units. 295€–850€ double; 750€–950€ junior suite; 1,000€–16,500€ suite. AE, DC, MC, V. Parking 50€. Bus: 4, 17, 33, or 70. **Amenities:** 3 restaurants; 2 bars; babysitting; children's programs; concierge; exercise room; outdoor pool; room service; spa. *In room:* A/C, TV/DVD, CD player, hair dryer, minibar, MP3 docking station, Wi-Fi (22€ per 24 hr.).

In Centro

EXPENSIVE

Hotel Tornabuoni Beacci ★ Near Piazza Santa Trìnita, this hotel occupies the three top floors of a 16th-century Strozzi family *palazzo*. Its public rooms have been furnished in an old Florentine style, with parquet floors, a fireplace, old paintings, murals, and rugs. Though renovated, it still has an air of old-fashioned gentility. The roof terrace is for late-afternoon drinks or breakfast; in summer, dinner, typically Florentine and Italian dishes, is also served here (except Aug, when it's closed). The guest rooms are moderately well furnished, and top-floor rooms, though a bit cramped, open onto views of the rooftops. The loveliest part of the place is a cozy reading room with a 1600s tapestry and a fireplace.

Via Tornabuoni 3, 50123 Firenze. ✆ **055-212645.** Fax 055-283594. www.tornabuonihotels.com. 28 units. 130€–280€ double; 210€–350€ suite. Rates include buffet breakfast. AE, DC, MC, V. Parking 24€–30€. Bus: C1, C2, 6, 11, or 36. **Amenities:** Restaurant; bar; babysitting; concierge; room service; Wi-Fi (3€ per hr., in lobby). *In room:* A/C, TV, hair dryer, minibar.

Palazzo Magnani Feroni ★★ A luxurious Renaissance palace from the 16th century, a 5-minute walk from Ponte Vecchio, has been converted from a nobleman's residence to a gem of boutique hotel with a dozen suites. Painstaking attention has been paid to the restoration, and the palace contains period furnishings. The suites themselves combine luxury and charm with modern conveniences. At dusk you can enjoy a drink on a panoramic terrace watching the sun set over Florence.

Breakfast is served in the spacious Murano Hall, lit by an original Murano crystal chandelier that once hung in the Palazzo Farnese in Rome. Each suite comes with a living room and a lush bathroom clad in marble with Bulgari beauty products.

Borgo San Frediano 5, 50124 Firenze. ✆ **055-2399544.** Fax 055-2608908. www.palazzo magnaniferoni.com. 12 units. 150€–550€ suite. Rates include breakfast. Parking: 42€. Bus: 6, 11, 36, or 68. **Amenities:** Bar; airport transfers (60€); babysitting; concierge; exercise room; room service. *In room:* A/C, TV/DVD/CD player, minibar, Wi-Fi (2€ per hr.).

INEXPENSIVE

Hotel Cellai ★★★ 🎁 In the heart of the historic zone, this 18th-century building is decorated in a 19th-century style. Small sofas and armchairs are placed here and there on the terra-cotta floors, creating the aura of a country manse. Most of the midsize to spacious bedrooms are in black-and-cream hues. Headboards are made of intertwined canes of black wood set in thick golden frames or padded and lined with a fabric in a black-and-white Kashmir floral pattern—or even padded in black with a shape evoking the black hats of the guards in pictures of Pinocchio's book for children.

Via 27 Aprile 14, 52R 50129 Firenze. ✆ **055-489291.** Fax 055-470387. www.hotelcellai.it. 55 units. 89€–189€ double. Rates include buffet breakfast. AE, DC, MC, V. Parking nearby 25€. Bus:

7, 20, 32, or 33. **Amenities:** Babysitting; bikes; room service. *In room:* A/C, TV, hair dryer, minibar, Wi-Fi (15€ per 24 hr.).

Near Piazza della Signoria
EXPENSIVE

In Piazza della Signoria ★★ 🏠   This B&B is a rare find lying only a few steps from the landmark square of Florence in a four-story *palazzo* that dates from the 14th century. Restoration was carried out with meticulous care by Alessandro and Sonia, who cater to lovers of Florentine art and elegance. Each room is uniquely furnished with antiques, and they are spacious and well lit, the most desirable of which overlook the piazza itself. Accommodations are named for a famous personality associated with Florence—Machiavelli, Giotto, even Dante or Beatrice. The Michelangelo Room, for example, has the original 18th-century wall frescoes.

Via dei Magazzini 2, 50122 Firenze. ✆ **055-2399546.** Fax 055-2676616. www.inpiazzadella signoria.com. 13 units. 160€–280€ double. Rates include buffet breakfast. AE, DC, MC, V. Parking 28€–30€. **Amenities:** Babysitting. *In room:* A/C, TV, CD player, hair dryer, Wi-Fi (free).

Relais Uffizi ★ 🏠   Next door to the Uffizi, this appropriately named inn is a real find and an unbeatable value. The restored 15th-century villa is imbued with homelike comfort and old-fashioned style, with antiques used liberally throughout the hotel. Attractively furnished midsize to spacious bedrooms open onto the landmark Piazza della Signoria, and the entrance is through the charming little walking lane, Chiasso del Buco. Bedrooms all contain marble bathrooms, and the most preferred rooms contain canopied beds. Considering its location, it's amazing that the Relais Uffizi isn't better known.

Chiasso del Buco 16, 50122 Firenze. ✆ **055-2676239.** Fax 055-2657909. www.relaisuffizi.it. 10 units. 100€–220€ double; 180€–260€ suite. Rates include buffet breakfast. AE, MC, V. Parking 30€. Bus: C1, C2, 23, or 71. **Amenities:** Bar; airport transfers (50€); babysitting; room service. *In room:* A/C, TV, hair dryer, minibar, Wi-Fi (free).

MODERATE

Best Western Hotel Rivoli ★   In the heart of Florence, only a few steps from Piazza della Signoria, this government-rated four-star hotel was originally a Franciscan monastery. The public areas and hallway have been returned to their original splendor, with coffered ceilings, cross-vaults, arches, and stone pillars. Bedrooms are elegantly furnished, and most of them overlook the inner garden and patio, with its open-air whirlpool and Jacuzzi. All of the rooms are tranquil and comfortable, some of them having a private balcony or terrace. The Carrera-marbled bathroom is furnished with everything from robes to scales and slippers.

Via della Scala 33, 50123 Firenze. ✆ **055-27861.** Fax 055-294041. www.hotelrivoli.it. 80 units. 104€–350€ double; 194€–500€ suite. Rates include buffet breakfast. AE, DC, MC, V. Parking 23€. Bus: 1, 2, 17, 22, or 23. **Amenities:** Restaurant; bar; airport transfers 20€; babysitting; concierge; Jacuzzi; room service. *In room:* A/C, TV, hair dryer, minibar, Wi-Fi (5€ per 24 hr.).

Near Piazza del Duomo
VERY EXPENSIVE

Savoy Hotel ★★ ☺   Everything is reborn at Florence's most legendary hotel, which opened in 1896. It's just a notch below the Westin Excelsior and the Grand in luxury, but it offers a great location for sightseers. Refined Italian elegance is the hallmark of this landmark, and its original architecture has been preserved through all its renovations. The art, however, seems to have been purchased by the yard. The corner accommodations are the most spacious and have the best views. Units on the second and fourth floors have small terraces.

Piazza della Repubblica 7, 50123 Firenze. ✆ **055-27351.** Fax 055-2735888. www.roccoforte hotels.com. 102 units (some with shower only). 520€–850€ double; from 1,300€ suite. Rates include buffet breakfast. AE, DC, MC, V. Parking 35€–50€. Bus: 22. **Amenities:** Restaurant; bar; babysitting; concierge; children's programs; exercise room; room service; Wi-Fi (25€ per 24 hr.). *In room:* A/C, TV, hair dryer, minibar.

EXPENSIVE

Hotel Calzaiuoli ★ Midway between the Duomo and the Uffizi, this hotel enjoys a fabulous location. Although the building is old (it was a home in the 1800s) and the location is historic, the interior has been modernized in a minimalist contemporary style. Its *pietra serena* (sandstone) staircase remains, however. This four-story hotel has an elevator to bring guests to their soundproof rooms, which are medium-size, with functional modern furnishings and good beds. Some rooms look out over the festive street scene (with its associated noise) or out back (either over the rooftops to the Bargello and Badia Towers or up to the Duomo's cupola). The recently renovated bathrooms are immaculately kept.

Via dei Calzaiuoli 6, 50123 Firenze. ✆ **055-212456.** Fax 055-268310. www.calzaiuoli.it. 45 units (half with shower only). 190€–350€ double. Rates include buffet breakfast. AE, DC, MC, V. Parking nearby 30€. Bus: 22, 36, or 37. **Amenities:** Airport transfers (45€); babysitting; room service. *In room:* A/C, TV, hair dryer, minibar, Wi-Fi (3€ per hr.).

MODERATE

Grand Hotel Cavour ★ Opposite the Bargello, this 13th-century palace stands on one of Florence's noisiest streets (even double-glazed windows can't quite block out the sounds). Check out the coved main lounge, with its frescoed ceiling and crystal chandelier, and the chapel now used as a dining room (the altar and confessional are still there). The guest rooms are traditional and comfortable but a little claustrophobic, though the bathrooms have more than enough shelf space. Every floor has a shared bathroom specially fitted for travelers with disabilities. At the front desk, the professional English-speaking staff can organize city tours upon request. The roof terrace, dubbed Michelangelo, offers incredible views.

Via del Proconsolo 3, 50122 Firenze. ✆ **055-266271.** Fax 055-218955. www.albergocavour.it. 105 units (some with shower only). 128€–300€ double; from 175€ triple. Rates include buffet breakfast. AE, DC, MC, V. Valet parking 40€. Bus: 14, 23, or 71. **Amenities:** Restaurant; babysitting; exercise room; room service; spa. *In room:* A/C, TV, hair dryer, minibar, Wi-Fi (free).

INEXPENSIVE

Albergo Firenze ✦ Finding an affordable hotel in overrun Florence seems to grow harder by the year, but this one is a find lying in the historic center only 150m (492 ft.) from the Duomo on one of the oldest city squares. Its exact age is unknown, but it received a wholesale renovation in 2006. Rising five floors, the Albergo stands next to a tower house where Dante's wife was born. The entrance is a bit bleak, but the bedrooms are comfortable if simply furnished.

Piazza Donati 4 (Via del Corso), 50122 Firenze. ☎ **055-268301.** Fax 055-212370. www.hotel firenze-fi.it. 57 units. 128€ double; 163€ triple. Rates include buffet breakfast. MC, V. Parking nearby 28€. Bus: 11 or 12. **Amenities:** Wi-Fi (2€ per 30 min., in lobby). *In room:* A/C, TV, hair dryer.

Hotel Colomba 🦋   On the third floor of an 18th-century building—there's an elevator—this good value hotel lies only 150m (490 ft.) from the Duomo. It combines modern comforts with Tuscan hospitality. The bedrooms are much more spacious than the usual European standard. Each is installed with soundproof glass, and seven of the units open onto views of the historic district. Guests are encouraged to use the library and reading room, with its collection of art books. A bar lounge is open 24 hours a day, and the breakfast room features an abundant buffet that is adjusted seasonally.

Via Cavour 21, 50100 Firenze. ☎ **055-289139.** Fax 055-265-285323. www.hotelcolomba.com. 14 units. 90€–160€ double. Rates include buffet breakfast. AE, DC, MC, V. Parking 23€. Bus: 1, 7, 10, or 17. **Amenities:** Bar; room service. *In room:* A/C, TV, hair dryer, minibar, Wi-Fi (free).

La Residenza del Proconsolo ★ 📱   This is one of the most elegant B&Bs in Florence, lying in front of the Duomo in the heart of the old city. The residence is on the second floor of a restored building from the 15th century, once the home of a noble family. The decor is in the Tuscan Renaissance style, called "arte povera," suggesting exposed wooden beams and terra-cotta flooring. In such an antique setting such modern conveniences as soundproof windows and a hydro-massage have been installed. The rooms are furnished with style, many beds draped in the four-poster style.

Via del Proconsolo 18, 50122 Firenze. ☎ **055-264-5657.** Fax 055-217501. www.proconsolo.com. 5 units. 96€–155€ double. Rates include continental breakfast. MC, V. Parking 30€. Bus: C1 or C2. *In room:* A/C, TV, minibar, Wi-Fi (free).

Pensione Maria Luisa de' Medici ★ 📱   This is an accommodations oddity with a lot of style and artistic flair, run by Angelo Sordi and his Welsh partner, Evelyn Morris. Charging some of the most affordable prices in Florence, they know how to take the bleakness out of a little *pensione.* The rooms are graced with frescoed portraits of the various Medici and filled with rare lamps, tables, and chairs, along with comfortable beds. The corridors are like a baroque museum of the 17th century, making for one of Florence's most unusual B&Bs. Bedrooms are most often spacious and can be shared with up to four guests. Reception is reached by a hike up three flights of stairs.

Via del Corso (btw. Via del Proconsolo and Via dei Calzaiuoli), 50122 Firenze. ☎ **055-280048.** 9 units. 95€ double. Rates include continental breakfast. No credit cards. Bus: C1, C2, 14, or 23. **Amenities:** Room service. *In room:* Hair dryer, no phone.

Residenza dei Pucci ★★ 📱   You get a room with a view of the cathedral's dome here, though it takes a bit of neck craning to take it in. It's not the view alone that sustains this elegantly restored 19th-century structure, a short walk from such attractions as the Uffizi and the Accademia. Large, high-ceilinged bedrooms are beautifully furnished with refined fabrics, and carpets are made of coconut fiber. The top-floor family suite is the most lavish accommodations, offering deluxe living in the heart of Florence. Each room is individually furnished, with lavish use made of French tapestries, four-poster beds, and marble bathrooms (only two have a full tubs, the rest have showers).

Via dei Pucci 9, 50122 Firenze. ✆ **055-281886.** Fax 055-264314. www.residenzadeipucci.com. 12 units. 80€–170€ double; 120€–250€ suite for 4. Rates include buffet breakfast. AE, DC, MC, V. Parking 25€. Bus: 1, 6, 14, or 17. **Amenities:** Room service. *In room:* A/C, TV, hair dryer, Wi-Fi (7€ per 24 hr.).

Near the Ponte Vecchio
VERY EXPENSIVE

Gallery Hotel Art ★   The Ferragamo family has long been celebrated for set-ting styles in Florence. Founding father Salvatore was known as shoemaker to the stars. One of the family's latest ventures is this unique boutique hotel near the Ponte Vecchio, which successfully combines the occasional antique with a sleek modern design sensibility. Its art theme stretches from the public areas to the pinstriped guest rooms. The rectilinear armchairs are in suede and pigskin, and the books in the library (over 400 volumes) were hand selected (often first edi-tions of English classics). The good-size bedrooms sport contemporary design, with leather headboards, fine linens, and Bulgari products in the well-main-tained, tiled bathrooms.

Vicolo dell'Oro 5, 50123 Firenze. ✆ **055-27263.** Fax 055-268557. www.lungarnohotels.com. 74 units. 310€–480€ double; from 660€ suite. Rates include buffet breakfast. AE, DC, MC, V. Parking 35€. Bus: 1, 10, 11, or 17. **Amenities:** Restaurant; bar; babysitting; exercise room; room service; sauna; Wi-Fi (free, in lobby). *In room:* A/C, TV, hair dryer, minibar.

MODERATE

Casa Howard ★★   This hotel lies in a restored *palazzo* next to the Santa Maria Novella Pharmacy, from which the hotel secures the most divine pome-granate and mint soaps. The midsize rooms are a bit quirky, with stylized themes: If you're the intellectual type, you'll enjoy the Library Room, which is filled with wall-to-wall reading. Favorite rooms include the Fireplace Room, with two pic-ture windows. The three different rooms that comprise the Oriental Room are filled with objects collected by the owners in Asia, including a gigantic lacquer red shower. The Black and White Room lives up to its name, right down to a zebra armchair, and the small, cozy Hidden Room is dressed in sensual red. The best unit is the Drawing Room, with an ancient Venetian mosaic marble floor with picture windows.

Via della Scala 18, 50123 Firenze. ✆ **06-6992-4555.** www.casahoward.com. 13 units. 110€–260€ double. AE, DC, MC, V. Parking nearby 25€. Bus: C1, C2, 6, 9, 11, 36, 37, or 68. **Amenities:** Bar; babysitting; concierge; room service. *In room:* A/C, TV, hair dryer, Wi-Fi (free).

Hotel Torre Guelfa ★★   One reason to stay in this atmospheric, renovated hotel is to drink in the 360-degree view from the hotel's 13th-century tower, the tallest privately owned tower in Florence's *centro storico*. Although you're just two steps from the Ponte Vecchio (and equidistant from the Duomo), you'll want to put sightseeing on hold and linger in your comfy canopied iron bed; your room is made even more inviting by pastel-washed walls and paisley carpeting. (For a view similar to the medieval tower's, ask for room no. 15 with its huge private terrace.)

Borgo SS. Apostoli 8 (btw. Via dei Tornabuoni and Via Per Santa Maria), 50123 Firenze. ✆ **055-2396338.** Fax 055-2398577. www.hoteltorreguelfa.com. 22 units. 110€–250€ double; 160€–260€ suite. Rates include buffet breakfast. AE, MC, V. Parking nearby 30€. Bus: C1, C2, 6, 11, 36, or 37. **Amenities:** Bar; babysitting; room service; Wi-Fi (2€ per hr., in lobby). *In room:* A/C, TV, hair dryer, minibar.

INEXPENSIVE

Hotel Cestelli   This small hotel in a restored 12th-century palace occupies a rare corner in the heart of Florence 100m (330 ft.) from the Ponte Vecchio and a block from the Arno. In the 16th century, it was home to the bishop of Florence, and it once housed a relative of Lorenzo il Magnifico. Because of its shortage of plumbing, it is granted only one star by the government. But because of its location, maintenance, and comfort, it is highly recommendable, run by a Florentine and Japanese couple that houses you at a very reasonable price. The rooms are spacious and warmly decorated, and much of the old style is still evoked with antiques, prints, and paintings. No two rooms are alike, and some of the doubles are big enough for three or four family members.

Borgo Santissimi Apostoli 25, 50123 Firenze. ⓒ/fax **055-214213.** www.hotelcestelli.com. 8 units (3 with bathroom). 70€–100€ double with bathroom; 50€–80€ double without bathroom; 80€–115€ suite with bathroom. MC, V. Parking 30€. Bus: C1, C2, or D. *In room:* No phone.

Near Piazza Santa Maria Novella & the Train Station

VERY EXPENSIVE

Grand Hotel ★★   The Grand is a bastion of luxury, and its Belle Epoque lounges are truly grand. The guest rooms have a refined elegance meant to evoke 15th-century Florence, with silks, brocades, frescoes, and real or reproduction antiques; the most desirable units overlook the Arno. The large bathrooms, adorned in two types of Italian marble, are filled with amenities such as plush bathrobes, separate phone lines, and designer bidets.

Piazza Ognissanti 1, 50123 Firenze. ⓒ **800/325-3589** in the U.S. and Canada, or 055-27161. Fax 055-217400. www.luxurycollection.com/grandflorence. 107 units. 430€–1,248€ double; from 2,800€ suite. AE, DC, MC, V. Parking from 45€. Bus: 6 or 17. **Amenities:** Restaurant; 2 bars; airport transfers 83€; babysitting; concierge; exercise room; room service. *In room:* A/C, TV, hair dryer, minibar, Wi-Fi (15€ per 24 hr.).

Grand Hotel Villa Medici ★★   This old-time favorite occupies an 18th-century Medici palace 2 blocks southwest of the train station. Of all the government-rated five-star hotels of Florence, it is the only one with its own pool and health club. Most rooms have twin beds. The most peaceful units front the garden, but during the day there's noise from the convent school next door. We prefer the sixth-floor accommodations because they open onto terraces. Out back is a private garden, not Florence's finest, but with one of the only pools in town.

Via il Prato 42, 50123 Firenze. ⓒ **055-277171.** Fax 055-2381336. www.villamedicihotel.com. 103 units. 170€–500€ double; 350€–600€ junior suite; from 500€ suite. AE, DC, MC, V. Parking 30€–50€. Bus: 1, 9, 14, 17, 23, 36, or 37. **Amenities:** Restaurant; babysitting; exercise room; outdoor pool; room service; sauna. *In room:* A/C, TV, hair dryer, minibar, Wi-Fi (3€ per hr.).

J.K. Place ★★★ 🎁   An artistic statement of refinement and taste, this hotel is unique in Florence—in fact, it calls itself "a museum of the soul, an archive of experiences." Close to the Piazza Santa Maria Novella, the Florentine house blends an elegant atmosphere of the past with modern conveniences. Statues, grace notes, and even fireplaces aglow in chilly weather help create a cozy, intimate ambience. Bedrooms are beautifully designed units containing the likes of four-poster beds and Louis XVI fireplaces, evoking the home of an aristocrat in Florence's past life. Breakfast is served in the courtyard covered with glass, and on the top floor is a terrace for relaxing.

Piazza Santa Maria Novella 7, 50123 Firenze. ℂ **055-264-5181.** Fax 055-265-8387. www.jkplace. com. 20 units. 350€–500€ double; 650€–1,000€ suite. Rates include buffet breakfast. AE, DC, MC, V. Parking 35€. Bus: 14 or 23. **Amenities:** Bar; babysitting; concierge; room service; access to nearby spa. *In room:* A/C, TV/DVD, hair dryer, minibar, Wi-Fi (free).

Westin Excelsior ★★★ ☺   This luxury address is one of the first choices for those who like glamour and glitz. The sumptuousness will bowl you over (if the high prices don't get you first). Near the Ponte Vecchio and the Uffizi, the hotel boasts the best service in town. Part of the hotel was once owned by Carolina Bonaparte, Napoleon's sister; the old *palazzi* were unified in 1927 and decorated with colored marbles, walnut furniture, Oriental rugs, and neoclassical frescoes. The opulent guest rooms have 19th-century Florentine antiques, sumptuous fabrics, "Heavenly Beds," and two-line phones. Accommodations come in a variety of configurations. The rooms on the top floor have balconies overlooking the Arno and the Ponte Vecchio.

Piazza Ognissanti 3, 50123 Firenze. ℂ **888/625-5144** in the U.S. and Canada, or 055-27151. Fax 055-210278. www.starwoodhotels.com. 171 units. 273€–993€ double; from 2,250€ junior suite. AE, DC, MC, V. Parking 30€. Bus: 6 or 17. **Amenities:** Restaurant; bar; babysitting; concierge; children's programs; exercise room; room service. *In room:* A/C, TV, hair dryer, minibar, Wi-Fi (16€ per 24 hr.).

EXPENSIVE

Montebello Splendid ★★   Full of charm and grace, this government-rated five-star boutique hotel is a hit. Enter a splendid garden in front of this restored palace, with a columned Tuscan-style *loggia,* and be ushered into a regal palace with Italian marble, stuccowork, and luminous niches. The decor provides a serene and harmonious setting, all in impeccably good taste. Each of the midsize to spacious bedrooms is individually decorated and soundproof—with a lavish use of parquet, marble, soft carpeting, and elegant fabrics—and deluxe beds and first-class bathrooms are clad in marble and equipped with hydromassages, among other features.

Via Garibaldi 14, 50123 Firenze. ℂ **055-27471.** Fax 055-2747700. www.montebellosplendid. com. 61 units. 216€–580€ double; 450€–920€ suite. Rates include buffet breakfast. AE, DC, MC, V. Parking 30€. Bus: 13. **Amenities:** Restaurant; bar; babysitting; concierge; exercise room; room service. *In room:* A/C, TV, hair dryer, Wi-Fi (10€ per 24 hr.).

MODERATE

Hotel Ariele   A block from the Arno, the Ariele is a corner villa that has been converted into a roomy *pensione.* The late-1700s building is architecturally impressive, with large salons and lofty ceilings. The furnishings, however, combine the antique with the functional. The guest rooms are a grab bag of comfort; you can still get a good night's sleep even if the beds are a bit old (they're still firm). Although breakfast is the only meal served, the staff will provide you with the names of some restaurants nearby, where the hotel's guests receive discounts.

Via Magenta 11, 50123 Firenze. ✆ **055-211509.** Fax 055-268521. www.hotelariele.it. 39 units (10 with shower only). 90€–170€ double; 110€–200€ triple. Rates include buffet breakfast. AE, DC, MC, V. Parking 12€. Bus: 1, 12, or 26. **Amenities:** Bar; babysitting; room service; Wi-Fi (free, in lobby). *In room:* A/C, TV, hair dryer.

Hotel Bellettini 🍴 The *palazzo* was built in the 1300s, with a history of inn-keeping at least 300 years old. This place is so traditional—with terra-cotta floors, beamed ceilings, and touches of stained glass—that you expect Henry James or Elizabeth Barrett Browning to check in at any minute. The rooms are plain (some are almost stark) but comfortable, with queen-size or double beds. Many have sweeping views of Florence. Only two rooms per floor share the corridor bathrooms, so you'll rarely have to wait in line. A small, charming annex, less than a 2-minute walk from the hotel's main core, contains five of the best rooms in the hotel.

Via De' Conti 7, 50123 Firenze. ✆ **055-213561.** Fax 055-283551. www.hotelbellettini.com. 32 units, 28 with bathroom (shower only). 59€–110€ double without bathroom, 65€–145€ double with bathroom. Rates include buffet breakfast. AE, DC, MC, V. Parking 25€. Bus: 1, 9, 14, 17, 23, 36, or 37. **Amenities:** Bar; room service; Wi-Fi (free, in lobby). *In room:* A/C, TV (in annex), minibar.

Hotel Malaspina A 10-minute walk north of the Duomo, this three-story hotel occupies a 19th-century structure (before that, it was a dorm for students at a nearby dentistry school). The interior has been renovated and filled with traditional furniture that fits gracefully into the high-ceilinged public rooms and midsize to large guest rooms. The windows are big, and floors are covered in glazed or terra-cotta tiles.

Piazza Indipendenza 24, 50129 Firenze. ✆ **055-489869.** Fax 055-474809. www.malaspinahotel. it. 31 units (some with shower only). 110€–230€ double; 130€–298€ triple. Rates include buffet breakfast. AE, DC, MC, V. Parking 25€–30€. Bus: 1, 20, or 23. **Amenities:** Babysitting; bikes. *In room:* A/C, TV, hair dryer, minibar, Wi-Fi (free).

Hotel Vasari ★ 🍴 This inn enjoys a rather literary history; for several years, it was the home of 19th-century French poet Alphonse de La Martine. Built in the 1840s as a home, it was a run-down hotel until 1993, when its owners poured money into its renovation and upgraded it. Its three stories are connected by elevator, and the rooms are comfortable, albeit somewhat spartan. Nonetheless, the beds are firm and the linen is crisp. The tiled bathrooms are small but immaculate. Some of the public areas retain their elaborate vaulting.

Via B. Cennini 9–11, 50123 Firenze. ✆ **055-212753.** Fax 055-294246. www.hotelvasari.com. 27 units (shower only). 155€ double; 210€ triple. Rates include buffet breakfast. AE, DC, MC, V. Parking 15€. Bus: 4, 7, 10, 13, 14, 23, or 71. **Amenities:** Bar; babysitting; room service; Wi-Fi (free, in lobby). *In room:* A/C, TV, hair dryer, minibar.

INEXPENSIVE

Hotel Albion ★★ 🎁 A true gem. Housed in a lovely 19th-century English neoclassical *palazzo*, the family owned Hotel Albion is the sort of place you'll come back to again and again. The rooms, some of which have balconies, are charmingly simple and spotless, and the hallways, reception area, and breakfast room are decorated with the family's eclectic art collection. The location, a short walk from the train station at Santa Maria Novella, the Duomo, and other major attractions, is ideal. But the big draw here is the service. Owner Massimo and his daughter Sara will happily reserve museum tickets for you long before you arrive and provide outstanding restaurant advice (and take care of the reservations).

Via il Prato 22R, 50123 Firenze. ✆ **055-214171.** www.hotelalbion.it. 80€–166€ double. Rates include continental breakfast. AE, MC, V. **Amenities:** Babysitting; bikes. *In room:* A/C, TV, hair dryer, Wi-Fi (free).

Hotel Annabella ☺   Near the Santa Maria Novella rail station, within an easy walk of the Duomo, this is a well-run and relatively undiscovered family hotel. It's installed in a turn-of-the-20th-century *palazzo.* At the second-floor reception, Mrs. Vittoria and her son Simone welcome you to Florence and will house you well in this elevator building. There is nothing overly adorned here, but the rooms are nicely furnished, each one midsize with comfortable beds resting on tile floors and including such extras as writing desks. Each unit comes with a small bathroom with shower. Many of the rooms are large enough to house three or four guests, making them ideal for families.

Via Fiume 5, 50123 Firenze. ✆ **055-281877.** Fax 055-2396814. www.hotelannabella.it. 15 units. 75€–185€ double; 90€–225€ triple. AE, DC, MC, V. Parking 20€. Bus: 1, 6, 11, or 17. **Amenities:** Bar; babysitting; room service. *In room:* A/C, TV, hair dryer, Wi-Fi (5€ per 4 hr.).

Hotel Anna's 🔥   As the low-cost Locanda Anna, this little *pensione* attracted budget-conscious Frommer's readers for years. Now it's been completely refurbished and turned into a government-rated two-star hotel with modern conveniences. It's close to the train station of Santa Maria Novella and the major monuments of Florence, most of which lie within walking distance. Loretta Bernardi and her son, Matteo, welcome you to this little bastion of comfort and hospitality. Sitting atop the heart of the 19th-century Palazzo Barbera, bedrooms here are fully renovated, with modern furnishings and a tasteful decor, complete with a small bathroom with shower. Most units come with a writing desk.

Via Faenza 56, 50123 Firenze. ✆ **055-2302714.** Fax 055-2647780. www.hotelannas.com. 7 units. 60€–130€ double; 3rd bed 20€. AE, DC, MC, V. Bus: C1, C2, 6, 9, 11, 36, 37, or 68. *In room:* A/C, TV, hair dryer, Wi-Fi (free).

Hotel Mario's ★ 🔥   Two blocks from the rail station, this is a winning choice. It's on the first floor of an old building that has been a hotel since 1872, when the *Room with a View* crowd started arriving in search of the glory of the Renaissance. This spotless, homelike place has been completely restored and furnished in Florentine style. Although you'll find cheaper inns in Florence, the service and hospitality make Mario's worth your euros. The guest rooms aren't large but are furnished with taste; wrought-iron headboards frame firm beds. Several rooms open onto a small private garden. The bathrooms are neat, with shelf space. Breakfast is the only meal served; fresh flowers and fruit are put out daily.

Via Faenza 89, 50123 Firenze. ✆ **055-216801.** Fax 055-212039. www.hotelmarios.com. 16 units (shower only). 98€–165€ double; 119€–220€ triple. Rates include buffet breakfast. AE, DC, MC, V. Valet parking 28€–30€. Bus: 10, 13, or 17. **Amenities:** Bar. *In room:* A/C, TV, hair dryer, minibar.

Stella Mary Hotel 🔥   Near the train station in the heart of Florence, this well-kept hotel on the third floor (second floor to Europeans) of a classic Florentine-style building (serviced by an elevator) is run by English-speaking Vittoria Tubi. The location is a 3-minute walk from either the train station or the San Lorenzo market and its landmark church. The midsize to spacious bedrooms are well furnished, each comfortable and neatly kept, with a private bathroom with shower. The best rooms also contain a bathtub and a private balcony. There is no nightly curfew.

Via Fiume 5, 50123 Firenze. ✆ **055-215694.** Fax 055-264206. www.hotelstellamary.com. 15 units. 65€–130€ double; 85€–153€ triple. Rates include buffet breakfast. AE, MC, V. Parking in nearby garage 25€. Bus: 14 or 17. **Amenities:** Bar; room service. *In room:* A/C, TV, Wi-Fi (4.50€ per hr.).

Near Piazza San Marco

EXPENSIVE

Carolus Hotel ★ This hotel lies inside an ancient neoclassical *palazzo*. Within easy reach of the city's major monuments and its best shops, the Carolus was recently renovated, its midsize and well-furnished bedrooms much improved with upgraded furniture. Accommodations open onto many of the best-known churches and monuments of Florence, with the hills of Fiesole on view in the background. Everything is decorated with sleek modern Italian styling.

Via XXVII Aprile 3, 50129 Firenze. ✆ **055-2645539.** Fax 055-2645550. www.carolushotel.com. 53 units. 83€–320€ double; 160€–390€ triple. Rates include buffet breakfast. AE, DC, MC, V. Parking in garage 26€. Bus: 1, 7, or 25. **Amenities:** Bar; babysitting; room service. *In room:* A/C, TV, hair dryer, minibar, Wi-Fi (free).

MODERATE

Antica Dimora Firenze ★ 🎁 A stay here is somewhat like living in a private Florentine home. It's small but choice and you must check in by 7pm before the staff heads home. You're given a key to the front door, in addition to one to your room. The place is tastefully and comfortably decorated with a lavish use of pastels throughout, which brightens the rooms considerably. The most desirable accommodations contain a private terrace. Close to the church of San Marco, the *residenza* is in an old palace dating from the 17th century, but it has been restored to its historical splendor.

Via San Gallo 72, 50129 Firenze. ✆ **055-4627296.** Fax 055-4634450. www.anticadimorafirenze. it. 6 units. 100€–150€ double. Rates include buffet breakfast. No credit cards. Parking nearby 20€. Bus: 5, 15, or 20. **Amenities:** Bar. *In room:* A/C, TV/DVD, hair dryer, minibar.

Hotel Casci ☺ This is a well-run little hotel 183m (600 ft.) from the rail station and 91m (300 ft.) from Piazza del Duomo. As one reader wrote, "For location, location, location, there's nothing better in Florence." It dates from the 15th century, and some of the public rooms (such as the breakfast room) feature the original frescoes. Gioacchino Rossini, the famous composer of *The Barber of Seville* and *William Tell*, lived here from 1851 to 1855. The hotel is both traditional and modern. The guest rooms are comfortably furnished, and every year, four or five units are upgraded and renovated. The few units overlooking the street are soundproof. Some very spacious rooms in the rear can comfortably house four to five overnighters.

Via Cavour 13, 50129 Firenze. ✆ **055-211686.** Fax 055-2396461. www.hotelcasci.com. 24 units. 80€–150€ double; 100€–190€ triple; 120€–230€ quad. Rates include buffet breakfast. AE, DC, MC, V. Parking 25€. Bus: 1, 7, 25, or 33. Closed Jan 25–31. **Amenities:** Bar; babysitting; Internet (free, in lobby). *In room:* A/C, TV/DVD, hair dryer, minibar, Wi-Fi (free).

Hotel Morandi alla Crocetta ★ 👜 This charming small hotel 2 blocks from the Accademia is run by Paolo Antuono. Although built in 1511 as a convent, it contains everything needed for a *pensione* and is on a back street near a university building. The rooms (small to medium in size) have been tastefully restored, filled with framed 19th-century needlework, beamed ceilings, and antiques. In the best Tuscan tradition, the tall windows are sheltered from the sun with heavy draperies. You register in an austere salon filled with Persian carpets.

Via Laura 50, 50121 Firenze. ✆ **055-2344747.** Fax 055-2480954. www.hotelmorandi.it. 10 units (shower only). 110€–220€ double; 130€–295€ triple. AE, DC, MC, V. Parking 20€. Bus: 6, 7, 10, 17, 31, or 32. **Amenities:** Room service. *In room:* A/C, TV, hair dryer, minibar, Wi-Fi (8€ per 24 hr.).

Loggiato dei Serviti ★ The amazing thing about this hotel is that it accepts paying guests at all—you'd think it could house a museum. But here you can wander through the premises of what was built in 1527 by Antonio da Sangallo as a monastery (a symmetrical foil for the Ospedale degli Innocenti across the square); it has been a hotel since the early 1900s. Once a run-down student hotel, it was transformed and upgraded. The guest rooms contain modern amenities but have been artfully designed to emphasize the building's origins, with beamed or vaulted ceilings, terra-cotta floors, and antique furnishings.

Piazza SS. Annunziata 3, 50122 Firenze. ✆ **055-289592.** Fax 055-289595. www.loggiatodei servitihotel.it. 38 units (some with shower only). 95€–180€ double; from 160€ suite. Rates include buffet breakfast. AE, DC, MC, V. Parking 24€–30€. Bus: 1, 7, or 17. **Amenities:** Bar. *In room:* A/C, TV, hair dryer, minibar, Wi-Fi (free).

Orto de'Medici This hotel is within a 10-minute walk of the Duomo, yet this residential neighborhood seems a world away from the crush in the tourist district. The hotel occupies four high-ceilinged floors of a 19th-century apartment building, and its elegantly faded public rooms evoke the kind of family run *pensione* you'd expect in a Merchant/Ivory film. The homey rooms contain nice Florentine decorative touches and an eclectic array of semiantique furniture. The tiny tiled bathrooms are neatly kept.

Via S. Gallo 30, 50129 Firenze. ✆ **055-483427.** Fax 055-461276. www.ortodeimedici.it. 31 units (some with shower only). 89€–259€ double; 119€–289€ triple. Rates include buffet breakfast. AE, DC, MC, V. Parking in nearby garage 30€. Bus: 1, 6, 7, 10, 11, 17, 25, 33, 67, or 68. **Amenities:** Bikes; room service. *In room:* A/C, TV, hair dryer, minibar, Wi-Fi (in some, free).

INEXPENSIVE

Hotel Cimabue ★ This hotel was built in 1904 as a Tuscan-style *palazzo*, and the most charming guest rooms are the six with original frescoed ceilings. Four of these are one floor above street level, and the other two are on the ground floor. Rooms have comfortable beds and range from small to medium in size. The bathrooms are not spacious but have adequate shelf space. The hotel was recently renovated and has turn-of-the-20th-century antiques that correspond to the building's age. Its Belgian-Italian management extends a warm multicultural welcome.

Via B. Lupi 7, 50129 Firenze. ✆ **055-471989.** Fax 055-4630906. www.hotelcimabue.it. 16 units (shower only). 59€–210€ double. Rates include buffet breakfast. AE, DC, MC, V. Parking 24€. Bus: 17. **Amenities:** Babysitting; room service. *In room:* A/C (in most units), TV, hair dryer, Wi-Fi (free).

Hotel Europa Two long blocks north of the Duomo, this hotel occupies a 16th-century building. The Europa has been family run since 1925. Despite the antique look of the simple exterior, much of the interior has been modernized, although it contains plenty of homey touches. All but four of the guest rooms overlook the back, usually opening onto a view of Giotto's campanile and Brunelleschi's dome; those facing the street are noisier but benefit from double-glazed windows. The rooms are small but decently furnished, with tiny but well-organized bathrooms.

Via Cavour 14, 50129 Firenze. ✆ **055-2396715.** Fax 055-268984. www.webhoteleuropa.com. 20 units (shower only). 77€–160€ double. Rates include buffet breakfast. AE, MC, V. Parking in nearby garage 24€. Bus: 1, 7, 25, or 33. **Amenities:** Bar; babysitting; room service. *In room:* A/C, TV, fridge, hair dryer, Wi-Fi (free).

Piccolo Hotel 🏄 Conveniently located near the railway station and all the top sights, this town-house hotel offers an intimate atmosphere. You'll feel at home, thanks to Ms. Angeloni, the English-speaking manager, who's a fount of advice about the city. Rooms are medium in size; some have balconies, while all have simple, tasteful furniture and floral bed linens. Bathrooms are a little small but well organized and neat. The only meal served is the generous buffet breakfast, but the hotel is surrounded by good restaurants.

Via S. Gallo 51, 50129 Firenze. ✆ **055-475519.** Fax 055-474515. www.piccolohotelfirenze.com. 10 units (shower only). 75€–100€ double; 90€–120€ triple. Rates include buffet breakfast. AE, MC, V. Parking nearby 15€. Bus: 1, 7, 11, or 17. **Amenities:** Bar; babysitting; bikes; room service. *In room:* A/C, TV, Wi-Fi (free).

On or near Piazza Massimo d'Azeglio

Piazza Massimo d'Azeglio is a 10- to 15-minute walk northeast of the historic core.

VERY EXPENSIVE

Hotel Regency ★★★ The Regency is a bastion of taste and exclusivity. It lies a bit apart from the shopping-and-sightseeing center, but it's only a 15-minute stroll from the cathedral and can be quickly reached by taxi or bus. This intimate hideaway, filled with stained glass, paneled walls, and reproduction antiques, offers exquisite accommodations, including some special rooms on the top floor with terraces. Accommodations boast numerous extras, such as double glazing, thick wool carpeting, coffered or beamed ceilings, rich fabrics, and private thermostats.

Piazza Massimo d'Azeglio 3, 50121 Firenze. ✆ **055-245247.** Fax 055-2346735. www.regency-hotel.com. 34 units. 200€–500€ double; 400€–881€ suite. Rates include buffet breakfast. AE, DC, MC, V. Parking 30€. Bus: 6, 31, or 32. **Amenities:** Restaurant; bar; airport transfers (80€); babysitting; concierge; room service. *In room:* A/C, TV, hair dryer, minibar, Wi-Fi (10€ per hr.).

EXPENSIVE

Hotel J and J ★★ A 5-minute walk from Santa Croce, this is a charming hotel. It was built in the 16th century as a monastery and you'll find many sitting areas throughout, including a flagstone-covered courtyard with stone columns and a salon with vaulted ceilings and preserved ceiling frescoes. The guest rooms combine an unusual mix of modern furniture with the original beamed ceilings. The suites usually contain sleeping lofts, and some have rooftop balconies overlooking Florence's historic core. Most of the rooms are spacious.

Via di Mezzo 20, 50121 Firenze. ✆ **055-26312.** Fax 055-240282. www.jandjhotel.net. 20 units. 105€–230€ double; 185€–280€ junior suite; 215€–340€ suite. Rates include buffet breakfast.

AE, DC, MC, V. Parking 30€. Bus: C1 or C2. **Amenities:** Bar; babysitting; room service; Wi-Fi (free, in lobby). *In room:* A/C, TV, hair dryer, minibar.

INEXPENSIVE

Albergo Losanna   The Losanna, a family run place off Viale Antonio Gramsci, offers utter simplicity and cleanliness, as well as insight into a typical Florentine atmosphere—the hotel seemingly belongs in the 1800s. The rooms are homey and well kept, although the private bathrooms are cramped, without enough shelf space. The hall bathrooms are large and quite adequate—you rarely have to wait in line.

Via Vittorio Alfieri 9, 50121 Firenze. ✆ **055-245840.** Fax 055-2480264. www.albergolosanna. com. 8 units, 3 with bathroom (shower only). 38€–45€ double without bathroom, 45€–65€ with bathroom; 65€ triple without bathroom, 75€–85€ with bathroom. AE, MC, V. Parking 20€. Bus: 6, 31, or 32. *In room:* No phone.

Near Piazza Santa Croce

EXPENSIVE

Plaza Hotel Lucchesi ★   Often a favorite with tour groups, this hotel dates from 1860 but has been renovated many times since. It lies along the Arno, a 10-minute walk from the Duomo and a few paces from Santa Croce. Its interior decor includes lots of glossy mahogany, acres of marble, and masses of fresh flowers. The guest rooms, ranging from medium to spacious, are well kept and comfortable. Twenty of them open onto balconies with views.

Lungarno della Zecca Vecchia 38, 50122 Firenze. ✆ **055-26236.** Fax 055-2480921. www.plaza lucchesi.it. 97 units (some with shower only). 134€–415€ double; 251€–485€ suite. Rates include buffet breakfast. AE, DC, MC, V. Parking 27€. Bus: C1, C2, 13, 14, or 23. **Amenities:** Restaurant; babysitting; concierge; room service. *In room:* A/C, TV/DVD (in some), hair dryer, minibar, Wi-Fi (free).

MODERATE

Residenza Casanuova ★ ✐   A recently renovated mansion from 1871, this is one of the best B&Bs in Florence, enjoying a prime location near Piazza Santa Croce. It's filled with all the modern conveniences yet retains its original antique architectural style. English-speaking Beatrice and Massimiliano Gorgi are the young and hospitable owners, who will do much to make a stay memorable for their guests. The residence occupies the entire second floor of the building with a terrace open to views of the monuments and hills of Florence, on which guests often sit to enjoy the sunset and a glass of Tuscan wine. Rooms have lots of individual character and a warm decor.

Villa della Mattonaia 21, 50121 Firenze. ✆ **055-2343413.** Fax 338-5450758. www.residenza casanuova.it. 5 units. 98€–169€. Rates include buffet breakfast. MC, V. Bus: 6, 14, 23, or C2. *In room:* A/C, TV, fridge, hair dryer.

Ritz Hotel ★ 📦   Along the Arno, the Ritz of Florence has nothing to do with the pricey palaces of London or Paris. This Ritz is a family run hotel that has been given a new lease on life by its owners, who have upgraded it and turned it into a reasonably priced alternative in a high-priced city. They have restored and redecorated, offering well-furnished, medium-size bedrooms, many with carpets, others with wood and marble. It's a short walk to the Ponte Vecchio or the Uffizi, and the Ritz enjoys a location right on the river, with nice views.

Lugarno Zecca Vecchia 24, 50122 Firenze. © **055-2340650.** Fax 055-240863. www.hotelritz. net. 32 units (some with shower only). 70€–180€ double; 140€–280€ suite. Rates include buffet breakfast. AE, DC, MC, V. Parking 25€. Bus: 23. **Amenities:** Bar; babysitting; Internet (free, in lobby); room service. *In room:* A/C, TV, hair dryer, minibar.

INEXPENSIVE

Locanda de' Ciompi ★ 🛏️   In the Santa Croce neighborhood, this is a real discovery. A tiny inn, it has been installed in a restored building from the 17th century. All of the individually decorated bedrooms are furnished in an antique Florentine style, offering both comfort and charm, each coming with a private bathroom. Except for one room, all the bathrooms are en suite. In room no. 2, the bathroom is private but outside the door. Color is used effectively here, with a blue room or a green room, even a beautiful pink room. Most of the accommodations open onto views of Florentine cityscapes.

Via Pietrapiana 28, 50121 Firenze. © **055-2638034.** Fax 055-2638037. www.locandadeciompi. it. 5 units. 70€–120€ double. Rates include continental breakfast. MC, V. Parking 25€–30€. **Amenities:** Room service. *In room:* A/C, TV, minibar (in some).

Across the Arno

Hotel Villa Carlotta ★ 🛏️   This hotel from the Edwardian age was built as a villa and bought in the 1950s by Carlotta Schulmann. Her lavish renovations have transformed it into one of Florence's most charming smaller hotels. It's still very homey and stands in a residential neighborhood. Rooms have silk wallpaper and bedspreads, reproduction antiques, safes, and crystal chandeliers; each has a view of the garden. The bathrooms are exceedingly well maintained. The hotel is only a 10-minute walk from the Ponte Vecchio; by taxi, it's a 5-minute ride.

Via Michele di Lando 3, 50125 Firenze. © **055-2336134.** Fax 055-2336147. www.hotelvilla carlotta.it. 32 units (some with shower only). 94€–320€ double; 125€–385€ triple. Rates include buffet breakfast. AE, DC, MC, V. Free parking. Bus: 11, 36, or 37. **Amenities:** Restaurant; bar; babysitting; bikes; room service. *In room:* A/C, TV, hair dryer, minibar, Wi-Fi (free).

UNA Hotel Vittoria ★★ 🛏️   Is this a boutique hotel or a disco? You're not sure as you enter and are immediately sucked into the world of "wonder boy" designer Fabio Novembre. The modern, innovative modular design comes at you instantly in a series of swirls, rings, and spirals. A floor-to-ceiling floral mosaic encases the reception desk. The bedrooms are adorned with black-leather walls and fiber-optic lights. The sleek lines of the decor are so avant-garde that they appear to have been created deep into the 21st century. Depending on your concept of privacy, you'll either love or hate the bathrooms, which are located right by the doorway to each room and encased in crystal, so that all your charms can be displayed to an arriving room-service waiter.

Via Pisana 59, 50143 Firenze. © **055-22771.** Fax 055-22772. www.unahotels.it. 84 units. 152€–502€ double. AE, DC, MC, V. Parking 20€. Bus: 6. **Amenities:** Restaurant; bar; babysitting; bikes; children's programs; concierge; room service; Wi-Fi (3€ per 30 min., in lobby). *In room:* A/C, TV, hair dryer, minibar.

Near Piazzale Michelangiolo

Villa La Vedetta ★★ 🛏️   This deluxe boutique hotel lies beside Piazzale Michelangiolo, with the most exceptional view of the Arno (and the monuments of Florence) of any hotel in town. A glamorous and sophisticated atmosphere prevails here, in a villa surrounded by gardens and reached by a tree-lined road. Behind its neoclassical facade, the hotel successfully blends contemporary and antique styles. Each individually decorated bedroom is luxurious, with parquet floors, fine marble bathrooms, and often a four-poster bed. A total of six units—two suites and four doubles—are housed in the equally distinguished annex. The hotel's Bellavista Suite is acclaimed as the largest in the hotel; it occupies two levels.

Viale Michelangiolo 78, 50125 Firenze. ✆ **055-681631.** Fax 055-6582544. www.villalavedetta hotel.com. 18 units. 299€–599€ double; from 649€ suite. AE, DC, MC, V. Free parking. Bus: 12. **Amenities:** Restaurant; bar; babysitting; exercise room; Jacuzzi; outdoor pool; room service; sauna; Wi-Fi (free, in lobby). *In room:* A/C, TV, hair dryer, minibar.

WHERE TO DINE

The Florentine table has always been set with the abundance of the Tuscan countryside. That means the region's best olive oil and wine (such as chianti), wonderful fruits and vegetables, fresh fish from the coast, and game in season. Meat lovers all over Italy sing the praise of *bistecca alla fiorentina,* an inch-thick juicy steak on the bone, often served with white Tuscan beans. Tuscan cuisine (with the exception of some of its hair-raising specialties) is simply flavored, without rich spices, and based on the hearty produce from the hills. Florentine restaurants aren't generally as acclaimed by gourmets as those of Rome, although good, moderately priced places abound.

In Centro
EXPENSIVE

Buca Lapi TUSCAN This cellar restaurant (under the Palazzo Antinori) opened in 1880 and is big on glamour, good food, and fun. The vaulted ceilings are covered with travel posters from all over the world. The cooks know how to turn out the classic dishes of the Tuscan kitchen with finesse, and there's a long table of interesting fruits, desserts, and vegetables. (Skip the international fare.) Pastas are homemade: Two favorites are flavored with a ragout of wild boar or duck. Specialties include *ribollita* (thick vegetable soup) and *bistecca alla fiorentina.* In season, the *fagioli toscani all'olio* (Tuscan beans in native olive oil) is a delicacy. For dessert, try crêpes suzette or the local choice, *zuccotto,* a dome-shaped ice-cream cake studded with almonds and rich in chocolate. The wine list is full of reasonably priced Tuscan and chianti wines.

Via del Trebbio 1R. ✆ **055-213768.** www.bucalapi.com. Reservations required for dinner. Main courses 15€–40€. AE, MC, V. Mon–Sat 7–10:30pm. Closed 2 weeks in Aug. Bus: 6, 11, 36, or 37.

Fuor d'Acqua ★★ SEAFOOD Arguably, this is the best seafood restaurant in Florence, a 10-minute walk from the center. The catch of the day is brought in from Viareggio on the coast and is among the freshest in inland Tuscany. Many serious Florentine foodies don't like the catch of the day disguised under a lot of heavy sauces; they prefer their fish grilled simply, with virgin olive oil, salt, and fresh lemon providing the extra flavor. Perhaps you'll follow their example. A wide variety of raw fish is served as a starter. Most of the pasta dishes are made with fresh seafood, our two favorites being spaghetti *trabaccolara,* with mixed fresh fish, and risotto with red shrimp. A house specialty, and it's a most worthy dish, is baked scampi with radicchio. For the catch of the day, always ask Alessio Ferri, the maitre d' and one of the owners, for advice on what to order.

Via Pisana 37R. © 055-222299. www.fuordacqua.it. Reservations required. Main courses 16€–40€. AE, MC, V. Mon–Sat 8–11pm. Bus: 6.

MODERATE

Cantinetta Antinori ★ 🏠 FLORENTINE/TUSCAN   Behind the severe stone facade of the 15th-century Palazzo Antinori is one of Florence's most popular restaurants and one of the city's few top-notch wine bars. It's no wonder the cellars are so well stocked: Antinori is the oldest (600 years), most distinguished wine company in Tuscany, Umbria, and Piedmont. You can sample these wines by the glass at the stand-up bar or by the bottle as an accompaniment to the meals served at wooden tables in the dining room, decorated with floor-to-ceiling racks of aged and dusty wine bottles. You can eat a meal or just snacks. The food is standard but satisfying, and many of the ingredients come directly from the Antinori farms. Especially good are two beef specialties—tender slices of beef with pecorino cheese from Castello della Sala or Tuscan entrecôte of beef grilled to perfection and served with roast potatoes. One of the best pasta specialties is with a wild boar ragout.

Piazza Antinori 3. © 055-292234. www.cantinetta-antinori.com. Reservations recommended. Main courses 12€–27€. AE, DC, MC, V. Mon–Fri 12:30–2:30pm and 7–10:30pm. Closed Aug and Dec 24–25. Bus: 6, 11, 14, 36, 37, or 68.

Frescobaldi Wine Bar ★ TUSCAN   On one of the corners of Piazza Signoria, this stylish wine bar and restaurant is the creation of those wine producers, the Frescobaldi family, which has been doing wonders with the grape for 7 centuries. Their showcase 80-seat restaurant decorated with stone wood, along with terra-cotta-colored walls and *trompe l'oeil* tapestries. Beside it is a wine bar with a shorter menu.

Raw materials are exquisitely handled by the kitchen staff, which turns out such delights as fresh sea bass baked with tomatoes, olives, and onions, or beef cheeks braised in a red chianti wine and served with cannellini beans. Another specialty is roast pork shank and baby onions. For a starter, try the steamed prawns with a celery salad with poached quail egg or an octopus and potato salad.

Via de'Magazzini 2-4R, Piazza della Signoria. © 055/284724. Reservations recommended in formal restaurant. Main courses 11€–20€; 3-course fixed menu 50€. MC, V. Tues–Sat noon–2:30pm and Mon–Sat 7–11pm. Closed Aug 10–31 and Jan 1–6. Bus: C1 or C2.

Oliviero TUSCAN   This small but smart and luxurious dining room maintains the finest traditions of Tuscan cookery; highly select fresh ingredients are used in the seasonal menu with such delights as ravioli with mortadella and pumpkin on a fondue of pecorino cheese and white truffles. We've come across such appetizers as octopus salad with basil, string beans, and tomatoes; fried mussels and squash blossoms; and Tuscan ham with figs and bread coated with virgin olive oil. We also enjoy *pici* pasta with savory tomato sauce, fresh garlic, and spicy red peppers, followed by a grilled Tuscan sirloin steak, flavored with sage and rosemary and covered in a perfect chianti sauce. For dessert, try the green-fig mousse with almonds and chocolate.

Via delle Terme 51R. © 055-287643 or 055-212421. www.ristorante-oliviero.it. Reservations required. Main courses 12€–30€. AE, DC, MC, V. Mon–Sat 7:30–11:30pm. Closed 3 weeks in Aug. Bus: 14, 23, or 71.

Where to Dine in Florence

Stazione S. M. Novelle

Piazza della Indipendenza

Piazza della Stazione

Santa Maria Novella

Piazza dell'Unita Italiana

SANTA MARIA NOVELLA

Piazza Santa Maria Novella

Ognissanti

Piazza d'Ognissanti

Arno River

Piazza Goldoni

Galleria Corsini

Ponte alla Carraia

Santa Trinita

Piazza Trinita

Palazzo Strozzi

CENTRO

Piazza del Carmine

V. S. Monaca

Santa Maria della Carmine

Santo Spirito

OLTRARNO

Ponte Santa Trinita

Ponte Vecchio

Piazza S. Spirito

Piazza dei Pitti

Casa Guidi

Santa Felicità

Pitti Palace

GIARDINO DI BOBOLI (BOBOLI GARDENS)

Forte di Belvedere

ⓘ Information

Venice

Florence

Rome

0   100 Mi
0 100 Km

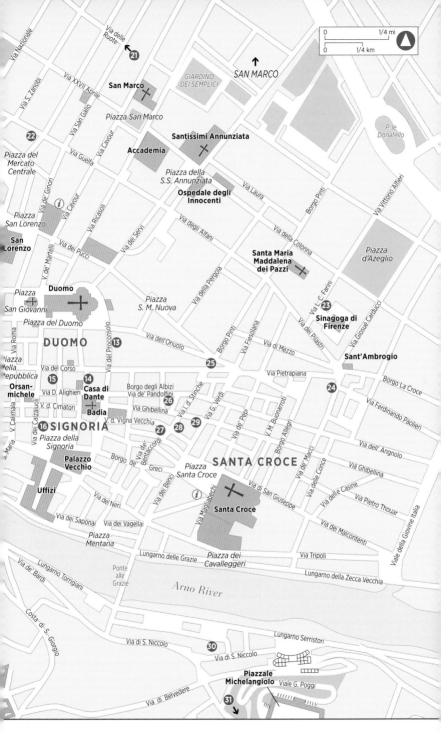

Via delle Ruote

㉑

Via Nazionale

Via XXVII Aprile

Via S. Zanobi

San Marco

Via S. Gallo

Piazza San Marco

GIARDINO DEI SEMPLICI

↑ SAN MARCO

P. le Donatello

Via Guelfa

㉒

Via Cavour

Accademia

Santissimi Annunziata

Piazza della S.S. Annunziata

Via Laura

Borgo Pinti

Via Vittorio Alfieri

Piazza del Mercato Centrale

Ospedale degli Innocenti

Via de' Ginori

ⓘ

Via Cavour

Via Ricasoli

Via dei Servi

Via degli Alfani

Santa Maria Maddalena dei Pazzi

Via della Colonna

Piazza d'Azeglio

Piazza San Lorenzo

San Lorenzo

V. de' Martelli

Via dei Pucci

Via della Pergola

Via L. C. Farini

Via de' Pilastri

Via Giosuè Carducci

㉓

Sinagoga di Firenze

Via de' Fiesolana

Via di Mezzo

Sant'Ambrogio

Piazza del Duomo

Duomo

Piazza San Giovanni

Piazza S. M. Nuova

Via dell'Oriuolo

Borgo Pinti

Via de' Pilastri

DUOMO

Via Roma

Via del Corso

㉝

Via del Proconsolo

㉕

Via Pietrapiana

Borgo La Croce

㉔

Via Ferdinando Paolieri

Piazza della Repubblica

Orsan-michele

⑮

⑭

Casa di Dante

Via D. Alighieri

Borgo degli Albizi

Via de' Pandolfini

㉖

Via I. d. Stinche

Via G. Verdi

Via de' Pepi

V. M. Buonarroti

Via dell'Angnolo

Via dei Calzaiuoli

V. d. Cimatori

Badia

V. d. Vigna Vecchia

Via Ghibellina

㉗ ㉘ ㉙

Via Ghibellina

SIGNORIA

⑯

Piazza della Signoria

Palazzo Vecchio

Borgo de' Greci

Via de' Bentaccordi

SANTA CROCE

Via di San Giuseppe

Borgo Allegri

Via de' Macci

Via delle Conce

Via delle Casine

Via Pietro Thouar

Uffizi

Via dei Neri

Via de' Bardi

Via Magliabechi

ⓘ

Piazza Santa Croce

Santa Croce

Via dei Malcontenti

Viale della Giovine Italia

Via dei Saponai

Via dei Vagellai

Piazza Mentana

Via Tripoli

Lungarno delle Grazie

Piazza dei Cavalleggeri

Lungarno della Zecca Vecchia

Lungarno Torrigiani

Ponte alle Grazie

Arno River

Costa di S. Giorgio

Lungarno Serristori

Via di S. Niccolo

㉚

Via di S. Niccolo

Piazzale Michelangiolo

Viale G. Poggi

Via di Belvedere

㉛ ↓

INEXPENSIVE

Osteria Antica Mescita ✦ TUSCAN   This *trattoria* might get by on its setting alone, located in a crypt from the 10th century behind the Church of San Niccolò. Fortunately, the food—good, simple Tuscan fare—is also worthy. Upstairs under vaulted ceilings, you might have to sit next to people you don't know. On the lower level tables are arranged as in a cantina, with rustic wooden furniture. The owners, the Prosperi family, give you a warm welcome into their little eatery where no one goes away hungry.

Traditional starters from the Tuscan kitchen include *ribollita* (broad beans and black cabbage soup) or else *papa al pompodoro* (a soup made of bread and tomatoes). Hearty fare includes a classic Florentine-style tripe; boar stew with fresh herbs; or rabbit in a white wine sauce. The famous white navy beans of Tuscany, laced with garlic, accompany most main dishes. For dessert, why not the chocolate semolina pie?

From March to November outdoor seating is available on a street leading to the Piazzale Michelangelo.

Via San Niccolò 60R, San Niccolò. ✆ **055-2342836.** www.osteriasanniccolo.it. Reservations recommended. Main courses 6€–20€; fixed-price 2-course lunch 10€. MC, V. Mon–Thurs noon–3pm and 7pm–midnight; Fri–Sat noon–3pm and 7pm–1:30am. Bus: 13, 23, or 71.

Near Piazza del Duomo

INEXPENSIVE

Le Mossacce ✦ FLORENTINE/TUSCAN   The 35-seat Le Mossacce is midway between the Bargello and the Duomo. It opened in the early 1900s, and within its 300-year-old walls, hardworking waiters serve a wide range of excellent Florentine and Tuscan specialties, such as *ribollita*, baked lasagna, and heavily seasoned baked pork. *Bistecca alla fiorentina* is a favorite—and you'll be hard-pressed to find it at a better price. Pasta buffs rightly claim that the cannelloni here is among Florence's finest—these baked pasta tubes are stuffed with spinach, a savory tomato sauce, and seasoned ground meat. For dessert, try the excellent *castagnaccio,* a cake baked with chestnut flour. Ask the waiters for advice and trust them; we had a great meal this way.

Via del Proconsolo 55R. ✆ **055-294361.** www.trattorialemossacce.it. Main courses 9€–18€. AE, DC, MC, V. Mon–Fri noon–2:30pm and 7–9:30pm. Closed Aug. Bus: 14.

Vecchia Firenze FLORENTINE/TUSCAN   Housed in a 14th-century palace with an elegant entrance, this *trattoria* combines atmosphere and budget meals. Some tables are in the courtyard; others are in the vaulted dining rooms or the stone-lined cantina downstairs (usually reserved for groups). The place caters to students and working people, who eat here regularly and never tire of its simple but hearty offerings, such as a creamy risotto with mushrooms or large-size ravioli flavored with butter and fresh sage. With a minimum of artifice, chefs regale you with such dishes as grilled sea bass with tartar sauce, grilled sirloin steak with pepper sauce, or tenderloin of beef Rossini in a gooseliver sauce. Almost any kind of meat you select can be grilled on a barbecue.

Borgo degli Albizi 18. ✆ **055-2340361.** www.vecchiafirenze.eu. Main courses 8€–18€; pizzas 7€–11€. AE, DC, MC, V. Tues–Sun noon–3pm and 7–10pm. Bus: 14, 23, or 71.

Near Piazza della Signoria

MODERATE

Paoli ★★ ITALIAN/TUSCAN   This restaurant is one of the best located in Florence. Paoli, between the Duomo and Piazza della Signoria, was opened in 1824 by the Paoli brothers in a building dating in part from the 13th century. It has a wonderful medieval-tavern atmosphere, with arches and ceramics stuck into the fresco-adorned walls. The pastas are homemade, including a house specialty, green handmade gnocchi with Gorgonzola cheese. The chef does a superb chicken breast with curry and rice pilaf or else veal piccata with lemon zest. A recommended side dish is *piselli alla fiorentina* (garden peas). The ultrafresh vegetables are often served with olive oil, which your waiter will loudly proclaim as the world's finest.

Via dei Tavolini 12R. ✆ **055-216215.** Reservations required. Main courses 8€–22€. AE, DC, MC, V. Daily noon–3pm and 7–11pm. Closed 3 weeks in Aug. Bus: 16 or 17.

INEXPENSIVE

Da Pennello 🍴 FLORENTINE/ITALIAN   This informal *trattoria*—also called Casa di Dante—offers many Florentine specialties on its a la carte menu and is known for its wide selection of antipasti; you can make a meal out of these delectable hors d'oeuvres. The ravioli is homemade, and one pasta specialty (loved by locals) is *spaghetti carrettiera,* with tomatoes and pepperoni. To follow that, you can have filet mignon in green-pepper sauce. Sometimes it's best to order the daily specials, which are made with food bought fresh that day at the

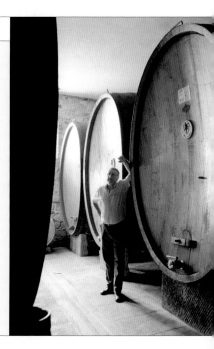

🎁 Focaccia & Chianti on the Run

Owned by the Castello di Verrazzano, one of Chianti's best-known wine-producing estates, the **Cantinetta del Verrazzano,** Via dei Tavolini 18–20R (✆ **055-268590;** www.verrazzano.com), helped spawn a revival of stylish wine bars as convenient spots for fast-food breaks. It promises a delicious self-service lunch or a snack of focaccia, plain or studded with peas, rosemary, onions, or olives; buy it hot by the slice or ask for *farcite* (sandwiches filled with prosciutto, arugula, cheese, or tuna). A glass of full-bodied chianti priced at 3.50€ each makes this the perfect respite. Summer hours are Monday through Saturday from 8am to 4pm; winter hours are Monday to Saturday from 8am to 9pm.

market. A Florentine cake, *zuccotto*, rounds out the meal. Da Pennello is on a narrow street near Dante's house, about a 5-minute walk from the Duomo. Called "The Painter" in English, its walls are hung with art, and it used to attract such local guys as Cellini and Andrea del Sarto.

Via Dante Alighieri 4R. ☏ **055-294848.** Fax 055-21455. www.ristoranteilpennello.it. Main courses 7€–18€; fixed-price menus from 25€. AE, DC, MC, V. Tues–Sat noon–3pm and 7–10pm and Sun noon–3pm. Closed 1st 3 weeks in Aug and Dec 24–Jan 2. Bus: 14, 22, or 23.

Il Cavallino ITALIAN/TUSCAN   A local favorite since the 1930s, Il Cavallino is on a tiny street (which probably won't even be on your map) leading off Piazza della Signoria at its northern end. Two of the three dining rooms have vaulted ceilings and peach-colored marble floors; the main room looks out over the piazza. Menu items are typical hearty Tuscan fare, including an assortment of boiled meats in green herb sauce, veal scaloppini with asparagus, chicken breast Medici style, and the inevitable Florentine spinach, which comes encased in a crepe with ricotta. The portions are large. Most diners prefer the house wine, but a limited selection of bottled wines is also available. Reservations must be made by faxing 055-214555; the restaurant does not take phone reservations.

Piazza della Signoria 28. ☏ **055-215818.** www.ristorantifiorentini.com. Reservations required (see above). Main courses 9€–20€; fixed-price menus 20€–25€. AE, MC, V. Mar–Oct daily noon–3pm and 7–10pm; Nov–Feb Thurs–Tues noon–3pm, Thurs–Mon 7–10:30pm. Bus: C1 or C2.

Near the Ponte Vecchio
MODERATE

Buca dell'Orafo ★★★ 🍴 FLORENTINE   This is an authentic neighborhood restaurant whose cuisine is firmly rooted in Tuscan traditions and inspired by whatever happens to be in season. Accessible via an alley beneath a vaulted arcade adjacent to Piazza del Pesce, it's named after the *orafo* (goldsmith shop) that occupied its premises during the Renaissance. The place is usually stuffed with regulars, who appreciate that the chef has made almost no concessions to international palates. Pastas are homemade, a specialty being *maltagliati* with a tomato-and-beef sauce and a serving of pecorino cheese. Florentine tripe and beefsteak are enduring favorites, as is *stracotto e fagioli* (beef braised in chopped vegetables and red wine), served with beans in tomato sauce.

Via dei Girolami 28R. ☏ **055-213619.** Main courses 12€–35€. MC, V. Tues–Sat 12:30–2:30pm and 7:30–10:30pm. Closed Aug and 2 weeks in Dec. Bus: C1 or C2.

Near Piazza Santa Maria Novella & the Train Station
EXPENSIVE

Buca Mario ★ FLORENTINE   In business for a century, Buca Mario is one of Florence's most famous cellar restaurants, in the 1886 Palazzo Niccolini. While diners sit at tables beneath vaulted ceilings, the waiters (some of whom have worked in the U.S.) will make suggestions from an array of fine-textured homemade pastas, veal stew cooked in white wine, or filet of lamb sautéed with garlic and rosemary, followed by a tempting selection of desserts, including *Torta della Nonna* (grandmother cake), a lemon-and-almond cake. Locals like to begin with that Florentine classic, ribollita (a thick soup of bread and black cabbage).

The pasta specialty is *cappellacci* (a kind of ravioli) filled with ricotta and spinach and flavored with butter and fresh sage. There's a wonderful exuberance about the place, but in the enigmatic words of one longtime patron, "It's not for the fainthearted."

Piazza Ottaviani 16R. *©* **055-214179.** www.bucamario.it. Reservations recommended. Main courses 10€–27€. AE, MC, V. Daily 7:30–10:30pm; Sun 12:30–2:30pm. Bus: 6, 9, 11, 36, 37, or 68.

Don Chisciotte ★★ ITALIAN/SEAFOOD   One floor above street level in a Florentine *palazzo,* this soft-pink dining room is known for its creative cuisine and a changing array of fresh fish that emerges with a flourish from the kitchens. Flavors are often enhanced by an unusual assortment of fresh herbs, vegetables, and fish stocks. Some of the best items on the menu include squid filled with ricotta, Sardinian cheese, and truffles served with a cream of artichoke sauce, or *cappellacci di branzino* (a kind of ravioli filled with sea bass) served on an asparagus purée. One especially delectable dish is scampi with truffles. You can begin with such antipasti as stockfish with pumpkin flowers.

Via Ridolfi 4R. *©* **055-475430.** www.ristorantedonchisciotte.it. Reservations recommended. Main courses 15€–30€. AE, DC, MC, V. Tues–Sat 1–2:30pm; Mon–Sat 8–10:30pm. Closed Aug. Bus: 20.

Sabatini ★★ FLORENTINE/INTERNATIONAL   Locals and visitors alike extol Sabatini as the finest of the city's typically Florentine restaurants. To celebrate our annual return here, we order the same main course we had on our first visit: boiled Valdarno chicken with a savory green sauce. Back then we complained to the waiter that the chicken was tough. He replied, "But, of course!" Florentines like chicken with muscle, not the hothouse variety so favored by Americans. Having eaten a lot of Valdarno chicken since then, we're more appreciative of Sabatini's dish. But on subsequent visits, we've found some of the other main courses more delectable, such as the veal scaloppine with artichokes, sole meunière, classic beefsteak Florentine, and spaghetti Sabatini (a cousin of spaghetti carbonara but enhanced with fresh tomatoes). American-style coffee is served, following the Florentine cake called *zuccotto.*

📎 Take a Gelato Break

Opened in the 1930s and today run by the third generation of the Vivoli family, the **Gelateria Vivoli** ★★, Via Isola delle Stinche 7R (*©* 055-292334; www.vivoli. it), on a back street near Santa Croce, produces some of Italy's finest ice cream and provides the gelati for many of Florence's restaurants.

Buy a ticket first and then select your flavor. Choose from blueberry *(mirtillo),* fig *(fico),* melon *(melone),* and other fruits in season, as well as chocolate mousse *(mousse al cioccolato)* or coffee ice cream flavored with espresso. A special ice cream is made from rice *(gelato di riso).* You can also choose from a number of flavors of *semifreddi—* an Italian ice cream with a base of cream instead of milk. The most popular flavors are *mandorla* (almond), *marengo* (a type of meringue), and *zabaglione* (eggnog). Others are *limoncini alla crema* (candied lemon peels with vanilla ice cream) and *aranciotti al cioccolato* (candied orange peels with chocolate ice cream). Prices range from 3€ to 11€, and it's open Tuesday to Saturday 7:30am to 1am, and Sunday 9am to 9pm (closed Jan and 3 weeks in Aug).

Via de'Panzani 9A. ℗ **055-211559.** www.ristorantesabatini.it. Reservations recommended. Main courses 12€–24€. AE, DC, MC, V. Tues–Sun 12:30–2:30pm and 7:30–11pm. Bus: C1 or C2.

Trattoria Garga ★★ FLORENTINE/TUSCAN   Some of the most creative cuisine in Florence is served here, about midway between the Ponte Vecchio and Santa Maria Novella. The thick Renaissance walls contain paintings by both Florentine and American artists, including those painted by owners Giuliano Gargani and his Canadian wife, Sharon, along with their son, Andrea. Both operatic arias and heavenly aromas emerge from a postage stamp–size kitchen. Many of the Tuscan menu items are so unusual that Sharon's bilingual skills are put to good use: octopus with peppers and garlic, boar with juniper berries, grilled marinated quail, and "whatever strikes the mood" of Giuliano. One dish has earned a lot of publicity: *tagliolini magnifico,* made with angel-hair pasta, orange and lemon rind, mint-flavored cream, and Parmigiano-Reggiano. One of the most delectable pastas is spaghetti cooked with fresh tomatoes, shrimp, oranges, and chili peppers.

Via del Moro 48R. ℗ **055-2398898.** www.garga.it. Reservations required. Main courses 12€–30€. AE, MC, V. Tues–Sun 7:30–11pm. Bus: C1, C2, 11, 36, 37, or 68.

MODERATE/INEXPENSIVE

La Carabaccia ★ 🎭 FLORENTINE   Two hundred years ago, a *carabaccia* was a workaday boat, shaped like a hollowed-out half onion and used on the Arno to dredge silt and sand from the bottom. This restaurant still features the Medicis' favorite *zuppa carabaccia,* a creamy white-onion soup with croutons (not in the French style, the chef rushes to tell you). You can, of course, eat more than onions here, sampling such specialties as paper-thin slices of beef on a nest of radicchio and Parmesan. You might choose the soup of the day, followed by one of four or five pastas, such as green gnocchi with Parmesan zabaione and truffle slices or *bavette* (a pasta) served with broccoli and a sea bass ragout. Two recommendable specialties include pork filets with sweet-and-sour onions, or prime sirloin with porcini mushrooms. The homemade breads are irresistible (especially the onion variety).

Via Palazzuolo 190R. ℗ **055-214782.** www.trattorialacarabaccia.com. Reservations recommended. Main courses 9€–22€. AE, DC, MC, V. Daily noon–3pm and 7–11pm. Bus: C1, C2, 11, 36, 37, or 68.

Le Fonticine ★ BOLOGNESE/TUSCAN   Today the richly decorated interior contains all the bounty of an Italian harvest, as well as the second passion of Signor Bruci's life: his collection of original modern paintings. The first passion, as a meal here reveals, is the cuisine that he and his wife produce from recipes she collected from her childhood in Bologna. Proceed to the larger of the two dining areas; along the way you can admire dozens of portions of fresh pasta decorating the table of an exposed grill. At the far end of the room, a wrought-iron gate shelters the extensive wine collection. The food, served in copious portions, is both traditional and delicious. Try such specialties as a creamy gnocchi with porcini mushrooms, and *taglierini* Fonticine with truffles and a mushroom sauce. The chef does a wonderful saltimbocca (veal fried in white wine and topped with sage).

Via Nazionale 79R. ℗ **055-282106.** www.lefonticine.com. Reservations recommended for dinner. Main courses 6€–15€. AE, MC, V. Tues–Sat noon–2:30pm and 7–10pm. Closed Aug and 2 weeks at Christmas. Bus: 12, 25, 31, 33, or 70.

Sostanza ★ 🍴 FLORENTINE Sostanza, the city's oldest (opened in 1869) and most revered *trattoria,* is where working people go for excellent moderately priced food. In recent years, however, it has also begun attracting a more sophisticated set, despite its somewhat funky atmosphere. (Florentines call the place *Troia,* a word that means "trough" but also suggests a woman of easy virtue.) The small dining room has crowded family tables, but when you taste what comes out of the kitchen, you'll know that fancy decor would be superfluous. Specialties include breaded chicken breast, a succulent T-bone, and tripe Florentine-style (cut into strips and then baked in a casserole with tomatoes, onions, and parmigiano).

Via della Porcellana 25R. 📞 **055-212691.** Reservations recommended. Main courses 9€–25€. No credit cards. June–July and Nov–Mar Mon–Fri 12:30–2pm and 7:30–9:45pm; Apr–May and Sept–Oct Mon–Sat 12:30–2pm and 7:30–9:45pm. Closed Aug and 2 weeks at Christmas. Bus: 12.

Trattoria Antellesi ★ 🍴 TUSCAN Occupying a 15th-century historic monument just steps from the Medici Chapels and a 4-minute walk from the railway station, this place is devoted almost exclusively to well-prepared versions of time-tested Tuscan recipes. The restaurant changes its menu every 3 weeks, based on whatever is seasonal and fresh at the food market (Mercato San Lorenzo), which lies a short walk away. Dishes might include fresh fish (generally on Fri), and a superb *bistecca alla fiorentina* (local beefsteak). Culinary creations are sometimes simple, sometimes complex, including such dishes as filet of salmon with a celery purée or *bottarga* (salted fish roe) with potatoes gratinée and zucchini. One of the best pastas is *tagliolini* with black truffles. Expect a wide selection of high-quality Italian wines, mostly Tuscan. A special dessert is *budino di castagna* (chestnut pudding).

Via Faenza 9R. 📞 **055-216990.** Reservations recommended. Main courses 7€–30€. AE, DC, MC, V. Daily noon–3pm and 7–10:30pm. Bus: 1, 6, 7, 11, 17, 33, 67, or 68.

Near Piazza San Marco
EXPENSIVE

Taverna del Bronzino ★ TUSCAN It's a bit of an event to dine in the converted studio of a 16th-century Renaissance artist. You can do so in style where Santi di Tito, a student of Bronzino's, once painted. Against a backdrop of classic simplicity, you are served fine food from a menu that changes every week, based on the best produce in any given season. The waiters are among the most helpful in the city and will recommend the daily delights. In fair weather select a table on the patio, shaded by an arbor, or else dine inside under a vaulted ceiling. Start with one of the daily antipasti, guaranteed fresh. In season Tuscan asparagus appears in a creamy risotto. Among the main courses likely to be featured all year are grilled beefsteak with black truffles or rare carpaccio of beef with Parmesan shavings.

Via delle Ruote 27R, near Piazza Indipendenza. 📞 **055-495220.** www.tavernadelbronzino.com. Reservations required. Main courses 13€–25€. AE, DC, MC, V. Mon–Sat 12:30–2:30pm and 7:30–10:30pm. Closed Aug. Bus: 12 or 91.

INEXPENSIVE

Il Vegetariano 🍴 VEGETARIAN This is Florence's only strictly vegetarian dining room. It is far from luxurious—you sit at wooden bench tables with other diners—but its menu of veggie and vegan plates is tasty, fresh, and well prepared, as well as most affordable. After finding a space and saving it with your coat, scan the blackboard menus—one for antipasti, another for first courses, another for main courses, and a final one for *dolci*, or desserts. Write down your selections on pads of paper provided. Then line up cafeteria style for your food. The constantly changing menu, based on the best vegetables of any season, offers a good variety of dishes.

Typical plates include two types of whole-wheat risotto—one with yellow squash, another with radicchio. You can also order a Tunisian-style couscous with vegetables; an eggplant and cheese pie; or a *pizza rustica* with ricotta, tomatoes, olives, and mushrooms. A batch of fresh salads is made daily, including one with spinach, bean sprouts, and fresh onions in a soy sauce. One of the homemade desserts is likely to include a yogurt, walnut, and almond cake.

Via della Ruote 30R (off Via Santa Reparata near Piazza Indipendenza). ℰ **055-475-030.** www. il-vegetariano.it. Reservations not accepted. Main courses 5€–9€. No credit cards. Tues–Fri 12:30–2:30pm and 7:30–10:30pm; Sat–Sun 7:30–10:30pm. Closed 3 weeks in Aug and Dec 24–Jan 1. Bus: 4, 12, or 20.

I' Toscano TUSCAN   Bouquets of flowers liven up this restaurant's plain interior, but despite the understated setting, the place is a magnet for foodies who appreciate its Tuscan specialties. Menu items change with the seasons but are often at their best in late autumn and winter, when mixed platters with slices of wild boar, venison, partridge, and (when available) pheasant are a worthy substitute for the antipasti that tempt visitors the rest of the year. Always popular are the spinach-stuffed ravioli and the several forms of gnocchi or *tagliatelle*. Veal, turkey, pork, and Florentine beefsteaks are also offered.

Via Guelfa 70R. ℰ **055-215475.** www.itoscano.it. Reservations recommended at dinner. Main courses 8€–20€. MC, V. Wed–Mon noon–2:45pm and 7–10:30pm. Closed 1 week in Aug. Bus: 6, 11, or 14.

Near Piazza Santa Croce

MODERATE/INEXPENSIVE

La Giostra ★★ 🏠 TUSCAN   The host with the most, Prince Dimitri Kunz d'Asburgo Lorena, with a title left over from the days of the Austro-Hungarian empire, along with his twin sons, welcomes you to this enclave of fine dining. You get not just old-world charm here, but also a regionally based repertoire of imaginative associations of flavors. Everything seems to taste of Tuscany's pungent bounty. We'd dine here just to sample the pasta courses, especially a divine concoction of homemade *tagliatelle* with pine nuts, basil, and tomato sauce. The chefs are adept in their use of mushrooms and truffles. Truffles appear in such "worthy-of-a-king" dishes as *taglierini* with the white truffle of Umbria. Pigeon is baked with bay leaves, and there is also homemade potato gnocchi with ricotta and spinach.

Borgo Pinti 12R (off Piazza Salvemini). ℰ **055-241341.** www.ristorantelagiostra.com. Reservations required. Main courses 15€–35€. AE, DC, MC, V. Daily 12:30–3pm and 7pm–1am. Bus: C1, C2, 14, 23, 71, or 80.

Osteria del Caffè Italiano ★ 🍴 TUSCAN   Housed in the 13th-century Palazzo Salviati, this *trattoria* is the brainchild of Umberto Montano. The front room is warmed by burnished wood paneling and made even more welcoming when you see the prices. Beneath a wrought-iron chandelier hanging from the vaulted 6m (20-ft.) ceiling, you can sample delicious choices from the short menu. Look for the fresh *mozzarella di bufala,* specially couriered from a private supplier in Naples (not available June–Aug). Or come back in the evening to dine in the elegant restaurant in the back room and splurge with excellently prepared main courses from the grill and a more serious sampling of wine. Try such specialties as Florentine T-bone steak with white beans or else beef stew with a Chianti Classico, or ravioli filled with polenta stuffed with potatoes, flavored with fresh thyme, and served in a pecorino cheese sauce.

Don't miss Montano's handsome **Caffè Italiano,** Via Condotta 12, off Via dei Calzaiuoli (✆ **055-289020;** www.caffeitaliano.it; bus: 14, 23, or 71), which offers a delicious lunch and dinner to standing-room-only crowds (come early). It's open Monday to Wednesday 8am to 8pm, Thursday to Saturday 8am to midnight, and Sunday 11am to 8pm.

Via Isola delle Stinche 11–13R (2 blocks west of Piazza Santa Croce). ✆ **055-289368.** www.osteria caffeitaliano.com. Reservations recommended. Main courses 10€–22€; fixed-price menu 50€. MC, V. Tues–Sun 12:30–3pm and 7:30–11pm. Bus: C1, C2 or 14.

Ristorante Simon Boccanegra TUSCAN   Near Piazza Santa Croce, this restaurant continues to win devotees with its hearty, filling regional food, served in a setting that blends modern and antique styles. Savor such well-crafted dishes as homemade cannelloni with mozzarella and sun-dried tomatoes with an eggplant sauce; or black *tagliatelle* with squid ink, scallops, and broccoli (although this dish may not be for the faint of heart). Perhaps the Medicis themselves dined on homemade pasta with shellfish and other "fruits of the sea," or baked turbot with artichokes. Desserts are homemade fresh daily and are usually quite luscious.

Via Ghibellina 124. ✆ **055-2001098.** www.boccanegra.com. Reservations recommended. Main courses 10€–18€. AE, DC, MC, V. Mon–Sat noon–2:30pm and 7pm–midnight. Bus: C1, C2, 13, 23, or 71.

Ruth's KOSHER JEWISH   For your kosher food fix, Ruth's will welcome you into a Santa Croce setting with a modern decor and wooden furniture. Most of the dishes are inspired by the Mediterranean, notably Morocco and Tunisia. The food is backed up by a kosher wine list, mostly Italian and Israeli vintages. The restaurant lies next to the synagogue of Florence and a store selling kosher products.

Start with such appetizers as marinated fried eggplant or salmon carpaccio, perhaps the pasta or homemade soup of the day. Pizza is also on the menu, including one made with four different cheeses. For a main course, you can enjoy Ruth's fish dish of the day or else a vegetable couscous, perhaps falafel. The desserts are tempting, especially the Jewish cheesecake, apple strudel, or sweet blintzes.

Via Luigi Carlo Farini 2A. ✆ **055-2480888.** www.kosheruth.com. Reservations recommended. Main courses 7€–18€. AE, MC, V. Sun–Fri 12:30–3pm; daily 7:30–10pm. Bus: 6, 14, 23A, or C1.

Teatro del Sale ★ 🍴 FLORENTINE   This unique establishment is a private club, theater, lounge, grocery store, and, yes, even a restaurant. It costs only 5€ annually for foreigners who don't plan to settle permanently in Florence to join the private club, which bills itself as "your home in Florence." The main attraction is the food, of course, served in an informal dining hall and laid out buffet-style. Dishes are not quite as refined as Cibrèo's, but are nonetheless quite wonderful. Chef Fabio Picchi serves an array of delights, including baked mackerel with virgin olive oil and vinegar, a tuna-and-garbanzo salad with fresh celery, tasty cinnamon-flavored polenta, or homemade pasta that depends only on butter and Parmesan cheese for its succulent flavor. Nightly performances, ranging from jazz to poetry readings, are presented at dinner.

Via del Macci 111R. ✆ **055-2001492.** www.edizioniteatrodelsalecibreofirenze.it. Reservations required for dinner. Lunch buffet 20€; dinner buffet with show 30€. AE, DC, MC, V. Tues–Sat 9am–midnight. Closed July 26–Sept 5. Bus: C1, C2, 13, 23, or 71.

Trattoria Pallottino FLORENTINE/TUSCAN   Less than a block from Piazza Santa Croce, on a narrow street, this distinctive restaurant contains two sometimes-cramped dining rooms. Flickering candles illuminate a timeless Italian scene where the staff works hard, usually with humor and style. Menu specialties are succulent antipasti; penne with Gorgonzola and arugula; potato *tortelloni* (a kind of big ravioli) with walnut sauce; *peposa* (a slab of beef marinated for at least 4 hr. in a rich broth of ground black pepper, olive oil, and tomatoes), and *spaghetti giaccheraia* (with spicy red chilies, olive oil, and tomatoes). Dessert might be vanilla custard drizzled with a compote of fresh fruit.

Isola delle Stinche 1R. ✆ **055-289573.** www.trattoriapallottino.com. Reservations recommended at dinner. Main courses 8€–20€. AE, DC, MC, V. Tues–Sun 12:30–2:30pm and 7:30–10:30pm. Bus: 14, 23, or 71.

> ### Taking to the Hills: A Dining Secret
>
> On Sunday nights, many of Florence's best restaurants are closed. For years we've driven 5km (3 miles) south to the town of Arcetri to dine at **Omero**, Via Pilan de Giullari 11R (✆ **055-220053;** www.ristorante omero.it). This is a small, rustic place, but every dish is perfumed with flavor. We can never resist the lip-smacking *pollo shiacciato* (grilled chicken). On a second visit, you're treated like a long-lost family friend. It's closed Tuesday and in August.

Across the Arno

MODERATE

Mamma Gina ★ TUSCAN   Mamma Gina is a rustic restaurant that prepares fine foods in the traditional manner. Although it's run by a corporation that operates other restaurants around Tuscany, this place is named after its founding matriarch, whose legend has continued despite her death in the 1980s. A few of the savory menu items are chicken breast with cognac and mushrooms, fresh rigatoni with a cream-cheese sauce, and risotto with anglerfish and prawns. This is an ideal spot for lunch after visiting the Pitti Palace.

Borgo San Jacopo 37R. ✆ **055-2396009.** www.mammagina.it. Reservations required for dinner. Main courses 9€–20€. AE, DC, MC, V. Mon–Sat noon–2:30pm and 7–10:30pm. Closed 3 weeks in Aug. Bus: D.

Trattoria Cammillo TUSCAN   On the ground floor of a former Medici palace, the Cammillo is one of the most popular (and perhaps the finest) of the Oltrarno neighborhood's dining spots. Its most serious rival is Mamma Gina (listed above). Cammillo has been pleasing clients since it opened in those horrible months of 1945 at the close of World War II. Of course, the Florentine cognoscenti write it off as "filled with tourists" and "old-fashioned." But it has its enduring habitués, of which we number ourselves. Begin with crostini, warm bread slices topped with mashed chicken livers, and follow with all sorts of earthy Italian dishes, including braised veal shank (*osso buco*) with porcini mushrooms, or stewed wild boar flavored with fresh herbs. Chicken breast with truffles and parmigiano has long been a succulent specialty. Florentines like the golden mixed fry of tiny meatballs, brains, sweetbreads, and zucchini flowers. The savory breast of squab remains a delight, as does the Florentine rib steak, always a satisfying choice.

Borgo San Jacopo 57R (btw. the Ponte Vecchio and Ponte Santa Trinita). © **055-212427.** Reservations recommended at dinner. Main courses 10€–35€. AE, MC, V. Thurs-Mon noon-2:30pm and 7-11pm. Closed 1 week at Christmas and 2 weeks in Aug (dates vary). Bus: C1 or C2.

INEXPENSIVE

Fuori Porta ★ 👜 TUSCAN   This is the city's best enoteca (wine tavern). As the name translates, it means "outside the gates," yet it's only a 15-minute taxi or bus ride from the landmark Piazza della Signoria, the historic core of Florence. The wine list ranks at the top in Florence, yet the prices are more than reasonable. Many of the finest selections are available by the glass. Discerning palates also appreciate the Tuscan fare, which is soul food to the Florentines. Two succulent pasta dishes are *taglierini* (flat noodles) with fresh mushrooms and linguine with an arugula pesto. We especially like the loaves of bread that arrive freshly baked from the oven and are most often served with mozzarella and vine-ripened tomatoes.

Via del Monte alle Croce 10R. © **055-2342483.** www.fuoriporta.it. Reservations recommended. Main courses 7€–13€. AE, MC, V. Daily 12:30-3:30pm and 7pm-12:30am. Bus: 13 or 23.

Dining in Florence.

At Artimino

MODERATE

Da Delfina ★ 👜 TUSCAN   Even on a short visit to Florence, give yourself a break and dip at least once into the countryside of Tuscany for a meal. Our candidate for an outing is this family-run restaurant in the medieval walled village of Artimino, a 15-minute train ride from the center of Florence. Based on the freshest of local ingredients, the food has a wonderful, earthy taste, and some of it comes from the nearby fields, including nettles, mushrooms, and wild herbs. If you arrive in fair weather, request a table on the terrace with its classic view of the Tuscan landscape. The chefs turn out some of the region's best homemade pasta dishes and delectable sausages. We'd visit just for a plate of the aged salami with its intense, meaty flavor. Raw fava beans appear with pecorino sheep-milk cheese, and homemade pasta with wild mushrooms should win an award. Baby goat (*capretto*) is roasted to perfection in the oven.

Via della Chiesa 1, Artimino. ✆ **055-8718074.** www.dadelfina.it. Reservations recommended. Main courses 10€–20€. MC, V. Wed–Sun 12:30–2:30pm; Tues–Sat 8–10:30pm. From Santa Maria Novella station in Florence, take the Signa train. At Signa, take a taxi for the 5-min. ride to Da Delfina.

WHAT TO SEE & DO

Florence was the fountainhead of the Renaissance, the city of Dante and Boccaccio. For 3 centuries, the city was dominated by the Medici family, patrons of the arts, and masters of assassination. But it's chiefly through Florence's incomparable artists that we know of the apogee of the Renaissance: Ghiberti, Fra Angelico, Donatello, Brunelleschi, Botticelli, Leonardo da Vinci, and Michelangelo.

In Florence, you can trace the transition from medievalism to the age of "rebirth." For example, all modern painters owe a debt to an ugly, unkempt man named Masaccio (Vasari's "Slipshod Tom"), who died at 27. Modern painting began with his frescoes in the Brancacci Chapel in Santa Maria del Carmine, which you can see today. Years later, Michelangelo painted a more celebrated Adam and Eve in the Sistine Chapel, but even this great artist never realized the raw humanity of Masaccio's *Adam and Eve Expelled from Paradise*.

Group tourism has so overwhelmed this city that in 1996, officials demanded that organized tour groups book their visits in advance and pay an admission fee. No more than 150 tour buses are allowed into the center at one time (considering how small Florence is, even that's a stretch). Today there are more than seven tourists for each native Florentine, and that isn't counting the day-trippers, who rush off to Venice in the late afternoon. But despite all its traffic and inconveniences, Florence is still one of the world's greatest art cities.

CafTours, Via degli Alfani 151R (✆ **055-283200;** www.caftours.com), runs morning tours of the major attractions of Florence, departing daily year-round at 9:30pm and lasting 3 hours. The departure point is Piazza Stazione at the corner of Piazza dell'Unità. The tour costs 45€ and includes transport, guide,

---

Attractions Open in the Afternoon

Most stores close for long lunch breaks, and many of the museums close for the day at 2pm or earlier (the last entrance is at least 30 min. before closing) and are closed on Monday. The **Uffizi,** the **Accademia,** the **Palazzo Vecchio,** the **Duomo** and the **Duomo Museum,** the **Campanile di Giotto,** the baptistery, **Santa Croce,** the **Pitti Palace, Cappella Brancacci,** the **Roman Amphitheater, Museo Archeologico (Fiesole),** and the **Boboli Gardens** are among the attractions that remain open during *il riposo* (afternoon closing).

Stop by the tourist office for an up-to-date listing of museum hours.

Churches and **markets** are good alternatives for afternoons because they usually remain open until 7pm (however, many churches, too, close for the long lunch break). The open-air **Mercato San Lorenzo** gets the lunch crowd; the stalls are open Monday through Saturday from 9am to 6pm.

and museum admissions. Highlights of the tour include the Duomo, the baptistery, and the Galleria dell'Accademia, containing Michelangelo's *David*. You're driven to the Piazzale Michelangolo for a panoramic view of the heart of Florence.

Walking Tours of Florence, Via dei Sassetti 1 (𝄞 **055-2645033;** www.italy. artviva.com), are the best—fun, with small groups and well-informed guides. Reservations are required. The classic offering is the 3-hour "Original Florence Walk" for 25€ per person, which takes in all the highlights, including the Duomo and Piazza della Signoria. Other walks include a 2-hour "Masterpieces of the Uffizi" for 39€ and a 1½-hour "Evening Walk" for 30€. Tours of Tuscany, including bike tours, are also offered.

A street musician.

The Top Museums

Bargello Museum (Museo Nazionale del Bargello) ★★   A short walk from Piazza della Signoria, this is a 1255 fortress palace whose dark underground chambers resounded with the cries of the tortured when it served as the city's jail and town hall during the Renaissance. Today the Bargello is a vast repository of some of the most important Renaissance sculpture, including works by Michelangelo and Donatello.

Here you'll see **another Michelangelo *David*** (referred to in the past as *Apollo*), chiseled perhaps 25 to 30 years after the statuesque figure in the Accademia. The Bargello *David* is totally different, effete when compared to its stronger brother. The armory here displays Michelangelo's grape-capped and drunk *Bacchus* (one of his earlier works, carved when he was 22), who's tempted by a satyr. Among the more significant sculptures is Giambologna's *Winged Mercury* (ca. 1564), a Mannerist masterpiece looking as if it's ready to take flight.

The Bargello displays two versions of Donatello's ***John the Baptist* ★**, one emaciated and the other a younger and much kinder-looking man. Donatello was one of the outstanding and original talents of the early Renaissance, and in this gallery you'll learn why. His **St. George ★** is a work of heroic magnitude. According to an oft-repeated story, Michelangelo, upon seeing it for the first time, commanded it to "March!" **Donatello's bronze *David* ★★** in this salon is truly remarkable; it was the first attempt at a free-standing nude since the Romans stopped chiseling. As depicted, David is narcissist (a stunning contrast to Michelangelo's later-day virile interpretation). For the last word, however, we'll have to call back our lady of the barbs, Mary McCarthy, who wrote: "His *David*, wearing nothing but a pair of fancy polished boots and a girlish bonnet, is a transvestite's and fetishist's dream of alluring ambiguity."

Look for at least one more work: another *David*, this one by Andrea del Verrocchio, one of the finest of the 15th-century sculptors. The Bargello also contains a large number of terra cottas by the della Robbia clan.

What to See & Do In Florence

Stazione S. M. Novelle

Via Guelfa

Via Cennini

Via Faenza

Via Flume

Via Nazionale

Via Panicale

Piazza della Stazione

Piazza dell'Unita Italiana

Via S. Antonino

Santa Maria Novella

Via D. Orti Oricellari

Via dell' Albero

Via Della Scala

Via Palazzuolo

Via de' Panzani

Via de' Giglio

SANTA MARIA NOVELLA

Piazza Santa Maria Novella

Via dei Cerretani

Borgo Ognissanti

Via della Porcellana

Ognissanti

Via delle B. Donne

Via de' Pecori

Piazza d'Ognissanti

Lungarno Vespucci

Via de' Fossi

Via del Moro

Via degli Strozzi

Via de' Tornabuoni

Palazzo Strozzi

Arno River

Piazza Goldoni

Via della Vigna Nuova

Via del Parione

CENTRO

Via Porta Rossa

Ponte alla Carraia

Galleria Corsini

Santa Trinita

Piazza Trinita

Via Pellicceria

Lungarno Corsini

Borgo S.S. Apostoli

Lungarno Guicciardini

Lungarno Acciaiuoli

Piazza del Carmine

Via Santo Spirito

Ponte Santa Trinita

Ponte Vecchio

Via S. Monaca

OLTRARNO

Borgo S. Jacopo

Via Por

Santa Maria della Carmine

Via Sant' Agostino

Santo Spirito

V. Vellutini

Piazza S. Spirito

Via Maggio

Via Guicciardini

Santa Felicità

Via de' Serragli

Via Mazzetta

Piazza dei Pitti

☐ **CASA GUIDI**

Borgo Tegolaio

Via Romana

Pitti Palace

GIARDINO DI BOBOLI (BOBOLI GARDENS)

Forte di Belveder

ⓘ Information

San Marco

Via S. Zanobi

Via XXVII Aprile

Piazza San Marco

San Marco ⑨

Via San Gallo

Via Guelfa

Via Cavour

GIARDINO DEI SEMPLICI

↑ *SAN MARCO*

0 — 1/4 mi
0 — 1/4 km

Piazza del Mercato Centrale

⑤

⑥

Piazza San Lorenzo

San orenzo ⑦

Santissimi Annunziata

Accademia ⑩

Piazza della S.S. Annunziata

⑪
⑫ **Ospedale degli Innocenti**

⑬

Via Laura

Borgo Pinti

Via degli Alfani

Via della Colonna

Via Vittorio Alfieri

Piazza d'Azeglio

V. de' Ginori

Via Ricasoli

ⓘ ⑧

Via Cavour

Via dei Servi

Via dei Pucci

V. de' Martelli

Via della Pergola

Santa Maria Maddalena dei Pazzi

Via L. C. Farini

⑭ **Sinagoga di Firenze**

Via de' Pilastri

Via Giosuè Carducci

Piazza ⑧
San Giovanni

Piazza ⑧ **Duomo** ②⑥ ②⑤

Piazza S. M. Nuova

Piazza del Duomo ②⑦

DUOMO

Via del Proconsolo

Via dell'Oriuolo

Borgo Pinti

Via Fiesolana

Via di Mezzo

Sant'Ambrogio

Via Roma

iazza ella epubblica

Via del Corso

Borgo degli Albizi

Via Pietrapiana

Orsan-michele

Via D. Alighieri

Casa di Dante

Via de' Pandolfini

V. d. Cimatori

Badia ②④

V. d. Vigna Vecchia

Via Ghibellina

Via d. Stinche

Via G. Verdi

Via de' Pepi

V. M. Buonarroti

Borgo Allegri

⑮

Via de' Macci

Via dell'Angnolo

Via Ghibellina

V. Calimala

SIGNORIA

Piazza della Signoria ②③

Via de' Calzaiuoli

②② **Palazzo Vecchio**

Borgo de' Greci

Via de' Bentaccordi

Piazza Santa Croce

⑰

ⓘ ⑯

SANTA CROCE

Via di San Giuseppe

Via delle Conce

Via delle Casine

Via Pietro Thouar

②① **Uffizi**

②⓪

Via del Neri

Via dei Benci

Via Magliabechi

Santa Croce

Via dei Saponai

Via dei Vagellai

Via dei Malcontenti

⑲ Piazza Mentana

Lungarno delle Grazie

Piazza dei Cavalleggeri

Via Tripoli

Lungarno della Zecca Vecchia

Lungarno Torrigiani

Via de' Bardi

Ponte alle Grazie

Arno River

Lungarno Serristori

Via di S. Niccolo

Via di S. Niccolo

Via di Belvedere

Piazzale Michelangiolo

Viale G. Poggi

⑱

Venice •

0 — 100 Mi
0 — 100 Km

45° N.

Florence •

★ **Rome**

40° N.

10° E.

Via del Proconsolo 4. ℂ **055-2388606.** www.firenzemusei.it. Admission 4€. Daily 8:15am–1:50pm. Closed 2nd and 4th Mon and 1st, 3rd, and 5th Sun of each month; Jan 1; May 1; and Christmas. Bus: A, 14, or 23.

Galleria dell'Accademia ★★ This museum boasts many paintings and sculptures, but they're completely over-shadowed by one work: Michelangelo's colossal *David* ★★★, unveiled in 1504 and now the world's most famed sculpture. It first stood in Piazza della Signoria but was moved to the Accademia in 1873 (a copy was substituted) and placed beneath the rotunda of a room built exclusively for its display. When he began work, Michelangelo was just 29. One of the most sensitive accounts we've ever read of how Michelangelo turned the 5m (17-ft.) "Duccio marble" into *Il Gigante* (the Giant) is related in Irving Stone's *The Agony and the Ecstasy*. Stone describes a Michelangelo "burning with marble fever," who set out to create a *David* who "would be Apollo, but considerably more; Hercules, but considerably more; Adam, but considerably more; the most fully real-

Donatello's bronze *David* at the Bargello.

ized man the world had yet seen, functioning in a rational and humane world." For his 500th birthday in 2004, David was given a bath to wash away the accumulated dirt and grime of centuries. The statue now has a bit more shine and polish.

David is so overpowering in his majesty that many visitors head here just to see him and leave immediately afterward. However, the hall leading up to him is lined with other Michelangelos, notably his quartet of celebrated **Prisoners** or **Slaves** ★★. The statues are presumably unfinished, although art historians have found them more dramatic in their current state as they depict the struggles of figures to free themselves from stone. Michelangelo worked on these statues, originally intended for the tomb of Pope Julius II, for 40 years because he was never pleased with them. The gallery also displays Michelangelo's statue of St. Matthew, which he began carving in 1504.

The Accademia also owns a gallery of paintings, usually considered to be of minor importance (works by Santi di Tito, Granacci, and Albertinelli, for example). Yet there are masterpieces here as well, notably Lo Scheggia's 1440s *Cassone Adimari*, a panel from a wedding chest.

Warning: The wait to get in to see *David* can be up to an hour or more, so we highly recommend making reservations in advance (ask the concierge at your hotel or call ℂ **055/294-883**). If you don't have a reservation, try getting there before the museum opens in the morning or an hour or two before closing time. Via Ricasoli 60. ℂ **055-2388612.** www.firenzemusei.it. Admission 6.50€. Tues–Sun 8:15am–6:50pm. Bus: C1, C2, D, or 12.

Museo Galileo ★ 🏛 Since 1927, this museum has been a repository of ancient instruments and devices of historical and scientific interest, including Galileo's telescope. The most important exhibit is the **Medici Collection ★**, which displays scientific instruments owned by the Medicis, including the objective lens of the telescope with which Galileo discovered the satellites around Jupiter. Other exhibits include a planetary clock by Lorenzo della Volpaia, plus exhibits relating to 5 centuries of scientific collecting by the once-powerful Tuscan family of Lorraine. Dozens of other displays relate to instruments used in the early studies of mathematics, physics, meteorology, and electricity.

Piazza dei Giudici. ℂ **055-265311.** www.museogalileo.it. Admission 8€, free for kids 5 and under. June–Sept Mon and Wed–Fri 9:30am–5pm, Tues and Sat 9:30am–1pm; Oct–May Mon and Wed–Sat 9:30am–5pm, Tues 9:30am–1pm. Bus: 13, 23, or 62.

Palazzo Pitti & the Boboli Gardens (Giardini di Boboli) ★★ The massive bulk of the **Palazzo Pitti** is one of Europe's greatest artistic treasure-troves, with the city's most extensive coterie of museums embracing a painting gallery second only to the Uffizi. It's a cavalcade of the works of Titian, Rubens, Raphael, and Andrea del Sarto. Built in the 16th century (Brunelleschi was probably the architect), this was once the residence of the powerful Medici family. It's located across the Arno (a 5-min. walk from the Ponte Vecchio).

Of the several museums in this complex, the most important is the first-floor **Palatine Gallery (Galleria Palatina)** ★★, which houses one of Europe's great art collections and shows masterpieces hung one on top of the other as in the days of the Enlightenment. If for no other reason, you should come for its Raphaels. After passing through the main door, proceed to the Sala di Venere (Venus), where you'll find Titian's *La Bella,* of rich and illuminating color (entrance wall), and his portrait of Pietro Aretino, one of his most distinguished works. On the opposite wall are Titian's *Concert of Music,* often attributed to Giorgione, and his portrait of Julius II.

In the Sala di Apollo (on the opposite side of the entrance door) are Titian's **Man with Gray Eyes ★★**, an aristocratic, handsome romanticist; and his luminously gold **Mary Magdalene ★**, covered only with her long hair. On the opposite wall are van Dyck portraits of Charles I of England and Henrietta of France. This salon also contains some of the grandest works of Andrea del Sarto, notably his *Holy Family* and his *Deposition.*

In the Sala di Marte (entrance wall) is an important *Madonna and Child* by Murillo of Spain and the Pitti's best-known work by Rubens, *The Four Philosophers.* Rubens obviously had so much fun with this rather lighthearted work that he painted himself in on the far left (that's his brother, Filippo, seated). On the left wall is one of Rubens's most tragic and moving works, **Consequences of War ★**, an early *Guernica,* painted in his declining years.

In the Sala di Giove (entrance wall) are Andrea del Sarto's *John the Baptist* in his youth and Fra Bartolomeo's *Descent from the Cross.* On the third wall (opposite the entrance) is the Pitti's second famous Raphael, **La Velata ★**—the woman under the veil, known as La Fornarina, is his bakery-girl mistress.

In the following gallery, the Sala di Saturno, look to the left on the entrance wall to see Raphael's *Madonna of the Canopy.* On the third wall near the doorway is the greatest Pitti prize, Raphael's **Madonna of the Chair ★★**, his best-known interpretation of the Virgin and what's probably one of the six most celebrated paintings in all Europe. In the Sala dell'Iliade (to your left on the entrance wall) is a work of delicate beauty, Raphael's rendition of a pregnant woman. On the left wall is Titian's *Portrait of a Gentleman,* which he was indeed. (Titian is the second big star in the gallery.) Other masterpieces are in the smaller rooms that follow, notably the Sala dell'Educazione di Giove, home to the 1608 *Sleeping Cupid* that "the divine" Caravaggio painted in Rome while escaping charges of murder in Malta.

The **Royal Apartments (Appartamenti Reali)** ★ boast lavish reminders of when the Pitti was a private residence. This was once the home of the kings of Savoy, when they presided over a unified Italy. You can see these apartments in all their baroque sumptuousness, including a flamboyant decor and works of art by del Sarto and Caravaggio.

The **Modern Art Gallery (Galleria d'Arte Moderna; ℂ 055-2388616)** can easily be skipped if you're exhausted after all those Titians. Nevertheless, it contains an important collection of 19th-century proto-Impressionist works of the Macchiaioli school, embracing many romantic and neoclassical pieces. Even if you don't like the art, the incredible view from the top floor is worth the visit.

The opulence of the Galleria Palatina at the Pitti Palace.

The **Gallery of Costume (Galleria del Costume),** in the Palazzina della Meridiana wing of the Modern Art gallery, traces the history of dress over 2 centuries, from the tight corsets and wide panniers of the 18th century to the beginning of the loose flapper dresses in the 1920s. Some of the costumes are even older.

The ground-floor **Museum of Silver (Museo degli Argenti)** ★ displays the household wares of the Medicis, everything from precious ivory, silver, and rare gems to Lorenzo the Magnificent's celebrated collection of vases. These precious stone vases spawned a vogue for *pietra dura* (precious stonework) in the 19th century (the English called it Florentine mosaic). One writer called the entire collection here "a camp glorification of the Medici." Many of the exhibits are in dubious taste. The Museo degli Argenti has a separate number to call for information (ℂ **055-2388709**).

Behind the Pitti Palace are the **Boboli Gardens (Giardini di Boboli)** ★★, Piazza Pitti 1 (ℂ **055-2388786**), through which the Medicis romped. These Renaissance gardens were laid out by Triboli, a great landscape artist, in the 16th century. Although plans were drawn up for them in 1549, they weren't completed until 1656 and weren't open to the public until 1766. The Boboli is ever popular for a stroll or an idyllic interlude in a pleasant setting. You can climb to the top of the Fortezza di Belvedere for a dazzling view of the city. The gardens are filled with fountains and statuary, such as *Venus* by Giambologna in the "Grotto" of Buontalenti. Our favorite? An absurd Mannerist piece depicting Cosimo I's court jester posing as a chubby Bacchus riding a turtle, next to the **Vasari Corridor** (see below for the Uffizi).

After a visit to the Boboli, wander over to the adjoining site, **Giardino Bardini,** a 14th-century garden spread over a 4-hectare (10-acre) site. The gardens, originally designed in 1309, reopened in 2005 after a 30-year slumber following a drawn-out legal wrangle. The government finally took over the gardens and began a 5-year restoration program. Views here are just as good as at Boboli, and Bardini also contains a temple, grottoes, an English-style copse of holly and oak, and a baroque staircase bordered by Bengal roses.

Piazza Pitti, across the Arno. ✆ **055-2388614.** www.polomuseale.firenze.it. Palatina and Modern Art Gallery 8.50€; 7€ for both Argenti and Boboli Gardens. Galleria Palatina, Appartamenti Reali, and Modern Art Gallery Tues–Sun 8:15am–6:50pm. Boboli Gardens and Museo degli Argenti Nov–Feb daily 8:15am–4:30pm; Mar daily 8:15am–5:30pm; Apr–May and Sept–Oct daily 8:15am–8:30-pm; June–Aug daily 8:15am–6:50pm. Closed the 1st and last Mon of each month. Ticket office closes 1 hr. before the gardens. Bus: C1, C2, 11, 36, 37, or 68.

St. Mark's Museum (Museo di San Marco) ★★   This state museum is a handsome Renaissance monastery whose cell walls are decorated with frescoes by the mystical **Fra Angelico,** one of Europe's greatest 15th-century painters. In the days of Cosimo de' Medici, San Marco was built by Michelozzo as a Dominican convent. It contained bleak, bare cells, which Angelico and his students brightened considerably with some of the most important works by this pious artist of Fiesole, who portrayed recognizable landscapes in vivid colors.

After buying a ticket, you enter the **Cloister of St. Anthony (Chiostro di Sant'Antonio),** designed by Michelozzo. Turn right in the cloister to enter the **Ospizio dei Pellegrini,** a virtual Fra Angelico gallery filled with painted panels and altarpieces. Here you'll see one of his better-known paintings, *The Last Judgment* ★★ (1431), depicting people with angels on the left dancing in a circle and lordly saints towering overhead. Hell, as it's depicted on the right, is infested with demons, reptiles, and sinners boiling in a stew. Much of hell was

created by Angelico's students; his brush was inspired only by the Crucifixion, Madonnas, and bambini, or landscapes, of course. Henry James claimed that Angelico "never received an intelligible impression of evil; and his conception of human life was a perpetual sense of sacredly loving and being loved." Here also are his *Deposition* (ca. 1440), an altarpiece removed from Santa Trìnita, and his *Madonna dei Linaiuoli,* commissioned by the flax workers' guild. Other works to look for are Angelico's panels from the life of Christ.

Detail from Fra Angelico's *The Last Judgment* at St. Mark's Museum.

Now you can enter the courtyard, where a sign points the way to the **Chapter House (Capitolare),** to the right of a large convent bell. Here you can see a large *Crucifixion and Saints* painted in 1442 by Fra Angelico. Returning to the courtyard, follow the sign into the **Refectory (Refettorio)** to see a *Last Supper* by Domenico Ghirlandaio, who taught Michelangelo how to fresco. This work is rather realistic, with the faces of the saints evoking a feeling of impending doom.

From the courtyard, you can go up to the second floor to view the highlight of the museum: Fra Angelico's *The Annunciation* ★★★. The rest of the floor is taken up with dorm cells, 44 small cells once used by the Dominicans (nos. 12–14 were once occupied by Savonarola and contain portraits of the reformer by Bartolomeo, who was plunged into acute melancholy by the jailing and torturing of his beloved teacher). Most of the cells were frescoed by Angelico and his students from 1439 to 1445, and depict scenes from the Crucifixion.

Piazza San Marco 1. ℘ **055-2388608.** www.firenzemusei.it. Admission 4€. Mon–Fri 8:15am–1:50pm; Sat 8:15am–6:50pm; Sun 8:15am–4:50pm. Ticket office closes 30 min. before the museum. Closed 2nd and 4th Mon and 1st, 3rd, and 5th Sun of the month; Jan 1; May 1; and Christmas. Bus: 7, 10, 11, 17, or 33.

Uffizi Gallery (Galleria degli Uffizi) ★★★   When Anna Maria Ludovica, the last Medici grand duchess, died in 1737, she bequeathed to the people of Tuscany a wealth of Renaissance and even classical art. The paintings and sculptures had been accumulated by the powerful grand dukes during 3 centuries of rule that witnessed the height of the Renaissance. The collection is housed in an impressive *palazzo* commissioned by Duke Cosimo de' Medici in 1560 and initiated by Giorgio Vasari to house the Duchy of Tuscany's administrative offices (*uffizi* means offices).

After several renovations following a terrorist bomb in 1993, the Uffizi has a new look. A lobby has been added so that visitors don't have to wait in line outside; the galleries at the upper two floors are three times their previous size; the *trompe l'oeil* painting in the Loggiato sull'Arno has been restored to its original beauty; and walking down this hall, looking through the windows, you'll have enchanting views of Florence. There's also a bookstore.

You can buy tickets in advance through **Firenze Musei** (℘ **055-294-883;** www.firenzemusei.it) and **www.selectitaly.com**, which has a full catalog of the museum's works on the Web. Any hotel in Florence that has a concierge can also make reservations for you, cutting down on the lines and hassle.

The Uffizi is nicely grouped into periods or schools to show the development and progress of Italian and European art.

Room 2: Here you'll meet up with those rebels from Byzantium, Cimabue and his pupil Giotto, with their Madonnas and bambini. Because the Virgin and Child seem to be the overriding theme of the earlier Uffizi artists, it's enlightening just to follow the different styles over the centuries, from the ugly, almost midget-faced babies of the post-Byzantine works to the red-cheeked chubby cherubs that glorified the baroque. One of the great works in the center of the salon is Giotto's masterful *Ognissanti Maestà* ★★ (1310).

Room 3: Look for Simone Martini's *Annunciation,* full of grace; the halo around the head of the Virgin doesn't conceal her pouty mouth.

Room 7: Fra Angelico of Fiesole, a 15th-century painter lost in a world peopled with saints and angels, makes his Uffizi debut with (naturally) *Madonna and Bambino.* Fra Angelico's *Coronation of the Virgin* is also in this salon.

Room 8: Here you'll find Fra Filippo Lippi's superior ***Coronation of the Virgin*** ★, as well as a galaxy of charming Madonnas. Lippi was a rebel among the brethren.

Rooms 10 to 14: These are the **Botticelli rooms,** with his finest works. Botticelli ("Little Barrels") was the nickname of the great master of women in flowing gowns, Sandro Filipepi. Many come to contemplate his "Venus on the Half Shell": This supreme conception of life (more formally known as the ***Birth of Venus*** ★★★) really packs 'em in. Also check out *Minerva Subduing the Centaur,* which brought about renewed interest in mythological subjects. Botticelli's ***Allegory of Spring,*** or ***Primavera*** ★★, is a gem; it depicts Venus in a citrus grove with Cupid hovering over her head and Mercury looking out of the canvas to the left. Before leaving the room, look for Botticelli's *Adoration of the Magi,* in which you'll find portraits of the Medici (the vain man at the far right is Botticelli, with golden curls and a yellow robe), and his allegorical *Calumny.*

Room 15: Here you'll come across one of Leonardo da Vinci's unfinished paintings, the brilliant ***Adoration of the Magi*** ★★. Also here hangs Leonardo's *Annunciation,* reflecting the early years of his genius with its twilight atmosphere and each leaf painstakingly in place. The splendid Renaissance palace that he designed is part of the background.

Room 19: This room is devoted to Perugino, especially his *Madonna* and his *Portrait of Francesco delle Opere,* and to Luca Signorelli's *Holy Family.* Signorelli was taught by his master, Piero della Francesca, to convey depth and perspective, as illustrated by this work.

A detail of the three Graces from Botticelli's *Allegory of Spring (Primavera)* at the Uffizi Gallery.

Room 20: This room takes you into the world of German artists who worked in Florence, notably Lukas Cranach and Dürer, both intrigued with the Adam and Eve theme.

Room 21: You'll see the beginnings of important Venetian painting here, with works by Giambellino and Giorgione. The best example is Giovanni Bellini's *Sacred Allegory.*

Room 22: This room contains a cavalcade of works by northern Europeans, particularly Flemish and German works, especially Hans Holbein the Younger's ***Portrait of Sir Richard Southwell.***

Room 23: Correggio's ***Rest on the Flight to Egypt*** ★ (1515) dominates this room, but the finest pieces are by Andrea Mantegna (1489): ***Epiphany, Circumcision,*** and ***Ascension*** ★★.

Room 25: The star here is Michelangelo's magnificent ***Holy Family*** ★★ (1506–08). This is one of the few panel paintings by the great artist, still glowing with color, although its nudes are hardly as shocking as they once were. Michelangelo also designed the elaborate frame.

Room 26: This salon displays one of Raphael's most celebrated works, *Madonna of the Goldfinch* (1505). The work was painted in the Leonardo-esque style for the wedding of a friend. Also showcased here are the artist's portraits of *Pope Leo X with Cardinals Giulio de' Medici, Luigi de' Rossi,* and *Pope Julius II,* as well as Raphael's self-portrait. This room is also devoted to works by Andrea del Sarto's star Mannerist pupils, Rosso Fiorentino and Pontormo, and by Pontormo's adopted son, Bronzino.

Room 28 and the rest: Masterpieces in the salons include two Venuses by Titian, Veronese's *Martyrdom of St. Justina,* Tintoretto's *Leda and the Swan,* Rubens's *Portrait of Philip IV of Spain* and *Judith and Holofernes,* and Caravaggio's *Adolescent Bacchus* and *The Head of Medusa.*

Michelangelo's *Holy Family* at the Uffizi Gallery.

Vasari Corridor (Corridoio Vasariano): This corridor, commissioned from Vasari by Cosimo I after the Uffizi's completion, is an aboveground "tunnel" running along the rooftops of the Ponte Vecchio buildings and connecting the Uffizi with Cosimo's residence in the Palazzo Pitti (Pitti Palace) on the other side of the Arno (see earlier). The corridor is lined with portraits and self-portraits by a stellar list of international masters, including Bronzino, Rubens, Rembrandt, and Ingres. Access to the corridor is highly limited; plan to make your reservation months in advance if you wish to see it during your Uffizi tour (see below).

Piazzale degli Uffizi 6. ✆ **055-294883.** www.polomuseale.firenze.it. Admission 10€. Tues–Sun 8:15am–7pm (last entrance 45 min. before closing). Bus: C1, C2, 14, or 23.

Reserving Tickets for the Uffizi & Other Attractions

The endless lines outside the Italian museums are a fact of life. But new reservation services can help you avoid waiting, at least for some of the major museums.

Select Italy offers the possibility to reserve your tickets for the Uffizi, Boboli Gardens, Galleria dell'Accademia, and many other attractions in Florence (plus Rome and Venice). The cost varies from 16€ to 37€, depending on the museum, and several combination passes are available. Contact Select Italy at ✆ **800/ 877-1755,** or buy online at www.select italy.com.

If you're already in Florence and don't want to waste a half-day waiting in line, call **Firenze Musei** (✆ **055-2654321;** www.firenzemusei.it). The service operates Monday to Friday 8:30am to 6:30pm, and Saturday to 12:30pm. Requests must be made a minimum of 5 days in advance; you pick up the tickets at the museum booth on the day your visit has been approved. There's a service charge of 3€, plus, of course, the regular price of the museum admission.

If your hotel has a concierge, don't be shy about asking what he can do to get you tickets.

The Duomo, Campanile & Baptistery

In the heart of Florence, at **Piazza del Duomo** and **Piazza San Giovanni** (named after John the Baptist), is a complex of ecclesiastical buildings that form a triumvirate of top sights.

Il Duomo (Cattedrale di Santa Maria del Fiore) ★★★   The Duomo, graced by Filippo Brunelleschi's red-tiled dome, is the crowning glory of Florence and the star of the skyline. Before entering, take time to view the exterior, with its geometrically patterned bands of white, pink, and green marble; this tricolor mosaic is an interesting contrast to the sienna-colored fortresslike *palazzi* around the city. The Duomo is one of the world's largest churches and represents the flowering of the "Florentine Gothic" style. Construction stretched over centuries: Begun in 1296, it was finally consecrated in 1436, although finishing touches on the facade were applied as late as the 19th century.

Volunteers offer **free tours** of the cathedral every day except Sunday from 10am to 12:30pm and 3 to 5pm. Most of them speak English; if there are many of you and you want to confirm tour availability, call ✆ **055-2710757** (Tues–Fri, mornings only). Looking rather professorial and kindly, they can be found sitting at a table along the right (south) wall as you enter the Duomo. They expect no payment, but a nominal donation to the church is always appreciated. They also organize tours of Santa Croce and Santa Maria Novella.

Brunelleschi's efforts to build the **dome ★★★** (1420–36) could be the subject of a Hollywood script. At one time before his plans were accepted, the architect was tossed out on his derrière and denounced as an idiot. He eventually won the commission by a clever "egg trick," as related in Giorgio Vasari's *Lives of the Painters,* written in the 16th century: The architect challenged his competitors to make an egg stand on a flat piece of marble. Each artist tried to make the egg stand, but each failed. When it was Brunelleschi's turn, he took the egg and cracked its bottom slightly on the marble and thus made it stand upright. Each of the other artists said he could've done the same thing, if he'd known he could crack the egg. Brunelleschi retorted that they also would've known how to vault the cupola if they had seen his model or plans.

His dome, a "monument for posterity," was erected without supports. When Michelangelo began to construct a dome over St. Peter's, he paid tribute to Brunelleschi's earlier cupola in Florence: "I am going to make its sister larger, yes, but not lovelier." You can climb 463 spiraling steps to the ribbed dome for a view that's well worth the trek (however, you can climb only 414 steps and get the same view from Giotto's campanile, below).

Inside, the overall effect of the cathedral is bleak because much of the decoration has been moved to the Duomo Museum (see below). However, note the restored frescoes covering the inside of the cupola; begun by Giorgio Vasari and completed by Federico Zuccari, they depict the Last Judgment. The three stained-glass windows by Ghiberti on the entrance wall are next to Uccello's giant clock using the heads of the four prophets. Some of the stained-glass windows in the dome were based on designs by Donatello (Brunelleschi's friend) and Ghiberti (Brunelleschi's rival).

Also in the cathedral are some terra cottas by Luca della Robbia. In 1432 Ghiberti took time out from his "Gates to Paradise" for the baptistery (see below) and designed the tomb of St. Zenobius. Excavations in the depths of the cathedral have brought to light the remains of the ancient Cathedral of Santa Reparata (tombs, columns, and floors), which was probably founded in the 5th century and transformed in the following centuries until it was demolished to make way for the present cathedral. The entrance to the excavations is via a stairway near the front of this cathedral, to the right as you enter. Look for the sign SCAVI DELLA CRIPTA DI SANTA REPARATA (Excavation of the Crypt of Santa Reparata).

Incidentally, during excavations in 1972, Brunelleschi's tomb was discovered, and new discoveries indicate the existence of a second tomb nearby. It's speculated that Giotto's tomb, which has never been found, might be in the right nave, beneath the campanile bearing his name.

Piazza del Duomo. (*?* **055-2302885.** www.opera duomo.firenze.it. Cathedral free admission; excavations 3€; cupola 8€. Duomo Mon–Wed and Fri 10am–5pm; Thurs 10am–3:30pm; Sat 10am–4:45pm (1st Sat of each month 10am–3:30pm); Sun 1:30–4:45pm. Cupola Mon–Fri 8:30am–7pm; Sat 8:30am–5:40pm. Bus: C1 or C2.

The Duomo, featuring Brunelleschi's dome.

Giotto's Bell Tower (Campanile di Giotto) ★★   If we can believe the accounts of his contemporaries, Giotto was the ugliest man ever to walk the streets of Florence. It's ironic, then, that he left to posterity Europe's most beautiful campanile, rhythmic in line and form. That Giotto was given the position of *capomastro* and grand architect (and pensioned for 100 gold florins for his service) is remarkable in itself because he's famous for freeing painting from the confinements of Byzantium. He designed the campanile in the last 2 or 3 years of his life and died before its completion.

The final work was carried out by Andrea Pisano, one of Italy's greatest Gothic sculptors (see his bronze doors on the baptistery). The "Tuscanized" Gothic tower, with bands of the same colored marble as the Duomo, stands 84m (274 ft.) high; you can climb 414 steps to the top for a panorama of the sienna-colored city. After Giotto's death, Pisano and Luca della Robbia did some fine bas-relief and sculptural work, now in the Duomo Museum (see below).

If you can make the tough climb up (and up and up) the cramped stairs, the **view** ★★★ from the top of Giotto's bell tower is unforgettable, sweeping over the city, the surrounding hills, and Medici villas.

Piazza del Duomo. (*?* **055-2302885.** www.operaduomo.firenze.it. Admission 6€. Daily 8:30am–7:30pm. Last admission 40 min. before closing. Closed Jan 1, Easter, Sept 8, and Christmas. Bus: C1 or C2.

Baptistery (Battistero San Giovanni) ★★★   Named after the city's patron saint, Giovanni (John the Baptist), the octagonal baptistery dates from the 11th and 12th centuries. It's the oldest structure in Florence and is a highly original interpretation of the Romanesque style, with bands of pink, white, and green marble to match the Duomo and campanile.

Visitors from all over the world come to gape at its three sets of **bronze doors** ★★★. In his work on two sets of the doors (the east and the north), Lorenzo Ghiberti reached the pinnacle of his artistry in quattrocento (early 1400s) Florence. To win his first commission on the north doors, the 23-year-old sculptor had to compete against formidable opposition such as Donatello, Brunelleschi (architect of the Duomo's dome), and Siena-born Jacopo della Quercia. Upon seeing Ghiberti's work, Donatello and Brunelleschi conceded defeat. By the time he had completed the work on the north doors, Ghiberti was around 44. The gilt-covered panels (representing scenes from the New Testament, including the Annunciation, the Adoration, and Christ debating the elders in the temple) make up a flowing narration in bronze. To protect them from the elements, the originals are now in the Duomo Museum (see below), but the copies are works of art unto themselves.

After Ghiberti's long labor, the Florentines gratefully gave him the task of sculpting the east doors (directly opposite the Duomo entrance). Given carte blanche, he designed his masterpiece, choosing as his subject familiar scenes from the Old Testament, such as Adam and Eve at the creation. This time Ghiberti labored over the rectangular panels from 1425 to 1452 (he died in 1455). Upon seeing the finished work, Michelangelo is said to have exclaimed, "These doors are fit to stand at the gates of Paradise," and so they've been nicknamed the "Gates of Paradise" ever since. Ghiberti apparently agreed: He claimed that he personally planned and designed the Renaissance— all on his own.

Shuttled off to adorn the south entrance and to make way for Ghiberti's "Gates of Paradise" were the baptistery's oldest doors, by Andrea Pisano, mentioned earlier for his work on Giotto's bell tower. For his subject, the Gothic sculptor represented the "Virtues" as well as scenes from the life of John the Baptist, whom the baptistery honors. The door was completed in 1336. On the interior (walk through Pisano's door—no charge) the dome is adorned with 13th-century mosaics, dominated by a figure of Christ. Mornings are reserved for worship.

Piazza San Giovanni. ℰ **055-2302885.** www. operaduomo.firenze.it. Admission 4€. Mon–Sat 12:15–7pm; Sun 8:30am–2pm. Last admission 30 min. before closing. Bus: C1 or C2.

The baptistery, with its glittering bronze doors by Lorenzo Ghiberti.

Duomo Museum (Museo dell'Opera del Duomo) ★★ This museum, across from the Duomo but facing the apse of Santa Maria del Fiore, is beloved by connoisseurs of Renaissance sculpture. It houses the sculpture that was removed from the campanile and the Duomo, to protect the pieces from the weather and from visitors who want samples. A major attraction is **Michelangelo's unfinished *Pietà*** ★★, in the middle of the stairs. It was carved between 1548 and 1555, when the artist was in his 70s. In this vintage work, a figure representing Nicodemus (but said to have Michelangelo's face) is holding Christ. The Florentine intended it for his own tomb, but he's believed to have grown disenchanted with it and attempted to destroy it. The museum has a Brunelleschi bust, as well as della Robbia terra cottas. The premier attraction is the restored **panels of Ghiberti's "Gates of Paradise"** ★★★, which were removed from the baptistery. In gilded bronze, each is a masterpiece of Renaissance sculpture, perhaps the finest low-relief perspective in all Italian art.

You'll see bits and pieces from what was the old Gothic-Romanesque fronting of the cathedral, with ornamental statues, as conceived by the original architect, Arnolfo di Cambio. One of Donatello's early works, **St. John the Evangelist,** is here—not his finest hour, but anything by Donatello is worth looking at. One of his most celebrated works, the ***Magdalene*** ★★, is in the room with the *cantorie* (see below). This wooden statue once stood in the baptistery and had to be restored after the 1966 flood. Dating from 1454 to 1455, it's stark and penitent.

A good reason to come here is to see the **marble choirs (*cantorie*) of Donatello and Luca della Robbia** ★★. (The works face each other and are in the first room you enter after climbing the stairs.) The della Robbia choir is more restrained, but it still "praises the Lord" in marble, with clashing cymbals and sounding brass that constitute a reaffirmation of life. In contrast, the dancing cherubs of Donatello's choir are a romp of chubby bambini. Of all Donatello's

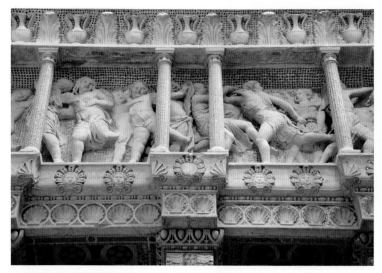

A detail from the della Robbia marble choirs at the Duomo Museum.

works, this one is the most lighthearted. But, in contrast, lavish your attention on Donatello's **Zuccone,** one of his masterpieces, created for Giotto's bell tower.

Piazza del Duomo 9. (*) **055-2302885.** www.operaduomo.firenze.it. Admission 6€. Mon–Sat 9am–7:30pm; Sun 9am–1:45pm. Last admission 40 min. before closing. Closed Jan 1, Easter, Sept 8, and Christmas. Bus: C1 or C2.

On or near Piazza Della Signoria

The L-shaped **Piazza della Signoria** ★★, though never completed, is one of Italy's most beautiful squares. It was the center of secular life in the days of the Medici and is today a virtual sculpture gallery. Through it pranced church robbers, connoisseurs of entrails, hired assassins seeking employment, chicken farmers from Valdarno, book burners, and many great men (including Machiavelli, on a secret mission to the Palazzo Vecchio, and Leonardo da Vinci, trailed by his entourage).

On the square is the controversial **Fountain of Neptune** (1560–75), with the sea god surrounded by creatures from the deep, as well as frisky satyrs and nymphs. It was designed by Ammannati, who later repented for chiseling Neptune in the nude. But Michelangelo, to whom Ammannati owed a great debt, judged the fountain inferior. Florentines used to mock it as *Il Biancone* (Big Whitey). Actually, the Mannerist bronzes around the basin aren't at all bad; many might have been designed by a young Giambologna.

Near the fountain is a **small disk in the ground,** marking the spot where Savonarola was executed. This zealous monk was a fire-and-brimstone reformer who rivaled Dante in conjuring up the punishment that hell would inflict on sin-

ners. His chief targets were Lorenzo the Magnificent and the Borgia pope, Alexander VI, who excommunicated him. Savonarola whipped the Florentine faithful into an orgy of religious fanaticism but eventually fell from favor. Along with two other friars, he was hanged in the square in 1498. Afterward, as the crowds threw stones, a pyre underneath the men consumed their bodies. It's said that the reformer's heart was found whole and grabbed up by souvenir collectors. His ashes were tossed into the Arno.

For centuries, Michelangelo's *David* stood in this square, but it was moved to the Accademia in the 19th century. The work that you see on the square today is an inferior copy, commonly assumed by many first-timers to be Michelangelo's original. Near the towering statue stands Baccio Bandinelli's *Heracles* (1534). Bandinelli, however, was no Michelangelo, and his statue has been denounced through the centuries; Cellini dismissed it as a "sack of melons."

The 14th-century **Loggia della Signoria** (or **Loggia dei Lanzi**) ★★ houses a gallery of sculpture often depicting violent scenes.

The Fountain of Neptune in the Piazza della Signoria.

The most famous piece is a rare work by Benvenuto Cellini, the goldsmith and tell-all autobiographer. Critics have claimed that his exquisite but ungentlemanly *Perseus* ★★★, holding up the severed head of Medusa, is the most significant Florentine sculpture since Michelangelo's *Night* and *Day.* Three other well-known pieces are Giambologna's bronze **statue of Duke Cosimo de' Medici on horseback,** celebrating the man who subjugated all Tuscany under his military rule; his *Rape of the Sabines,* an essay in three-dimensional Mannerism; and his *Hercules with Nessus the Centaur,* and a chorus line of half a dozen Roman Vestal wallflowers.

Palazzo Vecchio ★★   The secular "Old Palace" is Florence's most famous and imposing *palazzo.* Gothic master builder Arnolfo di Cambio constructed it from 1299 to 1302, although it wasn't until 1540 that Cosimo I and the Medicis called it home. Its most remarkable architectural feature is the 94m (308-ft.) tower, an engineering feat that required supreme skill at the time. Today the Palazzo is occupied by city employees, but much is open to the public.

The 16th-century **Hall of the 500 (Salone dei Cinquecento),** the most outstanding part of the palace, is filled with Vasari and company frescoes as well as sculpture. A tragic loss to Renaissance art, the frescoes originally done by Leonardo da Vinci in 1503 melted when braziers were brought in to speed up the drying process. The ever-inventive Leonardo had used wax in his pigments, and, of course, the frescoes melted under the heat. As you enter the hall, look for Michelangelo's *Victory* ★, depicting an insipid-looking young man treading on a bearded older man (it has been suggested that Michelangelo put his own face on that of the trampled man). This statue (1533–34) was originally intended for the tomb of Pope Julius but was later acquired by the Medicis.

Later you can stroll through the rest of the palace, examining its apartments and main halls. You can also visit the private apartments of Eleanor of Toledo, the

The Palazzo Vecchio, in the Piazza della Signoria.

> ## The Ponte Vecchio
>
> Spared by the Nazis in their bitter retreat from the Allied advance in 1944, the "Old Bridge" at Via Por Santa Maria and Via Guicciardini is the last remaining medieval *ponte* spanning the Arno (the Germans blew up the rest). It was again threatened in the 1966 flood, when the waters of the Arno swept over it and washed away a fortune in jewelry from the goldsmiths' shops flanking the bridge.
>
> The Ponte Vecchio was built in 1220, probably on the Roman site of a bridge for the Via Cassia, the ancient road running through Florence on its way to Rome. Vasari claims that Taddeo Gaddi reconstructed it in 1354, and Vasari himself designed the corridor running over it (see the Uffizi entry, earlier in this chapter). Once home to butchers, it was cleared of this stench by Ferdinand de' Medici, who allowed these "vile arts" to give way to goldsmiths and jewelers, who have remained ever since.
>
> Today the restored Ponte Vecchio is closed to vehicular traffic. The little shops continue to sell everything from the most expensive of Florentine gold to something simple—say, a Lucrezia Borgia poison ring.

Spanish wife of Cosimo I, and a chapel begun in 1540 and frescoed by Bronzino. The palace displays the original of **Verrocchio's bronze putto** (1476) from the courtyard fountain, called both *Winged Cherub Clutching a Fish* and *Boy with a Dolphin*. You'll also find a 16th-century portrait of Machiavelli that's attributed to Santi di Tito. Donatello's bronze group, ***Judith Slaying Holofernes*** ★ (1455), once stood on Piazza della Signoria but was brought inside. The salons, such as a fleur-de-lis apartment, have their own richness and beauty.

Following his arrest, Savonarola was taken to the Palazzo Vecchio for more than a dozen torture sessions, including "twists" on the rack. The torturer pronounced Savonarola his best customer.

Piazza della Signoria. © **055-2768224.** www.museicivicifiorentini.it. Admission 6€. Fri–Wed 9am–7pm; Thurs 9am–2pm. Ticket office closes 1 hr. before palace. Bus: C1, C2, or 23.

Near Piazza San Lorenzo

Piazza San Lorenzo and its satellite, Piazza Madonna degli Aldobrandini, are lively and colorful. A huge market, the Mercato Centrale, forms around the church of San Lorenzo, continuing all the way to the area of San Marco. For details, see "Shopping," later in this chapter.

Basilica di San Lorenzo ★★ This is Brunelleschi's 1426 Renaissance church, where the Medicis attended services from their nearby palace on Via Larga, now Via Camillo Cavour. Critic Walter Pater found it "great rather by what it designed or aspired to do, than by what it actually achieved." Most visitors flock to see Michelangelo's New Sacristy with his *Night* and *Day* (see the Medici Chapels, below), but Brunelleschi's handwork deserves some time, too.

Built in the style of a Latin cross, the church is distinguished by harmonious grays and rows of Corinthian columns. The **Old Sacristy** (**Vecchia Sacrestia;** walk up the nave and then turn left) was designed by Brunelleschi and decorated in part by Donatello (view his terra-cotta bust of St. Lawrence). The Old Sacristy is often cited as the first and finest work of the early Renaissance. Even more intriguing are the two bronze 1460 pulpits of Donatello, among his last works, a project carried out by students following his death in 1466. Scenes depict Christ's passion and resurrection.

After exploring the Old Sacristy, go through the first door (unmarked) on your right, and you'll emerge outside. A sign will point to the entrance of the **Medici Laurentian Library** ★★ (**Biblioteca Medicea Laurenziana;** ✆ **055-210760;** www.bml.firenze.it), which you enter at Piazza San Lorenzo 9. Designed by Michelangelo to shelter the expanding collection of the Medicis, the library is a brilliant example of Mannerist architecture, its chief attraction a curving flight of stone steps. Michelangelo worked on it in 1524, but the finishing touches were completed in 1578 by Vasari and Ammannati. Michelangelo, however, designed the reading benches. The library is filled with some of Italy's greatest manuscripts, many of which are handsomely illustrated. In the rare book collection are autographs by Petrarch, Machiavelli, Poliziano, and Napoleon. You're kept at a distance by protective glass, but it's well worth the visit.

Piazza San Lorenzo. ✆ **055-210760.** Free admission. Mon, Wed, and Fri 8am–5:30pm. Bus: 1, 6, 7, 11, 17, 33, 67, or 68.

Medici Chapels (Cappelle Medicee) ★★ The Medici tombs are adjacent to the Basilica of San Lorenzo (see above). You enter the tombs, housing the "blue-blooded" Medici, in back of the church by going around to Piazza Madonna degli Aldobrandini. First you'll pass through the baroque **Chapel of the Princes (Cappella dei Principi),** that octagon of death often denounced for its "trashy opulence." In back of the altar is a collection of Italian reliquaries.

Hidden gem: Discovered in a sepulchral chamber beneath the Medici Chapels with access via a trapdoor and a winding staircase was **Michelangelo's only group of mural sketches** ★. Apparently, he had used the walls as a giant doodling sheet. The drawings include a sketch of the legs of Duke Giuliano, Christ risen, and the *Laocoön,* the Hellenistic figure group. Fifty drawings, done in charcoal on plaster walls, were found. You can ask for a free ticket to view the sketches at the ticket office for the chapels.

The real reason you come here is to see the **New Sacristy (Nuova Sacrestia)** ★★★, designed by Michelangelo as a gloomy mausoleum. "Do not wake me; speak softly here," Michelangelo wrote in a bitter verse. Working from 1521 to 1534, he created the Medici tombs in a style that foreshadowed the baroque. Lorenzo the Magnificent—a ruler who seemed to embody the qualities of the Renaissance itself and was one of the greatest names in the history of the Medici family—was buried near Michelangelo's uncompleted *Madonna and Child* group, a simple monument evoking a promise unfulfilled.

Ironically, the finest groups of sculpture were reserved for two Medici "clan" members, who (in the words of Mary McCarthy) "would better have been forgotten." Both are represented by Michelangelo as armored, idealized princes of the Renaissance. In fact, Lorenzo II, duke of Urbino, depicted as "the thinker," was a deranged young man (just out of his teens when he died). Michelangelo wasn't working to glorify these two Medici dukes. Rather, he was chiseling for posterity. The other two figures on Lorenzo's tomb are most often called ***Dawn*** and ***Dusk,*** with morning represented as a woman and evening as a man.

The two best-known figures, showing Michelangelo at his most powerful, are ***Night*** and ***Day*** ★★★ at the feet of Giuliano, the duke of Nemours. *Night* is chiseled as a woman in troubled sleep, and *Day* is depicted as a man of strength awakening to a foreboding world. These figures weren't the works of Michelangelo's innocence.

Piazza Madonna degli Aldobrandini 6. ☎ **055-2388602.** www.polomuseale.firenze.it. Admission 6€. Daily 8:15am–1:50pm. Closed 2nd and 4th Sun, and 1st, 3rd, and 5th Mon of each month. Bus: 1, 6, 7, 11, 17, 33, 67, or 68.

Palazzo Medici-Riccardi ★   This palace, a short walk from the Duomo, was the home of Cosimo de' Medici before he took his household to the Palazzo Vecchio. At the apogee of the Medici power, it was adorned with some of the world's greatest masterpieces, such as Donatello's *David.* Built by Michelozzo in the mid–15th century, the brown stone building was also the scene, at times, of the court of Lorenzo the Magnificent. Art lovers visit today chiefly to see **Benozzo Gozzoli's mid-15th-century frescoes ★★** in the **Medici Chapel** (not to be confused with the Medici Chapels, above). Gozzoli's frescoes, depicting the journey of the Magi, form his masterpiece—they're a hallmark in Renaissance painting. Although he takes a religious theme as his subject, the artist turned it into a gay romp, a pageant of royals, knights, and pages with fun mascots such as greyhounds and even a giraffe. It's a fairy-tale world come alive, with faces of the Medicis and local celebrities who were as famous as Madonna in their day but are known only to scholars today.

Another gallery, which you enter via a separate stairway, was frescoed by Luca Giordano in the 18th century, but his work seems merely decorative. The apartments, where the prefect lodges, aren't open to the public.

Via Camillo Cavour 1. ☎ **055-2760340.** www.palazzo-medici.it. Admission 7€. Thurs–Tues 9am–7pm. Bus: 1, 6, 11, or 17.

A detail from Michelangelo's New Sacristy in the Medici Chapels.

On or near Piazza Della Santissima Annunziata

Lovely **Piazza della Santissima Annunziata** is surrounded on three sides by arcades. In the center is an equestrian statue of Grand Duke Ferdinand I, by Giambologna. The Hospital of the Innocents stands on the eastern side. Once Brunelleschi wanted to create a perfectly symmetrical square here, but he died before his plans could be realized. The piazza is a popular student hangout.

Archaeology Museum (Museo Archeologico) ★★   This museum, a short walk from Piazza della Santissima Annunziata, houses one of Europe's most outstanding Egyptian and Etruscan collections in a palace built for Grand Duchess Maria Maddalena of Austria. The Etruscan-loving Medicis began that collection, although the Egyptian loot was first acquired by Leopold II in the 1830s. Its Egyptian mummies and sarcophagi are on the first floor, along with some of the better-known Etruscan works. Pause to look at the lid to the coffin of a fat Etruscan (unlike the blank faces staring back from many of these tombs, this man's countenance is quite expressive).

One room is graced with three bronze Etruscan masterpieces, among the rarest objets d'art of these relatively unknown people. They include the *Chimera,* a lion with a goat sticking out of its back. This was an Etruscan work of the 5th century B.C., found near Arezzo in 1555. The lion's tail—in the form of a venomous reptile—lunges at the trapped beast. The others are *Minerva* and an *Orator,* ranging from the 5th to the 1st centuries B.C. Another rare find is a Roman bronze of a young man, the so-called *Idolino,* fished from the sea at Pesaro. The statue has always been shrouded in mystery; it might have been a Roman statue sculpted around the time of Christ. The François vase on the ground floor, from 570 B.C., is celebrated. A prize in the Egyptian department is a wood-and-bone chariot, beautifully preserved, that astonishingly dates from a tomb in Thebes from the 14th century B.C.

Via della Colonna 36. (℃ **055-23575.** www.firenzemusei.it. Admission 3€. Mon 2–7pm; Tues–Thurs 8:30am–7pm; Wed and Fri–Sun 8:30am–2pm. Bus: 6, 31, or 32.

Hospital of the Innocents (Ospedale degli Innocenti)   Opened in 1445, this was the world's first hospital for foundlings, although the Medici and Florentine bankers weren't known for welfare benefits. The building and the loggia with its Corinthian columns were conceived by Brunelleschi and marked the first architectural bloom of the Renaissance in Florence. On the facade are terracotta medallions done in blues and opaque whites by Andrea della Robbia, depicting babes in swaddling clothes.

Still used as an orphanage, the building no longer has its "lazy Susan," where Florentines used to deposit unwanted *bambini,* ring the bell, and then flee. It does contain an art gallery, and notable among its treasures is a terra-cotta *Madonna and Child,* by Luca della Robbia, plus works by Sandro Botticelli. One of its most important paintings is Domenico Ghirlandaio's **Adoration of the Magi** (the chubby bambino looks a bit pompously at the Wise Man kissing his foot).

Piazza della Santissima Annunziata 12. (℃ **055-2491708.** www.istitutodeglinnocenti.it. Admission 4€. Daily 10am–7pm. Bus: 6, 31, or 32.

On Piazza Santa Maria Novella

Hardly the most beautiful or tranquil square, **Piazza Santa Maria Novella** overflows with traffic from the rail station. Vendors, backpackers, beggars, and buses and taxis vie for precious space. Visitors will want to tolerate this chaos for only one reason: to see the basilica.

Basilica di Santa Maria Novella ★★   Near the rail station is one of Florence's most distinguished churches, begun in 1278 for the Dominicans. Its geometric facade, with bands of white and green marble, was designed in the late 15th century by Leon Battista Alberti, an aristocrat and true Renaissance man (philosopher, painter, architect, poet). The church borrows from and harmonizes the Romanesque, Gothic, and Renaissance styles.

In the left nave as you enter, the third large painting is the great Masaccio's *Trinità* ★, a curious work that has the architectural form of a Renaissance stage setting but whose figures (in perfect perspective) are like actors in a Greek tragedy. A special treasure is the *Madonna* by Masaccio. In this painting you can see the beginning of the use of perspective. If you view the church at dusk, you'll see the stained-glass windows in the fading light cast kaleidoscope fantasies on the opposite wall.

Head straight up the left nave to the **Gondi Chapel (Cappella Gondi)** for a look at Brunelleschi's wooden *Christ on the Cross* ★, said to have been carved to compete with Donatello's same subject in Santa Croce (see below). According to Vasari in *Lives of the Artists,* when Donatello saw Brunelleschi's completed crucifix, he dropped his apron full of eggs intended for their lunch.

"You have symbolized the Christ," Donatello is alleged to have said. "Mine is an ordinary man." (Some art historians reject this story.)

In 1485, Ghirlandaio contracted with a Tornabuoni banker to adorn the sanctuary behind the main altar with frescoes illustrating scenes from the lives of Mary and John the Baptist. Michelangelo, a teenager at the time, is known to have studied under Ghirlandaio (perhaps he even worked on this cycle).

In the north transept, a staircase leads to the remarkable **Strozzi Chapel (Cappella Strozzi)** ★, honoring St. Thomas Aquinas. Decorated between 1350 and 1357 by Nardo di Cione and Andrea Orcagna, it depicts Dante's *Purgatorio* and *Inferno.* On the left wall is *Paradiso.*

If time remains, you might want to visit the **cloisters,** going first to the Green Cloister and then to the Spanish Chapel frescoed by Andrea di Bonaiuto in the 14th century (one panel depicts the Dominicans in triumph over wolves).

Basilica di Santa Maria Novella.

A view of the Duomo, dominated by Brunelleschi's dome.

Piazza Santa Maria Novella. (☎) **055-282187.** Church free admission; Spanish Chapel and cloisters 3.50€. Church Mon–Thurs 9am–5pm. Spanish Chapel and cloisters Sat and Mon–Thurs 9am–5pm. Bus: C1, C2, 6, 9, 11, 36, 37, or 68.

On or near Piazza Santa Croce

Every street leading to the famed **Piazza Santa Croce** seems to be lined with shops selling leather goods. The square has been an integral part of Florentine life for centuries, beginning when Franciscan friars used to preach here. The piazza used to be the playing field for *calcio* (soccer), and a marble disk in the center marks the center line of pitch. Today it's still devoted to popular gatherings such as games, events, and jousts.

○ Catching the View from Piazzale Michelangiolo

For a view of the wonders of Florence below and Fiesole above, climb aboard bus no. 12 or 13 at the Ponte alle Grazie (the first bridge east of the Ponte Vecchio) for a 15-minute ride to **Piazzale Michelangiolo,** an 1865 belvedere overlooking a view seen in many a Renaissance painting and on many a modern-day postcard. It's reached along Viale Michelangelo. It's best at dusk, when the purple-fringed Tuscan hills form a frame for Giotto's bell tower, Brunelleschi's dome, and the towering hunk of stones that stick up from the Palazzo Vecchio.

Another copy of **Michelangelo's** *David* dominates the square and gives the *piazzale* (wide piazza) its name. Crown your trip with a gelato at the **Gelateria Michelangelo** ((☎) **055-2342705**), open daily from 6am to 2am.

Warning: At certain times during the day, the square is overrun with tour buses and peddlers selling trinkets and cheap souvenirs. If you go at these times, often midday in summer, you'll find that the view of Florence is still intact—but you might be struck down by a Vespa or crushed in a crowd if you try to enjoy it.

Basilica di Santa Croce ★★   Think of this as Tuscany's Westminster Abbey. This church shelters the tombs of everyone from Michelangelo to Machiavelli, from Dante (he was actually buried at Ravenna) to Galileo, who at the hands of the Inquisition "recanted" his concept that the earth revolves around the sun. Just as Santa Maria Novella was the church of the Dominicans, Santa Croce, said to have been designed by Arnolfo di Cambio, was the church of the Franciscans.

In the right nave (the first tomb) is the Vasari-executed **monument to Michelangelo,** whose 89-year-old body was smuggled back to his native Florence from its original burial place in Rome, where the pope wanted the corpse to remain. Along with a bust of the artist are three allegorical figures representing the arts. In the next memorial, a prune-faced Dante, a poet honored belatedly in the city that exiled him, looks down. Farther on, still on the right, is the tomb of Niccolò Machiavelli, whose *The Prince* (about Cesare Borgia) became a virtual textbook in the art of wielding power. Nearby is Donatello's lyrical bas-relief, *The Annunciation.*

The **Trecento frescoes ★★** are reason enough for visiting Santa Croce—especially those by Giotto to the right of the main chapel. Once whitewashed, the Bardi and Peruzzi chapels were "uncovered" in the mid–19th century in such a clumsy fashion that they had to be drastically restored. Although badly preserved, the frescoes in the **Bardi Chapel (Cappella Bardi)** are most memorable, especially the deathbed scene of St. Francis. The cycles in the **Peruzzi Chapel (Cappella Peruzzi)** are of John the Baptist and St. John. In the left transept is Donatello's once-controversial wooden crucifix—too gruesome for some Renaissance tastes, including that of Brunelleschi, who is claimed to have said: "You [Donatello] have put a rustic upon the cross." (Brunelleschi's "answer" to the Donatello version here can be seen in Santa Maria Novella, above.) Incidentally, the **Pazzi Chapel (Cappella Pazzi),** entered through the cloisters, was designed by Brunelleschi, with terra cottas by Luca della Robbia.

Inside the monastery, the Franciscan fathers established the **Leather School (Scuola del Cuoio) ★** at the end of World War II. The purpose of the school was to prepare young boys technically to specialize in Florentine leatherwork. The school has flourished and produced many fine artisans who continue their careers here. Stop in and see the work when you visit the church.

Piazza Santa Croce 16. © **055-2466105.** www.santacroceopera.it. Church free admission; cloisters and church museum 5€. Church Mon–Sat 9:30am–5pm; Sun 1–5pm. Museum and cloisters Mon–Sat 9:30am–5:30pm; Sun 1–5:30pm. Bus: C1, C2, 13, 23, or 71.

Inside the Basilica Santa Croce.

La Sinagoga di Firenze.

Buonarroti's House (Casa Buonarroti) ★   A short walk from Santa Croce is the house that Michelangelo bought for his nephew, Leonardo. It was Leonardo's son, named after Michelangelo, who turned the house into a virtual museum to his great-uncle, hiring artists and painters to adorn it with frescoes. Turned into a museum by his descendants, the house was restored in 1964. It contains some fledgling work by the artist, as well as some models by him. Here you can see his *Madonna of the Stairs,* which he did when he was 16 (maybe younger), as well as a bas-relief that he did later, the *Battle of the Centaurs.* The casa is enriched by many of Michelangelo's drawings and models, shown to the public in periodic exhibits. A curiosity among them is the wooden model for the San Lorenzo facade that Michelangelo designed but never constructed.

Via Ghibellina 70. ✆ **055-241752.** www.casabuonarroti.it. Admission 6.50€. Wed–Mon 10am–5pm. Bus: 14 or 23.

A Synagogue

La Sinagoga di Firenze   The synagogue is in the Moorish style, inspired by Constantine's Byzantine church of Hagia Sophia. Completed in 1882, it was badly damaged by the Nazis in 1944 but has been restored to its original splendor. A museum is upstairs, exhibiting, among other displays, a photographic record of the history of the ghetto that remained in Florence until 1859.

Via Farini 6. ✆ **055-245252.** www.firenzebraica.it. Admission 5€. Apr–Sept Mon–Thurs 10am–6pm; Fri 10am–2pm; Sat–Sun closed. Oct–May Mon–Thurs 10am–3pm; Fri 10am–2pm; Sat–Sun closed. Closed Jewish holidays. Bus: 6, 31, or 32.

SHOPPING

Skilled craftsmanship and traditional design unchanged since the days of the Medicis have made this a serious shopping destination. Florence is noted for its hand-tooled **leather goods** and various **straw merchandise,** as well as superbly crafted **gold jewelry.**

The whole city strikes many visitors as a gigantic department store. Entire neighborhoods on both sides of the Arno offer good shops, though those along the medieval Ponte Vecchio (with some exceptions) are generally too touristy.

Florence isn't a city for bargain shopping, however. Most visitors interested in gold or silver jewelry head for the **Ponte Vecchio** and its tiny shops. It's difficult to tell one from another, but you really don't need to because the merchandise is similar. If you're looking for a charm or souvenir, these shops are fine. But the heyday of finding gold jewelry bargains on the Ponte Vecchio is long gone.

The street for antiques is **Via Maggio;** some of the furnishings and objets d'art here are from the 16th century. Another major area for antiques shopping is **Borgo Ognissanti.** Florence's Fifth Avenue is **Via dei Tornabuoni,** the place to head for the best-quality leather goods, for the best clothing boutiques, and for stylish but costly shoes. Here you'll find everyone from Armani to Ferragamo.

The better shops are largely along Tornabuoni, but there are many on **Via della Vigna Nuova, Via Porta Rossa,** and **Via degli Strozzi** as well. You might also stroll on the *lungarno* along the Arno. For some of the best buys in leather, check out **Via del Parione,** a short, narrow street off Tornabuoni.

Shopping hours are generally Monday 4 to 7:30pm and Tuesday to Saturday 9 or 10am to 1pm and 3:30 or 4 to 7:30pm. During summer, some shops are open Monday morning. However, don't be surprised if shops are closed for several weeks in August, or even for the entire month.

Shopping A to Z

ANTIQUES   There are many outlets for antiques in Florence, many clustered along **Via Maggio** (ouch—those high prices!). If you're in the market for such expensive purchases or if you just like to browse, try these stores.

Chic **Adriana Chelini,** Via Maggio 28 (© **055-213471**), specializes in 17th- and 18th-century furniture, from small to large pieces. It also carries some paintings and porcelain and glass items from later periods. The **Bottega San Felice,** Via Maggio 39R (© **055-215479**), offers many intriguing items from the 19th century, sometimes in the style known as Charles X. The shop also sells more modern pieces, such as many Art Deco items and Biedermeier pieces.

Said to be the oldest antiques dealer in Italy, **Galleria Luigi Bellini** ★★, Lungarno Soderini 5 (© **055-214031**), offers unusual,

 often one-of-a-kind selections of Florence antiques, paintings, and other objets d'art. The merchandise is tasteful and well chosen, but not cheap. The founding father of the outlet, Mario Bellini, is one of the most respected names in Florentine antiques and the founder of the international antiques biennial.

The eclectic **Paolo Romano,** Borgo Ognissanti 20R (© **055-293294**), carries furniture, accessories, and objets d'art from the 17th to the 19th centuries.

Shopping along Via dei Tornabuoni.

263

BOOKS Artistic books are found at **FMR,** Via delle Belle Donne 41R (✆ **055-283312;** www.babelefirenze.com), the domain of the locally known Franco Maria Ricci, who enjoys a worldwide reputation for his exquisite art books, particularly strong on the Renaissance. He also sells an exquisite selection of handmade papers. Another well-chosen selection of art books is found at **Libreria Salimbeni,** Via Matteo Palmieri 14R (✆ **055-2340904;** www.libreriasalimbeni.com). **Paperback Exchange,** Via della Oche 4R (✆ **055-293460;** www.papex.it), enjoys a central location, literally in the shadow of the Duomo. It has the largest collection of books in English, both used and new, in Florence.

CERAMICS & POTTERY **Richard Ginori ★**, Via De' Rondinelli 17R (✆ **055-210041;** www.negozirichardginori.com), has one of the most intriguing assortments of china and tableware, often in amusing designs and bright colors. In business since 1735, the shop features a changing array of merchandise from all parts of Italy. Sometimes you'll find good buys here in Murano (Venice) glassware.

DEPARTMENT STORES The best outlet is **La Rinascente,** Piazza della Repubblica 2 (✆ **055-219113;** www.rinascente.it), right in the heart of Florence. This is where frugal but taste-conscious Florentines go to shop. Their clothing for men and women features some of the big names but also talented and lesser known Italian designers. You'll also find good buys in china, perfumes, and jewelry, along with a "made in Tuscany" department that sells everything from terra-cotta vases to the finest virgin olive oils. Another good store is **Coin,** Via Calzaiuoli 56R (✆ **055-280531;** www.coin.it), which is particularly noted for offering good prices on fashionable ready-to-wear items.

FABRICS & EMBROIDERY In business for more than half a century, **Casa dei Tessuti,** Via de' Pecori 20–24R (✆ **055-215961;** www.casadeitessuti.com), has a huge, high-quality selection of linen, silk, wool, and cotton.

FASHION At **Loretta Caponi,** Piazza Antinori 4R (✆ **055-213668;** www.lorettacaponi.com), the arched ceiling and gilt trim create a perfect atmosphere in which to browse a wonderful selection of slip dresses, robes, linens, and children's wear in luxurious silks, velvets, and cottons.

Mariposa, Lungarno Corsini 18–20R (✆ **055-284259**), offers women's and men's fashions from such famous designers as Krizia, Ungaro, Rocco Barocco, Missoni, and Mimmina. Foreign customers are often granted a 20% discount on tax-free items.

Max Mara, Via del Pecori 23R (✆ **055-2396590;** www.maxmara.com), features high-quality women's clothes, with classic elegance and even a touch of flamboyance. The selection covers everything from hats and coats to suits and slacks.

Like Milan, many of the biggest names in fashion are centered in Florence, including the flagship store for **Gucci ★★★**, Via de Tournabuoni 73R (✆ **055-2645432;** www.gucci.com). Saddle maker Guccio Gucci (1881–1953) founded his first shop in Florence with almost no capital. On his dying day, he was objecting to his sons opening their first overseas boutique in New York, claiming that Americans would have no interest in Gucci leather products. How wrong he was. Not an Asian rip-off, Gucci leather products sold here, from classy shoes to clothing for both men and women, are the real thing.

Florence is the home not only of Gucci but also of **Pucci.** The descendant of a Florentine family famous since the Renaissance, Marchese Emilio Pucci di Barsento, a debonair Italian aristocrat, burst onto the fashion world in the 1950s with his rich colors, supple fabrics, and dramatic prints, as well as his couture collection that would cover some of the most celebrated women in the world, including Jacqueline Kennedy. Pucci led the postwar emergence of the casually chic jet-setter, adorning his fans with what came to be known as "the Italian look." It was a Pucci-designed flag that Apollo 15 carried to the moon. Pucci fashion today is undergoing a revival, directed by Julio Espada, and is on display at its shop at Via de Tournabuoni 20R (𝄐 **055-2658082;** www.emiliopucci.com).

For that **Armani** look, patronize the outlets of that often rude, arrogant, but brilliantly talented workaholic Giorgio Armani at Via de Tournabuoni 48 (𝄐 **055-219041;** www.giorgioarmani.com); a branch at Piazza degli Strozzi 16R (𝄐 **055-284315**) offers less expensive items. The relaxed Armani designs for women are inspired by his menswear (for example, he uses menswear fabrics in his sophisticated, unstructured jackets and suits for women). And, of course, for men, an Armani suit is what you wear to the most special of occasions.

On a much more democratically priced level, **Enrico Coveri,** Lung'Arno Guicciardini 19 (𝄐 **055-264259;** www.coveri.com), is celebrated as *il signore in rosso,* "the man in red," known as the urban cowboy of fashion. Women loved his "women in red look," and now Coveri fully expects thousands of fashionable young men to burst out in similarly flaming red wardrobes—long jackets, red pants, woolen sweaters, T-shirts, and even red mink coats. Get this: a red mink backpack.

GLASS The small **Cose del '900,** Borgo Sant' Jacopo 45R (𝄐 **055-283491;** www.italianglassconnection.com), is full of glass items of every description from 1900 to 1950: shot glasses, drinking glasses, centerpieces, and many Art Deco pieces.

Dating from the era of the grand dukes, the art of grinding and engraving glass is still carried out at **Paola Locchi,** Via Burchiello 10 (𝄐 **055-229416;** www.locchi.com), with exquisite skill and craftsmanship. Seemingly every kind of engraved object is sold, some of it of stupendous size. You can even find engraved goblets that decorated the banqueting tables of the ancients.

GLOVES The place to go for gloves is **Madova** ★★, Via Guicciardini 1R (𝄐 **055-239-6526;** www.madova.com), at the base of Ponte Vecchio. The family owners, the Donnini brood, have been turning out exquisite leather gloves since 1919. The shop is the only one in Europe that produces and sells strictly leather gloves. They continue to research new styles and colors for their huge assortment. If you check out a basket on the counter, you can come up with a glove containing an almost imperceptible defect at a fraction of the price of the regular gloves.

HERBAL REMEDIES/BATH & BODY PRODUCTS The **Antica Farmacia del Cinghiale** ★★, Piazza del Mercato Nuovo 4R (𝄐 **055-282128;** www.farmaciadelcinghiale.it), in business for some 3 centuries, is an *erboristeria* (herbalist/health food shop), dispensing herbal teas and fragrances along with herbal potpourris. A pharmacy is also here.

The **Officina Profumo Farmaceutica di Santa Maria Novella ★**, Via della Scala 16N (✆ **055-216276;** www.smn ovella.it), is the most fascinating pharmacy in Italy. Northwest of Santa Maria Novella, it opened in 1612 and offered a selection of herbal remedies created by friars of the Dominican order. Those closely guarded secrets have been retained, and many of the same elixirs are still sold today. A wide selection of perfumes, scented soaps, shampoos, and potpourris, along with creams and lotions, is also sold. The store is closed for 2 weeks in August.

Soaps for sale at the Antica Farmacia del Cinghiale.

HOUSEWARES   **Ceramiche Ricceri,** Via dei Conti 14R (✆ **055-291296;** www.riccericeramica.com), has an unusual collection of terra-cotta tableware that it obtains from the town of Imruneta, 9.5km (6 miles) south of Florence. The region is known for its gray clay with a high content of aluminum and iron. This makes a very strong pottery for pitchers, platters, and the like.

JEWELRY   Proceed with caution. You'll find some stunning antique pieces and, if you know how to buy, some good values.

Tiffany, Via dei Tornabuoni 25R (✆ **055-215506;** www.tiffany.com), draws a well-heeled patronage, looking for a branch of the fabled jewelry store in New York.

Lo Spillo ★, Borgo San Jacopo 72R (✆ **055-293126**), means "the Pin" in Italian. Surely this is the smallest shop in town. It's also as pretty as a jewel box itself. Owner Sofia Casalini is the most charming jeweler in Florence, and she knows every piece and its origin, ranging from Art Nouveau earrings to platinum-and-diamond rings. The less expensive jewelry sells for under 70€, but prices could range much higher, of course.

Modern 18-carat white gold jewelry—sometimes accented with diamonds—is the specialty at **Elisabetta Fallaci,** Ponte Vecchio 22 (✆ **055-213192**), all made in Florence. Another well-respected jewelry store, **Gioielleria Ponte Vecchio,** lies a few steps away, at Ponte Vecchio 10R (✆ **055-294981**).

LEATHER   Universally acclaimed, Florentine leather is still the fine product that it always was—smooth and well shaped, often in vivid colors.

Beltrami, Via della Vigna Nuova 70R (✆ **055-287779;** www.beltrami firenze.it), sells fine leather goods as well as expensive evening clothes, heavyweight silk scarves, and fashions of the best quality. This is one of several Beltrami shops in the area. High fashion, high prices, and high quality are what you'll find here, but prices are significantly lower than what you'll pay for Beltrami in the United States.

Sergio Bojola, Via dei Rondinelli 25R (✆ **055-211155;** www. bojola.it), a leading name in leather, has distinguished himself in Florence by the variety of his selections, in both synthetic materials and beautiful leathers.

You'll find first-class quality and craftsmanship at **Cellerini** ★★, Via del Sole 37R (📞 **055-282533;** www.cellerini.it), one of the city's master leather workers. Silvano Cellerini has been called a genius in leather. Original purses, shoulder bags, suitcases, accessories, wallets, and even a limited number of shoes (for both women and men) are sold.

Leonardo Leather Works, Borgo dei Greci 16A (📞 **055-292202;** www.leonardoleather.com), concentrates on leather and jewelry. Leather goods include wallets, bags, shoes, boots, briefcases, clothing, travel bags, belts, and gift items, with products by famous designers. The jewelry department has a large assortment of gold chains, bracelets, rings, earrings, and charms.

Pollini, Via Por Santa Maria 42R, near the Ponte Vecchio (📞 **055-288672;** www.pollini.com), offers a wide array of stylized merchandise, including shoes for men and women, suitcases, clothing, and belts.

MARKETS Intrepid shoppers head for the **Mercato della Paglia** ★★ or **Mercato Nuovo** (**Straw Market** or **New Market**), 2 blocks south of Piazza della Repubblica. It's called Il Porcellino by the Italians because of the bronze statue of a reclining wild boar, a copy of the one in the Uffizi; tourists pet its snout (which is well worn) for good luck. The market stands in the monumental heart of Florence, an easy stroll from the Palazzo Vecchio. It sells not only straw items but also leather goods (not the best quality), along with typical Florentine merchandise: frames, trays, hand embroidery, table linens, and hand-sprayed and -painted boxes in traditional designs. From mid-March to early November, this market is open daily 9am to 8pm; off-season hours are Tuesday to Sunday 9am to 7:30pm.

Even better bargains await those who make their way through the pushcarts to the stalls of the open-air **Mercato Centrale** (**Mercato San Lorenzo;** www.sanlorenzofirenze.it), in and around Borgo San Lorenzo, near the rail station. If you don't mind bargaining, which is imperative, you'll find an array of merchandise such as raffia bags, Florentine leather purses, sweaters, gloves, salt-and-pepper shakers, straw handbags, and art reproductions. It's open Monday to Saturday from 9am to 6:30pm.

MOSAICS Florentine mosaics are universally recognized. At **Le Pietre nell'Arte,** Piazza Duomo 36R (📞 **055-212587;** www.scarpellimosaici.it),

FLORENTINE high fashion
AT A DISCOUNT

Not every Florentine walking around in Prada or Fendi paid the top euro. Locals secretly guard addresses where high fashion—admittedly last year's offerings—prevails. It's worth the drive to the town of Montevarchi, some 30km (19 miles) from the center of Florence, to do a little Italian outlet shopping. Stand in line and get a numbered ticket to take a look at the discounted Prada selections at **I Pellettieri d'Italia,** Località Levanella SS69, Montevarchi (📞 **055-9199822**). It sells everything from elegant shoes to nifty little handbags, all at 50% discounts. Try to avoid weekends, which are overcrowded.

Renzo and Leonardo Scarpelli are a father-and-son team of artists who turn out some of the most beautiful mosaics in Florence, following an art form started in the Renaissance with the Medici family. Their "stone paintings" are collectors' items and highly valued. Their workshop only a 10-minute walk from their shop, and visits can be arranged.

At **Pitti Mosaici,** Piazza Pitti 23R (✆ **055-282127;** www.pitti mosaici.it), the mosaic artistry reflects generations of family tradition.

PAPER & STATIONERY   Giulio Giannini & Figlio ★, Piazza Pitti 37R (✆ **055-212621;** www.giuliogiannini.it), has been a family business for more than 150 years and is Florence's leading stationery store. Foreigners often snap up the exquisite merchandise for gift giving later in the year.

The specialty at **Il Papiro,** Via Cavour 49R (✆ **055-215262;** www. ilpapirofirenze.it), is parti-colored marbleized paper that's skillfully incorporated into everything from bookmarks to photo albums (which make valued wedding gifts). More unusual are the marbleized wood (like music boxes) and leather items (couture-style purses and bags), as well as the marbleized fabric. The staff is charming, and the prices are reasonable, considering the high quality. There are branches at Via Porta Rossa 76R (✆ 055-216593) and Lugarno Acciaiuoli 42R (✆ 055-2645613).

Opened in 1774 and still run by descendants of the original founders, **J Pineider,** Piazza della Signoria 13R (✆ **055-281747;** www.pineider. com), is the oldest store in Florence specializing in printing and engraving. The most aristocratic-looking greeting cards, business cards, stationery, and invitations come from this outfit. Because most orders take between 2 and 3 weeks to fill, you can arrange to have the final product shipped home. The store also stocks a wide range of gifts, such as beautifully crafted diaries, stationery, desk sets for your favorite CEO, address books, photo albums, and etchings of vistas unique to Florence.

Scriptorium, Via dei Servi 5R (✆ **055-211804;** www.scriptorium firenze.com), offers wonderful hand-sewn notebooks, journals, and photo albums made of thick paper and bound with soft leather covers.

PRINTS & ENGRAVINGS   Ducci, Lungarno Corsini 24R (✆ **055-214550;** www.duccishop.com), hawks the best selection of historical prints and engravings covering the history of Florence from the 13th century. Also available are marble fruit, wooden items, and Florentine boxes covered with gold leaf.

Giovanni Baccani, Via della Vigna Nuova 75R (✆ **055-214467**), has long been a specialist in this field. Everything that it sells is old. "The Blue Shop," as it's called, offers a huge array of prints and engravings, often of Florentine scenes. Tuscan paper goods are also sold.

SHOES   Casadei, Via dei Tornabuoni 33R (✆ **055-287240;** www.casadei. com), is an interesting shop that is painted white; its pillars make the room look like a small colonnade. This shop is one of four Casadei shops (others are in Milan, Ferrara, and Rimini). Locally produced women's shoes, boots, and handbags are sold.

Salvatore Ferragamo ★★, Via dei Tornabuoni 14R (✆ **055-292123;** www.ferragamo.com), has long been one of the most famous names in shoes. The headquarters of this famed manufacturer were installed

here in the Palazzo Ferroni, on the most fashionable shopping street of Florence, before World War II broke out. Ferragamo sells shoes for men and women, along with elegant boutique items such as men's and women's clothing, scarves, handbags, ties, and luggage.

SILVER Pampaloni, Via Porta Rossa 99R (✆ **055-289094;** www. pampaloni.com), is headed by Gianfranco Pampaloni, a third-generation silversmith. The business was launched in 1902, and some of the classic designs turned out back then are still being made.

Shoes and bags are the big draws at Salvatore Ferragamo.

FLORENCE AFTER DARK

Evening entertainment in Florence isn't an exciting prospect, unless you simply like to walk through the narrow streets or head toward Fiesole for a truly spectacular view of the city at night. The typical Florentine begins an evening early at one of the cafes listed below.

From late April or early May to mid-June, the city welcomes classical musicians for its **Maggio Musicale** festival of cantatas, madrigals, concertos, operas, and ballets, many of which are presented in Renaissance buildings. Schedule and ticket information is available from **Maggio Musicale Fiorentino/Teatro Comunale,** Corso Italia 16, 50123 Firenze (✆ **055-213535**). Tickets cost 25€ to 100€. For further information, visit the theater's website at www.maggio fiorentino.com.

The Performing Arts

Teatro Comunale di Firenze/Maggio Musicale Fiorentino ★★★, Corso Italia 16 (✆ **055-27791;** www.maggiofiorentino.it), is Florence's main theater, with opera and ballet seasons presented September through December and a concert season January through April. This theater is also the venue for the Maggio Musicale (see above), Italy's oldest and most prestigious festival.

Teatro della Pergola, Via della Pergola 18 (✆ **055-22641;** www.teatro dellapergola.com), is Florence's major legitimate theater, but you'll have to understand Italian to appreciate most of its plays. Plays are performed year-round except during the Maggio Musicale, when the theater becomes the setting for many of the festival events. Tickets cost 15€ to 30€. The box office is open from Monday to Friday 9:30am to 6:45pm, and Saturday 10am to 1:30pm.

Teatro Verdi, Via Ghibellina 99 (✆ **055-212320;** www.teatroverdionline. it), is a venue for prestigious dance and classical music events. Major operatic and ballet performances are often presented here as well, often by big-name performers. Tickets cost 20€ to 65€. The box office is open from Monday to Saturday 10am to 1pm and 4 to 7pm.

Many cultural presentations are performed in churches. These might include open-air concerts in the cloisters of the **Badia Fiesolana** in Fiesole or at the **Ospedale degli Innocenti,** on summer evenings only. Orchestral offerings, performed by the Regional Tuscan Orchestra, are often presented at **Santo Stefano al Ponte Vecchio.**

Live-Music Clubs

Riding the crest of great popularity is **Universale,** Via Pisana 77 (✆ **055-221122;** www.universalefirenze.it), attracting a diverse group ranging in age from 20 to 50. If you want nonstop action and a freewheeling and fun-loving atmosphere, it's the best show in town. Guests start arriving at 8pm to enjoy the balcony restaurant or the pizzeria on the main floor. By 11pm, a live band occupies the main floor stage for an hour's performance before a DJ takes over for disco music until 3am nightly. Entrance usually ranges from 18€ to 25€.

In the cellar of an antique building in the historic heart of town, **Full-Up,** Via della Vigna Vecchia 23–25R (✆ **055-293006;** www.fullupclub.com), attracts college students who appreciate the club's two-in-one format. One section contains a smallish dance floor with recorded dance music; the other is a somewhat more restrained piano bar. The place can be fun, and even an older crowd feels at ease. It's open Wednesday to Saturday 11pm to 4am, charging a 13€ to 25€ cover.

Red Garter, Via dei Benci 33R (✆ **055-2344904**), right off Piazza Santa Croce, has an American Prohibition–era theme and features everything from rock to bluegrass. The club is open Monday to Thursday 8:30pm to 1am, and Friday to Sunday 9pm to 2am (closed Mon in winter). Beer and drink prices start at 3.50€. Cover is 10€ to 15€.

Within a 10-minute cab ride from Piazza del Duomo, **Tenax,** Via Pratese 46A (✆ **055-308160;** www.tenax.org), is the premier venue for live rock-'n'-roll and grunge-rock bands in Tuscany, with individual musical styles varying widely, and each drawing a widely different crowd of loyal fans. Bands come from throughout Italy and the rest of Europe, but whenever they're not playing, a DJ will provide high-energy, highly danceable recorded music instead. Shows begin nightly except Monday at 11pm and continue to around 4am. The cover is 20€ to 25€ and includes the first drink.

Cafes

Café Rivoire ★, Piazza della Signoria 4R (✆ **055-214412;** www.rivoire.it), offers a classy and amusing old-world ambience with a direct view of the statues on one of our favorite squares in the world. You can sit at one of the metal tables on the flagstones outside or at one of the wooden tables in a choice of inner rooms filled with marble detailing and unusual oil renderings of the piazza outside. If you don't want to sit at all, try the bar, where many colorful characters talk, flirt, or gossip. There's a selection of small sandwiches, omelets, and ice creams, and the cafe is noted for its hot chocolate.

The oldest and most beautiful cafe in Florence, **Gilli's,** Via Roma 1, adjacent to Piazza Repubblica 39R, Via Roma 1 (✆ **055-213896;** www.gilli.it), is a few minutes' walk from the Duomo. It was founded in 1789, when Piazza della Repubblica had a different name. You can sit at a brightly lit table near the bar or

Cafe in Florence.

retreat to an intricately paneled pair of rooms to the side and enjoy the flattering light from the Venetian-glass chandeliers. Daily specials, sandwiches, toasts, and hard drinks are sold, along with an array of "tropical" libations.

The waiters at **Giubbe Rosse,** Piazza della Repubblica 13–14R (© **055-212280;** www.giubberosse. it), still wear the Garibaldi red coats, as they did when this place was founded in 1888. It has always been known as a literary cafe, where intellectuals and writers met to discuss politics and literature. It survived the Mussolini era and continues to attract an artsy crowd. You can enjoy coffee, drinks, and also salads and sandwiches surrounded by turn-of-the-20th-century chandeliers and polished granite floors. Light lunches and full American breakfasts are specialties.

Procacci ★, Via de Tornabuoni 64R (© **055-211656**), is a little charmer of a cafe and bar on the chic shopping street of Florence. A city tradition since 1885, it has attracted the movers and shakers in Florentine couture. We once encountered Emilio Pucci here, who warned us, "Don't write anything about me. I'm too famous already!" This is a marvelously old-fashioned kind of food shop and bar known for its house special, a panini *tartufati,* a dainty glazed roll shaped like an egg and filled with the world's most delectable white truffle paste. You can also enjoy a creamy brie with a nut sauce or else foie gras or smoked salmon. Ask for a glass of prosecco while surveying the food on the shelves, everything from Sicilian orange marmalade (which we consider Italy's finest) to the rarest of balsamic vinegars. Hours are Monday to Saturday 10am to 8pm.

Bars & Pubs

At **Angels,** Via del Proconsolo 29–31 (© **055-2398762;** www.ristoranteangels. it), at first you'll think you've been transported to Miami, Florida. Only a short distance from the Duomo, the American bar here is the best place in Florence for a midnight martini, attracting a crowd mostly in its 30s. The decor is minimalist with stark white chairs. Techno music often rules the night. The on-site restaurant serves traditional Tuscan dishes. The ritzy bar of Florence is the **ORVM,** in the Westin Excelsior, Piazza Ognissanti 3 (© **055-27151;** www.westinflorence. com). On the ground floor of the deluxe hotel, it can be entered through the lobby or through another door on the Arno River side. It has been completely redecorated in a tasteful Art Deco design with two impressive orange chandeliers casting a warm light over the brown leather and wood furnishings. The most popular time to visit is 7 to 9pm daily, when there is live background music. The cocktail menu has the classics but many innovative drinks as well. ORVM is open daily 11am to 1am.

The **Dublin Pub,** Via Faenza 27R (© **055-2741571;** www.dublinpub.it), is very much an Irish pub, with an Italian accent. Along with Fiddler's Elbow (see below), few other places in Tuscany mingle the Celtic and Mediterranean souls as seamlessly. Neither offers live music, but there's an ongoing medley of recorded music, often Irish. The pub serves Irish grub and Irish whiskey along with

Guinness and Irish coffee—and lots and lots of beer. It's a rollicking, congenial spot near the Santa Maria Novella rail station.

After an initial success in Rome, **Fiddler's Elbow,** Piazza Santa Maria Novella 7R, near the rail station (📞 **055-215056;** www.thefiddlerselbow.com), an Irish pub, has invaded this city and quickly become one of its most popular watering holes. Here you can get a pint of authentic Guinness.

La Dolce Vita, Piazza del Carmine 6R (📞 **055-284595;** www.dolcevita florence.com), draws the beautiful people. It's a see-and-be-seen type of place, lying south of the Arno and west of the historic core. You come here to drink, gossip, and look ever so chic. So you can see how you're doing, the owners have wisely covered the walls in mirrors.

Dance Clubs

At **Space Electronic,** Via Palazzuolo 37 (📞 **055-293082;** www.space electronic.net), the decor consists of wall-to-wall mirrors and an imitation space capsule that goes back and forth across the dance floor. If karaoke doesn't thrill you, head to the ground-floor pub, which stocks an ample supply of imported beers. On the upper level is a large dance floor with a wide choice of music and a high-energy row of laser beams. This place attracts a lot of foreign students who want to hook up with Florentine men and women on the prowl. The disco opens Tuesday to Sunday at 10pm and usually goes until 3am. The 15€ cover includes the first drink.

Yab, Via Sassetti 5R (📞 **055-215160;** www.yab.it), is in the historic core of the city. It has been renovated and now offers an ultramodern decor, with dinner served after 9:30pm. Recorded music ranges from punk to rock, from funk to garage. Partly because it isn't well air-conditioned, it closes between May and October. Otherwise, hours are Monday and Thursday through Saturday from 7:30pm to 4am. The cover is 20€, which includes the first drink, or 30€, which includes the cover and dinner.

Gay & Lesbian Clubs

ArciGay/Lesbica (aka Azione Gay e Lesbica), Italy's largest and oldest gay organization, has a center in Florence at Via Pisana 32R (📞 **055-220250;** www. azionegayelesbica.it). It's open for visits Monday to Thursday 6 to 8pm.

A SIDE TRIP TO FIESOLE ★

For more extensive day trips see chapter 7, "Tuscany, Umbria & the Marches." But Fiesole, once an Etruscan settlement, is a virtual suburb of Florence and its most popular outing. Florentines often head for these hills when it's just too hot in the city. Bus no. 7, leaving from Piazza San Marco, will take you here in 25 minutes and give you a breathtaking view along the way. You'll pass fountains, statuary, and gardens strung out over the hills like a scrambled jigsaw puzzle.

Exploring the Town

In Fiesole you won't find anything as dazzling as the Renaissance treasures of Florence; the town's charms are more subtle. Fortunately, all major sights branch out within walking distance of the main square, **Piazza Mino da Fiesole,** beginning with the **Cattedrale di San Romolo (Duomo).** At first this cathedral might seem austere, with its concrete-gray Corinthian columns and Romanesque

The Cattedrale di San Romolo (Duomo) in Fiesole.

arches. But it has its own beauty. Dating from A.D. 1000, it was much altered during the Renaissance, and in the Salutati Chapel are important sculptural works by Mino da Fiesole. It's open daily from 7:30am to noon and 4 to 7pm.

Bandini Museum (Museo Bandini)   This ecclesiastical museum, around to the side of the Duomo, belongs to the Fiesole Cathedral Chapter, established in 1913. On the ground floor are della Robbia terra-cotta works, as well as art by Michelangelo and Pisano. On the top floors are paintings by the best Giotto students, reflecting ecclesiastical and worldly themes, most of them the work of Tuscan artists of the 14th century.

Via Dupré 1. ✆ **055-5961293.** www.fiesolemusei.it. Admission (includes admission to Roman Theater and Archaeological Museum, below) 10€. Mar–Oct daily 10am–7pm; Nov–Feb Wed–Mon 10am–2pm.

Museum of the Franciscan Missionaries (Museo Missionario Francescano Fiesole) ★   The hardest task you'll have in Fiesole is to take the steep goat-climb up to the Convent of San Francesco. You can visit the Gothic-style Franciscan church, built in the first years of the 1400s and consecrated in 1516. Inside are many paintings by well-known Florentine artists. In the basement of the church is the ethnological museum. Begun in 1906, the collection has a large section of Chinese artifacts, including ancient bronzes. An Etruscan-Roman section contains some 330 archaeological pieces, and an Egyptian section also has numerous objects.

Via San Francesco 13. ✆ **055-59175.** Free admission (but a donation is expected). Church daily 8am–1pm and 3–8pm. Museum Mon–Fri 10am–noon and 3–5pm (to 7pm in summer); Sat–Sun 3–5pm. Bus: 7.

Roman Theater and Archaeological Museum (Teatro Romano e Museo Archeologico) ★   On this site is the major surviving evidence that Fiesole was an Etruscan city 6 centuries before Christ and later a Roman town. In the 1st century B.C., a theater was built, and you can see the restored remains today. Near the theater are the skeleton-like ruins of the bathrooms, which might have been built at the same time. Try to visit the Etruscan-Roman museum, with its many interesting finds that date from the days when Fiesole, not Florence, was supreme (a guide is on hand to show you through).

Via Portigiani 1. © **055-5961293.** Admission (includes admission to Bandini Museum, above) 10€. For hours, see the Bandini Museum, above. Bus: 7.

Where to Stay

Pensione Bencistà This has been the villa of the Simoni family for years. It was built around 1300, with additions made about every 100 years after that. In 1925, Paolo Simoni opened the villa to paying guests, and today it's run by his son, Simone Simoni. Its position, high up on the road to Fiesole, is commanding, with an unmarred view of the city and the hillside villas. The spread-out villa has many lofty old rooms furnished with family antiques. They vary in size and interest. In chilly weather, guests meet one another in the evening in front of a huge fireplace. It's a 10-minute bus ride from the heart of Florence.

Via Benedetto da Maiano 4, Fiesole, 50014 Firenze. ©/fax **055-59163.** www.bencista.com. 40 units, 184€ double. Rates include half board. MC, V. Free parking. Bus: 7. Closed Nov 9–Mar 15. **Amenities:** Restaurant; bar; babysitting; Internet (free, in lobby); room service. *In room:* Hair dryer.

Villa San Michele ★★★ This is an ancient monastery of unsurpassed beauty in a memorable setting on a hill below Fiesole, a 15-minute walk south of the center. It was built in the 15th century, damaged in World War II, and then restored. The facade and loggia were reportedly designed by Michelangelo. A curving driveway, lined with blossoming trees and flowers, leads to the entrance, and a 10-arch-covered loggia continues around the view side of the building to the Italian gardens at the rear. Most of the guest rooms open onto the view; the others face the inner courtyard. Each is unique, some with iron or wooden canopy beds, antique chests, ecclesiastical paintings, candelabra, and statues. In the old friars' cells, the units are rather austerely decorated in the spirit of their former role. The Michelangelo Suite is the grand choice, a spacious room with a marble fireplace and a large whirlpool.

Via Doccia 4, Fiesole, 50014 Firenze. © **055-5678200.** Fax 055-5678250. www.villasan michele.com. 46 units. 860€–1,070€ double; from 2,450€ suite. Rates include full American breakfast. AE, DC, MC, V. Closed Nov 7–Mar 31. Bus: 7. **Amenities:** Restaurant; bar; babysitting; bikes; concierge; exercise room; outdoor heated pool; room service. *In room:* A/C, TV, DVD (in some), CD player (in some), hair dryer, minibar, Wi-Fi (10€ per day).

Where to Dine

You might also want to dine at the fine restaurant of the **Villa San Michele** (see above).

Trattoria le Cave di Maiano TUSCAN This former farmhouse is at Maiano, a 15-minute ride east from the heart of Florence and just a short distance south of Fiesole. The rustically decorated family run *trattoria* is a garden restaurant, with stone tables and large sheltering trees. We highly recommend the antipasti and homemade green tortellini. For a main course, there's golden grilled chicken or savory herb-flavored roast lamb. For side dishes, we suggest fried polenta, Tuscan beans, and fried potatoes. As a final treat, the waiter will bring you homemade ice cream with fresh raspberries.

Via Cave di Maiano 16. © **055-59133.** www.trattoriacavedimaiano.it. Reservations required. Main courses 9€–22€. AE, MC, V. Daily 12:30–2:30pm and 7:30–10:30pm. Closed 1 week in Feb.

7

TUSCANY, UMBRIA & THE MARCHES

T he Tuscan landscapes look just like Renaissance paintings, with rolling plains of grass, cypress trees, and olive groves; ancient walled hill towns; and those fabled Chianti vineyards.

Tuscany (Toscana) was where the Etruscans first appeared in Italy. The Romans followed, absorbing and conquering them. By the 11th century, the region had evolved into a collection of independent city-states, such as Florence and Siena, each trying to dominate the others. Many of the cities reached the apogee of their economic and political power in the 13th century. The Renaissance reached its apex in Florence, but was slow to come to Siena, which remains a gem of Gothic glory.

Tuscany might be known for its Renaissance artists, but the small region of **Umbria,** at the heart of the Italian peninsula, is associated mainly with saints. Christendom's most beloved saints were born here, including St. Francis of Assisi, founder of the Franciscans. Also born here were St. Valentine, a 3rd-century bishop of Terni, and St. Clare, founder of the Order of Poor Clares.

However, Umbrian painters also contributed to the glory of the Renaissance. Il Perugino, whose lyrical works you can see in the National Gallery of Umbria in Perugia, is one such example.

Umbria's countryside, also the subject of countless paintings, remains as lovely as ever today: You'll pass through a hilly terrain dotted with chestnut trees, interspersed with fertile plains of olive groves and vineyards.

For more in-depth coverage of both regions, you might want to pick up a copy of *Frommer's Florence, Tuscany & Umbria* (John Wiley & Sons, Inc.).

THE CHIANTI ROAD ★★

The Chianti Road (La Chiantigiana), as the S222 is known, twists and turns narrowly through the hilly terrain of Tuscany's famous wine region. Chianti, once associated with cheap, sweet Italian wines, has finally captured the attention of connoisseurs with well-crafted classicos and *riservas*. This is the result of improved attention to growth and vinification techniques over the last 2 decades.

The Castello di Verrazzano winery in Chianti.
PREVIOUS PAGE: **Wine bottles in Chianti, Tuscany.**

Poppies in bloom along the Chianti Road.

The entire area of Chianti is only 48km (30 miles) from north to south and 32km (20 miles) at its widest point. You could rent a bike or scooter for your tour, but you'd have to cope with hills, dust, and the driving habits of "road king" Italians. Renting an easily maneuverable small car is preferable, but even with an auto, you still must deal with road-hogging buses and flying Fiats. On the plus side, a car will let you stop at vineyards along the dirt lanes that stray from the main road, an option not provided by any bus tour. Still, be prepared for hairpin turns, ups and downs, and unidentified narrow lanes.

Signs touting DEGUSTAZIONE or VENDITA DIRETTA lead you to wineries that are open to the public and offer tastings. However, you should call ahead and try to make appointments at the wineries in this area. In other words, don't just show up. See also the "Tuscany & Umbria" entry in "The Best Winegrowing Regions," in chapter 1, "The Best of Italy."

Essentials

GETTING AROUND By far the best way to explore the region is by car, but you can also do it by bike. You can reach the central town of Greve by a Autolinee Chianti Valdarno which runs buses from Florence to the Chianti region. The trip takes 50 minutes and costs 3.50€ one-way. Call ℭ **055-47821** for information. Once you're in Greve, go to **Marco Ramuzzi,** Via Italo Stecchi 23 (ℭ **055-853037;** www.ramuzzi.com), and rent a mountain bike for 20€ per day or a scooter for 30€ to 65€ per day. Renters must be 18 or over and must leave a passport, a driver's license, and the number of a valid credit card. Armed with a map from the tourist office, you can set out, braving the winding roads of Chianti country.

Touring the Wineries

Leaving Florence, get on S222 off autostrada E35 and head south. At Petigliolo, 4km (2½ miles) south of the city, turn left and follow the signs to the first attraction along the road—not a winery, but the vine-clad **Santo Stefano a Tizzano,**

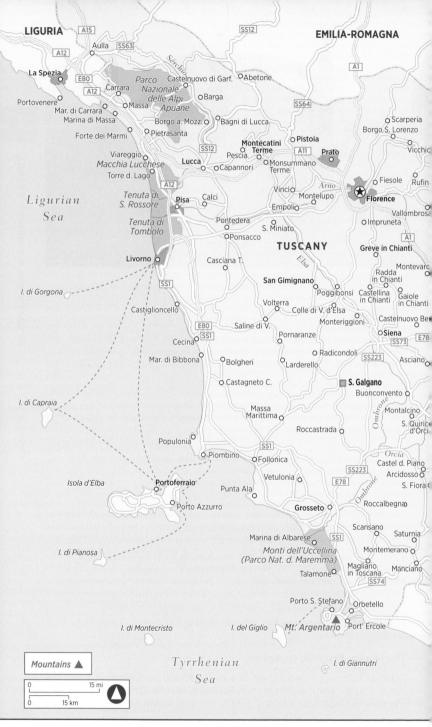

Tuscany & Umbria

SS16

Forlì

SS67

A14

SS9

Rimini

SAN
MARINO

E45

Riccione

S. Marino

SS16

Pesaro

Fano

*Adriatic
Sea*

Monte Falterona,
Campigna, e Foreste
Casentinesi

Camaldoli

Stia

Poppi

La Verna

Bibbiena

Urbino

E78

A14

Ancona

Caprese Mich.

THE
MARCHES

SS71

Sansepolcro

Arno

Arezzo

E45

Monterchi

Città
di Castello

SS76

A1

Mt. Cucco

Mte. S. Savino

Castiglion Fio.

Macerata

Lucignano

Cortona

Umbertide

Gubbio

SS326

SS71

Gualdo-Tadino

Tolentino

Sinalunga

Tevere

Camerino

SS77

Castiglione
del Lago

*Lago
Trasimeno*

Perugia

SS3

Nocera Umbra

SS78

Montepulciano

Pienza

A1

Assisi

Mt. Subasio

Chianciano Terme

Chiusi

UMBRIA

Torgiano

SS75

Spello

SS77

Sarteano

Deruta

Foligno

Cetona

Città d. Pieve

Marsciano

E45

Montefalco

Trevi

*Parco dei
Monti Sibillini*

Radicofani

Piano Grande

obadia S. Salvatore

SS2

SS3

*Parco Naturale
Regionale*

Castell'Azzara

Paglia

Acquapendente

SS448

Todi

Spoleto

Cáscia

SS4

oyana

Sorano

Bolsena

Orvieto

*Parco Nazionale
del Gran Sasso*

Pitigliano

SS2

Bagnoregio

Tevere

Amelia

Fiora

*Lago di
Bolsena*

SS71

Lugnano

Terni

Piediluco

674

Montefiascone

Narni

Nera

*Parco Nazional del Gran
Sasso e Monti della Laga*

Vulci

Orte

SS3

Rieti

VITERBO

SS2

L'Aquila

SS1

SS1B

arquinia

LAZIO

SS2

SS3

A1

To Rome
↓

ABRUZZI

Venice

0   100 Mi
0 100 Km

45° N.

Tuscany

Umbria

Rome

40° N.

10° E

a Romanesque church. Nearby, 18km (11 miles) from Florence, stands the 11th-century **Castello di Tizzano** (✆ **055-495380**), the prestigious centerpiece of sprawling vineyards and a consortium of farms producing Chianti Classico under the Gallo Nero label. *Note:* To visit here, you ***must*** call ahead and ask for an appointment, as you should at all wineries. We cannot emphasize this strongly enough. Many readers who arrived unannounced have been denied visits here or at other wineries in the region, particularly during busy times, such as the autumn grape harvest. If you've called ahead, and it's a slower season, you may be allowed to visit the 15th- and 16th-century cellars. If supplies are available for retail, you might be able to purchase some chianti or vin santo and the estate's award-winning olive oil.

About 2km (1¼ miles) farther along S222 is **San Polo in Chianti,** at the heart of Italy's iris industry. So many flowers grow in this region that there's an **Iris Festival** in May (dates vary according to weather patterns and the growing season). Far removed from the bustle and hordes of Florence, San Polo seems like a lonely time capsule, with a building that once belonged to the powerful Knights Templar. A church of ancient origins stands here, **San Miniato in Rubbiana,** which, if you believe the inscription, was consecrated in 1077 by the bishop of Fiesole.

At San Polo, turn left and follow the signs back to S222 and the village of **Strada in Chianti,** 14km (8½ miles) from Florence. *Strada,* which means "street," seems a strange name for a town; locals claim that the name came from an old Roman road that ran through here. The **Castello di Mugano,** one of the best preserved in Tuscany, stands guard over the region.

Continue along La Chiantigiana until reaching the isolated village of **Vicchiomaggio,** 19km (12 miles) from Florence, where an 11th-century castle once hosted the illustrious Leonardo da Vinci. You'll be following in his footsteps by visiting the **Fattoria Castello di Vicchiomaggio** (✆ **055-854078**; www.vicchiomaggio.it), open Monday to Friday 10:30am to 1pm and 2:30 to 6:30pm. Here you can sample and buy wines, homegrown olive oil, vin santo, and grappa. Overall, the estate controls more than 120 hectares (300 acres), 28 hectares (70 acres) of which are devoted to vineyards.

Nearby, 1.6km (1 mile) north of the hamlet of Greve, lies the hamlet of **Verrazzano,** a name that's more familiar to New Yorkers than to Tuscans because of the famous bridge bearing the name of Giovanni da Verrazzano. He left the land of the grape and set to sea in the service of François I of France. In 1524, he was the first European colonial to sail into the harbor of New York and the island of Manhattan; he disappeared without a trace on his second voyage to Brazil.

His birthplace still stands on a hilltop overlooking Greve (4km/2½ miles from Greve, to be precise; take the route marked Via San Martino in Valle in the direction of Siena to reach it). **Castello di Verrazzano** (✆ **055-854243**; www.verrazzano.com) is centered in a 10th-century tower surrounded by other buildings from the 15th and 16th centuries. If you call ahead to make a reservation, the castle is open Monday to Friday from 8am to 5pm. (Try to schedule your trip for 11am any day Mon–Sat, when you can join a tour.) Visits through the ancient caves usually include a sampling of the estate's great red and white wines, as well as complimentary platters of salami, cheese, and almond-scented cookies. You can buy bottles of any of the wines. Unless the staff is rushed, you might get instructions on how to become a wine snob. If you didn't make reservations,

The Chianti Region

↑ *To Florence*

Bagno a Ripoli

Galluzzo

San Piero a Ema

Grassina

Chiesanuova

Ugolino

Impruneta

San Casciano
in Val di Pesa

La Chiantigiana
SS222

**S. Stefano
a Tizzano**

Castello di Tizzano

San Polo in Chianti

Strada
in Chianti

Spedaluzzo

**Castello di
Vicchiomaggio**

Le Bolle

Figline
Valdamo

SS2

**Castello di
Uzzano**

Castello di Verrazzano

Badia a
Passignano

San Cresci

Montefioralle

Dudda

**Castello di
Querceto**

Lucolena di Sotto

ⓘ **Greve in
Chianti**

Fontodi

Sambuca

Rignana

Lucolena

Tavernelle in
Val di Pesa

Castello Vignamaggio

Panzano
in Chianti

Lámole

Barberino
Val di Pesa

San Donato
in Poggio

Piazza

**Castello di
Volpaia**

Villa

Badia a Coltibuono

Monsanto

Pietrafitta

Villa Strozzi-Sonnino

← *To San Gimignano*

SS429

Radda
in Chianti

Vertine

Gaiole in Chianti

Poggibonsi

Castellina
in Chianti

San Giusto

Barbischio

Fonterutoli

**Castello di
Ama**

Meleto

SS408

Castagnoli

Colle di
Val d'Elsa

SS2

Lecchi

San Sano

**Castello
di Brolio**

Monteriggioni

SS222

Quercegrossa

Monti

SS484

**Fattoria dei
Pagliaresi**

**Fattoria della
Aiola**

🍇 Vineyard

ⓘ Information

0   2 mi

0   2 km

Area of Detail

Venice

Florence

Rome

0   100 Mi

0   100 Km

45° N.

40° N.

10° E

Arno River

A1

you'll find that on S222 heading south toward Greve is a *punto vendita* (sales outlet) open daily during daylight hours.

Lying just a mile to the west of Greve in Chianti is a little find off the beaten path. The small hilltop village of **Montefioralle** ★ is the ancestral home of Amerigo Vespucci (1454–1512), the mapmaker and navigator for whom America was named. It is said that Vespucci's niece, Simonette, was the model for *Venus* in Botticelli's celebrated *Primavera*. This village is sleepy except in mid-September when it hosts the Rassegna del Chianti Classico wine festival.

Consider spending at least an hour of your time here, exploring this partially restored hamlet, with some of its octagonal walls still standing, along with its old tower houses and two Romanesque churches, Santo Stefano and Pieve di San Cresci a Montefioralle.

A signposted and potholed gravel road beyond Montefioralle continues for about 30 minutes to **Badia a Passignano** (© **055-8071278;** www.osteriadi passignano.com), a 212-hectare (530-acre) property set in the midst of some of the best vineyards for producing Chianti Classico. In 1049, the Vallombrosian Order, a reformed branch of the Benedictines, moved in at this property. St. Giovanni Gualberto, who established the order here, died in 1073, and his relics are still preserved in the abbey. The original Romanesque church where the saint was buried was given a baroque overlay in the 16th century. Ridolfo di Ghirlandio decorated the monks' refectory with one of his three representations of *The Last Supper* (1476). The order was suspended in 1866 when, following the unification of Italy, the government outlawed monastic orders and appropriated the property. The on-site castle tower is from the 19th century. Antinori, one of the most famous wine producers in Italy and a legend since 1385, purchased the estate in 1987.

Badia a Passignano.

tuscan tours: BIKING, HORSEBACK RIDING & MORE

Florence-based **I Bike Italy ★** (📞 **055-0123994;** www.ibikeitaly.com) offers guided single-day rides in the Tuscan countryside, past olive groves, vineyards, castles, and vine-covered estates. Tours begin daily in Florence at 9:30am in front of the agency office on Via de'Lamberti 1. The company provides a shuttle service to carry you in and out of the city and also provides 21-speed bicycles, helmets, water bottles, and a bilingual guide to show you the way, fix flats, and so on. Tours cover a scenic 24 to 48km (15- to 30-mile) stretch, at an average speed of 5kmph (3¼ mph), and return to Florence around 5pm. The cost is 80€ per person, with lunch included.

Ciclismo Classico (📞 **800/866-7314** in the U.S.; www.ciclismoclassico.com) has more than a decade of experience leading biking and walking tours in Italy. From May to September, the outfit runs several guided tours through Tuscany, always van supported, or will help you arrange a do-it-yourself bike trip. Six- to 15-day trips usually include Italian and cooking lessons, along with wine tasting and cultural itineraries. Groups average 10 to 18 people, with all ages and ability levels welcome.

U.S.-based **Custom Tours in Tuscany** (📞 **847/432-1814;** www.customtoursin tuscany.com), with up to 10 bilingual staff members familiar with Tuscany's art and culture, can customize a daylong tour around your personal interests. Its staff can help you visit Florence's monuments, guide you through its "secret" alleyways, and show you where to buy antiques, gold, leather, extra-virgin olive oil, or linens at unbeatable prices. Its Tuscan day tours include visits to Lucca, Siena, San Gimignano, and Pietrasanta. They begin and end in Florence, where you should plan to do a lot of walking; outside Florence, the guide accompanies you in your own rented car or arranges for a car and driver. Fees are US$695 per day for Florence tours or US$795 for tours in the countryside (6–7 hr.), for one or two people. Extra persons are US$50 each. The company requires that payments be made in U.S. dollars. Transport, meals, highway tolls, mileage fee for longer trips ($95), museum admissions, and gratuities aren't included.

Only 20km (12 miles) from Florence in Pontassieve is the **Vallebona Ranch** (📞 **055-8397246;** www.vallebona.it), where Western riding is the tradition. You can choose from lessons; full-day horseback rides returning daily to the six guest rooms (shared bathrooms) at the centuries-old farmhouse (1-week package with full board 510€ per person, double occupancy); or weeklong inn-to-inn treks that begin and end at Vallebona (860€ per person, double occupancy).

You can visit the *bottega* (small store) on the grounds to purchase wines from the Badia's vineyards and tour the historic cellars. La Bottega lies in an 18th-century building near the abbey gate. Next to the shop is a good restaurant, l'Osteria di Passignano. The *bottega* is open Monday to Saturday 9:30am to 7:30pm, and the *osteria* is open 12:15 to 2:30pm and 7:30 to 10pm. Call for an appointment if you want to see the interior of the monastery, usually open on Sunday.

The road continues to **Greve in Chianti,** the region's unofficial capital, on the banks of the Greve River. Tuscany's grandest **wine fair** takes place here every September. Its central square is the funnel-shaped **Piazza del Mercatale,** with a statue honoring Giovanni da Verrazzano. Greve's castle long ago burned to the ground, but on Piazzetta Santa Croce you can visit the parish church, **Santa Croce,** containing a Bicci di Lorenzo triptych depicting the Annunciation. Greve is filled with enoteche (wine shops), but we find it far more adventurous to buy from the wineries themselves.

Six kilometers (3¾ miles) from Greve, along the road signposted FIGLINE VAL D'ARNO, you'll find a tranquil estate, the **Castello di Querceto,** Via A. François 2 (② **055-85921;** www.castellodiquerceto.it). It boasts more than 50 hectares (125 acres) of vineyards producing several grades of red Chianti and La Corte (made from the same Sangiovese grapes) and at least two whites (especially Le Giuncaie di Vernaccia). It's centered on a verdant park with an 11th-century castle that can be viewed only from the outside; the interior is not open to visitors. The staff is proud to show off the winery and cellars and will sell you wine, olive oil, and regional produce. Reservations are required.

About 9.5km (6 miles) south of Greve is **Fontodi,** Via San Leolino 89 (② **055-852005;** www.fontodi.com), accessible via S222, near the village of Panzano, less than a kilometer (½ mile) southeast of Sant'Eufrosino. Here you'll find 62 hectares (155 acres) of vineyards radiating from a stone villa built between the 18th and 19th centuries, plus wine tastings and sales of several grades of Chianti and a reputable table wine known as Flaccianello della Pieve. Reservations are required; send a fax to **055-852537.** Visits are possible Monday to Friday 8am to noon and 1:30 to 5:30pm.

South of Greve on S222 is another highlight: **Vignamaggio ★**, Via Petriolo 5 (② **055-854661;** www.vignamaggio.com), boasting a beautiful Renaissance villa that was once the residence of La Gioconda (Lisa Gherardini). With her enigmatic smile, she sat for the most famous portrait of all time, Leonardo da Vinci's *Mona Lisa,* now in Paris's Louvre. You can tour the gardens (some of the

The gardens at Vignamaggio.

most beautiful in Tuscany) Monday and Thursday if you call in advance for a reservation. (The classical statues and towering hedges served as a backdrop for Kenneth Branagh's 1993 *Much Ado About Nothing*.) In 1404, the wine of this estate became the first red to be referred to as "Chianti." This is a private villa, and you can come here for a wine tasting, served along with snacks; it costs 25€ to 45€, depending on your selection. Lovely, moderately priced apartments are available for rent here as well.

From Greve, continue 6km (3¾ miles) south along the winding Chianti-giana to one of the most enchanting spots in the Chianti, the little agricultural village of **Panzano.** It's worth a walk around the grounds and parts of its medieval castle, which once witnessed battles between Florence and Siena. The village women make the finest embroidery around, and you might want to buy some from the locals. If you're so charmed by Panzano that you want to spend the night, contact the owners of the **Torre Guelfa** hotel in Florence (www.hoteltorre guelfa.com; ✆ **055-2396338;** fax 055-2398577) and ask about their **Villa Rosa di Boscorotondo,** Via San Leolino 59, Panzano (✆ **055-852577;** fax 055-8560835; www.resortvillarosa.it).

Farther south is the delightful hill town of **Castellina in Chianti ★**, with a population of only 3,000. Once a fortified Florentine outpost against the Sienese, it fell to Sienese-Aragónese forces in 1478. But when Siena collapsed in 1555 to Florentine forces, sleepy little Castellina was left to slumber for centuries. That's how the town has preserved its quattrocento (15th-c.) look, with its once-fortified walls virtually intact. Although *bottegas* here sell Chianti and olive oils, you're better off delaying your purchases until later because you're on the doorstep of some of the finest wineries in Italy.

After Castellina, detour from S222 and head east along a tortuous road to **Radda in Chianti,** with a population of 1,700. Radda is surrounded by the rugged region of Monti del Chianti and was the ancient capital of Lega del Chianti. The streets of the village still follow their original plan from the Middle Ages. The main square with its somber **Palazzo Comunale,** bearing a fresco from the 1400s, will make you feel as if you've traveled back in time.

Another winery is in the hamlet of Rentennano, near the village of Monti. Here the **Fattoria San Giusto a Rentennano** (✆ **0577-747121;** www.fattoria sangiusto.it) is the site of a 12th-century cellar that sits beneath a 15th-century villa. The centerpiece, 30 hectares (76 acres) of vineyards, produces two grades of Chianti, as well as a simple table wine (Percarlo), which connoisseurs find surprisingly full of flavor. Tastings are possible, but only with a reservation and only for a minimum of three to four people. Hours are May to October Monday to Friday 9am to 1pm and 2 to 7pm, and Saturday by appointment only.

After a meal, continue 10km (6¼ miles) east to the market town of **Gaiole in Chianti,** with a population of 5,000. You'll come to a local cooperative, the **Agricoltori Chianti Geografico,** Via Mulinaccio 10 (✆ **0577-749489;** www. Chiantigeografico.it), a branch of one of the region's largest associations of wine-growers (more than 200). About 2km (1¼ miles) north of Gaiole in Chianti, it contains a modern wine-pressing facility with a prodigious output of (red) Chianti Classico and (white) Valdarbia. The local vin santo is made of trebbiano and malvasia grapes left to dry before pressing and then fermented in small oak barrels for about 4 years. The cooperative sells wine by the glass or the bottle, as well as olive oil, the Chianti Colli Senesi, and the (white) Galestro wines produced on its lands near Siena. Visits are possible only by appointment.

Many other wineries in the area are easily reached by car from Gaiole. One of the best is the towering **Castello di Brolio** ★★ (© 0577-7301; www.ricasoli.it), 10km (6¼ miles) south along S484. This is the home of the Barone Ricasoli Wine House, famous since the 19th century for Ricasoli's experiments aimed at improving the quality of Chianti. Known as the Iron Baron, he inherited the property in 1829; in time he became one of the creators of a unified Italy and was elected its second prime minister. The property's history dates from 1141, when Florentine monks came here to live at a site whose vineyards date from 1005. Caught up many times in the bombardments between the warring forces of Florence and Siena, the castle was later torn down, but then authorities in Florence ordered that it be reconstructed. Visiting hours are Saturday to Thursday from 9am to noon and 3 to 6pm; admission is 5€ and a tasting costs 15€. Free tastings are offered only to groups of five or more. A cantina sells the award-winning wines.

Wine with a view at the Ristoro di Lamole restaurant in Chianti.

If you backtrack, taking S408 to Siena, you can follow the signposts about 10km (6¼ miles) north to the **Fattoria della Aiola** (© 0577-322615; fax 0577-322509; www.aiola.net), near the hamlet of Vagliagli, 20km (12 miles) southwest of Gaiole. Site of a ruined medieval castle (only a wall and a moat remain) and a 19th-century villa (not open to the public), it features 36 hectares (90 acres) of vineyards that produce Chianti, Sangiovese, grappa, and Spumante "Aioli Brut" (a sparkling wine similar to champagne). The winery even produces olive oil and vinegar. This place receives a lot of visitors (including tour buses), so advance reservations or at least a phone call before arriving is a good idea.

Where to Stay Along the Chianti Road

The atmospheric Tuscan inns along the Chianti Road are wonderful, and it's a good idea to break up a visit between Florence and Siena with a night at one of them. The best places to stay are Greve, Radda, Gaiole, and Castellina (our favorite). Many of these inns are also noted for their good food and wine. Even if you're not a guest, you might visit for a meal.

Albergo del Chianti ★ 🍴   At the edge of Greve's main square, with a facade and foundation as old as the square itself (more than 1,000 years), is this charming small inn with views over the countryside. Each cozy, simple guest room is painted a different color and is done in rustic Tuscan style with a wrought-iron bedstead. Aside from breakfast, dinner is the only meal served (only to hotel guests). The Bussotti family takes good care of you in the restaurant; in warm weather, the food is served in a beautiful Mediterranean garden.

Piazza G. Matteotti 86, 50022 Greve in Chianti. © **055-853763.** Fax 055-853764. www.albergo delChianti.it. 16 units. 72€–110€ double. Rates include buffet breakfast. MC, V. **Amenities:** Restaurant; bar; babysitting; outdoor pool; room service. *In room:* A/C, TV, hair dryer, minibar, Wi-Fi (free).

Badia a Coltibuono ★★ 🎁   The on-site monastery here, standing on 809 hectares (2,000 acres) of land, is 1,000 years old. Benedictine monks lived here until 1810. The farmhouse villa has been extensively restored and is now open to overnight guests, who can sleep in comfort and wander the ancient abbey garden. There's even a rectangular pool at the center of the garden. Guests are housed in either five renovated monks' cells or else a trio of more charming and more spacious bedrooms. Most of the rooms open onto panoramic vistas of the Chianti countryside. Many of the bedrooms have special features such as the dressing room in no. 1 or a coffered wooden ceiling and the large wrought-iron bed in no. 11. The cloisters of the original building as well as massive fireplaces have been retained. Tuscan wines and a fine regional cuisine are served at the on-site restaurant.

Località Badia a Coltibuono, 53013 Gaiole in Chianti. © **0577-744832.** Fax 0577-744839. www. coltibuono.com. 8 units. 160€–190€ double. Rates include buffet breakfast. Free parking. AE, MC, V. **Amenities:** Restaurant; bar; children's center; outdoor pool. *In room:* A/C, no phone.

Borgo Argenina ★   From the flagstone terrace of Elena Nappa's hilltop B&B (she bought the whole medieval village), you can see the farmhouse where Bertolucci filmed his gorgeous *Stealing Beauty* in 1996. Against remarkable odds (she'll regale you with the anecdotes), she has created the rural retreat of her dreams—and yours, too. Elena's design talents (she was a fashion stylist in Milan) are amazing, and the guest rooms boast antique wrought-iron beds, handmade quilts, hand-stitched lace curtains, and timeworn terra-cotta tiles. The bathrooms are made to look old-fashioned, although the plumbing is modern. The place isn't easy to find, so English-speaking Elena will fax you directions when you reserve.

Località Argenina (San Marcellino Monti), 53013 Gaiole in Chianti. © **0577-747117.** Fax 0577-747228. www.borgoargenina.it. 7 units. 170€–240€ double; 240€–480€ apt. Rates include buffet breakfast. MC, V. Ask for directions when reserving. **Amenities:** Room service. *In room:* Hair dryer, minibar.

Castello di Spaltenna ★   One of the region's unique luxury hotels is on a hill above Gaiole. Opened during the Middle Ages as a monastery, it retains some medieval flair, despite several enlargements and modifications. In the compound are a small medieval chapel, two soaring towers, and several stone-sided annexes, one housing some of the junior suites. The guest rooms are cozy and traditionally furnished, with all the modern conveniences. Look for wrought-iron or wooden headboards and terra-cotta floors whose tiles might be as much as 1,000 years old. Some rooms have fireplaces, and all enjoy views over the peaceful countryside and classic cypress trees. Hiking, horseback riding, and tennis are available nearby. Dining is either indoors by candlelight in the old cloister or outdoors on a terrace.

Pieve di Spaltenna, 53013 Gaiole in Chianti. (☎) **0577-749483.** Fax 0577-749269. www.spaltenna. it. 38 units. 195€–330€ double; 460€–540€ suite. Rates include buffet breakfast. Free parking. AE, DC, MC, V. Closed Jan 7–Mar 31. **Amenities:** Restaurant; bar; babysitting; bikes; exercise room; 2 pools (1 heated indoor); room service; sauna; outdoor tennis court (lit). *In room:* A/C, TV, hair dryer, minibar, Wi-Fi (free).

Hotel Colle Etrusco Salivolpi ★ 🏠 In a classic farm setting that looks as if it's straight out of a Renaissance painting, the family run Salivolpi is only a 15- to 20-minute drive from Siena, or 30 minutes from Florence. The simple Tuscan-style guest rooms are spread across three buildings, each beautifully maintained and decorated with regional antiques. The bathrooms are spotless.

Via Fiorentina 89, 53011 Castellina in Chianti. (☎) **0577-740484.** Fax 0577-740998. www.hotel salivolpi.com. 19 units (15 with shower only). 80€–110€ double. AE, MC, V. **Amenities:** Bar; bikes; outdoor pool; Wi-Fi (free, in lobby). *In room:* TV, hair dryer.

Podere Terreno ★ 🏠 This is one of the best examples of *agriturismo* (lodging on a working farm) in Tuscany. Robert Melosi and his Paris-born wife, Marie-Sylvie Haniez, welcome you. They sensitively restored a 16th-century farmhouse and today welcome houseguests to share communal dinners with them. The former kitchen is now a dining room where guests take their meals at a long table. Wooden beams, terra-cotta floors, and rustic but comfortable accommodations are provided. Each room has a private bathroom with shower. The tasteful units are graced with painted metal bedsteads, and each bedroom is named for a local grape. The old farmstead is enveloped by vineyards. Special features include a wine-tasting cantina and a small "spa," with massages and a summer-only Jacuzzi.

Rte. S22, 53107 Radda in Chianti (4.5km/3 miles north of town). (☎) **0577-738312.** Fax 0577-738400. www.podereterreno.it. 6 units. 150€ double. Rates include half board (breakfast and dinner). AE, MC, V. **Amenities:** Restaurant; bar. *In room:* No phone.

Tenuta di Ricavo ★★ This place is a fantasy of what a Tuscan inn should look like. In fact, it's like a medieval village of stone houses. On nippy nights, guests gather near the fireplace in the atmospheric bar. The innkeepers rent beautifully furnished and kept guest rooms, each with a well-maintained bathroom. Surrounding the compound are 178 hectares (445 acres) of woodlands, with paths that are ideal for taking long walks or riding a mountain bike.

Località Ricavo 4, 53011 Castellina in Chianti (3km/2 miles north of town). (☎) **0577-740221.** Fax 0577-741014. www.ricavo.com. 23 units (shower only). 140€–246€ double; 280€–400€ suite. Rates include buffet breakfast. Free parking. AE, MC, V. Closed Nov–Mar. **Amenities:** Restaurant; babysitting; exercise room; 2 outdoor pools; room service; Wi-Fi (5€ per hr., in lobby). *In room:* TV, hair dryer, minibar.

Villa Bordoni ★★★ 🏠 One of our favorite stopovers along the Chianti Road is this restored wisteria-covered inn and restaurant, a bold creative statement of two Scottish expats, David and Catherine Gardner. A stay in one of its rustic, chic bedrooms and a gourmet dinner at its intimate restaurant is one of the highlights of the wine country. Originally a 16th-century villa with an olive mill and chapel, today this vineyard-ringed hotel evokes an English country house with beautifully furnished bedrooms, filled with Italian antiques and original wood-beamed ceilings.

Via San Cresci, 31–32 Località Mezzuola, 50022 Greve in Chianti. (☎) **055-8547453.** Fax 055-8519114. www.villabordoni.com. 12 units. 190€–310€ double; 260€–490€ suite. Rates include buffet breakfast. Free parking. AE, MC, V. **Amenities:** Restaurant; bar; babysitting; exercise room; outdoor pool; room service. *In room:* A/C, TV/DVD, hair dryer, minibar, Wi-Fi (in some, free).

Villa Casalecchi Almost as elegant as the Tenuta di Ricavo (listed above), this government-rated four-star hotel is built into a hill. You arrive on the hilltop and enter into the top floor. The hotel is composed of a trio of buildings; the main structure is an elegant villa whose 16 units are spread across two floors. The guest rooms range from small to medium, each furnished in part with 18th-century reproductions and often with canopied beds. The bathrooms are rather small. There's an elegant restaurant, offering outdoor dining in the evergreen garden in summer. The staff will help you arrange outings to nearby wineries on bike or horseback.

Località Casalecchi 18, 53011 Castellina in Chianti. © **0577-740240.** Fax 0577-741111. www.villa casalecchi.it. 25 units. 110€–210€ double. Rates include buffet breakfast. AE, DC, MC, V. Free parking. Closed Nov–Mar. **Amenities:** Restaurant; bar; babysitting; bikes; outdoor pool; room service; outdoor tennis court. *In room:* A/C (in some), TV, hair dryer, minibar.

Where to Dine Along the Chianti Road

Some of the best food in Italy is served in Chianti, and all dishes are accompanied by the wine of the region.

Antica Trattoria La Torre ★ TUSCAN This old, family-run dining room is on the town's main square in an 18th-century building, next to a medieval tower. The kitchen depends on the harvest from the field, stream, and air to keep its cooks busy. The Tuscan game, the fowl (such as pigeon and guinea), and the local beef are the finest in the area. The Florentine beefsteak alone is worth the trip. Other typical dishes are delicious *ribollita* (hearty vegetable soup), pasta with game sauce, and meat grilled over charcoal with mushrooms. The best dessert is the homemade pine-nut cake.

Piazza del Comune 15, Castellina in Chianti. © **0577-740236.** www.anticatrattorialatorre.com. Reservations required in summer and weekends. Main courses 7€–20€. AE, MC, V. Sat–Thurs noon–2:30pm and 7–9:30pm. Closed Sept 1–10 and Feb 15–Mar 10.

Borgo Antico ★ 🍴 TUSCAN Opened more than 30 years ago in a 200-year-old compound of farmhouses and barns, this country inn hauls in fresh produce from nearby farms every morning. The pastas are made fresh on the premises, and the specialty is *pappardella* (wide noodles) made with chestnut flour and served with a wild-boar sauce. The desserts, especially such relatively simple concoctions as crema cotta and tiramisu, are wonderful. The Florentine-style beefsteaks are among the best in the region, tender and loaded with Mediterranean herbs and olive oil. The turkey filet grilled with olive oil and the veal scallops with lemon juice or wine are worth the drive. As you dine, you'll enjoy views of the nearby slopes of Monte San Michele.

The Maruntis rent three simple guest rooms. The solid-stone-wall facade and old-time setting more than compensate for the lack of luxuries. Each has a private bathroom, although in one case it's outside the bedroom. Doubles are 60€. No breakfast is served.

Via Case Sparse 115, Lucolena (16km/10 miles northeast of Greve). © **055-851024.** www.ilborgo antico.it. Reservations recommended. Main courses 10€–22€. AE, DC, MC, V. Mar–Oct Wed–Mon noon–2:30pm and 7–9:30pm; Nov–Dec and Feb Fri–Sat 7–9:30pm, Sat–Sun noon–3pm. Closed Jan 5–Feb 15.

Bottega del Moro ★ TUSCAN/SEAFOOD Our favorite restaurant in Greve's center occupies an old stone blacksmith's shop. (Locals referred to the blacksmith as "the Moor" because of the charcoal that blackened his face, and ever since, the nickname "Lair of the Moor" has been associated with this restaurant.) It specializes in light Tuscan fare that goes easy on the olive oil. The cooking, based on fine seafood and local farm products, is very good indeed. Try the sautéed red tuna steak with crispy vegetables or calamari stuffed with sea bream and zucchini. Other specialties include linguine sautéed with shrimp and served with broccoli and black beans or goose breast flavored with honey. The unusual modern paintings in the two dining rooms are by a well-known local artist, Alvaro Baragli. A flowering terrace provides limited extra seating on the square during clement weather.

Piazza Trieste 14R, Greve in Chianti. ℂ **055-853753.** www.labottegadelmoro.it. Reservations required. Main courses 8€–18€. AE, DC, MC, V. Tues–Sun noon–3pm and 7–11pm. Closed 2 weeks in Nov.

Il Vignale TUSCAN This rustic yet elegant place is the area's best family run dining room, turning out home-style Tuscan cuisine that's flavorful and prepared with fresh ingredients. Every day something new appears, and the cuisine is quite creative. You can start with a typical *crostini* (similar to a small bruschetta, with different kinds of prosciutto on top). Among the main courses are home-made soups and pastas, such as *tagliatelle* (flat noodles) with wild-boar sauce. In autumn, some of the region's finest game dishes are offered, and you can order roast lamb stuffed with artichokes and aromatic herbs. Guests can enjoy a table on the restaurant's wisteria terrace that opens onto a panoramic view.

In the Relais Vignale, Via Pianigiani 9. ℂ **0577-738094.** www.vignale.it. Reservations recommended. Main courses 10€–26€. AE, DC, MC, V. Daily 12:30–3pm and 7:30–9:30pm. Closed Nov–Mar.

Montagliari ★ 🏠 TUSCAN Associated with a local vineyard, Montagliari is full of rustic charm and serves authentic regional fare. Tables are set out in a garden, and the place is decorated like an old Tuscan farmhouse. The specialty here is wild-boar cacciatore. You can also order roasted lamb or rabbit with potatoes, penne with raw chopped tomatoes and homegrown basil, tortellini stuffed with minced meat, or roasted lamb in the age-old style of the Tuscan hills.

Via di Montagliari 29, Panzano (btw. Montagliari and Greve, 1km/½ mile north of Panzano). ℂ **055-852014.** www.montagliari.it. Reservations recommended. Main courses 10€–18€. AE, DC, MC, V. Tues–Sun 12:30–2:30pm and 7:30–9:30pm.

LUCCA ★★★

72km (45 miles) W of Florence, 21km (13 miles) E of Pisa, 336km (208 miles) N of Rome

In 56 b.c., Caesar, Crassus, and Pompey met in Lucca and agreed to rule Rome as a triumvirate. By the time of the Roman Empire's collapse, Lucca was virtually the capital of Tuscany. Periodically in its valiant, ever-bloody history, this town was an independent principality, enjoying fame and prestige. Now, however, Lucca is largely bypassed by time and travelers, rewarding those who venture off the beaten track.

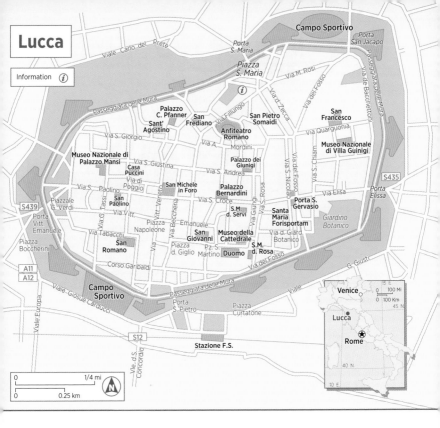

Lucca

Information (i)

In the late 1600s, Lucca's third and final set of city walls was erected. This girdle of ramparts is largely intact and is one of the major reasons to visit the town, where the architecture ranges from Roman to Liberty.

Today, Lucca is best known for its *olio d'oliva lucchese,* the quality olive oil produced in the region outside the town's walls. Shoppers will be delighted to find a number of upscale boutiques here as well, testimony to an affluence not dependent on tourism. Thriving, cosmopolitan, and perfectly preserved, Lucca is a sort of Switzerland of the south: The banks have latticed Gothic windows, the shops look like well-stocked linen cupboards, children play in landscaped gardens, and geraniums bloom from the roofs of medieval tower houses.

Essentials

GETTING THERE At least 20 **trains** travel daily between Florence and Lucca. The trip takes 1¼ hours and costs 5.50€ each way. The rail station is about .5km (¼ mile) south of Lucca's historic core, a short walk from the city's ramparts. For rail information, call ⓒ **892021.** If you don't have a lot of luggage, you can walk into the center; otherwise, most of the city's buses (notably, nos. 1, 2, and 3) and lots of taxis stand ready to take you there.

Biking Lucca's city walls.

The **Lazzi bus** company (✆ **0583-584877;** www.lazzi.it) operates buses traveling between Florence and Lucca. They take less time than the train (50 min.–1 hr.), and, unlike the train, they carry passengers to a point within the city walls. Bus transit between Florence and Lucca costs 6€. Buses pick up passengers in front of the rail station in Florence and drop them off in Lucca at both the rail station and the historic core at Piazzale Verdi, near the tourist office.

If you have a **car,** from Florence take the A11 highway through Prato, Pistoia, and Montecatini. If you're in Pisa, take S12.

VISITOR INFORMATION   The Lucca **tourist office** (www.luccaturismo.it), on Piazza Santa Maria 35 (✆ **0583-919931**), is open daily 9am to 7:30pm April to October, and from November to March Monday to Saturday 9am to noon and 3 to 6pm.

GETTING AROUND   Lucca is a great place to rent a bike, especially because you can ride along the ancient city walls. Try **Bibiclette Poli,** Piazza Santa Maria 42 (✆ **0583-493787;** www.biciclettepoli.com), which is open daily from 8:30am to 7:30pm, except for Sunday and Monday morning in winter. Expect to pay about 3.50€ per hour or 18€ for a whole day to rent a good mountain bike.

SPECIAL EVENTS   Sleepy Lucca comes to life in July during the classical music festival, the **Summer Festival.** Venues spring up everywhere, and the tourist office keeps a list. On July 12, residents don medieval costumes and parade through the city, with the revelry continuing late into the night.

In Puccini's hometown, you'll find a devotion to opera, and in October and November his work is showcased at the **Teatro Comunale del Giglio,** Piazza di Giglio (✆ **0583-465320;** fax 0583-465339; www.teatrodelgiglio.it). More classical music performances fill the town in September during the **Settembre Lucchese Festival,** highlighted by Volto Santo feast day on September 13. The crucifix bearing the "face" of Christ (normally housed in a chapel in the Duomo) is hauled through town in a candlelit procession to commemorate its miraculous journey to Lucca. The last 2 weeks of September also bring an **agricultural market** to Piazza San Michele, featuring Lucca's wines, honeys, and olive oils.

One of Italy's top **antiques markets** is held the third Saturday and Sunday of every month in Piazza Antelminelli and the streets around the Duomo. (Hotel and restaurant reservations are always harder to get on these weekends.)

Exploring the Town

The **city walls** ★★ enclose the old town; they're the best-preserved Renaissance defense ramparts in Europe. The present walls, measuring 35m (115 ft.) at the base and soaring 12m (40 ft.) high, replaced crumbling ramparts built during the Middle Ages. They comprise a city park more than 4km (2½ miles) long but only about 18m (60 ft.) wide, filled with leafy trees. The shady paved paths of Lucca's formidable bastions are always filled with couples strolling hand in hand, families on outings, old men playing cards, and hundreds of people on bikes. You can enter from one of 10 bastions; try the one behind the tourist office at **Piazzale Verdi.** For orientation, you might want to walk completely around the city on the ramparts, the **Passeggiata delle Mura,** a distance of 4km (2½ miles).

Besides the major sights below, worth seeking out is the **Roman Amphitheater (Anfiteatro Romano),** at Piazza Anfiteatro, reached along Via Fillungo. You can still see the outlines of its arches in its outer walls, and within the inner ring only the rough form remains to evoke what must've been. Once the theater was adorned with many-hued Tuscan marble, but greedy builders hauled off its materials to create some of the many churches of Lucca, including San Michele and the Duomo. The foundations of the former grandstands, which once rang with the sound of Tuscans screaming for gladiator blood, now support an ellipse of houses from the Middle Ages. The theater is from the 2nd century A.D.

If you want to catch a glimpse of Lucca life, find a chair at one of the cafes and pass the day away. In July and August, you can come to the **Piazza Guidiccioni** nearby and see a screening of the latest hit movies in the open air.

Cattedrale di San Martino (Duomo) ★★
The Duomo is the town's main monument, dating from 1060, although the present structure was mainly rebuilt during the following centuries. The facade is exceptional, evoking the Pisan-Romanesque style but with enough originality and idiosyncrasies to distinguish it from the Duomo at Pisa. Designed mostly by Guidetto da Como in the early 13th century, the west front contains three wide ground-level arches, surmounted by three scalloped galleries with taffylike twisting columns tapering in size.

The main relic inside (in some ways the religious symbol of Lucca itself) is the **Volto Santo ★**, a crucifix carved by Nicodemus (so tradition has it) from the Cedar of Lebanon. The face of Christ was supposedly chiseled onto the statuary.

The main art treasure lies in the sacristy: the **tomb of Ilaria del Carretto Guinigi ★★**, sculpted by Jacopo della Quercia. Ilaria was a local aristocrat and the wife of Paolo Guinigi; she died in 1405 while still young. Her marble effigy, in regal robes and guarded by her dog, rests atop the sarcophagus; the diffused mauve afternoon light casts a ghostly glow on her face. (Long-term plans include moving the tomb to the Duomo Museum.) Also in the sacristy is the superb Domenico Ghirlandaio *Madonna and Saints* altarpiece (1494).

Adjacent to the Duomo is the **Duomo Museum** (**Museo della Cattedrale; ✆ 0583-490530;** admission 4€; Mar–Oct daily 10am–6pm, Nov–Feb Mon–Fri 10am–2pm and Sat–Sun 10am–5pm). Here you'll find some rather dusty-looking memorabilia and mostly minor artworks, with the exception of Matteo Civitali's late-15th-century choir screen (removed from the cathedral in 1987) and Jacopo della Quercia's majestic early-15th-century sculpture *St. John the Evangelist*.

Piazza San Martino. ✆ **0583-957068.** www.museocattedralelucca.it. Free admission to cathedral; sacristy and inner sanctum 4€. Apr–Oct daily 10am–6pm; Nov–Mar Mon–Fri 10am–2pm, Sat–Sun 10am–5pm. Closed Dec 25, Jan 1, and Easter.

National Picture Gallery and Palazzo Mansi Museum (Pinacoteca Nazionale e Museo di Palazzo Mansi)   This palace was built for the powerful Mansi family, whose descendants are still some of the movers and shakers in town. Although Tuscany has far greater art collections, there are some treasures, notably a portrait of Princess Elisa by Marie Benoist. Elisa Bonaparte (1777–1820), who married into a local wealthy family, the Bacceocchis, was "given" the town by her brother Napoleon in 1805 when he made her princess of Lucca and Piombino. Unlike her profligate sister, Pauline Borghese in Rome, Elisa was a strong woman with a remarkable aptitude for public affairs (she laid out Piazza Napoleone, among other accomplishments). The collection is enriched by lesser works from Lanfranco, Luca Giordano, and Tintoretto, among others. There's a damaged Veronese, but Tintoretto's *Miracle of St. Mark Freeing the Slave* is amusing—the patron saint of Venice literally divebombs from heaven to save the day.

Via Galli Tassi 43. ✆ **0583-55570.** Admission 4€. Tues–Sat 8:30am–7pm; Sun 8:30am–1pm. Closed Dec 25, Jan 1, and May 1.

San Frediano ★   Romanesque in style, this is one of Lucca's most important churches, built in the 12th and 13th centuries when the town enjoyed its greatest glory. The severe white facade is relieved by a 13th-century mosaic of Christ ascending, and the campanile (bell tower) rises majestically. The interior is dark, and visitors often speak in whispers. But the bas-reliefs on the Romanesque font add a note of comic relief: Supposedly depicting the story of Moses, among other themes, they show Egyptians in medieval armor chasing after the Israelites. Two tombs in the basilica (in the fourth chapel on the left) were the work of celebrated Sienese sculptor Jacopo della Quercia.

Piazza San Frediano. ✆ **0583-493627.** Free admission. Mon–Sat 9am–noon and 3–5pm; Sun 9am–noon and 3–6pm.

San Michele in Foro ★   This church often surprises first-timers, who mistake it for the Duomo. Begun in 1143, it's the most memorable example of the style and flair that the Lucchese brought to the Pisan-Romanesque school of architecture. The exquisite west front, employing the scalloped effect, is spanned by seven ground-level arches and then surmounted by four tiers of galleries, utilizing imaginatively designed columns. Dragon-slaying St. Michael, wings outstretched, rests on the friezelike peak of the final tier. Inside, seek out a Filippo Lippi painting, *Saints Sebastian, Jerome, Helen, and Roch*, on the far wall of the right transept. If you're here in September, the piazza outside, which was the old Roman forum, holds a daily colorful open market selling everything from olive oil to souvenirs of Tuscany.

Piazza San Michele. ✆ **0583-48459.** Free admission. Daily 9am–noon and 3–5:30pm.

Detail from the mosaics at San Frediano in Lucca.

Where to Stay

Albergo San Martino  Enclosed within the great walls of Lucca and around the corner from the Duomo, this budget inn opens onto a tiny square. As a hotel, it enjoys one of the best locations in Lucca, and its prices are reasonable. Bedrooms for the most part are midsize and comfortably furnished. There is a homelike aura to the place, and the buffet breakfast is bountiful.

Via della Dogana 9, 55100 Lucca. 🕿 **0583-469181.** Fax 0583-991940. www.albergosanmartino. it. 10 units. 80€–110€ double; 120€–160€ suite. AE, MC, V. Parking 15€. **Amenities:** Bar; bikes. *In room:* A/C, TV, minibar, Wi-Fi (free).

Locanda l'Elisa ★★★ This Relais & Châteaux member is the region's most elegant hotel, 3km (2 miles) south of the city walls. In the mid–19th century, it was the home of an army officer who was the intimate companion of Napoleon's sister Elisa, who lived across the road. Today, both lovers' villas are upscale hotels (Elisa's is now La Principessa). Behind a dignified neoclassical facade, Locanda l'Elisa offers verdant gardens, a worthy collection of antiques, discreet service, and large, plush guest rooms.

Via Nuova per Pisa 1952, 55050 Massa Pisana (Lucca). 🕿 **0583-379737.** Fax 0583-379019. www. locandalelisa.it. 10 units. 70€–340€ double; 100€–390€ junior suite. AE, DC, MC, V. Free parking. Bus: 54. **Amenities:** Fine conservatory-style restaurant (Il Gazebo, see below); bar; babysitting; outdoor pool; room service. *In room:* A/C, TV, hair dryer, minibar, Wi-Fi (4.50€ per hr.).

Palazzo Alexander ★★ In the historic district, a stone's throw from San Michele in Foro, this former abode of Lucchesi nobles in the 12th century has been sensitively restored and now is the *hotel de charme* in town. A boarding school in the 1800s, it has been turned into four floors of rooms and apartments, all with private, modern bathrooms (some with whirlpool tubs). The style in both the bedrooms and public areas is classic Lucchese with antique wood floors in all the bedrooms and fine marble and other local stone in the bathrooms and public areas. High ceilings, brocaded chairs, and damask upholstery contribute to the atmosphere.

Via S. Giustina 48, San Michele, 55100 Lucca. ✆ **0583-583571.** Fax 0583-583610. www.hotel palazzoalexander.it. 15 units. 100€–170€ double. Rates include buffet breakfast. AE, DC, MC, V. Parking 15€. **Amenities:** Bar; bikes. *In room:* A/C, TV, hair dryer, Wi-Fi (free).

Piccolo Hotel Puccini ★ 🔥   Your best bet within the city walls is this palace built in the 1400s, across from the house where Puccini was born (Puccini's music often plays in the lobby). Right off Piazza San Michele and one of the most enchanting spots in Lucca, this little hotel is better than ever now that an energetic couple has taken over. Intimate and comfortable, the rooms are beautifully maintained, with freshly starched curtains, good beds, crisp linens, and tasteful furnishings. Some windows open onto the small square in front with a bronze statue of the great Puccini.

Via Di Poggio 9, 55100 Lucca. ✆ **0583-55421.** Fax 0583-53487. www.hotelpuccini.com. 14 units. 95€ double; 110€ triple. AE, DC, MC, V. Free parking nearby. **Amenities:** Bar; babysitting; bikes; room service. *In room:* TV, hair dryer.

Villa Marta   With only a dozen or so rooms, this former 19th-century hunting lodge feels much like a private home, albeit a romantic one with an outdoor pool and large garden. Antique furnishings, wood beams, and terra-cotta floorings evoke the 19th century, but the hotel boasts all modern amenities. A buffet is served in the garden in summer. The lodge lies only a 20-minute drive from Lucca.

Via del Ponte Guasperini 873, 55100 Lucca. ✆ **0583-370101.** Fax 0583-379999. www.albergo villamarta.it. 15 units. 59€–229€ double. Rates include buffet breakfast. AE, MC, V. Free parking. **Amenities:** Restaurant; bar; babysitting; bikes; outdoor pool; room service. *In room:* A/C, TV, hair dryer, minibar, Wi-Fi (5€ per hr.).

Where to Dine

Don't forget to drop in at the **Antico Caffè di Simo,** Via Fillungo 58 (✆ **0583-496234;** www.caffedisimo.it), where Puccini used to come to eat and drink and perhaps dream about his next opera. At this historic cafe you can order the best gelato in town while taking in the old-time aura of faded mirrors, brass, and marble. The cafe is open Tuesday to Sunday 8am to 8pm.

Buca di Sant'Antonio ★★ TUSCAN   On a difficult-to-find alley near Piazza San Michele is Lucca's finest restaurant. The 1782 building was constructed on the site of a chapel (Buca di Sant'Antonio). The cuisine is refined and inspired, respecting the traditional but also daring to be innovative. Menu items include homemade ravioli stuffed with ricotta and pulverized zucchini; pork ragout, stewed rabbit with olives, and roast Tuscan goat with roast potatoes and braised greens. Try the house-special dessert, *semifreddo Buccellato* (partially melted ice cream with local red berries).

Via della Cervia 3. ✆ **0583-55881.** www.bucadisantantonio.com. Reservations recommended. Main courses 13€–20€. AE, DC, MC, V. Tues–Sun 12:30–3pm; Tues–Sat 7:30–10:30pm. Closed 1st week of July and 2nd week of Jan.

Da Giulio in Pelleria LUCCHESE   This cavernous restaurant holds fast to local traditions and time-honored recipes, with dishes such as great minestrones, pastas, veal, hearty soups, and chicken dishes served in robust portions. Some regional dishes might be a little too adventurous for some tastes, such as *cioncia* (calf snout and herbs). Other food items include a Lucchese specialty, *farinata,* a soup with a base of minestrone and white flour; cuttlefish with beets; lamb with olives; and a fabulous almond torte for dessert.

Via delle Conce 45. ℂ **0583-55948.** Reservations recommended. Main courses 10€–32€. AE, MC, V. Tues–Sat 6:30–11:30pm; Sat 12:30–2:30pm. Closed Dec 25, 26, and 31, and Jan 1.

Giglio ★ REGIONAL/TUSCAN   In regional appeal and popularity, this place is rivaled only by the Buca di Sant'Antonio (see above). The secret to its appeal might be its rustic decor (including 16th-c. architectural detailing), its attentive staff, and its fine interpretations of time-honored recipes. Menu items usually include steaming bowls of *minestra di farro* (vegetable soup with pasta), followed by homemade pasta with zucchini and shrimp sauce; fried chicken with mushrooms; or grilled tuna with fresh tomatoes.

Piazza del Giglio 2. ℂ **0583-494058.** www.ristorantegiglio.com. Reservations recommended. Fixed-price lunch 13€–20€; main courses 7€–16€. AE, DC, MC, V. Thurs–Tues noon–2:30pm; Thurs–Mon 7:30–10pm. Closed 2 weeks in Feb and Nov 20–Dec 6.

Il Gazebo ★ ITALIAN/TUSCAN   Set in one of Tuscany's most elegant hotels, 3km (2 miles) south of Lucca's center, the restaurant is a re-creation of an English conservatory. The wraparound windows in the almost-circular room offer garden views. The service, as you'd expect in a Relais & Châteaux, is impeccable. Menu items include upscale versions of Luccan recipes, such as *farro Lucchese,* a red-bean soup with locally grown greens. Other dishes include skewers of lobster with olives and pearl onions, smoked swordfish with grilled eggplant, and ravioli stuffed with herbed eggplant and served with prawn sauce. Each is prepared with refinement and skill. The chefs also serve vegetarian and low-cholesterol dishes.

In the Locanda l'Elisa, Via Nuova per Pisa 1952. ℂ **0583-379737.** www.locandalelisa.it. Reservations recommended. Main courses 16€–32€; fixed-price menus 110€–120€. AE, V. Apr–Nov Mon–Sat 12:30–2pm and 7:30–10:30pm; Dec–Mar Mon–Sat 7:30–10:30pm. Closed Jan–Feb 10. Bus: 54.

Trattoria da Leo TUSCAN   In this unpretentious family-run spot, almost no one speaks English (although there's a menu in English). This is a pleasant *trattoria* in a 16th-century building close to Piazza San Michele. The decor of the dining rooms (one large, one very small) is vaguely 1930s. The savory menu items include an array of dishes such as ravioli with pine nuts, fresh tomatoes and basil, or else spaghetti with a spicy tomato sauce flavored with chopped garlic and parsley. A shank of pork is served with roast potatoes, and a dish with small pieces of stewed veal comes with olives and polenta.

Via Tegrimi 1. ℂ **0583-492236.** www.trattoriadaleo.it. Reservations recommended. Main courses 7€–12€. No credit cards. Daily noon–2:30pm and 7:30–10:30pm. Closed Sun Nov–Feb (except 3rd Sun of each month).

Shopping

The sunny, scenic hills around Lucca have been famous since the days of the Romans for producing fabulous amber-colored olive oil. You won't have to look far to find it—every supermarket, butcher shop, and delicatessen in Lucca sells a huge variety, in glass or metal containers. But if you want to travel into the surrounding hills to check out the production of this heart-healthy product, the best-known company selling its products on rustic Tuscan farms is **Maionchi,**

Via Tofori 81, in the hamlet of Capannori (© **0583-978194;** www.fattoria maionchi.it), 18km (11 miles) northeast of Lucca.

Take a stroll along the town's top shopping streets, **Via Fillungo** and **Via del Battistero.** The best gift/souvenir shops are **Insieme,** Via Vittorio Emanuele 70 (© **0583-419649**), and **Incontro,** Via Buia 9 (© **0583-491225;** www.lincontrolucca.it), which places a special emphasis on Lucca's rustically appealing porcelain, pottery, tiles, and crystal.

If you're in town on the right weekend, check out the wonderful **antiques market.**

PISA ★★

76km (47 miles) W of Florence, 333km (206 miles) NW of Rome

Few buildings in the world have captured imaginations as much as the Leaning Tower of Pisa, the most instantly recognizable building in the Western world (except, perhaps, for the Eiffel Tower). Perhaps visitors are drawn to it as a symbol of the fragility of people—or at least the fragility of their work. The Leaning Tower is a powerful landmark. It draws hordes of day-trippers every midday.

There's more to Pisa than just the tower. In addition to other historic sights, there are the modern busy streets surrounding the university and the market. You'll find a town resounding with the exuberance of its student population and its residents as they make the purchases of everyday life.

Essentials

GETTING THERE Both domestic and international flights arrive at Pisa's **Galileo Galilei Airport** (© **050-849111;** www.pisa-airport.com). From the airport,

The Leaning Tower of Pisa.

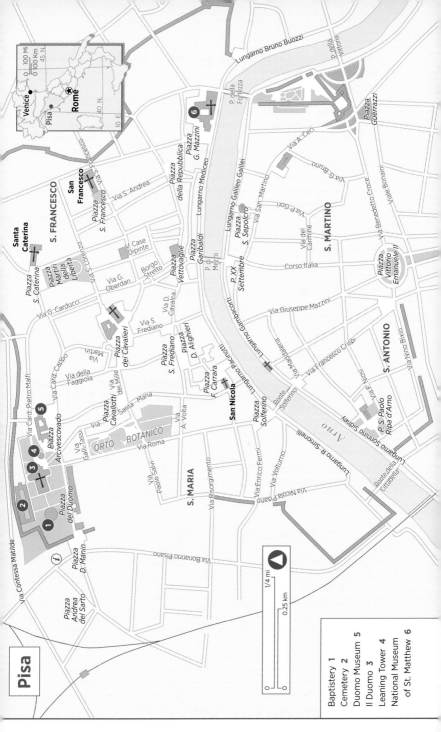

Pisa

Baptistery **1**
Cemetery **2**
Duomo Museum **5**
Il Duomo **3**
Leaning Tower **4**
National Museum of St. Matthew **6**

0 100 Km
0 100 Mi

Venice
Pisa
Rome

S. FRANCESCO

Santa Caterina

San Francesco

Piazza S. Francesco

Piazza S. Caterina

Via S. Andrea

Via S. Francesco

Piazza della Repubblica

Piazza G. Mazzini

Lungarno Bruno Buozzi

P. della Vittoria

P. della Fortezza

Piazza Guerrazzi

Via A. Ceci

Via G. Bruno

Lungarno Mediceo

Lungarno Galileo Galilei

Via San Martino

Via P. Gori

S. MARTINO

Via Benedetto Croce

Viale Bonaini

Piazza Vittorio Emanuele II

Corso Italia

Piazza Sepolcro

S. Sepolcro

Piazza Garibaldi

P. di Mezzo

P. XX Settembre

Via del Carmine

Via Giuseppe Mazzini

S. ANTONIO

Via Nino Bixio

Via S. Lorenzo

Case Dipinte

Borgo Stretto

Piazza Vettovaglie

Via G. Oberdan

Via G. Carducci

Piazza Martiri della Libertà

Via D. Cavalca

Via S. Frediano

Piazza dei' Cavalieri

Via Cavallotti

Via Card. Cappo

Via Martiri

Via della Faggiola

Via Card.-Pietro-Malfi

Piazza S. Frediano

Piazza D. Alighieri

Piazza F. Carrara

Lungarno Pacinotti

Lungarno Gambacorti

Via Maddalena

Via Francesco Crispi

P.S. Paolo Ripa d'Arno

Lungarno Sonnino Sidney

Arno

Ponte Solferino

San Nicola

Piazza Solferino

Via A. Volta

Santa Maria

Piazza Cavallotti

Via Galli-Tassi

ORTO BOTANICO

Via Roma

Piazza Arcivescovado

Piazza del Duomo

Via Contessa Matilde

Piazza D. Manin.

Piazza Andrea del Sarto

Via Bonanno Pisano

Via Nicola Pisano

Via Enrico Fermi

Via Risorgimento

Via Paolo Salvi

Via Volturno

S. MARIA

Ponte della Cittadella

0 0.25 km
0 1/4 mi

299

trains depart every 15 to 30 minutes, depending on the time of the day, for the 5-minute trip into Pisa. As an alternative, "LAM Rossa," a bus, leaves the airport every 40 minutes for the city.

Trains link Pisa and Florence every 1½ hours for the 1-hour trip, costing 6€ one-way. Trains running along the seacoast link Pisa with Rome and require about 3 hours travel time. Depending on the time of day and the speed of the train, one-way fares are 18€ to 61€. In Pisa, trains arrive at the **Stazione Pisa Centrale,** Piazza Stazione (© **892021** for information in Italy), about a 30-minute walk from the Leaning Tower. Otherwise, you can take bus LAM rossa, which runs every 20 minutes, from the station to the heart of the city. A ticket costs 1€ and is valid for 60 minutes, 1.50€ if you buy it on board.

If you're **driving,** leave Florence by taking the autostrada west (A11) to the intersection (A12) going south to Pisa. Travel time is about an hour each way.

VISITOR INFORMATION   There is a **tourist office** at Piazza Vittorio Emanuele (© **050-42291;** www.pisaunicaterra.it), open Monday to Saturday 9am to 7pm and Saturday 9am to 4pm.

SPECIAL EVENTS   On summer evenings, **free classical music concerts** are presented on the steps of the Duomo. Music aficionados from all over the world can be seen sprawled on the lawn. Concerts are also presented in the Duomo (with an admission fee), which is known for its phenomenal acoustics. The tourist office has details.

The best time to be in Pisa is the last Sunday in June, when Pisans stage the **Gioco del Ponte,** their annual tug-of-war that revives some of their pomp and ceremony from the Middle Ages. Each quadrant of the city presents richly costumed parades. Also in June is the **Festa di San Ranieri,** when Pisans honor their patron saint by lining the Arno with torches on the 16th and then staging a boat race on the 17th.

Exploring the City

In the Middle Ages, Pisa reached the apex of its power as a maritime republic before falling to its rivals, Florence and Genoa. As is true of most cities at their zenith, Pisa turned to the arts and made contributions in sculpture and architecture. Its greatest legacy remains at **Piazza del Duomo,** where you'll find the top three attractions: the Duomo, the baptistery, and the campanile (that famous Leaning Tower).

A 6€ **combination ticket** (you can buy it at any of the included attractions) allows you to visit two of these three sights: the baptistery, the cemetery, and the Duomo Museum. For 10€, you can visit the five major attractions: the baptistery, the Duomo, the cemetery, the Duomo Museum, and the Museum of Preliminary Frescoes.

Baptistery (Battistero) ★★★   Begun in 1153, the baptistery is like a Romanesque crown. Its most beautiful feature is the exterior, with its arches and columns, but you should visit the interior to see the hexagonal pulpit (1255–60) by Nicola Pisano. Supported by pillars resting on the backs of three marble lions, the pulpit contains bas-reliefs of the Crucifixion, the Adoration of the Magi, the presentation of the Christ Child at the temple, and the Last Judgment (many angels have lost their heads over the years). Column statues represent the Virtues. At the baptismal font is a contemporary *John the Baptist* by a local sculptor. The echo inside the baptistery shell has enthralled visitors for years.

The interior of Pisa's Baptistery.

Piazza del Duomo. ℰ **050-3872210.** www.opapisa.it. Admission 5€. Nov–Feb daily 10am–5pm; Mar and Oct daily 9am–6pm; Apr–Sept daily 8am–8pm. Bus: LAM rossa.

Cemetery (Camposanto) ★★ This cemetery was designed by Giovanni di Simone in 1278, but a bomb hit it in 1944 and destroyed most of the famous frescoes that had covered the inside. (The fresco sketches are displayed at the Museo dell'Opera del Duomo; see review below.) Recently it has been partially restored. It's said that the crusaders shipped earth from Calvary here on Pisan ships (the city was a great port before the water receded). The cemetery is of interest because of its sarcophagi, statuary, and frescoes. One room contains three of the frescoes from the 14th century that were salvaged from the bombing: *The Triumph of Death, The Last Judgment,* and *The Inferno,* with the usual assortment of monsters, reptiles, and boiling caldrons. *The Triumph of Death* is the most interesting, with its flying angels and devils. In addition, you'll find lots of white-marble bas-reliefs, including Roman funerary sculpture.

Piazza del Duomo. ℰ **050-3872210.** www.opapisa.it. Admission 5€. Nov–Feb daily 10am–5pm; Mar and Oct daily 9am–6pm; Apr–Sept daily 8am–8pm. Bus: LAM rossa.

Duomo Museum (Museo dell'Opera del Duomo) ★★ This museum exhibits works of art removed from the monumental buildings on the piazza. The heart of the collection, on the ground floor, consists of sculptures spanning the 11th to the 13th centuries. A notable treasure is an Islamic griffin from the 11th century, a bronze brought back from the Crusades as booty. For decades it adorned the cupola of the cathedral before being brought here for safekeeping. The most famous exhibit is the *Madonna and the Crucifix,* by Giovanni Pisano, carved from an ivory tusk in 1299. Also exhibited is the work of French goldsmiths, presented by Maria de' Medici to Archbishop Bonciani in 1616.

Upstairs are paintings from the 15th to the 18th centuries. Some of the textiles and embroideries date from the 15th century; another section of the museum

Pisa's sprawling Duomo.

is devoted to Egyptian, Etruscan, and Roman works. In the 19th century, Carlo Lasinio restored the Camposanto frescoes (see above) and made a series of etchings of each. These etchings were widely published, influencing the pre-Raphaelite artists of the time. When the Camposanto was bombed in 1944, the etchings were destroyed, but Lasinio's legacy provided an enduring record of them.

Piazza Arcivescovado. ✆ **050-3872210.** www.opapisa.it. Admission 5€. Nov–Feb daily 10am–5pm; Mar daily 9am–6pm; Apr–Sept daily 8am–8pm; Oct daily 9am–7pm. Bus: LAM rossa.

Il Duomo ★★   This cathedral was designed by Buscheto in 1063. In the 13th century, Rainaldo erected the unusual facade with its four layers of open-air arches diminishing in size as they ascend. It's marked by three bronze doors, rhythmic in line, that replaced those destroyed in a disastrous 1595 fire. The most artistic is the original south Door of St. Ranieri, the only one to survive the fire; it was cast by Bonnano Pisano in 1180.

In the restored interior, the chief treasure is the polygonal pulpit by Giovanni Pisano, finished in 1310. It was damaged in the fire and finally rebuilt (with bits of the original) in 1926. It's held up by porphyry pillars and column statues symbolizing the Virtues, and the relief panels depict biblical scenes. The pulpit is similar to an earlier one by Giovanni's father, Nicola Pisano, in the baptistery across the way.

There are other treasures, too, including Galileo's lamp (which, according to tradition, the Pisa-born astronomer used to formulate his laws of the pendulum). At the entrance to the choir pier is a painting that appears to be the work of Leonardo. Actually St. *Agnes and Lamb* was done in the High Renaissance style by the great Andrea del Sarto. In the apse you can view a 13th-century mosaic, *Christ Pancrator,* finished in 1302 by Cimabue (it survived the great fire).

Piazza del Duomo 17. ✆ **050-3872210.** www.opapisa.it. Admission 2€; free Nov–Feb. Nov–Feb daily 10am–12:45pm and 2–5pm; Oct 10am–7pm; Mar 10am–6pm; Apr–Sept daily 10am–8pm. Sightseeing visits are discouraged during Mass and religious rites. Bus: LAM rossa.

Leaning Tower of Pisa (Campanile) ★★★ ☺   In 1174, Bonnano began construction of this eight-story marble campanile, intended as a free-standing bell tower for the Duomo (see above). A persistent legend is that he deliberately intended the tower to lean. Another legend is that Galileo let objects of different weights fall from the tower, timing their descent to prove his theories of bodies in motion. The real story is that the tower began to tilt sometime after the completion of the first three stories; only then did its builders discover that the foundation wasn't rock solid, but water-soaked clay. Construction was suspended for a century and was eventually resumed, with completion in the late 14th century. The tower currently leans at least 4m (14 ft.) from perpendicular. If it stood straight, it would measure about 55m (180 ft.) tall.

From 1990 until 2001, the tower was closed because of dangerous conditions. Since that time, to stabilize its tilt, tons of soil were removed from under the foundation, and lead counterweights were placed at the monument's base.

Piazza del Duomo 17. ℭ **050-3872210.** Fax 050-560505. www.opapisa.it. Admission 15€. Only a group of 40 admitted at a time. Children 7 and under not admitted. Dec–Jan daily 10am–4:40pm; Nov and Feb daily 9:30am–5:30pm; Mar 9am–5:30pm; Apr–Sept daily 8:30am–-8pm; Oct 9am–7pm. Bus: LAM rossa.

National Museum of St. Matthew (Museo Nazionale di San Matteo) ★ This well-planned museum contains a good assortment of paintings and sculptures, many from the 13th to the 16th centuries. You'll find statues by Giovanni Pisano; Simone Martini's *Madonna and Child with Saints,* a polyptych; Nino Pisano's *Madonna del Latte (Madonna of the Milk),* a marble sculpture; Masaccio's *St. Paul,* painted in 1426; Domenico Ghirlandaio's two *Madonna and Saints* depictions; and works by Strozzi and Alessandro Magnasco.

Piazzetta San Matteo 1 (near Piazza Mazzini). ℭ **050-541865.** Admission 5€. Tues–Sat 9am–7pm; Sun 9am–1pm. Closed Mon. Bus: LAM verde or 13.

Where to Stay

Amalfitana ★ 🍴 In the 15th century, this hotel—which stands in the historic center only 250m (820 ft.) from the Leaning Tower—was a monastery attached to the Church of San Leonardo. You can still see its facade with an ancient portal and tranquil cloister. The old building was converted into a hotel in 1992. The small to midsize bedrooms here are simply though comfortably furnished. The hotel has a little garden and a welcoming, inviting staff.

Via Roma 44, 56126 Pisa. ℭ **050-29000.** Fax 050-25218. www.hotelamalfitana.it. 21 units. 80€ double. Rates include continental breakfast. AE, MC, V. Free parking on street. Bus: 4. **Amenities:** Room service. *In room:* A/C, TV, hair dryer.

Grand Hotel Bonanno This well-run hotel is at the top of the pack among moderate choices. The location is only 800m (2,625 ft.) from the Duomo and the Leaning Tower. In a city of great architecture, the structure is rather undistinguished, but it's quite cozy inside. Some of the well-furnished rooms open onto private balconies, and the floors are either parquet or else fitted with carpets. Bedrooms are midsize, and furnished in a sleek, modern style that never rises above a good motel standard.

Via Carlo Francesco Gabba 7, 56122 Pisa. ℭ **050-524030.** Fax 050-532072. www.grandhotel bonanno.it. 89 units. 77€–160€ double; 105€–180€ junior suite. Rates include buffet breakfast. AE, MC, V. Free parking. **Amenities:** Restaurant; bar; babysitting; bikes; room service. *In room:* A/C, TV, hair dryer, minibar, Wi-Fi (free).

NH Cavalieri   A generic chain-run property that hosts lots of business travelers, this seven-story hotel opens onto a view of the train station and its piazza. The guest rooms are filled with timeworn furniture, fine mattresses, paneling, and lots of glass. The best ones, on the fifth floor, have balconies with good views. Parking is often possible in the square in front of the station or in a nearby garage.

Piazza della Stazione 2, 56125 Pisa. © **888/726-528** in the U.S., or 050-43290. Fax 050-502242. www.nh-hotels.com. 100 units. 97€–152€ double; 217€–257€ suite. Rates include buffet breakfast. AE, DC, MC, V. Parking 16€. **Amenities:** Restaurant; bar; babysitting; room service. *In room:* A/C, TV, hair dryer, minibar, Wi-Fi (6€ per hr.).

Relais dell'Orlogio ★★★   At last Pisa has a hotel worthy of its status as a worldwide tourist destination. Surpassing both the NH Cavalieri and Royal Victoria in style and glamour, Relais dell'Orlogio is a boutique hotel of charm and grace. It is also Pisa's most tranquil, lying near the heartbeat Piazza dei Cavalieri, just 200m (656 ft.) from the Arno River. This historic mansion was constructed as a fortified tower in the 13th century. There was great respect shown for the style of the original building in its modernization; for example, many of the wooden beams were retained in the bedrooms. The midsize bedrooms are furnished with Italian flair and style.

Via della Fagiola Uguccione 12–14, 56126 Pisa. © **050-830361.** Fax 050-551869. www.hotelrelais orologio.com. 21 units. 290€–430€ double; 570€–840€ suite. Rates include buffet breakfast. AE, DC, MC, V. Parking 30€. **Amenities:** Restaurant; bar; airport transfers (60€); babysitting; Jacuzzi; room service; Wi-Fi (free, in lobby). *In room:* A/C, TV, hair dryer, minibar.

Royal Victoria ★   This isn't Pisa's most luxurious hotel, but it's a favorite for traditionalists, thanks to its sense of history. It occupies several medieval towers and houses. Adjacent to the Arno and within walking distance of most of the jewels in Pisa's crown, it was opened in 1839 by ancestors (five generations ago) of the genteel manager, Nicola Piegaja, who runs the place with his brother and oversees the most helpful staff in town. The guest rooms are old-fashioned and well kept. The best units are the three with balconies.

Lungarno Pacinotti 12, 56126 Pisa. © **050-940111.** Fax 050-940180. www.royalvictoria.it. 48 units, 40 with private bathroom. 80€ double without bathroom; 100€–150€ double with bathroom; 190€ junior suite. Rates include buffet breakfast. AE, DC, MC, V. Bus: LAM rossa. Parking 20€. **Amenities:** Bar; babysitting; bikes; room service; Wi-Fi (2.50€ per hr., in lobby). *In room:* A/C (in some units), TV, hair dryer.

Where to Dine

Antica Trattoria Da Bruno PISAN   For around half a century, Da Bruno has flourished in this spot near the Leaning Tower. It's one of Pisa's finest restaurants, although it charges moderate tabs. It serves old-fashioned but market-fresh dishes of the Pisan kitchen, including hare with *pappardelle, zuppa alla pisana* (thick vegetable soup), and grilled salt cod with chickpeas. Other specialties include wild boar with olives and polenta.

Via Luigi Bianchi 12. © **050-560818.** www.ristorante.dabruno.it. Reservations recommended for dinner. Main courses 12€–24€. AE, DC, MC, V. Wed–Mon noon–3pm and 7–11pm. Bus: 4.

Emilio PISAN/ITALIAN   Because of its well-prepared food and its proximity to Piazza del Duomo, this place is always packed. Inside, a large, high window, similar to one you'd find in a church, filters light down upon the brick-walled interior. The menu features a fresh assortment of antipasti, spaghetti with clams, risotto with mushrooms, fish dishes such as *branzino all'isolana* (oven baked with tomatoes and vegetables), and Florentine beefsteaks. In season, try one of the game dishes with polenta. Grilled fish is always perfectly prepared. The chef's dessert specialty is *crema di limoncello,* a mousse prepared with lemon liqueur.

Via Cammeo 44. ✆ **050-562141.** Reservations required. Main courses 7€–16€; fixed-price menu 15€–25€. AE, DC, MC, V. Daily noon–3:30pm. Bus: LAM rossa.

Shopping

On the second weekend of every month, an **antiques fair ★★** runs through Borgo Largo and Piazza dei Cavalieri. Virtually everything from the Tuscan hills is for sale, from fresh virgin olive oil to what one dealer told us was the "original" *Mona Lisa* (not the one hanging in the Louvre).

If you're not in town for the antiques fair, head for the stalls at **Piazza delle Vettovaglie,** just off Via Borgo Stretto (bus: LAM verde), which has a market on Wednesdays and Saturdays. You'll find everything from old clothing to fresh Tuscan food products. You can skip the restaurants for lunch and eat here; an array of little *trattorie* will fill you up at an affordable price. You can also pick up the makings for a picnic to enjoy later in the Tuscan hillsides.

Intriguing stores line **Via Borgo Stretto,** an arcaded street where mimes and street performers often entertain the shoppers.

SAN GIMIGNANO ★★★

42km (26 miles) NW of Siena, 52km (32 miles) SW of Florence

This gem of the Middle Ages preserves 13 of its noble towers, giving it a "skyscraper" skyline. The approach to the walled town is dramatic today, but once it must have been fantastic. In the heyday of the Guelph and Ghibelline conflict, **San Gimignano** (aka San Gimignano dalle Belle Torri/San Gimignano of the Beautiful Towers) had as many as 72 towers. Its fortresslike severity is softened by the subtlety of its harmonious squares. Many of its palaces and churches are enhanced by Renaissance frescoes; San Gimignano could afford to patronize major painters.

With its beauty and authenticity, the town is packed with tourists during the day in the high season. Stay overnight, if you can, so that you can enjoy the late afternoon or early evening and get a sense of the town without the crowds. Go to one of the tasting rooms for a sample of the famous Vernaccia, the light white wine bottled in the region.

Shopping in San Gimignano.

San Gimignano

Sant'Agostino
Pza. S. Agostino
Via Bagnaia
Museo Etrusco
San Iacopo
Porta S. Iacopo
Via Folgore da S. Gimignano
Porta S. Matteo
San Pietro
Via 20 Settembre
Via Bigazzino
Via delle Fonti
Porta delle Fonti
Via delle Romite
Palazzo Pesciolini
Via S. Matteo
Via Capassi
Palazzo Cancelleria
Torre Salvacci
Rocca
❶
Pza. del Duomo
Pza. Pecori
Palazzo del Podestà
San Loreno in Ponte
❹
❷ ❸
Pza. della Cisterna
Via del Castello
Via S. Stefano
Arco dei Becci
Palazzo Tortoli
Via d. Innocenti
Porta Quercecchio
Via di Quercecchio
Via Berignano
Via S. Giovanni
Via Piandorella
Via di Bonda
Porta S. Giovanni
Piazzale dei Martiri di Montemaggio

Venice
0 100 Mi
0 100 Km
45 N.
San Gimingano
Rome
40 N.
10 E.

0 .... 1/8 mi
0 .... 0.125 km

Civic Museum **3**
Duomo Collegiata o Basilica
  di Santa Maria Assunta **1**
Museo di Criminologia **4**
Sacred Art Museum **2**

Essentials

GETTING THERE The **rail station** nearest to San Gimignano is at Poggibonsi, serviced by regular trains from Florence and Siena. At Poggibonsi, buses depart from the front of the rail station at frequent intervals, charging 3€ each way to the center of San Gimignano. For information, call ☏ **0577-204246.**

    Buses operated by TRA-IN (☏ **0577-204111;** www.trainspa.it) service San Gimignano from Florence with a change at Poggibonsi (trip time: 85 min.); the one-way fare is 9€. TRA-IN also operates service from Siena; the one-way fare is 6€. In San Gimignano, buses stop at Piazzale Montemaggio, outside the Porta San Giovanni, the southern gate. You'll have to walk into the center because vehicles aren't allowed in most of the town's core.

If you have a **car,** leave Florence (1½ hr.) or Siena (1 hr., 10 min.) by the Firenze-Siena autostrada and drive to Poggibonsi, where you'll need to cut west along a secondary route (S324) to San Gimignano. There are parking lots outside the city walls.

VISITOR INFORMATION   The **Associazione Pro Loco,** Piazza del Duomo 1 (✆ **0577-940008;** www.sangimignano.com), is open daily November through February from 9am to 1pm and 2 to 6pm, and March to October 9am to 1pm and 3 to 7pm.

Exploring the Town

In the town center is the **Piazza della Cisterna,** so named because of the 13th-century cistern in its heart. Connected with the irregularly shaped square is its satellite, **Piazza del Duomo ★★,** whose medieval architecture of towers and palaces is almost unchanged. It's the most beautiful spot in town. On the square, the **Palazzo del Popolo ★** was designed in the 13th century, and its **Torre Grossa,** built a few years later, is believed to have been the tallest "skyscraper" (about 53m/178 ft. high) in town (see the entry for the Civic Museum below for information on how to climb this tower).

Civic Museum (Museo Civico) ★   This museum is installed upstairs in the Palazzo del Popolo (town hall). Most notable is the **Dante Salon (Sala di Dante),** where the poet supporter of the White Guelph spoke out for his cause in 1300. Look for one of the masterpieces of San Gimignano: *La Maestà* (a Madonna enthroned), by Lippo Memmi (later touched up by Gozzoli). The first large room upstairs contains the other masterpiece: a *Madonna in Glory,* with Sts. Gregory and Benedict, painted by Pinturicchio. On the other side of it are two depictions of the *Annunciation,* by Filippino Lippi. On the opposite wall, note the magnificent Byzantine Crucifix by Coppo di Marcovaldo.

Passing through the Museo Civico, you can scale the **Torre Grossa** and be rewarded with a bird's-eye view of this most remarkable town. The tower, the only one you can climb, is open during the same hours as the museum.

In the Palazzo del Popolo, Piazza del Duomo 1. ✆ **0577-990312.** Admission 5€ adults, 4€ students and children 17 and under. Mar–Oct daily 9:30am–7pm; Nov–Feb daily 10am–5:30pm.

Duomo Collegiata o Basilica di Santa Maria Assunta ★   Residents of San Gimignano still call this a Duomo (cathedral), even though it was demoted to a "Collegiata" after the town lost its bishop. Don't judge this book by its cover, though. The facade—dating from the 12th century—was never finished, which causes the building to look plain and austere on the outside, but it is richly decorated inside.

To escape the burning Tuscan sun, retreat inside to a world of tiger-striped arches and a galaxy of gold stars. Head for the north aisle, where in the 1360s Bartolo di Fredi depicted scenes from the Old Testament. Two memorable ones are *The Trials of Job* and *Noah with the Animals.* Other outstanding works by this artist are in the lunettes off the north aisle, including a medieval view of the cosmography of the Creation. In the right aisle, panels trace scenes from the life of Christ: the kiss of Judas, the Last Supper, the Flagellation, and the Crucifixion. Seek out Bartolo's horrendous *Last Judgment,* one of the most perverse paintings in Italy. Abandoning briefly his rosy-cheeked Sienese Madonnas, he depicted distorted and suffering nudes, shocking at the time.

The chief attraction here is the **Chapel of Santa Fina (Cappella Santa Fina),** designed by Giuliano and Benedetto da Maiano. Michelangelo's fresco

Two of San Gimignano's towers.

teacher, Domenico Ghirlandaio, frescoed it with scenes from the life of a local girl, Fina, who became the town's patron saint. Her deathbed scene is memorable. According to accounts of the day, the little girl went to the well for water and accepted an orange from a young swain. When her mother scolded her for her wicked ways, she was so mortified that she prayed for the next 5 years, until St. Anthony called her to heaven.

Spend a few minutes in the small **Sacred Art Museum (Museo d'Arte Sacra),** to the left of the Duomo (enter from Piazza Pecori and an arch to the left of the Duomo's entrance). The collection features a *Madonna and Child* triptych painted by Bartolo di Fredi, some illuminated choir books, medieval tombstones, and wooden sculptures. If you're rushed, it can be missed.

Piazza del Duomo. ✆ **0577-940316.** Church free admission; chapel 3€ adults, free for children 5 and under. Mar–Oct daily 9:30am–7pm; Nov–Feb Mon–Sat 9:30am–5pm, Sun 1–5pm.

Museo della Tortura   In this Tuscan chamber of horrors, some of the most appalling instruments of torture are on display. In case you don't know just how the devices worked, descriptions are provided in English. The museum has a definite political agenda (including some pointed commentary on the continued use of capital punishment in the United States). The exhibits, such as cast-iron chastity belts, reveal some of the sexism inherently involved in torture devices, with the revelation that many have been updated for use around the world today, from Africa to South America. These include the garrote, that horror of the Inquisition trials of the 1400s. Fittingly enough, this chilling sight is housed in what locals call the Torre del Diavolo (Devil's Tower). This is one spot where it might be best not to bring the little ones.

Porta San Giovanni 123. ✆ **0577-940526.** www.museodellatortura.it. Admission 12€, free for children 5 and under. Apr–Oct daily 10am–8pm; Nov–Mar daily 10am–6pm.

Where to Stay

You can learn about additional choices and see pictures of all the hotels by going to www.sangimignano.com.

Hotel Belsoggiorno ⚐   This hotel, though no longer the town's best, is still a good, affordable alternative. Although the Gigli family has run it since 1886, there's not as much old-fashioned charm as you'd think. The rear guest rooms and dining room open onto the lower pastureland and the bottom of the village. The medium-size rooms have cheap, functional furniture and beds verging on the oversoft, but the management is quite friendly. The best 10 rooms are those with private balconies. In summer, you'll be asked to take your meals at the hotel, which is no great hardship because the cuisine is excellent. The medieval-style **dining room** boasts murals depicting a wild-boar hunt (see "Where to Dine," below).

Via San Giovanni 91, 53037 San Gimignano. © **0577-940375.** Fax 0577-907521. www.hotel belsoggiorno.it. 22 units. 95€–120€ double; 120€–170€ suite. Rates include continental breakfast. AE, DC, MC, V. Parking 15€. Closed mid-Nov to Dec 27 and mid-Feb to mid-Mar. **Amenities:** Restaurant (reviewed below); bar. *In room:* A/C, TV, hair dryer, minibar (in some).

Hotel Leon Bianco ★　This restored 11th-century villa is San Gimignano at its best—the front rooms look out over medieval Piazza della Cisterna, and the rear rooms have a sweeping view of the Elsa Valley. The guest rooms are all different (one is rustically romantic, with vaulted ceilings and alcoves of rough brick) and range from small to medium, with tidy bathrooms. The sunny roof terrace is a good place to order breakfast or relax.

Piazza della Cisterna, 53037 San Gimignano. © **0577-941294.** Fax 0577-942123. www.leon bianco.com. 25 units (some with shower only). 85€–150€ double. Rates include buffet breakfast. AE, DC, MC, V. Parking 15€. **Amenities:** Bar; exercise room; Jacuzzi; room service. *In room:* A/C, TV, hair dryer, minibar, Wi-Fi (in some, free).

Hotel Pescille　This hotel conveys a sense of sleepy rural Tuscany, and although the blasé staff sometimes draws complaints, you might appreciate the tranquillity. About 3.2km (2 miles) from town, it's surrounded by vineyards and olive trees. The guest rooms are outfitted in an old-time style, often with country-side views. All are comfortable and charming, but the most striking is the Tower Room, overlooking San Gimignano's towers. Sixteen rooms have balconies.

Località Pescille, 53037 San Gimignano. © **0577-940186.** Fax 0577-943165. www.pescille.it. 42 units (shower only). 90€–200€ double; from 150€–220€ suite. Rates include buffet breakfast. AE, DC, MC, V. Closed Nov to early Apr. Head 3.2km (2 miles) north of San Gimignano, following the signs to Castel S. Gimignano and Volterra. **Amenities:** Bar; babysitting; outdoor pool; room service; outdoor tennis court. *In room:* A/C, TV, hair dryer (in some), minibar.

La Collegiata ★★★　Outside of town and surrounded by a park of Tuscan cypresses, this elegant, refined choice offers the finest accommodations in the San Gimignano area, even surpassing Relais Santa Chiara (see below). The villa dates from 1587, when it housed Capuchin monks. The redbrick Renaissance structure has been beautifully converted to receive guests, who live here far better than the monks. You can walk to the building through a beautifully planted Italian garden. After checking in, you can go for a dip in an open-air swimming pool and enjoy the Tuscan landscape so beloved by painters. The cloister opens into the reception area, a wine bar, a coffee shop, sitting rooms, and a reading room. Bedrooms are beautifully furnished, often with such decorative touches as mullioned windows or small balconies. Most of those on the first floor open onto the inner courtyard.

Località Strada 27, 53037 San Gimignano. © **800/735-2478** or 0577-943201. Fax 0577-940566. www.lacollegiata.it. 22 units. 230€–535€ double; from 500€ suite. AE, MC, V. Free parking. Closed Nov–Mar. **Amenities:** Restaurant; babysitting; bikes; exercise room; outdoor pool; Wi-Fi (free, in lobby). *In room:* A/C, TV, hair dryer, minibar.

L'Antico Pozzo ★★ This is the top inn within the historic city walls. A 15th-century *palazzo* converted to a hotel in 1990, it has a medieval atmosphere and lovely antique touches, yet it provides all the modern comforts. Accommodations vary in size and decor, but none are small. Throughout, the furnishings are 19th-century wooden pieces, and the firm beds have cast-iron frames. "Superior" doubles have 17th-century ceiling frescoes. The smaller "standard" rooms on the third floor have wood floors and a view of the Rocca and a few towers. The other rooms overlook the street or the rear terrace, where breakfast is served in summer.

Via San Matteo 87, 53037 San Gimignano (near Porta San Matteo). ✆ **0577-942014.** Fax 0577-942117. www.anticopozzo.com. 18 units (some with shower only). 110€–180€ double; 145€–195€ triple. Rates include buffet breakfast. AE, DC, MC, V. Parking 20€ in nearby garage or lot. Closed Jan 9–Feb 10. **Amenities:** Bar; babysitting; concierge; room service. *In room:* A/C, TV, hair dryer, minibar, Wi-Fi (free).

Relais Santa Chiara ★★ This comfortable, upscale hotel lies on private grounds in a residential neighborhood about a 10-minute walk south of the medieval ramparts. It's surrounded by elegant gardens, and its spacious public rooms contain Florentine terra-cotta floors and mosaics. The guest rooms are furnished in precious brierwood and walnut. Some enjoy views of the countryside; others overlook the hotel's garden. There's no restaurant, but the hotel serves a buffet breakfast and lunchtime snacks in summer.

Via Matteotti 15, 53037 San Gimignano. ✆ **0577-940701.** Fax 0577-942096. www.rsc.it. 41 units (some with shower only). 125€–240€ double; 195€–290€ suite. Rates include buffet breakfast. AE, DC, MC, V. Free parking. Closed Nov 23–Mar 20. **Amenities:** Bar; babysitting; Jacuzzi; outdoor pool; room service; Wi-Fi (3€ per 24 hr., in lobby). *In room:* A/C, TV, hair dryer, minibar.

Where to Dine

San Gimignano produces its own white wine, **Vernaccia.** You'll find one of the widest selections in town, as well as samplings of Chianti from throughout Tuscany, at **Da Gustavo,** Via San Matteo 29 (✆ **0577-940057**). The Beccuci family runs this wine shop, which has been thriving here since 1946. There's an informal stand-up bar where you can order by the glass. If you don't see what you're looking for on the shelves, ask—someone will probably haul it out from a storeroom the moment you mention its name.

Dorandò ★★ TUSCAN Between Piazza Duomo and Piazza Cisterna, this elegant restaurant in a 14th-century building in the heart of town is the supreme choice for dining. Three dining rooms with vaulted roofs and imposing stone walls form the backdrop, the walls decorated with original paintings from local artists. The inventive cuisine features the local products of Tuscany. The menu is seasonally adjusted to keep it market fresh. The dishes reflect the robust flavors of regional produce, including such appetizers as red onion soup with toasted almonds and pecorino cheese or else a vegetable and mushroom soup served with a quail egg. Main dish specialties include *pici* (a Tuscan spaghetti) served with guinea hen ragout or a filet of pork with a bittersweet apple purée.

Vicolo dell'Oro 2. ✆ **0577-941-862.** www.ristorantedorando.it. Reservations required. Main courses 8€–25€. MC, V. Daily noon–2:30pm and 7–9:30pm. Closed Mon Feb–Easter and Dec–Jan.

Ristorante Belsoggiorno TUSCAN Its windows and terrace overlook the countryside, and its kitchen uses only fresh ingredients from nearby farms. Two of the most appealing specialties (available only late summer to late winter) are roasted wild boar with red wine and mixed vegetables, and *pappardelle* pasta, garnished with a savory ragout of pheasant. Other pastas are *pappardelle* with roasted hare, and risotto with herbs and seasonal vegetables. The main courses stress vegetable garnishes and thin-sliced meats that are simply but flavorfully grilled over charcoal, and breads are homemade and baked on-site. Many dishes hearken back to medieval recipes.

In the Hotel Belsoggiorno, Via San Giovanni 91. © **0577-940375.** www.hotelbelsoggiorno.it. Reservations recommended. Main courses 16€–18€; fixed-price menu 50€. AE, DC, MC, V. Thurs–Tues 12:30–2:30pm and 7:30–10pm. Closed mid-Nov to Dec 27 and mid-Feb to mid-Mar.

Ristorante Le Terrazze TUSCAN   One of this restaurant's two dining rooms boasts stones laid in the 1300s, and the other offers lots of rustic accessories and large windows overlooking the old town and the Val d'Elsa. The food features an assortment of produce from nearby farms. The soups and pastas make fine beginnings, and specialties of the house include such delectable items as sliced filet of wild boar with polenta and Chianti, goose breast with walnut sauce, *zuppa San Gimignanese* (a hearty minestrone), Florentine-style steaks, and *risotto con funghi porcini* (risotto with porcini mushrooms). A superb dessert is vin santo, accompanied by an almond cookie called a *cantucci.*

In La Cisterna, Piazza della Cisterna 24. © **0577-940328.** www.hotelcisterna.it. Reservations required. Main courses 10€–20€. AE, DC, MC, V. Mar 18–Oct daily 12:30–2:30pm and 7:30–10pm; Nov–Jan 6 Mon and Wed–Sun 12:30–2:30pm and 7:30–9:30pm. Closed Jan 7–Mar 17.

SIENA ★★★

34km (21 miles) S of Florence, 230km (143 miles) NW of Rome

All medieval towers, piazzas and dreamy country views—Siena is a miniature masterpiece of a city and Florence's age-old rival. The UNESCO-listed center brings you back to the Middle Ages at the Gothic Duomo and vast Piazza del Campo, the backdrop for the thunderous Palio horse race in summer. More than anything, the simple pleasures captivate you here—eating rustic Tuscan fare in family-run *osterie*; sampling Chianti wines from nearby vineyards; and watching wistfully as sunset bathes the city the colors of a fresco painter's palette.

Things to Do   Strolling aimlessly in Siena is a joy, up alleys and staircases affording snapshot views over tiled rooftops and undulating countryside. The fan-shaped **Piazza del Campo,** where the redbrick **Palazzo Pubblico**'s campanile rises 320 feet, is the city's medieval centerpiece. Contemplate the frescoes of Sienese master Ambrogio Lorenzetti in the **Museo Civico** and the Gothic **Duomo**'s filigree stonework and black-and-white striped marble. Step inside to see the extravagantly gilded dome, frescoed **Baptistery** and the **Museo dell'Opera Metropolitana**'s religious art treasures.

Nightlife & Entertainment   As Siena lights up, locals take their evening *passeggiata* (stroll). Join them for gelato or a glass of full-bodied Chianti on **Piazza del Campo, Piazza del Mercato,** and **Piazza del Sale.** Cafes and cocktail bars attract a fashion-conscious crowd on **Banchi di Sopra.** For a younger, livelier scene, try the tiny pubs, live music bars and clubs on **Via di Pantaneto** and **Via dei Termini.** Choose among 1,500 Tuscan wines in **Enoteca Italiana**'s atmospheric 16th-century vaults and inner courtyard.

Restaurants & Dining A simple lunch in Siena: arugula and local pecorino drizzled with thick extra virgin-olive oil, hand-rolled *pici* pasta in a garlicky sauce, accompanied by a good value Chianti. Find convivial *osterie* and alfresco *trattorias* on **Via dei Rossi** and **Via del Casato di Sotto.** Authentic Sienese fare from roast rabbit to *fagioli all'uccelletto* (white bean and sausage stew) is served in **Via del Porrione**'s rustic-chic restaurants. Pop into **Osteria Le Logge** for the best veal steaks in town.

Relaxation Pack up local goodies like pecorino and fennel-infused *finocchiona* salami and head off into the rolling, cypress-studded **Tuscan countryside** for a picnic. Wild poppies stud the cornfields in springtime. To the north, the vineyards of **Chianti Country** invite lazy strolls, bike rides, and wine tasting. It seems like time is standing still in sleepy, fairy-tale villages such as **Pienza** and hilltop **San Gimignano,** whose 14 mismatched towers are visible from afar.

Essentials

GETTING THERE The **rail** link between Siena and Florence is sometimes inconvenient because you often have to change and wait at other stations, such as Empoli. But trains run every hour from Florence, costing 7€ one-way. You arrive at the station at Piazza Carlo Rosselli. This is an awkward half-hour climb uphill to the monumental heart of the city. However, bus no. 13A will take you to Piazza Gramsci near the center. For information and schedules, call ✆ **892021.**

TRA-IN, Piazza La Lizza (✆ **0577-204225;** www.trainspa.it), offers bus service from all of Tuscany in air-conditioned coaches. The one-way fare between Florence and Siena is 7€. The trip takes 1¼ hours (actually faster than taking the train, and you'll be let off in the city center). Ticket offices are open Monday to Friday 6am to 7:30pm, Saturday and Sunday 7am to 7:30pm.

If you have a **car,** head south from Florence along the Firenze-Siena autostrada, a superhighway linking the two cities, going through Poggibonsi. (It has no route number; just follow the green autostrada signs for Siena.)

Piazza del Campo.

Trying to drive into the one-way and pedestrian-zoned labyrinth that is the city center just isn't worth the headache. Siena's parking (℃ **0577-228711;** www.sienaparcheggi.com) is now coordinated, and all the lots charge 1.50€ per hour (although almost every hotel has a discount deal with the nearest lot wherein parking for hotel guests is either free or discounted by 40% or more). Lots are well signposted, just inside several of the city gates.

VISITOR INFORMATION The **tourist office** is at Piazza del Campo 56 (℃ **0577-280551;** www.terresiena.it). It's open daily 9am to 7pm. The office will give you a good free map.

Exploring the Medieval City

There's much to see here. Start in the heart of Siena, the shell-shaped **Piazza del Campo ★★★**, described by Montaigne as "the finest of any city in the world." Pause to enjoy the **Fonte Gaia,** which locals sometimes call the Fountain of Joy. It was inaugurated to great jubilation throughout the city, with embellishments by Jacopo della Quercia. The present sculptured works are reproductions—the badly beaten-up original ones are found in the town hall. The square is truly stunning, designed like a sloping scallop shell; you'll want to linger in one of the cafes along its edge.

Baptistery (Battistero) ★ The Gothic facade was left unfinished by Domenico di Agostino in 1355. But you don't come here to admire that—you come for the frescoes inside, many of which are lavish, intricate, and devoted mainly to depictions of the lives of Christ and St. Anthony.

The star of the place, however, is a **baptismal font** (1417–30), one of the greatest in all Italy. The foremost sculptors of the early Renaissance from both Florence and Siena helped create this masterpiece. Jacopo della Quercia created *Annunciation to Zacharias,* Giovanni di Turino crafted *Preaching of the Baptist* and the *Baptism of Christ,* and Lorenzo Ghiberti worked with Giuliano di Ser

Horses race through Siena during the Palio.

313

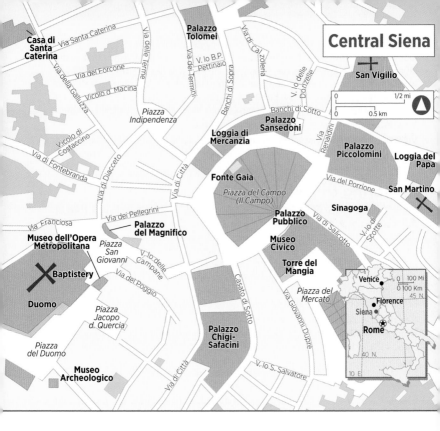

Central Siena

Andrea on the masterful *Arrest of St. John.* Our favorite is Donatello's *Feast of Herod,* a work of profound beauty and perspective.

Piazza San Giovanni (behind the Duomo). ℭ **0577-283048.** www.operaduomo.siena.it. Admission 3€. Mar 1–15 and Oct–Nov daily 9:30am–7:30pm; Mar 16–Sept 30 daily 9:30am–8pm; Nov–Feb daily 10am–5pm. Closed Jan 1 and Dec 25. Bus: 1.

Civic Museum (Museo Civico) & Torre del Mangia ★★★ The Museo Civico, in the Palazzo Pubblico (1288–1309), is filled with important artworks by some of the leaders in the Sienese school of painting and sculpture.

In the **Globe Room (Sala del Mappomondo)** is Simone Martini's earliest-known work (ca. 1315) and his masterpiece, *La Maestà* ★★, the Madonna enthroned with her Child, surrounded by angels and saints. The other remarkable Martini fresco (on the opposite wall) is the equestrian portrait of Guidoriccio da Fogliano, general of the Sienese Republic, in ceremonial dress.

The next room is the **Peace Room (Sala della Pace),** frescoed from 1337 to 1339 by Ambrogio Lorenzetti. The frescoes, perhaps the single most important piece of secular art to survive from medieval Europe, compose the **Allegory of Good and Bad Government and Their Effects on the Town and Countryside ★★★**. In this depiction, the most notable figure of the Virtues surrounding the king is La Pace (Peace). To the right of the king and the Virtues is a representation of Siena in peaceful times. On the left, Lorenzetti showed his opinion of "ward heelers," but some of the sting has inadvertently been taken out of the frescoes because the evil-government scene is badly damaged. These were propaganda frescoes in their day, commissioned by the party in power, but they're now viewed as among the most important of all secular frescoes to come down from the Middle Ages.

Accessible from the courtyard of the Palazzo Pubblico is the **Torre del Mangia,** the most prominent architectural landmark on the skyline of Siena. Dating from the 14th century, it soars to a height of 102m (335 ft.). The tower takes its name from a former bell ringer, a sleepy fellow called *mangiaguadagni* ("eat the profits"). Surprisingly, it has no subterranean foundations. If you climb this needlelike tower (more than 500 steps!), you'll be rewarded with a drop-dead-gorgeous view of the red-tile roofs of the city and the surrounding Tuscan landscape. In the Middle Ages, this was Italy's second-tallest tower (Cremona has Siena beat). The tower is open the same hours as the Civic Museum and charges 6€ for you to climb it.

In the Palazzo Pubblico, Piazza del Campo. ℂ **0577-226230.** Admission 8€. Mid-Mar to Oct daily 10am–7pm; Nov to mid-Mar daily 10am–6pm. Tower mid-Oct to Feb daily 10am–4pm; Mar to mid-Oct daily 10am–7pm. Bus: 1, 2, or 5.

Duomo Museum (Museo dell'Opera Metropolitana) ★★ This museum houses paintings and sculptures created for the Duomo. On the ground floor is much interesting sculpture, including works by Giovanni Pisano and his assistants. But the real draw hangs on the next floor: Duccio's fragmented *La Maestà* ★★ (1308–11), a Madonna enthroned, one of Europe's greatest late-medieval paint-

The Duomo.

ings. The majestic panel was an altarpiece by Duccio di Buoninsegna for the cathedral, filled with dramatic moments illustrating the story of Christ and the Madonna. A student of Cimabue, Duccio was the first great name in the school of Sienese painting. Upstairs are the collections of the treasury, and on the top floor is a display of paintings from the early Sienese school.

Piazza del Duomo 8. ℂ **0577-283048.** www.opera duomo.siena.it. Admission 6€. Mar 1–15 and Oct–Nov daily 9:30am–7:30pm; Mar 16–Sept 30 daily 9:30am–8pm; Nov–Feb daily 10am–5pm. Bus: 1.

Il Duomo ★★★ At Piazza del Duomo, southwest of Piazza del Campo, stands an architectural fantasy. With its colored bands of marble, the Sienese Duomo is an original and exciting building, erected in the Roman-esque and Italian Gothic styles in the 12th century. The dramatic facade, designed in part by Giovanni Pisano, dates from the 13th century, as does the Romanesque campanile.

The zebralike interior of black-and-white stripes is equally stunning. The floor consists of various inlaid works of art depicting both biblical and mythological sub-jects (many are roped off to preserve the rich-ness in design). Numerous artists worked on the floor, notably Domenico Beccafumi. The octagonal 13th-century pulpit ★★★ is by Nicola Pisano (Giovanni's father), one of the most significant Italian sculptors before the dawn of the Renaissance. The Siena pulpit is his masterpiece; it reveals in relief such scenes as the slaughter of the innocents and the Crucifixion. The elder Pisano finished the pulpit in 1268, aided by his son and others. Its pillars are supported by four marble lions, reminiscent of the Pisano pulpit at Pisa.

In the chapel of the left transept (near the library) is a glass box containing an arm that tradition maintains is the one John the Baptist used to baptize Christ; the box also

A fountain in Il Campo in Siena.

contains Donatello's bronze of John the Baptist. To see another Donatello work in bronze (a bishop's grave marker), look at the floor in the chapel to the left of the pulpit's stairway. Some of the designs for the inlaid wooden stalls in the apse are by Riccio. A representational blue starry sky twinkles overhead.

In 1999 a room under the Duomo was discovered, containing 13th-century frescoes depicting scenes from both the Old and New Testaments. It's called the Cripta, though technically it's not a crypt but is quite fascinating considering it lay unknown for centuries.

Inside the Duomo is the **Piccolomini Library** ★★, founded by Cardinal Francesco Piccolomini (later Pius III) to honor his uncle (Pius II); the library is renowned for its cycle of frescoes by the Umbrian master Pinturicchio. His fres-coes are well preserved, although they date from the early 16th century. In Vasa-ri's words, the panels illustrate "the history of Pope Pius II from birth to the minute of his death." Raphael's alleged connection with the frescoes, if any, is undocumented. In the center is an exquisite *Three Graces,* a Roman copy of a 3rd-century-B.C. Greek work from the school of Praxiteles.

Piazza del Duomo. ✆ **0577-283048.** www.operaduomo.siena.it. Duomo and library 3€. Duomo Nov–Mar 15 daily 8am–1pm and 2:30–5pm (Mar 16–Oct to 7:30pm). Library Nov–Feb daily 10am–6:30pm; Mar 1–15 and Oct–Nov daily 10:30am–7:30pm; Mar 16–Sept daily 10:30am–8pm. Closed Sun mornings, Jan 1, and Dec 25. Bus: 1.

National Picture Gallery (Pinacoteca Nazionale) ★★   Housed in a 14th-century *palazzo* near Piazza del Campo is the National Gallery's collection of the Sienese school of painting, which once rivaled that of Florence. Displayed are some of the giants of the pre-Renaissance, with most of the paintings covering the period from the late 12th century to the mid–16th century.

The principal treasures are on the second floor, where you'll contemplate the artistry of Duccio in **rooms 3 and 4.** Duccio was the first great Sienese mas-ter. **Rooms 5 to 8** are rich in the art of the 14th-century Lorenzetti brothers, Ambrogio and Pietro. Ambrogio is represented by an *Annunciation* and a *Cruci-fix,* but one of his most celebrated works, carried out with consummate skill, is an almond-eyed *Madonna and Bambino* surrounded by saints and angels. Pietro's most important entry is an altarpiece, *Madonna of the Carmine,* made for a Siena church in 1329. Simone Martini's *Madonna and Child* (1321) is damaged but one of the best-known paintings here.

In the salons that follow are works by Giovanni di Paolo (*Presentation at the Temple*), Sano di Pietro, and Giovanni Antonio Bazzi (called Il Sodoma, allegedly because of his sexual interests). Of exceptional interest are the cartoons of Mannerist master Beccafumi, from which many of the panels in the cathedral floor were created.

In the Palazzo Buonsignori, Via San Pietro 29. ✆ **0577-281161.** www.spsae-si.beniculturali.it. Admission 4€. Mon 9am–1pm; Tues–Sat 8:15am–7:15pm; Sun 8:30am–1:30pm. Closed Jan 1, May 1, and Dec 25. Bus: 54.

Ospedale di Santa Maria della Scala ★   In 1997, when the hospital moved to more modern quarters, the city of Siena found itself in possession of a treasure-trove of medieval and Renaissance art not seen for centuries except by patients. Storerooms below were filled with priceless archaeological treasures. How did a hospital acquire such art? Since its founding in the 14th century, Santa Maria della Scala was once one of the biggest landowners in Tuscany and a major patron of the arts, commissioning works from some of the finest artists in the province. Wealthy Sienese also left bequests to the hospital. Even the ceiling of an underground staircase contained a fresco by Ambrogio Lorenzetti. The **frescoes ★** created by Domenico di Bartolo from 1440 to 1441 are particularly evocative, richly colored, and filled with stunning details. (Pieces of a marble fountain by Jacopo della Quercia were also discovered.) Underground storerooms have been converted to display archaeological treasures. Although it can currently be visited by the public, it is very much a "work in progress" and will be so for years. Currently, its most impressive gem is the **Pilgrims Hall ★★**, a vast hall near the main entrance. This stunning hall is adorned with a marvelous cycle of 1300s frescoes depicting major events in the history of the city. Below you can wander among funeral urns, busts, and ancient burial tablets.

Piazza del Duomo 2. ✆ **0577-224811.** www.santamariadellascala.com. Admission 6€ without reservations, 5.50€ with reservations, free for children 10 and under. Daily 10:30am–6:30pm.

Permanent Italian Library of Wine (Enoteca Italica Permanente) Owned and operated by the Italian government, this showcase for the finest wines of Italy whets the palate of even the most demanding wine lover. An unusual architectural setting is designed to show bottles to their best advantage. The place lies just outside the entrance to an old fortress, at the bottom of an inclined ramp, behind a massive arched doorway. Marble bas-reliefs and wrought-iron sconces, along with regional ceramics, are set into the high brick walls of the labyrinthine corridors, the vaults of which were built for Cosimo de' Medici in 1560. There are several sunny terraces for outdoor wine tasting, an indoor stand-up bar, and voluminous lists of available vintages for sale by the glass or the bottle. Special wine tastings for groups may be booked for 10€ for two wines or 13€ for three. Count yourself lucky if the bartender will agree to open an iron gate for access to the subterranean wine exposition; in the lowest part of the fortress, illuminated display racks contain bottles of recent vintages.

Fortezza Medicea. ✆ **0577-228811.** www.enoteca-italiana.it. Free admission. Mon–Sat noon–1am. Bus: C.

St. Catherine's Sanctuary (Santuario e Casa di Santa Caterina) Of all the personalities associated with Siena, the most enduring legend surrounds St. Catherine, acknowledged by Pius XII in 1939 as Italy's patron saint. Born in 1347 to a dyer, the mystic was instrumental in persuading the papacy to return to Rome from Avignon. The house where she lived, between Piazza del Campo and San Domenico, has been turned into a sanctuary; it's really a church and an oratory, with many artworks. On the hill above is the 13th-century **Basilica di San Domenico,** where a chapel dedicated to St. Catherine was frescoed by Il Sodoma.

Costa di San Antonio. ✆ **0577-288175.** www.caterinati.org. Free admission (a donation is expected). Daily 9am–12:30pm and 3–6pm. Bus: 1.

Where to Stay

You'll definitely need hotel reservations if you're here for the Palio. Make them far in advance and secure your room with a deposit. If it looks as if Siena is full, you might want to check out some of the nearby accommodations in the Chianti region, north of Siena (see "The Chianti Road," earlier in this chapter). The **Siena Hotels Promotion** booth on Piazza Madre Teresa di Calcutta 5 (✆ **0577-288084;** www.hotelsiena.com); will help you find a room for a small fee.

VERY EXPENSIVE

Certosa di Maggiano ★★ This early-13th-century Certosinian monastery lay in dusty disrepair until 1969, when Anna Grossi Recordati fell in love with the property and set out on a long process of renovation and restoration. Now affiliated with Relais & Châteaux, it's an intimate, plush retreat. The stylish public rooms fill the spaces in what used to be the ambulatory of the central courtyard, and the complex's medieval church still holds Mass on Sunday. The individually decorated guest rooms are spacious, with antiques, art objects, and sumptuous beds; one has a private walled garden. The hotel isn't easy to find; there are some signs, but you might want to phone ahead for directions. The staff can help you arrange for guided tours, wine tastings, and many other outings. Most guests take a taxi into the historic center of town, but there's also a shuttle.

Strada di Certosa 82, 53100 Siena. ✆ **0577-288180.** Fax 0577-288189. www.certosadimaggiano. com. 17 units. 370€–660€ double; 750€–1,270€ suite. Rates include American buffet breakfast. AE, MC, V. Parking 30€. Closed Nov–Mar. Children 11 and under are not accepted. **Amenities:** Restaurant; bar; babysitting; bikes; exercise room; Internet (5€ per hr., in lobby); outdoor heated pool; room service; outdoor tennis court (lit). *In room:* A/C, TV, hair dryer, minibar.

Grand Hotel Continental ★★ A few steps from Piazza del Campo and the Duomo, this restored 1816 majestic building is the first government-rated five-star hotel to open in the heart of Siena. After a faithful renovation of a palace designed by the baroque architect Giovanni Fontana, this deluxe and rather posh nest is for big spenders. The restoration revealed magnificent frescoes from the 1600s and decorative touches from the 19th century. Furnished with elegance and refinement, the midsize to spacious accommodations contain tiled bathrooms. Panoramic junior suites on the top level have a terrace; other junior suites contain a studio area on a loft level. Many rooms open onto views of the Duomo and are decorated with frescoes.

Banchi di Sopra 85, 53100 Siena. ✆ **0577-56011.** Fax 0577-5601555. www.royaldemeure.com. 51 units. 430€–580€ double; from 750€ junior suite, from 900€ suite. AE, DC, MC, V. Parking 45€. **Amenities:** Restaurant; bar; babysitting; room service; outdoor tennis court (lit). *In room:* A/C, CD player (in some), Wi-Fi (10€ per 24 hr.).

EXPENSIVE

Villa Scacciapensieri ★   This is one of Tuscany's lovely 19th-century villas, where you can stay in a personal, if timeworn, atmosphere. Standing on the crest of a hill about 3km (2 miles) from Siena, the villa is approached by a private driveway under shade trees. Although it's not exactly state of the art, it positively oozes tradition. The guest rooms vary widely in style and comfort, and your opinion of this hotel might depend on your room. If your accommodations open onto the rear, you'll have a view of the sweet hills of Chianti. You won't be staying within the historic walls here, but two local buses pass by the hotel entrance every 15 minutes or so during the day (the ride into town takes 10 min.). You might want to simply take a taxi into the old town.

Via di Scacciapensieri 10, 53100 Siena. ⓒ **0577-41441.** Fax 0577-270854. www.villa scacciapensieri.it. 31 units (some with shower only). 150€–305€ double; 250€–330€ suite. Rates include continental breakfast. AE, DC, MC, V. Free parking. Closed Dec 8–Mar 20. Bus: 3 or 8. **Amenities:** Restaurant; bar; babysitting; bikes; outdoor pool; room service; outdoor tennis court. *In room:* A/C, TV, hair dryer, minibar, Wi-Fi (in some, free).

MODERATE

Hotel Garden   One of the really pleasant places to stay outside Siena, less than 1.6km (1 mile) north of the old city's fortifications, boasts an 18th-century core built as a villa by a Sienese aristocrat and expanded in the 1970s with an annex. Located on the ledge of a hill, with lovely gardens, the Hotel Garden commands a view of Siena and the countryside that has been the subject of many a painting. Its outstanding features are its garden and reasonable prices. The villa contains 24 guest rooms, high-ceilinged but less luxurious than the units in the modern annex. Although the hotel doesn't lie within the historic walls, a local bus stops nearby every 10 minutes or so during the day; walking takes about 20 minutes.

Via Custoza 2, 53100 Siena. ⓒ **0577-567111.** Fax 0577-46050. www.gardenhotel.it. 122 units. 109€–250€ double. Rates include buffet breakfast. AE, DC, MC, V. Bus: 6 or 10. Free parking. **Amenities:** Restaurant; bar; babysitting; outdoor pool; room service; outdoor tennis court (lit). *In room:* A/C, TV, hair dryer, minibar, Wi-Fi (3€ per hr.).

Hotel Santa Caterina   This 18th-century villa is beautifully preserved, featuring original terra-cotta floors, sculpted marble fireplaces and stairs, arched entryways, beamed ceilings, and antique wooden furniture. Lorenza Capannelli runs this place, and she thinks of her guests as an extended family. The grounds include a terraced garden overlooking the valley south of Siena. When booking, ask for one of the 12 guest rooms with a garden view. Each room is filled with antique reproductions and chestnut furnishings.

Via Enea Silvio Piccolomini 7, 53100 Siena. ⓒ **0577-221105.** Fax 0577-271087. www.hscsiena.it. 22 units. 105€–195€ double; 120€–225€ triple. Rates include buffet breakfast. AE, DC, MC, V. Parking 15€ nearby (6 spaces). Bus: 1 or 2. **Amenities:** Bar; concierge; room service. *In room:* A/C, TV, hair dryer, minibar.

Palazzo Ravizza ★★   This is an elegant small hotel, housed in a converted building from the 19th century. Every guest room has a few antiques along with ceiling frescoes. Some rooms open onto a view of the garden. Each comes with a supremely comfortable bed and mattress, along with a small but tidily kept bathroom. The hotel is within a short walk of Piazza del Campo, outside the center of town but still within the walls. Free parking is a real plus.

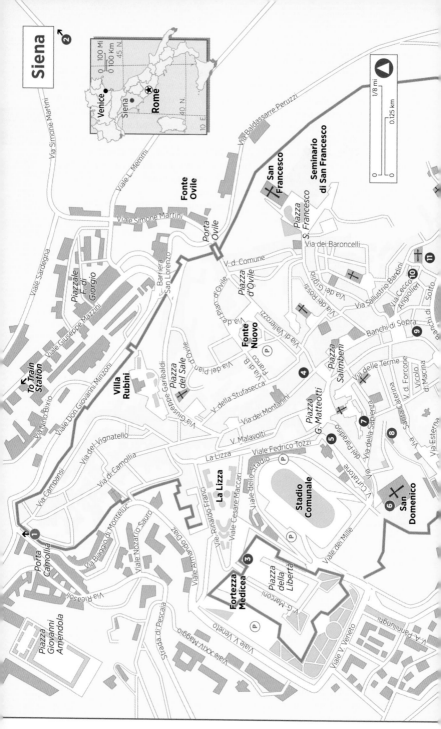

Siena

To Train Station

Porta Camollia

Piazza Giovanni Amendola

Via Riccasoli

Via Campansi

Via di Biaggio di Montelucc

Via Nino Bixio

Via del Vignatello

Via di Camollia

Viale Don Giovanni Minzoni

Viale Giuseppe Mazzini

Piazzale F. di Giorgio

Viale Sardegna

Via Simone Martini

Viale L. Memmi

Viale Simone Martini

Barriera San Lorenzo

Porta Ovile

Fonte Ovile

Via Baldassarre Peruzzi

San Francesco

Piazza S. Francesco

Seminario di San Francesco

Via dei Baroncelli

V. d. Comune

Piazza d'Ovile

Via dei Pian. d'Ovile

Fonte Nuovo

Via di Vallerozzi

Via dei Rossi

Via del Giglio

Via Sallustio Bandini

Via Cecco Angiolieri

Banchi di Sopra

Banchi di Sotto

Villa Rubini

Via Giuseppe Garibaldi

Piazza del Sale

Via del Pian. d'Ovile

Via di la Franco

Via della Stufasecca

Via dei Montanini

Piazza Salimbeni

Via delle Terme

Vicolo. d'Macina

Via d. Forcone

V. d. Macina

Piazza G. Matteotti

V. Malavolti

La Lizza

Viale Federico Tozzi

V. del Paradiso

V. Curtatone

Via della Sapienza

Santa Caterina

Via Esterna

La Lizza

Via Rinaldo Franci

Viale Cesare Maccari

Viale dello Stadio

Stadio Comunale

San Domenico

Viale dei Mille

Fortezza Medicea

Viale Nazario Sauro

Viale Amerigo Diaz

Piazza della Libertà

V. G. Marconi

Piazza della Libertà

Strada di Pescaia

Viale XXIV Maggio

Viale V. Veneto

V. A. Pantaleoni

Viale V. Veneto

Venice

Siena

Rome

0   100 Mi
0   100 Km

45° N.

40° N.

10° E.

0   1/8 mi
0   0.125 km

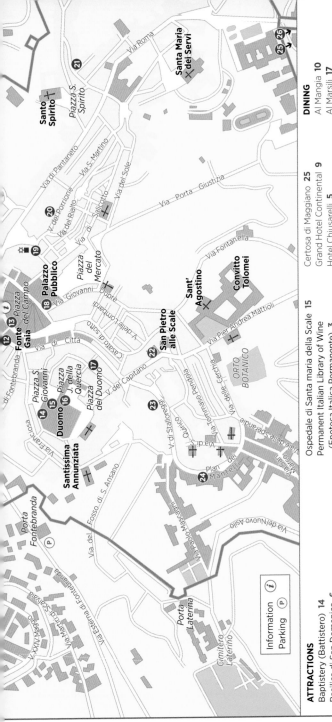

ATTRACTIONS

Baptistery (Battistero) **14**
Basilica di San Domenico **6**
Civic Museum (Museo Cívico) & Torre del Mangia **18**
Duomo Museum (Museo dell' Opera Metropolitana) **16**
Fonte Gaia **13**
Il Duomo **2**
National Picture Gallery (Pinacoteca Nazionale) **22**
Ospedale di Santa maria della Scale **15**
Permanent Italian Library of Wine (Enoteca Italica Permanente) **3**
St. Catherine's Sanctuary (Sanctuario e Casa di Santa Caterina) **8**

ACCOMMODATIONS

Albergo Bernini **7**
Albergo Cannon d'Oro **4**
Antica Torre **21**
Certosa di Maggiano **25**
Grand Hotel Continental **9**
Hotel Chiusarelli **5**
Hotel Duomo **23**
Hotel Garden **1**
Hotel Santa Caterina **26**
Palazzo Ravizza **24**
Piccolo Hotel Etruria **11**

DINING

Al Mangia **10**
Al Marsili **17**
Da Guido **12**
La Taverna di Nello (Nello La Taverna) **19**
Osteria Le Logge **20**

Information ⓘ
Parking Ⓟ

321

Pian dei Mantellini 34, 53100 Siena. ☎ **0577-280462.** Fax 0577-221597. www.palazzoravizza.it. 38 units. 130€–220€ double; 225€–300€ suite. Rates include continental breakfast. AE, DC, MC, V. Free parking. Bus: 3. **Amenities:** Restaurant; bar; concierge; room service. *In room:* A/C, TV, hair dryer, minibar (in suite), Wi-Fi (free).

INEXPENSIVE

Albergo Bernini 🏃 In the historic center of Siena, accordion-playing Mauro and his wife, Nadia, welcome you to the second floor of an old building that has other tenants. The beds, for the most part, rest under beamed ceilings. The furnishings are minimalist but comfortable. Maintenance levels are high and the hotel is well kept. Scattered antiques are placed about, lending an old-fashioned aura. All-new plumbing has been installed, and guests are granted access to the rooftop terrace for panoramic vistas of Siena and the Tuscan hills in the distance.

Via della Sapienza 15 (near San Domenico Church), 53100 Siena. ☎/fax **0577-289047.** www. albergobernini.com. 9 units, 4 with bathroom. 65€ double without bathroom, 85€ with bathroom. Children 11 and under stay free in parent's room. MC, V. Bus: 3, 9, or 10. **Amenities:** Room service. *In room:* A/C (in some).

Albergo Cannon d'Oro 🏃 Rated only two stars by the government, this hotel is installed in a restored palace from the 1400s that was once owned by Ghinibaldo di Saracino and his wife, Sapia Salvani, featured in Dante's *Divine Comedy.* But there have been a lot of changes since medieval times. With almost no public amenities, the plainly furnished yet comfortable bedrooms are the draw. A few architectural remnants of the *palazzo* remain, including terra-cotta floors and stone walls from the Middle Ages. Except for a wall print here or a mirror there, the decor is minimalist. Sometimes an antique chest of drawers will add a grace note. The location is on the shop-filled Via Montanini 200m (656 ft.) from the Piazza del Campo, very close to the bus station.

Via Montanini 28, 53100 Siena. ☎ **0577-44321.** Fax 0577-280868. www.cannondoro.com. 30 units. 60€–105€ double; 77€–135€ triple. Rates include buffet breakfast. AE, DC, MC, V. Parking 15€. *In room:* Ceiling fan, TV, Wi-Fi (free).

Antica Torre ★ The Landolfo family extends a warm welcome to international visitors. This restored 17th-century tower within the city walls is in the southeastern sector of town, a 10-minute walk from Piazza del Campo. Small and graceful, the tower sits on top of a centuries-old potters' workshop that's now the breakfast room. Take a stone staircase to the small but comfortable guest rooms, each with some Tuscan antiques, iron-filigree headboards, and marble floors. Try for one of the accommodations on the top floors for a panoramic view of the medieval city and the rolling Tuscan hills.

Via di Fieravecchia 7, 53100 Siena. ☎/fax **0577-222255.** www.anticatorresiena.it. 8 units (shower only). 80€–115€ double. AE, DC, MC, V. Free parking on street nearby. **Amenities:** Bar; Internet (free, in lobby). *In room:* A/C, TV, hair dryer.

Hotel Chiusarelli Near Piazza San Domenico, the Chiusarelli is in an ocher-colored 1870 building with Ionic columns and Roman caryatids supporting a second-floor loggia. The interior has been almost completely renovated, and each functional, nondescript guest room contains a modern bathroom. Ask for a room in back to escape the street noise. The hotel is just at the edge of the old city, a 5-minute walk from the Campo and a half-block from the bus station. It's not the prettiest area, but it's convenient.

Viale Curtatone 15, 53100 Siena. ℂ **0577-280562.** Fax 0577-271177. www.chiusarelli.com. 49 units. 92€–138€ double; 130€–208€ junior suite. Rates include buffet breakfast. AE, MC, V. Parking 15€. Bus: 9, 10, or 17. **Amenities:** Restaurant; bar; bikes; room service. *In room:* A/C, TV, hair dryer, Wi-Fi (5€ per 3 hr.).

Hotel Duomo   With a fabulous location within the historic walls just south of its namesake, this hotel is in a 12th-century *palazzo*. Once the barracks for medieval troops, the only reminders are the central staircase and the brickwork in the basement. The carpeted guest rooms are of a modest size but not cramped, and the modern furnishings are tasteful. If you want to secure one of the 13 rooms with Duomo views, ask when booking. The best choices are nos. 61 and 62, with terraces overlooking the Duomo.

Via Stalloreggi 38, 53100 Siena. ℂ **0577-289088.** Fax 0577-43043. www.hotelduomo.it. 23 units (shower only). 105€–150€ double; 140€–200€ triple. Rates include buffet breakfast. AE, DC, MC, V. Free parking nearby. Bus: 1. **Amenities:** Babysitting; room service; Wi-Fi (free, in lobby). *In room:* A/C, TV, hair dryer.

Piccolo Hotel Etruria ★ 🍴   This small family-run hotel could thumb its nose at the big corporate chains; it offers equally comfortable modern luxuries with twice the character at a fourth of the price. In both the main building and the annex across the street, the guest rooms have tiled floors, wood-toned built-in furnishings with stone-topped desks and end tables, leather strap chairs, and quite decent beds. The rooms aren't very spacious, but they aren't small either. The only real drawback is that the hotel closes from 1 to 7am.

Via Donzelle 3, 53100 Siena. ℂ **0577-288088.** Fax 0577-288461. www.hoteletruria.com. 13 units (shower only). 80€–110€ double; 90€–138€ triple. AE, MC, V. Closed Dec 17–27. Bus: 1, 2, 3, 9, or 10. **Amenities:** Room service. *In room:* A/C, TV, hair dryer.

Poste Regie ★ 📷   If you have a car, you can escape tourist-clogged Siena and find lodgings in a romantic old B&B 21km (13 miles) to the west in a tiny, hillside village called Ancaiano. The villa, built in 1888, is the ancestral home of the Peruzzis and was once the local grocery store and bar. The house has now been converted into a romantic-looking B&B, with antiques—all comfortable and cozy. The Peruzzi family is environmentally conscious, using energy-saving lightbulbs and collecting rainwater for their vegetable garden. Guests lounge in the double hammock in the garden or barbecue some steaks for dinner. Other than a private bathroom, there are no in-room amenities.

Via della Montagnola 68, Ancaiano, 53018 Sovicille. ℂ **349-4754995.** Fax 0577-45387. www. posteregie.com. 4 units. 75€–80€ double. Extra bed 25€. Rates include continental breakfast. No credit cards. *In room:* No phone.

Where to Dine
EXPENSIVE/MODERATE

Al Mangia TUSCAN/INTERNATIONAL   Al Mangia, one of the historic center's most appealing restaurants, offers outside tables overlooking the town hall. It was constructed more or less continuously between 1100 and the late 1600s. The food is artfully cooked and presented by a relatively formal staff, with excellent menu items changing with the seasons. Look for *pici alla Sienese* (thick noodles made only with flour and water) with a sauce of fresh tomatoes, tarragon, and cheese; spicy spaghetti with baby spring onions and sausages; *filetto alla terra* *di Siena* (grilled steak with a chianti-and-tarragon sauce); and grilled lamb ribs with balsamic vinegar. The homemade desserts include *Cassatina di mascarpone e pinoli con cascata di cioccolata* (Cassata cake with mascarpone cheese and pine nuts, served with chocolate syrup).

Piazza del Campo 43. ✆ **0577-281121.** www.almangia.it. Reservations recommended. Main courses 15€–28€. AE, DC, MC, V. Daily noon–3:30pm and 7–10pm. Closed Thurs in winter. Bus: 1, 2, or 5.

Al Marsili SIENESE/ITALIAN   This beautiful restaurant stands between the Duomo and Via di Città. You dine beneath crisscrossed ceiling vaults whose russet-colored brickwork was designed centuries ago. The antipasti offer some unusual treats, such as polenta with chicken-liver sauce; a medley of the best of Siena's cold cuts; and smoked venison, wild boar, and goose blended into a pâté. The wide selection of first courses ranges from the typical vegetable soup of Siena *(ribollita alla senese)* to a risotto with four cheeses. Pasta specialties include *pici all'aglione* (fresh Sienese pasta with a garlic and tomato sauce) or else *conchiglie alla rustica* (a shell pasta in a spinach and sausage sauce). For a main dish, you might try guinea hen cooked with pine nuts, almonds, and prunes. The *panna cotta* is a cream pudding with fresh berries, and the *dolce Marsili* is a soft cake flavored with coffee and mascarpone cream.

Via del Castoro 3. ✆ **0577-47154.** www.ristorantealmarsili.it. Reservations recommended. Main courses 12€–22€. AE, DC, MC, V. Tues–Sun 12:30–2:30pm and 7:30–10:30pm. Bus: 1, 2, or 5.

Osteria Le Logge ★★ SIENESE/TUSCAN   This *trattoria* deserves its longtime popularity. At the end of the 19th century, this place was a pharmacy, dispensing creams and medicines to cure the ill. Today it has been transformed into a bastion of superb cuisine in a refined and old-fashioned atmosphere. The menu, changed daily, overflows with freshness and flavor. Try the wild-boar stew with spicy tomato sauce or the delectable baked duck stuffed with fennel or grapes. In autumn, try the *pappardelle* with game sauce. The tender veal steaks are among the best in town, and you can also order *taglierini* pasta with black-truffle sauce. Save room for one of the desserts, which are made fresh each morning.

Via del Porrione 33. ✆ **0577-48013.** www.giannibrunelli.it. Reservations recommended. Main courses 11€–23€. AE, DC, MC, V. Mon–Sat noon–2:45pm and 7–10:30pm. Closed Jan 7–31.

INEXPENSIVE

Da Guido SIENESE/INTERNATIONAL   Da Guido is a medieval Tuscan restaurant about 30m (98 ft.) off the promenade near Piazza del Campo. It's decked out with crusty old beams, aged brick walls, arched ceilings, and iron chandeliers. Our approval is backed up by the testimony of more than 300 prominent people who have left autographed photos to adorn the walls of the three dining rooms. Meals seem to taste best when begun with selections from the antipasti table. Pastas that appeal to anyone who loves the taste of spring vegetables include *rustici alla Guido* (spaghetti laced with mushrooms, truffles, and fresh asparagus). Some of the best meat dishes are grilled over the kitchen's charcoal grill and include spicy chicken breast with rosemary, sage, garlic, and Tabasco sauce; and *bistecca alla Guido*, steak grilled simply with a sauce of olive oil and rosemary.

Vicolo Pier Pettinaio 7. ✆ **0577-280042.** www.ristoranteguido.com. Reservations required. Main courses 9€–26€. AE, MC, V. Daily 12:30–3pm and 7:30–10pm. Bus: 1.

La Taverna di Nello (Nello La Taverna) TUSCAN/VEGETARIAN   On a narrow stone-covered street half a block from Piazza del Campo, this 1930s restaurant offers a tavern decor with brick walls, lanterns, racks of wine bottles, and sheaves of corn hanging from the ceiling. Best of all, you can view the forgelike kitchen with its crew of uniformed cooks busily preparing your dinner from behind a row of hanging copper utensils. Specialties include a salad of fresh radicchio, green lasagna ragout-style, and risotto with porcini mushrooms. Freshly made pasta is served every day; perhaps it will be ravioli in a velvety sauce of artichokes and cream. Your waiter will gladly suggest a local vintage. The restaurant's wine bar offers more than 150 vintages from the south of Tuscany.

Via del Porrione 28. (©) **0577-289043.** Reservations required. Main courses 8€–18€. MC, V. Mon-Sat noon–3pm and 7–10:30pm. Closed Jan. Bus: 1, 2, or 5.

Shopping

Although Siena's shopping scene can't compete with that in Florence, you'll still find a good selection of stores and boutiques. The best is **Martini Marisa,** Via del Capitano 5 (© **0577-226438**), purveyor of gift items, local stoneware, and porcelain.

Specializing in older jewelry, **Antichità Saena Vetus ★**, Via di Città 53 (© **0577-42395**), also handles modern furniture and paintings from the 1700s and 1800s, and always has smaller pieces reasonably priced for the bargain hunter.

More contemporary is the intricately crafted knitwear at **Il Telaio,** Chiasso del Bargello 2 (© **0577-47065**). Most of the stock includes artfully tailored women's jackets, scarves, and jumpers, although there's a small collection of pullovers for men. Focusing on smaller leather goods, **Mercatissimo della Calzatura e Pelletteria,** Viale Curtatone 1 (© **0577-45310**), is the largest store of its type in Siena. You'll find discounted prices on upscale Italian-made leather goods (handbags, suitcases, briefcases, and men's and women's shoes), and there's an inventory of tennis and basketball sneakers imported from Asia.

A farm on the outskirts of Pienza.

Siena merchants also sell some of Tuscany's finest wines. Virtually every street corner has an outlet for local chianti (sold in individual bottles and sometimes four-packs and six-packs). Many of the finer bottles are wrapped in the distinctive straw sheathing. For the largest selection, head to the **Enoteca Italica Permanente** (p. 317). A Tuscan gourmet's delight, the **Enoteca San Domenico,** Via del Paradiso 56 (© **0577-271181;** www.enotecasandomenico. it), sells regional wines and grappa by the bottle, plus pasta, virgin olive oils, sauces, jams, and assorted sweets.

A Side Trip to Pienza

This jewel of a Renaissance town 24km (15 miles) from Montalcino and 53km (33 miles) from Siena is easy to reach from Montalcino (to the west) by bus. (A rental car will make your life easier.)

When looking for a place to film *Romeo and Juliet* in 1968, director Franco Zefferelli found the perfect backdrop in Pienza, so he bypassed "fair Verona" as the obvious choice. Pienza was also used in the Oscar-winning epic *The English Patient.* Although it appears as a medieval town on film, Pienza is more noteworthy as a testament to the ambitions and ego of a quintessential Renaissance man. Pope Pius II (of Siena's illustrious Piccolomini family) was born here in 1405 when the town was called Corsignano, and in 1459 (a year after he was elected pope), he commissioned Florentine architect Bernardo Rossellino to level the medieval core of the town and create the first stage of what would be the model High Renaissance city. He renamed it Pienza, in his own honor.

The grand scheme didn't get very far (the pope died in 1464), but what has remained is perfectly preserved and has become a UNESCO-protected site. The graceful **Piazza Pio II ★★★** is the star of the town. Visit its **Palazzo Piccolomini** (the pope's residence, lived in by descendants of the Piccolomini family until 1968) and the **Duomo;** then walk behind the Duomo for sweeping views of the dormant Mount Amiata and the wide Val d'Orcia. The piazza is also the location for the **tourist office,** Piazza Dante Alighieri 18 (©/fax **0578-748359;** www. ufficioturisticodipienza.it). Ask about free guided tours of the town during summer.

You can see most of the town in half a day. It takes about 5 minutes to cover Pienza's main drag, **Corso Rossellino,** whose food stores specialize in the gourmet products from this bountiful corner of Tuscany, namely wines, honey, and pecorino cheese (also known as *cacio*). Cheese tasting is more popular than wine tasting here, and stores offer their varieties of *fresco* (fresh), *semistagionato* (partially aged), *pepperocinato* (dusted with hot peppers), or *tartufi* (truffles). Taste as much cheese as you will, but by all means save room for lunch at the reasonably priced **Dal Falco,** Piazza Dante Alighieri 7 (© **0578-748551;** www.ristorante dalfalco.it), closed Friday. A meal of homemade *pici* pasta and a savory grilled meat will cost around 18€, main courses 7€ to 20€. There are also fixed-price menus from 35€ to 40€. Upstairs are six simple doubles with a bathroom for 64€, with breakfast 75€.

Montepulciano ★★★

13km (8 miles) E of Pienza, 967km (40 miles) SE of Siena, 124km (76 miles) SE of Florence

The great wine beloved by epicures, the garnet-colored *Vino Nobile,* put the medieval hamlet of Montepulciano on the map. In his 17th-century poem "Bacchus in Tuscany," Francesco Redi called it "the king of wines," and his praise still

The steep, winding streets of Montepulciano.

holds true today. The town is surrounded by fortifications and walls designed by Antonio da Sangallo the Elder in 1511 for Cosimo I.

Views over the surrounding vineyards are remarkable, as Montepulciano is Tuscany's loftiest hill town at 605m (1,985 ft.). The area inside the walls is car free. Before checking out individual attractions, climb its serpentine main street—locals call it simply "Corso," although it has several names. The street proceeds on a north-south axis, and part of the fun of walking it is to duck down its offshoot and steeply graded alleyways left over from the Middle Ages.

At the summit of Corso, you can reach the main square, Piazza Grande, dominated by the Palazzo Comunale and the Duomo. Here you can begin your tour of the individual attractions.

Although Montepulciano has many fine hotels, it can be explored on a day trip from Pienza (see above). From Florence, take the A1 south to the Chianciano Terme exit, then S146 in the direction of Chianciano for 18km (11 miles). From Siena, head south on the S2 to San Quírico d'Orcia, then follow S146 through Pienza to Montepulciano.

EXPLORING THE TOWN

Centro Storico

Duomo CENTRO STORICO   To the world, the Duomo presents a stark, austere facade—in fact, it was not completed. On this monumental square, it is a poor cousin but contains treasures inside, even though the interior is also a bit sparse for our more lavish taste in cathedrals. If for nothing else, we always visit just to gaze at the masterpiece of the Sienese artist, Taddeo di Bartolo. Hanging in a triptych above the high altar, his *Assumption of the Virgin* is so poignant we stand in awe of it, fascinated by the artist's use of colors in subtle pinks, blood orange, eggplant purple, and amber gold—glowing, yet discordant as intended by di Bartolo. The monumental altarpiece was created in 1401. There are scattered sculptures by Michelozzo as well.

Piazza Grande (off Via Ricci). No phone. Free admission. Daily 9am–12:30pm and 3:15–7pm.

Palazzo Neri-Orselli (Museo Civico)   This is the showcase of the treasures of Montepulciano, everything housed in this Sienese-Gothic palazzo. A collection of some 200 Tuscan paintings range from the 13th to the 17th centuries. Its two most important paintings are *St. Francis* by Margaritone da Arezzo and the lush *Coronation of the Virgin* by Jacopo de Mino. There are many other treasures as well, including 15th-century illuminated choir books, enameled terra cottas by Andrea della Robbia (master of such art), Etruscan funerary urns, and a lot of the other booty the town acquired by one means or the other over the centuries. It's grandma's attic with an artistic bent.

Via Ricci 10 (off Piazza Grande). (✆) **0578-717300.** www.museisenesi.org. Admission 5€ adults, 3€ ages 17 and under. Tues–Sun 10am–1pm and 3–7pm.

Palazzo Nobili-Tarugi   Facing the Duomo or cathedral in the center of town, this *palazzo* is believed to have been designed by Antonio da Sangallo the Elder as a sort of architectural dream fantasy, with half-moon arches, Ionic columns, and a great portico and entryway with pilasters adorning the walled-in upper story. The open loggia on the ground floor is a masterpiece of architecture. Out front is a much-photographed 1520 fountain that incorporates two Etruscan columns and is topped by two griffins, plus two stately lions that bear the Medici coat of arms. The interior can't be visited.

Piazza Grande (off Via Ricci). No phone.

Piazza Grande   In the bull's-eye center, and at the highest point in town, this square goes by the official name of Piazza Vittorio Emanuele, but everybody calls it "Piazza Grande." It is dominated by the Duomo and enveloped with Renaissance *palazzo,* the chief of these being the Gothic town hall, the rather austere **Palazzo Comunale,** the work of Michelozzo, the Florentine artist who designed it in the 15th century. He was clearly inspired by the Palazzo Vecchio in Florence. If you climb the Town Hall clock tower, you'll be rewarded with one of the most magnificent vistas in all of Tuscany.

Piazza Grande. ✆ **0578-7121.** Admission to tower 2€. Mon–Sat 10am–5pm.

West Montepulciano
Tempio di San Biagio ★★   This masterpiece of High Renaissance architecture was the greatest achievement of architect Antonio da Sangallo, who finished it in 1529. He was obviously inspired by Bramante's design for St. Peter's in Rome. Built on a Greek cross plan, in the popular style of its day, it was constructed to house a much-venerated statue of the Madonna. Crowned by its dome, the church has two campaniles, or bell towers—one left unfinished. If viewed in the right sunlight, the golden yellow travertine structure shines like gold itself.

Via di San Giagio (1km/½ mile west of city via Porta al Prato, lying below the town walls). No phone. Free admission. Daily 9am–12:30pm and 3:30–7:30pm.

WHERE TO STAY
Centro Storico
Albergo Duomo   Taking its name from the adjacent Duomo (cathedral), this is a family-run favorite. The old-fashioned hotel is entered through a courtyard and up a couple of flights of stairs. The small to midsize bedrooms are decorated in a tasteful yet simple Tuscan *arte povera* style, all with well-maintained private bathrooms. Cast-iron frame beds, large wooden armoires, and a few simple modern pieces comprise the furnishings.

Via San Donato 14 (next to the Duomo, off Piazza Grande), 53045 Montepulciano. ✆/fax **0578-757473.** www.albergoduomomontepulciano.it. 13 units. 90€–110€ double; 110€–120€ triple. Rates include buffet breakfast. AE, DC, MC, V. Free parking. *In room:* A/C, TV, hair dryer, minibar.

Il Borghetto ★   This historic and rather rustic hostelry lies in a converted 16th-century building, with most of its small to midsize bedrooms opening onto panoramic views. Modern amenities have been installed in a historic atmosphere, with many of the old brick floors intact. For the most part, Tuscan antiques are used extensively.

Via Borgo Buio 7 (at Via di Gozzano), 53045 Montepulciano. ✆ **0578-757535.** Fax 0578-757387. www.ilborghetto.it. 17 units. 105€ double; 152€ suite. AE, DC, MC, V. Parking 10€. *In room:* A/C, TV, hair dryer.

Il Marzocco Down a notch or two from San Biagio, this inn appeals more to traditionalists, as it's been housing wayfarers since the early 20th century. Most of the rooms are spacious and furnished in a combination of Victorian and modern. The best units have large terraces opening onto views. In spite of some renovations, the patina of another era still lingers.

Piazza Savonarola 18 (off Via Grachiano nel Corso), 53045 Montepulciano. © **0578-757262.** Fax 0578-757530. www.albergoilmarzocco.it. 16 units. 90€ double; 120€ triple. Rates include continental breakfast. AE, DC, MC, V. Free parking. **Amenities:** Bar. *In room:* A/C, TV, hair dryer, minibar, Wi-Fi (free).

Mueble Il Riccio In one of the oldest palaces in this part of Tuscany, dating from 1280, this historic building—much altered over the years—has been converted to receive guests. Reached after a two-story climb (no elevator), the hotel has as its grace note a rooftop terrace with vistas over the agriculturally rich Valdichiana Valley. The comfortable bedrooms are midsize, but bathrooms are small. More impressive is the courtyard at the entrance with its tiled floor and pointed arches supported on travertine columns holding up an upper gallery with Ionic pillars.

Via Talosa 21 (off Piazza Grande), 53045 Montepulciano. ©/fax **0578-757713.** www.ilriccio. net. 6 units. 100€ double. Rates include buffet breakfast. AE, DC, MC, V. Free parking. *In room:* A/C, TV, minibar.

San Biagio The town's leading inn is installed in an ancient but restored nobleman's house. Lying only 50m (164 ft.) from the church of San Biagio in the historic center, it is furnished in a traditional Tuscan style, both tasteful and comfortable. All rooms have a balcony for picture-postcard views. A special feature is the indoor swimming pool built in the classical style of ancient Pompei.

Via San Bartolomeo 2, 53045 Montepulciano. © **0578-717233.** Fax 0578-716524. www. albergosanbiagio.it. 27 units. 95€–120€ double; 115€–150€ triple. Rates include buffet breakfast. MC, V. Free parking. **Amenities:** Restaurant; bar; babysitting; Jacuzzi; indoor heated pool; room service. *In room:* A/C, TV, hair dryer, minibar.

WHERE TO DINE

Fattoria Pulcino TUSCAN At a point 3km (2 miles) southwest of the center, a 16th-century farmhouse has been turned into a mammoth dining room with long communal tables serving the finest fare in the area, including bottles of the celebrated *Vino Nobile.* In fair weather, terrace dining is a feature. The family owners (not the friendliest crew) sell their own Pulcino extra-virgin olive oil and wine produced at the rate of 65,000 bottles a year. Grilled free-range chicken and succulent Florentine steaks are the specialties. You can also order polenta in a meat sauce or *tagliatelle* with fresh mushrooms.

> ### Tasting the Noble Wine
>
> Since Montepulciano is known worldwide for its wine, *Vino Nobile di Montepulciano,* a visit to a *cantine* is in order. Winegrowers have organized a consortium, **Conforzio del Vino Nobile di Montepulciano** (www.consorziovino nobile.it). At the Palazzo del Capitano on Piazza Grande in the center of town, you can visit its showroom and tasting center and sample the vintages of every member Monday to Friday 1 to 6pm, Saturday 2 to 6pm.

S146 per Chianciano 35 (on the road to Chianciano). ℰ **339-1403162.** www.pulcino ristorante.com. Reservations recommended. Main courses 12€–22€; degustation menu 25€. AE, DC, MC, V. Apr–Oct daily noon–3pm and 7pm–midnight; Nov–Mar Mon–Fri noon–3pm; Sat–Sun noon–3pm and 7pm–midnight.

Il Cantuccio POLIZIANA/ETRUSCAN   Believe it or not, the chefs here actually prepare some menu items based on ancient Etruscan recipes—for example, *pollo e coniglio all'Etrusca,* a combination platter of Etruscan-style chicken and rabbit. Most of the dishes served in this long dining room with a roaring fire in winter are Poliziana, referring to the local regional cookery. Favorite dishes include tagliatelle in a duck ragout or perfectly grilled Florentine steak with Tuscan white beans and roast potatoes, climaxed by a ricotta torte, a forerunner of cheesecake.

Via delle Cantine 1–2 (off Via Gracciano nel Corso). ℰ **0578-757870.** www.ristoranteilcantuccio. com. Reservations recommended. Main courses 9€–22€. AE, DC, MC, V. Tues–Sun noon–3pm and 7–10:30pm. Closed 2 weeks in early Nov and 1st 2 weeks of July.

West of Town

La Grotta TUSCAN/POLIZIANA   Across the street from the landmark church of San Biagio, this is an old-fashioned tavern setting decorated with arched and brick ceilings, serving tasty specialties, most of it recently harvested from the countryside. We return again and again to taste such robust, regional fare as pasta with guinea fowl ragout, lamb in a crust of aromatic herbs, pork filet flavored with coffee beans and served with a carrot-and-onion flan, and wild boar braised with plums.

Località San Biagio 15 (lies 1km/½ mile west of center). ℰ **0578-757479.** Reservations recommended. Main courses 12€–18€. AE, DC, MC, V. Thurs–Tues noon–3pm and 7pm–midnight. Closed Jan 10–Mar 10.

AREZZO ★

81km (50 miles) SE of Florence

The most landlocked of all the towns of Tuscany, Arezzo was originally an Etruscan settlement and later a Roman center. The city flourished in the Middle Ages before its capitulation to Florence.

The walled town grew up on a hill; but large parts of the ancient city, including native son Petrarch's house, were bombed during World War II before the area fell to the Allied advance in the summer of 1944. Apart from Petrarch, famous sons of Arezzo have included Vasari, the painter/architect remembered chiefly for his history of the Renaissance artists, and Guido of Arezzo (sometimes known as Guido Monaco), who gave the world the modern musical scale before his death in the mid–11th century.

Today, Arezzo looks a little rustic, as if the glory of the Renaissance has long passed it by. But this isn't surprising when you consider that it lost its prosperity when Florence annexed it in 1348. Arezzo might look a bit down at the heels, but it really isn't. The city has one of the biggest jewelry industries in western Europe. Little firms on the outskirts turn out an array of rings and chains, and bank vaults overflow with gold ingots. However, Arezzo's inner core, which most visitors want to explore, didn't share in this gold and looks as if it needs a rehab.

If Arezzo looks familiar to you, you might've seen it in Roberto Benigni's wonderful *Life Is Beautiful,* which was partially filmed here.

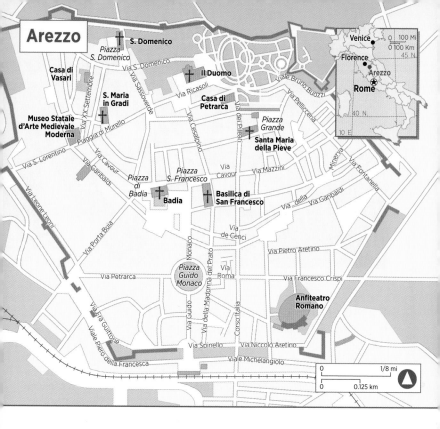

Essentials

GETTING THERE A **train** comes from Florence at intervals of 20 to 60 minutes throughout the day. The trip takes between 40 and 60 minutes, costing 6€ to 13€ one-way, depending on its speed. In Arezzo, trains depart and arrive at the **Stazione Centrale,** Piazza della Repubblica (✆ 892021). Because there are no direct trains from Siena to Arezzo, rail passengers from Siena are required to make a transfer at Chiusi. Therefore, unless it happens to be Sunday (see below), it's better to travel by bus if your point of origin is Siena.

From Monday to Saturday **TRA-IN** (✆ **0577-204111;** www.trainspa.it) runs seven buses a day from Siena to Arezzo, a trip taking 2 hours and costing 8€ one-way.

If you have a **car** and are in Rome, head north on A1; from Florence, head south on A1. In both directions, the turnoff for Arezzo is clearly marked.

VISITOR INFORMATION The **tourist office** is on Via Ricasoli 1 (✆ **0575-377829;** www.apt.arezzo.it). From November to March, it's open daily 10am to 6pm; April to October, hours are daily 9:30am to 6:30pm.

SPECIAL EVENTS A major event on the Arezzo calendar is the **Giostra del Saracino,** staged the third Sunday of June and the first Sunday of September on Piazza Grande. In a tradition unbroken since the 13th century, horsemen in medieval costumes reenact the lance-charging joust ritual. The most dangerous aspect of the tournament involves the use of medieval-style balled whips, a tradition depicted in countless movies like *Ivanhoe.*

A market along Arezzo's streets.

Exploring the Town

Stop by **Piazza Grande** to see the medieval and Renaissance palaces and towers that flank it, including the 16th-century loggia by Vasari.

Basilica di San Francesco ★★   This Gothic church was finished in the 14th century for the Franciscans. Inside is a Piero della Francesca masterpiece, a restored fresco cycle called **Legend of the True Cross ★★★**. His frescoes are remarkable for their grace, clearness, dramatic light effects, well-chosen colors, and ascetic severity. Vasari credited della Francesca as a master of the laws of geometry and perspective, and Sir Kenneth Clark called Piero's frescoes "the most perfect morning light in all Renaissance painting." The frescoes depict the burial of Adam, Solomon receiving the queen of Sheba at the court (the most memorable scene), the dream of Constantine with the descent of an angel, and the triumph of the Holy Cross with Heraclius, among other subjects. Because of worldwide interest in these frescoes, you must now make reservations to get in to see them, as only two dozen visitors are admitted every half-hour. After that time is up, visitors are then ushered out to make room for more. To make reservations, call ✆ **0575-352727** or go to www.pierodellafrancesca.it.

Piazza San Francesco. ✆ **0575-20630.** Free admission. Daily 8:30am–noon and 2–6pm. Guided 30-min. visits to the frescoes 6€. Mon–Sat 9am–6pm; Sun 10am–5:30pm.

House of Vasari (Casa di Vasari)   This house was purchased by the artist (and the first art-history writer) in 1540. There are works by Vasari himself, but it's apparent that his fame rests on his *Lives of the Artists* more than it does on his actual artwork. His best works are *Virtue, Envy, and Fortune* and *Deposition*. Other works displayed are by Santi di Tito, Alessandro Allori, and Il Poppi.

Via XX Settembre 55. ✆ **0575-409050.** Admission 2€. Wed–Sat and Mon 8:30am–7pm; Sun 8:30am–1pm.

Il Duomo   The Duomo was built in the pure Gothic style, rare for Tuscany. It was begun in the 13th century, but the final touches (on the facade) weren't applied until the outbreak of World War I. Its art treasures include stained-glass windows

(1519–23) by Guillaume de Marcillat and a main altar in the Gothic style. Its main treasure, though, is **Mary Magdalene** ★, a Piero della Francesca masterpiece.

Piazza del Duomo. ✆ **0575-23991.** Free admission. Daily 7am–12:30pm and 3–6:30pm.

Petrarch's House (Casa di Petrarca)   A short walk away from Santa Maria della Pieve, this house was rebuilt after World War II damage. Born at Arezzo in 1304, Petrarch was a great Italian lyrical poet and humanist who immortalized his love, Laura, in his sonnets. Actual mementos are few, but the house displays books, engravings, sketches, and even some furnishings from Petrarch's time.

Via dell'Orto 28A. ✆ **0575-24700.** Free admission (ring the bell to enter). Mon–Fri 10am–noon and 3–5pm; Sat 10am–noon. Closed Aug 1–25 and Dec 20–Jan 7.

Santa Maria della Pieve ★   This Romanesque church boasts a front of three open-air loggias, with each pillar designed uniquely. The 14th-century bell tower is known as "the hundred holes" because it's riddled with windows. Inside, the church is bleak and austere, but there's a notable polyptych, *The Virgin with Saints,* by one of the Sienese Lorenzetti brothers (Pietro), painted in 1320.

Corso Italia 7. ✆ **0575-22629.** Free admission. Mon–Sat 8am–1pm and 3–7pm; Sun 8am–1pm and 3–6:30pm.

Where to Dine

Buca di San Francesco ★ ARETINE/ITALIAN   Located in the historic core, the city's finest restaurant is in the cellar of a 14th-century *palazzo;* it's decorated with medieval references and strong Tuscan colors of sienna and blue. Menu items—some based on centuries-old recipes—include *pollo del Valdarno arrosto* (roast chicken from the Arno valley) flavored with anise, homemade *tagliolini* with tomatoes and ricotta, and calves' liver with onions. A popular first course is green noodles with a rich meat sauce, oozing with creamy cheese and topped with a hunk of fresh butter. All ingredients are fresh, many of the staples are produced in-house, and even the olive oil is from private sources not shared by other restaurants.

Via San Francesco 1. ✆ **0575-23271.** www.bucadisanfrancesco.it. Reservations recommended. Main courses 8.50€–15€. AE, DC, MC, V. Wed–Sun 7–9:30pm; Wed–Mon noon–2:30pm. Closed 2 weeks in July.

Shopping

Arezzo hosts one of Europe's biggest gold-jewelry industries. In the center of town, around **Piazza Grande,** are dozens of antiques shops carrying these shiny wares.

If you happen to be in Arezzo the first Saturday and Sunday of the month, don't miss the **antiques street market.** It was started some 3 decades ago by the Italian antiques expert Ivan Bruschi. For 2 days, this little town becomes a center of interest for antiques connoisseurs, with more than 500 stalls scattered all over the Piazza San Francesco to Piazza Vasari (also known as Piazza Grande), going through Piazza della Libertà.

ELBA

179km (111 miles) SW of Florence, 231km (143 miles) NW of Rome, 86km (53 miles) S of Livorno, 12km (7½ miles) off the eastern coast of Piombino

Right off the Italian mainland, the island of Elba is the gem of the Tuscan archipelago. It's much smaller than Sicily or Sardinia, yet it's the third-largest Italian island, measuring about 27×18km (17×11 miles). Except for its mountainous interior, with old mining villages, the sea seems ever present in Elba.

In all, there are 146km (91 miles) of coastline with 50 small sandy beaches and plenty of hidden coves. The landscape is typically Mediterranean, with silvery olive trees and hill-climbing vineyards under sun-baked skies (the climate is rather dry).

Italy has far more glamorous islands, including Capri and Ischia, attracting the rich and famous, whereas Elba tends to draw more middle-class families, especially the Italians themselves and hordes of Germans who descend from July to September.

The Greeks discovered Elba long before the Etruscans, who eventually surrendered it to the Romans when Elba became part of the Roman Empire. In the Middle Ages the Elbani were ruled by the Pisans, but in the 1500s the island was menaced by Barbary pirates. The Medicis took over in the latter 16th century.

In 1814, Napoleon Bonaparte reigned over Elba when he was sent here on his first exile from France. Although only here a year or so, he made vast improvements, including modernizing agriculture and improving the roads. Still proud of its associations with such a towering historical figure, Elba preserves two Napoleonic villas that can be visited.

Swimming is possible here from mid-May to September.

Essentials

GETTING THERE Most visitors take the ferry from Piombino on the western coast of Italy to the port of Portoferraio, the capital of Elba. The two major ferry companies are **Moby Lines** (© **199-30-30-40** in Piombino, or 0565-914133 in Portoferraio; www.mobylines.it) and **Toremar** (© **0565-31100** in Piombino, or 0565-918080 in Portoferraio; www.toremar.it).

Trip time to Elba is about 1 hour, and one-way tickets from Piombino to Portoferraio is 20€ per passenger. Cars cost 43€ to 50€, depending on the time of year and the size of the vehicle. Toremar also offers a faster hydrofoil service (40 min.), costing 15€ to Portoferraio.

Toremar also runs boats to Elba's minor ports, including Cavo, Rio Marina, and Porto Azzurro. No cars are transported on the *aliscafo,* or hydrofoil. Boats depart hourly from April to August, pared back to six to eight daily off season.

GETTING AROUND The coastal road is quite good, and if you didn't bring a car over by ferry you can rent one at **Happy Rent,** Viale Elba 7 (© **0565-914665;** www.renthappy.it) in Portoferraio. Many visitors prefer to rent a scooter or bike from **Two Wheels Network,** Viale Elba 32 (© **0565-914666;** www.twn-rent. it), both outlets in Portoferraio. Depending on the season, bikes cost 15€ to 18€ per day, with scooters going for 24€ to 35€.

ATL (© **800-317709;** www.atl.livorno.it) runs buses from Portoferraio to most of the major towns, leaving from the main terminal at Viale Elba 20 in Portoferraio. One-way tickets cost 1.20€ to 3.10€, depending on the distance, or you can purchase a day pass for 7€.

VISITOR INFORMATION The main **tourist office** is in Portoferraio at Viale Elba 4 (© **0565-914671;** www.aptelba.it), open Monday to Saturday 8am to 1pm and 3 to 6pm. If you've arrived without a reservation (not a good idea in summer), head for **Associazione Albergatori Isola d'Elba,** Calata Italia 43 (© **0565-915555;** www.albergatorielbani.it), in Portoferraio. It is open Monday to Friday 9am to 5pm and Saturday 9:30am to noon and 3 to 6pm.

The Forte della Stella stands guard over the port.

Exploring the Island

PORTOFERRAIO   Elba's capital is a busy boat-clogged harbor, filled with the comings and goings of thousands of visitors in summer. It's not the loveliest spot on Elba at which to base a vacation by the sea, as other resorts offer far more idyllic settings. Off season, however, hotel closings elsewhere make Portoferraio the best bet. The best beach nearby is **Le Viste;** it's little and rocky but sign-posted from the rear side of the sheer cliff behind Villa dei Mulini (see below).

Walk through an ancient gateway of town, **Porta al Mare,** into the old city. The chief attraction of the upper level of town is **Villa dei Mulini,** Piazzale Napoleone (✆ **0565-915846**), once the official residence of Napoleon and his court for 9 months. The structure was created from two joined windmills (*mulino* means windmill in Italian). Inside you can visit the exiled emperor's apartments, including period furniture, weapons, paintings, Napoleon's library, and a garden with a panoramic view over the gulf. Admission is 3€, and visits are Monday to Saturday 9am to 7pm, Sunday 9am to 1pm. A cumulative ticket, costing 11€, gets you inside Napoleon's summer place (see below).

In 1548 the Medici grand duke, Cosimo I, founded Portoferraio, creating the **Medici Fortress** that towers over the town to guard the port from attack. To the west is Forte del Falcone, and to the east, above the lighthouse, stands Forte della Stella. The fortress is open Monday and Wednesday to Saturday 9am to 7pm; Sunday 9am to 1pm. Admission is 3€.

As you descend toward the docks, you'll pass two churches, including **Chiesa della Misericordia** (✆ **0565-914009**), which has a death mask of Napoleon. Built in 1677, the church also contains other mementos of the emperor. The other church is **Santissimo Sacramento** (no phone), dating from 1551. On the left as you enter the church, note the Votive Temple dedicated to Elban soldiers who died in World War I.

OUTSIDE PORTOFERRAIO   The major attraction on the island is **Villa San Martino ★★** (✆ **0565-914688**), Napoleon's summer villa at San Martino, 5km (3 miles) to the south. When the road divides at Bivio Boni, take the route going west (the villa is signposted).

It was here in this summer villa, and in Portoferraio, that Napoleon ruled over the small principality of Elba following his abdication on April 11, 1814. Only 45 years old, the Corsican was impatient, launching many projects to keep his mind occupied.

In late February 1815, he left Elba to begin the famous "Hundred Days" that culminated in the Battle of Waterloo. He was never to return to Elba but was exiled next to Saint Helena.

The neoclassical facade of the villa was added long after Napoleon's departure by Prince Demidoff, a distant relative who bought the house and upgraded it into a museum. The frescoes inside the villa are by the painter Ravelli.

Inside the gallery is a statue of Galathea attributed to Canova (Pauline Bonaparte Borghese, Napoleon's sister, once posed nude for Canova). In the Egyptian Room are mementos of Napoleon's campaign in Egypt with *trompe l'oeil* desert scenes. Hours are Monday and Wednesday to Saturday 9am to 8pm, and Sunday 9am to 2pm costing 6€; see details on cumulative ticket by referring to Villa dei Mulini, above.

Back at Bivio Boni you can take the road east to **Terme San Giovanni** (© **0565-914680;** www.termelbane.com), which features massages, seaweed body wraps, sulfurous mud baths, and spa treatments costing from 10€ to 85€.

Armed with a map from the tourist office, you can seek out the best beaches in this part of the island, including **Acquaviva, Sanzone, Viticcio, Magazzini, Ottone,** and **Bagnaia.**

PORTO AZZURRO   On the east coast of Elba, Porto Azzurro lies 14km (9 miles) from Portoferraio. Porto Azzurro was the old Spanish capital of the island; the remaining fortress from 1603 is a prison today. Originally called Porto Longone, this little resort and port is the southern terminus of the ferry lines. Most of its life revolves around the harbor, which in summer is filled with both yachts and fishing boats. Some of the best sandy beaches on island are found around here.

En route to Porto Azzurro you can stop at the ruins of **Delle Grotte,** a sign-posted Roman villa constructed during the 1st century B.C. in a perfect opus reticulatum. Here an ornamental pool stretches toward the sea. Admission is free; it's open from Easter to September (no set hours).

Far more intriguing and colorful than Porto Azzurro itself is the mountain town of **Capoliveri ★,** which lies 8km (5 miles) to the southwest. On a peninsula, this is a naturally fortified town with twisting, closely knit streets. You'll want to spend an hour or so walking about before settling on terracelike Piazza Matteotti, with its cavernlike bars.

Marciana Marina ★   In western Elba on the north coast 20km (12 miles) from Portoferraio, this small town is the island's oldest settlement. It is also one of the island's prettiest villages. Dating from Roman times, it was fortified in the 12th century by its Pisan rulers. High on a hill, it overlooks a deep valley studded with olive and fig trees as well as lush vineyards.

You can wander for 2 hours through its small squares shaded by trees, climbing the step-stone streets that are stacked like pancakes atop one another.

For your culture fix, pop into the **Communal Archeologic Museum,** Via del Pretorio (© **0565-901215**), which is divided into four sections, beginning with the prehistoric and Etruscan period on the island and continuing through the Roman era with many dozens of artifacts. Charging 2€ for admission, the museum is open in May to September Friday and Saturday and Monday to Wednesday 9am to 1pm and 4 to 7:30pm; Sunday 9am to 1pm. Closed Thursday.

Marciana Marina.

Where to Stay

Visitors without cars may want to lodge directly in Portoferraio. But in the summer, the best resort hotels, those closer to better beaches, are in the outskirts of town at Picchiaie, 7.5km (4½ miles) to the southeast; at Biodola, 9km (5½ miles) to the west; and at Ottone, 11km (6¾ miles) to the southeast.

Acquamarina   In a residential area about a 10-minute walk from the center, this is the best hotel within the town itself. It fronts the gulf and has direct access to a sandy beach below. The hotel is no great style setter, but it offers comfortably furnished and spacious bedrooms, the best of which have a balcony or terrace with a view of the sea. The Mediterranean-style building in pastel colors rises three floors.

Località Padulella Ovest, 57037 Portoferraio. ⓒ/fax **0565-914057.** www.villaombrosa.it. 36 units. 42€–51€ per person double. Rates include buffet breakfast. AE, DC, MC, V. Free parking. Closed Nov to mid-Mar. **Amenities:** Bar; babysitting; room service. *In room:* A/C, TV, hair dryer, minibar.

Biodola ★   The Hermitage (see below) nearby is a far better resort, but Biodola is a worthy competitor. Biodola Bay is the most exclusive yacht-filled body of water on Elba. Both the Hermitage and Biodola lie 8km (5 miles) from Portoferraio. The hotel also opens onto one of the best beaches of Elba, and is surrounded by well-landscaped gardens. Its on-site sporting facilities are among the best on Elba. Bedrooms are midsize and furnished in a standard but tasteful Mediterranean beach style—nothing special, but cozy and comfortable nonetheless. The restaurant and bar on the beach is one of its major attractions.

Località Biodola, 57037 Portoferraio. ⓒ **0565-974812.** Fax 0565-969852. www.biodola.it. 100€– 233€ per person double; 182€–328€ per person suite. Rates include half board. AE, DC, MC, V. Free parking. Closed Nov–Mar. **Amenities:** Restaurant; bar; babysitting; 6-hole golf course; 2 outdoor freshwater pools; room service; 8 outdoor tennis courts; Wi-Fi (free, in lobby). *In room:* A/C, TV, hair dryer, minibar.

Hermitage ★★   Relais delle Picchiaie is more intimate, inviting, and tranquil, but the Hermitage is the highest-rated hotel on the island and the most luxurious if you're seeking a big resort. It is the grande dame of resorts, having opened in the 1950s, but it's made many improvements in the last half-century and has stayed abreast of the times. Overlooking a bay—the so-called "Gold Coast" of Elba—the hotel lies only a few steps from the sea and opens onto its own private beach. It's surrounded by landscaped gardens filled with such growth as holm oaks or strawberry trees. There are 32 rooms in the main building, but we infinitely prefer one of the luxurious villas with balconies set in a private park overlooking the sea. Although charmingly furnished in a Mediterranean resort style, the bedrooms are only midsize, though each is comfortable and tasteful.

Località Biodola, 57037 Portoferraio. ☎ **0565-9740.** Fax 0565-969984. www.hotelhermitage.it. 130 units. 122€–325€ per person double; 250€–535€ per person suite. Rates include half board. AE, DC, MC, V. Free parking. Closed Nov–Mar. **Amenities:** 3 restaurants; 3 bars; babysitting; children's center; exercise room; 6-hole golf course; 3 outdoor seawater pools; room service; spa; 9 outdoor tennis courts; watersports equipment/rentals. *In room:* A/C, TV, hair dryer, minibar.

Relais delle Picchiaie ★★★ This is the ultimate romantic getaway on the island and our favorite lodging, though admittedly it's not as grand as the Hermitage nearby. Small and intimate, it's a hotel of charm and grace. The Relais was a great house in the 19th century, around which the modern hotel complex has risen. The hotel stands on top of a landscaped hill in a setting of pine trees and oaks, a position that opens onto panoramic views in all directions. It is the most tranquil oasis on island, surrounded by oleander, geraniums, and lavender. The midsize rooms are the best decorated on the island, with sleek, contemporary Italian furnishings and fabrics.

Località Picchiale, 57037 Portoferraio. ☎ **0565-933110.** Fax 0565-933186. www.relaisdelle picchiaie.it. 49 units. 95€–220€ per person double; 145€–350€ per person suite. Rates include half board. AE, DC, MC, V. Free parking. Closed Oct 4–Apr 30. **Amenities:** Restaurant; bar; bikes; exercise room; outdoor freshwater pool; room service; spa; outdoor tennis court (lit). *In room:* A/C, TV, hair dryer, minibar, Wi-Fi (free).

Villa Ombrosa ☺ Acquamarina has a slight edge in style, service, and food, but Villa Ombrosa is the second-best choice if you're seeking a room in Portoferraio itself. The villa also has the advantage of being open all year. Located close to the sea and the center of town, the villa is only a short walk from Le Ghiaie beach. Most of the bedrooms open onto balconies with a sea view. The midsize bedrooms are modern, bright, and airy, though furnished in a sort of standard model style. Families often check in here because some rooms can be connected through a communicating door. Hopefully you'll be here when group bookings don't dominate.

Via Alcide de Gasperi 9, 57037 Portoferraio. ☎ **0565-914363.** Fax 0565-915672. www.villa ombrosa.it. 38 units. 80€–300€ double. Rates include half board. AE, DC, MC, V. Free parking. **Amenities:** Restaurant; bar; babysitting; room service. *In room:* A/C, TV, hair dryer, Wi-Fi (2€ per hr.).

Villa Ottone ★★ 🎁 Set in a beautiful park on the sea, this hotel grew from the core of a 19th-century villa owned by Conti Toscanelli. East of the bay of Portoferraio, it is an escapist's retreat, far removed from the tourist bustle. Although all the furnishings don't live up to the grandeur of the setting, some of the public rooms have painted ceilings and frescoes. The hotel was greatly expanded in the 1970s to add more rooms, and many of these newer units have been stylishly furnished with wicker or antique reproductions. Bedrooms in the more modern rooms open onto small balconies with a view of the sea. If you're on a honeymoon seeking an escape, ask for one of the attic bedrooms, which are romantically furnished under beamed ceilings.

Località Ottone, 57037 Portoferraio. ✆ **0565-933042.** Fax 0565-933257. www.villaottone.com. 80 units. 130€–345€ per person double; 185€–650€ per person suite. Rates include half board. AE, DC, MC, V. Free parking. Closed Oct 9–May 13. **Amenities:** 3 restaurants; 3 bars; babysitting; exercise room; outdoor freshwater pool; room service; spa; outdoor tennis court; Wi-Fi (free, in lobby). *In room:* A/C, TV, hair dryer, minibar.

Where to Dine

Da Lido ELBAN/SEAFOOD   In the center of Portoferraio, this is a rustic, family-run restaurant. The cooks focus on the catch of the day, particularly crustaceans, and prepare homemade pastas and fresh, seasonal vegetables. The fish soup is one of the best in town, and the winning pasta dish is *straccetti all'astice* (with lobster). Another fish specialty is *stoccafisso alla riese* (stockfish prepared with anchovies, capers, onions, peppers, and olives), everything stewed in a kettle. The dessert specialty is an island favorite—*schiaccia briaca* (a cake made with walnuts, raisins, hazelnuts, and pine nuts mixed with Aleatico, Elba's most famous wine).

Salita del Falcone 2. ✆ **0565-914650.** www.ristorantelido.org. Reservations recommended. Main courses 12€–24€. AE, DC, MC, V. Daily 12:30–2:30pm and 7:30–10:30pm. Closed mid-Dec to mid-Feb.

La Barca SEAFOOD/ELBAN   Locals rub elbows and lift forks with visitors in this simple, small *trattoria.* At "The Boat," you can eat outside in fair weather, an awning shading you from the burning sun. You can pick your own dinner from the catch of the day. You pay by the pound (prices vary daily), and tell the chef how you want it cooked—grilled, baked, or fried. Fish appears in other specialties too, including a baked codfish with chickpeas, and black rice studded with seafood. Pastas are also a temptation, including spaghetti with dried tuna eggs, and *gnocchi all'Elbana,* a local potato dumpling pasta with a savory tomato sauce and pesto.

Via Guerrazzi 60–62. ✆ **0565-918036.** Reservations recommended. Main courses 12€–26€. AE, DC, MC, V. Sept–Jan and Mar–June Mon–Sat 12:30–2:30pm and 7:15–10:30pm; July–Aug daily noon–2:30pm and 7pm–midnight. Closed mid-Jan to mid-Feb.

Stella Marina ELBAN/SEAFOOD   Marina's decor, wine *carte,* and service give it the slight edge over Da Lido and La Barca as the best restaurant in town. Especially desirable in summer are awning-shaded tables outside. Inside you can peruse the menu against the backdrop of a marine decor. The fish is invariably very fresh, and the chefs consistently turn out a reliable cuisine. Start, perhaps, with *crudo di pesce,* which is sliced raw fish—the Elban version of sushi. The risotto with lobster is the best on the island, and care goes into the succulent homemade pastas such as *paccheri* with a capon ragout. A classic favorite, and worthy of praise, is baked sea bass with fresh tomatoes and black olives. Only the lobster dishes have a high price tag; most main courses are moderately priced.

Vittorio Emanuele II 2. ✆ **0565-915983.** www.ristorantestellamarina.com. Reservations recommended. Main courses 8€–50€. AE, DC, MC, V. July–Aug Tues–Sat noon–2:30pm, Mon–Sat 7–11:30pm; Sept–June Tues–Sun noon–2:30pm and 7–10:30pm. Closed 2 weeks in Aug and 2 weeks in Feb.

GUBBIO ★★

40km (25 miles) NE of Perugia, 217km (135 miles) N of Rome, 92km (57 miles) SE of Arezzo, 55km (34 miles) N of Assisi

Gubbio is one of the best-preserved medieval towns in Italy. It has modern apartments and stores on its outskirts, but once you press through that, you feel like you're back in the Middle Ages. The best-known streets of its medieval core are **Via XX Settembre, Via dei Consoli, Via Galeotti,** and **Via Baldassini.** All these are in the old town (Città Vecchia), set against the slopes of Monte Ingino.

Because Gubbio is off the beaten track (near Umbria's border with The Marches), it remains a fairly sleepy backwater today except for the intrepid shoppers who drive here to shop for ceramics (see "Exploring the Old Town," below). Gubbio is almost as well known for ceramics as is Deruta. The last time Gubbio entered the history books was in 1944, when 40 hostages were murdered by the Nazis. Today, the central **Piazza dei Quaranta Martiri** is named for and honors those victims.

Essentials

GETTING THERE   Gubbio doesn't have a rail station, so **train** passengers headed for Gubbio from other parts of Italy get off at Fossato di Vico, 19km (12 miles) away, and then transfer to one of the frequent buses that make the short trip on to Gubbio. One-way bus transfers to Gubbio from Fossato di Vico cost 6€.

APM (🕻 **800-512141;** www.apmperugia.it) runs 17 buses a day from Perugia to Gubbio. Trip time is about 65 minutes, and a one-way ticket costs 6.50€. Buses arrive and depart from Piazza 40 Martiri (no phone), in the heart of town.

If you have a **car** and are coming from Rome, follow A1 to Orte and then take S3 north 142km (88 miles) to its intersection with S298 at Scheggia. Go southwest on S298 for 13km (8 miles) to Gubbio. From Florence, take A1 south to Orte and then follow the directions above. From Perugia, this turnoff is 40km (25 miles) northeast on the S298.

VISITOR INFORMATION   The **tourist office,** on Via Repubblica 15 (🕻 **075-9220693**), is open from October to February Monday to Friday 8:30am to 2pm and 3 to 6pm, and Saturday 9am to 1pm and 3 to 6pm; March to September hours are Monday to Friday 8:30am to 2pm and 3:30 to 6:30pm, and Saturday 9am to 1pm and 3:30 to 6:30pm. Year-round, it's open Sunday 9:30am to 12:30pm and 3 to 6pm.

SPECIAL EVENTS   The biggest annual bash is the **Corso dei Ceri ★** on May 15, one of Italy's top traditional festivals. It starts out with solemn ceremonies in the Piazza Grande in the morning and then turns into a wild free-for-all as teams compete in races with giant candles, ringing bells, and vases hurled into the crowds to shatter, all culminating in a giant seafood banquet and a religious procession.

The last Sunday in May brings the **Palio della Balestra,** a traditional crossbow competition accompanied by an evening procession through the streets with lots of colorful medieval costumes.

The **Gubbio Festival** brings acclaimed international performers to town for 3 weeks of performances in late July; the town also stages free classical concerts in the ruins of the Roman theater.

Exploring the Old Town

If the weather is right, you can take a cable car up to **Monte Ingino** (🕻 **075-9273881**), at a height of 820m (2,690 ft.), for a panoramic view of the area. A round-trip ticket costs 5€. Call ahead for scheduling because operating hours vary dramatically from month to month.

In Gubbio, you can set about exploring a town that knew its golden age in the 1300s. Begin at **Piazza Grande,** the most important square. Here you can

Gubbio.

visit the Gothic **Palazzo dei Consoli ★** (© **075-9274298**), housing the famed bronze *tavole eugubine,* a series of tablets as old as Christianity that were discovered in the 15th century. The tablets contain writing in the mysterious Umbrian language. The museum has a display of antiques from the Middle Ages and a collection of not-very-worthwhile paintings. It's open daily April to October from 10am to 1pm and 3 to 6pm, and November to March from 10am to 1pm and 2 to 5pm. Admission is 5€.

The other major sight is the **Ducal Palace (Palazzo Ducale) ★**, Via Ducale (© **075-9275872**), built for Federico of Montefeltro. It's open Tuesday to Sunday 8:30am to 7:30pm; admission is 5€ (closed Dec 25 and Jan 1).

After visiting the palace, you can go inside **Il Duomo,** Via Ducale (© **075-9272138**), across the way. The cathedral is a relatively unadorned pink Gothic building with some stained-glass windows from the 12th century. It has a single nave. Inside, several arches support the ceiling. Of particular interest is the wood cross above the altar, an exquisite example of the Umbrian school of the 13th century. It's open daily from 9am to 12:30pm and 3:30 to 8:30pm, and admission is free.

Shopping is the major reason many visitors flock here. Gubbio's fame as a ceramics center had its beginnings in the 14th century. In the 1500s, the industry rose to the height of its fame. Sometime during this period, Mastro Giorgio pioneered a particularly intense iridescent ruby red that awed his competitors. Today, pottery workshops are found all over town, with beautiful flowery plates lining the walls of shop doorways. You can't miss them.

Two of the best outlets are in the town center: **Ceramiche Rampini ★**, at Via Leonardo da Vinci 94 (© **075-9272963;** www.rampiniceramiche.com), where you can visit the workshop, and the Rampini store, at Via dei Consoli 52 (© **075-9274408**). Its largest competitor, **Il Mastro Giorgio ★**, Piazza della Signoria 3 (© **075-9271574**), opens its factory at Via Tifernate 10 (© **075-9273616**), about 1km (½ mile) from the center, to visitors who phone in advance.

Gubbio is known for more than pots and vases: Its replicas of medieval crossbows *(balestre)* are prized as children's toys and macho decorative ornaments by aficionados of such things. If you want to add a touch of medieval authenticity to your den or office, head for **Medioevo,** Ponte d'Assi

(📞 **075-9272596**). Your souvenir will cost from 13€ for a cheap version to as much as 75€ for something much more substantial.

Where to Stay

Palace Hotel Bosone ★   This hotel once housed Dante Alighieri when it was owned by a patrician Gubbian family, the Bosone clan. Set at the meeting point of a flight of stone steps and a narrow street in the upper regions of town, it was built in the 1300s, enlarged during the Renaissance, and converted from a private home into a hotel in 1974. Ever since, it has been welcoming guests into its generally spacious stone-trimmed rooms; the Renaissance suites boast stucco ceilings and 17th-century frescoes.

Via XX Settembre 22, 06024 Gubbio. 📞 **075-9220688.** Fax 075-9220552. www.hotelbosone. com. 30 units (shower only). 65€–150€ double; 169€–240€ suite. Rates include buffet breakfast. AE, DC, MC, V. Free self-parking nearby. Closed Jan 24–Mar 1. **Amenities:** Restaurant; bar; babysitting; bikes; room service. *In room:* A/C, TV, hair dryer, minibar, Wi-Fi (free).

Park Hotel ai Cappuccini ★★   This is the leading hotel of Gubbio, with the best facilities and the finest service in the area. The hotel grew from the ruins of a Capuchin monastery—hence, its name. The entire structure has been reconstructed and renovated or often rebuilt in most cases. Set in the middle of a park, the hotel is still surrounded by the ancient garden of the friars. The bedrooms, ranging from midsize to spacious, have all the modern amenities and are the best accessorized in town. The on-site restaurant serves a superb international and regional cuisine.

Via Tifernate 06024. 📞 **075-9234.** Fax 075-9220323. www.parkhotelaicappuccini.it. 93 units. 240€–310€ double; from 350€ suite. Rates include buffet breakfast. AE, DC, MC, V. Free parking. **Amenities:** Restaurant; bar; babysitting; exercise room; indoor heated pool; room service; spa; outdoor tennis court (lit). *In room:* A/C, TV, hair dryer, minibar, Wi-Fi (4€ per hr.).

Relais Ducale ★★   This modern hotel occupies the guest quarters of the dukes of Urbino, between the Palazzo Ducale and Piazza Grande. Hanging gardens shaded by palms and scented by jasmine offer views over the city's main square, its *palazzi*, and a panorama. The elegant, spacious guest rooms boast parquet floors, damask bedspreads and curtains, and the occasional historical touch (stone vaulted ceilings) or modern luxury (heated towel racks and Jacuzzis in some rooms). Rooms on the upper floors have terrific views.

Via Galeotti 19, 06024 Gubbio. 📞 **075-9220157.** Fax 075-9220159. www.relaisducale.com. 31 units (shower only). 65€–180€ double; 125€–275€ suite. Rates include buffet breakfast. AE, DC, MC, V. **Amenities:** Restaurant (w/outdoor dining on the main town square); bar; babysitting; room service; Wi-Fi (free, in lobby). *In room:* A/C, TV, hair dryer, minibar.

San Marco 🍴   Its unpromising location on the busiest corner in town is the San Marco's only drawback. Otherwise, this is a worthwhile hotel near a municipal parking lot. Built of stone in stages between 1300 and the 1700s, it contains an arbor-covered terrace and traditionally furnished guest rooms that are comfortable and well maintained, with small bathrooms.

Via Perugina 5, 06024 Gubbio. 📞 **075-9220234.** Fax 075-9273716. www.hotelsanmarcogubbio. com. 63 units (about half with shower only). 80€–110€ double. Rates include buffet breakfast. AE, DC, MC, V. Parking 15€. **Amenities:** Restaurant; bar; room service; Wi-Fi (free, in lobby). *In room:* A/C, TV, hair dryer.

Villa Montegranelli Hotel ★   The area's most tranquil retreat isn't in Gubbio—it's in this restored 18th-century manor house with a distant view of the town. The guest rooms are beautifully furnished, often with antiques, and the bathrooms are modern. The public rooms have been restored in keeping with their original architecture of wood ceilings and stone walls. The staff is among the most helpful and efficient in the area, providing such thoughtful extras as a basket of fresh fruit in your room every day. Even if you can't stay here, consider calling ahead and visiting its restaurant for an excellent meal.

Loc. Monteluiano, 06024 Gubbio (3km/2 miles southwest of Gubbio). ✆ **075-9220185.** Fax 075-9273372. www.hotelvillamontegranelli.it. 21 units. 90€–120€ double; 140€–170€ suite. Rates include buffet breakfast. AE, DC, MC, V. Free parking. **Amenities:** Restaurant; bar; babysitting; room service; Wi-Fi (free). *In room:* A/C, TV, hair dryer, minibar.

Where to Dine

You can also dine at the Hotel Relais Ducale's refined **Caffè Ducale** or at the restaurant of the **Villa Montegranelli** (see above).

Federico de Montefeltro ITALIAN/UMBRIAN   Named after the feudal lord who built the ducal palace, this restaurant stands beside steeply inclined flagstones in the oldest part of the city. Inside is a pair of tavern-style dining rooms ringed with exposed stone and pinewood planking. Many of the specialties are based on ancient regional recipes, although the selection of tasty antipasti covers the traditions of most of the Italian peninsula. A classic dish is grilled beef in apple balsamic vinegar. Other tempting items include platters garnished with truffles, roast suckling pig, several types of polenta, and a homemade pasta in a creamy truffle sauce. Fresh fish is offered on Friday. A local version of unleavened bread fried in oil is part of the meal.

Via della Repubblica 35. ✆ **075-9273949.** www.federicodamontefeltro.it. Reservations recommended. Main courses 8€–15€. AE, DC, MC, V. Fri–Wed noon–2:30pm and 7–10:30pm.

Taverna del Lupo ★ ITALIAN/UMBRIAN   This is the most authentically medieval restaurant in Gubbio. Built in the 1200s, with unusual rows of tiles, it contains ceilings supported by barrel vaults and ribbing of solid stone, from which hang iron chandeliers. For such a relatively modest place, the menu is sophisticated and filled with the rich bounty from this part of Italy, each dish deftly prepared by a talented staff. Choose from a guinea fowl with juniper, supreme of pheasant, rich minestrones, or many of the pork, veal, and beef dishes that are distinctly Tuscan. A local favorite that's addictive is gnocchi filled with cheese and porcini mushrooms.

Via Giovanni Ansidei 21. ✆ **075-9274368.** www.tavernadellupo.it. Reservations recommended. Main courses 10€–26€. AE, DC, MC, V. Sept–June Tues–Sun noon–3pm and 7pm–midnight; July–Aug daily noon–3pm and 7pm–midnight.

PERUGIA ★★

81km (50 miles) SE of Arezzo, 188km (117 miles) N of Rome, 155km (96 miles) SE of Florence

Perugia was one of a dozen major cities in the mysterious Etruscan civilization, and here you can peel away the epochs. One of the town gates is called the **Arco di Augusto (Arch of Augustus).** The loggia spanning the arch dates from the

Renaissance, but the central part is Roman. Builders from both periods used the Etruscan foundation, which was the work of architects who laid stones to last.

Today the city, home to luscious Perugina chocolate, is the capital of Umbria. It has retained much of its Gothic and Renaissance charm, although it has been plagued with wars and swept up in disastrous events. The city is home to universities and art academies, and it attracts a young, vibrant crowd—some of whom can be seen in one of the zillions of local bars, pizzerias, music shops, or cafes enjoying the famous chocolate *baci* (kisses). To capture the essence of the Umbrian city, you must head for **Piazza IV Novembre** in the heart of Perugia. During the day, the square is overrun, so try to go late at night when the old town is sleeping. That's when the ghosts come out to play.

Essentials

GETTING THERE Perugia has **rail** links with Rome and Florence, but connections can be awkward. Usually, two trains per day from Rome connect in Foligno, where, if you miss a train, you might face a wait of an hour or more. If possible, try to get one of the infrequent direct trains that take 3 hours or an ES (Eurostar train) that cuts the trip to 2 hours. A one-way ticket from Rome costs 12€ to 35€. Most trains from Florence are direct. A one-way fare ranges from 11€ to 21€. For information and schedules, call ☎ **892021.** The train station is away from the main historic center of town, at Piazza Vittorio Veneto. Bus no. G runs to Piazza Italia, which is as close as you can get to the center.

A daily **bus** arrives in Perugia, pulling into Piazza Partigiani, a short walk from the city's historic core. One-way fares from Rome (from Stazione Tiburtina) are 17€, and the trip takes 2½ hours. The several buses that pull into Perugia from Florence charge 12€ each way for a trip that takes 2 hours. For information and schedules, call the bus company, **Sulga,** at ☎ **800-099661,** www.sulga.it. Buses that operate exclusively in Perugia use Piazza Italia as their central base, departing and arriving there.

If you have a **car** and are coming from either Rome or Florence, Autostrada del Sole (A1) takes you to the cutoff east to Perugia. Just follow the signs. From Siena, S73 winds its way to Perugia and connects with the autostrada. If you arrive by car, you can drive to your hotel to unload your baggage; after that, you'll be directed to a parking lot on the outskirts.

VISITOR INFORMATION The **tourist office,** at Piazza Matteotti 18 (☎ **075-5736458**), is open Monday to Saturday 8:30am to 6:30pm, and Sunday 8:30am to 1:30pm.

SPECIAL EVENTS The hottest time to visit Perugia is during Italy's foremost jazz festival, **Umbria Jazz ★★**, in mid-July. Jazz heavies such as Sonny Rollins and Keith Jarrett have performed here. For tickets and schedules, call ☎ **075-5732432** (www.umbriajazz.com). Tickets cost 13€ to 130€.

The weeklong **Eurochocolate Festival ★** is held annually from mid- to late October in Perugia. You can witness a chocolate-carving contest, when the scraps from the massive blocks are yours for the sampling and entire multiple-course menus are created around the chocolate theme. Half-day lessons from visiting chefs are also available. For details, call the tourist office (see above).

Exploring the City

The central **Piazza IV Novembre ★★** is one of the most beautiful squares in Italy. In the heart of the piazza is the **Grand Fountain (Fontana Maggiore) ★★**, built

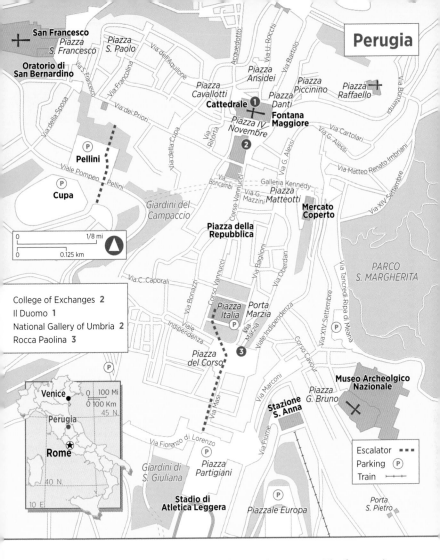

Perugia

San Francesco
Piazza S. Francesco
Piazza S. Paolo
Piazza S. Paolo
Oratorio di San Bernardino
Piazza Ansidei
Piazza Cavallotti
Piazza Piccinino
Piazza Raffaello
Cattedrale ❶
Piazza Danti
Fontana Maggiore
Piazza IV Novembre
Pellini ⓟ
College of Exchanges ❷
Cupa ⓟ
Giardini del Campaccio
Galleria Kennedy
Piazza Matteotti
Mercato Coperto
Piazza della Repubblica
PARCO S. MARGHERITA
0   1/8 mi
0   0.125 km

College of Exchanges **2**
Il Duomo **1**
National Gallery of Umbria **2**
Rocca Paolina **3**

Piazza Italia
Porta Marzia ⓟ
❸
Piazza del Corso
ⓟ
Museo Archeolgico Nazionale
Piazza G. Bruno
Stazione S. Anna

Venice •
0   100 Mi
0   100 Km
45° N.
Perugia •
Rome ★
40° N.
10° E

Piazza Partigiani
Giardini di S. Giuliana
Stadio di Atletica Leggera
Piazzale Europa
Porta S. Pietro

Escalator ▪▪▪
Parking ⓟ
Train ┣━━━┫

in the late 1270s by a local architect, a monk named Bevignate. The fountain's artistic triumph stems from the sculptural work by Nicola Pisano and his son, Giovanni. Along the lower basin is statuary symbolizing the arts and sciences, Aesop's fables, the months of the year, the signs of the zodiac, and scenes from the Old Testament and Roman history. On the upper basin (mostly the work of Giovanni) is allegorical sculpture, including a figure that represents Perugia, as well as sculptures of saints, biblical characters, and even 13th-century local officials. The fountain emerged spectacularly from a major restoration in 1999, gleaming white as new.

Most of the other major attractions either open onto Piazza IV Novembre or lie only a short distance away.

An escalator will take you from the older part of Perugia at the top of the hill and the upper slopes to the lower city. During construction, the old **Rocca Paolina ★** fortress, Via Marzia, was rediscovered, along with buried streets. The fortress had been covered over to make the gardens and viewing area at the end of Corso Vannucci in the last century. The old streets and street names have been cleaned up, and the area is well lighted, with an old wall exposed and modern sculpture added. The fortress was built in the 1500s by Sangallo. The Etruscan gate, **Porta Marzia,** is buried in the old city walls and can be viewed from Via Baglioni Sotterranea. This street lies in the fortress and is lined with houses, some from the 1400s. The escalator to the Rocca operates daily from 6am to 1am; the Rocca is open daily from 8am to 7pm.

The Arco di Augusto.

College of Exchanges (Collegio del Cambio) ★

During the Middle Ages, this section of the sprawling Palazzo dei Priori was conceived as a precursor of today's commodities exchanges, where grains, cloth, foodstuffs, gold, silver, and currencies were exchanged by the savvy merchants of Perugia. Today, its artistic and architectural appeal is largely centered on the **Hall of the Audience (Sala dell'Udienza) ★★**, a meeting room whose frescoes were painted by Perugino and his assistants, one of whom was a 17-year-old Raphael.

On the ceiling, Perugino represented the planets allegorically. The Renaissance master peopled his frescoes with the Virtues, sibyls, and such biblical figures as Solomon. But his masterpiece is his own countenance. It seems rather ironic that the oft-sentimental Perugino could be realistic (at least for once), even depicting his chubby face and double chins resting under a red cap. Another room of interest is the **Chapel of S. J. Battista (Cappella di S. J. Battista),** which contains many frescoes painted by a pupil of Perugino, G. Nicola di Paolo.

Corso Vannucci 25, street level of the Palazzo dei Priori (see National Gallery, below). ✆ **075-5728599.** www.collegiodelcambio.it. Admission 4.50€. Mar–Oct daily 9am–12:30pm and 2:30–5:30pm; Nov–Feb Tues–Fri 9am–2pm, Sat 9am–12:30pm. Closed New Year's Day, May Day, and Christmas.

Il Duomo (Cathedral of San Lorenzo) ★

The basilica was built in the Gothic style and dates from the 14th and 15th centuries. Its exterior is rather raw looking, as if the builders had suddenly been called away and never returned. In the **Cappella di San Bernardino,** you'll find *Descent from the Cross,* by Frederico Barocchio. In the **Cappella del Sacramento** hangs Luca Signorelli's *Madonna,* an altarpiece created in 1484. Signorelli was a pupil of della Francesca.

Piazza IV Novembre. ✆ **075-5723832.** Free admission. Church and *cappella* daily 7am–12:30pm and 4–6:45pm.

National Gallery of Umbria (Galleria Nazionale dell'Umbria) ★★

Opposite Il Duomo is the Palace of the Priors (Palazzo dei Priori), one of the finest secular buildings in Italy, dating from the 13th century and containing both the National Gallery and the Collegio del Cambio (see above). The facade holds bronze copies of the 13th-century griffin (symbol of Perugia) and the Guelph (papal) lion, both holding the massive chains once used to close the city gates of Siena. These chains were looted from Siena when Perugia scored a military victory over the town in 1358. You can walk up the stairway (the Vaccara) to the pulpit. By all means, explore the interior, especially the vaulted *Sala dei Notari,* frescoed with stories of the Old Testament and from Aesop.

On the *palazzo's* second and third floors is the **National Gallery of Umbria,** containing the most comprehensive collection of Umbrian art from the 13th to 19th centuries. Among the earliest paintings of interest (room 2) is a *Virgin and Child* (1304), by Duccio di Buoninsegna, the first important master of the Sienese school. A *Madonna and Child* (1405), by Gentile da Fabriano, one of the gems of the collection, is in room 6. In room 11, you'll see a masterpiece by Piero della Francesca, the *Polyptych of Sant'Antonio,* an altarpiece from the mid–15th century. Guarded by a medley of saints, the Virgin is enthroned in a classical setting.

No one is exactly sure who painted the eight panels in room 15. Dating from 1473, the *Miracles of St. Bernardino of Siena* was created in a workshop of the time. Both Perugino and Francesco di Giorgio Martini might have worked on these panels.

In room 15 are works of native son Perugino, among them his *Adoration of the Magi,* from 1475. Perugino was the master of Raphael. He was often accused of sentimentality, and today Perugino doesn't enjoy the popularity that he did at the peak of his career. However, he remains a key Renaissance painter, noted for his landscapes, as exemplified by the 1517 *Transfiguration* in room 23. You'll also find art by Pinturicchio, who studied under Perugino and whose most notable work was the library of Siena's Duomo.

3rd floor of the Palazzo dei Priori, Corso Vannucci 19. ✆ **075-5741410.** www.gallerianazionaleumbria.it. Admission 6.50€. Tues–Sun 8:30am–7:30pm. Bus: 4, 6, or 7.

Where to Stay

Brufani Palace ★ This deluxe hotel is Perugia's finest choice. At the top of the city, part of this deluxe hotel was built by Giocomo Brufani in 1884 on the ruins of the ancient Rocca Paolina. This site, known to the ancient Romans, later served as a papal address. The Brufani combined with the much larger Palace Hotel Bellavista to form the hotel you see today. The Bellavista was built in the late 1800s as a home for a prominent English family, the Collinses, who eventually married into the aristocratic Brufanis. Now there's a wedding again with the marriage of the two structures. Many of the guest rooms open onto wonderful views of the countryside. Some of the grander rooms have antiques and frescoed ceilings; all are elegant and filled with modern

The escalator from the lower part of Perugia to the older section of the city.

luxuries. The best accommodations are on the second and third floors. Avoid cramped cell nos. 129 and 229, however.

Piazza Italia 12, 06121 Perugia. ℰ **075-5732541.** Fax 075-5720210. www.brufanipalace.com. 94 units. 125€–385€ double; 400€–980€ suite. AE, MC, V. Parking 31€. **Amenities:** Restaurant; bar; babysitting; exercise room; Jacuzzi; indoor heated pool; room service; sauna. *In room:* A/C, TV, hair dryer, minibar, Wi-Fi (6€ per hr.).

Fortuna Perugia 🖉 Here's a chance to stay at a government-rated four-star hotel in the heart of town that in 1996 deliberately "downgraded" itself to three-star status and lowered its prices. It dates from the 13th century but has been extensively reconstructed over the years. Today, arched leaded-glass doors lead to an interior of hardwood floors and tasteful art. The guest rooms have sleek contemporary styling (often blond woods and flamboyant fabrics) and are filled with modern amenities. Even better than the rooms are the views, some of which might have inspired Perugino himself. The hotel has a rooftop terrace opening onto the tile roofs of the town and the Umbrian landscape. When the weather is good, guests have their cappuccinos and croissants here.

Via Bonazzi 19, 06123 Perugia. ℰ **075-5722845.** Fax 075-5735040. www.hotelfortunaperugia. com. 52 units. 99€–147€ per person double; 134€–173€ per person triple. AE, DC, MC, V. Parking 20€ nearby. **Amenities:** Bar; babysitting; Internet (free, in lobby); room service. *In room:* A/C, TV, hair dryer, minibar.

Hotel La Rosetta From humble beginnings, this is now one of Perugia's leading inns. Since this Perugian landmark opened in 1927, it has expanded from a seven-room *pensione* to a labyrinthine complex (it's the big hangout for the musicians in town for the jazz festival). Guest rooms vary from cramped to palatial, with curving Empire bed frames in some and modular units in others. With its frescoed ceiling, suite no. 55 has been declared a national treasure. (The bullet holes that papal mercenaries shot into the ceiling in 1848 have been artfully preserved.) Each unit is peaceful, clean, and comfortable, though the bathrooms could be better outfitted.

Piazza Italia 19, 06121 Perugia. ℰ/fax **075-5720841.** 90 units. 60€–84€ per person double. Rates include buffet breakfast. AE, DC, MC, V. Parking 20€. **Amenities:** Restaurant; bar; babysitting; room service. *In room:* A/C, TV, hair dryer, minibar.

Locanda della Posta ★ This time-honored inn enjoys the town's most central location, in the heart of Corso Vannucci, the main drag. Goethe and Hans Christian Andersen slept here—in fact, this used to be the only hotel in Perugia. It sits behind an ornate facade sculpted in the 1700s. The della Posta's views might not be grand, but it's nostalgic and inviting. The guest rooms are generally spacious, with fabric-covered walls, Art Nouveau floral prints, and sturdy wood furnishings.

Corso Vannucci 97, 06121 Perugia. ℰ **075-5728925.** Fax 075-5732562. www.locandadellaposta. com. 40 units. 150€–190€ double; 170€–230€ suite. Rates include buffet breakfast. AE, DC, MC, V. Parking 25€ in nearby garage. **Amenities:** Bar; babysitting; room service. *In room:* A/C, TV, hair dryer, minibar, Wi-Fi (free).

Sangallo Palace Hotel ★ Rivaled only by the Brufani, this palace in the historic zone is a contemporary classic, up-to-date and favored by local business travelers. A roomy interior and a lobby of marble columns and fine furnishings are immediately welcoming. The halls are lined with reproductions of the works of Perugino, and over each bed is a framed reproduction of a Perugino or

Pinturicchio. The guest rooms boast such luxuries as extrawide beds, and some open onto panoramic views of the countryside.

Via L. Masi 9, 06121 Perugia. © **075-5730202.** Fax 075-5730068. www.sangallo.it. 100 units (some with shower only). 89€–178€ double; 110€–222€ triple. Rates include buffet breakfast. AE, DC, MC, V. Parking nearby 15€. **Amenities:** Restaurant; bar; babysitting; exercise room; indoor heated pool; room service; Wi-Fi (2.50€ per hr., in lobby). *In room:* A/C, TV, hair dryer, minibar.

Where to Dine

Antica Trattoria San Lorenzo UMBRIAN This family-run spot is known for its fresh ingredients, culinary flair, and elegant presentation. The restaurant is in an antique building, whose interior is decorated in part with marble that came from the Duomo. In the canteen you can sample some 700 different labels of wine. Our favorite appetizer is filet of chicken with black truffles and porcini mushrooms. After that you might follow with pasta *mezza luna* ("half-moon" pasta tossed with duck in a tomato-and-bacon sauce) or ravioli stuffed with stockfish and chickpeas. The chef's grandest specialty is filet of suckling pig with wild prunes and a beer sauce. Many desserts make use of the famed chocolate of Perugia, and none are finer than the chocolate-and-hazelnut soufflé.

Piazza Danti 19A. © **075-5721956.** www.anticatrattoriasanlorenzo.com. Reservations recommended. Main courses 8€–28€; fixed-price menus 13€–20€. AE, DC, MC, V. Mon–Sat 12:30-3:30pm and 7:30–11:30pm.

Il Falchetto ★★ UMBRIAN/ITALIAN This restaurant, a short walk from Piazza Piccinino (where you can park), has flourished in this 19th-century building since 1941. The dining room in the rear has the most medieval ambience, with stone walls dating from the 1300s. In summer you might like a table outside; during Umbria Jazz, it's like having free seats to the concerts on Piazza IV Novembre. Many dishes adhere to traditional themes such as ravioli stuffed with mushrooms, served with a truffle sauce; or wild-boar goulash served with polenta. One special dish is *falchetti* (gnocchi with ricotta and spinach); another is filet of beef in a black-truffle sauce. The restaurant also serves some of the best Umbrian wines.

Via Bartolo 20. © **075-5731775.** www.ilfalchetto.it. Reservations recommended. Main courses 8€–20€. AE, DC, MC, V. Tues–Sun 12:30-3pm and 7:30-10:30pm.

La Taverna ★ UMBRIAN One of Umbria's most innovative restaurants, La Taverna occupies a medieval house and offers the best regional cuisine. Its entrance is at the bottom of one of the narrowest alleys in town, in the heart of the historic center. (Prominent signs indicate its position off Corso Vannucci.) Three dining rooms, filled with exposed masonry, oil paintings, and a polite staff, radiate from the high-ceilinged vestibule. The best menu choices include a tangy soup of fava beans and artichokes or else ravioli with black truffles, pine nuts, and Parmesan cheese. Yet another dish to try is filet of tuna cooked in a pepper crust. For something really local and good, order the Colfiorito lamb and grilled local pecorino cheese.

Via delle Streghe 8. © **075-5724128.** www.ristorantelataverna.com. Reservations recommended. Main courses 10€–25€. AE, MC, V. Tues–Sun 12:30-2:30pm and 7:30–11pm.

Osteria del Bartolo ★★ MEDITERRANEAN In the heart of the city, one of Perugia's finest restaurants lies a short stroll from the Maggiore Fountain. Chef Umberto Bava and his staff extend a hearty welcome to visitors and invite them to partake of refined cuisine. Whenever possible they use the produce of the region, turning out dishes rich in olive oil, fresh tomatoes, garden-fresh basil, fish, and an array of luscious vegetables. One of their daily soups might be studded with the rare and delicate Norcia black truffle of the region. Lamb appears baked in a pastry case with fresh herbs and served with potatoes seasoned with hazelnut oil. For dessert, delight in a dark Perugia chocolate mousse with a basil-flavored cream.

Via Bartolo 30. ℰ **075-5716027.** Reservations required. Main courses 8€–17€. MC, V. Thurs–Tues 7:30–11:30pm; Sun 12:30–3pm.

Osteria del Gambero ★★ SEAFOOD/UMBRIAN Behind the Duomo, Perugia's best restaurant is found in a palace from the 15th century in the historic core of Perugia. The decor is rustic with simple wooden furniture, but the taste sensations of chef/owner Guglielmo Gamberini are sublime. Patrons are visibly charmed by the creative cuisine, which is marked by a fearless freedom in choice of flavors and market-fresh products. All breads, pastas, and desserts are home-made. Start perhaps with veal liver pâté with spiced pears and pure chocolate. Main courses are likely to feature *tagliatelle* with wild mushrooms, broccoli, and bacon; or else wild-herb *tortelli* with pigeon breast and sautéed fresh sage. Among other delights are sea bass with prawns in a ginger sauce and loin of lamb confit baked in foil with a mustard-seed sauce. Among the better desserts is a chocolate-and-cardamom cake with coffee caramel and a mint sorbet.

Via Baldeschi 8A. ℰ **075-5735461.** www. osteriadelgambero.it. Reservations required. Main courses 13€–50€; fixed-price menus 30€–32€. MC, V. Tues–Sun 7–11pm; Sun 12:30–2:20pm. Closed June 15–30 and Jan 15–30.

Shopping

The most famous foodstuff in town comes from one of Italy's best-loved manufacturers of chocolates and bonbons, **Perugina** ★. Displays of the foil-wrapped chocolates crop up at tobacco shops, supermarkets, newspaper kiosks, and sometimes gas stations around the city. The selection includes *cioccolato al latte* (milk chocolate) and its darker counterpart, *cioccolato fondente*, both sold in everything from mouth-size morsels *(baci)* to romance-size decorative boxes. One always-reliable place to buy is from the factory itself, which offers tours to those who phone in advance. The **Fabbrica Nestlé Perugina** ★ (ℰ **075-52761;** www.nestle.it), 5km (3 miles) west of Perugia's historic

Perugia's ancient streets.

core, forms the centerpiece of the hamlet of San Sisto. It's open Monday to Friday 9am to 1pm and 2 to 5pm (Sat–Sun by arrangement). Admission is free. Call to book your visit.

Looking for ceramics and souvenirs that'll last longer than chocolate? Head for one of Perugia's most intriguing shops, **La Bottega del Vasaio,** Via Baglioni 32 (✆ **075-5723108;** www.labottegadelvasaio.com).

If you're searching for fashion, particularly the cashmere garments that are tailored and often designed in Perugia, consider a trip 6km (3¾ miles) south to the village of Ponte San Giovanni. One of the largest inventories of cashmere garments (coats, suits, dresses, and sweaters) for men and women is stockpiled at **Big Bertha,** Via Industria 19, Ponte San Giovanni (✆ **075-5997572**).

Perugia After Dark

Begin your evening by joining Italy's liveliest *passeggiata* (a promenade at dusk) along **Corso Vannucci,** a pedestrian strip running north to south. Everyone, especially the students, seems to stroll here. Many drop into one of the little cafes or enoteches for a drink. If you do a cafe hop or wine-bar crawl, you can sample as many as 150 wines from 60 Umbrian vineyards—if you can stay on your feet for that long!

One cafe outshines the rest: chandelier-lit **Sandri Pasticceria,** Corso Vannucci 32 (✆ **075-5724112;** www.pasticceriasandri.it), offering drinks, cakes, pastries, and sandwiches. You can also order full meals, including eggplant parmigiano and veal cutlet Milanese. It's another outlet for the city's famous chocolates.

If you've got a hankering to go dancing, the best bet within Perugia's town center is **Velvet Fashion Cafe,** Viale Roma 20 (✆ **075-5721321;** www.velvet fashioncafe.com), which attracts a relatively young (in their 20s) crowd that dances every night except Monday from 9pm to 3am. There's no cover charge, but someone will probably urge you to buy at least one drink before the night is over. Another competitor, and one more favored by night owls in their 30s and 40s, is **Disco Gradisca,** Via Montalcino 2C, Ponte Valleceppi (✆ **075-5928611;** www.gradisca.tv). It lies almost immediately adjacent to the Ponte Valleceppi exit off the SuperStradale (superhighway) E45, about 8km (5 miles) east of Perugia. Charging 18€ for entrance, which includes one free drink, it's open only Saturday 9pm to at least 5am.

ASSISI ★★★

177km (110 miles) N of Rome, 24km (15 miles) SE of Perugia

Ideally placed on the rise to Mount Subasio, watched over by the medieval Rocco Maggiore, the purple-fringed Umbrian hill town of Assisi retains a mystical air. The site of many a pilgrimage, Assisi is forever linked in legend with its native son, St. Francis. The gentle saint founded the Franciscan order and shares honors with St. Catherine of Siena as the patron saint of Italy. But he's remembered by many, even non-Christians, as a lover of nature (one legend relates how he preached to an audience of birds). Dante compared him to John the Baptist.

Socializing on the Corso Vannucci.

St. Francis put Assisi on the map, and making a pilgrimage here is one of the highlights of a visit to Umbria. Today, Italy's Catholic youth flock here for religious conferences, festivals, and reflection. But even without St. Francis, the hill town merits a visit for its sights and architecture. Tourists and pilgrims pack the town in summer, and at Easter or Christmas you're likely to be trampled underfoot. We've found it best and less crowded in spring or fall.

Essentials

GETTING THERE   Although there's no **rail station** in Assisi, the city lies within a 30-minute bus or taxi ride from the rail station in nearby Santa Maria degli Angeli. From Santa Maria degli Angeli, buses depart at 15-minute intervals for Piazza Matteotti in the heart of Assisi. One-way fares are 1€. If you're coming to Assisi from Perugia by train, expect to pay around 2.50€ one-way. If you're coming from Rome, expect to pay 9.50€ to 30€ each way, depending on the train. Rail fares between Florence and Assisi are about 12€ each way. For more information call ℂ **892021.**

Frequent **buses** connect Perugia with Assisi (run by APM; ℂ **075-5731707;** www.apmperugia.it). The trip takes 1 hour and costs 4€ one-way; a ticket costs 5€ if you buy it on board. One bus a day arrives from Rome (run by SULGA; ℂ **800-099661** in Italy; www.sulga.it); it takes about 3 hours and costs 21€ one-way. Two buses pull in from Florence (also run by SULGA), taking 2½ hours and costing 14€ one-way.

If you have a **car,** you can make the trip from Perugia in 30 minutes by taking S3 southwest. At the junction of S147, just follow the signs toward Assisi. But you'll have to park outside the town's core because those neighborhoods are usually closed to traffic. (***Note:*** The police officer guarding the entrance to the old town will usually let motorists drop off luggage at a hotel in the historic zone, with the understanding that you'll eventually park in a lot on the outskirts of town. Likewise, delivery vehicles are allowed to drop off supplies in the town's pedestrian zones daily from 10am–noon and 4–6pm.)

VISITOR INFORMATION   The **tourist office** at Piazza del Comune 10 (ℂ **075-8138680;** www.regioneumbria.eu) is open Monday to Saturday 8am to 2pm and 3 to 6pm and Sunday 9am to 1pm.

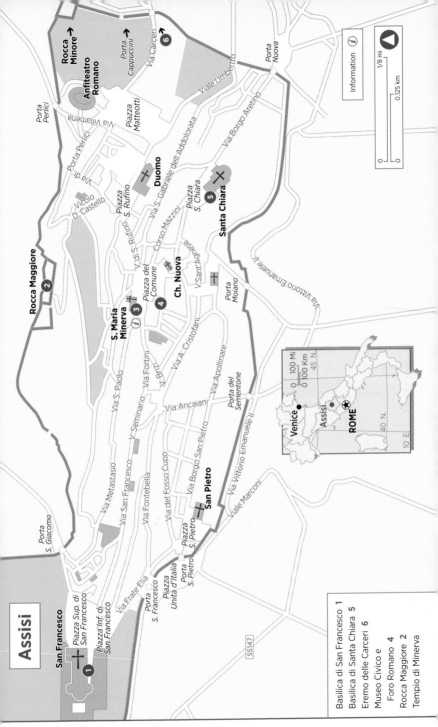

Assisi

San Francesco

Piazza Sup. di San Francesco

Piazza Inf. di San Francesco

Rocca Maggiore

Porta S. Giacomo

Via Frate Elia

Via S. Paolo

Via Metastasio

Via San Francesco

V. Seminario

Via Fortini

Porta S. Francesco

Piazza Unità d'Italia

Porta S. Pietro

San Pietro

Piazza S. Pietro

Via Fontebella

Via del Fosso Cupo

Via Borgo San Pietro

Via Ancaiani

Via A. Cristofani

Brizi

Via Apollinare

Porta del Sementone

Via Vittorio Emanuele II

Viale Marconi

SS147

S. Maria Minerva

Piazza del Comune

Ch. Nuova

V.Sant'Agnese

V.Sant'Agnese

Corso Mazzini

Porta Moiano

Santa Chiara

Piazza S. Chiara

Via Vittorio Emanuele II

V. di S. Rufino

Piazza S. Rufino

Duomo

Via S. Gabriele dell'Addolorata

Via Borgo Aretino

Vicolo D. Castello

Via di Porta Perlici

Porta Perlici

Porta Perlici

Via Villamena

Piazza Matteotti

Anfiteatro Romano

Rocca Minore →

Porta Cappuccini →

Via Carceri →

6

Viale Umberto I

Porta Nuova

Information ⓘ

0 ⎯ 1/8 mi
0 ⎯ 0.125 km

Venice
Assisi
ROME
0 ⎯ 100 Mi
0 ⎯ 100 Km
45° N.
40° N.
10° E

Basilica di San Francesco **1**
Basilica di Santa Chiara **5**
Eremo delle Carceri **6**
Museo Civico e
   Foro Romano **4**
Rocca Maggiore **2**
Tempio di Minerva

353

SPECIAL EVENTS May brings the **Calendimaggio** spring festival, with processions, medieval contests of strength and skill, late-night partying in 14th-century costumes, and singing duels on the main piazza. This annual event takes place from Thursday to Saturday after May 1.

Exploring the Town

Piazza del Comune, in the heart of Assisi, is a dream for lovers of architecture from the 12th to the 14th centuries. On the square is a pagan structure, with six Corinthian columns, called the **Temple of Minerva (Tempio di Minerva),** from the 1st century B.C. With Minerva-like wisdom, the people of Assisi turned the interior into a baroque church so as not to offend the devout. Adjoining the temple is the 13th-century **Tower (Torre)** built by Ghibelline supporters. The site is open daily from 7am to noon and 2:30pm to dusk.

Basilica di Santa Chiara (St. Clare) ★★ The basilica is dedicated to "the little plant of Blessed Francis," as St. Clare liked to describe herself. Born in 1193 into one of the noblest families of Assisi, Clare gave all her wealth to the poor and founded, together with St. Francis, the Order of the Poor Clares. She was canonized by Pope Alexander IV in 1255.

Many of the frescoes that once adorned this basilica have deteriorated and fallen away as time has rolled by, but much remains that is worthy of note. Upon entering, your attention will be caught by the striking *Crucifix* behind the main altar, a painting on wood dating from the time of the church itself (ca. 1260). The work is by "the Master of St. Clare," who's also responsible for the beautiful icons on either side of the transept. In the left transept is an oft-reproduced fresco of the Nativity from the 14th century. The basilica houses the remains of St. Clare, as well as the crucifix under which St. Francis received his command from above.

The closest bus stop is near Porta Nuova, the eastern gate to the city at the beginning of Viale Umberto I. The bus doesn't have a number; it departs from the depot in Piazza Matteotti for its first run to the train station at 5:35am and concludes its final run at 11:59pm. Buses arrive at half-hour intervals.

Warning: The custodian turns away visitors in shorts, miniskirts, plunging necklines, and backless or sleeveless attire.

Piazza di Santa Chiara 1. ℭ **075-812282.** Free admission. Nov–Mar daily 6:30am–noon and 2–6:30pm; Apr–Oct daily 6:30am–noon and 2–7pm.

Basilica di San Francesco (St. Francis) ★★★ This important basilica, with both an upper church (1230–53) and a lower church (1228–30), houses some of the most important **cycles of frescoes** in Italy, including works by such pre-Renaissance giants as Cimabue and Giotto. The basilica and its paintings form the most significant monument to St. Francis, a focal point of both high art and intense spirituality.

On the entrance wall, you can enjoy **Giotto's celebrated frescoes of St. Francis** ★★★ preaching to the birds. In the nave is the cycle of 27 additional frescoes, some by Giotto, although the authorship of the entire cycle is uncertain. Many of these are almost surrealistic (in architectural frameworks), like a stage set that strips away the walls and allows you to see the actors inside. In the cycle, you can see pictorial evidence of the rise of humanism that led to Giotto's and Italy's split away from the rigidity of Byzantium.

The upper church also contains a damaged Cimabue masterpiece, his **Crucifixion** ★. Time and earthquakes have robbed the fresco of its former radiance, but its power and ghostlike drama remain, at least on video. The cycle of badly damaged frescoes in the transept and apse are other works by Cimabue and his helpers.

The **lower church** was speedily reopened after the quakes, with only marginal damage. Reached by the entrance in Piazza Inferiore on the south side of the basilica, it's dark and mystical (if you're lucky enough to find a moment of calm btw. the arrival of fender-to-fender tour buses) and almost entirely covered with **frescoes ★★★** by the greatest pre-Renaissance painters of the 13th and 14th centuries. Look for Cimabue's faded but masterly *Virgin and Child* with four angels and St. Francis looking on from the far right; it's often reproduced in detail as one of Cimabue's greatest works. On the other side is the *Deposition from the Cross,* a masterpiece by Sienese artist Pietro Lorenzetti, plus a *Madonna and Child* with St. John and St. Francis (stigmata showing). In a chapel honoring St. Martin of Tours, Simone Martini of Siena painted a cycle of frescoes, with great skill and imagination, depicting the life and times of that saint. Finally, under the lower church is the **crypt of St. Francis,** with some relics of the saint. In the past, only scholars and clergymen were allowed access to the vaults containing these highly cherished articles, but now anyone can visit. Some of the items displayed are the saint's tunic, cowl, and shoes, and the chalice and communion plate used by him and his followers.

Insider tip: The Franciscan community affiliated with the basilica offers free guided tours by English-speaking friars Monday to Saturday 9:30am to noon and 2 to 5:30pm (to 4:30pm in winter). Stop by the office just left of the entrance to the lower church in Piazza Inferiore (✆ **075-815228**). Tours don't go into the basilica itself to avoid disrupting worshipers (although the friar will tell you lots about the church), but do visit other sites and explore the life of St. Francis and today's religious community.

From the lower church, you can also visit the **Treasury ★★** and the **Perkins Collection.** The Treasury shelters precious church relics, often in gold and silver, and even the original gray sackcloth worn by St. Francis before the order adopted the brown tunic. The Perkins Collection is a limited but rich exhibit donated by a U.S. philanthropist who had assembled a collection of Tuscan/Renaissance works, including paintings by Luca Signorelli and Fra Angelico. The Treasury and the Perkins Collection are open April to October Monday to Saturday from 9:30am to 5:30pm. Admission is free, but donations are accepted.

Piazza San Francesco. ✆ **075-819001.** www.sanfrancescoassisi.org. Free admission. Daily 8:30am–6:30pm.

Duomo di San Rufino ★   Built in the mid–12th century, the Duomo is graced with a Romanesque facade, greatly enhanced by rose windows. This is one of the finest churches in the hill towns, as important as the one at Spoleto. Adjoining it is a bell tower (campanile). The church's interior was remodeled in the baroque

---

A San Francesco Warning: Cover Up!

The church has a strict dress code: Entrance to the basilica is absolutely forbidden to those in shorts or miniskirts or showing bare shoulders. You must remain silent and cannot take any photographs in the Upper Church. The same dress code applies at the Basilica of St. Clare.

Basilica di San Francesco.

style in the 16th century, an unfortunate decision that destroyed the purity that the front suggests. St. Francis and St. Clare were both baptized here. The church was spared any damage during the quakes.

Piazza San Rufino. ☏ **075-812712.** www.assisimuseodiocesano.com. Church free admission; crypt and museum 3.50€. Mar 16–Oct 15 daily 10am–1pm and 3–6pm; Oct 16–Mar 15 daily 10am–1pm and 2:30–5:30pm.

Great Fortress (Rocca Maggiore) ★★ The Great Fortress sits astride a hill overlooking Assisi. It's worth the visit, if only for the panoramic view of the Umbrian countryside from its ramparts. The present building (now in ruins) dates from the 14th century, and the origins of the structure go back beyond time. The dreaded Cardinal Albornoz built the medieval version to establish papal domination over the town. A circular rampart was built in the 1500s by Pope Paul III.

Reached by an unmarked stepped street opposite the basilica. ☏ **075-8155234.** Admission 5€. Daily 10am–dusk.

Prisons' Hermitage (Eremo delle Carceri) ★★ This "prison," from the 14th and 15th centuries, is not a penal institution but a spiritual retreat. It's believed that St. Francis retired to this spot for meditation and prayer. Out back is the Tree of Birds, a moss-covered, gnarled *Quercus ilex* (live oak) more than 1,000 years old, where St. Francis is believed to have blessed the birds. After the blessing, they flew in the four major compass directions to symbolize that Franciscans would spread from Assisi all over the world. The friary contains some faded frescoes. One of the handful of friars who still inhabit the retreat will show you through. (In keeping with the Franciscan tradition, they're completely dependent on donations for their support.)

About 4km (2½ miles) east of Assisi, on Via Eremo delle Carceri. ☏ **075-812301.** www.eremo carceri.it. Free admission (donations accepted). Old refectory daily 9am–noon and 2:30–4:30pm; Tree of Birds Easter–Nov daily 6:30am–7:15pm; Dec–Apr daily 6:30am–sunset.

Where to Stay

Space in Assisi tends to be tight, so book as far in advance as possible.

Albergo Ristorante del Viaggiatore ⚑ This budget choice offers a great deal. The ancient town house has been totally renovated, although the stone walls and arched entryways of the lobby hint at its age. The high-ceilinged guest rooms are spacious and contemporary, with cramped bathrooms.

Via San Antonio 14, 06081 Assisi. ℰ **075-816297.** Fax 075-813051. www.albergodelviaggiatore. com. 12 units (shower only). 100€–120€ double. Rates include continental breakfast. DC, MC, V. Parking 10€. **Amenities:** Restaurant; bar; Wi-Fi (free, in lobby). *In room:* A/C, TV, hair dryer.

Hotel dei Priori   Opened in 1923, this hotel occupies one of the town's most historic buildings, dating from the 16th century, when it was known as the Palazzo Nepis. A homey, somewhat old-fashioned atmosphere prevails. Marble staircases and floors, terra cotta, vaulted ceilings, and stone-arched doors remain from its heyday. Antiques and tasteful prints in both the guest rooms and the public areas add grace notes, along with a collection of Oriental rugs. Many of the rooms are a bit small, but each has a comfortable bed and a tidy bathroom. Regrettably, the staff could be much more helpful.

Corso Mazzini 15, 06081 Assisi. ℰ **075-812237.** Fax 075-816804. www.assisi-hotel.com. 34 units. 90€–180€ double; 120€–200€ suite. Rates include continental breakfast. AE, DC, MC, V. Parking 10€ nearby. **Amenities:** Restaurant (closed Jan–Feb); bar; babysitting; room service; Wi-Fi (free, in lobby). *In room:* A/C, TV/DVD, hair dryer, minibar.

Hotel Giotto ★   The Giotto is up-to-date and well run, built at the edge of town on several levels and opening onto panoramic views. Some of the foundations are 500 years old, although it is hard to tell because of frequent modernizations. It offers spacious, modern public rooms and comfortable guest rooms; bright colors predominate, although many rooms look tatty. The small bathrooms still manage to offer adequate shelf space. There are small formal gardens and terraces for meals or sunbathing.

Via Fontebella 41, 06082 Assisi. ℰ **075-812209.** Fax 075-816479. www.hotelgiottoassisi.it. 87 units (shower only). 140€–160€ double; from 225€ suite. Rates include buffet breakfast. AE, DC, MC, V. Free parking. **Amenities:** Restaurant; bar; babysitting; outdoor pool; room service; spa. *In room:* A/C, TV, minibar.

Hotel Sole ⚘   For Umbrian hospitality and a general down-home feeling, the Sole is a winner. The severe beauty of rough stone walls and ceilings, terra-cotta floors, and marble staircases pays homage to the past, balanced by big-cushioned chairs in the TV lounge and contemporary wrought-iron beds and well-worn furnishings in the guest rooms. Some rooms are across the street in an annex. The hotel shows some wear and tear, but the price is right, the location is central, and the **restaurant** is a good choice even if you aren't a guest (you might want to take the meal plan, if you are).

Corso Mazzini 35, 06081 Assisi. ℰ **075-812373.** Fax 075-813706. www.assisihotelsole.com. 38 units (shower only). 65€ double; 85€ triple. Half board (Apr–Nov) 53€ per person. AE, DC, MC, V. Parking 10€ nearby. **Amenities:** Restaurant (closed Dec–Mar); bar; room service. *In room:* TV, hair dryer (in some).

Ròseo Hotel Assisi ★★   At last, Assisi—never known for its good hotels—has a front-ranking charmer. The Grand offers the most comfortable and best-furnished rooms in town. The suites come with a hydromassage tub and a balcony opening onto a panoramic view. The Grand's roof garden terrace is the hotel's most dramatic feature. The on-site restaurant **Giotto & Leonardo** (see below) is also one of the best in town, featuring homemade pastas, delicious truffles, and other succulent ingredients, plus the finest wines from the

Umbrian hills. Some visitors make the 40-minute walk into the center; others use the city bus.

Via G. Renzi 2, 06081 Assisi. ☎ **075-81501.** Fax 075-815272. www.roseohotelassisi.com. 155 units (some with tub only; some with shower only). 100€–200€ double. Rates include buffet breakfast. AE, DC, MC, V. Free parking. **Amenities:** 2 restaurants; 2 bars; babysitting; exercise room; indoor heated pool; room service; spa. *In room:* A/C, TV, hair dryer, minibar, Wi-Fi (free).

St. Anthony's Guest House   This is not a traditional hotel, but a religious guesthouse. This special place provides economical, comfortable rooms in a medieval villa-turned-guesthouse operated by the Franciscan Sisters of the Atonement and located on the upper ledges of Assisi. The guest rooms are small and basic, and so are the bathrooms.

Via Galeazzo Alessi 10, 06081 Assisi. ☎ **075-812542.** Fax 075-813723. atoneassisi@tiscali.it. 21 units (shower only). 60€ double; 80€ triple. Rates include continental breakfast. No credit cards. Parking 3€. Closed Nov–Feb. *In room:* Ceiling fans, no phone.

Where to Dine

You might also want to try the wonderful restaurants at the **Hotel Sole** and the **Albergo Ristorante del Viaggiatore** (see above).

Giotto ★★ UMBRIAN   This restaurant is in the Ròseo Hotel Assisi. Preference of seating is given to residents of the hotel, so it's imperative that nonguests nail down reservations. The chefs here work hard in a meticulous search for typical regional dishes. They are dedicated to rediscovering the flavors of the past, ranging from homemade pastas to virgin olive oil to the delectable truffles that abound in the land of St. Francis. These succulent ingredients of the region are enhanced by the highly prized wines from the Umbrian hills. Menu specialties might change with the season but are likely to include Strangozzi (homemade pasta) with a truffle sauce, saddle of lamb with aromatic herbs and a pistachio crust with a vegetable cake, or else *quadrucci* pasta with chickpeas grown around Spello.

Via Fratelli Canonichetti. ☎ **075-81501.** Reservations required. Fixed-price menu 30€. AE, DC, MC, V. Daily 7–10pm.

La Fortezza ★★ 🍴 UMBRIAN   Up a stepped alley from Piazza del Comune, this lovely restaurant has been family run for 40 years and is prized for its high quality and reasonable prices. An exposed ancient Roman wall to the right of the entrance establishes the antiquity of this *palazzo* with brick-vaulted ceilings; the rest dates from the 13th century. Truffles are an important ingredient in many dishes, such as a homemade pasta or else guinea fowl cooked in a truffle crust. The delicious homemade pastas are prepared with sauces that follow the season's fresh offerings, while the roster of meats skewered or roasted on the grill (*alla brace*) ranges from veal and lamb to duck. La Fortezza also rents seven rooms upstairs. A double room costs 58€ to 80€.

Via della Fortezza 2B. ☎ **075-812993.** Fax 075-8198035. www.lafortezzahotel.com. Reservations recommended. Main courses 8€–14€. MC, V. Fri–Wed 12:30–3pm and 7–10:30pm. Closed Feb.

Ristorante Buca di San Francesco UMBRIAN/ITALIAN   Evocative of the Middle Ages, this restaurant occupies a cave near the foundation of a 12th-century palace. Menu items change often, based on the availability of ingredients, but you're likely to find homemade *tagliatelle* with truffles; *umbricelli* (big noodles) with asparagus sauce; cannelloni with ricotta, spinach, and tomatoes;

carlaccia (baked crepes) stuffed with cheese, prosciutto, and roasted veal; and *piccione alla sisana* (roasted pigeon with olive oil, capers, and aromatic herbs). There are about 100 seats in the dining room and another 60 in the garden overlooking Assisi's historic center.

Via Brizi 1. *℘* **075-812204.** Reservations recommended. Main courses 9€–20€. AE, DC, MC, V. Tues–Sun noon–2:30pm and 7-10pm. Closed July 1-15 and Jan 6-Feb 6.

SPOLETO ★

129km (80 miles) N of Rome, 48km (30 miles) SE of Assisi, 209km (130 miles) S of Florence, 64km (40 miles) SE of Perugia

Hannibal couldn't conquer it, but Gian Carlo Menotti did—and how! Before Maestro Menotti put Spoleto on the tourist map in 1958, it was known mostly to art lovers, teachers, and students. Today huge crowds flood this Umbrian hill town to attend performances of the world-famous **Spoleto Festival,** usually held in June and July. Menotti searched and traveled through many towns of Tuscany and Umbria before making a final choice. When he saw Spoleto, he fell in love with it—quite understandably.

Essentials

GETTING THERE **Trains** arrive several times a day from Rome. The fastest are ES (Eurostar) trains; they're a bit more expensive than ordinary trains. The one-way fare from Rome to Spoleto is 8€ to 21€. The fastest train takes about 90 minutes; those requiring connections can take 2½ hours. Trains also run several times a day between Perugia and Spoleto; the ride lasts about an hour and costs 5€ to 16€ each way. The **rail station** in Spoleto (*℘* **892021**) is at Piazza Polvani, just outside the historic heart. Notice the gigantic statue in front by artist Alexander Calder. SSIT bus no. D will take you from the station into Piazza della Libertà in the town center for 1€. Buy your ticket for the Circolare at the bar in the rail station, perhaps along with an espresso.

If you have a **car** and are coming from Perugia or Assisi, continue along S3, heading south to the junction of Foligno, where you can pick up Hwy. 75 for the rest of the route into Spoleto. Driving time from Assisi is about 30 minutes.

VISITOR INFORMATION The **tourist office** is at Piazza della Libertà 7 (*℘* **0743-238920;** www.visitspoleto.it). From April to October, it's open Monday to Saturday 9am to 1pm and 4 to 7pm, and Sunday 9am to 1pm; November to March, hours are Monday to Saturday 9am to 1pm and 3:30 to 6:30pm, and Sunday 9am to 1pm.

SPECIAL EVENTS The **Spoleto Festival ★★★** is an internationally acclaimed event. It's held annually, most often in June and July, and attracts the elite of the operatic, ballet, and theatrical worlds from Europe and America. Tickets for most events cost 13€ to 100€, plus a 15% handling charge. For tickets in advance, contact the **Spoleto Festival,** Piazza della Libertà 10, 06049 Spoleto (*℘* **0743-776444**). Visit online at **www.festivaldispoleto.com**. Once in Spoleto, you can get tickets at the Piazza della Libertà. Make your hotel reservations well in advance.

Exploring the Town

Spoleto was known to St. Francis and Lucrezia Borgia (she occupied the Rocca dell'Albornoz, the 14th-c. castle towering over the town). The town is filled with palaces, medieval streets, and towers built for protection at the time when visitors weren't as friendly as they are today. There are churches, churches, and more churches—some, such as San Gregorio Maggiore, were built in the Romanesque style in the 11th century.

The tourist center of town is **Piazza del Duomo** with its **Duomo.** A walk along Via del Ponte brings you to the **Ponte delle Torri ★★**, with nine towering pylons separating stately arches. The bridge is 80m (264 ft.) high and 232m (760 ft.) long, spanning a gorge. It's believed to date from the 13th century and is one of the most photographed sights in Spoleto. Goethe praised it when he passed this way in 1786.

If you have a car, continue up the hill from Spoleto around a winding road (about 8km/5 miles) to **Monteluco,** an ancient spot 762m (2,500 ft.) above sea level, where you'll enjoy a sweeping view. Monteluco is peppered with summer villas. The monastery here was once frequented by St. Francis of Assisi.

Il Duomo ★★   The cathedral is a hodgepodge of Romanesque and medieval architecture, with a 12th-century campanile. Its facade is of exceptional beauty, renowned for its 1207 mosaic by Salsterno. You should visit the interior, if for no other reason than to see the cycle of **frescoes** (1467–69) in the chapel by Filippo Lippi. His son, Filippino, designed the tomb for his father, but a grave robber hauled off the body one night 2 centuries later. The keeper of the apse will be happy to unlock it for you. These frescoes, believed to have been carried out largely by students, were the elder Lippi's last work; he died in Spoleto in 1469. As friars went in those days, Lippi was a bit of a swinger; he ran off with a nun, Lucrezia Buti, who later posed as the Madonna in several of his paintings.

Piazza del Duomo. ✆ **0743-44307.** Free admission. Apr–Oct daily 8am–12:30pm and 3–6:30pm; Nov–Mar daily 8am–noon and 3–5:30pm.

Roman Amphitheater (Teatro Romano) & Archaeological Museum (Museo Archeologico)   A setting for performances during the Spoleto Festival, the **Roman Amphitheater** dates from the 1st century A.D., and excavations began on it in 1891. For the same ticket, you can also visit the **Archaeological Museum** nearby, with a warrior's tomb dating from the 7th century B.C. Among the exhibits is Les Poletina, two tablets inscribed around 241 B.C.

Via S. Agata. ✆ **0743-225531.** Admission to both 4€. Daily 8:30am–7:30pm.

Sant'Eufemia & Diocese Museum (Museo Diocesano)   The **Sant'Eufemia** church was built in the 11th century. Note the gallery above the nave where women were required to sit; a holdover from the Eastern Church, it's one of the few such galleries in Italy. In the courtyard, double stairs lead to the **Museo Diocesano,** noted for its Madonna paintings, including one from 1315. Room 5 contains Filippino Lippi's 1485 *Madonna and Child with Sts. Montano and Bartolomeo.*

Via Saffi 13, btw. Piazza del Duomo and Piazza del Mercanto. ✆ **0743-48942** (museum). Admission to both 3€. Apr–Oct Mon–Sat 10am–1pm and 3–6pm, Sun 10am–6pm; Nov–Mar Mon–Sat 10am–1pm and 3–5pm, Sun 10am–5pm.

Where to Stay

Spoleto offers an attractive range of hotels, but when the crowds flood in at festival time, the going's rough. (One year a group of students bedded down on Piazza del Duomo.) In an emergency, the **tourist office** (see "Essentials," above) can offer a list of where to stay in a private home at a moderate price, but it's

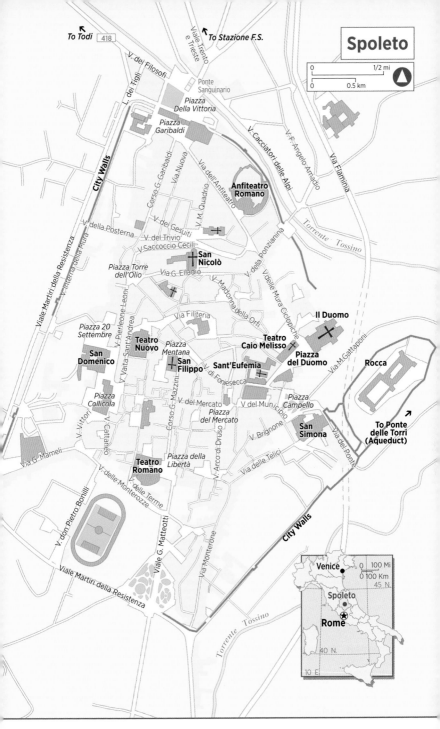

Spoleto

To Todi [418]
To Stazione F.S.

Viale Trento e Trieste
V. dei Filosofi
L. dei Tigli
Ponte Sanguinario
Piazza Della Vittoria
Piazza Garibaldi
V. Cacciatori delle Alpi
V.-F.-Angelo-Amadio
Via Flaminia

City Walls

Corso-G.-Garibaldi
Via Nuova
Via-V.-M.-Quadrio
Via dell'Anfiteatro
Anfiteatro Romano

V. della Posterna
V. Interna della Mura
V. dei Gesuiti
V. del Trivio
V. Saccoccio Cecili
San Nicolò
Via G. Elladio
Piazza Torre dell'Olio
Via Madonna della Orfi
V. delle Mura Ciclopiche
V. della Ponzianina
Torrente Tossino

Via Filiteria
Piazza 20 Settembre
V. Pierleone-Leoni
V. Vata Sant'Andrea
Teatro Nuovo
Piazza Mentana
San Filippo
Sant'Eufemia
Teatro Caio Melisso
Il Duomo
Piazza del Duomo
Via-M.-Gattaponi
Rocca

San Domenico
Corso-G.-Mazzini
V. di Fontesecca
Piazza Campello
To Ponte delle Torri (Aqueduct)

Piazza Collicola
V. Vittori
V. Cattaneo
V. del Mercato
V. del Municipio
Piazza del Mercato
V. Brignone
San Simona
V. del Ponte

Via G. Mameli
V. Arco-di-Druso
Piazza della Libertà
V. delle Telici
City Walls

Teatro Romano
V. delle Terme
V. delle Monterozze
V. Monterone
V. Montefone

V. don Pietro Bonilli
Viale G. Matteotti
Viale Martiri della Resistenza

Torrente Tossino

0 1/2 mi
0 0.5 km

Venice
Spoleto
Rome
0 100 Mi
0 100 Km
45 N.
40 N.
10 E

imperative to lock up your reservation well in advance. Many of the private rooms are often rented well ahead to artists appearing at the festival. Innkeepers will raise their prices as high as the market will bear at festival time.

Albornoz Palace Hotel ★ 🎁   No hotel in Spoleto has such first-class amenities and such artistic flair. The owners view their hotel as a statement of modern art, and they invite artists here from all over the world to display their work to art lovers, most often the guests themselves. Not only is the family's prestigious collection on exhibit, but a constantly changing array of contemporary art is displayed in the bedrooms, the corridors, and the public lounges. Bedrooms are large and designed in some futuristic modern style, but very comfortable, including state-of-the-art bathrooms. Accommodations open onto views over Spoleto, Monteluco, and the surrounding hills, or else the garden in back.

Viale Matteotti, 06049 Spoleto. ✆ **0743-221221.** Fax 0743-221600. www.albornozpalace.com. 96 units. 94€–150€ double; 161€–172€ suite. Rates include buffet breakfast. AE, DC, MC, V. Free parking. **Amenities:** Restaurant; bar; babysitting; outdoor pool; room service. *In room:* A/C, TV, hair dryer, minibar, Wi-Fi (2€ per hr.).

Hotel Charleston ★   This tile-roofed, sienna-fronted building is from the 17th century and today serves as a pleasant hotel in the historic center. It's a solid, reliable choice, with wood-beamed ceilings, terra-cotta floors, and open fireplaces. Each of the large guest rooms has a ceiling accented with beams of honey-colored planking. Many have been updated with new furnishings and bathrooms.

Piazza Collicola 10, 06049 Spoleto. ✆ **0743-220052.** Fax 0743-221244. www.hotelcharleston.it. 21 units (some with shower only). 69€–135€ double. Rates include buffet breakfast. AE, DC, MC, V. Parking 10€. **Amenities:** Bar; bikes; room service; sauna; Wi-Fi (6€ per hr., in lobby). *In room:* A/C, TV, hair dryer, minibar.

Hotel Clarici   The Clarici is rated only third class by the government, but it's airy and modern, the best of the budget bets. The hotel doesn't emphasize style, but focuses on the creature comforts: soft, low beds; built-in wardrobes; steam heat; and an elevator. Fourteen rooms open onto private balconies. There's a large terrace for sunbathing or sipping drinks.

Piazza della Vittoria 32, 06049 Spoleto. ✆ **0743-223311.** Fax 0743-222010. www.hotelclarici.com. 24 units (shower only). 63€–110€ double. Rates include continental breakfast. AE, MC, V. Parking 6€. Bus: D. **Amenities:** Bar; room service. *In room:* A/C, TV, hair dryer, minibar, Wi-Fi (free).

Hotel Gattapone ★★ 🎁   The stunning Gattapone is our first choice in town. It occupies two side-by-side stone 17th-century cottages among the clouds; it clings to the cliffs high on a twisting road leading to the ancient castle and the 13th-century Ponte delle Torri. It feels isolated and surrounded by nature, but it's only a 2-minute stroll to the Duomo. The interiors maximize views of the valley and the remarkable 14th-century arched bridge a few hundred feet away. The rooms are uniquely furnished, with comfortable beds, antiques, and plenty of space.

Via Del Ponte 6, 06049 Spoleto. ✆ **0743-223447.** Fax 0743-223448. www.hotelgattapone.it. 15 units. 120€–230€ double. Rates include continental breakfast. AE, DC, MC, V. Free parking. **Amenities:** Babysitting; bikes; room service; Wi-Fi (free, in lobby). *In room:* A/C, TV, hair dryer, minibar.

Hotel San Luca ★   Occupying a restored building from the 19th century, this hotel is the most up-to-date in town, filled with ambience and style. Wherever you turn, there's a grace note of the past, such as a roof garden and a spacious courtyard with a 1602 fountain. All the elegant and soundproof guest rooms are spacious and furnished in a sober yet comforting style with all the amenities. The bathrooms are particularly welcoming, with extras such as phones and towel warmers. Many rooms are also fitted with a Jacuzzi tub. The public rooms respect the style of the building with period furniture. A garden solarium is a nice touch.

Via Interna delle Mura 21, 06049 Spoleto. ℰ **0743-223399.** Fax 0743-223800. www.hotelsan luca.com. 35 units. 110€–240€ double; 210€–300€ suite. Rates include buffet breakfast. AE, DC, MC, V. Parking 13€. **Amenities:** Bar; babysitting; bikes; room service. *In room:* A/C, TV, hair dryer, minibar, Wi-Fi (2€ per hr.).

Palazzo Dragoni ★★   Near Piazza del Duomo, this is a lovingly renovated 16th-century palace once inhabited by the aristocracy of Spoleto. Skillfully converted into a hotel—more like a residence—it is one of the most atmospheric choices in the area. It's filled with antiques and beautiful fabrics that are in harmony with the architecture. The rooms on the lower floors are the most evocative of palace living. We prefer room nos. 3, 6, 8, and 10 because of their antiques, decorated ceilings, and views. Avoid the cramped and viewless no. 16. Breakfast is served on an open-air loggia with a panoramic view.

Via del Duomo 13, 06049 Spoleto. ℰ **0743-222220.** Fax 0743-222225. www.palazzodragoni.it. 15 units (shower only). 130€ double; 160€ suite. Rates include buffet breakfast. MC, V. Free parking. **Amenities:** Babysitting; room service. *In room:* A/C, TV, hair dryer, minibar, Wi-Fi (free).

Vecchio Molino ★ 🎒   If you have a car, you may want to drive 9.5km (6 miles) outside Spoleto to a site on the Clitunno River in the village of Fonti del Clitunno. This undiscovered gem is in the heart of the Umbrian countryside, next to a Paleo-Christian temple from the 4th century A.D. The landscape here has been celebrated by poets from Plinius the Young to Lord Byron. The inn incorporates the ruins of an ancient corn mill, including old grinding stones from the 15th century. You can walk through tree-shaded gardens along the river's bank. The interior is rustic, the rooms decorated with dark furnishings and handcrafted wool bedspreads. We prefer room nos. 2, 4, and 10, opening onto the garden. Avoid nos. 15, 16, and 19, opening onto the parking lot.

Via del Tempio 34, Loc. Pissignano, Campello sul Clitunno, 06042 Spoleto. ℰ **0743-521122.** Fax 0743-275097. www.vecchio-molino.it. 13 units (shower only). 115€ double; 120€–150€ suite. AE, DC, MC, V. Closed Nov–Mar. **Amenities:** Babysitting; room service. *In room:* A/C, minibar.

Where to Dine

Il Tartufo ★★ UMBRIAN   At Il Tartufo, near the amphitheater, you might be introduced to the Umbrian *tartufo* (truffle)—if you can afford it. It's served in the most expensive appetizers and main courses at Spoleto's oldest restaurant. This excellent tavern serves at least nine regional specialties using the black *tartufo*. A popular pasta dish (and a good introduction for neophyte palates) is *strengozzi al tartufo*. Or you might want to start with an omelet, such as *frittata al tartufo*. Main dishes are well prepared, including such items as guinea fowl stuffed with potatoes and porcini mushrooms or *maltagliati* (pasta) with braised artichokes and tomatoes. For such a small restaurant, the menu is large.

Piazza Garibaldi 24. ℰ **0743-40236.** www.ristoranteiltartufo.it. Reservations recommended. Main courses 9€–21€; fixed-price menu 35€. AE, DC, MC, V. Tues–Sun noon–3pm; Tues–Sat 7:30–10:30pm. Closed Jan 20–31 and 1 week in June.

Ristorante Apollinare UMBRIAN   The dining room was created from an ancient church whose origins date from the 12th century. Today the atmosphere is intimate and elegant. A dining tradition since 1991, the restaurant serves imaginative, carefully conceived dishes. Roasted guinea fowl comes with artichokes flavored with balsamic vinegar, and a delectable pigeon appears in a casserole. Eel from Trasimeno Lake is smoked and served as an appetizer. *Stringozzi,* the local pasta, is served with the black truffles of the region. Other specialties include grilled beef filet with truffles and artichokes or sea bass and shrimp roulades flavored with olive oil and fresh ginger.

In the Hotel Aurora, Via Sant'Agata 14. (℃) **0743-223256.** www.ristoranteapollinare.it. Reservations required. Main courses 8€–16€; fixed-price menus 25€–35€. AE, DC, MC, V. Apr–Oct daily 12:30–2:30pm and 7–10:45pm; Nov–Mar Wed–Mon 12:30–2:30pm and 7–10:45pm.

A Side Trip to Todi ★

For years, Todi lay slumbering in the Umbrian sun. Then the world moved in. The University of Kentucky keeps voting it "the most livable town in the world." This has brought a moneyed class from America rushing in to buy decaying castles and villas, hoping to convert them into holiday homes. And Todi has imitated Spoleto and now stages an **Umbria Music Fest,** attracting ballet, theatrical, and operatic stars during the first 10 days of September.

Taking S418 out of Spoleto for 45km (28 miles) northwest will lead you to what the excitement is all about. At Acquasparta, get on A3 northwest. Soon you'll come to this well-preserved medieval village, today a retreat for wealthy artists and diplomats. The setting is simply lovely.

Upon arrival, you'll enter the walled town through one of its three gates, named for the destinations of the roads leading away: **Rome** in the southwest wall, **Perugia** in the north, and **Orvieto** in the southeast. The remains of original Roman and Etruscan walls are also evident just inside the Rome gate. The central square, **Piazza del Popolo,** was built over a Roman forum. It contains the 12th-century Romanesque-Gothic **cathedral** and three beautiful palaces: the **Palazzo del Popolo,** built in 1213; the **Palazzo del Capitano,** dating from 1292; and the 14th-century **Palazzo dei Priori,** with its trapezoidal tower. Each summer, all three (and the piazza) are filled with the wares of the **National Exhibit of Crafts (Mostra Nazionale dell'Artigianato).**

Todi's cathedral.

Also on view are **Santa Maria della Consolazione,** standing guard over Todi with its domes and exquisite stained glass, and the 13th-century **San Fortunato,** in the **Piazza della Repubblica,** burial site of the town's most famous citizen, the monk/medieval poet Jacopone. To the right of the church, a path leads uphill to the ruins of a 14th-century castle known as **La Rocca.** From here, a walk up the Viale della Serpentina will reward you with a bird's-eye view of the surrounding valley. If the climb seems a bit much, check the view from **Piazza Garibaldi.**

Today the artisans of Todi are renowned for their woodwork. Examples of historical as well as contemporary craft are available for perusal or purchase, especially during the **National Exhibit of Crafts** along Piazza del Popolo.

Our favorite place to stay is **Tenuta di Canonica,** Località La Canonica 75–76 (© **075-8947545;** fax 075-8947581; www.tenutadicanonica.com), lying 5km (3 miles) northwest of Todi. Here Maria and Daniele Fano have converted a brick farmhouse and former medieval tower into a dining room with exposed stone walls, brick floors, and high ceilings. Their dining room is only for guests of their 11 attractively furnished bedrooms, costing 160€ to 195€ for a double and 200€ to 250€ for a junior suite, including breakfast. There is also an outdoor pool. The inn is closed from December 1 to March 31.

ORVIETO

121km (75 miles) N of Rome, 76km (47 miles) SW of Perugia, 113km (70 miles) SW of Assisi

Built on a pedestal of volcanic rock above vineyards in a green valley, Orvieto is the Umbrian hill town closest to Rome and is often visited by those who don't have the time to explore other spots in Umbria. It lies on the Paglia, a tributary of the Tiber, and sits on an isolated rock some 315m (1,035 ft.) above sea level. Crowning the town is its world-famed cathedral, still a pilgrimage destination for Catholics and art lovers the world over.

The most spectacularly sited hill town in Umbria (but not the most spectacular town), Orvieto was founded by the Etruscans, who were apparently drawn to it because of its good defensive possibilities. Likewise, long after its days as a Roman colony, it became a papal stronghold. It was a natural fortress, because its cliffs rise starkly from the valley below, even though Orvieto, when you finally reach it, is relatively flat. Although the tall, sheer cliffs on which the town stands saved it from the incursion of railroads and superhighways, time and traffic vibrations have caused the soft volcanic rock to disintegrate so that work is imminently necessary to shore up the town.

Orvieto is known for its white wine; the best place to enjoy it is at a wine cellar at Piazza del Duomo 2 as you contemplate the cathedral's facade. Like many of Italy's popular hill towns, once the day-trippers have rolled out of town on the last bus, quiet descends on its streets and narrow Medieval alleys, making for a perfect time to explore the ancient city the Etruscans called *Velzna.*

Essentials

GETTING THERE   Twelve **trains** a day arrive in Orvieto from Perugia but require a change of trains in Orte or Terontola. Because of frequent stops, the trip takes 2½ hours. A one-way ticket costs 7.50€. From Florence, the trains make the trip in 2 hours, with a one-way ticket costing 12€ to 24€ (depending on the train). From Rome, the train takes 1 hour and costs 7.50€ to 35€ each way. Orvieto's rail station (**892021** for rail information in Italy) lies below the town in the valley. To get to the town center, take a small funicular that operates daily between 7:15am and 8:30pm, then bus no. A, departing at intervals of 40 minutes or less throughout the day and most of the night. One-way fares on either the funicular or bus cost 1€. For information, call the tourist office (see below).

If you have a **car** and are coming from Rome, drive for about 90 minutes (around 121km/75 miles north along A1) to Orvieto. From Perugia, head 42km (26 miles) south on S3bis to Todi, then take S448 for 25km (16 miles) southwest to the intersection of S205; drive 9km (5½ miles) to Orvieto.

VISITOR INFORMATION   The **tourist office,** Piazza dell'Erba 1 (**0763-393453;** www.orvietoturismo.it), is open Monday to Friday 8am to 2pm and 4 to 7pm, Saturday and Sunday 10am to 1pm and 3 to 6pm.

Exploring The Town

Emilio Greco Museum (Museo Emilio Greco)
This museum opened in 1991 to house a major art collection donated to the city by eminent sculptor Emilio Greco. A devoted advocate of civic pride and an internationally recognized sculptor best remembered in Orvieto for his bronze doors in the front of the Duomo (see below), he died in 1996 in his mid-80s. You'll find 32 Greco sculptures and 60 graphic works (including lithographs, etchings, and drawings). The modern museum was designed by architect Giulio Savio on the ground floor of a 14th-century *palazzo*.

In the Palazzo Soliano, Piazza del Duomo. **0763-342477.** Admission 6.50€. Apr–Sept daily 9:30am–7pm; Oct–Mar daily 9:30am–1pm and 2–6pm.

Il Duomo ★★★
Erected on the site of two older churches and dedicated to the Virgin, the Duomo was begun in 1288 (maybe even earlier) to commemorate the Miracle of Bolsena. This alleged miracle came out of the doubts of a priest who questioned the transubstantiation (the incarnation of Jesus Christ in the Host). However, as the story goes, at the moment of consecration, the Host started to drip blood. The priest doubted no more, and the Feast of Corpus Christi was launched.

The cathedral is known for its **elaborately adorned facade ★★★**, rich statuary, marble bas-reliefs, and mosaics. Pope John XXIII proclaimed that, on Judgment Day, God would send his angels down to earth to pick up this facade and transport it back to heaven. The modern bronze portals are controversial, and many art historians journey from around the world to see them. Installed in 1970, they were the work of eminent sculptor Emilio Greco, who took as his theme the Misericordia, the seven acts of corporal charity. One panel depicts Pope John XXIII's famous visit to the prisoners of Rome's Queen of Heaven jail in 1960. Some critics have called the doors "outrageous"; others have praised them as "one of the most original works of modern sculpture." You decide.

The west facade, divided into three gables, boasts richly sculptured marble based on designs of Lorenzo Maitani of Siena. Four wall surfaces around the three doors are adorned with bas-reliefs, also based on Maitani designs. Maitani worked on the facade until his death in 1330. The bas-reliefs depict scenes from the Bible, including the Last Judgment. After Maitani's death, Andrea Pisano took over, but the actual work carried on until the dawn of the 17th century.

Inside, the nave and aisles are constructed in alternating panels of black and white stone. You'll want to seek out the **Cappella del Corporale,** with its

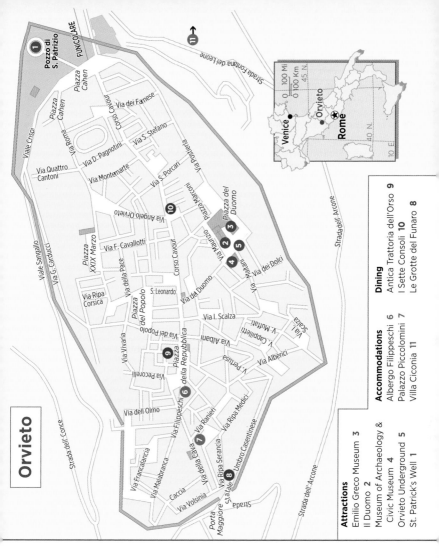

Orvieto

Attractions

Emilio Greco Museum **3**
Il Duomo **2**
Museum of Archaeology &
Civic Museum **4**
Orvieto Underground **5**
St. Patrick's Well **1**

Accommodations

Albergo Filippeschi **6**
Palazzo Piccolomini **7**
Villa Ciconia **11**

Dining

Antica Trattoria dell'Orso **9**
I Sette Consoli **10**
Le Grotte del Funaro **8**

mammoth silver shrine based on the design of the cathedral facade. This 1338 masterpiece, richly embellished with precious stones, was the work of Ugolino Vieri of Siena and was designed to shelter the Holy Corporal from Bolsena (the cloth in which the bleeding Host was wrapped). The most celebrated chapel is the **Cappella di San Brizio,** which contains newly restored frescoes of the *Last Judgment* and the *Apocalypse* ★★ by Luca Signorelli, who was called in to complete them (they were begun by Fra Angelico). Michelangelo was said to have been inspired by the frescoes at the time he was contemplating the Sistine Chapel. The masterpiece was produced between 1499 and 1503, and cost $4.4 million to renovate. Only 25 persons at a time are allowed to see the chapel.

Piazza del Duomo. ℂ **0763-342477.** www.opsm.it. Admission 2€. Nov–Mar daily 9:30am–5:30pm; Apr–June and Oct daily 9:30am–7:30pm; July–Sept daily 9:30am–6:30pm.

Museum of Archaeology & Civic Museum (Musei Archeologici Faina e Civico) This museum across from the cathedral contains many Etruscan artifacts found in and around Orvieto. In addition to the stone sarcophagi, terra-cotta portraits, and vials of colored glass left by the Etruscans, it exhibits many beautiful Greek vases. Three of the most intriguing objects are amphorae attributed to one of the finest of the Attic vase painters, Exekias (550–540 B.C.). They were found in a necropolis near Orvieto and are a gauge of the wealth of this former city-state.

In the Palazzo Faina, Piazza del Duomo 29. ✆ **0763-341511.** www.museofaina.it. Admission 4.50€ adults, 3€ students, seniors, and children 7-12. Mar–Oct daily 9:30am–6pm; Nov–Feb Tues–Sun 10am–5pm.

Orvieto Undergound ★★ Just steps from the Duomo lies one of Orvieto's most fascinating—and only recently accessible—features. The soft volcanic tufa on which the city is built is laced with an extensive network of manmade caves, some of which date from the Etruscans. Interest in the caves was first sparked in the 1970s, when a large chunk of the *rupe* (cliff) of Orvieto fell away in a landslide and exposed a section of the caves. Speleologists have identified at least 1,200 such caves, which served various purposes through the years—from sacred places to storerooms to olive mills to hideouts for a city under siege—in the Middle Ages and as recently as World War II. Orvieto Underground offers hour-long, guided tours (in English) of a portion of these caves, during which guides explain the geological formation of the region as well as the functions of the caves over the millennia.

Piazza del Duomo 24 (Tourist Information Office). ✆ **0763-340688** or 339-7332764. www. orvietounderground.it. Admission 5.50€. Tours daily at 11am, 12:15, 4 and 5:15pm (Sat–Sun only in Feb). Closed Dec 25.

Pozzo di San Patrizio (St. Patrick's Well) ★★ St. Patrick's Well is an architectural curiosity, and in its day it was an engineering feat. Pope Clement VII ordered the well built when he feared that Orvieto might come under siege and its water supply might be cut off. The well was entrusted to the design of Antonio da Sangallo the Younger in 1527. It's some 61m (200 ft.) deep and about 13m (42 ft.) in diameter, cut into volcanic rock. Two spiral staircases, with about 250 steps, lead into the wells. These spiral ramps never meet.

Viale Sangallo, off Piazza Cahen. ✆ **0763-343768.** Admission 5€. May–Aug daily 9am–8pm; Mar–Apr, Sept–Oct daily 9am–7pm; Jan–Feb, Nov–Dec daily 10am–5pm.

Where to Stay

Albergo Filippeschi 🏷 If you're searching for a bargain, head here. Managed by its family owners, the Filippeschi is the most affordable property in the center. It occupies a historic mansion and has been restored with a certain style and grace by gutting a decaying structure and modernizing it. The guest rooms are generally spacious and, though lacking style, contain small refrigerators.

Via Filippeschi 19, 05019 Orvieto. ✆/fax **0763-343275.** www.albergofilippeschi.it. 15 units (shower only). 95€–115€ double. Rates include buffet breakfast. AE, DC, MC, V. Parking 13€ nearby. **Amenities:** Bar; room service. *In room:* A/C, TV, hair dryer, minibar, Wi-Fi (free).

Palazzo Piccolomini ★★ 🏷 A hotel since 1998, this inn was carved from a 16th-century Renaissance palazzo. Today it is the best hotel in Orvieto. Looking very pretty in pink, this was the Orvieto home of the illustrious Tuscan family that gave us two popes. The building has emerged from a complete refurbishment that kept the historical shell and its grand dimensions of vaulted ceilings and wide halls, while creating a quasi-minimalist ambience with cool terra-cotta floors and white slipcovered furniture. The rooms are elegant but simple, with dark-wood furnishings and canopied beds. Ground-floor rooms have high-vaulted ceilings; those on the upper floors have nice views. The best room is the corner double no. 311.

Piazza Ranieri 36, 05018 Orvieto. © **0763-341743.** Fax 0763-391046. www.hotelpiccolomini.it. 31 units. 154€ double; 244€–280€ suite. Rates include buffet breakfast. AE, MC, V. Parking 10€. **Amenities:** Restaurant; bar; babysitting; room service; Wi-Fi (free, in lobby). *In room:* A/C, TV, hair dryer, minibar.

Villa Ciconia ★ This beautiful 16th-century villa (the best hotel in the environs) sits in a 3.2-hectare (8-acre) park at the confluence of the Chain and Paglia rivers, 4km (2½ miles) from Orvieto. It has the thick walls, terra-cotta floors, and beamed ceilings typical of its era. Huge chestnut beams run more than 12m (39 ft.) along the ceiling of the lobby, and the main dining room features a great stone fireplace and a lacuna ceiling with ornate molding and frescoes around the walls. The spacious guest rooms have park views and period furnishings. You can use a nearby (1km/¾ mile from the hotel) public sports center, which has an indoor Olympic-size pool, indoor and outdoor red-clay tennis courts, and horseback riding.

Via dei Tigli 69, 05019 Orvieto. © **0763-305582.** Fax 0763-302077. www.hotelvillaciconia.com. 12 units. 100€–180€ double. Rates include buffet breakfast. AE, MC, V. **Amenities:** Restaurant; bar; babysitting; Jacuzzi; outdoor pool; room service. *In room:* A/C, TV, hair dryer, minibar.

Where to Dine

Antica Trattoria dell'Orso ★ UMBRIAN/ABRUZZESE The *tagliolini fatti in casa* (Umbria's homemade spaghetti-like specialty) is best served here *alla campagnola* ("country style," with zucchini, eggplant, and onions). Any of the fresh pastas are a "must-try" at this unassuming *trattoria* full of locals, partly free of tourists because of its location, a little too far off the beaten path (it's a 10-min. stroll from the Duomo). The ingredients of fresh market offerings and homegrown herbs help confirm the impression of a day in the country. Even the simplest dish (a frittata of asparagus or potatoes) is full of flavor and bears the masterful touch of chef Gabriele di Giandomenico and his Neapolitan partner, Ciro Cristiano.

Via della Misericordia 18–20. © **0763-341642.** Reservations recommended. Main courses 12€–20€. AE, DC, MC, V. Wed–Sun noon–2:30pm and 7:30–10pm. Closed mid-Jan to mid-Feb and 3 weeks in July.

I Sette Consoli ★★ MEDITERRANEAN In a dining room that was once the sacristy of the 18th-century church next door, Orvieto's finest cuisine is served at this Michelin-starred restaurant. We prefer the place in fair weather when we can sit in the garden, open only on summer nights, looking out onto the rear of Orvieto's monumental cathedral. Inventiveness and a solid culinary technique form a magic combination here. One of the most typical Umbrian regional dishes is young pigeon or rabbit, cooked to perfection in the oven and served with vegetables gathered in the fields. Rabbit also appears cooked with bacon and served in a leek sauce with crunchy potato strings. Ravioli stuffed with duck and served in a nut sauce is another commendable dish. Our favorite is lamb chops stuffed with foie gras in a sesame crust.

Piazza Sant'Angelo 1A. © **0763-343911.** www.isetteconsoli.it. Reservations required. Main courses 13€–25€. AE, DC, MC, V. Thurs–Tues 12:30–3pm and 7:30–10pm. Closed Sun night in winter and last 2 weeks in Feb.

Le Grotte del Funaro UMBRIAN/PIZZA   The cuisine is the type of fare Umbrian grandmothers have served for generations—fresh, flavorful, and nutritious, with no attempt to be creative. The setting, however, is a surprisingly dry cave below the city center that includes many eerie references to other times. No one seems to have any idea how long the cave has been in use (the staff believes it was part of the storerooms used by the ancient Etruscans). Homemade pastas are flavored with mushrooms and Umbrian truffles. One authentic recipe, not recommended if you're watching your cholesterol, is *lombrichelle* (a homemade pasta) with *lardo di colonnata* (pork lard) and Umbrian pecorino cheese. The lard is aged in marble quarries in the town of Colonnata, where it is placed with spices. Our preferred meat dishes are sautéed filet of beef with truffles or wild boar with wine and fresh herbs, served with polenta.

Via Ripa Serancia 41. © **0763-343276.** www.grottedelfunaro.it. Reservations recommended. Main courses 9€–19€. MC, V. Tues–Sun noon–3pm and 7pm–midnight.

Shopping

Orvieto's local white wine, **Orvieto Classico,** is made from grapes that thrive in the local chalky soil and are sometimes fermented in caves around the countryside. You'll be able to buy glasses of the fruity wine ("liquid gold") at any tavern in town, but if you want to haul a bottle or two back to your own digs, try the town's best wine shop, **Foresi,** Piazza del Duomo 2 (© **0763-341611**).

You'll find a wide selection of hand-carved wooden items at **Michelangeli,** Via Gualverio Michelangeli 3 (© **0763-342660;** www.michelangeli.it), where you can find everything from full-scale furniture to an ornate cup and bowl.

Antonia Carraro, Corso Cavour 101 (© **0763-342870**), is a fabulous place to stock up for a picnic or just to buy locally made breads, olive oils, cheeses, salamis, wines, and biscotti.

Orvieto is also known for its pottery, with the majority of shops lining both sides of Via del Duomo.

THE MARCHES (LE MARCHE)

"A new Tuscany in the making," proclaim the Sunday travel supplements. An exaggeration, perhaps, but the Marches are indeed on the rise in world tourism, with Raphael's Renaissance city of Urbino drawing the most international visitors.

Along the Adriatic, the Marches is riddled with umbrella-laden sandy beaches. Inland is a pastoral of farmland and craggy hills as the landscape moves toward the Apennines Mountains. If your time is limited, focus your itinerary on Urbino, with a day for Ascoli Piceno if you can spare it.

The Marches form the eastern seaboard of central Italy with the regions of Emilia-Romagna (Bologna) to the north and Abruzzo to the south. The countryside is sparsely inhabited, and you'll need a car to get about freely as public transportation, including rail lines, is severely limited.

Urbino ★★

101km (63 miles) NE of Perugia, 107km (66 miles) NE of Arezzo, 35km (22 miles) W of Pesaro, 70km (43 miles) S of Rimini

Locals are not modest—but are somewhat accurate—in hailing Urbino as "the ideal Renaissance city." In a secluded mountain setting, it basks in its former

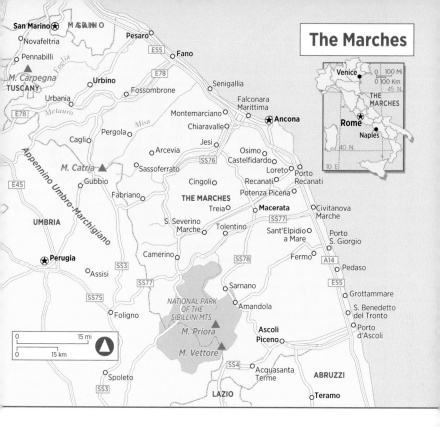

The Marches

glory but is not as culturally isolated today as it might have been. The hub of the town is the animated triangle of **Piazza della Repubblica,** lying in a dip between the twin humps of a hill. Its Università di Urbino is one of the oldest in the world, founded in 1564. Its student population and never-ending stream of art-conscious international travelers lend the town a cosmopolitan air.

The flowering of Urbino occurred during the Renaissance reign of Federico da Montefeltro (1444–82), a great supporter of arts and letters. Under his patronage, Urbino reached the zenith of its power and influence, almost without rival in western Europe. His son, Guidobaldo, continued in his father's footsteps.

Also, Urbino was home to two celebrated native sons. Raffaello Sanzio (1483–1520), more popularly known as Raphael, came from here, as did Donato Bramante (1444–1514). Bramante introduced the early Renaissance style to Milan and the High Renaissance style to Rome, where his most famous design was St. Peter's Basilica.

This mellow old artistic city was once surrounded by walls, the outlines of which can still be traced. Many old palaces are more or less still standing as they did in the days when Urbino was plagued with Gothic wars. These bastions of history have earned Urbino the honor of being on the UNESCO list of World Heritage Sites.

ESSENTIALS

GETTING THERE From Pesaro (see below), buses operated by **Amibus** (✆ **0722-376711;** www.amibus.it) run to Urbino, taking 55 minutes and costing

Urbino's Piazza della Repubblica.

3€ one-way. You can purchase tickets aboard. Because of winding mountain roads, motorists often choose to approach Urbino from Pesaro by heading south along A14 to Fano. Once here, cut southwest along E78 until you reach the signposts leading north into Urbino's center.

VISITOR INFORMATION Across from Palazzo Ducale, the **tourist office** at Piazza Rinascimento 1 (✆ **0722-2613;** www.turismo.pesarourbino.it) is open daily 9am to 7pm.

EXPLORING THE CITY

A tour of Urbino with some major stopovers (see below) will take 5 to 6 hours, not counting time out for lunch. On even the most rushed of visits, be sure to head for the following highlights.

Casa Natale di Raffaello   Raphael lived in this 15th-century house with his father, Giovanni Sanzio, until he turned 14. The museum is filled with period furnishings and mementos, including coins, books, and portraits. In the room where the painter was born, a fresco by the young artist, *Madonna and Child,* has been preserved. Some art critics attribute this painting to Raphael's father.

Via Raffaello 57. ✆ **0722-320105.** Admission 3€. Mar–Oct Mon–Sat 9am–1pm and 3–7pm, Sun 10am–1pm; Nov–Feb Mon–Sat 9am–2pm, Sun 10am–1pm.

Oratorio di San Giovanni Battista   Two adjacent churches now stand at this site. The chief treasures of the first church—dating from the 14th century—are its **frescoes ★** by the Salimbene brothers, who depicted scenes from the life of St. John the Baptist. The painters allegedly created their sketches from the blood of a freshly killed lamb. Built in the 16th century, the second church contains a nave with a colossal statue of St. Joseph from the 18th century. The very beautiful **stucco crib ★** is a life-size work that was the masterpiece of the artist Federico Brandani (1522–75).

Via Barocci. ✆ **347-6711181.** Admission 2.50€. Daily 10am–12:30pm, Mon–Sat 3–5:30pm.

Palazzo Ducale ★★★ and Galleria Nazionale delle Marche ★★ The greatest palace ever built in the Marches, this imposing monument was constructed by the Dalmatian architect Luciano Laurana between 1465 and 1482. It is a vision of harmonious design, a symphony of elegance, and home to the Galleria Nazionale delle Marche.

Come here to gaze upon some of the greatest collections of Renaissance art in all of Italy, rivaled only by some in Florence. There is a memorable *Madonna* by Verrocchio, and Uccello painted the *Profanation of the Host* in 1465, a work that frequents the pages of art history books. The great Piero della Francesca left behind a *Madonna of Senigallia* and a *Flagellation of Christ.* The *Ideal City,* a masterpiece of perspectivist wizardry, is often credited to him as well, though some art historians attribute it to Laurana.

The most important painting in the collection is Raphael's *The Mute One.* It is the portrait of a gentlewoman—her face, like Mona Lisa's smile, is usually called enigmatic by art historians. Painted in 1507, the picture now resides behind Plexiglas, having been stolen in 1975 and returned to Urbino in good condition 2 years later in one of the country's most sensational art thefts.

We like to save the best for last: The ducal study is decorated with stunning inlays often attributed to Botticelli. The inlays are mounted on panels and depict well-known men. Just van Gand, who painted the gallery's *Gathering of the Apostles,* also painted some of the portraits here.

Piazza Duca Federico 107. ✆ **0722-322625.** www.palazzoducaleurbino.it. Admission 4€ adults, 2€ ages 18–25, free for ages 17 and under. Mon 8:30am–2pm; Tues–Sun 8:30am–7:15pm.

WHERE TO STAY

Albergo San Domenico ★★ One of the most prestigious addresses in the Marches, this first-class *albergo* abuts the Church of San Domenico, with which it shares a wall. In fact, from the fourth floor of the hotel you can look through a window down into the church. A 4-minute walk from the main square of town, the hotel is the most convenient in Urbino, located across from the Ducal Palace. The hotel is imbued with comfort, elegance, and taste, having been carved from a 15th-century convent between the cathedral and the university. Bedrooms are large and furnished with thoughtful extras for your comfort, such as armchairs equipped for shiatsu massage.

Piazza Rinascimento 3, 61029 Urbino. ✆ **0722-2626.** Fax 0722-2727. www.viphotels.it. 31 units. 120€–210€ double; 220€–395€ suite. AE, DC, MC, V. Parking 9€–15€. **Amenities:** Restaurant; bar; babysitting; bikes; exercise room; room service. *In room:* A/C, TV, hair dryer, minibar, Wi-Fi (5€ per hr.).

San Giovanni 🍴 In the heart of the old town, San Giovanni is modesty itself compared to San Domenico, but its simply furnished, well-maintained, and comfortable accommodations offer the best value in Urbino. Many bedrooms open onto panoramic views of the town, especially room nos. 26 to 30. The hotel has a low-cost pizzeria and restaurant on the ground floor of the restored medieval building. Most of the bedrooms are fairly spacious, although the bathrooms are small with only showers. To reach it from the landmark Piazza della Repubblica, head to town on Via Mazzino, turning right at the signpost.

Via Barocci 13, 61029 Urbino. ✆ **0722-2827.** Fax 0722-329055. www.albergosangiovanni urbino.it. 31 units, 17 with bathroom. 50€ double without bathroom; 68€ double with bathroom. No credit cards. Parking 10€. Closed July and Christmas week. **Amenities:** Restaurant. *In room:* No phone.

The Palazzo Ducale in Urbino.

WHERE TO DINE

Nene ITALIAN   This rustic country cottage serves good food from a hillside 2km (1¼ miles) west of the town center. Expect traditional dishes that are well prepared and served by a hospitable staff in a welcoming environment. All of the dishes feature ingredients that change with the season. Nene's patrons flock here to feast on homemade fare such as gnocchi with Gorgonzola and pistachios, or grilled polenta (some of the best we've ever had). Stewed wild boar is a specialty. From ravioli to *pappardelle,* the homemade pastas are the best in the area. Filet of beef and various poultry dishes are prepared with flair, as is the array of freshly made desserts that are offered daily.

Strada Rossa Crocicchia. ✆ **0722-2996.** www.neneurbino.com. Reservations recommended. Main courses 8€–20€. AE, DC, MC, V. Tues–Sun 12:30–2:30pm and 7:30–10:30pm.

Vecchia Urbino ★ ITALIAN   The town's finest dining room, in the center of the ancient Lavagine quarter, is reached along narrow lanes. The restaurant boasts the ambience of a rustic yet elegant country inn. Vecchia Urbino, which opened in 1985, is a family-run concern that enjoys a devoted local clientele with educated palates. Gabriele and Eugenia Monti use organic ingredients when possible, and you'll delight in their offerings of fresh game, black and white truffles, savory cheese, and extra-virgin olive oils used in the salads, pasta, and meat dishes. Freshwater fish is shipped in from the seaside town of Fano. Rabbit is marinated in white wine and stuffed with a mixture of lard and fresh rosemary. Their lasagna—with a hand-rolled pasta and a sauce of chicken giblets, pork, veal, and other meats blended with a white sauce made in a bain-marie (double boiler) to gently heat the mixture—is absolutely a personal favorite.

Via dei Vasari 3-5. ✆ **0722-4447.** www.vecchiaurbino.it. Reservations required. Main courses 10€–26€. AE, DC, MC, V. Wed–Mon noon–3pm and 7–11pm.

Pesaro

216km (134 miles) NE of Perugia, 148km (92 miles) S of Ravenna, 122km (76 miles) N of Ancona, 315km (196 miles) E of Florence

In medieval times, Pesaro formed part of the Pentapolis, one of the five major seaports of the Adriatic. Those glory days are over, but Pesaro is still thriving—a more minor port today, but one known as a seaside resort and the birthplace of Gioacchino Rossini.

Pesaro is not big on major monuments, but it is worth a 3-hour stroll through its old quarter and along its beaches. If you're in town at nightfall, order a seafood dinner by the shore.

In early August, Pesaro's annual **Rossini Opera Festival** (✆ **0721-38001;** www.rossinioperafestival.it), featuring the composer's large repertoire of bel canto operas, draws music lovers from around the world.

To avoid literally hundreds of sunbathing Italian families in summer, head for the more secluded beach of **Baia Flaminia** just to the north of town.

ESSENTIALS

GETTING THERE   If you're approaching Pesaro from the north, you can take one of 35 trains per day from the seaside resort of Rimini. Travel time is half an hour, and the train costs 3.50€ one-way. From the west, 26 trains arrive daily from Bologna, taking 2 hours and costing 9.50€ one-way. Amibus (✆ **0722-376711;** www.amibus.it) runs frequent buses to Urbino from the Pesaro train station; 3€ buys you a one-way ticket for the trip, which takes just under an hour. Motorists can drive from Urbino to Pesaro by heading east on S423. The drive is 55km (34 miles) long.

VISITOR INFORMATION   Past Piazza del Popolo, the **tourist office,** Via Trieste 164 (✆ **0721-69341;** www.turismo.pesarourbino.it), is open daily 9am to 1pm and 3 to 6pm.

EXPLORING THE TOWN

The wide main square, **Piazza del Popolo,** occupies the heart of Pesaro. Cafes flank this piazza, which is dominated by a landmark fountain adorned with tritons and sea horses. The massive **Palazzo Ducale** was built in the 15th century by Alessandro Sforza. Scheduled events and exhibitions occasionally take place inside; otherwise, you can admire its facade.

The chief attraction in town is the **Musei Civici** ★, Via Toschi Mosca 29 (✆ **0721-387474;** www.museicivicipesaro.it). You can browse through one of Italy's finest collections of **Renaissance and baroque pottery** ★, much of it striking for its spontaneous, almost modern, use of color and design. Displayed inside is Giovanni Bellini's splendid *Coronation of the Virgin* polyptych ★. The altarpiece was painted in the 1470s and dominates all of the other art here, even the fiery *Fall of the Giants* by Guido Reni. Marco Zoppo left a *Pietà,* with a dead Christ so sensuous in his muscles it only added to the speculation that the artist was a practicing necrophiliac. Since Pesaro is known for its ceramics, a fine collection makes its home here: Especially impressive is a Medusa, with her trademark reptilian coiffure, by local artist Ferruccio Mengaroni.

Admission to the Musei Civici is 4€ for adults 27 and older, 2€ for ages 15 to 26, and free for children 14 and under. It's open all year Tuesday to Sunday 10am to 1pm and 3:30 to 7pm; Wednesday, Thursday, and Sunday 10am to 1pm.

Opera devotees flock to **Casa Rossini,** Via Rossini 34 (✆ **0721-387357**), where the great Rossini was born in 1792. This is a modest shrine to the composer of *The Barber of Seville* and three dozen or so other works, including *The Silken Ladder*. Universally honored, Rossini died in 1868. The museum displays photographs, signed opera scores, theatrical memorabilia, even Rossini's piano. Admission is 4€ adults, 2€ ages 15 to 26, and free for children 14 and under. It's open mid-September to May, Tuesday, Friday, and Saturday 10am to 1pm and 3:30 to 7pm; Wednesday, Thursday, and Sunday 10am to 1pm. June to mid-September Tuesday, Friday, and Saturday 10am to 1pm and 4:30 to 7:30pm; Wednesday 10am to 1pm; Thursday 10am to 1pm and 9 to 11pm; Sunday 4:30 to 7:30pm.

WHERE TO STAY

Hotel Vittoria ★★★   The town's luxury hotel, opened in 1908, perches on the main seaside promenade with a view of the Adriatic. The hotel has long been known for its elegance, comfort, and first-rate service—in fact, everyone from Pirandello to the Rothschilds, from Agnelli to Sting, has been coddled here. Vittoria was designated as one of Italy's "Hundred Historical Hotels." The only hotel in the Marches to receive this honor, it has also been consistently rated as one of the 20 best hotels in the country. The main lounge sets the stellar tone, with Grecian columns and a 16th-century fireplace. A lovely bar and tearoom open onto a famous seaside terrace where lunch is served in fair weather. Bedrooms are richly furnished with antiques, original paintings, and elaborate high beds, often in gold leaf.

Piazzale Libertà 2, 61100 Pesaro. ✆ **0721-34343.** Fax 0721-65204. www.viphotels.it. 27 units. 122€–318€ double; 220€–395€ suite. AE, DC, MC, V. Parking 12€. **Amenities:** Restaurant; American bar; bikes; children's center; exercise room; Jacuzzi; outdoor heated pool; room service; sauna. *In room:* A/C, TV, hair dryer, minibar, Wi-Fi (5€ per hr.).

Villa Serena ★ 🏠   Enjoying the most tranquil setting of the local hotels, this restored 17th-century villa in the neighborhood of Muraglia occupies its own park on a hilltop 4km (2½ miles) east of Pesaro and 4.8km (3 miles) west of the sea. Your welcoming hosts, the Pinto family, are the most hospitable in the area. Staying with them is like being a guest in an elegant private home of yesteryear. Furnished with antiques, the bedrooms are generally spacious and comfortably appointed with thoughtful extras to make your stay enjoyable. We prefer this oasis to the better-known and more expensive hotels nearby.

Via San Nicola 6/3, 61100 Pesaro. ✆ **0721-55211.** Fax 0721-55211. www.villa-serena.it. 8 units. 118€–170€ double; 130€–190€ suite. AE, DC, MC, V. Free parking. **Amenities:** Restaurant; bar; babysitting; outdoor pool; room service. *In room:* A/C, TV, hair dryer, minibar.

WHERE TO DINE

Da Alceo ★★ SEAFOOD   On the ground floor of the Hotel Le Terrazze, Da Alceo stands 5km (3 miles) east of the center of Pesaro along the "road to the sea" leading to Fano. It attracts gourmets from throughout the region to its well-run precincts with first-class service. The fish is the freshest around, and the varied menu boasts first-rate ingredients prepared with both skill and flair. Try such delights as baked "peter fish" with fresh vegetables, or scampi in a champagne sauce. The homemade pasta (*passatelli*) is served with scampi and monkfish. Monkfish, one of the most popular seafoods in Le Marche, is also served with

Pesaro's harbor.

potatoes and black olives. Always ask about what was "just caught"—the fresh fish can be prepared either grilled or sautéed, as you like it.

Strada Panoramica Ardizio 119. 🕿 **0721-51360.** www.ristorantealceo.it. Reservations recommended. Main courses 10€–28€; fixed-price menu 50€. AE, DC, MC, V. Tues–Sat 12:30–2pm and 8–11pm; Sun 12:30–2pm.

Ancona

139km (87 miles) NE of Perugia, 87km (54 miles) SE of Urbino, 76km (46 miles) S of Pesaro

Jutting out into the Adriatic, Ancona—one of the major ports along that sea—was the ancient gateway for thousands of visitors passing through to eastern countries like Greece, Slovenia, and Croatia.

Built in the form of an amphitheater on the slopes of a rocky promontory, Ancona drew its share of attention and was bombarded by the Austrians in 1915 and then by Allied forces in 1944. An earthquake leveled part of the old town in 1972. Throw in a major New Orleans–caliber flood or two, and you wonder how all the major monuments have remained standing.

But in spite of its past adversity, today's Ancona is prospering as more than just a stopover between ferry boats. Ancona is the chief town of the Marches, outranking both Urbino and Pesaro. Many travelers spend their layover in Ancona at the sparkling **Passetto Beach,** with its blue waters and family friendly sands (but not *the* sandiest along the east coast).

ESSENTIALS

GETTING THERE Ancona is a major transportation hub for the Marches, with rail links to both Milan (5 hr.) and Rome (3–4 hr.). Many visitors approach Ancona on a train from Pesaro. An amazing 40 trains per day make the 45-minute run that costs 3.50€ to 13€ one-way. The train from Venice takes 5 hours, costing 27€ to 76€ one-way. Motorists heading south along the Adriatic coast approach Ancona from Pesaro, following S16 and E55 (it's signposted).

VISITOR INFORMATION   Offering good maps, the **tourist office** at Via Gramsci 2A (✆ **320-0196321**), is open April to December Monday to Friday 10am to 1pm and 4 to 8pm, and Saturday from 10am to 1pm.

EXPLORING ANCONA

As a remnant of Ancona's illustrious past, the **Arco di Traiano** ★, built to honor the emperor Trajan, who constructed the port in A.D. 115, still stands at the northern end of Lungomare Vanvitelli. The sculptural reliefs have gone with the wind, but the arch is still one of the best preserved along the Adriatic.

At the center of the port stands the **Loggia dei Mercanti,** constructed in the 15th-century Venetian Gothic style. This was the merchants' exchange, the work of a Dalmatian, Giorgio Orsini, and the best monument to Ancona's heyday as a great maritime city.

Duomo ★   Dedicated to St. Cyriacus, the 4th-century martyr and patron saint of Ancona, this cathedral is Romanesque with both Byzantine and Lombard architectural features. It crowns Monte Guasco, which in the days of antiquity held a famous temple dedicated to Venus. The cathedral is reached by climbing a steep garden staircase, *Scalone Nappi* (you can also take bus 11 from Piazza Cavour). Inside, the marble columns were actually those that once held up the Temple of Venus. Note the carved altar screen from the 12th century. However, the glory of the church is not inside, but on its facade, which is fronted by a majestic Gothic porch made of pink stone and held up by two fierce lions.

Piazzale del Duomo. ✆ **071-52688.** Free admission. Mon–Sat 8am–noon and 3-7pm (closes at 6pm in winter).

Museo Archeologico Nazionale delle Marche   Installed in the landmark Palazzo Ferretti, this museum, one of the major repositories of art in the Marches, is stuffed with prehistoric and archaeological relics of the region. Look for exceptional Greek vases, sculpture, and metalwork left by Greek traders. Greek jewelry was unearthed early in the 20th century, and the collection includes bronze incense-burning pots, the most famous of which, the Ionian Dinos of Amandola, date from the 5th century B.C.

Via Ferretti 6. ✆ **071-202602.** Admission 4€. Tues–Sun 8:30am-7:30pm.

The World War II memorial at Passetto Beach in Ancona.

Pinacoteca Civica Francesco Podesti ★   This is one of the finest art galleries in the Marches. We come here mainly to see the works of Carlo Crivelli, who has the dubious distinction of being called "one of the tidiest of all Renaissance artists." In his *Madonna with Bambino,* look for his trademark: a depiction of apples and cucumbers hanging overhead. The collection includes minor works by big names such as Titian and Lorenzo Lotto, both of whom are also represented by their own versions of the Madonna. There is even a modest collection of art from the 20th century.

Via Ciriaco Pizzecolli. ✆ **071-2225045.** Admission 5€ adults, 3.50€ ages 16–25, free for those 15 and under. Tues–Fri 9am–7pm; Sat 10am–6pm; Sun 10am–1pm and 4–6pm.

WHERE TO STAY

Grand Hotel Palace ★   The town's best hotel in the port area opened in 1968 and has been much renovated and improved since those days. Fronting the harbor in the city center, it offers a roof garden terrace where breakfast is served—guests can take in the view from the best vantage point in Ancona. The hotel is the epitome of taste and elegance, with classic decor in its public and private rooms, which are often filled with antiques and luxurious touches like beds dressed in damask. Try, if possible, for a room with a view of the port. Bedrooms are midsize—each with a small bathroom (half with showers, the others with tubs).

Lungomare Vanvitelli 24, 60121 Ancona. ✆ **071-201813.** Fax 071-2074832. www.hotelancona.it. 40 units. 160€ double; 300€ suite. Rates include buffet breakfast. AE, DC, MC, V. Parking 21€. Closed Dec 23–Jan 1. **Amenities:** Bar; babysitting; room service. *In room:* A/C, TV, hair dryer, minibar, Wi-Fi (free).

WHERE TO DINE

La Moretta 1897 ★ SEAFOOD/ITALIAN   In the historic medieval center, this classic *trattoria* offers the port's finest dining against a background of wood-paneled walls and top-notch service. The family run *trattoria* secures some of the finest ingredients for its dishes, including fresh fish from the Adriatic and the agricultural bounty of the countryside. We always gravitate here just to devour its *brodetto all'anconetana,* which is the typical local fish soup. This might be followed with *maccheroncino in salsa righera* (homemade long pasta with fresh fish and a "fruits of the sea" sauce). Another local favorite is *racchiusi di mare* (a kind of ravioli stuffed with fish). A final specialty is Adriatic sea bass baked in parchment paper.

Piazza Plebiscito 52. ✆ **071-202317.** www.trattoriamoretta.com. Reservations recommended. Main courses 8€–18€. AE, DC, MC, V. Mon–Sat 12:15–3pm and 5:30–11pm. Closed Jan 1–8.

Ascoli Piceno

175km (109 miles) SE of Perugia, 122km (76 miles) S of Ancona

It's the city of travertine, a stone used harmoniously in Ascoli Piceno's medieval and Renaissance buildings and its hundred towers. This romantic architecture has earned the town the title of "Little Siena." Ringed by steep hills, Ascoli Piceno lies in a valley where the Castellano and Tronto rivers meet. One of the gems of the Marches, the town was the metropolis of the Piceno, a Latin tribe that once controlled much of the region bordering the Adriatic. You can drive around this "remembrance of things past," but its *centro storico* (central historic district) is for pedestrians only.

Allow about 4 hours to explore the town, much of which can be appreciated from the outside, even if you never duck into a church or a museum (although there are plenty of those, too).

The city's past is honored in numerous festivals, including the **Tournament of St. Emidio,** the patron saint of Ascoli Piceno. Hundreds of citizens don medieval clothing for jousting tournaments and torch-lit processions on the first Sunday in August. Six sections of town stage their own fierce competition evocative of the more famous Palio at Siena.

ESSENTIALS

GETTING THERE   Most travelers by train go through the gateway of San Benedetto del Tronto, lying 39km (24 miles) to the east near the coast. At San Benedetto trains arrive from Ancona frequently, a one-way fare costing 4.50€. From here trains run to Ascoli Piceno every half-hour, costing 2.50€.

Buses from San Benedetto are more crowded than trains and passage takes an hour; we do not recommend them. For motorists, Ascoli Piceno is usually approached by drivers heading down the Adriatic coast, perhaps after a stopover in Ancona (see above). Once you reach San Benedetto del Tronto, cut inland along S4 for the final run into Ascoli.

VISITOR INFORMATION   In the heart of town, the **tourist office** is situated at Piazza Arringo 7 (✆ **0736-253045**), open Monday to Friday 8:30am to 1:30pm and 3 to 7pm, Saturday 9am to 1pm and 3 to 7pm, and Sunday 9am to 1:30pm.

EXPLORING THE TOWN

Start at **Piazza del Popolo ★★**, the main square in the heart of the *centro storico.* Elongated and beautifully proportioned, it's surrounded by impressive Gothic and Renaissance mansions and riddled with imposing arcades.

To get your bearings, stop for a coffee or a drink at **Caffè Meletti ★**, Piazza del Popolo 20 (✆ **0736-259626;** www.caffemeletti.com); founded in 1904, it is the most famous watering hole in the Marches today. Silvio Meletti first served his now-famous *anisette* liqueur at this cafe, and it was introduced to the world in the classic 1960 film *I delfini* by Citto Maselli. In summer the cafe is open daily from 7am to midnight (closed Mon in winter).

Dominating the square is **Palazzo dei Capitani ★** (✆ **0736-244975**), the former town hall, erected in the 13th century. Visitors can walk inside for a look at its 16th-century arcaded courtyard.

At the narrow end of the square, the Romanesque-Gothic **Chiesa di San Francesco ★** is open daily from 8am to noon and 3:30 to 7:30pm. Admission is free. The church has several Lombard architectural features and a wood crucifix rescued from a 1535 fire. Over the south door is a statue of Pope Julius II. In spite of its Gothic bays and towers resting under a low dome, the church's look is austere. The southern end of the facade links with the **Loggia dei Mercanti ★**, constructed in the 1500s by local wool merchants.

The **Duomo,** or cathedral, of Ascoli Piceno stands on Piazza Arringo and combines classical, Romanesque, and baroque architectural features. The facade is from the 1530s, built to the design of Cola dell'Amatrice, but the transept was once a Roman basilica. The octagonal dome actually was first constructed in the 8th century. The Duomo is richly decorated with frescoes. Stairs lead down into the Cripta di Sant'Emidio, which houses the tomb of the city's patron saint. Adjacent to the cathedral stands the squat **baptistery** from the 12th century. Free admission; the complex is open daily from 7am to 12:30pm and 5:30 to 7:30pm.

Also standing on Piazza Arringo is the **Pinacoteca Civica** (© 0736-298213), open daily from 9am to 7pm, for an admission of 8€. Housed in the massive Palazzo Arringo, the gallery features some of the most famous paintings in the Marches, with works by Carlo Crivelli (1430–94), who married the solidity of Renaissance geometry with late Gothic decorative opulence, and Cola dell'Amatrice, who designed the facade of the Duomo.

Afterward, a stroll through the historic center is in order. The main street, **Corso Mazzini ★**, is lined with historic *palazzi*, many from the Middle Ages. Also filled with mansions, **Via dei Soderini** was the main artery in medieval days. Feudal towers can also be seen along this street. Allow time to dart off down a few of its intriguing side streets.

WHERE TO STAY

Hotel Pennile   In spite of its unhelpful staff, this is the best hotel in town. Rooms are comfortably and tastefully furnished. Il Pennile stands in a tranquil residential area outside the *centro storico* in a grove of olive trees. With its fitness center and other facilities, the hotel is also the best equipped in town. Bathrooms are small with showers only, but are functionally adequate. It's fine for an overnight, but we wouldn't want to linger here.

Via Spalvieri, 63100 Ascoli Piceno. © **0736-41545.** Fax 0736-342755. www.hotelpennile.it. 33 units. 70€ double; 80€ triple. Rates include buffet breakfast. AE, DC, MC, V. Free parking. **Amenities:** Bar; exercise room; room service. *In room:* A/C, TV, hair dryer, minibar, Wi-Fi (free).

Hotel Residenza Cento Torri ★★   This exclusive hotel was created from the stables of a patrician *palazzo* dating from the 13th century. That such luxury can be made from former stables is amazing. The hotel lies in the ancient core of town, within walking distance of Piazza del Popolo in the heart of town. All of the individually designed bedrooms have been furnished with sophisticated designer taste, and the latest in modern accessories installed. From the parquet floors to the soft upholstery to the romantic canopied beds, this is a pocket of posh. Breakfast is served in the winter garden under a pyramidal glass roof.

Via Mazzoni 6, 63100 Ascoli Piceno. © **0736-255123.** Fax 0736-251646. www.centotorri.com. 14 units. 128€–225€ double; 295€–420€ suite. Rates include buffet breakfast. AE, DC, MC, V. Free parking. **Amenities:** Bar; babysitting; room service; spa; Wi-Fi (free, in lobby). *In room:* A/C, TV, hair dryer, minibar.

WHERE TO DINE

Gallo d'Oro ★ ITALIAN/ASCOLANA   In the historic center of town, the best restaurant in the area is housed in a small villa from the 1950s, with a classic decor of terra-cotta floors and wooden panels and chairs. Some 100 diners can pile in here and select a table on one of two floors, but in summer you can also dine outside in the courtyard. You can order the best and most authentic regional specialties here, more so than at any other restaurant in town. Our favorite is the *fritto misto all'ascolana* (a mixed fry of stuffed olives, fresh artichokes, and tender, succulent lamb cutlets). Other delectable menu items include homemade pasta with tomatoes and porcini mushrooms, or else risotto with pecorino cheese, black pepper, broccoli rabe, and crispy sausage.

Corso Vittorio Emanuele 54. © **0736-253520.** Reservations recommended. Main courses 8€–21€. AE, DC, MC, V. Mon–Fri 12:30–2:30pm; Mon–Sat 7:30–10:15pm. Closed Aug 15–31.

BOLOGNA & EMILIA-ROMAGNA

I n the northern reaches of central Italy, the region of Emilia-Romagna is known for its gastronomy and for its art cities, Modena and Parma. Here, such families as the Renaissance dukes of Ferrara rose in power and influence, creating courts that attracted painters and poets.

Bologna, the region's capital, stands at the crossroads between Venice and Florence and is linked by express highways to Milan and Tuscany. By basing yourself in this ancient university city, you can branch out in all directions: north for 52km (32 miles) to Ferrara; southeast for 50km (31 miles) to the ceramics-making town of Faenza; northwest for 40km (25 miles) to Modena, with its Romanesque cathedral; or farther northwest for 55km (34 miles) to Parma, the legendary capital of the Farnese family duchy in the 16th century. Ravenna, famed for its mosaics, lies 74km (46 miles) east of Bologna on the Adriatic Sea.

Most of our stops in this region lie on the ancient Roman road, **Via Emilia,** which began in Rimini and stretched to Piacenza, a Roman colony that often attracted invading barbarians. This ancient land (known to the Romans as Aemilia, and to the Etruscans before them) is rich in architecture (Parma's cathedral and baptistery) and in scenic beauty (the green plains and the slopes of the Apennines). Emilia is one of Italy's most bountiful farming districts and sets a table highly praised in Europe, both for its wines and for its imaginatively prepared pasta dishes.

BOLOGNA ★★

52km (32 miles) S of Ferrara, 151km (94 miles) SW of Venice, 378km (234 miles) N of Rome

A relic from Dante's era and Europe's oldest student city, Bologna *La Dotta* ("the learned") lives on in its redbrick towers and stately colonnades. Red, along with nicknames, is something you'll see a lot of in Bologna *La Rossa* ("the red"). It's the color of the city's greatest gift to students everywhere—spaghetti Bolognese—and what the predominantly socialist Bolognesi see whenever a political debate is raging. Heading to nearby Florence? Make sure the less touristy Bologna *La Grassa* ("the fat")—Italy's gourmet capital—gets equal time.

Things to Do   Bologna's red-tiled roofs tumble out before you like a red carpet from the 12th-century leaning **Tower of the Asinelli.** All streets lead to the city's lively hub, **Piazza Maggiore,** dominated by the unfinished **Basilica di San Petronio.** It's been that way since the 16th century, when the pope halted work to stop it outdoing Rome's St. Peter's. Head to the **Manifattura della Arti** to visit the **Museo d'Arte Moderna di Bologna,** Bologna's version of London's Tate Modern.

Shopping   Raining outside? Not a problem for the style-conscious Bolognesi—the shopping streets in the city's **historic center** are covered in intricately decorated porticoes. Embrace the Bolognesi gourmet obsession and stop into hole-in-the-wall delicatessens to buy tasty wedges of **Parmesan** and the local *mortadella* **sausage.** Do your shopping before lunch—once food is served, the

PREVIOUS PAGE: **Bologna's Baptistery.**

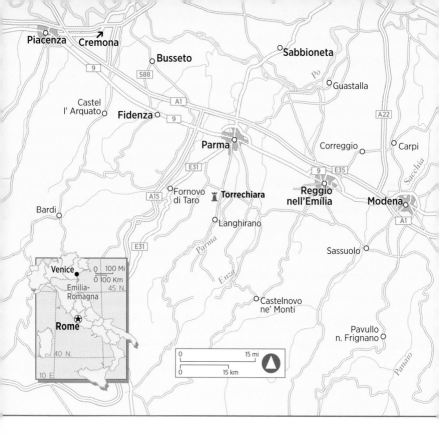

shops shut and the streets empty. For big department stores, try the **Via Rizzoli,** the city's central thoroughfare.

Nightlife & Entertainment   Like denim-clad pigeons, the young perch on the steps of **Neptune Fountain,** while their elders gather in local cafes. Everyone ends up drinking in the fading sunlight on the **Piazza Maggiore.** Start your evening the local way with a leisurely *passeggiata* stroll around the square. Bologna's cultured minds get a workout at the **Teatro Comunale,** the city's main arts venue, before gathering under vaulted 15th-century ceilings at cool, low-lit bars in the student quarter around **Via Zamboni.**

Eating & Drinking   Bologna and the Emilia Romagna region have given the world not only spaghetti Bolognese but also pasta shapes of tortellini and *tagliatelle* fame. Make a reservation at **Diana,** the city's favorite restaurant, to taste true Bologna. White-jacketed waiters have been serving regional dishes like *tortellini en brodo,* stuffed tortellini parcels in a steaming broth, to discerning Bolognese diners since the 1920s. Wash it down with a glass of sparkling red Lambrusco from the vineyards outside the city.

Essentials

GETTING THERE   The international **Aeroporto Guglielmo Marconi** (② **051-6479615;** www.bologna-airport.it) is 6km (3¾ miles) north of the town

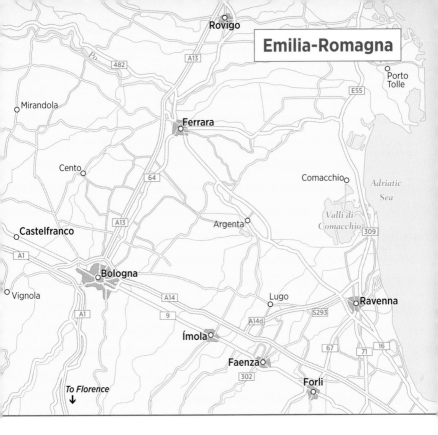

center and served by such domestic carriers as Alitalia and Meridiana; all the main European airlines have connections through this airport. An **Aerobus** (marked AEROBUS) runs daily every 20 minutes from the airport to the air terminal at Bologna's rail station. A one-way ticket costs 5€.

Bologna's **Stazione Centrale rail station** is at Piazza Medaglie d'Oro 2 (✆ **892021**). Trains arrive hourly from Rome (trip time: 3½ hr.). There are also high-speed trains from Rome to Bologna (trip time 2 hr., 20 min.). A one-way fare costs 23€ to 80€. From Milan, trip time is 2 hours, 10 minutes, costing 12€ to 56€ one-way. Bus nos. A, 25, and 30 run between the station and the historic core of Bologna, Piazza Maggiore.

If you have a **car** and are coming from Florence, continue north along A1 until reaching the outskirts of Bologna, where signs direct you to the city center. From Milan, take A1 southeast along the Apennines. From Venice or Ferrara, follow A13 southwest. From Rimini, Ravenna, and the towns along the Adriatic, cut west on A14.

VISITOR INFORMATION The **tourist office** is at Piazza Maggiore 1, open daily 9am to 7pm. There are two other offices, one at the railway station, Piazza Medaglie d'Oro 2, and the other one at the airport. Hours at the rail station are Monday to Saturday 9am to 7pm, and Sunday 9am to 3pm. The central number to call for all tourist information is ✆ **051-239660,** and the website is www.bolognaturismo.info.

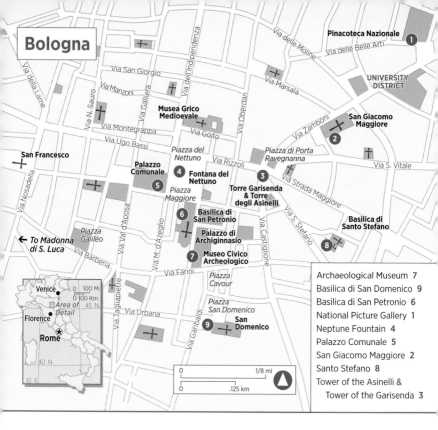

Archaeological Museum	**7**
Basilica di San Domenico	**9**
Basilica di San Petronio	**6**
National Picture Gallery	**1**
Neptune Fountain	**4**
Palazzo Comunale	**5**
San Giacomo Maggiore	**2**
Santo Stefano	**8**
Tower of the Asinelli & Tower of the Garisenda	**3**

GETTING AROUND   Bologna is easy to cover on foot; most of the major sights are in and around Piazza Maggiore. However, if you don't want to walk, **city buses** leave for most points from Piazza Nettuno or Piazza Maggiore. Free maps are available at the storefront office of the **ATC** (Azienda Trasporti Comunali) at Piazza XX Settembre (✆ **051-290290;** www.atc.bo.it). You can buy tickets at one of many booths and tobacconists in Bologna. The ATC Customer Service Office is at Via IV Novembre 16A, open Monday to Saturday from 7:45am to 7:45pm. Tickets cost 1€ and last 60 minutes. A **citypass**—a booklet of 10 tickets, each valid for 1 hour—costs 8.50€. There is also a 1-day ticket, valid for 24 hours, that costs 3€. Once on board, you must have your ticket validated or you'll be fined up to 150€.

Taxis are on radio call at ✆ **051-372727** or 051-534141.

Exploring the City

On Piazza del Nettuno (adjacent to Piazza Maggiore) stands the **Neptune Fountain (Fontana di Nettuno)** ★★, which has gradually become a symbol of the city, although it was designed in 1566 by a Frenchman named Giambologna (the Italians altered his name). Viewed as irreverent by some, "indecent" by the Catholic Church, and magnificent by those with more liberal tastes, this 16th-century fountain depicts Neptune with rippling muscles, a trident in one arm, and a heavy foot on the head of a dolphin. The church forced Giambologna to manipulate Neptune's left arm to cover his monumental endowment. Giambologna's defenders denounced this as "artistic castration." Around his feet are four highly erotic cherubs, also with dolphins. At the base of the fountain, four very sensual sirens spout streams of water from their breasts.

Archaeological Museum (Museo Civico Archeologico) ★ This museum houses one of Italy's major Egyptian collections, as well as important discoveries dug up in Emilia. As you enter, look to the right in the atrium to see a decapitated marble torso, said to be Nero's. One floor below street level, a new Egyptian section presents a notable array of mummies and sarcophagi. The chief attraction in this collection is a cycle of bas-reliefs from Horemheb's tomb. On the ground floor, a new wing contains a gallery of casts, displaying copies of famous Greek and Roman sculptures. On the first floor are two exceptional burial items from Verrucchio (Rimini). Note the wood furnishings, footrests, and throne of tomb 89, decorated with scenes from everyday life and ceremonial parades.

Upstairs are cases of prehistoric objects, tools, and artifacts. Etruscan relics constitute the best part of the museum, especially the highly stylized *Askos Benacci,* depicting a man on a horse that's perched on yet another animal. Also displayed are terra-cotta urns, a vase depicting fighting Greeks and Amazons, and a bronze Certosa jar from the 6th century B.C. The museum's greatest treasure is Phidias's head of Athena Lemnia, a copy of the 5th-century-B.C. Greek work.

Via dell'Archiginnasio 2. ℰ **051-2757211.** www.comune.bologna.it. Free admission. Tues–Fri 9am–3pm; Sat–Sun 10am–6:30pm. Bus: A, B, 11, 13, or 14.

Basilica di San Domenico ★ The basilica dates from the 13th century but has undergone many restorations. It houses the beautifully crafted **tomb of St. Domenico,** in front of the Cappella della Madonna. The sculptured tomb, known as an *area,* is a Renaissance masterpiece, a joint enterprise of Niccolò Pisano, Guglielmo (a friar), Niccolò dell'Arca, Alfonso Lombardi, and the young

Bologna's Palazzo Communale.

Detail from the tomb of St. Domenico.

Michelangelo. Observe the gaze and stance of Michelangelo's *San Procolo,* which appears to be the "rehearsal" for his later *David.* The **choir stalls ★** were carved by Damiano da Bergamo, another friar, in the 16th century.

Piazza San Domenico 13. (✆ **051-6400411.** Free admission. Daily 8am–12:30pm and 3:30–6:30pm. Bus: 16, 30, 38, 39, or 52.

Basilica di San Petronio ★★   Sadly, the facade of this enormous Gothic basilica honoring the patron saint of Bologna was never completed. Legend has it that the construction was curtailed by papal decree when the Vatican learned that the Bologna city fathers had planned to erect a basilica larger than St. Peter's. Although the builders went to work in 1390, after 3 centuries the church was still not finished (nevertheless, Charles V was crowned emperor here in 1530). Jacopo della Quercia of Siena did grace the central door with a masterpiece Renaissance sculpture. Inside, the church could accommodate the traffic of New York's Grand Central Terminal. The central nave is separated from the aisles by pilasters shooting up to the ceiling's flying arches. Of the 22 art-filled chapels, the most interesting is the **Bolognini Chapel (Cappella Bolognini),** the fourth on the left as you enter; it's embellished with frescoes representing heaven and hell. The purity and simplicity of line represent some of the best of the Gothic in Italy.

Piazza Maggiore. (✆ **051-225442.** Free admission. Daily 7:30am–12:30pm and 3–6pm. Bus: 11, 13, 14, 17, 18, 19, 20, or 25.

National Picture Gallery (Pinacoteca Nazionale di Bologna) ★★   The most significant works of the school of painting that flourished in Bologna from the 14th century to the heyday of the baroque have been assembled under one roof in this second-floor *pinacoteca.* The gallery also houses works by other major Italian artists, such as Raphael's *St. Cecilia in Estasi.* Guido Reni (1575–1642) of Bologna steals the scene with his *St. Sebastian* and *Pietà,* along with his penetrating *St. Andrea Corsini, The Slaying of the Innocents,* and idealized *Samson the Victorious.* Other Reni works are *The Flagellation of Christ, The Crucifixion,* and his masterpiece, *Ritratto della Madre* (a revealing portrait of his mother that must surely have inspired Whistler). Then seek out Vitale de Bologna's (1330–61) rendition of St. George slaying the dragon—a theme in European art that parallels *Moby-Dick* in America. Also displayed are works by Francesco Francia, and especially noteworthy is a polyptych attributed to Giotto.

Via Belle Arti 56. ✆ **051-4209411.** www.pinacotecabologna.it. Admission 4€ adults, free for children 18 and under. Tues–Sun 9am–7pm. Closed holidays. Bus: 20, 28, 36, 37, 89, or 93.

Palazzo Comunale ★   Built in the 14th century, this town hall has seen major restorations but retains its splendor. Enter through the courtyard; then proceed up the steps on the right to the **Communal Collection of Fine Arts (Collezioni Comunali d'Arte;** www.iperbole.bologna.it), which includes many paintings from the 14th- to 19th-century Emilian school. Another section, the **Museum of Giorgio Morandi** (**Museo di Giorgio Morandi;** www.museomorandi.it), is devoted to the works of this famed Bolognese painter (1890–1964). His subject matter (a vase of flowers or a box) might have been mundane, but he transformed

FACTORY OF the arts

For decades, no visitor went to the northwest corridor of old Bologna, home to tobacco factories, saltworks, and slaughterhouses. Today, lying only a 15-minute walk from the heart of Bologna, it has become a center of art, boutiques, and chic restaurants and cafes. The district between Via Don Minzoni and Via Riva di Reno is now called **Manifattura della Arti,** or Factory of the Arts.

At its core is the **Museo d'Arte Moderna di Bologna** (nicknamed Mambo), Via Don Minzoni 14 (✆ **051-649-6611;** www. mambo-bologna.org), hailed as the Bologna version of London's Tate Modern. Admission is 6€ for adults, 4€ for ages 6 to 17, and free for children 5 and under; hours are Tuesday to Wednesday, Friday to Sunday 10am to 6pm; Thursday 10am to 10pm. The museum showcases its permanent collection of Italian art, but also is home to traveling exhibitions of the avant-garde. On-site is **Ex Forno** (✆ **051-649-3896;** www.mambo-bologna.org), one of the best places in Bologna for a light lunch, featuring such dishes as salade niçoise or *risotto al funghi* (mushroom risotto), costing from 10€ per platter.

Experimental music and dance performances are showcased at the theater of the **Centro di Musica e Spettacolo** at Via Azzo Gardino 65A (✆ **051-209-2400;** www.muspe.unibo.it/cimes), sponsored by the University of Bologna.

Near Mambo is a striking red stucco silo housing **Cineteca,** Via Azzo Gardino 65 (✆ **051-219-5311;** www.cinetecadi bologna.it), an art and film house with two theaters. Festivals are devoted to every artist from actor Sean Penn to the notorious director Pier Paolo Pasolini, who was killed in Rome by a male hustler. The film center operates a nearby gallery, **Sala Espositiva della Cineteca,** Via Riva di Reno 72, displaying movie photographs, vintage movie posters, and other cinema memorabilia in a former tobacco factory.

Among the many boutiques in the district is **Daniele Ancarani,** Via Porta Nova 8A (✆ **051-272745;** www.daniele ancarani.it), one of the best designer stores in Bologna.

As you wander the district, you'll find plenty of cafes and bars where you can take a break, including **Bar Planet,** Via Porta Nova 16 (✆ **051-236300**), a cyber-cafe where you can order sandwiches and wine by the glass. Or else try the tea and chocolate shop of **Strega Te,** Via Porta Nova 7A (✆ **051-222564;** www. stregate.it). Our preferred choice of pizza in Bologna is served at **Café du Midi,** Via Porta Nova 4 (✆ **051-224485**). Order the Parma ham–topped pizza fresh from a wood oven, and the day is yours.

The main doorway to the Basilica di San Petronio.

these objects into works of art of startling intensity and perception. Some of his finest works are landscapes of Grizzana, a village where he spent many lazy summers working and drawing. There's also a reconstruction of his studio.

Piazza Maggiore 6. ⓒ **051-2031111.** Free admission. Tues–Sun 10am–6pm. Closed holidays. Bus: 11, 17, 25, 27, 30, or 86.

San Giacomo Maggiore (St. James) ★ This church was a Gothic structure in the 13th century but, like so many others, was altered and restored at the expense of its original design. Still, it's one of Bologna's most interesting churches, filled with art treasures. The **Bentivoglio Chapel (Cappella Bentivoglio)** is the most sacred haunt, although time has dimmed the luster of its frescoes. Near the altar, seek out a *Madonna and Child* enthroned, one of the most outstanding works of Francesco Erancia. The holy pair is surrounded by angels and saints, as well as by a half-naked Sebastian to the right. Nearby is a sepulcher of Antonio Bentivoglio, designed by Jacopo della Quercia, who labored so long over the doors to the Basilica of San Petronio. In the **Chapel of Santa Cecilia (Cappella di Santa Cecilia),** you'll discover important frescoes by Francia and Lorenzo Costa.

Piazza Rossini. ⓒ **051-225970.** Free admission. Daily 7am–noon and 3:30–6:30pm. Bus: C.

Santo Stefano ★   From the leaning towers (see below), head up Via Santo Stefano to see four churches linked together. A church has stood on this site since the 5th century, converted from a Temple of Isis. Charlemagne stopped here to worship on his way to France in the 8th century.

The first church you enter is the 11th-century **Church of the Crucifix (Chiesa del Crocifisso),** relatively simple with only one nave and a crypt. To the left is the entrance to **Santo Sepolcro,** a polygonal temple dating principally from the 12th century. Under the altar is the tomb of San Petronio (St. Petronius), modeled after the Holy Sepulcher in Jerusalem and adorned with bas-reliefs. Continuing left, you enter the churches of **Santi Vitale e Agricola.** The present building, graced with three apses, also dates from the 11th century. To reenter Santo Sepolcro, take the back entrance, this time into the **Courtyard of Pilate (Cortile di Pilato),** onto which several more chapels open. Legend has it that the basin in the courtyard was the one in which Pontius Pilate washed his hands after condemning Christ to death. (Actually, it's a Lombard bathtub from the 8th c.) Through the courtyard entrance to the right, proceed into the Romanesque **cloisters** from the 11th and 12th centuries. The names on the lapidary wall honor Bolognese war dead.

Via Santo Stefano 24. ⓒ **051-223256.** www.abbaziasantostefano.it. Free admission. Daily 9am–noon and 3:30–6:30pm. Bus: 11, 13, 19, 25, 27, 29, or 30.

Torre degli Asinelli & Tower of the Garisenda ★★   Built by patricians in the 12th century, these leaning towers, the virtual symbol of Bologna, keep defying gravity year after year. In the Middle Ages, Bologna contained dozens of these skyscraper towers. The towers were status symbols: The more powerful the family was, the taller its tower was. The smaller one, the Garisenda, is only 49m (162 ft.) tall, but because the Garisendas didn't prepare a solid foundation, it sways tipsily to the south, about 3m (11 ft.) from perpendicular. In 1360, part of the tower was lopped off because it was viewed as a threat to public safety. Access to the Garisenda still isn't allowed. The taller one, the Asinelli (102m/334 ft. tall, a walk-up of nearly 500 steps), inclines almost 2.5m (7½ ft.). The reward for scaling the Asinelli is a panoramic view of the red-tile roofs of Bologna and the green hills beyond.

After visiting the towers, stroll what must be the most architecturally elegant street in Bologna, **Via Strada Maggiore,** with its colonnades and mansions.

Piazza di Porta Ravegnana. Admission 3€. Summer daily 9am–6pm (to 5pm off season). Bus: 13, 14, 19, 25, or 27.

Where to Stay

Bologna hosts four to six trade fairs a year, during which hotel room rates rise dramatically. Some hotels announce their prices in advance; others wait to see what the market will bear. At trade fair times (dates vary yearly; check with the tourist office), business clients from throughout Europe book the best rooms, and you'll be paying a lot of money to visit Bologna.

An important note on parking: Much of central Bologna is closed to cars without special permits from 7am to 8pm daily (including Sun and holidays). When booking a room, be prepared to present your car registration number, which the hotel will then provide to the police to ensure that you are not fined for driving in a restricted area. Also, ask about parking facilities as well as the most efficient route to take to reach your hotel, because many streets in central Bologna are permanently closed to traffic. A permit is required to park in the center; hotel guests can purchase one through their hotel, if offered.

VERY EXPENSIVE

Grand Hotel Majestic ★★★   The Majestic boasts a location near Bologna's main square and is a superb atmospheric choice, a favorite of celebrities. Its four-story facade is crafted of the same reddish brick that distinguishes many of the city's older buildings, and the interior is noted for its wall and ceiling frescoes. In fact, the restaurant frescoes were painted by the Carracci brothers in the 16th century, and part of an old Roman road can be seen on the way to the breakfast room. The rooms are elegantly appointed featuring Venetian style furniture and a Murano-glass chandelier. The 4th floor refurbishment has enriched the hotel with a

The Tower of the Asinelli and the Tower of the Garisenda.

new range of junior suites and deluxe rooms. The style in this case is 18th-century French. They're generally spacious, with the fourth-floor units being the largest. There's also an excellent restaurant, I Carracci.

Via dell'Indipendenza 8, 40121 Bologna. ℭ **051-225445.** Fax 051-234840. www.duetorrihotels. com. 109 units. 265€–560€ double; from 790€ suite. Rates include buffet breakfast. AE, DC, MC, V. Parking 32€. **Amenities:** Restaurant; bar; airport transfers (30€); babysitting; bikes; exercise room; room service; spa. *In room:* A/C, TV, hair dryer, minibar, Wi-Fi (free).

Royal Hotel Carlton ★★   Some claim that the Carlton, only a few minutes' walk from many of the national monuments, is the best hotel in Bologna, but we feel the honor goes to the Grand Hotel Majestic (see above). The Hilton-style Carlton is a rather austere place with a triangular garden, catering mainly to business travelers. It's modern all the way, with a balcony and a picture window for each room, although the views aren't particularly inspiring. The guest rooms range from medium to large, each with a comfortable bed.

Via Montebello 8, 40121 Bologna. ℭ **051-249361.** Fax 051-249724. www.monrifhotels.com. 240 units. 450€–490€ double; from 800€ suite. Rates include buffet breakfast. AE, DC, MC, V. Parking 15€–20€ in garage; free outside. Bus: A, C, E, 11, 17, or 21. **Amenities:** Restaurant; bar; babysitting; exercise room; room service; spa. *In room:* A/C, TV, hair dryer, minibar, Wi-Fi (10€ per 24 hr.).

EXPENSIVE

Albergo Al Cappello Rosso   If you need a break from rustic charm, this is the hotel for you, dating from 1375 and located just 50m (164 ft.) from Piazza Maggiore. In the 14th century, the "Red Hat" in the hotel's name referred to the preferred headgear of the privileged tradesmen who stayed here. Now the hotel has been revamped into an ultramodern place with no hint of its past. The guest rooms tend to be modular, small to medium in size and each with a good bed. Breakfast is the only meal served.

Via dei Fusari 9, 40123 Bologna. ℭ **051-261891.** Fax 051-227179. www.alcappellorosso.it. 32 units. 109€–365€ double; 209€–435€ suite. Rates include buffet breakfast. AE, DC, MC, V. Parking 25€. Bus: A, B, D, E, or 30. **Amenities:** Babysitting; bikes; room service; Wi-Fi (free, in lobby). *In room:* A/C, TV, hair dryer, minibar.

Art Hotel Novecento ★★   This has become one of our favorite personality inns of Bologna, its design evoking the Continent of the prewar 1930s, the hey-day of elegant travel. Although it turns to the past for its inspiration, it is completely up-to-date in its amenities. Ideal for a romantic weekend, the inn lies in the very heart of Bologna. The building itself is in the so-called Viennese Secession style, taking inspiration from flower motifs and the works of the painter Gustav Klimt. Each of the midsize bedrooms is decorated in an individual style. Regardless of your room assignment, you can count on a great

Reserving Winery Tours

Emilia's most famous wine is Lambrusco, 50 million bottles of which are produced every year near Modena and Reggio Emilia. Less well known but also highly rated are the Colli Piacentini wines, one of the rising stars for which is **Cantine Romagnoli,** Via Genova 20, Villò di Vigolzone 29020 (ℭ **0523-870129;** www.cantineromagnoli.it). If you'd like to venture out into the countryside, you should call ahead and make an appointment for a tour and tasting, and get directions.

bed and a beautiful bathroom—you even get a bathrobe. The hotel's breakfast is the best in town.

Piazza Galilei, 40126 Bologna. ℂ **051-7457311.** Fax 051-7457322. www.bolognarthotels.it. 25 units. 154€–425€ double; 275€–590€ suite. Rates include buffet breakfast. AE, DC, MC, V. Parking 26€. Bus: 25 or 37. **Amenities:** Bar; bikes; room service; Wi-Fi (free, in lobby). *In room:* A/C, TV, hair dryer, minibar.

Hotel Commercianti ★ 📷   This hotel, beside San Petronio in the pedestrian area of Piazza Maggiore, is near the site of the Domus (the first seat of the town hall) for the commune of Bologna in the 12th century. Recent restorations have uncovered original wooden features, which you can see in the hall and the rooms in the old tower. Despite the centuries-old history, the atmosphere is bright, and all modern luxuries are offered. The guest rooms, most small or medium in size, are decorated with antique furniture.

Via de' Pignattari 11, 40124 Bologna. ℂ **051-7457511.** Fax 051-7457522. www.bolognarthotels.it. 34 units (half with shower only). 154€–425€ double; 275€–590€ suite. Rates include buffet breakfast. AE, DC, DISC, MC, V. Parking 30€. Bus: 25 or 37. **Amenities:** Bar; babysitting; bikes; room service. *In room:* A/C, TV, hair dryer, minibar, Wi-Fi (free).

Hotel Corona d'Oro 1890 ★   This *palazzo*, home of the noble Azzoguidi family in the 15th century, preserves the architectural features of various periods, from the Art Nouveau in the hall to the medieval coffered ceiling in the meeting room to the frescoes (coats of arms and landscapes) in the rooms. The good-size guest rooms are decorated according to various periods. The bathrooms are small but well equipped. The hotel is a short distance from Piazza Maggiore.

Via Oberdan 12, 40126 Bologna. ℂ **051-7457611.** Fax 051-7457622. www.bolognarthotels.it. 40 units (shower only). 164€–378€ double; 284€–492€ suite. Rates include buffet breakfast. AE, DC, DISC, MC, V. Parking 30€. Bus: 25 or 37. **Amenities:** Bar; babysitting; bikes; room service. *In room:* A/C, TV, minibar, Wi-Fi (free).

MODERATE

Art Hotel Orologio ★   This charming small hotel faces the *orologio* (clock) on the civic center in the heart of medieval Bologna, with a view of Piazza Maggiore and the Podestà Palace. The guest rooms all have modern furnishings with wrought-iron bed frames. Most are small but provide reasonable comfort, including tidy bathrooms. This is the ideal place for those who want a historical atmosphere without forfeiting modern comforts.

Via IV Novembre 10, 40123 Bologna. ℂ **051-7457411.** Fax 051-7457422. www.bolognarthotels.it. 35 units (some with shower only). 144€–435€ double; 264€–600€ suite. Rates include buffet breakfast. AE, DC, DISC, MC, V. Parking 30€. Bus: 25 or 37. **Amenities:** Bar; airport transfers (20€); babysitting; bikes; room service. *In room:* A/C, TV, hair dryer, minibar, Wi-Fi (free).

Hotel Porta San Mamolo Bologna ★★   In the heart of Bologna, this government-rated three-star hotel has some bedrooms that date back 3 centuries. But everything is up-to-date and modern today in this restored building that lies only a 10-minute walk from Piazza Maggiore. Our favorite spot here is a traditional courtyard and winter garden where breakfast is served. Bedrooms are midsize, streamlined, and modern, with a slightly romantic aura. Refined fabrics and the latest technology are set off by the delicate pastel colors of the walls. Best are the rooms on the top floor with a terrace opening onto panoramic views of Bologna.

Vicolo del Falconi 6–8, 40124 Bologna. ✆ **051-583056.** Fax 051-3311739. www.hotel-portasan mamolo.it. 43 units. 140€–170€ double; 220€ suite. AE, DC, MC, V. Parking 20€. Bus: A, B, E, or 30. **Amenities:** Bikes; room service; Wi-Fi (free, in lobby). *In room:* A/C, TV, fridge, hair dryer.

Hotel Regina   A good, plain choice with moderate comfort, the Regina dates from the 1800s, but has kept abreast of the times. The guest rooms range from small to medium but come with comfortable furnishings. The bathrooms are a bit cramped. The staff is helpful, and the maids keep everything spotless.

Via dell'Indipendenza 51, 40121 Bologna. ✆ **051-248878.** Fax 051-9914309. www.zanhotel.it. 61 units (shower only). 70€–349€ double. Rates include buffet breakfast. AE, DC, MC, V. Parking 20€. Bus: A, C, 11, or 20. **Amenities:** Bar; babysitting; room service. *In room:* A/C, TV, hair dryer, minibar.

Hotel Roma ★ 🍴   This is one of the best buys in Bologna; it also enjoys one of the most scenic locations (despite the heavy traffic). Most of the guest rooms are roomy yet old-fashioned, with large closets, comfortable armchairs, and excellent beds with fine linen. The best units are on the top floor, where there's a terrace overlooking the city rooftops.

Via Massimo d'Azeglio 9, 40123 Bologna. ✆ **051-226322.** Fax 051-239909. www.hotelroma.biz. 86 units. 150€ double; 240€ suite. AE, DC, MC, V. Parking 16€. Bus: A, B, 11, 14, or 17. **Amenities:** Restaurant; babysitting; bikes; room service. *In room:* A/C, TV, hair dryer, minibar, Wi-Fi (8€ per 24 hr.).

Hotel Touring   On the edge of the historic district, near the Church of San Domenico and Piazza Maggiore, Touring is a refurbished 1955 hotel offering comfort at an affordable price. Bedrooms are midsize and tastefully appointed, with shiny wood furnishings and faux-marble ceramic flooring. Bathrooms are tiled in white with deep sinks—sometimes a double sink—as well as roomy shower stalls and gilt-framed mirrors. Try for accommodations on the third or fourth floor where your room will often come with a balcony. The hotel's best feature is a roof terrace opening onto panoramic vistas of the *centro storico* (central historic district).

Via De'Mattuiani 1–2, 40124 Bologna. ✆ **051-584305.** Fax 051-334763. www.hoteltouring.it. 36 units. 113€–240€ double; 165€–350€ suite. Rates include buffet breakfast. AE, MC, V. Parking 21€. Bus: 30. **Amenities:** Babysitting; bikes; room service. *In room:* A/C, TV, hair dryer, Wi-Fi (free).

Il Convento dei Flori di Seta ★★   A small 15th-century convent is now one of the most sought after addresses in Bologna, following its beautiful and sensitive restoration. The nuns of yesterday would hardly recognize the hip, modern styling that prevails today. The location in the south of Bologna is a 10-minute walk from the center. With its brick walls and vaulted ceiling, the original architecture has been preserved, even with the installation of modern conveniences. Discretion and privacy are the hallmarks of this place. The bedrooms are comfortably and stylishly furnished in a modern style of minimal chic. Four of the rooms have been fashioned out of the aisle of apse of the convent church. Six of the bedrooms lie on the upper floor.

Via Orfeo 34, 40124 Bologna. ✆ **051-272039.** Fax 051-2759001. www.ilconventodeifioridiseta. com. 10 units. 140€–170€ double; 185€–215€ junior suite; 300€ suite. Rates include continental breakfast. AE, DC, MC, V. Parking 25€. Bus: C. **Amenities:** Bar; concierge; Jacuzzi; room service; sauna. *In room:* A/C, TV, Wi-Fi (free).

INEXPENSIVE

Albergo delle Drapperie ★ 🍴   In the oldest part of the city, the Quadrilatero, the Albergo is the latest version of the long-standing Hotel Apollo.

Completely restored since its use as a traditional guesthouse in 1800, it's been given a new lease on life as the most upmarket B&B in this historic zone. The hotel is ideal for sightseeing, located only 100m (328 ft.) from the landmark Piazza Maggiore. The style, as is to be expected, is traditional with much use of wood and Italian tiles, even frescoes on the ceilings. Bedrooms are comfortably appointed, often featuring exposed wooden beams.

Via della Drapperie 5, 40124 Bologna. ☏ **051-223955.** Fax 051-238732. www.albergodrapperie. com. 21 units. 75€–140€ double; 100€–165€ triple. AE, MC, V. **Amenities:** Wi-Fi (free, in lobby). *In room:* A/C, TV, minibar.

Where to Dine

EXPENSIVE/MODERATE

After dinner, many restaurant patrons skip the dessert course and head for **Gelatauro,** Via San Vitale 98 (☏ **051-230049;** www.gelatauro.com), run by three brothers. Bologna's best ice-cream vendor is known for its organic gelato, including one divine concoction made from Sicilian oranges. One ice cream is flavored with such fresh herbs as jasmine and bergamot.

Bitone ★★ EMILIAN   When this long-revered restaurant opened in 1834, it was a stop for stagecoaches en route to Florence. For years, its owner, Caesar Chiari, had stayed abreast of the times and changing culinary tastes. The chefs bring imagination and enthusiasm to their cuisine, and dishes are invariably cooked to perfection. The antipasti selections are among the best in Bologna, including a mousse made with mortadella and ricotta, or else tender prosciutto from Langhirano. The pasta selections are sublime, including various versions of tortellini. A classic veal cutlet Bolognese always appears on the menu, as do succulent lamb cutlets. Florentine beefsteak, the finest in Italy, also appears regularly on the menu, and it's always a succulent cut.

Via Emilia Levante 111, San lazzaro. ☏ **051-546110.** www.ristorantebitone.it. Main courses 25€–30€; fixed-price menu 65€. AE, DC, MC, V. Wed–Sun noon–2pm and 8–11pm. Closed Aug.

Da Cesari ★ BOLOGNESE   In business for more than a century, this rustic, two-floor restaurant stands in the heart of the historic district. Since 1956, the Da Cesari family has been on hand to welcome you and feed you well, luring you with its classic Bolognese cuisine. The dishes overflow with fresh ingredients deftly handled by the kitchen staff. We could order the pumpkin-stuffed ravioli with butter and Parmesan once a week. Prepared with consummate skill are such appetizers as cheese flan with Parmesan sauce and white truffles, or else salmon-and-sea-bass carpaccio with an orange vinaigrette. Main courses are hearty, including a homemade green pasta with a sauce studded with sausage, or else filet of beef with a balsamic vinaigrette sauce.

Via de' Carbonesi 8 (south of Piazza Maggiore). ☏ **051-237710.** www.da-cesari.it. Reservations required. Main courses 12€–20€; degustation menu 38€. DC, MC, V. Mon–Sat 12:30–2:30pm and 7–11pm. Closed 3 weeks in Aug and Jan 1–7. Bus: 20, 29, 38, or 39.

Diana ★ REGIONAL/INTERNATIONAL   Occupying a late medieval building in the heart of town, the Diana has been popular since 1920. This restaurant offers three gracefully decorated dining rooms and a verdant terrace. It was named in honor of the goddess of the hunt because of the many game dishes it served when it first opened. In recent years, although game is still featured in season, the restaurant has opted for a staple of regional and international cuisine, all competently prepared. Begin with one of the city's most delicious appetizers: *spuma di mortadella,* a pâté made of mortadella sausage served on dainty white toast. You'll never eat American-style bologna again.

Via dell'Indipendenza 24. ℂ **051-231302.** www.ristorantedianabologna.com. Reservations recommended. Main courses 12€–24€. AE, DC, MC, V. Tues–Sun noon–2:30pm and 7–10:30pm. Closed Jan 1-10 and Aug 1-28. Bus: 11 or 27.

I Portici ★★ BOLOGNESE/ITALIAN   In the I Portici Hotel, close to the railroad station, lies one of Bologna's most distinguished restaurants. It has a chic contemporary black-and-white decor and attracts a discerning group of gourmet-minded diners who insist on the best. Chef Guido Haverkook delivers both in his imaginative recipes and in his shopping for only the finest ingredients. His flavors celebrate the naturalness of Italian-grown produce.

He offers an ever-changing menu that might include such antipasti as filet of sole with potato salad with a pesto of wild garlic and lemon-flavored sour cream or else lime-flavored rooster tempura with lamb's lettuce. Four pastas are offered nightly, perhaps a blue lobster risotto with spring vegetables. The chef shines brightly in his main dishes, including medallions in a juniper bean sauce on a Jerusalem artichoke purée or grilled house-smoked tuna with cherry tomatoes.

Via Indipendenza 69. ℂ **051-42185.** www.iporticihotel.com. Reservations required. Main courses 16€–26€, fixed-price lunch 30€, 7-course tasting menu 85€. Tues–Sat 12:30–2:30pm and 7:30–11pm. Closed Aug. Bus: 215, 36, 68, 81, or 87.

Montegrappa da Nello ★ 🏠 BOLOGNESE/INTERNATIONAL   This wonderful *trattoria* is one of the few restaurants still doing classic Bolognese cuisine. Hosts Franco and Ezio Bolini insist that all the produce be fresh. The menu's signature dish is *tortellini Montegrappa,* a pasta favorite served in cream-and-meat sauce. The restaurant is also known for its fresh white truffles and porcini mushrooms. A good example is the *graminia,* a very fine white spaghetti presented with mushrooms, cream, and pepper. A heavenly salad is made with truffles, mushrooms, parmigiano, and artichokes. ***Note:*** *Graminia* is also served with cream and sausage.

Via Montegrappa 2. ℂ **051-236331.** www.ristorantedanello.com. Reservations recommended for dinner. Main courses 10€–17€. AE, DC, MC, V. Tues–Sun noon–3pm and 7–11:30pm. Closed 1 week in Jan and all of Aug. Bus: 20, 28, or A.

Ristorante al Pappagallo ★★★ BOLOGNESE   Foodies might disagree on which is the very best restaurant in Bologna, but this upscale choice is always at or near the top of everyone's list. It has drawn a faithful following for decades; in past years, it has hosted Einstein, Hitchcock, and Toscanini (not at the same time). "The Parrot," still going strong, is on the ground floor of a Gothic mansion across from the 14th-century Merchants' Loggia (a short walk from the leaning towers). Some of the best specialties, each a tantalizing dish, include rabbit ravioli with smoked ricotta; guinea fowl breast glazed with white grapes; duck liver marinated in balsamic vinegar, and green *tagliatelle* pasta with squid and fresh asparagus. The menu also features some low-calorie offerings.

Piazza della Mercanzia 3C. ℂ **051-232807.** www.alpappagallo.it. Reservations recommended. Main courses 10€–24€. AE, DC, MC, V. Mon–Sat 12:30–2:30pm and 7:30–10:30pm. Closed Sat June–Aug and Dec 24–Jan 2. Bus: 11, 13, 14, or 19.

INEXPENSIVE

Enoteca Italiana, Via Marsala 2/B (ℂ **051-235989;** www.enotecaitaliana.it), is an inviting and aromatic shop-cum–wine bar on a side street just north of

Piazza Maggiore. You can stand at the bar and sip a local wine while enjoying a sandwich. For a movable feast, you can stock up on ham, salami, and cheese at the deli counter, and enjoy a picnic at the nearby Neptune fountain. It's open Monday to Saturday from 7:30am to 8pm.

On a stroll through the **Pescherie Vecchie,** the city's market area near the Due Torri, you can assemble a meal. Along the Via Drapperie and adjoining streets, salumerias, cheese shops, bakeries, and vegetable markets are heaped high with attractive displays. The stalls of Bologna's other food market, the **Mercato delle Erbe,** Via Ugo Bassi 2, www.mercatodelleerbe.it, are open Monday to Wednesday and Friday and Saturday 7:15am to 1pm and 5 to 7:30pm, Thursday and Saturday 7:15am to 1pm.

Bar Roberto at Via Orefici 9/A (© **051-232256**), near Bologna's central market, turns out delicious homemade pastries that attract a loyal breakfast clientele.

Drogheria della Rosa ★ BOLOGNESE/ITALIAN   Some of the best homemade pastas, for which Bologna is famous, are served here at a typical meal—and not just tortellini, which was invented in the city. A mixed clientele of all ages patronizes the premises of chef/owner Emanuele Addone, who installed his restaurant in a former pharmacy, the original doors and window frames still intact. In the historic center, the look is one of a rustic *trattoria*. The produce is market fresh, the cooking superb, and the wine cellar has several hundred choices. Start perhaps with *culatello,* a prized cured ham, or else a classic *tortelli,* which is stuffed with zucchini blossoms. An eggplant ravioli comes with fresh tomatoes and basil, and vegetable pie is laced with a Parmesan cream sauce. Sautéed lamb with fresh rosemary is given extra flavor by the balsamic vinegar of Modena, or roast breast of guinea fowl with spicy honey.

Via Cartoleria 10. © **051-222529.** www.drogheriadellarosa.it. Reservations recommended. Main courses 9€–15€. MC, V. Mon–Sat 12:30–3pm and 8–10:30pm. Closed Aug 10–27 and 1st week of Jan. Bus: 11 or 19.

Marco Fadiga Bistrot ★★ 🏛 CREATIVE ITALIAN   Not all chefs in Bologna specialize in the classic recipes of yesterday. Marco Fadiga is the most acclaimed chef in the city, and he's known for inventive dishes with unusual flavor combinations. In the historic center, Fadiga operates a casually chic bistro decorated with Tintin pictures and old champagne crates, along with a scattering of graffiti. Look for his daily specials posted on a chalkboard menu. We are dazzled by his appetizers—perhaps prawns in a vinaigrette of mango, dried tomatoes, or fresh basil; or else an artichoke-and-squid salad with a nutty vinaigrette. You can also savor such dishes as *tagliolini* pasta with Savoy cabbage and shrimp, or else ravioli stuffed with creamed peas (also served with shrimp).

Via Rialto 23C. © **051-220118.** www.marcofadigabistrot.com. Reservations required. Main courses 10€–16€. AE, MC, V. Tues–Sat 7:30pm–midnight. Bus: 11, 13, or 14.

Osteria dell'Orsa ITALIAN   The restaurant, which offers some of the best *ragù alla bolognese* in town, occupies a 15th-century building near the university. Most diners opt for the high-ceilinged, medieval-looking main floor, though an informal cantina-like cellar room is open for additional seating. You won't go wrong if you preface a meal with any kind of pasta labeled *bolognese*. Other options are homemade *tagliolini,* veal cutlet *fiorentina,* and tortellini with cheese, ham, and mushroom sauce. If you feel adventurous, you can always try grilled donkey meat *(somarello).*

Via Mentana 1F. ☎ **051-231576.** www.osteriadellorsa.com. Reservations recommended. Main courses 6€–15€. AE, DC, MC, V. Daily noon–3pm and 7pm–12:30am. (closes 1 hr. earlier Sat–Sun). Bus: C.

A STANDOUT RESTAURANT IN NEARBY IMOLA

San Domenico ★★★ ITALIAN   Foodies from all over travel to the unlikely village of Imola to savor the offerings of what some food critics (ourselves included) consider the best restaurant in Italy. The cuisine is sometimes compared to France's modern creations. However, owner Gian Luigi Morini claims his delectable offerings are nothing more than adaptations of festive regional dishes, except that they're lighter, more subtle, and served in manageable portions. A tuxedo-clad member of his talented young staff will escort you to a table near the tufted leather banquettes. Meals include heavenly concoctions made with the freshest ingredients. You might select such temptations as braised lobster tail with a sweet paprika sauce, truffles, and a sea bass ravioli, or baked pigeon with black truffles and a fava bean sauce, perhaps grilled rack of lamb in an olive sauce with caramelized cauliflower. Signor Morini has collected some of the best vintages in Europe for the past 30 years, with some bottles of cognac dating from the time of Napoleon.

Via Gaspare Sacchi 1, Imola (34km/21 miles southeast of Bologna). ☎ **0542-29000.** www.san domenico.it. Reservations required. Main courses 30€–50€; fixed-price lunch 60€, dinner 120€. AE, DC, MC, V. Tues–Sun 12:30–2:30pm; Tues–Sat 8–10:30pm. Closed Sun (June–Aug), Jan 1–10, and 1 week in Aug.

Shopping

Galleria Marescalchi, Via Mascarella 116B (☎ **051-245710;** www.marescalchi. it), features traditional art, offering paintings and prints for view or sale by native son Morandi and Italian modern master De Chirico, as well as Chagall and Magritte.

Pastries at Atti.

THE WORLD'S GREATEST china shop

Faenza, 58km (36 miles) southeast of Bologna, has lent its name to a form of ceramics called faience, which originated on the island of Majorca, off Spain's coast. Faenza potters found inspiration in the work coming out of Majorca, and in the 12th century they began to produce their own designs, characterized by brilliant colors and floral decorations. The art reached its pinnacle in the 16th century, when the "hot-fire" process was perfected, during which ceramics were baked at a temperature of 950°C (1,742°F).

The legacy of this fabled industry is preserved at the **International Museum of Ceramics (Museo Internazionale delle Ceramiche),** Via Campidori 2 (✆ **0546-697311;** www.micfaenza.org), called "the world's greatest china shop." Housed here are works from the artisans of Faenza as well as from around the world, including pre-Columbian pottery from Peru. Of exceptional interest are Etruscan and Egyptian ceramics and a wide-ranging collection from the Orient, dating from the Roman Empire.

Deserving special attention is the section devoted to modern ceramic art, including works by Matisse and Picasso. On display are Picasso vases and a platter with his dove of peace, a platter in rich colors by Chagall, a "surprise" from Matisse, and a framed ceramic plaque of the Crucifixion by Georges Rouault. Another excellent work is a ceramic woman by Dante Morozzi. Even the great Léger tried his hand at ceramics.

Open from October to March, Tuesday to Friday 9:30am to 1:30pm, and Saturday and Sunday from 9:30am to 5:30pm; April to September, hours are Tuesday to Sunday 9:30am to 7pm. Admission is 6€. It's closed New Year's Day, May 1, August 15, and Christmas.

Faenza ceramics.

An array of breads, pasta, and pastries makes **Atti,** Via Caprarie 7 (✆ **051-220425;** www.paoloatti.com), tempting whether you're hungry or not. Among the pastries are the Bolognese specialty *certosino,* a heavy loaf resembling fruitcake, and an assortment of *gastronomie* (delectable heat-and-serve starters and main courses made fresh at the shop). If you want chocolate, head to **Majani,** Via De' Carbonesi 5 (✆ **051-234302**), which claims to be Italy's oldest sweets shop, having made and sold confections since 1796. A wide assortment of chocolates awaits you, accompanied by several types of cookies; at Easter, the shop also makes chocolate eggs, rabbits, and lambs. **Roccati,** Via Clavature 17A (✆ **051-261-964;** www.roccaticioccolato.com), is run by a husband-and-wife team that is still celebrated for the *gianduja* chocolate their ancestors made for the princes of Savoy. In their open-air laboratory, you can see these heavenly delights being created. When you bite into their cognac-filled chocolates, you'll think you've entered Paradise before your time. At **Tamburini ★**, Via Caprarie 1 (✆ **051-234726;** www.tamburini.com), one of Italy's most lavish food shops, you can choose from an impressive array of meats and fish, soups and salads, vegetables, and sweets, as well as fresh pasta to prepare at home.

If you have hard-to-fit feet, walk to **Piero,** Via delle Lame 56 (✆ **051-558680;** www.pierocalzature.it), for attractive footwear for men and women in large sizes, ranging up to European size 53 for men (American size 20) and size 46 for women (American size 14). Bruno Magli quickly made a name for himself after opening his first shoe factory in 1934. Today, a **Bruno Magli** shop selling leather bags, jackets, and coats for men and women—in addition to shoes—is at Galleria Cavour 9 (✆ **051-266915**).

The Veronesi family has been closely tied to the jewelry trade for centuries. Now split up and competing among themselves, the various factions are represented by **F. Veronesi & Figli,** Piazza Maggiore 4 (✆ **051-224835;** www.veronesi 1893.it), which offers contemporary jewelry, watches, and silver using ancient designs; and **Giulio Veronesi,** with locations at Piazza di Re Enzo 1H (✆ **051-234237;** www.giulioveronesi.it) and Galleria Cavour 1 (✆ **051-234196**), which sells modern jewelry and Rolex watches.

Bologna After Dark

Because Bologna has a large population of students, it has a vibrant, diverse nightlife scene, including lots of cafes that are packed with a young crowd. The Via del Pratello and, near the university, Via Zamboni and Via delle Belle Arti and their surrounding areas are the usual haunts of night owls. You can usually find a place for a drink, a shot of espresso, or a light meal as late as 2am.

Café de Paris, Piazza del Francia 1C (✆ **051-234980;** www.cafedeparis bologna.org), is another hot spot, attracting a young crowd. It has some of the best bartenders in Bologna, and serves light, tasty, and market-fresh platters of food throughout the day and night, costing from 15€ to 20€.

Facing the Duomo is **Bar Giuseppe,** Piazza Maggiore 1 (✆ **051-264444**), serving some of the best espresso and gelato in town. It stretches for at least a block beneath the arcades facing the Piazza Maggiore. The best dry martinis in town are served at **Nu Lounge Bar,** Via de'Musei 6 (✆ **051-222532;** www. nu-lounge.com), attracting a post-30 crowd of fashionistas last seen munching on those addictive Calabrian green olives.

At 10:30pm, make your way to the cellars of a 16th-century *palazzo* near the university at **Cantina Bentivoglio** at Via Mascarella 4B (✆ **051-265416;** www.cantinabentivoglio.it). That's when you'll hear some of the best jazz in Bologna. It is open daily from 8pm to 2am. It is also open for lunch Monday to Friday from 12:15 to 2:45pm.

Cassero, Via Don Minzoni 18 (✆ **051-6494416;** www.cassero.it), is Bologna's most popular gay bar, with a noisy, discolike atmosphere and floor shows. The biggest attraction here is the setting—the club occupies one of Bologna's medieval gates, the top of which serves as a roof garden and open-air dance floor in good weather. Cassero is also the Bologna headquarters of Arcigay and Arcilesbiche, a gay and lesbian center organizing cultural meetings and entertainment. Thursday is set aside for women, on Friday theatrical performances of interest to the gay and lesbian community take place, and on Sunday disco fever takes over (events vary widely and are scheduled at different times). Wednesday and Saturday are disco nights; beer night is the first Friday of every month.

Osteria de Poeti, Via Poeti 1B (✆ **051-236166;** www.osteriadepoeti. com), is Bologna's oldest *osteria* and has been in operation since the 16th century.

The brick-vaulted ceilings, stone walls, and ancient wine barrels provide just the sort of ambience you would expect to find in such a historic establishment. Stop in to enjoy the live jazz and folk music that's on tap most nights (closed Mon).

During July and August, the city authorities transform the **parks** along the town's northern tier into an Italian version of a German *biergarten* (beer garden), complete with disco music under colored lights. Vendors sell beer and wine from indoor/outdoor bars set up on the lawns, and others hawk food and souvenirs. Events range from live jazz to classical concerts. Ask any hotelier or the tourist office for the schedule of midsummer events, or try your luck by taking either a taxi or (much less convenient) bus no. 25, 35, or 38 from the main station to Arena Parco Nord.

The **Teatro Comunale,** Largo Respighi 1 (✆ **051-529958;** www.tcbo.it), is the venue for major cultural presentations, including opera, ballet, and orchestral presentations. During the 1970s, Luciano Pavarotti traveled from his home in Modena to perform operas at this 1763 landmark.

Music lovers flock to the Sala Mozart at the **Accademia Filarmonica di Bologna,** Via Guerrazzi 13 (✆ **051-222997;** www.accademiafilarmonica.it), to hear performances by Haydn, Brahms, Vivaldi, and, of course, Mozart himself. The boy genius was only 14 years old when he earned a diploma in composition at this academy in 1770.

FERRARA ★

417km (259 miles) N of Rome, 52km (32 miles) N of Bologna, 100km (62 miles) SW of Venice

When Papa Borgia (Pope Alexander VI) was shopping for a third husband for the apple of his eye, darling Lucrezia, his gaze fell on the influential house of Este. From the 13th century, this great Italian family had dominated Ferrara, building up a powerful duchy and a reputation as patrons of the arts. Alfonse d'Este, son of the shrewd but villainous Ercole I, the ruling duke of Ferrara, was an attractively virile candidate for Lucrezia's much-used hand. (Her second husband was murdered, perhaps by her brother, Cesare, who was the apple of nobody's eye—with the possible exception of Machiavelli. Her first marriage, a political alliance, was to Giovanni Sforza, but it was annulled in 1497.)

Although the Este family might have had reservations (after all, it was common gossip that the pope "knew" his daughter in the biblical sense), they finally consented to the marriage. As the duchess of Ferrara, a position she held until her death, Lucrezia bore seven children. But one of her grandchildren, Alfonso II, wasn't as prolific and left the family without a male heir. The greedy eye of Pope Clement VIII took quick action, gobbling up the city as his personal fiefdom in the waning months of the 16th century. The great house of Este went down in history, and Ferrara sadly declined under the papacy.

Incidentally, Alfonso II was a dubious patron of Torquato Tasso (1544–95), author of the epic *Jerusalem Delivered,* a work that was to make him the most celebrated poet of the Late Renaissance. The legend of Tasso (who's thought to have been insane, paranoid, or at least tormented) has steadily grown over the centuries. It didn't need any more boosting, but Goethe fanned the legend through the Teutonic lands with his late-18th-century drama *Torquato Tasso.* It's said that Alfonso II at one time made Tasso his prisoner.

Ferrara is still relatively undiscovered, but it's richly blessed, with much of its legacy intact. Among the historic treasures are a great cathedral and the Este Castle, along with enough ducal palaces to make for a fast-paced day of sightseeing. Its palaces, for the most part, have long been robbed of their furnishings, but the faded frescoes, the paintings that weren't carted off, and the palatial rooms are reminders of the vicissitudes of power.

Modern Ferrara is one of the most health-conscious places in all Italy. Bicycles outnumber the automobiles on the road, and more than half of the citizens get exercise by jogging. In fact, it's almost surreal: Enclosed in medieval walls under a bright sky, everywhere you look, you'll find the people of Ferrara engaged in all sorts of self-powered locomotion. Beware of octogenarian cyclists whizzing by you with shopping bags flapping in the wind.

Essentials

GETTING THERE   Getting to Ferrara by **train** is fast and efficient because it's on the main line between Bologna and Venice. A total of 39 trains a day originating in Bologna pass through. Trip time is 40 minutes, and the fare is about 9€ one-way. Some 29 trains arrive from Venice (1½ hr.). The fare costs 6.50€ to 30€ depending on the train and the class of service. Ravenna is an hour away, with hourly departures all day. For more information, call © **892021.**

If you have a **car** and are coming from Bologna, take A13 north. From Venice, take A4 southwest to Padua and continue on A13 south to Ferrara.

VISITOR INFORMATION   The helpful **tourist office** is at Castello Estense, Piazza del Castello (© **0532-299303;** www.ferrarainfo.com), open Monday to Saturday from 9am to 1pm and 2 to 6pm, Sunday 9:30am to 1pm and 2 to 5pm.

SPECIAL EVENTS   Not quite as dramatic as its counterpart in Siena, Ferrara's **Palio di San Giorgio** is a popular event held in the Piazza Ariostea the last Sunday of May. Two-legged creatures run first, in races for young men and young women. They are followed by donkeys and, in the main event, horses ridden bareback by jockeys representing Ferrara's eight traditional districts.

During the summer, the streets of Ferrara seem like one great theater. Some excellent jazz and classical concerts are the main events of **Estate a Ferrara,** an outdoor festival that begins in early July and runs until late August, when the festivities are augmented by street musicians, mimes, and orators, who partake in the **Busker's Festival.**

Exploring the Town

Ferrara's **medieval walls,** massive enough to be topped with trees and lawns, encircle the city with an aerie of greenery. The wide paths are ideal for biking, jogging, and strolling; they provide wonderful views of the city and surrounding farmland. Many hotels offer guests free use of bikes, or you can rent them from the lot outside the train station.

Casa Romei ★   This 15th-century palace near the Este tomb was the property of Giovanni Romei, a friend and confidant of the fleshy Duke Borso d'Este, who made the Este realm a duchy. Giovanni was later set to marry one of the Este princesses, although we don't know if it was for love or power or both. In later years, Lucrezia and her gossipy coterie, riding in the ducal carriage drawn by white horses, descended on the Romei house, perhaps to receive Borgia messengers from Rome. Its once-elegant furnishings have been carted off, but the chambers (many with terra-cotta fireplaces) remain, and the casa has been filled with frescoes and sculpture.

Via Savonarola 30. © **0532-234100.** Admission 3€ adults, free for ages 17 and under. Tues–Sun 8:30am–7:30pm. Bus: 1 or 9.

Ferrara

ATTRACTIONS
Casa Romei 8
Castello Estense 4
Il Duomo 7
Museo Civico
 d'Arte Antica 10
Museo del Duomo 8
Palazzo dei Diamanti 1

ACCOMMODATIONS
Hotel Duchessa Isabella 3
Hotel Europa 5
Locanda Borgonuovo 6
Ripagrande Hotel 11

DINING
La Provvidenza 2
La Romantica 12

Castello Estense ★ A moated four-towered castle (lit at night), this proud fortress began as a bricklayer's dream near the end of the 14th century, although its face has been lifted and wrenched about for centuries. It was home to the powerful Estes, where the dukes went about their ho-hum daily chores: trysting with their own lovers, murdering their wives' lovers, beheading or imprisoning potential enemies, whatever. Today it's used for the provincial and prefectural administration offices, and you can view many of its once-lavish rooms—notably the **Salon of Games (Salone dei Giochi), the Salon of Dawn (Salone dell'Aurora),** and a **Ducal chapel** that once belonged to Renata di Francia, daughter of Louis XII. Parisina d'Este, wife of Duke Niccolò d'Este III, was murdered with her lover, Ugolino (the duke's illegitimate son), in the dank prison below the castle, creating the inspiration for Browning's "My Last Duchess."

Largo Castello. ⓒ **0532-299233.** www.castelloestense.it. Admission 8€ adults, 6€ children ages 11–18, free for ages 10 and under. Tues–Sun 9:30am–4:45pm. Bus: 1, 2, 4, or 9.

Civic Museum of Ancient Art (Museo Civico d'Arte Antica) The Schifanoia Palace was built in 1385 for Albert V d'Este and was enlarged by Borso d'Este (1450–71). The Museum of Ancient Art was founded in 1758 and transferred to its present site in 1898. At first, only coins and medals were exhibited, but then the collection was enhanced by donations of archaeological finds, antique bronzes, Renaissance plates and pottery, and other collections.

Art lovers are lured to the **Salon of the Months (Salone dei Mesi)** to see the astrological wall cycle, which represents the 12 months. Each month is subdivided into three horizontal bands: The lower band shows scenes from the daily life of courtiers and people, the middle shows the relative sign of the zodiac, and the upper depicts the triumph of the classical divinity for that myth. Humanist Pellegrino Prisciani conceived the subjects of the cycle, although Cosmé Tura, the official court painter, was probably the organizer of the works. Tura was the founder of the Ferrarese School, to which belonged, among others, Ercole de' Roberti and Francesco del Cossa, who painted the March, April, and May scenes. The frescoes are complex, leading to varied interpretations of their meaning.

In the Palazzo Schifanoia, Via Scandiana 23. ℭ **0532-244949.** Admission 6€ adults, free for those 17 and under. Tues–Sun 9am–6pm. Closed Mon and major holidays. Bus: 1 or 9.

Il Duomo ★★   A short stroll from the Este Castle, the 12th-century Duomo weds the delicate Gothic with a more virile Romanesque. Its outstanding feature is its **triple facade ★★** with a magnificent porch. Over the tympanum, the Last Judgment is depicted in stone in a style evocative of a French Gothic cathedral. The lunette over the main door is a sculpture by Nicholaus, depicting St. George. There are two splendid tiers of galleries on the upper section of the south side. Never finished, the bell tower (campanile) was built to the designs of Leon Battista Alberti. The interior of this massive structure is heavily baroque. In decades to come, more artisans would be called in to festoon the cathedral with *trompe l'oeil.* Very little of the original decoration can be seen.

Piazza Cattedrale. ℭ **0532-207449.** Free admission but donation appreciated. Daily 7:30am–noon and 3–6:30pm. Bus: 2 or 3C.

Museo del Duomo ★   In its new location, the Duomo Museum is worth a visit just to see works by Ferrara's most outstanding 15th-century painter, Cosmé Tura. Aesthetically controversial, the big attraction is Tura's St. George slaying the dragon to save a red-stockinged damsel in distress. Opposite is an outstanding Jacopo della Quercia work of a sweet, regal Madonna with a pomegranate in one hand and the Christ child in the other. Also from the Renaissance heyday of Ferrara are some bas-reliefs, notably a Giano *bifronte* (a mythological figure looking at the past and the future), along with some 16th-century *arazzi* (tapestries) woven by hand.

Via San Romano 1–9. ℭ **0532-244949.** Admission 6€, free for those 17 and under. Tues–Sun 9am–1pm and 3–6pm. Bus: 2 or 3C.

Palazzo dei Diamanti ★   The Palazzo dei Diamanti, another jewel of Este splendor, is so named because of the 9,000 diamond-shaped stones on its facade. Of the handful of museums here, the **National Picture Gallery (Pinacoteca Nazionale)** is the most important. It houses the works of the Ferrarese artists—notably the trio of old masters, Tura, del Cossa, and Roberti. The collection covers the chief period of artistic expression in

A detail from the Salon of Months' astrological wall cycle in the Civic Museum of Ancient Art.

Castello Estense.

Ferrara from the 14th to the 18th century. Next in importance is the **Civic Gallery of Modern Art (Galleria d'Arte Moderna),** which sponsors the most important contemporary art exhibits in town. The other three museums in the *palazzo* aren't really worth your time.

Corso Ercole d'Este 21. ℂ **0532-205844** or 0532-244949. www.palazzodiamanti.it. Admission to Pinacoteca 6€; Civic Gallery of Modern Art 11€. Pinacoteca Tues–Sat 9am–2pm (to 7pm Thurs); Sun 9am–1pm. Civic Gallery of Modern Art daily 9am–7pm, when exhibits are staged. Bus: 3C.

Where to Stay

Hotel Duchessa Isabella ★   Despite readers' complaints about staff attitude, this remains the town's leading inn. It opened in 1990 as a government-rated five-star hotel, named after the Este family's most famous ancestor, Isabella. The soundproof guest rooms are identified by the names of the flowers whose colors they most closely resemble. This might strike you as a bit gaudy if you end up in a room with pink pillows and satin. Each boasts a sense of history and is outfitted with modern amenities, plus plush bathrooms. As a courtesy to guests, free horse-drawn tours are offered by the hotel—a romantic orientation to Ferrara and some of its most significant landmarks.

Via Palestro 68–70, 44100 Ferrara. ℂ **0532-202121.** Fax 0532-202638. www.duchessaisabella.it. 27 units. 299€ double; from 418€ suite. Rates include buffet breakfast. AE, DC, MC, V. Free parking. Closed Aug. Bus: 1, 2, 3, or 9. **Amenities:** Restaurant; babysitting; bikes; room service. *In room:* A/C, TV, fax, hair dryer, minibar.

Hotel Europa   This is the leading moderately priced choice in town. In the 1600s, this palace was built near the Castello Estense. It was transformed into one of the most prestigious hotels in town in 1861, but during World War II, portions of the rear were bombed and then repaired in a less grandiose style. The government-rated three-star place continues today, with a well-trained staff, reasonable prices, and guest rooms that are clean and comfortable, with antique furnishings and modern comforts. A handful of rooms overlook the *corso* (they retain ceiling frescoes from the original construction).

Corso della Giovecca 49, 44100 Ferrara. ✆ **0532-205456.** Fax 0532-212120. www.hoteleuropa ferrara.com. 43 units (shower only). 95€–125€ double; 125€–160€ suite. Rates include buffet breakfast. AE, DC, MC, V. Parking 10€. Bus: 1, 2, 3, or 9. **Amenities:** Bar; bikes; room service. *In room:* A/C, TV, hair dryer, minibar, Wi-Fi (free).

Locanda Borgonuovo ★ ★ 👔 This is Ferrara's most elegant B&B, installed in a former 17th-century monastery near the Castello d'Estense. Your host is Filippo Orlandini, who has turned the space into an accommodating and stylish hostelry. His most frequent guests are actors and musicians from the local theater who prefer this place to all others in town. Rooms are spacious and fashionably decorated, often with antiques and with comfortable beds. The best unit has a kitchenette, but those accommodations are usually rented to those seeking longer stays. In fair weather, breakfast is served in the garden in back of this medieval *palazzo.* Reserve well in advance, because this is a very preferred address.

Via Cairoli 29, 44100 Ferrara. ✆ **0532-211100.** Fax 0532-246328. www.borgonuovo.com. 4 units (shower only). 80€–110€ double; apt 180€ for 4, 200€ for 5. AE, MC, V. Parking 10€. **Amenities:** Babysitting; bikes; room service; Wi-Fi (free, in lobby). *In room:* A/C, TV, hair dryer, minibar.

Ripagrande Hotel ★ The Ripagrande, one of the town's unusual hotels, occupies a Renaissance palace in the center of town inside the city wall. Coffered ceilings, walls in Ferrarese brickwork, 16th-century columns, and a wide staircase with a floral cast-iron handrail characterize the entrance hall. Inside are two Renaissance courtyards decorated with columns and capitals. Half of the guest rooms are junior suites with sleeping areas connected to an internal stairway. The rooms are spacious, with tasteful furnishings, which are often antique reproductions. Some of the units are trilevel, with a garretlike bedroom above. The most desirable are on the top floor, opening onto terraces overlooking the red-tile roofs.

Via Ripagrande 21, 44100 Ferrara. ✆ **0532-765250.** Fax 0532-764377. www.ferrarahotel ripagrande.it. 40 units. 110€–250€ double; 170€–260€ junior suite. Rates include buffet breakfast. AE, DC, MC, V. Bus: 2, 3, 6, 9, or 11. Parking 25€. **Amenities:** Restaurant; bar; babysitting; bikes; room service. *In room:* A/C, TV, hair dryer, minibar.

Where to Dine

On a nice day, you might put together a picnic to enjoy atop Ferrara's medieval walls. Buy what you need on the **Via Cortevecchia,** a narrow brick street near the cathedral where locals shop for food. It's lined with salumerias, cheese shops, and bakeries. The nearby **Mercato Comunale,** at the corner of Via Santo Stefano and Via del Mercato, is crowded with food stalls and open until 1pm Monday to Saturday, and 3:30 to 7:30pm Friday.

La Provvidenza ★ ★ FERRARESE/ITALIAN This first-rate restaurant stands on the same street as the Palazzo dei Diamanti. It has a farm-style interior, with a little garden where you can dine in fair weather. The antipasti table is the finest we've sampled in Ferrara. Hearty eaters should order a pasta, such as ravioli stuffed with pumpkin, before tackling the main course, perhaps perfectly grilled and seasoned veal chops. Other specialties are *pasticcio alla Ferrarese* (macaroni mixed with a mushroom and meat sauce laced with creamy white sauce) and *fritto misto di carne* (mixed grill). Dessert choices are wide and luscious.

Corso Ercole d'Este 92. ✆ **0532-205187.** www.laprovvidenza.com. Reservations required. Main courses 10€–22€. AE, DC, MC, V. Tues–Sat noon–2:30pm and 7:30–10:30pm; Sun noon–2:30pm. Bus: 3 or 9.

Wine bottles at Enoteca Al Brindisi.

La Romantica ★ 🍴 FERRARESE   One of this city's most delightful dining experiences is in what used to be the stables of a 17th-century merchant's house. In a bright, fashionable decor, the well-trained chefs dazzle your palate with one taste sensation after another. Here is a chance to dine on several rare regional recipes, including pasta in a tomato-cream sauce (*cappellacci di zucca*) given added flavor by walnuts and Parmesan cheese. Other excellent dishes include black *tagliolini* with clams and sea urchins, or else a steamed tuna steak with a mustard sauce. Filet of beef with Gorgonzola sauce and pine nuts is yet another sublime dish.

Via Ripagrande 36. (📞 **0532-765975.** www.trattorialaromantica. com. Reservations recommended. Main courses 9€–18€. MC, V. Thurs–Tues 12:30–2:30pm and 7:30–10:30pm; Mon 7:30–10:30pm.

Shopping

Ferrara has a rich tradition of artisanship dating from the Renaissance. You can find some of the best, albeit expensive, products in the dozen or so antiques stores in the historic center.

You find beautifully designed, colorful ceramics at **La Marchesana,** Via Cortevecchia 38A (📞 **0532-240535;** www.lamarchesana.it).

Enoteca Al Brindisi, Via Adelardi 11 (📞 **0532-471225;** www.albrindisi. net), stockpiles the fruits of the Ferrarese harvest in historically evocative settings. Every month Tuesday through Sunday 9am to 1pm, the **open-air antiques and handicraft markets** feature lots of junk amid the increasingly rare treasures. The markets are conducted in Piazza Municipale (mostly antiques and bric-a-brac) and Piazza Savonarola (mainly handicrafts and bric-a-brac).

Ferrara After Dark

During July and August, concerts and temporary art exhibits are offered as part of the **Estate a Ferrara** program. The tourist office can provide a schedule of events and dates, which vary from year to year. During the rest of the year, you can rub elbows with fellow drinkers, and usually lots of students, at a refreshingly diverse collection of bars, pubs, and discos. The **Enoteca Al Brindisi,** Via Adelardi 11 (📞 **0532-471225;** www.albrindisi.net), claims, with some justification, to be the oldest wine bar in the world, with a tradition of uncorking bottles dating from the early 1400s. Wine begins at around 3€ per glass and seems to taste best when accompanied by a few of the dozen panini (sandwiches).

RAVENNA & ITS DAZZLING MOSAICS ★★★

74km (46 miles) E of Bologna, 145km (90 miles) S of Venice, 130km (81 miles) NE of Florence, 365km (226 miles) N of Rome

Ravenna is one of the most unusual towns in Emilia-Romagna. Today you'll find a sleepy town with memories of a great past, luring hordes of tourists to explore what remains. As the capital of the Western Roman Empire (from A.D. 402), the Visigoth Empire (from A.D. 473), and the Byzantine Empire under Emperor Justinian and Empress Theodora (A.D. 540–752), Ravenna became one of the greatest cities on the Mediterranean.

Ravenna achieved its cultural peak as part of the Byzantine Empire between the 6th and the 8th centuries, and it is known for the many well-preserved mosaics created during that time—the finest in all Western art and the most splendid outside Istanbul. Although it now looks much like any other Italian city, the low Byzantine domes of its churches still evoke its Eastern past.

Essentials

GETTING THERE   With frequent **train** service that takes only 1¼ hours from Bologna, Ravenna can easily be visited on a day trip; one-way fare is 6.50€. There's also frequent service from Ferrara, which connects to Venice; one-way fare from Ferrara is 5.80€. The train station is a 10-minute walk from the center at Piazza Fernini (✆ **892021**). The tourist office (below) has rail schedules and more details.

If you have a **car** and are coming from Bologna, head east along A14. From Ferrara, take the S16.

VISITOR INFORMATION   The helpful **tourist office** is at Via Salara 8 (✆ **0544-35404;** www.turismo.ravenna.it). It's open Monday to Saturday 8:30am to 7pm, and Sunday from 10am to 6pm. Stop in here for a good map, free bicycle rental, and a combination ticket to the city's attractions.

SPECIAL EVENTS   If you're here in June and July, you can enjoy the **Ravenna Festival Internazionale.** Tickets begin at 10€ but go much higher. For information, call ✆ **0544-249211;** for tickets, call ✆ **0544-249244** (Teatro Alighieri). A **Dante Festival** is held the second week in September, sponsored by the church of San Francesco.

Exploring the Town

You can see all the sights in 1 busy day. The center of Ravenna is **Piazza del Popolo,** which has a Venetian aura. To the south, off the colonnaded Piazza San Francesco, you can visit the **Tomba di Dante** on Via Dante Alighieri. After crossing Piazza dei Caduti and heading north along Via Guerrini, you reach the **Battistero Neoniano** at Piazza del Duomo. Directly southeast and opening onto Piazza Arcivescovado is the **Museo Arcivescovile** and the **Chapel of San Andrea.**

Then you can head back to the tourist office, cutting west along Via San Vitale. This will take you to the **Basilica di San Vitale** and the **Mausoleum of Galla Placidia** behind the basilica. Nearby is the **Museo Nazionale di Ravenna** along Via Fiandrini (adjacent to Via San Vitale). To cap off your day, you can take bus no. 4 or 44 from the rail station or Piazza Caduti to visit the **Basilica di Sant'Apollinare in Classe,** reached along Via Romeo Sud.

If you're planning on seeing more than one sight, the most economical choice is to buy a **combination ticket** to visit these four monuments for 8.50€: the Battistero Neoniano, Church of San Vitale, Mausoleum of Galla Placidia, and Basilica di Sant'Apollinare. The ticket is available at the individual sights. For more information on these sights, call ✆ **0544-35404.**

Archepiscopal Museum & Chapel of San Andrea (Museo Arcivescovile e Cappella di San Andrea) ★   This twofold attraction is housed in the

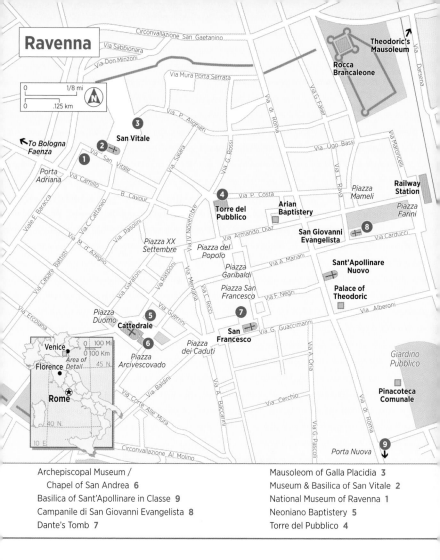

Ravenna

To Bologna
Faenza

Theodoric's
Mausoleum

Rocca
Brancaleone

Porta
Adriana

San Vitale

Railway
Station

Torre del
Pubblico

Arian
Baptistery

Piazza
Mameli

Piazza
Farini

Piazza XX
Settembre

Piazza del
Popolo

San Giovanni
Evangelista

Piazza
Garibaldi

Sant'Apollinare
Nuovo

Piazza San
Francesco

Palace of
Theodoric

Piazza
Duomo

Cattedrale

San
Francesco

Giardino
Pubblico

Piazza
dei Caduti

Piazza
Arcivescovado

Venice

Florence

Rome

Area of
Detail

Pinacoteca
Comunale

Porta Nuova

Archepiscopal Museum /
    Chapel of San Andrea **6**
Basilica of Sant'Apollinare in Classe **9**
Campanile di San Giovanni Evangelista **8**
Dante's Tomb **7**

Mausoleom of Galla Placidia **3**
Museum & Basilica of San Vitale **2**
National Museum of Ravenna **1**
Neoniano Baptistery **5**
Torre del Pubblico **4**

6th-century Archbishop's Palace. In the museum, the major exhibit is an ivory throne carved for Archbishop Maximian, from around the mid–6th century. In the chapel (oratory) dedicated to St. Andrea are brilliant mosaics. Pause in the antechamber to look at an intriguing mosaic above the entrance, an unusual representation of Christ as a warrior, stepping on the head of a lion and a snake; tough but haloed, he wears partial armor. The chapel, built in the shape of a cross, contains other mosaics that are "angelic," both figuratively and literally. Busts of saints and apostles stare down at you with the ox-eyed look of Byzantine art. **Note:** At press time this monument was closed for renovations; check its status upon your arrival.

In the Archbishop's Palace, Piazza Arcivescovado. ✆ **0544-541688.** Admission 8.50€. Apr–Sept daily 9am–7pm; Mar and Oct daily 9:30am–5:30pm; Nov–Feb daily 10am–5pm. Bus: 1 or 11.

Basilica di Sant'Apollinare in Classe ★★   About 6km (3¾ miles) south of the city, this church dates from the 6th century and was consecrated by Archbishop Maximian. Dedicated to St. Apollinare, the bishop of Ravenna, the early basilica stands side by side with a campanile, symbols of faded glory now resting in a lonely low-lying area. Inside is a central nave flanked by two aisles, the latter containing tombs of ecclesiastical figures in the Ravenna hierarchy. The floor (once carpeted with mosaics) has been rebuilt. Along the central nave are frescoed tablets. Two dozen marble columns line the approach to the apse, where you'll find the major reason for visiting the basilica: The **mosaics** are exceptional, rich in gold and turquoise, set against a background of top-heavy birds nesting in shrubbery. St. Apollinare stands in the center, with a row of lambs on either side lined up as in a processional; the 12 lambs symbolize the Apostles.

Via Romea Sud. ✆ **0544-473569.** Admission 8.50€. Apr–Sept daily 9am–7pm; Mar and Oct daily 9:30am–5:30pm; Nov–Feb daily 10am–5pm. Bus: 4 or 40 from rail station (every 20 min.) or Piazza Caduti.

Dante's Tomb (Tomba di Dante)   Right off Piazza Garibaldi, the final monument to Dante Alighieri, "the divine poet," isn't much to look at, graced with a marble bas-relief. But it's a far better place than he assigned to some of his fellow

The Basilica di Sant'Apollianre in Classe.

Detail from mosaics in the Mausoleum of Galla Placidia.

Florentines. The author of the *Divine Comedy*, in exile from his hometown, died in Ravenna on September 14, 1321. To the right of the small temple is a mound of earth in which Dante's urn went "underground" from March 1944 to December 1945 because it was feared that his tomb might suffer from the bombings. Near the tomb is the 5th-century church of **San Francesco** (worth a look for its mosaicked crypt, now underwater and filled with goldfish) the site of the poet's funeral. Via Dante Alighieri. ✆ **0544-33662.** Free admission. Daily 10am–6:30pm.

Mausoleum of Galla Placidia ★★   This 5th-century chapel is so unpretentious that you'll think you're in the wrong place. But inside it contains some exceptional **mosaics** dating from antiquity, though they might not look it. Translucent panels bring the mosaics alive in all their grace and harmony, vivid with peacock blue, moss green, Roman gold, eggplant, and burnt orange. The mosaics in the cupola literally glitter with stars. Popular tradition claims that the cross-shaped structure houses the tomb of Galla Placidia, sister of Honorius, Rome's last emperor. Galla, who died in Rome in A.D. 450, is one of history's most powerful women. She became virtual ruler of the Western world after her husband, Ataulf, king of the Visigoths, died (when she was named regent for Valentinian III, who was only 6 at the time of his father's death).

Via Fiandrini Benedetto. ✆ **0544-541688.** www.ravennamosaici.it. Admission 8.50€. Apr–Sept daily 9am–7pm; Mar and Oct daily 9:30am–5:30pm; Nov–Feb daily 10am–5pm. Bus: 10 or 11.

Museum & Basilica of San Vitale (Museo e Basilica di San Vitale) ★★★   This octagonal domed church dates from the mid–6th century. The **mosaics ★** inside—in brilliant greens and golds, lit by light from translucent panels—are among the most celebrated in the Western world. Covering the apse is a mosaic of a cleanshaven Christ astride the world, flanked by saints and angels. To the right is a mosaic of Empress Theodora and her court, and to the left is the figure of the man who married this courtesan/actress, Emperor Justinian, and his entourage.

Via San Vitale 17. ✆ **0544-215193.** www.ravennamosaici.it. Admission 8.50€. Apr–Sept daily 9am–7pm; Mar and Oct daily 9am–5:30pm; Nov–Feb daily 9:30am–5pm. Bus: 10 or 11.

National Museum of Ravenna (Museo Nazionale di Ravenna)   This museum contains archaeological objects from the early Christian and Byzantine periods: icons, fragments of tapestries, medieval armaments and armory, sarcophagi, ivories, ceramics, and bits of broken pieces from the stained-glass windows of San Vitale.

Via Fiandrini (adjacent to Via San Vitale). ☎ **0544-543711.** Admission 4€. Tues–Sun 8:30am–7:30pm. Bus: 10 or 11.

Neoniano Baptistery (Battistero Neoniano)   This octagonal baptistery was built in the 5th century, and in the center of the cupola is a tablet showing John the Baptist baptizing Christ. The circle around the tablet depicts in dramatic mosaics of deep violet-blues and sparkling golds the 12 crown-carrying Apostles. The baptistery originally served a cathedral that no longer stands. (The present-day Duomo was built in the mid–18th c. and is of little interest except for some unusual pews.) Beside it is a campanile from the 11th century, perhaps earlier.

Piazza del Duomo. ☎ **0544-215201.** www.ravennamosaici.it. Admission to all sights 8.50€. Apr–Sept daily 9am–7pm; Mar and Oct daily 9:30am–5:30pm; Nov–Feb daily 10am–5pm. Closed Christmas and New Year's Day. Bus: MB.

Where to Stay

Albergo Cappello ★★ 🏨   With a history dating from 1885, this is Ravenna's most charming boutique hotel. It's small but choice, housed in a meticulously restored palace from the 1300s, although much altered over the years. It boasts such classic features as 15th-century frescoes gracing the corridor. Even though it's old, it was overhauled completely in 1998 when it entered the modern world with up-to-date amenities, although the wine cellar and the architectural style of the splendid rooms were retained. The various color schemes inspired the names of the rooms: Yellow Gem, Green Gold, Rose and Roses. Painted beamed ceilings and terra-cotta floors are grace notes from another time, but the furnishings are modern, either contemporary in style or else reproductions of antiques.

Via IV Novembre 41, 48100 Ravenna. ☎ **0544-219813.** Fax 0544-219814. www.albergocappello.it. 7 units. 130€–200€ double; 180€–240€ suite. Rates include buffet breakfast. AE, MC, V. Parking 13€. **Amenities:** Restaurant; wine bar; room service. *In room:* A/C, TV, hair dryer, Wi-Fi (free).

Hotel Bisanzio 🏨   This member of the Best Western chain offers small to midsize guest rooms in a pleasantly renovated modern setting. Guest rooms have attractive Italian styling, some with mottled batik wall coverings. The uncluttered breakfast room has softly draped windows, and you have use of a garden. The hotel is ideally situated for exploring Ravenna's main sites on foot.

Via Salara 30, 48100 Ravenna. ☎ **0544-217111.** Fax 0544-32539. www.bisanziohotel.com. 38 units. 114€–170€ double. Rates include buffet breakfast. AE, DC, MC, V. Parking 15€. **Amenities:** Bar; babysitting; room service. *In room:* A/C, TV, hair dryer, minibar, Wi-Fi (free).

Hotel Centrale Byron   This Art Deco–inspired hotel is a few steps from Piazza del Popolo and is named for Lord Byron, who shared a nearby palace with his mistress (and her husband!). The lobby is an elegant combination of white marble and brass detailing. The long, narrow public rooms include an alcove sitting room. The small guest rooms are simply but comfortably furnished, but the bathrooms are a bit cramped.

Via IV Novembre 14, 48100 Ravenna. ☎ **0544-212225.** Fax 0544-34114. www.hotelsravenna.it. 54 units (shower only). 80€–110€ double. Rates include buffet breakfast. AE, DC, MC, V. Parking 15€. **Amenities:** Bar; room service. *In room:* A/C, TV, hair dryer, minibar, Wi-Fi (free).

NH Ravenna   This hotel, built in 1950 in the postwar cracker-box style with a bunkerlike facade, contains a conservative decor of stone floors and lots of paneling. Ravenna doesn't have many first-class accommodations, so this chain

The beach outside of Ravenna.

member has become a favorite of business travelers. Although the guest rooms are not style setters, they are of a decent size and have well-kept bathrooms.

Piazza Mameli 1, 48100 Ravenna. © **800/221-2626** in the U.S., or 0544-35762. Fax 0544-216055. www.nh-hotels.it. 84 units. 99€–210€ double; 159€–265€ suite. Rates include buffet breakfast. AE, DC, MC, V. Parking 15€. **Amenities:** Restaurant; bar; babysitting; bikes; room service; Wi-Fi (free, in lobby). *In room:* A/C, TV, hair dryer, minibar.

Where to Dine

San Domenico (p. 398), in the nearby town Imola, is one of the finest restaurants in Italy and is well worth the 48km (30-mile) drive.

A walk through Ravenna's lively food market, the **Mercato Coperto,** will introduce you to the bounty of the land. It's near the center of town on Piazza Andrea Costa and is open Monday to Saturday 7am to 2pm, and on Friday also 4:30 to 7:30pm.

Bella Venezia ROMAGNOLA/ITALIAN   Despite the name, the only Venetian dish prepared is delicious *fegato alla veneziana* (liver fried with onions). The repertoire is almost exclusively regional, with such dishes as risotto, *cappelletti alla romagnola* (cap-shaped pasta stuffed with ricotta, roasted pork loin, chicken breast, and nutmeg, and served with meat sauce), and *garganelli* pasta served with whatever happens to be in season (baby asparagus, mushrooms, or peas). All pastas are made by hand, and the place is family run and very old Italy. One of the best specialties is shrimp from the lagoon with polenta; the chefs also make a savory fish soup. The Bella Venezia is a few steps from Piazza del Popolo and next to the Hotel Centrale Byron (see above).

Via IV Novembre 16. © **0544-212746.** www.bellavenezia.it. Reservations required. Main courses 10€–18€. AE, DC, MC, V. Mon–Sat 12:15–2:30pm and 7:30–10pm. Closed Dec 23–Jan 23.

Ristorante La Gardèla ★ 🐟 EMILIA-ROMAGNA/SEAFOOD   Considering the quality of the food and the first-rate ingredients, this is Ravenna's best restaurant buy. A few steps from one of Ravenna's startling leaning towers, La Gardèla is spread out over two levels, with paneled walls lined with racks of wine bottles. The waiters bring out an array of typical but savory dishes, including spinach ravioli with poppy seeds, and *spezzatino alla contadina* (roast veal with potatoes, tomatoes, and herbs). Ravioli is stuffed with truffles, and one of the best pasta dishes, *tagliatelle,* is offered with porcini mushrooms. The chefs prepare more fresh fish than ever, most often from the Adriatic.

Via Ponte Marino 3. © **0544-217147.** www.ristorantelagardela.com. Reservations recommended. Fixed-price menus 18€–30€. AE, DC, MC, V. Fri–Wed noon–2:30pm and 7–10pm. Closed Jan 25–30.

Ristorante Villa Antica ★ INTERNATIONAL/EMILIAN/ SEAFOOD   This appealing spot keeps prices under control while combining solid technique and inventiveness. The most delightful pasta is homemade *passatelli* with scampi and porcini mushrooms. Another choice dish is ravioli filled with ricotta and spinach and served with an arugula pesto. A final most worthy dish is baked turbot with fresh vegetables, black olives, and cherry tomatoes. There is also a very good collection of wines.

Via Faentina 136. © **0544-500522.** www.villaantica.it. Reservations recommended. Main courses 8€–28€. AE, DC, MC, V. Wed–Mon noon–2:30pm and 7pm–1am.

Shopping

One of the best places to admire (and buy) mosaics is the **Studio Akomena,** Via Chartres 3 (© **0544-554700;** www.akomena.com). Replicas of Christ, the Madonna, the saints, and penitent sinners appear in all their majesty amid more secular forms whose designs were inspired by Roman gladiators or floral and geometric motifs. Virtually anything can be shipped. **Scianna,** Via di Roma 34A (© **0544-37556;** www.ravennamosaic.it), is a worthy competitor.

Ravenna After Dark

Beside the **Marina di Ravenna,** you'll find a handful of pubs and dance clubs. Our favorite is the **BBK,** Lungomare Cristoforo Colombo 171 (© **0544-438494;** www.bbkbeach.com), an open-air dance club featuring recorded tunes: It attracts a crowd that's mainly in their 20s and early 30s. The BBK is open only in June, July, and August.

Further entertainment is offered by the **Teatro Alighieri,** Via Mariani 2 (© **0544-249244;** www.teatroalighieri.org), which sponsors free summer concerts in the various squares and churches around town.

MODENA ★

40km (25 miles) NW of Bologna, 403km (250 miles) NW of Rome, 130km (81 miles) N of Florence

After Ferrara fell to Pope Clement VIII, the Este family established a duchy at Modena in the closing years of the 16th century. This city in the Po Valley possesses many great art treasures evoking its more glorious past. On the food front,

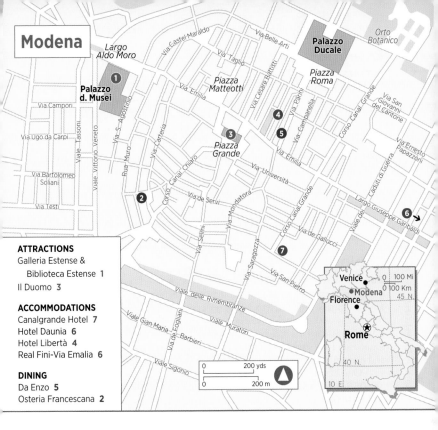

Modena

Largo
Aldo Moro

Via Castel Maraldo

Via Belle Arti

**Palazzo
Ducale**

Orto
Botanico

❶

**Palazzo
d. Musei**

Via Taglio

Piazza
Matteotti

Via Emilia

Piazza
Roma

Via San
Giovanni
del Cantone

Via Campori

Via Ugo da Carpi

Viale Tassoni

Viale Vittorio Veneto

Via S. Agostino

Rua Muro

Via Cartera

Piazza
Grande

❸

❹

❺

Via Emilia

Corso Canal Grande

Via Ernesto
Papazzoni

Via Bartolomeo
Soliani

Via Testi

Corso Canal Chiaro

Via de Servi

Via Università

Caduti di Guerra

Largo Giuseppe Garibaldi

❷

Via Selmi

Via Saragozza

Via de Gallucci

Corso Canal Grande

Via Mondatora

❼

❻

ATTRACTIONS
Galleria Estense &
 Biblioteca Estense **1**
Il Duomo **3**

Viale delle Rimembranze

Via San Pietro

Venice

Modena
Florence

0   100 Mi
0   100 Km

45° N.

ACCOMMODATIONS
Canalgrande Hotel **7**
Hotel Daunia **6**
Hotel Libertà **4**
Real Fini-Via Emalia **6**

Viale Gian Maria

Via di Cogliani

Viale Muratori

Via di Barbieri

Rome

DINING
Da Enzo **5**
Osteria Francescana **2**

Viale Sigonio

0   200 yds
0   200 m

40° N.

10° E.

Modena's chefs enjoy an outstanding reputation in hard-to-please gastronomic circles. Traversed by the ancient Roman road, Via Emilia, Modena also is a hot spot for European art connoisseurs.

Modena is an industrial zone blessed with Italy's highest per-capita income, and it can seem as sleek as the sports cars it produces. This is partially because of its 20th-century face-lift—the city was largely rebuilt following World War II bombings. These factors create a stark contrast to both the antiquity and the poverty so noticeable in other regions. Modena is home to automobile and racing giants Ferrari, Maserati, and De Tomaso, and is known for producing Lambrusco wine and balsamic vinegar. Modena was also the hometown of the late, great opera singer Luciano Pavarotti.

Many visitors who care little about antiquities come here to do business with the Ferrari or Maserati car plants (both off-limits to the general public). You can visit a showroom, the **Galleria Ferrari,** Via Dino Ferrari 43 in Maranello (✆ **0536-943204;** www.galleria.ferrari.com), a suburb of Modena, which displays engines, trophies, and both antique and the latest Ferrari cars. It's open May to September daily 9:30am to 7pm, October to April daily 9:30am to 6pm, charging an admission of 13€ for adults and 9€ for youth ages 6 to 10. From the bus station on Via Bacchini in Modena, a bus marked MARANELLO departs hourly during the day. Ask at the tourist office (see below) for details and a map.

Essentials

GETTING THERE   There are good **train** connections to and from Bologna (one train every 30 min.); trip time is 20 minutes, and a one-way fare is 3.30€. Trains arrive from Parma once per hour (trip time: 40 min.); the one-way fare is 4.60€. For information and schedules, call ℰ **892021.**

If you have a **car** and are coming from Bologna, take A1 northeast until you see the turnoff for Modena.

VISITOR INFORMATION   The **tourist office** is on Via Scudari 8 (ℰ **059-2032660;** http://turismo.comune.modena.it). It's open Monday 3 to 6pm, Tuesday to Saturday 9am to 1pm and 3 to 6pm, and Sunday 9:30am to 12:30pm.

All of Modena seems to be a stage during 1 week each year at the end of June or beginning of July, when vendors, artists, mimes, and other performers take to the streets for the **Settimana Estense;** festivities culminate in a parade in which the town turns out in Renaissance attire.

Exploring the City

Galleria Estense & Biblioteca Estense ★★   The **Galleria Estense** is
noted for its paintings from the Emilian or Bolognese school from the 14th to the 18th centuries. The nucleus of the collection was created by the Este family in the heyday of their duchies in Ferrara and then Modena. Some of the finest work is by Spanish artists, including a miniature triptych by El Greco and a portrait of Francesco I d'Este by Velázquez. Other works are Bernini's bust of Francesco I and paintings by Correggio, Veronese, Tintoretto, Carracci, Reni, and Guercino.

One of the greatest libraries in southern Europe, the **Biblioteca Estense** (ℰ **059-222248;** www.cedoc.mo.it) contains around 500,000 printed works and 13,000 manuscripts. An assortment of the most interesting volumes is kept under glass for visitors to inspect. Of these, the most celebrated is the 1,200-page *Bible of Borso d'Este,* bordered with stunning miniatures.

In the Palazzo dei Musei, Piazza Sant'Agostino 48 (off Via Emilia). ℰ **059-4395711.** www.galleria estense.beniculturali.it. Gallery admission 4€. Library 2.60€. Gallery Tues–Sun 8:30am–7pm. Library Mon–Thurs 8:30am–9:15pm; Fri 8:30am–6:45pm; Sat 8:30am–1:45pm. Bus: 7 or 11.

Il Duomo ★★   One of the glories of the Romanesque in northern Italy, Modena's cathedral was founded in 1099 and designed by an architect named Lanfranco. The cathedral, consecrated in 1184, was dedicated to St. Geminiano, the patron saint of Modena, a 4th-century Christian and defender of the faith. Towering from the rear is the **Ghirlandina,** a 12th- to 14th-century campanile, 87m (285 ft.) tall. Leaning slightly, the bell tower guards the replica of the Secchia Rapita (stolen bucket), garnered as booty from the defeated Bolognese.

The facade of the Duomo features a 13th-century rose window by Anselmo da Campione. It also boasts Wiligelmo's main entry, with pillars supported by lions, as well as Wiligelmo bas-reliefs depicting scenes from Genesis. The south door, the "Princes' Door," was designed by Wiligelmo in the 12th century and is framed by bas-reliefs illustrating scenes in the saga of the patron saint. You'll find an outside pulpit from the 15th century, with emblems of the Evangelists.

Inside, there's a vaulted ceiling, and the overall effect is gravely impressive. The Modenese restored the cathedral during the first part of the 20th century, so its present look resembles the original design. The gallery above the crypt is an outstanding piece of sculpture, supported by four lions. Two hunchbacks hold up

An illuminated manuscript at the Biblioteca Estense.

the pulpit. And the crypt, where the body of the patron saint was finally taken, is a forest of columns; here you'll find Guido Mazzoni's *Holy Family* group in terra cotta, completed in 1480. Visits are not allowed during Masses.

Corso Duomo. © **059-216078.** www.duomodimodena.it. Free admission. Daily 7:30am–12:30pm and 3:30–7pm. Bus: 6 or 11.

Where to Stay

Canalgrande Hotel ★   Situated in the old town, the Canalgrande is housed in a 300-year-old stucco palace and has more atmosphere and charm than the more highly rated Real Fini. The Canalgrande boasts elaborate mosaic floors, Victorian-era furniture, elaborately carved and frescoed ceilings, and chandeliers. French doors open onto a beautiful garden with a central flowering tree that's always full of chirping birds (ask for a room facing it). The guest rooms are decorated in pastels and boast marble bathrooms. Some of the best rooms open onto balconies; the ones on the garden side are quieter.

Corso Canalgrande 6, 41100 Modena. © 059-217160. Fax 059-221674. www.canalgrandehotel.it. 74 units (some with shower only). 132€–200€ double; 208€–295€ suite. Rates include buffet breakfast. AE, DC, MC, V. Parking 15€. Bus: 7, 12, or 14. **Amenities:** Restaurant; bar; room service. *In room:* A/C, TV, hair dryer, minibar.

Hotel Daunia   Away from the city center, Daunia boasts an exterior in a modified 18th-century design. Inside, it's modern Italian all the way, with gleaming brass, polished woods, eclectic contemporary furniture, and marble and tiled floors. The bar is a pleasant place for a drink, but the breakfast room has a claustrophobic cafeteria feel. The guest rooms are comfortable but seem bare, with light-colored walls and neutral fabrics contrasting with the dark wood furnishings.

In an unusual arrangement, the hotel restaurant, **Il Patriarca,** is on the far side of the city center (around 3km/2 miles from the hotel).

Via del Pozzo 158, 41100 Modena. © 059-371182. Fax 059-374807. www.hoteldaunia.it. 42 units (shower only). 95€ double. Rates include buffet breakfast. AE, DC, MC, V. Free parking. Bus: 7, 12, or 14. **Amenities:** Restaurant (3km/1¾ miles from the hotel); bar; room service. *In room:* A/C, TV, hair dryer, minibar.

Hotel Libertà   A modern hotel wrapped in an aged exterior, this lodge is steps from the cathedral and the Palazzo Ducale. Marble and terra-cotta floors run throughout. The guest rooms favor floral wallpapers and blond-wood furniture; some top-floor rooms are made cozy by sloping ceilings with skylights. Each room provides a good night's sleep. Several restaurants are close, and the staff will make recommendations.

Via Blasia 10, 41100 Modena. ℂ **059-222365.** Fax 059-222502. www.bestwestern.com. 51 units (shower only). 119€–180€ double; from 150€ suite. Rates include buffet breakfast. AE, DC, DISC, MC, V. Parking 20€. Bus: 4 or 7. **Amenities:** Bar; concierge; room service. *In room:* A/C, TV, hair dryer, minibar, Wi-Fi (free).

Real Fini-Via Emilia   We prefer the Canalgrande (see above) because it has more atmosphere and personal charm, but Real Fini is the top choice for most visiting businesspeople. The hotel offers the largest and best-accessorized rooms in town. The hotel is imbued with sleek modern Italian styling. The Fini name is famous in this part of Italy, having been launched in 1912 as a little Modena deli. The food company, Fini, was sold to Kraft in 1989, but the name lives on among the string of cafeterias labeled Fini along the Autostrada del Sole in Italy.

Via Emilia Est 441, 41100 Modena. ℂ **059-2051511.** Fax 059-364804. www.hotelrealfini.it. 90 units. 118€–275€ double; 199€–350€ suite. AE, DC, MC, V. Parking 20€. **Amenities:** Bar; baby-sitting; exercise room; room service; sauna. *In room:* A/C, TV, hair dryer, minibar, Wi-Fi (3€ per hr.).

Where to Dine

To put together a wonderful picnic, pick your way through the food stalls of the outdoor market on **Via Albinelli,** open weekdays from 6:30am to 2pm and Saturday afternoons in summer from 5 to 7pm.

Da Enzo MODENSE   The local favorite in Modena, this popular *trattoria* lies one floor above street level in an old building in the historic center's pedestrian zone. The chef here prepares classic regional dishes, including the famous *zampone* or stuffed pigs' trotters. Rabbit appears on the menu in the autumn, and the pastas are homemade, including several kinds of *tortellini*. *Pappardella* (wide noodles) is another favorite, as is an array of grilled or boiled meats liberally seasoned with fresh herbs and balsamic vinegar. If your doctor isn't looking, try *cotechino,* a delicious, rich, and tasty pork sausage, although it's very fatty.

Via Coltellini 17. ℂ **059-225177.** Reservations Fri–Sat at dinner. Main courses 18€–30€. AE, MC, V. Tues–Sun 12:30–2pm; Tues–Sat 7:30–10:30pm.

Osteria Francescana ★★ INTERNATIONAL/VEGETARIAN   In a city known for having some of the most demanding palates in Italy, chef Massimo Bottura satisfies. The iconoclastic chef doesn't seem to care whether he earns Michelin stars. He's more content to please his customers with his exciting food, which he serves on mismatched plates purchased in New York. Bottura's return to Italy followed a decade of work with Alain Ducasse, who, upon discovering Bottura's food, whisked him away to cook at his three-star Louis XV restaurant in Monte Carlo. Now released and "my own man" again, Bottura has taken all he learned from Ducasse and has used it to forge his own style and unique dishes. One reviewer called his cream sauce "edible gold." He still makes his heavenly *Modenese tortellini* based on his grandmother's recipe, but every other dish is his own invention. Try also his suckling pig with a red-wine sauce or his veal cheek with creamed potatoes.

Balsamic vinegar for sale in Modena.

Via Stella 22. ✆ **059-210118.** www.osteriafrancescana.it. Reservations required. Main courses 18€–30€; fixed-price menu 90€–160€. AE, DC, MC, V. Mon–Fri 12:30–2pm; Mon–Sat 8–10:30pm. Closed Aug.

Shopping

Consider picking up a bottle or two of the item that changed salad forever: balsamic vinegar. Right in the city center, **Fini,** Corso Canalchiaro 139 (✆ **059-223320;** www.store.hotelrealfini.it), sells bottles of Modena's aromatic variety, plus other fabulous food products.

Modena After Dark

Opera arrives in winter at the **Teatro Comunale,** Corso Canal Grande 85 (✆ **059-2033010** for reservations; www.teatrocomunalemodena.it), and the summer brings a major opera festival.

Stroll through the neighborhood to the spot where everyone seems to gravitate on long, hot evenings, the **Parco Amendola,** south of Modena's historic core, filled with ice-cream stands, cafes, and bars.

PARMA ★

457km (283 miles) NW of Rome, 97km (60 miles) NW of Bologna, 121km (75 miles) SE of Milan

Parma, straddling Via Emilia, was the home of Correggio, Il Parmigianino, Bodoni (of typeface fame), and Toscanini, and has also given us prosciutto and parmigiano cheese. Parma rose in influence and power in the 16th century as the seat of the Farnese duchy, and is still one of the most prosperous cities in Italy.

Upon the extinction of the male Farnese line, Parma came under the control of the French Bourbons. Its most beloved ruler, Marie-Louise, widow of Napoleon and niece of Marie Antoinette, arrived in 1815 after the Congress of Vienna awarded her this duchy. Marie-Louise became a great patron of the arts, and much of the collection she acquired is on display at the Galleria Nazionale (see "Exploring the City," below). Rising unrest in 1859 forced her abdication, and, in 1860, following a plebiscite, Parma was incorporated into the kingdom of Italy.

The city has also been a mecca for opera lovers such as Verdi, the great Italian composer whose works include *Il Trovatore* and *Aïda*. He was born in the small village of Roncole, north of Parma, in 1813. In time, his operas echoed through the Teatro Regio, the opera house that was built under the orders of Marie-Louise. Because of Verdi, Parma became a center of music, and even today the opera house is jampacked in season.

Essentials

GETTING THERE Parma is served by the Milan-Bologna **rail** line, with 30 trains a day arriving from Milan (trip time: 1½ hr.); the one-way fare starts at 9€. From Bologna, 52 trains per day arrive in Parma (1 hr.); the one-way fare is around 6.50€. There are nine connections a day from Florence (2 hr.); the one-way fare begins at 20€. For information and schedules, call ✆ **892021.**

If you have a **car** and are starting out in Bologna, head northwest along A1.

VISITOR INFORMATION The **tourist office** at Via Melloni 1A (✆ **0521-218889;** http://turismo.comune.parma.it) is open Monday 9am to 1pm and 3 to 7pm, Tuesday to Saturday 9am to 7pm, and Sunday 9am to 1pm.

Exploring the City

The gravel paths, wide lawns, and splashing fountains of the **Parco Ducale,** across the river from the Palazzo Pilotta, provide a nice retreat from Parma's more crowded areas.

Abbey of St. John (San Giovanni Evangelista)

Behind the Duomo is this church of unusual interest. After admiring the baroque front, pass into the interior to see yet another cupola by Correggio. From 1520 to 1524, the High Renaissance master depicted the *Vision of San Giovanni.* Vasari, author of *Lives of the Artists* and a contemporary of Correggio, liked it so much that he became completely carried away in his praise, suggesting the "impossibility" of an artist conjuring up such a divine work and marveling that it could actually have been painted "with human hands." Correggio also painted a St. John with pen in hand, in the transept (over the door to the left of the main altar). Il Parmigianino, the second Parmesan master, did some frescoes in the chapel at the left of the entrance. You can visit the **abbey,** the **school,** the **cloister,** and a **pharmacist's shop,** where monks made potions for some 6 centuries, a practice that lasted until the closing years of the 19th century. Mortars and jars, some as old as the Middle Ages, line the shelves.

Piazzale San Giovanni 1. ✆ **0521-235311.** www.monasterosangiovanni.it. Free admission to church and cloisters; 2€ for the pharmacist's shop. Daily 8–11:45am and 3–5:30pm; pharmacist's shop Tues–Sun 8:30am–1:30pm. Bus: 15.

Arturo Toscanini Birthplace and Museum (Casa Natale e Museo di Arturo Toscanini)

This is the house where the great conductor was born in 1867. Toscanini was the greatest orchestral conductor of the first half of the 20th century and one of the most astonishing musical interpreters of all time. He spent his childhood and youth in this house, which has been turned into a museum with interesting mementos and a library containing all the recorded works he conducted. No more than 25 people at a time are permitted inside.

Via Rodolfo Tanzi 13. ✆ **0521-285499.** www.museotoscanini.it. Admission 2€. Wed–Sat 9am–1pm and 2–6pm; Sun 2–6pm. Bus: 21.

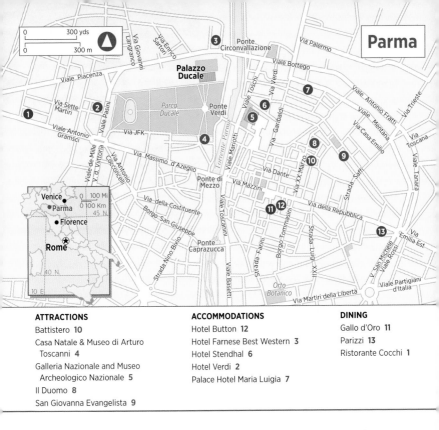

Parma

Baptistery (Battistero) ★★★　Among the greatest Romanesque buildings in northern Italy, the baptistery was the work of Benedetto Antelami. The project was begun in 1196, although the date it was completed is unclear. Made of salmon-colored marble, it's spanned by four open tiers (the fifth is closed off). Inside, the baptistery is richly frescoed with biblical scenes: a *Madonna Enthroned* and a *Crucifixion*. But it's the sculpture by Antelami that's the most worthy treasure and that provides the basis for that artist's claim to fame.

Piazza del Duomo 7. (ℓ) **0521-235886.** www.cattedrale.parma.it. Admission 6€. Daily 9am–12:30pm and 3–6:30pm. Bus: 11.

Il Duomo ★★　Built in the Romanesque style in the 11th century, with 13th-century Lombard lions guarding its main porch, the dusty pink Duomo stands side by side with a campanile constructed in the Gothic-Romanesque style and completed in 1294. The facade of the cathedral is highlighted by three open-air loggias. Inside, two darkly elegant aisles flank the central nave. The octagonal cupola was frescoed by a master of light and color, Correggio (1494–1534), one of Italy's greatest painters of the High Renaissance. His fresco, *Assumption of the Virgin*, foreshadows the baroque. The frescoes were painted from 1522 to 1534. In the transept to the right of the main altar is a somber Romanesque bas-relief, *The Deposition from the Cross*, by Benedetto Antelami, each face bathed in tragedy. Made in 1178, the bas-relief is the best-known work of the 12th-century artist, who was the most important sculptor of the Romanesque in northern Italy.

Piazza del Duomo. ✆ **0521-235886.** www. cattedrale.parma.it. Free admission. Daily 9am–12:30pm and 3–7pm. Bus: 11.

National Gallery (Galleria Nazionale) & National Archaeological Museum (Museo Archeologico Nazionale) ★★ Palazzo della Pilotta once housed the Farnese family in Parma's heyday as a duchy in the 16th century. Badly damaged by bombs in World War II, it has been restored and turned into a palace of museums.

The **National Gallery** offers a limited but well-chosen selection of the works of Parma artists from the late 15th

Detail from the exterior of the Baptistery.

to 19th centuries, notably paintings by Correggio and Parmigianino. In one room is an unfinished head of a young woman attributed to Leonardo da Vinci. Correggio's *Madonna della Scala* (of the stairs), the remains of a fresco, is also displayed. But his masterpiece is *St. Jerome with the Madonna and Child.* Imbued with delicacy, it represents age, youth, and love—a gentle ode to tenderness. In the next room is Correggio's *Madonna della Scodella* (with a bowl), with its agonized faces. You'll also see Correggio's *Coronation,* a golden fresco that's a work of great beauty, and his less successful *Annunciation.* One of Parmigianino's best-known paintings is *St. Catherine's Marriage,* with its rippling movement and subdued colors.

You can also view **St. Paul's Chamber (Camera di San Paolo),** which Correggio frescoed with mythological scenes, including one of Diana. The chamber faces onto Via Macedonio Melloni. On the same floor as the National Gallery is the **Farnese Theater (Teatro Farnese),** a virtual jewel box, evocative of Palladio's theater at Vicenza. Built in 1618, the structure was bombed in 1944 and has been restored. Admission to the theater is included in the admission to the gallery; however, if you want to visit only the theater, it costs 2€.

Also in the *palazzo* is the **National Archaeological Museum.** It houses Egyptian sarcophagi; Etruscan vases; Roman- and Greek-inspired torsos; Bronze Age relics; and its best-known exhibit, the Tabula Alimentaria, a bronze-engraved tablet dating from the reign of Trajan and excavated at Velleia in Piacenza.

In the Palazzo della Pilotta, Piazzale della Pilotta 15. ✆ **0521-233309** (National Gallery) or 0521-233718 (Archaeological Museum). www.gallerianazionaleparma.it. National Gallery admission 6€. Archaeological Museum admission 2€. National Gallery Tues–Sun 8:30am–1:45pm. Archaeological Museum Oct–May Tues–Sat 9am–1pm, Sun 3–5pm; June–July and Sept Sun 9:30am–12:30pm and 4–7pm; Aug Sun 9:30am–12:30pm. Bus: 1, 7, 8, 9, 10, or 13.

Where to Stay

Hotel Button 🔑 The Button is a local favorite, one of the best bargains in the town center, lying just off Piazza Garibaldi. This is a family-owned and -run hotel, and you're made to feel welcome. The guest rooms are simply but comfortably furnished and generally spacious, although the decor is dull. The bathrooms are a bit cramped but tidy, containing shower stalls. There's room service but no restaurant, and the bar never closes.

Strada San Vitale Borgo Salina 7 (off Piazza Garibaldi), 43100 Parma. ℰ **0521-208039.** Fax 0521-238783. www.hotelbutton.it. 40 units (shower only). 97€–115€ double; 115€–142€ triple. Rates include continental breakfast. AE, DC, MC, V. Parking 15€. Closed July 18–Aug 17. Bus: 8. **Amenities:** Bar; babysitting; room service. *In room:* A/C, TV, hair dryer, Wi-Fi (free).

Hotel Farnese Best Western   This hotel is in a quiet area convenient to the town center, the airport, and fairs. The guest rooms, ranging from small to medium, are furnished in Italian marble. The tiled bathrooms are kept tidy.

Via Reggio 51A, 43100 Parma. ℰ **800/780-7234** in the U.S. and Canada, 800-820080 toll-free in Italy, or 0521-994247. Fax 0521-992317. www.farnesehotel.it. 76 units. 110€–250€ double. Rates include buffet breakfast. AE, DC, MC, V. Free parking outdoors; 9€ indoors. Bus: 11. **Amenities:** Restaurant; bar; babysitting; bikes; exercise room; room service. *In room:* A/C, TV, hair dryer, minibar, Wi-Fi (3.50€ per hr.).

Hotel Stendhal   The Stendhal sits on a square near the opera house, a few minutes' walk from many of the important sights and 6 blocks south of the station. The guest rooms are well maintained and furnished with contemporary pieces that are reproductions of various styles, ranging from rococo to provincial. Try for one of the traditional-looking rooms with classic furnishings.

Via Bodoni 3, 43100 Parma. ℰ **0521-208057.** Fax 0521-285655. www.hotelstendhal.it. 62 units (23 with shower only). 110€–220€ double. Rates include continental breakfast. AE, DC, MC, V. Parking 15€. **Amenities:** Restaurant; bar; babysitting; room service; Wi-Fi (free, in lobby). *In room:* A/C, TV, hair dryer, minibar.

Hotel Verdi ★   Facing the Ducal Gardens, this Art Nouveau hotel preserves the elegance of its era while meeting the needs of today's visitors. The guest rooms feature parquet floors, brierwood furnishings, and fine linens. The adjacent Santa Croce restaurant offers a refined yet cordial atmosphere resplendent with period art, furnishings, and lighting in which to savor traditional cuisine and fine Italian wines. In summer, a brick courtyard, alive with greenery, allows you to dine outdoors. During the day, you can walk through the **Ducal Gardens (Parco Ducale),** landscaped by the French architect Petitot and decorated with statues by another Frenchman, Boudard.

Via Pasini 18, 43100 Parma. ℰ **0521-293539.** Fax 0521-293559. www.hotelverdi.it. 20 units (shower only). 110€–220€ double; 180€–250€ suite. AE, DC, MC, V. Free parking. Bus: 9, 11, or 12. **Amenities:** Bar; babysitting; bikes; concierge; room service. *In room:* A/C, TV, hair dryer, minibar, Wi-Fi (5€ per 24 hr.).

Palace Hotel Maria Luigia ★   This hotel caters especially to business travelers. Bold colors create an up-to-date mood, and the comfortable, modern rooms are attractive, with amenities such as soundproof walls. All the bedrooms and suites have recently been redecorated in styles ranging from classical to modern. The penthouse rooms contain large windows opening onto panoramic cityscapes. The bar looks over a pleasant patio-garden.

Viale Mentana 140, 43100 Parma. ℰ **0521-281032.** Fax 0521-2311126. www.palacemarialuigia. com. 102 units. 96€–310€ double; 345€–460€ suite. Rates include buffet breakfast. AE, DC, MC, V. Parking 20€. Bus: 6, 7, 10, or 18. **Amenities:** Restaurant; bar; babysitting; exercise room; room service. *In room:* A/C, TV, hair dryer, minibar, Wi-Fi (in some; 3€ per hr.).

Where to Dine

The chefs of Parma are acclaimed throughout Italy. Of course, Parmigiano-Reggiano has added just the right touch to millions of Italian meals, and the word *parmigiana* is quite familiar to American diners.

At the atmospheric **Enoteca Fontana,** Strada Farini 24A (✆ **0521-286037**), open Tuesday to Saturday (closed Aug) 9am to 3pm and 4:30 to 9pm, you can stand at the ancient old bar or take a seat at one of the long communal tables. Sample from a list of hundreds of wines from Emilia-Romagna, many of them from the immediate region. You might decide to order a light meal, too, from the short menu of panini, ham-and-cheese platters, and pastas.

The most popular pizzeria in Parma is open late (although it's closed Mon) and is almost always crowded. You might have to wait at **Pizzeria La Duchessa,** Piazza Garibaldi 1 (✆ **0521-235962**), especially if you want an outdoor table, but the pizzas are fabulous, especially when washed down with a carafe of Lambrusco.

Maxim's, in the Palace Hotel Maria Luigia (see above), is also worth seeking out, whether you're staying in the hotel or not.

Gallo d'Oro ★ 🍴 PARMIGIANA   This is our favorite *trattoria*. It has an unpretentious decor with flea-market items such as antique cinema posters and old-fashioned toys. Downstairs is a bodega where locals pile in to taste the wine of the region, especially Lambrusco, which seems to go with anything served in Modena. Start with *salumi misti,* a variety of locally cured hams. All the pasta dishes are homemade, including *tortelli ripieni* (pasta stuffed with cottage cheese and fresh spinach). For a main course, we recommend the tender roasted lamb stuffed with bread, cheese, and eggs. A Parma classic is the chicken breast rolled with delectable prosciutto and parmigiano and offered in a white-wine sauce.

Borgo della Salina 3. ✆ **0521-208846.** Reservations recommended. Main courses 7€–15€. AE, DC, MC, V. Mon–Sat noon–3pm and 7–midnight; Sun noon–3pm.

Parizzi ★★★ PARMIGIANA/ITALIAN   In the historic center of town, the building that houses Parizzi dates from 1551, when it first opened as an inn; the current restaurant was opened in 1958 by the father of the present owner. Seated under the skylit patio, you'll enjoy rich cuisine that's among the best in this region of Italy. After you're shown to a table, a cart filled with antipasti is wheeled before you, containing shellfish, stuffed vegetables, and marinated salmon. Then you might be tempted by *culatello,* cured ham made from sliced haunch of wild boar; a pasta served with a sauce of herbs and Parmigiano-Reggiano; a parmigiano soufflé with white truffles; or pheasant ravioli with black truffles.

Strada della Repubblica 71. ✆ **0521-285952.** www.ristoranteparizzi.it. Reservations required. Main courses 18€–28€; 6-course degustation menu 65€. AE, DC, MC, V. Tues–Sun noon–2:30pm and 7:30–10:30pm. Closed 3 weeks in Aug and Jan 8–15.

Parma Rotta ★ 🍴 PARMIGIANA   If you don't mind driving 1.6km (1 mile) out of town along the road to Langhirano, this is a Parma classic. It's the best neighborhood *trattoria* we know for sampling some of the hearty and flavor-filled dishes of the region, such as sautéed duck breast—slightly rare—served with a combination fruit-and-vegetable flavoring. No one knows for sure how old the building housing the restaurant is, but everything has had a century or so to mellow out. The spit-roasted lamb or the roast smoked pork is reason enough to come out here, although we're also fond of the grilled beef cooked in a wood-stoked oven. For a first course, many locals prefer *tortelli di erbetta,* pasta stuffed with fresh greens. There is also a wide selection of homemade desserts.

Via Langhirano 158. (C) **0521-966738.** www.parmarotta.com. Reservations recommended. Main courses 10€–25€. AE, DC, MC, V. Tues–Sat noon–2:30pm and 8–10:30pm. Bus: 7.

Ristorante Cocchi ★★★ 🍴 PARMIGIANA Local foodies claim this out-of-the-way restaurant serves the best cuisine in town, although there is disagreement. The Hotel Daniel, in which it is situated, is rather plain, and the location is on the far side of the ring road enveloping the city. When you arrive, you may think you're at the wrong address, but press on for an amazing culinary discovery.

Start with *strolghino,* a thin salami made from lean leg meat. It's carved tableside and is delectable. The rice dishes are without equal in town. *Savarin* is Parmesan- and risotto-filled "envelopes" of cooked ham, veal *polpettini,* and a porcini ragout. The *bomba Di Riso* is marinated pigeon that has been braised and deboned. These ingredients are layered inside a rice-lined dome and baked. Other meat, pasta, and poultry dishes, each delectable, are also offered.

16A Viale Gramsci. (C) **0521-995-147.** www.hoteldaniel.biz. Reservations required. Main courses 9€–20€. AE, DC, MC, V. Sun–Fri noon–2:30pm and 7:30–10pm. Closed Sat.

Shopping

Parma's most famous food product—parmigiano (Parmesan) cheese, the best being Parmigiano-Reggiano—is savored all over the world. Virtually every corner market sells thick wedges of the stuff, but if you're looking to buy your cheese in a special setting, head for the **Salumeria Garibaldi,** Via Garibaldi 42 ((C) **0521-235606**). You might also take a walk through the city's **food market** at Piazza Ghiaia, near the Palazzo della Pilotta; it's open Monday through Saturday 8am to 1pm and 3 to 7pm.

Hoping to learn more about the region's famous hams and cheeses? There are well-funded bureaucracies in Parma whose sole functions are to encourage the world to use greater quantities of the city's tastiest products. They can arrange tours and visits to the region's most famous producers. For information about Parma cheeses, contact the **Consorzio del Parmigiano Reggiano,** Via dei Mercati 9 ((C) **0521-292700;** www.parmigiano-reggiano.it). For insights into the dressing and curing of Parma hams, contact the **Consorzio del Prosciutto di Parma,** Via dell'Arpa 8B ((C) **0521-246211;** www.prosciuttodiparma.com).

Cheese and sausages for sale at Salumeria Garibaldi.

Enoteca Fontana, Strada Farini 24A ((C) **0521-286037**), sells bottles from virtually every vineyard in the region, and the staff is extremely knowledgeable.

Parma After Dark

Life in Parma extends beyond munching on strips of salty ham and cheese. The **Teatro Regio,** Via Garibaldi 16, near Piazza della Pace ((C) **0521-039399;** www.teatroregio parma.org), is the site of concerts throughout the year.

If you'd like to sample a glass or two of great wine, head for the bar section of a spot recommended in the "Where to Dine" section, above: the **Enoteca Fontana,** Strada Farini 24A (© **0521-286037**).

At **Bacco Verde,** Via Cavalloti 33 (© **0521-230487**), sandwiches, glasses of beer, and a wide selection of Italian wines are dispensed in a cramped but convivial setting ringed with antique masonry.

In the mood for dancing? Head for **Dadaumpa,** Via Emilio Lepido 48 (© **0521-483813;** www.dadaumpa.com), a stylish and lighthearted venue for dance tunes.

VENICE

9

Venice is a preposterous monument to both the folly and the obstinacy of humankind. It shouldn't exist, but it does, much to the delight of thousands of visitors, gondoliers, lace makers, hoteliers, restaurateurs, and glass blowers.

Centuries ago, in an effort to flee barbarians, Venetians left dry land and drifted out to a flotilla of "uninhabitable" islands in the lagoon. Survival was difficult enough, but no Venetian has ever settled for mere survival. The remote ancestors of the present inhabitants created the world's most beautiful city. To your children's children, however, Venice might be nothing more than a legend. The city is sinking at an alarming rate of about 2½ inches per decade, and at the same time, the damp climate, mold, and pollution are contributing to the city's decay. Estimates are that, if no action is taken soon, one-third of the city's art will deteriorate within the next decade or so. Clearly, Venice is in peril. One headline proclaimed, "The Enemy is at the Gates."

But for however long it lasts, Venice, decaying or not, will be one of the highlights of your trip through Italy. It lacks the speeding cars and roaring Vespas of Rome; instead, you make your way through the city either on foot or by boat. It would be ideal if it weren't for the hordes of tourists that descend every year, overwhelming the squares and making the streets almost impossible to navigate. In the summer heat of the Adriatic, the canals become a smelly stew. Steamy and overcrowded July and August are the worst times to visit; May, June, September, and October are much better.

Although Venice is one of the world's most enchanting cities, you do pay a price, literally and figuratively, for all this beauty. Everyone leaves complaining about the outrageous prices, which can be double what they are elsewhere in the country. Since the 19th century, Venice has thrived on its visitors, but these high prices have forced out many locals. They've fled across the lagoon to dreary Mestre, an industrial complex launched to help boost the regional economy.

Today the city is trying to undo the damage that its watery environs and tourist-based economy have wrought. In 1993, after a 30-year hiatus, the canals were dredged in an attempt to reduce water loss and reduce the stench brought in with the low tides. In an effort to curb the other 30-year-old problem of residential migration to Mestre, state subsidies are now being offered to the citizens of Venice as an incentive to not only stay, but also to renovate their crumbling properties.

"Lately, there's been a resurgence, a great influx of artists, actors, and creative people," said author Andrea di Roblilant. "In other words, those droves that left the city of the Doges by the boatload are now paddling back, adding oomph to local restaurants, refurbishing hotels, and injecting the city with huge doses of modernism."

Unwilling to even dream of defeat, Venice has, in fact, commissioned new works by internationally famed architects, including Lawrence Nield, Vittorio

PREVIOUS PAGE: **The Bridge of Sighs (Ponte dei Sospiri).**

Boats tied along one of Venice's canals.

Gregotti, Santiago Calatrava, and David Chipperfield. With an eye to the future, the city unveiled its ultramodern Grand Canal Bridge in 2006, connecting the Piazzale Roma with the Santa Lucia train station.

ESSENTIALS
Arriving

The arrival scene at unattractive **Piazzale Roma** is filled with nervous expectation; even the most veteran traveler can become confused. Whether arriving by train, bus, car, or airport limo, everyone walks to the nearby docks (less than a 5-min. walk) to select a method of transport to his or her hotel. The cheapest way is by *vaporetto* (public motorboat); the more expensive is by gondola or motor launch (see the section "Getting Around," later in this chapter).

BY PLANE You can now fly nonstop from North America to Venice on Delta. You'll land at the **Aeroporto Marco Polo** (✆ 041-2606111; www.venice airport.it) at Mestre, north of the city on the mainland. The **Consorzio Motoscafi** (✆ 041-5222303; www.motoscafivenezia.it) operates a *moto-scafo* (shuttle boat) service that can deliver you from the airport directly to the center of Venice at Piazza San Marco in about 30 minutes. The boats wait just outside the main entrance, and the fare begins at 100€ for up to six passengers (if there are only two of you, find some fellow travelers to share the ride and split the fare with you). If you've got some extra euros to spend, you can arrange for a **private water taxi** by calling ✆ 041-5222303. The cost of the ride to the heart of Venice is 105€.

Buses from the airport are less expensive, though they can only take you as far as Piazzale Roma; from there you will need to take a *vaporetto* to reach your hotel. The **Azienda Trasporti Veneto Orientale** (✆ 041-383672; www.atvo.it) shuttle bus links the airport with Piazzale Roma for

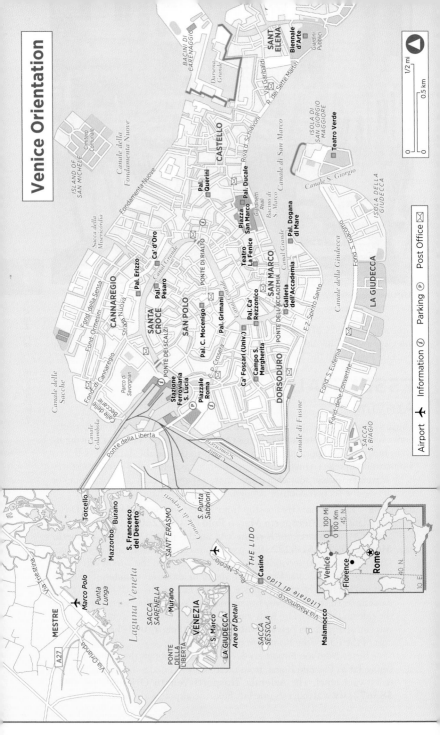

Venice Orientation

ISLAND OF SAN MICHELE

Cimitero Comunale

Canale della Fondamenta Nuove

BACINI DI CARENAGGIO

Darsena Grande

SANT ELENA

Biennale d'Arte

Giardini Pubblici

Via Garibaldi

R. dei Sette Martiri

CASTELLO

Pal. Querini

Pal. Ducale

Piazza San Marco

Giardinetti Reali

Canale di San Marco

Canale S. Giorgio

ISOLA DI SAN GIORGIO MAGGIORE

Teatro Verde

Canale della Fondamenta Nuove

Sacca della Misericordia

CANNAREGIO

Fond. della Sensa

Fond. Ormesini

Strada Nuova

Ca' d'Oro

Pal. Erizzo

Canal Grande

PONTE DI RIALTO

Pal. Pesaro

Teatro La Fenice

Pal. Dogana di Mare

Bacino di S. Marco

Pal. Dogana di Mare

SAN MARCO

Canal Grande

ISOLA DELLA GIUDECCA

Canale delle Sacche

Fond. di Cannaregio

Parco di Savorgnan

Fond. delle Beccarie

SANTA CROCE

SAN POLO

Pal. C. Mocenigo

Pal. Grimani

C. P. Crosera

Ca' Foscari (Univ.)

Campo S. Margherita

Pal. Ca' Rezzonico

Galleria dell'Accademia

PONTE DELL'ACCADEMIA

DORSODURO

F.Z. Spirito Santo

Fond. S. Giacomo

Canale della Giudecca

LA GIUDECCA

Fond. S. Eufemia

Fond. delle Convertite

SACCA S. BIAGIO

Canale di Fusina

PONTE DEI SCALZI

Stazione Ferroviaria S. Lucia

Piazzale Roma

Canale delle Sacche

Canale Colombola

Ponte della Libertà

Canal Scomenzera

Torcello

Burano

Mazzorbo

S. Francesco del Deserto

SANT'ERASMO

Canal di Tre porti

S. Punta Sabbioni

Laguna Veneta

MESTRE

A27

Via Orlanda

Via Triestina

Marco Polo

Punta Lunga

SACCA SERENELLA

Murano

PONTE DELLA LIBERTÀ

VENEZIA

S. Marco

LA GIUDECCA

Area of Detail

SACCA SESSOLA

THE LIDO

RIVA S. NICOLÒ

Casinò

Litorale di Lido

Via Malamocco

Malamocco

Venice

Florence

Rome

100 Mi

100 Km

45 N

40 N

10 E

Airport ✈   Information ①   Parking ℗   Post Office ✉

1/2 mi

0.5 km

430

3€. The trip takes about 20 minutes, and departures are about every 30 minutes daily 8:20am to 12:20am. Even cheaper is a local bus company, **ACTV** (*©* **041-2424;** www.actv.it), whose bus no. 5 makes the run for 3€. The ACTV buses depart every half-hour and take about a half-hour to reach Piazzale Roma.

BY TRAIN   Trains pull into the **Stazione di Santa Lucia,** at Piazzale Roma (*©* **892021** in Italy only). Travel time is about 5 hours from Rome, 3½ hours from Milan, 4 hours from Florence, and 2 hours from Bologna. The *vaporetto* departs near the station's main entrance. There's also a **tourist office** at the station (*©* **041-5298711**), open daily 8am to 6:30pm.

BY CAR   The autostrada links Venice with the rest of Italy, with direct routes from such cities as Trieste (driving time: 1½ hr.), Milan (3 hr.), and Bologna (2 hr.). Bologna is 151km (94 miles) southwest of Venice, Milan is 266km (165 miles) west, Trieste is 156km (97 miles) east, and Rome is 526km (327 miles) southwest.

From the mainland, follow the signs leading to Venice, going to the Ponte della Libertà along S11, which links Venice to the mainland. The small island of Tronchetto appears on your right as the bridge comes to an end. Here you'll find the parking garages of Venice.

One of the most prominent garages is the **Garage San Marco,** Piazzale Roma 467F (*©* **041-5232213;** www.garagesanmarco.it), near the *vaporetto,* gondola, and motor launch docks. The charge is 26€ for 12 hours or 30€ for 24 hours for any kind of car. From spring to fall, this municipal parking lot is nearly always filled. Bookings can only be made through the website www.garagesanmarco.it. You're more likely to find parking on **Isola del Tronchetto** (*©* **041-5207555;** www.veniceparking.it), which costs 21€ per day. From Tronchetto, take *vaporetto* no. 2 to Piazza San Marco. If you have heavy luggage, you'll need a water taxi. Parking is also available at Mestre.

Visitor Information

Visitor information is available at the **Azienda di Promozione Turistica,** San Marco 71/F (*©* **041-5298711;** www.turismovenezia.it). Year-round hours are daily 9am to 3:30pm. Posters around town with exhibit and concert schedules are more helpful. Ask for a schedule of the month's special events and an updated list of museum and church hours because these can change erratically and often. There is also another tourist office at the airport open daily from 9am to 9pm (*©* **041-5298711**).

Anyone between the ages of 14 and 29 is eligible for a **Rolling Venice pass,** entitling you to discounts for museums, restaurants, stores, language courses, hotels, and bars. The Rolling Venice pass is valid until December 31 of the year in which it is purchased. It costs 4€ and can be picked up at any tourist office in Venice.

Venice's Castello neighborhood.

Another pass, the VeniceCard is valid for 3 days, costing 48€. It offers free use of public transport on land and water and free admission to all of the city's civic museums. The pass is sold at all tourist offices.

City Layout

Venice lies 4km (2½ miles) from the Italian mainland (connected to Mestre by the Ponte della Libertà) and 2km (1¼ miles) from the open Adriatic. It's an archipelago of 118 islands. Most visitors, however, concern themselves only with **Piazza San Marco** and its vicinity. In fact, the entire city has only one piazza, which is San Marco (all the other squares are campos). Venice is divided into six districts *(sestieri)*: **San Marco, Santa Croce, San Polo, Castello, Cannaregio,** and **Dorsoduro.**

Many of Venice's so-called streets are actually canals *(rios)*—more than 150 in all, spanned by a total of 400 bridges. Venice's version of a main street is the **Grand Canal (Canal Grande),** which snakes through the city. Three bridges cross the Grand Canal: the white marble **Ponte Rialto,** the wooden **Ponte Accademia,** and the stone **Ponte degli Scalzi.** The Grand Canal splits Venice into two unequal parts.

South of Dorsoduro, which is south of the Grand Canal, is the **Canale della Guidecca,** a major channel separating Dorsoduro from the large island of La Guidecca. At the point where Canale della Guidecca meets the **Canale di San Marco,** you'll spot the little **Isola di San Giorgio Maggiore,** with a church by Palladio. The most visited islands in the lagoon, aside from the **Lido,** are **Murano, Burano,** and **Torcello.**

If you really want to tour Venice and experience that hidden, romantic *trattoria* on a nearly forgotten street, bring along a map that details every street and that has an index on the back.

A broad street running along a canal is a *fondamenta,* a narrower street running along a canal is a *calle,* and a paved road is a *salizzada, ruga,* or *calle larga.* A *rio terra* is a filled canal channel now used as a walkway, and a *sottoportego* is a passage beneath buildings. When you come to an open-air area, you'll often

A maniac must've numbered Venice's buildings. Before you set out for a specific place, get detailed instructions and have someone mark it on your map. Don't depend on street numbers; try to locate the nearest cross street. Because signs and numbers have decayed over 6 centuries, it's best to look for signs posted outside rather than for a number.

Every building has a street address and a mailing address. For example, a business at Calle delle Botteghe 3150 (3150 Botteghe St.) will have a mailing address of San Marco 3150 because it's in the San Marco *sestiere*, and all buildings in each district are numbered continuously from 1 to 6,000. (To confuse things, several districts have streets of the same name, so it's important to know the *sestiere*.) In this chapter, we give the street name first, followed by the mailing address.

encounter the word *campo*—that's a reference to the fact that such a place was once grassy, and in days of yore cattle grazed there.

The Neighborhoods in Brief

This section will give you some idea of where you might want to stay and where the major attractions are.

SAN MARCO Welcome to the center of Venice. Napoleon called it "the drawing room of Europe," and it's one crowded drawing room today. It has been the heart of Venetian life for more than 1,000 years. **Piazza San Marco (St. Mark's Square)** is dominated by **St. Mark's Basilica.** Just outside the basilica is the **campanile** (bell tower), a reconstruction of the one that collapsed in 1902. Around the corner is the **Palazzo Ducale (Doge's Palace),** with its **Bridge of Sighs.** Piazza San Marco is lined with some of the world's most overpriced cafes, including **Florian's** (opened 1720) and **Quadri** (opened 1775). The most celebrated watering hole, however, is away from the square: the overrated **Harry's Bar,** founded by Giuseppe Cipriani but made famous by Hemingway. In and around the square are some of the most convenient hotels in Venice (though not necessarily the best) and an array of expensive tourist shops and *trattorie.*

CASTELLO The shape of Venice is often likened to that of a fish. If so, Castello is the tail. The largest and most varied of the six *sestieri,* Castello is home to many sights, such as the **Arsenale,** and some of the city's plushest hotels, such as the **Danieli.** One of the neighborhood's most notable attractions is the Gothic **Santa Giovanni e Paolo (Zanipolo),** the Pantheon of the doges. Cutting through the *sestiere* is **Campo Santa Maria Formosa,** one of Venice's largest open squares.

The most elegant street is **Riva degli Schiavoni,** which runs along the Grand Canal; it's lined with some of the finest hotels and restaurants and is one of the city's favorite promenades.

CANNAREGIO This is Venice's gateway, the first of the six *sestieri.* At its heart is the **Santa Lucia Railway Station** (1955). It also shelters about a third of the population, some 20,000 residents. The area embraces the old **Jewish Ghetto,** the first one on the Continent. Jews began to move here at the beginning of the 16th century, when they were segregated from the rest of the city.

Impressions

Wonderful city, streets full of water, please advise.
—Robert Benchley

From here, the word *ghetto* later became a generic term used all over the world. Attractions in this area include the **Ca' d'Oro,** the finest example of the Venetian Gothic style; the **Madonna dell'Orto,** a 15th-century church known for its Tintorettos; and **Santa Maria dei Miracoli,** with a Madonna portrait supposedly able to raise the dead. Unless you're coming for one of these attractions, this area doesn't offer much else because its hotels and restaurants aren't the best. Some of the cheapest lodging is found along **Lista di Spagna,** to the left as you exit the train station.

SANTA CROCE This area is on the opposite side of the Grand Canal from Cannaregio, between Piazzale Roma and a point just short of the Ponte di Rialto. It's split into two rather different neighborhoods. The eastern part is in the typically Venetian style and is one of the least crowded parts of Venice, although it has some of the Grand Canal's loveliest *palazzi* (palaces). The western side is more industrialized and isn't very interesting to explore.

SAN POLO This is the heart of commercial Venice and the smallest of the six *sestieri.* It's reached by crossing the Grand Canal at **Ponte di Rialto (Rialto Bridge).** The shopping here is much more reasonable than that around Piazza San Marco. One of the major sights is the **Erberia,** which Casanova wrote about in his 18th-century biography. Both wholesale and retail markets still pepper this ancient site. At its center is **San Giacomo di Rialto,** the city's oldest church. The district also encloses the **Scuola Grande di San Rocco,** a repository of the works of Tintoretto. **Campo San Polo** is one of the oldest and widest squares and one of the principal venues for Carnevale. San Polo is also filled with moderately priced hotels and a large number of *trattorie,* many specializing in seafood. In general, the hotels and restaurants are cheaper here than along San Marco, but not as cheap as those around the train station in Cannaregio.

DORSODURO The least populated of the *sestieri,* this funky neighborhood is filled with old homes and half-forgotten churches. Dorsoduro is the southernmost section of the historic district (from San Marco, take the Accademia Bridge across the Grand Canal). Its major sights are the **Accademia Gallery** and the **Peggy Guggenheim Foundation.** It's less trampled than the areas around the Rialto Bridge and Piazza San Marco. Its most famous church is **La Salute,** whose first stone was laid in 1631. The **Zattere,** a broad quay built after 1516, is one of Venice's favorite promenades. Cafes, *trattorie,* and *pensioni* (boardinghouses) abound in the area.

GETTING AROUND

You can't hail a taxi—at least, not on land—so get ready to walk and walk and walk. Of course, you can break up your walks with *vaporetto* or boat rides, which are great respites from the packed (and we mean *packed*) streets in summer.

However, note that in autumn, the high tide (*acqua alta*) is a real menace. The squares often flood, beginning with Piazza San Marco, one of the city's lowest points. Many visitors and locals wear knee-high boots to navigate their way. In fact, some hotels maintain a storage room full of boots in all sizes for their guests.

A cafe on Campo Santa Margherita in the Dorsoduro section.

By Public Transportation

Much to the chagrin of the once-ubiquitous gondoliers, Venice's **motorboats** (*vaporetti*) provide inexpensive and frequent, if not always fast, transportation in this canal city. The *vaporetti* are called "water buses," and they are indeed the "buses" of Venice because traveling by water is usually faster than traveling by land. The service is operated by **ACTV (Azienda del Consorzio Trasporti Veneziano),** Isola Nova del Tronchetto 32 (✆ **041-2424;** www.actv.it). An *accelerato* is a vessel that makes every stop; a *diretto* makes express stops. The average fare is 6.50€. Note that in summer, the *vaporetti* are often fiercely crowded. Pick up a map of the system at the tourist office. They run daily up and down the Grand Canal, with frequent service 7am to midnight and then hourly midnight to 7am.

The Grand Canal is long and snakelike and can be crossed via only three bridges, including the one at Rialto. If there's no bridge in sight, the trick in getting across is to use one of the *traghetti* **gondolas** strategically placed at key points. Look for them at the end of any passage called Calle del Traghetto. They're under government control, so the fare is only .60€.

Venice Connected (www.veniceconnected.it) is an online reservation system to smooth your stay in the city by allowing you to make reservations for certain public tourism services. When items are purchased 15 days in advance of your visit, discounts are granted. You can book public transportation, certain civil museums such as the Doge's Palace, toilet services, and car parking in municipal garages at the entrance to the city. On the website, you can click on a bar for online purchases and then enter your dates of travel onto an electronic calendar. Patrons can then use the tabs at the top of each date to choose among the various sites. Payments are made by credit card. You'll be issued a voucher containing a code (PNR), a summary of your purchased services. For information about Venice Connected call ✆ **041-2424.**

By Motor Launch (Water Taxi)

Motor launches (*taxi acquei*) cost more than public *vaporetti*, but you won't be hassled as much when you arrive with your luggage if you hire one of the many private ones. You might or might not have the cabin of one of these sleek vessels to yourself because the captains fill their boats with as many passengers as the law allows before taking off. Your porter's uncanny radar will guide you to one of the inconspicuous piers where a water taxi waits.

The price of a transit by water taxi from Piazzale Roma (the road/rail terminus) to Piazza San Marco is 65€ for 5 passengers, plus 10€ for each additional passenger. The captains adroitly deliver you, with luggage, to the canal-side entrance of your hotel or on one of the smaller waterways within a short walking distance of your destination. You can also call for a water taxi; try the **Consorzio Motoscafi** at ℰ **041-5222303.**

By Gondola

You and your gondolier have two major agreements to reach: the price and the length of the ride. If you aren't careful, you're likely to be taken on both counts. It's a common sight to see a gondolier huffing and puffing to take his passengers on a "quickie," often reducing an hour to 15 minutes.

The average rate is 80€ for 40 minutes. A 40€ surcharge is applied for each additional 20 minutes. The actual fare depends on how well you stand up to the gondolier. Many gondoliers offer rates beginning at 110€ for up to 50 minutes. Prices go up after 8pm. In fairness to them, we must say that their job is hard and has been overly romanticized: They row boatloads of tourists across hot, smelly canals with such endearments screamed at them as, "No sing, no pay!" And these fellows have to make plenty of euros while the sun shines because their work ends when the first cold winds blow in from the Adriatic. Speaking of winds, many visitors get very seasick in a gondola on the open water on a windy day.

Two major stations where you can hire gondolas are **Piazza San Marco** (ℰ **041-5200685**) and **Ponte di Rialto** (ℰ **041-5224904**).

[FastFACTS] VENICE

Consulates The **U.K. Consulate** is at Piazzale Donatori di Sangue 2/5, Mestre (ℰ **041-5055990;** www.fco.gov.uk), open Monday to Friday 10am to 1pm. The **United States, Canada,** and **Australia** have consulates in Milan, about 3 hours away by train (see "Milan," in chapter 11).

Currency Exchange There are many banks in Venice where you can exchange money. You might try the **Banca Intesa,** Campo Manin, San Marco 4216 (ℰ **041-5296811;** www.intesasanpaolo.com; *vaporetto:* San Marco), or Banco San Marco, Calle Larga San Marco, San Marco 383 (ℰ **041-5293711;** www.bancosanmarco.it; *vaporetto:* San Marco). Hours are Monday to Friday 8:30am to 1:30pm and 2:45 to 4:15pm. ATMs are located on most main thoroughfares and in front of banks.

Dentists & Doctors Your best bet is to have your hotel set up an appointment with an English-speaking dentist or doctor. The American Express office and the British Consulate also have lists. Also see "Hospitals," below.

Drugstores If you need a pharmacist in the middle of the night, go to any drugstore, even a closed one. A list of after-hours pharmacies will be posted on the door. These drugstores operate on a rotational system of late nights. A well-recommended central one is **Antica Farmacia al Mondo,** Piscina Frezzeria, San Marco 1676 (✆ **041-5225813;** *vaporetto:* San Marco).

Emergencies   Call ✆ **113** for the police, ✆ **118** for an ambulance, or ✆ **115** to report a fire.

Hospitals   Get in touch with the **Ospedale Civile Santi Giovanni e Paolo,** Campo Santi Giovanni e Paolo in Castello (✆ **041-5294111;** *vaporetto:* San Toma), staffed with English-speaking doctors 24 hours.

Internet   For laptop links or international calls, head for **Venetian Navigator,** Calle Casselleria, Castello 5300 (✆ **041-2771056;** www.venetian navigator.com; *vaporetto:* San Marco), which lies near Piazza San Marco in the heart of Venice. You can search the Web with an American-style keyboard, send a fax, download pictures from your digital camera, and even burn CDs and DVDs. You

can purchase a card to use the facilities, costing 3€ for 15 minutes or 8€ for up to an hour.

Laundry & Dry Cleaning   A convenient coin-operated laundromat and dry-cleaning enterprise is **Lavanderia Gabriella,** Calle Fiubera, San Marco 985 (✆ **041-5221758;** *vaporetto:* San Marco), behind Piazza San Marco. Its washing machines are available daily 8am to 12:30pm in winter and 8am to 7pm in summer, and its dry-cleaning facilities are open Monday to Saturday 8am to 12:30pm in winter, 3 to 7pm in summer.

Police   See "Emergencies," above.

Safety   The curse of Venice is the pickpocket. Violent crime is rare. But because of the overcrowding in *vaporetti* and on the narrow streets, it's easy to pick pockets. Purse snatchers are commonplace as well. They can dart out of nowhere, grab a purse, and disappear in seconds down some dark alley. Keep valuables

locked in a safe in your hotel, if one is provided.

Telephone   See "Staying Connected" in chapter 18 for full details on how to call Venice from home and how to place international calls once you're here. The **city code** for Venice is **041;** use this code for all calls—even within Venice itself (and you must now include the zero every time, even when calling from abroad).

Toilets   These are available at Piazzale Roma and various other places, but they aren't as plentiful as they should be. A truly spotless one is at the foot of the Accademia Bridge. Often you'll have to rely on the restrooms in cafes, although you should buy something, perhaps a light coffee, because, in theory, the toilets are for customers only. Most museums and galleries have public toilets. You can also use the public toilets at the Albergo Diurno, Via Ascensione, just behind Piazza San Marco. Remember, *signori* means men and *signore* means women.

WHERE TO STAY

Venice has some of the most expensive hotels in the world, but we've also found some wonderful lesser known moderately priced places, often on hard-to-find streets. However, Venice has never been known as an inexpensive destination.

Because of their age and lack of uniformity, Venice's hotels offer widely varying rooms. For example, it's entirely possible to stay in a hotel generally considered "expensive" while paying only a "moderate" rate—if you'll settle for a less desirable room. Many "inexpensive" hotels and boardinghouses have two or three rooms in the "expensive" category. Usually these are more spacious and open onto a view. Also, if an elevator is essential for you, always inquire in advance; not every building has one.

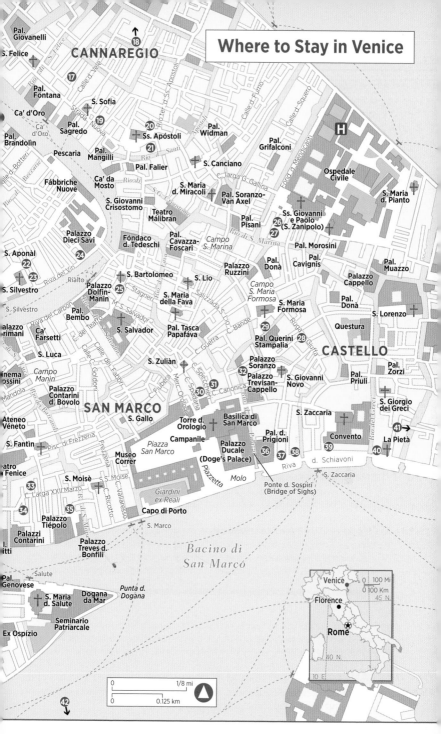

Where to Stay in Venice

CANNAREGIO

Pal. Giovanelli
S. Felice
Pal. Fontana
Ca' d'Oro
Pal. Sagredo
Pal. Brandolin
Pescaria
Pal. Mangilli
Ca' da Mosto
Fábbriche Nuove
S. Sofia
Ss. Apóstoli
Pal. Falier
Pal. Widman
Pal. Grifalconi
S. Canciano
S. Maria d. Miracoli
Pal. Soranzo-Van Axel
Ospedale Civile
S. Maria d. Pianto
H
Palazzo Dieci Savi
S. Giovanni Crisostomo
Teatro Málibran
Pal. Cavazza-Foscari
Fóndaco d. Tedeschi
Pal. Pisani
Ss. Giovanni e Paolo (S. Zanipolo)
Pal. Morosini
S. Aponàl
S. Silvestro
Riva del Vin
S. Bartolomeo
Palazzo Dolfin-Manin
Campo S. Marina
Palazzo Ruzzini
Pal. Donà
Pal. Cavignis
Pal. Muazzo
Palazzo Cappello
S. Lio
Campo S. Maria Formosa
Pal. Donà
S. Lorenzo
alazzo rimani
Ca' Farsetti
Pal. Bembo
S. Salvador
S. Maria della Fava
Pal. Tasca Papafáva
S. Maria Formosa
Questura
S. Luca
inema ossini
Campo Manin
Palazzo Contarini d. Bovolo
S. Zuliàn
Pal. Querini Stampalia
CASTELLO
Pal. Zorzi
Ateneo Véneto
SAN MARCO
S. Gallo
Torre d. Orologio
Campanile
Palazzo Soranzo
Palazzo Trevisan-Cappello
S. Giovanni Novo
Pal. Priuli
S. Giorgio dei Greci
S. Fantin
Museo Corrèr
Basilica di San Marco
Palazzo Ducale (Doge's Palace)
Pal. d. Prigioni
S. Zaccaria
Convento
La Pietà
atro Fenice
S. Moisè
Piazza San Marco
Piazzetta
Molo
Riva d. Schiavoni
S. Zaccaria
Ponte d. Sospiri (Bridge of Sighs)
C. Larga XXII Marzo
Palazzo Tiépolo
Capo di Porto
S. Marco
Giardini ex Reali
Palazzi Contarini itti
Palazzo Treves d. Bonfili
Bacino di San Marcó
Pal. Genovese
Salute
S. Maria d. Salute
Dogana da Mar
Punta d. Dogana
Seminario Patriarcale
Ex Ospízio

Venice
Florence
Rome
0 — 100 Mi
0 — 100 Km
45° N.
40° N.
10° E

0 — 1/8 mi
0 — 0.125 km

CARNEVALE

Venetians are once more taking to the open piazzas and streets for the pre-Lenten holiday of **Carnevale.** The festival traditionally marked the unbridled celebration that preceded Lent, the period of penitence and abstinence before Easter. It lasts about 5 to 10 days and culminates the Friday to Tuesday before Ash Wednesday (dates vary).

In the 18th-century heyday of Carnevale, well-heeled revelers came from all over Europe to take part in the festivities. Masks became ubiquitous, affording anonymity and pardoning 1,000 sins. They permitted the fishmonger to attend the ball and dance with the baroness. The doges condemned the festival and the popes denounced it, but nothing could dampen the Venetian Carnevale spirit until Napoleon arrived in 1797 and put an end to the festivities.

Resuscitated in 1980 by local tourism powers to fill the winter months, Carnevale is calmer now, though just barely. In the 1980s, it attracted seemingly the entire student population of Europe, backpackers who slept in the piazzas and train station. Politicians and city officials adopted a middle-of-the-road policy that helped establish Carnevale's image as neither a free-for-all outdoor party nor a continuation of the exclusive private balls in the Grand Canal *palazzi* available to only a very few.

Each year the festival opens with a series of lavish balls and private parties, most of which aren't open to the public. But the candlelit **Doge's Ball (Ballo del Doge)** is a dazzling exception, traditionally held the Saturday before Shrove Tuesday in the 15th-century Palazzo Pisani Moretta on the Grand Canal. Historical costumes are a must, and you can rent them. Of course, this ball isn't exactly cheap—the price for 2011 was around 1,200€ per person including dinner—and you can expect it to rise for future years because organizers plan to make the ball even more extravagant. If you're interested in finding out more and arranging for a costume rental, contact Antonia Sautter at the Ballo del Doge at ☎ **041-2413802** or 041-5224426 (fax 041-5287543).

Even if you don't attend a ball, there's still plenty of fun in the streets. You'll find a patchwork of musical and cultural events, many of them free of charge, that appeal to all tastes, nationalities, ages, and budgets. At any time, musical events are staged in any of the city's dozens of piazzas—from reggae to zydeco to jazz to chamber music—and special art exhibits are mounted at numerous museums and galleries. The recent involvement of international corporate sponsors has met with a mixed reception, but it seems to be the wave of the future.

Carnevale is not for those who dislike crowds. The crowds are what it's all about. All of life becomes a stage, and everyone is on it. Whether you spend months creating an elaborate costume

The cheapest way to visit Venice is to book into a *locanda* (small inn), which is rated below the *pensione* in official Italian hotel lingo. Standards are highly variable in these places, many of which are dank, dusty, and dark. The rooms even in many first-class hotels are often cramped because space has always been a problem in Venice. It's estimated that in this "City of Light," at least half of the rooms in any category are dark, so be duly warned. Those with lots of light and opening onto the Grand Canal carry a hefty price tag.

or grab one from the countless stands set up around town, Carnevale is about giving in to the spontaneity of the magic and surprise around every corner, the mystery behind every mask. Masks and costumes are everywhere, with the emphasis on the historical, because Venice's Carnevale is a chance to relive the glory days of the 1700s, when Venetian life was at its most extravagant. Groups travel in coordinated getups that range from a contemporary passel of Fellini-esque clowns to the court of the Sun King in all its wigged-out glory. You might see the Three Musketeers riding the *vaporetto;* your waiter might appear dressed as a nun. The places to be seen in costume are the cafes lining Piazza San Marco. Don't expect to be seated at a full-view window seat unless your costume is straight off the stage of the local opera house. The merrymakers carry on until Shrove Tuesday, when the bells of San Francesco della Vigna toll at midnight. But before they do, the grand finale involves fireworks over the lagoon.

The city is the quintessential set, the perfect venue; Hollywood could not create a more evocative location. This is a celebration about history, art, theater, and drama. Venice and Carnevale were made for each other.

In 2000, Venetians passed a law permitting families to house paying guests without getting involved in a lot of red tape. As a result, many aging *palazzi,* closed to the public for centuries, have since been reopened. Today, many of these *palazzi* are among the best small hotels in Venice, offering anywhere from six to a dozen rooms. The competition they are generating has forced many established institutions to polish up their dusty rooms and improve their service.

The most difficult times to find rooms are during the February Carnevale, around Easter, and from June to September. Because of the tight hotel situation, it's advisable to make reservations as far in advance as possible (months in advance for summer, and even a year in advance for Carnevale). The reservation must be guaranteed by a credit card or else by sending a down payment equivalent of 1 night's accommodations with a money order or bank draft. After those peak times, you can virtually have your pick of rooms. If you ask at the reception desk, most hotels will grant you a 10% to 15% discount in winter (Nov–Mar 15). But getting this discount could require a little negotiation. A few hotels close in January if there's no prospect of business.

If you arrive without a reservation, go to one of the **Venezia Sì reservation booths** throughout the area at the train station, the municipal parking garage at Piazzale Roma, the airport, and the information point on the mainland where the highway comes to an end. The main office is at Piazzale Roma (© **199-173309;** www.veneziasi.it). To get a room, you'll have to pay a deposit that's then rebated on your hotel bill. Depending on the hotel classification, deposits are 15€ to 50€ per person. All hotel booths are open daily 9am to 11pm.

If you plan a longer stay in Venice, consider contacting **Venetian Apartments** (© **020/31784180** in London; www.venice-rentals.com), which offers 100 apartments of varying degrees of luxury in Venice. The range is from studios to one-, two-, or three-bedroom apartments, even four bedrooms in some cases for larger families. Rentals begin at 895€ per week, going up to 3,350€ per week, and most bookings are on a Saturday-to-Saturday basis.

See "The Neighborhoods in Brief," earlier in this chapter, to get an idea of where you might want to stay, whether in less touristy San Polo or in Dorsoduro, or in the thick of things (and crowds, too) in and around Piazza San Marco.

Near Piazza San Marco

VERY EXPENSIVE

Gritti Palace ★★★   The Gritti, in a stately Grand Canal setting, is the renovated *palazzo* of 15th-century doge Andrea Gritti. Even after its takeover by ITT Sheraton, it's still a bit starchy and has a museum aura (some of the furnishings are roped off), but for sheer glamour and history, only the **Cipriani** (p. 456) tops it. (Stay at the Cipriani for quiet, isolation, and more recreational facilities, but stay here for a central location and service that's just as good.) The Gritti evokes a well-tailored, well-upholstered private home of a Venetian nobleman—discreet, tranquil, and horrendously upscale, providing a shelter for billionaires. Guests here are more pampered than those at the **Danieli** (p. 446), the Gritti's closest rival.

The variety of guest rooms seems almost limitless, from elaborate suites to small singles. But throughout, the elegance is evident, as exemplified by the gilt mirrors, the antiques, and the hand-painted 18th-century-style furnishings.

Campo Santa Maria del Giglio, San Marco 2467, 30124 Venezia. © **800/325-3589** in the U.S., or 041-794611. Fax 041-5200942. www.gritti.hotelinvenice.com. 91 units. 300€–1,390€ double; 1,400€–3,070€ suite. AE, DC, MC, V. *Vaporetto:* Santa Maria del Giglio. **Amenities:** Restaurant; bar; babysitting; concierge; room service. *In room:* A/C, TV, DVD/CD player (in some), hair dryer, minibar, Wi-Fi (15€ per 24 hr.).

Palazzo Sant'Angelo ★★★ 🛍   This is the first hotel with its main entrance on the Grand Canal to open in more than a century. Formerly a private palace, the hotel is awash in Venetian silk fabrics and antique furnishings. A three-story property, it houses guests in the 21st century the way Venice welcomed its 19th-century luminaries, such as George Sand or Henry James. Its interior bedrooms open onto courtyard gardens; its suites offer views of the Grand Canal between the Rialto and Accademic bridges. All the rooms are sumptuous, the suites in particular, featuring red-and-gold silk wall coverings as well as antiques.

San Marco 3488–3489, 30124 Venezia. ℭ **041-2411452.** Fax 041-2411557. www.palazzosant angelo.com. 14 units. 220€–680€ double; 440€–880€ suite. Rates include buffet breakfast. AE, DC, MC, V. *Vaporetto:* Sant'Angelo. **Amenities:** Bar; babysitting; room service. *In room:* A/C, TV, hair dryer, minibar, Wi-Fi (3€ per hr.).

EXPENSIVE

Hotel Concordia ★   The Concordia, in a russet-colored building with stone-trimmed windows, is the only hotel with rooms overlooking St. Mark's Square (only a few do, and they command a high price). A series of gold-plated marble steps takes you to the lobby, where you'll find a comfortable bar area, good service, and elevators to whisk you to the labyrinthine halls. The (quite small) guest rooms are decorated in a Venetian antique 18th-century style, with Murano chandeliers, coordinated fabrics, hand-painted furnishings, and red-marble bathrooms.

Calle Larga, San Marco 367, 30124 Venezia. ℭ **041-5206866.** Fax 041-5206775. www.hotelconcordia. com. 57 units (some with shower only). 150€–420€ double; 210€–470€ suite. Rates include buffet breakfast. AE, DC, MC, V. *Vaporetto:* San Marco. **Amenities:** Restaurant; bar; airport transfers (150€); babysitting; room service. *In room:* A/C, TV, hair dryer, minibar, Wi-Fi (free).

Hotel Saturnia International ★   The Saturnia is one of Venice's most successful adaptations of a 14th-century *palazzo.* You're surrounded by richly embellished beauty: a grand hall with a wooden staircase, iron chandeliers, fine paintings, and beamed ceilings. The individually styled guest rooms are generally spacious and furnished with chandeliers, Venetian antiques, tapestry rugs, gilt mirrors, and carved ceilings. A few on the top floor have small balconies; others overlook the garden in back.

Calle Larga XXII Marzo, San Marco 2399, 30124 Venezia. ℭ **041-5208377.** Fax 041-5207131. www. hotelsaturnia.it. 95 units (a few with tub or shower only). 138€–492€ double; 252€–666€ junior suite. Rates include buffet breakfast. AE, DC, MC, V. *Vaporetto:* San Marco. **Amenities:** Restaurant; babysitting; room service. *In room:* A/C, TV, hair dryer, minibar, Wi-Fi (in some, 2€ per 3 hr.).

Hotel Violino d'Oro ★   On the 18th-century Palazzo Barozzi is a restored three-story hotel, a choice boutique hotel on a small *campiello* or square with a marble fountain, lying on the heavily trafficked route from San Marco to the Accademia. The midsize guest rooms are handsomely furnished with well-kept bathrooms. Grace notes are evident in the gilt decoration on marble-top desks and the Murano chandeliers. Two rooms and the junior suite open onto private terraces.

Campiello Barozzi, San Marco 2091, 30124 Venezia. ℭ **041-2770841.** Fax 041-2771001. www. violinodoro.com. 26 units. 117€–400€ double. Rates include buffet breakfast. AE, DC, MC, V. *Vaporetto:* San Marco Vallaresso. **Amenities:** Bar; babysitting; room service. *In room:* A/C, TV, hair dryer, minibar, Wi-Fi (12€ per 24 hr.).

Palazzo del Giglio ★★   For years, this salmon-fronted town house was marketed as an integral part of the Gritti Palace, one of the most expensive and legendary hotels in Europe, which is next door. Thanks to the ownership of its actual premises by an entity not associated with the Gritti Palace, the Palazzo del Giglio staged a minirevolt, and reestablished itself as a completely independent, government-rated four-star entity in its own right. The result is a comfortable, even plush hotel that would have achieved five-star status except for its lack of a restaurant and additional facilities. Bedrooms are not outfitted as plushly or as elegantly as those at the nearby Gritti Palace, but each of its accommodations is comfortable, elegant, and airy.

Campo S. Maria del Giglio, San Marco 2462, 30124 Venezia. © **041-2719111.** Fax 041-5205158. www.hotelgiglio.com. 24 units. 110€–290€ double; 250€–420€ suite. Rates include breakfast. AE, MC, V. *Vaporetto:* Santa Maria del Giglio. **Amenities:** Bar; room service. *In room:* A/C, TV, hair dryer, Wi-Fi (free).

Splendid Hotel   On the site of a 16th-century inn, Starhotels, the Italian independent hotel group, has taken five 18th-century buildings and turned them into a sleek modern hotel, at least inside. Totally refurbished, the government-rated, four-star property lies between Piazza San Marco and the Rialto Bridge in the heart of Venice. The interior is decorated in beige with splashes of wisteria, black, and red. The midsize to large bedrooms overlook either the canal or the hotel's *campiello,* a courtyard with a retractable glass ceiling. In addition, there is a ground-floor library by the courtyard, and on the rooftop is a terrace with a solarium and a hot tub. The bedrooms have been restored in the traditional Venetian style, but with modern amenities, featuring parquet floors, the walls embellished with hand-painted wisteria decorations.

San Marco Mercerie 760, 30124 Venezia. © **041-5200755.** Fax 041-5286498. www.starhotels. com. 165 units. 160€–590€ double; from 460€ suite. AE, DC, MC, V. *Vaporetto:* Rialto. **Amenities:** Restaurant; bar; babysitting; concierge; room service. *In room:* A/C, TV, CD player (in some), hair dryer, minibar, Wi-Fi (12€ per 24 hr.).

MODERATE

Hotel Do Pozzi ★   A short stroll from Piazza San Marco, this place feels more like a country tavern than a hotel. Its original structure is 200 years old, and it opens onto a paved courtyard with potted greenery. The sitting and dining rooms are furnished with antiques (and near-antiques) intermixed with utilitarian modern decor. Half the guest rooms open onto the street and half onto a view of an inner garden where breakfast is served in summer. Some have Venetian styling with antique reproductions; others are in a more contemporary and more sterile vein. A major refurbishment has given a fresh touch to the bathrooms.

Via XXII Marzo, San Marco 2373, 30124 Venezia. © **041-5207855.** Fax 041-5229413. www.hotel dopozzi.it. 35 units (some with shower only). 98€–280€ double. Rates include buffet breakfast. AE, DC, MC, V. *Vaporetto:* Santa Maria del Giglio. **Amenities:** Bar; babysitting; room service; Wi-Fi (12€ per 24 hr., in lobby). *In room:* A/C, TV, hair dryer, minibar.

INEXPENSIVE

Bed and Breakfast Corte Campana ★ ✦   This was the family home of Marco Scurati, occupying the third floor of an old apartment building only 60m (195 ft.) from Piazza San Marco. One guest likened it to a place where Lucy Honeychurch from *A Room with a View* would have stayed in Venice. There are only a handful of bedrooms, so reservations are important. On the downside, occupants of the bedrooms must share a bathroom. Each room is spacious and beautifully furnished, and the best unit opens onto a private terrace.

Calle del Remedio, 4410 Castello, 30122 Venezia. ©/fax **041-5233603.** www.cortecampana. com. 3 units. 90€–150€ double. MC and V accepted only for bookings; payment must be made in cash. *Vaporetto:* San Marco. **Amenities:** Internet (free, in lobby). *In room:* A/C, TV, hair dryer.

Ca' Dei Dogi ★★ 🎁   This small *albergo* (Italian hotel) in a tranquil pocket of Venice is reached down a maze of narrow alleyways, just a surprisingly short walk from the Bridge of Sighs and the Doge's Palace. At night you can sit out on the rooftop patio listening to the gondoliers singing beneath the bridge. This remarkable find combines luxury and value, two elements that rarely, if ever, come together in Venice. The most idyllic accommodations include a small alcove and overlook the ducal palace. Each of the midsize bedrooms are individually decorated, the details of the decor carefully chosen for both taste and comfort. Much altered over the years, the palace itself dates from the 15th century. Next door to the hotel, Taverna dei Dogi offers typically Venetian fare such as risotto with black cuttlefish flavored with orange. In summer, it offers outdoor dining in a garden.

Corte Santa Scolastica, Castello 4242, 30122 Venezia. 🕾 **041-2413759.** Fax 041-5285403. www. cadeidogi.it. 6 units. 140€–260€ double. MC, V. *Vaporetto:* San Zaccaria. **Amenities:** Restaurant; bar; babysitting; room service. *In room:* A/C, TV, hair dryer, minibar.

Hotel Ai Do Mori ★ ✏   This 1450s town house lies about 10 paces from tourist central. You'll have to balance your need for space with your desire for a view (and your willingness to climb stairs because there's no elevator). The lower-level rooms are larger but don't have views; the third- and fourth-floor rooms are cramped but have sweeping views over the basilica's domes. Most of the units have a charming view on San Marco basilica and the bell tower, and the best room on the top floor has a private terrace overlooking Venice. The building is frequently upgraded by owner Antonella Bernardi. The furniture in the guest rooms is functional and modern, bathrooms are well maintained, and most of the street noise is muffled by double-paned windows.

Calle Larga San Marco, San Marco 658, 30124 Venezia. 🕾 **041-5204817.** Fax 041-5205328. www.hotelaidomori.com. 11 units. 50€–150€ double. MC, V. *Vaporetto:* San Marco. *In room:* A/C, TV, hair dryer.

Locanda Armizo ★ 🎁   This is a glorified B&B and a real discovery with one of the most gracious hosts in Venice, Massimiliano. He has taken an antique home of a former Venetian merchant and converted it into this little inn decorated in a typically Venetian style. The word *armizo* means "mooring" in old Venetian. The location is only a 2-minute walk from the Rialto Bridge and close to the Grand Canal where ancient ships indeed used to moor. Bedrooms have reproductions of Venetian antiques and are immaculately kept and midsize.

Campo San Silvestro–San Polo 1104, 30100 Venezia. 🕾 **041-5206473.** Fax 041-2960384. www. locandaarmizo.com. 6 units. 69€–189€ double; 90€–280€ junior suite. Rates include continental breakfast. AE, MC, V. *Vaporetto:* San Silvestro. **Amenities:** Babysitting. *In room:* A/C, TV, hair dryer, minibar, Wi-Fi (free).

Locanda Ca le Vele ★ 🎁   One of the many—and also one of the best—little inns to spring up in postmillennium Venice opens onto the Santa Sofia Canal, within easy walking distance of the Rialto Bridge and St. Mark's Square. Its charm is of another day, although its facilities are completely modern. Bedrooms are comfortably elegant and furnished tastefully in the classic Venetian style of exposed rafter beams, damasks, marbles, and Murano glass chandeliers.

Ca le Vele, 30131 Venezia. 🕾 **041-2413960.** Fax 041-2414280. www.locandalevele.com. 6 units. 80€–180€ double; 100€–190€ triple; 130€–220€ quad; 150€–240€ suite. AE, DC, MC, V. *Vaporetto:* Ca d'Oro. **Amenities:** Room service. *In room:* A/C, TV, hair dryer, minibar, Wi-Fi (free).

Locanda Fiorita ★ 🍴 In a red-painted *palazzo,* parts of which date from the 1700s, this is a little charmer and both a winning and affordable place to stay. At the close of the century, new management took over and massively renovated the place. Everything was given a kind of faux Venetian style of the 1700s. The location is on a postage-stamp square off Campo Santo Stefano. If available, ask for room no. 1 or 10, which offer a little patio beneath a glorious wisteria vine best enjoyed in the spring. Bedrooms have style and a certain Venetian flair, giving you much comfort either in the main building or in an annex. Six other equally good bedrooms lie in a nearby annex.

San Marco 3457 (on Campiello Novo), 30124 Venezia. 🕭 **041-5234754.** Fax 041-5228043. www.locandafiorita.com. 16 units. 80€–170€ double. Rates include buffet breakfast. AE, MC, V. *Vaporetto:* Sant'Angelo. **Amenities:** Babysitting; room service. *In room:* A/C, TV, hair dryer, Wi-Fi (free).

Castello/Riva Degli Schiavoni

VERY EXPENSIVE

Hotel Danieli ★★★ The Cipriani is more exclusive and isolated, and the Gritti coddles its guests a bit more, but the Danieli is clearly number three among the fabulous *palazzi* hotels of Venice. Comparisons between the Danieli and the Gritti are inevitable. Whereas the Gritti Palace is imperial and dignified, the Danieli is elegant, *beau geste,* and fun. The Danieli sprawls, whereas the Gritti is intimate. The Danieli was built as a showcase by Doge Dandolo in the 14th century and in 1822 was transformed into a "hotel for kings." The atmosphere is luxurious; even the balconies opening off the main lounge are illuminated by stained-glass skylights. The rooms range widely in price, dimension, decor, and vistas (those opening onto the lagoon cost a lot more but are also susceptible to the noise of Riva degli Schiavoni). You're housed in one of three buildings: a modern structure (least desirable), a 19th-century building, and the 14th-century Venetian Gothic Palazzo Dandolo (most desirable).

Riva degli Schiavoni, Castello 4196, 30122 Venezia. 🕭 **800/325-3535** in the U.S. and Canada, or 041-5226480. Fax 041-5200208. www.starwoodhotels.com. 233 units. 300€–1,140€ double; from 790€ suite. AE, DC, MC, V. *Vaporetto:* San Zaccaria. **Amenities:** Restaurant; bar; airport transfers (195€); babysitting; concierge; room service; Wi-Fi (15€ per 24 hr.). *In room:* A/C, TV, hair dryer, minibar.

Londra Palace ★★ It's no Danieli, but the Londra is a gabled manor on the lagoon, a few yards from Piazza San Marco. The hotel's most famous guest was Tchaikovsky, who wrote his *Fourth Symphony* in room no. 108 in December 1877; he also composed several other works here. The cozy reading room is reminiscent of an English club, with leaded windows and paneled walls with framed blowups of some of Tchaikovsky's sheet music. The guest rooms are luxurious, often with lacquered Venetian furniture. Romantics ask for one of the two Regency-style attic rooms with beamed ceilings. The best units are on the fifth floor, with beamed ceilings and private terraces.

Riva degli Schiavoni, Castello 4171, 30122 Venezia. 🕭 **041-5200533.** Fax 041-5225032. www. hotelondra.it. 53 units. 275€–595€ double; 485€–699€ junior suite. Rates include buffet breakfast. AE, DC, MC, V. *Vaporetto:* San Zaccaria. **Amenities:** Restaurant; bar; babysitting; concierge; room service. *In room:* A/C, TV, hair dryer, minibar, Wi-Fi (free).

EXPENSIVE

Locanda Vivaldi ★ 🎁   Here is a rare chance to immerse yourself in a cliché of Venetian charm. The house of the composer Antonio Vivaldi (1678–1741) has been converted into a hotel. The most original and influential Italian composer of his day, Vivaldi was *maestro de' concerti* in Venice from 1716 to 1738, when he lived at this house. In keeping with the spirit of the maestro, the Locanda has been decorated with baroque ornamentation. Bedrooms are lush, evoking a time gone by but with modern conveniences such as tiled bathrooms.

Riva degli Schiavoni, 4152–4153, 30122 Venezia. ✆ **041-2770477.** Fax 041-2770489. www.locanda vivaldi.it. 22 units (some with shower only). 160€–525€ double; 300€–770€ junior suite. Rates include buffet breakfast. AE, DC, MC, V. *Vaporetto:* San Zaccaria. **Amenities:** Rooftop restaurant (May–Oct); bar; concierge; room service. *In room:* A/C, TV, minibar, Wi-Fi (free).

Metropole Hotel ★★   One of our favorite hotels in Venice is a government-rated four-star boutique hotel with roots that go back to its days as the orphanage that employed Vivaldi to teach music to some of its students from 1704 to 1738. What you get here is a grand and genuine Venetian *palazzo*, redolent with the grandiose trappings of Europe's 19th-century sense of adventure. The facade of the hotel faces the Venetian lagoon; its inner recesses ramble back through a hidden garden that's almost mystically beautiful. Each of the bedrooms is outfitted in an individual style that reflects the aesthetic traditions of Imperial Venice, usually with antiques, some with tapestries, and the soft pastel palettes of 18th-century Venice.

Castello, Riva degli Schiavone 4149, 30122 Venezia. ✆ **041-5205044.** Fax 041-5223679. www. hotelmetropole.com. 70 units. 210€–473€ double; 315€–538€ junior suite; 400€–1,025€ suite. Rates include buffet breakfast. AE, DC, MC, V. *Vaporetto:* San Zaccaria. **Amenities:** Restaurant; bar; babysitting; concierge; room service; Wi-Fi (free, in lobby). *In room:* A/C, TV, hair dryer, minibar.

MODERATE

Albergo Al Piave ★ ☺   For Venice, this centrally located hotel is a real bargain, and the Puppin family welcomes you with style. Although the hotel is rated only one star by the government, its level of comfort is far above that, and its decor and ambience are inviting. Even some guests who can afford to pay more select Piave for its cozy warmth. Rare for a hotel of this category, you get orthopedic mattresses, found under the floral bedspreads. The most desirable accommodations open onto small terraces with views of Venice. The best deal for a family is one of the suites containing two bedrooms that share a bathroom. There are also some stylish apartments with kitchenettes.

Ruga Giuffa, Castello 4838–4840, 30122 Venezia. ✆ **041-5285174.** Fax 041-5238512. www.hotel alpiave.com. 15 units (shower only). 110€–210€ double; 140€–260€ suite for 3. Rates include continental breakfast. AE, DC, MC, V. *Vaporetto:* San Zaccaria. *In room:* A/C, TV, fridge, hair dryer, Wi-Fi (free).

Hotel Ca' Formenta   Set at the border of "touristic Venice" and a working-class neighborhood where foreign visitors aren't often spotted, this is a four-story, friendly, and completely unpretentious hotel. It has absolutely no glamour, and few amenities, but thanks to the staff, it is imbued with enormous amounts of charm. The only public area is the modern, granite-trimmed bar/reception and lobby area, where the receptionist might pour you a (stiff) drink if you want it, and dispense everything from advice to free directions. The high ceilings in the bedrooms reflect the building's 15th-century origins. Other than that, each unit is small, efficiently decorated, colorful, and contemporary looking, each with a private bathroom containing a shower. In spite of its offbeat location, the hotel lies only a 5-minute walk from St. Mark's Square.

Via Garibaldi, Castello 1650, 30122 Venezia. ⓒ **041-5285494.** Fax 041-5204633. www.hotel caformenta.it. 14 units. 94€–295€ double; 134€–320€ junior suite. Rates include buffet breakfast. AE, DC, MC, V. *Vaporetto:* Arsenale. **Amenities:** Bar; Wi-Fi (free, in lobby). *In room:* A/C, hair dryer, minibar.

La Residenza ★★   In a 14th-century building that looks a lot like a miniature Doge's Palace, this little hotel is on a residential square where children play soccer and older people feed the pigeons. You'll pass through a stone vestibule lined with ancient Roman columns before ringing another doorbell at the bottom of a flight of stairs. First an iron gate and then a door will open into an enormous salon filled with antiques, 300-year-old paintings, and some of the most marvelously preserved walls in Venice. The guest rooms are far less opulent, with contemporary pieces and good beds. The choice rooms are usually booked far in advance, especially for Carnevale.

Campo Bandiera e Moro, Castello 3608, 30122 Venezia. ⓒ **041-5285315.** Fax 041-5238859. www.venicelaresidenza.com. 15 units (shower only). 71€–200€ double. Rates include continental breakfast. MC, V. *Vaporetto:* Arsenale. **Amenities:** Concierge. *In room:* A/C, TV, minibar, Wi-Fi (free).

Locanda La Corte ★ 🏨   In the Castello quarter, this handsomely renovated inn lies close to the Campo SS. Giovanni e Paolo. It is housed in a 16th-century palace that has been beautifully restored with comfortable furnishings, well-chosen fabrics, elegant furniture, and much comfort from the beds to the private bathrooms. Many rooms rest under wooden beamed ceilings, and the beds are decorated in the typically Venetian style with satin headboards. In fair weather, breakfast is served in a courtyard with trees and flowers. The Locanda overlooks a small canal with its own entrance for those who wish to arrive by water taxi.

Castello 6317, 30122 Venzia. ⓒ **041-2411300.** Fax 041-2415982. www.locandalacorte.it. 18 units. 72€–235€ double; 135€–250€ junior suite. Rates include buffet breakfast. AE, DC, MC, V. *Vaporetto:* Fondamenta Nuove. **Amenities:** Bar; babysitting; room service. *In room:* A/C, TV, hair dryer, minibar, Wi-Fi (free).

Residenza Ca' Bauta ★ 🏨   A real discovery, this gem occupies the second floor of the 15th-century former Muazzo family palace, only a few steps from Campo SS. Giovanni e Paolo. It is within walking distance of the action, Piazza San Marco, yet is more remotely located in the Castello residential neighborhood. The former reception salon of the palace has been turned into a grand lounge, from which all the bedrooms radiate. Bedrooms are beautifully maintained and handsomely decorated with Versace-style prints. Ask for room no. 203 with its private terrace.

Castello-Calle Muazzo 6457, 30122 Venezia. ⓒ **041-2413787.** Fax 041-5212313. www.cabauta. com. 6 units. 90€–210€ double; 120€–280€ junior suite. Rates include buffet breakfast. AE, DC, MC, V. *In room:* A/C, TV, hair dryer, minibar.

INEXPENSIVE

Alloggi Barbaria ⚓ Away from the frantic tourist scene, this is a friendly little hotel that's completely undiscovered though it lies only a 15-minute walk from Piazza San Marco. Giorgio and Fausto welcome you to their little inn, which is an ideal starting point for exploring the islands in the lagoon—Torcello, Burano, and Murano. Rooms are simply furnished but spacious, well maintained, and comfortable.

Castello 6573, 30122 Venezia. ✆ **041-5222750.** Fax 041-2775540. www.alloggibarbaria.it. 8 units. 60€–120€ double; 90€–140€ triple. Rates include continental breakfast. AE, DC, MC, V. *Vaporetto:* Ospedale. **Amenities:** Wi-Fi (13€ per 24 hr.). *In room:* A/C, TV, hair dryer, minibar.

Near the Ponte di Rialto

The center of this neighborhood is the bustling Rialto Market itself. This area is a mixed bag, with plenty of decaying apartment houses alongside tourist sights. There are some fine shops and restaurants, but also some of the worst tourist traps in Venice. Our recommendations will steer you in the right direction.

VERY EXPENSIVE

Hotel Ca' Sagredo ★★★ A stay at this sumptuously restored 15th-century palace is like enveloping yourself in the *Serenissima*. No hotel in Venice has the grand opulence of this gem, which is actually a National Monument opening onto the Grand Canal and the historical Rialto Market. Ca' Sagredo is a private palazzo, a noble residence, a museum, and a member of Small Luxury Hotels of the World.

The former ballrooms and bedrooms are filled with paintings by some of the most celebrated of Venetian artists, including Pietro Longhi and Tiepolo. Most of the bedrooms and suites open onto a view of the canal, and each is decorated differently and most luxuriously with a refined elegance unmatched in the city. You'll feel like an 18th-century Venetian nobleman, living in such opulence. In the chic L'Alcova Restaurant, you dine by candlelight on an original cuisine based on local Venetian traditions.

Campo Santa Sofia 4198/99, 30121 Venezia. ✆ **041-2413111.** Fax 06-2413521. www.casagredo hotel.com. 42 units. 190€–650€ double; 450€–900€ junior suite; from 650€ suite. Rates include buffet breakfast. AE, DC, MC, V. *Vaporetto:* Ca' d'Oro. **Amenities:** Restaurant; bar; airport transfers (100€); babysitting; concierge; exercise room; room service. *In room:* A/C, TV/DVD, hair dryer, minibar, Wi-Fi (14€ per 24 hr.).

MODERATE

Da Bruno ⚓ Between Piazza San Marco and the Rialto Bridge, this small, two-story hotel has been owned and run by the Sartore clan for some three generations. You escape from a busy shopping street into the soothing confines of this affordable hotel with an intimate bar lying off the lobby. Since 1956, the hotel has catered to various generations of travelers, some of whom send their sons and daughters. Rooms are completely modernized because the hotel was virtually restructured in 2002. The midsize bedrooms are furnished with reproductions of antique Venetian furniture and are most inviting and beautifully maintained.

Salizada San Lio 5726A Castello, 30122 Venezia. ✆ **041-5230452.** Fax 041-5221157. www.hotelda bruno.com. 32 units. 72€–230€ double; 100€–265€ triple. Rates include buffet breakfast. AE, DC, MC, V. *Vaporetto:* Rialto. **Amenities:** Bar; room service. *In room:* A/C, TV, hair dryer, minibar, Wi-Fi (free).

Hotel Marconi This old relic is still going strong, although its heyday was in the 1930s. The Marconi, less than 15m (50 ft.) from the Rialto Bridge, was built in 1500 when Venice was at the height of its supremacy. The drawing-room furnishings would be appropriate for visiting archbishops, and the Maschietto family operates everything efficiently. Only four of the lovely old guest rooms open onto the Grand Canal, and these are the most eagerly sought after—and the most expensive. The rooms vary from small to medium, each with a comfortable bed, and the small bathrooms are tiled. Meals are served in a room with Gothic chairs, but in fair weather the sidewalk tables facing the Grand Canal are preferred by many.

Riva del Vin, San Polo 729, 30125 Venezia. ✆ **041-5222068.** Fax 041-5229700. www.hotel marconi.it. 26 units. 105€–340€ double; 125€–500€ triple. Rates include buffet breakfast. AE, DC, MC, V. *Vaporetto:* Rialto. **Amenities:** Babysitting; room service. *In room:* A/C, TV, hair dryer, minibar, Wi-Fi (6€ per hr.).

Locanda Sturion ★ 📖 The facade of this building seems familiar. Then you recognize it from a painting by Carpaccio hanging in the Galleria dell'Accademia. In 1290, the Venetian doges commissioned this site where foreign merchants could stay for the night. After long stints as a private residence, the Sturion continues to cater to visitors. A private entrance leads up four steep flights of marble steps, past apartments, to a labyrinth of cozy, clean, but not overly large guest rooms. Most have views over the terra-cotta rooftops of the neighborhood; two open onto Grand Canal views. Furnishings are with Venetian pieces based on 18th-century designs, along with damasklike wallpaper and parquet floors. The breakfast room is homelike—almost like a parlor, with red brocaded walls, a Venetian chandelier, and a trio of windows over the canal.

Calle del Sturion, San Polo 679, 30125 Venezia. ✆ **041-5236243.** Fax 041-5228378. www.locanda sturion.com. 11 units. 80€–365€ double; 100€–420€ triple. Rates include buffet breakfast. AE, MC, V. *Vaporetto:* Rialto. **Amenities:** Babysitting; room service. *In room:* A/C, TV, hair dryer, minibar, Wi-Fi (free).

Residenza Goldoni ★ 📖 Near Ponte di Rialto, this small, charming, and much-renovated inn is one of the gems of the area. Although in a noisy, busy part of the city, all the bedrooms are soundproof. The interior is intimate and inviting, with a touch of elegance. Andrea and Papà Ferruccio are on hand to offer suggestions to ease you into Venetian life. Breakfast is served in your room. Each guest room comes with a small private bathroom—some with shower, others with tub. The bedrooms are spread over four floors, and the furnishings are in the Louis Philippe style. If you can get them, go for the two rooms on the fourth floor, one resting in wooden beams and the other opening onto a terrace.

San Marco 5234, 30124 Venezia. ✆ **041-2410086.** Fax 041-2774728. www.residenzagoldoni. com. 12 units. 75€–250€ double; 95€–320€ suite. Rates include breakfast in room. AE, DC, MC, V. *Vaporetto:* Rialto. **Amenities:** Room service. *In room:* A/C, TV, hair dryer, minibar.

In Cannaregio

This is one of our favorite sections because it affords a chance to see some of the local life. Otherwise, you'd think that nobody lived here except tourists. Nearly a third of the shrinking population of Venice calls Cannaregio home.

EXPENSIVE

Ai Mori d'Oriente ★ This well-run establishment is attractive, moderately priced, well maintained, and totally modern, even though it was originally a 16th-century Venetian *palazzo* before massive renovations. The hotel lays claim to one of the more tranquil parts of Venice, the *sestiere* of the Cannaregio district, near the Jewish Ghetti (the oldest in the world) and Tintoretto's home. There is elegance and style throughout Ai Mori d'Oriente in its use of antiques and old-fashioned Venetian fabrics.

Fondamenta della Sensa, Cannaregio 3319, 30121 Venezia. 55 units. ☎ **041-711001.** Fax 041-714209. www.hotelaimoridoriente.it. 89€–500€ double; 200€–600€ suite. AE, DC, MC, V. *Vaporetto:* S. Marcuola/Casino or Madonna dell'Orto. **Amenities:** Bar; babysitting; room service. *In room:* A/C, TV/DVD, hair dryer, minibar, Wi-Fi (19€ per 24 hr.).

Boscolo Grand Hotel dei Dogi ★★ 🏠 Once an embassy and later a convent, this is one of the hotel secrets of Venice, definitely a hidden gem. On the northern tier of Venice, dei Dogi looks across the lagoon to the mainland. As you sit in the beautiful garden of rose bushes, you will think that you've arrived at a Venetian Shangri-La. The hotel lies just a short stroll down the canal from the Church of Madonna dell'Orto, where Tintoretto lies buried. Bedrooms are elegantly decorated in a palatial Venetian style, with gilt and polish. Some 18th-century frescoes often decorate the walls of the bedrooms, as do antique mirrors, swag draperies, and doors intricately inlaid with veneer.

Fondamenta Madonna dell'Orto 3500, 30121 Venezia. ☎ **041-2208111.** Fax 041-722278. www.boscolohotels.com. 76 units. 153€–390€ double; from 352€ junior suite. AE, DC, MC, V. *Vaporetto:* Madonna dell'Orto. **Amenities:** Restaurant; bar; babysitting; room service; spa. *In room:* A/C, TV, hair dryer, minibar.

Locanda Ai Santi Apostoli ★ ☺ If you can't afford the Gritti but you still fantasize about living in a *palazzo* overlooking the Grand Canal, near the Rialto, here's your chance. This inn isn't cheap, but it's a lot less expensive than the palaces nearby. The hotel is on the top floor of a 15th-century building, and the guest rooms, though simple, are roomy and decorated in pastels, and they often contain antiques. Naturally, the two rooms opening onto the canal are the most requested. Extra beds can often be set up in the rooms to accommodate children. This is one of three 14th- or 15th-century Venetian palaces still owned by the family that built it.

Strada Nuova, Cannaregio 4391, 30131 Venezia. ☎ **041-5212612.** Fax 041-5212611. www.locanda santiapostoli.com. 11 units (shower only). 200€–350€ double; 300€–450€ double with Grand Canal view; 400€–450€ suite. AE, DC, MC, V. *Vaporetto:* Ca' d'Oro. **Amenities:** Babysitting. *In room:* A/C, TV, hair dryer, minibar, Wi-Fi (8€ per hr.).

Residenza Cannaregio ★ 🏠 Lying in a charming, tranquil corner of Venice, this little stunner has a dramatically modern interior in spite of its ancient origins as a monastery from the 17th century. By the 19th century it had become a *squero*, a place where gondolas are built. All its former roles have been wiped away in a complete renovation of this *residenza*, with its several lounge rooms, a popular American bar (Il Grappolo), and a first-class restaurant, along with a magnificent Venetian garden. Resting under beamed ceilings, the guest rooms are like garrets with style, comfort, and drama. The use of wood, wrought iron, Venetian tiles, and ancient stones creates a certain architectural distinctiveness.

Cannaregio 3210A, 30121 Venezia. ☏ **041-5244332.** Fax 041-2757952. www.residenzacannaregio.it. 66 units. 89€–409€ double; 139€–449€ suite. Rates include American-style buffet breakfast. AE, DC, MC, V. *Vaporetto:* San Alvise. **Amenities:** Restaurant; bar; babysitting; room service. *In room:* A/C, TV, minibar, Wi-Fi (10€ per 24 hr.).

MODERATE

Hotel Abbazia   The benefit of staying here is that there's no need to transfer onto any *vaporetto*—you can walk from the rail station, about 10 minutes away. This hotel was built in 1889 as a monastery for barefoot Carmelite monks, who established a verdant garden in what's now the courtyard; it's planted with sub-tropical plants that thrive, sheltered as they are from the cold Adriatic winds. You'll find a highly accommodating staff and comfortable but very plain guest rooms with well-kept bathrooms. Twenty-five rooms overlook the courtyard, ensuring quiet in an otherwise noisy neighborhood. ***Note:*** The hotel is only inexpensive if you specifically request one of the cheaper accommodations.

Calle Priuli ai Cavaletti, Cannaregio 68, 30121 Venezia. ☏ **041-717333.** Fax 041-717949. www.abbaziahotel.com. 49 units (some with shower only). 80€–270€ double; 200€–300€ junior suite. Rates include buffet breakfast. AE, DC, MC, V. *Vaporetto:* Ferrovia. **Amenities:** Room service. *In room:* A/C, TV, hair dryer, minibar, Wi-Fi (free).

Hotel Giorgione ★★   This modernized hotel in a converted 18th-century warehouse comes as a surprise. Its lounges under large wooden beams evoke an old-fashioned style, although the rooms are up-to-date with fine furnishings and tasteful decorative accessories. The most desirable rooms front a brick-built courtyard with a little pool, an elegant retreat from the tourist masses going by the door outside. Some of the better units have canopied draperies on the headboards, along with reproductions of classic 18th-century Venetian pieces, giving you not only comfort but a little style as well. The suites are also romantically decorated in the classic Venetian style, with half-testers and beautiful, embroidered fabrics. Everyone wants room no. 105 with its small patio planted with flowers.

Campo SS. Apostoli, Cannaregio 4587, 30131 Venezia. ☏ **041-5225810.** Fax 041-5239092. www.hotelgiorgione.com. 76 units (some with shower only). 100€–240€ double; from 200€ suite. Rates include buffet breakfast. AE, DC, MC, V. *Vaporetto:* Ca' d'Oro. **Amenities:** Bar; babysitting; room service; Wi-Fi (10€ per 24 hr.). *In room:* A/C, TV, hair dryer.

Santa Croce

The eastern part of Santa Croce is rarely visited by most visitors, but it represents a slice of authentic Venetian life. Although Santa Croce sprawls all the way to Piazzale Roma, its heart is the Campo San Giacomo dell'Orio.

MODERATE

Hotel San Cassiano-Ca' Favretto ★   The hotel's gondola pier affords views of the lacy Ca' d'Oro, Venice's most beautiful building. The hotel is a 16th-century palace (it contained the studio of 19th-c. painter Giacomo Favretto), and the owner has worked to preserve the original details, such as a 6m (20-ft.) beamed ceiling in the entrance. Fifteen of the conservatively decorated guest rooms overlook one of two canals, and many are filled with antiques or high-quality reproductions.

Calle della Rosa, Santa Croce 2232, 30135 Venezia. ☏ **041-5241768.** Fax 041-721033. www.sancassiano.it. 35 units. 94€–430€ double. Rates include buffet breakfast. AE, DC, MC, V.

Vaporetto: San Stae. **Amenities:** Bar; babysitting; room service; Wi-Fi (3€ per hr.). *In room:* A/C, TV, hair dryer.

INEXPENSIVE

Albergo Marin 🏆   Since the 1930s this little gay-friendly hotel has been a "secret address" known to savvy travelers trying to escape the high prices of Venice. The place is a simple, no-frills hotel and not a haven for devotees of Venetian aesthetics. What it does it does very well: provide an affordable, decent, and comfortable bed for the night. It's more for travelers who like to explore Venice all day, returning to the hotel just to sleep in one of the midsize bedrooms. The location is a 5-minute walk from the train station at Santa Lucia.

Ramo delle Chioverete 670B, Santa Croce, 30135 Venezia. ☎ **041-718022.** Fax 041-721485. www.albergomarin.it. 60€–200€ double. Rates include continental breakfast. AE, DC, MC, V. *Vaporetto:* Ferrovia. **Amenities:** Wi-Fi (free, in lobby). *In room:* A/C, TV, hair dryer.

In San Polo

MODERATE

Oltre il Giardino ★ 🏨   This little inn in the San Polo district is surrounded by a beautiful walled garden filled with olive trees and magnolias. The house was once owned by Alma, the widow of Gustav Mahler (1860–1911), the celebrated Bohemian and Austrian composer and conductor. The house where Alma lived in the 1920s lies next to a small canal just a stone's throw from the Church of the Frari. The bedrooms are tastefully and individually furnished, with paintings or portraits from the family's personal collection. Our favorite is the Green Suite, with a door leading to a private patch of garden; it also has a separate sitting room with a double sofa bed.

Fondamenta Contarini, San Polo 2542, 30125 Venezia. ☎ **041-2750015.** Fax 041-795452. www. oltreilgiardino-venezia.com. 6 units. 150€–250€ double; 200€–350€ junior suite; 250€–500€ suite. Rates include buffet breakfast. AE, DC, MC, V. *Vaporetto:* San Tomà. **Amenities:** Babysitting; room service. *In room:* A/C, TV, hair dryer, minibar.

In Dorsoduro

On the opposite side of the Accademia Bridge from San Marco, Dorsoduro is one of our favorite neighborhoods, with a real flavor of the city and a dash of funky chic. Accommodations are limited but rather special and full of character.

EXPENSIVE

Ca' Pisani ★★ 🏨   The style of this boutique hotel, located near the Accademia gallery, evokes the 1930s and 1940s, but the setting is a former Venetian nobleman's residence from the end of the 16th century. Accommodations come in a wide variety of sizes, ranging from standard doubles to spacious suites. The design is unusual for Venice in that it concentrates on the avant-garde trends that blossomed "between the wars." The lobby, for example, recalls the forms of futurism, with a wealth of marble and walnut wood. The walls in the bedrooms evoke the graphics of Mondrian. Our favorites are the two studios with loft sleeping areas. The rooms are equipped with modern technology such as electric curtains and remote-control door openings. The bathrooms are under "starlight," creating the effect of small shining stars. A roof terrace solarium opens onto the rooftops of Venice.

Dorsoduro 979A, 30123 Venezia. ℂ **041-2401411.** Fax 041-2771061. www.capisanihotel.it. 29 units. 159€–415€ double; 232€–495€ suite. Rates include buffet breakfast. AE, DC, MC, V. *Vaporetto:* Accademia. **Amenities:** Restaurant; bar; babysitting; room service; sauna. *In room:* A/C, TV, hair dryer, minibar, Wi-Fi (free).

DD724 ★★ 🏠 Steps away from the Peggy Guggenheim Museum and the Accademia Gallery, this one-of-a-kind hotel is the brainchild of hotelier Chiara Bocchini. The odd name comes from the hotel's location in the Dorsoduro area. A house of charm and grace, it is a luxurious choice and is ideal for a romantic getaway. Abstract paintings by contemporary artists hang in the tiny lobby. Breakfast is cooked individually for each guest. Under wooden beamed ceilings, each bedroom is one of a kind with velvet armchairs and Signoria di Firenze linens. Every detail seems to have been taken care of, including careful attention to lighting design.

Dorsoduro 724, 30123 Venezia. ℂ **041-2770262.** Fax 041-2960633. www.dd724.it. 7 units. 155€–420€ double; 325€–530€ suite. Rates include breakfast. AE, DC, MC, V. *Vaporetto:* Accademia. **Amenities:** Bar; babysitting; concierge; room service. *In room:* A/C, TV/DVD, CD player, hair dryer, minibar, Wi-Fi (free).

Palazzina Grassi ★★ 🏠 During the shooting of *The Tourist,* Johnny Depp chose this brand-new hotel in a restored 16th-century building that was once a Roman bath. The palazzina itself is a layer cake of ancient medieval design opening on the Grand Canal. Classical references abound in the hotel's public areas, including a restored central colonnade. The hotel boasts a magnificent collection of Modernist glass from Murano masters in the sparkling space designed by Philippe Starck. Horsehair chairs and old Vuitton suitcases are nostalgic reminders of another day in travel. A total of 286 mirrors by Bellini coinhabit the common areas. Bedrooms are like private enclaves, all in white, creams, and steel. Of the four suites, the most desirable is 201 with its floor-to-ceiling windows overlooking the city's ancient palazzi. Try one of the prosecco cocktails in the *molto romantico* bar, or a platter of sublime ravioli in the canal-fronting restaurant.

Calle Grassi, San Marco 3247, 30124 Venezia. ℂ **800/337-4685** in the U. S. or Canada, or 041-5284644. www.designhotels.com. 26 units. 290€–535€ double, 500€–1,200€ suite. Rates include buffet breakfast. AE, DC, MC, V. *Vaporetto:* San Samuele. **Amenities:** Restaurant; bar; concierge; room service. *In room:* A/C, TV, hair dryer, minibar, Wi-Fi (free).

MODERATE

Locanda San Barnaba ★ 🍴 Unpretentious yet exceedingly charming, this 16th-century *palazzo* (open for business after a 9-year hiatus) opened as a hotel in the unfortunate year of 1939 as Europe went to war. Its most winning architectural feature is its deluxe *piano nobile* on the second floor. This is a spacious salon, adorned with frescoes and surrounded by stained-glass windows. The large bedrooms are simply yet comfortably furnished. One of the staff told us, "We aimed for the pure essence of an old-fashioned Italian inn." Bedrooms are designed to evoke themes of long ago—the lover's nest, the philosopher's refuge, the artist's studio, or the playwright's chamber.

Calle del Traghetto, Dorsoduro 2785–2786, 30123 Venezia. ℂ **041-2411233.** Fax 041-2413812. www.locanda-sanbarnaba.com. 13 units (half with shower only). 120€–180€ double; 160€–210€ suite. Rates include buffet breakfast. AE, DC, MC, V. *Vaporetto:* Carezzonico. **Amenities:** Bar; room service. *In room:* A/C, TV, hair dryer.

Pensione Accademia ★★ 🗡 The Accademia is the most patrician of the *pensioni,* in a villa whose garden is bounded by the junction of two canals. Until the 1930s this was the seat of the Russian consulate. The interior features Gothic-style paneling, Venetian chandeliers, and Victorian-era furniture, and the upstairs sitting room is flanked by two large windows. This place has long been a favorite of the *Room with a View* crowd of Brits and scholars; it's often booked months in advance. The guest rooms are airy and bright, decorated in part with 19th-century furniture.

Fondamenta Bollani, Dorsoduro 1058, 30123 Venezia. ✆ **041-5210188.** Fax 041-5239152. www. pensioneaccademia.it. 27 units (shower only). 140€–285€ double; 200€–320€ junior suite. Rates include buffet breakfast. AE, DC, MC, V. *Vaporetto:* Accademia. **Amenities:** Bar; babysitting; concierge; room service. *In room:* A/C, TV, hair dryer, Wi-Fi (10€ per hr.).

INEXPENSIVE

Antica Locanda Montin ★ 🎒 The Montin is an old-fashioned Venetian inn whose adjoining restaurant is one of the area's most loved. The guest rooms are cozy and quaint. Only a few units have private bathrooms, and in-room extras are scarce aside from a phone. Most guests have to share the small corridor bathrooms, which are barely adequate in number, especially if the house is full. The inn is a bit difficult to locate (it's marked by only a small carriage lamp etched with the name) but is worth the search.

Fondamenta di Borgo, Dorsoduro 1147, 31000 Venezia. ✆ **041-5227151.** Fax 041-5200255. www. locandamontin.com. 11 units, 6 with bathroom. 60€–120€ double without bathroom; 70€–160€ double with bathroom. Rates include continental breakfast. AE, DC, MC, V. *Vaporetto:* Accademia. **Amenities:** Restaurant; bar. *In room:* A/C (in most).

Ca'della Corte ★ 🎒 Just 3 minutes from Piazzale Roma, this 16th-century Venetian *palazzo* with its own courtyard has been completely renovated and modernized inside to receive paying guests in elegant trappings. Modern amenities were added, though the four-story building retains its original architectural features. Rooms are spacious—some are large enough for a family of four—and furnished with traditional Venetian pieces. Large windows open onto views of old *palazzo* and of gardens. Your breakfast is brought to your room each morning.

Corte Surian, Dorsoduro 3560, 30123 Venezia. ✆ **041-715877.** Fax 041-722345. www.cadella corte.com. 10 units. 90€ double; 110€–220€ suite. Rates include buffet breakfast. AE, MC, V. **Amenities:** Babysitting; room service. *In room:* A/C, TV, hair dryer, minibar, Wi-Fi (free).

Pensione La Calcina ★ This *pensione* is still touting the fact that British author John Ruskin lodged here in 1876 when he wrote the memorable *Stones of Venice.* He stayed in room no. 2, which is not surprisingly the most frequently requested. Massively restored, the little inn is still attracting visitors seeking to discover the stones of Venice for themselves. Following in Ruskin's footsteps has been a series of writers and artists over the years, the type that used to be called "bohemians." The most desirable units overlook Giudecca Canal as it leads to Palladio's 16th-century creation of Redentore (Church of the Redeemer). The outdoor floating terrace is a summer mecca. All the bedrooms are nicely and comfortably furnished, each slightly different.

Dorsoduro 780 (on Zattere al Gesuati), 30123 Venezia. ✆ **041-5206466.** Fax 041-5227045. www.lacalcina.com. 29 units (shower only). 110€–240€ double without canal view, 150€–310€ with canal view. Rates include buffet breakfast. AE, DC, MC, V. *Vaporetto:* Zattera. **Amenities:** Bar; Internet (free, in lobby); room service. *In room:* A/C, TV, hair dryer, minibar, Wi-Fi (free).

On Isola di San Clemente

EXPENSIVE

San Clemente Palace ★★★ 🎁   Set on one of the most remote islands in the Venetian lagoon, a 6.8-hectare (17-acre) outpost that has traditionally been the site of fresh water for mariners, this is the most unusual hotel development project in Venice's recent history. Its origins date from 1131, when a church was built as the starting point for soldiers and pilgrims setting out on the Crusades. In the 19th century, the island erupted into a building frenzy that resulted in a sprawling complex of grim, institutional buildings that functioned as both an asylum and a hospital. Today, the site functions as a full-fledged and upscale resort—one of the few of its kind in Venice. Access to and from the piers near the Piazza San Marco is provided by frequent, free motorboat service, but it's a bumpy and, in winter, bone-chilling ride. At least 80 of the 200 units at this hotel are suites. All units have very high ceilings, many of them more than 4m (13 ft.) high, plush upholsteries, and fine reproductions of antique furniture.

Isola di San Clemente 1, San Marco 30124 Venezia. ✆ **041-2445001.** Fax 041-2445800. www. sanclemente.thi.it. 200 units. 180€–495€ double; from 350€ junior suite; from 600€ suite. Rates include buffet breakfast. AE, DC, MC, V. **Amenities:** 3 restaurants; bar; babysitting; concierge; exercise room; 3-hole golf course; outdoor pool; spa; 2 outdoor tennis courts (lit). *In room:* A/C, TV, hair dryer, minibar, Wi-Fi (15€ per 24 hr.).

On Isola Della Giudecca

Even though this is traditionally a blue-collar neighborhood, it contains one of the grandest pockets of posh in northeast Italy, the Cipriani. You are isolated if you stay here (and can afford it), but just across the water from Piazza San Marco.

VERY EXPENSIVE

Cipriani ★★★   For old-world Venetian splendor, check into the Gritti or Danieli. But for chic, contemporary surroundings, flawless service, and refinement at every turn, the Cipriani is in a class by itself. Set in a 16th-century cloister on the island of Giudecca (reached by private hotel launch from St. Mark's Sq.), this pleasure palace was opened in 1958 by Giuseppe Cipriani, founder of Harry's Bar. The rooms range in design from tasteful contemporary to grand antique; all have splendid views and are sumptuous. We prefer the corner rooms, which are the most spacious and elaborately decorated.

Isola della Giudecca 10, 30133 Venezia. ✆ **041-5207744.** Fax 041-5203930. www.hotelcipriani. com. 95 units. 950€–1,370€ double; 1,730€–2,140€ junior suite; 2,470€–8,550€ suite. Rates include full American breakfast. AE, DC, MC, V. *Vaporetto:* Zitelle. Closed Nov 8–Apr 1. **Amenities:** 2 restaurants; 3 bars (including a piano bar); airport transfers (170€); babysitting; children's center; concierge; exercise room; Olympic-size outdoor heated pool; room service; sauna; spa; outdoor tennis court. *In room:* A/C, TV/DVD, hair dryer, minibar, Wi-Fi (free).

EXPENSIVE

Hilton Molino Stucky Venice ★★★   On Giudecca Island, across from Piazza San Marco, a former flour mill and grainery has been turned into a pocket of posh, one of Venice's newest landmarks. All its stunningly contemporary bedrooms open onto panoramic views, best enjoyed from the ninth-floor Skyline Bar. You can also enjoy afternoon tea in a secluded private courtyard. In addition, a spectacular rooftop pool with a fitness center rounds out the amenities. Outfitted with the latest

Venice International Film Festival is second only to Cannes for sheer glamour. It brings together stars, directors, producers, and filmmakers from all over the world during the first week or so of September. Films are shown more or less constantly between 9am and 3am in various areas of the Palazzo del Cinema on the Lido. Although many of the seats are reserved for jury members, the public viewers can also attend any film if seats are available. And there's always great people-watching all over the city. For information call **La Biennale di Venezia** (𝒞 **041-5218711**; www.la biennale.org).

technology, the bedrooms contain picture-book windows, restored timber-beamed ceilings, and are furnished with Venetian fabrics along with marble-clad bathrooms. The flagship restaurant, Aromi, features a contemporary Mediterranean cuisine in a romantic atmosphere with a panoramic terrace opening a view of Venice and the Giudecca Canal.

Giudecca 810, 30133 Venezia. 𝒞 **041-2723311.** Fax 041-2723490. www.molinostuckyhilton.com. 379 units. 249€–534€ double; from 699€ suite. AE, DC, MC, V. *Vaporetto:* Palanca. **Amenities:** 2 restaurants; 3 bars; airport transfers (110€); babysitting; concierge; exercise room; Jacuzzi; rooftop heated pool; room service; sauna. *In room:* A/C, TV, hair dryer, minibar, MP3 docking station, Wi-Fi (22€ per 24 hr.).

Near Piazzale Roma

INEXPENSIVE

Palazzo Odoni ★ 👜   This restored Gothic palace from the 15th century lies a few steps from Piazzale Roma and the Santa Lucia railway station. It is family run by the descendants of owners who took it over five generations ago. Modern comforts have been added without ruining the Gothic architectural features of this place, which is decorated with antiques, tapestries, and Murano glass. All the bedrooms are spacious and romantically decorated, and all the private bathrooms have been completely redone. There are almost no common areas, however.

Santa Croce 151, Fondamenta Minotto, 30135 Venezia. 𝒞 **041-2759454.** Fax 041-0993073. www.palazzoodoni.it. 10 units. 90€–235€ double; 125€–295€ junior suite. Rates include buffet breakfast. MC, V. *Vaporetto:* Piazzale Roma. **Amenities:** Bar; room service; Wi-Fi (10€ per hr., in lobby). *In room:* A/C, TV, hair dryer, minibar.

On the Lido

If you can balance it, you can have a beach vacation on the Lido with time out for sightseeing in the heart of Venice.

VERY EXPENSIVE

Hotel Excelsior ★★★   This luxe palace caters to the most pampered beach crowd in Europe. When the Excelsior was built, it was the world's biggest resort hotel, and its presence helped make the Lido fashionable. Today it offers the most luxury on the Lido. Its guest rooms range in style and amenities, but all have walk-in closets. The good-size bathrooms boast deluxe toiletries and deep tubs.

9

VENICE | Where to Stay

Most of the social life takes place around the angular pool or on the flowered terraces leading up to the cabanas on the sandy beach.

Lungomare Marconi 41, 30126 Venezia Lido. *(C)* **800/325-3589** in the U.S. and Canada, or 041-5260201. Fax 041-5267276. www.ho10.net. 196 units. 300€–1,500€ double; 1,130€–3,800€ suite. Rates include buffet breakfast. AE, DC, MC, V. Closed Nov–Mar. *Vaporetto:* Lido, then bus A, B, or C. **Amenities:** 2 restaurants; 3 bars; babysitting; bikes; children's center; concierge; exercise room; outdoor pool; room service; sauna; 6 outdoor tennis courts (lit); Wi-Fi (15€ per 24 hr., in lobby). *In room:* A/C, TV, hair dryer, minibar.

EXPENSIVE

Albergo Quattro Fontane ★   The Quattro Fontane is one of the most charming hotels on the Lido. The trouble is, a lot of people know that, so it's likely to be booked. This former summer home of a 19th-century Venetian family is most popular with the British, who seem to appreciate the homey atmosphere, the garden, the helpful staff, and the rooms with superior luxuries, not to mention the good food served at tables set under shade trees. Many of the guest rooms are furnished with antiques, and all have tile or terrazzo floors and excellent beds.

Via Quattro Fontane 16, 30126 Lido di Venezia. *(C)* **041-5260227.** Fax 041-5260726. www.quattro fontane.com. 59 units. 220€–500€ double. Rates include buffet breakfast. AE, DC, MC, V. Closed Nov–Apr 20. *Vaporetto:* Lido, then bus A, B, or C. **Amenities:** Restaurant; bar; babysitting; bikes; room service; outdoor tennis court. *In room:* A/C, TV, hair dryer, minibar.

MODERATE

Hotel Belvedere ☺   The modernized Belvedere has been a family favorite since 1857. Right across from the *vaporetto* stop, the hotel is open year-round, unusual for the Lido, and offers simply furnished rooms, each with a good bed and tiled bathroom. In summer, guests can use the hotel's cabanas on the Lido.

Piazzale Santa Maria Elisabetta 4, 30126 Lido di Venezia. *(C)* **041-5260115.** Fax 041-5261486. www.belvedere-venezia.com. 31 units (shower only). 80€–319€ double; 100€–382€ triple. Rates include buffet breakfast. DC, MC, V. *Vaporetto:* Lido. **Amenities:** Restaurant; bar; room service; Wi-Fi (free, in lobby). *In room:* A/C, TV, hair dryer.

Hotel Helvetia   This 19th-century building, on a side street near the lagoon side of the island, is an easy walk from the *vaporetto* stop. The quieter guest rooms face away from the street, and rooms in the older wing have Belle Epoque high ceilings and attractively comfortable furniture. The newer wing has a more conservative style. Breakfast is served, weather permitting, in a flagstone-covered wall garden behind the hotel.

Gran Viale S. Maria Elisabetta 4, 30126 Lido di Venezia. *(C)* **041-5260105.** Fax 041-5268903. www.hotelhelvetia.com. 60 units. 60€–275€ double; 105€–330€ triple. Rates include continental breakfast. AE, DC, MC, V. Closed Jan to mid-Apr. *Vaporetto:* Lido. **Amenities:** Bar; babysitting; room service. *In room:* A/C, TV, hair dryer.

WHERE TO DINE

Venice is surrounded by a rich agricultural district and plentiful vineyards, and of course, there's fresh seafood. Venice's restaurants are among the most expensive in Italy, but we've found some wonderful moderately priced *trattorie*.

Near Piazza San Marco

VERY EXPENSIVE

Quadri ★★★ VENETIAN/INTERNATIONAL   One of Europe's most famous restaurants, Quadri is even better known as a cafe (p. 501). Its elegant premises open onto Piazza San Marco, where a full orchestra often adds to the magic. Many diners come just for the view and are often surprised by the high-quality cuisine and impeccable service (and the whopping tab). The skills of Quadri's chef are considerable. He's likely to tempt you with such appetizers as sea bass puff pastry or else smoked breast of goose with a pomegranate sauce. A pear salad is served with arugula and Parmesan cheese with a raspberry vinaigrette. For your main course, you can feast on filet of beef in a chestnut sauce with braised red chicory or grilled lamb cutlets with Venetian artichokes and a mint sauce. Filet of hake comes under an aromatic crust with anchovies and baby broccoli.

Piazza San Marco, San Marco 121. ℭ **041-5289299.** www.quadrivenice.com. Reservations required. Main courses 19€–38€. AE, DC, MC, V. Apr–Oct daily noon–2:30pm and 7–10:30pm; Nov–Mar Tues–Sun noon–2:30pm and 7–10:30pm. *Vaporetto:* San Marco.

EXPENSIVE

Antico Martini ★★★ VENETIAN/INTERNATIONAL   Antico Martini elevates Venetian cuisine to its highest level (although we still give Harry's a slight edge). Elaborate chandeliers glitter and gilt-framed oil paintings adorn the paneled walls. The courtyard is splendid in summer. An excellent beginning is the smoked salmon with caviar. One of the best pasta dishes is black *tagliolini* with fresh zucchini, or the always reliable smoked breast of wild duck. The chefs are better at regional dishes than international ones. Other menu items include pasta with scampi and mushrooms, scallops with basil and polenta, *pappardelle* with scampi and sweet peppers, and sea bass filet with wild fennel. The restaurant has one of the city's best wine lists, featuring more than 350 choices. The yellow Tocai is an interesting local wine and is especially good with fish dishes.

Campo San Fantin, San Marco 1983. ℭ **041-5224121.** www.anticomartini.com. Reservations required. Main courses 21€–44€. AE, DC, MC, V. Daily noon–11:30pm. *Vaporetto:* San Marco or Santa Maria del Giglio.

Centrale Restaurant & Lounge VENETIAN/MEDITERRANEAN   Only a 1-minute walk from Piazza San Marco in the center of Venice, this restaurant lies in a historic *palazzo* dating from 1659. The facade is pierced with three showcase windows and entered on Piscina Frezzeria on foot; there is an antique door opening onto the canal Rio dei Barcaroli, should you arrive by gondola. The location is also just 30m (100 ft.) from the La Fenice opera house. Spike Lee or other celebrities visiting Venice might be seen lingering for hours (at least until the un-Venetian hour of 2am), enjoying after-theater cocktails in the lounge, with its bamboo, screen, spider-web metal chairs, and a backlit crystal bar over busy fabrics. The flavorful cuisine features such delights as duck carpaccio with crunchy spinach and a walnut sauce, filet of suckling pig with black truffle in a baked Wellington crust, or black ravioli filled with sea bass.

Piscina Frezzeria, San Marco 1659B. ℭ **041-2960664.** www.centrale-lounge.com. Reservations required. Main courses 21€–34€. AE, DC, MC, V. Daily 6:30pm–2am. *Vaporetto:* San Marco.

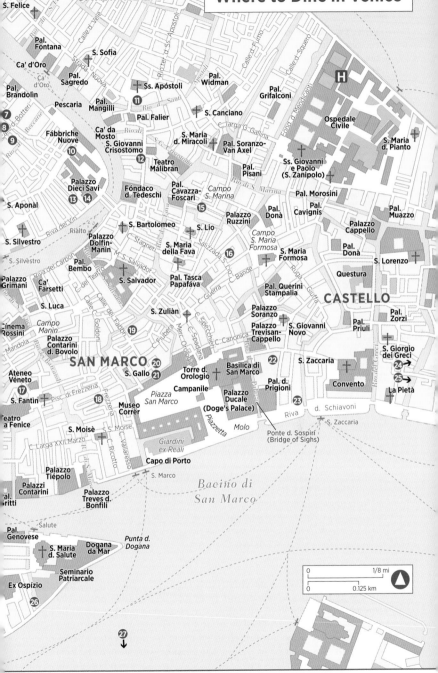

Where to Dine in Venice

CANNAREGIO

S. Felice

Pal. Fontana

Ca' d'Oro

Pal. Sagredo

Pal. Brandolin

Pescaria

Pal. Mangilli

S. Sofia

Ss. Apóstoli

Pal. Widman

Pal. Grifalconi

H Ospedale Civile

S. Maria d. Pianto

7

8

9

Fábbriche Nuove

10

Ca' da Mosto

Pal. Falier

11

S. Canciano

S. Maria d. Miracoli

Pal. Soranzo-Van Axel

S. Giovanni Crisostomo

12

Teatro Málibran

Pal. Pisani

Ss. Giovanni e Paolo (S. Zanipolo)

Palazzo Dieci Savi

13 **14**

Fóndaco d. Tedeschi

Pal. Cavazza-Foscari

15

Campo S. Marina

Pal. Morosini

S. Aponàl

S. Bartolomeo

S. Lio

Palazzo Ruzzini

Pal. Donà

Pal. Cavignis

Pal. Muazzo

Palazzo Cappello

S. Silvestro

Rialto

Palazzo Dolfin-Manin

S. Maria della Fava

16

Campo S. Maria Formosa

S. Maria Formosa

Pal. Donà

S. Silvestro

Pal. Bembo

S. Salvador

Pal. Tasca Papafáva

Questura

S. Lorenzo

Palazzo Grimani

Ca' Farsetti

Pal. Querini Stampalia

CASTELLO

S. Luca

Campo Manin

Cinema Rossini

Palazzo Contarini d. Bovolo

S. Zuliàn

19

Palazzo Soranzo

Palazzo Trevisan-Cappello

S. Giovanni Novo

Pal. Priuli

Pal. Zorzi

Ateneo Véneto

SAN MARCO

20

S. Gallo

21

Torre d. Orologio

Basilica di San Marco

22

S. Zaccaria

S. Giorgio dei Greci

24

S. Fantin

18

Museo Corrèr

Campanile

Piazza San Marco

Palazzo Ducale (Doge's Palace)

Pal. d. Prigioni

Convento

25

La Pietà

Teatro a Fenice

S. Moisè

Piazzetta

23

S. Zaccaria

d. Schiavoni

S. Zaccaria

C. Larga XXII Marzo

S. Marco

Molo

Riva

Ponte d. Sospiri (Bridge of Sighs)

Palazzo Tiépolo

Giardini ex Reali

Capo di Porto

Palazzi Contarini

Palazzo Treves d. Bonfili

S. Marco

Bacino di San Marco

Pal. Genovese

Salute

S. Maria d. Salute

Dogana da Mar

Punta d. Dogana

Seminario Patriarcale

Ex Ospízio

26

27

0   1/8 mi

0   0.125 km

461

Fishy Business

Venice's restaurants specialize in the choicest seafood from the Adriatic—but the fish dishes are *very* expensive. On most menus, the price of fresh grilled fish *(pesce alla griglia)* commonly refers to the *etto* (per 100g) and thus is a fraction of the real cost. Have the waiter estimate it before you order, to avoid a shock when your bill comes.

The fish merchants at the Mercato Rialto (Venice's main open-air market) take Monday off, which explains why so many restaurants are closed on Monday. Those that are open on Monday are selling Saturday's goods—beware!

Trattoria La Colomba ★ VENETIAN/INTERNATIONAL   This is one of Venice's most distinctive *trattorie*, with its history going back at least a century. Modern paintings adorn the walls; they change periodically and are usually for sale. Menu items are likely to include at least five daily specials based on Venice's time-honored cuisine, as well as risotto with pumpkin and monkfish, and *baccalà mantecato* (milk-simmered dry cod seasoned with onions, anchovies, and cinnamon and served with polenta). The fruits and vegetables used are mostly grown on the lagoon islands.

Piscina Frezzeria, San Marco 1665. ✆ **041-5221175.** Reservations recommended. Main courses 20€–40€; degustation menu 50€. AE, DC, MC, V. Daily noon–3pm and 7–11pm; Thurs–Tues 7–11pm. *Vaporetto:* San Marco or Rialto.

MODERATE

Osteria alle Testiere ★ 🏠 VENETIAN/ITALIAN   This little 24-seat restaurant has its priorities in order: good, fresh food at affordable prices. Nothing is spent on fancy white linen—the tables are covered in butcher paper. In such a tavern setting, you'll be tempted by an array of well-prepared dishes paired with a carefully selected wine list. Among menu temptations, tuna steak flavored with juniper berries is a delight, as is the potato gnocchi with calamari and a cinnamon flavor. *Gnocchetti* with baby squid turned out to be a savory and tasty dish, as was the whitefish of the day baked with aromatic fresh herbs. For another main course, the scampi was heaven-sent, given extra flavor by a sprinkle of cinnamon, a dash of hot pepper, and freshly chopped tomatoes.

Castello 5801 (on Calle del Mondo Novo). ✆ **041-5227220.** www.osterialletestiere.it. Reservations recommended. Main courses 16€–25€. MC, V. Tues–Sat noon–2pm and 7–10pm. Closed Aug and Dec 20–Jan 15. *Vaporetto:* San Marco or Rialto.

Ristorante Noemi VENETIAN   The decor of this simple place includes a multicolored marble floor in abstract patterns and swag curtains covering big glass windows. The restaurant opened in 1927, named for the matriarch of the family that continues to own it. Specialties, many bordering on *nuova cucina,* include thin black spaghetti with cuttlefish in its own sauce; salmon crepes with cheese; filet of sole Casanova, with a velouté of white wine, shrimp, and mushrooms; and *tagliolini* with shrimp and tomatoes. For dessert, try the special lemon sorbet, made with sparkling wine and fresh mint.

Calle dei Fabbri, San Marco 912. ✆ **041-5225238.** www.ristorantenoemi.com. Reservations recommended. Main courses 10€–19€; 2-course fixed-price menu 24€; 3-course fixed-price menu 30€. AE, DC, MC, V. Daily 11:30am–1am. *Vaporetto:* San Marco.

Trattoria da Fiore ★ 🍴 VENETIAN   Don't confuse this *trattoria* with the well-known and much more expensive Osteria da Fiore. Start with the house specialty, *penne alla Fiore* (prepared with olive oil, garlic, and seven in-season vegetables), and you might be happy to call it a night. Or skip right to another popular specialty, *fritto misto,* comprising more than a dozen varieties of fresh fish and seafood. The *zuppa di pesce* is a soup stocked with mussels, crab, clams, shrimp, and chunks of fresh tuna. This is a great place for an afternoon snack or a light lunch at the Bar Fiore next door (daily 10:30am–10:30pm).

Calle delle Botteghe, San Marco 3461. ✆ **041-5235310.** www.dafiore.it. Reservations suggested. Pasta dishes 14€–18€; main courses 18€–28€. MC, V. Wed–Mon noon–3pm and 7–10pm. Closed Jan 15–30 and Aug 1–15. *Vaporetto:* Accademia.

Castello/Riva degli Schiavoni
EXPENSIVE

Al Covo ★★ VENETIAN/SEAFOOD   Al Covo has a special charm because of its atmospheric setting, sophisticated service, and the fine cooking of Cesare Benelli and his Texas-born wife, Diane. Look for a reinvention of a medieval version of fish soup, roast lamb chops with mint sauce and lentils, roast codfish with prunes and fresh rosemary, soft-shell crabs fried with potatoes and onion rings, and homemade potato gnocchi with baby calamari and spider crab roe. Al Covo prides itself on not having any freezers, guaranteeing that all food is fresh every day.

Campiello della Pescaria, Castello 3968. ✆ **041-5223812.** www.ristorantealcovo.com. Reservations recommended for dinner. Main courses 16€–33€; fixed-price menus 52€. MC, V. Fri–Tues 12:45–2:15pm and 7:30–10pm. *Vaporetto:* Arsenale.

MODERATE/INEXPENSIVE

Al Nuovo Galeon 🍴 VENETIAN   Sometimes it's a good idea to go where your waiter takes his family to eat on his day off. Such a choice might be this restaurant in the Castello neighborhood with a typical Venetian square outside. With its two dining rooms, it's decorated just like the interior of a 16th-century ship. The location is a 15-minute walk east of Piazza San Marco. The chef prepares good-value,

---

Something Sweet

If you're in the mood for some tasty gelato, head to the **Gelateria Paolin,** Campo Stefano Morosini (✆ **041-5225576**), which offers 20 flavors. It has stood on the corner of this busy square since the 1930s, making it Venice's oldest ice-cream parlor. April to October, it's open daily 8am to midnight; November to March, hours are daily 8am to 8:30pm.

One of the city's finest pastry shops is the **Pasticceria Marchini,** Spadaria,

San Marco 676 (✆ **041-5229109;** www. pasticceriamarchini.com), whose cakes, muffins, and pastries are the stuff of childhood memories for many locals. The pastries include traditional versions of *torte del Doge,* made from almonds and pine nuts; *zaleti,* made from a mix of cornmeal and eggs; and *bigna,* akin to *zabaglione,* concocted from chocolate and cream. It's open Wednesday to Monday 9am to 8:30pm.

---

wholesome food made with market-fresh ingredients. Specialties include scampi in *saorone* (fried scampi marinated in a sweet-and-sour sauce with lightly sautéed onions), or else a filet of turbot with curried vegetables. Our favorite is a large platter of seafood with such delights as spider crab, octopus, squid, sea bass, shrimp, and a couple of fish we don't recognize. You can also order linguine with clams, salt cod with polenta, or fried calamari. A lovely starter is either the salmon or sea bass carpaccio.

Via Garibaldi 1308, Castello. ✆ **041-5204656.** www.ilnuovogaleon.com. Reservations recommended. Main courses 12€–20€. AE, MC, V. Wed–Sun 12:30–2:30pm and 7:30–10pm. Closed Dec 9–Jan 22. *Vaporetto:* Ciardini.

Do Leoni ★★ VENETIAN/INTERNATIONAL This restaurant offers a view of a 19th-century equestrian statue ringed with heroic women taming (you guessed it) lions. The menu is something to savor. The chef isn't afraid to dip into Venice's culinary attic at times for inspiration—take the boneless sardines fried and left to marinate in onions before being served with fresh pine nuts and Cyprus sultanas. The risottos and pastas are delectable. Begin perhaps with the fried shrimp on polenta perfumed with garlic, or clams and mussels with croutons. Savor such main dishes as roast saddle of lamb with eggplant, filet of grouper with Swiss chard and an orange hollandaise mousse, or homemade *tagliatelle* with spider crab. If weather permits, you can dine out on the piazza.

In the Londra Palace, Riva degli Schiavoni, Castello 4171. ✆ **041-5200533.** www.londrapalace. com. Reservations required. Main courses 16€–38€. AE, DC, MC, V. Restaurant daily 12:30–2:30pm and 7:30–11pm. Bar daily 11am–12:30am. *Vaporetto:* San Zaccaria.

Nuova Rivetta 🐟 SEAFOOD Nuova Rivetta is an old-fashioned *trattoria* where you get good food at a good price. The most popular dish is *frittura di pesce,* a mixed fish fry that includes squid or various other "sea creatures" from the day's market. Other specialties are gnocchi stuffed with spider crab, *pasticcio* of fish (a main course), and spaghetti flavored with squid ink. The most typical wine is sparkling prosecco, whose bouquet is refreshing and fruity with a slightly sharp flavor; it has long been one of the most celebrated wines of the Veneto.

Campo San Filippo, Castello 4625. ✆ **041-5287302.** Reservations required. Main courses 8€–18€. MC, V. Tues–Sun noon–10pm. Closed July 20–Aug 20. *Vaporetto:* San Zaccaria.

Ristorante Corte Sconta VENETIAN/SEAFOOD   Corte Sconta is behind a narrow storefront that you'd ignore if you didn't know about this place. This modest restaurant boasts a multicolored marble floor, plain wooden tables, and not much of an attempt at decoration. It has become well known as a gathering place for artists, writers, and filmmakers. It's a fish restaurant, serving a variety of grilled creatures (much of the "catch" largely unknown in North America). The fish is flawlessly fresh; the gamberi, for example, is placed live on the grill. A great start is marinated salmon with arugula and pomegranate seeds in olive oil. Two pasta specialties include *tagliolini* with lobster, wild fennel, and fresh spinach; or spaghetti in black squid ink with scallops. If you don't like fish, a beef filet is available.

Calle del Pestrin, Castello 3886. © **041-5227024.** Reservations required. Main courses 16€–28€. MC, V. Tues–Sat 12:30–2pm and 7:30–9:30pm. Closed Jan 7–Feb 7 and July 20–Aug 18. *Vaporetto:* Arsenale or San Zaccaria.

Near the Ponte di Rialto
MODERATE

Fiaschetteria Toscana ★ ✦ VENETIAN   The service at this hip restaurant might be uneven and the staff might be frantic, but lots of local foodies come here to celebrate special occasions or to soak in the see-and-be-seen ambience. The dining rooms are on two levels, the upstairs of which is somewhat more claustrophobic. In the evening, the downstairs is especially appealing with its romantic candlelit ambience. Menu items include *frittura della Serenissima* (a mixed platter of fried seafood with vegetables), a succulent ravioli filled with lobster and broccoli, and freshly caught fish from the North Adriatic along with tender and well-flavored Tuscan beefsteak.

Campo San Giovanni Crisostomo, Cannaregio 5719. © **041-5285281.** www.fiaschetteriatoscana.it. Reservations required. Main courses 15€–35€; degustation menu 45€. MC, V. Wed 7:30–10:30pm; Thurs–Mon 12:30–2:30pm and 7:30–10:30pm. Closed July 25–Aug 20. *Vaporetto:* Rialto.

Il Milion VENETIAN/ITALIAN   With a tradition more than 300 years old and a location near the rear of San Giovanni Crisostomo, this restaurant is named after the book written by Marco Polo, *Il Milion,* describing his travels. In fact, it occupies a town house once owned by members of the explorer's family. The bar, incidentally, is a favorite with some of the gondoliers. The menu items read like a who's who of Venetian platters, each fresh and well prepared. Examples are veal kidneys, calves' liver with fried onions, grilled sardines, spaghetti with clams, risotto with squid ink, and *fritto misto* of fried fish. Menu items also include *Spaghetti alla Scogliera* (with seafood) and *tagliolini* with scampi and artichokes. The staff is charming and friendly.

Corte Prima al Milion, Cannaregio 5841. © **041-5229302.** www.ilmilion.com. Reservations recommended. Main courses 8€–22€. AE, MC, V. Nov–Mar Thurs–Tues noon–3pm and 6:30–11pm; Apr–Oct daily noon–3pm and 6:30–11pm. Closed Aug 5–20. *Vaporetto:* Rialto.

Il Sole sulla Vecia Cavana ★ 🎁 SEAFOOD/VENETIAN/ITALIAN   This restaurant is off the tourist circuit and well worth the trek through the winding streets. A *cavana* is a place where gondolas are parked, a sort of liquid garage, and the site of this restaurant was such a place in the Middle Ages. When you enter, you'll see brick arches, stone columns, terra-cotta floors, framed modern paintings, and a photo of 19th-century fishermen relaxing after a day's work. The menu specializes in seafood, such as a mixed grill from the Adriatic, fried scampi,

465

fresh sole, squid, three types of risotto (each with seafood), and a spicy zuppa di pesce. *Antipasti di mare alla veneziana* is an assortment of just about every kind of seafood. The food is authentic and seems prepared for the Venetian palate—not necessarily for the visitor's.

Rio Terà SS. Apostoli, Cannaregio 4624. ℗ **041-5287106.** www.veciacavana.it. Reservations recommended. Main courses 12€–28€. AE, MC, V. Tues–Sun noon–2:30pm and 7–10:30pm. *Vaporetto:* Ca' d'Oro.

L'Osteria di Santa Marina ★ ▥ VENETIAN/ITALIAN   Near Ponte di
Rialto, this discovery is the domain of Agostino Doria and Danilo Baldan, the latter a Cipriani alum. Together they have forged their own place with a combination of a rustic yet classic decor. In a warm, cozy setting, you feel right at home as you partake of their savory cuisine. Come here with a hearty appetite; it will be satisfied. The cuisine is light, full flavored, and impertinently inventive as evoked by the lasagna served crepe-style with fresh shrimp and purple radicchio. The ravioli with turbot and mussels in a crayfish sauce has subtly intermingled flavors. All the pasta is homemade. Another standout dish is the shrimp in *saor* (confit) with a smattering of chopped leeks and ginger, and the veal cheek braised with potatoes. Or else you might try the sautéed soft-shell crabs and artichokes, or the John Dory filet baked with vegetables au gratin.

Camo Santa Marina 5911. ℗ **041-5285239.** Reservations recommended. Main courses 14€–25€. MC, V. Mon 7:30–9:30pm; Tues–Sat 12:30–2:30pm and 7:30–9:30pm. Closed Jan 10–25 and 2 weeks in Aug. Vaporetto: Rialto.

Osteria Antico Giardinetto ★ ITALIAN/MEDITERRANEAN   A 5-minute
walk from the Rialto Fish Market brings you to this family-run *trattoria* with its cozy open-air garden where chef-owner Virgilio Iezzi welcomes you. Freshly caught fish and well-flavored vegetarian dishes are prepared to order, and all kinds of succulent pastas and tempting desserts are homemade daily. Dishes likely to become your favorites are the spider crab with an arugula salad or *tagliolini* with scallops and artichokes. A dish to be savored is the pumpkin gnocchi with scampi and red chicory. For something really authentic, try the vermicelli with cuttlefish in an ink salad. The chef specialty that wins the most praise is sea bass baked in a salt crust to retain its juices and flavor.

Calle dei Morti 2253, Santa Croce 30135. ℗ **041-722882.** Reservations recommended. Main courses 15€–25€. MC, V. Tues–Sun noon–2:30pm and 6–11:30pm. Closed Jan. *Vaporetto:* San Stae.

Poste Vecie ★ SEAFOOD   This charming restaurant is near the Rialto open-air market and connected to the rest of the city by a small, privately owned bridge. It opened in the early 1500s as a post office, and the kitchen used to serve food to fortify the mail carriers. Today it's the oldest restaurant in Venice, with a pair of intimate rooms (both graced with paneling, murals, and 16th-c. mantelpieces) and a courtyard. Menu items include fresh fish from the nearby markets; a salad of shellfish and exotic mushrooms; *tagliolini* flavored with squid ink, crabmeat, and fish sauce; and the *pièce de résistance, seppie* (cuttlefish) *à la veneziana* with polenta. If you don't like fish, calves' liver or veal shank with ham and cheese is also well prepared.

Pescheria Rialto, San Polo 1608. ℗ **041-721822.** www.postevecie.com. Reservations recommended. Main courses 16€–34€. AE, DC, MC, V. Wed–Mon noon–3pm and 7–10:30pm. *Vaporetto:* Rialto.

Trattoria alla Madonna VENETIAN   No, this place has nothing to do with *that* Madonna. It opened in 1954 in a 300-year-old building and is one of Venice's most characteristic *trattorie,* specializing in traditional Venetian recipes and grilled fresh fish. A good beginning might be the antipasto *frutti di mare.* Pastas, polentas, risottos, meats (including *fegato alla veneziana,* liver with onions), and many kinds of irreproachably fresh fish are widely available.

Calle della Madonna, San Polo 594. ℂ **041-5223824.** www.ristoranteallamadonna.com. Reservations recommended but not always accepted. Main courses 17€–26€. AE, MC, V. Thurs–Tues noon–3pm and 7:15–10pm. Closed Dec 24–Jan and Aug 4–17. *Vaporetto:* Rialto.

In Santa Croce

MODERATE

Trattoria Antica Besseta ★ SEAFOOD/VENETIAN   If you manage to find this place (go with a good map), you'll be rewarded with true Venetian cuisine at its most unpretentious. Head for Campo San Giacomo dell'Orio; then negotiate your way across infrequently visited piazzas and winding alleys. Push through saloon doors into a bar area filled with modern art. The dining room is hung with paintings and illuminated with wagon-wheel chandeliers. The food depends on what looked good in the market that morning, so the menu could include roast chicken, fried scampi, fritto *misto,* spaghetti in sardine sauce, various roasts, and a selection from the day's catch.

Campo SS. de Ca' Zusto, Santa Croce 1395. ℂ **041-721687.** www.anticabesseta.it. Reservations required. Main courses 14€–27€. AE, DC, MC, V. Thurs–Mon noon–2:30pm; Wed–Mon 7–10:30pm. *Vaporetto:* Rive di Biasio.

In San Polo

VERY EXPENSIVE

Osteria da Fiore ★★★ 📱 SEAFOOD   The breath of the Adriatic seems to blow through this place, although how the wind finds this little restaurant tucked away in a labyrinth is a mystery. The imaginative fare depends on the availability of fresh fish and produce. If you love seafood, you'll find everything from scampi to *granceola* (a type of spider crab). In days gone by, we've sampled fried calamari, risotto with scampi, *tagliata* with rosemary, *masenette* (tiny green crabs that you eat shell and all), and *canoce* (mantis shrimp). For your wine, we suggest prosecco, with a distinctive golden color and a bouquet that's refreshing and fruity.

Calle del Scaleter, San Polo 2202. ℂ **041-721308.** www.dafiore.net. Reservations required. Main courses 35€–46€. AE, DC, MC, V. Tues–Sat 12:30–2:30pm and 7:30–10pm. Closed Aug 5–25 and Dec 25–Jan 15. *Vaporetto:* San Tomà or San Silvestro.

MODERATE

Al Pesador VENETIAN   If you want to blend in with the locals, head just 100m (195 ft.) from the Rialto Bridge to this little *trattoria* in San Polo. The location is right off Campo San Giacometo, a charming square where many young people and young-at-heart Venetians hang out devouring bottles of wine from the Veneto. Around the corner from the square stands Al Pesador, where in-the-know diners go for food and drink. This is a trendy spot for well-prepared but nonfussy food such as lasagna with leeks or turbot in a fish sauce. Turbot also appears imaginatively with chestnuts and grapefruit. You can also order various versions of carpaccio—tuna, scorpion fish, or wild sea bass. The dessert specialty, chocolate cake with prune sauce, is scrumptious.

San Polo 125. ✆ **041-5239492.** www.alpesador.it. Reservations required. Main courses 14€–25€. AE, MC, V. Apr–Oct Tues–Sun 10am–2am; Nov–Mar Tues–Sun 11am–3:30pm and 6pm–2am. *Vaporetto:* Rialto.

Antiche Carampane VENETIAN/SEAFOOD   Venetians might call this little *trattoria molto romantic.* In a tranquil little corner just past Campo San Polo, it takes its name from the slang word for the prostitutes who worked their trade around here in medieval times. Today it attracts politicians and show business personalities who are drawn to its intimate atmosphere and a menu based on classic Venetian dishes, most often freshly caught seafood. Start with the antipasti of the house, a large platter of fresh seafood to be consumed raw like sushi or cooked. In fair weather, dine on the terrace enjoying such dishes as spaghetti with crab or baked filet of turbot in a citrus sauce, even fried soft-shell crabs. Finish with the chef's divine chocolate mousse.

San Polo 1911. ✆ **041-5240165.** www.antichecarampane.com. Reservations recommended. Main courses 16€–23€. AE, DC, MC, V. Tues–Sat 12:30–2:30pm and 7:30–10:30pm. *Vaporetto:* San Silvestro. Closed Jan 10–21 and 2 weeks in Aug.

In Dorsoduro

EXPENSIVE

Lineadombra ★★ 🏛 INTERNATIONAL   Venice doesn't look entirely as it did at the time of the doges. There is such a thing as Nouveau Venice, as exemplified by this modern restaurant with sleek contemporary lines. In Dorsoduro, it faces the Canale della Giudecca. In fair weather, you can sit out on the deck on cushy chairs. Here you will enjoy one of the most scenic spots in Venice behind the Church of the Salute. The chefs blend their creativity and imagination, turning out a mouthwatering range of freshly made dishes. The best of these include grilled scallops with a zucchini, yogurt, and a saffron sauce, or else *tortelloni* filled with spinach and ricotta. Baked turbot comes with a velvety sauce made with fresh asparagus. Every dish is a feast for the eye and palate, especially a *millefeuille* of scampi with onions and green apples.

Ponte dell'Umilta, Dorsoduro 19. ✆ **041-2411881.** www.ristorantelineadombra.com. Reservations required. Main courses 23€–40€. AE, DC, MC, V. Wed–Mon 12:30–3pm and 7:30–10pm. Closed Nov.15–Mar 10. *Vaporetto:* Salute.

MODERATE

Locanda Montin ★ INTERNATIONAL/ITALIAN   This mellow old inn offers the most authentic Venetian dining in the city. The Montin opened after World War II and has hosted Ezra Pound, Jackson Pollock, Mark Rothko, and the artist friends of the late Peggy Guggenheim. More recent visitors have included everybody from Brad Pitt to Mick Jagger. It's owned and run by the Carretins, who have covered the walls with paintings donated by or bought from their many friends and guests. The arbor-covered garden courtyard is filled with regulars, many of whom allow their favorite waiter to select their meal. The frequently changing menu includes a variety of salads, grilled meats, and fish caught in the Adriatic. Desserts might include *semifreddo di fragoline,* a tempting chilled liqueur-soaked cake, capped with whipped cream and wild strawberries.

Fondamenta di Borgo, Dorsoduro 1147. ✆ **041-5227151.** www.locandamontin.com. Reservations recommended. Main courses 16€–28€. MC, V. Thurs–Tues 12:30–2:30pm; Thurs–Mon 7:30–10pm. *Vaporetto:* Accademia.

INEXPENSIVE

La Piscina MEDITERRANEAN   Located in the **Pensione La Calcina** (p. 455) hotel, the doors to this historic cafe and restaurant reopened in 2003 after a long slumber. With a terrace built over a canal, the dramatic and scenic setting is an ideal venue for a typical light Mediterranean cuisine, focusing on sumptuous salads, tantalizing one-plate meals, seasonal vegetables, and appetizing starters. This kitchen provides top-quality produce and generous portions. Menu items include spaghetti with black squid ink, linguine with *branzino* (a type of sea bass) and zucchini, and swordfish carpaccio. The chef has rigid rules: no canned products, no preservatives, and nothing prepared ahead of time and frozen.

In Pensione La Calcina, Dosoduro 780. ✆ **041-2413889.** www.lacalcina.com. Reservations recommended. Main courses 10€–19€. AE, DC, MC, V. Tues–Sun noon–2:30pm and 7–9:30pm. *Vaporetto:* Accademia.

Muro Vino e Cucina INTERNATIONAL   In the heart of the Rialto Market, close to the Rialto Bridge, this restaurant is one of the few in Venice that aims for high modernism—all polished steel and sharp angles. The bar is downstairs, with the restaurant on the second floor opening onto a view. This place continues to please us year after year with such dishes as lasagna with spinach and a beef ragout, or gnocchi with a red pesto-and-fava-bean sauce. Another local favorite is beef roulades stuffed with olives and served with risotto. For starters, try the zucchini stuffed with baked sea bass, Mediterranean herbs, and quail eggs. The chef uses only fresh produce from the local market.

San Polo 222. ✆ **041-523-7495.** www.murovinoecucina.it. Reservations recommended. Main courses 9€–15€. AE, DC, MC, V. Mon–Sat 9am–3pm. *Vaporetto:* Rialto.

On Isola della Guidecca

VERY EXPENSIVE

Fortuny ★★★ ITALIAN   The grandest of the hotel restaurants, Cipriani's Fortuny offers a sublime but relatively simple cuisine, with the freshest of ingredients used by one of the best-trained staffs along the Adriatic. This isn't the place to bring the kids—in fact, children 7 and under aren't allowed in the evening (a babysitter can be arranged). You can dine in the formal room with Murano chandeliers and Fortuny curtains when the weather is nippy, or on the terrace overlooking the lagoon. Freshly made pasta is a specialty, and it's among the finest we've sampled. Try the *taglierini verdi* with noodles and ham au gratin. Chef's specialties include mixed fried scampi and squid with tender vegetables, and sautéed veal filets with spring artichokes.

In the Hotel Cipriani, Isola della Giudecca 10. ✆ **041-5207744.** www.hotelcipriani.com. Reservations required. Jacket required for men, tie recommended. Main courses 25€–46€. AE, DC, MC, V. Daily 12:30–3pm and 8–10:30pm. Closed Nov 8–Mar 31. *Vaporetto:* Zitelle.

EXPENSIVE

Harry's Dolci ★ INTERNATIONAL/ITALIAN   From the quay-side windows of this chic place, you can watch seagoing vessels, from yachts to lagoon barges.

White napery and uniformed waiters grace a modern room, where no one minds if you order only coffee and ice cream or perhaps a selection from the large pastry menu (the zabaglione is divine). Popular items are carpaccio Cipriani, chicken salad, club sandwiches, gnocchi, and house-style cannelloni. The dishes are deliberately kept simple, but each is well prepared.

Sestiere Giudecca 773, Isola della Giudecca. ✆ **041-5285777.** www.cipriani.com. Reservations recommended, especially Sat–Sun. Main courses 30€–33€. AE, DC, MC, V. Daily noon–3pm and 7–10:30pm. Closed Nov–Mar. *Vaporetto:* Santa Eufemia.

MODERATE

Cip's Club ★ VENETIAN/ITALIAN

On the island of Giudecca, site of the plush Hotel Cipriani, this is a hot spot for dining. It's reached by private launch from the Piazza San Marco and makes for a delightful afternoon lunch. Cip's is informal and much more reasonable in price than Ristorante Cipriani. Tables are set out with an incredible view toward San Marco. The menu makes the most of local ingredients and delights with such dishes as homemade cannelloni with a delicate filling of robiola cheese and zucchini, or else *pappardelle* with basil in a sauce of roast scampi and zucchini. Specialties include roast monkfish flavored with rosemary and served with stewed fresh vegetables, or breast of guinea fowl in a traditional liver sauce, served with polenta soufflé.

Seafood, a Venice specialty.

In the Hotel Cipriani, Isola della Giudecca 10. ✆ **041-5207744.** www.hotelcipriani.com. Reservations required. Main courses 21€–46€. AE, DC, MC, V. Daily 7:30–11:30pm. Closed Nov 8–Mar 31. *Vaporetto:* Zitelle.

On the Lido

EXPENSIVE

Favorita SEAFOOD   Occupying two rustic dining rooms and a garden, Favorita is a Lido favorite. It has thrived since the 1920s, operated by the Pradel family, now in its third generation of ownership. Their years of experience contribute to flavorful, impeccably prepared seafood and shellfish, much of it grilled. Try the *trenette* (spaghetti-like pasta) with baby squid and eggplant, potato-based gnocchi with crabs from the Venetian lagoon, and grilled versions of virtually every fish in the Adriatic, including eel, sea bass, turbot, and sole.

Via Francesco Duodo 33, Lido di Venezia. ✆ **041-5261626.** Main courses 28€–32€; fixed-price menus 55€–60€. AE, DC, MC, V. Wed–Sun 12:30–2:30pm; Tues–Sun 7:30–10:30pm. *Vaporetto:* Lido.

INEXPENSIVE

Ristorante Belvedere VENETIAN   Outside the big hotels, the best food on the Lido is served at the Belvedere, across from the *vaporetto* stop. It attracts a lot of locals, who come here knowing that they can get some of the best fish along the Adriatic. The main dining room is attractive, with cane-backed bentwood chairs and big windows. In back is a busy cafe with its own entrance.

Piazzale Santa Maria Elisabetta 4, Lido di Venezia. ✆ **041-5260115.** www.belvedere-venezia. com. Reservations recommended. Main courses 8€–18€. DC, MC, V. Tues–Sun noon–2:30pm and 7–9:30pm. Closed Nov 4–Easter. *Vaporetto:* Lido.

SEEING THE SIGHTS

Venice appears to have been created specifically to entertain its legions of callers. Ever since the body of St. Mark was smuggled out of Alexandria and entombed in the basilica, the city has been host to a never-ending stream of visitors, famous, infamous, and otherwise. Venice has perpetually captured the imagination of poets and artists. Wordsworth, Byron, and Shelley addressed poems to the city, and it has been written about or used as a setting by many contemporary writers.

In the pages ahead, we explore the city's great art and architecture. But, unlike Florence, Venice would reward its guests with treasures even if they never ducked inside a museum or church. Take some time just to stroll and let yourself get lost in this gorgeous city.

Piazza San Marco ★★★

Piazza San Marco was the heart of Venice in the heyday of its glory as a seafaring republic. If you have only 1 day for Venice, you need not leave the square: Some of the city's major attractions, such as St. Mark's Basilica and the Doge's Palace, are centered here or nearby.

The traffic-free square is a source of bewilderment and interest. If you rise at dawn, you can almost have the piazza to yourself; as you watch the sun come up, the sheen of gold mosaics glistens with a mystical beauty. At midafternoon the tourists reign supreme, and it's not surprising in July to witness a scuffle over a camera angle. At sunset, when the two Moors in the Clock Tower strike the end of another day, lonely sailors begin a usually frustrated search for those hot spots that characterized the Venice of yore. Deeper into the evening, as strollers parade by, stop for an espresso at the Caffè Florian and sip while listening to the orchestra play.

Thanks to Napoleon, the square was unified architecturally. The emperor added the Fabbrica Nuova facing the basilica, thus bridging the Old and New Procuratie on either side. Flanked with medieval-looking palaces, Sansovino's Library, elegant shops, and colonnades, the square is now finished—unlike Piazza della Signoria in Florence.

If Piazza San Marco is Europe's drawing room, then the piazza's satellite, **Piazzetta San Marco ★**, is Europe's antechamber. Hedged in by the Doge's Palace, Sansovino's Library, and a side of St. Mark's, the tiny square faces the Grand Canal. Two tall granite columns grace the square. A winged lion, representing St. Mark, surmounts one. A statue of a man taming a dragon, supposedly the dethroned patron saint Theodore, tops the other. Both columns came from the East in the 12th century.

During Venice's heyday, dozens of victims either lost their heads or were strung up here, many of them first subjected to torture that would've made the Marquis de Sade flinch. One, for example, had his teeth hammered in, his eyes gouged out, and his hands cut off before being strung up. Venetian justice became notorious throughout Europe. If you stand with your back to the canal,

Piazza San Marco and the Campanile.

looking toward the south facade of St. Mark's, you'll see the so-called *Virgin and Child of the Poor Baker,* a mosaic honoring Pietro Fasiol (also Faziol), a young man unjustly sentenced to death on a charge of murder.

To the left of the entrance to the Doge's Palace are four porphyry figures representing two Roman emperors (East and West) and their corresponding vice-emperors.

Campanile di San Marco ★★   One summer night in 1902, the bell tower of St. Mark's, suffering from years of rheumatism in the damp Venetian climate, gave out a warning sound that sent the fashionable coffee drinkers in the piazza below scurrying for their lives. But the campanile gracefully waited until the next morning, July 14, before tumbling into the piazza. The Venetians rebuilt their belfry, and it's now safe to climb to the top. Unlike Italy's other bell towers, where you have to brave narrow, steep spiral staircases to reach the top, this one has an elevator so you can get a pigeon's view. It's a particularly good vantage point for viewing the cupolas of the basilica.

Piazza San Marco. ☎ **041-5224064.** www.basilicasanmarco.it. Admission 8€. Oct–Mar daily 9:30am–3:45pm; Apr–June daily 9am–7pm; July–Sept daily 9am–9pm. *Vaporetto:* San Marco.

Clock Tower (Torre dell'Orologio)   The two Moors striking the bell atop this Renaissance clock tower, soaring over the Old Procuratie, are one of the most characteristic Venetian scenes. The clock under the winged lion not only tells the time but is a boon to the astrologer: It matches the signs of the zodiac with the position of the sun. If the movement of the Moors striking the hour seems slow in today's fast-paced world, remember how many centuries the poor wretches have been at their task without time off. The Moors originally

Piazza San Marco

represented two European shepherds, but after having been reproduced in bronze, they've grown darker with the passing of time. As a consequence, they came to be called Moors by the Venetians.

Pigeons flock to Piazza San Marco.

The base of the tower has always been a favorite *punto di incontro* ("meet me at the tower") for Venetians and is the entrance to the ancient **Mercerie** (from the word for merchandise), the principal souklike retail street of both high-end boutiques and trinket shops that zigzags its way to the Rialto Bridge. Piazza San Marco. ℭ **041-5209070.** www. museicivicivenezianai.it. Admission 12€, including booking fee and guide, and entrance to Correr Civic Museum and Ducal Palace. Reservations required. Children 11 and under not admitted. Tours in English Mon–Wed 10 and 11am, Thurs–Sun 2 and 3pm. *Vaporetto:* San Marco.

Ducal Palace & Bridge of Sighs (Palazzo Ducale & Ponte dei Sospiri) ★★★ You enter the Palace of the Doges through the magnificent 15th-century **Porta della Carta** ★★ at the piazzetta. This Venetian Gothic *palazzo* gleams in the tremulous light somewhat like a frosty birthday cake in pinkish-red marble and white Istrian stone. Italy's grandest civic structure, it dates from 1309, although a 1577 fire destroyed much of the original building. That fire made ashes of many of the palace's masterpieces and almost spelled doom for the building itself because the new architectural fervor of the post-Renaissance was in the air. However, sanity prevailed. Many of the greatest Venetian painters of the 16th century contributed to the restored palace, replacing the canvases or frescoes of the old masters.

If you enter from the piazzetta, past the four porphyry Moors, you'll be in the splendid Renaissance courtyard, one of the most recent additions to a palace that has benefited from the work of many architects with widely varying tastes. To get to the upper loggia, you can take the **Giants' Stairway (Scala dei Giganti),** so called because of the two Sansovino statues of mythological figures.

If you want to understand something of this magnificent palace, the history of the 1,000-year-old Maritime Republic, and the intrigue of the government that ruled it, search out the infrared **audio guide** at the entrance, which costs 7€. Unless you can tag along with an English-language tour group, you may otherwise miss out on the importance of much of what you're seeing.

After climbing the Sansovino stairway, you'll enter some get-acquainted rooms. Proceed to the **Sala di Anti-Collegio,** housing the palace's greatest works, notably Veronese's *Rape of Europa,* to the far left on the right wall. Tintoretto is well represented with his *Three Graces* and his *Bacchus and Ariadne.* Some critics consider the latter his supreme achievement. The ceiling in the adjoining **Sala del Collegio** bears allegorical paintings by Veronese. As you proceed to the right, you'll enter the **Sala del Senato o Pregadi,** with its allegorical painting by Tintoretto in the ceiling's center.

It was in the **Sala del Consiglio dei Dieci,** with its gloomy paintings, that the dreaded Council of Ten (often called the Terrible Ten, for good reason) assembled to decide who was in need of decapitation. In the antechamber, bills of accusation were dropped in the lion's mouth.

The excitement continues downstairs. You can wander through the once-private apartments of the doges to the grand **Maggior Consiglio,** with Veronese's allegorical *Triumph of Venice* on the ceiling. The most outstanding feature, however, is over the Grand Council chamber: Tintoretto's *Paradise,* said to be the world's largest oil painting. Paradise seems to have an overpopulation problem, perhaps reflecting Tintoretto's too-optimistic point of view (he was in his 70s when he began this monumental work and died 6 years later). The second grandiose hall, which you enter from the grand chamber, is the **Sala dello Scrutinio,** with paintings telling of Venice's past glories.

Reentering the Maggior Consiglio, follow the arrows on their trail across the **Bridge of Sighs (Ponte dei Sospiri)** ★★, linking the Doge's Palace with the Palazzo delle Prigioni. Here you'll see the cellblocks that once lodged the prisoners who felt the quick justice of the Terrible Ten. The Terrible Ten was a series of state inquisitors appointed by the city of Venice to dispense justice to the citizens. This often meant torture even for what could be viewed as a minor infraction. The reputation of the Terrible Ten for the ferocity of their sentences became infamous in Europe. The "sighs" in the bridge's name stem from the sad laments of the numerous victims forced across it to face certain torture and possible death. The cells are somber remnants of the horror of medieval justice.

If you're intrigued by the palace, you might want to check out the **"Secret Trails of the Palazzo Ducale" ("Itinerari Segreti del Palazzo Ducale").** These 18€ guided tours are so popular that they've recently been introduced in English (reserve in advance at the ticket-buyers' entrance or by calling ☏ **041-5209070**). These tours are daily at 9:55, 10:45, and 11:35am. You'll peek into otherwise restricted quarters and hidden passageways of this enormous palace, such as the doge's private chambers and the torture chambers where prisoners were interrogated. The tour is also offered in Italian daily at 9:30 and 11:10am.

Piazzetta San Marco. ☏ **041-2715911.** www.museicivicveneziani.it. Admission (including entrance to Correr Civic Museum and Clock Tower [reservation required for tower]) 12€. Nov–Mar; 14€ Apr–Nov. Apr–May daily 9am–7pm; June–Oct daily 8:30am–6:30pm; Nov–Mar daily 9am–6pm. Closed Dec 25 and Jan 1. *Vaporetto:* San Marco.

St. Mark's Basilica (Basilica di San Marco) ★★★

Dominating Piazza San Marco is the Church of Gold (Chiesa d'Oro), one of the world's greatest and most richly embellished churches, its cavernous candlelit interior gilded with mosaics added over some 7 centuries. In fact, it looks as if it had been moved intact from Istanbul. The basilica is a conglomeration of styles, although it's particularly indebted to Byzantium. Like Venice, St. Mark's is adorned with booty from every corner of the city's once far-flung mercantile empire: capitals from Sicily, columns from Alexandria, porphyry from Syria, and sculpture from old Constantinople.

The basilica is capped by a dome that, like a spider plant, sends off shoots—in this case, a quartet of smaller-scale bulbed cupolas. Spanning the facade is a loggia, surmounted by replicas of the four famous St. Mark's horses, the *Triumphal Quadriga*. The facade's rich marble slabs and mosaics depict scenes from the lives of Christ and St. Mark. One of the mosaics re-creates the entry of the evangelist's body into Venice—according to legend, St. Mark's body, hidden in a pork barrel, was smuggled out of Alexandria in A.D. 828 and was shipped to Venice. The evangelist dethroned Theodore, the Greek saint who until then had been the patron of the city that had outgrown him.

In the **atrium** are six cupolas with mosaics illustrating scenes from the Old Testament, including the story of the Tower of Babel. The interior of the basilica, once the private chapel and pantheon of the doges, is a stunning wonderland of marbles, alabaster, porphyry, and pillars. You'll walk in awe across the undulating multicolored ocean floor, patterned with mosaics.

To the right is the **baptistery,** dominated by the Sansovino-inspired baptismal font, upon which John the Baptist is ready to pour water. If you look back at the aperture over the entry, you can see a mosaic of the dance of Salome in front of Herod and his court. Salome, wearing a star-studded russet-red dress and three white fox tails, is dancing under a platter holding John the Baptist's head. Her glassy face is that of a Madonna, not an enchantress.

After touring the baptistery, proceed up the right nave to the doorway to the oft-looted **treasury** (*tesoro*) ★. Here you'll find the inevitable skulls and bones of some ecclesiastical authorities under glass, plus goblets, chalices, and Gothic candelabra. The entrance to the **presbytery** is nearby. In it, on the high altar, the

Basilica di San Marco

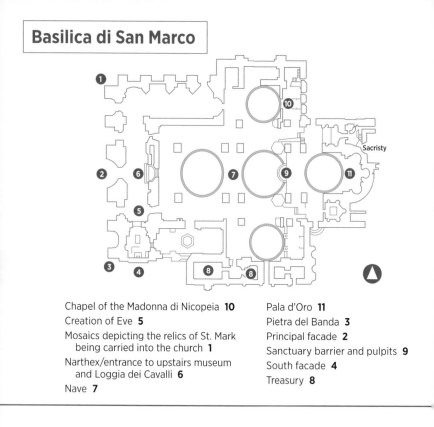

Chapel of the Madonna di Nicopeia **10**
Creation of Eve **5**
Mosaics depicting the relics of St. Mark being carried into the church **1**
Narthex/entrance to upstairs museum and Loggia dei Cavalli **6**
Nave **7**

Pala d'Oro **11**
Pietra del Banda **3**
Principal facade **2**
Sanctuary barrier and pulpits **9**
South facade **4**
Treasury **8**

alleged sarcophagus of St. Mark rests under a green marble blanket and is held by four Corinthian alabaster columns. Behind the altar is the rarest treasure at St. Mark's: the Byzantine-style **Pala d'Oro ★★★**, a golden altar screen measuring 3×1m (10×4 ft.). It's set with 300 emeralds, 300 sapphires, 400 garnets, 100 amethysts, and 1,300 pearls, plus rubies and topazes accompanying 157 enameled rondelle and panels. Second in importance is the 10th-century *Madonna di Nicopeia,* a bejeweled icon taken from Constantinople and exhibited in its own chapel to the left of the high altar.

After leaving the basilica, head up the stairs in the atrium to the **Marciano Museum** and the **Loggia dei Cavalli.** The star of the museum is the world-famous *Triumphal Quadriga ★★,* four horses looted from Constantinople by Venetian crusaders during the sack of that city in 1204. These horses once surmounted the basilica but were removed because of pollution damage, and were subsequently restored. This is the only *quadriga* (a quartet of horses yoked together) to have survived from the

---

A St. Mark's Warning

A dress code for men and women prohibiting shorts, bare arms and shoulders, and skirts above the knee is strictly enforced at all times in the basilica. You *will* be turned away. In addition, you must remain silent and cannot take photographs.

A detail from the mosaics in St. Mark's Basilica.

classical era, believed to have been cast in the 4th century. Napoleon once carted these much-traveled horses off to Paris for the Arc de Triomphe du Carrousel, but they were returned to Venice in 1815. The museum, with its mosaics and tapestries, is especially interesting, but also be sure to walk out onto the loggia for a view of Piazza San Marco.

Piazza San Marco. *C* **041-5225205.** www.basilicasanmarco.it. Basilica free admission; treasury 3€; presbytery 2€; Marciano Museum 4€. Basilica and presbytery daily 9:45am–5pm. Marciano Museum daily 9:45am–4:45pm. *Vaporetto:* San Marco.

The Grand Canal (Canal Grande) ★★★

Paris has its Champs-Elysées, and New York City has its Broadway—but Venice, for sheer uniqueness, tops them all with its Canal Grande. Lined with *palazzi* (many in the Venetian Gothic style), this great road of water is filled with *vaporetti,* motorboats, and gondolas. The boat moorings look like peppermint sticks. The canal begins at Piazzetta San Marco on one side and Longhena's La Salute church opposite. At midpoint, the Rialto Bridge spans it. Eventually, the canal winds its serpentine course to the rail station.

Some of the most impressive buildings along the Grand Canal have been converted into galleries and museums. Others have been turned into cooperative apartments, but often the lower floors are now deserted because of rising waters. (Venetian housewives aren't as incurably romantic as foreign visitors. A practical lot, these women can be seen stringing up their laundry to dry in front of thousands of tourists.)

The best way to see the Grand Canal is to board *vaporetto* no. 1 (push and shove until you secure a seat at the front of the vessel). Settle yourself in, make sure that you have your long-distance viewing glasses, and prepare yourself for a view that can thrill even the most experienced world traveler.

477

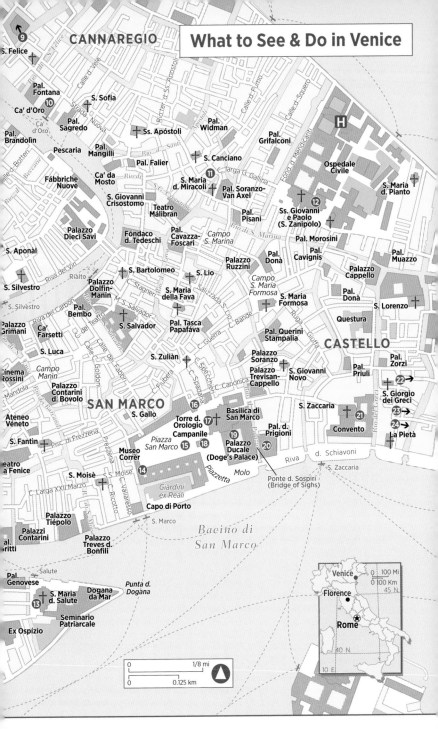

What to See & Do in Venice

CANNAREGIO

S. Felice

Pal. Fontana

Ca' d'Oro

S. Sofia

Pal. Sagredo

Ca' d'Oro

Pal. Brandolin

Pescaria

Pal. Mangilli

Ss. Apóstoli

Pal. Widman

Pal. Grifalconi

H

Ospedale Civile

S. Maria d. Pianto

Pal. Falier

S. Canciano

Ca' da Mosto

S. Maria d. Miracoli

Pal. Soranzo-Van Axel

S. Giovanni Crisostomo

Teatro Málibran

Pal. Pisani

Ss. Giovanni e Paolo (S. Zanipolo)

Pal. Morosini

Fábbriche Nuove

Palazzo Dieci Savi

Fóndaco d. Tedeschi

Pal. Cavazza-Foscari

Campo S. Marina

Pal. Donà

Pal. Cavignis

Pal. Muazzo

S. Aponàl

Palazzo Cappello

S. Silvestro

S. Silvestro

Palazzo Dolfin-Manin

S. Bartolomeo

S. Lio

S. Maria della Fava

Campo S. Maria Formosa

S. Maria Formosa

Pal. Donà

S. Lorenzo

Pal. Bembo

S. Salvador

Pal. Tasca Papafáva

Questura

Palazzo Grimani

Ca' Farsetti

Pal. Querini Stampalia

CASTELLO

S. Luca

S. Zuliàn

Palazzo Soranzo

S. Giovanni Novo

Pal. Zorzi

Cinema Rossini

Campo Manin

Palazzo Contarini d. Bovolo

Palazzo Trevisan-Cappello

Pal. Priuli

22

S. Giorgio dei Greci

Ateneo Véneto

SAN MARCO

S. Gallo

16

Torre d. Orologio

17

Basilica di San Marco

S. Zaccaria

21

23

24

La Pietà

S. Fantìn

Campanile

19

Palazzo Ducale (Doge's Palace)

Pal. d. Prigioni

20

Convento

Teatro a Fenice

Museo Corrèr

15

Piazza San Marco

18

S. Moisè

14

S.S. Moisè

Piazzetta

Molo

Riva d. Schiavoni

S. Zaccaria

Giardini ex Reali

Ponte d. Sospiri (Bridge of Sighs)

Palazzo Tiépolo

Capo di Porto

S. Marco

Palazzi Contarini

Palazzo Treves d. Bonfili

Bacino di San Marco

Pal. Genovese

Salute

S. Maria d. Salute

Dogana da Mar

Punta d. Dogana

13

Seminario Patriarcale

Ex Ospízio

Venice

Florence

Rome

100 Mi
100 Km

45 N.

40 N.

10 E

0   1/8 mi
0   0.125 km

Museums & Galleries

Venice is a city of art. Decorating its *palazzi* and adorning its canvases were artists such as Giovanni Bellini, Carpaccio, Titian, Giorgione, Lotto, Tintoretto, Veronese, Tiepolo, Guardi, Canaletto, and Longhi, to name just the important ones. You'll even come across some modern surprises, such as those in the Guggenheim Collection.

Academy Gallery (Gallerie dell'Accademia) ★★★ The pomp and circumstance, the glory that was Venice, lives on in this remarkable collection of paintings spanning the 13th to 18th centuries. The hallmark of the Venetian school is color and more color. From Giorgione to Veronese, from Titian to Tintoretto, with a Carpaccio cycle thrown in, the Accademia has samples of its most famous sons—often their best works. Here we highlight only some of the most renowned master-pieces for the first-timer in a rush.

A bronze horse on the loggia of St. Mark's Basilica.

You'll first see works by such 14th-century artists as Paolo and Lorenzo Veneziano, who bridged the gap from Byzantine art to Gothic (see the latter's *Annunciation*). Next, you'll view Giovanni Bellini's *Madonna and Saint* (poor Sebastian, not another arrow) and Carpaccio's fascinating yet gruesome work of mass crucifixion. As you move on, head for the painting on the easel by the window, attributed to the great Venetian artist Giorgione. On this canvas he depicted the Madonna and Child, along with the mystic St. Catherine of Siena and John the Baptist (a neat trick for Catherine, who seems to have perfected transmigration to join the cast of characters).

Two of the most important works with secular themes are Mantegna's armored *St. George,* with the slain dragon at his feet, and Hans Memling's 15th-century portrait of a young man. A most unusual *Madonna and Child* is by Cosmè Tura, the master of Ferrara, who could always be counted on to give a new twist to an old subject.

The Madonnas and bambini of Giovanni Bellini, an expert in harmonious color blending, are the focus of another room. None but the major artists could stand the test of a salon filled with the same subject, but under Bellini's brush each Virgin achieves her individual spirituality. Giorgione's *Tempest,* displayed here, is the single most famous painting at the Accademia. It depicts a baby suckling from the breast of its mother, while a man with a staff looks on. What might've emerged as a simple pastoral scene by a lesser artist comes

Boats make their way along the Grand Canal.

forth as rare and exceptional beauty. Summer lightning pierces the sky, but the tempest seems to be in the background, far away from the foreground figures, who are menaced without knowing it.

You can see the masterpiece of Lorenzo Lotto, a melancholy portrait of a young man, before coming to a room dominated by Paolo Veronese's *The Banquet in the House of Levi*. This painting began as a Last Supper but was considered a sacrilege in its day, so Veronese was forced to change its name and pretend that it was a secular work. (Impish Veronese caught the hot fire of the Inquisition by including dogs, a cat, midgets, Huns, and drunken revelers in the mammoth canvas.) Four large paintings by Tintoretto, noted for their swirling action and powerful drama, depict scenes from the life of St. Mark. Finally, painted in his declining years (some have suggested in his 88th year, before he died from the plague) is Titian's majestic *Pietà*.

After an unimpressive long walk, search out Canaletto's *Porticato*. Yet another room is heightened by Gentile Bellini's stunning portrait of St. Mark's Square, back in the days (1496) when the houses glistened with gold in the sun. All the works in this salon are intriguing, especially the re-creation of the Ponte de Rialto and a covered wood bridge by Carpaccio.

Also displayed is the cycle of narrative paintings that Vittore Carpaccio did of St. Ursula for the Scuola of Santa Orsola. The most famous is no. 578, showing Ursula asleep on her elongated bed, with a dog nestled on the floor nearby, as the angels come for a visitation. Finally, on the way out, look for Titian's *Presentation of the Virgin*, a fitting farewell to this galaxy of great Venetian art.

Campo della Carità, Dorsoduro. ✆ **041-5222247.** www.gallerieaccademia.org. Admission 7.50€. Mon 8:15am–2pm; Tues–Sun 8:15am–7:15pm. Closed Jan 1, May 1, and Dec 25. *Vaporetto:* Accademia.

Ca' d'Oro ★★★   The only problem with the use of this building as an art museum is that the Ca' d'Oro is so opulent that its architecture and decor compete with the works. It was built in the early 1400s, and its name translates as "House of Gold," although the gilding that once covered its facade eroded away long ago, leaving softly textured pink and white stone carved into lacy

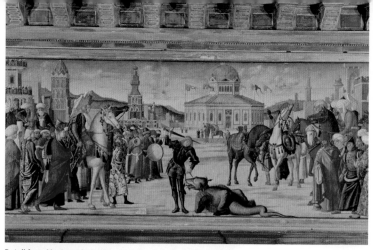

Detail from Mantegna's *St. George* at the Gallerie dell'Accademia.

Gothic patterns. Historians compare its majesty to that of the Ducal Palace. The building was meticulously restored in the early 20th century by philanthropist Baron Franchetti, who attached it to a smaller nearby *palazzo* (Ca' Duodo), today part of the Ca' d'Oro complex. The interconnected buildings contain the baron's valuable private collection of paintings, sculpture, and furniture, all donated to the Italian government during World War I.

You enter into a stunning courtyard, 46m (150 ft.) from the *vaporetto* stop. The courtyard has a multicolored patterned marble floor and is filled with statuary. Proceed upstairs to the *palazzo*. One of the gallery's major paintings is Titian's voluptuous *Venus*. She coyly covers one breast, but what about the other?

In a niche reserved for the masterpiece of the Franchetti collection is Andrea Mantegna's icy-cold *St. Sebastian,* the central figure of which is riddled with what must be a record number of arrows. You'll also find works by Carpaccio.

For a delightful break, step out onto the *palazzo*'s loggia, overlooking the Grand Canal, for a view up and down the aquatic waterway and across to the Pescheria, a timeless vignette of an unchanged city.

Cannaregio 3931-3932. ℂ **041-5238790.** www.cadoro.org. Admission 6€. Mon 8:15am-2pm; Tues-Sun 8:15am-7:15pm. Closed Jan 1, May 1, and Dec 25. *Vaporetto:* Ca' d'Oro.

The Five Major Landmarks

Time and again, you'll think you know where you're going, only to wind up on a dead-end street or at the side of a canal with no bridge to get to the other side. Just remind yourself that Venice's complexity is an integral part of its charm, and getting lost is part of the fun.

Fortunately, around the city are yellow signs whose arrows direct you toward one of five major landmarks: **Ferrovia** (the train station), **Piazzale Roma**, the **Rialto** (Bridge), **San Marco** (Piazza), and the **Accademia** (Bridge). You'll often find these signs grouped together, with their arrows pointing off in different directions.

Ca' Rezzonico ★★ This 17th- and 18th-century palace along the Grand Canal is where Robert Browning set up his bachelor headquarters and eventually died in 1889. Pope Clement XIII also stayed here. It's a virtual treasure house, known for its baroque paintings and furniture. First you enter the **Grand Ballroom** with its allegorical ceiling, and then you proceed through lavishly embellished rooms with Venetian chandeliers, brocaded walls, portraits of patricians, tapestries, gilded furnishings, and touches of chinoiserie. At the end of the first walk is the **Throne Room,** with its allegorical ceilings by Giovanni Battista Tiepolo.

On the first floor you can walk out onto a **balcony** for a view of the Grand Canal as the aristocratic tenants of the 18th century saw it. Another group of rooms follows, including the library. In these salons, look for a bizarre collection of paintings: One, for example, depicts half-clothed women beating up a defenseless naked man (one Amazon is about to stick a pitchfork into his neck, while another looks to crown him with a violin). In the adjoining room, another woman is hammering a spike through a man's skull.

Upstairs is a survey of 18th-century Venetian art. As you enter the main room from downstairs, head for the **first salon** on your right (facing the canal), which contains the best works, paintings from the brush of Pietro Longhi. His most famous work, *The Lady and the Hairdresser,* is the first canvas to the right on the entrance wall. Others depict the life of the idle Venetian rich. On the rest of the floor are bedchambers, a chapel, and salons, some with badly damaged frescoes, including a romp of satyrs.

Fondamenta Rezzonico, Dorsoduro 3136. © **041-2410100.** www.museicivicivenez iani.it. Admission 7€. Nov–Mar Wed–Mon 10am–5pm; Apr–Oct Wed–Mon 10am–6pm. Closed Jan 1, May 1, and Dec 25. *Vaporetto:* Ca' Rezzonico.

Giorgione's *Tempest* at the Gallerie dell'Accademia.

Correr Civic Museum (Museo Civico Correr) ★★ This museum traces the development of Venetian painting from the 14th to 16th centuries. On the second floor are the red-and-maroon robes once worn by the doges, plus some fabulous street lanterns and an illustrated copy of *Marco Polo in Tartaria.* You can see Cosmè Tura's *Pietà,* a miniature of renown from the genius in the Ferrara School. This is one of his more gruesome works, depicting a bony, gnarled Christ sprawled on the lap of the Madonna. Farther on, search out Schiavone's *Madonna and Child* (no. 545), our candidate for ugliest bambino ever depicted on canvas (no wonder his mother looks askance).

One of the most important rooms boasts three masterpieces: a *Pietà* by

Antonello da Messina, a *Crucifixion* by Flemish Hugo van der Goes, and a *Madonna and Child* by Dieric Bouts, who depicted the baby suckling at his mother's breast in a sensual manner. The star attraction of the Correr is the **Bellini salon,** which includes works by founding padre Jacopo and his son, Gentile. But the real master of the household was the other son, Giovanni, the major painter of the 15th-century Venetian school (look for his *Crucifixion* and compare it with his father's treatment of the same subject). A small but celebrated portrait of St. Anthony of Padua by Alvise Vivarini is here, along with works by Bartolomeo Montagna. The most important work is Vittore Carpaccio's *Two Venetian Ladies,* although their true gender is a subject of much debate. In Venice, they're popularly known as "The Courtesans." A lesser work, *St. Peter,* depicting the saint with the daggers piercing him, hangs in the same room.

The water entrance to the Ca' d'Oro.

The entrance is under the arcades of Ala Napoleonica at the west end of the square.

In the Procuratie Nuove, Piazza San Marco. ℂ **041-2405211.** www.museiciviciveneziani.it. Admission (including entrance to the Ducal Palace and Clock Tower [reservation required for tower]; see earlier) 13€. Apr–Oct daily 10am–7pm; Nov–Mar daily 10am–5pm. Closed Dec 25 and Jan 1. *Vaporetto:* San Marco.

Naval History Museum (Museo Storico Navale) & Arsenale ★ The Naval History Museum is filled with cannons, ships' models, and fragments of vessels dating to the days when Venice was supreme in the Adriatic. The prize exhibit is a gilded model of the *Bucintoro,* the great ship of the doge that surely would've made Cleopatra's barge look like an oil tanker. In addition, you'll find models of historic and modern fighting ships, fishing and rowing craft, and a collection of 24 Chinese junks, as well as a number of maritime ex-votos (religious paintings in the form of triptychs or altarpieces) from churches of Naples.

A Note on Museum Hours

As throughout Italy, visiting hours in Venice's museums are often subject to major variations, both in hours and in days. Many visitors who have budgeted only 2 or 3 days for Venice often express disappointment when, for some unknown reason, a major attraction closes abruptly, sometimes for the entire day. When you arrive, check with the tourist office for a list of the latest open hours.

If you walk along the canal as it branches off from the museum, you'll arrive at the Ships' Pavilion, where historic vessels are displayed (about 250m/820 ft. from the museum and before the wooden bridge). Proceeding along the canal, you'll soon reach the Arsenale, Campo dell'Arsenale, guarded by stone lions, Neptune with a trident, and other assorted ferocities. You'll spot it readily enough because of its two towers flanking the canal. In its day, the Arsenale turned out galley after galley at speeds usually associated with wartime production.

Campo San Biagio, Castello 2148. ℭ **041-2441399.** Admission 1.60€. Mon–Fri 8:45am–1:30pm; Sat 8:45am–1pm. Closed holidays. *Vaporetto:* Arsenale.

Palazzo Grassi ★★ If Peggy Guggenheim's museum (see below) doesn't satisfy your hunger for modern art, you can visit this collection of contemporary art amassed by luxury goods magnate François Pinault. He'd originally wanted to open the museum in Paris, but ran into bureaucratic snags. Opening onto the Grand Canal, the *palazzo* was designed in the 1740s by famed architect Giorgio Massari. This was the last palace erected in Venice before the fall of the Republic.

The famous Japanese architect Tadao Ando turned the palace into a modern museum for Pinault's impressive collection of art. At any given time 200 pieces of art, less than a tenth of Pinault's vast collection, can be exhibited. Palazzo Grassi is especially rich in postwar artists, including controversial Damien Hirst, Agnes Martin, Cindy Sherman, and Bruce Nauman.

Campo Samuo Samuele 3231. ℭ **041-5231680.** Fax 041-5286218. www.palazzograssi.it. Admission 15€ adults, 10€ 18 and under. Wed–Mon 10am–7pm. *Vaporetto:* San Samuele or Sant' Angelo.

Peggy Guggenheim Collection (Collezione Peggy Guggenheim) ★★★
This is one of the most comprehensive and brilliant, modern art collections in the Western world, and it reveals both the foresight and the critical judgment of its

A lion, the symbol of Venice, guards the Arsenale.

The sculpture garden at the Peggy Guggenheim Collection.

founder. The collection is housed in an unfinished *palazzo,* the former Venetian home of Peggy Guggenheim, who died in 1979. In the tradition of her family, Peggy Guggenheim was a lifelong patron of contemporary painters and sculptors. In the 1940s, she founded the avant-garde Art of This Century Gallery in New York, impressing critics not only with the high quality of the artists she sponsored, but also with her methods of displaying them.

As her private collection increased, she decided to find a larger showcase and selected Venice. Today you can wander through the home and enjoy art in an informal and relaxed way.

Max Ernst was one of Peggy Guggenheim's early favorites (she even married him), as was Jackson Pollock (she provided a farmhouse where he could develop his technique). Displayed here are works not only by Pollock and Ernst, but also by Picasso (see his 1911 cubist *The Poet*), Duchamp, Chagall, Mondrian, Brancusi, Delvaux, and Dalí, plus a garden of modern sculpture with Giacometti works (some of which he struggled to complete while resisting the amorous intentions of Marlene Dietrich). Temporary modern art shows sometimes are presented during winter. Since Guggenheim's death, the collection has been administered by the Solomon R. Guggenheim Foundation, which also operates New York's Guggenheim Museum. In the new wing are a museum shop and a cafe, overlooking the sculpture garden.

In the Palazzo Venier dei Leoni, Calle Venier dei Leoni, Dorsoduro 701. (✆ **041-2405411.** www. guggenheim-venice.it. Admission 12€ adults, 7€ children/students, free for children 11 and under. Wed–Mon 10am–6pm. *Vaporetto:* Accademia.

Punta della Dogana ★   A 17th-century Customs house, the last *palazzo* to be built in Venice before the fall of the Republic, has been converted into exhibition rooms of a stunning collection of modern art. Major temporary exhibitions are showcased here, most of the art based in whole or in part from the fabulous collection of billionaire François Pinault (he owns Christie's). This tycoon beat out the Guggenheim Foundation to secure this building. The walls were gutted to reveal brick, which forms the backdrop of Pinault's 2,500-piece collection. Some of the world's leading contemporary artists are exhibited here, including Jeff Koons, Sigmar Polke, Cindy Sherman, Richard Prince, Cy Twombly, and Takashi Murakami. Emerging talents are also displayed in these temporary shows. On site is the Palazzo Grassi Café, ideal for a light lunch or snack. Open from 10am to 7pm, it also is one of the most romantic places in Venice to have afternoon tea.

Campo San Samuele. © **041-199-139-139.** www.palazzograssi.it. Admission 15€, free for children 10 and under. Wed–Mon 10am–7pm. *Vaporetto:* S. Samuele.

Churches & Guild Houses

Much of the great art of Venice lies in its **churches** and *scuole* (guild houses or fraternities). Most of the guild members were drawn from the rising bourgeoisie. The guilds were said to fulfill both the material and the spiritual needs of their (male) members, who often engaged in charitable works in honor of the saint for whom their *scuola* was named. Many of Venice's greatest artists, including Tintoretto, were commissioned to decorate these guild houses. Some created masterpieces that you can still see today. Narrative canvases that depicted the lives of the saints were called *teleri*.

Madonna dell'Orto ★   At this church, a good reason to walk to this remote northern district, you can pay your final respects to Tintoretto. The brick structure with a Gothic front is famed not only because of its paintings by that artist, but also because the great master is buried in the chapel to the right of the main altar. At the high altar are his *Last Judgment* (on the right) and *Sacrifice of the Golden Calf* (left), with monumental paintings curving at the top like a Gothic arch. Over the doorway to the right of the altar is Tintoretto's portrayal of the presentation of Mary as a little girl at the temple. The composition is unusual in that Mary isn't the focal point; rather, a pointing bystander dominates the scene.

The first chapel to the right of the main altar contains a masterly work by Cima de Conegliano, showing the presentation of a sacrificial lamb to the saints (the plasticity of St. John's body evokes Michelangelo). In the first chapel on the left, as you enter, notice the photo of Giovanni Bellini's *Madonna and Child.* The original, which was noteworthy for its depiction of the eyes and mouths of the mother and child, was stolen in 1994; the photograph was installed in its place. Two other pictures in the apse are *The Presentation of the Cross to St. Peter* and *The Beheading of St. Christopher.*

A gondola on the Canal Grande passing by the Basilica San Giorgio Maggiore.

Campo dell'Orto, Cannaregio 3512. ℂ **041-2750462.** www.madonnadellorto.org. Admission 3€. Mon–Sat 10am–5pm. Closed holidays. *Vaporetto:* Madonna dell'Orto.

San Giorgio degli Schiavoni ★★ At the St. Antonino Bridge (Fondamenta dei Furlani) is the second important guild house to visit. Between 1502 and 1509, Vittore Carpaccio painted a pictorial cycle here of exceptional merit and interest. His works of **St. George and the Dragon ★** are our favorite art in all Venice and certainly the most delightful. For example, in one frame St. George charges the dragon on a field littered with half-eaten bodies and skulls. Gruesome? Not at all. Any moment you expect the director to call "Cut!" The pictures relating to St. Jerome are appealing but don't compete with St. George and his ferocious dragon.

Calle dei Furiani, Castello. ℂ **041-5228828.** Admission 4€. Nov–Mar Tues–Sat 9:15am–12:30pm and 4:45–6pm, Sun 9:15am–12:30pm; Apr–Oct Tues–Sat 9:30am–12:30pm and 3:30–6:30pm, Sun 9:30am–12:30pm. Last entrance 30 min. before closing. *Vaporetto:* San Zaccaria.

San Giorgio Maggiore ★ This church, on the little island of San Giorgio Maggiore, was designed by the great Renaissance architect Palladio—perhaps as a consolation prize because he wasn't chosen to rebuild the burned-out Doge's Palace. The logical rhythm of the Vicenza architect is played here on a grand scale. But inside it's almost too stark because Palladio wasn't much on gilded adornment. The chief art hangs on the main altar: two epic paintings by Tintoretto, the *Fall of Manna* to the left and the far more successful *Last Supper* to the right. It's interesting to compare Tintoretto's *Cena* with that of Veronese at the Accademia. Afterward, you might want to take the elevator (for 5€) to the top of the belfry for a view of the greenery of the island itself, the lagoon, and the Doge's Palace across the way. It's unforgettable.

Isola San Giorgio Maggiore, across from Piazzetta San Marco. ℂ **041-5227827.** Free admission. May–Sept daily 9:30am–12:30pm and 2:30–6:30pm; Oct–Apr daily 9:30am–12:30pm and 2:30–4:30pm.

San Giorgio Maggiore.

Closed for Mass on Sun and feast days 10:45am–noon. *Vaporetto:* Take the Giudecca-bound *vaporetto* on Riva degli Schiavoni and get off at the 1st stop, right in the courtyard of the church.

San Rocco ★★★   Of all Venice's *scuole,* none are as richly embellished as this, filled with epic canvases by Tintoretto. Born Jacopo Robusti in 1518, Tintoretto became known for paintings of mystical spirituality and phantasmagoric light effects. By a clever trick, he won the competition to decorate this darkly illuminated early-16th-century building. He began painting in 1564, and the work stretched on until his powers as an artist waned; he died in 1594. The paintings sweep across the upper and lower halls, mesmerizing you with a kind of passion play. In the grand hallway, they depict New Testament scenes, devoted largely to episodes in the life of Mary (the **Flight into Egypt** is among the best). In the top gallery are works illustrating scenes from the Old and New Testaments, the most renowned being those devoted to the life of Christ. In a separate room is Tintoretto's masterpiece: his mammoth **Crucifixion.** In it, he showed his dramatic scope and sense of grandeur as an artist, creating a deeply felt scene that fills you with the horror of systematic execution, thus transcending its original subject matter. (**Movie trivia:** Watch Woody Allen try to pick up Julia Roberts in *Everyone Says I Love You* while she studies the Tintorettos in San Rocco—if you can get past the idea of Roberts as an art historian.)

Campo San Rocco, San Polo. ✆ **041-5234864.** www.scuolagrandesanrocco.it. Admission 7€ adults, free for ages 17 and under. Daily 9:30am–5:30pm. Closed Easter, Dec 25, and Jan 1. Ticket office closes 30 min. before last entrance. *Vaporetto:* San Tomà.

Santa Maria della Salute ★★   Like the proud landmark it is, La Salute, the pinnacle of the baroque movement in Venice, stands at the mouth of the Grand Canal overlooking Piazzetta San Marco and opening onto Campo della Salute. One of Venice's most historic churches, it was built by Longhena in the 17th century (work began in 1631) as an offering to the Virgin for delivering the city

Tintoretto's paintings adorn the ceiling of San Rocco.

from the plague. Longhena, almost unknown when he got the commission, dedicated half a century to working on this church and died 5 years before the long-lasting job was completed. Surmounted by a great cupola, the octagonal basilica makes for an interesting visit: It houses a small art gallery in its sacristy (tip the custodian), which includes a marriage feast of Cana by Tintoretto, allegorical paintings on the ceiling by Titian, a mounted St. Mark, and poor St. Sebastian with his inevitable arrow.

Campo della Salute, Dorsoduro. ℂ **041-2743911.** Free admission (but offering is expected); sacristy 2€. Mar–Nov daily 9am–noon and 3–6pm (5:30pm Dec–Feb). *Vaporetto:* Salute.

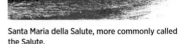

Santa Maria della Salute, more commonly called the Salute.

Santa Maria Gloriosa dei Frari ★★

Known simply as the Frari, this Venetian Gothic church is only a short walk from the San Rocco and is filled with great art. The best work is Titian's **Assumption** over the main altar—a masterpiece of soaring beauty depicting the ascension of the Madonna on a cloud puffed up by floating cherubs. In her robe, but especially in the robe of one of the gaping saints below, "Titian red" dazzles as never before.

On the first altar to the right as you enter is Titian's second major work here: **Madonna Enthroned,** painted for the Pesaro family in 1526. Although it lacks the power and drama of the **Assumption,** it nevertheless is brilliant in its use of color and light effects. But Titian surely would turn redder than his Madonna's robes if he could see the latter-day neoclassical tomb built for him on the opposite wall. The kindest word for it: large.

Facing the tomb is a memorial to Canova, the Italian sculptor who led the revival of classicism. To return to more enduring art, head to the sacristy for a 1488 Giovanni Bellini triptych on wood; the Madonna is cool and serene, one of Bellini's finest portraits of the Virgin. Also, see the almost primitive-looking woodcarving by Donatello of St. John the Baptist.

Campo dei Frari, San Polo. ℂ **041-2750462.** www.basilicadeifrari.it. Admission 3€. Mon–Sat 9am–6pm; Sun 1–6pm. Closed holidays and Sun July–Aug. *Vaporetto:* San Tomà.

Santi Giovanni e Paolo ★★

This great Gothic church (also known as Zanipolo) houses the tombs of many doges. It was built during the 13th and 14th centuries and contains works by many of the most noted Venetian painters. As you enter (right aisle), you'll find a retable by Giovanni Bellini (which includes a St. Sebastian filled with arrows). In the Rosary Chapel are Veronese ceilings depicting New Testament scenes, including *The Assumption of the Madonna.* To the right of the church is one of the world's best-known equestrian statues, that of Bartolomeo Colleoni, sculpted in the 15th century by

Andrea del Verrochio. The bronze has long been acclaimed as his masterpiece, although it was completed by another artist. The horse is far more beautiful than the armored military hero, who looks as if he had just stumbled on a three-headed crocodile.

To the left of the pantheon is the **Scuola di San Marco,** with a stunning Renaissance facade (it's now run as a civic hospital). The church requests that Sunday visits be of a religious nature rather than for sightseeing.

Campo SS. Giovanni e Paolo, Castello 6363. ✆ **041-5235913.** Admission 2.50€. Mon–Sat 9am–6:30pm. *Vaporetto:* Rialto or Fondamenta Nuove.

San Zaccaria ★★   Behind St. Mark's is this Gothic church with a Renaissance facade, filled with works of art, notably Giovanni Bellini's restored *Madonna Enthroned,* painted with saints (second altar to the left). Many have found this to be one of Bellini's finest Madonnas, and it does have beautifully subdued coloring, although it appears rather static. Many worthwhile works lie in the main body of the church, but for a view of even more of them, apply to the sacristan for entrance to the church's museum, housed in an area once reserved exclusively for nuns. Here you'll find works by Tintoretto, Titian, Il Vecchio, Anthony van Dyck, and Bassano. The paintings aren't labeled, but the sacristan will point out the names of the artists. In the Sisters' Choir are five armchairs in which the Venetian doges sat. And if you save the best for last, you can see the faded frescoes of Andrea del Castagno in the shrine honoring San Tarasio.

Campo San Zaccaria, Castello. ✆ **041-5221257.** Admission 1€ to crypt and treasury; church free admission. Mon–Sat 10am–noon; daily 4–6pm. *Vaporetto:* San Zaccaria.

Titian's *Assumption* at the Frari.

The Frari (Santa Maria Gloriosa dei Frari).

The Lido ★★

For centuries, the Lido drew artists and the literati, but they are long gone. Today the resort area is complete with deluxe hotels, a casino, and stratospheric prices.

But don't expect the Lido of days gone by. It is well past its heyday. A chic crowd still checks into the Excelsior Palace and the Hotel Des Bains, but the beach strip is overrun with tourists and opens onto polluted waters. (For swimming, guests use their hotel pools, although they still stroll along the Lido sands and enjoy the views.) Even if you aren't planning to stay in this area, you should come over and explore for an afternoon. There's no denying the appeal of a beach so close to one of the world's most romantic cities, even if it is unfit for swimming. The strips of beachfront in front of the big hotels on the Lido are technically considered private, and the public is discouraged from using the facilities. But because you can use the beachfront on either side of their property, no one seems to really care about shooing nonguests away.

If you don't want to tread on the beachfront property of the rarefied hotels (which have huts lining the beach like those of some tropical paradise), you can try the **Lungomare G. d'Annunzio (Public Bathing Beach)** at the end of the Gran Viale (Piazzale Ettore Sorger), a long stroll from the *vaporetto* stop. You can book cabins (*camerini*) and enjoy the sand. Rates change seasonally.

Located on the Lido is one of the oldest Jewish cemeteries in Europe. Established in 1386, it still has the oldest surviving gravestone, that of Shemuel ben Shimshon, who died in 1389. The **Venice Jewish Cemetery** was abandoned for 200 years and almost completely inaccessible for decades. This once-crumbling cemetery has been restored and is now open to visitors. If you'd like to explore it, contact the Jewish Museum at ✆ **041-715359** or www.museoebraico.it to arrange a visit. Tickets cost 8.50€, and guided tours last about an hour. In winter the cemetery is sometimes closed depending on weather conditions.

Verrochio's statue of Bartolomeo Colleoni, in the Castello.

San Zaccaria, in the Castello.

To reach the Lido, take *vaporetto* no. 1, 6, or 51 (the ride takes about 15 min.). The boat departs from a landing stage near the Doge's Palace.

The Ghetto ★★

The Ghetto of Venice, called the **Ghetto Nuovo,** was instituted in 1516 by the Venetian Republic in the Cannaregio district. It's considered to be the first ghetto in the world and also the best kept. The word *geto* comes from the Venetian dialect and means "foundry" (originally there were two iron foundries here where metals were fused). At one time, Venetian Jews were confined to a walled area and obliged to wear red or yellow marks sewn onto their clothing and distinctive-looking hats. The walls that once enclosed and confined the ghetto were torn down long ago, but much remains of the past.

There are five synagogues in Venice, each built during the 16th century and each representing a radically different aesthetic and the cultural differences among the groups of Jews who built them. The oldest is the **German Synagogue (Sinagoghe Grande Tedesca),** restored after the end of World War II with funds from Germany. Others are the **Spanish Synagogue (Sinagoghe Spagnola),** the oldest continuously functioning synagogue in Europe; the **Italian Synagogue (Sinagoghe Italiana);** the **Levantine-Oriental Synagogue (Sinagoghe Levantina,** also known as the **Turkish Synagogue**); and the **Canton Synagogue (Sinagoghe del Canton).**

The best way to visit the synagogues is to take one of the guided tours departing from the **Museo Comunità Ebraica,** Campo di Ghetto Nuovo 2902B (✆ **041-715359;** www.museoebraico.it). It contains a small but worthy collection of artifacts pertaining to the Jewish community of Venice and costs 8.50€ for adults. From June to September, the museum is open Sunday to Friday 10am to 7pm; hours October to May are Sunday to Friday 10am to 6pm. However, the museum is by no means the focal point of your experience: More worthwhile are the walking tours that begin and end here, costing 8.50€, with free entrance to the museum. The 50-minute tours incorporate a brisk commentary and a stroll through the neighborhood, including visits to the interiors of three of the five synagogues (the ones that you visit depend on various factors). From June to September, the tours depart hourly Sunday to Friday 10:30am to 5:30pm (Oct–May to 4:30pm).

SHOPPING

Venetian glass and lace are known throughout the world. However, selecting quality products in either craft requires a shrewd eye because there's much that's tawdry and shoddily crafted. Some of the glassware hawked isn't worth the cost of shipping it home. Yet other pieces represent some of the world's finest artistic and ornamental glass. Murano is the island famous for its handmade glass. However, you can find little glass-animal souvenirs in shops all over Venice.

For lace, head out to Burano, where the latest of a long line of women put in painstaking hours to produce some of the finest lace in the world.

Shopping Strolls

All the main shopping streets, even the side streets, are touristy and overrun. The greatest concentration of shops is around **Piazza San Marco** and the **Rialto Bridge.** Prices are much higher at San Marco, but the quality of merchandise is also higher. There are two major shopping strolls in Venice.

First, from **Piazza San Marco** you can stroll west toward spacious **Campo Morosini.** You just follow one shop-lined street all the way to its end (although the name will change several times). Begin at Salizzada San Moisè, which becomes Via 22 Marzo and then Calle delle Ostreghe before it opens onto Campo Santa Maria Zobenigo. The street then narrows and changes to Calle Zaguri before widening into Campo San Maurizio, finally becoming Calle Piovan before reaching Campo Morosini. The only deviation from this tour is a detour down Calle Vallaressa, between San Moisè and the Grand Canal, which is one of the major shopping arteries with some of the biggest designer names in the business.

The other great shopping stroll wanders from Piazza San Marco to the Rialto in a succession of streets collectively known as the **Mercerie.** It's virtually impossible to get lost because each street name is preceded by the word *merceria,* such as Merceria dell'Orologio, which begins near the clock tower in Piazza San Marco. Many commercial places, mainly shops, line the Mercerie before it reaches the Rialto, which then explodes into one vast shopping emporium.

Shopping A to Z

ANTIQUES   Antichita Santomanco ★, Corte Contarina, San Marco 1567 (✆ **041-5236643**), is for the well-heeled serious collector. It deals in antique furniture, jewels, silver, prints, and old Murano glass. The outlet also specializes in Russian and English silver work, old prints, period glass and jewelry, and assorted bric-a-brac. Of course, the merchandise is ever changing, but you're likely to pick up some little heirloom item in the midst of the clutter. Many of the items date from the Venetian heyday of the 1600s.

ART   Imagina, Ponte dei Pugni, Dorsoduro (✆ **041-2410625;** www.imagina cafe.it), is the first cafe/gallery to open in the city of Venice. Shaped like a white cube, the building showcases a gallery that stays abreast of what's new and cutting edge in the arts in Venice. The lounge bar changes its personality throughout the day. In the morning it's a place where art patrons drop in for a cappuccino and a brioche, sitting back in designer armchairs and flipping through newspapers and fashion magazines. At lunch the chef prepares tasty panini and fresh, crisp salads. This is the time to check out the latest art exhibitions. The place is also a photography gallery. In the evening the cafe takes on a party atmosphere, as fashionable young Venetians and art lovers turn up to drink chilled prosecco and talk about developing trends in modern art.

BOOKS The most centrally located bookstore is the **Libreria Sansovino,** Bacino Orseolo, San Marco 84 (*€* **041-5222623**), to the north of Piazza San Marco. It carries both hard- and softcover books in English.

BRASS Founded in 1913, **Valese Fonditore ★★**, Calle Fiubera, San Marco 793 (*€* **041-5227282;** www.valese.it), serves as a showcase for one of the most famous of the several foundries with headquarters in Venice. Many of the brass copies of 18th-century chandeliers produced by this company grace fine homes in the United States and become valuable family heirlooms. Some of the most appealing objects are the 50 or 60 replicas of the brass sea horses that grace the sides of many of the gondolas. A pair of medium-size ones, each about .3m (11 in.) tall, begins at 150€.

CARNEVALE MASKS Venetian masks, considered collectors' items, originated during Carnevale, which takes place the week before the beginning of Lent. In the old days there was a good reason to wear masks during the riotous Carnevale—they helped wives and husbands to be unfaithful to one another and priests break their vows of chastity. Things got so out of hand that Carnevale was banned in the late 18th century. But it came back, and the masks went on again.

Making Carnevale masks at Mondonovo.

You can find shops selling masks practically on every corner. As with glass and lace, however, quality varies. Many masks are great artistic expressions, while others are shoddy and cheap. The most sought-after is the *Portafortuna* (luck bringer), with its long nose and birdlike visage. *Orientale* masks evoke the heyday of the Serene Republic and its trade with the Far East. The *Bauta* was worn by men to assert their macho qualities, and the *Neutra* blends the facial characteristics of both sexes. The list of masks and their origins seems endless.

The best place to buy Carnevale masks is **Mondonovo,** Rio Terrà Canal, Dorsoduro 3063 (✆ **041-5287344;** www.mondonovomaschere.it), where talented artisans labor to produce copies of both traditional and more modern masks, each of which is one of a kind and richly nuanced with references to Venetian lore and traditions. Prices range from 40€ for a fairly basic model to 1,830€ for something that you might display on a wall as a piece of art.

FABRICS   Select outlets in Venice sell some of the greatest fabrics in the world. **Norelene,** Calle della Chiesa, Dorsoduro 727 (✆ **041-5237605**), sells lustrous hand-printed silks, velvets, and cottons, plus wall hangings and clothing.

Venetia Studium is at Calle Larga XXII Marco, San Marzo 2403 (✆ **041-5229281;** www.venetiastudium.com). For years, Lino Lando worked to crack the secret of fabled designer Mariano Fortuny's plissé (finely pleated silk). Eventually he found the secret. The result can now be yours in his selection of silk accessories, scarves, Delphos gowns, and even silk lamps.

Gaggio Arredamento Emma, San Marco, San Stefano 3441–3451 (✆ **041-5228574**), offers unique items, the most stunning of which are velvets and artistic fabrics with filigree, all inspired by the deep colors and designs of Fortuny. The fabrics are very Venetian and very decadent. You can purchase these fabrics by the meter, or they can be fashioned into clothing, shawls, cushions, or whatever.

Yet another Fortuny-inspired outlet is **Vittorio Trois,** Campo San Maurizio, San Marco 2666 (✆ **041-5222905**). Trois was selected to receive a priceless legacy. The great Mariano Fortuny revealed his exquisite printing techniques to a friend of Trois, the late Contessa Gozzi, and she passed them on to Trois, who made a business of them. Today you can buy the same Fortuny patterns that stunned your grandparents on their visit to Venice decades ago. The radiant designs look like brocade and are sold by the yard.

FASHION   **La Coupole,** Calle Larga XXII Marzo, San Marco 2255 (✆ **041-5231273**), is a large outlet for a stylish assortment of designers from throughout Europe.

Silks for sale at Venetia Studium.

The most visible of several members of a citywide chain, it sells women's clothing from top designers.

By accident we stumbled on **Caberlotto,** San Salvador, San Marco 5114 (ⓒ **041-5229242;** www.caberfurs.com), with a stunning collection of classic apparel for both women and men, all in jewel-like colors. Head here to see the rich collection of Loro Piana shawls, cashmere sweaters, scarves, and other apparel.

GIFTS The **Bac Art Studio,** San Vio, Dorsoduro 862 (ⓒ **041-2412716;** www.bacart.com), sells paper goods, but it's mainly a graphics gallery, noted for its selection of engravings, posters, and lithographs of Venice at Carnevale time. For the most part, items are reasonably priced, and it's clear that a great deal of care has gone into the choice of merchandise.

GLASS Venice is crammed with glass shops: It's estimated that there are at least 1,000 in San Marco alone. Unless you go to a top-quality dealer, you'll find that most stores sell both shoddy and high-quality glassware, and often only the most trained eye can tell the difference. A lot of "Venetian glass" isn't from Venice at all, but from the Czech Republic. (Of course, the Czech Republic has some of the finest glassmakers in Europe, so that might not be bad either.) Buying glass boils down to this: If you like an item, buy it. It might not be high quality, but high quality can cost thousands.

The art glass sold by **Venini ★★★**, Piazzetta Leoncini, San Marco 314 (ⓒ **041-5224045;** www.venini.com), has caught the attention of collectors from all over the world. Many of its pieces, including anything-but-ordinary lamps, bottles, and vases, are works of art representing the best of Venetian craftsmanship. Its best-known glass has a distinctive swirl pattern in several colors, called a *venature.* This shop is known for the refined quality of its glass, some of which appears almost transparent. Much of it is very fragile, but the shop learned long ago how to ship it anywhere safely. To visit the furnace, call ⓒ **041-2737211.**

L'Isola, Campo San Moisè, San Marco 1468 (ⓒ **041-5231973;** www.lisola.com), is the shop of Carlo Moretti, one of the world's best-known contemporary artisans working in glass. You'll find all his signature designs in decanters, glasses, vases, bowls, and paperweights.

Galleria Marina Barovier ★★, Salizzada San Samuele, San Marco 3216 (ⓒ **041-5236748;** www.barovier.it), sells some of the most creative modern glass sculptures in Italy. Since it was opened in the early 1980s by its founder, Marina Barovier, in the suburb of Mestre, it has grown until it's now viewed as one of the most glamorous art galleries in the world of glass-making. Especially sought after are sculptures by master glassmakers Luco Tagliapietra and American artist Dale Chihuly, whose chandeliers represent amusing or dramatic departures from traditional Venetian forms. Anything sold can be shipped.

At **Vetri d'Arte,** Piazza San Marco 140 (ⓒ **041-5200205**), you can find moderately priced glass jewelry for souvenirs and gifts, as well as a selection of pricier crystal jewelry and porcelain dolls.

Luco Tagliapietra, one of the masters of Venetian glass blowing, has his works distributed by **Domus Vetri d'Arte,** Fondamenta Vetrai 82, Murano (ⓒ **041-739215**). This artisan, with his cutting-edge sense of design, began blowing glass at age 12 and by age 21 was recognized as a master—some even called him a genius in glass. Unlike some Venetian glassmakers, inspired by ancient Greece and Rome, Tagliapietra roams the world for inspiration, finding it even in some Native American cultures.

JEWELRY Since 1846, **Missiaglia** ★★★ Piazza San Marco, San Marco 125 (*©* **041-5224464**), has been the supplier to savvy shoppers from around the world seeking the best jewelry. Go here for a classic piece, such as handcrafted jewelry with a Venetian twist—everything from a gold gondolier oar pin to a diamond-studded fan brooch with an ebony Carnevale mask. The specialty is precious and semiprecious gemstones set in white or yellow gold.

Art glass for sale at Venini.

For antique jewelry, there's no shop finer than **Codognato,** Calle Ascensione, San Marco 1295 (*©* **041-5225042;** www.attiliocodognato. it). Some of the great heirloom jewelry of Europe is sent here when estates are settled.

LACE Most lace vendors center on Piazza San Marco. Although the price of handmade Venetian lace is high, it's still reasonable considering the painstaking work that goes into the real thing. Authentic hand-tatted lace is cheaper in Venice than it is elsewhere, and it's even cheaper on the island of Burano, where stores don't have to pay high-priced Venetian rents. But no one ever called handmade Burano lace a bargain, even on its home turf.

Regardless of where you buy lace, however, make sure it's the real thing. The lace shops are like the glassware outlets, selling the whole gamut from the shoddy to the exquisite. Much of it—even on Burano—is shoddy, and a lot of it isn't handmade in Venice but machine-made in Taiwan. Shop carefully and know what you're buying. If a price seems too good to be true, it probably is.

LEATHER **Bottega Veneta,** Calle Vallaresso, San Marco 1337 (*©* **041-5202816;** www.bottegaveneta.com), is primarily known for its woven leather bags. They're sold elsewhere, but the prices are said to be less at the company's flagship outlet in Venice. The shop also sells women's shoes, suitcases, wallets, belts, and accessories.

Furla, Mercerie del Capitello, San Marco 4954 (*©* **041-5230611;** www.furla.com), is a specialist in women's leather bags, but sells belts and gloves as well. Many of the bags are stamped with molds, creating alligator- and lizardlike textures. You'll also find costume jewelry, silk scarves, briefcases, and wallets.

MARKETS If you're looking for some bargain-basement buys, head to one of the shops lining the **Rialto Bridge.** The shops there branch out to encompass fruit and vegetable markets as well. The Rialto isn't the Ponte Vecchio in Florence, but for what it offers it isn't bad, particularly if your euros are running short. You'll find a wide assortment of merchandise, from angora sweaters to leather gloves. The quality is likely to vary, so plunge in with your eyes open.

PAPER   Florence is the major center in Italy for artistic paper, especially marbleized paper. However, craftsmen in Venice still make marble paper by hand, sheet by sheet. The technique offers unlimited decorative possibilities and the widest range of colors. Each sheet of handmade paper is one of a kind.

Il Papiro ★★, Calle del Piovan, San Marco 2764 (✆ **041-5223055;** www.ilpapirofirenze.it), carries absolutely gorgeous stationery, plus photo albums, address books, picture frames, diaries, and boxes covered in artfully printed paper. It is also the best outlet for purchasing leather-bound blank and lined journals, a unique gift.

Stylish **Piazzesi** ★★★, Campiello della Feltrina, San Marco 2511 (✆ **041-5221202;** www.legatoriapiazzesi.it), claims to be Italy's oldest purveyor of writing paper (opened 1900). Some of its elegant lines of stationery require as many as 13 artisans to produce. Most of the production is hand blocked, marbleized, stenciled, or accented with dyes that are blown onto each of the sheets with a breath-operated tube. If you want impressive paper for your social thank-you notes or wedding invitations, Piazzesi will undoubtedly have it in stock. Also look for papier-mâché masks and commedia dell'arte–style statues representing age-old professions such as architects, carpenters, doctors, glassmakers, church officials, and notaries. Seeking something more modern? Consider any of the whimsically decorated containers for CDs and computer disks.

Another elegant choice for marble paper and upscale stationary is **Il Mercante Veneziano,** Castello 2139 (✆ **041-5205990**). It's the domain of Roberto Bizuitti, an artist whose reproductions of old maps, diaries, appointment books, and household articles evoke the feel, the look, and the aura of their original 18th-century antecedents. Look for inventories of playing cards, chessboards, and the most opulent-looking photo albums in Venice.

WOOD SCULPTURES   A unique outlet in Venice is **Livio de Marchi,** San Samuele, San Marco 3157 (✆ **041-5285694;** www.liviodemarchi.com). De Marchi and his staff can take almost any item, from cowboy boots to a Vespa to a woman's handbag, and sculpt it in wood in hyperreal detail. Even if you don't buy anything, just stop in to take a look at these stunning items sculpted from wood.

VENICE AFTER DARK

For such a fabled city, Venice's nightlife is pretty meager. Who wants to hit the nightclubs when strolling the city is more interesting than any spectacle staged inside? Ducking into a cafe or bar for a brief interlude, however, is a good way to break up your walk. Although Venice offers gambling and a few other diversions, it is pretty much an early-to-bed town. Most restaurants close at midnight.

The best guide to what's happening is **"Un Ospite di Venezia,"** a free pamphlet (part in English, part in Italian) distributed by the tourist office every 15 days. It lists any music and opera or theatrical presentation, along with art exhibits and local special events.

The interior of Teatro La Fenice.

At least 10 of Venice's historic churches host **concerts,** with a constantly changing schedule. These include the Chiesa di Vivaldi, the Chiesa della Pietà, and the Chiesa Santa Maria Formosa. Many concerts are free; others charge an admission that rarely exceeds 30€. For information about what's going on, call © **041-5208722,** or log on to www.unospitedivenezia.it.

The Performing Arts

Teatro La Fenice Campo San Fantin, San Marco 1965 ★★★ (© **041-786511;** www.teatrolafenice.it), reopened in 2004 after renovations in the wake of a 1996 fire. The Teatro has a total of 1,076 seats, and the stage curtain was donated by Italian fashion designer Laura Biagiotti. Tickets and subscriptions can be purchased in person from the HelloVenezia box office at Piazzale Roma and the Teatro La Fenice box office in Campo San Fantin, San Marco 1965. The box office in Piazzale Roma is open daily 6:30am to 8pm. The theater box office in Campo San Fantin is open daily 10am to 6pm.

The **Teatro Goldoni** ★, Calle Goldoni, near Campo San Luca, San Marco 4650B (© **041-2402011;** www.teatrostabileveneto.it), honors Carlo Goldoni (1707–93), the most prolific and one of the best of the Italian playwrights. The theater presents a changing repertoire of productions, often plays in Italian but musical presentations as well. The box office is open Monday to Saturday 10am to 3pm and 6:30pm. During performance days it is also open on Saturday 10am to 1pm and 3 to 6:30pm. Tickets cost 7€ to 27€.

Cafes

All the cafes on Piazza San Marco offer a simply magical setting, several with full orchestras playing in the background. But you'll pay shockingly high prices (plus a hefty music charge) to enjoy a drink or a snack while you soak in the atmosphere. Prepare yourself for it, and splurge on a beer, a cappuccino, or an ice cream, anyway. It'll be the most memorable 15€ to 20€ (that's *per person*) that you'll drop on your trip.

Venice's most famous spot is **Caffè Florian ★★★**, Piazza San Marco, San Marco 56–59 (*(C)* **041-5205641;** www.caffeflorian.com), built in 1720 and elaborately decorated with red banquettes, elaborate murals under glass, and Art Nouveau lighting. The Florian has hosted everyone from Casanova to Lord Byron and Goethe. Light lunch is served noon to 3pm, and an English tea is served 3 to 6pm, when you can select from a choice of pastries, ice creams, and cakes. It's open Thursday to Tuesday 10am to 11pm. It's closed the week before Christmas and January 7 to January 13.

Previously recommended as a restaurant (p. 459), **Quadri ★★★**, Piazza San Marco, San Marco 120–124 (*(C)* **041-5289299;** www.quadrivenice.com), stands on the opposite side of the square from Florian's and is as elegantly decorated in antique style. It should be: It was founded in 1638. Wagner used to drop in for a drink when he was working on *Tristan und Isolde*. The bar was a favorite with the Austrians during their long-ago occupation. From April to October, it's open daily 9am to 11:30pm; off-season hours are Tuesday to Sunday 9am to 11:30pm (it's closed the first week of Dec and the first week of Jan).

The 18th-century **Gran Caffè Lavena,** Piazza San Marco, San Marco 133–134 (*(C)* **041-5224070;** www.lavena.it), is a popular but intimate cafe under the piazza's arcades. During his stay in Venice, Richard Wagner was a frequent customer; he composed some of his greatest operas here. This cafe has one of the most beautifully ornate glass chandeliers in town. The best tables are near the plate-glass window in front, although there's plenty of room at the stand-up bar as well. It's open daily 9:30am to 12:30am, until 11pm in winter (closed Jan and Tues in winter).

Although **Gran Caffè Chioggia,** Piazza San Marco, San Marco 8–12 (*(C)* **041-5285011**), isn't the only cafe whose entrance opens onto the piazza, it's the only one with a view of the Venetian lagoon (off to one side). Starting around 8am and continuing, with reasonable breaks, until 1:30am, music here might

The Art Nouveau entrance to Teatro Goldoni.

Musicians play at Quadri on Piazza San Marco.

begin with the kind of piano music you'd expect in a bar and end with a jazz trio. Don't expect a full-fledged restaurant: The only food served is light platters and sandwiches. Drinks include whiskey with soda, beer, and endless cups of coffee.

The hippest cafe in Venice today is funky little **Cip's ★**, on Isola della Giudecca within the Cipriani Hotel (© **041-5207744**; www.hotelcipriani.it). Pronounced *chips* (as in potato), this cafe with its summer terrace frames one of the grandest views of Piazza San Marco. If you arrive between May and August, ask for a Bellini, made from prosecco and white-peach purée. You can also order the best bitter chocolate gelato in Venice here. Cip's also serves terrific international and Venetian dishes (p. 470). It closes from November 8 to March 31. To reach the place, take the *vaporetto* to Zittelle.

Bars & Pubs

Want more in the way of nightlife? All right, but be warned: The Venetian bar owners might sock it to you when they present the bill.

In addition to the specific recommendations below, you might **barhop around San Francesco Vigna,** where there is a plethora of local watering holes.

The most famous of all the watering holes of Ernest Hemingway is **Harry's Bar,** Calle Vallaresso, San Marco 1323 (© **041-5285777**; www.cipriani.com). Harry's is known for inventing its own drinks and exporting them around the world, and it's said that carpaccio, the delicate raw-beef dish, was invented here. Fans say that Harry's makes the best Bellini in the world, although many old-time visitors still prefer a vodka martini. (Even Hemingway ordered a Bellini once, although he later called it a drink for sissies, suggesting that it might be ideal for Fitzgerald.) Harry's Bar is now found around the world, but this is the original (the others are unauthorized knockoffs). Celebrities frequent the place during the various film and art festivals. From April to October, Harry's is open daily 10:30am to 11pm.

Bar Ducale, Calle delle Ostreghe, San Marco 2354 (© **041-5210002**), occupies a tiny corner of a building near a bridge over a narrow canal. Customers stand at the zinc bar facing the carved 19th-century Gothic-reproduction shelves.

Mimosas are the specialty, but sandwiches are also offered. It's ideal for an early evening cocktail as you stroll about. Bar Ducale is open daily 7:30am to 9pm.

Close to the Rialto Bridge is **Devil's Forest,** Calle Stagneri, San Marco 5185 (*C* **041-5200623;** www.devilsforest.com), an authentic English pub where you'll find a comfortable balance between the English- and Italian-speaking worlds. A comforting roster of beers and ales is on tap (Guinness, Harp, Kilkenny, and a line of German beers). It's open daily 11am to midnight.

A rival of Devil's Forest, **Olandese Volante (the Flying Dutchman),** Campo San Lio, Castello 5658 (*C* **041-5289349**), is another English-style pub with lots of wood paneling. A young, heavy-drinking crowd patronizes this place, mainly for beer, although fast food is also served.

Do Leoni (p. 464) is in the Londra Palace hotel, Riva degli Schiavoni, Castello 4171 (*C* **041-5200533**). While sipping your cocktail, you'll enjoy a view of a 19th-century bronze statue, the lagoon, and the foot traffic along the Grand Canal. A piano player entertains Wednesday to Monday. Do Leoni is open daily 12:30 to 2:30pm and 7:30 to 10:30pm (bar 10:30am–12:30am).

Wine Bars

The temperamental Francesco (when he's in a good mood) feeds his faithful habitués at **La Cantina,** Campo San Felice, Cannaregio 3689 (*C* **041-5228258**). Patrons fill up the tables to sample slices of raw fish from the Adriatic, some of the best cured salami in Venice, and tasty cheeses. His *crostini*—especially tongue piled high under fresh horseradish shavings—wins deserved raves from food critics. Salted beef with smoked ricotta and chopped pickle is another local favorite.

FUELED BY *cicchetti*

Madrid has its tasca hopping, London has its pub-crawling, and Venice has its cantina or *cicchetti* crawl. Venetians thrive on small glasses of wine and bar snacks consumed in these little wine bars.

Drop in to **Enoteca Mascareta,** Castello, Calle Lunga Santa Maria Formosa 5183 (*C* **041-5230744**), for its wines but also its superb meats and cheese offered with crusty, freshly baked bread. In a setting of copper kettles and wooden kegs, **Cantina do Mori,** San Polo, Calle del Do Mori 429 (*C* **041-5225401**), serves some of the best little sandwiches in Venice. The cantina also prepares delectable tapas, some made from oxtail and others made from cured bacon called *speck*.

The Lilliputian **Osteria da Pinto,** San Polo, Campo de le Becarie 367

(*C* **041-5224599**), is known for preparing the best *baccalà mantecato* in the city. This is a creamy paste of salt cod beaten with olive oil to form a paste, which is then spread across *crostini*.

Finally, the best for last: **Vecio Fritolin,** Santa Croce, Calle della Regina 2262 (*C* **041-5222881;** www.veciofritolin.it), one of the last remaining *fritolin* (fry shops) that used to pepper Venice. A small blonde woman from northern Italy has brought new life to this *fritolin,* and her *fritto misto,* or mixed fried seafood, is the best that you are likely to encounter on a trip to Venice.

Mascareta, Calle Lunga Santa Maria Formosa, Castello 5183 (*©* **041-5230744**), is a showcase for a rich assortment of Italian wines. Especially prevalent are reds and whites from the Veneto, Sicily, Pulia, and Tuscany, beginning at 3€ per glass. There's room for only about 20 people at the cramped tables in this antique building. If you're hungry, you can order simple, cheap platters of cold food. It's open Friday to Tuesday 7pm to 2am.

At **Vino Vino,** Ponte della Veste, San Marco 2007A (*©* **041-2417688**), you can choose from more than 350 Italian and imported wines (available by the glass or by bottle). This place is loved by everyone from snobs to young people to almost-broke tourists. It offers wines by the bottle or the glass, including Italian grappas. Popular and supercheap Venetian dishes are served, including pastas, beans, *baccalà* (codfish), and polenta, including quail with polenta, rabbit baked with thyme, and filet of sea bass with a pink-peppercorn sauce and fresh dill. Main dishes range from 10€ to 22€. The two rooms are always jammed like a *vaporetto* in rush hour, and there's takeout service if you can't find a place. It's open daily 11:30am to 11:30pm.

Dining & Dancing

Near the Accademia, **Il Piccolo Mondo,** Calle Contarini Corfu, Dorsoduro 1056A (*©* **041-5200371;** www.piccolomondo.biz), is open during the day but comes alive with dance music at night. The crowd is often young. It's open daily 11pm to 4am, but the action actually doesn't begin until after midnight. Cover, including the first drink, is 10€ Thursday and Friday, and 15€ Saturday.

Casinos

Venice is home to two casinos. Regardless of where you happen to drop your euros, know that shorts and sneakers are forbidden. You must be at least 18 to enter. Both casinos offer slot machines, but more interesting are the roulette wheels, where minimum bets are 5€ and maximum wagers 200€.

Vendramin Calergi Palace ★★, Cannaregio 2040–30121 Venezia (*©* **041-5297111;** www.casinovenezia. it), is Italy's most elegant casino. A frequent visitor, Gabriele D'Annunzio, called it "a sculpted cloud resting on water." Historically, the Renaissance *palazzo* was once a home to the doges and later a town mansion where Richard Wagner died in 1883. Opening onto the Grand Canal, the casino offers French roulette, blackjack, Caribbean poker, and chemin de fer. Gala dinners and even classical music concerts are occasionally offered in the garden in summer.

The water entrance to Vendramin-Calergi Palace.

Men must wear a jacket (available for rent on-site). Entrance is 10€. From June 16 to August 31 the opening hours are: Sunday to Thursday 4pm to 2:30am, Friday and Saturday 4pm to 3am. A free shuttle from Piazzale Roma runs every 10 minutes during open hours.

Ca'Noghera ★, Via Paliaga 4–8 (© **041-2695888;** www.casinovenezia.it), is the first American-style casino to open in the north of Italy, lying on the mainland opposite the Marco Polo airport. The Vendramin-Calergi is a glorious antique; in contrast, C'Noghera is as modern as the 21st century. Expect the standard games of chance such as roulette, blackjack, and Caribbean-style poker, but also the latest electronic games. The Theater Arena hosts concerts, shows, and fashionable catwalks, and a restaurant serves first-class international specialties. Entrance is 10€. From June 16 to August 31 the opening hours are: Sunday to Thursday 4pm to 2:45am, Friday and Saturday 4pm to 3:45am. A free shuttle service runs from the Piazzale Roma during casino hours. Dress here is informal.

MURANO, BURANO & TORCELLO

If you take a boat from the Grand Canal near San Marco to Murano, Burano, and Torcello, it can take hours. But in about 20 minutes or so, you can head north from Piazza San Marco, coming to the Campo di Santa Maria Formosa and continuing north until you reach the *vaporetto* stop at Fondamenta Nuove. Here you can catch the *vaporetto* to Murano or the other islands and cut down traveling time considerably. You can spend more time seeing the sights instead of taking a long boat trip with seemingly endless stops.

Murano ★★

For centuries, glass blowers on the island of Murano have turned out those fantastic chandeliers that Victorian ladies used to prize so highly. They also produce heavily ornamented glasses so ruby red or so indigo blue that you can't tell whether you're drinking blackberry juice or pure-grain alcohol. Happily, the glass blowers are still plying their trade, although increasing competition (notably from Sweden) has compelled a greater degree of sophistication in design.

Murano remains the chief expedition from Venice, but it's not the most beautiful nearby island. (Burano and Torcello are far more attractive.)

You can combine a tour of Murano with a trip along the lagoon. To reach Murano, take **vaporetto no. 5 or 41** at Riva degli Schiavoni, a short walk from Piazzetta San Marco. The boat docks at the landing platform at Murano where the first furnace awaits conveniently. It's best to go Monday to Friday 10am to noon if you want to see some glass-blowing action.

TOURING THE GLASS FACTORIES & OTHER SIGHTS

As you stroll through Murano, you'll find that the factory owners are only too glad to let you come in and see their age-old crafts. While browsing the showrooms, you'll need stiff resistance to keep the salespeople at bay. Bargaining is expected. Don't—repeat, *don't*—pay the marked price on any item. That's merely the figure at which to open negotiations.

However, the prices of made-on-the-spot souvenirs aren't negotiable. For example, you might want to buy a horse streaked with blue. The artisan takes a piece of incandescent glass, huffs, puffs, rolls it, shapes it, snips it, and behold—he has shaped a horse. The showrooms of Murano also contain a fine assortment of Venetian crystal beads, available in every hue. You might find some of the best work to be the experiments of apprentices.

While on the island, you can visit the Renaissance *palazzo* housing the **Museo del Vetro di Murano,** Fondamenta Giustinian 8 (☏ **041-739586;** www.musei civiciveneziani.it), which contains a spectacular collection of Venetian glass. From April to October, it's open Thursday to Tuesday from 10am to 6pm (to 5pm Nov–Mar). Admission is 6.50€. It is closed January 1, May 1, and December 25.

If you're looking for something different, head to **San Pietro Martire,** Fondamente Vetrai (☏ **041-739704**), which dates from the 1300s but was rebuilt in 1511 and is richly decorated with paintings by Tintoretto and Veronese. Its proud possession is a *Madonna and Child Enthroned,* by Giovanni Bellini, plus two superb altarpieces by the same master. The church lies right before the junction with Murano's Grand Canal, about 225m (750 ft.) from the *vaporetto* landing stage. It's open daily 9am to noon and 3 to 6pm; it's closed for Mass on Sunday morning.

Even more notable is **Santa Maria e Donato,** Campo San Donato (☏ **041-739056**), open Monday through Saturday from 9am to noon and 3:30 to 7pm, with time variations for Sunday Mass. Dating from the 7th century but reconstructed in the 1100s, this building is a stellar example of Venetian Byzantine style, despite its 19th-century restoration. The interior is known for its mosaic floor (a parade of peacocks and eagles, as well as other creatures) and a 15th-century ship's keel ceiling. Over the apse is an outstanding mosaic of the Virgin against a gold background from the early 1200s.

WHERE TO STAY

Locanda Conterie ★ 🎁   At long last there is a place to stay on the glass-blowing island of Murano. Its obvious appeal is to devotee of Murano glass, but other visitors seeking a retreat from the tourist hordes of Venice will find it an oasis. This little hotel, created by a family of glassmakers, is a restored villa located near the Museo del Vetro (glass museum). All midsize bedrooms are furnished with tasteful pieces, more minimalist than most of the Venetian baroque on "mainland" Venice. Each room comes with a simple tiled bathroom with shower.

Calle Conterie 21, 30141 Venezia. ☏ **041-5275003.** Fax 041-5274245. www.locandaconterie. com. 26 units. 68€–180€ double; 115€–200€ triple; 130€–230€ quad. Rates include buffet breakfast. MC, V. *In room:* A/C, Wi-Fi (5€ per hr.).

WHERE TO DINE

Ai Vetrai VENETIAN   Ai Vetrai entertains and nourishes its guests in a large room not far from the Canale dei Vetrai. If you're looking for fish prepared in the local style, with the widest selection on Murano, this is it. Most varieties of

Street painters capture the colors on Burano.

crustaceans and fish are available on the spot. However, if you phone ahead and order food for a large party, as the Venetians sometimes do, the owners will prepare what they call "a noble fish." You might begin with spaghetti in green clam sauce and follow with *griglia misto di pesce*, a dish that combines all the seafood of the Adriatic, or other types of grilled or baked fish with vegetables.

Fondamenta Manin 29. © **041-739293.** Reservations recommended. Main courses 10€–18€. AE, DC, MC, V. Daily 9am–4pm; Fri-Sun 6–10:30pm. Closed Jan 10–31. *Vaporetto:* 41.

Burano ★★

Burano became world famous as a center of lace making, a craft that reached its pinnacle in the 18th century. The visitor who can spare a morning to visit this island will be rewarded with a charming fishing village far removed in spirit from the grandeur of Venice but only half an hour away by ferry. **Boats** leave from Fondamenta Nuove, overlooking the Venetian graveyard (which is well worth the trip all on its own). To reach Fondamenta Nuove, take *vaporetto* **no. 52** from Riva degli Schiavoni. To reach Burano from Fondamenta Nuove take vaporetto LN.

EXPLORING THE ISLAND

Once at Burano, you'll discover that the houses of the islanders come in varied colors: sienna, robin's egg or cobalt blue, barn red, butterscotch, and grass green.

Check out the **Scuola di Merletti di Burano,** Piazza Galuppi 187 (© **041-730034;** www.merlettoitaliano.com), in the center of the village at Piazza Baldassare Galuppi. From November to March, the museum is open Wednesday to Monday 10am to 4pm (to 5pm Apr–Oct). Admission is 4€ adults, 2.50€ seniors and children. The Burano School of Lace was founded in 1872 as part of a movement aimed at restoring the age-old craft that had earlier declined, giving way to such lace-making centers as Chantilly and Bruges. On the second floor you can see the lace makers, mostly young women, at their painstaking work, and you can purchase hand-embroidered or handmade lace items.

After visiting the lace school, walk across the square to the **Duomo** and its leaning **campanile** (inside, look for the *Crucifixion,* by Tiepolo). See it while you can, because the bell tower is leaning so precariously that it looks as if it might topple at any moment.

WHERE TO DINE

Osteria ai Pescatori SEAFOOD   This is your finest choice on Burano. This restaurant opened 200 years ago in a building that was antique even then. Today, Paolo Torcellan and his wife serve a cuisine prepared with gusto. The place has gained a reputation as the preserver of a type of simple restaurant unique to Burano. Patrons often take the *vaporetto* from other sections of Venice (the restaurant lies close to the boat landing) to eat at the plain wooden tables set up indoors or on the small square in front. Specialties feature all the staples of the Venetian seaside diet, such as fish soup, *risotto di pesce,* pasta seafarer style, *tagliolini* in squid ink, and a wide range of crustaceans, plus grilled, fried, and baked fish. Dishes prepared with local game are also available, but you must request them well in advance. Your meal might include a bottle of fruity wine from the region. **Warning:** No one ever won any congeniality contests around here.

Piazza Baldassare Galuppi 371. ℂ **041-730650.** Reservations recommended. Main courses 7€–25€. DC, MC, V. Wed–Mon noon–3pm and 6–9:30pm. Closed Jan. *Vaporetto:* LN.

Torcello ★★

Of all the islands of the lagoon, Torcello, the so-called Mother of Venice, offers the most charm. If Burano is behind the times, Torcello is positively antediluvian. You can stroll across a grassy meadow, traverse an ancient stone bridge, and step back into that time when the Venetians first fled from invading barbarians to create a city of Neptune in the lagoon.

To reach Torcello, take ***vaporetto* LN** from Fondamenta Nuove. Fondamenta Nuove is in the Cannaregio district of Venice, it is not on Murano. The trip from Fondamenta Nuove to Torcello takes 1 hour.

Warning: If you go to Torcello on your own, don't listen to the gondoliers who hover at the ferry quay. They'll tell you that the cathedral and the locanda are miles away. Actually, they're both reached after a leisurely 12- to 15-minute stroll along the canal.

EXPLORING THE ISLAND

Torcello has two major attractions: a church with Byzantine mosaics good enough to make Empress Theodora at Ravenna turn as purple with envy as her robe, and a locanda that converts day-trippers into inebriated angels of praise (see "Where to Dine," below). First the spiritual nourishment, then the alcoholic sustenance.

Cattedrale di Torcello, also called **Santa Maria Assunta Isola di Torcello** ★ (ℂ **041-2960630**), was founded in A.D. 639 and subsequently rebuilt. It stands in a lonely grassy meadow beside an 11th-century campanile. The attractions here are its **Byzantine mosaics ★★**. Clutching her child, the weeping Madonna in the apse is a magnificent sight, and on the opposite wall is a powerful *Last Judgment.* Byzantine artisans, it seems, were at their best in portraying hell and damnation. In their *Inferno,* they've re-created a virtual human stew with the fires stirred by wicked demons. Reptiles slide in and out of the skulls of cannibalized sinners. The church is open daily: March to October 10:30am to 6pm (to 5pm Nov–Feb). Admission is 4€.

WHERE TO DINE

Locanda Cipriani ★★ VENETIAN   This place is operated by the same folks behind the Hotel Cipriani and Harry's Bar (actually, by the very cosmopolitan Bonifacio Brass, nephew of Harry Cipriani). This artfully simple locanda is deliberately rustic, light-years removed from the family's grander venues. Menu items are uncompromisingly classic, with deep roots in family tradition. A good example is *filetto di San Pietro alla Carlina* (filet of John Dory in the style of Carla, a late and much-revered matriarch, who made the dish for decades using tomatoes and capers). Also look for carpaccio Cipriani, *risotto alla Torcellana* (with vegetables and herbs from the family's garden), fish soup, *tagliolini verdi gratinati,* and a roster of veal, liver, fish, and beef dishes.

For years the Locanda's six bedrooms have attracted those seeking an exclusive, remote retreat in an authentic Venetian inn unlike any other in the city. The price is 180€ per person with half board. Bedrooms are air-conditioned with a phone, hair dryer, minibar, and safe.

Piazza San Fosca 29, Isola di Torcello. ℂ **041-730150.** www.locandacipriani.com. Reservations recommended. Main courses 24€–34€. AE, DC, MC, V. Wed–Mon noon–3pm; Fri–Sat 7–9:30pm. Closed Jan–Feb 5. *Vaporetto:* LN.

9

VENICE

Murano, Burano & Torcello

THE VENETO & THE DOLOMITES

10

Venice doesn't have a monopoly on art or architectural treasures. Of the cities of interest that you can easily reach from Venice, in the area known as the Veneto, three cities tower above the rest: **Verona,** home of the eternal lovers Romeo and Juliet; **Padua,** the city of Mantegna, with frescoes by Giotto; and **Vicenza,** the city of Palladio, with streets of Renaissance *palazzi* and hills studded with villas.

In order of interest, we'd rank the three in that order. Outside of Venice, Verona is the most beautiful city in the region for wandering. Padua's many art treasures, including Giotto frescoes, give it a nod over Vicenza, which lures those who are mainly interested in touring Palladio's villas. If time remains, you can also explore the **Riviera del Brenta,** with its Venetian *palazzi,* and such historic old cities as **Treviso** and **Bassano del Grappa.**

If you have even more time, you can venture farther afield to the limestone **Dolomites (Dolomiti),** one of Europe's greatest natural attractions. Some of these peaks in the northeastern Italian Alps soar to 3,200m (10,500 ft.). The Dolomiti are a year-round destination, with two high seasons: midsummer, when the hiking is great, and winter, when the skiers slide in. In places, the Dolomiti form fantastic shapes, combining to create a primordial landscape, with mountain chains resembling the teeth of a giant dragon. Clefts descend precipitously along jagged rocky walls; at other points a vast, flat tableland, spared nature's fury, emerges.

Travelers with an extra day or so to spare might first want to postpone their Dolomite adventure for a detour to **Trieste,** the unofficial capital of **Friuli–Venezia Giulia.** It was Venice's main rival in the Adriatic from the 9th century to the 15th century. Even though Trieste doesn't boast Venice's charm, it is still one of Italy's most interesting ports, with Habsburg monuments at its core and the world's largest accessible cave on its outskirts.

THE RIVIERA DEL BRENTA ★★

The **Brenta Canal,** running from Fusina to Padua, functioned as a mainland extension of Venice during the Renaissance, when wealthy merchants began using the area as a retreat from the city's summer heat. Dubbed the Riviera del Brenta, the 17km (11-mile) stretch along the banks of the canal from Malcontenta to Stra is renowned for its gracious villas, 44 of which are still visible. Meticulous readers of Shakespeare will remember that in *The Merchant of Venice,* Portia's home is a villa at Belmont along the Brenta.

The region's primary architect was **Andrea di Pietro,** known as **Palladio** (1508–80), who designed 19 of the villas. Inspired by ancient Roman architecture, Palladio's singular design—square, perfectly proportioned, functionally elegant—became the standard by which villas were judged. His designs are familiar to Americans as the basis for most state capitols and for Jefferson's Monticello.

PREVIOUS PAGE: **View of the Dolomites.**

Essentials

GETTING THERE   You can tour the Brenta Riviera by **buses** leaving from Venice headed for Padua. The buses, operated by the **ACTV** line (✆ **041-2424;** www.actv.it), depart from the Venetian company's ticket office in Piazzale Roma daily every 15 to 30 minutes starting at 6:10am. A one-way ticket to Villa Foscari is 5€ and a one-way fare to the Villa Pisani is 5.20€.

By **car,** note that all villas open to the public are on the north bank of the canal along S11 headed west out of Venice toward Padua. At the APT in Venice, you can pick up the guide *Riviera del Brenta Venezia,* offering information on the villas and a map of their locations between Malcontenta and Stra.

VISITOR INFORMATION   Contact the **APT tourist office** of Villa Widmann, Via Nazionale 420, Mira (✆ **041-424973**). From May to September, it's open Tuesday to Sunday 10am to 6pm; April and October Tuesday to Sunday 10am to 5pm; and November to March only Saturday and Sunday 10am to 5pm.

Touring the Villas

The villa closest to Venice that's open for tours is the **Villa Foscari (Villa La Malcontenta)** ★, Via dei Turisti 9, Malcontenta (✆ **041-5470012** or 041-5203966), www.lamalcontenta.com, on Rte. S11 about 4km (2½ miles) west of where the canal empties into the Venetian Lagoon. It was constructed by Palladio for the Foscari family in 1560. A Foscari wife was exiled here for some alleged misdeed, and the unhappiness surrounding the incident gave the name Malcontenta ("unhappy one") to the villa and its village. It's open April to October Tuesday through Saturday 9am to noon, with a 10€ admission. The villa is also open Tuesday and Saturday 9am to noon. It is closed from November to April.

In Stra, 32km (20 miles) west of Venice on Rte. S11, stands the **Villa Pisani (Villa Nazionale;** ✆ **049-502074;** www.villapisani.beniculturali.it). Built in

One of the rooms in the Villa Foscari.

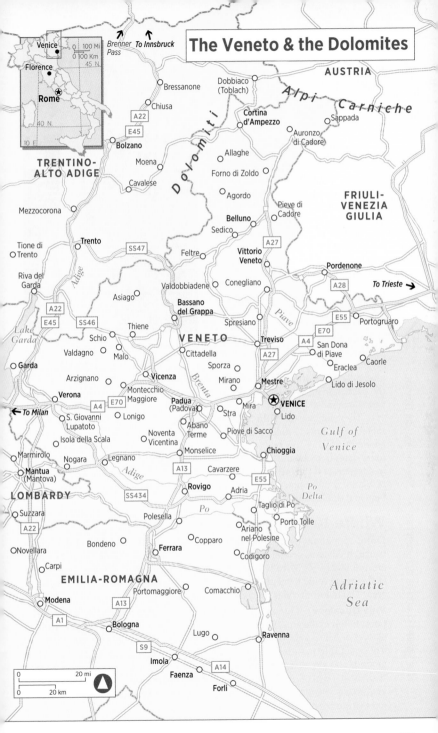

The Veneto & the Dolomites

AUSTRIA

Venice
Florence
Rome

TRENTINO-
ALTO ADIGE

Brenner Pass
To Innsbruck

Bressanone
Chiusa
A22
E45
Bolzano
Moena
Cavalese

Dobbiaco
(Toblach)

Alpi Carniche

Sappada

Cortina
d'Ampezzo
Auronzo
di Cadore

Allaghe
Forno di Zoldo
Agordo

Dolomiti

FRIULI-
VENEZIA
GIULIA

Mezzocorona

Tione di
Trento

Trento

SS47

Riva del
Garda

A22
E45
SS46

Adige

Asiago

Pieve di
Cadore

Belluno
Sedico
Feltre

Vittorio
Veneto

A27

Pordenone

A28

To Trieste →

*Lake
Garda*

Thiene

Schio
Valdagno
Malo

Garda

Arzignano

Verona

A4
E70

S. Giovanni
Lupatoto
Isola della Scala

Marmirolo

Nogara

Mantua
(Mantova)

LOMBARDY

Valdobbiadene
Conegliano

Bassano
del Grappa
Spresiano

VENETO

Cittadella
Sporza
Mirano

Vicenza

Montecchio
Maggiore
Lonigo

Padua
(Padova)

Stra
Mira

Legnano

Adige

A13

Noventa
Vicentina

Monselice

Cavarzere

Treviso

A27

E55

Portogruaro

E70
A4

San Dona
di Piave
Eraclea

Caorle

Lido di Jesolo

Mestre

VENICE

Lido

*Gulf of
Venice*

Abano
Terme
Piove di Sacco

Chioggia

E55

*Po
Delta*

Suzzara

A22

Bondeno

Novellara

Carpi

Modena

A1

Rovigo

Adria

Polesella

Copparo

Ferrara

Po

Ariano
nel Polesine

Codigoro

Taglio di Po

Porto Tolle

EMILIA-ROMAGNA

Portomaggiore

Comacchio

*Adriatic
Sea*

A13

Bologna

S9

Imola

Faenza

A14

Forlì

Lugo

Ravenna

→ To Milan

SS434

0 100 Mi
0 100 Km
45° N.
40° N.
10° E

0 20 mi
0 20 km

1720 as a palatial retreat for Doge Alvise Pisani, it became the Italian home of Napoleon and later served as the initial meeting site of Mussolini and Hitler. Given this historical context, it's no surprise that the villa is the largest and grandest. A reflecting pool out front gives added dimension, and a small army of statues stands guard over the premises. The highlights of a visit are the magnificent Giambattista Tiepolo frescoes, painted on the ballroom ceiling to depict the *Glory of the Pisani Family,* in which family members are surrounded by angels and saints. The villa is open Tuesday to Sunday 9am to 8pm April to September, and until 4pm October to March. Admission is 7.50€ for both the park and the museum but only 4.50€ to explore just the park.

The Villa Pisani.

There are other villas you can visit along the Riviera, each with a stately private home whose owners appreciate and fiercely protect the unique nature of their property. These structures don't follow the gracefully symmetrical rhythms of Palladio: Each appears to be a larger version of the *palazzi* lining Venice's Grand Canal. Although most villas welcome the occasional appropriately respectful visitor, do call in advance before you drop in.

These include the **Villa Sagredo,** Via Sagredo (✆ **049-503174;** www.villa sagredo.it), 1km (½ mile) northwest of the hamlet of Vigonovo. In a suitably gnarled garden, it was built on ancient Roman foundations, and the form it has today dates from around 1700, the result of frequent rebuilding. You must reserve in advance, and the owners prefer scheduled visits Tuesday to Friday 5 to 10pm or Saturday and Sunday 2 to around 8pm. A restaurant and a bar serve simple food and drink. Admission is free.

Where to Stay

Dolo, 15 minutes by car from Venice or Padua, is at the midpoint of the Brenta Canal. It contains several villas from the 17th and 18th centuries, most of which are still inhabited. **Mira** is 10 minutes from Venice and 20 minutes from Padua at the most scenic bend of the Brenta; it's no wonder that several villas lie in the area. The following villas welcome overnight guests.

Villa Ducale ★ This villa, built in 1884 by Count Giulio Rocca, is one of the finest hotels in the area. Restored to its original grandeur, it's graced with Murano glass chandeliers, elaborate frescoes, luxurious fabrics, and antique furnishings. The beautifully outfitted, midsize to spacious bedrooms overlook the statue-filled grounds and are extremely comfortable.

Riviera Martiri della Libertà 75, 30031 Dolo. ✆ **041-5608020.** www.villaducale.it. 11 units. 90€–180€ double; 125€–210€ suite. AE, DC, MC, V. Free parking. **Amenities:** Restaurant; babysitting; room service. *In room:* A/C, TV, hair dryer, minibar.

The Riviera del Brenta

THE VENETO & THE DOLOMITES

Villa Margherita ★★   This 17th-century villa is on a particularly scenic bend of the Brenta. It features marble columns and fireplaces, marble and terra-cotta floors, frescoes and stucco, a sunny breakfast room, and guest rooms that blend individualized traditional elegance with modern comfort. The rooms come in various shapes and sizes, each with first-rate linen and well-kept bathrooms. An immense park opens up behind the villa.

Via Nazionale 416–417, 30030 Mira, Venezia. ✆ **041-4265800.** Fax 041-4265838. www.villa-margherita.com. 19 units. 102€–180€ double; 152€–205€ junior suite. Rates include buffet breakfast. AE, DC, MC, V. **Amenities:** Bar; babysitting; room service. *In room:* A/C, TV, hair dryer, minibar, Wi-Fi (10€ per 24 hr.).

Where to Dine

Trattoria Nalin VENETIAN/SEAFOOD   Most of the Riviera del Brenta's restaurants focus on seafood, and this one is no exception. In a century-old building, the restaurant has flourished as a family-run enterprise since the 1960s. It's adjacent to the canal near the town center, and you'll probably gravitate to the terrace, where potted shrubs and flowers bloom in summer. The specialties vary with whatever happens to be in season but are likely to include *tagliatelle con salsa di calamaretti* (with squid sauce), *spaghetti al nero* (with octopus ink), crabs from the Venetian lagoon, and variations on polenta and risotto.

Via Nuovissimo 29, Mira. ✆ **041-420083.** www.trattorianalin.it. Reservations recommended. Main courses 16€–24€. AE, DC, MC, V. Tues–Sun noon–2:30pm; Tues–Sat 7:30–10pm. Closed Aug and Dec 25–Jan 10.

PADUA ★

40km (25 miles) W of Venice, 81km (50 miles) E of Verona, 233km (144 miles) E of Milan

Padua (Padova) no longer looks as it did when Richard Burton's Petruchio tamed Elizabeth Taylor's Katerina in the Zeffirelli adaptation of *The Taming of the Shrew.* However, it remains a major art center of the Veneto. Many visitors stay in more affordable Padua and commute to pricey Venice. With its high-rises and urban blight, Padua doesn't have the beauty of Venice, but its inner core has a wealth of attractions. Its university, Italy's second oldest, adds life and vibrancy, even though visitors and professors such as Dante and Galileo haven't been seen here in a while.

Essentials

GETTING THERE The **train** is best if you're coming from Venice, Milan, or Bologna. Trains depart for and arrive from Venice once every 30 minutes (trip time: 30 min.). Trains to and from Milan run every hour (trip time: 2½ hr.). Trains from Venice to Padua cost 2.90€ to 18€, depending on the train. Trains from Milan to Padua cost 13€ to 40€, depending on the train. For information and schedules, call *C* **892021** in Italy. Padua's main rail terminus is at Piazza Stazione, north of the historic core and outside the 16th-century walls. A bus will connect you to the center.

Buses from Venice arrive every 30 minutes (trip time: 45 min.), costing 4.30€ one-way. There are also connections from Vicenza every 30 minutes (trip time: 30 min.) at 3.60€ one-way. Padua's bus station is at Via Trieste 42 (*C* **049-8206844;** www.sitabus.it), near Piazza Boschetti (buses depart from Piazza Boschetti), 5 minutes from the rail station.

By **car,** take A4 west from Venice.

VISITOR INFORMATION The **tourist office** is at Galleria Pedrocchi (*C* **049-8767927;** www.turismopadova.it). It's open Monday to Saturday 9am to 12:30pm and 3 to 7pm. There's another tourist office at the train station (*C* **049-8752077**), open Monday to Saturday 9am to 7pm and Sunday 9:15am to 12:30pm.

Exploring the City

A university that grew to fame throughout Europe was founded here as early as 1222. The **University of Padua,** www.unipd.it, has remained one of the great centers for learning in Italy. The physics department counts Galileo among its past professors, and Petrarch lectured here. Today its buildings are scattered around the city. The historic main building is called **Il Bo,** after an inn on the site that used an ox as its sign. The chief entrance is on Via Otto Febbraio. Of particular interest is an anatomy theater, which dates from 1594 and was the first of its kind in Europe. For 5€, you can join an English-language guided tour of the university. On Tuesday, Thursday, and Saturday, tours depart at 10 and 11am; on Monday, Wednesday, and Friday, they start at 3, 4, and 5pm. For details, contact the Servizio Cerimoniale dell'Università di Padova at *C* **049-8273047.**

If you're on a tight schedule, concentrate on the Cappella degli Scrovegni (Giotto frescoes) and the Basilica di Sant'Antonio.

The Padova Card, a combination ticket valid for admission to all of Padua's museums, is good for 48 hours and costs 15€. It is available at the tourist office, the train station, or any of the city's museums. There is also a Padova Card available for 72 hours, costing 20€.

Basilica di Sant'Antonio ★★ This basilica was built in the 13th century and dedicated to St. Anthony of Padua, who's interred within. It's a synthesis of styles, with mainly Romanesque and Gothic features. Spired minarets combine with more traditional bell towers (campaniles) to lend an Eastern appearance. The **interior** ★★ is richly frescoed and decorated, filled with pilgrims touching the saint's marble **tomb in the Saints Chapel** ★★, a Renaissance masterpiece. One of the more unusual relics is in the treasury: the 7-centuries-old, still-uncorrupted tongue of St. Anthony.

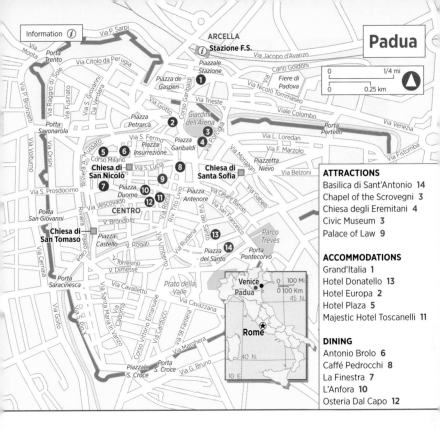

Information ⓘ

Via P. Sarpi

ARCELLA

Padua

ⓘ Stazione F.S.

Via Jacopo d'Avanzo

Via Monta

Porta
Trento

Via Citolo da Perugia

Piazzale
Stazione

Carlo Goldoni

0   1/4 mi

Via P. Bronzetti

Via Raggio d'Sole

Via P. Bronzetti

Via Volturno

Piazza de
Gasperi

Fiere di
Padova

Via Nicolò Tommaseo

0   0.25 km

Via S. Giovanni
Da Verdara

Via Trieste

Viale Colombo

Via Venezia

Porta
Savonarola

Piazza
Petrarca

Via Giotto

Via Fusinato

Porta
Portello

Via Volterno

Via Orsini

Via S. Fermo

Piazza
Insurrezione

Piazza
Garibaldi

Via L. Loredan

Via F. Marzolo

Via Fistomba

Chiesa di
San Nicolò

Via S. Lucia

Piazzetta
Nievo

Via Belzoni

Via S. Prosdocimo

Chiesa di
Santa Sofia

Via Morgagni

Porta
San Giovanni

Piazza
Duomo

Piazza
Antenore

Via Cesare Battisti

Via Gabelli

CENTRO

Via Vescovado

Via Roma

Via Tito Livio

Via San Francesco

Chiesa di
San Tomaso

V. Brondolo

Piazza
Castello

V. Rogati

Via del Santo

Via Rudena

Parco
Treves

Piazza
del Santo

Porta
Pontecorvo

V. Torresino

V. Dimesse

Prato della
Valle

Via Umberto I

Porta
Saracinesca

Via Cavalletto

Via Cavazzana

Venice
Padua

100 Mi
0 100 Km

45 N.

Via Cernaia

Via Santa Maria in Vanzo

Piazza (X)

Via Cadore

Via Corso Vittorio Emanuele

Via Carducci

Via 58 Fanteria

Rome

Via Marghera

40 N.

Via Goito

Piazzale
S. Croce

Porta
S. Croce

Via G. Bruno

10 E

ATTRACTIONS

Basilica di Sant'Antonio 14
Chapel of the Scrovegni 3
Chiesa degli Eremitani 4
Civic Museum 3
Palace of Law 9

ACCOMMODATIONS

Grand'Italia 1
Hotel Donatello 13
Hotel Europa 2
Hotel Plaza 5
Majestic Hotel Toscanelli 11

DINING

Antonio Brolo 6
Caffé Pedrocchi 8
La Finestra 7
L'Anfora 10
Osteria Dal Capo 12

The great art treasures are the **Donatello bronzes ★★** at the main altar, with a realistic crucifix towering over the rest. Seek out as well the **Donatello relief** depicting the removal of Christ from the cross (at the back of the high altar), a unified composition expressing in simple lines and with an unromantic approach the tragedy of Christ and the sadness of the mourners.

Among his other innovations, Donatello restored the lost art of the **equestrian statue ★★** with the well-known example in front of the basilica. Although the man it honors (Gattamelata) is of little interest to art lovers, the 1453 statue is of prime importance. The large horse is realistic because Donatello was a master of detail. He cleverly directs the eye to the commanding face of the Venetian military hero, nicknamed "Spotted Cat." Gattamelata was a dead ringer for the late Sir Laurence Olivier.

Piazza del Santo 11. ⓒ **049-8242811.** www.basilicadelsanto.org. Free admission. Daily 6:30am–6:30pm. Bus: 3, 8, 12, or 18.

Chapel of the Scrovegni (Cappella degli Scrovegni) ★★★   This modest chapel is the best reason for visiting Padua because it contains remarkable **Giotto frescoes ★★★**. Sometime around 1305 and 1306, Giotto did a cycle of more than 35 frescoes, which, along with those at Assisi (see chapter 7), form the basis of his claim to fame. Like an illustrated storybook, the frescoes unfold biblical scenes. The third bottom panel (lower level on the right) is most often

Donatello's bronze *Madonna and Child.*

A detail from the Giotto frescoes.

reproduced; it depicts Judas kissing a most skeptical Christ. On the entrance wall is Giotto's *Last Judgment,* in which hell wins out for sheer fascination. The master's representation of the *Vices and Virtues* is bizarre; it reveals the depth of his imagination in personifying nebulous evil and elusive good. One of the most dramatic panels depicts the raising of Lazarus from the dead—a masterfully balanced scene, rhythmically ingenious for its day. The swathed and cadaverous Lazarus, however, looks indecisive on whether he'll rejoin the living. The **Virgin ★** on the altar is by the Tuscan sculptor Giovanni Pisano.

Piazza Eremitani 8, off Corso Garibaldi. ℂ **049-2010020.** www.cappelladegliscrovegni.it. Admission 13€ adults, 6€ children 6–17. Daily 9am–7pm. Bus: 3, 8, 12, or 18.

Chiesa degli Eremitani ★   One of Padua's tragedies occurred when this church was bombed on March 11, 1944. Before that, it housed one of the greatest treasures in Italy, the **Ovetari Chapel (Cappella Ovetari),** with the first significant cycle of **frescoes ★** by Andrea Mantegna (1431–1506). The church was rebuilt, but alas, you can't resurrect 15th-century frescoes. To the right of the main altar are the fragments left after the bombing. The best fresco saved is a panel depicting the dragging of St. Christopher's body through the streets. Note also the *Assumption of the Virgin.* Like Leonardo da Vinci, the artist had a keen eye for architectural detail. In the chancel chapel are some magnificent **frescoes ★★** attributed to Guarineto, a Venetian student of Giotto.

Piazza Eremitani 9. ℂ **049-8756410.** Free admission (donations accepted). Mon–Sat 8am–6pm; Sun and religious holidays 10am–1pm and 4–7pm. Bus: 3, 8, 12, or 18.

Civic Museum (Musei Civici Eremitani) ★   This picture gallery is filled with minor works by major Venetian artists, some dating from the 14th century. Look for a wooden crucifix by Giotto and two miniatures by Giorgione. Other works are Giovanni Bellini's *Portrait of a Young Man* and Jacopo Bellini's miniature *Descent into Limbo,* with its childlike devils. The 15th-century Arras tapestry is also on display. Other works are Veronese's *Martyrdom of St. Primo and St.*

Feliciano, plus Tintoretto's *Supper in Simone's House* and *Crucifixion,* probably the finest single painting in the gallery.

Piazza Eremitani 8. ✆ **049-8204551.** Admission included with entry to Cappella degli Scrovegni and to Palace of Law; separate visit 12€. Tues–Sun 9am–7pm. Bus: 3, 8, 10, or 12.

Palace of Law (Palazzo della Ragione) ★   This *palazzo,* dating from the early 13th century, is among the most remarkable buildings of northern Italy. It sits in the marketplace, ringed with loggias and with a roof shaped like the hull of a sailing vessel. Climb the steps and enter the grandiose **Salone,** an 82m (270-ft.) assembly hall containing a gigantic 15th-century wooden horse. The walls are richly frescoed with symbolic paintings that replaced the frescoes by Giotto and his assistants that were destroyed by fire in 1420.

Via VIII Febbraio, btw. Piazza delle Erbe and Piazza dell Frutta. ✆ **049-8205006.** Admission 4€. Feb–Oct Tues–Sun 9am–7pm; Nov–Jan Tues–Sun 9am–6pm. Bus: 3, 8, 12, or 18.

Where to Stay

Grand'Italia ★★   This is the town's finest hotel, surpassing the position long held by the Hotel Plaza. Rated four stars by the government, it lies in a restored building in the heart of the city near the train station. It was built in 1909 as a *palazzo* in the then-innovative Art Nouveau style, an architecture still in evidence in its terraces, verandas, and balconies. Before the opening of this hotel, the innkeeping at Padua was rather dismal. The Cinel family took over the building and succeeded in bringing back its former luster. The elegant reception hall sets the grace note for the entire hotel. Two living rooms on the second floor, decorated with stucco and gilt, reproduce the Deco style of two rooms of the Louvre in Paris. Bedrooms aren't neglected either. Each is roomy and decorated in a fashionable modern style, with many conveniences, including a hydromassage in the suites.

Corso del Popolo 81, 35131 Padova. ✆ **049-8761111.** Fax 049-8750850. www.hotelgranditalia.it. 61 units. 130€–235€ double; 200€–340€ suite. Rates include buffet breakfast. AE, DC, MC, V. Parking nearby 15€. **Amenities:** Bar; babysitting; room service. *In room:* A/C, TV, hair dryer, minibar, Wi-Fi (free).

Hotel Donatello   The Donatello is a renovated hotel with an ideal location in front of St. Anthony's. Its facade is pierced by an arched arcade, and the chandeliers of its lobby combine with the checkerboard marble floor to create a hospitable ambience. The guest rooms are reasonably comfortable, if unremarkable, and most come with private balconies overlooking the basilica.

Via del Santo 102–104, 35123 Padova. ✆ **049-8750634.** Fax 049-8750829. www.hoteldonatello. net. 44 units (some with tub, some with shower). 198€ double; 231€ triple. AE, DC, MC, V. Free parking. Closed Dec 7–Jan 7. Bus: 3, 8, or 12. **Amenities:** Bar; room service; Wi-Fi (free, in lobby). *In room:* A/C, TV, hair dryer, minibar.

Hotel Europa   The Europa was built in 1971 and looks its age, but it's still a good buy. The compact, serviceable guest rooms have built-in furnishings and open onto small balconies. The public rooms are enhanced by cubist murals, free-form ceramic plaques, and furniture placed in conversational groupings.

Largo Europa 9, 35137 Padova. ✆ **049-661200.** Fax 049-661508. www.hoteleuropapadova. com. 64 units (shower only). 120€–180€ double; 200€–250€ junior suite. Rates include continental breakfast. AE, DC, MC, V. Parking 14€–25€. **Amenities:** Restaurant; bar; room service. *In room:* A/C, TV, hair dryer, minibar.

Hotel Plaza   Popular with business travelers, the Plaza is one of Padua's leading inns. The guest rooms are comfortable, attractive, and well maintained. They're the most spacious and up-to-date in town, offering modern bathrooms. The hotel staff is efficient and helpful.

Corso Milano 40, 35139 Padova. ℃ **049-656822.** Fax 049-661117. www.plazapadova.it. 142 units (shower only). 230€ double; 350€ suite. Rates include buffet breakfast. AE, DC, MC, V. Parking 20€. Bus: 5, 7, or 10. **Amenities:** Fine restaurant; bar; babysitting; bikes; exercise room; room service. *In room:* A/C, TV, hair dryer, minibar, Wi-Fi (22€ per 24 hr.).

Majestic Hotel Toscanelli ★★   This 1946 family-run hotel has wrought-iron balconies and stone-edged French windows on its facade, plus a Renaissance well and dozens of potted shrubs out front. It's centrally located; you can walk to all the major attractions from here. The inviting breakfast room is surrounded by a garden of green plants. The midsize to spacious guest rooms have elegant cherrywood pieces crafted by Tuscan artisans, along with mahogany and white-marble touches. Furnishings are tasteful, with good lighting, adequate desk space, and plush carpets. The staff is attentive and helpful.

Via dell'Arco 2, 35122 Padova. ℃ **049-663244.** Fax 049-8760025. www.toscanelli.com. 32 units (25 with shower only). 139€–195€ double; 189€–295€ suite. Rates include buffet breakfast. AE, DC, MC, V. Parking 19€. Bus: 8. **Amenities:** Bar; babysitting; room service. *In room:* A/C, TV, hair dryer, minibar, Wi-Fi (free).

Where to Dine

Hailed as Europe's most elegant coffeehouse when it opened in 1831, **Caffè Pedrocchi ★★**, Via 8 Febbraio 15 (℃ **049-8781231;** www.caffepedrocchi.it), off Piazza Cavour, is a neoclassical landmark. On sunny days, you might want to sit on one of the two stone porches; in winter, you'll have plenty to distract you inside. The sprawling bathtub-shaped travertine bar has a brass top and brass lion's feet; the velvet banquettes have maroon upholstery, red-veined marble tables, and Egyptian Revival chairs. It's open Tuesday to Sunday 8am to midnight.

Antico Brolo ★★ ITALIAN   Across from the ornate Teatro de Padova (Civic Theater), this is the city's best restaurant. Even though the 16th-century dining room evokes the Renaissance, many patrons prefer a table in the garden, where candlelit tables are set on a terrace. The cuisine follows the tenets of most of Italy, with special emphasis on seasonal ingredients and the traditions of the Veneto and Emilia-Romagna. For a starter, try the imaginative octopus and potato pie with olives and sautéed pumpkin flowers. Especially delicious are the made-on-the-premises *garganelli* (similar to the tubular shape of penne) with garlic sauce, onion soup baked in a crust, chateaubriand with balsamic vinegar, and grilled fish. The perfect dessert is *zuppa inglese,* a cream-enriched equivalent to zabaglione.

Corso Milano 22. ℃ **049-664555.** www.anticobrolo.it. Reservations recommended. Main courses 16€–34€. AE, MC, V. Tues–Sun 12:30–2:30pm and 7:30pm–midnight. Closed Aug 10–20. Bus: 5, 7, or 10.

L'Anfora ★ ITALIAN   This is the favorite *osteria* (tavern) of savvy foodies, and they recommend it to visitors seeking a dining room of character and atmosphere with affordable prices. The chefs continue in the cooking traditions of their founders, consistently turning out a reliable cuisine of deftly prepared dishes based on market-fresh ingredients. You can savor the town's best *pasta e fagioli* (a country-style pasta-and-bean soup that's like a stew). A savory spaghetti is studded with succulent mussels. Want something authentic to the town's kitchens? Try the squid stew with creamy polenta. Two other specialties include beef braised with red wine or pan-seared salmon filet with a honey and balsamic vinaigrette.

Via dei Soncin 13. (C) **049-656629.** www.osterianfora.it. Reservations recommended. Main courses 5.50€–14€. AE, MC, V. Mon–Sat noon–midnight. Closed 2 weeks in Aug and Jan 1–7.

La Finestra ★★ ITALIAN   It's smart, trendy, and sophisticated, and its take on modern Italian cuisine is the key to its success. Owners Carlo and Hélène will treat you right and feed you well. Even though they often adhere to a traditional regional cuisine, they do so with so much flair you might not recognize the dish.

In the historic center, a few steps from the Duomo, you can begin with such delights as sea scallops with pumpkin seeds, purée of fava beans and fresh rosemary, or even a crispy strudel filled with escarole and ricotta. Five pastas always appear on the menu but each comes with unusual ingredients, perhaps ravioli stuffed with braised duck and a lentil sauce. For your main, select such inventive creations as seared tuna with braised onions and a saffron sauce or roast pork shank with porcini mushrooms and an apple horseradish compote.

Via dei Tadi 15. (C) **049/650313.** www.ristorantefinestra.it. Reservations recommended. Main courses 9€–18€. AE, MC, V. Tues–Thurs 7–11pm; Fri–Sat 12:30–3pm and 7–11pm, Sun 12:30–3pm. Closed Jan 1–7 and Aug 8–29.

Osteria Dal Capo 🏠 VENETO Locals jealously guard this little gem of a *trattoria,* lying in the center of the former Jewish Ghetto of Padua. For years, Veneto classics have been the feature, and the recipes are traditional (not much experimenting here). But the pasta e *fagioli* (homemade pasta with beans) is one of the best around. Other homemade pastas include *taglioni* with ricotta and fresh vegetables. Want something really regional? Try the stewed donkey with polenta that is crisp on the outside, moist inside. For something perhaps a bit more appetizing, opt for the herb-flavored baked lamb. The place is also a fine bargain.

Via Soncin 45. (C) **049/663105.** Reservations recommended. Main courses 7€–17€. AE, DC, MC, V. Mon 7–11pm; Tues–Sat 12:30–3pm and 7–11pm.

Shopping

Padua is an elegant town where you'll find a wide roster of upscale consumer goods and luxury items, and less emphasis on souvenirs and handicrafts. For insights into the good life *alla Padovese,* trek through the neighborhood around the landmark **Piazza Insurrezione,** especially the **Galleria Borghese,** a conglomeration of shops off Via San Fermo.

Droves of shoppers head to the **Prato delle Valle** on the third Sunday of every month, when more than 200 antiques and collectibles vendors set up shop for the day. The square, one of the largest in all Europe, also hosts a smaller **weekly market** on Saturday. Shoes from nearby Brenta factories are the prevalent product, but the range of goods offered remains eclectic.

The outdoor markets (Mon–Sat) in the twin **Piazza delle Erbe** (for fresh produce) and **Piazza della Frutta** (dry goods), flanking the enormous Palazzo della Ragione, are some of Italy's best.

Specialty shops include **Roberto Callegari,** Via Davila 8 ((C) **049-8763131;** www.robertocallegari.com), Padua's leading jewelry store, and **L'Antiquario Gemmologo,** Via Davila 6 ((C) **049-664195;** www.lantiquario gemmologo.eu), run by Callegari's brother. He sells antique silver and also has an

Shopping on the Piazza delle Erbe.

outstanding collection of jewelry next door. If you found the designer shops of Venice too pricey, you'll encounter the same merchandise by walking along **Via San Fermo,** where you'll find Prada, Armani, Gucci, Hermès, Max Mara, and the like.

Padua After Dark

You can hang out with students in town at any of the crowded cafes along **Via Cavour,** or walk over to the wine and beer dives around **Piazza della Frutta** to find out where most of the college crowd is being cool. But other than a quiet stroll through the town's historic core, there's little happening in the city.

We like to spend an evening in Padua at one of the city's wine bars or *enoteches.* The oldest wine bar is **Enoteca Severino,** Via del Santo 44 (✆ **049-650697). La Corte dei Leoni,** Via Pietro d'Abano 1 (✆ **049-8750083**), is more of a restaurant, but it offers live music on weekends.

For dancing in Padua, try **Disco Extra Extra,** Via Ciamician Giacomo 5 (✆ **049-620044**).

PALLADIO'S VICENZA ★★

203km (126 miles) E of Milan, 68km (42 miles) W of Venice, 52km (32 miles) NE of Verona

In the 16th century, Vicenza was transformed into a virtual laboratory for the architectural experiments of Andrea di Pietro, known as **Palladio** (1508–80). One of the greatest architects of the High Renaissance, he was inspired by the classical art and architecture of ancient Greece and Rome. Palladio peppered the city with *palazzi* and basilicas, and the surrounding hills with villas for patrician families.

The architect was particularly important to England and America. In the 18th century, Robert Adam was inspired by him, as is reflected by many country homes in England. Then, through the influence of Adam and others even earlier, the spirit of Palladio was brought to America (examples are Jefferson's Monticello and plantation homes in the antebellum South). Palladio even lent his name to this architectural style, Palladianism, which is identified by regularity of form, imposing size, and an adherence to lines established in the ancient world. Visitors arrive in Vicenza today principally to see the works left by Palladio; for this reason, the city was designated a UNESCO World Heritage Site in 1994.

Federico Faggin, inventor of the silicon chip, was born here, and many local computer-component industries now prosper on Vicenza's outskirts; its citizens earn one of the highest average incomes in the country.

Essentials

GETTING THERE   From Padua (our last stopover), trains are frequent (trip time: 25 min.), a one-way fare costing 3€ to 17€, depending on the train. There are also frequent connections from Milan (trip time: 2½ hr.), at 11€ to 32€ one-way. For information and schedules, call *②* **892021** in Italy. Vicenza's rail station is at Piazza Stazione (Campo Marzio), at the southern edge of Viale Roma.

By **car,** take A4 west from Venice toward Verona, bypassing Padua.

VISITOR INFORMATION   The **tourist office,** at Piazza Matteotti 12 (*②* **0444-320854;** www.vicenzae.org), is open daily 9am to 1pm and 2 to 6pm.

Exploring the World of Palladio

Basilica Palladiana ★★   This basilica was partially designed by Palladio. The loggias rise on two levels; the lower tier has Doric pillars and the upper has Ionic pillars. In its heyday, this building was much frequented by the Vicentino aristocrats, who lavishly spent their gold on villas in the neighboring hills. They met here in a kind of social fraternity, perhaps to talk about the excessive sums being spent on Palladio-designed or -inspired projects. The original basilica was done in the Gothic style and served as the Palazzo della Ragione (Hall of Justice). The roof collapsed following a 1945 bombing but was rebuilt. Although there aren't any treasures inside, two or three times a year art exhibits are held here.

The stage of the Olympic Theater.

Beside the basilica is the 13th-century **Torre Bissara** ★, soaring almost 82m (270 ft.). Across from the basilica is the **Loggia del Capitanio (Captain of the Guard)** ★, designed by Palladio in his waning years.

Piazza dei Signori. *©* **0444-323681.** Free admission. Tues–Sun 9am–5pm. *Note:* Closed for renovations early 2011; check locally.

Civic Museum (Museo Civico) ★

This museum is in one of the most outstanding buildings by Palladio. Begun in the mid–16th century, it wasn't finished until the late 17th century, during the baroque period. Visitors come chiefly to view its excellent collection of Venetian paintings on the second floor. Works by lesser-known artists (Paolo Veneziano, Bartolomeo Montagna, and Jacopo Bassano) hang alongside paintings by giants such as Tintoretto *(Miracle of St. Augustine)*,

The Basilica Palladiana.

Veronese *(The Cherub of the Balustrade),* and Tiepolo *(Time and Truth).*

In the Palazzo Chiericati, Piazza Matteotti 37–39. *©* **0444-321348.** www.museicivicivicenza.it. Admission 8€, including entry to the Olympic Theater. Sept–July 4 Tues–Sun 9am–5pm; July 5–Aug Tues–Sun 10am–7pm.

Olympic Theater (Teatro Olimpico) ★★

Palladio's masterpiece and last work—ideal for performances of classical plays—is one of the world's greatest theaters still in use. It was completed in 1585, 5 years after Palladio's death, by Vincenzo Scamozzi, and the curtain went up on the Vicenza premiere of Sophocles's *Oedipus Rex*. The arena seating area, in the shape of a half-moon, is encircled by Corinthian columns and balustrades. The simple proscenium abuts the arena. What's ordinarily the curtain in a conventional theater is here a permanent facade, U shaped, with a large central arch and a pair of smaller ones flanking it. The permanent stage set represents the ancient streets of Thebes, combining architectural detail with *trompe l'oeil*. Above the arches (to the left and right) are rows of additional classic statuary on pedestals and in niches. Over the area is a dome, with *trompe l'oeil* clouds and sky, giving the illusion of an outdoor Roman amphitheater.

Piazza Matteotti 11. *©* **0444-222800.** www.teatrolimpicovicenza.it. Admission 8€, including entry to the Civic Museum. Sept–July 3 Tues–Sun 9am–4:30pm; July 4–Aug Tues–Sun 9am–7pm.

Santa Corona

This much-altered Gothic church was founded in the mid–13th century. Visit it to see **Giovanni Bellini's *Baptism of Christ*** ★★ (fifth altar on the left). In the left transept, a short distance away, is another of Vicenza's well-known artworks, this one by Veronese, depicting the **Three Wise Men paying tribute to the Christ child** ★★. The high altar with its intricate marble work is also worth a look. A visit to Santa Corona is more rewarding than a trek to the Duomo, which is only of passing interest.

LA CITTÀ DEL palladio

His name was Andrea di Pietro, but his friends called him Palladio. In time, he became the most prominent architect of the Italian High Renaissance, living and working in his beloved Vicenza. Despite the destruction of 14 of his buildings during World War II air raids (luckily, they were photographed and documented before their demise), this city remains a living museum of his architectural achievements. Vicenza eventually became known as La Città del Palladio.

Palladio was born in Padua in 1508, where he was apprenticed to a stone carver, but he fled in 1523 to Vicenza, where he lived until his death in 1580. In his youth, he journeyed to Rome to study the architecture of the Roman Vitruvius, who had a profound influence on him. Returning to Vicenza, Palladio perfected the "Palladian style," with its use of pilasters and a composite structure on a gigantic scale. The "attic" in his design was often surmounted by statues. One critic of European architecture wrote, "The noble design, the perfect proportions, the rhythm, and the logically vertical order invites devotion." Palladio's treatise on architecture, published in four volumes, is required reading for aspiring architects.

By no means was Palladio a genius, in the way the Florentine Brunelleschi

was. No daring innovator, Palladio was more like an academician who went by the rules. Although all his buildings are harmonious, there are no surprises in them. One of his most acclaimed buildings is the **Villa Rotonda** in Vicenza, a cube with a center circular hall crowned by a dome. On each external side is a pillared rectangular portico. The classical features, though dry and masquerading as a temple, captured the public's imagination. This same type of villa soon appeared all over England and America.

The main street of Vicenza, **Corso Andrea Palladio,** honors the man who spent much of his life building villas for the wealthy. The street is a textbook illustration of the great architect's work (or that of his pupils), and a walk along the Corso is one of the most memorable in Italy.

Via Santa Corona. ℂ **0444-321924.** Free admission. Tues–Sun 8:30am–noon and 2:30–6pm; Mon 4–6pm.

Villa Rotonda ★★   This is Palladio's most famous villa, featuring his trademark design inspired by the Roman temples. It's listed as a UNESCO World Heritage Site. The interior lacks the grand decor of many lesser-known villas, but the exterior is the focus anyway, having inspired Christopher Wren's English country estates, Jefferson's Monticello, and the work of a slew of lesser-known architects designing U.S. state capitols and southern antebellum homes. The building was begun by Palladio in 1567, although he died (1580) before it was finished; Scamozzi completed the project in 1592. If you aren't here during the limited open hours, you can still view it clearly from the road.

Via della Rotonda 25. ℂ **0444-321793.** www.villalarotonda.it. Admission 10€ to interior; 5€ to grounds. Interior Wed and Sat 10am–noon and 3–6pm. Grounds Tues–Sun 10am–noon and 3–6pm. Closed Nov 5–Mar 14.

Villa Valmarana "Ai Nani" ★★   The most magnificent thing about this 17th-century villa, built by Palladio disciple Mattoni, is the series of frescoes by Giambattista Tiepolo that taken together create an elaborate mythological world. In the garden, you'll find miniature statues, which are the *nani* (dwarves) referred to in its name. Winter tours, available by appointment, require a group of 10 or more.

Via Dei Nani 8. ☏ **0444-321803.** www.villavalmarana.com. Admission 8€. Mar 9–Nov 7 Tues–Sun 10am–noon and 3–6pm; Nov 8–Mar 7 Sat–Sun 10am–noon and 2–4:30pm.

Where to Stay

Due Mori ★   This 1883 palace is not only the most historic hotel in town, but also predictably the most atmospheric. The *palazzo* dates from the 19th century and lies in the center of town. After many long years, it was restored to its original luster in 2002. The traditionally furnished bedrooms, often filled with antiques, are stylistic and beautifully furnished, including many Art Nouveau pieces. Private bathrooms have been installed in all but three units. Except for a phone, in-room amenities are lacking.

Contrà Do Rode 24, Vicenza 36100. ☏ **0444-321886.** Fax 0444-326127. www.hotelduemori. com. 30 units. 55€ double without bathroom, 80€ with bathroom. MC, V. Parking 15€. **Amenities:** Bar. *In room:* Hair dryer, Wi-Fi (free).

Hotel Campo Marzio   This contemporary and rather elegant hotel is ideally situated in a peaceful part of the historic center, adjacent to a park and a 5-minute walk from the rail station. The guest rooms have undergone a complete renovation, and the sunny lobby has a conservatively comfortable decor that extends into the rooms. The tiled bathrooms are small but well equipped. *Note:* Superior rooms have hydromassage tubs and are soundproof.

Viale Roma 21, 36100 Vicenza. ☏ **0444-545700.** Fax 0444-320495. www.hotelcampomarzio. com. 35 units. 103€–270€ double. Rates include buffet breakfast. AE, DC, MC, V. Free parking. **Amenities:** Restaurant; babysitting; bikes; room service. *In room:* A/C, TV, hair dryer, minibar, Wi-Fi (5€ per hr.).

Hotel Cristina   The Cristina is a cozy place near the city center, with an inside courtyard where you can park. The refurbished decor consists of lots of marble, parquet flooring, and exposed paneling, coupled with comfortable furniture in the public rooms. The high-ceilinged guest rooms are also well furnished, although some are small. The hotel is strongly committed to improving the environment. In 2007 it was awarded the prestigious Ecolabel for its efforts in energy, water saving, and waste reduction.

Corso San Felice e Fortunato 32, 36100 Vicenza. ☏ **0444-323751.** Fax 0444-543656. www. hotelcristinavicenza.it. 33 units (shower only). 90€–170€ double. Rates include buffet breakfast. AE, DC, MC, V. Parking 8€. **Amenities:** Room service; bikes. *In room:* A/C, TV, hair dryer, minibar, Wi-Fi (15€ per 24 hr.).

Where to Dine

Antica Trattoria Tre Visi ★ VICENTINO/INTERNATIONAL   This restaurant opened as a tavern in the early 1600s. After many variations, it settled on its current name ("The Three Faces") more than a century ago, in honor of the rulers of Austria, Hungary, and Bavaria, all of whom wielded political influence in the Veneto. The decor is rustic, with a fireplace, ceramic wall decorations, baskets of fresh fruit, tavern chairs, and an open kitchen. Along with the good selection of regional wines, you can enjoy dishes such as *baccalà alla vicentina* (salt codfish), *zuppa di fagioli* (bean soup), and spaghetti with duck sauce. Another specialty is *capretto alla gambellari* (kid marinated for 4 days in wine, vinegar, and spices, and then roasted). The best-known dessert is the traditional *pincha alla vicentina,* made with yellow flour, raisins, and figs.

Corso Palladio 25. ℰ **0444-324868.** www.ristorantetrevisi.com. Reservations required. Main courses 7€–14€. AE, DC, MC, V. Daily 12:30–2:30pm; Tues–Sat 6–10:30pm.

Antico Ristorante Agli Schioppi ★ VENETO   In the heart of the historic center, in a restored building from 1897, this is the finest restaurant in Vicenza. Fresh ingredients are the hallmark of the cuisine, that and generous portions and an emphasis on taste and flavor. The menu features a variety of regional dishes, including *bigoli* (a kind of local spaghetti). Specialties include risotto with wild mushrooms and zucchini flowers; black ravioli filled with prawns in a tomato stock; or loin of veal with a tuna sauce. In addition to succulent, hearty dishes, the wine *carte* features 80 different vintages. An unusual but tasty dessert is cornmeal cake with fig mustard.

Contra' Piazza del Castello 26. ℰ **0444-543701.** www.ristoranteaglischioppi.com. Reservations recommended. Main courses 8€–15€. AE, DC, MC, V. Mon–Sat 12:30–3pm; Mon–Fri 7–10pm.

Vicenza After Dark

In Vicenza you can enjoy music presented in settings of architectural splendor. The outdoor **Teatro Olimpico,** Piazza Matteotti 3 (ℰ **0444-222800;** www.olimpico. vicenza.it), hosts cultural events from April to late September. For information about the actual programs being presented, call the theater. Look for a changing program of classic Greek tragedy (*Oedipus Rex* is an enduring favorite), Shakespearean plays (sometimes translated into Italian), chamber music concerts, and dance recitals. You can pick up schedules and buy tickets at the gate daily from 11am to 7pm. Tickets are 15€ to 40€ and can be bought at the gate Tuesday to Sunday 9am to 4:30pm.

   More esoteric, and with a shorter season, is a series of concerts scheduled in June, the **Concerti in Villa.** Every year, it includes chamber music performed in or near villas (often privately owned) in the city's outskirts. Look for orchestras set up on loggias or under formal pediments, and audiences sitting on chairs in gardens or inside. Note that these depend on the whims of both local musicians and villa owners. Contact the tourist office (see "Essentials," above) for details.

VERONA ★★★

114km (71 miles) W of Venice, 502km (311 miles) NW of Rome, 81km (50 miles) W of Padua

Verona was the setting for the most famous love story in the English language, Shakespeare's *Romeo and Juliet.* A long-forgotten editor of an old volume of the Bard's plays once wrote, "Verona, so rich in the associations of real history, has even a greater charm for those who would live in the poetry of the past." It's not known if a Romeo or a Juliet ever existed, but the remains of Verona's actual past are much in evidence today. Its Roman antiquities are unequaled north of Rome.

   In its medieval golden age under the despotic Scaligeri princes, Verona reached the pinnacle of its influence and prestige, developing into a town that, even today, is among the great cities of Italy. The best-known member of the ruling Della Scala family, Cangrande I, was a patron of Dante. His sway over Verona has been compared to that of Lorenzo the Magnificent over Florence.

Verona stands in contrast to Venice, even though both are tourist towns. Despite the day-trippers, most of the people walking the streets of Verona are actually residents, not visitors. For a city that hit its peak in the 1st century A.D., Verona is doing admirably well. However, stick to the inner core and not the newer sections, which are blighted by industry and tacky urban development.

Essentials

GETTING THERE   A total of 36 daily trains make the 2-hour run between Venice and Verona, costing 6.15€ to 28€ one-way, depending on the train. From Milan, there are even more connections, taking 2 hours to Verona, a one-way ticket costing 8€ to 24€. The trip from Rome on a high-speed train costs 64€ in second class, 87€ in first class. Rail arrivals are at Verona's **Stazione Porta Nuova,** Piazza XXV Aprile, south of the centrally located Arena and Piazza Brà; call ✆ **892021** in Italy for information. At least six **bus** lines service the area, arriving at Piazza XXV (✆ **045-8057811**).

By **car,** take A4 west from Venice to the cutoff marked Verona Sud. From points north or south, take A22 and get off at the exit marked Verona Nord.

VISITOR INFORMATION   The **main tourist office** is at Piazza Brà (✆ **045-8068680;** www.tourism.verona.it). Hours are Monday to Saturday 8:30am to 7pm and Sunday 9am to 1pm and 2 to 5pm.

SPECIAL EVENTS   Opera festivals on a scale more human and accessible than those in cities such as Milan are presented in Verona annually between July and August. The setting is the ancient **Arena di Verona ★**, a site that's grand enough to accommodate as many elephants as might be needed for a performance of *Aïda*. Schedules change every year, so for more information and tickets, call ✆ **045-8005151;** www.arena.it. Prices of tickets vary with view lines and whatever is being staged, but usually they are 23€ to 198€.

For tickets and information on the opera or ballet in Verona, **Keith Prowse Global Tickets** has a U.S. office (✆ **212/398-4175;** www. keithprowse.com) from which you can buy tickets before you go. The office can mail vouchers or fax a confirmation to allow you to pick up the tickets half an hour before curtain call.

Teatro Romano is known for its Shakespeare Festival in July. In recent years, it has included a week of English-language performances by the Royal Shakespeare Company. Festival performances begin in late May and June with jazz concerts. In July and August, there are also a number of ballets (such as Prokofiev's *Romeo and Juliet*) and modern dance performances. Check for a current schedule at ✆ **045-8077631** or with the tourist office.

Exploring the City

Verona lies along the Adige River. The city is most often visited on a quick half-day excursion but deserves more time—it's meant for wandering and contemplation. But if you're rushed, head first to the old city.

Opening onto **Piazza dei Signori ★★**, the handsomest in Verona, is the **Palazzo del Governo,** where Cangrande extended the shelter of his hearth and home to the fleeing Florentine Dante Alighieri. A marble statue of the "divine poet" stands in the center of the square, with an expression as cold as a Dolomite icicle, but unintimidated pigeons perch on his pious head. Facing Dante's back is the late-15th-century **Loggia del Consiglio,** frescoed and surmounted by five statues. Five arches lead into Piazza dei Signori.

Verona

ATTRACTIONS
Arche Scaligere **13**
Arena di Verona **21**
Basilica de Sant'
  Anastasia **6**
Basilica San Zeno
  Maggiore **1**
Castelvecchio **2**
Duomo **3**
Giardino Giusti **5**
Juliet's House **17**
Juliet's Tomb **22**
Loggia del Consiglio **13**
Palazzo del Governo **13**
Roman Theater &
  Archaeological Museum **4**
Romeo's House **10**
San Fermo **23**

ACCOMMODATIONS
Colomba d'Oro **20**
Due Torri Hotel Baglioni **8**
Hotel Accademia **16**
Hotel Aurora **14**
Hotel Gabbia d'Oro **9**
Hotel Giulietta e Romeo **19**

DINING
Antiche Sere **7**
Arche **12**
Ristorante 12 Apostoli **15**
Ristorante Il Desco **18**
Ristorante Re Teodorico **11**

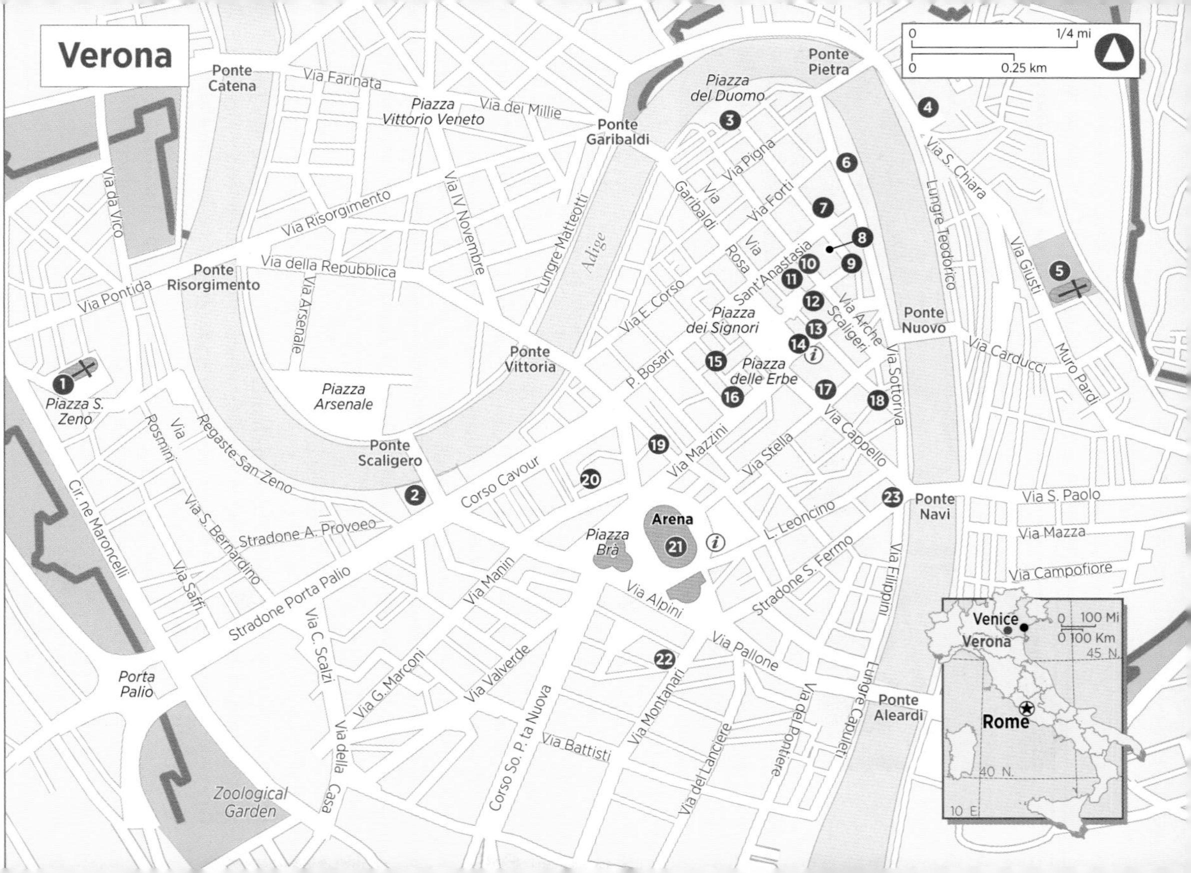

Piazza dei Signori.

The **Arche Scaligere** are outdoor tombs surrounded by wrought-iron gates that form a kind of open-air pantheon of the Scaligeri princes. One tomb, that of Cangrande della Scala, rests directly over the door of the 12th-century **Santa Maria Antica.** The mausoleum contains many Romanesque features and is crowned by a copy of an equestrian statue (the original is now at the Castelvecchio). The tomb nearest the door is that of Mastino II; the one behind it, and the most lavish of all, is that of Cansignorio.

Piazza delle Erbe (Square of the Herbs) ★★ is a lively square, flanked by palaces, that was formerly the Roman city's forum. Today, it's the fruit-and-vegetable market, milling with Veronese shoppers and vendors. In the center is a fountain dating from the 14th century and a Roman statue dubbed *The Virgin of Verona.* The pillar at one end of the square, crowned by a chimera, symbolizes the many years Verona was dominated by Venice. Important buildings include the early-14th-century **House of Merchants (Casa dei Mercanti);** the **Torre Gardello,** built by one of the Della Scala princes; the restored former **city hall** and the **Torre Lamberti,** soaring about 79m (260 ft.); the baroque **Palazzo Maffei;** and the **Casa Mazzanti.**

From the vegetable market, you can walk down **Via Mazzini,** the most fashionable street in Verona, to **Piazza Brà,** with its neoclassical town hall and Renaissance *palazzo,* the **Gran Guardia.**

Arena di Verona ★★

The elliptical amphitheater on Piazza Brà, resembling Rome's Colosseum, dates from the 1st century A.D. Four arches of the "outer circle" and a complete "inner ring" still stand, which is remarkable because an earthquake hit this area in the 12th century. From mid-July to mid-August, it's the setting for an opera house, where more than 20,000 people are treated to performances of music by Verdi and Mascagni. The acoustics are perfect, even after all these centuries, and performances still can be conducted without microphones. Attending an outdoor evening performance here can be one of the highlights of your visit. In one season alone, you might be able to hear *Macbeth, Madam Butterfly, Aïda, Carmen, Rigoletto,* and Verdi's *Requiem.*

Piazza Brà. ✆ **045-8005151.** www.arena.it. Admission 6€ adults, 1€ children 8–13; 1€ the 1st Sun of each month. Tues–Sun 8:30am–7:30pm (on performance days 9am–3pm); Mon 1:30–6:30pm.

Basilica di Sant'Anastasia ★   Verona's largest church was built from 1290 to 1481. Its facade isn't complete, yet it's the finest representation of Gothic design in the city. Many artists in the 15th and 16th centuries decorated the interior, but few of the works are worthy of being singled out. The exception is the **Pellegrini Chapel (Cappella Pellegrini),** with terra-cotta reliefs by the Tuscan artist Michele, and the **Giusti Chapel (Cappella Giusti),** with a fresco by Pisanello representing St. George preparing to face his inevitable dragon. The patterned floor is especially impressive. As you enter, look for two *gobbi* (hunchbacks) supporting holy-water fonts. The church also has a beautiful **campanile** from the 1300s that's richly decorated with sculpture and frescoes.

Piazza Sant'Anastasia. ✆ **045-8004325.** Admission 3€. Apr–Oct Mon–Sat 9am–6pm, Sun 1–6pm; Nov–Mar Tues–Sat 1:30am–4pm, Sun 1–5pm.

Basilica San Zeno Maggiore ★★   This near-perfect Romanesque church and campanile built between the 9th and 12th centuries offers a stunning entrance: two pillars supported by puce-colored marble lions and surmounted by a rose window called the **Ruota della Fortuna (Wheel of Fortune).** On either side of the portal are bas-reliefs depicting scenes from the Old and New Testaments, as well as a mythological story portraying Theodoric as a huntsman lured to hell (the king of the Goths defeated Odoacer in Verona). The panels on the bronze doors, nearly 50 in all, are a remarkable achievement of medieval art, sculpted perhaps in the 12th century. They reflect a naive handling of their subject (see John the Baptist's head resting on a platter). The artists express themselves with such candor they achieve the power of a child's storybook. The interior, somber and severe, contains a major Renaissance work at the main altar: a triptych by Andrea Mantegna, showing an enthroned Madonna and Child with saints. Although not remarkable in its characterization, it reveals the artist's genius for perspective.

Piazza San Zeno. ✆ **045-8006120.** Admission 3€. Apr–Oct Mon–Sat 8:30am–6pm, Sun 1–6pm; Nov–Mar Tues–Sat 10am–1pm, Sun 1–5pm.

Castelvecchio ★★   Built on the order of Cangrande II in the 14th century, the Old Castle stands beside the Adige River (head out Via Roma) near the Ponte Scaligero, a bridge bombed by the Nazis and subsequently reconstructed. This former seat of the Della Scala family has been turned into an art museum, with important paintings from the Veronese school and other masters of northern Italy. Fourteenth- and 15th-century sculptures are on the ground floor, and on the upper floor you'll see masterpieces of painting from the 15th to the 18th centuries.

In the **Sala Monga** is Jacopo Bellini's *St. Jerome,* in the desert with his lion and crucifix. Two sisterlike portraits of Saint Catherina and Veneranda by Vittore Carpaccio grace the **Sala Rizzardi Allegri.** The Bellini family is

The Arena di Verona.

also represented by a lyrical *Madonna con Bambino,* painted by Giovanni, a master of that subject.

Between the buildings is the most provocative equestrian statue we've ever seen, that of Cangrande I, grinning like a buffoon, with a dragon sticking out of his back. In the **Sala Murari della Corte Brà** is one of the most beguiling portraits in the castle—Giovanni Francesco Caroto's smiling red-haired boy. In the **Sala di Canossa** are Tintoretto's *Madonna Nursing the Child* and *Nativity,* and Veronese's *Deposition from the Cross* and *Pala Bevilacqua Lazise.*

In the **Sala Bolognese Trevenzuoli** is a rare self-portrait of Bernardo Strozzi, and in the **Sala Avena,** among paintings by the most famous Venetian masters, such as Gianbattista and Giandomenico Tiepolo and Guardi, hangs an almost satirical portrait of an 18th-century patrician family by Longhi.

Corso Castelvecchio 2. ✆ **045-8062611.** Admission 6€. Tues–Sun 8:30am–7:30pm; Mon 1:30–7:30pm. Last admission at 6:30pm. Bus: 21, 22, 23, 24, 31, or 32.

Duomo ★ Verona's cathedral is less interesting than San Zeno Maggiore but still merits a visit. It was begun in the 12th century but not completed until the 17th. A blend of Romanesque and Gothic, its facade contains (lower level) 12th-century sculptured reliefs by Nicolaus depicting scenes of Roland and Oliver, two of the legendary dozen knights attending Charlemagne. In the left aisle (first chapel) is Titian's ***Assumption,*** the stellar work of the Duomo. The other major work is the **rood screen** in front of the presbytery, with Ionic pillars, designed by Sammicheli.

Piazza del Duomo. ✆ **045-8008813.** www.cattedralediverona.it. Admission 3€. Daily 7am–6:30pm.

Giardino Giusti ★ One of Italy's oldest and most famous gardens, the Giardino Giusti, was created at the end of the 14th century. These well-manicured Italian gardens, studded with cypress trees, form one of the most relaxing and coolest spots in Verona for strolls. You can climb up to the "monster balcony" for an incomparable view of the city.

The layout of the gardens was designed by Agostino Giusti. All its 16th-century characteristics—the grottoes, statues, fountains, box-enclosed flower garden, and maze—have remained intact. In addition to the flower displays, you can admire statues by Lorenzo Muttoni and Alessandro Vittoria, Roman remains, and the great cypress mentioned by Goethe. The gardens, with their adjacent 16th-century *palazzo,* form one of Italy's most interesting urban complexes. The maze of myrtle hedges reproduces the 1786 plan of the architect Trezza. Its complicated pattern

The balcony at Juliet's House (Casa di Giulietta).

and small size make it one of the most unusual in Europe. The gardens lie near the Roman Theater, a few minutes' walk from the heart of the city.

Via Giardino Giusti 2. ☎ **045-8034029.** Admission 5€. Apr–Sept daily 9am–7pm (to sunset off season).

Juliet's House (Casa di Giulietta)   There's no evidence that any family named Capulet lived here, but that hasn't stopped millions of visitors from flocking to this contrived sight. People see the small home, with its balcony and courtyard, and immediately imagine Romeo saying, "But, soft! What light through yonder window breaks? It is the east, and Juliet is the sun!" The house was acquired by the city in 1905. Many locals believe that in the 19th century it was a bordello. You'll notice that the right breast on a bronze statue of Juliet is much more brightly polished than the left. That's the result of a tradition (having nothing to do with Shakespeare) that calls for visitors to rub the breast as they pass.

So where did Juliet's heartthrob live? At the so-called **Romeo's House (Casa di Romeo),** Via Arche Scaligeri 2, said to have been the home of the Montecchi family, the model for Shakespeare's Montagues. It's been turned into a very good, atmospheric, and affordable restaurant called the **Osteria dal Duca** (☎ **045-594474**).

Via Cappello 23. ☎ **045-8034303.** Admission 4€. Mon 1:30–6:45pm; Tues–Sun 8:30am–6:45pm.

Juliet's Tomb (Tomba di Giulietta) ✋   The so-called Juliet's tomb is sheltered in a Franciscan monastery, which you enter on Via Luigi da Porto, off Via del Pontiere. "A grave? O, no, a lantern . . . For here lies Juliet, and her beauty makes this vault a feasting presence full of light." Don't you believe it! Still, the cloisters, near the Adige River, are graceful. Adjoining the tomb is a museum of frescoes, dedicated to G. B. Cavalcaselle.

Via del Pontiere 35. ☎ **045-8000361.** Admission 3€; free 1st Sun of each month. Mon 1:45–7:30pm; Tues–Sun 8:30am–7:30pm.

Roman Theater (Teatro Romano) & Archaeological Museum (Museo Archeologico) ★   The Teatro Romano, built in the 1st century A.D., now stands in ruins at the foot of St. Peter's Hill. For nearly 25 years, a Shakespearean festival has been staged here in July and August; of course, a unique theatergoing experience is to see *Romeo and Juliet* or *Two Gentlemen of Verona* in this setting. The theater is across the Adige River (take the Ponte di Pietra). After seeing the remains of the theater, you can take a rickety elevator to the 10th-century Santi Siro e Libera church towering over it. In the cloister of St. Jerome is the Archaeological Museum, with interesting mosaics and Etruscan bronzes.

Rigaste Redentore 2. ☎ **045-8000360.** Admission 3€ adults, 1€ children 8–13; free 1st Sun of each month. Mon 1:30–7:30pm; Tues–Sun 8:30am–7:30pm. Last admission at 6:30pm.

San Fermo ★   This 11th-century Romanesque church forms the foundation of the 14th-century Gothic building surmounting it. Through time, it has been used by both the Benedictines and the Franciscans. The interior is unusual, with a single nave and a splendid roof constructed of wood and exquisitely paneled. The most important work inside is Pisanello's frescoed ***Annunciation,*** to the left of the main entrance (at the Brenzoni tomb). Delicate and graceful, the work reveals the artist's keen eye for architectural detail and his bizarre animals.

Stradone San Fermo. ☎ **045-8007287.** Admission 3€. Mon–Sat 10am–4pm; Sun 1–5pm. Closed Mon Nov–Mar and Tues–Sun 1–1:30pm.

Where to Stay

Hotel rooms tend to be scarce during the County Fair in March and during the opera and theater season in July and August.

VERY EXPENSIVE

Byblos Art Hotel ★★★ In the Valpolicella countryside, 7km (4½ miles) from Verona, is the most fashionable and stylish hotel in the province, the creation of Dino Facchini, owner of the fashion label Byblos and a world-class art collector. She has turned this 15th-century Venetian villa into a bastion of elegance and deluxe living—called a "hybrid of a contemporary art museum and a grand palace resort." Her style permeates the place—for example, she replaced frolicking rococo bambini with photographs of naked young women (some in red wigs). The hotel is the most theatrical in Italy. Each room has its own style and is harmoniously decorated, but you'll never know what your room's decor will be until you enter.

Via Cedrare 78, 37029 Corrubbio di Negarine. Lies 7km (4½ miles) north of Verona off SPIA. *☎* **045-6855555.** Fax 045-6855500. www.byblosarthotel.com. 60 units. 267€–429€ double; 365€–660€ junior suite; 660€–1,243€ suite. Rates include buffet breakfast. AE, DC, MC, V. Parking 15€. **Amenities:** Restaurant; bar; airport transfers (60€); babysitting; bikes; exercise room; outdoor pool; spa. *In room:* A/C, TV, hair dryer, minibar, Wi-Fi (20€ per 24 hr.).

EXPENSIVE

Due Torri Hotel Baglioni ★★★ This is the inn of choice for the discerning. The Baglioni began as the 1400s home of the Scaligeri dynasty. During the 18th and 19th centuries, it hosted VIPs such as Czar Alexander I. In the 1950s, legendary hotelier Enrico Wallner transformed the palace into a hotel with a stunning collection of antiques. In 2010 the hotel was richly restored. Many antiques remain in the public areas and guest rooms—a range of Directoire, Empire, Louis XVIII, and Biedermeier. Most rooms are generous in size, and the Portuguese marble bathrooms come with deluxe toiletries.

Piazza Sant'Anastasia 4, 37121 Verona. *☎* **045-595044.** Fax 045-8004130. www.baglionihotels. com. 88 units. 315€–572€ double; from 650€ suite. Rates include breakfast. AE, DC, MC, V. Parking 30€. **Amenities:** Restaurant; bar; airport transfers (42€); babysitting; concierge; room service. *In room:* A/C, TV, hairdryer, minibar, Wi-Fi (free).

Hotel Gabbia d'Oro ★★ Gabbia d'Oro is sweet and romantic on first impression, particularly for first-time visitors to Europe. But if you look closely, it borders on cutesy, with lots of faux antiquing (by contrast, Due Torri Hotel Baglioni, above, is the real thing). Opened in 1990 in an 18th-century *palazzo*, this was the first hotel in years to give the Baglioni some competition. Small and discreet, it contains many of the building's original grandiose frescoes, its beamed ceiling, and (in the cozy bar area) much of the carved paneling. The interior courtyard has potted plants, flowering shrubs, and tables devoted to drinking and dining in clement weather. Guest rooms boast framed engravings, antique furniture, and (in some) narrow balconies with wrought-iron detailing overlooking the street or the courtyard.

Corso Porta Borsari 4A, 37100 Verona. *☎* **045-8003060.** Fax 045-590293. www.hotelgabbia doro.it. 27 units. 220€–400€ double; 300€–900€ suite. AE, DC, MC, V. Parking 30€. **Amenities:** Bar; babysitting; room service. *In room:* A/C, TV, hair dryer, minibar, Wi-Fi (free).

MODERATE

Colomba d'Oro ★   A few steps from the Arena, Colomba d'Oro was built as a villa in the 1600s and later transformed into a monastery. During the 18th and 19th centuries, it served as an inn for travelers and employees of the postal service, and eventually grew into this large hotel. The building is efficiently organized and has an atmosphere somewhere between traditional and contemporary. Behind soundproof windows, the guest rooms are nicely appointed with matching fabrics and comfortable furniture. Some bathrooms are clad in marble.

Via C. Cattaneo 10, 37121 Verona. ℂ **045-595300.** Fax 045-594974. www.colombahotel.com. 51 units (11 with shower only). 136€–242€ double; 190€–290€ suite. Rates include continental breakfast. AE, DC, MC, V. Parking 23€. **Amenities:** Room service. *In room:* A/C, TV, hair dryer, minibar, Wi-Fi (1€ per hr.).

Hotel Accademia ★   An inn has stood on this spot in the historic center of Verona since 1797. Today's welcoming hotel is a restored version of an 1880 classic town house opening onto Via Mazzini, the most exclusive shopping street in Verona. The decor is classic with patterned fabrics and dark wood furnishings. Lying only 3 blocks from the Arena di Verona, the hotel rises four floors.

Bedrooms come in an wide array of choices, including two dozen with king-size beds, plus 40 superior class doubles that also include junior suites. For those who want to live more stylishly, there are seven elegantly furnished suites. One of the best buffet breakfasts in town is served here.

Via Scala 12, 37121 Verona. ℂ **045-596222.** Fax 065-8008440. www.accademiavr.it. 94 units. 133€–234€ double, 236€–312€ suite. **Amenities:** Restaurant; bar; babysitting; concierge; room service. *In room:* A/C, TV, hair dryer, minibar, Wi-Fi (free).

INEXPENSIVE

Hotel Aurora   Creaky with age, this landmark budget hostelry still endures. The foundations of this tall and narrow hotel were already at least 400 years old when the building was constructed in the 1500s. Owners completed a radical renovation that improved all the hidden systems (structural beams, electricity, plumbing) but retained hints of the building's antique origins. The Aurora is set behind a sienna-colored facade on a square that's transformed every morning, at around 7:30am, into Verona's busiest emporium of fruits and vegetables. Views from all but a few of the simply furnished guest rooms encompass a full or partial look at the activity in the square. The rooms are small, with cramped bathrooms, but the beds are comfortable.

Piazzetta XIV Novembre 2 (off Piazza Erbe), 37121 Verona. ℂ **045-594717.** Fax 045-8010860. www.hotelaurora.biz. 18 units (shower only). 110€–160€ double; 130€–200€ triple. Rates include buffet breakfast. AE, DC, MC, V. Free parking on street; 15€ in public lot (a 10-min. walk). **Amenities:** Babysitting. *In room:* A/C, TV, hair dryer.

Hotel Giulietta e Romeo   This place makes a slightly saccharine use of Shakespeare's great love story as its theme. Most of the rooms in this once-stately *palazzo* look out over the Roman arena. In honor of the maiden Juliet, the hotel maintains at least one marble balcony that might be appropriate in a modern-day revival of the great play. The guest rooms are tastefully modernized, not overly large, and have burnished hardwoods, comfortable furnishings, and lighting that you can actually read by, plus marble-sheathed bathrooms.

Vicolo Tre Marchetti 3, 37121 Verona. ☏ **045-8003554.** Fax 045-8010862. www.giulietta
eromeo.com. 30 units (22 with shower only). 98€–230€ double; 138€–230€ triple. Rates include
buffet breakfast. AE, DC, MC, V. Parking 19€. **Amenities:** Babysitting; room service. *In room:* A/C,
TV, hair dryer, minibar, Wi-Fi (free).

A HOTEL ON THE OUTSKIRTS

Villa del Quar ★★   This is a patrician villa complex constructed over 14th-
century foundations and in Verona-Nord, 7km (4¼ miles) north of the heart of
Verona. Its pristine elegance evokes that of a Tuscan villa farther south. At this
Relais & Châteaux property, buildings are arranged around a large courtyard and
garden. Once allowed to fall into ruin, the complex today is beautifully restored
and set on a 2.8-hectare (7-acre) property. From your window, you'll have views
of the Valpolicella Valley, famous for its wines that have been praised by everybody from Dante to Hemingway. All the rooms are traditionally furnished in an
antique neoclassical style, and some units are equipped with hydromassage tubs.

Via Quar 12, 37020 Pedemonte (Verona). ☏ **045-6800681.** Fax 045-6800604. www.hotel
villadelquar.it. 28 units. 300€–410€ double; from 415€ suite. AE, MC, V. Free parking. Closed Nov
3–Mar 15. **Amenities:** Restaurant; bar; babysitting; exercise room; outdoor pool; room service;
spa; Wi-Fi (free, in lobby). *In room:* A/C, TV, fax, minibar.

Where to Dine

EXPENSIVE

Arche ★★   ITALIAN/REGIONAL/SEAFOOD   This classic restaurant is
among the finest in Verona. We give the top honor to Il Desco (see below), but
Arche is a close runner-up. It was founded in 1879 by the great-grandfather of
owner Giancarlo Gioco, and the seafood dishes are based on recipes passed
down from generation to generation, including some discovered in ancient cook-
books. Giancarlo and his wife, Paola, insist on market-fresh fish, with sole, sea
bass with porcini mushrooms, and scampi among the favorites. Specialties
include giant ravioli filled with sea bass with a foie gras sauce and truffles, or else
breast of smoked duck with Parmesan cheese and baby greens. The furnishings
in this 1420s building are set off by candlelight and fresh flowers.

Via Arche Scaligere 6. ☏ **045-8007415.** www.ristorantearche.com. Reservations required. Main
courses 15€–49€. AE, DC, MC, V. Tues–Sat 12:30–3pm; Mon–Sat 8–10:30pm. Closed Jan 6–28.

Ristorante Il Desco ★★★ VERONESE/ITALIAN   The tops in Verona, Il
Desco is a handsome restaurant occupying a renovated *palazzo* that's one of the
city's civic prides. The menu steers closer to the philosophy of *cuisine moderne*
than anyplace in town. The freshest ingredients are used in the specialties: filet
of John Dory with radishes in a sherry-and-almond sauce, sea bass filet with porcini mushrooms, suckling pig with black truffles and morels, or risotto with red
beets and raw squid marinated in lime. The wine cellar is superb, and the sommelier will help if you're unfamiliar with regional vintages.

Via Dietro San Sebastiano 7. ☏ **045-595358.** www.ildesco.com. Reservations recommended.
Main courses 32€–45€; tasting menu 130€; 4-course fixed-price menu 60€, 6-course 90€. AE,
DC, MC, V. Tues–Sat 12:30–2pm and 7:30–10:30pm. Closed 2 weeks in June and Dec 25–Jan 7.

MODERATE

Ristorante Re Teodorico ★ REGIONAL/INTERNATIONAL   Ristorante
Re Teodorico is perched high on a hill at the edge of town, with a panoramic view

The market at Piazza delle Erbe.

of Verona and the Adige. From its entrance, you descend a cypress-lined road to the ledge-hanging restaurant suggestive of a lavish villa. Tables are set out on a flagstone terrace edged with classical columns and an arbor of red, pink, and yellow flowering vines. Some notable, well-prepared specialties include potato-and-herb soup with crisp bacon, followed by baked turbot with artichokes and cherry tomatoes or goose leg with aromatic herbs and horseradish. A special delight is ravioli filled with fresh asparagus and served in a mushroom-cream sauce.

Piazzale Castel San Pietro 1. © **045-8349990.** www.ristorantereteodorico.com. Reservations required. Main courses 17€–28€. AE, MC, V. Thurs–Tues noon–3pm; Thurs–Sat and Mon–Tues 7–10pm. Closed Jan 1–24.

Ristorante 12 Apostoli ★★ REGIONAL/ITALIAN   Operated by the two Gioco brothers, this is Verona's oldest restaurant, in business for 250 years. It's a festive place, steeped in tradition, with frescoed walls and two dining rooms separated by brick arches. Giorgio, the artist of the kitchen, changes his menu daily, while Franco directs the dining room. To begin, we recommend the tempting *antipasti alla Scaligera*. Along with considering the tantalizing meat courses, you might also try one of the pasta dishes, especially the ravioli that comes stuffed with fresh pumpkin or else ricotta cheese and fresh truffles. For dessert, try the homemade cake.

Vicolo Corticella San Marco 3. © **045-596999.** www.12apostoli.it. Reservations recommended. Main courses 12€–28€. AE, DC, MC, V. Tues–Sun 12:30–2:30pm; Tues–Sat 7–10pm. Closed 1st week in Jan and June 15–July 5.

INEXPENSIVE

Veronica Antica VERONESE   This is a local restaurant on the ground floor of a town house a short block from the river, across from a cobblestone arcade similar to the ones used in Zeffirelli's *Romeo and Juliet*. This place attracts locals, not just tourists. It's made even more romantic at night by a hanging lantern that dimly illuminates the street. Their dishes are hearty and robust, and specialties include *tagliatelle* with wild boar sauce; *cappellacci* (a kind of ravioli) with porcini mushrooms; or a delectable array of cold meats served with polenta.

10

THE VENETO & THE DOLOMITES

Verona

Via Sottoriva 10. ☎ **045-8004124.** www.osteriaveronaantica.it. Reservations recommended. Main courses 7.50€–16€; fixed-price menu 10€. MC, V. Daily noon–2:30pm and 7–11pm.

Shopping

The byword for shopping in Verona is *elegance,* and shops feature the fashions being touted in Milan and Rome. Don't look for touristy products or rustic crafts and souvenirs; instead, look for more upscale versions of all-Italian fashion and accessories. A worthwhile shop for men is **Class Uomo,** Via San Rocchetto 13B (☎ **045-595775;** www.classuomo.it), and, for both genders, there's the classic **Armani,** Via Cappello 25 (☎ **045-594727;** www.armanijeans.com).

You'll find a concentration of vendors selling antiques or old bric-a-brac in the streets around **Sant'Anastasia,** or head to **Piazza delle Erbe** for a more-or-less constant roster of merchants in flea market–style kiosks selling dusty, and often junkier, collectibles of yesteryear, along with herbs, fruits, and vegetables.

Verona After Dark

Oenophiles will be in their element when they discover the unmatched 80,000-bottle selection at **Bottega del Vino,** Vicolo Scudo di Francia 3 (off Via Mazzini; ☎ **045-8004535;** www.bottegavini.it). This atmospheric *bottega* opened in 1890, and the old-timers who spend hours in animated conversation seem to have been here ever since. The atmosphere and conviviality are reason enough to come by for a tipple at the well-known bar, where five dozen wines are available by the glass. Regulars, journalists, and local merchants often fill the few wooden tables at mealtimes, ordering simple and affordable but excellent dishes, such as homemade risottos.

Put on your dancing shoes and head for **Disco Berfis Club,** Via Lussemburgo 1 (☎ **045-508024;** www.berfis.com), where the rhythms echo what's being broadcast in New York and Milan.

Gays and lesbians can call **Circolo Pink,** Via Scrimiari 7 (☎ **045-8012854;** www.circolopink.it), to get details on gay cultural activities, parties, or newly opened bars. You can call the hot line only Tuesday and Thursday 9 to 11pm and Saturday 4 to 6pm. It is closed in August.

TREVISO ★

31km (19 miles) N of Venice

Treviso is known to culinary fans for the cherries grown in its environs and the creation of tiramisu ("pick me up"), a delicious blend of ladyfingers, mascarpone cheese, eggs, cocoa, liqueur, and espresso. Art aficionados know Treviso for its many works by Tomaso da Modena.

Treviso also attracts those interested in fashion who know it as the birth-place of Benetton. Many come here to browse and window-shop the dozens of stores selling fashion and Italian leather goods. Visitors often pass through Treviso on their way to the wine route (see "The Wine Roads from Treviso," below). But Treviso also draws connoisseurs, those who love the Veneto region so much that they are willing to devote a day of their travels exclusively to Treviso. In recent years, the town has begun to emerge as Italy's newest center for artists, fashion designers, filmmakers, and art lovers.

ATTRACTIONS	ACCOMMODATIONS
Duomo **6**	Cà del Galletto **1**
Episcopal Seminary	Hotel Al Fogher **3**
(Seminario Vescovile) **4**	
Museo Civico **2**	**DINING**
Piazza dei Signori **9**	Beccherie **8**
San Nicolò **5**	Toni del Spin **7**
Santa Caterina **10**	Toulà-Da Alfredo **11**

Essentials

GETTING THERE   There are 50 **trains** a day from Venice, a trip of 30 minutes that costs 2.40€ one-way. Treviso's station is at Piazza Duca d'Aosta on the southern end of town. For rail information and schedules, call ℂ **892021** in Italy.

The station at Lungosile Mattei 21 gets **buses** on the La Marca bus line (ℂ **0422-577311;** www.lamarcabus.it) from Bassano del Grappa nine times daily, a trip of 1 hour costing 5€ one-way. From Padua, buses arrive every 30 minutes; the trip takes 1 hour, 10 minutes, and costs 5€ one-way. The ACTV line (ℂ **0422-541281;** www.actv.it) runs two buses an hour from Venice, a 30-minute trip for 4€. The ACTV office in Treviso is at Lungo Sile Mattei Antonio 29.

By **car,** take A11 from Venice through Mestre for 10km (6¼ miles); head northeast on A4 for 5km (3 miles), and then take Rte. S13 for 16km (10 miles) north to Treviso.

VISITOR INFORMATION   The **tourist office** is on Via S. Andrea 3 (ℂ **0422-547632;** www.turismo.provincia.treviso.it). Opening hours are Monday 9am to 1pm, Tuesday to Friday 9am to 1pm and 2 to 6pm, Saturday 9am to 1pm and 3 to 6pm, and Sunday 9:30am to 12:30pm and 3 to 6pm.

San Nicolò.

Exploring the Town

The huge Romanesque-Gothic **San Nicolò** ★, Via San Nicolò (℗ **0422-3247**), boasts some important treasures, including its ornate vaulted ceiling with 14th-century frescoes by Tomaso da Modena on its columns. Even more impressive is the **Dominican Chapter (Capitolo dei Dominicani)** of the **Episcopal Seminary (Seminario Vescovile),** next door to the church. Here Modena captured in 40 portraits the diverse personalities of a series of Dominican monks seated at their desks. There's no admission fee, and both buildings are open daily 8am to noon and 3:30 to 6pm.

No longer a church, the renovated **Santa Caterina,** Piazzetta Mario Botter, houses the frescoes composing Modena's depiction of the Christian legend of the Ursula Cycle, with its 11,000 virgins all accounted for. A little museum on-site displays ecclesiastical artifacts but you can skip it if you're rushed. Charging 3€ for admission, it is open Tuesday to Sunday 9am to 12:30pm and 2:30 to 6pm.

More intriguing is the **Museo Civico,** Borgo Cavour 24 (℗ **0422-658442;** www.museicivicitreviso.it), housing the strange *Il Castragatti (The Cat Fixer),* by Sebastiano Florigero; a *Crucifixion* by Bassano; and the fresco *San Antonio Abate,* by Pordenone. Hours are Tuesday to Sunday 9am to 12:30pm and 2:30 to 6pm. Admission is 3€.

You can visit the **Duomo,** Piazza del Duomo at Via Canoniche 2 (℗ **0422-545720**), Monday to Saturday 7:15am to noon and 3:30 to 7pm, and Sunday 7:30am to 1pm and 3:30 to 8pm. It contains more frescoes by Pordenone, as well as an *Annunciation* by Titian. The crypt is open after 10:30am.

A stroll through **Piazza dei Signori** ★ offers views of several interesting Romanesque buildings, including the municipal **bell tower,** the **Palazzo Trecento** ★, and the **Loggia dei Cavalieri** on Via Martiri della Libertà.

Where to Stay

Cà del Galletto   This thoroughly modern hotel offers comfortable soundproof guest rooms with serviceable but attractive furnishings. Deluxe rooms also include Jacuzzis. The bathrooms are small but tidily organized. An enclosed garden allows you outdoor privacy in the city.

Via Santa Bona Vecchia 30, 31100 Treviso. ✆ **0422-432550.** Fax 0422-432510. www.hotelcadel galletto.com. 58 units (about half of the rooms have Jacuzzi tubs, half have showers). 87€–160€ double. Rates include buffet breakfast. AE, DC, MC, V. Free parking. Bus: 51. **Amenities:** Restaurant; bar; babysitting; bikes; exercise room; outdoor heated pool; room service; sauna; outdoor tennis court (lit). *In room:* A/C, TV, hair dryer, minibar, Wi-Fi (free).

Hotel Al Fogher ★ We especially recommend this Best Western, a business favorite of wine merchants, just north of the medieval fortifications of Treviso. The decor contrasts antique statuary with modern art prints and marble with glass bricks. The top floor has a panoramic terrace where guests congregate for views over the countryside.

Viale della Repubblica 10, 31100 Treviso. ✆ **800/528-1234** in the U.S., or 0422-432950. Fax 0422-430391. www.alfogher.com. 55 units. 69€–149€ double; 170€ suite. Rates include buffet breakfast. AE, DC, MC, V. Free parking. **Amenities:** Restaurant; bar; bikes; concierge; room service. *In room:* A/C, TV, hair dryer, minibar, Wi-Fi (in some, free).

NEARBY ACCOMMODATIONS

Villa Abbazia ★★ 🗄 This is a great little hotel where wine and food lovers often stay in the historic center of Follina (58km/36 miles north of Treviso). The hotel is in a building that dates from the 16th century. A visit here is like staying in a private home with its own lush garden. Every spacious bedroom is architecturally different with a unique decor, but all are romantic in concept. Sometimes a room will open onto a private terrace. We prefer a room in the main building, but there are equally good units in the annex, a 19th-century Liberty villa. The villa lies along the route of vineyards producing white wines. The staff rents good bikes to guests, with route maps across the relatively flat terrain.

Piazza IV Novembre 3, 31051 Follina (Treviso). ✆ **0438-971277.** Fax 0438-970001. www.hotel abbazia.it. 18 units. 165€–330€ double; 400€–600€ suite. Rates include buffet breakfast. AE, DC, MC, V. Parking 15€. **Amenities:** Restaurant; bar; babysitting; bikes; Jacuzzi; room service. *In room:* A/C, TV, hair dryer, minibar, Wi-Fi (3€ per hr.).

Where to Dine

Beccherie VENETIAN This stone-sided building still evokes the era of its construction (1830). The cuisine and the flavorings of the dishes vary with the seasons and include such midwinter game dishes as *faraona in salsa peverada* (guinea hen in peppery sauce) and the spring/summer favorite *pasticcio di melanzane* (eggplant casserole). In between, look for enduring traditions such as fried crabs from the Venetian lagoon served with herb-flavored polenta, salt cod Vicenza-style, fiery hot pastas, roasted chicken, or *pasta e fagioli* with radicchio.

Piazza Ancilotto 10. ✆ **0422-540871.** www.anticoristorantebeccherie.it. Reservations recommended. Main courses 8€–24€. AE, DC, MC, V. Tues–Sun 12:30–2pm; Tues–Sat 7:30–10pm. Closed July 15–31.

Toni del Spin ★ 🍴 TREVISANA In the center of Treviso, this is a typical *trattoria* serving good food at affordable prices. Some excellent dishes of the northern Italian kitchen appear on the menu. Against a rustic backdrop, you can peruse the menu for such delights as risotto with fresh asparagus. A local favorite—perhaps an acquired taste for foreigners—is the *baccalà* (dried codfish)

THE wine roads **FROM TREVISO**

The gently rolling foothills of the Dolomites around Treviso are known for producing fine wines. For a view of the ancient vines, take a drive along the two highways known as the **Strade dei Vini del Piave** in honor of the nearby Piave River. Both begin at the medieval town of **Conegliano,** where the tourist office is at Via XX Settembre, 61 (✆ **0438-21230;** www.turismo.provincia.treviso.it), open from Wednesday to Friday 9am to 12:30pm and 3 to 6pm, Saturday and Sunday 9am to 12:30pm.

You won't find route numbers associated with either of these wine roads, and each is badly signposted en route, beginning in central Conegliano. The less interesting is the **Strada del Vino Rosso (Red Wine Road),** running through 40km (25 miles) of humid flatlands southeast of Conegliano. Significant points en route include the scenic hamlets of Oderzo, Motta, and Ponte di Piave.

Much more scenic and evocative is the **Strada del Vino Bianco (White Wine Road),** or, more specifically, the **Strada del Prosecco,** meandering through the foothills of the Dolomites for about 39km (24 miles) northwest of Conegliano, ending at Valdobbiadene. It passes through particularly prestigious regions famous for their sparkling prosecco, a quality white meant to be drunk young, with the characteristic taste and smell of ripe apples, wisteria, and acacia honey. The most charming of the hamlets you'll encounter (blink an eye and you'll miss them) are San Pietro di Feletto, Follina, and Pieve di Soligno. Each is awash with family-run cantinas, kiosks, and roadside stands, all selling the fermented fruits of the local harvest and offering platters of prosciutto, local cheese, and crusty bread.

cooked in milk with olive oil and onions and baked to perfection in the oven. It comes with a helping of polenta, as does a perfectly roasted and aromatic duck. Other delights include *tagliatelle* with duck sauce, or risotto with mushrooms and radicchio. Summer meals are served under an arbor, and local wines are featured, of course.

Via Inferiore 7. ✆ **0422-543829.** www.ristorantetonidelspin.com. Reservations recommended. Main courses 8€–20€. AE, DC, MC, V. Tues–Sat 12:30–2:30pm; Mon–Sat 7:30–10:30pm.

Toulà-Da Alfredo ★ INTERNATIONAL/ TREVISANA   This restaurant launched what's now a chain known throughout Italy for its food and service. It offers regional dishes whose inspiration varies with the seasonality of ingredients and the chef's intelligent takes on local traditions. In one of the two Art Nouveau dining rooms, you can order superb versions of green *tagliolini* with ham au gratin; veal cheeks with red radicchio and mashed potatoes, or spaghetti with fish roe and cherry tomatoes. One specialty is spicy *tagliolini* with lobster.

Porcini mushrooms with pasta.

The Strada del Vino Bianco.

The best hotel for establishing a base here is in Conegliano. The **Canon d'Oro,** Via XX Settembre 131, 31015 Conegliano (📞 **0438-34246;** www.hotelcanondoro. it), occupies a 15th-century building near the rail station and charges from 118€ for a double or 165€ for a junior suite, and 225€ for a suite.

If you're looking for a bite to eat in Conegliano, try our favorite restaurant,

Tre Panoce, Via Vecchia Trevigiana 50 (📞 **0438-60071;** www.trepanoce.it). Occupying a 16th-century stone building, it charges around 32€ for full meals that include a celebration of whatever is in season (wine not included). Your pasta could be flavored with radicchio, fresh mushrooms, wild herbs, or local cheese. Tre Panoce is in the hills above Conegliano, 1km (½ mile) from the town center. It's open from Tuesday to Saturday noon to 2:30pm and 8 to 10pm (closed Aug). The most formal restaurant in town is **Al Salisà,** Via XX Settembre 2 (📞 **0438-24288;** www.ristorantealsalisa.com), in a stone building with 12th-century foundations. The excellent menu includes roasted veal with wild herbs, sea bass with seasonal vegetables and basil-flavored white-wine sauce, and fettuccine with wild duck. Expect to spend 28€ and up for a meal. It's open Thursday to Monday noon to 2:30pm and 7:30 to 10:30pm; Tuesday noon to 2:30pm.

Via Collato 26. 📞 **0422-540275.** www.toula.it. Reservations required Fri–Sat. Main courses 11€–34€. AE, DC, MC, V. Tues–Sun noon–2:30pm; Tues–Sat 8–10:30pm. Closed 3 weeks in Aug.

Shopping

The city is known for its production of wrought-iron and copper utensils, and the best place to find these goods is **Morandin,** Via Palestro 50 (📞 **0422-543651;** www.morandinregali.com).

The cherries grown in the surrounding area ripen in June. At that time, you can buy them at all local markets, especially the **open-air market** on Tuesday and Saturday morning sprawling across Via Pescheria. Otherwise, one of the best selections is found at **Pam** supermarket, Piazza Borsa 18 (📞 **0422-583913**).

BASSANO DEL GRAPPA ★

37km (23 miles) N of Venice

At the foot of Mount Grappa in the Valsugana Valley, this hideaway along the Brenta River draws Italian vacationers because of its proximity to the mountains and its panoramic views. Bassano is best known for its liquor, grappa, a brandy usually made from grape pomace left in a wine press, but it's also known for pottery, porcini mushrooms, white asparagus, and radicchio.

Essentials

GETTING THERE   There's direct **train** service from Trent 16 times a day, a 2-hour journey costing 5.50€ one-way. There are also trains requiring a change at Castelfranco from Padua. From Padua, 10 trains per day make the 1-hour trip for 3.40€; from Venice, 19 trains arrive daily, taking 1 hour and 20 minutes for 4.50€. Call ☎ **892021** for information and schedules.

There are many more **buses** to Bassano than trains. The **FTV** bus line (☎ **0444-223115;** www.ftv.vi.it) offers service hourly from Vicenza (trip time: 1 hr.) for 4€ one-way. **SITA** (☎ **049-8206811;** www.sitabus.it) arrives from Padua every 30 minutes; the trip takes 1 hour and costs 6.50€.

By **car** from Asolo, take S248 for 11km (7 miles) west. From Padua, take the S47 north to Bassano. From Vicenza, take the S47 north and the S53 east. From Verona, take the S47 north and the A4 east.

VISITOR INFORMATION   The **tourist office** is at Largo Corona d'Italia 35, off Via Jacopo del Ponte (☎ **0424-524351;** www.comune.bassano.vi.it or www.vicenzae.org); it hands out the *Bassano News,* a monthly information and accommodations guide with a town map. The office is open daily 9am to 1pm and 2 to 6pm.

Exploring the Town

The village is lovely and the liquor is strong, but there aren't a lot of specific sights. Bassano's best-known landmark is the **Ponte dei Alpini,** a covered wooden bridge over the Brenta, which has been replaced numerous times because of flooding, but each version is faithful to the original 1209 design.

Housing numerous paintings by Basano, the **Civic Museum (Museo Civico)** ★, in Piazza Garibaldi at Via Museo 12 (☎ **0424-519450;** www.museo bassano.it), also has works by Canova, Tiepolo, and others. It's open Tuesday to Saturday 9am to 6:30pm, Sunday 10:30am to 1pm and 3:30 to 6:30pm with an admission of 5€; check to see if it is open before heading here. That ticket will also admit you to the **Palazzo Sturm,** Via Schiavonetti (☎ **0424-524933**), home of the **Ceramics Museum,** featuring 4 centuries of finely crafted regional pottery. It is open Tuesday to Saturday 9:30am to 1pm and 3 to 6pm, and Sunday 10:30am to 1pm and 3 to 6pm. Admission is 5€.

If you don't get sick from overindulging on grappa, you might want to pick some up to take home. The best-known distillery is the 18th-century **Nardini,** Via Ponte Vecchio 2 (☎ **0424-227741;** www.nardini.it), next to the Ponte degli Alpini, where juniper, pear, peach, and plum versions supplement the grape standard. Other grappa shops are **Poli,** Via Gamba 6 (☎ **0424-524426;** www. poligrappa.com), and **Bassanina,** Via Angarano 22 (☎ **0424-30924;** www. bassanina.it). Because you're in the heart of grappa country, you can also find good smaller labels such as Folco Portinari, Maschio, Jacopo de Poli, Rino Dal Tosco, Da Ponte, and Carpene Malvolti.

Where to Stay

Al Castello ✦   Opened in the heart of town by the Cattapan family more than 25 years ago, this is a simple hotel outfitted to provide you with a comfortable stay at a bargain rate. This antique town house has been renovated but retains a classical style. The guest rooms are on the small side, but each is comfortable. The tiled bathrooms are a bit cramped.

Piazza Terraglio 19, 36061 Bassano del Grappa. ©/fax **0424-228665.** www.hotelalcastello.it. 11 units (shower only). 70€–100€ double. AE, MC, V. Free parking. **Amenities:** Bar; room service. *In room:* A/C, TV, hair dryer.

Best Western Hotel Palladio ★

This is the Belvedere's sibling (they're 457m/1,499 ft. apart), but you'd never guess they were related. This hotel's facade is modern, with cut stone and stepped glass panels. The interior is contemporary as well, and the lobby boasts a curved wood-and-brass counter and modern recessed lighting. The guest rooms are modern and streamlined, small to medium in size.

Via Gramsci 2, 36061 Bassano del Grappa. © **0424-523777.** Fax 0424-524050. www.bonotto.it. 66 units. 70€–136€ per person double. Rates include buffet breakfast. AE, DC, MC, V. Parking 15€. **Amenities:** Bar; babysitting; concierge; exercise room; room service. *In room:* A/C, TV, hair dryer, minibar, Wi-Fi (3€ per hr.).

Bonotto Hotel Belvedere ★

This has been the town's leading hotel since it opened in the 15th century as a place to rest and change horses before traveling on to Venice. Today it is outranked by the hotel Ca' Sette. The third-floor rooms attest to the hotel's age, with rustic exposed beams. All the guest rooms incorporate classical, Venetian, and Bassanese styles. The hotel recently added five superior doubles and renovated 14 others. The public rooms are luxurious, with Oriental rugs and tapestries, fresh flowers, and curvaceous wooden furniture covered with rich fabrics. The lounge houses a baby grand piano, a fireplace, and a wooden ivy-covered balcony.

Piazzale Generale Giardino 14, 36061 Bassano del Grappa. © **0424-529845.** Fax 0424-529849. www.bonotto.it. 87 units. 180€–212€ double; 360€ suite. Rates include buffet breakfast. AE, DC, MC, V. Parking 13€; free on street. **Amenities:** Restaurant; bar; babysitting; concierge; room service; Wi-Fi (free, in lobby). *In room:* A/C, TV, hair dryer, minibar.

Ca' Sette ★★

The most tranquil and luxurious hotel in the area lies 1km (½ mile) north of center. A contemporary design overlay has been given to a villa that was constructed in 1700. Napoleon's troops sequestered the villa during the Battle of Brenta. Originally, the Sette family, the owners, constructed this villa to escape the stifling summer heat of Venice. You can wander the well-manicured grounds, admiring the fountains, walking through an olive grove, or sitting by a little lake. Bedrooms are spacious and done in a rather somber, though elegant style. The villa still contains frescoed ceilings in spite of its modern touches, and some of the accommodations still have their stone walls and old wooden beams. Since you're a bit isolated, you'll appreciate the **restaurant,** which uses the freshest local ingredients along with a well-chosen and reasonably priced wine list.

Via Cunizza da Romano 4, 36061 Bassano del Grappa. © **0424-383350.** Fax 0424-393287. www.ca-sette.it. 19 units. 180€–250€ double; from 320€ suite. Rates include buffet breakfast. AE, DC, MC, V. Free parking; 10€ in garage. **Amenities:** Restaurant; bar; babysitting; bikes; room service. *In room:* A/C, TV, hair dryer, minibar, Wi-Fi (free).

ON THE OUTSKIRTS

Villa Palma ★

This 18th-century villa lies 5km (3 miles) from Bassano. Renovations preserved features such as its beamed and vaulted brick ceilings. The guest rooms are individualized by mixing antiques, carpets, and tapestries to create a comfortable yet elegant atmosphere. Most rooms are spacious, and all have excellent mattresses and fine linen. Some bathrooms have sauna showers or Jacuzzis.

Via Chemin Palma 30, 36065 Mussolente. ☎ **0424-577407.** Fax 0424-87687. www.villapalma.it. 21 units. 110€ double; 180€ junior suite. Rates include buffet breakfast. AE, DC, MC, V. Free parking. **Amenities:** Restaurant; babysitting; bikes; Jacuzzi; room service. *In room:* A/C, TV, hair dryer, minibar, Wi-Fi (free).

Where to Dine

Al Sole-da Tiziano ★ VENETIAN   Gian-Franco Chiurato's successful restaurant occupies this cavernous early-19th-century *palazzo,* where both dining rooms are decorated with local ceramics. The cuisine is rooted in the Veneto's traditions and celebrates two annual crops: In springtime, look for the region's distinctive white asparagus blended into pastas and risottos, used as a garnish for main courses, and often featured as a refreshing course on its own. In autumn and winter, look for similar variations on mushrooms, especially porcini, which are absolutely addictive, with game birds and venison. The rest of the year other specialties include *tortellini* stuffed with aromatic herbs and Morlacco cheese, or else roast duck with a pomegranate sauce.

Via Jacopo Vittorelli 41. ☎ **0424-523206.** Reservations recommended. Main courses 12€–24€. AE, MC, V. Tues–Sun noon–3pm and 7:30–10pm. Closed July 20–Aug 20.

TRIESTE ★

116km (72 miles) NE of Venice, 667km (414 miles) NE of Rome, 407km (252 miles) E of Milan

Remote Trieste, a shimmering city with many neoclassical buildings, is perched on the half-moon Gulf of Trieste, which opens into the Adriatic. Trieste has had a long history, with many changes of ownership. The Habsburg emperor Charles VI declared it a free port in 1719, but by the 20th century it was an ocean outlet for the Austro-Hungarian Empire. After World War I and a secret deal among the Allies, Trieste was ceded to Italy. In 1943, Trieste again fell to foreign troops—this time the Nazis, who were ousted by Tito's Yugoslav army in 1945. In 1954, after much negotiation, the American and British troops withdrew as the Italians marched in, with the stipulation that the much-disputed Trieste would be maintained as a free port. Today that status continues. Politics, as always, dominates the agenda here. There's racial tension, and many Italian Fascists and anti-Slav parties are centered in Trieste.

Trieste has known many glamorous literary associations, particularly in the pre–World War II years. As a stop on the Orient Express, it became a famed destination. Dame Agatha Christie came this way, as did Graham Greene. James Joyce, eloping with Nora Barnacle, arrived in 1904. Out of money, Joyce got a job teaching at the Berlitz School and lived in Trieste for nearly 10 years. He wrote *A Portrait of the Artist as a Young Man* here and might have begun his masterpiece *Ulysses* here as well. Poet Rainer Maria Rilke also lived in the area. Author Richard Burton, known for his *Arabian Nights* translations, lived in Trieste from 1871 until he died about 20 years later.

Trieste, squashed between Slovenia and the Adriatic, has been more vulnerable to conditions following the collapse of Yugoslavia than any other city in Italy. Civil war and turmoil have halted the flow of thousands who used to cross the border to buy merchandise—mainly jeans and household appliances. The port has also suffered from crises in the shipbuilding and steel industries. Trieste remains Italy's insurance capital, and one-fourth of its population of 250,000 residents is retired (it has the highest per-capita retiree population in Italy).

Piazza dell'Unità d'Italia.

Essentials

GETTING THERE Trieste is serviced by an **airport** at **Ronchi dei Legionari** (© **0481-773224;** www.aeroporto.fvg.it), 35km (22 miles) northwest of the city. **Alitalia** (© **800/223-5730;** www.alitalia.it) has daily flights to and from Rome. **Lufthansa** (© **800/645-3880** in the U.S., or 199-400-044 in Italy) offers daily flights from Trieste to Munich.

Trieste lies on a direct **rail** link from Venice. Trip time from Venice is 2½ hours, and a one-way ticket is 10€ to 24€. The station is on Piazza della Libertà (© **892021**), northwest of the historic center. It's better to fly, drive, or take the train to Trieste. Once here, you'll find a network of **local buses** servicing the region from Corso Cavour (© **800-016675** toll-free in Italy).

By **car,** follow A4 northeast from Venice until you reach the end at Trieste.

VISITOR INFORMATION The **tourist office,** Piazza Unità di Italia (© **040-3478312;** www.turismofvg.it), is open Monday to Saturday 9am to 6pm, and Sunday 9am to 1pm.

Exploring the City

The heart of Trieste is the neoclassical **Piazza dell'Unità d'Italia ★**, Italy's largest square that fronts the sea. Opening onto the square is the town hall with a clock tower, the Palace of the Government, and the main office of the Lloyd Triestino ship line. Flanking it are numerous cafes and restaurants, popular at night with locals who sip an aperitif and promenade along the seafront esplanade.

After visiting the main square, you might want to view Trieste from an even better vantage point. Head up the hill for another cluster of attractions—you can take an antiquated **tram** leaving from Piazza Oberdan and get off at Obelisco. At the **belvedere,** the city of the Adriatic will spread out before you.

Miramare Castle (Castello di Miramare).

Cathedral of St. Just (Cattedrale di San Giusto)   Dedicated to the patron saint of Trieste, who was martyred in A.D. 303, this basilica was consecrated in 1330, incorporating a pair of churches that had been separate until then. The front is Romanesque style, enhanced by a rose window. Inside, the nave is flanked by two pairs of aisles. To the left of the main altar are the best of the Byzantine mosaics in Trieste (note especially the blue-robed Madonna and child). The main altar and the chapel to the right contain much-photographed mosaics. To the left of the basilica entrance is a campanile from the 14th century, which you can scale for a view of Trieste and its bay. At its base are preserved the remains of a Roman temple from the 1st century A.D. You might prefer to take a taxi up to the cathedral and then walk a leisurely 15 minutes back down. From the basilica you can also stroll to the nearby St. Just Castle (see below).

Piazza Cattedrale, Colle Capitolino. ✆ **040-309666.** Free admission. Daily 7:30am–7pm.

Miramare Castle (Castello di Miramare) ★   Overlooking the Bay of Grignano, this castle was built by Archduke Maximilian, the brother of Franz Josef, the Habsburg emperor of Austria. Maximilian, who married Princess Charlotte of Belgium, was the commander of the Austrian navy in 1854. In an ill-conceived move, he and "Carlotta" sailed to Mexico in 1864, where he became the emperor in an unfortunate, brief reign. He was shot in 1867 in Querétaro, Mexico. His wife lived until 1927 in a château outside Brussels, driven insane by the Mexican episode. On the ground floor, you can visit Maximilian's bedroom (built like a ship's cabin) and Charlotte's, as well as an impressive receiving room and more parlors, including a *chinoiserie* salon.

   Enveloping the castle are magnificently designed grounds (the **Parco di Miramare**), ideal for pleasant strolls. In July and August, a **sound-and-light presentation** in the park depicts Maximilian's tragedy in Mexico. Tickets begin at 10€.

Viale Miramare, Grignano (8km/5 miles NW of town). ✆ **040-224143.** www.castello-miramare. it. Admission 6€. Daily 9am–6:30pm. Bus: 36.

St. Just Castle (Castello di San Giusto)   Constructed in the 15th century by the Venetians on the site of a Roman fort, this fortress maintained a sharp eye on the bay, watching for unfriendly visitors arriving by sea. From its

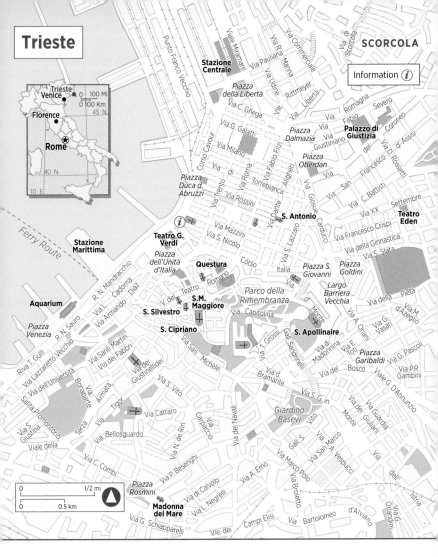

bastions, panoramic views of Trieste unfold. Inside is a museum with a collection of arms and armor.

Piazza Cattedrale 3. ✆ **040-309362.** Castle 4€; museum 5€. Castle daily 9am–sunset. Museum Tues–Sun 9am–1pm.

Where to Stay

Filoxenia 🛥   Next door to the historic church of S. Nicolò of the Greeks, this family-run hotel offers an affordable choice in a high-priced city. The hotel lies about a 5-minute walk from the central station and is close to the sea. Some bedrooms are very small, but most are midsize, each with simple yet comfortable furnishings. Maintenance is good, and pictures with mythological themes are used for decoration. Like the sea lapping up on Greek islands, the predominant color is blue.

Via Mazzini 3, 34121 Trieste. ✆ **040-3481644.** Fax 040-661371. www.filoxenia.it. 20 units. 80€–120€ double; 95€–140€ triple. AE, DC, MC, V. Parking 15€ nearby. **Amenities:** Restaurant; bar; room service. *In room:* A/C, TV, hair dryer, Wi-Fi (free).

Grand Hotel Duchi d'Aosta ★

This remains the traditional favorite among upscale travelers to Trieste who want to stay in the center of the city. This glamorous hotel began about 200 years ago as a restaurant for the dock workers who toiled nearby. In 1873, one of the most beautiful facades in Trieste—a white neoclassical shell with delicate carving, arched windows, and a stone crown of heroic sculptures—was erected over the existing building. The design is very much that of an 18th-century palace, enhanced by views over the fountains and lamps of the square and the sea beyond it, while the Victorian public rooms give it a 19th-century ambience. Each guest room boasts antiqued walls and tasteful furniture.

Piazza Unità d'Italia 2, 34121 Trieste. ✆ **040-7600011.** Fax 040-366092. www.magesta.com. 55 units (some with shower only). 188€–330€ double; 290€–666€ suite. Rates include buffet breakfast. AE, DC, MC, V. Parking 22€. **Amenities:** Restaurant; bar; babysitting; indoor heated pool; room service; spa. *In room:* A/C, TV, hair dryer, minibar, Wi-Fi (free).

Hotel Greif Maria Theresia ★★

In the exclusive Barcola district, a 5-minute drive from the city center, this restored villa is the number-one choice for your Trieste layover. It now surpasses the top position long held by the Grand Hotel Duchi d'Aosta (see above). Overlooking the Gulf of Trieste, the building is stylishly furnished and decorated, with exceedingly comfortable and soundproof bedrooms. Service is efficient, and housekeeping is first-rate. The hotel also has more facilities than any other in the area.

Viale Miramare 109, Barcola, 34136 Trieste. ✆ **040-410115.** Fax 040-413053. www.greifgroup.net. 36 units. 320€–400€ double; 700€ junior suite. AE, DC, MC, V. Free parking. **Amenities:** Restaurant; bar; exercise room; indoor heated pool; room service; sauna; Wi-Fi (free, in lobby). *In room:* A/C, TV, hair dryer, minibar.

A Room with No View: The Grotta Gigante

In the heart of the limestone plateau called Carso surrounding Trieste, you can visit the **Grotta Gigante ★** (✆ 040-327312; www.grottagigante.it), an enormous cavern that's one of the most interesting phenomena of speleology. First explored in 1840 via the top ceiling entrance, this huge room, some 116m (380 ft.) deep, was opened to the public in 1908. It's the biggest single-room cave ever opened to visitors and one of the world's largest underground rooms. You can visit only with a guide on a 40-minute tour. Near the entrance is the Man and Caves Museum.

Daily tours of the cave are given April to September 10am to 6pm every half-hour, and October and March 10am to 4pm every hour. From November to February, tours are given every hour from 10am to noon and 2 to 4pm. Tours cost 11€ for adults, 8€ for children 6 to 16, free for children 5 and under. If you're driving, take Strada del Friuli beyond the white marble Victory Lighthouse as far as Prosecco. On the freeway, you can take the exit at Prosecco. By public transport, take the tram from Piazza Oberdan, and then bus no. 42 to Prosecco.

Where to Dine

Al Granzo ★ SEAFOOD   The people of Trieste still flock here today to enjoy seafood, often based on the same recipes that the founding fathers, a trio of brothers, have been serving since 1923. It's one of Trieste's leading seafood restaurants, serving flavor-filled versions of that curious mix of Italian, Austrian, and Yugoslav cuisines known as Triestino. Menu items include *brodetto,* a traditional bouillabaisse spiced with saffron and other herbs; vermicelli with black mussels; and risotto with seafood. Fresh fish are displayed on crushed ice in a wagon, and there's an impressive selection of fresh *contorni* (vegetables, sold individually). A suitable wine would be a local Tocai Friulano, aromatic and somewhat tart. Dessert might be homemade strudel.

Piazza Venezia 7. ℰ **040-306788.** www.algranzo.it. Reservations recommended. Main courses 8€–20€; fixed-price menu 24€–55€. AE, DC, MC, V. Thurs–Tues noon–3pm; Mon–Tues and Thurs–Sat 7:30–10:30pm.

Antica Trattoria Suban ITALIAN/CENTRAL EUROPEAN   This tavern is 4km (2½ miles) north of Trieste in the district of San Giovanni, on a spacious terrace opening onto a hill view. The landscape contains glimpses of the Industrial Age, but the brick-and-stone walls, the terrace, and the country feeling are still intact. The restaurant is run by descendants of the founding family, and the cuisine is both hearty and delicate, drawing its inspiration from northeastern Italian, Slavic, Hungarian, and Germanic traditions. A tantalizing appetizer is filet of smoked deer with fresh radicchio and grana cheese, with a side of fresh artichokes. A succulent pasta dish is homemade "pocket pasta" filled with spinach and sausage. Dishes include a flavorful risotto with herbs, beef with garlic sauce, a perfectly prepared chicken Kiev, veal croquettes with parmigiano and egg yolks, crepes stuffed with basil and roasted veal, and haunch of veal with roasted potatoes. The chef's handling of grilled meats is adept, and the rich pastries, such as the honey strudel, are worth the calories.

Via Comici 2, at San Giovanni. ℰ **040-54368.** www.suban.it. Reservations recommended. Main courses 9€–22€. AE, DC, MC, V. Thurs–Tues 7:30–10pm; Sat–Sun noon–3pm. Closed 2 weeks in Aug.

Ristorante Harry's Grill ★ INTERNATIONAL   This restaurant is related to the famous Harry's Bar in Venice, having been founded in 1972 by Arrigo Cipriani. In Trieste's most upscale hotel, this restaurant manages to be both elegant and relaxed, where you can have an American-style martini followed by a simple plate of pasta or a full meal. The big lace-covered curtains complement the paneling, the polished brass, and the blue Murano chandeliers. In summer, tables are set up in the traffic-free piazza. The outdoor terrace, sheltered by a canopy, has a separate area for bar patrons. The Mediterranean-inspired cuisine is good but not great and includes fresh shrimp with oil and lemon, pasta and risotto dishes, boiled salmon in sauce, calves' liver with onions, *bigoli* (fat spaghetti) with duck meat, and beef filet with red-wine sauce. The adjoining bar is one of the most popular rendezvous spots in town.

In the Grand Hotel Duchi d'Aosta, Piazza dell'Unità d'Italia 2. ℰ **040-660606.** www.duchi.eu. Reservations required. Main courses 17€–28€. AE, DC, MC, V. Daily 12:30–2:30pm and 7:30–10:30pm.

Shopping

Trieste is a great place to shop for antiques. Look for examples of both Biedermeier and Liberty (Italian Art Nouveau) furniture and accessories, and wander at

Candy on display at La Bomboniera.

will through the city's densest collection of antiques dealers, the neighborhood around **Piazza dell'Unità d'Italia.** Dealers to look out for are **Davia,** Via dell'Annunziata 6 (✆ **040-304321**), specializing in antique engravings; and **Fulvio Rosso,** Via Armando Diaz 13 (✆ **040-306226**), specializing in crystal and porcelain from the turn of the 20th century.

Fine leather and suede goods fill **Christine Pelletterie,** Piazza della Borsa 15 (✆ **040-366212**), where women can find well-crafted shoes, bags, and pants.

Offering both casual and formal attire, **Max Mara,** Corso Italia 20 (✆ **040-636723;** www.maxmara.com), features impeccable women's designs, plus shoes and bags.

The 130-year-old **La Bomboniera ★,** Via XXX Ottobre 3 (✆ **040-632752**), is a candy store as beautifully wrapped as the chocolates it sells, with etched glass, carved walnut shelves, and an elaborate glass chandelier. Besides fine chocolates, it offers traditional sweets and pastries of the region, as well as a few Austro-Hungarian specialties.

Trieste After Dark

Trieste's most impressive theater, the **Teatro Verdi,** Corso Cavour via San Carlo (✆ **040-6722111;** www.teatroverdi-trieste.com), has been compared to a blend of the Vienna State Opera and Milan's La Scala. Built in 1801 and massively renovated in the mid-1990s, it presents classical concerts and operas throughout the year. Tickets range from 22€ to 130€.

The town's loveliest cafe, almost adjacent to the above-mentioned theater, is the **Caffè Tommaseo,** Piazza Tommaseo 4-C (✆ **040-362666**). The bar adjoining **Ristorante Harry's Grill** (see above) is also a popular watering hole.

CORTINA D'AMPEZZO: GATEWAY TO THE DOLOMITES ★★

161km (100 miles) N of Venice, 411km (255 miles) NE of Milan

This chic resort town is your best center for exploring the snowy Dolomiti. Its reputation as a tourist mecca dates from before World War I, but its recent growth has been phenomenal, spurred by the 1956 Olympics held here. Cortina d'Ampezzo draws throngs of nature lovers in summer and both Olympic-caliber and neophyte skiers in winter. (Expect high hotel prices in July–Aug, as well as in the 3 months of winter, Nov–Jan.)

Cortina is in the middle of a valley ringed by enough Dolomite peaks to cause Hannibal's elephants to throw up their trunks and flee in horror. Regardless of which road you choose for a drive, you'll find the scenery rewarding. And Cortina sets an excellent table, inspired by the cuisine of both Venice and Tirol.

Essentials

GETTING THERE   Frequent **trains** run between Venice and Calalzo di Cadore (trip time: 2½ hr.), 31km (19 miles) south of Cortina. You proceed the rest of the way by bus. For information about schedules, call ✆ **892021.** About 14 to 16 **buses** a day connect Calalzo in Cadore with Cortina. Buses arrive at the Cortina bus station on Via Stazione (✆ **0436-2741**). *Note:* Trains from Venice to Calalzo in Cadore cost 8€ one-way.

By **car,** take A27 north from Venice and then follow the S51 into Cortina.

VISITOR INFORMATION   The **tourist office,** at Piazzetta San Francesco 8 (✆ **0436-3231;** www.infodolomiti.it), is open daily 9am to 12:30pm and 3:30 to 6:30pm.

Exploring the Peaks of the Dolomites

One of the main attractions in Cortina is to take a **cable car** "halfway to the stars," as the expression goes. On one of them, at least, you'll be just a yodel away from the Pearly Gates: the **Freccia nel Cielo ("Arrow of the Sky").** From July

3 to September 12 and December 3 to mid-April beginning at 9am, cars depart from the base behind Cortina's Olympic Stadium every 20 minutes (call ✆ **0436-5052** for departures the rest of the year; www.frecciandelcielo. com). Round-trip cost is 25€ in winter and 31€ in summer. An ascent to the summit of the cable car run requires two changes en route and an uphill ride through three separate cable car segments. The first station is Col Druscie, at 1,753m (5,752 ft.); the second is Ra Valles, at 2,447m (8,027 ft.); the top is Tofana di Mezzo, at 3,214m (10,543 ft.). At Tofana on a clear day, you can see as far as Venice.

Part of the Alps, the snowy peaks of the **Dolomiti** stretch along Italy's northwestern tier, following the line of the Austrian border between the valleys of the Adige and Brenta rivers.

Although the highest peak is the Marmolada (about 3,350m/11,000 ft.

The mountains surrounding Cortina.

above sea level), the range contains 18 peaks in Italian territory that rise above 3,050m (10,000 ft.). Escaping from the often intense heat of other parts of the country, Italians travel here to breathe the Dolomiti's cool mountain air and to ski and play in resorts such as Cortina.

The mix of limestone and porphyry, combined with the angle of the sun, contributes to the peaks' dramatic coloration. Most pronounced in the morning and at dusk, their colors range from soft pinks to brooding russets. When the sun shines directly overhead, the hues fade to a homogenized dull gray. Fortunately for tourists, trekkers, and skiers, the climate isn't as bone-chilling as it is in the Alpine regions of western Italy and in the Alps of the Tirol, farther north.

Throughout the Dolomiti, networks of **hiking trails** are clearly marked with signs, and local tourist offices (as well as most hotel staffs) can help you choose a good hike that suits your time and ability level. Maps of hiking trails are broadly distributed, and any tourist office can refer you to the nearest branch of the Associazione Guide Alpine. If you decide to ramble across the Dolomiti, you'll need stout shoes, warm clothing, and a waterproof jacket (storms erupt quickly at these altitudes). Rustically charming *refugi* (mountain huts) offer the opportunity for an overnight stay or just a rest. (While you're hiking, please don't pick the wildflowers because many of them, including the Austrian national flower, the edelweiss, are endangered species. Picking flowers or destroying vegetation is punishable by stiff fines.)

Skiing & Other Outdoor Pursuits

DOWNHILL SKIING The **Faloria-Cristallo area** surrounding Cortina is known for its 30km (19 miles) of slopes and 16km (10 miles) of fresh-snow runs. At 1,223m (4,014 ft.) above sea level, Cortina's altitude isn't particularly forbidding (at least, compared with other European ski resorts), and though snowfall is *usually* abundant from late December to early March, a holiday in November or April might leave you without adequate snow. Die-hard Cortina enthusiasts usually compensate for that, at least during the tail end of the season, by remaining only at the surrounding slopes' higher altitudes (there's lots of ski-ability at 2,743m/9,000 ft.) and traversing lower-altitude snowfields by cable car.

As Italy's premier ski resort, Cortina boasts more than 50 cable cars, and lifts spread out across the valley of the Boite River. The surrounding mountains contain about two dozen restaurants, about 145km (90 miles) of clearly designated ski trails, and a virtually unlimited number of off-piste trails for cross-country enthusiasts. Cortina boasts plenty of sunshine, a relative lack of crowds, and an array of slopes that will suit intermediate, advanced intermediate, and novice skiers alike. During winter, ski lifts are open daily 9am to between 4 and 5pm, depending on the time of sunset.

Cortina boasts eight distinct ski areas, each with its own challenges and charms. Regrettably, because they sprawl rather disjointedly across the terrain, they're not always easy to interconnect. The most appealing are the **Tofana-Promedes, Forcella Rossa,** and **Faloria-Tondi** complexes. The **Pocol, Mietres,** and **Socepres** areas are for novices; the **Cinque Torri** is good for intermediates; and the outlying **Falzarego** is a long, dramatic, and sometimes terrifying downhill jaunt not recommended for anyone except a very competent skier.

Despite the availability of dozens of cable cars originating outside the town center along the valley floor, Cortina's most dramatic cable cars are the **Freccia**

Cortina.

nel Cielo ("Arrow of the Sky"), the region's longest and most panoramic (see above), and the **F**; www.funiviefaloria.com **univia Faloria** (**Faloria chairlift**; ℭ **0436-2517**). It departs from Piazzale Marconi (bus station). Both of these cable cars are patronized even by visitors who'd never dream of skiing. A single round-trip ticket for the chairlift is 21€—although if you plan on spending time in Cortina, it's almost always more economical to buy a ski pass.

Ski passes are issued for from 1 to 21 days. They can include access to just the lifts around Cortina (about 50) or to all the ski lifts in the Dolomiti (around 464). By far the better value is the more comprehensive pass. This **Dolomiti Super Ski Pass** allows you unlimited access to a vast network of chairlifts and gondolas over Cortina and the mountains flanking at least 10 other resorts. The single-day pass is 37€ to 46€, but the daily cost goes down as you increase the days of the pass. For example, depending on the season, a 7-day pass is 198€ to 247€ and a 21-day pass is 496€ to 563€. The Cortina-only pass sells for about 10% less, but few people opt for it. Children 7 and under ski free.

Included in any pass is free transport on any of Cortina's bright-yellow ski buses that run the length of the valley in season, connecting the many cable cars. Depending on snowfall, the two ski lifts mentioned above, as well as most of the other lifts in Cortina, are closed from around April 25 to July 15 and September 15 to around December 1. For information, call ℭ **0436-862171.**

CROSS-COUNTRY SKIING The trails start about 3km (2 miles) north of town. Some, but not all, run parallel to the region's roads and highways. For information about their location, instruction, and rental of equipment, contact the **Scuola Italiana di Sci Snowboard** in Cortina (ℭ **0436-2911**; www.scuolascicortina.com).

ICE-SKATING In winter, two rinks operate in the **Stadio Olimpico del Ghiaccio,** Via dello Stadio (ℭ **0436-881818**). One of the two operates throughout

THE VENETO & THE DOLOMITES

Cortina d'Ampezzo

summer, but the other is converted to a concrete surface suitable for in-line skating. Regardless of the season, you'll pay 9€. Skates are included in the price. Children 11 and under pay 8€.

Where to Stay

If you're looking for the chance to live with a Dolomite family in comfort and informality, ask the tourist office for its list of private homes that take in paying guests (the office won't make the reservations for you, however; you have to do it yourself). Even though nearly 5,000 hotel beds are available, it's best to reserve ahead, especially in August and December 20 to January 7.

Hotel Ancora ★ This evocative hotel from 1826 is the domain of the empress of the Dolomiti, Flavia Bertozzi, who gathered its antique sculptures and objets d'art during her trips throughout Italy. The Ancora attracts sporting guests from all over the world, hosts modern art exhibits and classical concerts, and boasts terraces with outdoor tables and umbrellas (the town center for sipping and gossiping). Garlanded wooden balconies encircle the five floors. Most guest rooms open onto these porches, and all are well furnished, comfortable, and inviting; many have sitting areas.

Corso Italia 62, 32043 Cortina d'Ampezzo. (℘ **0436-3261.** Fax 0436-3265. www.hotelancora cortina.com. 49 units. Summer 126€–230€ per person double, 156€–340€ per person suite; winter 150€–208€ per person double, 177€–318€ per person suite. Rates include half board. AE, DC, MC, V. Free parking. Closed after Easter to June and Nov–Dec 4. **Amenities:** Restaurant; bar; babysitting; room service. *In room:* TV, hair dryer, minibar.

Hotel Corona 🦪 For anyone interested in modern Italian art, a stop here is an event—the walls are hung with dozens of works. Many of the most important artists of Italy (and a few from France) from 1948 to 1963 are represented by paintings, sculptures, and ceramic bas-reliefs acquired by manager Luciano Rimoldi. The guest rooms are cozy, with varnished pine and local artifacts. The tiled bathrooms are compact. Rimoldi is also a ski instructor (he once coached Princess Grace in her downhill technique) and was head of the Italian ice-hockey team during the 1988 Winter Olympics, where one of his former pupils, Alberto Tomba, began his Olympic domination of Alpine events.

Via Val di Sotto 12, 32043 Cortina d'Ampezzo. (℘ **0436-3251.** Fax 0436-867339. www.hotel coronacortina.it. 46 units (17 with shower only). 60€–160€ per person double. Rates include continental breakfast. AE, DC, MC, V. Closed Apr–June and Sept–Dec 3. **Amenities:** Restaurant; babysitting; room service. *In room:* TV, hair dryer, minibar.

Hotel de la Poste ★★ Long a celebrity favorite, this is the most traditional hotel of Cortina, with a history dating from 1835 when it received guests arriving in horse-drawn carriages. It was founded by the Manaigo family, which still runs it today, keeping up with modern conveniences while maintaining its old-fashioned comforts. In the center of town, it was built like a Tyrolean mountain chalet, with open wooden balconies and terraces encircling the building, giving bedrooms sun porches. The midsize to spacious bedrooms are furnished with antiques or reproductions, and the hotel is justly renowned for its dining and drinking facilities.

Piazza Roma 14, 32043 Cortina d'Ampezzo. (℘ **0436-4271.** Fax 0436-868435. www.delaposte. it. 83 units. 101€–294€. Rates include buffet breakfast. AE, DC, MC, V. Closed Apr to mid-June and Oct to mid-Dec. **Amenities:** 2 restaurants; bar; room service. *In room:* TV, hair dryer, minibar.

Hotel Menardi ★ 🎁 This eye-catcher in the upper part of Cortina looks like a great country inn, with wooden balconies and shutters. Its rear windows open onto a flowery meadow and a view of the Dolomite crags. The inn is 100 years old and is run by the Menardi family, which still knows how to speak the old Dolomite tongue, Ladino. The regular guest rooms are decorated in the Tyrolean fashion, each with its own distinct personality; bathrooms are on the small side. Rooms in the annex are more modern and stylish, and this is also the site of a wellness center with a Jacuzzi and steam bath, plus massages.

Via Majou 110, 32043 Cortina d'Ampezzo. © **0436-2400.** Fax 0436-862183. www.hotelmenardi.it. 51 units. Winter 110€–160€ double per person, summer 90€–150€ per person. Rates include half board. AE, DC, MC, V. Parking 10€. Closed Apr 12–May 28 and Sept 22–Dec 3. **Amenities:** Bar; babysitting; Jacuzzi; room service; sauna. *In room:* TV, hair dryer, Wi-Fi (5€ per hr.).

Miramonti Majestic Grand Hotel ★★ Built in 1893, this hotel, one of the grandest in the Dolomites, is a short distance from the center of town. The rustic interior is filled with warm colors, lots of exposed timbers, and the most elegant crowd in Cortina. The well-furnished guest rooms look like those of a private home, complete with matching accessories, built-in closets, and all the modern extras. The bathrooms boast deluxe toiletries. Suites have a fireplace and Jacuzzi. From December 18 to January 8, there is a minimum stay requirement of 7 days.

Via Peziè 103, 32043 Cortina d'Ampezzo. © **0436-4201.** Fax 0436-867019. www.miramonti majestic.it. 108 units. 185€–600€ per person double; 520€–850€ per person suite. Rates include half board. AE, DC, MC, V. Parking 42€ in garage; free outside. Closed Apr–June and Sept–Nov. Hotel shuttle to/from town center every 30 min. (8:30am–11pm). **Amenities:** Restaurant; bar; babysitting; Jacuzzi; indoor panoramic heated pool; room service; spa; outdoor tennis court (lit). *In room:* A/C, TV, hair dryer, minibar.

Where to Dine

Da Beppe Sello 🍴 ALPINE/INTERNATIONAL/ITALIAN This down-to-earth and reasonably priced restaurant is in a Tyrolean-style hotel at the edge of the village. Named for the hotel founder's two nicknames, Joseph (Beppe) Menardi (Sello), it's a bastion of superb regional cuisine. Scan the menus for *casunziei* (ravioli filled with red beets), the specialty of Cortina. Okay, so it's an Austrian, but so was Cortina for 4 centuries until World War I came along. Menu items include venison filet with pears, polenta, and *marmellata di mirtilli* (marmalade made from an Alpine berry like a huckleberry or blueberry); *pappardelle* with rabbit sauce; *tagliolini* with porcini mushrooms; roast chicken with bay leaves; and filet steak flavored with bacon. You get to keep your plate as a souvenir.

Via Ronco 68. © **0436-3236.** www.beppesello.it. Reservations recommended. Main courses 15€–27€. AE, MC, V. High season daily 12:30–2pm and 7:30–10pm; low season Wed–Mon 12:30–2pm and 7:30–10pm. Closed Apr–May 20 and Sept 20–Dec 3.

El Toulà ★ ITALIAN/VENETIAN Located 3km (2 miles) east of Cortina toward Pocol, this restaurant offers an elegant setting. This restaurant is a wood-framed structure with picture windows and a terrace. The cuisine is a celebration of regional produce, as exemplified by artichoke hearts with melted Fonduta cheese and poppy seeds as an appetizer, followed by fusilli pasta with radicchio and crispy sausage. Another specialty is pork filet with air-cured ham (Speck) served with an apple purée.

Località Ronco 123. ☎ **0436-3339.** www.toula.it. Reservations required. Main courses 13€–38€. AE, DC, MC, V. Tues–Sun noon–3pm and 8–11pm. Closed Easter to late July and Sept–Nov.

The Great Dolomite Road ★★★

Stretching from Cortina d'Ampezzo in the east to Bolzano in the west, the **Great Dolomite Road (Grande Strada delle Dolomiti)** follows a circuitous route of about 109km (68 miles) and ranks among the grandest scenic drives in all Europe. The first panoramic pass you'll cross is **Falzarego,** about 18km (11 miles) from Cortina and 2,103m (6,900 ft.) above sea level. The next great pass is **Pordoi,** at about 2,240m (7,350 ft.) above sea level, the loftiest point. (You can get out of your car and ride a cable car, the Funicolare Porta Vescovo, btw. the roadside parking lot and the mountain's summit. At both ends, you'll find Alpine-style restaurants, hotels, and cafes. Cable cars depart at 30-min. intervals throughout daylight hours. For fares and more information, contact the tourist office in Cortina.) In spring, edelweiss grows in the surrounding fields; in winter, virtually everything except the surface of the road is blanketed in snow. After crossing the pass, you'll descend to the little resort of **Canazei,** and then much later pass by sea-blue **Carezza Lake.**

TRENT ★

232km (144 miles) NE of Milan, 101km (63 miles) N of Verona

A northern Italian city that basks in its former glory, the medieval Trent (Trento) on the left bank of the Adige is famous as the host of the Council of Trent (1545–63). Beset with difficulties, such as the rising tide of "heretics," the Ecumenical Council convened at Trent, leading to the Counter-Reformation. Trent lies on the main rail line from the Brenner Pass, and many visitors like to stop off here before journeying farther south into Italy.

Although it has an Alpine setting, Trent still has a definite Italian flavor. As capitals of provinces go, Trent is rather sleepy and provincial. It hasn't been overly commercialized and is still richly imbued with a lot of architectural charm, with a small array of attractions. Nonetheless, it makes a good refueling stop for those exploring this history-rich part of Italy.

Essentials

GETTING THERE   Trent lies on the **rail line** for Bologna, Verona, the Brenner Pass, and Munich; trains pass through day and night. The trip from Milan takes 2¾ hours; from Rome, it's 7 hours. Five trains per day make the 3½-hour run from Venice. For rail information and schedules, call ☎ **892021** in Italy.

Both the train and the bus stations lie between the Adige River and the public gardens of Trent. The heart of town is to the east of the Adige. From the station, turn on Via Pozzo, which becomes Via Orfane and Via Cavour before reaching the city's heartbeat, Piazza del Duomo.

By **car,** take A22 north from Verona or south from Bolzano.

VISITOR INFORMATION   The **tourist office,** on Via Manci 2 (☎ **0461-216000;** www.apt.trento.it), is open daily 9am to 7pm.

The two most important wine-producing regions of northwestern Italy are the Alto Adige (also known as the Bolzano or Sudtirol region) and Trento. The loftier of the two, the Alto Adige, grows an Italian version of the Gewürztraminers (a fruity white) that are more often found in Germany, Austria, and Alsace. Venerable winegrowers include **Alois Lageder** (founded in 1855), Tenuta Loüwengang, Vicolo dei Conti, in the hamlet of Magré (✆ **0471-809500**; www.aloislageder.eu); and **Schloss Turmhof**, Entiklar, Kurtatsch, 39040 (✆ **0471-880122**). The Trentino area, a short distance to the south, is one of the leading producers of chardonnay and sparkling wines fermented by using methods developed centuries ago.

Exploring the City

Trent is loaded with old-fashioned charm and Alpine flair. For a quick glimpse of the old town, head for **Piazza del Duomo ★**, dominated by the **Cattedrale di San Virgilio.** Built in the Romanesque style and much restored over the years, it dates from the 12th century. A medieval crypt under the altar holds a certain fascination, and the ruins of a 6th-century Christian basilica were recently discovered beneath the church. You're entitled to visit these remains by paying your admission to the **Diocese Museum (Museum Diocesano) ★**, facing the cathedral (✆ **0461-234419;** www.museodiocesanotridentino.it), with its religious artifacts on display relating to the Council of Trent, which met in the Duomo from 1545 to 1563. The museum is open Wednesday to Monday 9:30am to 12:30pm and 2 to 5:30pm; it costs 4€. The Duomo is open daily 6:30am to noon and 2 to 6pm. In the center of the square is a mid-18th-century **Fountain of Neptune (Fontana di Nettuno).**

The Nardis waterfall.

The ruling prince-bishops of Trent, who held sway until they were toppled by the French in the early 19th century, resided at the medieval **Castello del Buonconsiglio ★** (✆ **0461-233770;** www.buonconsiglio.it), reached from Via Bernardo Clesio 3. The castle is open Tuesday to Sunday with this schedule: November 8 to May 3 from 9:30am to 5pm, and May 4 to November 7 from 10am to 6pm. Admission is 7€.

Trent makes a good base for exploring **Monte Bondone,** a sports resort about 35km (22 miles) from the city center; **Paganella,** slightly more than 19km (12 miles) from Trent (the summit is nearly 2,133m/7,000 ft. high); and the **Brenta Dolomiti.** The last excursion, which requires at least a

The Fountain of Neptune (Fontana di Nettuno).

day for a good look, will reward you with some of the finest mountain scenery in Italy. En route from Trent, you'll pass by **Lake Toblino** and then travel a winding road past jagged boulders. A 10-minute detour from the main road at the turnoff to the Genova valley offers untamed scenery. Take the detour at least to the thunderous **Nardis waterfall.** A good stopover point is the little resort of **Madonna di Campiglio.**

If you don't have time to drive around, you'll get a breezy view over Trent and a heart-thumping aerial ride as well by taking the **cable car** from Ponte di San Lorenzo near the train station up to Sardagna, a village on one of the mountainsides that enclose the city. You might want to pack sandwiches and enjoy an Alpine picnic on one of the grassy meadows nearby. The cable car (☎ **0461-232154**) runs daily every 30 minutes (every 15 min. during peak hours) from 7am to 10:30pm, and the fare is 2.30€ for an all-day ticket. A single ticket costs .90€.

Where to Stay

Albergo Accademia ★ 🎒 This Alpine inn behind the Renaissance Santa Maria Maggiore is made up of three buildings that have been joined to create an attractive hotel. One of the structures is believed to be of 11th- or 12th-century origin, based on a brick wall similar to the city walls found during renovation work. According to legend, the older part of the Accademia housed church leaders who attended the Council of Trent in the 16th century. The guest rooms are done in light natural wood, and a suite at the top of the house has a terrace with a view of the town and mountains. The rooms are comfortable and cozy, each with a compact bathroom.

Vicolo Colico 4, Trento. ☎ **0461-233600.** Fax 0461-230174. www.accademiahotel.it. 43 units (shower only). 150€–180€ double; 200€–210€ junior suite. Rates include buffet breakfast. AE, DC, MC, V. Closed Dec 24–Jan 6. Free parking. **Amenities:** Restaurant; bar; room service; Wi-Fi (2€ per hr., in lobby). *In room:* A/C, TV, hair dryer, minibar.

Grand Hotel Trento ★★ This *fin de siècle* monument is the finest hotel in the area and the only luxe choice in the city itself. It offers luxuries such as a beauty center that no other hotel does. A renovation has restored this traditional choice to some of the glory it knew in its heyday. Natural woods, bright colors, tasteful furnishings, and artwork enliven the atmosphere in a hotel filled with modern conveniences. The bedrooms are the most spacious in town, with rich fabrics, heavy draperies, thick carpets, and wood-trimmed furnishings along with ample bathrooms with tub or shower. A skylit piano bar and lounge is one of the most inviting after-dark venues in Trento. Coffered ceilings, fireplaces, antiques, and frescoes take you back to the Trent of yesterday.

Via Alfieri 1–3, 38100 Trento. ✆ **0461-271000.** Fax 0461-271001. www.grandhoteltrento.com. 136 units. 120€–200€ double; 196€–260€ suite. Rates include buffet breakfast. AE, DC, MC, V. Parking 10€. **Amenities:** Restaurant; bar; babysitting; room service; spa. *In room:* A/C, TV, hair dryer, minibar, Wi-Fi (4€ per hr.).

Hotel Buonconsiglio   Built shortly after World War II and massively reno-vated in the 1990s, this is an immaculate hotel with pleasant rooms and an English-speaking staff. It's on a busy street near the rail station and has a slight edge over the Accademia (see above). In the lobby is a collection of abstract modern paintings. Each guest room is soundproof to keep out traffic noise and has a well-kept bathroom.

Via Romagnosi 14–16, 38100 Trento. ✆ **0461-272888.** Fax 0461-272889. www.hotelbuonconsiglio. it. 46 units (with shower only). 75€–109€ double; 140€–160€ suite. Rates include buffet break-fast. AE, DC, MC, V. Parking 12€. **Amenities:** Bar; room service. *In room:* A/C, TV, hair dryer, minibar, Wi-Fi (6€ per 24 hr.).

Where to Dine

It's almost a requirement to stroll down Trent's Renaissance streets with a gelato from **Gelateria Torre Verde di Zanella** on Via Suffragio 2 (✆ **0461-232039**). Many flavors are made from fresh local fruits in season.

Orso Grigio ITALIAN/TRENTINE   This elegant restaurant is about 30m (98 ft.) from Piazza Fiera, in a building whose origins might date from the 1500s. When you see the immaculate table linen, well-cared-for plants, and subdued lighting, you'll know something is going right. The menus are seasonal to take advantage of the finest fresh produce. Starters include potato pie with salami and cheese or else carpaccio of salted beef with asparagus and Grana cheese. *Rufioli* (a green *tortellini*) and *squazet con polenta* (Trentine-style fried tripe) are two regional specialties. Finish with chocolate mousse. The wines of the province are a special feature here.

Via degli Orti 19. ✆ **0461-984400.** www.orsogrigio.it. Reservations recommended. Main courses 8€–20€. AE, DC, MC, V. Mon–Sat 12:30–2:30pm and 7:30–10pm.

Osteria a Le Due Spade ★★ TRENTO/TYROLEAN   Situated just 50m (164 ft.) from the cathedral, this restaurant was established back in 1545. The antique choice is appropriately decorated in an old-fashioned country style, with tables decked out in lace, beautiful glass and cutlery, and wood paneling, even an old-fashioned stove. Since the restaurant has only eight tables, reservations are essential. Expect impeccable service and a warm welcome, and also some first-rate food, much of it harvested from the surrounding region itself. The chefs show their skills in such dishes as a half-moon-shaped potato ravioli filled with regional cheese and topped with black truffles, or else deer filet cooked over mountain hay and served with a creamy yellow polenta. All of the pasta dishes are homemade daily, and often black truffles provide a tantalizingly deluxe touch. Filet of suckling pig with a cheese fondue is a regional delight.

Via Don Archangelo Rizzi 11. ℂ **0461-234343.** www.leduespade.com. Reservations recommended. Main courses 16€–24€. AE, DC, MC, V. Tues–Sat noon–2:30pm; Mon–Sat 7:30–10pm.

Restaurant Chiesa ★ 🎁 TRENTINE/ITALIAN   This restaurant offers the largest array of dishes we've ever seen made with apples. Owner Allesandro recognized that Eve's favorite fruit, which grows more abundantly around Trent than practically anywhere else, was the base of dozens of traditional recipes. Specialties include risotto with apple, liver pâté with apple, perch filet with apple, and a range of other well-prepared specialties (not all of which contain apples).

Via Livio Marchetti 9. ℂ **0461-238766.** www.ristorantechiesa.it. Reservations recommended. Main courses 10€–20€. AE, DC, MC, V. Mon–Sat noon–2:30pm and 7:30–10pm.

Shopping

The most memorable food-and-wine shop in town is the **Enoteca del Corso,** Corso 3 Novembre 64 (ℂ **0461-916424**), with wines from the region and everywhere else in Italy, as well as the salamis, olives, cheeses, and other salty tidbits that go well with them. Another outlet for the reds and whites produced throughout the Trentino and the rest of Italy is the **Grado 12,** Largo Carducci 12 (ℂ **0461-982496**).

MILAN, LOMBARDY & THE LAKE DISTRICT

Among the most progressive of all the Italians, the Lombards have charted an industrial empire unequaled in Italy. Often the dream of the poor and jobless in the south is to go to Milan for the high wages and the good life, although thousands end up finding neither. Lombardy isn't all about manufacturing, however. Milan is filled to the brim with important attractions, and nearby are old Lombard art cities such as Bergamo and Mantua.

Conquerors from barbarians to Napoleon have marched across the plains of Lombardy, and even Mussolini came to his end here. He and his mistress (both already dead) were strung up in a Milan square as war-weary residents vented their rage.

The **Lake District,** with its flowery promenades, lemon trees, villas, parks, and crystal-blue waters, is an old-fashioned resort area, with some grand old hotels. The lakes themselves—notably Garda, Como, and Maggiore—form one of the most enchanting splashes of scenery in northern Italy. They've attracted poets and writers from Goethe to d'Annunzio. After World War II, the Italian lakes seemed to be largely the domain of matronly English and German types. In our more recent swings through the district, however, we've seen a new, younger crowd, particularly at resorts such as Limone on Lake Garda. Even if your time is limited, you'll want to have at least a look at Lake Garda.

MILAN ★★★

572km (355 miles) NW of Rome, 140km (87 miles) NE of Turin, 142km (88 miles) N of Genoa, 257km (160 miles) W of Venice

With two million inhabitants, Milan (Milano) is Italy's most dynamic city. Milan is Italy's window on Europe, its most sophisticated and high-tech metropolis, devoid of the dusty history that sometimes paralyzes modern developments in Rome and Florence or the watery rot that seems to pervade Venice.

Part of the work ethic that has catapulted Milan into the 21st century might stem from the Teutonic origins of the Lombards (originally from northwestern Germany), who occupied Milan and intermarried with its population after the collapse of the Roman Empire. In the 14th century, the Viscontis, through their wits, wealth, and marriages to the royalty of England and France, made Milan Italy's strongest city, economically. And Milan initiated a continuing campaign of drainage and irrigation of the Po Valley that helped to make it one of the world's most fertile regions.

In the 1700s, Milan was dominated by the Habsburgs, a legacy that left it with scores of neoclassical buildings in its inner core and an abiding appreciation for music and (perhaps) work. In 1848, it was at the heart of the northern Italian revolt against its Austro-Hungarian rulers and, with Piedmont, was at the center

PREVIOUS PAGE: **Villas along Lake Como.**

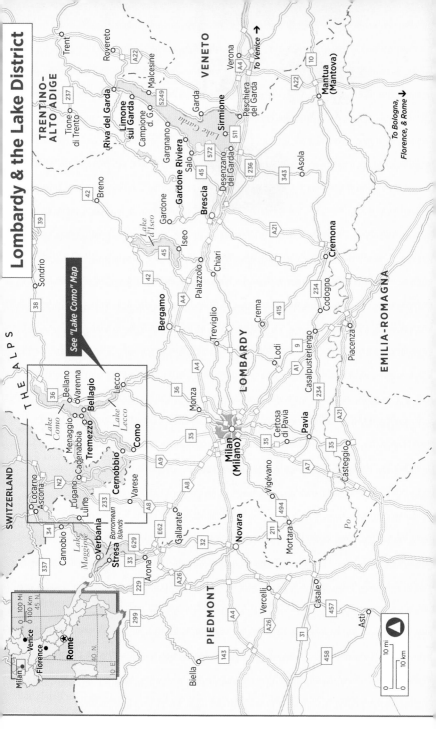

Lombardy & the Lake District

SWITZERLAND

THE ALPS

TRENTINO-ALTO ADIGE

VENETO

LOMBARDY

PIEDMONT

EMILIA-ROMAGNA

See "Lake Como" Map

Lake Como

Lake Lecco

Lake Maggiore

Lake d'Iseo

Lake Garda

Borromean Islands

To Venice →

To Bologna, Florence, & Rome →

Trent

Rovereto

Tione di Trento

Riva del Garda

Limone sul Garda

Campione d. G.

Malcesine

Gargnano

Gardone Riviera

Salò

Desenzano del Garda

Garda

Sirmione

Peschiera del Garda

Verona

Mantua (Mantova)

Asola

Breno

Gardone

Brescia

Iseo

Palazzolo

Chiari

Bergamo

Crema

Cremona

Codogno

Piacenza

Treviglio

Lodi

Casalpusterlengo

Casteggio

Pavia

Certosa di Pavia

Monza

Milan (Milano)

Vigévano

Mortara

Novara

Gallarate

Varese

Como

Cernobbio

Tremezzo

Bellagio

Varenna

Bellano

Lecco

Menaggio

Cadenabbia

Lugano

Luino

Locarno

Ascona

Cannobio

Verbania

Stresa

Arona

Sondrio

Vercelli

Casale

Asti

Biella

Sorico

Novara

Santa Tione

Switzerland · **Venice** · **Milan** · **Florence** · **Rome**

237 · A22 · 39 · 38 · 42 · 237 · S249 · 45 · 572 · S11 · A22 · 10 · A4 · 236 · 343 · A21 · 42 · 45 · A4 · 415 · 234 · 9 · 234 · A21 · 36 · 35 · A1 · 35 · A7 · A8 · A9 · E62 · 233 · 629 · 33 · 229 · 299 · 337 · 34 · N2 · A26 · 32 · 211 · 494 · 31 · A26 · A4 · 143 · 458 · 457 · 35

0 100 MI
0 100 KM

45° N

40° N

10 E

0 10 mi
0 10 km

Inside Pucci, one of Milan's many designer boutiques.

of the 19th-century nationalistic passion that swept through Italy and culminated in the country's unification. During this same period, Milan (through the novelist Manzoni) was encouraging the development of a Pan-Italian dialect.

Today, Milan is a commercial powerhouse and, partly because of its 400 banks and major industrial companies, Italy's most influential city. It's the center of publishing, silk production, TV, advertising, and fashion design; it also lies close to Italy's densest collection of automobile-assembly plants, rubber and textile factories, and chemical plants. Milan also boasts La Scala, one of Europe's most prestigious opera houses; a major university; and world-renowned annual trade fairs.

With unashamed capitalistic style, Milan has purchased more art than it has produced and has attracted an energetic group of creative intellects. To make it in Milan, in either business or the arts, is to have made it to the top of the pecking order. If you came to Italy to find sunny piazzas and lazy bright afternoons, you won't find them amid the fogs and rains of Milan. You will, however, have placed your finger on the pulse of modern Italy.

Essentials

GETTING THERE Milan has two airports: the **Aeroporto di Linate,** 7km (4¼ miles) east of the inner city; and the **Aeroporto Malpensa,** 45km (27 miles) west of the center. Malpensa is used for most transatlantic flights, whereas Linate is used for flights within Italy and Europe. For general airport and flight information, call ✆ **02-74852200.**

Delta (✆ **800/241-4141;** www.delta.com) flies nonstop from New York's JFK to Milan, and from Atlanta's Hartsfield-Jackson International Airport to Milan. **Alitalia** (✆ **800/223-5730** in the U.S., or 800/361-8336 in Canada; www.alitaliausa.com) offers nonstop flights into Milan only from New York (JFK). **British Airways** (✆ **800/AIRWAYS** [247-9297]; www.britishairways.com) has flights from London to Milan.

Malpensa Express trains whisk arrivals from Malpensa airport to the Cadorna station in the heart of Milan in about 45 minutes. They run every 30 minutes daily from 5:30am to midnight. A one-way ticket costs 11€ for adults and 6€ for children 4 to 12 years old. Tickets are available at Milan Cadorna Ferrovie Nord Milano railway station on the left side, front platform 1 and 2 (daily 6am–8:30pm) or at Malpensa Airport Terminal 1, Malpensa Express Ticket Office (Mon–Sat 6:30am–10pm, Sun and holidays 6:30am–10:30pm). For information, call ✆ **199-151152** between 7am and 8pm, or visit www.malpensaexpress.it.

Buses run between Linate and the Centrale station (7€) every 30 minutes daily 6:10am to 11:30pm. A bus (73) also runs between Piazza San Babila and

Linate airport every 20 minutes daily from 6am to 12:55am. Buses run from Malpensa to Stazione Centrale daily every 30 to 45 minutes, costing 7.50€ one-way. Service is from 5:30am to 1:20am. For information about buses from Linate to Milan, call *②* **02-58587237.** For information about buses from Malpensa to Milan and vice versa, call *②* **02-58583185.** This is much cheaper than taking a taxi, which could run you a whopping 90€.

Milan is serviced by the finest **rail connections** in Italy. The main rail station for arrivals is Mussolini's mammoth **Stazione Centrale,** Piazza Duca d'Aosta (*②* **892021**), where you'll find the National Railways information office open daily 7am to 9pm. One train per hour arrives from Genoa (trip time: 1½ hr.), costing 17€ one-way. Trains from Turin to Milan take 1 hour, 55 minutes, costing 10€ to 28€ one-way. The new high-speed train (Frecciarossa) from Turin takes only 1 hour, costing 31€ to 44€ one-way. Twenty-five trains arrive daily from Venice (trip time: 3 hr.), costing 30€ to 42€ one-way. Trains from Florence to Milan take 3½ hours, costing 28€ to 38€ one-way. The high-speed train (Frecciarossa) from Florence takes only 1 hour and 45 minutes, costing 52€ to 70€ one-way. Trains from Rome to Milan take 6 hours and 35 minutes, with the high-speed train (Frecciarossa) taking 3½ hours. A one-way ticket costs 89€ to 114€, depending on the train. The station is directly northeast of the heart of town; trams, buses, and the Metro link the station to Piazza del Duomo in the very center.

If you're **driving** to Milan, A4 is the principal east-west route for Milan, with A8 coming in from the northwest, A1 from the southeast, and A7 from the southwest. A22 is another major north-south artery, running just east of Lake Garda. But once you arrive, put your car in a garage and keep it there. Don't even try to drive around the crowded, confusing main tourist areas of Milan.

VISITOR INFORMATION   The **Informazione e accoglienza turistica Milano,** on Piazza del Duomo 19A (*②* **02-77404343;** www.visitamilano.it), is open Monday to Saturday 8:45am to 1pm and 2 to 6pm, and Sunday 9am to 1pm and 2 to 6pm in summer (it closes 1 hr. early in winter). There's also a branch at Stazione Centrale (*②* 02-77404318), open Monday to Saturday 9am to 6pm, and Sunday 9am to 1pm and 2 to 5pm.

GETTING AROUND   The **subway** system is extensive and efficient, covering most of Milan; in addition, there are buses and trams, making it fairly easy to navigate. Regular tickets cost 1€ and are sold at Metro stations and newsstands. Some subway tickets are good for continuing trips on city buses at no extra charge, but they must be used within 75 minutes of purchase. You must stamp your ticket when you board a bus or tram, or risk incurring a fine.

The tourist office and all subway ticket offices sell a **travel pass** for 3€ for 1 day, or 5.50€ for 2 days, good for unlimited use on the city's tram, bus, and subway network. For information on transportation in Milan, call A.T.M. (*②* **800-808181** toll-free in Italy; daily 7:30am–7:30pm).

To phone a **taxi,** dial *②* **02-4040,** 02-8585, or 02-8383; fares start at 3€, with a nighttime surcharge of 6.10€.

Don't try to drive within the relatively small Cerchia dei Navigli, where all the major attractions are located. It's easy to walk to everything in this area.

American Express   The **American Express** office is at Via Larga 4 (✆ **02-721041;** www.americanexpress.com; Metro: Duomo); it's open Monday to Friday 9am to 5:30pm.

Consulates   The **U.S. Consulate,** Via Principe Amedeo 2–10 (✆ **02-290351;** Metro: Turati), is open Monday to Friday 8:30am to noon. The **U.K. Consulate** is at Via San Paolo 7 (✆ **02-723001;** www.ukinitaly.fco.gov.uk; Metro: Duomo), open Monday to Friday 9am to 1pm and 2 to 5pm. The **Australian Consulate** is at Via Borgogna 2 (✆ **02-777041;** Metro: San Babila), open Monday to Thursday 9am to noon and 2 to 4pm, and Friday 9am to noon.

Emergencies   For the **police,** call ✆ **112;** for an **ambulance,** call ✆ **118;** for any **emergency,** call ✆ **113.** About a 5-minute ride from the Duomo, the **Ospedale Maggiore Policlinico,** Via Francesco Sforza 35 (✆ **02-55031;** www.policlinico.mi.it; Metro: Crocetta), has English-speaking doctors. You can find an all-night **pharmacy** by phoning ✆ **800-801185** toll-free in Italy. The pharmacy (✆ **02-6690735;** Metro: Centrale) at the Stazione Centrale never closes.

Where to Stay

In Milan, you'll find some deluxe hotels and an abundance of first- and second-class hotels, most of which are big on comfort but short on romance. In the third- and fourth-class bracket and on the *pensione* (boardinghouse) level are dozens of choices, although the budget hotels in Milan are not nearly as nice as those in Italy's other major cities. If you can afford it, spend more on your hotel in Milan and opt for budget accommodations in Rome, Florence, and Venice, which have clean, comfortable, and often architecturally interesting third- and fourth-class hotels and *pensioni.*

VERY EXPENSIVE

Bulgari Hotel ★★★   Bulgari, the Italian jewelry maker, has made an impressive debut with the opening of this bastion of luxury where casual, streamlined elegance and minimalist design prevail. Once a late-19th-century convent, the Bulgari sits on a cul-de-sac in a garden setting, just a 5-minute walk from La Scala. Fabulous materials were used for its inner decor, including black matte marble from Zimbabwe. With their heavy doors and bleached oak walls, most bedrooms face the garden. The standard rooms are a bit small, but comfortable, and the larger accommodations are fit for Sophia Loren.

Via Privata Fratelli Gabba 7B, 20121 Milan. ✆ **02-8058051.** Fax 02-8058-05222. www.bulgari hotels.com. 58 units. 500€–850€ double; from 1,500€ suite. AE, DC, MC, V. Parking 50€. Metro: Montenapoleone. **Amenities:** Restaurant; bar; airport transfers (150€); concierge; exercise room; indoor heated pool; room service; spa. *In room:* A/C, TVDVD, CD player, minibar, MP3 docking station, Wi-Fi (10€ per hr.).

Four Seasons Hotel Milano ★★★   There is a saying in Milano that guests go to the Principe di Savoia to make their fortunes, but they come to the Four Seasons to spend them. This five-star hotel opened in 1993 on a side street opening onto Via Montenapoleone's upscale boutiques, near the Duomo. The building was first a 15th-century monastery, then the residence of the Habsburg-appointed governor of northern Italy in the 1850s, and later the site of luxury apartments. The medieval facade, many of the frescoes and columns, and the original monastic details were incorporated into a modern edifice accented with bronze, stone floors, glass, pearwood cabinetry, Murano chandeliers, and acres of Fortuny fabrics. The guest rooms are cool, conservative, sleek, and spacious, with a sense of understated luxury. The staff can arrange tee times at several area golf courses.

Via Gesù 8, 20121 Milano. ✆ **02-77088.** Fax 02-77085000. www.fourseasons.com. 118 units. 500€–820€ double; 790€–880€ junior suite; from 1,300€ suite. AE, DC, MC, V. Parking 51€. Metro: Montenapoleone or San Babila. **Amenities:** 2 restaurants; babysitting; children's programs; concierge; exercise room; room service. *In room:* A/C, TV/DVD, CD player, hair dryer, minibar, Wi-Fi (22€ per 24 hr.).

The Gray ★★ This modern designer hotel opened in 2003 between the Duomo and La Scala. Setting a whimsical note is a swing hanging in the lobby: a full-size mattress upholstered in fuchsia and silk shantung, suspended by four grosgrain-wrapped steel cords. A wall is lined by Makassar ebony displaying silver leaves. Fashionistas checking in here are dazzled by such unique features as virtual pictures playing on screen-walls, moving carpets encased in the floors, private workout rooms in some guest rooms, and large round tubs featuring TVs on their rims. Designer Guido Ciompi created 21 different rooms for 21 different experiences. In one of the bi-level accommodations, a counterbalanced bed is suspended from the ceiling on steel cables. As for the minimalist bedrooms, comfort reigns supreme. The headboards? Only white leather or ostrich will do.

Via San Raffaele 6, 20121 Milano. ✆ **02-7208951.** Fax 02-866526. www.sinahotels.com. 21 units. 280€–680€ double; from 600€ junior suite. Rates include buffet breakfast. AE, DC, MC, V. Parking 58€. **Amenities:** Restaurant; bar; babysitting; concierge; room service. *In room:* A/C, TV/DVD, CD player, hair dryer, MP3 docking station, Wi-Fi (5€ per hr.).

Hotel Principe di Savoia ★ The Principe was built in 1927 to fill the need for a luxurious hotel near Stazione Centrale. It offers solid comfort, fine service, and contemporary amenities in an opulent old-world setting of crystal, detailed plasterwork, fine carpets, and polished marble. The guest rooms are spacious, decorated in a 19th-century Lombard style but offering high-tech efficiency. All contain leather chairs and other stylish furniture. The front rooms face the rowdy traffic of Piazza della Repubblica, but the ones in back are more tranquil, opening onto the Alps.

Piazza della Repubblica 17, 20124 Milano. ✆ **800/325-3535** in the U.S., or 02-62301. Fax 02-6595838. www.hotelprincipedisavoia.it. 404 units. 199€–850€ double; from 595€ suite. AE, DC, MC, V. Parking 60€. Metro: Repubblica. Tram: 1, 4, 11, 29, or 30. **Amenities:** 2 restaurants; bar; babysitting; concierge; exercise room; Jacuzzi; indoor heated pool; room service; sauna. *In room:* A/C, TV/DVD, CD player, hair dryer, minibar, Wi-Fi (27€ per 24 hr.).

Park Hyatt Milan ★★★ This deluxe chain's first Italian property, adjoining the Galleria, is installed in a 130-year-old *palazzo* near La Scala and the Duomo. Manolo-shod fashionistas have discovered this hotel and are seen passing by the lobby's 9m (30-ft.) floating glass dome. Ceilings are high, and the luxury living is top-notch. Massive travertine and elegant fabrics are found in the public rooms and spacious bedrooms, each custom designed and beautifully furnished. Bathrooms are, in essence, almost the same size as the bedrooms and even contain a minibar. The Hyatt is also one of the most high-tech hotels in Italy, from Technofitness center machines and a spa to state-of-the art Bang & Olufsen video systems.

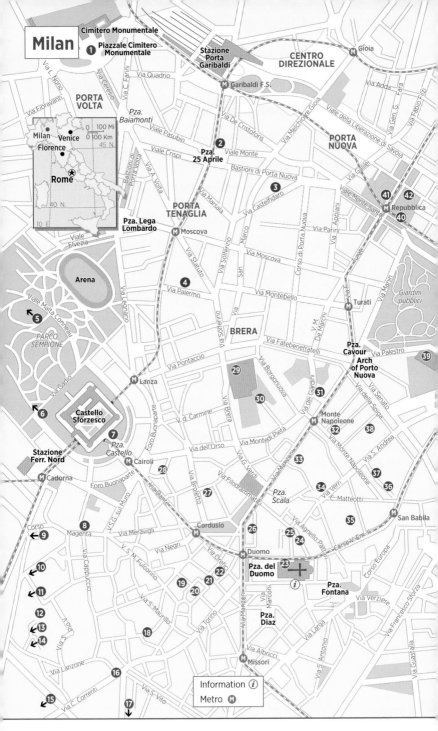

Milan

Cimitero Monumentale

❶ **Piazzale Cimitero Monumentale**

Via L. Nono
Via C. Farini
Via Ceresio
Via Quadrio

PORTA VOLTA

Via Fioravanti
Via Fioravanti

Milan
Venice
Florence
Rome

0   100 Mi
0   100 Km
45° N.

40° N.

10° E

Stazione Porta Garibaldi

Ⓜ Garibaldi F.S.

CENTRO DIREZIONALE

Ⓜ Gioia
Via Adda
Via G. Fara
Via Fabio Filzi

Via De Cristoforis
Viale della Liberazione di Savoia
Viale Monte Gioia

PORTA NUOVA

Pza. Baiamonti
Viale Pasubio
Viale Crispi

❷ **Pza. 25 Aprile**
Viale Monte
Bastioni di Porta Nuova

Via A. Volta
Via Marsala

❸

Via Castelfidato
Corso di Porta Nuova

Via Appiani
Via Parini

Via Galilei
Via Monte Santo

❹❶ Ⓜ **Repubblica**
❹❷
❹⓪

PORTA TENAGLIA

Pza. Lega Lombardo

Ⓜ **Moscova**

Via Statuto
Via Solferino
Via S. Marco
Via Moscova

Bastioni di Porta Nuova

Arena

Viale Malta Comneno

❺

PARCO SEMPIONE

Via Gadio

❻

❹ Via Palermo
Via Montebello

Via Leopardi

BRERA

Ⓜ **Turati**

Giardini pubblici

Via Manin

Via Fatebenefratelli
V. M. De Marchi

Pza. Cavour
Arch of Porto Nuova

Via Palestro
❸❾

Ⓜ **Lanza**

❷❾
❸⓪

Via Pontaccio
Foro Buonaparte
V. d. Carmine
Via Brera

Via Borgonuova
Via dei Giardini
❸❶

Castello Sforzesco

❼

Pza. Castello

Ⓜ **Cairoli**

❷❽

Via dell'Orso
Via Monte di Pietà
Via G. Verdi

Ⓜ **Monte Napoleone**
❸❽

Via Monte Napoleone
Via della Spiga
Via S. Andrea

❸❼
❸❻

Stazione Ferr. Nord

Ⓜ **Cadorna**

V.S.G. sul Muro
Foro Buonaparte
Via Dante
Via Broletto
Via Filodrammatici

❷❼
Via G. Verdi

Pza. Scala

❸❸

Via Verri
C. Matteotti

Corso
❾

Via Cappuccio
Via Meravigli
Via Negri
V. S. M. Fulcorino

Magenta

❽

Via S. Maurilio

Ⓜ **Cordusio**

❷❻
Via Orefici

Via Agnello
Via Agnello
❸❺

Corso V. En. II

Ⓜ **San Babila**
Corso Europa

❷❺
❷❹

❿
⓫

❷❷
❷❶

Ⓜ **Duomo**

❷❸

Pza. del Duomo
ⓘ

Pza. Fontana

Via Verziere

⓬
⓭
⓮

Via Torino

❶❾
❷⓪

Via Marconi

Pza. Diaz

Via Larga

Via S. Antonio
Via Francesco Sforza
Via Guastalla

❶❽

Via Lanzone

⓰

Via S. Vito

Via Albricci
Ⓜ **Missori**

Via C. Correnti

⓯

⓱

| Information | ⓘ |
| Metro | Ⓜ |

Attractions

Ambrosiana Library & Picture Gallery **20**
Basilica di San Ambrogio &
  San Ambrogio Basilica Museum **13**
Basilica di Sant'Eustorgio **17**
Brera Picture Gallery **29**
Civic Gallery of Modern Art **39**
Il Duomo & Baptistery **23**
Leonardo da Vinci National Museum of
  Science & Technology **14**
Monumental Cemetery **1**
Museo Bagatti Valsecchi **32**
Museo Poldi-Pezzoli **33**
Museum of Ancient Art **7**
Santa Maria delle Grazie
  (The Last Supper) **9**
Teatro degli Arcimboldi **43**
Torre Branca **6**

Accommodations

Antica Locanda dei Mercanti **12**
Antica Locanda Leonardo **8**
Antica Locanda Solferino **3**
Ariston **16**
Bulgari Hotel **30**
Casa Mia **40**
Enterprise Hotel **5**
Four Seasons Hotel Milano **38**
The Gray **25**
Hotel Gran Duca di York **19**
Hotel Principe di Savoia **42**
Hotel Rovello **28**
Hotel Star **27**
Park Hyatt Milan **26**
Pierre Milano **11**
Spadari al Duomo **21**
Straf **24**
St. George **46**
Town House 31 **48**
Westin Palace **41**

Dining

Acanto **42**
Al Tempio d'Oro **44**
Armani / Nobu **31**
A Santa Lucia **35**
Boeucc Antico Ristorante **34**
Cracco **22**
Gold **47**
Il Luogo di Aimo e Nadia **10**
Joia **45**
Just Cavalli Café **7**
La Libera **4**
La Magolfa **17**
Paper Moon **36**
Tano Passami L'Olio **15**
10 Corso Como Café **2**
Trattoria Bagutta **37**
Trattoria Milanese **18**

Via Tommaso Grossi, 20121 Milano. ℰ **02-88211234.** Fax 02-88211235. www.hyatt.com. 117 units. 480€–676€ double; 700€ junior suite; from 955€ suite. AE, DC, MC, V. Valet parking 50€. Metro: Duomo. **Amenities:** 2 restaurants; bar; airport transfers 135€–340€; babysitting; bikes; concierge; exercise room; room service; spa. *In room:* A/C, TV, hair dryer, minibar, Wi-Fi (15€ per 24 hr.).

Town House 31 ★ ★ 🏨   Small and discreet, this restored 19th-century town house in one of the city's finest residential areas is like an elegant and refined B&B. It's also a multicultural atmosphere, filled with objects from around the world, mostly African bric-a-brac and Chinese furnishings. A courtyard leads to the serene interior, one of Milan's best alternatives for those who shy from chain-formatted bedroom factories. Everything is carefully selected: the coconut fiber carpets, the powerful hair dryers, even the "herbal pillows." The best rooms have terraces, but they must be requested when booking.

Via Carlo Goldoni 31, 20129 Milano. ℰ **02-70156.** Fax 02-713167. www.townhouse.it. 19 units. 173€–560€ double; 236€–616€ junior suite. Rates include buffet breakfast. AE, DC, MC, V. Parking 20€–40€ nearby. Metro: Stazione Centrale. **Amenities:** Bar; airport transfers (90€); babysitting; concierge; room service. *In room:* A/C, TV, hair dryer, minibar, Wi-Fi (free).

Westin Palace ★   The Palace stands aloof on a hill near the rail station, with a formal car entrance, a facade boasting tiers of balconies, and an opulent lobby. Geared primarily to business travelers, the Palace is also a fine choice for vacationers and hosts the occasional visiting celeb. The midsize to spacious guest rooms are furnished with pastel upholstery and reproductions of Italian antiques, as well as video games, voice mail, and the supercomfortable beds for which Starwood Hotels are known. The elegant bathrooms are in pink and green marble, and 10 units have private Turkish baths.

Piazza della Repubblica 20, 20124 Milano. ℰ **800/325-3535** in the U.S., 800-780-525 toll-free in Italy, or 02-63361. Fax 02-63366337. www.starwoodhotels.com. 228 units. 220€–800€ double; from 1,086€ suite. AE, DC, MC, V. Parking 50€. Metro: Repubblica. **Amenities:** Restaurant; airport transfers 110€–160€; babysitting; children's center; concierge; exercise room; room service; sauna. *In room:* A/C, TV, hair dryer, minibar, Wi-Fi (15€ per 24 hr.).

EXPENSIVE

Enterprise Hotel ★ ★ 🏨   In spite of its dull-sounding name, this is one of the most innovative of the postmillennium newcomers to Milan's hotel scene. Design and comfort go hand in hand here. Attracting both commercial and leisure travelers, the hotel lies 2km (1¼ miles) from the historic district in a bustling commercial zone. Bedrooms are both stylish and functional and of minimalist design with all of the required amenities, such as state-of-the-art bathrooms. In the 1930s this was a printing house, and much of its industrial past is clearly visible, but this only adds to its recycled allure. Skilled artisans added such touches as tons of Venetian marble. Fine fabrics and designer furniture abound.

Corso Sempione 91, 20154 Milano. ℰ **02-318181.** Fax 02-31818811. www.enterprisehotel.com. 123 units. 125€–760€ double; 199€–1,310€ suite. Rates include buffet breakfast. AE, DC, MC, V. Parking 18€. Tram: 1, 19, or 33. **Amenities:** Restaurant; 2 bars; babysitting; concierge; exercise room; room service. *In room:* A/C, TV, hair dryer, minibar, Wi-Fi (free).

Pierre Milano ★ 🏨   This is a little undiscovered gem. In the central section of the city, close to the Sant'Ambrogio, a church of the Middle Ages, the Pierre is luxury on a small scale. Few hotels in Milan were thought out so well. It's the choice (to borrow from a Marlene Dietrich lyric) "for the laziest gal in town." It's all electronic: A touch of a button and you can turn off your lights, receive messages on your television, and even open or close the draperies in your bedroom. Rooms are beautifully, even luxuriously furnished, with tasteful fabrics and silks and an inviting medley of contemporary and antique furnishings. Each room is individually decorated, and contains a luxurious first-rate tiled bathroom.

Via de Amicis 32, 20123 Milano. ✆ **02-72000581.** Fax 02-8052157. www.hotelpierremilano.it. 51 units (shower only). 160€–300€ double; 230€–560€ suite. AE, DC, MC, V. Parking 26€ per day. Closed Aug. Metro: Sant'Ambrogio. **Amenities:** Restaurant; concierge; room service. *In room:* A/C, TV, hair dryer, minibar, Wi-Fi (free).

Spadari al Duomo ★★ 🎁   A group of artists and architects pooled their talents to create this unique hotel filled with individually decorated and personalized rooms. Even the fireplace in the reception hall is stunning, hand-worked in Trani marble, with a spiral motif in Verona red marble. In the bedrooms all the furniture—including the beds and dressing tables—was specially designed. In the small American bar, paintings create an aura of spaciousness, and the room is filled with fantasy landscapes. The breakfast room is frescoed, and there is a stunning winter garden. Located near the Duomo, the hotel enjoys a bull's-eye central location.

Via Spadari 11, 20123 Milano. ✆ **02-72002371.** Fax 02-8611184. www.spadarihotel.com. 43 units. 198€–290€ double; from 290€ suite. AE, DC, MC, V. Parking 30€. Rates include buffet breakfast. Metro: Duomo. **Amenities:** Bar; concierge; room service. *In room:* A/C, TV, minibar, Wi-Fi (free).

Straf ★★ 🎁   Hidden behind a 2-century-old facade, this hotel is close to La Scala and the deluxe shopping street, Via Montenapoleone. The landmark Duomo lies outside your door. Its burnished brass and black stone create a minimalist aura for the jet set who check in, making it one of the hottest hotel addresses in town. Stylish and comfortable, the bedrooms are elegant. The special rooms are five units equipped for chromotherapy and aromatherapy, with Japanese auto-massage chaise longue. Even the less-grand accommodations will still make you feel fashionable. The architect, Vincenzo De Cotiis, used scratched mirrors, burnished brass, iron, and black stone, among other materials, to create the aura.

Via San Raffaele 3, 20121 Milano. ✆ **02-805081.** Fax 02-89095294. www.straf.it. 66 units. 297€–506€ double; 726€ suite. AE, DC, MC, V. Parking 48€. Metro: Duomo. **Amenities:** Restaurant; bar; babysitting; concierge; exercise room; room service; Wi-Fi (5€ per hr., in lobby). *In room:* A/C, TV, hair dryer, minibar.

MODERATE/INEXPENSIVE

AC Milano Hotel ★ 🔥   One guest after a stay here concluded the hotel was "for women who look like Donatella Versace and the men who love them." A 10-minute, 3.2km (2-mile) tram ride from the center, the hotel is part of the AC chain of moderately priced hotels—and it's one of the best. AC hotels stress affordable prices and a minimalist design. This gray stone monolith has some rooms opening onto the Cimitero Monumentale. If that's a turnoff for you, check in elsewhere. Bedrooms are well designed with dark-wood floors and shojilike screens on the closet doors. Extras include a library in the lobby and a small fitness center in the basement.

Via Tazzoli 2, 20154 Milano. ✆ **02-20424211.** Fax 02-20424212. www.ac-hotels.com. 158 units. 110€–283€ double; 370€–467€ suite. Rates include buffet breakfast. AE, DC, MC, V. Parking 25€. Metro: Garibaldi. **Amenities:** Restaurant; bar; airport transfers 40€–95€; babysitting; concierge; exercise room; room service. *In room:* A/C, TV, hair dryer, minibar, Wi-Fi (17€ per 24 hr.).

Antica Locanda dei Mercanti   This eccentric choice won't please everybody, but it has its devotees. Located in the historic district, this reasonably priced but sophisticated hotel is an offbeat choice with charm. It remains a favorite with many movers and shakers in Milan's fashion industry. In 1996, former model Paola Ora gutted the second floor of this late-19th-century building and installed a streamlined hotel, custom-designing each room. The furnishings are upholstered in fine fabrics and the bathrooms are sheathed in marble. Some rooms have canopied beds, and all feature fresh flowers, books, and magazines. Don't be startled by the monumental, severe-looking entrance or the businesslike appearance of three of the building's four floors, most of which are occupied by crafts studios for the jewelry industry.

Via San Tommaso 6, 20123 Milano. ✆ **02-8054080.** Fax 02-8054090. www.locanda.it. 14 units (shower only). 185€–275€ double. MC, V. Parking 25€. Tram: 1, 14, or 24. Metro: Cairoli, Cordusio, or Duomo. **Amenities:** Airport transfers (35€–95€); babysitting; concierge; room service. *In room:* Hair dryer, Wi-Fi (free).

Antica Locanda Leonardo ★ 🎒   In the historic district of Milan, the building that houses this inn dates from the late 1890s. Leonardo da Vinci and Bramante patronized other establishments on this street that no longer exist. Even though it's in the city center, it enjoys the most tranquil location of the moderate or inexpensive hotels. The hotel is made more delightful by its inner courtyard and gardens—at times when you hear the birds chirping you'll forget you're in Milan. We love it in spring when the wisteria bursts into bloom. Bedrooms, many opening onto balconies, are midsize and traditionally and tastefully furnished. Each room is decorated in a different style—rococo, Liberty, flowery, or contemporary.

Corso Magenta 78, 20123 Milano. ✆ **02-48014197.** Fax 02-48019012. www.anticalocanda leonardo.com. 20 units. 165€–245€ double; 285€ triple. Rates include continental breakfast. AE, DC, MC, V. Parking 20€–25€. **Amenities:** Bar; bikes; room service. *In room:* A/C, TV, hair dryer, Wi-Fi (free).

Antica Locanda Solferino ★★   When this hotel opened in 1976, the neighborhood was a depressed backwater. Today it's an avant-garde community of actors, writers, and poets, and this inn deserves some of the credit. It got off to a great start soon after opening when editors from GQ stayed here while working on a fashion feature. Since then, countless celebs and fashion-industry types have either stayed in the old-fashioned rooms or dined in the ground-floor restaurant. Each guest room is unique, furnished with Daumier engravings and Art Nouveau or late-19th-century pieces, as well as well-kept bathrooms, half of which contain a Jacuzzi. Reserve as far in advance as possible.

Via Castelfidardo 2, 20121 Milano. ✆ **02-6570129.** Fax 02-6571361. www.anticalocandasolferino. it. 11 units. 180€–400€ double. Rates include breakfast. AE, DC, MC, V. Parking 20€ nearby. Metro: Moscova or Repubblica. **Amenities:** Room service. *In room:* A/C, TV, hair dryer, Wi-Fi (free).

Ariston ★ 🎒   Located near the Duomo, the first-ever "ecohotel" in Milan boasts all-natural or nontoxic materials, including mattresses, fibers, and paints. The cleaning products are biodegradable, and only recycled paper products are used throughout the hotel. Air purifiers protect guests from outdoor pollutants. Even the drinks, which include a wide range of herbal teas, are made with purified water; and naturally, the breakfast buffet offers organic foods. The bedrooms are exceedingly comfortable. For the convenience of its guests, Ariston provides complimentary bikes and free Internet access in both guest rooms and the lobby.

Largo Carrobbio 2, 20123 Milano. ☏ **02-72000556.** Fax 02-72000914. www.aristonhotel.com. 52 units. 155€–290€ double; 230€–320€ triple. Rates include buffet breakfast. AE, DC, MC, V. Metro: Duomo. Parking 25€. **Amenities:** Bikes; Internet (free, in lobby). *In room:* A/C, TV, fridge, Wi-Fi (18€ per 24 hr.).

Casa Mia ✦   This small, attentive hotel is one of the best maintained and comfortable (for the price) in the area of Central Station, and it lies within easy access to all of Milan. The small, family-run hotel is on the second floor of a modern building. Bedrooms are simply furnished, ranging from small to midsize with tiny bathrooms. The staff is welcoming and helpful.

Viale Vittorio Veneto 30, 20124 Milano. ☏ **02-6575249.** Fax 02-92877803. www.casamiahotel.it. 15 units. 55€–160€ double; 75€–215€ triple. Rates include continental breakfast. AE, MC, V. Parking 25€. Metro: Repubblica. **Amenities:** Bar; room service. *In room:* A/C, TV, hair dryer, Wi-Fi (free).

Hotel Gran Duca di York ★★   This longtime favorite, with its pleasantly furnished and well-kept rooms, just keeps getting better. When it was built by the Catholic Church in the 1890s, the Liberty-style *palazzo* housed dozens of priests from the Duomo. Among them was the cardinal of Milan, who later became Pope Pius XI. Today, anyone can rent accommodations, which range from small to medium in size and offer private tile bathrooms. You'll find a bar in an alcove of the severely elegant lobby, replete with a suit of armor and leather-covered armchairs.

Via Moneta 1A (Piazza Cordusio), 20123 Milano. ☏ **02-874863.** Fax 02-8690344. www.ducadiyork.com. 33 units. 170€–248€ double. Rates include buffet breakfast. AE, MC, V. Parking 30€. Closed Aug. Metro: Cordusio or Duomo. **Amenities:** Bar; room service; Wi-Fi (free, in lobby). *In room:* A/C, TV, hair dryer, minibar.

Hotel Rovello   The location is ideal, close to the Santa Maria delle Grazie, near La Scala, between Castello Sforzesco and Piazza Duomo. The hotel is serviceable and a top choice, charging affordable prices in an expensive district. The guest rooms are not overly adorned but are furnished in a minimalist yet comfortable style in a centuries-old building. Many original details, such as wooden beams in the ceilings, have been retained, although the furnishings are modern. Hardwood floors, orthopedic mattresses, and small dressing areas in some units are part of this hotel's charm, along with well-kept bathrooms with showers. It's not luxurious but is highly commendable.

Via Rovello 18, 20121 Milano. ☏ **02-86464654.** Fax 02-72023656. www.hotel-rovello.it. 10 units. 120€–220€ double; 150€–260€ triple. Rates include continental breakfast. AE, DC, MC, V. Parking 30€. Bus: 1, 2, 3, 4, 12, 14, 18, 19, 20, 24, or 27. Metro: Cordusio. **Amenities:** Bar; room service. *In room:* A/C, TV, hair dryer.

Hotel Star   The Ceretti family welcomes guests to its well-run little hotel, a few blocks from La Scala and the Duomo. The lobby has been brightened, and the guest rooms are pleasant, if plain. They range from small to midsize, each with a comfortable bed and double-glass windows that cut down on street noise. All rooms contain bathrooms, and 15 units include a personal sauna and a hydromassage tub; the others contain a hydromassage shower.

Via dei Bossi 5, 20121 Milano. 🄲 **02-801501.** Fax 02-861787. www.hotelstar.it. 30 units (some with shower only). 104€–215€ double. Rates include buffet breakfast. AE, MC, V. Parking 25€. Closed Aug and Christmas. Metro: Cordusio or Duomo. **Amenities:** Room service; Wi-Fi (free, in lobby). *In room:* A/C, TV, hair dryer, minibar.

Sabotino ★ ✦   This charmingly funky hotel is popular with fashionable photographers and others seeking good value in the center of town near La Scala, a 10-minute walk from the cathedral. Its main attraction is a large terrace where you can sit out, enjoying drinks, the view, and the flowers. The atmosphere is homelike, and the rooms, though small, are comfortably furnished with a sort of Italian kitsch. Accommodations are decorated with art, and both the public and private bathrooms, each with shower, are well maintained. Breakfast is not included in the price, but there are many cafes outside the doorstep of this hotel.

Viale Sabotino 16, 20135 Milano. 🄲 **02-58308797.** Fax 02-58310400. www.hotelsabotino.com. 15 units. 100€ double. AE, DC, MC, V. Tram: 9, 24, 29, or 30. *In room:* TV, Wi-Fi (free).

St. George ★★   This richly furnished deluxe hotel with monochrome interiors seems evocative of this city of fashion and industry, attracting both the commercial traveler and the discerning visitors who wants to enjoy the pleasures of Milan. In the heart of Milan's business district, the modern, concrete building lies near some of the finest shops. The rooms reflect the latest in stylish contemporary design, with double-glazed windows, "armored" doors, and individually controlled air-conditioning. If you'll pay more, you can request an elegantly appointed superior room with a separate living room with work desk and panoramic views overlooking the Duomo. The manager claims that the entire hotel—paintings, color schemes, even the breakfast menu—was designed to give the visitor an "Italian experience."

Viale Tunisis 9, 20124 Milano. 🄲 **02-29516375.** Fax 02-2043852. www.hotelst.george.it. 50 units. 98€–170€ double; 180€–226€ suite. Rates include buffet breakfast. Parking: 25€. AE, DC, MC, V. Metro: Porta Vanazia. Closed 2 weeks in Aug. **Amenities:** Bar; airport transfers (45€–105€); babysitting; concierge. In room: A/C, TV, hair dryer, minibar, Wi-Fi (5€ per 24 hr.).

Where to Dine

VERY EXPENSIVE

Armani/Nobu ★★ JAPANESE   This innovative Japanese cuisine, long enjoyed by foodies in such cities as London and New York, has invaded Milan. Yes, that was one of the restaurant's founders, Robert De Niro, we spotted dining here. The kitchen staff is as brilliant and finely tuned as its New York or London cousins. Sushi chefs create not just sushi but gastronomic pyrotechnics. Elaborate preparations lead to perfectly balanced flavors. Patrons don't seem to mind the high prices that go with these incredibly fresh fish dishes. Where can you find a good sea urchin tempura in Milano but at Nobu? Specialties include lobster in peppercorn sauce with wasabi, prawns in a spicy sauce, or filet of salmon in a teriyaki sauce. If you don't like fish, you might opt for such dishes as chicken in teriyaki sauce. You can order light snacks and drinks on the ground floor.

Via Pisoni 1. 🄲 **02-72318645.** www.armaninobu.it. Reservations required. Average meal cost 45€–90€ per person, without drinks. Tasting menu 160€. AE, DC, MC, V. Mon–Sat noon–2:30pm; daily 7:30–11:30pm. Closed Dec 25–Jan 9. Metro: Montenapoleone.

Il Luogo di Aimo e Nadia ★★★ 🎒 ITALIAN/CREATIVE MEDITERRA-NEAN   Some of the most creative cookery in Milan is offered at this somewhat remote outpost of fine cuisine in an avant-garde modern setting. Tastes, fragrances, and colors are innovatively combined on the platter with polish; only top-quality, fresh ingredients are used. The sommelier is often cited as the best in Lombardy, and the wine list is just one reason to dine here. The chef's risotto with zucchini flowers, truffles, and porcini mushrooms also merits the trek across town. Some of the most enticing items on the menu include a soup of red mullet with Tuscan artichokes, endive, and pine nuts, or sea bass flavored with lemon grass and Sicilian capers. You might also try homemade fusilli (pasta) with a sauce made with Venus clams, mussels, and fresh tomatoes.

Via Montecuccoli 6. ℰ **02-416886.** www.aimoenadia.com. Reservations essential. Main courses 26€–55€; 5-course fixed-price menu 90€; 9-course fixed-price menu 110€. AE, DC, MC, V. Mon-Fri 12:30–2pm; Mon-Sat 7:30–10:30pm. Closed 3 weeks in Aug and Jan 1–10. Metro: Primaticcio.

EXPENSIVE

Acanto ★★ LOMBARD/ITALIAN   This is our choice for a romantic dinner in Milan. The subdued lighting that makes even Godzilla look good and the beautifully lit garden set the mood for an inspired cuisine that respects Lombard tradition but is infused with a world of flavor influenced by the Mediterranean. Nothing but the finest seasonal fare appears on the menu. The chef has a lightness of touch in his dishes, which, although completely filling and satisfying, will hardly put on the pounds. Pasta dishes are prepared with a certain artistry and have great flavor, including spaghetti with clams, fennel, and a spicy bread; or else *agnolotti* filled with smoked eggplant and small mozzarella dumplings. Inventive main courses reflect Lombard's bounty, as evoked by such dishes a tempura of squid, prawns, and sole filets with zucchini in a sweet-and-sour sauce; spit-roasted shoulder of suckling pig flavored with Szechuan peppers, and veal filet wrapped in Savoy cabbage and served with parsnip chips. A spectacular dessert is the chestnut sponge cake with a pomegranate sorbet.

In the Principe di Savoia Hotel, Piazza della Repubblica 17. ℰ **02-6230.** www.hotelprincipedi savoia.com. Reservations recommended. Main courses 24€–52€; fixed-price menus 50€–90€. AE, DC, MC, V. Daily 12:30–3pm and 7–11pm. Metro: Repubblica. Tram: 1, 4, 11, 29, or 30.

Cracco ★ MILANESE/ITALIAN   Mr. Cracco, who until 2007 was associated with the most famous deli in Milan (Peck's), has branched out on his own to create this specialty restaurant. Amid shimmering marble and modern Italian paintings, an efficient staff serves his sublime cuisine based on market-fresh ingredients. Of course, he prepares one of the most classic versions of risotto Milanese, but he also does his own imaginative version—risotto with zesty peppers, ginger, and anchovies. Black cod is glazed with honey and flavored with coffee, an imaginative dish. A sea urchin salad is a specialty, as is a concoction of layers of marinated egg yolk with smoked sea bass. The wine cellar has 1,800 kinds of wines from around the world.

Via Victor Hugo 4. ℰ **02-876774.** www.ristorantecracco.it. Reservations required. Main courses 36€–48€; fixed-price menus 130€–160€. AE, DC, MC, V. Tues-Fri 12:30–2pm and Mon-Sat 7:30–10pm. Closed Dec 23–Jan 11 and 3 weeks starting Aug 15. Metro: Duomo.

Gold ★★ ITALIAN/MEDITERRANEAN   It's not just gold in its namesake but in the color of its decor, something you might find in Las Vegas. Those on the see-and-be-seen circuit flock to this chic bistro and restaurant established by designers Domenico Dolce and Stefano Gabbana, a 5-minute stroll from their Milan showroom in the Porta Venezia sector. The establishment houses a second-floor gourmet restaurant, a bar, a casual ground-floor bistro, and a small food store selling gourmet items. The interior has retro touches such as raw-cut marble walls evoking Frank Lloyd Wright, and a menu that comes in a gold eel-skin cover. Some of the dishes are inspired by Dolce's native Sicily. The cuisine is sublime, a seductive repertoire that brings out the intrinsic flavors of produce instead of disguising it. In the restaurant feast on such dishes as spaghetti with broccoli, clams and almonds, or rack of lamb baked in a crispy crust. In the bistro sample a delectable eggplant parmigiana, or else grilled swordfish with capers, lemon zest, and cherry tomatoes. One of our favorites is filet of tuna with black rice and a sweet soy sauce.

Via Poerio 2A (entrance at Piazza Risorgimento). ✆ **02-7577771.** www.dolcegabbana.it. Reservations required. Main courses 8€–25€ in bistro, 16€–30€ in restaurant. AE, DC, MC, V. Bistro daily noon–midnight. Restaurant Wed–Sat 7:30–11pm. Closed Aug and 1 week at Christmas. Bus: 54 or 61. Metro: Palestro.

Joia ★★★ VEGETARIAN Vegetarian restaurants abound, but it's rare to find a haute cuisine vegetarian restaurant. Back in 1989, a group of vegetarians interested in good food got together to form this restaurant, which in 1996 won the award for best vegetarian restaurant in Europe. That was a long time ago, but standards have been maintained, or even improved as newer and more imaginative recipes are found.

Chef Pietro Leemann honed his culinary skills on the continent before going to China and Japan, where he learned new ways to reveal the true essence of produce, concentrating on color, taste, and freshness. He learned to create "architecture of ingredients" on your plate. The menu is ever changing but special dishes are likely to include "Prosperity"—Swiss cheese ravioli with an herb pesto; "The Fifth Taste" (grilled cannelloni stuffed with endive), and "Equilibrium" (a tart made with potatoes and flap mushrooms). The simple no-frills decor invites you to dine on wooden chairs and fine white tablecloths spread over small tables. The location lies 1.7 km (1 mile) northeast of the city center near the Giardini Pubblici Indro Montanelli.

Via Panfilo Castaldi 18. ✆ **02-29522124.** www.joia.it. Reservations recommended. Main courses 18€–30€. AE, DC, MC, V. Mon–Sat noon–2:30pm and 7:30–11:30pm. Closed Dec 25–Jan 6 and 3 weeks in Aug. Metro: Repubblica.

Paper Moon ★ NORTHERN ITALIAN Just 750m (2,440 ft.) from the Duomo, this fashionable restaurant was launched in 1977 and has since spread to New York, Tokyo, and Istanbul. In Milan, its home base, it attracts celebrities from the world of fashion, entertainment, and sports. The space is sleek and modern, the walls covered with black-and-white photographs, an elegant decor for a finely honed cuisine using market-fresh ingredients. Paper Moon is also one of the most fashionable pizzerias in Milan. No pizza is more elegant or more expensive than the pie with a white-truffle sauce. Come here to discover the radiantly authentic flavors of *pappardelle* (wide noodles) with a tomato-and-cream sauce, or else sautéed wild mushrooms with polenta. Vincenza-style stockfish is simmered in milk and also served with polenta.

Take a Gelato Break

In the Brera neighborhood, you'll find the **Gelateria Toldo**, Via Sacchi Giuseppe 6 (ⓒ **02-86460863**; Metro: Cairoli), where the gelato is wonderfully creamy and many of the sorbetto selections are so fruity and fresh that you can pretend they're healthy.

Via Bagutta 1. ⓒ **02-76022297**. www.papermoonrestaurant.com. Reservations recommended. Main courses 12€–40€. AE, MC, V. Mon–Sat 12:30–3pm and 7:30pm–12:30am. Closed 10 days in Aug. Metro: San Babila.

Tano Passami L'Olio ★ 🍴 MEDITERRANEAN   The name of this restaurant translates as "Tano, pass me the oil." Owners Tano Simonato and his wife, Nadia, stock more than three dozen different types of regional olive oils, many from Lombardy itself. Striking out against butter-and-cream chefs, they are devotees of the olive branch, using a different type of oil for each course served here. When the virgin oil meets fresh, seasonal ingredients, a first-class cuisine emerges. The cuisine reflects imagination and flair, beginning with the raw Italian filet of beef with a honey-and-goat-cream sauce, or else truffles with pears, goat cheese, and truffle ice cream. The highly personal cuisine also features a saddle of venison with fig sauce and chocolate powder; saddle of lamb under an almond-and-mint crust or medallions of monkfish with a caramelized caper crust with foie gras and truffles.

Via Eugenio Villoresi 16. ⓒ **02-8394139**. www.tanopassamilolio.it. Reservations required. Main courses 26€–36€. AE, DC, MC, V. Mon–Sat 8–11pm. Closed Dec 24–Jan 6 and Aug. Metro: Romolo.

MODERATE

Boeucc Antico Ristorante INTERNATIONAL/MILANESE   This restaurant, opened in 1696, is a trio of rooms in an elegant old palace, within walking distance of the Duomo and the major shopping streets. Throughout you'll find soaring stone columns and modern art. In summer, guests gravitate to a terrace for open-air dining. You might enjoy ravioli with lobster and scampi; salmon steak flavored with green peppercorns, or swordfish in a sauce made of capers and white wine. In season, sautéed zucchini flowers garnish many dishes.

Piazza Belgioioso 2. ⓒ **02-76020224**. www.boeucc.it. Reservations required. Main courses 13€–28€. AE. Mon–Fri 12:40–2:30pm; Sun–Fri 7:40–10:30pm. Closed Dec 25–Jan 4, Easter, and Aug. Metro: Duomo, Montenapoleone, or San Babila.

Just Cavalli Café ★★ 🍴 MEDITERRANEAN   Milano's trendy restaurants are getting more and more sophisticated: Take this see-and-be-seen enclave at the foot of Torre Branca at Parco Sempione, where a creative cuisine is served. Enveloped by a beautiful garden, in a building made of steel and glass, Just Cavalli was conceived by fashion designer Roberto Cavalli. Every season the decor changes—leopard-skin sofas (imitation, of course) one season, Asian prints the next. When you see goldfish swimming in a bowl—and that's your centerpiece—you know what to expect. But then again, do you? Flavors are combined in surprising ways on this innovative menu—for example, sautéed filet of turbot with almond crunches served with a fennel-and-orange sauce. Other full-flavored dishes include lamb cutlets with sautéed artichokes and fresh tomatoes stuffed with goat cheese, or else salmon rolls served with green beans in a balsamic vinegar sauce.

Via Camoens. ✆ **02-311817.** www.justcavallihollywood.it. Reservations recommended. Main courses 14€–34€. AE, DC, MC, V. Daily 8pm–3am. Metro: Cadorna.

10 Corso Como Café ✦ ITALIAN/INTERNATIONAL   In the Brera, the hottest cafe is the domain of Carla Sozzani. It's part of her stylish bazaar at Corso Como 10, which also includes an art gallery, a music room, a boutique, and a bookstore. It pushes the envelope of chic, attracting a big fashion-industry crowd, yet it isn't overpriced. The minimalist decor of cast iron, stained glass, and steel is Milanese modern at its best. Oh, yes, the food. Of course, everyone likes to stay fashionably thin here, so expect a selection of Mediterranean sushi or sashimi and beautifully flavored Italian fresh vegetables and fish tempura. The pastas have distinctive and original flavors, including one with toasted pine nuts and fresh marjoram. This trendsetter also offers a wide selection of teas from all over the world. On Saturday and Sunday, an American-style brunch is served until 5pm.

Corso Como 10. ✆ **02-29013581.** www.10corsocomo.com. Reservations recommended. Main courses 14€–30€. AE, DC, MC, V. Mon 6pm–12:30am; Tues–Fri noon–12:30am; Sat 11am–2am; Sun 11am–12:30am. Metro: Garibaldi.

Trattoria Bagutta ★ INTERNATIONAL   This is Milan's most traditional *trattoria,* drawing an artsy crowd. Dating from 1927, the Bagutta is known for the caricatures (framed and frescoed) covering its walls. Of the many bustling dining rooms, the rear one with its picture windows is most enticing. The food draws from the kitchens of Lombardy and Tuscany for inspiration. On the menu are assorted antipasti, and main-dish specialties include fried squid and scampi; rigatoni with cream, peas, and a beef ragout; linguine with shrimp in tomato-cream sauce; and *scaloppine alla Bagutta* (veal baked with fresh tomatoes, mozzarella, and lettuce).

Via Bagutta 14. ✆ **02-76002767.** www.bagutta.it. Reservations required. Main courses 14€–30€. AE, DC, MC, V. Mon–Sat 12:30–2:30pm and 7:30–10:30pm. Closed Dec 24, Jan 6, and Aug. Metro: San Babila.

INEXPENSIVE

Al Tempio d'Oro ITALIAN/MEDITERRANEAN   This restaurant near the central rail station offers inexpensive and well-prepared meals. The chef tempts you with stockfish with olives, pine nuts, cherry tomatoes, and polenta; or else a winning spaghetti Tempio d'Oro (with Genovese pesto, cream, tomatoes, and, yes, beer). Spaghetti is also served with salmon, mascarpone, cream, and vodka. Other rewarding offers include potato gnocchi with saffron sauce; penne with fresh swordfish, tomatoes, eggplant, and basil; or else swordfish cooked in the oven with fresh salmon and rose pepper. The crowd is relaxed, and ceiling columns contribute to an atmosphere somewhat like that of a beer hall.

Via delle Leghe 23. ✆ **02-26145709.** www.altempiodoro.it. Main courses 6€–14€. MC, V. Mon–Sat 8pm–2am. Closed 2 weeks in Aug. Metro: Pasteur.

A Santa Lucia ★ MEDITERRANEAN/SEAFOOD   This festive place is decked out with photographs of pleased celebs, who attest to the skill of the kitchen. You can order such specialties as savory fish soup (a meal in itself), fried baby squid, or well-prepared sole. *Spaghetti alla vongole* evokes the tang of the sea with its succulent clam sauce. A signature pasta is *rigatoni strascicati* (pasta with tomatoes, fresh basil, and hot chili peppers). Pizza also reigns supreme: Try either the calzone or the traditional pie, both *alla napoletana*.

Via San Pietro all'Orto 3. ℂ **02-76023155.** www.asantalucia.it. Reservations recommended. Main courses 12€–30€. AE, DC, MC, V. Daily noon–3pm and 7pm–1am. Closed Aug. Metro: San Babila.

La Libera 🍴 MILANESE/PIZZA/ITALIAN   In the Brera district, only a short walk from Castello Sforzesco, this *trattoria* appears more like a beer cellar with a kitchen, an unlikely setting for an establishment that serves such good and reasonably priced food. The lobby and bar contain the original furniture from 1900. Architects and journalists are often the chief and most loyal patrons. The chefs are talented, and they wisely change their menu seasonally. Locals come here at night for the pizzas, including one pie specialty, pesto with toasted pine nuts. Some dishes have imaginative though harmonious flavors you might not normally link together—take the pumpkin risotto and squid fritters, for example. You might begin with a delectable artichoke soup and follow with either swordfish roulades au gratin or else beef filet with porcini mushrooms.

Via Palermo 21. ℂ **02-8053603.** www.lalibera.it. Reservations required. Main courses 8€–17€. AE, DC, MC, V. Daily 7:30pm–12:30am. Metro: Moscova.

La Magolfa 🍴 PIZZERIA/INTERNATIONAL   La Magolfa, one of the city's dining bargains, offers a great value in pizzas and pastas. The building is a country farmhouse whose origins date from the 1500s, although the restaurant only opened in 1960. It's likely to be crowded with young people, as is every other restaurant in Milan that offers such value. If you don't mind its location away from the center of town (in Zona Ticinese in the southern part of the city), you'll be treated to some hearty food and gargantuan helpings. A general air of conviviality reigns.

Via Magolfa 15. ℂ **02-8321696.** Pastas 6€–10€; pizza 5€–11€. MC, V. Daily noon–2:30pm and 7pm–2am. Metro: Porta Genova.

Trattoria Milanese ★ 🍴 MILANESE/LOMBARD   West of the Duomo, this traditional *trattoria* has been a local favorite since 1933. In a narrow lane in a historic district of Milan, it is most convenient for dining as you tour the sights of the historic core. Local businesspeople crowd in at lunch, sharing the long tables with Milanese families. Giuseppe and Antonella Villa, your hosts, see that you're fed well on all the classic dishes of the Lombard larder. We like to begin with the *minestrone alla milanese* made with whatever fresh vegetables are in season, the smoky flavor coming from pancetta (cured pork belly). The *risotto alla milanese* is classic, simple, and good, cooked with bone marrow and the richest-tasting beef stock flavored with Parmesan, taking its beautiful golden hues from saffron. Two classic dishes are the *osso buco alla milanese* (on-the-bone shin of veal cooked slowly with wine and vegetables) and their *cotoletta alla milanese* (breaded veal sautéed to a golden brown).

Via Santa Marta 11. ℂ **02-86451991.** Reservations required. Main courses 8€–19€. AE, DC, MC, V. Wed–Mon noon–3pm and 7pm–midnight. Closed July 18–Aug and Dec 25–Jan 7. Metro: Cordusio.

ON THE OUTSKIRTS

Antica Osteria del Ponte ★★ ITALIAN   One of our favorite restaurants in the area is 29km (18 miles) outside Milan (see the directions later in this review).

A country inn since the 18th century, this *osteria* is one of Lombardy's most acclaimed restaurants. The Santin family chefs are some of the best in Lombardy, turning out a classic risotto with saffron, Parmesan cheese, and crispy raw ham. You might also try the shrimp marinated with olive oil and lemon sauce, served with caviar and a touch of vanilla. For a regal taste treat, try the baked goose stuffed with foie gras.

From the center of Milan, take the S494 Vigevanese until you reach Abbiategrasso; then cross the bridge over the Naviglio Canal. At the first traffic light, turn right and follow the directions to Novara/Magenta. Go straight for 3km (2 miles) until you come to an intersection with a signpost marking the way to Cassinetta di Lugagnano. Turn left and follow this sign to the restaurant.

Piazza G. Negri 9, Cassinetta di Lugagnano. ℂ **02-9420034.** www.anticaosteriadelponte.it. Reservations required. Main courses 18€–42€; fixed-price menu 85€. AE, DC, MC, V. Tues–Sat noon–2pm and 8–10pm. Closed Aug and Dec 25–Jan 10.

Exploring the City

With its spired cathedral, the **Piazza del Duomo** lies at the heart of Milan. The city is encircled by three "rings," one of which is the **Cerchia dei Navigli,** a road that more or less follows the outline of the former medieval walls. The road runs along what was formerly a series of canals—hence the name Navigli. All the major attractions, including Leonardo's *Last Supper,* La Scala, and the Duomo, lie in this ring, which is easily navigated on foot.

The second ring, known both as **Bastioni** and **Viali,** follows the outline of the Spanish Walls from the 16th century. It's now a tram route (29 or 30). A much more recent ring is the **Circonvallazione Esterna,** connecting with the main roads coming into Milan.

In the Cerchia dei Navigli, one of Milan's most important streets, **Via Manzoni,** begins near the Teatro alla Scala and takes you to **Piazza Cavour,** a key point for the traffic arteries. The **Arch of Porta Nuova,** a remnant of the medieval walls, marks the entrance to Via Manzoni. To the northwest of Piazza Cavour is the **Giardini Pubblici,** and to the northwest of these gardens is **Piazza della Repubblica.** From this square, Via Vittorio Pisani leads into **Piazza Duca d'Aosta,** site of the cavernous Stazione Centrale.

At Piazza Cavour, you can head west on Via Fatebenefratelli into the **Brera** district, whose major attraction is the Pinacoteca di Brera. This district has become a major center in Milan for offbeat shopping and after-dark diversions.

For a quick overview of Milan, visit the **Torre Branca,** Via Camoens, Parco Sempione (ℂ **02-3314120;** www.branca.it; admission 4€; Metro: Cadorna), called "the Eiffel Tower of Milan." Reopened to the public after years of closure, the tower is functioning once again. The 108m (354-ft.) structure offers elevators that carry you to the top. Once there you can take in a 360-degree view of Milan, ranging from the Duomo to one of Prime Minister Silvio Berlusconi's many villas. The tower was designed by Gió Ponti in the 1930s. From mid-October to mid-April it is open Wednesday 10:30am to 12:30pm and 4 to 6:30pm; Saturday 10:30am to 1pm, 3 to 6:30pm, and 8:30pm to midnight; and Sunday 10:30am to 2pm and 2:30 to 7pm. From mid-April to mid-October it is open Tuesday and Thursday 9:30pm to midnight; Wednesday 10:30am to 12:30pm, 4 to 6:30pm, and 9:30pm to midnight; Friday 2:30 to 6pm, and 9:30pm to midnight; and Saturday and Sunday 10:30am to 2pm, 2:30 to 7:30pm, and 9:30pm to midnight.

Crowds in the Piazza del Duomo.

The entire trip lasts 10 minutes. At the end, treat yourself to a cocktail at Just Cavalli, a cafe below the tower (see above).

THE TOP ATTRACTIONS

Despite its modern architecture and industry, Milan is still a city of great art. Serious art lovers should budget at least 2 days here. If your schedule is frantic, see the Duomo, the Brera Picture Gallery, and one of the most important galleries of northern Italy, the Ambrosiana Library and Picture Gallery.

Ambrosiana Library & Picture Gallery (Biblioteca-Pinacoteca Ambrosiana) ★★   Near the Duomo, the Ambrosiana Library and Picture Gallery were founded in the early 17th century by Cardinal Federico Borromeo. On the second floor, the **Picture Gallery** contains a remarkable collection of art, mostly from the 15th to the 17th centuries. Most notable are *Madonna and Angels* by Botticelli; works by Bruegel (which have impressive detail and are among the collection's best pieces); paintings by Lombard artists, including Bramantino's *Presepe,* in earthy primitive colors; a curious miniature *St. Jerome with Crucifix,* by Andrea Solario; and works by Bernardino Luini. One of the museum's highlights is room 10, with 10 magnificent **cartoons by Raphael ★★★**, which he prepared for the frescoes of the School of Athens in the Vatican. Another room contains a collection of reproductions from the drawings of Leonardo da Vinci's *Codex Atlanticus.* The museum owns a remarkable portrait that Leonardo did of the musician Gaffurio. The **Library** contains many medieval manuscripts, which are shown for scholarly examination only.

Piazza Pio XI 2. ✆ **02-806921.** www.ambrosiana.eu. Admission 15€ adults, 10€ seniors and children 17 and under. Mon–Fri 9am–5pm. Metro: Duomo or Cordusio.

Brera Picture Gallery (Pinacoteca di Brera) ★★★   This is one of Italy's finest galleries, boasting an exceptional collection of works by both Lombard and

Venetian masters. Like a Roman emperor, Canova's nude Napoleon, with a toga draped over his shoulder, stands in the courtyard (fittingly, a similar statue ended up in the duke of Wellington's house in London).

Among the notable pieces, the *Pietà*, by Lorenzo Lotto, is a work of great beauty, as is Gentile Bellini's *St. Mark Preaching in Alexandria* (finished by his brother, Giovanni). Seek out Andrea Mantegna's *Virgin and the Cherubs*, from the Venetian school, and Tintoretto's eerie *Finding of the Body of St. Mark*. Three of the most important prizes are **Mantegna's *Dead Christ* ★★★**, **Giovanni Bellini's *La Pietà* ★★**, and **Carpaccio's *St. Stephen Debating* ★★**.

Other paintings include Titian's *St. Jerome,* as well as such Lombard art as Bernardino Luini's *Virgin of the Rose Bush* and Andrea Solario's *Portrait of a Gentleman.* One of the greatest panels is Piero della Francesca's *Virgin and Child Enthroned with Saints and Angels* and the *Kneeling Duke of Urbino in Armor.* Another work to seek out is the *Christ* by Bramante. One wing, devoted to modern art, offers works by such artists as Boccioni, Carrà, and Morandi. One of our favorite paintings is **Raphael's *Wedding of the Madonna* ★★**, which has a dancelike quality. The moving *Last Supper at Emmaus* is by Caravaggio.

Via Brera 28. ✆ **02-722631**. www.brera.beniculturali.it. Admission 11€. Tues–Sun 8:30am–7:15pm. Metro: Lanza or Montenapoleone.

Il Duomo & Baptistery ★★★ Milan's impressive lacy Gothic cathedral, 146m (479 ft.) long and 87m (284 ft.) wide at the transepts, ranks with St. Peter's in Rome and the cathedral at Seville, Spain, as among the world's largest. It was begun in 1386 and has seen numerous architects and builders (even Milan's conqueror, Napoleon, added his ideas to the facade). This imposing structure of marble is the grandest and most flamboyant example of the Gothic style in Italy. Ethereal and colossal, its **exterior ★★★** is a wonder to behold, with its belfries, statues, gables, and pinnacles.

Built in the shape of a Latin cross, the Duomo's interior is divided by soaring pillars into five naves. The overall effect is like a marble-floored Grand Central Terminal (that is, in space), with far greater dramatic intensity. In the **crypt** rests the tomb of San Carlo Borromeo, the cardinal of Milan. To experience the Duomo at its most majestic, you must ascend to the **roof** or **visita ai terrazzi ★★★**, on which you can walk through a forest of pinnacles, turrets, and marble statuary. Alfred, Lord Tennyson rhapsodized about the panorama of the Alps as seen from this roof. A gilded Madonna towers over the tallest spire.

If you're really interested in antiquity, you might want to explore the **Baptistery (Battistero Paleocristiano),** which you enter through the cathedral. This is a subterranean ruin lying beneath the cathedral's piazza

Caravaggio's *Last Supper at Emmaus.*

Milan's Duomo.

that dates from the 4th century. It's believed that this is the site where Ambrose, the first bishop and the patron saint of the city, baptized the future St. Augustine.

Piazza del Duomo. ✆ **02-86463456.** www.duomomilano.it. Cathedral free admission; roof via stairs 5€, roof via elevator 8€; crypt free; baptistery 1.50€. Cathedral daily 7am–7pm. Roof daily 9am–5:30pm. Crypt daily 9am–noon and 2:30–6pm. Baptistery Tues–Sun 9:30am–5pm. Metro: Duomo.

Santa Maria delle Grazie & The Last Supper ★★   This Gothic church was erected by the Dominicans in the mid–15th century, and a number of its outstanding features, such as the cupola, were designed by the great Bramante. But visitors from all over the world flock here to gaze on a mural in the convent next door. In what was once a refectory, the incomparable Leonardo da Vinci adorned one wall with *The Last Supper (Il Cenacolo Vinciano)* ★★★.

Commissioned by Ludovico the Moor, the 8.5×4.5m (28×15-ft.) mural was finished about 1497; it began to disintegrate almost immediately and was repainted in the 1700s and the 1800s. Its gradual erosion makes for one of the most intriguing stories in art. In 1943, it narrowly escaped being bombed, but the bomb demolished the roof; the painting was exposed to the elements for 3 years before a new roof was built. The current restoration has been controversial, drawing fire from some art critics (as has the Sistine Chapel restoration). The chief restorer of *The Last Supper,* Pinin Brambilla Barcilon, said that the Sistine Chapel was a "simple window wash" compared with the Leonardo.

It has been suggested that all that's really left of the original *Last Supper* are a "few isolated streaks of fading color"—that everything else is the application and color of artists and restorers who followed. What remains, however, is Leonardo's "outline," and even that is suffering badly. As an Italian newspaper writer put it: "If you want to see *Il Cenacolo,* don't walk—run!" A painting of grandeur, the composition portrays Christ at the moment he announces to his shocked apostles that one of them will betray him. Vasari called the portrait of Judas "a study in perfidy and wickedness."

The Last Supper by Leonardo da Vinci at Santa Maria delle Grazie.

Only 25 viewers are admitted at a time, reservations are a must, and you're required to pass through antechambers to remove pollutants from your body. After viewing the painting, for 15 minutes only, you must walk through two additional filtration chambers as you exit.

Piazza Santa Maria delle Grazie 2 (off Corso Magenta). ℭ **02-4987588.** www.grazieop.it. Free admission to church; 8€ for reservation to see *The Last Supper.* Church Mon–Sat 7:30am–noon and 3–7pm; Sun 3:30–6:30pm. *The Last Supper* viewings Tues–Sun 8:15am–6:45pm. Reservations required for *The Last Supper;* call Mon–Sat 8am–7pm and leave your name. Metro: Cadorna or Conciliazione.

MORE ATTRACTIONS

Basilica di Sant'Ambrogio ★★   From the basilica that St. Ambrose constructed on this site in the 4th century A.D.—when he was bishop of Milan and when the city, in turn, was briefly the capital of the Western Roman Empire—he had a profound effect on the development of the early church. Little remains of Ambrose's original church, but the 11th-century structure built in its place and renovated many times is remarkable. It has a striking atrium, lined with columned porticos and opening to the brick facade, with two ranks of loggias and, on either side, a bell tower. Look carefully at the door on the left, where you'll see a relief of St. Ambrose. This church set a standard for Lombard Romanesque architecture that you'll see imitated many times in your travels throughout the region. In the apse are interesting mosaics from the 12th century. The Lombard tower at the side dates from 1128, and the facade, with its two tiers of arches, is impressive. In the church is the **Museo della Basilica di Sant'Ambrogio,** which contains some frescoes, 15th-century wood paneling, silver and gold objects originally for the altar, paintings, sculpture, and Flemish tapestries.

Piazza Sant'Ambrogio 15. ℭ **02-86450895.** www.santambrogio-basilica.it. Free admission to basilica; 3€ to museum. Basilica Mon–Sat 7am–noon and 2:30–7pm; Sun 7am–8pm. Museum Tues–Sun 10am–noon and 3–5pm. Closed Aug. Metro: Sant'Ambrogio.

Basilica di Sant'Eustorgio ★ Originally this 4th-century basilica was the tomb of the Three Wise Men, or the Three Kings. Inside, its greatest treasure is the **Portinari Chapel (Cappella Portinari),** designed by the Florentine Michelozzo in Renaissance style. The chapel is frescoed and contains a bas-relief of angels at the base of the cupola. In the center is an intricately carved tomb containing the remains of St. Peter Martyr, supported by 13th-century marble statuary by Balduccio of Pisa. The basement has a Roman crypt. The bell tower—the first tower clock in the world—dates from 1305 and was built in the romantic style by patrician Milanese families.

Piazza Sant'Eustorgio 1. *©* **02-58101583** basilica, or 02-89402671 museum. www.santeustorgio. it. Free admission to basilica; chapel and museum 6€ adults, 3€ students and seniors, 1€ children 14 and under. Daily 10am–6pm. Metro: Genova.

Civic Gallery of Modern Art (Galleria Civica d'Arte Moderna) This sumptuous palace (the site of many local weddings) houses an important collection of late-19th-century and early-20th-century art, mostly from 1850 to 1918. The palace was built from 1790 to 1793 by noted architect Leopold Pollack and served as the Milanese home of both Napoleon and Eugène de Beauharnais (son of Josephine from her first marriage). The exhibit space is divided into three collections (the Carlo Grassi, the Vismara, and the Marino Marini), all showing the development of Impressionism and modernism in the Italian and the Lombard school of painting. Major emphasis is given to the works of Marino Marini, a 20th-century sculptor. Other artists include Picasso, Matisse, Rouault, Renoir, Modigliani, Corot, Millet, Manet, Cézanne, Bonnard, and Gauguin.

In the Villa Reale (Villa Comunale), Via Palestro 16. *©* **02-76002819.** www.gam-milano.com. Free admission. Tues–Sun 9am–1pm and 2–5:30pm. Metro: Palestro.

GET THEE TO A renaissance monastery

Certosa (Charter House) of Pavia ★, Viale Certosa 48, Certosa di Pavia (*©* **0382-925613**), marks the pinnacle of the Renaissance statement in Lombardy. The Carthusian monastery is 31km (19 miles) south of Milan and 8km (5 miles) north of Pavia. Founded in 1396 but not completed until years later, it is one of the most harmonious structures in Italy. The facade, studded with medallions and adorned with colored marble and sculptures, was designed in part by Amadeo, who worked on it in the late 15th century. Inside, much of its rich decoration is achieved by frescoes reminiscent of an illustrated storybook.

Through an elegantly decorated portal, you enter the cloister, noted for its exceptional terra-cotta decorations and continuous chain of elaborate "cells," attached villas with their own private gardens and *loggia.*

Admission is free, but donations are requested. It's open Tuesday to Sunday 9 to 11:30am and 2:30 to 5:30pm. Trains leave Milan bound for Pavia once every hour, costing 3.50€. If you're driving, take Rte. S35 south from Milan or A7 to Binasco, and then continue on S35 to Pavia and its Certosa.

Leonardo da Vinci National Museum of Science & Technology (Museo Nazionale della Scienza e della Tecnica Leonardo da Vinci) ★ ☺ If you're a fan of Leonardo da Vinci, you'll want to visit this vast museum complex, where you could spend practically a week. For the average visitor, the most interesting section is the Leonardo da Vinci Gallery, which displays copies and models from the Renaissance genius. There's a reconstructed convent pharmacy, a monastic cell, and collections of antique carriages and even sewing machines. You'll also see exhibits relating to astronomy, telecommunications, watchmaking, goldsmithery, motion pictures, and the subject of classic physics.

Via San Vittore 21. ℂ 02-485551. www.museoscienza.org. Admission 8€ adults, 6€ children and seniors, free for children 2 and under. Tues–Fri 9:30am–5pm; Sat–Sun 9:30am–6:30pm. Metro: Sant'Ambrogio. Bus: 50, 58, or 94.

Monumental Cemetery (Cimitero Monumentale) ★ This cemetery has catered for more than 100 years to the whims of Milan's elite. The only requirements for burial here are that you're dead and that when you were alive, you were able to afford a plot. Some families have paid up to 28,000€ just for the privilege of burying their dead here. The graves are marked not only with brass plates or granite markers but also with Greek temples, obelisks, or such original works as an abbreviated version of Trajan's Column.

This outdoor museum has become such an attraction that a superintendent has compiled an illustrated guidebook—a sort of "Who Was Who." Among the cemetery's outstanding sights is a sculpted version of *The Last Supper*. Several fine examples of Art Nouveau sculpture dot the hillside, and there's a tasteful example of Liberty-style (Italy's version of Art Nouveau) architecture in a tiny chapel designed to hold the remains of Arturo Toscanini's son, who died in 1906. Among the notables buried here are Toscanini himself and novelist Alessandro Manzoni. In the Memorial Chapel is the tomb of Salvatore Quasimodo, who won the 1959 Nobel Prize in literature. Here also rest the ashes of Ermann Einstein, father of the scientist. In the Palanti Chapel is a monument commemorating the 800 Milanese citizens slain in Nazi concentration camps. (A model of this monument is displayed in New York's Museum of Modern Art.) The cemetery is a few blocks east of Stazione Porta Garibaldi, in the urban congestion of Milan, 3km (2 miles) north of Il Duomo.

Piazzale Cimitero Monumentale 1. ℂ **02-88465600.** www.monumentale.net. Free admission. Tues–Sun 8am–6pm. Metro: Garibaldi. Tram: 14.

Museo Bagatti Valsecchi ★ 🏛 In the heart of Milan, in a restored *palazzo,* this is a private foundation set up by Bagatti Valsecchi heirs to display the family's collections and its artworks. The restored interiors are filled with paintings, woodcarvings, antiques, armor, ceramic and glass wares, rare objects in gold and ivory, and tapestries, a rich, fascinating collection. Every room is embellished with beautiful items. As the museum shows, family members were key players in the revival of Lombard Renaissance. The owners' preference is for collections including furnishings and paintings executed in the late 15th and early 16th centuries. Temporary exhibitions and concerts are staged here in summer.

Via Santo Spirito 10. ℂ **02-76006132.** www.museobagattivalsecchi.org. Admission 8€ (Wed 4€) adults, 4€ kids 6–14 and students, free for children 5 and under. Tues–Sun 1–5:45pm. Tram: Via Manzoni.

Museo Poldi-Pezzoli ★★   This fabulous museum displays its treasures in a sumptuous, elegant salon setting of antique furnishings, tapestries, frescoes, and Lombard woodcarvings (it's much like visiting the Frick Collection in New York or the Isabella Stewart Gardner Museum in Boston). The remarkable collection includes paintings by many of the old masters of northern and central Italy, such as Andrea Mantegna's *Madonna and Child,* Giovanni Bellini's *Cristo Morto,* and Filippo Lippi's *Madonna, Angels, and Saints* (with superb composition). Antonio Pollaiolo's *Portrait of a Lady* is a gorgeous portrait of haunting originality. One room is devoted to Flemish artists, and there's a collection of ceramics and also one of clocks and watches.

Via Manzoni 12. (℗ **02-794889.** www.museopoldipezzoli.it. Admission 8€. Tues–Sun 10am–6pm. Closed Jan 1, Easter, Apr 25, May 1, Aug 15, Nov 1, and Dec 8, 25–26. Metro: Duomo or Montenapoleone.

Museum of Ancient Art (Museo d'Arte Antica) ★   The Castle Sforzesco is an ancient fortress rebuilt by Francesco Sforza, who launched another governing dynasty. It's believed that both Bramante and Leonardo contributed architectural ideas to the fortress. Following extensive World War II bombings, it was painstakingly restored and continues its activity as a Museum of Ancient Art. On the ground floor are sculptures from the 4th century A.D., medieval art mostly from Lombardy, and armor. The most outstanding exhibit, however, is **Michelangelo's *Rondanini Pietà,*** on which he was working the week he died. In the rooms upstairs, besides a good collection of ceramics, antiques, and bronzes, is the important picture gallery, rich in paintings from the 14th to the 18th centuries. Included are works by Lorenzo Veneziano, Mantegna, Lippi, Bellini, Crivelli, Foppa, Bergognone, Cesare da Sesto, Lotto, Tintoretto, Cerano, Procaccini, Morazzone, Guardi, and Tiepolo.

In the Castello Sforzesco, Piazza Castello. (℗ **02-88463703.** www.milanocastello.it. Admission 3€, free for ages 17 and under. Tues–Sun 9am–5:30pm. Metro: Cairoli.

Shopping

Milan is one of Europe's top shopping cities, with a large concentration of sophisticated, high-style boutiques—and that's only fitting because Milan is the dynamo of the Italian fashion industry. Dolce & Gabbana, Ferré, Krizia, Moschino, Prada, Armani, and Versace have all catapulted to international stardom from design studios based here.

Most shops are closed all day Sunday and Monday (although some open on Mon afternoon). Some stores open at 9am, unless they're very chic, and then they're not likely to open until 10:30am. They remain open, for the most part, until 1pm and then reopen between 3:30 and 7:30pm.

The best time for the savvy shopper to visit Milan is for the **January sales,** when *saldi* (sale) signs appear in the windows. Sales usually begin in mid-January and, in some cases, extend all the way through February. Prices in some emporiums are cut by as much as 50% (but don't count on it). Of course, items offered for sale are most often last season's merchandise, but you can get some good buys. Items bought on sale can't be returned.

THE TOP SHOPPING AREAS

THE GOLDEN TRIANGLE We recently met a well-heeled shopper who spent the better part of her vacation in Italy shopping for what she called "the most unbelievable variety of shoes, clothes, and accessories in the world." A walk on the fashion subculture's focal point, **Via Montenapoleone ★★★**, heart of the **Golden Triangle,** will quickly confirm that impression. It's one of Italy's three great shopping streets. But expect high prices and service that's based on the salesperson's impression of how much money you plan to spend.

Milan is a shopper's paradise.

CORSO BUENOS AIRES Bargain hunters leave the Golden Triangle and head for a mile-long stretch of **Corso Buenos Aires,** where you can find style at more affordable prices. Start off at **Piazza Oberdan,** the square closest to the heart of Milan. Clothing abounds on Corso Buenos Aires, especially casual wear and knockoffs of designer goods. But you'll find a vast array of merchandise, from scuba-diving equipment to soft luggage. Saturdays are unbelievably crowded here.

THE BRERA DISTRICT You'll find more bargains in the **Brera,** the name given to a sprawling shopping district around the Brera Museum. This area is far more attractive than Corso Buenos Aires and has often been compared to New York's Greenwich Village because of its cafes, shops, antiques stores, and art students. Skip the main street, **Via Brera,** and concentrate on the side streets, especially **Via Solferino, Via Madonnina,** and **Via Fiori Chiari.** To get here, start by the La Scala opera house and continue to walk along Via Verdi, which becomes Via Brera. Running off from Via Brera to the left is the pedestrian-only Via Fiori Chiari, good for bric-a-brac and even some fine Art Deco and Art Nouveau pieces. Via Fiori Chiari will lead to another traffic-free street, Via Madonnina, which has some excellent clothing and leather-goods buys. Via Madonnina connects with busy Corso Garibaldi. This will take you to Via Solferino, the third-best shopping street. In addition to traditional clothing and styling, a lot of eye-catching but eccentric modern clothing is sold here.

The best time to visit the Brera area is for the **Mercatone dell'Antiquariato,** which takes place on the third Saturday of each month (it's especially hectic at Christmastime) along Via Brera in the shadow of La Scala. Artists and designers, along with antiques dealers and bric-a-brac peddlers, turn out in droves.

SHOPPING A TO Z

BOOKS The **American Bookstore,** Via Camperio 16 (✆ **02-878920;** Metro: Cairoli), will probably have that novel you're looking for or the scholarly volume on Milanese artwork you should've reviewed before your trip. It stocks only English-language books and periodicals.

DEPARTMENT STORE & MALL   La Rinascente ★, Piazza del Duomo (℃ **02-88521;** www.rinascente.it; Metro: Duomo), bills itself as Italy's largest fashion department store. In addition to clothing, the basement carries a wide variety of giftware, including handwork from all regions of Italy. On the seventh floor are many restaurants and a beautiful food market. The restaurants on the seventh floor are open daily noon to midnight.

One of Milan's most famous landmarks, the huge **Galleria Vittorio Emanuele II** ★, Corso Vittorio Emanuele II, is reminiscent of a rail station, and the architectural details are impressive, with vaulted glass ceilings merging in a huge central dome, decorative window and door casings, elaborate bas-reliefs, huge arched frescoes, wrought-iron globe lamps, and a decorative tile floor. You can browse in shops that include a Prada boutique and a Rizzoli bookstore, or grab a coffee.

FASHION   There's always **Il Salvagente,** Via Fratelli Bronzetti 16 (℃ **02-76110328;** www.salvagentemilano.it; tram: 12; bus: 60 or 62), for the fashion-conscious shopper with a limited budget. On the second floor is the selection of men's clothing; the women's wear, including sweaters, clothes, shoes, and belts, is on the main floor. Here you'll find Versace gowns at cut-rate prices. Of course, it'll be last year's style or something that didn't sell, but who'll ever know?

Ermenegildo Zegna, Via Montenapoleone 27E (℃ **02-76006437;** www.zegna.com; Metro: Montenapoleone), offers a complete range of menswear, beginning with the Sartorial line of suits, jackets, trousers, and accessories. The "soft line" is dedicated to a younger customer, and the sportswear collection and yachting line allow you to wander the globe with the right apparel. The shop also offers a "made-to-measure" service with a selection of 300 fabrics per season. They can make an outfit in about 4 weeks and then ship it to any destination.

Giorgio Armani ★★★, Via Montenapoleone 2 (℃ **02-76003234;** www.giorgioarmani.com; Metro: Montenapoleone), houses the sleek style we've come to expect in a large showroom vaguely reminiscent of an upscale aircraft hangar. Armani's trademark look incorporates unstructured clothing draped loosely over firm bodies—elegant upholstery for elegant people. The big news coming from Armani is the success of a new Giorgio Armani at Via Manzoni 31 (℃ **02-72318600;** Metro: Montenapoleone), a three-story megacomplex at the northern end of Milan's Golden Triangle. Armani has told the press, "I want there to be a sense of discovery and surprise every 15 meters throughout the store." It boasts everything from Emporio Armani clothing to an Italian outpost of the famed Nobu sushi restaurants. The store's displays are brilliant.

Gianfranco Ferré ★★, Via Sant'Andrea 15 (℃ **02-794864;** www.gianfrancoferre.com; Metro: Montenapoleone), is the only outlet in Milan for the famous designer whose fashions are worn by some of the world's most elegant women. The range is wide, from soft knitwear to sensual evening dresses, along with refined leather accessories. Next door to the women's shop is an outlet for the designer's men's clothing. It's closed in August (summer closing times may vary).

Prada.

Prada ★★★, Via della Spiga 18 (✆ **02-780465**; www.prada.com; Metro: Montenapoleone), has the best leather goods and other stylish accessories in Milan for women; it's a fashion industry phenomenon. Other Prada outlets include **Galleria Vittorio Emanuele 63** (✆ **02-876979**; Metro Duomo), Via Montenapoleone 6 (✆ 02-76020273; Metro: San Babila), and Corso Venezia 3 (✆ 02-76001426; Metro: San Babila).

GIFTS   In the tiny **G. Lorenzi,** Via Montenapoleone 9 (✆ **02-76022848**; www.glorenzi.it; Metro: Montenapoleone), in San Babila, you'll find everything you were looking for in the way of small gifts—and a lot of stuff you've never seen. Many are one-of-a-kind items, but they mainly sell knives and razors.

10 Corso Como, Corso Como 10 (✆ **02-29013581**; www.10 corsocomo.com; Metro: Garibaldi), is the creation of Carla Sozzani, who discovered candlelight and futons back in the 1970s. Today she runs the city's hippest lifestyle shop, selling an eclectic range of merchandise from clothing to household goods in a former coach-repair shop. The outlet also offers a courtyard cafe, a restaurant, and a gallery.

GLASS   If you're not going to include Venice in your Italian shopping itinerary, you can patronize **Venini ★★**, Montenapoleone 9 (✆ **02-76000539**; www.venini.com; Metro: Montenapoleone). This is the Milanese branch of this world-famous Venetian glassmaker. The outlet in Milan stocks one of the most comprehensive collections of Venini's wares outside Venice itself. Look for heirloom vases, precious glasses, and a stunning collection of plates and bowls.

JEWELRY & SILVER   At **Mario Buccellati ★★★**, Via Montenapoleone 23 (✆ **02-76002153**; www.mariobuccellati.it; Metro: Montenapoleone), you'll find Italy's best-known and most expensive silver and jewels. The designs of the cast-silver bowls, tureens, and christening cups are nothing short of rhapsodic.

LEATHER GOODS & SHOES   The prices on the merchandise at **Alfonso Garlando,** Via Madonnina 1 (✆ **02-86463733**; www.alfonsogarlando.it; Metro: Cairoli), range to the very expensive, but the shop's size and its lack of concern for a stylish showroom guarantee a reasonable choice at a reasonable price. It sells shoes for men and women but not children.

Gucci ★★★, Via Montenapoleone 5 (☏ **02-771271;** www.gucci. com; Metro: Montenapoleone), is the Milanese headquarters for the most famous leather-goods distributor in Italy. Its shoes, luggage, and wallets for men and women; handbags; and leather accessories usually have the colors of the Italian flag (olive and crimson) stitched in the form of a fairly discreet ribbon across the front.

At **Salvatore Ferragamo ★★★**, Via Montenapoleone 3 (☏ **02-76000054;** www.salvatoreferragamo.com; Metro: Montenapoleone), the label is instantly recognizable and the quality is high. Rigidly controlled by

TOP designer fashions ON THE CHEAP

Many fashion-conscious visitors flock to Milan not to shop at Prada or outfit themselves in Armani, but to purchase designer "seconds," knockoffs that look amazingly like the real thing, or last season's fashions—all at heavily discounted prices.

The wares of designer hotshots are best showcased at **Il Salvagente,** Via Bronzetti 16 (☏ **02-76110328;** www.salvagentemilano.it), a legendary shop where you'll find women screaming with glee or fighting each other for slashed-down prices on Alberta Ferretti, Marni, Armani, Prada, and others. At sales times (usually from early Jan into early Feb and once more in late June and July), prices are often cut by an astonishing 30% to 70%. Of course, you must shop wisely, as returns are forbidden. This outlet is the most famous designer discounter in all of Italy. Forget the drab ambience and even expect some clothing to have been worn on the runways. Not all garments are in A-1 condition.

Another outlet, **Biffi,** Corso Genova 6 (☏ **02-8311601;** www.biffi.com), is one of Milan's oldest and most trendsetting boutiques, with discounts galore. Pick up a stylish scarf or a fur hat, as the fashion range is cutting edge and avant-garde. The labels of new designers are included along with Fendi, plus a tempting selection of accessories. This old-world shop

has been run by generations of the Biffi clan. An eclectic range of clothing from such designers as Eley Kishimoto to Jean-Paul Gaultier hangs from the racks. Marni ready-to-wear is displayed in its own miniboutique, and there's also a branch for men just across the street (Metro: Sant'Ambrogio).

A final outlet for designer discounts is **D Magazine Outlet,** Via Montenapoleone 26 (☏ **02-76006027;** www.dmagazine.it), lying on the main and very expensive shopping street of Milan. But it offers plenty of discounts from names such as Fendi and Armani, along with other Continental big names. We recently visited the shop with a Milanese fashion-conscious woman who admits to being a "Moschino faddie." She found several worthy purchases from Milan's "bad boy" of fashion, much of the merchandise conveying his wild and wacky sense of fashion, especially his parodies of Chanel designs. Designer names from Japan, England, and other countries are also for sale (Metro: Montenapoleone).

an extended second generation of the original founders, it's still a style setter. This branch offers shoes, luggage, accessories for women and men, leather jackets, and a small selection of clothing.

LINENS   You'll find some great buys (as much as 50% off) in linens at the company headquarters of **Frette ★**, Via Montenapoleone 21 (𝄢 **02-783950;** www.frette.com; Metro: Montenapoleone). Frette is one of the finest names in Italian linens, so this is an exceptional deal, especially if you're looking for damask tablecloths in the vibrant colors of Italy—everything from apple green to sunflower yellow.

PAPER & STATIONERY   **Papier,** Via San Maurilio 4 (𝄢 **02-865221;** www. papier-milano.it; Metro: Missori), is the premier address for stationery, including "extreme paper" (plasticized and plaited paper given a metallic sheen evoking fabric). Banana-leaf pages from Thailand and Nepal are sold, as are hairy coconut sheets resembling the real thing.

PERFUME   In the Brera district, **Profumo,** Via Brera 6 (𝄢 **02-72023334;** Metro: Duomo), sells some of Italy's most exotic perfumes for women, plus cologne and after-shave lotions for men.

PRINTS & ENGRAVINGS   **Raimondi di Pettinaroli,** Corso Venezia 6 (𝄢 **02-76002412;** www.pettinaroli.it; Metro: San Babila), is the finest shop in Milan for antique prints and engravings, plus reprints of old engravings made from the original copperplates. Of particular interest are the engravings of Italian cityscapes during the 19th century, many of them treasures worth framing after you return home.

Milan After Dark

As in Rome, many of the top nightclubs in Milan shut down for the summer, when the cabaret talent and the bartenders pack their bags and head for the hills or the seashore. However, Milan is a big city, and there are always plenty of after-dark diversions. This metropolis is also one of Europe's cultural centers.

The interior of La Scala.

THE PERFORMING ARTS   The most complete list of cultural events appears in the large Milan newspaper, the left-wing *La Repubblica.* Try for a Thursday edition, which usually has the most complete listings.

The world's most famous opera house is **La Scala ★★★**, Piazza della Scala (Metro: Duomo). After 3 years of renovation, La Scala reopened in late 2004 with a production of *Europa Riconosciuta* by Antonio Salieri, Mozart's envious antagonist. The long-forgotten opera had been commissioned for the house's original opening in 1778, and had gone unproduced since that time—many critics felt with good reason. La Scala is now fully restored, with a technologically advanced stage and a splendid auditorium. Critics have raved about the new acoustics. There are now three moveable stages and 200 added seats. Tickets are hard to come by and should be arranged as far in advance as possible. Costing from 12€ to 187€, tickets can be purchased at **Biglietteria Centrale,** in the Galleria del Sagrato, Piazza Duomo (*©* **02-72003744;** daily noon–6pm; Metro: Duomo). For more information, go to www.teatroallascala.org.

Other operas are staged at the modern 2,500-seat auditorium, **Teatro degli Arcimboldi,** Zona Bicocca, Viale dell'Innovazione (*©* **899-500022;** www.teatroarcimboldi.it), on the northern outskirts of Milan. It lies alongside a university campus and dreary housing developments. You have to take the Metro to the Zara stop and from there take a tram (no. 7) to the auditorium.

Tickets cost 20€ to 155€. The opera house is closed in midsummer (late July and all of Aug). The new season begins every year on December 7, although the program for the upcoming season is announced the previous September.

Conservatorio, Via del Conservatorio 12 (*©* **02-7621101;** www.consmilano.it; Metro: San Babila), in the San Babila neighborhood, features the finest in classical music. Year-round, a cultured Milanese audience enjoys high-quality programs of widely varied classical concerts. Tickets cost 15€ to 35€.

Piccolo Teatro, Via Rivoli 2, near Via Dante (☎ **848-800304** in Italy only; www.piccoloteatro.org; Metro: Cordusio), hosts a wide variety of Italian-language performances. Its director, Giorgio Strehler, is acclaimed as one of the most avant-garde and talented in the world. The theater lies between the Duomo and the Castle of the Sforzas. It's sometimes hard to obtain seats. It's closed in July and August. Tickets cost 10€ to 55€.

LIVE-MUSIC CLUBS At **Le Scimmie,** Via Ascanio Sforza 49 (☎ **02-89402874;** www.scimmie.it; bus: 59), bands play everything from funk to blues to creative jazz. They also serve food, and a 10€ cover includes the first drink. Doors open Tuesday to Sunday around 8pm, and music is presented 9:30pm to around 3am.

CAFES Boasting a chic crowd of garment-district workers and shoppers, **Caffè Cova** ★, Via Montenapoleone 8 (☎ **02-76000578;** www.pasticceriacova. it; Metro: Montenapoleone), has been around since 1817, serving pralines, chocolates, brioches, and sandwiches. The more elegant sandwiches contain smoked salmon and truffles. Sip your espresso from fragile gold-rimmed cups at one of the small tables in an elegant inner room or while standing at the prominent bar. It's closed in August and on Sunday year-round. Closing time is in the early evening.

Sant'Ambroeus, Corso Matteotti 7 (☎ **02-76000540;** www.sant ambroeusmilano.it; Metro: Montenapoleone), is the best pastry and coffee shop in Milan. Some of the most discerning of the Milanese visit this cafe daily for their caffeine fix, and the espresso will give you a jolt even if you've stayed up all night. Designers from the Dolce & Gabbana firm often hang out here. For the very best taste sensation, opt for the cafe's Ambrogetto chocolate. The cafe opens early for breakfast and serves until 8pm daily.

BARS & PUBS Decorated a bit like a 19th-century bohemian parlor, **Al Teatro,** Corso Garibaldi 16 (☎ **02-864222;** Metro: Garibaldi), is a popular bar across from the Teatro Fossati. It opens Tuesday to Sunday at 5pm and closes (after several changes of ambience) at 2am. Most of the time the crowd seems perfectly happy to drink, gossip, and flirt. In addition to coffee and drinks, it serves toasts and tortes. In fine weather, tables are set out on Corso Garibaldi.

Bar Giamaica, Via Brera 32 (☎ **02-876723;** www.jamaicabar.it; Metro: Lanza or Borgonvovo), is loud and bustling, with a gruff but humorous style. Everyone on staff has worked here forever. If you want only a drink, you'll have lots of company among the office workers who jostle around the tiny tables of this standing-room-only bar. The bar opens at 8am Monday to Saturday and remains open until around 2am; it's closed 1 week in mid-August.

Despite its name, the **Grand Hotel l'Osteria,** Via Ascanio Sforza 75 (☎ **02-89511586;** www.osteriagrandhotel.it; bus: 59), doesn't rent rooms or even pretend to be grand. Instead, it's a large animated restaurant, which frequently offers live music. In summer, the crowds can move quickly from the smoky interior into a sheltered garden. Most visitors come here only for a drink, but if you're hungry you can get a moderately priced meal. The place is open Tuesday to Sunday 8pm to midnight. There's usually no cover.

Milan's first brewery is **Birrificio Lambrate,** Via Porpora, at the corner of Via Adelchi (☎ **02-70638678;** www.birrificiolambrate.com; Metro: Lambrate). The beer is made on the premises in three steel kettles. It's open Monday to Friday 12:30 to 2:30pm, and Monday to Saturday 6pm to 2am.

DANCE CLUBS & NIGHTCLUBS Usually packed with a good-looking crowd, **Hollywood,** Corso Como 15 (✆ **02-6598996;** www.discotecahollywood. it; Metro: Garibaldi or Moscova), is small and has a sound system that's so good that you might get swept up in the fun of it all. It's open Tuesday to Sunday 10:30pm until at least 3am, with a 15€ to 20€ cover that includes the first drink.

WINE BARS Open until late, **La Salumeria del Vino,** Via Cadore 30 (✆ **02-55184931;** www.lasalumeriadelvino.it; bus: 84), is one of the best of the Milanese wine bars, with outdoor tables when the weather is warm. They have a wide selection of reasonably priced Italian wines, plus a number of small Italian dishes. It's open Monday to Saturday 7:30pm to 1:30am.

GAY & LESBIAN CLUBS **Nuova Idea International ★★**, Via de Castillia 30 (✆ **02-69007859;** www.lanuovaidea.com; Metro: Garibaldi), is the largest, oldest, and most fun gay disco in Italy, very much tied to Milan's urban bustle. It prides itself on mimicking the large all-gay discos of northern Europe, and it draws young and not-so-young men. There is a large video screen and occasional live entertainment. It is open Tuesday and Sunday 9:30pm to 1:30am, Thursday and Friday 10:30pm to 3am, and Saturday 10pm to 4am. Cover is 10€ on Tuesday and Thursday, 13€ on Friday, 18€ on Saturday, and 12€ on Sunday.

BERGAMO ★★

50km (31 miles) NE of Milan, 601km (373 miles) NW of Rome

Bergamo is one of the most characteristic Lombard hill towns. Many of the town's stone fortifications were built on Roman foundations by the medieval Venetians, who looked on Bergamo as one of the gems of their trading network during several centuries of occupation. Set on a hilltop between the Seriana and the Brembana valleys, Bergamo lies in the Alpine foothills.

The Upper Town, 274m (900 ft.) above sea level, is buttressed by and terraced on the original Venetian fortifications. About .8km (½ mile) downhill is the Lower Town (usually identified by residents simply as "Bergamo"), with many 19th-century and early-20th-century buildings lining its wide streets. This modern metropolis and industrial center contains the bus and rail stations, most of the hotels, and the town's commercial and administrative center.

Essentials

GETTING THERE **Trains** arrive from Milan once every hour, depositing passengers in the center of the Lower Town at Piazza Marconi. The trip takes an hour and costs 3.60€. For information about rail connections in Bergamo, call ✆ **892021.**

The **bus station** in Bergamo is across from the train station. For information or schedules, call ✆ **02-33910794.** Buses arrive from Milan once every 30 minutes and cost 6.50€ one-way.

If you have a **car** and are coming from Milan, head east on A4.

VISITOR INFORMATION The **tourist office,** on Città Alta, Via Gombito 13 (✆ **035-242226;** www.turismo.bergamo.it), is open daily 9am to 12:30pm and 2 to 5:30pm.

Exploring the Upper Town (Città Alta)

Bergamo's cable car.

The higher you climb, the more rewarding the view will be. The **Upper Town (Città Alta) ★★★** is replete with narrow circuitous streets, old squares, splendid monuments, and imposing and austere medieval architecture. To reach the Upper Town, take bus no. 1 or 3, and then walk for 10 minutes up Viale Vittorio Emanuele, or take the cable car.

The heart of the Upper Town is **Piazza Vecchia ★**, which has witnessed most of the town's upheavals and a parade of conquerors ranging from Attila to the Nazis. On the square are the Palazzo della Ragione (town hall), an 18th-century fountain, and the Palazzo Nuovo of Scamozzi (town library).

A vaulted arcade connects Piazza Vecchia with **Piazza del Duomo.** Opening onto the latter is the cathedral of Bergamo, which has a baroque overlay.

Basilica di Santa Maria Maggiore & Baptistery ★   Built in the Romanesque style, the church was founded in the 12th century but much later was given a baroque interior and a disturbingly busy ceiling. Displayed are exquisite Flemish and Tuscan tapestries incorporating such themes as the Annunciation and the Crucifixion. The choir, designed by Lotto, dates from the 16th century. In front of the main altar is a series of inlaid panels depicting themes such as Noah's Ark and David and Goliath.

Facing the cathedral is the **baptistery,** dating from Giovanni da Campione's design in the mid–14th century, but it was rebuilt at the end of the 19th century.

Piazza Duomo. ℂ **035-223327.** Free admission. Nov–Mar Mon–Fri 9am–12:30pm and 2:30–5pm, Sat 9am–12:30pm and 2:30–6pm, Sun 9am–12:45pm and 3–6pm; Apr–Oct daily 9am–12:30pm and 2:30–6pm.

Colleoni Chapel (Cappella Colleoni) ★★   This Renaissance chapel honors the inflated ego of the Venetian military hero Bartolomeo Colleoni, with an inlaid marble facade reminiscent of Florence. It was designed by Giovanni Antonio Amadeo, who's chiefly known for his creation of the Certosa in Pavia (see "Get Thee to a Renaissance Monastery," earlier in this chapter). For the condottiere, Amadeo built an elaborate tomb, surmounted by a gilded equestrian statue. (Colleoni, who was once the ruler of the town and under whose watch the town fell to the Republic of Venice, which he then served, was also the subject of one of the world's most famous equestrian statues, now standing on a square in Venice.) The tomb sculpted for his daughter, Medea, is much less elaborate. Giovanni Battista Tiepolo painted most of the frescoes on the ceiling.

Piazza Duomo. ℂ **035-210061.** Free admission. Mar–Oct Tues–Sun 9am–12:30pm and 2–6:30pm; off season Tues–Sun 9am–12:30pm and 2–4:30pm.

Exploring the Lower Town (Città Bassa)

Carrara Academy Gallery (Galleria dell'Accademia Carrara) ★★   Filled with a wide-ranging collection of the works of homegrown artists, as well as Venetian and Tuscan masters, the academy draws art lovers from all over the world. The most important works are on the top floor—head here first if your time is limited. The Botticelli portrait of Giuliano de' Medici is well known, and one room contains three versions of Giovanni Bellini's favorite subject, the *Madonna and Child*. It's interesting to compare his work with that of his brother-in-law, Andrea Mantegna, whose *Madonna and Child* is also displayed, as is Vittore Carpaccio's *Nativity of Maria,* seemingly inspired by Flemish painters.

Farther along, you encounter a most original treatment of the old theme of the Madonna and Child, this one by Cosmè Tura of Ferrara. Also displayed are three tables of a predella by Lotto and his *Holy Family with St. Catherine* (wonderful composition), as well as Raphael's *St. Sebastian.* The entire wall space of another room is taken up with paintings by Moroni (1523–78), a local artist who seemingly did portraits of everybody who could afford one. In the salons to follow, such foreign masters as Rubens, van der Meer, and Jan Bruegel are represented, along with Guardi's architectural renderings of Venice and Longhi's continuing parade of Venetian high society.

Piazza Giacomo Carrara. ℓ **035-399640.** www.accademiacarrara.bergamo.it. Admission 5€ adults, 3€ children 6–12, free for children 5 and under. June–Sept Tues–Fri and Sun 10am–9pm, Sat 10am–11pm; Oct–May Tues–Fri 9:30am–5:30pm, Sat–Sun 10am–6pm.

Where to Stay

Hotel Agnello d'Oro ⚜ This is an intimate 17th-century country inn in the heart of the Città Alta. It's an atmospheric setting for good food or a serviceable room. When you enter the cozy reception lounge, ring an old bell to bring the owner away from the kitchen. The guest rooms come in different shapes and sizes, although most are quite small (as are the attached bathrooms); each has a comfortable bed, either a double or a twin.

Via Gombito 22, 24129 Bergamo. ℓ **035-249883.** Fax 035-235612. www.agnellodoro.it. 20 units (most with shower only). 85€ double. Rates include buffet breakfast. AE, MC, V. Bus: 1, then funicular. **Amenities:** Restaurant; bar. *In room:* TV, hair dryer.

Hotel Cappello d'Oro This Best Western affiliate lies in a renovated 150-year-old corner building on a busy street in the center of the Città Bassa. The public rooms and guest rooms are functional, high-ceilinged, and clean. The rooms are adequately but rather plainly furnished and are accompanied by compact tiled bathrooms. If you need a parking space, reserve it with your room.

Viale Papa Giovanni XXIII 12, 24121 Bergamo. ℓ **800/780-7234** in the U.S. and Canada, or 035-2289011. Fax 035-242946. www.hotelcappellodoro.it. 91 units. 140€–180€ double; 250€–290€ suite. Rates include buffet breakfast. AE, DC, MC, V. Parking 20€. **Amenities:** Restaurant; bar; exercise room; room service; sauna. *In room:* A/C, TV, hair dryer, minibar, Wi-Fi (free).

Hotel Excelsior San Marco ★ This 4-decade-old hotel at the edge of a city park is about midway between the Città Alta and the Città Bassa, both of which might be visible from the balcony of your room. The lobby features comfy leather chairs and ceiling frescoes depicting the lion of St. Mark. The guest rooms are attractively furnished and comfortable, most midsize to spacious and all with modernized bathrooms.

Piazza della Repubblica 6, 24122 Bergamo. ℓ **035-366111.** Fax 035-223201. www.hotelsan marco.com. 163 units (some with shower only). 175€–250€ double; 250€–390€ suite. Rates include buffet breakfast. AE, DC, MC, V. Parking 20€. **Amenities:** Restaurant; bar; babysitting; exercise room; room service; sauna. *In room:* A/C, TV, hair dryer, minibar, Wi-Fi (free).

Where to Dine

Colleoni dell'Angelo ★ BERGAMASCA/NORTHERN ITALIAN   Pierangelo Cornaro deserves the local fame he enjoys. His historic restaurant in the 11th-century Palazzo Bramante fronts one of the most beautiful squares (designed by Bramante) in the old city. A taverna for 4 centuries, Colleoni once fascinated the fabled Le Corbusier with its architecture. The decor consists of a large fresco of the winged lion of Venice along with antique Asian carpets, marble floors, and even crossed battle axes and suits of armor. Begin with one of the chef's home-made pastas or else a risotto. Skillfully prepared main courses include homemade macaroni sautéed with scorpion fish, clams, and sun-dried cherry tomatoes; veal kidney with sweet garlic; or theme-glazed medallions of lamb served with aspara-gus flavored with Parmesan cheese. The rack of lamb is baked under an aromatic herb crust and served with potato pie. In summer, guests can dine outside.

Piazza Vecchia 7, Bergamo Alta. ✆ **035-232596.** www.colleonidellangelo.com. Reservations recommended. Main courses 12€–29€; fixed-price menus 55€–70€. AE, DC, MC, V. Tues–Sun noon–2:30pm and 7:15–10:30pm. Closed Jan 7–20 and 1 week in Aug.

Ol Giopi e la Margi ★★ 🍴 BERGAMASCA/NORTHERN ITALIAN   Dar-win Foglieni is the finest chef in Bergamo, operating out of this traditional coun-try-style restaurant with a rustic decor 2.5km (1½ miles) east of the historic center, off Piazza Sant'Anna. Chef Darwin is warm and welcoming, and will feed you well from his large repertoire of dishes, each made with market-fresh ingre-dients. Always expect delightful surprises to emerge from the kitchen, such as roasted country rabbit flambéed with grappa and served with an Indian country polenta, or a potato-and-nettle *gnocchetti* with fried sausage and apple slices. Another specialty is risotto with sweet Gorgonzola cheese, pears, and walnuts. We'd walk a mile (even more) for a piece of his walnut cake with chocolate mousse.

Via Borgo Palazzo 27. ✆ **035-242366.** www.giopimargi.eu. Reservations required. Main courses 12€–23€; fixed-price menus 40€–46€. MC, V. Tues–Sun 12:30–3pm; Tues–Sat 7:30–11pm. Closed Jan 1–15 and Aug.

Bergamo After Dark

The opera season lasts from September to November, with a drama being staged from then until April at the **Teatro Donizetti,** Piazza Cavour (✆ **035-4160611;** www.gaetano-donizetti.com). The tourist office (under "Essentials," above) will provide a pamphlet of upcoming events.

If you want to visit a *birreria* (beer hall), head for **Via Gombito** in the Città Alta. It's lined with places to drink. One of the most popular joints is **Papageno Pub,** Via Colleoni 1B (✆ **035-236624;** www.papagenopub.com), which makes the best sandwiches and bruschetta in town.

MANTUA ★★

40km (25 miles) S of Verona, 153km (95 miles) SE of Milan, 469km (291 miles) NW of Rome, 145km (90 miles) SW of Venice

Mantua (Mantova) had a flowering of art and architecture under the Gonzaga dynasty, which held sway over the city for nearly 4 centuries. Originally an Etrus-can settlement and then a Roman colony, it has known many conquerors, including the French and the Austrians in the 18th and 19th centuries. Virgil, the great Latin poet, has remained its most famous son (he was born outside the city in a place called Andes). Verdi set *Rigoletto* here, Romeo (Shakespeare's creation, that is) took refuge here, and writer Aldous Huxley called Mantua "the most romantic city in the world."

Mantua is imposing and at times even austere. It's very much a city of the past, and its historic center is gloriously traffic-free.

Essentials

GETTING THERE Mantua has excellent **train** connections because it lies on direct lines to Milan, Cremona, Modena, and Verona. Nine trains arrive daily from Milan, taking 2¼ hours and costing 8.80€ one-way. From Cremona, trains arrive every hour (trip time: 1 hr.), costing 4.60€ one-way. The train station is on Piazza Don Leoni (© 892021). Take bus no. 3 from outside the station to get to the center of town.

Most visitors arrive by train, but Mantua has good **bus** connections with Brescia; 24 buses a day make a 1¾-hour journey at a cost of 7€ one-way. The bus station is on Via Mutilati Caduti del Lavoro (© 0376-230346).

If you have a **car** and are in Cremona, continue east along Rte. S10.

VISITOR INFORMATION The **tourist office,** at Piazza Mantegna 6 (© 0376-432432; www.turismo.mantova.it), is open daily 9am to 5pm.

Exploring the Town

The best shopping is at the **open-air market** that operates only on Thursday morning at Piazza delle Erbe and Piazza Sordello. Here you can find a little bit of everything, from cheap clothing (often designer knockoffs) to bric-a-brac. The place is like an outdoor traveling department store.

Basilica di Sant'Andrea & Campanile ★ Built to the specifications of Leon Battista Alberti, this church opens onto Piazza Mantegna, just off Piazza delle Erbe, where you'll find fruit vendors. The actual work was carried out by a pupil of Alberti's, Luca Fancelli. However, before Alberti died in 1472, it's said that, architecturally speaking, he knew that he had "buried the Middle Ages." The church wasn't completed until 1782, when Juvara crowned it with a dome.

As you enter, check out the first chapel to your left, which contains the tomb of the great Mantegna (the paintings are by his son, except for the *Holy Family* by the old master himself). The sacristan will light it for you. In the crypt, you'll encounter a representation of one of the more fanciful legends in the history of church relics: St. Andrew's claim to possess the blood of Christ, "the gift" of St. Longinus, the Roman soldier who's said to have pierced his side. Beside the basilica is a 1414 **campanile** (bell tower).

Piazza Mantegna. © **0376-328504.** Free admission to the church, 1€ to the crypt. Mon–Sat 7:30am–noon; daily 3–7pm.

Museo di Palazzo Ducale ★★★ The ducal apartments of the Gonzagas, with more than 500 rooms and 15 courtyards, are the most remarkable in Italy, certainly when judged from the standpoint of size. Like Rome, the compound wasn't built in a day, or even a century. The earlier buildings, erected to the specifications of the Bonacolsi family, date from the 13th century. The 14th and early 15th centuries saw the rise of the **Castle of St. George (Castello di San Giorgio),** designed by Bartolino da Novara. The Gonzagas also added the **Palatine Basilica of Santa Barbara (Basilica Palatina di Santa Barbara),** by Bertani.

Over the years, the historic monument of Renaissance splendor has lost many of the art treasures collected by Isabella d'Este during the 15th and 16th centuries in her efforts to turn Mantua into *la città dell'arte*. Her descendants, the Gonzagas, sold the most precious objects to Charles I of England in 1628, and 2 years later most of the remaining rich collection was looted during the sack of Mantua. Even Napoleon did his bit by carting off some of the objects still there.

What remains of the painting collection is still superb, including works by Tintoretto and Sustermans and a "cut-up" Rubens. The display of classical statuary is impressive, gathered mostly from the various Gonzaga villas at the time of Maria Theresa of Austria. Among the more inspired sights are the **Zodiac Room (Sala dello Zodiaco);** the **Hall of Mirrors (Salone degli Specchi),** with a vaulted ceiling from the beginning of the 17th century; the **River Chamber (Sala del Fume);** the **Apartment of Paradise (Appartamento del Paradiso);** the **Apartment of Troia (Appartamento di Troia),** with frescoes by Giulio Romano; and a scale reproduction of the **Holy Staircase (Scala Santa)** in Rome. The most interesting and best-known room in the castle is the **Bridal Chamber (Camera degli Sposi),** frescoed by Andrea Mantegna. Winged cherubs appear over a balcony at the top of the ceiling. Look for a curious dwarf and a mauve-hatted portrait of Christian I of Denmark. There are many paintings by Domenico Fetti, along with a splendid series of nine tapestries woven in Brussels based on cartoons by Raphael. A cycle of frescoes on the age of chivalry by Pisanello has recently been discovered. A tour guide will point out the many highlights.

Piazza Sordello 40. Ⓒ **0376-352100.** www. mantovaducale.beniculturali.it. Admission 6.50€. Tues–Sun 8:15am–7:15pm. Last admission 1 hr. before closing.

The Hall of Mirrors in the Palazzo Ducale.

Palazzo Te ★★ This Renaissance palace is known for its frescoes by Giulio Romano and his pupils. Fun-loving Federigo II, one of the Gonzagas, had it built as a place where he could slip away to see his mistress, Isabella Boschetto. The name, Te, is said to have been derived from the word *tejeto,* which in the local dialect means "a cut to let the waters flow out." This was once marshland drained by the Gonzagas for their horse farm.

The frescoes in the various rooms, dedicated to everything from horses to Psyche, rely on mythology for subject matter. The **Room of the Giants (Sala dei Giganti),** the best known, has a scene depicting Heaven venting its rage on the giants who had moved threateningly against it. Federico's motto was "What the lizards lack is that which tortures me," an obscure reference to the reptile's cold blood as opposed to his hot blood. The **Cupid and Psyche Room (Sala di Amore e Psiche)** forever immortalizes the tempestuous love affair of these swingers; it's decorated with erotic frescoes on the theme of the marriage of Cupid and Psyche, two other "hot bloods."

Viale Te 13. ✆ **0376-323266.** www.palazzote.it. Admission 9€, free for children 10 and under. Tues–Sun 9am–6pm; Mon 1–6pm. Last admission 30 min. before closing. Closed Jan 1, May 1, and Dec 25.

Where to Stay

Casa Poli ★ The town's best lodgings are found in a three-story, classic *palazzo* from the 19th century, lying on the main street of town in the historic center. Some of the bedrooms open onto the street, the others fronting an inviting courtyard. The decor is elegant, yet minimalist, with modern comforts. Natural fabrics, contemporary furnishings, dark wooden floors, and a sophisticated design characterize the midsize to spacious bedrooms.

Corso Garibaldi 32, 46100 Mantova. ✆ **0376-288170.** Fax 0376-362766. www.hotelcasapoli.it. 34 units. 109€–200€ double; 220€–240€ triple. Rates include buffet breakfast. AE, DC, MC, V. Parking 20€. Bus: 1. **Amenities:** Bar; bikes; room service. *In room:* A/C, TV, hair dryer, minibar, Wi-Fi (free).

Mantegna Hotel ✦ This inn is in a commercial section of town, a few blocks from one of the entrances to the old city. The lobby is accented with gray and red marble slabs, along with enlargements of details of paintings by Mantegna. About half of the guest rooms look out over a sunny rear courtyard, though the rooms facing the street are fairly quiet. They're small to midsize, each with a small bathroom.

Via Fabio Filzi 10, 46100 Mantova. ✆ **0376-328019.** Fax 0376-368564. www.hotelmantegna.it. 40 units (shower only). 120€–140€ double; from 140€ suite. Rates include buffet breakfast. AE, DC, DISC, MC, V. Free parking. Closed Dec 24–Jan 3. **Amenities:** Bar; babysitting; room service; Wi-Fi (free, in lobby). *In room:* A/C, TV, hair dryer.

Rechigi Hotel Near the center of the old city stands the Rechigi. The lobby is warmly decorated with modern paintings and contains an alcove bar. The owners maintain the property well and have decorated the guest rooms in good taste. Most comfortably furnished rooms are medium in size.

Via P. F. Calvi 30, 46100 Mantova. ✆ **0376-320781.** Fax 0376-220291. www.rechigi.com. 60 units (shower only). 130€–230€ double; from 160€ suite. AE, DC, MC, V. Parking 20€. **Amenities:** Bar; babysitting; room service. *In room:* A/C, TV, hair dryer, minibar.

Where to Dine

The local specialty is **donkey stew (stracotto di asino).** Legend claims that you're not a man until you've sampled it.

Il Cigno Trattoria dei Martini MANTOVANO   This *trattoria* overlooks a cobblestone square in the old part of Mantua. The exterior is a faded ocher, with wrought-iron cross-hatched window bars within sight of the easy parking on the piazza outside. After passing through a large entrance hall studded with frescoes, you'll come to the bustling dining rooms. The menu offers both freshwater and saltwater fish and dishes such as *agnoli* (a form of pasta) in a light sauce or risotto. One succulent pasta, *tortelli di zucca,* is stuffed with pumpkin.

Piazza Carlo d'Arco 1. ✆ **0376-327101.** Reservations recommended. Main courses 16€–28€. AE, DC, MC, V. Wed–Sun 12:30–1:45pm and 7:40–9:45pm. Closed Jan 1–5 and Aug.

L'Aquila Nigra (The Black Eagle) ★★ MANTOVANO/ITALIAN   This restaurant is in a Renaissance mansion on a narrow passageway by the Bonacolsi Palace. The foundations were laid in the 1200s, but the restaurant dates from 1984. In the elegant rooms, you can choose from such dishes as pike from the Mincio River, served with *salsa verde* (green sauce) and polenta, as well as other regional specialties, such as fried freshwater shrimp with zucchini, eel marinated in vinegar (one of the most distinctive dishes of Mantua), *tortelli di zucca* (with a pumpkin base), or breast of guinea fowl with a carrot sauce.

Vicolo Bonacolsi 4. ✆ **0376-327180.** www.aquilanigra.it. Reservations recommended. Main courses 22€–25€; fixed-price 3-course menu 50€, 5-course menu 70€. DC, MC, V. Tues–Sat noon–2pm and 8–10pm (also Sun noon–2pm Apr–May and Sept–Oct). Closed 2 weeks in Aug.

Ristorante Pavesi ★ 🎁 MANTOVANO/ITALIAN   The Pavesi is located under an ancient arcade on Mantua's most beautiful square. The walls partially date from the 1200s, although the restaurant goes back only before World War II. It's an intimate family-run place with hundreds of antique copper pots hanging from the single-barrel vault of the plaster ceiling; tables spill out into the square in summer. The antipasti table is loaded with delicacies, and specialties include *agnoli* (a form of *tortellini*) with meat, cheese, sage, and butter, as well as *risotto alla mantovana* (with pesto). Also try the roast filet of veal (deboned and rolled) and a blend of *fagioli* (white beans) with onions.

Piazza Erbe 13. ✆ **0376-323627.** www.ristorantepavesi.com. Reservations recommended. Main courses 13€–20€; 4-course menu 25€. AE, DC, MC, V. Wed–Mon noon–2:30pm and 7–10:30pm. Closed Feb.

Mantua After Dark

The major cultural venue is the **Teatro Sociale di Mantova,** Piazza Cavallotti, off Corso Vittorio Emanuele (✆ **0376-323860;** www.teatrosocialemantova.it). Tickets cost 18€ to 65€. You might also catch a chamber music series in April and May. The season runs October to June.

If you're just looking for a fun place for a drink, head for **Leoncino Rosso,** Via Giustiziati 33 (✆ **0376-323277**), behind Piazza Erbe. This *osteria* opened in 1750 and hasn't changed some of its recipes (such as tortellini with nuts or pumpkin) since then. It's closed August and 2 weeks in January.

LAKE GARDA ★★★

The easternmost of the northern Italian lakes, Lake Garda is also the largest, 52km (32 miles) long and 19km (12 miles) at its widest. Sheltered by mountains, its scenery, especially the part on the western shore that reaches from Limone to Salò, seems almost Mediterranean; you'll see olive, orange, and lemon trees, and even palms. The almost-transparent lake is ringed with four art cities: Trent to the northeast, Brescia to the west, Mantua to the south, and Verona to the east.

The lake's eastern side is more rugged and less developed, but the resort-studded western strip is probably best for first-timers. On the western side, a circuitous road skirts the lake through one molelike tunnel after another. You can park your car at several secluded belvederes and take in the panoramic lakeside views (or stop and take a cruise on the lake; see "Getting Around," below). In spring, the scenery is splashed with color as everything from wild poppies to oleander burst into bloom.

Essentials

GETTING THERE   Eight buses a day make the 1-hour trip from Trent to Riva del Garda, costing 5€ one-way. For information and schedules, call the Auto-stazione on Viale Trento in Riva at ✆ **0464-552323.** The nearest train station is at Rovereto, a 20-minute ride from Riva. Frequent buses make the 20-minute trip from the train station to Riva, costing 4€ one-way.

If you have a **car** and are coming from Milan or Brescia, A4 east runs to the southwestern corner of the lake. From Mantua, take A22 north to A4 west. From Verona and points east, take A4 west.

GETTING AROUND   For getting around Lake Garda, you'll need a **car.** Most drivers take the road along the western shore, S45bis, north to Riva del Garda. For a less-congested drive, try heading back down the lake along its eastern shore on the Gardesana Orientale (S249). S11 runs along the south shore.

The twisting roads following the shores of Lake Garda would be enough to rattle even the most experienced driver. Couple the turns, dimly lit tunnels, and emotional local drivers with convoys of tour buses and trucks that rarely stay in their lane, and you have one of the more frightening drives in Italy. Use your horn around blind curves, and be warned that Sunday is especially risky because everyone on the lake and from the nearby cities seems to take to the roads after a long lunch with lots of heady wine.

Both **ferries** and **hydrofoils** operate on the lake from Easter to September. For schedules and information, contact **Navigazione Lago di Garda** at ✆ **800-551801;** www.navigazionelaghi.it (its main office in Desenzano). For timetables and information, call ✆ **800-551801** toll-free in Italy. Ferries connect Riva's harbor, Porto San Nicola, with the major lakeside towns, such as Gardone (trip time: 2½ hr.), costing 9€ one-way; Sirmione (trip time: 4 hr.), 11€ one-way; and Desenzano (trip time: 4 hr., 20 min.), 12€ one-way.

These ferries provide the best opportunity for admiring the lake's beauty and are quite a bargain. Following the same routes, at about the same times, are a battalion of hydrofoils, which cut the travel time to each of the destinations in half. Transit on any of them requires a supplement of

1.50€ to 4€, depending on the distance you intend to travel. If you want to admire the lake from a waterside vantage, a well-recommended mode of attack is to travel in one direction via conventional ferry and return to Riva del Garda by hydrofoil. From early November to late February, there's no transportation offered in or out of Riva del Garda's port, or anywhere else along the lake's northern tier; only very limited transportation options are available from Desenzano, in the south.

Riva del Garda ★

Riva del Garda is the lake's oldest, most traditional resort. It consists of an expanding new district and an old town, the latter centered at **Piazza III Novembre.**

ESSENTIALS

GETTING THERE   Riva del Garda is linked to the Brenner-Modena motorway (Rovereto Sud/Garda Nord exit) and to the railway (Rovereto station); it is near Verona's airport.

VISITOR INFORMATION   The tourist office is at Largo Medaglie d'Oro 5 (✆ **0464-554444;** www.gardatrentino.it) and is open as follows: May to September daily 9am to 7pm; October to April daily 9am to 6pm.

EXPLORING THE RESORT

Situated on the northern banks of the lake, between the Benacense plains and towering mountains, Riva offers the advantages of both the Riviera and the Dolomites. Its climate is classically Mediterranean—mild in winter and moderate in summer. Vast areas of rich vegetation combine with the deep blue of the lake. Many people come for the healthy air and climate; others come for business conferences, meetings, and fairs. Riva is popular with tour groups from Germany and England.

Riva is the windsurfing capital of Italy. Windsurfing schools offer lessons and also rent equipment. The best one is **Sailing du Lac,** Viale Rovereto 44 (✆ **0464-552453;** www.sailingdulac.com), closed November to Easter. It has full rentals, including life jackets, wet suits, and boards, costing from 45€ per day.

If you'd like to explore the area by bike, go to **Super Bike Girelli,** Viale Damiano Chiesa 21 (✆ **0464-556602**), where rentals cost 15€ per day.

Most of the town's shopping consists of unremarkable souvenirs, but a large **open-air market,** the best on Lake Garda, comes to town on the second and fourth Wednesdays of every month. It mainly sprawls along Viale Dante, Via Prati, and Via Pilati. You can buy virtually anything, from Alpine handicrafts to busts of Mussolini. While you're shopping, drop in at the **Pasticceria Copat di Fabio Marzari,** Viale Dante 37 (✆ **0464-551885**), for delectable pastries.

On the harbor, at Piazza III Novembre, you'll see the town's highest building, a 13th-century watchtower, the **Tower of Appanale (Torre d'Appanale).** It isn't open for visits, but the angelic-looking trumpeter adorning its pinnacle has been adopted as the symbol of the town itself. There's also a severe-looking castle, **La Rocca,** Piazza Battisti 3 (✆ **0464-573869**). Built in 1124 and owned at various times by both the ruling Scaligeri princes of Verona and the Viennese Habsburgs (who used it as a prison), La Rocca has been turned into a **Civic Museum (Museo Civico La Rocca),** which you might visit on a rainy day to see its exhibits of local artworks and attractions reflecting local traditions. Admission is 2€; it's open from March to October Tuesday to Sunday 10am to 12:30pm and 1:30 to 6pm.

WHERE TO STAY

Feeling Hotel Luise ★★   The Bertolini family launched it as a small hotel and restaurant in 1958, renovating and enlarging it in 2004. Today it's surrounded by a large garden and a big swimming pool. Guests sit on comfortable sofas in the lounge admiring sculptures by Jacopo Foggini and an exhibition of baggage labels that date back 2 centuries. Rooms are comfortable but furnished in a rather minimalist style, a light, airy feeling with natural beechwood parquet floors and harmonious colors.

Viale Rovereto 9, 38066 Riva del Garda. ⓒ **0464-550858.** Fax 0464-554250. www.feeling hotelluise.com. 68 units. 79€–219€ double; 169€–269€ junior suite. Rates include buffet breakfast. AE, DC, MC, V. Free parking. **Amenities:** Restaurant; bar; babysitting; bikes; outdoor pool; room service. *In room:* A/C, TV, hair dryer, minibar, Wi-Fi (5€ per hr.).

Hotel Sole ★ 🍴   This large 15th-century *palazzo* with arched windows and colonnades enjoys the most scenic location on the waterfront and offers luxuries that you'd expect from a more expensive hotel. The character and the quality of the guest rooms vary considerably, but most have lake views and some have balconies. Some are almost suites, with living-room areas; the smaller ones are less desirable. The staff can help you arrange bike trips and steer you toward the best watersports on the lake.

Piazza III Novembre 35, 38066 Riva del Garda. ⓒ **0464-552686.** Fax 0464-552811. www.hotel sole.net. 52 units. 48€–95€ per person double; 94€–146€ per person suite. Rates include buffet breakfast. AE, DC, MC, V. Parking 10€. **Amenities:** Restaurant; bar; babysitting; bikes; room service; sauna; Wi-Fi (free, in lobby). *In room:* TV, hair dryer, minibar.

Hotel Venezia ★ 🍴   This is one of the most attractive budget hotels in town. The main section of the Venezia's angular modern building is raised on stilts above a private parking lot set back from the lakefront promenade. The complex is surrounded by trees on a quiet street bordered with flowers and private homes. The guest rooms are pleasantly furnished and well maintained, each with a compact bathroom. Breakfast is served on the open-air sunroof.

Via Franz Kafka 7, 38066 Riva del Garda. ⓒ/fax **0464-552216.** www.rivadelgarda.com. 21 units (shower only). 110€–130€ double. Rates include continental breakfast. AE, DC, MC, V. Closed Nov–Easter. **Amenities:** Outdoor pool. *In room:* A/C, TV, hair dryer.

WHERE TO DINE

Al Volt ★ TRENTINO   In the historic center of the resort, this elegant, old-style restaurant lies in a converted palace from the 15th century. It is one of the leading places to dine at Riva del Garda. The chefs are basically inspired by the recipes of the Trentino–Alto Adige area, which includes some recipes from Austria, which used to be the military power in the area. The culinary traditions of yesteryear live on, and the chefs take full advantage of the rich bounty of the surrounding agricultural lands. You might begin with homemade *tagliolini* in a savory ragout sauce and follow with veal cutlets in a radicchio sauce, or perhaps tuna filet sautéed with vermouth sauce. Beef cheeks are delectable in a cabernet sauvignon wine sauce with a vegetable ratatouille.

Via Fiume 73. ☎ **0464-552570.** www.ristorantealvolt.com. Reservations required. Main courses 12€–22€; fixed-price menus 38€–40€. AE, DC, MC, V. Tues–Sun noon–2pm and 7–10pm. Closed Feb 15–Mar 15.

Ancora ITALIAN   In spite of a staff that's often less than helpful, this *trattoria* is an enduring favorite among locals because of its affordable dishes. Downstairs is a restaurant with a maritime decor, but most diners in summer prefer the roof-top terrace. Your best bet is one of the fresh fish dishes from the lake, although the cooks prepare homemade pastas and meats as well. The restaurant is attached to a small hotel with a dozen comfortable rooms, which are among the most reasonable at the resort, costing 76€ to 94€ for a double.

Via Montanara 2. ☎ **0464-567099.** Reservations recommended. Main courses 12€–22€; fixed-price menus 20€–30€. AE, MC, V. Daily noon–2:30pm and 7pm–midnight. Closed Tues Oct–Mar.

Limone sul Garda ★

Limone sul Garda lies 10km (6 miles) south of Riva on the western shore of Lake Garda and is one of the liveliest resorts on the lake.

Limone snuggles close to the water at the bottom of a narrow, steep road, so its shopkeepers, faced with no building room, dug right into the rock. There are 4km (2½ miles) of beach for sunbathing, swimming, sailing, and windsurfing. The only way to get around is by walking, but that's part of the fun. You can enjoy tennis, soccer, and other sports, as well as the discos that seem to come and go every year.

If you're bypassing Limone, you might still want to make a detour south of the village to **Tignale,** in the hills. You can climb a modern highway to the town for a sweeping vista of Garda, one of the most scenic spots on the entire lake.

There's a **tourist office** in the City Hall, Via IV Novembre 2-C (☎ **0365-918987**); it's open Monday to Friday 9am to 1pm and 2:30 to 5:30pm from November to March, and daily 8:30am to 10pm from April to October.

WHERE TO STAY

Hotel Capo Reamol ★ ☺   You won't even get a glimpse of this 1960s hotel from the main highway because it nestles on a series of terraces well below road level. Pull into a roadside area indicated at 2km (1¼ miles) north of Limone; then follow the driveway down a steep, narrow hill. Its most dramatic feature is its pool set above the lake. The most desirable accommodations open onto terraces overlooking the lake, and the less attractive lie in an annex where the rooms are older but still have lake views. Guest rooms are well furnished and freshly decorated, ranging from midsize to spacious; some offer balconies overlooking the lake and the gravel beach.

Via IV Novembre 92, 25010 Limone sul Garda. ☎ **0365-954040.** Fax 0365-954262. www.hotel caporeamol.it. 58 units. 48€–83€ per person double; 61€–93€ per person junior suite. Rates include buffet breakfast. AE, DC, MC, V. Closed mid-Oct to Easter. Free parking. **Amenities:** Restaurant; bar; bikes; children's playground; exercise room; outdoor pool; spa; limited water-sports rentals; Wi-Fi (5€ per hr., in lobby). *In room:* A/C, TV, hair dryer, minibar.

Hotel Le Palme ★   Opening directly onto Lake Garda with a flowery terrace, this Venetian-style villa with period furniture stands in the shade of palm trees 2 centuries old. It offers well-furnished guest rooms, each individually decorated, and compact tiled bathrooms. The second floor has a comfortable reading room with a TV, and the third floor has a wide terrace.

Via Porto 36, 25020 Limone sul Garda. (𝒞 **0365-954681.** Fax 0365-954120. www.sunhotels.it. 28 units (shower only). 85€–155€ double. Rates include buffet breakfast. Minimum 3-day stay required. MC, V. Closed Nov–Easter. **Amenities:** Restaurant; bar; outdoor pool; room service. *In room:* A/C, TV.

Gardone Riviera ★★

On Lake Garda's western shore, 97km (60 miles) east of Milan, **Gardone Riviera** is a bustling resort with a number of good hotels and sporting facilities. Its lakeside promenade attracts a wide range of European visitors for most of the year. When it used to be chic for patrician Italian families to spend their vacations by the lake, many prosperous families built elaborate villas here and in neighboring Fasano, and many of these homes have been converted into inns. The town also has the major sightseeing attraction along the lake, d'Annunzio's Villa Vittoriale.

ESSENTIALS

GETTING THERE The resort lies 42km (26 miles) south of Riva on the west coast. During the day, buses from Brescia arrive every 30 minutes; the trip takes 1 hour and costs 5€ one-way. For schedule information, call (𝒞 **030-44061.**

VISITOR INFORMATION The **tourist office** is at Corso della Repubblica 8 ((𝒞 **0365-20347**). It's open Monday to Saturday 9am to 12:30pm, and Monday to Wednesday and Friday to Saturday 3 to 6pm.

EXPLORING THE TOWN

There are many scenic hiking trails and walking paths through the area; the staff at your hotel or the tourist office can help you choose a route that fits your available time and ability level. One easy day hike with charming scenery starts from the edge of the lake, near the town center, and goes 4.8km (3 miles) up a gentle hill to the north, taking you to the village of **San Michele.** There you'll find a cluster of ancient houses and a village church, with views over the surrounding landscapes.

If you want to get out on the lake, you can rent motorboats or sailboats at **Nautica Benaco,** along the lakefront of the village of Manerba del Garda ((𝒞 **0365-654074;** www.nauticabenaco.it), 14km (9 miles) from Gardone. You can rent a boat for a full day for 160€ to 210€, depending on the boat. Fuel is not included, and a deposit of 1,000€ is required.

> ## Wine Tasting
>
> This region produces everything from dry still reds to sparkling whites with a champagnelike zest. **Fratelli Berlucchi,** Via Broletto 2, Borgonato di Cortefranca, 25040 Brescia ((𝒞 **030-984451;** www.fratelli berlucchi.it), one of Italy's largest wineries, is especially happy to host visitors. If you'd like to drive around the countryside to taste wine and tour a vineyard, call to make an appointment and get detailed directions.

Villa Vittoriale ★ This villa was the home of Gabriele d'Annunzio (1863–1938), the poet and military adventurer, another Italian who believed in *la dolce vita,* even when he couldn't afford it. Most of the celebrated events in d'Annunzio's life occurred before 1925, including his love affair with Eleonora Duse and his bravura takeover as a self-styled commander of a territory being ceded to

Yugoslavia. In the later years of his life, until he died in the winter before World War II, he lived the grand life at his private estate on Garda.

The furnishings and decor passed for avant-garde in their day but now evoke the Radio City Music Hall of the 1930s. D'Annunzio's death mask is of morbid interest, and his bed with a "Big Brother" eye adds a curious touch of Orwell's *1984* (over the poet's bed is a faun casting a nasty sneer). The marble bust of Duse ("the veiled witness" of his work) seems sadly out of place, but the manuscripts and old uniforms perpetuate the legend. In July and August, d'Annunzio plays are presented at the amphitheater on the premises. Villa Vittoriale is a bizarre monument to a hero of yesteryear.

Via Vittoriale 12. ℂ **0365-296511.** www.vittoriale.it. Admission 8€ to grounds only; 13€ to grounds and villa. Summer daily 8:30am–8pm; winter daily 9am–5pm. Head out Via Roma, connecting with Via Colli.

WHERE TO STAY

You can also rent a luxury room at the **Villa Fiordaliso** (see below).

Bellevue Hotel 🏅   This villa, perched above the main road, offers many terraces surrounded by trees and flowers, and an unforgettable view. You can stay here on a budget, enjoying the advantages of lakeside villa life. The guest rooms come in a variety of shapes and sizes, each with a small bathroom.

Via Zanardelli 81, 25083 Gardone Riviera. ℂ **0365-290088.** Fax 0365-290080. www.hotel bellevuegardone.com. 30 units (shower only). 109€–130€ double. Rates include buffet breakfast. MC, V. Free parking. Closed Oct 8–Apr 4. **Amenities:** Restaurant; outdoor pool. *In room:* A/C, TV, hair dryer.

Grand Hotel ★★   This grande old dame is still the leading lady of Gardone. When it was built in 1881, this was the most fashionable hotel on the lake and one of the biggest resorts in Europe. Famous guests have included Winston Churchill, Gabriele d'Annunzio, and Somerset Maugham. It's only a rumor that Vladimir Nabokov was inspired to write *Lolita* after spotting a young girl here. The main salon's sculpted ceilings, parquet floors, and comfortable chairs make it an ideal spot for reading or watching the lake. For the most part, the guest rooms are spacious and traditionally furnished, always inviting (especially those balconies overlooking the lake).

Via Zanardelli 84, 25083 Gardone Riviera. ℂ **0365-20261.** Fax 0365-22695. www.gran gardone.it. 180 units. 170€–270€ double; 265€–330€ junior suite. Rates include buffet breakfast. Half board 35€ per person. AE, DC, MC, V. Parking 12€. Closed Oct 19–Mar. **Amenities:** Restaurant (plus buffet lunches on the garden terrace); bar; babysitting; Jacuzzi; outdoor heated pool; room service; sauna; Wi-Fi (10€ per hr., in lobby). *In room:* A/C, TV, hair dryer, minibar.

WHERE TO STAY NEARBY

The nearby town of **Fasano del Garda** is a satellite resort of Gardone Riviera, 2km (1¼ miles) to the north. Many prefer it to Gardone.

Hotel Villa del Sogno ★★★   This 1920s re-creation of a Renaissance villa offers sweeping views of the lake and spacious old-fashioned guest rooms (nine are air-conditioned). The rooms come in various shapes and sizes, and all are elegantly comfortable. The bathrooms are also well equipped, each with deluxe toiletries. This "Villa of the Dream" is far superior to anything in the area and offers a gorgeous, peaceful setting with extensive grounds. The baronial stairway of the interior and many of the ceilings and architectural details were crafted from beautiful woods.

Via Zanardelli 107, 25083 Gardone Riviera. ✆ **0365-290181.** Fax 0365-290230. www.villadel sogno.it. 31 units. 250€–420€ double; 470€–820€ suite. Rates include buffet breakfast. AE, DC, MC, V. Free parking. Closed Nov 4–Mar 31. **Amenities:** Restaurant; babysitting; Jacuzzi; outdoor pool; room service; sauna; outdoor tennis court. *In room:* A/C, TV, hair dryer, minibar, Wi-Fi (free).

WHERE TO DINE

Most visitors take their meals at their hotels. However, there are some good independent choices.

Ristorante La Stalla ☺ INTERNATIONAL   This charming restaurant, set in a garden ringed with cypresses on a hill above the lake, is frequented by local families. It occupies a handcrafted stone building with a brick-columned porch and outdoor tables. To get here, follow the signs toward Il Vittoriale (the building was commissioned by d'Annunzio as a horse stable) to a quiet residential street. Depending on what's at the market that day, the specialties might include a selection of freshly prepared antipasti, risotto with truffles or porcini mushrooms, or crepes fondue. Polenta is served with Gorgonzola and walnuts, or you might prefer beef filet in a green-peppercorn sauce. Sunday afternoon can be crowded.

Via dei Colli 14 Strada per Il Vittoriale. ✆ **0365-290444.** www.ristorantelastalla.it. Reservations recommended. Main courses 7€–25€. MC, V. Wed–Mon 12:30–2:30pm and 7:30–11:30pm. Closed Jan–Feb.

Villa Fiordaliso ★★★ ITALIAN   This deluxe restaurant is in a Liberty-style villa from 1903 with gardens stretching down to the lake. Many famous guests have dined here—none more notorious than Mussolini and his mistress, Claretta Petacci, who used it from 1943 until their deaths in 1945 (one of the hotel's suites is named after Claretta). Not only is it the most scenic and beautiful eatery on Lake Garda, but it also serves the finest cuisine. The chef gives his dishes a personal touch; the menu is likely to include a terrine of eel and salmon in herb-and-onion sauce, a timbale of rice and shellfish with curry, and several fish and meats grilled over a fire. Other specialties are ravioli with Bagoss (a salty regional cheese), sardines from a nearby lake baked in an herb crust, and scampi in a sauce of tomatoes and wild onions. This little bastion of fine food has impeccable service to match.

Today this famous villa is owned by Rosa Tosetti, who runs it beautifully and also offers guest rooms in a setting of cypresses, pine trees, and olive trees, near a private beach. Each room is exquisitely furnished. It was here that poet Gabriele D'Annunzio used to gaze out through the villa's stained-glass windows. The five standard rooms cost 350€ to 500€, with Claretta's suite costing 700€.

Corso Zanardelli 150, 25083 Gardone Riviera. ✆ **0365-20158.** www.villafiordaliso.it. Reservations required. Main courses 25€–36€; 7-course degustation menu 110€. AE, DC, MC, V. Wed–Sun 12:30–2pm and 7:30–10pm; Tues 7:30–10:30pm. Closed Nov 2–Mar 19.

Sirmione ★★

Perched at the tip of a narrowing strip on the southern end of Lake Garda, Sirmione juts out 4km (2½ miles) into the lake. Noted for its thermal baths (used to treat deafness), the town is a major resort, just north of the autostrada connecting Milan and Verona. As in many Lake District resorts, things come to life in spring, go full tilt in summer, and then wilt away again in autumn.

ESSENTIALS

GETTING THERE   Sirmione lies 6km (3¾ miles) from the A4 exit and 8km (5 miles) from Desanzano.

    Buses (operated by SAIA) run from Brescia and from Verona to Sirmione every hour (trip time from either, depending on traffic: 1 hr.). A one-way ticket from Brescia costs 5€, and from Verona, 4.50€. For information call ✆ **030-44915.**

    There's no rail service. The nearest train terminal is at Desenzano, on the Venice-Milan rail line. From here, there's frequent bus service to Sirmione; the bus trip takes 30 minutes and costs 5€ one-way.

VISITOR INFORMATION   The **tourist office** is at Viale Marconi 2 (✆ **030-916114**). From April to October, it's open daily 9am to 12:30pm and 3 to 6pm; November to March, hours are Monday to Saturday 9am to 12:30pm and Monday to Friday 3 to 6pm.

EXPLORING THE TOWN

Known for its beaches (which are invariably crowded in summer), Sirmione is Garda's major lakeside resort. The best beach is **Lido delle Bionde,** which you reach by taking Via Dante near the castle. Here vendors will rent you a chaise longue with an umbrella for 20€. If you're feeling more athletic, other vendors will hook you up with a **pedal boat** at 25€ per hour or a **kayak** at 23€ per hour.

    The resort is filled with souvenir shops, many hawking cheap trinkets aimed at the day-tripper. However, the best buys are found Friday 8am to 1pm when an **outdoor market** blossoms in Piazza Montebaldo. Vendors bring their wares here not only from nearby lake villages, but also from towns and villages to the south.

    The resort was a favorite of Gio-sué Carducci, the Italian poet who won the Nobel prize for literature in 1906. In Roman days it was frequented by another poet, the hedonistic Catullus, who died in 54 B.C. Today the **Grotte di Catullo ★**, on Piazzale Orti Manara (✆ **030-916157**), is the chief sight, an unbeatable combination of Roman ruins and a panoramic lake view. You can wander through the

The thermal baths in Sirmione.

remains of this once-great villa March to October Tuesday to Saturday 9:30am to 7pm, and Sunday 9am to 6pm, November to February Tuesday to Saturday 8:30am to 5pm and Sunday 8:30am to 2pm. Admission is 4€.

At the entrance to the town stands the moated 13th-century **Castello Scaligero ★**, Piazza Castello (✆ **030-916468**), which once belonged to the powerful Scaligeri princes of Verona. You can climb to the top and walk the ramparts. It's open year-round from Tuesday to Sunday 8:30am to 7pm. Admission is 4€.

WHERE TO STAY

During the peak summer season, you need a hotel reservation to bring a car into this crowded town. However, there's a large parking area at the town entrance. Accommodations are plentiful.

Flaminia Hotel ★ ✇   This is one of the best little hotels in Sirmione, with a number of modern facilities and amenities. It's right on the lakefront, with a terrace extending into the water. The guest rooms are made attractive by French doors opening onto private balconies. The rooms come in different shapes and sizes, each with a tiled bathroom. The lounges are furnished in a functional modern style.

Piazza Flaminia 8, 25019 Sirmione. ✆ **030-916078.** Fax 030-916193. www.hotelflaminia.it. 35 units. 125€–185€ double; 170€–300€ triple. Rates include buffet breakfast. AE, MC, V. Free parking. Closed Nov 7–Mar 19 and Dec 26–Jan 10. **Amenities:** Bar; babysitting; room service. *In room:* A/C, TV, hair dryer, minibar, Wi-Fi (free).

Grand Hotel Terme ★   This rambling hotel at the entrance of the old town is on the lake next to the Scaligeri Castle, and it boasts a lovely lakefront garden. Wide marble halls and stairs lead to well-furnished guest rooms ranging from medium in size to spacious, each with a lake view. The tiled bathrooms have deluxe toiletries.

Viale Marconi 7, 25019 Sirmione. ✆ **030-916261.** Fax 030-916568. www.termedisirmione.com. 58 units. 140€–470€ double; 474€–660€ suite. Rates include buffet breakfast. AE, DC, MC, V. Free parking. Closed Jan 6–Feb. **Amenities:** Restaurant; babysitting; exercise room; Jacuzzi; outdoor heated pool and indoor thermal pool; sauna; room service; spa; Wi-Fi (free, in lobby). *In room:* A/C, TV, hair dryer, minibar.

Villa Cortine Palace Hotel ★★   This first-class choice, whose original building dates from 1905, is set apart from the town and surrounded by sumptuous formal gardens. For serenity, atmosphere, professional service, and even good food, there's nothing to equal it in Sirmione. Today all but a handful of its guest rooms are in the new wing, and the reception area is located in the older building. Most rooms are medium to spacious, each with an excellent bathroom containing deluxe toiletries. Most units have balconies and lovely lake views. The formal drawing room boasts lots of gilt and marble—it's positively palatial.

Via Grotte 12, 25019 Sirmione. ✆ **030-9905890.** Fax 030-916390. www.hotelvillacortine.com. 52 units. 310€–680€ double; 540€–720€ suite. Rates include buffet breakfast. AE, DC, MC, V. Closed end of Oct to Easter. **Amenities:** 2 restaurants (plus barbecue lunches on the private beach); bar; babysitting; outdoor pool; room service; clay tennis court. *In room:* A/C, TV, hair dryer, minibar.

WHERE TO DINE

La Rucola ★★ ITALIAN/PIZZERIA   This restaurant lies down a small alley a few steps from the main gate leading into Sirmione. The building looks like a vine-laden, sienna-colored country house (actually, it was a stable 150 years ago). The menu includes fresh salmon, *langoustines* (small lobsters), such fish dishes as scallops with porcini mushrooms or sea bass with aromatic herbs, plus a more limited meat selection, such as roast pork shank on a white rabe purée with bitter cocoa. Meats, such as Florentine beefsteak, are most often grilled or flambéed. More innovative items include *gnocchetti di riso* with baby squid and squid ink, and sea bass over an artichoke omelet and seafood sausage. A good pasta dish is spaghetti with clams. From the wood-burning oven emerge nearly two dozen different types of pizza.

Vicolo Strentelle 5. ⓒ **030-916326.** www.ristorantelarucola.it. Reservations required for lunch, recommended for dinner. Main courses 25€–33€; fixed-price menu 90€. AE, DC, MC, V. Sat–Wed 12:30–2:30pm; Fri–Wed 8–10:30pm. Closed Jan–Feb 8.

Signori ★ NORTHERN ITALIAN/SEAFOOD   Although not quite of the high standard of la Rucola, this contemporary-style restaurant in the historic center runs a close second. In fair weather, it offers both indoor and outdoor seating, with a terrace projecting directly into the lake. Many locals dock their boats nearby to dine here on a creative cuisine based on first-rate seasonal products, especially seafood and locally grown vegetables. Fish from the lake is a special highlight. The chefs have a talent for sauces and combining ingredients. Start with *ravioli di lavarello alla Maggiorana* (freshwater fish ravioli with marjoram) or else the warm and cold lake-fish antipasti. A red-beet ravioli is prepared with river shrimp, and baked lake fish is also served more simply with lemon butter and capers. The most elegant offering is filet of sole stuffed with lobster.

Via Romagnoli 17. ⓒ **030-916017.** www.ristorantesignori.it. Reservations recommended. Main courses 17€–32€. AE, DC, MC, V. Tues–Sun 12:30–3:30pm and 7:30pm–midnight. Closed early Nov to early Dec.

LAKE COMO ★★★

More than 48km (30 miles) north of Milan, romantic and lovely Lake Como is a shimmering deep blue, spanning 4km (2½ miles) at its widest point. With its flower-filled gardens, villas built for the wealthy of the 17th and 18th centuries, and mild climate, it's among the most scenic spots in Italy. The best way to admire the lake's many faces is to take a boat tour and pull into selected ports of call en route for a meal, an espresso, a stroll, or some shopping or swimming.

One of the many villas along Lake Como.

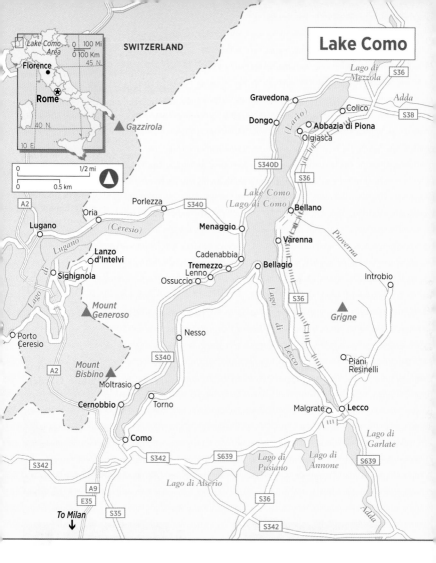

Essentials

GETTING THERE **Trains** arrive daily at Como from Milan every hour. The trip takes 40 minutes, and a one-way fare is 3.60€. The main station, **Stazione San Giovanni,** Piazzale San Gottardo (✆ **892021**), lies at the end of Viale Gallio, a 15-minute walk from the center (Piazza Cavour).

    The city of Como is 40km (25 miles) north of Milan; you can **drive** there via A9. Once at the Como, a small road (S583) leads to the resort of Bellagio.

GETTING AROUND Bus service connecting the major towns along the lake is offered by **SPT,** Piazza Matteotti (✆ **031-2769911;** www.sptlinea.it). A one-way fare from Como to the most popular resort of Bellagio is 3.50€, on bus no. 30 to Bellagio. Travel time depends on the traffic.

Como ★

At the southern tip of the lake, 40km (25 miles) north of Milan, Como is known for its silk industry. Most visitors at least pass through here to take a cruise on the lake (see below). But because Como is also an industrial city, this isn't the best place to stay (head instead to one of the more attractive resorts along the lake, such as Bellagio), unless you don't have your own car and are dependent on public transportation (in which case, it's the most convenient base).

For centuries, the town's economy has been linked to Milan. Como has been making silk since Marco Polo first returned with silkworms from China (since the end of World War II, however, Como has left the cultivation of silk to the Chinese and just imports the thread to weave into fabrics). Como's silk makers are major suppliers for the fashion designers of Milan, and big names like Giorgio Armani come here to discuss the patterns that they want with silk manufacturers.

ESSENTIALS

GETTING THERE See "Essentials," above.

VISITOR INFORMATION The **tourist office,** at Piazza Cavour 17 (© **031-269712;** www.lakecomo.it), is open Monday to Saturday 9am to 1pm and 2:30 to 6pm; from June to September, it is also open on Sunday 9:30am to 1pm.

EXPLORING THE CITY

The heart of Como is **Piazza Cavour,** with its hotels, cafes, and steamers departing for lakeside resorts. Immediately to the west, the **Public Gardens**

The gardens at the Villa Carlotta.

(**Giardini Pubblici**) make for a pleasant stroll, especially if you're heading for the **Tempio Voltiano,** Viale Marconi (✆ 031-574705), which honors native son Alessandro Volta, the physicist and pioneer of electricity. The temple contains memorabilia of his life and experiments. It's open April to September Tuesday to Sunday 10am to noon and 3 to 6pm, and October to March Tuesday to Sunday 10am to noon and 2 to 4pm. Admission costs 3€.

From Como, it's easy to take a cruise around the lake; boats departing from the town's piers make calls at every significant settlement along its shores. Stroll down to the **Lungo Lario,** adjacent to Piazza Cavour, and head to the ticket windows of the **Società Navigazione Lago di Como** (✆ 800-551801; www. navigazionelaghi.it). Between Easter and September, half a dozen ferries and almost as many high-speed hydrofoils embark for circumnavigations of the lake. One-way transit from Como to Colico at the northern end of the lake takes 4 hours by ferry and 90 minutes by hydrofoil, and includes stops at each of the towns en route. Transit each way costs 10€ to 14€, depending on which boat you take. One-way transit between Como and Bellagio takes 2 hours by ferry and 45 minutes by hydrofoil, and costs 8.20€ to 12€ per person. There's no service from Como between October and Easter.

Note: Be warned in advance that much of your view will be obscured by mists thrown up by the hydrofoils, so if you're taking this ride primarily for the view, the slower, cheaper boat is preferable.

To get an overview of the area, take the funicular at Lungolario Trieste (near the main beach at Villa Genio) to the top of **Brunate,** a hill overlooking Como and providing a panoramic view. Departures are every 30 minutes daily, costing 4.80€ round-trip. For information, call ✆ **031-303608.**

The best swimming is at the **Lido Villa Olmo,** Via Percernobbio 2 (✆ **031-570968**), a pool adjoining a sandy stretch of beach for sunbathing (May 20–Sept 15). Admission is 15€, and it's open daily 9am to 6pm.

Because this lakeside city has such a thriving silk industry, there's great shopping for scarves, blouses, lingerie, and neckties. Before you buy, you might be interested in knowing more about the history and techniques of the silk industry; if that's the case, head for the **Museo Didattico della Seta,** Via Castelnuovo 1 (✆ **031-303180;** www.museosetacomo.com; Tues–Fri 9am–noon and 3–6pm; bus: 7). Maintained by a local trade school, it displays antique weaving machines and memorabilia going back to the Renaissance concerning the world's most elegant fabric. The relatively expensive admission is 8€.

Not all the silk factories will sell retail to individuals, but the best of those that do include **Martinetti,** Via Torriani 41 (✆ **031-269053**).

Before rushing off on a boat for a tour of the lake, you might want to visit the **Cattedrale di Como** ★, Piazza del Duomo (✆ **031-265244**). Construction began in the 14th century in the Lombard Gothic style and continued on through the Renaissance until the 1700s. Frankly, the exterior is more interesting than the interior. Dating from 1487, the exterior is lavishly decorated with statues, including those of Pliny the Elder (A.D. 23–79) and the Younger (A.D. 62–113), whom one writer once called "the beautiful people of ancient Rome." Inside, look for the 16th-century tapestries depicting scenes from the Bible. The cathedral is open Monday to Saturday 7am to noon and 3 to 7pm.

On the other side of the Duomo lies the colorfully striped **Brolette (town hall)** and, adjoining it, the **Torre del Comune.** Both are from the 13th century.

If time remains, head down the main street, **Via Vittorio Emanuele,** where the five-sided **San Fedele ★**, a 12th-century church standing on Piazza San Fedele, rises 2 blocks south of the cathedral. It's known for its unusual pentagonal apse and a doorway carved with "fatted" figures from the Middle Ages. Farther along, you come to the **Museo Archeologico Paolo Giovio (Archaeological Museum Paolo Giovio),** Piazza Medaglie d'Oro Comasche (© **031-271343**), the virtual attic of Como, displaying artifacts collected by the city from prehistoric times through World War II. The museum is open Tuesday to Saturday 9:30am to 12:30pm and 2 to 5pm, and Sunday 10am to 1pm. Admission is 4€.

The art museum of Como is of passing interest: The small **Pinacoteca Palazzo Volpi,** Via Diaz 84 (© **031-269869**), has several old and wonderful paintings from the Middle Ages, most of which were taken from the monastery of Santa Margherita del Broletto. Two of the museum's best paintings are anonymous: that of St. Sebastian riddled with arrows (though appearing quite resigned to the whole thing) and a moving *Youth and Death.* The museum is open Tuesday to Saturday 9:30am to 12:30pm and 2 to 5pm, and Sunday 10am to noon. Admission is 4€.

After the museum, continue down Via Giovio until you come to the **Porta Vittoria,** a gate from 1192 with five tiers of arches. A short walk away, passing through a dreary commercial area leads you to Como's most interesting church, the 11th-century **Sant'Abbondio ★**, a Romanesque gem. From Porta Vittoria, take Viale Cattaneo to Viale Roosevelt, turning left onto Via Sant'Abbondio on which the church stands. Because of its age, it was massively restored in the 19th century. Heavily frescoed, the church has five aisles.

WHERE TO STAY

Hotel Barchetta Excelsior ★   This first-class hotel is at the edge of the main square in the commercial section of town. Major additions have been made to the 1957 structure, including an upgrading of the guest rooms, which are comfortably furnished, most with balconies overlooking the square and the lake. All of the medium-size to spacious accommodations are soundproof and some are reserved for nonsmokers. A few of the spotless bathrooms are fitted with Jacuzzis. There's a parking lot behind the hotel, plus a covered garage about 45m (148 ft.) away.

Piazza Cavour 1, 22100 Como. © **031-3221.** Fax 031-302622. www.hotelbarchetta.it. 84 units. 140€–220€ double; from 359€ suite. Rates include buffet breakfast. AE, DC, MC, V. Parking 15€. Closed Nov 25–Dec. **Amenities:** 2 restaurants; bar; babysitting; room service. *In room:* A/C, TV, hair dryer, minibar, Wi-Fi (10€ per hr.).

Terminus ★★   Such a fine hotel and such a dull, unattractive name. This is no run-of-the-mill railway station hotel, but a turn-of-the-20th-century Liberty-era building, Como's most prestigious address. From its "command" position overlooking Lake Como, the hotel has been completely refurbished, and its public rooms evoke the style of the villa of some long-ago Lombard nobleman. Rooms come in a variety of sizes, ranging from small singles to spacious suites, and even a romantic room in the tower, idyllic for a honeymoon. Some of the luxurious accommodations offer terraces opening onto lakeside views. Each comes with a first-rate bathroom with tub or shower. The taste level is high, with sofas upholstered in elegant silk fabrics, bright floral patterns, and highly polished wood surfaces, often walnut or cherry. The garden terrace is a mecca in summer, and the cuisine is among the finest in the Lombard tradition.

Lungo Lario Trieste 14, 22100 Como. ✆ **031-329111.** Fax 031-302550. www.albergoterminus.com. 40 units. 184€–360€ double; 430€–590€ suite. Rates include continental breakfast. AE, DC, MC, V. Parking 24€. **Amenities:** Restaurant; bar; babysitting; bikes; exercise room; room service; sauna. *In room:* A/C, TV, hair dryer, minibar, Wi-Fi (25€ per 24 hr.).

WHERE TO DINE

La Colombetta ★ SEAFOOD/ITALIAN   In the historic center, this restaurant—one of the resort's finest—is installed in an old church that dates from the early 14th century. There is a main high-ceilinged dining room, plus two smaller dining areas installed in what were former chapels of a medieval church. Many old favorites appear on the menu along with several innovative dishes. Sardinia is also represented on the menu by both wines and cuisine. For a truly tantalizing pasta, opt for the black *tagliolini* with mullet roe. You can also order sea bass cooked in a salt crust to preserve its aroma and juices. Other fish specialties include a homemade pasta studded with seafood and baked sea bream with radicchio and olives. One fish, called "gilthead," is cooked in Vernaccia, a wine imported from Sardinia. The dish is well crafted, and, in the words of our dining companion, "contains a bit of soul."

Via Diaz 40. ✆ **031-262703.** www.colombetta.it. Reservations recommended. Main courses 12€–38€. AE, DC, MC, V. Aug–Feb Mon–Sat 12:30–2:30pm and 7:30–11pm; Mar–July daily 12:30–2:30pm and 7:30–11pm. Closed Dec 23–Jan 3.

Ristorante Imbarcadero ★ LOMBARD/ITALIAN   Near the edge of the lake, this restaurant is filled with a pleasing blend of carved Victorian chairs, panoramic windows, and potted palms. The summer terrace set up on the square is ringed with shrubbery and illuminated with evening candlelight. First-class ingredients are deftly handled by the kitchen. The chef makes his own *tagliatelle,* or you might want to order ravioli stuffed with lake fish. The fish dishes are excellent, especially slices of sea bass with braised leek and aromatic vinegar, and sage-flavored Lake Como white fish. Among the meat selections, nothing quite equals the *tournedos* Rossini with black truffles.

Piazza Cavour 20. ✆ **031-270166.** www.ristoranteimbarcadero.it. Reservations recommended. Main courses 10€–26€; fixed-price menu 25€. AE, DC, MC, V. Daily 12:30–2:30pm and 7:30–10:30pm. Closed Jan 2–6.

Cernobbio ★★

Cernobbio, 5km (3 miles) northwest of Como and 53km (33 miles) north of Milan, is a small, chic resort frequented by wealthy Europeans, who come largely to check into its famous deluxe hotel, the 16th-century Villa d'Este. However, the town's idyllic setting on the lake is available to everyone, because there are a number of more affordable hotels as well. Call the tourist office for information about other options in the area.

WHERE TO STAY

Grand Hotel Villa d'Este ★★★   This is the grandest hotel on any of Italy's lakes. The Villa d'Este was built in 1568 as a lakeside home/pleasure pavilion for Cardinal Tolomeo Gallio. Designed in the neoclassical style by Pellegrino Pellegrini di Valsolda, it passed from owner to illustrious owner for 300 years until it became a hotel in 1873. The hotel remains a kingdom unto itself, a splendid palace surrounded by 4 hectares (10 acres) of some of the finest gardens in Italy.

The silken wall coverings of the Salon Napoleone were embroidered especially for the emperor's visit, and the Canova Room includes a statue of Venus by Canova himself. The frescoed ceilings, impeccable antiques, and attentive service create one of the world's most envied hotels. Each plush guest room is individually decorated with antiques. Some 27 of the hotel's 152 accommodations are in the Queen's Pavilion, an elegant annex built in 1856.

Via Regina 40, 22012 Cernobbio. ⓒ **031-3481.** Fax 031-348844. www.villadeste.it. 152 units. 490€–1,200€ double; from 1,320€ suite. Rates include buffet breakfast. AE, DC, MC, V. Free parking. Closed Nov 15–Mar 2. **Amenities:** 3 restaurants; 2 bars; babysitting; concierge; exercise room; 3 pools (heated outdoor, heated indoor, children's); room service; spa; 8 outdoor tennis courts (lit); limited watersports equipment. *In room:* A/C, TV, hair dryer, minibar.

Bellagio ★★★

Sitting on a promontory at the point where Lake Como forks, 77km (48 miles) north of Milan and 29km (18 miles) northeast of Como, Bellagio is one of the prettiest towns in Europe. A sleepy veil hangs over the arcaded streets and little shops. Bellagio has attracted wealthy visitors, even royalty, for centuries (Leopold I of Belgium used to own the 18th-c. Villa Giulia). It's not so aristocratic anymore, but it's still a thriving and lovely resort town, a 45-minute drive north of Como.

The narrow streets of Bellagio.

The **tourist office** is at Piazza Mazzini (ⓒ **031-950204;** www. bellagiolakecomo.com). April to October, it's open daily 9am to 12:30pm and 3 to 6pm; November to March, hours are Monday and Wednesday to Saturday 9am to 12:30pm and 3 to 6pm.

EXPLORING THE TOWN

To reach many of the places in Bellagio, you must climb streets that are really stairways. Its lakeside promenade blossoms with flowering shrubbery. From the town, you can take tours of Lake Como, enjoy watersports and tennis, or just lounge at the **Bellagio Lido** (the beach).

You'll probably spend a lot of your time just sunbathing and enjoying that glorious lakeside scenery. Most of the lakefront hotels have their own swimming **beaches.** (The swimmable lakefront section that's maintained by the Grand Hotel Villa Serbelloni is especially well maintained, but it's only for hotel guests.) Otherwise, you can walk 10 minutes north of the town center to swim in the lake at the free public facilities at **La Punta.** Anyone can rent either of the two **tennis courts,** for around 20€ an hour, at the Grand Hotel Villa Serbelloni, and you can visit that hotel's **fitness center** for about 35€.

If you're interested in a **boat tour,** in a motorized craft suitable for up to six passengers, **Barindelli Taxi Boats** (✆ 031-951380; www.barindellitaxiboats.it) will take your group for rides on the lake, priced at around 130€ per hour.

Shoppers gravitate to the clusters of **boutiques** along the Salita Serbelloni and the Salita Mella, in the town center. And although there's not a lot of raucous nightlife in this quiet town, you can always hang out at **La Divina Commedia,** on Salita Mella (✆ 031-951680).

If you're in the mood for a little sightseeing, check out the **gardens of the Villa Serbelloni ★**, Piazza della Chiesa (✆ 031-950204), the Bellagio Study and Conference Center of the Rockefeller Foundation (not to be confused with the Grand Hotel Villa Serbelloni by the water in the village). The landlord here used to be Pliny the Younger. The villa isn't open to the public, but you can visit the park on 1½-hour guided tours starting at 11am and 4pm. Tours are conducted mid-April to late-October, Tuesday to Sunday, at a cost of 8.50€; the proceeds go to local charities.

There's also a garden at the **Villa Melzi Museum and Chapel** (✆ 339-4573838; www.giardinidivillamelzi.it) Lungolario Marconi, which was built in 1808 for Duca Francesco Melzi d'Eril, vice president of the Italian republic founded by Napoleon. Franz Liszt and Stendhal are among the illustrious guests who've stayed here. The park has many well-known sculptures, and, if you're here in spring, you can enjoy the azaleas. Today it's the property of Conte Gallarti Scotti, who opens it April to October, daily 9am to 6pm. The museum contains an undistinguished collection of Egyptian sculptures. Admission is 6€. For further information, contact the tourist office (see above).

From Como, car ferries sail back and forth across the lake to **Cadenabbia** on the western shore, another lakeside resort with hotels and villas. Directly south of Cadenabbia on the run to Tremezzo, the **Villa Carlotta ★★** (✆ 0344-40405; www.villacarlotta.it) is the most-visited attraction on Lake Como, and with good reason. In a serene setting, the villa is graced with gardens of exotic flowers and blossoming shrubbery, especially rhododendrons and azaleas. Its beauty is tame, formal, and cultivated, indicative of the halcyon life available only to the very rich of the 19th century. Dating from 1847, the estate was named after a Prussian princess, Carlotta, who married the duke of Sachsen-Meiningen. Inside are a number of art treasures, including Canova's *Cupid and Psyche,* and neoclassical statues by Bertel Thorvaldsen, a Danish sculptor who died in 1844. There are also neoclassical paintings, furniture, and a stone-and-bronze table ornament that belonged to Viceroy Eugene Beauharnais. It's open March and October daily from 9am to noon and 2 to 4:30pm, and April to September daily from 9am to 6pm. Admission is 8.50€.

WHERE TO STAY

Grand Hotel Villa Serbelloni ★★   This lavish old hotel is grand indeed. It stands proud at the edge of town against a backdrop of hills, surrounded by gardens. The public rooms rekindle the spirit of the baroque: a drawing room with a painted ceiling, marble columns, a glittering chandelier, gilt furnishings, and a mirrored neoclassical dining room. The guest rooms are wide-ranging, from elaborate suites with recessed tile bathrooms, baroque furnishings, and lake-view balconies to more simple quarters. The most desirable rooms open onto the lake. You can sunbathe on the waterside terrace or doze under a willow tree.

Via Roma 1, 22021 Bellagio. ✆ **031-950216.** Fax 031-951529. www.villaserbelloni.com. 83 units. 385€–820€ double; 990€–1,050€ suite. Rates include buffet breakfast. AE, DC, MC, V. Parking 18€. Closed mid-Nov to Mar. **Amenities:** Restaurant; babysitting; children's center; exercise room; Jacuzzi; 2 pools (outdoor and heated indoor); room service; sauna; Wi-Fi (free, in lobby). *In room:* A/C, TV, hair dryer, minibar.

Hotel du Lac ★ This little charmer offers the most panoramic views of lake and mountain from its terraced roof garden. The Hotel du Lac was built 150 years ago, when the lake waters came up to the front door. Landfill has since created Piazza Mazzini, and today there's a generous terraced expanse of flagstones in front with cafe tables and an arched arcade. The guest rooms are comfortably furnished with a mixture of antiques and reproductions. You can bask in the sun or relax in the shade on the rooftop garden, opening onto panoramic views of the lake.

Piazza Mazzini 32, 22021 Bellagio. ✆ **031-950320.** Fax 031-951624. www.bellagiohoteldulac. com. 42 units (some with shower only). 160€–235€ double. Rates include buffet breakfast. MC, V. Parking 15€. Closed Nov–Mar. **Amenities:** Restaurant; bar; access to nearby fitness center and spa; room service; Wi-Fi (free, in lobby). *In room:* A/C, TV, hair dryer, minibar.

Hotel Florence The entrance to this green-shuttered villa is under a vaulted arcade near the ferry landing. Wisteria climbs over the iron balustrades of the lake-view terraces, and the entrance hall's vaulted ceilings are supported by massive timbers and granite Doric columns. The main section was built around 1720, although most of what you see today was added around 1880. The guest rooms are scattered amid spacious sitting and dining areas and often have high ceilings, antiques, and lake views.

Piazza Mazzini 45, 22021 Bellagio. ✆ **031-950342.** Fax 031-951722. www.hotelflorencebellagio. it. 30 units. 150€–200€ double; 230€–260€ suite. Rates include buffet breakfast. AE, DC, DISC, MC, V. Closed Nov–Mar. **Amenities:** Restaurant; bar; Jacuzzi; sauna; Wi-Fi (free, in lobby). *In room:* TV, hair dryer.

Tremezzo

Reached by frequent ferries from Bellagio, Tremezzo, 77km (48 miles) north of Milan and 29km (18 miles) north of Como, is another popular west-shore resort that opens onto a panoramic view of Lake Como. Around the town is a district known as Tremezzina, with lush citrus trees, palms, cypresses, and magnolias. Because Tremezzo lies in the middle of the western bank of Como, it's easy to use as a base for taking scenic drives either to the north of the lake or all the way south to the city of Como. From here, it's also easy to visit Villa Carlotta (see under "Bellagio," above), but accommodations in Tremezzo are much more limited than those in Bellagio.

The **tourist office** is at Via Regina 3 (✆ **0344-40493**). May to October, it's open Monday to Wednesday and Friday to Saturday 9am to noon and 3:30 to 6:30pm.

WHERE TO STAY

Grand Hotel Tremezzo ★★ Built in 1910 on a terrace several feet above the lakeside road, this hotel is one of the region's best examples of the Italian Liberty style. In 1990 most of it was discreetly modernized, with air-conditioning installed on two of the four floors (many guests still reject the air-conditioning in favor of the lakefront breezes). The high-ceilinged rooms are comfortable, traditionally furnished, and priced according to whether they have views of the lake (many of these have balconies) or the rear park and garden.

Via Regina 8, 22019 Tremezzo. © **0344-42491.** Fax 0344-40201. www.grandhoteltremezzo. com. 100 units. 240€–740€ double; 600€–1,400€ suite. Rates include buffet breakfast. AE, DC, MC, V. Parking 20€ in a garage; free outside. Closed Nov–Mar. **Amenities:** 2 restaurants; bar; babysitting; exercise room; Jacuzzi; 4 pools (1 heated indoor); room service; spa; outdoor tennis court (lit). *In room:* A/C, TV, DVD (in some), hair dryer, minibar, Wi-Fi (10€ per 24 hr.).

Hotel Bazzoni & du Lac ★ 🔑 This hotel is one of the best choices in a resort town filled with grand hotels that offer much less desirable guest rooms. There was an older hotel here during Napoleon's era, but it was bombed by the British 5 days after the official end of World War II. Today the reconstructed hotel is a collection of glass-and-concrete walls, with prominent balconies. The pleasantly furnished sitting rooms include antique architectural elements from older buildings. A summer restaurant near the entrance is constructed like a small island of glass walls.

Via Regina 26, 22019 Tremezzo. © **0344-40403.** Fax 0344-41651. www.hotelbazzoni.it. 140 units. 180€–200€ double. Rates include breakfast. AE, DC, MC, V. Closed Oct 10–Mar. Ferry from Bellagio or hydrofoil from Como. **Amenities:** 2 restaurants; bar; babysitting; Wi-Fi (3€ per hr.). *In room:* TV, hair dryer, minibar.

Hotel Villa Marie 🔑 Enjoying a lakeside location, this intimate 19th-century villa will house you well at an affordable price. Guests look out over the lake from the chaise longues in the garden and later retreat to their homey bedrooms, most of which also have lake views. Beds are comfortable, and the bathrooms, though small, are well appointed.

Via Regina 30, Tremezzo 20019. ©/fax **0344-40427.** www.hotelvillamarie.com. 13 units (shower only). 85€–120€ double; 140€–170€ suite. Rates include buffet breakfast. AE, DC, MC, V. Free parking. Closed Nov–Mar. **Amenities:** Outdoor pool. *In room:* TV, hair dryer, minibar.

WHERE TO STAY NEARBY

Grand Hotel Victoria ★★ Built in 1806, this is one of the best hotels on the lake. It has been renovated over the years, but lovely old touches remain, such as the ornate plasterwork of the ceiling vaults. The modern furniture and extras in the spacious guest rooms include bathroom tiling designed by Valentino. The beach in front of the hotel is one of the best spots on Lake Como for windsurfing, especially between 3 and 7pm. The staff can help you arrange tee times nearby.

Via Lungolago Castelli 9, 22017 Menaggio. © **0344-32003.** Fax 0344-32992. www.centro hotelslagocomo.it. 53 units. 130€–260€ double; from 180€ junior suite; 330€–560€ deluxe suite. Rates include buffet breakfast. AE, DC, MC, V. Free parking. Closed Nov–Feb. **Amenities:** Restaurant; bar; babysitting; outdoor pool; room service; outdoor tennis court; Wi-Fi (free, in lobby). *In room:* A/C, TV, hair dryer, minibar.

WHERE TO DINE

Al Veluu ★ LOMBARD/INTERNATIONAL Al Veluu, 1.6km (1 mile) north of the resort in the hills, is an excellent regional restaurant with plenty of relaxed charm and personalized attention. The terrace tables offer a panoramic sweep of the lake, and the rustic dining room with its fireplace and big windows is a welcome refuge in inclement weather. Most of the produce comes freshly picked from the garden; even the butter is homemade, and the best cheeses come from a local farmer. The menu is based on the flavorful cuisine of northern Italy: Examples are grilled fresh fish from the lake, *penne al Veluu* (with spicy tomato sauce), *risotto al Veluu* (with champagne sauce and fresh green peppers), and an unusual lamb pâté.

Via Rogaro 11, Rogaro di Tremezzo. ✆ **0344-40510.** www.alveluu.com. Reservations recommended. Main courses 16€–28€. AE, MC, V. Wed–Mon noon–2pm and 7–10pm. Closed Nov–Mar 15.

LAKE MAGGIORE ★★

The waters of Lake Maggiore wash up on the banks of Piedmont and Lombardy in Italy, but its more austere northern basin (Locarno, for example) lies in the mountainous region of Switzerland. It stretches more than 64km (40 miles) and is 10km (6¼ miles) at its widest. A wealth of natural beauty awaits you: mellowed lakeside villas, dozens of lush gardens, sparkling waters, and panoramic views. A veil of mist seems to hover at times, especially in early spring and late autumn.

Maggiore is a most rewarding lake to visit from Milan, especially because of the Borromean Islands in its center (most easily reached from Stresa). If you have time, drive around the entire basin; on a more limited schedule, you might find the resort-studded western shore the most scenic.

The Alps rise above Lake Maggiore.

Essentials

GETTING THERE The major resort of the lake, Stresa, is just 1 hour by **train** from Milan on the Milan-Domodossola line. Service is every hour, costing 6€ to 19€ one-way, depending on the train. For information and schedules, call ✆ **892021.**

If you have a **car** and are in Milan, take an 82km (51-mile) drive northwest along A8 (staying on E62 out of Gallarate until it joins S33 up the western shore of the lake) to Stresa.

GETTING AROUND S33 goes up the west side of the lake to Verbania, where it becomes S34 on its way to the Swiss town of Locarno, about 40km (25 miles) away. If you want to drive around the lake, you'll have to clear Swiss Customs before passing through such famed resorts as Ascona and Locarno. From Locarno you can head south again along the eastern, less touristy shore, which becomes SS. 493 on the Italy side. At Luino, you can cut off on S233 and then A8 to return to Milan, or continue along the lakeshore (the road becomes S629) to the southern point again, where you can get E62 back toward Milan.

Cruising Lake Maggiore on modern **boats** and fast **hydrofoils** is great fun. There's a frequent ferry service for cars and passengers between Intra (Verbania) and Laveno. Boats leave from Piazza Marconi along Corso Umberto I in Stresa. For boat schedules, contact the **Navigazione Sul Lago Maggiore,** Viale F. Baracca 1 (✆ **800-551801;** www.navigazione laghi.it), in the lakeside town of Arona.

Stresa ★★

On the western shore, 655km (406 miles) northwest of Rome and 82km (51 miles) northwest of Milan, Stresa has skyrocketed from a simple village of fisher folk to a first-class international resort. Its vantage on the lake is almost unparalleled, and its accommodations level is superior to that of other Maggiore resorts in Italy. The scene of sporting activities and an international **Festival of Musical Weeks** (beginning in Aug), the city swings into action in April, stays hopping all summer, and then quiets down at the end of September. For information, call Settimane Musicali (✆ **0323-31095** or 0323-30459; www.stresafestival.eu).

The **tourist office** is at Piazza Marconi 16 (✆ **0323-30150;** www.stresa online.com). It's open daily from 10am to 12:30pm and 3 to 6:30pm from June to September; in other months, hours are Monday to Saturday 10am to 12:30pm and 3 to 6:30pm.

Near the resort of Pallanza, north of Stresa, the **Botanical Gardens (Giardini Botanici) at Villa Taranto ★★**, Via Vittorio Veneto 111, Verbania-Pallanza (✆ **0323-556667;** www.villataranto.it), spread over more than 20 hectares (50 acres) of the Castagnola Promontory jutting out into Lake Maggiore. In this dramatic setting between the mountains and the lake, more than 20,000 species of plants from all over the world thrive in a cultivated institution begun in 1931 by a Scotsman, Capt. Neil McEacharn. Plants range from rhododendrons and azaleas to specimens from such faraway places as Louisiana. Seasonal exhibits include fields of Dutch tulips (80,000 of them), Japanese magnolias, giant water-lilies, cotton plants, and rare varieties of hydrangeas. The formal gardens are carefully laid out with ornamental fountains, statues, and reflection pools. Among the more ambitious creations is the elaborate irrigation system that pumps water from the lake to all parts of the gardens and the Terrace Gardens, complete with waterfalls and pool. From March 26 to November 1, the gardens are open daily 8:30am to 6:30pm, but close at 5pm in October. Admission is 9€ adults, 5.50€ children. You also can take a round-trip **boat ride** from Stresa, docking at the Villa Taranto pier adjoining the entrance to the gardens. The admission price includes the boat ride from Stresa.

WHERE TO STAY

Grand Hotel des Iles Borromées ★★★ On the edge of the lake in a flowering garden, this is Stresa's leading resort hotel. You can see the Borromean Islands from many rooms, which are furnished in an Italian/French Empire style, including rich ormolu, burnished hardwoods, plush carpets, and pastel colors. The hotel opened in 1863; Hemingway sent the hero of *A Farewell to Arms* here to escape World War I. The hotel also operates a 27-room Residenza in a separate building, where the prices are 20% lower and the rooms are decorated in a modern style.

Corso Umberto I 67, 28838 Stresa. ℰ **0323-938938.** Fax 0323-93832405. www.borromees.it. 175 units. 170€–400€ per person double; 260€–750€ per person junior suite; from 600€ per person suite. Rates include buffet breakfast. AE, DC, MC, V. Free parking. Closed Dec 4–Jan 15. **Amenities:** Restaurant; babysitting; exercise room; 3 heated pools (1 indoor and 2 outdoor); room service; spa; outdoor tennis court (lit). *In room:* A/C, TV, hair dryer, minibar, Wi-Fi (22€ per 24 hr.).

Hotel Moderno A block from the lake and boat-landing stage, the recently renovated Moderno lies in the center of Stresa. It dates from the turn of the 20th century, but renovations have rendered the building's original lines unrecognizable. The small guest rooms have a personalized decor, good beds, and compact bathrooms.

Via Cavour 33, 28838 Stresa. ℰ **0323-933773.** Fax 0323-933775. www.hms.it. 54 units (with shower only). 170€ double. Rates include breakfast. AE, DC, MC, V. Parking 10€. Closed Oct 22–Mar. **Amenities:** 2 restaurants; room service; Wi-Fi (2€ per hr., in lobby). *In room:* A/C, TV, hair dryer.

Hotel Villa Aminta ★ 🛏 Across from Isola Bella (see below), this hotel, only a 5-minute drive from the center, lies on a hill above the main road running along the shore. From its rooms, a panoramic view unfolds, and it is the most tranquil resort at Stresa. Villa Aminta stands above the drive. Rooms range from midsize to spacious, each tastefully and comfortably decorated. The highest-priced units are those with lake views (as opposed to garden views). The public rooms are splendidly decorated, and the restaurants enjoy a deserved reputation for their fine cuisine.

Via Sempione Nord 123, 28838 Stresa. ℰ **0323-933818.** Fax 0323-933955. www.villa-aminta.it. 68 units. 330€–550€ double; from 658€ suite. AE, DC, MC, V. Free parking. Closed Nov to mid-Apr. **Amenities:** 2 restaurants; babysitting; bikes; exercise room; outdoor heated pool; room service; spa; outdoor tennis court (lit). *In room:* A/C, TV, hair dryer, minibar, Wi-Fi (17€ per 24 hr.).

Regina Palace ★ We prefer the Grand Hotel des Iles Borromées, but this lakeside palace is still a wonderful choice, especially for traditionalists. The Regina was built in 1908 in a boomerang shape, with a central curve facing the lakefront. Inside, the Art Deco columns of illuminated glass are topped with gilded Corinthian capitals, and a wide marble stairwell is flanked with carved oak

lions. Guests have included George Bernard Shaw, Ernest Hemingway, and Princess Margaret. Lately, about half are American, many with the tour groups that stream through town. The rooms contain all the modern comforts; many have views of the Borromean Islands.

Corso Umberto I 33, 28049 Stresa. ⓒ **0323-936936.** Fax 0323-936666. www.regina-palace.it. 214 units. 240€–380€ double; from 460€ suite. Rates include buffet breakfast. AE, DC, MC, V. Parking 15€ in garage; free outside. Closed Nov–Mar. **Amenities:** 2 restaurants; concierge; Jacuzzi; 2 heated pools (1 indoor); room service; tennis court. *In room:* A/C, TV, hair dryer, minibar, Wi-Fi (free).

WHERE TO DINE

Ristorante Piemontese PIEDMONTESE/ITALIAN In the ancient heart of Stresa, this rustic *trattoria* with wooden furniture is a true lakeside restaurant—unsophisticated, intimate, and with a homelike atmosphere. Even so, many celebrated writers, painters, models, and actors have patronized it over the years and praised its food. The welcome is from the Belossi family, which offers you tables in spacious rooms with a garden where the scent is of strawberry grapes.

Market-fresh ingredients are deftly handled and turned into such dishes as grilled salmon with a truffle sauce or baked rack of lamb with aromatic herbs. One of the best pastas is spaghetti with sweet red peppers, onions, and fresh basil flavored with pecorino cheese. A regional specialty is gnocchi, potato dumplings with shrimp and fresh vegetables.

Via Mazzini 25. ⓒ **0323-30235.** www.ristorantepiemontese.com. Reservations recommended. Main courses 11€–17€; 3-course lunch menu 23€. AE, MC, V. Tues–Sun 12:30–2:30pm and 7–10pm. Closed Sun night Dec–Jan.

Taverna del Pappagallo 🍴 ITALIAN/PIZZA This formal little garden restaurant and tavern is operated by the Ghiringhelli brothers, who turn out some of the least expensive meals in Stresa—always served with a personal touch. Specialties include gnocchi, many types of scaloppine, *salamino allo spiedo e fagioli* (grilled sausage with beans), and *saltimbocca alla romana* (a veal-and-prosciutto dish). At night, pizza is king (try the pizza Regina).

Via Principessa Margherita 46. ⓒ **0323-30411.** www.tavernapappagallo.com. Reservations recommended. Main courses 7€–17€; pizzas 5€–10€. AE, DC, MC, V. Thurs–Tues 11:30am–2:30pm and 6:30–11pm.

The Borromean Islands ★★

In the middle of Lake Maggiore lie the **Borromean Islands,** a chain of tiny islands that were turned into sites of lavish villas and gardens by the Borromeo clan. Boats leave from Stresa about every 30 minutes in summer, and the trip takes 3 hours. The **navigation offices** at Stresa's center port (ⓒ **800-5511801;** www.navigazionelaghi.it) are open daily 7am to 7pm. The best deal is to buy an excursion ticket for 15€ entitling you to go back and forth to all three islands during the day.

Dominating the **Isola Bella (Beautiful Island)** ★★★ is the major sight: the 17th-century **Borromeo Palazzo** (ⓒ 0323-30556; www.borromeoturismo. it), where Napoleon reputedly slept. From the front, the figurines in the garden seem straight off the top of a wedding cake. On conducted tours, you're shown through the airy palace, whose views are remarkable. A special feature is the six grotto rooms, built piece by piece like a mosaic. In addition, there's a collection of

The Borromeo Palazzo.

quite good tapestries, with gory, cannibalistic animal scenes. Outside, the white peacocks in the garden enchant year after year. From March 20 to October 17, the palace and its grounds are open daily 9am to 5:30pm. Admission is 12€ adults, 5.50€ children 14 and under.

The largest of the chain, the **Isola Madre (Mother Island)** ★★ is visited chiefly for its **Botanical Garden (Orto Botanico).** You wander through a setting ripe with pomegranates, camellias, wisteria, rhododendrons, bougainvillea, hibiscus, hydrangea, magnolias, and even a cypress tree from the Himalayas. You can also visit the 17th-century **palace** (② **0323-1261;** www.borromeoturismo.it), which contains a rich collection of 17th- and 18th-century furnishings. Of particular interest is a collection of 19th-century French and German dolls belonging to Countess Borromeo and the livery of the House of Borromeo. The unique 18th-century marionette theater, complete with scripts, stage scenery, and devices for sound, light, and other special effects, is on display. Peacocks, pheasants, and other birds live and roam freely on the grounds. From March 20 to October 17, the palace is open daily 9am to 5:30pm. Admission to the palace and grounds is 10€.

Isola del Pescatori (Fishermen's Island) ★ doesn't have major sights or lavish villas, but in many ways it's the most colorful. Less a stage setting than its two neighbors, it's inhabited by fisher folk who live in cottages that haven't been converted to souvenir shops. It's a lovely place for a stroll.

Homes on Isola Bella, one of the Borromean Islands.

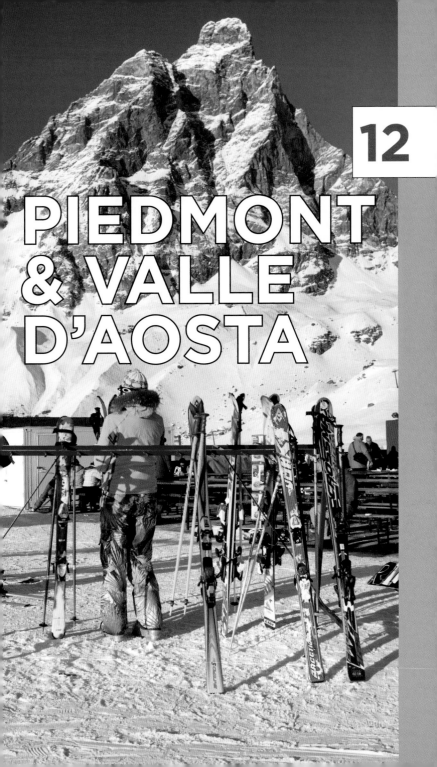

PIEDMONT & VALLE D'AOSTA

Snowcapped Alpine peaks; oleander, poplar, and birch trees; sky-blue lakes; river valleys and flowering meadows; the chamois and the wild boar; medieval castles; Roman ruins and folklore; the taste of vermouth on its home ground; Fiats and fashion—northwestern Italy is a fascinating area to explore.

The Piedmont (Piemonte) is largely agricultural, though its capital, Turin, is one of Italy's front-ranking industrial cities (with more mechanics per sq. ft. than any other place in Europe). The influence of France is strongly felt, both in the dialect and in the kitchen.

The Valle d'Aosta (really a series of valleys) traditionally has been associated with Piedmont, but in 1948 it was given wide-ranging autonomy. Most of the residents in this least-populated district of Italy speak French. Closing in Valle d'Aosta to the north on the French and Swiss borders are the tallest mountains in Europe, including Mont Blanc (4,809m/15,780 ft.), the Matterhorn (4,478m/ 14,690 ft.), and Monte Rosa (4,633m/15,200 ft.). The tunnels of Great St. Bernard and Mont Blanc connect France and Italy.

The region and the town of Turin drew the world's attention when they hosted the 20th Olympic Winter Games in 2006.

TURIN ★★

225km (140 miles) W of Milan, 174km (108 miles) NW of Genoa, 667km (414 miles) NW of Rome

In Turin (Torino), the capital of Piedmont, the Italian Risorgimento (unification movement) was born. While the United States was fighting its Civil War, Turin became the first capital of a unified Italy, a position it later lost to Florence. Turin was once the capital of Sardinia. Much of the city's history is associated with the House of Savoy, a dynasty that reigned for 9 centuries, even presiding over the Kingdom of Italy when Vittorio Emanuele II was proclaimed king in 1861. The family ruled, at times in name only, until the monarchy was abolished in 1946.

In spite of extensive bombings, Turin found renewed prosperity after World War II, largely because of the Fiat manufacturers based here (it has been called the Detroit of Italy). Many buildings were destroyed, but much of its 17th- and 18th-century look remains. Located on the Po River, Turin is well laid out, with wide streets, historic squares, churches, and parks. For years it has had a reputation as the least visited and least known of Italy's major cities, but it has become an increasingly dynamic center for industry and the arts.

PREVIOUS PAGE: **Skiers relaxing beneath the Matterhorn.**

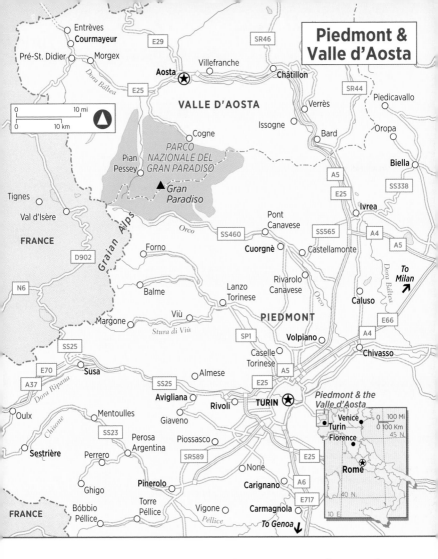

Piedmont &
Valle d'Aosta

Turin's biggest draw, the **Cattedrale di San Giovanni,** home to the **Shroud of Turin,** was damaged by fire in 1997. The Chapel of the Holy Shroud, where the silver reliquary that protects the controversial Christian symbol is usually on display, and the west wing of the neighboring Royal Palace sustained most of the damage. Luckily, the shroud had been moved into the cathedral itself because the dome of its chapel was being renovated.

Turin is one of Italy's richest cities, with some million Turinese, many of whom are immigrants who came here to get a piece of the pie. This "Car Capital of Italy" (also now home to high-tech and aerospace industries) is

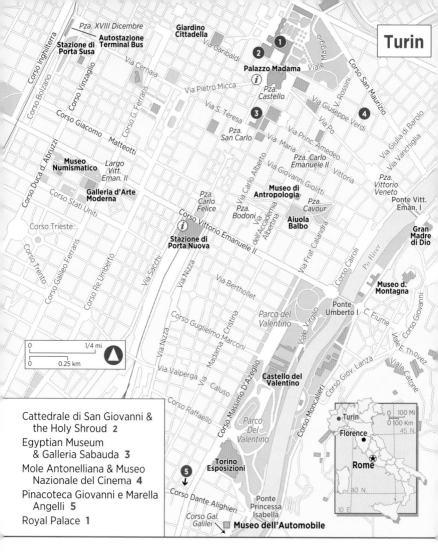

Turin

Pza. XVIII Dicembre

Autostazione
Terminal Bus

Stazione di
Porta Susa

Giardino
Cittadella

Via Garibaldi

Corso Inghilterra

Corso Bolzano

Corso Vinzaglio

Via Cernaia

Corso Giacomo

Matteotti

Via G. Ferraris

Via Pietro Micca

Palazzo Madama

Pza.
Castello

Via S. Teresa

Corso San Maurizio

V. Rossini

Via le Maggio

Corso Duca d'Abruzzi

Museo
Numismatico

Largo
Vitt.
Eman. II

Galleria d'Arte
Moderna

Corso Stati Uniti

Pza.
San Carlo

Via Maria

Via Princ. Amedeo

Via Giuseppe Verdi

Via Po

Via Giulia di Barolo

Via Vanchiglia

Corso Trieste

Corso Galileo Ferraris

Corso Trento

Corso Re Umberto

Pza.
Carlo
Felice

Corso Vittorio Emanuele II

Via Carlo Alberto

Via Giovanni Giolitti

Pza. Carlo
Emanuele II

Vittoria

Pza.
Vittorio
Veneto

Ponte Vitt.
Eman. I

Museo di
Antropologia

Pza.
Bodoni

Via dell'Accademia Albertina

Aiuola
Balbo

Pza.
Cavour

Via Frat Calandra

Corso Cairoli

Gran
Madre
di Dio

Stazione di
Porta Nuova

Via Sacchi

Via Nizza

Via Berthollet

Via Madama Cristina

Corso Guglielmo Marconi

Parco del
Valentino

Viale Virgilio

Ponte
Umberto I

C. Fiume

Po River

Museo d.
Montagna

Corso Giovanni

Viale E. Thovez

Viale Catone

Via Nizza

Via Valperga

Via Caluso

Corso Raffaello

Corso Massimo D'Azeglio

Castello del
Valentino

Corso Giov. Lanza

Corso Moncalieri

Parco
Del
Valentino

Torino
Esposizioni

Corso Dante Alighieri

Ponte
Princessa
Isabella

Corso Gal.
Galilei

Museo dell'Automobile

0   1/4 mi
0   0.25 km

Cattedrale di San Giovanni &
the Holy Shroud **2**

Egyptian Museum
& Galleria Sabauda **3**

Mole Antonelliana & Museo
Nazionale del Cinema **4**

Pinacoteca Giovanni e Marella
Angelli **5**

Royal Palace **1**

Turin
Florence
Rome
45° N.
40° N.
10° E
0   100 Mi
0   100 Km

surrounded by some hideous suburbs that are ever growing, but its Crocietta district is home to some of the most aristocratic residences in Italy, and its inner core is one of grace and harmony. Gianni Agnelli, former heir to the Fiat fortune, international playboy extraordinaire, and one of Italy's most influential power brokers, lived in Turin until his death in 2003. The city was also once the home of Antonio Gramsci, who staged "occupations" of the Fiat factory and later helped found the Italian Communist Party before dying in a Fascist prison. On a cultural note, Turin is the center of modern Italian writing; it was here that such major authors as Primo Levi, Cesare Pavese, and Italo Calvino were first published. Major exhibitions and shows are being booked all the time.

Essentials

GETTING THERE Alitalia flies into the **Caselle International Airport (Aeroporto Internazionale di Caselle;** $©$ **011-5676361;** www.aeroportoditorino.it), about 14km (8½ miles) north of Turin. It receives direct flights from 42 cities (13 domestic and 29 from major European centers); it's used by 21 carriers operating regular flights. Its Air Passenger Terminal is one of Europe's most technologically advanced, capable of handling up to three million passengers a year.

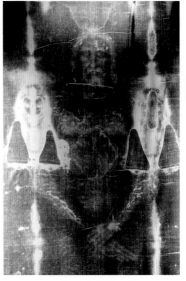

The Shroud of Turin.

Turin is a major **rail** terminus, with arrivals at **Stazione di Porta Nuova,** Corso Vittorio Emanuele (www.trenitalia.it), or **Stazione Centrale,** Corso Vittorio Emanuele II, in the heart of the city. For rail information and schedules, call $©$ **892021** in Italy. It takes 1¼ hours to reach Turin by train from Milan, but it takes anywhere from 7 to 11 hours to reach Turin from Rome, depending on the connection. The one-way fare from Milan is 10€; from Rome, fares start at 45€.

By **car** from France via the Mont Blanc Tunnel, you can pick up the autostrada (A5) at Aosta. You can also reach Turin by autostrada from both the French and the Italian Rivieras, and there's an easy link from Milan.

VISITOR INFORMATION Go to the office of **APT,** Piazza Castello (www.turismo torino.org), open daily 9am to 7pm. There's another office at the Porta Nuova train station open daily 9:30am to 7pm. There is also a tourist office at the airport open daily 8am to 11pm. For phone information, only one phone number is used: $©$ **011-535181.**

SPECIAL EVENTS Turin stages a major cultural fest every year: the month-long **Settembre Musica** in September, with dozens of classical music performances in various parts of the city. For details about this festival, write the **Assesorato per la Cultura,** Via San Francesco da Paola 3. However, if you're seeking information on the phone, call the APT tourist office number listed above.

Exploring the City

One of Turin's main arteries is **Corso Vittorio Emanuele II.** The railway station is on this boulevard; follow it east for a little less than a kilometer (about ½ mile) and you'll reach the Po River. Turin is also a city of fashion, and you might want to walk along the major shopping street, **Via Roma,** which begins north of the station and leads eventually to two squares that join each other, **Piazza Castello** and **Piazza Reale.**

In the middle of Via Roma is **Piazza San Carlo ★★**, the heartbeat of Turin. Begin your exploration here. Although it was heavily bombed during World War II, it's still the loveliest and most unified square in the city. Designed by Carlo di Castellamonte in the 17th century, it covers about 1.4 hectares (3½ acres). Some of the most prestigious figures in Italy once sat on this square, sipping coffee and plotting the unification of Italy. The two churches are **Santa Cristina** and **San Carlo.**

GTT, the Public Transportation Company of Turin, offers a **"Sightseeing Torino"** bus that takes visitors around the city with a guide. Tours depart from Piazza Castello and last 1 hour. For information, call Sightseeing Torino (✆ **011-535181** toll-free in Italy; www.torino.city-sightseeing.it), or visit the Sightseeing Torino center at Piazza Castello Monday to Saturday 7:15am to 7pm, and Sunday 10am to 4:30pm. Tickets cost 15€ for adults, 7.50€ for children; tours are daily from 10am to 6pm, every hour July to September 14; the rest of the year only on Saturday and Sunday every hour 10am to 6pm.

Cattedrale di San Giovanni & the Holy Shroud ★   This Renaissance cathedral, dedicated to John the Baptist, was swept by fire in 1997, with major damage sustained by Guarini's **Chapel of the Holy Shroud (Cappella della Sacra Sindone) ★★★**, the usual resting place of the relic in which Jesus Christ is believed to have been wrapped after his crucifixion (see "The Mystery of Turin's Holy Shroud," later). Fortunately, the shroud itself was undamaged. The garment made world headlines in 1998 when it was put on public display for the first time in 20 years. At its unveiling for only the fourth time in the 20th century, on the occasion of the cathedral's 500th anniversary, one million pilgrims traveled to Turin to see it. Most visitors to the cathedral must content themselves with a series of dramatically backlit photos of the relic near the entrance. The chapel is somberly clad in black marble, but, as if to suggest that better things await in the heavens, it ascends to an airy, light-flooded, six-tiered dome, one of the masterpieces of Italian baroque architecture.

The shroud itself is tucked away at the **Holy Shroud Museum (Museo della Sacra Sindone),** Via San Domenico 28 (✆ **011-4365832;** www.sindone.it), which is open daily from 9am to noon and 3 to 7pm, charging an admission of 6€.

Piazza San Giovanni. ✆ **011-4361540.** Free admission. Daily 9am–noon and 3–7pm. Bus: 63.

Egyptian Museum (Museo Egizio) & Galleria Sabauda ★★★   Two illustrious museums are in the Guarini-designed 17th-century Science Academy Building. The collection of the **Egyptian Museum** is world-class.

The Royal Papyrus on display at the Egyptian Museum.

THE mystery OF TURIN'S HOLY SHROUD

One of the world's greatest mysteries, the **Holy Shroud (Sacra Sindone)** is the most famous and controversial religious artifact on earth. The shroud is said to be the one that Joseph of Arimathea wrapped around the body of Christ when he was removed from the cross.

This 3.5m (12-ft.) length of linen reveals, in almost photographic detail, the agonized features of a man who suffered crucifixion. The face of the bearded man is complete with a crown of thorns, and the marks of a thonged whip and bruises are compatible with the torment of carrying a cross. No one has successfully put forth a scientific explanation as to why the imprints of the man on the cloth exist or even how its image became impregnated in the threads.

Turin didn't always possess this relic. First mentioned in the Gospel of Matthew, the shroud disappeared in history until it mysteriously turned up in Cyprus, centuries after the death of Christ. From Cyprus, it was taken to France, where it was first exhibited in 1354 and immediately denounced as a fraud by a French bishop. In 1578, the shroud was acquired by Duca Emanuele Filiberto, of the House of Savoy, who took it to Turin.

For centuries, the church didn't allow scientists to conduct dating tests of the shroud. The first scientific testing suggested that it was a fraud, probably from the 12th century. In 1988, three teams of scientists (from the United States, Britain, and Italy) each announced that the shroud was a clever forgery, and they estimated the time frame of its fabrication as between 1260 and 1390. Recent findings, however, propose a much earlier dating. Using calculations based on the fact that the shroud was involved in a fire in the 16th century, scientists now say that the shroud is roughly 1,800 years old—a date that could realistically make it the shroud of Christ. In 1997, Avinoam Danin, a plant expert at the University of Jerusalem, analyzed threads from the linen and detected traces of pollen in the flax. This pollen was believed to have dropped into the linen from flowers laid on the shroud. Danin stated that some of those species are found only in the Middle East.

The archbishop of Turin has presented the shroud to the Holy See, and the fact that the Vatican accepted it as a holy relic has increased some world belief in its validity. However, the Vatican has refrained from pronouncing it "the true shroud." The shroud remains encased in a silver casket. Only two keys can unlock the casket, one held by the archbishop of Turin and the other held by the Palatine cardinals, church seniors who are based permanently in the Vatican. The keys unlock only the casket—not the mystery of the shroud.

Of the statuary, those of Ramses II and Amenhotep II are best known. A room nearby contains a rock temple consecrated by Thutmose III in Nubia. In the crowded wings upstairs, the world of the pharaohs lives on—one of the prized exhibits is the Royal Papyrus, with its valuable chronicle of the Egyptian monarchs from the 1st to the 17th dynasty. The funerary art is exceptionally rare and valuable, especially the chapel built for Maia and his young wife, and an entirely reassembled tomb (of Kha and Merit, 18th dynasty), discovered in good condition at the turn of the 20th century.

Galleria Sabauda presents one of Italy's richest art collections, acquired over the centuries by the House of Savoy. The largest exhibit is of Piedmontese masters, but there are many fine examples of Flemish art as well. Of the latter, the best-known painting is Sir Anthony van Dyck's *Three Children of Charles I.* Other important works are Botticelli's *Venus,* Memling's *Passion of Christ,* Rembrandt's *Sleeping Old Man,* Duccio's *Virgin and Child,* Mantegna's *Holy Conversation,* Jan van Eyck's *The Stigmata of Francis of Assisi,* Veronese's *Dinner in the House of the Pharisee,* Bellotto's *Views of Turin,* paintings by Bruegel, and a section of the royal collections between 1730 and 1832.

In the Palazzo dell'Accademia delle Scienze, Via Accademia delle Scienze 6. ☎ **011-5617776** (Egyptian Museum), or 011-547440 (Galleria Sabauda). www.museoegizio.it. Egyptian Museum 7.50€; Galleria Sabauda 4.50€. Egyptian Museum Tues–Sun 9:30am–8:30pm in summer; Tues–Sun 8:30am–7:30pm off season. Galleria Tues and Fri–Sun 8:30am–2pm; Wed–Thurs 2–7:30pm. Both closed Jan 1 and Dec 25. Tram: 18.

Mole Antonelliana ★ & Museo Nazionale del Cinema ★★ A landmark in Turin, this curiosity of a building, constructed between 1863 and 1889, was at one time the tallest brick-built structure on earth. Its steep conelike roof supports several "layers" of classical temples stacked one on top of the other. Crowning it is the Turin "needle," a spire rising 168m (552 ft.) over the city. The original intention was to make this the synagogue of Turin. Today a film museum has been installed in the building. You can, however, skip the museum if you wish and take the elevator to an observation platform for one of the **grandest views ★★** in Piedmont. You can see as far away as the Alps on a clear day.

In the cinema museum the history of "the flickers" is traced from shadow puppets to kinescopes. Famous costumes are displayed, including the bowler worn by "The Little Tramp" (Chaplin), a dress Bette Davis wore in *What Ever Happened to Baby Jane?,* and the robe worn by Peter O'Toole in *Lawrence of Arabia.* Film clips are shown, including President Lyndon Johnson talking to Tom

Modigliani's *Reclining Nude* at the Pinacoteca Giovanni e Marella Agnelli.

Shopping along Turin's arcaded sidewalks.

Hanks in *Forrest Gump*. Most films are of the Hollywood variety, but world cinema is also shown, including films coming out of Cuba. Changing exhibitions add variety to the collection, including one we recently enjoyed of famous Italian divas of the screen from the silents to the present.

Via Montebello 20. ℗ **011-8138560.** www.museonazionaledelcinema.org. Admission to the museum and panoramic lift 12€. Tues–Fri and Sun 9am–8pm; Sat 9am–11pm. Bus: 68.

Palazzo Madama (Museo d'Arte Antica) ★ The *palazzo* has an unusual name, honoring Madama Reale (loosely, dowager duchess) Maria Cristina of France, widow of Vittorio Amedeo II of Savoy and mother of Charles Emmanuel II. The famous Sicilian architect Filippo Juvarra added a baroque facade. Today the complex houses a museum of ancient art, a bit of a misnomer since the bulk of the collection dates from the late Middle Ages. A spacious gallery boasts a Venetian state barge that once belonged to the kings of Sardinia. All in all, the collection contains some 30,000 items—paintings, sculptures, illuminated codices, majolica, porcelain, gold, silver, antique furniture, and fabrics that stretch over a period of 10 centuries. The renovated galleries spread over four floors and encompass 35 galleries, starting out at the moat level with medieval sculptures and stonework. In one of the castle's 15th-century towers, the **Torri Tesori ★★**, the most precious and representative works of the museum are shown, including the museum's greatest masterpieces, the *Portrait of a Man* by Antonello da Messina, as well as *Très belles Heures Notre Dame de Jean de Berry* codex illuminated by Jan van Eyck. Also on display here is a series of objets d'art from the late 16th and early 17th centuries from the *wunderkammer* of Charles Emmanuel I.

In the Palazzo Madama, Piazza Castello. ℗ **011-4433501.** www.palazzomadamatorino.it. Admission 7.50€. Tues–Sat 10am–6pm; Sat 10am–8pm. Bus: 11, 12, 51, or 55.

Pinacoteca Giovanni e Marella Agnelli ★ Fueled by Fiat money, the Agnelli family members were great art collectors, and the cream of their treasures is showcased in this daringly designed new museum by the famed Italian architect Renzo Piano. Every one of the paintings on display at this gallery is hailed as a masterpiece of world art—no Sunday painting here. As president of Fiat, Giovanni Agnelli not only manufactured cars, but he also roamed the world acquiring art masterpieces. The collection began as early as 1961. The Agnelli collection of Matisses is unparalleled in Italy, with works such as the 1943 *Tobaco Royal*. In contrast to the bright color of Matisse, you can see such masterpieces as Renoir's 1882 ***La Baigneuse Blonde (The Blonde Bather)*** ★, a milky-white nude. (This is one of the very best Renoirs.) The collection also includes six noteworthy Canalettos, Modigliani's ***Reclining Nude*** ★, some Picassos, plus countless others. Agnelli once said that he set out to put together an avant-garde collection, but time caught up with him; the collection today is classical instead.

Lingotto, Via Nizza 230. ✆ **011-0062008.** www.pinacoteca-agnelli.it. Admission 5€. Tues–Sun 10am–7pm. Bus: 1, 18, 34, or 35.

Royal Palace (Palazzo Reale)   The palace that the Savoys called home was begun in 1645. The halls, the columned ballroom by Palagi, the tea salon, and the Queen's Chapel are richly baroque in style. The original architect was Amedeo de Castellamonte, but numerous builders supplied ideas and effort before the *palazzo* was completed. As in nearly all ducal residences of that period, the most bizarre room is the one bedecked with flowering chinoiserie.

The **Throne Room** is of interest, as is the tapestry-draped **Banqueting Hall.** Le Nôtre, the famous Frenchman, mapped out the gardens, which also may be visited along with the Royal Armory (Armeria Reale), containing a large collection of arms and armor and many military mementos. Guided tours are offered (in Italian only) every 40 minutes.

Piazza Castello. ✆ **011-4361455.** Admission 6.50€. Tues–Sun 8:30am–6:30pm. Bus: 55.

Shopping

The most adventurous shopping is at the **Gran Balôn,** an old-fashioned flea market set up every second Sunday in Piazza della Repubblica (northwest of Piazza Castello; www.balon.it).

Some of the best-known drinks in the world are produced in Torino. For the best sampling, head for **Paissa,** Corso de Gasperi 29 (✆ **011-5628364**), where, among the wine and food items available, you'll find the best deals on Cinzano and Martini & Rossi vermouths.

Where to Stay

EXPENSIVE

Grand Hotel Sitea   In the elegant heart of Risorgimento Turin, this government-rated four-star hotel is most central, a few minutes walk from the Piazza Castello. In Turin, it's a landmark and a legend, having hosted a parade of celebrities, everyone from Nobel Prize winners to show business stars, since its opening early in the 20th century. Modernized and restored many times over the years, it exudes elegance, tradition, and charm today in a four-story, Liberty-style building, a few blocks from Porta Nuova station. Bedrooms are midsize to spacious and elegantly decorated in a classic, sober style. Rooms are completely up to date, containing everything from personal safes and soundproofing to hydromassage tubs. Carignano Restaurant is one of the finest hotel dining rooms in the area, featuring many Piedmontese specialties.

Via Carlo Alberto 35, 10123 Torino. ✆ **011-5170171.** Fax 011-548090. www.thi.it. 120 units. 171€–223€ double; from 324€ suite. Rates include buffet breakfast. AE, DC, MC, V. Parking 21€. Bus: 11, 12, 58, 58B, or 63. **Amenities:** Restaurant; bar; babysitting; airport transfers (45€); exercise room; room service; Wi-Fi (free, in lobby). *In room:* A/C, TV, hair dryer, minibar.

Le Meridien Art + Tech ★★

It's owned by the same chain as the Lingotto (see below), with the same designer (Renzo Piano), but we prefer this luxury hotel to its bigger sister. Art + Tech, like its larger chain member, was converted from a former Lingotto Fiat factory. We are especially fond of the track on the roof that was once employed by the auto giant to test new cars. Today it's available to clients for jogging. Spread across four floors, rooms are ultramodern in style, elegant, minimalist, and chic. The past and the future are combined here perhaps better than in any other hotel in Piedmont. Contemporary designers have furnished the spacious, high-ceilinged guest rooms with all the latest gadgetry and comforts.

Via Nizza 230, 10126 Torino. ✆ **011-6642000.** Fax 011-6642001. www.lemeridien.com. 142 units. 153€–170€ double; from 220€ suite. Rates include buffet breakfast. AE, DC, MC, V. Free parking. Bus: 1 or 35. **Amenities:** Restaurant; bar; airport transfers (50€); babysitting; exercise room; room service; Wi-Fi (13€ per 24 hr., in lobby). *In room:* A/C, TV, hair dryer, minibar.

Le Meridien Lingotto ★

A favorite of Fiat executives, this is a grand example of recycling an industrial building in the city. Built in 1995 and the largest hotel in Turin, it is a bastion of luxury, having been converted from an antique Fiat automobile factory by the famous Italian architect Renzo Piano. All of the good-size bedrooms are elegant in the latest contemporary style. The soundproof bedrooms are loft styled with floor-to-ceiling windows, cherrywood paneling, and furnishings personally selected by Piano.

Via Nizza 262, 10126 Torino. ✆ **800/543-4300** in the U.S. and Canada, or 011-6642000. Fax 011-6642001. www.starwoodhotels.com. 240 units. 140€–330€ double; from 360€ suite. Rates include buffet breakfast. AE, DC, MC, V. Parking 15€. Bus: 1 or 35. **Amenities:** Restaurant; bar; airport transfers (50€); babysitting; room service; spa; Wi-Fi (13€ per 24 hr., in lobby). *In room:* A/C, TV, hair dryer, minibar.

Victoria Hotel ★ 🔥

One of the city's best bargains, this worthy selection lies between the river and Via Roma. In honor of its namesake, it evokes a bit of the aura of a British manor. You'll think you're back in Devon as you sink in the public living room with its soft armchairs and floral print couches, opening onto a garden. The rooms come in various sizes with individualized decor, each with a midsize bathroom. In the more luxurious bedrooms, you get antiques and canopied beds, but even the standard rooms are well furnished and inviting.

Via Nino Costa 4, 10123 Torino. ✆ **011-5611909.** Fax 011-5611806. www.hotelvictoria-torino.com. 106 units. 180€–240€ double. Rates include buffet breakfast. AE, DC, MC, V. Bus: 15. **Amenities:** Babysitting; bikes; indoor heated pool; room service; spa. *In room:* A/C, TV, hair dryer, minibar, Wi-Fi (free).

MODERATE

Best Western Hotel Genio   In the center of Turin, next to the Porta Nuova station, this government-rated three-star hotel is a four-story structure. It was modernized from an 1873 building constructed right after the unification of Italy, and lies on the Corso Vittorio Emanuele II, one of the city's major arteries. The main shopping street, Via Roma, is nearby, and many attractions are within walking distance. Bedrooms range from midsize to spacious, each well lit and attractively furnished in a homelike way. The bedrooms are cozy and traditional, some furnished with canopy beds.

Corso Vittorio Emanuele II 47, 10125 Torino. ℂ **011-6505771.** Fax 011-6508264. www.hotelgenio. it. 128 units. 100€–240€ double; 295€ junior suite. Rates include buffet breakfast. AE, MC, V. Parking 18€. Bus: ST1, 11, 12, or 63. **Amenities:** Bar; room service. *In room:* A/C, TV, hair dryer, minibar, Wi-Fi (free).

Best Western Hotel Piemontese ★   The Piemontese is in a 19th-century building near the railway station, its facade covered with iron balconies and ornate stone trim. The guest rooms range from small to medium. All the rooms have a certain style in furnishings; many are in a contemporary mode but others are called the romantic rooms, resting under vaulted ceilings with elegant, traditional furnishings. Breakfast, taken in a sunny room, is the only meal served, but there are lots of restaurants nearby. *Note:* All rooms are soundproof and have either Jacuzzi tubs or hydromassage showers.

Via Berthollet 21, 10125 Torino. ℂ **011-6698101.** Fax 011-6690571. www.hotelpiemontese.it. 37 units. 85€–190€ double; 139€–250€ suite. Rates include buffet breakfast. Children 12 and under stay free in parent's room. AE, DC, MC, V. Parking 20€. Tram: 1, 9, or 18. **Amenities:** Bar; airport transfers (50€); babysitting; bikes; access to nearby fitness center w/pool; room service; Wi-Fi (free). *In room:* A/C, TV, hair dryer, minibar.

Hotel Dogana Vecchia ★★ 📖   This one is a bit funky but fun. The oldest hotel in Turin, Dogana Vecchia was built in the 18th century as the headquarters of the postal service. It was later converted to an inn, playing host to the likes of Verdi, Mozart, and Napoleon. The wood-paneled hall continues to evoke the Turin of a century ago. Today, you'll find midsize to spacious bedrooms, each recently renovated and rather charming, despite the faux baroque furnishings. The staff is the most helpful we've encountered in the city.

Via Corte D'Appello 4, 10122 Torino. ℂ **011-4366752.** Fax 011-4367194. www.hoteldogana vecchia.com. 64 units (shower only). 75€–170€ double. Rates include buffet breakfast. AE, DC, MC, V. Parking 20€. Bus: 63. Tram: 4. **Amenities:** Bar; room service; Wi-Fi (free, in lobby). *In room:* TV, hair dryer, minibar.

Hotel Due Mondi 🍴   Off Corso Vittorio Emanuele and within walking distance of the railway station and many restaurants, this little hotel is near the top of the list for those seeking old-fashioned yet affordable grace. Everything is smartly outfitted, often in dark patterns and woods. The best rooms are those on the third and fourth floors because they have been renewed. The bathrooms are well equipped, with a shower and a private little sauna in each.

Via Saluzzo 3, 10125 Torino. ℂ **011-6505084.** Fax 011-6699383. www.hotelduemondi.it. 42 units. 78€–182€ double; 120€–222€ suite. Rates include buffet breakfast. AE, DC, MC, V. Closed Aug 10–20. Parking nearby 18€. Bus: 52. Tram: 1 or 35. **Amenities:** Restaurant; room service. *In room:* A/C, TV, hair dryer, minibar, Wi-Fi (in most, 3€ per hr.).

Where to Dine

Instead of dining at one of the regular restaurants listed below, you might check out the enormous food emporium, **Eataly,** Via Nizza 230 (ℂ **011-195-06801;** www.eataly.it). Boasting nine separate eating areas, the three-story complex bills itself as the world's largest wine and food center. One shopper found the row of vine-ripe tomatoes "longer than the entire produce section at Wal-Mart," and noted that pastas come in hundreds of unpronounceable shapes and sizes lining the ceiling-high shelves.

If you choose to dine here, you'll find open-air kitchens serving everything from the best and most succulent of Florentine steaks to tortellini in a savory Bolognese sauce. The various restaurants—Il Pesce, I salumi e I Formaggi, La Carne, La Pasta, La Pizza, Le Verdure, L'Agrigelateria, Della Birra, Il Vino—serve high-quality food at affordable prices. The opening hours of the restaurants are: daily 11:45am to 3:45pm and 6:45 to 10:15pm.

EXPENSIVE

Al Garamond ★★ PIEDMONTESE   In a palace dating from the 19th century, this classically elegant dining room is renowned for its take on the specialties of Piedmont. The chef easily crosses the culinary bridge between traditional and creative cooking. Beautifully set tables overlook walls of ancient brick vaulting. There are dishes that are adventurous, but many recipes are time tested. Try the lobster ravioli with fresh tomatoes and squid ink or a homemade pasta with artichokes, mint, and shrimp. Your chicken might be cooked in beer and served with a cabbage sauce, or else you can opt for the spaghetti with fish roe, sun-dried tomatoes, and carrot juice. Even if you don't like licorice, we'd still go for a divine licorice mousse served with a white chocolate sauce.

Via Pomba 14. ℂ **011/8122781.** Reservations recommended. Main courses 15€–25€; degustation menus 38€–70€. AE, MC, V. Mon–Fri 12:30–2:30pm and 8–10:30pm; Sat 8–10:30pm. Closed 1st week of Jan and 3 weeks in Aug. Metro: Porta Nuove.

Del Cambio ★★ PIEDMONTESE/MEDITERRANEAN   At Del Cambio, you dine in a setting of white-and-gilt walls, crystal chandeliers, and gilt mirrors. Opened in 1757, it's the oldest restaurant in Turin. Statesman Camillo Cavour was a loyal patron, and his regular corner is immortalized with a bronze medallion. The chef, who has received many culinary honors, features white truffles in many of his specialties. The assorted fresh antipasti are excellent; the best pasta dish is the regional *agnolotti piemontesi.* Among the main dishes, the *agnolotti* with truffles and the beef braised in Barolo wine deserve special praise. The chef is rightly proud of such specialties as braised beef cheeks in Barolo red wine and polenta, filet of pork with red prawns and candied onions, and veal shank slow cooked in the oven with a fresh rosemary sauce.

Piazza Carignano 2. ℂ **011-543760.** www.thi.it. Reservations required. Main courses 15€–30€. AE, DC, MC, V. Sept–June Mon–Sat 12:30–2:30pm and 8–10:30pm; July–Aug Mon–Fri 12:30–2:30pm and 8–10:30pm. Closed Aug 4–28. Bus: 13, 15, or 55.

La Prima Moreno ★ PIEDMONTESE/MEDITERRANEAN   The owner, Mr. Grossi,

---

Wine Tasting

Reds with rich and complex flavors make up most of the wine output of this rugged high-altitude region near Italy's border with France. One of the most interesting vineyards is headquartered in a 15th-century abbey near the hamlet of Alba, south of Turin: **Renato Ratti Cantina,** Abbazia dell'Annunziata, La Morra, 12064 Cuneo (ℂ **0173-50185;** www.renatoratti.com). If you'd like to drive through the countryside for a wine-tasting and a vineyard tour, call to make an appointment and get detailed directions.

is proud of his vast selection of Italian and international wines, and his fine Piedmontese fare and innovative Mediterranean dishes. Even a simple fish salad with cherry tomatoes and fresh basil is made with flair. Only the best of regional beef goes into the beef filet with mushroom-laced cream sauce. Among the pasta dishes, try *gramigna* (homemade pasta) on a bed of funduta cheese with fresh chestnuts and pumpkin blossoms. You might follow with a main course of sea bass cooked with diced potatoes, green olives, and fresh young artichokes or a Florentine steak. All the desserts are made fresh daily: Count yourself lucky if the chef has prepared hazelnut chocolate mousse.

Corso Unione Sovietica 244. ℂ **011-3179657.** www.laprimamoreno.it. Reservations required. Main courses 16€–29€. AE, DC, MC, V. Daily 12:30–3:30pm and 8pm–1am. Tram: 4. Bus: 63.

Vintage 1997 ★★ PIEDMONTESE/SEAFOOD   Surpassed only by Del Cambio (see above), this restaurant looks like an English pub, but the food is unmistakably Italian. The "1997" in the name refers to the year the place opened, but it's already becoming entrenched in the minds of serious foodies. You can partake of the fish-tasting menu or enjoy the mainly meat-based Piedmontese fare, or else order rack of lamb in an almond crust. Tuna appears in a delectable starring role in chateaubriand of tuna with fresh spinach. Our favorite pasta is the tortelli stuffed with mozzarella and eggplant and served in a cherry tomato sauce. For dessert, the heavenly choice is chocolate flan with white-chocolate ice cream over which a rum sauce is drizzled.

Piazza Solferino 16. ℂ **011-535948.** www.vintage1997.com. Reservations required. Main courses 18€–36€; fixed-price menus 55€–90€. AE, DC, MC, V. Mon–Fri noon–3pm; Mon–Sat 8–11pm. Closed Aug and 1st week Jan. Tram: 4 or 10. Bus: 5 or 67.

MODERATE/INEXPENSIVE

Caffè Torino ITALIAN   Opened in 1903, this famous coffeehouse is the best re-creation in Turin of the days of Vittorio Emanuele. It's set on one of the most elegant squares in northern Italy and is decorated with faded frescoes, brass and marble inlays, and a somewhat battered 19th-century formality. Don't be surprised if the staff has all kinds of rules about where and when you can be seated. There's a stand-up bar near the entrance, a formal dining room off to the side, and a cafe area with tiny tables and unhurried service.

Piazza San Carlo 204. ℂ **011-545118.** Main courses 15€–24€. AE, DC, MC, V. Daily noon–2:45pm and 7–10:30pm. Tram: 13.

Da Mauro 🍴 ITALIAN/TUSCAN   Within walking distance of Piazza San Carlo, this place, the best of the town's affordable *trattorie*, is generally packed. The food is conventional but does have character; the chef borrows freely from most of the gastronomic centers of Italy, although the cuisine is mainly Tuscan. An excellent pasta specialty is the cannelloni. Most main dishes consist of well-prepared fish, veal, and poultry. The desserts are consistently enjoyable.

Via Maria Vittoria 21. ℂ **011-8170604.** Reservations not accepted. Main courses 12€–24€. No credit cards. Tues–Sun noon–2:30pm and 7:30–10pm. Closed July. Tram: 13, 15, 55, 56, or 61.

Micamale ★ PIEDMONTESE   A good cross section of Turin society, from students to businesspeople, have made this *trattoria* popular. It's known for its creative take on Piedmontese specialties and for its affordable prices. Dress is casual in its trio of rooms, which are decorated with iridescent gray walls, white tablecloths, and brown metal chairs. For your pasta fix, order the home-made "trofie," with pesto and green beans. Wild boar sausage is a favorite of the mountains, served flavored with basil and tomatoes. The chef's specialty is fillet of suckling pig stuffed with Scamorza cheese and scented with coffee (yes, that's right).

Via Corte d'Appello 13. (C) **011/4362288.** Reservations recommended. Main courses 9.50€–15€; fixed-price menus 18€–34€. AE, DC, MC, V. Mon–Fri noon–2:30pm and Mon–Sat 8–11pm. Closed 2 weeks in Aug. Bus: Star 2.

Porto di Savona ★ PIEDMONTESE   This venerable, rustic, old-style tavern served its first diners back in 1863. It's been going strong ever since. In spite of changes over the years, it still looks like a 19th-century dining room. The restau-rant is entered under the arcades of the sprawling piazza Vittorio Veneto. Patrons are seated family style at long wooden tables, as they were decades ago. Many of the dishes are from grandmother's attic, but each is well prepared with fresh ingredients. Start with cold veal with tuna sauce or else leek pie with eggs and Castelmagno cheese. For a main, opt for pork filet in pastry with a mustard sauce, or a traditional risotto with beans and sausage. Finish off with baked pears in a red-wine sauce.

Piazza Vittorio Veneto 2. (C) **011-8173500.** www.portodisavona.com. Main courses 8€–19€. AE, MC, V. Daily 12:30–2:30pm and 7:30–10:30pm. Bus: 68.

Ristorante C'Era una Volta ★ PIEDMONTESE   "Once Upon a Time" is a good introduction to classic Piedmontese cuisine. In an old-fashioned dining room, fixed-price meals feature an aperitif, a choice of seven or eight antipasti, and two first and two main courses, with vegetables, dessert, and coffee. The menu includes Piedmont's most typical dish, *bagna cauda,* raw vegetables dipped into a sauce made with garlic, anchovies, and olive oil. Also worth trying are the risotto with truffles from Alba and a truly delectable caramelized filet of beef with a Barolo wine sauce. Two pasta specialties are lasagna with shrimp and arti-chokes or ravioli stuffed with braised beef. From the cellar emerge 300 different types of wine, mainly from Piedmont and Tuscany.

Corso Vittorio Emanuele II 41. (C) **011-655498.** www.ristoranteceraunavolta.it. Reservations recommended. Main courses 12€–22€; fixed-price menu 35€. AE, MC, V. Mon–Sat 8–11pm. Bus: 52, 67, or 68. Tram: 9 or 18.

Turin After Dark

Turin is the cultural center of northwestern Italy, a major stopover for concert artists performing between Genoa and Milan. The daily newspaper of Piedmont, *La Stampa,* lists complete details of current cultural events.

Turin is home to one of the country's leading opera houses, the **Teatro Regio,** Piazza Castello 215 ((C) 011-88151; www.teatroregio.torino.it). Concerts and ballets are also presented here. The box office ((C) **011-8815241** or 011-8815242) is open Tuesday to Friday from 10:30am to 6pm, Saturday 10:30am to 4pm (closed Aug). Tickets cost 22€ to 300€. Opera and other classical produc-tions are presented in summer outside the gardens of the **Palazzo Reale.**

The last remaining government-subsidized (RAI) orchestra performs at Piazza Rossaro at the Auditorium Rai ((C) **011-8104653;** www.orchestrasin fonica.rai.it). Ticket prices vary with the performance.

The rest of the city's nightlife is like that of Milan, only smaller. A karaoke club is **Luca's,** Via Freidour 26B (✆ **011-7764604**), where sports talk and karaoke contests bring out the exhibitionism of cinematic hopefuls. One of Turin's leading discos is **Hennessy,** Strada Traforo del Pino 23, Pino Torinese (✆ **011-8998522;** www.hennessyclub.com), a large dance floor in a posh residential section on the eastern bank of the River Po. It's open Friday and Saturday 11pm to 4am.

Pick-Up, Via Barge 8 (✆ **011-4472204;** www.pick-up.it), is aptly named. This club has a motto that "you only live once—and we're not big on second comings," so they suggest you make the most of it at their stylish bar and dance club. This is a major hangout for hip Turinese, often university students. It's open Wednesday to Sunday 11pm to 4am.

Turin has several elegant cafes where you can pass the time sipping coffee, enjoying a cocktail, or simply people-watching. One of our favorites is **Al Bicerin Caffè,** Piazza della Consolata 5 (✆ **011-4369325;** www.bicerin.it), Turin's oldest cafe dating from 1763. Dumas, Nietzsche, and Puccini have all enjoyed its signature drink—coffee with the famous Giandujotti chocolate, served with whipped cream in the cozy, wood-paneled setting with marble-topped tables and the original 18th-century bar. The name Bicerin is Turinese for "something delicious." Right next door is **Il Bacaro Pane e Vino,** Piazza della Consolata 1 (✆ **011-4369064;** www.bacaropanevino.com), a little wine bar that offers the most delectable sandwiches in an Art Deco setting with subdued lighting. Full meals (some of them Venetian) are also available. For night owls, it stays open until 2am Tuesday through Sunday.

AOSTA ★

184km (114 miles) NW of Milan, 126km (78 miles) N of Turin, 745km (462 miles) NW of Rome

Founded by the Emperor Augustus, Aosta has lost much of its quaintness today. It's called the "Rome of the Alps," but that's just tourist propaganda. Aostans number about 40,000 now and live in the shadow of the peaks of Mont Blanc and San Bernardo. The economy is increasingly dependent on tourism.

Lying as it does on a major artery, Aosta makes for an important stop, either for overnighting or as a base for exploring Valle d'Aosta or taking the cable car to the Conca di Pila, the mountain that towers over the town.

Essentials

GETTING THERE   Thirteen **trains** per day run directly from Turin to Aosta (trip time: 2 hr.), costing 7.70€ one-way. From Milan, the trip takes 3½ hours and costs 14€ one-way; you must change trains at Chivasso. For information and schedules, call ✆ **892021.** The train station is at Piazza Manzetti, only a 5-minute stroll over to the Piazza Chanoux, the very core of AostaBy **car** from Turin, take A5 north until it ends, just east of Aosta.

VISITOR INFORMATION   The **tourist office** is at Piazza Chanoux 2 (✆ **0165-236627**), open June to September daily 9am to 1pm and 2:30 to 8pm; from October to May, hours are Monday to Saturday 9:30am to 1pm and 3 to 6:30pm, and Sunday 9:30am to 1pm.

View of the mountains surrounding Aosta.

Exploring Aosta

The town's Roman ruins include the **Arch of Augustus,** built in 24 B.C., the date of the Roman founding of the town. Via Sant'Anselmo, part of the old city from the Middle Ages, leads to the arch. Even more impressive are the ruins of a **Roman theater,** reached by the Porta Pretoria, a major gateway built of huge blocks dating from the 1st century B.C. The ruins are open year-round daily from 9am to 7pm; entrance is free. A **Roman forum** is today a small park with a crypt, lying off Piazza San Giovanni near the cathedral.

The town is also enriched by its medieval relics. The Gothic **Collegiata dei Santi Pietro e Orso,** directly off Via Sant'Anselmo (✆ **0165-262026**), was founded in the 12th century and is characterized by its landmark Romanesque steeple. You can explore the crypt, but the cloisters, with capitals of some three dozen pillars depicting biblical scenes, are more interesting. The church is open daily from 9am to 7pm.

A Side Trip to a Great Paradise

Aosta is a good base for exploring the **Great Paradise National Park (Parco Nazionale di Gran Paradiso)** ★★★, five lake-filled valleys that in 1865 were a royal hunting ground of Vittorio Emanuele II. Even back then, long before the term *endangered species* was common, he awarded that distinction to the ibex, a nearly extinct species of mountain goat. In 1919, Vittorio Emanuele III gave the property to the Italian state, which established a national park in 1922. The park encompasses some 3,626 sq. km (1,400 sq. miles) of forest, pastureland, and Alpine meadows, filled with not only ibex but also the chamois and other animals that roam wild.

The main gateway to the park is **Cogne,** a popular resort. The best time to visit is in June, when the wildflowers are at their most spectacular. You can get a sampling of this rare Alpine fauna by visiting the **Paradise Alpine Garden** (**Giardino Alpino Paradiso;** ✆ **0165-74147**), near the village of Valnontey, a mile south of Cogne. It's open from June 12 to September 12 daily from 10am to 5:30pm. Admission costs 3€, free for children 11 and under. For information about Great Paradise National Park, visit the **park headquarters** at Via della Rocca 47, Turin (✆ **011/8606211;** www.pngp.it), or visit the A.I.A.T. (tourist office) in Via Bourgeois 34, Cogne (✆ **0165-74040**). Cogne lies about 29km (18 miles) south of Aosta and is reached along S47/S507.

Where to Stay

Europe ★   One of the town's leading hotels, this is a government-rated four-star hotel lying in the historic center of Aosta. It is only a short walk to both the bus and train stations. The six-story modern building is already a landmark. The bedrooms are completely up to date and very contemporary, even though the decor is classic. Depending on the rate you're willing to pay, bedrooms range in size from small to medium. The public rooms are done in a wonderful traditional style, and the on-site restaurant serves a first-rate cuisine.

Piazza Narbonne 8, 11100 Aosta. ✆ **0165-236363.** Fax 0165-40566. www.hoteleuropeaosta.it. 63 units. 80€–110€ per person double. Rates include half board. AE, DC, MC, V. Parking 10€. **Amenities:** Restaurant; bar; Wi-Fi (3€ per hr., in lobby). *In room:* A/C, TV, fridge, hair dryer.

Hotel Le Pageot ✦   This hotel is one of the best values in town. It has a modern angular facade of brown brick with big windows and floors crafted from carefully polished slabs of mountain granite. The guest rooms are comfortable and functional, but not a lot more, and the bathrooms are small.

Via Giorgio Carrel 31, 11100 Aosta. ✆ **0165-32433.** Fax 0165-33217. www.lepageot.it. 20 units (shower only). 80€–90€ double. AE, MC, V. Parking nearby 5€. **Amenities:** Bar; room service. *In room:* A/C, TV, hair dryer, Wi-Fi (free).

Milleluci ★ 🏠   Back in the 1960s this family-run, government-rated four-star hotel was an Aostan farmstead that had been passed from generation to generation. It was converted into a chalet more evocative of the Swiss Alps, standing on a hillside close to Castello Jocteau, 1km (½ mile) north of the center. The public lounge sets the antique tone, with old wooden beams, a large brick hearth with a blazing fireplace in winter, and an Alpine-like bar that's a snug nest on a snowy night. Much attention was paid to the bedrooms, which range in size from generous to cozily cramped. Try for a room with a balcony opening onto the resort itself and the snowcapped mountain peaks beyond.

Località Porossan Roppoz 15, 11100 Aosta. ✆ **0165-235278.** Fax 0165-235284. www.hotel milleluci.com. 31 units. 140€ double without balcony; 150€–190€ double with balcony; 240€ suite. Rates include buffet breakfast. AE, DC, MC, V. Free parking. **Amenities:** Babysitting; exercise room; Jacuzzi; heated outdoor pool; room service; sauna. *In room:* TV, hair dryer, minibar, Wi-Fi (free).

Where to Dine

La Brasserie du Commerce ★ ITALIAN/AOSTAN   Forget the dreary name and come in and enjoy attentive service, a cozy ambience, and superbly prepared food based on market-fresh ingredients. In the heart of Aosta, near the Duomo, the restaurant has a classical but rustic regional decor, with a huge fresco domination the decor. The location is in a renovated palace from the 19th century. An appetite-whetting array of food is served, including such specialties as *pappardelle* (homemade pasta) with a cold boar sauce, or perhaps potato gnocchi with Speck (an Italian prosciutto). Starters include such temptations as pumpkin and fava bean soup. The chef's special achievement is wild boar braised in a red wine sauce with fresh rosemary.

Via de Tillier 10. ✆ **0165-35613.** www.brasserieducommerce.com. Reservations recommended. Main courses 8€–15€; 2-course set menu 20€; 3-course menu 30€. MC, V. Daily 11am–3pm and 7–11pm. Closed Oct–May.

Vecchia Aosta VALDOSTAN/INTERNATIONAL   The most unusual restaurant in Aosta lies in the narrow niche between the inner and outer Roman walls of the Porta Pretoria. It's in an old structure that, though modernized, still bears evidence of the superb building techniques of the Romans, whose chiseled stones are sometimes visible between patches of modern wood and plaster. Full meals are served on at least two levels in a labyrinth of nooks and isolated crannies. Menu highlights include *maltagliata* (homemade pasta) with porcini mushrooms; filet of beef in a cocoa crust with black olives, or potato dumplings with bleu d'Aosta cheese.

Piazza Porta Pretoria 4. ✆ **0165-361186.** www.vecchiaosta.it. Reservations recommended. Main courses 10€–20€; fixed-price menus 21€–28€. MC, V. Thurs–Tues noon–2:30pm and 7:30–10:15pm.

Vecchio Ristoro ★★ VALDOSTAN   In a converted mill, this restaurant takes full advantage of the region's bounty and towers above all others in Aosta and the surrounding area. The atmosphere alone is worth the visit, with its ceramic stove, dark-wood furnishings, and mellow ambience. Everything served here is created from scratch. Only the freshest ingredients go into the chef's rich, creative cuisine. The lasagna with porcini mushrooms and a black-truffle sauce is delectable, or else you might try chestnut dumplings with onion and a pumpkin and pecorino cheese sauce. You might also tuck into the eggplant pâté with fresh tomato jelly and pesto. Cappelliti is another pasta that's enlivened with mussels, other fish, basil, and fresh tomatoes. Nothing has quite the grandeur for a main course as the pastry and herb-encrusted loin of lamb from the Alps, or roast suckling pig with mustard sauce.

Via Tourneuve 4. ✆ **0165-33238.** www.ristorantevecchioristoro.it. Reservations required. Main courses 17€–25€; fixed-price menus 60€–70€. AE, DC, MC, V. Tues–Sat 9am–3pm; Mon–Sat 6pm–midnight. Closed June and Nov 1–10.

Shopping

Valle d'Aosta is known for its woodcarvings and wrought-iron work. For a sampling, head for the permanent craft exhibits in the arcades of **Piazza Chanoux,** the center of Aosta. You're not expected to pay the first price quoted, so test your bargaining skill. The market here swells during the last 2 days in January, when dozens of artisans from all around the Italian Alps appear en masse to sell their handicrafts. Count yourself lucky if you pick up some handmade lace from neighboring Cogne. It's highly valued for its workmanship.

Valdostan handicrafts can be found at **IVAT,** Via Xavier de Maistre 1 (© **0165-41462;** www.ivat.org), where sculpture, bas-relief, and wrought iron are offered. The shop owners can also provide you with a list of local furniture makers. Antique furniture and paintings are the domain of **Bessone,** Via Edouard Aubert 53 (© **0165-40853**).

Aosta After Dark

Sweet Rock Caffè, Viale Piccolo St. Bernardo 18 (© **0165-553251;** www. sweetrockcafe.com), caters to a 25-to-45 crowd, featuring rock and jazz with live music on occasion.

COURMAYEUR & ENTRÈVES: SKIING & ALPINE BEAUTY

Courmayeur ★★

Courmayeur, a 35km (22-mile) drive northwest of Aosta, is Italy's best all-around ski resort, with two "high seasons," attracting skiers in winter and other active types who come to play in the mountain scenery in summer. Its popularity was given a considerable boost with the opening of the Mont Blanc road tunnel feeding traffic from France into Italy (estimated trip time: 20 min.). This vital link between France and Italy was closed by a tragic fire in the spring of 1999, and the Mont Blanc tunnel didn't reopen until 2002. The tunnel is now hailed by engineers as "the safest in the world." For motorists coming from Italy into France, the toll for a car and its occupants is 36.80€ one-way and 45.90€ round-trip. The return half of the round-trip ticket must be used within 7 days of its issue. For more information within Italy, call © **0165-890411;** the website is www.tunnelmb.net.

With Europe's highest mountain in the background, Courmayeur sits snugly in a valley. Directly to the north of the resort is the Alpine village of Entrèves, sprinkled with a number of chalets (some of which take in paying guests).

ESSENTIALS

GETTING THERE There's **no direct train service;** you'll have to take the **Savda** bus (© **0165-361244;** www.savda.it) from Aosta (see above). Aosta's bus terminal, Via Carrel (© **0165-262027**), is adjacent to the train station. There's a bus every hour that costs 5€ each way or 7.50€ round-trip. Transit time is 1 hour. The last departure from Aosta is at 9:45pm.

By **car,** take S26 west from Aosta (toward Monte Bianco).

VISITOR INFORMATION The **tourist office** for Courmayeur is on Piazzale Monte Bianco (© **0165-842060;** www.courmayeur-montblanc.com), open daily from 9am to 12:30pm and 3 to 6:30pm.

FUN ON & OFF THE SLOPES

The **ski season** begins in mid-December and lasts until sometime in April, depending on snow conditions in the area. The skiing, although good, has little to attract experts, who head instead for Chamonix across Mont Blanc in France; Courmayeur is more for beginners and intermediates. **Lift tickets** in Courmayeur cost 42€ for 1 day, and 185€ for 5 days. For **snow reports** in and around Courmayeur, check www.courmayeur-montblanc.com.

Near Courmayeur, you can take one of the most unusual **cable cars** in Europe across Mont Blanc all the way to Chamonix, France. It's a ride across glaciers that's altogether frightening and thrilling. Departures on the **Funivie Monte Bianco** are from La Palud, near Entrèves. The three-stage cable car heads for the intermediate stations, Pavillon and Rifugio Torino, before reaching its peak at Punta Helbronner at 3,430m (11,254 ft.). At the latter, you'll be on the doorstep of the glacier and the celebrated 19km (12-mile) Vallée Blanche ski run to Chamonix, France. From Courmayeur to Chamonix, cable cars are available only from the end of June to the end of September. The round-trip price for the cable car ride is 95€. The return trip is by bus through the Mont Blanc tunnel. Departures are every 20 minutes, and service is daily from 8:30am to 12:40pm and 2 to 5pm. At the top are a bar, a snack bar, and a terrace for sunbathing. Bookings can be made at **Esercizio Funivie,** Frazione La Palude 22 (ⓒ **0165-89925;** www.montebianco.com).

Many nonskiing visitors come here just for the bracing mountain air and the panoramic views. The shopping is excellent, especially on **Via Roma,** and many of the most prestigious retailers in Milan or Rome maintain branches here.

In **summer** the scenery is gorgeous, with towering Mont Blanc in the distance. Some 52km (32 miles) southeast of Courmayeur is the **Parco Nazionale del Gran Paradiso,** once the private domain of King Vittorio Emanuele II (1820–78). For more information, see "A Side Trip to a Great Paradise," in "Aosta," above.

Skiing at Courmayeur.

WHERE TO STAY

Courmayeur has a number of attractive hotels, many of which are open seasonally. *Always* reserve ahead in high season, either summer or winter.

Expensive

Grand Hotel Royal e Golf ★★   This hotel sits dramatically above the heart of the resort town. It is a top choice, exceeded only by the more tranquil and elegant Hotel Pavillon, and the even grander Hotel Gran Baita (see both below). Much of its angular facade is covered with rocks, so it fits in neatly with the mountainous landscape. The guest rooms are decent, with streamlined bathrooms; fifth-floor rooms have private balconies. The rooms most requested are those with southern exposure, offering a great view of Mont Blanc; those on the north side open onto a valley.

Via Roma 87, 11013 Courmayeur. ✆ **0165-831611.** Fax 0165-842093. www.hotelroyalegolf.com. 85 units. 200€–300€ per person double; 250€–350€ per person suite. Rates include buffet breakfast. AE, DC, MC, V. Parking 20€ inside; free outside. Closed Apr 6–Dec 2. **Amenities:** Restaurant; bar; babysitting; exercise room; 9-hole golf course (Golf Club Courmayeur & Grandes Jorasses, which lies outside of town at Le Pont–Val Ferret); outdoor heated pool; room service; sauna. *In room:* A/C, TV, hair dryer, minibar.

Hotel Gran Baita ★★★   Courmayeur's grandest resort lies on the outskirts of town at the foot of Mont Blanc and is linked by courtesy bus to the center with its ski lifts. The landscape and backdrop are impressive, in the midst of rocks, medieval castles, and snowcapped peaks. Skiers flock here in winter and mountain visitors in summer, each lured by the elegant style, grand comfort, fine food, and impeccable service of this place. Bedrooms are beautifully maintained and tastefully equipped with traditional pieces, including furnishings, carpets, and decorative objects. Roomy bathrooms with up-to-date amenities appease the gilt-edged clientele. Jet-set celebrities can often be seen enjoying the modern spa, and the hotel's food and drinking facilities are the finest at the resort.

Strada Larzey 2, 11013 Courmayeur. ✆ **0165-844040.** Fax 0165-844805. www.standardhotels. net. 53 units. 270€–470€ double; 400€–650€ junior suite. Rates include half board. AE, DC, MC, V. Parking 18€ in garage; free outside. **Amenities:** Restaurant; bar; exercise room; 2 pools (heated indoor w/hydromassage tub and heated outdoor); room service; sauna; spa. *In room:* TV, hair dryer, minibar, Wi-Fi (free).

Hotel Pavillon ★★   This is one of the swankiest hotels in town, despite its small size. Designed like a chalet, the hotel is a 4-minute walk south of Courmayeur's inner-city pedestrian zone. The guest rooms feature leather-covered doors and conservative decor; all but two have private balconies. Accommodations range from midsize to spacious. The hotel is only a short walk from the funicular that goes to Plan Checrouit.

Strada Regionale 62, 11013 Courmayeur. ✆ **0165-846120.** Fax 0165-846122. www.pavillon.it. 50 units. Winter 260€–380€ double, 330€–480€ suite; off season 220€–360€ double, 310€–460€ suite. Rates include breakfast and dinner. AE, DC, MC, V. Valet parking 10€. Closed early May to early June and Oct to early Dec. **Amenities:** 2 restaurants; bar; babysitting; exercise room; Jacuzzi; indoor heated pool; room service; sauna; spa. *In room:* TV, hair dryer, minibar.

Inexpensive

Albergo del Viale   This old-style mountain chalet at the edge of town is under family ownership and has an inviting terrace with tables set under trees in fair weather. In chillier months, the rooms inside are cozy and pleasant. The guest rooms, though small, have an alpine charm, each with an efficient tiled bathroom. In winter, guests can gather in the taproom to enjoy après-ski life, drinking at pine tables and warming their feet before the open fire.

Viale Monte Bianco 74, 11013 Courmayeur. ℂ **0165-846712.** Fax 0165-844513. www.hoteldelviale.com. 23 units. 100€–160€ double. Rates include breakfast and dinner. AE, DC, MC, V. Parking 10€ inside; free outside. Closed May and Oct–Nov. **Amenities:** Restaurant; bar; room service. *In room:* TV, hair dryer, minibar.

Hotel Bouton d'Or   This family-owned hotel is named for the buttercups that cover the surrounding hills in summer. French windows lead from the guest rooms onto small balconies. The rooms are a bit cramped, but you'll find reasonable comfort for the price. All units come with well-kept bathrooms. The hotel is about 91m (300 ft.) from the most popular restaurant in Courmayeur, Le Vieux Pommier (see below), which is owned by the same family.

Strada Traforo del Monte Bianco 10 (off Piazzale Monte Bianco), 11013 Courmayeur. ℂ **0165-846729.** Fax 0165-842152. www.hotelboutondor.com. 35 units (shower only). 95€–160€ double; 120€–200€ apt for 3; 170€–270€ apt for 4. Rates include buffet breakfast. AE, DC, MC, V. Free parking. Closed Nov. **Amenities:** Bar; exercise room; room service; sauna. *In room:* TV, hair dryer, minibar, Wi-Fi (free).

Hotel Courmayeur   This centrally located inn is built so that most of its rooms have unobstructed views of the mountains. It's a small, unpretentious hotel with immaculate rooms and low prices. A number of the guest rooms, furnished in mountain chalet style, also have wooden balconies. There is a minimum stay of 2 weeks in winter.

Via Roma 158, 11013 Courmayeur. ℂ **0165-846732.** Fax 0165-845125. www.hotelcourmayeur.com. 26 units. Winter 525€–700€ per person for 1 week; off season 65€–110€ per person double. Rates include half board. AE, DC, MC, V. Free parking. Closed Sept 6–Dec 18 and Apr 11–May. **Amenities:** Restaurant; bar; babysitting; room service. *In room:* TV, hair dryer.

WHERE TO DINE

Cadran Solaire ★ VALDOSTAN   In the center of town is Courmayeur's most regional restaurant, named after the sundial *(cadran solaire)* embellishing the upper floor of its chalet facade. It's owned by Domenico Pugliese, whose La Maison de Filippo in Entrèves (see below) is Valle d'Aosta's most popular restaurant. Try to come for a before-dinner drink in the vaulted bar; in the 16th century, the room's massive stones were crafted into long spans using techniques that the Romans perfected. The rustically elegant dining room has a stone fireplace, a beamed ceiling, and plank floors. Specialties change with the season but are likely to include such exotic temptations as risotto alla Valdostana (rice cooked with Parmesan and fontina cheese) or else a thick *minestra di castagne e riso* (thick soup of rice cooked in milk with chestnuts). Among the mains, perhaps you'll go for a *carbonade* (salt-cured beef cooked with onions and red wine into a savory stew). Polenta is baked with layers of fontina cheese and served with a ragout of beef and sausage.

Via Roma 122. ℂ **0165-844609.** Reservations required. Main courses 10€–24€. AE, MC, V. Wed–Mon 12:30–2:30pm and 7:30–10:30pm. Closed May 1–31 and Nov.

Le Vieux Pommier FRENCH   The hacked-up trunk of the old apple tree that was cut down to build this place was erected inside and serves as the focal point

Courmayeur & Entrèves: Skiing & Alpine Beauty

(and namesake) of the restaurant, which is located on the main square. The exposed stone, the copper-covered bar, and the thick pine tables arranged in an octagon create a charming atmosphere. Today Alessandro Casale, the son of the founder, directs the kitchen, assisted by his wife, Lydia. Your meal might consist of three kinds of dried Alpine beef, followed by noodles in ham-studded cream sauce or an arrangement of three pastas or four fondues, including a regional variety with fontina, milk, and egg yolks. Then it's on to chicken supreme en papillote, or four or five unusual meat dishes cooked mountain style, right at your table. **Note:** The restaurant also rents out six well-furnished and medium-size bedrooms, costing 71€ for a double, 93€ for a triple, with breakfast included.

Piazzale Monte Bianco 25. © **0165-842281.** www.levieuxpommier.it. Reservations recommended. Main courses 9€–20€. DC, MC, V. Tues–Sun noon–2pm and 7–9:30pm. Closed Oct and 15 days in May.

COURMAYEUR AFTER DARK

Not to be confused with a less desirable bar of the same name at the end of the same street, the **American Bar,** Via Roma 43 (© **0165-846707**), is one of the most popular watering holes on the après-ski circuit. It's rowdy and sometimes outrageous, but often a lot of fun. Most guests end up beside either the open fireplace or at the long, crowded bar. The place is open all day every day, until 2am in ski season. A few doors down, the **Café della Posta,** Via Roma 51 (© **0165-842272**), the oldest cafe in Courmayeur, is as sedate as its neighbor is unruly. Many guests prefer to remain in the warmly decorated bar area, never venturing into the large salon with its glowing fireplace. The place changes its stripes throughout the day, opening as a morning cafe at 8:30am.

The view ascending the Val Veny cable car.

Entrèves ★

Even older than Courmayeur, Entrèves is an ancient community that's small and compact, a mountain village of wooden houses. Many visitors prefer its Alpine charm to the more bustling resort of Courmayeur; they ski the slopes at Courmayeur and enjoy its shopping, dining, and nightlife, but they retreat here to stay in a quieter, less congested setting. Entrèves is reached by a steep, narrow road. Many gourmets visit to enjoy the fare for which the village is known.

Just outside Entrèves on the main highway lies the **Val Veny cable car,** which skiers take in winter to reach the Courmayeur lift system.

Entrèves is 3km (2 miles) north of Courmayeur (signposted off Rte. 26). Buses from the center of Courmayeur run daily to Entrèves. For more information, contact Courmayeur's tourist office (✆ **0165-842060**).

WHERE TO STAY

La Grange ★ ✦   This will be one of the first buildings you see as you enter this Alpine village. A few foundation stones date from the 13th century, when the hotel was a barn. What you'll see today is a stone building whose balconies and gables are outlined against the hillside into which it's constructed. The Berthod family transformed a dilapidated property into a rustic and comfortable hotel in 1979. It's enthusiastically managed by Bruna Berthod Perri. The decor includes a collection of antique tools and a series of thick timbers, stucco, and exposed stone walls. The guest rooms are imbued with a cozy Alpine charm, each with a tiled bathroom. A rich breakfast is the only meal served.

Strada La Brenva 1, 11013 Courmayeur-Entrèves. ✆ **0165-869733.** Fax 0165-869744. www. lagrange-it.com. 22 units (shower only). 80€–150€ double; 150€–230€ suite. Rates include buffet breakfast. AE, DC, MC, V. Free parking. Closed May–June and Oct–Nov. **Amenities:** Bar; babysitting; exercise room; room service; sauna; Wi-Fi (3€ per hr., in lobby). *In room:* TV, hair dryer, minibar.

WHERE TO DINE

La Maison de Filippo ✦ VALDOSTAN   This colorful tavern is for those who enjoy a festive atmosphere and bountiful regional food. The three-story open hallway seems like a rustic barn, with an open, worn wooden staircase leading to the dining nooks. The outdoor summer beer garden has a full view of Mont Blanc. You pass by casks of nuts, baskets of fresh fruits, bowls of salad, fruit tarts, and loaves of fresh-baked bread. The menu features local specialties on an all-you-can-eat basis, earning the place the nickname "Chalet of Gluttony." A typical meal might begin with a selection of antipasti, followed by a large platter of about 15 varieties of sausage. Next comes a parade of pasta dishes such as ravioli or *tagliatelle* from the Aosta Valley. For a main course, you can pick everything from fondue to *camoscio* (chamois meat) to trout with almond-butter sauce.

Frazione Entrèves di Courmayeur. ✆ **0165-869797.** www.lamaison.com. Reservations required. Fixed-price menu 45€. MC, V. Wed–Mon 12:30–2:30pm and 8–10:30pm. Closed May 16–July 10 and Nov–Dec 4.

La Palud VALDOSTANA/SEAFOOD   Perfect for a cold windy day, this intimate restaurant serves hearty Alpine fare in the shadows of Mont Blanc. We're talking authentic Valle d'Aosta specialties like *polenta concia* with plenty of home-churned butter and fontina cheese. In season, the kitchen invariably prepares venison and fresh mountain ham. Locals flock here on Friday when a big shipment of fresh fish arrives from the Italian Riviera. Some of our favorite specialties are beef stew with polenta, or else *pappardelle* (wide noodles) with wild boar, porcini mushrooms, and Parma ham.

Strada La Palud 17. ✆ **0165-89169.** www.lapalud.it. Reservations recommended. Main courses 10€–22€; fixed-price menus 25€–33€. AE, MC, V. Thurs–Tues noon–3:30pm and 7:30–10:30pm. Closed Wed in summer.

13

GENOA & THE ITALIAN RIVIERA

For years the retreat of the wealthy, the Italian Riviera now enjoys a broad base of tourism. It's popular even in winter, although not for swimming (the average Jan temperature hovers around 10°C/50°F). The protection provided by the Ligurian Apennines looming in the background makes for balmy weather. Genoa, dividing the Riviera in two, is the capital of Liguria. It's a big, bustling port that has charm for those willing to take the time to seek out its treasures.

The winding coastline of the Rivieras, particularly the one stretching from the French border to San Remo, is familiar to moviegoers as the background for countless flicks about sports-car racing, jewel thieves, and spies. The Mediterranean landscape is dotted with pines, olives, citrus trees, and cypresses. The western Riviera—the **Riviera di Ponente (Setting Sun),** from the border to Genoa—is sometimes known as the Riviera of Flowers (Riviera dei Fiori) because of its profusion of blossoms. Starting at the French border, Ventimiglia is the gateway city to Italy. Along the way you'll encounter the first big resort, Bardighera, followed by San Remo, the major center of tourism. On the eastern Riviera—the **Riviera di Levante (Rising Sun)**—are three dramatically situated small resorts: Rapallo, Santa Margherita, and Portofino (the favorite of the yachting set). **Genoa** itself, with its proud maritime history, is a world apart from the easygoing seaside resorts that surround it: Brusque and clamorous, it is one of the most historic, fascinating, and least-visited cities in Italy.

The Ligurians are famous for ceramics, lace, silver and gold filigree, marble, velvet, olive wood, and macramé, and all the towns and villages of the region hold outdoor markets in the main square or on the waterfront. Haggling is a way of life, so good deals exist; English speakers should be warned that prices might not fall as low as they would if you were negotiating in the local dialect.

SAN REMO ★★

16km (10 miles) E of the French border, 137km (85 miles) SW of Genoa, 639km (396 miles) NW of Rome

San Remo has been known as a resort ever since Emperor Frederick William wintered in a villa here. In time, Empress Maria Alexandrova, wife of Czar Alexander II, showed up, trailed by a Russian colony that included Tchaikovsky, who composed the *Fourth Symphony* here in 1878. Alfred Nobel, the father of dynamite and the founder of the famous prizes in Stockholm, died here in 1896.

The flower-filled resort is today something of a mini-Vegas by the sea, complete with a casino, racetrack, 18-hole golf course, and the deluxe Royal Hotel. Its climate is the mildest on the western Riviera, and the town offers mile after mile of well-maintained beaches.

PREVIOUS PAGE: **San Remo.**

The beach at San Remo.

Essentials

GETTING THERE   San Remo lies on the coast between Ventimiglia and Imperia, 10km (6¼ miles) from each, and it's a major stop for many **trains.** A train leaves Genoa heading for the French border once per hour, stopping in San Remo. Rome is 8 hours by train from San Remo. For train information and schedules, call ✆ **892021.** If you have a **car,** A10, running east-west along the Riviera, is the fastest way to reach San Remo from the French border or Genoa.

VISITOR INFORMATION   The **tourist office** is on Largo Nuvoloni 1 (✆ **0184-507649;** www.rivieradeifiori.com), open Monday to Friday 9:30am to 1pm; on Monday and Wednesday it is also open 3 to 5pm.

Exploring the Resort

Even if you're just passing through San Remo, you might want to visit **La Città Vecchia** (also known as **La Pigna**), the old city atop the hill. Far removed in spirit from the burgeoning sterile-looking town down near the water, old San Remo blithely ignores the present, and its tiny houses on narrow, steep lanes capture the past. In the new town, the palm-flanked **Corso dell'Imperatrice** (aka the **Passeggiata dell'Imperatrice**) attracts promenaders; at one end of the *corso* (main promenade) stands the Russian Orthodox **San Basilio,** boasting onion-shaped domes. For a scenic view, drive to the top of **San Romolo** and **Monte Bignone** (1,300m/4,265 ft.).

Outside of town, you can visit **Bussana Vecchia (Old Bussana),** 8km (5 miles) west of San Remo (it's signposted). Too well inhabited to really be considered a ghost town, Bussana Vecchia is, however, a rather unofficial town. A substantial 1887 earthquake killed thousands of its residents and destroyed many buildings. The survivors, too frightened to stay, started a new Bussana 2km (1¼ miles) closer to the sea. The original town, with several buildings still standing, has gradually been taken over by artist-squatters who've revamped interior spaces (but not exteriors—no reason to draw that much attention to themselves) and hooked up water, electricity, and phones. They live off their art, so haggling can get you a good deal on a painting.

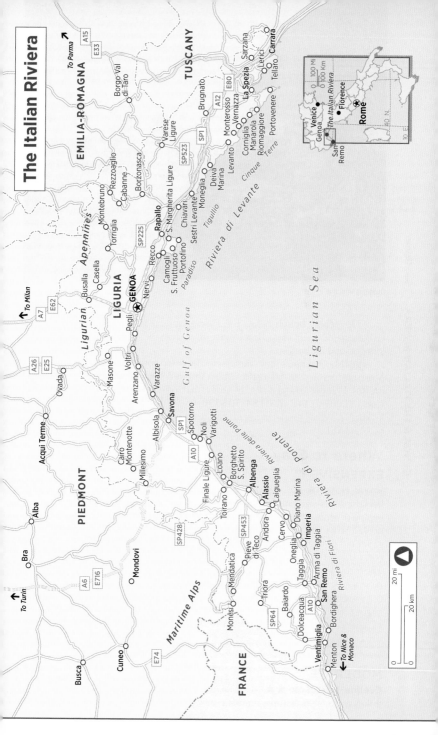

The Italian Riviera

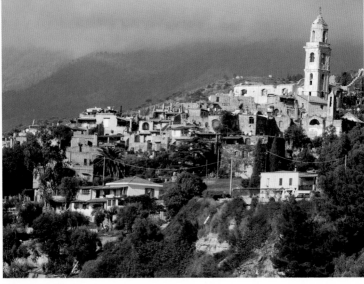

Bussana Vecchia.

The pebbly **beach** below the Passeggiata dell'Imperatrice is where many visitors spend their days. Beach huts offer showers, snack bars, beach chairs, lounges, and umbrellas.

Stylish boutiques line the town's busiest thoroughfare, **Via Matteotti.** Most are devoted to high-style Milan-inspired beachwear and slinky cocktail dresses. Wander up and down the street, making it a point to stop at **Annamode,** Corso Matteotti 141 (✆ **0184-505550;** www.annamode.it), which sells sporty-looking as well as formal garments for men and women, with labels such as Versace and YSL.

Where to Stay

EXPENSIVE

Royal Hotel ★ ☺ Though long past its heyday, this resort is a big name because of its size and facilities, including a private beach across the road. It's complete with terraces and gardens, a forest of palms, flowers, and hideaway nooks. Activity revolves around the garden terrace; no one really hangs out in the grand old public lounges. The guest rooms vary considerably: Some are tennis-court size with private balconies, many have sea views, and others face the hills. The furnishings range from traditional to modern. The luxurious fifth-floor rooms have the best views and are more expensive.

Corso Imperatrice 80, 18038 San Remo. ✆ **0184-5391.** Fax 0184-661445. www.royalhotel sanremo.com. 127 units. 279€–560€ double; 685€–1,645€ suite. Rates include buffet breakfast. AE, DC, MC, V. Free parking. Closed Nov 1–Feb 9. **Amenities:** 3 restaurants; 2 bars; babysitting; bikes; children's center; exercise room; minigolf; heated saltwater pool; room service; sauna; spa; 2 outdoor tennis courts (lit). *In room:* A/C, TV, hair dryer, minibar, Wi-Fi (7€ per 2 hr.).

MODERATE

Eveline-Portosole ★★ Our favorite hotel in San Remo has been a local tradition since 1948; with its dramatic new decor and romantic atmosphere, it has emerged as one of the area's most tranquil addresses and finest oases. One visitor described the hotel's warmth, friendly staff, and overall hospitality as "a cuddling experience." Each beautifully decorated room is unique and named after either flowers or the winds. Bedrooms are sumptuously decorated and often draped in fabrics. Some accommodations offer four-poster beds and others boast spacious terraces.

Corso Cavallotti 111, 18038 San Remo. ☏ **0184-503430.** Fax 0184-503431. www.eveline portosole.com. 22 units. 150€–387€ double; 337€–400€ suite. Rates include continental breakfast. AE, DC, MC, V. Free parking. Closed Jan 7–28. *In room:* A/C, TV, hair dryer, Wi-Fi (free).

Gran Hotel de Londres

Like the Royal, this hotel coasts along on past glories, but it's still a worthy choice. Built around 1900 as a two-story hotel, this place was later expanded into the imposing structure you see today. It's in a park with a sea view, within a 10-minute walk of the commercial district. The well-furnished interior is filled with framed engravings, porcelain in illuminated cases, gilt mirrors, and brass detailing. Many of the guest rooms, ranging from medium to spacious, have wrought-iron balconies.

Corso Matuzia 2, 18038 San Remo. ☏ **0184-65511.** Fax 0184-668073. www.londrahotelsanremo.it. 130 units. 140€–190€ per person double; from 320€ per person suite. Rates include buffet breakfast. AE, DC, MC, V. Free parking. Closed Sept 30–Dec 27. **Amenities:** Restaurant; bar; babysitting; saltwater pool; room service. *In room:* A/C (in half the rooms), TV, hair dryer, minibar, Wi-Fi (10€ per 24 hr.).

Hotel Miramare Continental Palace

A curved drive leads past palmettos to this traditional Liberty-style villa set behind semitropical gardens bordering a busy street. A private underpass gives direct access to the beach. After passing through the well-appointed public rooms, you'll discover a garden with a 300-year-old magnolia, sculptures, and plenty of verdant hideaways. The guest rooms are clean and comfortable, ranging from "too" small to medium; some are in a neighboring annex with garden views.

Corso Matuzia 9, 18038 San Remo. ☏ **0184-667601.** Fax 0184-667655. www.miramaresanremo.it. 59 units (shower only). 55€–135€ per person double; 300€–500€ suite. Rates include continental breakfast. AE, DC, MC, V. Free parking. **Amenities:** Restaurant; babysitting; exercise room; indoor heated saltwater pool; room service; sauna. *In room:* TV, minibar, Wi-Fi (12€ per 24 hr.).

Hotel Paradiso ✦

This once-private villa is now one of the most homelike accommodations in San Remo, in a residential area 100m (328 ft.) from the sea and a short walk from the heart of the resort. A hearty welcome is extended, and the Paradiso attracts a loyal following. Its garden setting provides for a tranquil oasis in a high-traffic city. The place is not elegant, and its decor is of another day, but it is exceedingly comfortable. Try for a room overlooking the sea, because these also come with flower-filled balconies. The bathrooms are tiled and roomy, containing old-fashioned tubs. Guests gather in the evening in the lounge for drinks, or else enjoy cocktails in the garden. A fixed-price menu is changed daily; it is reasonably priced and always offers some tempting Ligurian recipes.

Via Roccasterone 12, 18038 San Remo. ☏ **0184-571211.** Fax 0184-578176. www.paradisohotel.it. 40 units. 120€–220€ double. Rates include buffet breakfast. AE, DC, MC, V. Parking 10€. **Amenities:** Restaurant; bar; babysitting; heated pool; room service. *In room:* A/C, TV, hair dryer, minibar, Wi-Fi (free).

Suite Hotel Nyala ★ ☺   This comfortable hotel lies in what was, a century ago, the English-style park of a villa. Although it's in a residential neighborhood with some impressive antique villas, this is San Remo's most modern hotel. The accommodations are divided among three buildings connected with corridors. Most guest rooms have a view over the sea and a sun-filled terrace; about half are junior suites, with a separate sitting area and balconies. The rooms are tastefully decorated.

Via Solaro 134, 18038 San Remo. ⓒ **0184-667668.** Fax 0184-666059. www.nyalahotel.com. 80 units. 139€–300€ double; 149€–450€ suite. Rates include buffet breakfast. AE, DC, MC, V. Free parking. **Amenities:** Restaurant; 2 bars; bikes; children's center; outdoor freshwater pool; room service. *In room:* A/C, TV, hair dryer, minibar, Wi-Fi (in some; 20€ per 24 hr.).

INEXPENSIVE

Hotel Belsoggiorno   This centrally located hotel is near the Corso dell'Imperatrice, the main seaside walkway, and the beaches. Attractively furnished and inviting, it contains a large reception area, plenty of living rooms for lounging, and TV rooms. The guest rooms are contemporary and functional, if not exactly stylish. Nonetheless, they're quite comfortable, although the bathrooms are small. This hotel also provides a pleasant garden in which to sit and enjoy the sun and plants.

Corso Matuzia 41, 18038 San Remo. ⓒ **0184-667631.** Fax 0184-667471. www.belsoggiorno.net. 36 units (shower only). 84€–120€ double. Rates include continental breakfast. Half board 20€ per person. DC, MC, V. Free parking. **Amenities:** Babysitting; bikes; room service. *In room:* A/C, TV, hair dryer, minibar, Wi-Fi (free).

Hotel Mariluce 🥄   As you walk along the promenade away from the center, you'll note a flowering garden enclosed on one side by the walls of a Polish church; one wall is emblazoned with a gilded coat of arms. Behind the garden is the building that until 1945 was a refugee center that Poles throughout Europe used for finding friends and relatives. Today it's a reasonably priced hotel, a bargain for San Remo, offering sunny public rooms and simply furnished, small guest rooms with cramped, tiled bathrooms. A passage under the street leads from the garden to the beach.

Corso Matuzia 3, 18038 San Remo. ⓒ **0184-667805.** Fax 0184-667655. 23 units, 18 with bathroom (shower only). 90€–105€, 80€–95€ double without bathroom, 115€–125€ double with bathroom. DC, MC, V. Closed Oct–May (except Dec 25–Jan 10). **Amenities:** Room service. *In room:* No phone.

Where to Dine

VERY EXPENSIVE

Paolo e Barbara ★★★ LIGURIAN/ITALIAN   Named after the husband-and-wife team that owns it (the Masieris), this restaurant stands near the casino and has caught the imagination of San Remo. It specializes in traditional regional recipes plus a handful of innovative dishes. Meals tend to be drawn-out affairs, so allow adequate time. Menus are seasonally adjusted to take advantage of the best produce in any season. Care and craftsmanship go into each dish, beginning with such starters as an onion stuffed with tuna roe and mint. The seductive repertoire also features such dishes shrimp flambéed with whiskey and served with a saffron-laced paella; *tagliatelle* with calamari, white beans, and pesto; or seafood soup with shrimp, zucchini, fresh garlic, and fresh tomatoes.

Via Roma 47. © **0184-531653.** www.paolobarbara.it. Reservations recommended. Main courses 24€–60€; fixed-price lunch 49€; tasting menu (without wine) 85€. MC, V. July Fri–Sun 8–10pm; June 15–30 and Aug to mid-Sept 8–10pm; rest of the year Mon–Tues, Thurs, Sat–Sun 12:30–1:45pm and 8–10pm, Fri 8–10pm. Closed 2 weeks in Dec, 1 week in Jan.

EXPENSIVE

Da Giannino ★★ LIGURIAN/SEAFOOD   Long the market leader, this is still one of the finest dining rooms along the Italian Riviera. In a conservatively elegant setting, you can enjoy such specialties as warm seafood antipasti, a flavorful risotto laced with cheese and a pungently aromatic green sauce, and a selection of main courses that changes with the availability of ingredients. An exotic selection is marinated gratinéed cuttlefish. The wine list features many of the better vintages of both France and Italy. In the hot summer months it moves from the address below to an open space by a swimming pool, lying only a minute or so away, opening onto Via Anselmi.

Corso Cavallotti Felice 76. © **0184-504014.** Reservations required. Main courses 22€–32€. AE, DC, MC, V. Mon 7:30–10pm; Tues–Sat 12:30–2:30pm and 7:30–10pm.

INEXPENSIVE

Antica Trattoria Piccolo Mondo ★ 🍴 LUGURIAN/SEAFOOD   This colorful restaurant, crowded and boisterous, has long been a favorite of locals, lying on a narrow alley close to the waterfront in the less attractive business district of town. It opened in the 1920s when Mussolini was still in power and has survived wars and various other disasters. Its regional cuisine is market fresh. Pesto is used in many dishes, from soups to pastas. You might even try fresh anchovies here even if you didn't like them before. The antipasti is prepared fresh daily, and fresh vegetables, such as bell peppers, are stuffed with rice and shrimp. An octopus dish with potatoes is a far greater taste sensation than it sounds. Expect succulent pastas, such as *sciancui* (homemade pasta) slathered with pesto and studded with green beans, zucchini, and pine nuts.

Via Piave 7. © **0184-509012.** Reservations recommended. Main courses 15€–22€; 3-course fixed-price menu 15€. No credit cards. Tues–Sat 12:30–2:30pm and 7–10:15pm.

Magiargè ★ LIGURIAN   Motorists who are serious foodies often make a pilgrimage to the little seaside resort of Bordighera, 12km (7 miles) west of San Remo to dine at this old *osteria* in the historic center. Some of the best—and freshest—seafood along the coast is served here, and there is a fine *carte* of regional wines. With its wooden chairs and terra-cotta floors, the modestly priced restaurant is rustic. The chef turns out a first-rate cuisine, and is skilled at bringing together harmonious ingredients. Try the grilled calamari on a garbanzo puree or the homemade *tagliolini* served with fresh white fish and artichokes. A braised tuna steak appears with Tropea onions, or a savory stew of octopus and fava beans is also presented, as are fish meatballs served with a tomato sauce and mint.

Via Dritta 2. © **0184-262946.** www.magiarge.it. Reservations recommended. Main courses 10€–15€; fixed-price menus 18€–30€. MC, V. Sept–June Wed–Sun noon–2pm and 7:30–10pm; July–Aug daily 7:30–11pm.

San Remo After Dark

Most nightlife revolves around the **San Remo Casino,** Corso Inglesi 18 (© **0184-5951;** www.casinosanremo.it), in the center of town. For decades, visitors have dined in high style in the restaurant, reserved tables at the roof garden's cabaret, or tested their luck at the gaming tables. Like a palace, the pristine-looking casino stands at the top of a steep flight of stone steps above the main artery of town. Its showroom hosts a variety of fashion shows, concerts, and theatrical productions throughout the year. All gaming rooms are open daily from 2:30pm to 3:30am. You'll be required to show a passport, and men must wear jackets and ties. Admission is free. For the slot-machines section, open Sunday to Friday from 10am to 3am and Saturday from 2:30pm to 3:30am, there's no dress code. The casino restaurant is open nightly from 8 to 11:30pm, charging 30€ to 70€ per person for dinner. Its orchestra plays everything from waltzes to rock. The roof-garden cabaret is open year-round daily with shows beginning at 10:30pm. If you visit for drinks only (not dinner), the cost is 20€ or higher per drink.

You should also check out your hotel's bar or the bar in one of the grand hotels (especially the Royal; see above), whose bars are always open to well-dressed nonguests. You can always strike out for the cafes along **Via Matteotti,** which serve drinks until late at night.

GENOA ★★

142km (88 miles) SW of Milan, 501km (311 miles) NW of Rome, 193km (120 miles) NE of Nice

With its dizzying mix of the old and the new, of sophistication and squalor, Genoa is as multilayered as the hills it clings to. It's always been first and foremost a port city: It was an important maritime center for the Roman Empire, the boyhood home of Christopher Columbus, and later one of the largest and wealthiest cities of Renaissance Europe. It's easy to capture glimpses of these former glory days on the narrow lanes and dank alleyways of Genoa's port-side old town, where treasure-filled palaces and fine marble churches stand next to laundry-draped tenements. In fact, life within the old medieval walls seems frozen in time. The other Genoa, the modern city that stretches for miles along the coast and climbs the hills, is a city of international business, peaceful parks, and breezy belvederes from which you can enjoy views over this colorful metropolis and the sea that continues to define its identity.

The mix of old and new in Genoa's harbor.

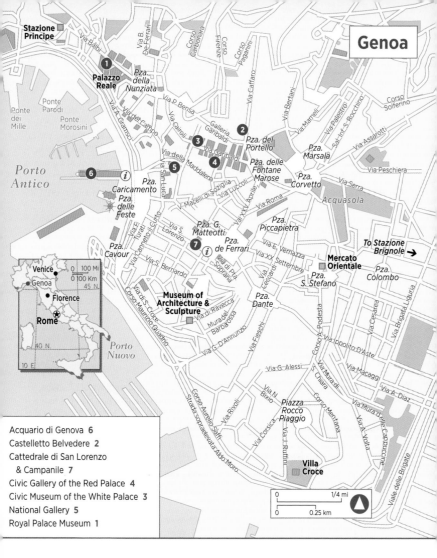

Genoa

Stazione Principe

① **Palazzo Reale**

Pza. della Nunziata

Ponte Parodi
Ponte dei Mille
Ponte Morosini

Porto Antico

Via Balbi
Via B. De-Ferrari
Corso Carbonara
Corso Firenze
Corso Paganini
Via Caffaro
Via Bertani
Via Mameli
Sal. Inf. S. Rocchino
Corso Solferino
Via Assarotti
Via P. Bensa
Galleria Garibaldi
② Pza. del Portello
Pza. Marsala
Via Peschiera
Via della Maddalena
③ Via Garibaldi
④
Pza. delle Fontane Marose
Pza. Corvetto
Via Serra
Acquasola
⑤
⑥ ⓘ Pza. Caricamento
Pza. delle Feste
Via S. Luca
V. Macelli di Soziglia
Via Luccoli
Via XXV Aprile
Via Roma
Pza. Piccapietra
To Stazione Brignole →
Pza. G. Matteotti
⑦ ⓘ Pza. de Ferrari
Via E. Vernazza
Via XX Settembre
Pza. Colombo
Pza. Cavour
Via S. Bernardo
Via di Pra Soprana
Mercato Orientale
Pza. S. Stefano
Pza. Dante
Via Cesarea
Via Brigata Liguria
Museum of Architecture & Sculpture
Via di Ravecca
Mura del Barbarossa
Via G. D'Annunzio
Corso A. Podesta
Via Ippolito D'Aste
Via Macaggi
Via A. Diaz
Via G. Alessi
S. Chiara
Via Mura di
Porto Nuovo
Strada sopraelevata Aldo Moro
Via Rivoli
Piazza Rocco Piaggio
Via N. Bixio
Corso Mentana
Via Mura delle Cappuccine
Viale delle Brigate
Via Corsica
Via T. Ruffini
Villa Croce
Via Mura di

Venice
Genoa ●
● Florence
Rome ★
0   100 Mi
0 100 Km
45 N.
40 N.
10 E.

Acquario di Genova **6**
Castelletto Belvedere **2**
Cattedrale di San Lorenzo
  & Campanile **7**
Civic Gallery of the Red Palace **4**
Civic Museum of the White Palace **3**
National Gallery **5**
Royal Palace Museum **1**

0 ————— 1/4 mi
0 ————— 0.25 km

Essentials

GETTING THERE   Alitalia and other carriers fly into the **Aeroporto Internazio-nale di Genova Cristoforo Colombo,** 6km (3¾ miles) west of the city center in Sestri Ponente (call ✆ **010-60151** for flight information; www.airport.genova.it).

Genoa has good **rail** connections with the rest of Italy; it lies only 1½ hours from Milan, 3 hours from Florence, and 1½ hours from the French border. Genoa has two major rail stations, **Stazione Principe** and **Stazione Brignole.** Chances are you'll arrive at the Principe, Piazza Acquaverde, nearest to the harbor and the old part of the city. The Brignole, on Piazza Verde, lies in the heart of the modern city. Both trains and municipally operated buses run between the two stations. For train information, call ☎ **892021.**

Genoa is right along the main **autostrada (A10)** that begins at the French border and continues along the Ligurian coastline.

There's a 20-hour **ferry** service to Genoa originating in Palermo (Sicily). The cost of an overnight cabin ranges from 151€ to 309€ per person, but chairs cost 103€ per person. Ferries also leave from Porto Torres (Sardinia) to Genoa, taking 8 hours; a cabin costs 79€ to 237€ per person, a chair only 41€ per person. For information, the number to call in Genoa is the **Stazione Marittima** at ☎ **010-2094591.**

VISITOR INFORMATION You'll find **information booths** dispensing tourist literature at the airport (☎ **010-6015247**) open daily 9am to 1pm and 1:30 to 5:30pm. There is another tourist office on Via Garibaldi 12R (☎ 010/557-2903), open daily 9am to 1pm and 2:30 to 6pm.

SAFETY The harbor, particularly after dark, isn't for the squeamish. If you go wandering, don't go alone and don't carry valuables. Genoa is rougher than Barcelona, more comparable to Marseille. A woman is likely to lose her purse not only in the harbor area but on any side street running downhill if she doesn't take precautions.

[FastFACTS] GENOA

Currency Exchange **Currency exchange** is available at **Cambiavalute Canepa,** Via Gramsci 217R (☎ **010-2462805;** www.cambiocanepa.com), open Monday to Friday from 8am to 6:30pm, and Saturday and Sunday 8:30am to 5:30pm. There are also exchange offices at the Principe rail station, open daily 7am to 10pm.

Emergencies For emergency assistance, dial ☎ **113** at any time from any phone in Genoa. For automobile trouble, call **ACI,** Soccorso Stradale, at ☎ **803116.**

Hospital The city's largest hospital, **Ospedale San Martino,** Largo Benzi Rosanna 10 (☎ **010-5551**), maintains a roster of emergency services and can link you with an appropriate specialist.

Pharmacy At least one of Genoa's pharmacies remains open 24 hours, based on a revolving schedule that changes from week to week. One of the largest of the city's pharmacies is **Pescetto,** Via Balbi 185R (☎ **010-261609**), across from the Principe rail station.

Taxi To call a **taxi,** dial ☎ **010-5966.**

Seeing the Sights

Like a half-moon, the port encircles the Gulf of Genoa. Its hills slope down to the water, so walking is an up- and downhill affair. Genoa invites exploring at random more than any other port city along Italy's western coastline. Broad traffic-filled boulevards give way to dark and twisting *vicoli,* or alleyways, which offer intrigue and interest at every turn (and danger at night from muggers). The center of the city's maritime life, the harbor in particular is worth a stroll. Sailors from many lands search for adventure and women in the little bars and cabarets occupying the back alleys.

Most of the section of interest lies between the two rail stations, **Stazione Principe,** on the western fringe of the town near the port, and **Stazione Brignole,** to the northeast, opening onto Piazza Verdi. A major artery is **Via XX Settembre,** running between Piazza Ferrari in the west and Piazza della Vittoria in the east. **Via Balbi** is another major artery, beginning east of Stazione Principe, off Piazza Acquaverde. Via Balbi ends at Piazza Nunziata.

From here, a short walk along Via Cairola leads to the most important street in Genoa, **Via Garibaldi,** the street of patricians, on which noble Genovese families erected splendid *palazzi* in late Renaissance times. The guiding hand behind the general appearance and most of the architecture was Alessi, who grew to fame in the 16th century (he studied under Michelangelo). Aside from the

Genoa's twisting alleyways.

art collections housed in the **Palazzo Bianco** and **Galleria Civica di Palazzo Rosso** (see below), the street contains a wealth of treasures. The **Palazzo Podesta,** no. 7, hides a beautiful fountain in its courtyard, and the **Palazzo Tursi,** no. 9, now housing the municipal offices, proudly displays artifacts of famous Genoans, such as letters written by Christopher Columbus and the violin of Niccolò Paganini (which is still played on special occasions). Palazzo Tursi is open Tuesday to Friday 9am to 7pm, Saturday and Sunday 10am to 7pm. Admission costs 8€.

The present harbor is the result of extensive rebuilding, following massive World War II bombardments that crippled its seaside. The best way to view the overall skyline is from a **harbor cruise.** Hour-long cruises on one of the boats in the fleet of the **Consorzio Liguria Via Mare** (© **010-265712;** www.liguria viamare.it) provide a close look at the harbor bustle and at the **Lanterna,** the 110m-tall (360-ft.) lighthouse built in 1544. Boats embark daily at 9:30am from Acquario di Genova. The cruises cost 7.50€.

Acquario di Genova ★★★ ☺   The largest aquarium in Europe and one of the biggest attractions in the country, this site explores the great richness of marine life. Opened as part of EXPO '92, to celebrate the 500th anniversary of Columbus's arrival in the New World, the 40-tank aquarium is styled like a mammoth ship ready to set sail. Allow at least 3 hours for this attraction, including the recent addition of a new exhibition center called the Big Blue Ship.

The different exhibits range the world, capturing marine life from the great coral reefs to the tropical rainforests of the Amazon River basin. Almost every known sea creature you'd want to meet (and some you wouldn't!) is on display. It's about a 15-minute walk from Stazione Principe.

Ponte Spinola. ℂ **010-2345678.** www.acquariodigenova.it. Admission 18€ adults, 12€ ages 4–12, free for ages 3 and under. Mon–Fri 9am–9:30pm; Sat–Sun 8:45am–9:30pm. Bus: 1, 12, or 13.

Cattedrale di San Lorenzo & Campanile ★★   Genoa is noted for its medieval churches, and this one towers over them all. A British shell fired during World War II almost spelled its doom, but the explosive never went off. The cathedral is distinguished by its bands of black-and-white marble adorning the **facade ★★** in the Pisan style. In its present form, it dates from the 13th century, although it was erected on the foundation of a much earlier structure. Alessi designed the dome, and the campanile (bell tower) dates from the 16th century. The **Chapel of John the Baptist (Cappella di San Giovanni) ★**, with interesting Renaissance sculpture, is said to contain the remains of the saint for whom it's named. Off the nave and in the vaults, the cathedral **treasury** contains a trove of artifacts acquired during Genoa's heyday as a mercantile empire. Some of the claims are a bit hard to believe, however (there's a crystal dish reputed to have been used for dinner service at the Last Supper and a blue chalcedony platter on which the head of John the Baptist was allegedly placed for its delivery to Salome). Other treasures include an 11th-century arm reliquary of St. Anne and a jewel-studded Byzantine Zaccaria Cross.

Piazza San Lorenzo, Via Tommaso Reggio 17. ℂ **010-265786.** Admission 4.50€. Mon–Sat 9am–noon and 3–6pm. Bus: 42.

The black-and-white marble facade of Cattedrale di San Lorenzo.

Genoa from on High

From Piazza Portello (at the eastern end of Via Garibaldi) a funicular climbs to the **Castelletto Belvedere**, which offers stunning views and refreshing breezes. The trip costs .70€ each way and runs daily from 7am to 12:30am.

A similar climb is via the **Granarolo** funicular, leaving from Piazza del Principe, behind the rail station, and ascending 305m (1,000 ft.) to Porto Granarolo, one of the gates in the city's 17th-century walls; there's a parklike belvedere in front. It costs 1.20€ each way and operates every 15 minutes daily from 5:40am to 8:40pm.

Civic Gallery of the Red Palace (Galleria Civica di Palazzo Rosso) ★

This 17th-century palace was once the home of the Brignole-Sale, a local aristocratic family that founded a Genovese dynasty. It was restored after having been bombed in World War II and now contains a good collection of paintings, with such exceptional works as *Giuditta* by Veronese, *St. Sebastian* by Guido Reni, and *Cleopatra* by Guercino. The best-known works are Sir Anthony van Dyck's portrait of Pauline and Anton Giulio Brignole-Sale from the original collection and the magnificent frescoes by Gregorio de Ferrari (*Spring* and *Summer*) and Domenico Piola (*Autumn* and *Winter*). There are also collections of ceramics and sculpture, and a display of gilded baroque statuary. Across from this red palace is the white palace, the Museo Civico di Palazzo Bianco (see below).

Via Garibaldi 18. ✆ **010-2476351.** Admission 8€. Tues–Fri 9am–7pm; Sat–Sun 10am–7pm. Bus: 17, 18, 19, 20, or 41.

Civic Museum of the White Palace (Museo Civico di Palazzo Bianco) ★

The duchess of Gallier donated this palace, along with her art collection, to the city. Although the palace dates from the 16th century, its appearance is the work of later architects and reflects the most recent advances in museum planning. The most significant paintings from the Dutch and Flemish schools include Gerard David's *Polittico della Cervara* and Memling's *Jesus Blessing the Faithful,* as well as works by Sir Anthony van Dyck and Peter Paul Rubens. A wide-ranging survey of European and local artists is presented, with paintings by Caravaggio, Zurbarán, and Murillo. You'll also find works by Bernardo Strozzi (a whole room) and Alessandro Magnasco (an excellent painting of a scene in a Genovese garden).

Via Garibaldi 11. ✆ **010-5572193.** Admission 8€. Tues–Fri 9am–7pm; Sat–Sun 10am–7pm. Bus: 17, 18, 19, 20, or 40.

National Gallery (Galleria Nazionale) ★

This gallery houses a major art collection. Its notable works include Joos van Cleve's *Madonna in Prayer,* Antonello da Messina's *Ecce Homo,* and Giovanni Pisano's *Giustizia.* The gallery is also known for its decorative arts (furniture, silver, and ceramics, among other items). The palace itself was designed for the Grimaldi family in the 16th century as a private residence, although the Spinolas took it over eventually.

In the Palazzo Spinola, Piazza della Pelliceria 1. ✆ **010-2705300.** www.palazzospinola.it. Admission 4€. Tues–Sat 8:30am–7:30pm; Sun 1:30–7:30pm. Bus: 17, 18, 19, 20, or 41.

Royal Palace Museum (Museo di Palazzo Reale) ★ A 5-minute walk from Stazione Principe, the Royal Palace was started in about 1650, and work continued until the early 18th century. It was built for the Balbi family, was sold to the Durazzos, and became one of the royal palaces of the Savoias in 1824. King Charles Albert modified many of the rooms around 1840. As in all Genovese *palazzi*, some of these subsequent alterations marred the original designs. Its gallery is filled with paintings and sculpture, works by van Dyck, Tintoretto, G. F. Romanelli, and L. Giordano. Frescoes and antiques from the 17th to the 19th centuries are displayed. Seek out, in particular, the **Hall of Mirrors** and the **Throne Room.**

Via Balbi 10. ☎ **010-2710236.** www.palazzorealegenova.it. Admission 4€. Tues–Wed 9am–1:30pm; Thurs–Sun 9am–7pm. Bus: 20 or 35.

Where to Stay

Generally, hotels in Genoa are second-rate, but some good finds await those who search diligently.

Warning: Avoid some of the cheap hotels and *pensioni* around the waterfront. Stick with our recommendations below, which are suitable even for women traveling alone.

EXPENSIVE

Bentley Hotel ★★★ If you want to wrap yourself in luxury, Genoa's latest five-star hotel is your finest choice. In what was the headquarters of Ilva, Italy's biggest iron and steel manufacturer, a posh bastion of charm and grace has been installed in one of Genoa's best examples of the complete makeover of a building. In the exclusive Carignano district, the hotel lies on a tree-flanked highway leading down to the Port of Genoa. The facade is a stunning display of German modernism, covered in green marble with plaster strips of sculpted friezes. Genoa hasn't had a five-star hotel since 1985 when Columbia di Principe closed. The bedrooms are classic studies in modern design, using warm colors of fabrics in platinum, titanium, silver gray, and copper. Bathrooms are in crystal white with antique brown marble walls. The most comfortable beds in Genoa rest on natural oak floors, the walls decorated with original photographs by some of the world's most renowned artists. If money is not an object, go for one of the very luxurious deluxe accommodations with panoramic rooms and far more living space.

Via Corsica 4, Carignano. ☎ **010/5315111.** Fax 010/5315800. www.bentley.thi.it. 99 units. 188€ double; 255€ junior suite; from 500€suite. AE, DC, MC, V. Parking 35€. Bus: 35. **Amenities:** Restaurant; bar; airport transfers (55€); babysitting; exercise room; Jacuzzi; indoor heated pool; room service; sauna; Wi-Fi (13 € per 24 hr.). *In room:* A/C, TV, hair dryer, minibar.

MODERATE

Bristol Palace ★ The late-19th-century Bristol boasts a number of features that'll make your stay in Genoa special, even though it's in the grimy heart of the old town. Its obscure entrance behind colonnades is misleading; the public rooms are decorated nicely with traditional pieces, although both the fabrics and the furnishings are beginning to show their age. The larger of the guest rooms have an old-fashioned elegance, often with chandeliers, Queen Anne desks, and padded headboards. All the soundproof rooms contain at least one antique and often several. The bathrooms are generally large; some come with whirlpool tubs. The hotel's stairway is one of the most stunning in Genoa.

Via XX Settembre 35, 16121 Genova. ℰ **010-592541.** Fax 010-561756. www.hotelbristolpalace. com. 133 units. 166€–470€ double; from 500€ suite. Rates include buffet breakfast. AE, DC, MC, V. Parking 25€. Bus: 17, 18, or 19. **Amenities:** Restaurant; bar; babysitting; Internet (free, in lobby); room service. *In room:* A/C, TV, hair dryer, minibar, Wi-Fi (in some; 7€ per 24 hr.).

Columbus Sea Hotel ★   One of the best moderately priced hotels in town, the Columbus Sea looks out at the cruise-ship terminal. It's warmer and more inviting inside than its cold, boxy exterior suggests, with guest rooms that are spacious for the most part, in muted colors with Oriental carpeting. The public rooms are more gracious, with a certain flair.

Via Milano 63, 16126 Genova. ℰ **010-265051.** Fax 010-255226. www.columbussea.com. 80 units (shower only). 95€–281€ double. Rates include buffet breakfast. AE, DC, DISC, MC, V. Free parking. Bus: 1, 3, 7, 8, 18, 19, 20, 30, or 34. **Amenities:** Restaurant; bar; babysitting; room service. *In room:* A/C, TV, hair dryer, minibar, Wi-Fi (15€ per 24 hr.).

Locanda di Palazzo Cicala ★★🏠   This restored 17th-century *palazzo* in the historic center opposite San Lorenzo Cathedral is the most romantic hotel in the city, and Genoa's only boutique hotel. The facade is graced with stucco and the remains of a medieval loggia overlooking Piazza Duomo. The interior has been restored with large, bright rooms with high arched ceilings and a scattering of antiques. Modern furnishings have been discreetly inserted against a backdrop of rich stucco work and architectural embellishments.

Piazza San Lorenzo 16, 16123 Genova. ℰ **010-2518824.** Fax 010-2467414. www.palazzocicala.it. 11 units. 179€–391€ double; 219€–445€ suite. Rates include buffet breakfast. AE, DC, MC, V. Parking nearby 16€. Bus: 18, 20, 35, or 37. **Amenities:** Babysitting; room service. *In room:* A/C, TV, hair dryer, minibar, Wi-Fi (free).

NH Plaza ★   A member of the NH chain, this hotel is newer than its modified classic facade would suggest. Near Piazza Corvetto, it was built in 1950 to replace an older hotel destroyed during a World War II air raid. In 1992, the hotel was renovated and enlarged, linking two former hotels, the Baglioni Eliseo and the Plaza. The rooms in the old Eliseo are generally more spacious than those in the Plaza (and better decorated). Elegant touches include mother-of-pearl inlay in the doors and marble bathrooms.

Via Martin Piaggio 11, 16122 Genova. ℰ **010-83161.** Fax 010-8391850. www.nh-hotels.it. 143 units (shower only). 109€–339€ double; from 299€ suite. Rates include buffet breakfast. AE, DC, MC, V. Parking 20€ nearby. Bus: 18, 34, or 37. **Amenities:** Restaurant; bar; babysitting; concierge; room service; Wi-Fi (5€ per 30 min.). *In room:* A/C, TV, hair dryer, minibar.

Villa Pagoda ★★ 🏠   Another romantic place to stay in the area, ideal for motorists, is this elegant Asian-styled villa built by a wealthy merchant hoping to lure his Chinese mistress west. Much of the original charm remains, including Murano chandeliers from Venice, Carrara marble, antiques, and beautiful silk fabrics. The villa stands in the garden suburb of Nervi, 11km (6¾ miles) to the east of Genoa. Each room is individually decorated with antiques or elegant reproductions; everything is tasteful and inviting.

Via Capolungo 15, 16167 Genova Nervi. ℰ **010-3726161.** Fax 010-321218. www.villapagoda.it. 17 units. 135€–275€ double; 285€–650€ suite. AE, DC, MC, V. Free parking. Bus: 517 from the center of Genoa. **Amenities:** Restaurant; bar; babysitting; outdoor freshwater pool; room service; outdoor tennis court. *In room:* A/C, TV, hair dryer, minibar, Wi-Fi (5€ per hr.).

INEXPENSIVE

Hotel Agnello d'Oro 🗡 This is one of Genoa's best bargains. When the Doria family owned this structure and everything around it in the 1600s, they carved their family crest on the walls near the top of the alley. The symbol was a golden lamb, and you can still see one at the point where the narrow street joins the busy boulevard leading to Stazione Principe. The hotel, named after the animal on the crest, is a 17th-century building that includes vaulted ceilings and paneling in the lobby. About half of the guest rooms are in a newer wing, but if you want the oldest ones, ask for room no. 6, 7, or 8.

Vico delle Monachette 6, 16126 Genova. ✆ **010-2462084.** Fax 010-2462327. www.hotelagnello doro.it. 38 units. 80€–120€ double. Rates include buffet breakfast. AE, DC, MC, V. Parking 20€. Bus: 18, 19, 20, 30, 32, or 41. **Amenities:** Bar; bikes; room service; Wi-Fi (free, in lobby). *In room:* A/C (in most), TV, hair dryer (in some), minibar.

Hotel Astoria Built in the 1920s but a hotel only since 1978, this place offers lots of polished paneling, wrought-iron accents, beige marble floors, and a baronial carved fireplace. The guest rooms are comfortably furnished and well maintained, with neatly kept bathrooms. The hotel sits on an uninspiring square that contains a filling station, and its view encompasses a traffic hub and many square blocks of apartment buildings.

Piazza Brignole 4, 16122 Genova. ✆ **010-873316.** Fax 010-8317326. www.hotelastoria-ge.com. 69 units. 120€–250€ double. Rates include breakfast. AE, DC, MC, V. Parking 15€. Bus: 18, 19, or 20. **Amenities:** Bar; room service. *In room:* A/C, TV, hair dryer, minibar, Wi-Fi (2€ per hr.).

Hotel Viale Sauli This hotel is on the second floor of a modern concrete office building, just off a busy shopping street. It's scattered over three floors, each reachable by elevator from the lobby. The high-ceilinged public rooms include a well-managed reception area. Enore Sceresini is the opera-loving owner, and his guests usually include businesspeople who appreciate cleanliness and comfort. Each guest room has marble floors and a spacious bathroom.

Viale Sauli 5, 16121 Genova. ✆ **010-561397.** Fax 010-590092. www.hotelsauli.it. 56 units (shower only). 75€–180€ double. Rates include breakfast. AE, DC, MC, V. Parking 20€ nearby. Bus: 33 or 37. **Amenities:** Bar; room service. *In room:* A/C, TV, hair dryer, minibar, Wi-Fi (free).

Where to Dine

Fast food is a Genoese specialty, and any number of storefronts dispense *focaccia,* the heavenly Ligurian raised bread stuffed with cheese and topped with herbs, olives, onions, and other vegetables.

Another Genovese favorite is *farinata,* a cross between a ravioli and a crepe, made from chickpea flour and stuffed with spinach and ricotta, lightly fried, and often topped with walnut-cream sauce. Locals say that this delicious concoction gets no better than at **Antica Sciamada,** Via San Giorgio 14R.

Da Giacomo ★ LIGURIAN Lots of foodies think that Da Giacomo is the best restaurant in Genoa. The service is excellent, as is the modern dining room, graced with plants. Ligurian cooking is dominated by the sea, and the menu begins with superb seafood antipasti, some of which is raw, carved with the exquisite care that you find in Tokyo. Meat, fish, and poultry dishes are prepared with unusual flair. Pesto accompanies many dishes, especially the pasta. (During the Crusades, it was reported that the Genovese contingent could always be identified by the aroma of pesto surrounding them.) Specialties include spaghetti with clams, zucchini, and tuna roe; whole-grain vermicelli with shrimp and vegetables; grilled squid with cherry tomatoes and basil; and finally, grilled filet of veal with a balsamic-cream sauce. Guests can choose from some of the finest regional wines in Italy, and the desserts are made fresh daily. There's also a piano bar where you can dance.

Corso Italia 1R. ☎ **010-311041.** www.ristorantedagiacomo.it. Reservations recommended. Main courses 16€–20€; fixed-price menu 45€–60€. AE, DC, MC, V. Mon–Fri 12:30–3pm and 8–11pm; Sat 8–11pm. Bus: 31.

Gran Gotto ★★★ SEAFOOD   This longtime favorite opened in 1937 and has been in the same family since. The emphasis is on seafood, but the meat and pasta dishes aren't neglected. The most typical offering is *trenette al pesto,* paper-thin noodles served with pesto. A succulent pasta dish is prepared with basil, shrimp, and pine nuts. The main dishes often feature the catch of the day, perhaps a white fish *(totanetti)* prepared with leeks and zucchini. The meat specialties are filet of lamb in a red-wine sauce and filet of Chianina beef with juniper berries and red-onion jam. The *zuppa di pesce* (fish soup) makes a wonderful lunch.

Viale Brigata Bisagno 69R. ☎ **010-583644.** Reservations recommended. Main courses 13€–25€. AE, DC, MC, V. Mon–Fri 12:30–2:30pm and 7:30–10:30pm; Sat 7:30–10:30pm. Closed Aug 12–31. Bus: 31.

I Tre Merli Antica Cantina ★ 🏠 GENOVESE   If you, like us, have a passion for drinking and dining in wine bars, your best bet in Genoa is this local favorite. A short distance from Via Aurea, it is recognized as a *vineria* of the highest quality, with a *carte* featuring 300 different wines, all stored in a converted 14th-century well. This is the same chain that offers four restaurants in Manhattan. You'll find it on a narrow street off Via Garibaldi. It has all the cozy trappings you'd associate with a wine bar: provincial tables and chairs, a mellow old stone floor, and walls of stone and red brick. You can sit at the bar or occupy one of the tables, selecting from a choice of local gastronomic specialties. These include such appetizers as octopus in aspic with an olive pâté, or paper-thin slices of marinated raw beef with grilled fresh cheese. Among the more tempting main courses are chestnut lasagna or stewed dried codfish Genovese style with pine nuts and aromatic herbs.

Vico Dietro il Coro della Maddalena 26R. ☎ **010-2474095.** www.itremerli.it. Main courses 12€–22€. AE, DC, MC, V. Mon–Fri 12:30–3pm and 7:30–11pm; Sat 7:30–11pm. Bus: 18 or 20.

Le Rune 🍴 LIGURIAN   This is a simple *trattoria* beloved by locals who know it for its fine take on regional cooking, using market-fresh ingredients. Often it's visited by opera-goers attending the nearby Teatro Carlo Felice. In the historic center of Genoa, the restaurant has four dining rooms, tables resting on terra-cotta floors. Try such specialties as roast sea bass with zucchini or beef filet served with green apples, porcini mushrooms, and duck liver. One of the best pasta dishes is *taglierini* with fresh scampi and mushrooms, or else you might try octopus *carpaccio* with potatoes and salted stockfish in a delectable walnut sauce. For us, the best dessert is the freshly made chocolate cake with a *zabaione* sauce.

Vico Domoculta 14R. ☎ **010-594951.** Reservations recommended. Main courses 9€–20€. MC, V. Mon–Fri 12:30–2:30pm and 7:30–10:30pm, Sun 7:30–10:30pm. Closed Sat. Bus: 20, 30, or 33.

Ristorante Saint Cyr LIGURIAN/PIEDMONTESE   At lunch, this place buzzes with talk of business deals; dinnertime brings a crowd of locals here to enjoy dishes adapted from regional recipes. Menu items change daily, although recent offerings featured rice with truffles and cheese, a timbale of fresh spinach, a charlotte of fish, and a variety of braised meats, each delicately seasoned. Specialties include *scamone* (a certain cut of beef) cooked in Barolo wine and *ravioli al sugo di carne* (with a sauce made from meat juices).

Piazza Marsala 4. ☎ **010-886897.** Reservations required. Main courses 14€–25€; 2-course fixed-price menu 35€. AE, DC, MC, V. Mon–Fri noon–3pm; Mon–Sat 8–11pm. Closed Dec 24–Jan 7 and 1 week in Aug. Bus: 33, 34, or 36.

Ristorante Zeffirino LIGURIAN   In a cul-de-sac off one of the busiest boulevards, this place has hosted everyone from Frank Sinatra and Luciano Pavarotti to the late Pope John Paul II and Liza Minnelli. At least 14 members of the Zeffirino family prepare the best pasta in the city, using recipes collected from all over Italy. These include lesser-known varieties such as *quadrucci, pettinati,* and *cappelletti,* as well as the more familiar *tagliatelle* and lasagna. Next, you can select from a vast array of meat and fish, along with 1,000 kinds of wine. Nothing is better than the grilled fish of the day, cooked to your specifications, or the tasty lobster.

Via XX Settembre 20. ☎ **010-591990.** www.zeffirino.com. Reservations recommended. Main courses 14€–35€; 2 fixed-price menus 40€ and 60€. AE, DC, MC, V. Daily noon–midnight. Bus: 14, 19, 20, 30, 33, or 44.

Shopping

Shopping in Genoa includes a good selection of apparel, antiques, jewelry, and foodstuff. Classic but contemporary **Berti,** Via XII Ottobre 94R (☎ **010-540026;** www.bertigenova.com), carries a line of Aquascutum items, as well as Italian-inspired creations by designers such as Antonio Fusco. Elegant **Pescetto,** Via Scurreria 8R (☎ **010-2473433;** www.pescetto.it), offers men's and women's designer outfits and fragrances, plus accessories such as leather bags and wallets.

On a street overrun with goldsmiths, the reputable **Codevilla,** Via della Orefici 53R (☎ **010-2472567;** www.luigicodevilla.it), fashions jewelry and small objects out of gold and silver, along with a wide variety of precious and semi-precious stones.

In the historic center of town, the **Dallai Libreria Antiquaria,** Piazza de Marini 11R (☎ **010-2472338**), handles first editions and rare books and prints from the 18th and 19th centuries.

Antique book for sale at Dallai Libreria Antiquaria.

Pecchioli, Via Pisa 13 (*℃* 010-3625082; www.pecchioli.it), sells upscale dinnerware and cookware of ceramic, crystal, and silver.

If you'd rather have a one-stop shopping excursion, **La Rinascente,** Via Ettore Vernazza 1 (*℃* 010-586995; www.rinascente.it), and **Coin,** Via XX Settembre 16A (*℃* 010-5705821; www.coin.it), are the two biggest department stores in town.

Mercato Orientale ★, the sprawling food market, might not be as exotic as it was back in its heyday of the 17th century, but it is still one of Europe's greatest and most colorful markets. It's also full of great photo opportunities: You can capture not only the bounty of the Ligurian countryside, including olives, fresh herbs, and citrus fruits, but also every known sea creature that's edible (many looking like they are

The entrance to the Teatro di Genova.

not for the faint of heart!). The market stands at the edge of the historic core of Genoa and Stazione Brignole on Via XX Settembre, close to Via Consolazione. We like to go early in the morning when it opens Monday through Saturday at 7am, although it is bustling and active until noon.

After you visit the market you can wander the streets just north of here, including **Via Colombo** and **Via San Vincenzo,** which are filled with shops that evoke the late Middle Ages. Each one is devoted to a different delight, from the finest of olive oils, canned pestos, and a series of bakeries and *pasticcerias* (pastry shops).

Most of Genova shops at a large mall, **Centro Commerciale Fiumara,** Via Fiumara, Genova Sampierdarena (www.fiumara.net), 10 minutes from the center. It boasts more than 110 stores, 20 restaurants, and a multiscreen cinema.

Genoa After Dark

In the performing arts, the outstanding venue is the national theater, **Teatro di Genova** ★, in residence in Teatro Carlo Felice, Passo Eugenio Montale 4 (*℃* 010-53811; www.carlofelice.it). With an international season, the theater presents Europe's leading playwrights, directors, and actors, as well as operas. Tickets are available at Galleria Cardinale Siri 6 (*℃* 010-589329) Tuesday to Saturday 11am to 6pm, and Sunday 1 to 4pm for matinees and 6 to 9pm for evening performances.

Another venue for concerts, dance events, and other shows is **Teatro della Corte,** Piazza Borgo Pila 42 (*℃* 010-5342200; www.teatrostabilegenova.it). Its ticket office is open Monday 10am to 7pm, Tuesday 8am to 9pm, Wednesday to Friday 10am to 9pm, Saturday 10am to 12:30pm and 3 to 9pm, and Sunday 3 to 6pm.

Warning: Keep your wits about you after dark in Genoa, especially in the labyrinthine alleys of the old medieval neighborhoods. The neighborhoods around the bus station and Piazza Matteotti are especially dubious; they're a center for the drug trade and prostitution.

You'll find enough discos to keep you occupied every night. The best of them is **Mako,** Via Podgora 17/R (☎ **010-367652;** www.makogenova.com), which has a piano bar, a disco, and a restaurant. On Friday and Saturday, a cover of 15€ is assessed.

Looking for a simple pint, some pub grub, and a dose of English humor? Head for the **Britannia Pub,** Vicolo della Casana, near Piazza de Ferrari (☎ **010-2474532**), where groups of friends fill a woodsy-looking setting.

RAPALLO ★

477km (296 miles) NW of Rome, 27km (17 miles) SE of Genoa, 161km (100 miles) S of Milan

Long known to the chic crowd that lives in the villas on its hillside, Rapallo occupies a remarkable site overlooking the Gulf of Tigullio. In summer the crowded heart of Rapallo takes on a carnival air, as hordes of sunbathers occupy the rocky sands along the beach. Other features that attract vacationers are an 18-hole golf course, as well as an indoor pool, a riding club, and a modern harbor.

Detail from the icon of the Virgin at the Montallegro Sanctuary.

You can also take a cable car or a bus to the **Montallegro Sanctuary (Santuario di Montallegro).** Inside this 16th-century church are some interesting frescoes and a curious Byzantine icon of the Virgin that allegedly flew here on its own from Dalmatia. The views over the sea and valleys are the main reason to come up here, and they're even more breathtaking from the summit of **Monte Rosa,** a short uphill hike away. There are many opportunities for summer **boat trips,** to Portofino and the Cinque Terre.

Rapallo's long history is often compared to Genoa's. It became part of the Repubblica Superba in 1229, but Rapallo had existed long before that. Its **cathedral** dates from the 6th century, when it was founded by the bishops of Milan. Walls once enclosed the medieval town, but now only the **Saline Gate** remains. Rapallo has also been the scene of many an international meeting, the most notable of which was the 1917 conference of wartime allies.

Today Rapallo is a bit past its heyday, although it was once one of Europe's most fashionable resorts, numbering among its residents Ezra Pound and D. H.

Lawrence. Other artists, poets, and writers have been drawn to its natural beauty, marred in part by a recent uncontrolled building boom brought on by tourism. At the innermost corner of the Gulf of Tigullio, Rapallo is still the most famous resort on the Riviera di Levante because of its year-round mild climate.

Essentials

GETTING THERE   Three **trains** from Genoa stop here each hour from midnight to 11pm, costing 2.40€ one-way. A train also links Rapallo with Santa Margherita every 30 minutes, costing 1.30€ one-way. For more information, dial ✆ **892021** in Italy. From Santa Margherita, a **bus** operated by ATP runs every 20 to 25 minutes to Rapallo, costing 1.20€ one-way and taking half an hour. The bus information office is at Piazza Vittorio Veneto in Santa Margherita (✆ **0185-288834;** www.tigulliotrasporti.it).

If you have a **car** and are coming from Genoa, go southeast along A12.

VISITOR INFORMATION   The **tourist office** at Lungomare Vittorio Veneto 7 (✆ **0185-230346**) is open Monday to Saturday 9:30am to 12:30pm and 2:30 to 5:30pm (summer daily 9:30am–12:30pm and 2:30–7:30pm).

Where to Stay

Excelsior Palace Hotel ★★★   Rapallo's most historic and elegant hotel is reigning once again over the Portofino Coast. Of course, Ernest Hemingway, the Duke of Windsor and Rita Hayworth no longer walk through the lobby, but the hotel has returned to some of the glory it knew when it opened in January 1901. Surrounded on three sides by the sea, this landmark fell into decay and closed in 1974. In its present incarnation, it was rebuilt inside and out, its original four floors becoming seven. The bedrooms are decorated sumptuously, all of them with a sea view. Its facilities are the best along the coast, including a beach club, panoramic swimming pool, "Beauty Farm" (spa), and its **Lord Byron restaurant,** celebrated for its Ligurian and Mediterranean cuisine.

Via San Michele di Pagana 8, 16035 Rapallo. ✆ **0185-230666.** Fax 0185-230214. www.excelsior palace.thi.it. 131 units. 130€–425€ double; from 820€ suite. Rates include buffet breakfast. AE, DC, MC, V. Parking 15€. **Amenities:** 2 restaurants; 2 bars; babysitting; exercise room; 2 freshwater pools (1 outdoor, 1 heated indoor); room service; spa. *In room:* A/C, TV, hair dryer, minibar, Wi-Fi (22€ per 24 hr.).

Hotel Miramare   On the water near a stone gazebo is this 1929 re-creation of a Renaissance villa, with exterior frescoes that have faded in the salt air. The gardens in front have been replaced by a glass extension that contains a dining area. The accommodations are well maintained and simple, comfortable, and high-ceilinged; many have iron balconies that stretch toward the harbor.

Lungomare Vittorio Veneto 27, 16035 Rapallo. ✆ **0185-230261.** Fax 0185-273570. www.miramare-hotel.it. 28 units (7 with shower only). 115€–170€ double. Rates include buffet breakfast. AE, DC, MC, V. Parking 10€. **Amenities:** Restaurant; babysitting; bikes; room service; Wi-Fi (free, in lobby). *In room:* A/C, TV, hair dryer, minibar.

Riviera ★ ✿   Ernest Hemingway came here in the winter of 1923 and wrote his famous short story "Cat in the Rain" at the hotel. Restored and modernized over the years, the Riviera is still going strong. An Art Nouveau–style building, the hotel stands along the waterfront, just steps from the railway station. The midsize bedrooms are comfortably furnished with wooden pieces resting on parquet floors. Some of the units open onto small balconies, and others are large enough to house small families.

Piazza 4 Novembre 2, 16035 Rapallo. ✆ **0185-50248.** Fax 0185-65668. www.hotelriviera rapallo.com. 20 units. 120€–165€ double; 145€–183€ junior suite. Rates include buffet breakfast. AE, DC, MC, V. Free parking. Closed Nov–Dec 14. **Amenities:** Restaurant; bar; babysitting; concierge; room service. *In room:* A/C, TV, hair dryer, minibar, Wi-Fi (free).

Where to Dine

Luca ★★ LIGURIAN   The most elegant restaurant at the resort offers the most refined cuisine. In the center of town, near the railway station, it opens onto Carlo Riva harbor. The big square dining room is adorned with a bright, nautical ambience with illuminated pictures of the port on its walls. The restaurant doesn't rest on its laurels but is continually improving and upgrading its cuisine. The market-fresh ingredients are deftly handled by the chefs. Try *taglierini* egg pasta with fresh tomatoes as well as the *totanini* (a local fish) cooked with fresh shrimp. The chefs are expert at combining different flavors, such as black gnocchi filled with shrimp and peas, or homemade lasagna with a fresh pesto sauce. The catch of the day is often oven baked and served with potatoes, olives, and pine nuts.

Via Langano 32. ✆ **0185-60323.** www.ristoranteluca.it. Reservations recommended. Main courses 10€–20€. MC, V. Wed–Mon noon–2:30pm and 6–11pm.

Ristorante da Monique SEAFOOD   This is one of the most popular seafood restaurants along the harbor, especially in summer, featuring a nautical decor and big windows overlooking the marina. As you'd expect, fish is the specialty, including seafood salad, fish soup, risotto with shrimp, spaghetti with clams or mussels, grilled fish, and both *tagliatelle* and scampi Monique. Some dishes might not always hit the mark, but you won't go wrong ordering the grilled fish.

Lungomare Vittorio Veneto 5. ✆ **0185-50541.** www.ristorantedamonique.com. Reservations recommended. Main courses 10€–20€. AE, DC, MC, V. Wed–Mon noon–2:30pm and 7:30–10pm. Closed Jan 7–Feb 10.

Ristorante Elite 🍴 SEAFOOD   This much-frequented restaurant is just up a busy avenue from the harbor; the pleasant room, hung with nautical items and paintings of local scenes, is a little less formal than the many seafood restaurants on the waterfront. Mainly fish is served; the offering depends on the catch of the day. Your dinner might consist of mussels marinara, minestrone Genovese style, risotto marinara, *trenette al pesto, scampi, zuppa di pesce,* turbot, or a mixed fish fry. A limited selection of standard meat dishes is available, too. At the peak of the midsummer invasion, the restaurant is likely to be open every day.

Via Milite Ignoto 19. ✆ **0185-50551.** www.eliteristorante.it. Reservations recommended. Main courses 10€–25€; 3 fixed-price menus at 21€, 26€, and 31€. AE, MC, V. Sept–June Thurs–Tues noon–2:30pm and 7:30–10pm; July–Aug daily noon–2:30pm and 7:30–10pm.

SANTA MARGHERITA LIGURE ★★

31km (19 miles) E of Genoa, 5km (3 miles) S of Portofino, 477km (296 miles) NW of Rome

Like Rapallo, Santa Margherita Ligure occupies a beautiful position on the Gulf of Tigullio. Its palm-fringed harbor is usually thronged with fun seekers, and the resort offers the widest range of accommodations in all price levels on the eastern Riviera. It has a festive appearance, with a promenade, flower beds, and palms swaying in the wind. As is typical of the Riviera, the town's sandy, pebbly beach is packed with a party crowd in fine weather. Santa Margherita Ligure is linked to Portofino by the narrow Corniche Road. The climate is mild, even in winter, drawing many retirees from northern Europe.

The town dates from A.D. 262. The official name of Santa Margherita Ligure was given to the town by Vittorio Emanuele II in 1863. Before that, it had many other names, including Porto Napoleone, an 1812 designation from Napoleon.

Essentials

GETTING THERE   Forty **trains** per day arrive from Genoa, costing 2.40€ one-way. The train station in Santa Margherita is at Piazza Federico Raoul Nobili. For more information, call ✆ **892021** in Italy. **Buses** run frequently between Portofino and Santa Margherita Ligure daily, costing 1.20€ one-way. You can also catch a bus in Rapallo to Santa Margherita for 1.20€; during the day one leaves every 20 to 25 minutes. For information, call ✆ **0185-288834.** If you have a **car,** take A12 southeast from Genoa. Servizio Marittimo del Tigullio **ferries** (✆ **0185-284670;** www.traghetti portofino.it) make hourly trips to both Rapallo and Portofino, the trip taking only 15 minutes to each resort.

The Corniche Road.

The **tourist office,** Via 25 Aprile 2B (✆ **0185-287485;** www.apttigullio.liguria.it), is open Monday to Saturday 9am to 12:30pm and 2:30 to 5:30pm.

Exploring the Town

Most visitors stroll along the palm-lined **waterfront** ★, with its array of fishing boats, yachts, marinas, and pebbly beaches. Many of the antique buildings are decorated with *trompe l'oeil* frescoes. The best cafes, and the best for people-watching, are on the two major sea-bordering squares, Piazza Vittorio Veneto and Piazza Martiri della Libertà.

Set in a scenic park, the **Villa Durazzo** ★, Via San Francesco 3 (✆ **0185-205449;** www.villadurazzo.it), is a 17th-century *palazzo* richly decorated with art, statues, tapestries, rare marbles, Venetian chandeliers, elaborate stucco work, and lacquered chinoiseries. On top of a hill overlooking the resort, it was the former living quarters of the Marquis Gio Luca Durazzo. The apartments on the second floor are especially beguiling and filled with antiques and paintings by 17th-century Genoese artists. With its rich vegetation the park is divided into three sections, one a romantic park, another an Italian garden, and finally, an English forest traversed by mosaic stone paths leading to a small orangery. Admission to Villa Durazzo costs 5.50€ adults, 3€ children 6 to 12, free for children under 6. Opening hours are: Summer: daily 9am to 1pm and 2:30 to 6:30pm. Winter: daily 9am to 1pm and 2 to 5pm.

Santa Margherita's other landmark of note is its **Basilica di Santa Margherita,** off the seafront on Piazza Caprera (✆ **0185-286555**). The interior is richly embellished, with Italian and Flemish paintings, along with relics of the saint for whom the town was named. Admission is free, and it's open daily from 8am to noon and 3 to 7pm.

Along the waterfront.

Where to Stay

VERY EXPENSIVE/EXPENSIVE

Grand Hotel Miramare ★★   The top hotel in town, this 1929 palace has kept up with the times better than has the Imperiale (see below). Its 1904 core was the home of Giacomo Costa, who transformed it into a hotel that attracted celebrities such as Sir Laurence Olivier and Vivien Leigh. It was from the terrace here in 1933 that Marconi succeeded in transmitting telegraph and telephone signals a distance of more than 145km (90 miles). Separated from a private stony beach by a busy boulevard, it's a 3-minute walk from the center of town. The guest rooms are classically furnished, with elegant beds. Even some of the standard rooms have large terraces with sea views.

Via Milite Ignoto 30, 16038 Santa Margherita Ligure. ☎ **800/223-6800** in the U.S., or 0185-287013. Fax 0185-284651. www.grandhotelmiramare.it. 84 units. 255€–445€ double; 610€–890€ suite. Rates include buffet breakfast. AE, DC, MC, V. Parking 25€–30€. **Amenities:** Restaurant; bar; babysitting; bikes; outdoor saltwater heated pool; room service; spa. *In room:* A/C, TV, hair dryer, minibar.

Imperiale Palace Hotel ★   The Imperiale looks like a gilded palace. Originally built in 1889 as a private villa, the palace was the setting for the signing of the Treaty of Rapallo, which marked the official ending of World War I. Although still regal, it's fading a bit, and the Miramare (see above) has overtaken it. It's built against a hillside at the edge of the resort, surrounded by semitropical gardens. The public rooms live up to the hotel's name, with vaulted ceilings, satin-covered antiques, ornate mirrors, and inlaid marble floors. The guest rooms vary widely, from royal suites to simple singles away from the sea. Many have elaborate ceilings, balconies, brass beds, chandeliers, and antique furniture, but others are rather sparse.

Via Pagana 19, 16038 Santa Margherita Ligure. ☎ **0185-288991.** Fax 0185-284223. www.hotel imperiale.com. 92 units. 320€–430€ double; 560€–850€ suite. Half board 65€–75€ per person extra. AE, DC, MC, V. Free parking. Closed Oct–Mar. **Amenities:** 2 restaurants; 2 bars; babysitting; exercise room; outdoor saltwater heated pool; room service; sauna. *In room:* A/C, TV, hair dryer, minibar.

MODERATE

Hotel Continental ★   The Continental is the only hotel in town that's right on the water, and the high-ceilinged public rooms give a glimpse of the gardens leading down to a private beach. The guest rooms are filled with comfortable, if somewhat faded, furnishings and often have French windows opening onto wrought-iron balconies. Try for a top-floor room in the main building (the annex contains lackluster lodgings). The view encompasses the curved harbor in the center of town.

Via Pagana 8, 16038 Santa Margherita Ligure. ☎ **0185-286512.** Fax 0185-284463. www.hotel-continental.it. 72 units. 120€–214€ double; 200€–470€ suite. Rates include buffet breakfast. AE, DC, MC, V. Parking 12€–18€. **Amenities:** Restaurant; bar; exercise room; room service; sauna; Wi-Fi (10€ per hr., in lobby). *In room:* A/C, TV, hair dryer, minibar.

Hotel Regina Elena ★   This pastel-painted Best Western hotel is along the scenic thoroughfare leading to Portofino. Guest rooms are modern, most opening onto a balcony with a sea view. Bathrooms are tidy. An annex in the garden contains additional units, but they're not as desirable. The hotel was built in 1908 and many turn-of-the-20th-century details remain, including a marble staircase. It's operated by the Ciana family, which has been receiving guests for almost 100 years.

Lungomare Milite Ignoto 44, 16038 Santa Margherita Ligure. ✆ **800/780-7234** in the U.S. and Canada, or 0185-287003. Fax 0185-284473. www.reginaelena.it. 104 units. 85€–300€ double with breakfast, 179€–380€ double with breakfast and dinner. AE, DC, MC, V. Parking 15€. **Amenities:** Babysitting; bikes; exercise room; Jacuzzi; outdoor heated pool; room service; Wi-Fi (10€ per hr., in lobby). *In room:* A/C, TV, hair dryer, minibar.

Park Hotel Suisse   Set in a garden above the town center, the Suisse features a panoramic view of the sea and harbor, which lie across the street. It has seven floors, all modern in design, with occasional deep private balconies that are like alfresco living rooms. The medium-size guest rooms that open onto the rear gardens, without a sea view, cost slightly less.

Via Favale 31, 16038 Santa Margherita Ligure. ✆ **0185-289571.** Fax 0185-1879900. www.park hotelsuisse.com. 80 units (shower only). 46€–110€ per person double. AE, DC, MC, V. Parking 12€. **Amenities:** 2 restaurants; babysitting; outdoor saltwater heated pool; room service. *In room:* A/C, TV, hair dryer, Wi-Fi (4€ per hr.).

INEXPENSIVE

Hotel Conte Verde 🏨   This renovated villa offers one of the warmest welcomes in town, with shuttered windows, flower boxes, and a small front garden where tables are set out for refreshments. Only 2 blocks from the sea, this third-class hotel has been revamped, and its guest rooms are simple but adequate, ranging from small to medium (the more spacious units also have terraces).

Via Zara 1, 16038 Santa Margherita Ligure. ✆ **0185-287139.** Fax 0185-284211. www.hotel conteverde.it. 31 units. 110€–230€ double. Rates include buffet breakfast. AE, DC, MC, V. Parking 15€. Closed Jan–Feb. **Amenities:** Bar; babysitting; exercise room; room service. *In room:* TV, hair dryer.

Hotel Jolanda   Since the 1940s, the Pastine family has welcomed visitors to its little hotel, a short walk from the sea on a peaceful little street. A patio serves as a kind of open-air living room. The guest rooms are comfortably furnished, ranging from small to medium.

Via Luisito Costa 6, 16038 Santa Margherita Ligure. ✆ **0185-287512.** Fax 0185-284763. www. hoteljolanda.it. 50 units. 104€–154€ per person standard double; 124€–164€ per person superior double; 144€–184€ per person suite. Rates include buffet breakfast. AE, DC, MC, V. Parking 20€. **Amenities:** Restaurant; bar; exercise room; Jacuzzi; room service; sauna. *In room:* A/C, TV, hair dryer, minibar, Wi-Fi (5€ per hr.).

Where to Dine

Ristorante il Faro ★ LIGURIAN/ITALIAN   The distinguished culinary background of the Fabbro family is reflected in one of the town's best restaurants. Roberto Fabbro sets a great table and feeds you well. The atmosphere is comfortable and cozy, and on any night 50 diners can be fed well. High-quality meats and fresh fish dishes are served with flair and style. Try the *gamberi alla Santa Margherita,* sweet grilled shrimp in light olive oil, lemon, and mint sauce. The sautéed fish from the Mediterranean is the way to go. Each dish is served with fresh vegetables cooked al dente, for the most part. The pastas are some of the resort's best, especially that Ligurian favorite *trenette,* with pesto made from the freshest and most aromatic basil.

Via Maragliano 24A. ☎ **0185-286867.** Reservations recommended. Main courses 12€–21€. AE, DC, MC, V. Wed–Mon noon–2:30pm and 7:30–10pm. Closed 2 weeks in Nov.

Trattoria Baicin 🐟 LIGURIAN   Husband-and-wife owners Piero and Car-mela Oppo make everything fresh daily, from fish soup to gnocchi, and still find time to greet diners at the door. You can get a glimpse of the sea if you sit at one of the tables out front. The owners/cooks are most happy preparing fish, which they buy fresh every morning; the sole, simply grilled, is especially good, and the *fritto misto di pesce* (fish fry) constitutes a memorable feast. Begin your meal with one of the pastas made that morning, especially if *trofie alla genovese* (gnocchi, potatoes, fresh vegetables, and pesto) is available.

Via Algeria 9. ☎ **0185-286763.** Main courses 9€–18€. AE, DC, MC, V. Tues–Sun noon–3pm and 7–10:30pm. Closed Jan 7–Feb 12.

Trattoria Cesarina SEAFOOD   This is a very nice *trattoria* beneath the arcade of a short but monumental street running into Piazza Fratelli Bandiere. In an atmosphere of bentwood chairs and discreet lighting, you can enjoy a variety of Ligurian dishes. Specialties include meat, vegetables, and seafood antipasti, along with such classic Italian dishes as *taglierini* with seafood and *pappardelle* (a flat noodle) in a fragrant sausage sauce, plus seasonal fish such as red snapper or dorado, best when grilled.

Via Mameli 2C. ☎ **0185-286059.** Reservations recommended, especially in midsummer. Main courses 12€–26€. AE, DC, MC, V. Mar–Dec Wed–Mon 12:30–2:30pm and 7:30–11pm; Jan–Feb Fri–Sun 12:30–2:30pm and 7:30–11pm. Closed Dec 21–30.

Santa Margherita Ligure After Dark

Nightlife here seems geared to sipping wine or cocktails on terraces with sea views, flirting with sunburned strangers, and flip-flopping along the town's sandy beachfront promenades. Folks congregate in the cafes that spill out into the town's two seaside squares, **Piazza Martiri della Libertà** and **Piazza Vittorio Veneto.** But if you want to put on your dancing shoes, head for **Disco Carillon,** Località Paraggi (☎ **0185-286721**), catering to dance and music lovers ages 20 to 40.

Looking for a completely unpretentious place to shoot some pool? Head for the **Old Inn Bar,** Piazza Mazzini 40 (☎ **0185-286041**), where you can play pool, drink bottled beers, and generally hang out with a crowd of young locals.

PORTOFINO ★★★

35km (22 miles) SE of Genoa, 171km (106 miles) S of Milan, 485km (301 miles) NW of Rome

Portofino is about 6km (3¾ miles) south of Santa Margherita Ligure, along one of the most beautiful coastal roads in Italy. Favored by the yachting set, the resort is in an idyllic location on a harbor, where the water reflects all the pastel-washed little houses. In the 1930s, it enjoyed a reputation with artists; over the next few decades, the town became known as a celebrity hide-out. Lots of famous names could be seen arriving by yacht, lounging poolside at the luxury hotels, and vacationing in private villas in the hills. And they do pour in—Portofino is almost too beautiful for its own good, and the crowds can be intense in the high season.

The thing to do in Portofino: Take a walk, preferably before sunset, leading toward the tip of the peninsula. When you come to the entrance of an old castle, **Castello Brown** (*C* **0185-267101;** www.castellobrown.it), step inside to enjoy a lush garden and the views of the town and harbor below; it's open daily from 10am to 7pm (to 5pm Oct–Apr), and admission is 4€. Continuing on, you'll pass old private villas, towering trees, and much vegetation before you reach the lighthouse (*faro*). Allow an hour at least. When you return to the main piazza, proceed to one of the two little bars, on the left side of the harbor, that rise and fall in popularity. Before beginning that walk to the lighthouse, however, you can climb the steps from the port leading to the little parish church of **San Giorgio,** built on the site of a sanctuary that Roman soldiers dedicated to the Persian god Mithras. From here you'll get a panoramic view of the port and bay.

In summer, you can also take **boat rides** around the coast to such points as San Fruttuoso. Or set out for a long hike on the paths crossing the Monte Portofino Promontory to the **Abbazia di San Fruttuoso,** about a 2-hour walk from Portofino. The tourist office provides maps.

Abbazia di San Fruttuoso.

Essentials

GETTING THERE   Take the **train** to Santa Margherita Ligure (see "Essentials," above); then continue the rest of the way by bus. ATP **buses** leave Santa Margherita Ligure once every 30 minutes bound for Portofino, costing 1.20€ one-way, and you can buy tickets aboard the bus. Call ℂ **0185-288834** for information and schedules. If you have a **car** and are in Santa Margherita, continue south along the only road, hugging the promontory, until you reach Portofino. In summer, traffic is likely to be heavy.

VISITOR INFORMATION   The **tourist office** is at Via Roma 35 (ℂ **0185-269024;** www.apttigullio.liguria.it). It's open daily in the summer from 10:30am to 1:30pm and 2:30 to 7:30pm; during the off season, it's open daily from 10am to 1pm and 1:30 to 5:30pm.

Where to Stay

Portofino just doesn't have enough hotels, and because of the high demand for rooms, they're all extremely expensive. In July and August, you might be forced to book a room in nearby Santa Margherita Ligure or Rapallo. Make your reservations as far in advance as possible.

Albergo Nazionale   At stage center right on the harbor, this old villa is modest yet well laid out. The suites are tastefully decorated, and the little lounge is a cozy gathering spot, with a brick fireplace, a coved ceiling, antique furnishings, and good reproductions. Most of the guest rooms, furnished in a mix of styles (hand-painted Venetian in some rooms), open onto a view of the harbor.

Vico Dritto 3, 16034 Portofino. ℂ **0185-269575.** Fax 0185-269138. www.nazionaleportofino.com. 12 units (shower only). 170€–400€ double. Rates include buffet breakfast. MC, V. Parking 20€ nearby. Closed Nov 23–Mar 10. **Amenities:** Room service; Wi-Fi (free, in lobby). *In room:* A/C, TV, hair dryer, minibar.

Eight Hotel Portofino ★   Only a 2-minute walk from the harbor, this chic little hotel lies on a tranquil back street and was created by joining two small town houses constructed in the 1800s. The four-story pink stucco building, so typical of Portofino, has been furnished with charming elegance. The bedrooms, often with canopied beds, are the epitome of taste and comfort, with parquet floors, natural fabrics, and painted wooden furniture. Some accommodations even have a Turkish bath, and there is a secluded garden out back.

Via del Fondaco 11, 16034 Portofino. ℂ **0185-26991.** Fax 0185-267139. www.eighthotels.it. 18 units. 300€–480€ double; 610€–810€ suite. Rates include buffet breakfast. AE, DC, MC, V. Closed Nov 7–Mar 7. Free parking. **Amenities:** Restaurant; bar; babysitting; bikes; concierge; Jacuzzi; room service. *In room:* A/C, TV, hair dryer, minibar, Wi-Fi (10€ per 24 hr.).

Hotel Eden   Just 46m (150 ft.) from the harbor in the heart of the village and set in a garden (hence its name), this hotel is a relatively moderately priced choice in an otherwise high-fashion resort town. Although it doesn't have a harbor view, there's a winning vista from the front veranda, where breakfast is served. The guest rooms are small and very simply furnished, although each has a comfortable bed. All have tidily kept bathrooms. *Warning:* Readers have complained that reservations sometimes aren't honored in high season.

Vico Dritto 20, 16034 Portofino. ☎ **0185-269091.** Fax 0185-269047. www.hoteledenportofino. com. 9 units (shower only). 140€–290€ double. Rates include buffet breakfast. AE, MC, V. Public parking 20€. **Amenities:** Bar; babysitting. *In room:* A/C, TV, hair dryer.

Hotel Splendido and Splendido Mare ★★★   This spectacular property, reached by a steep and winding road from the port, provides a luxury base. The four-story structure was built as a monastery during the Middle Ages, but has been a hotel since 1901. There are several levels of public rooms and terraces to maximize the views over the sea, which you'll also enjoy from the guest rooms. Each room is individually furnished. Some of the superior rooms are equipped with whirlpool tubs. The hotel has a 16-room annex down on the Piazzetta. It might look like a hostel on the outside, but the interior has the same glittering qualities as the main house. You can choose the Splendido Mare if you like to immerse yourself in village life, or retreat to the main house for more isolation.

Viale Baratta 16, 16034 Portofino. ☎ **800/223-6800** in the U.S., or 0185-267801. Fax 0185-267806. www.hotelsplendido.com. 66 units. 965€–1,505€ double; from 1,515€ suite. Rates at the Splendido Mare 610€–930€ double; from 1,100€ suite. AE, DC, MC, V. Rates at Splendido include half board; rates at Splendido Mare include buffet breakfast. Parking 22€. Closed Oct 18–Apr 22. **Amenities:** 2 restaurants; 2 bars; babysitting; concierge; exercise room; heated saltwater pool; room service; sauna; outdoor tennis court (lit). *In room:* A/C, TV/DVD, hair dryer, minibar, Wi-Fi only in Hotel Splendido (free).

Where to Dine

Da U'Batti SEAFOOD   Informal and colorful, this place is on a narrow cob-blestone-covered piazza a few steps above the port. A pair of barnacle-encrusted anchors hanging above the arched entrance hint at the seafaring specialties that have become the restaurant's trademark. Owner/sommelier Giancarlo Foppiano serves delectable dishes, which might include a soup of "hen clams," rice with shrimp or crayfish, or fish grilled with bay leaves and citrus. There is a good selection of grappa, as well as French and Italian wines.

Vico Nuovo 17. ☎ **0185-269379.** Reservations recommended. Main courses 15€–31€. AE, DC, MC, V. Tues–Sun noon–3pm and 8–11:30pm. Closed Nov to mid-Jan.

Delfino ★★ SEAFOOD   Opened in the 1800s on the village square that fronts the harbor, Delfino is Portofino's most fashionable dining spot (along with Il Pitosforo, below). It has a kind of rustic, informal chic and offers virtually the same type of food as Il Pitosforo, including *troffiette al pesto* (a regional pasta with basil, oil, and pine-nut sauce). The fish dishes are the best bets: *zuppa di pesce* (a soup made of fresh-caught fish with a secret spice blend) and spaghetti with shrimp, sole, squid, and other seafood. The chef also prides himself on his sage-seasoned *vitello all'uccelletto,* roast veal with a gamy taste. Try to get a table near the front so that you can enjoy (or at least be amused by) the parade of visitors and villagers.

Piazza Martiri Dell'olivetta 40. ☎ **0185-269081.** www.delfino-portofino.it. Reservations recommended Sat. Main courses 17€–33€. AE, DC, MC, V. Jan–Oct daily noon–3pm and 7–11pm.

Il Pitosforo ★★ LIGURIAN/ITALIAN   You have to climb some steps to reach this place, which draws raves when the meal is served and gasps when the tab is presented. Although it's not blessed with an especially distinguished decor, its position right on the harbor gives it all the natural charm it needs. Try the delectable Ligurian fish soup, *zuppa di pesce,* or go for the bouillabaisse. The pastas are especially tasty and include *lasagne al pesto*. Fish dishes feature mussels *alla marinara* and *paella valenciana* for two, and saffron-flavored rice studded with seafood and chicken. Some meat and fish dishes are grilled over hot stones; others are grilled over charcoal.

Molo Umberto I 9. ℂ **0185-269020.** www.delfino-portofino.it. Reservations required. Main courses 38€–52€. AE, DC, MC, V. Wed–Sun 7:30–11pm. Closed Oct–Feb.

Portofino After Dark

James Jones, the American novelist (1921–77) known mainly for his bestseller *From Here to Eternity* (1951), once called the snug little **La Gritta American Bar,** Calata Marconi 20 (ℂ **0185-269126**) "the nicest waterfront bar this side of Hong Kong." It is indeed very attractive, very friendly, and far enough along the harbor-side quay to be a little less hectic than other establishments. Stop by for a cocktail, coffee, or other libation (the floating terrace out front is perfect for a drink at sunset). Light fare, such as omelets and salads, is available and affordable. The crowd is often an interesting mix of celebrities, tourists, and U.S. Navy personnel—this is a legendary watering hole from way back. It's open in summer daily 9pm to 3am (in winter Fri–Wed).

Jolly American Bar, Calata Marconi 10 (ℂ **0185-269105**), is a chic place that draws the yachting crowd. The three-quarter-round banquettes inside are plush and comfortable, and unusual nautical engravings adorn the walls. From June to September, it's open daily 10am to 3am; October to May, hours are 10am to 3am Wednesday to Monday.

Portofino at night.

THE CINQUE TERRE ★★

Monterosso: 8km (5 miles) E of Genoa, 10km (6¼ miles) W of La Spezia

Among olive and chestnut groves on steep, rocky terrain overlooking the gulf of Genoa, the communities of Corniglia, Manarola, Riomaggiore, and Vernazza offer a glimpse into another time. These rural villages, inaccessible by car, make up an agricultural belt where garden and vineyard exist side by side. Together with their "city cousin" Monterosso, they're known as the Cinque Terre (five lands). The northernmost town, Monterosso, is the tourist hub of the region, with traffic, crowds, and the only notable glimpse of contemporary urban life here.

The area is best known for its culinary delights, culled from forest, field, and sea. Here the land yields an incredible variety of edible mushrooms. Oregano, borage, rosemary, and sage grow abundantly. The pine nuts essential to pesto are easily collected from the forests, as are chestnuts for making flour, and olives for the oil that is the base of all dishes. Garlic and leeks flavor sautéed dishes, and beets turn up unexpectedly in ravioli and other dishes. Fishing boats add their rich hauls of anchovies, mussels, squid, octopus, and shellfish. To pair with the cuisine, vineyards produce Sciacchetra, a DOC wine, rarer than many other Italian varieties because of the low 25% yield characteristic of the vermentino, bosco, and albarola grapes from which it's derived.

Most visitors explore the villages by excursion boat. To avoid the crowds and really get to know the region, take a hike along the walking paths that meander scenically for miles across the hills and through the forests.

Vineyards cling to the steep hills in Cinque Terre.

❶ Crinale Footpath
❷ Azzurro Footpath

The Cinque Terre

Brugnato

SP1

A12

E80

SP10

Beverino

SP34

San Cipriano

Montale

Pignone

SP1

Levanto

SP38

Pian di Barca

SP43

Sanctuary of Soviore

Ricco del Golfo di Spezia

SP17

To Pisa

SP10

❶ M. Malpertuso

SP15

Monterosso

Sanctuary of Reggio

Buon Viaggio

❷

M. Marvede

Vernazza

San Bernardino

SP51

SP1

Punta Mesca

Corniglia

Sanctuary of Salute Volastra

La Spezia

Gulf of Genoa

Manarola

Sanctuary of Montenero

Riomaggiore

Gulf of Spezia

Telegrafo

Biassa

Fezzano

Schiara

Ligurian Sea

Portovenere

Venice

0 100 Mi

0 100 Km

45 N.

Cinque Terre

Florence

Rome

40 N.

10 E

Isola Palmaria

I. del Tino

Essentials

GETTING THERE Hourly **trains** run from Genoa to La Spezia, a trip of 1½ hours, where you must backtrack by rail to any of the five towns that you want to visit. From La Spezia there are regular trains to the little towns of Cinque Terre. Once at Cinque Terre, local trains at the rates of one every 2 to 3 hours go between the five towns. Be careful, however, as some stop only in Monterosso and Riomaggiore. Don't expect views—the entire ride is within tunnels. For more information, dial ✆ **892021** in Italy.

If you have a **car** and are coming from Genoa, take A12 and exit at Monterosso. A gigantic parking lot accommodates visitors, who then travel between the towns by rail, boat, or foot. You can also park at other some other villages, including Manarola and Riomaggiore. The **Navigazione Golfo dei Poeti** plies the waters between Monterosso and Manarola or Riomaggiore eight times daily from April to October. For information and schedules, call ✆ **0187-732987,** or go to www.navigazionegolfodeipoeti.it. A one-way ferry ticket from Monterosso to Manarola costs 11€.

VISITOR INFORMATION The **APT office** for the five villages is in Monterosso, Via Fegina 38 (✆ **0187-817506;** www.cinqueterre.it). It's open Monday to Saturday 10am to 1pm and 2 to 6:30pm, and Sunday 10am to 1pm.

Exploring the Coast

Fourteen **walking trails** are laid out for exploring the wilds of the area; they're also a viable way to go from town to town. Walk these trails carefully and get local advice. Some are relatively easy, but others require the endurance of an Olympic athlete.

The easiest route if you want only a short, scenic walk without a major workout is to start at Riomaggiore and stroll to Manarola; it's an easy walk, and the trails are in good shape. If you continue on from Manarola to Corniglia, it's still pretty easy walking, but the trail begins to deteriorate slightly. From Corniglia to Vernazza is a steep walk that takes about 1½ hours, with the trail worsening as you go. The final section from Vernazza to Monterosso is a strenuous 2-hour climb on a narrow trail that's not at all well maintained. All these routes offer gorgeous scenery along the way.

The only sandy **beach** in the Cinque Terre is the crowded strand in **Monterosso,** where you can rent a

Corniglia, perched above the sea.

beach chair from a vendor for about 7€. **Guvano Beach** is an isolated pebbly strand that stretches just north of Corniglia and is popular with nudists. You can clamber down to it from the Vernazza-Corniglia path, but the drop is steep and treacherous. A weird alternate route takes you through an unused train tunnel, which you enter from a point near the north end of Corniglia's train station; you must ring the bell at the gated entrance and wait for the custodian, who will charge you 5€ for passage through the dimly lit 1.6km-long (1 mile) gallery that emerges onto the beach at the far end. There's a long rocky beach to the south of **Corniglia,** easily accessible by some downhill scrambles from the Corniglia-Manrola path. **Riomaggiore** has a tiny crescent-shaped beach reached by a series of stone steps on the south side of the harbor.

Where to Stay

IN CORNIGLIA

Albergo & Ristorante Cecio 🍴 Outside of the village on the road to Vernazza is one of the most durable inns in the area, an ideal spot for lodging or food during your Cinque Terre sojourn. This stone house, once the private home of an olive grower and his family, has been turned into a B&B, with four small, but comfortably furnished, bedrooms in the main building, plus another half-dozen scattered throughout the village. We prefer the accommodations in the main structure, because they open onto views of the water and the town itself. All have well-maintained private bathrooms. Even if you're not a guest, consider the on-site *ristorante,* where in fair weather, diners request a table on the flower terrace. Local seafood prepared according to old Ligurian recipes predominates on the menu.

Via Serra 58, 19010 Corniglia. ⓒ **0187-812043.** Fax 0187-812138. www.cecio5terre.com. 12 units (shower only). 60€ double. DC, MC, V. Closed Nov–Feb except for some weekend openings. **Amenities:** Restaurant; bar; room service. *In room:* No phone.

IN MONTEROSSO

A Cà du Gigante ★ 🎁
One of our favorite nests along Cinque Terrace is this little B&B. Linked with the excellent restaurant, **Miky** (see below), it offers newly furnished bedrooms that, although small, have Italian styling and flair, along with much comfort. Attached to each is a small tiled bathroom with shower, which is immaculately kept. Unlike many hotels along this coast, this inn is open year-round.

Via IV Novembre 11, 19017 Monterosso. ⓒ **0187-817401.** Fax 0187-817375. www.ilgigantecinque terre.it. 6 units. 90€–180€ double; 190€–220€ triple. Rates include buffet breakfast. Free parking. AE, DC, MC, V. Closed Jan 7 to mid-Feb. **Amenities:** Restaurant; bar; room service. *In room:* A/C, TV, fridge.

Hotel Baia
Opened in 1911, this hotel features a private beach and pleasant guest rooms where the whitewashed furniture lends an illusion of size and space. Each comes with a good bed and a small bathroom. What the hotel doesn't offer is air-conditioning or shuttle service, but the train station is steps away.

Lungomare Fegina 88, 19016 Monterosso. ⓒ **0187-817512.** Fax 0187-818322. www.baiahotel.it. 29 units (shower only). 110€–180€ double; 150€–200€ triple; 160€–220€ quad. Rates include buffet breakfast. AE, MC, V. Closed Nov to mid-Mar. Parking 12€. **Amenities:** Restaurant; bar; babysitting; room service; Wi-Fi (2.50€ per hr., in lobby). *In room:* TV, hair dryer, minibar.

Hotel Pasquale
This small hotel sits right by the beach, offering both intimacy and privacy because its few guest rooms are spread out across four floors. It's modern and has been decorated like a private Genovan home. Bedrooms are small but comfortable, each furnished with a tiled bathroom. The bar/restaurant is reminiscent of an Italian coffee shop, with gleaming marble floors, glass cases, dark-wood wainscoting, and a service counter accented with a brass rail and foot guard.

Via Fegina 4, 19016 Monterosso. ⓒ **0187-817477.** Fax 0187-817056. www.pasini.com. 15 units (shower only). 150€–200€ double; 185€–240€ triple. Rates include buffet breakfast. AE, MC, V. **Amenities:** Restaurant (for groups only); bar. *In room:* A/C, TV, hair dryer, minibar, Wi-Fi (6€ per 15 hr.).

Hotel Porto Roca ★★
You give up direct beach access to stay here, but it's a small price to pay for accommodations as gracious as these. The hotel is set on a cliff offering panoramic views of the village and harbor, and every corner is filled with antiques, knickknacks, and art. The guest rooms range from medium to spacious, each with a well-kept bathroom. The terrace is alive with lush greenery and an assortment of blossoming white flowers that complement the blue of the bay. The restaurant serves local seafood, and its large dining room offers privacy through the placement of columns and Liberty-style glass screens. In the bar,

furniture clusters create cozy pockets for chatting. Its fanciful fireplace adds warmth on cool days.

Via Corone 1, 19016 Monterosso. ℂ **0187-817502.** Fax 0187-817692. www.portoroca.it. 43 units. 170€–295€ double; from 550€ suite. Rates include buffet breakfast. AE, MC, V. Closed Nov–Mar. **Amenities:** Restaurant; babysitting; room service; sauna; Wi-Fi (7€ per hr., in lobby). *In room:* A/C, TV, hair dryer, minibar.

IN MANAROLA

Hotel Marina Piccola   With 10 rooms spread across five floors, this former home is a hotel as vertical as the town that houses it. There's a rustic charm to the small but serviceable guest rooms, which feature wrought-iron beds, old prints, and brass lamps.

Via Birolli 120, 19010 Manarola. ℂ **0187-920103.** Fax 0187-920966. www.hotelmarinapiccola. com. 13 units (shower only). 115€ double. Rates include continental breakfast. AE, DC, MC, V. Closed Nov. **Amenities:** Restaurant; bar. *In room:* A/C, TV, hair dryer.

IN MONTEROSSO

Casa dei Limoni   Set on a hill overlooking the town of Monterosso al Mare, this B&B is one of the finest in the area. The restored old farmhouse retains much of the original decor, though modern comforts have been added. Each of the comfortably furnished bedrooms opens onto view of the sea. At ground level, a beautiful terrace overlooks an ancient lemon grove. Olive trees and vineyards also surround the property.

Via Saviore 6, Località Balanello, 19016 Monterosso al Mare. ℂ **0187-818349.** www.casadei limoni.com. 6 units. 150€–170€ double; 230€ junior suite. Rates include buffet breakfast. MC, V. Parking 15€. *In room:* A/C, TV, fridge (in some), hair dryer.

IN RIOMAGGIORE

Villa Argentina   Perched at the top of a ridge overlooking the town, about a 5-minute steep hike with stairs from the center, this is a snug little retreat. It makes up in comfort what it lacks in style and decor. Request one of the units with balconies opening onto the port and the sea. Works of local artists are used for decor in the public rooms, and there is also a breeze-swept terrace, shaded by an arbor, with a bar area. Bedrooms are tiled but contain relatively simple furnishings. In lieu of air-conditioning, there is a ceiling fan in each room.

Via de Gasperi 170, 19017 Riomaggiore. ℂ **0187-920213.** Fax 0187-760531. www.villargentina. com. 15 units. 94€–139€ double. Rates include buffet breakfast. AE, MC, V. Parking 15€. **Amenities:** Bar; room service. *In room:* TV, hair dryer, minibar, no phone, Wi-Fi (free).

IN VERNAZZA

Albergo Barbara 🎁   Your window in this pleasant *pensione* will open onto one of the most enchanting views along the Cinque Terre. On the harbor square, Giuseppe and his Swiss wife, Patricia, run the inn. The place is simply furnished but clean, with adequate corridor bathrooms. Each bedroom is also equipped with its own sink. Try for room no. 8, which offers a particularly stunning vista, or for one of the larger doubles with a view. Breakfast isn't served but there are cafes nearby.

Piazza Marconi 30, Vernazza, Cinque Terre 19018. ℂ/fax **0187-812398.** www.albergobarbara.it. 10 units, 8 with private bathroom. 50€ double without bathroom; 60€–100€ double with bathroom. Major credit cards accepted to hold reservations only; payment is by cash only. Closed Dec–Feb 20. *In room:* No phone, Wi-Fi (free).

Where to Dine

IN CORNIGLIA

De Mananan ★ 🍴 SEAFOOD/LIGURIAN   The locals aren't quite sure when this old house in hilltop Corniglia was built. But of one thing they are certain: The couple that runs the place cooks and serves some of the best and most reasonably priced food along Cinque Terre. The small restaurant is found in the old cellars of this former home. The vegetables are grown along the coastline, and the fish freshly plucked from the sea. Dishes are prepared from old Ligurian recipes handed down from generation to generation. The moment you enter the dining room, you are greeted with the aromatic and basil-infused aroma of pesto, a sauce that will appear later whipped into your homemade pasta. Try the savory platter of steamed mussels, although we gravitate to the grilled catch of the day.

Via Fieschi 117, Corniglia. ✆ **0187-821166.** Reservations recommended. Main courses 12€–25€. AE, DC, MC, V. Wed–Mon 12:30–2:30pm and 7:30–9:30pm.

IN MONTEROSSO

Miky Ristorante ★ 🍽 LIGURIAN/SEAFOOD   Our favorite dining spot in Cinque Terre is this charming venue overlooking the sea. Stylish and sophisticated, it offers first-rate food using market-fresh ingredients. The choice of antipasti is the best in the area, and it's followed with a selection of succulent pastas homemade that day including linguine with lobster. Most diners revel in the freshly caught fish right off the coast. You can also select from the daily display of lobster and shellfish in a "boat" showcase. The fish is cooked according to old-fashioned Ligurian traditions, either salt-roasted or baked in a wood-burning stove. The fish soup deserves an award. Finish off with one of their homemade cakes.

Via Fegina 104. ✆ **0187-817401.** www.ristorantemiky.it. Reservations recommended. Main courses 10€–32€. AE, DC, MC, V. Daily noon–3pm and 7–10pm. Closed Tues in winter.

IN MANAROLA

Marina Piccola LIGURIAN   This simple and unpretentious restaurant is next to the inn of the same name (see "Where to Stay," above), right on the water. For a Ligurian palate tantalizer, try *cozze ripieni,* mussels cooked in white wine and served with butter sauce. Fresh sardines are a crowd-pleaser, and another homemade pasta, *trenette,* comes flavored with some of the best-tasting pesto on the coast. Grilled fish is the favorite for a main dish—always fresh and perfectly prepared, seasoned simply, as is the Ligurian style. Service can be a bit gruff.

Via Birolli 120. ✆ **0187-920103.** www.hotelmarinapiccola.com. Reservations recommended. Main courses 13€–24€. AE, DC, MC, V. Wed–Mon noon–3pm and 7–11pm.

IN RIOMAGGIORE

La Lanterna ★ LIGURIAN/SEAFOOD   Opening onto a terrace above Riomaggiore's boat-clogged harbor, this is one of the best seafood restaurants along the coast. You can even look out as local fishermen haul in the day's catch. The great appetizer here, beloved of locals, is the succulent seafood antipasti,

which comes in both small and large platters, the latter enough for a meal. Well-prepared pastas lure you into such dishes as gnocchi with fresh seafood or spaghetti with succulent mussels. The most exotic pasta on the menu is spaghetti with sea urchins (an acquired taste for some).

Via San Giacomo 46. © **0187-920589.** www.lalanterna.org. Reservations recommended. Main courses 8€–25€. Fixed-price menu 35€. AE, DC, MC, V. Daily noon–midnight. Closed Nov–Dec 6.

Seafood pasta at La Lanterna.

IN VERNAZZA

**Il Gambero Rosso ★ ** LIGURIAN/SEAFOOD   Opened over 100 years ago, this restaurant overlooks the sea at the harbor. Ask for a table on the terrace to make the most of this setting. The food is typically Ligurian, with house specialties such as ravioli stuffed with fresh fish. The wonderful porcini mushrooms that are harvested in the area figure into some dishes. Many of the recipes were passed from mother to daughter for generations, and a lot of the flavoring is based on the use of herbs and other ingredients that grow in the hills. The pesto is made with the best olive oil and mixed with basil, grated cheese, pine nuts, and fresh marjoram. Try the local fish of the day, which is baked with fresh tomatoes or potatoes. A recommended pasta is *trofie,* which is small and hand rolled like a tiny croissant; it's served with cubed potatoes, sliced green beans, and a basil-laced pesto.

Piazza Marconi 7. © **0187-812265.** www.ristorantegamberorosso.net. Reservations recommended Sat–Sun. Main courses 10€–25€. AE, MC, V. Tues–Sun 12:30–3pm and 7:30–10pm. Closed Nov–Feb.

14

CAMPANIA: NAPLES, POMPEII & THE AMALFI COAST

Campania is in many ways Italy's most memorable and beautiful region. It forms a fertile crescent around the bays of **Naples** and **Sorrento** and stretches inland into a landscape of limestone rocks dotted with patches of fertile soil. The geological oddities of Campania include a smoldering and dangerous volcano (famous for having destroyed **Pompeii** and **Herculaneum**), sulfurous springs that belch steam and smelly gases, and lakes that ancient myths refer to as the gateway to Hades. Its seaside highway is the most beautiful, and probably the most treacherous in the world, combining danger at every hairpin turn with some of Italy's most reckless drivers. Despite this, Campania is a captivating region, sought out by native Italians and visitors alike for its combination of earth, sea, and sky. Europe's densest collection of ancient ruins is here, each celebrated by classical scholars as among the very best of its kind.

The ancient Romans dubbed the land "Campania Felix" (pleasant countryside) and constructed hundreds of villas there. In some ways, the beauty of Campania contributed to the decay of the Roman Empire, as emperors, their senators, and their courtiers spent more time pursuing its pleasures and abandoning the cares of Rome's administrative problems. Even today, seafront land here is so desirable that hoteliers have poured their life savings into buildings that are sometimes bizarrely cantilevered above rock-studded cliffs. Despite an abundance of such hotels, they tend to be profitably overbooked in summer.

Campania is famous for its pizza.
PREVIOUS PAGE: A view of Positano from above.

Although residents of Campania sometimes stridently defend the cuisine, it's not the most renowned in Italy. The region's produce, however, is superb, its wine is heady, and its pizzas are memorable.

Today Campania typifies the conditions that northern Italians label "the problem of the south." Although the inequities are the most pronounced in Naples, the entire region outside the resorts along the

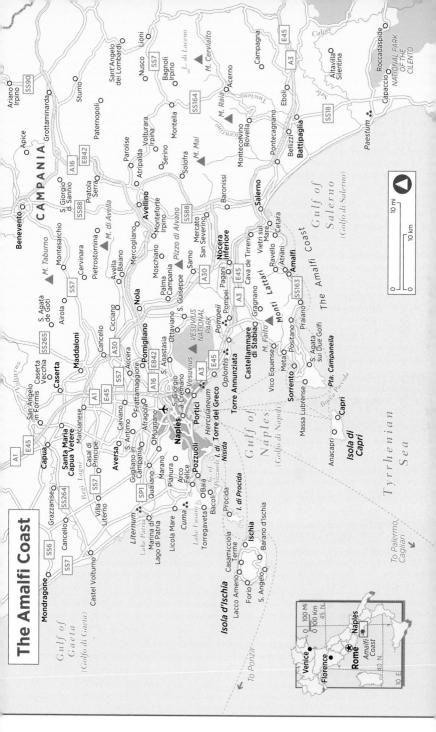

The Amalfi Coast

coast has a lower standard of living and education, higher crime rates, and less-developed standards of healthcare than the more affluent north.

When the English say "see Naples and die," they mean the city and the bay, with majestic Vesuvius in the background. When the Germans use the expression, they mean the **Amalfi Drive.** Indeed, several motorists die each year on the dangerous coastal road, which is too narrow to accommodate the stream of summer traffic, especially the large tour buses that almost sideswipe one another as they try to pass. When driving along the coast, you sometimes find it difficult to concentrate on the road because of the view. The drive, remarked André Gide, "is so beautiful that nothing more beautiful can be seen on this earth."

Sorrento and **Amalfi** are in the vanguard, with the widest range of facilities; **Positano** has more snob appeal and is popular with artists; and **Ravello** is still the choice of the discriminating few who desire relative seclusion. The gorgeous island of **Capri** (accessible by ferry from Sorrento or Naples) was known to emperors before international travelers discovered it. But the popularity of the resort-studded Amalfi Coast is a more recent phenomenon. It was discovered by German officers during World War II, and then later by American and English servicemen. When the war was over, many of these servicemen returned, often bringing their families. In time, the fishing villages became major tourism centers, with hotels and restaurants in all price ranges.

In addition to the stunning scenery and the lovely seaside towns, there are some world-class sightseeing attractions—the haunting ruins of **Pompeii** and the Greek temples of the ancient city of **Paestum** are among the highlights of all Italy.

NAPLES ★★

219km (136 miles) SE of Rome, 263km (163 miles) W of Bari

Naples (Napoli) is Italy's most controversial city: You'll either love it or hate it. It's louder, more intense, more unnerving, but perhaps ultimately more satisfying than almost anywhere else in Italy.

To foreigners unfamiliar with the complexities of all the "Italys" and their regional types, the Neapolitan is still the quintessence of the country and easy to caricature ("O Sole Mio," "Mamma Mia," bel canto). If Sophia Loren (a native who moved elsewhere) evokes the Italian woman for you, you'll find more of her look-alikes here than any other city. Naples also gave the world Enrico Caruso. Since 1995 the historic core of Naples has been listed as a World Heritage Site by UNESCO. Its setting on the Bay of Naples was hailed as idyllic.

Naples is the third most popular city in Italy and shares all of the troubles of such a huge, sprawling metropolis, including a high crime rate. Muggings are common, so be alert, of course, to your surroundings. Avoid wearing flashy or expensive jewelry, and keep wallets and handbags securely on your person.

Lately Naples has received a lot of bad press because of its garbage problem. Much of the beauty of the city is marred by mounds of trash seemingly piled everywhere, though largely outside of the most heavily tourist-trod areas. The Mafia is to blame, claim many Neapolitans, because its members control many aspects of city life, including sanitation. Local leaders have attacked the problem

The view from Naples's waterfront.

of trash on TV, but as of this writing, not much progress has been made toward a massive cleanup of this still beautiful but "trashed" city.

Essentials

GETTING THERE Domestic flights from Rome and other Italian cities put you into **Aeroporto Capodichino,** Via Umberto Maddalena (℡ **081-7896259;** www.gesac.it), 6km (3¾ miles) north of the city. To get to Piazza Garibaldi from the airport take the bus called Alibus. The bus fare is 1.10€; a **taxi** runs from 25€. Domestic flights are available on Alitalia, AirOne, and Meridiana. Flying time is 1½ hours from Milan, 1¼ hours from Palermo or Venice, and 50 minutes from Rome. ANM also makes the Alibus bus service from Piazza Municipio and Piazza Garibaldi to the airport. Departures are every 30 minutes daily from 6:30am to 11:30pm. An Alibus airport ticket costs 4€.

Frequent **trains** connect Naples with the rest of Italy. One or two trains per hour arrive from Rome, costing from 21€. EuroStar trains (marked ES) make limited stops, but Alta Velocità (AV) are high speed. Regular trains take from 2 to 2½ hours between Rome and Naples, the AV train takes only 1 hour. It's also possible to reach Naples from Milan in about 5 hours; cost is from 98€ one-way.

The city has two main rail terminals: **Stazione Centrale,** at Piazza Garibaldi, and **Stazione Mergellina,** at Piazza Piedigrotta. Most travelers will arrive at Stazione Central. For general rail information, call ℡ **892021** in Italy. The cost is .55€ per minute, plus .30€ per call fee.

Although driving *in* Naples is a nightmare, **driving** *to* Naples is easy. The Rome-Naples autostrada (A2) passes Caserta 29km (18 miles) north of Naples. The Naples–Reggio di Calabria autostrada (A3) runs by Salerno, 53km (33 miles) north of Naples.

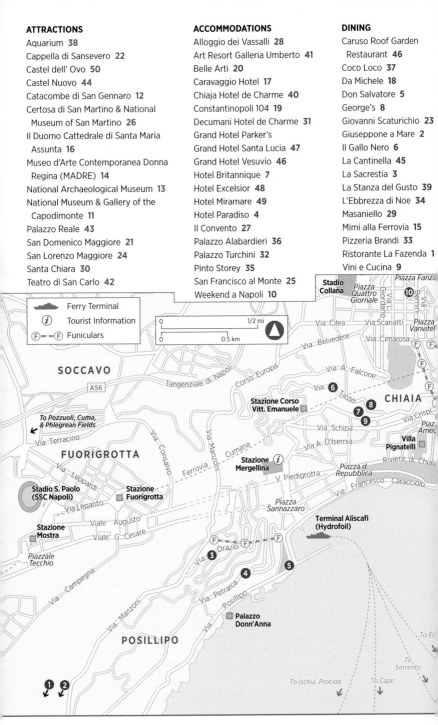

ATTRACTIONS

Aquarium **38**
Cappella di Sansevero **22**
Castel dell' Ovo **50**
Castel Nuovo **44**
Catacombe di San Gennaro **12**
Certosa di San Martino & National
   Museum of San Martino **26**
Il Duomo Cattedrale di Santa Maria
   Assunta **16**
Museo d'Arte Contemporanea Donna
   Regina (MADRE) **14**
National Archaeological Museum **13**
National Museum & Gallery of the
   Capodimonte **11**
Palazzo Reale **43**
San Domenico Maggiore **21**
San Lorenzo Maggiore **24**
Santa Chiara **30**
Teatro di San Carlo **42**

ACCOMMODATIONS

Alloggio dei Vassalli **28**
Art Resort Galleria Umberto **41**
Belle Arti **20**
Caravaggio Hotel **17**
Chiaja Hotel de Charme **40**
Constantinopoli 104 **19**
Decumani Hotel de Charme **31**
Grand Hotel Parker's
Grand Hotel Santa Lucia **47**
Grand Hotel Vesuvio **46**
Hotel Britannique **7**
Hotel Excelsior **48**
Hotel Miramare **49**
Hotel Paradiso **4**
Il Convento **27**
Palazzo Alabardieri **36**
Palazzo Turchini **32**
Pinto Storey **35**
San Francisco al Monte **25**
Weekend a Napoli **10**

DINING

Caruso Roof Garden
   Restaurant **46**
Coco Loco **37**
Da Michele **18**
Don Salvatore **5**
George's **8**
Giovanni Scaturichio **23**
Giuseppone a Mare **2**
Il Gallo Nero **6**
La Cantinella **45**
La Sacrestia **3**
La Stanza del Gusto **39**
L'Ebbrezza di Noe **34**
Masaniello **29**
Mimi alla Ferrovia **15**
Pizzeria Brandi **33**
Ristorante La Fazenda **1**
Vini e Cucina **9**

Ferry Terminal
Tourist Information
Funiculars

1/2 mi
0.5 km

Stadio Collana
Piazza Quattro Giornale
Piazza Fanza
Via L Giordano
Piazza Vanviteli

SOCCAVO
A56
Tangenziale di Napoli
Corso Europa
Via Cilea
Via Scariatti
Via Belvedere
Via Cimarosa
Via A. Falcone
Via Tasso
Stazione Corso Vitt. Emanuele
CHIAIA
To Pozzuoli, Cuma, & Phlegrean Fields
Via Terracino
Via Schipa
Via Crispi
Via A. D'Isernia
FUORIGROTTA
Cumana
Piaz Amed
Villa Pignatelli
Via Leopardi
Via Consalvo
Via Manzoni
Ferrovia
Stazione Mergellina
V. Piedigrotta
Piazza d. Repubblica
Riviera di Chiaja
Stadio S. Paolo (SSC Napoli)
Via Lepanto
Stazione Fuorigrotta
Via Francesco Caracciolo
Piazza Sannazzaro
Stazione Mostra
Viale Augusto
Viale G. Cesare
Terminal Aliscafi (Hydrofoil)
Piazzale Tecchio
Via Campegna
Via Orazio
Via Manzoni
Via Petrarca
Via Posillipo
Palazzo Donn'Anna
To Ec
POSILLIPO
To Sorrento
To Ischia, Procida
To Capri

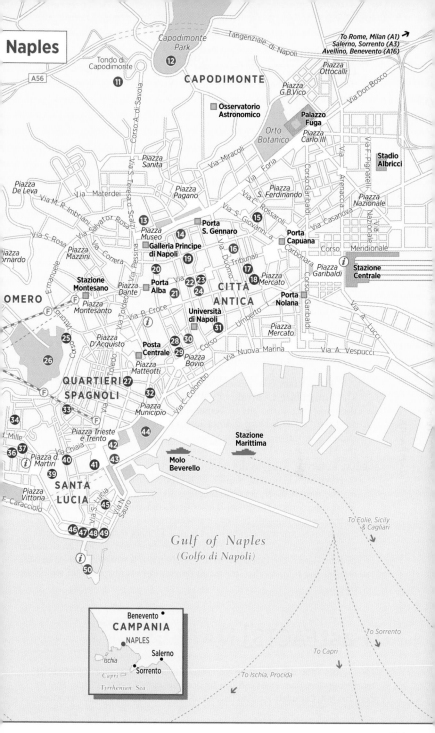

Naples

CAPODIMONTE

Capodimonte Park

Tondo di Capodimonte

Tangenziale di Napoli

To Rome, Milan (A1)
Salerno, Sorrento (A3)
Avellino, Benevento (A16)

Piazza Ottocalli

Piazza G.B.Vico

Osservatorio Astronomico

Palazzo Fuga

Orto Botanico

Piazza Carlo III

Stadio Albricci

Piazza De Leva

Piazza Sanita

Via Miracoli

Via Foria

Piazza Nazionale

Piazza Pagano

Piazza S. Ferdinando

Porta S. Gennaro

Porta Capuana

Piazza Mazzini

Galleria Principe di Napoli

Piazza Museo

Porta Alba

CITTÀ ANTICA

Piazza Mercato

Porta Nolana

Stazione Montesano

Piazza Dante

Piazza Montesanto

Università di Napoli

Piazza Garibaldi

Stazione Centrale

Piazza Mercato

OMERO

Piazza D'Acquisto

Posta Centrale

Piazza Bovio

Piazza Matteotti

QUARTIERI SPAGNOLI

Piazza Municipio

Via Nuova Marina

Via A. Vespucci

Piazza Trieste e Trento

Stazione Marittima

Molo Beverello

Piazza d. Martiri

SANTA LUCIA

Piazza Vittoria

To Eolie, Sicily & Cagliari

Gulf of Naples
(Golfo di Napoli)

To Sorrento

To Capri

To Ischia, Procida

CAMPANIA

Benevento

NAPLES

Salerno

Ischia

Sorrento

Capri

Tyrrhenian Sea

699

From Sicily, you can take a **ferry** to Naples that's run by **Tirrenia Lines,** Via Pontile Vittorio Veneto 1, Porto di Palermo (℡ **892-123;** www. tirrenia.it), in the port area of Palermo. A one-way ticket costs 50€ to 55€, depending on the season, per person for an armchair and 133€ to 149€ per person for a first-class cabin for the 10½-hour trip.

VISITOR INFORMATION   The **Ente Provinciale per il Turismo,** at Piazza dei Martiri 58 (℡ **081-413788;** bus: C25), is open Monday to Friday 9am to 2pm. There are **other offices** at Stazione Centrale (℡ **081-268779;** Metro: Garibaldi) and at Stazione Mergellina (℡ **081-7612102**). These offices are open Monday to Saturday 8:30am to 8pm, Sunday 8:30am to 2pm.

GETTING AROUND   The **Metropolitana** line will deliver you from Stazione Centrale in the east all the way to Stazione Mergellina and even to the suburb of Pozzuoli. Get off at Piazza Piedigrotta if you want to take the funicular to Vomero. The Metro uses the same tickets as buses and trams.

If you survive the **taxi** driver's reckless driving, you'll have to do battle over the bill. Cabdrivers may claim that the meter is broken and assess the cost of the ride, always to your disadvantage. Some legitimate surcharges are imposed, such as night drives and extra luggage. However, many drivers deliberately take the scenic route to run up costs. In repeated visits to Naples, we've never yet been quoted an honest fare. We no longer bother with the meter; we estimate what the fare should be, negotiate with the driver, and take off into the night. If you want to take a chance, you can call a radio taxi at ℡ **081-5520399** or 081-5707070.

As for **driving** around Naples, we have one word: *Don't.*

Funiculars take passengers up and down the steep hills of Naples. The **Funicolare Centrale** (℡ **800-568866;** www.metro.na.it) connects the lower part of the city to Vomero. Daily departures (6:30am–12:30am) are from Piazzetta Duca d'Aosta just off Via Roma. Be careful not to get stranded by missing the last car back. The same tickets valid for buses and the Metro are good for the funicular.

SPECIAL EVENTS   **Maggio dei Monumenti (May of Monuments)** is sponsored by the Council of Naples, with events occurring every weekend during the month. Each year the theme is slightly different. One of the most interesting parts of this event is a series of guided walks through the historic district, even through the city's underground passages. May is also the month for a variety of exhibits and fairs. Chamber music recitals, concerts, operettas, performances of classic Neapolitan songs, and even soccer matches and horse races add to the celebration. If you're in Naples in May, consult the tourist office for a full program of events, some of which are free.

[Fast FACTS] NAPLES

Consulates   The **U.S. Consulate** is on Piazza della Repubblica 1 (℡ **081-5838111;** Metro: Mergellina; tram: 1). Its consular services are open Monday to Friday 8am to noon. The **U.K. Consulate** is at Via Dei Mille 40 (℡ **081-4238911;** Metro: Amedeo), open Monday to Friday 9:30am to 12:30pm and 2 to 4pm. The **Canadian Consulate** is at Via Carducci 29 (☎ **081-401338;** Metro: Amedeo), open Monday to Friday 9am to 1:30pm. Citizens of **Australia** and **New Zealand** will need to go to the embassies or consulates in Rome (see chapter 18).

Drugstores   If you need a drugstore, try **Farmacia Helvetia,** Piazza Garibaldi 11, near Stazione Centrale (☎ **081-5548894;** Metro: Garibaldi).

Emergencies   If you have an emergency, dial ☎ **113** to reach the police. For medical care, dial ☎ **118,** but only in an emergency. To find the local **Guardia Medica Permanente,** ask for directions at your hotel.

Seeing the Sights

If you arrive by train at Stazione Centrale, in front of **Piazza Garibaldi,** you'll want to escape from that horror by taking one of Naples's major arteries, **Corso Umberto,** in the direction of the Santa Lucia district. Along the water, many boats, such as those heading for Capri and Ischia, leave from **Porto Beverello** (not within walking distance—take a taxi).

Many people confine their visit to the bayside **Santa Lucia** area and perhaps another section to see an important museum. Most of the major hotels lie along **Via Partenope,** which looks out on the Gulf of Naples and the Castel dell'Ovo. To the west is the **Mergellina** district, site of many restaurants and dozens of apartment houses. The far western section of the city is known as **Posillipo.**

One of the most important squares is **Piazza del Plebiscito,** north of Santa Lucia. The Palazzo Reale opens onto this square. A satellite is **Piazza Trento e Trieste,** with its Teatro San Carlo and entrance to the famed Galleria Umberto I. To the east is the third-most-important square, **Piazza Municipio.** From Piazza Trento e Trieste, you encounter the main shopping street, **Via Toledo/Via Roma,** on which you can walk as far as Piazza Dante. From that square, take Via Enrico Pessina to the most important museum, located on **Piazza Museo Nazionale.**

THE TOP MUSEUMS

Carthusian Monastery of San Martino (Certosa di San Martino) & National Museum of San Martino (Museo Nazionale di San Martino) ★★

Magnificently situated on the grounds of the Castel Sant'Elmo, this museum was founded in the 14th century as a Carthusian monastery. It fell into decay until the 17th century, when it was reconstructed by architects in the Neapolitan baroque style. The marble-clad **church** ★★ has a ceiling painting of the *Ascension* by Lanfranco in the nave, along with *12 Prophets* by Giuseppe Ribera, who also did the *Institution of the Eucharist* on the left wall of the choir (Lanfranco painted the *Crucifixion* and Guido Reni painted the *Nativity* at the choir's back wall). In the church treasury is Luca Giordano's ceiling fresco of the *Triumph of Judith* (1704) and Ribera's masterful *Descent from the Cross.*

Now a **museum** ★ for the city of Naples, the church displays two stately carriages, historical documents, ships' replicas, china and porcelain, silver, Campagna paintings of the 18th and 19th centuries, military costumes and armor, and a lavishly adorned crib by Cuciniello. The vast collection of *presepi* (Neapolitan Christmas crèches) includes a cast of thousands of peasants and holy figures that

The Castel Sant'Elmo.

have come out of the workshops of Naples's greatest craftsmen over the past 4 centuries. A balcony opens onto a panoramic view of Naples and the bay, as well as Vesuvius and Capri. Many people come here just to drink in the view. The colonnaded cloisters have curious skull sculptures on the inner balustrade.

Next to the monastery is the star-shaped **Castel Sant'Elmo** (✆ **081-5784120**), built by the Angevins in a strategic position above the city from 1329 to 1343. It was enlarged in the 16th century and today offers a magnificent 360-degree panorama of Naples and its bay. Admission is 5€.

Largo San Martino 5 (in the Vomero district). ✆ **081-5781769.** Admission 6€. Carthusian Monastery Tues–Sat 9am–2pm, Sun 9am–1pm. National Museum Mon–Tues and Thurs–Sat 8:30am–7:30pm, Sun 9am–7:30pm. Metro: Vanvitelli.

National Archaeological Museum (Museo Archeologico Nazionale) ★★★ With its Roman and Greek sculpture, this museum contains one of Europe's most valuable archaeological collections—particularly notable are the select Farnese acquisitions, and the mosaics and sculpture excavated at Pompeii and Herculaneum. The building dates from the 16th century and was turned into a museum 2 centuries later by Charles and Ferdinand IV of Bourbon.

The nude statues of Armodio and Aristogitone on the ground floor are outstanding. The spear-bearing nude *Doryphorus*, copied from a work by Polyclitus the Elder and excavated at Pompeii, enlivens another room. Also see the gigantic but weary *Farnese*

The famed "Beware of the Dog" mosaic, taken from the ruins at Pompeii.

Hercules, a statue of remarkable boldness discovered in Rome's Baths of Caracalla. It's a copy of an original by Lysippus, the 4th-century-B.C. Greek sculptor for Alexander the Great. On a more delicate pedestal is the decapitated but exquisite *Venus* (Aphrodite). The *Psyche of Capua* shows why Aphrodite was jealous. And the *Group of the Farnese Bull* presents a pageant of violence from the days of antiquity; the statue was discovered at the Baths of Caracalla and is a copy of a 2nd- or 3rd-century-B.C. Hellenistic statue. The marble group depicts a scene in the legend of Amphion and Zethus, who tied Dirce, wife of Lycus of Thebes, to the horns of a rampaging bull.

The mezzanine galleries are devoted to mosaics excavated from Pompeii and Herculaneum. These include scenes of cockfights, dragon-tailed satyrs, an aquarium, and *Alexander Fighting the Persians,* the finest of all. On the top floor are some of the celebrated bronzes dug out of the Pompeii volcanic mud and the Herculaneum lava. Of particular interest is a Hellenistic portrait of Berenice, a comically drunken satyr; a statue of a sleeping satyr; and Mercury on a rock.

Piazza Museo Nazionale 18–19. ✆ **081-4422149.** Admission 6.50€. Mon and Wed–Sat 9am–7pm; Sun 9am–8pm. Metro: Piazza Cavour or Museo.

National Museum & Gallery of the Capodimonte (Museo e Gallerie Nazionale di Capodimonte) ★★★ This museum and gallery, two of Italy's finest, are housed in the 18th-century Capodimonte Palace, built in the time of Charles III and set in a park. Seven Flemish tapestries were made according to the designs of Bernart van Orley. They show grand-scale scenes from the Battle of Pavia (1525), in which more than 25,000 forces of François I of France lost to those of Charles V. Van Orley obviously considered war not a horror but a romantic ballet.

One of the picture gallery's greatest possessions is Simone Martini's *Coronation,* depicting the brother of Robert of Anjou being crowned king of Naples by the bishop of Toulouse. You'll want to linger over the great Masaccio's *Crucifixion,* a bold expression of grief. The most important room is literally filled with the works of Renaissance masters, notably an *Adoration of the Child,* by Luca Signorelli; a *Madonna and Child,* by Perugino; a panel by Raphael; a *Madonna and Child with Angels,* by Botticelli; and, the most beautiful, Fra Filippo Lippi's *Annunciation and Saints.*

A detail from Fra Filippo Lippi's *Annunciation and Saints.*

Look for Andrea Mantegna's *St. Eufemia* and portrait of Francesco Gonzaga, his brother-in-law Giovanni Bellini's *Transfiguration,* and Lotto's *Portrait of Bernardo de Rossi* and *Madonna and Child with St. Peter.* In one room are Raphael's *Holy Family and St. John* and a copy of his celebrated portrait of Pope Leo X. Two choice sketches are Raphael's *Moses* and Michelangelo's *Three Soldiers*. Displayed farther on are the Titians, with Danae taking the spotlight from Pope Paul III.

Another room is devoted to Flemish art: Pieter Bruegel's *Blind Men* is outstanding and his *Misanthrope* is devilishly powerful. Other foreign works include Joos van Cleve's *Adoration of the Magi*. You can climb the stairs for a view of Naples and the bay, a finer landscape than you'll see inside.

The State Apartments downstairs deserve inspection. Room after room is devoted to gilded mermaids, Venetian sedan chairs, ivory carvings, a porcelain chinoiserie salon, tapestries, the Farnese armory, and a glass and china collection.

In the Palazzo Capodimonte, Parco di Capodimonte (off Amedeo di Savoia), Via Miano 2. 📞 **081-7499111.** Admission 7.50€. Thurs–Tues 8:30am–7:30pm. Bus: R4.

MORE ATTRACTIONS

Aquarium (Acquario) The Aquarium is in a municipal park, Villa Comunale, between Via Caracciolo and the Riviera di Chiaia. Established by a German naturalist in the 1800s, it's the oldest aquarium in Europe and displays about 200 species of marine plants and fish found in the Bay of Naples. (They must be a hardy lot.)

Inside Villa Comunale, Viale Acquario 1. 📞 **081-5833263.** Admission 1.55€ adults, 1€ children ages 5–12. Mar–Oct Mon–Sat 9am–6pm, Sun 10am–6pm; Nov–Feb Mon–Sat 9am–5pm, Sun 9am–2pm. Bus: 140, 152, C9, or C10.

Cappella di Sansevero If you want the best example of how baroque can be ludicrously over the top, hauntingly beautiful, and technically brilliant all at once, search out the nondescript entrance to one of Italy's most fanciful chapels. This 1590 chapel is a festival of marbles, frescoes, sculpture—in relief and in the round—masterfully showing off the technical abilities and storytelling of a few relatively unknown Neapolitan baroque masters. At the center is Giuseppe Sammartino's remarkable alabaster *Veiled Christ* (1753), depicting the dead Christ lying on pillows under a transparent veil.

Three wall sculptures stand out as well: Francesco Celebrano's 1762 relief of the *Deposition* behind the altar, Antonio Corradini's allegory of *Modesty* (a marble statue of a woman whose nudity is covered only by a decidedly immodest clinging veil), and Francesco Queirolo's virtuoso allegory of *Disillusion,* represented by a man struggling with a rope net carved entirely of marble.

Via F. de Sanctis 19 (near Piazza San Domenico Maggiore). 📞 **081-5518470.** www.museo sansevero.it. Admission 7€. Wed–Sat and Mon 10am–5:30pm; Sun 10am–1:30pm. Metro: Dante.

Castel dell'Ovo This 2,000-year-old fortress, the name of which means Castle of the Egg, overlooks the Gulf of Naples. The site was important centuries before the birth of Christ and was fortified by early settlers. In time, a major stronghold to guard the bay was erected by Virgil, who was said to have built it on an enchanted egg of mystical powers on the floor of the ocean. Legend has it that if the egg breaks, Naples will collapse.

Actually, most of the fortress was constructed by Frederick II and later expanded by the Angevins. Although there's little to see here today, the Castel dell'Ovo is one of the most historic spots in Naples, perhaps the site of the original Greek settlement of Parthenope. In time, it became the villa of Lucullus, the

Roman general and philosopher. By the 5th century, the villa had become the home in exile for the last of the Western Roman emperors, Romulus Augustulus. You can still see columns of Lucullus's villa in the dungeons. The view from here is worth your time. The interior of the fortress is not open to the public except for special exhibits.

Porto Santa Lucia (follow Via Console along the seafront from Piazza del Plebiscito to Porto Santa Lucia; Castel dell'Ovo is at the end of the promontory). ℂ 081-246334. Admission depends on exhibit. Mon–Sat 8am–5pm; Sun 8am–2pm. Call for schedules. Bus: C82 or R2.

The Castel dell'Ovo.

Catacombs of San Gennaro (St. Januarius) ★ A guide will show you through this two-story underground cemetery, dating from the 2nd century and boasting frescoes and mosaics. You enter the catacombs on Via di Capodimonte (head down an alley alongside the Madre del Buon Consiglio Church). These wide tunnels lined with early Christian burial niches grew around the tomb of an important pagan family; they became a pilgrimage site when the bones of San Gennaro himself were transferred here in the 5th century. Along with several well-preserved 6th-century frescoes, there's a depiction of San Gennaro (A.D. 400s), whose halo sports an alpha and an omega and a cross—symbols normally reserved exclusively for Christ's halo. The tour passes you through the upper level of tunnels, including several small early basilicas carved from the *tufo* rock. The cemetery remained active until the 11th century, but most of the bones have since been blessed and reinterred in ossuaries on the lower levels (closed to the public). The catacombs survived the centuries intact, but those precious antique frescoes suffered some damage when these tunnels served as an air raid shelter during World War II.

Via di Capodimonte 13. ℂ 081-7411071. www.catacombedinapoli.it. Admission 8€. Tours are every hour Mon–Sat 10am–5pm and Sun 10am–1pm. Bus: R4 or C63.

Frescoes in the catacombs of San Gennaro.

Il Duomo Cattedrale di Santa Maria Assunta ★★   Built largely in the Gothic style, the cathedral of Naples was consecrated in 1315. Over the years it has witnessed many changes, including a new facade in the 1800s. Inside are found 110 ancient granite columns, supporting the Latin Cross–style architecture.

Lavish art and decoration adorn the interior, including the monumental **Cappella di San Gennaro ★★**, honoring the city's patron saint. In this chapel the art of the Neapolitan baroque reached its zenith. The chapel is said to contain the blood of the saint. According to tradition, the cathedral contains two vials of the saint's blood, which is said to liquefy and boil three times annually (the first Sun in May, Sept 19, and Dec 16).

Another chapel of great beauty is the **Cappella Capece Minutolo ★★**, with its stunning frescoes from the 1200s. From the cathedral you have access to **Santa Restituta ★★**, the oldest basilica in Naples, dating from the 4th century. Try to pay a final visit to the **baptistery of San Giovanni in Fonte ★★**, which was founded in the 4th century and is the oldest baptistery in the West. It is decorated with damaged mosaics from the 5th century.

Via del Duomo 147. ☎ **081-449097.** www.duomodinapoli.it. Free admission to the cathedral, but the archaeological zone is 3€. Mon–Sat 8am–12:30pm and 4:30–7:30pm; Sun 8am–1:30pm and 5–7:30pm. Metro: Piazza Cavour.

Museo d'Arte Contemporanea Donna Regina (MADRE) ★   This old city has not been associated with modern art—until now. Naples's newest museum was the creation of Portuguese architect Alvaro Siza, who renovated the three floors of Palazzo Donnaregina to provide this showcase for an international collection of works of contemporary artists such as native-born Francesco Clemente. Clemente's pastel-hued fresco covers gallery walls on two floors and squeezes through a white well in the upper room. It's rather erotic, with bare-chested sirens and "floating phalluses." One section is devoted to "Neo-Geos," a group of New York City artists that emerged in the early '80s. Check out the garish raft, enshrining the jeweled suit of a cult figure (Elvis?). There's even an Elizabeth Taylor silkscreen photo painting by Andy Warhol, part of his "Death and Disaster" series.

Other featured artists include Bombay-born Anish Kapoor, one of the protagonists of English sculpture in the 1980s; San Francisco–born Richard Serra, hailed as one of the most innovative artists in the history of modern art; and German-born Rebecca Horn, who has expressed herself in everything from sculpture to performing in movies.

Via Settembrini 79. ☎ **081-19313016.** www.museomadre.it. Admission 7€ adults, 3.50€ ages 6–18, free for 5 and under; free admission for all Mon. Mon and Wed–Sun 10am–7pm. Bus: 3S. Metro: Cavour.

Castel Nuovo ★★   The New Castle was built in the late 13th century on orders from Charles I, king of Naples, as a royal residence for the House of Anjou. It was badly ruined and virtually reconstructed in the mid–15th century by the House of Aragón. The castle is distinguished by a trio of imposing round battle towers at its front; between two of the towers, guarding the entrance, is a triumphal arch designed by Francesco Laurana to commemorate the 1442 expulsion of the Angevins by the forces of Alphonso I. It's a masterpiece of the Renaissance. The castle is the home of the **Museo Civico,** housing a wealth of art from the castle itself. The artistic highlight is the **Cappella Palatine ★**, the only surviving segment of the Angevin castle. Note the carved portal from the 15th century and a lovely rose window. Giotto decorated the original chapel, but nearly all of his art has vanished with time. But other art remains, including a **tabernacle ★★** by Domenico Gagini and two depictions of the Virgin with her Bambino by Francesco Laurana. More-modern art is found on the third floor.

Piazza del Municipio. ✆ **081-7955877.** Free admission. Mon–Sat 9am–7pm. Bus: R2.

Royal Palace (Palazzo Reale) ★　This palace was designed by Domenico Fontana in the 17th century, and the eight statues on the facade are of Neapolitan kings. Located in the heart of the city, the square on which the palace stands is one of Naples's most architecturally interesting, with a long colonnade and a church, San Francesco di Paolo, that evokes the style of the Pantheon in Rome. Inside the Palazzo Reale you can visit the royal apartments, adorned in the baroque style with colored marble floors, paintings, tapestries, frescoes, antiques, and porcelain. Charles de Bourbon, son of Philip IV of Spain, became king of Naples in 1734. A great patron of the arts, he installed a library here, one of the finest in the south, with more than 1,250,000 volumes.

Piazza del Plebiscito 1. ✆ **081-5808111.** Admission 4.50€. Thurs–Tues 9am–8pm. Bus: R2 or R3.

San Domenico Maggiore ★　This massive Gothic edifice was built from 1289 to 1324 and then was rebuilt in the Renaissance and early baroque eras. Upon entry from the apse end, you'll see that the body of the church was overhauled in neo-Gothic style in the 1850s. Walk down the left aisle (which is on your right because you're coming in from the wrong end) to the last chapel, where you'll find Luca Giordano's *Crowning of St. Joseph.* Now turn around to attack the church from the proper direction.

The first chapel on the right aisle is a Renaissance masterpiece of design and sculpture by Tuscans Antonio and Romolo da Settignano. The third chapel on the right contains frescoes from 1309 by Roman master Pietro Cavallini (a contemporary of Giotto). The seventh chapel on the right is the **Crucifixion Chapel (Cappella del Crocifisso),** with some Renaissance tombs and a copy of the 12th-century *Crucifixion* painting that spoke to St. Thomas Aquinas. Next door, the theatrical **sacristy** has a ceiling fresco by Francesco Solimena (1706) and small caskets containing the ashes of Aragónese rulers and courtiers, lining a high shelf. What acts like a right transept was actually a preexisting church grafted onto this one, the **Chiesa Antica di Sant'Angelo a Morfisa,** today an oversize chapel containing finely carved Renaissance tombs.

On Piazza San Domenico is another of Naples's baroque spires, this one a 1737 confection called the **Guglia di San Domenico** by Domenico Antonio Vaccaro.

Piazza San Domenico Maggiore 8A. ✆ **081-459298.** Free admission. Daily 9am–noon and 4:30–7pm. Metro: Dante.

San Lorenzo Maggiore　The greatest of Naples's layered churches was built in 1265 for Charles I over a 6th-century basilica, which lays on many ancient remains. The interior is pure Gothic, with tall pointed arches and an apse off of

A detail from the exterior of San Lorenzo Maggiore.

which radiate nine chapels. Aside from some gorgeously baroque chapels of inlaid marbles, the highlight is Tino da Camaino's **canopy tomb of Catherine of Austria ★** (1323–25).

San Lorenzo preserves the best and most extensive (still rather paltry) **remains of the ancient Greek and Roman cities ★** currently open to the public. The church foundations are the walls of Neapolis's basilican law courts. In the **cloisters** are excavated bits of the Roman city's treasury and marketplace. In the **crypt** are the rough remains of a Roman-era shop-lined street, a Greek temple, and a medieval building.

Piazza San Gaetano Via Tribunali 316. ℂ **081-2110860.** www.sanlorenzomaggiorenapoli.it. Admission to church free; *scavi* (ruins) 4.50€. Mon–Sat 9am–5:30pm; Sun 9am–1:30pm. Bus: 110.

Santa Chiara ★ On a *palazzo*-flanked street, this church was built on orders from Robert the Wise, king of Naples, in the early 14th century. It became the church for the House of Anjou. Although World War II bombers heavily blasted it, it has been restored somewhat to its original Gothic look. The light-filled interior is lined with chapels, each of which contains some leftover bit of sculpture or fresco from the medieval church. The best three pieces line the wall behind the High Altar. In the center is the towering multilevel tomb of Robert the Wise d'Angiò, sculpted by Giovanni and Pacio Bertini in 1343. To its right is Tino di Camaino's tomb of Charles, duke of Calabria; on the left is the 1399 monument to Mary of Durazza. In the choir behind the altar are more salvaged medieval remnants of frescoes and statuary, including bits of a Giotto *Crucifixion*.

Wine Tasting

The wines produced in the harsh, hot landscapes of Campania seem stronger, rougher, and, in many cases, more powerful than those grown in gentler climes. Among the most famous are the Lacryma Christi (Tears of Christ), a white that grows in the volcanic soil near Naples, Herculaneum, and Pompeii; Taurasi, a potent red; and Greco di Tufo, a pungent white laden with the odors of apricots and apples. One of the most frequently visited vineyards is **Mastroberardino**, Via Manfredi 75–81, Atripalda, 83042 Avellino (ℂ **0825-614111;** www.mastroberardino.com), which is reached by taking the A16 east from Naples. If you'd like to spend a day outside the city, driving through the countryside and doing a little wine tasting, call to make an appointment.

You have to exit the church and walk down its left flank to enter this next sight—the 14th-century **Cloisters of the Order of the Clares (Chiostri dell'Ordine di Santa Chiara)** ★★★. In 1742, Domenico Antonio Vaccaro lined the four paths to the center of the cloisters' courtyard that are supported by columns plated with colorfully painted majolica tiles. Interspersed among the columns are tiled benches. In the **museum** are a scattering of Roman and medieval remains.

On the piazza outside is one of Naples's several baroque spires, the **Guglia dell'Immacolata,** a tall pile of statues and reliefs sculpted in 1750.

Via Santa Chiara 49C. ✆ **081-5526280.** www.santachiara.info. Church free admission; cloisters 5€. Mon–Sat 9:30am–1pm and 2:30–5:30pm; Sun 9:30am–1pm. Bus: E1.

Where to Stay

EXPENSIVE

Caravaggio Hotel ★ 🎁 A restored *palazzo* from the 1600s sits on a small square in back of the cathedral. It takes its name from the artist Caravaggio, who painted *Sette Opere della Misericordia,* displayed in the chapel opposite the entrance to the hotel. The sensitive restoration respected the architectural style of the building, although modern conveniences such as hydromassage showers and Internet access were added. The midsize bedrooms are modern, each with a small bathroom with tub or shower, some with hydromassage showers. The breakfast buffet is especially generous, with meats and cheese purchased from regional farms in Campania.

Piazza Cardinale Sisto Riario Sforza 157, 80139 Napoli. ✆ **081-2110066.** Fax 081-4421578. www.caravaggiohotel.it. 18 units. 190€ double; 240€ suite. Rates include buffet breakfast. AE, DC, MC, V. Parking 20€–25€. Metro: Piazza Cavour. **Amenities:** Bar; Wi-Fi (free, in lobby). *In room:* A/C, TV, minibar.

Spend time exploring Naples's streets.

Costantinopoli 104 ★★ 🎁   You'd never know you were in Naples, as this converted Art Nouveau palace seems like a country villa once you're inside. In the historic core of Naples, the building still retains much of its architectural styling, including its original stained-glass windows. Each of the midsize to spacious bedrooms is individually decorated. About half the bedrooms contain showers, the rest tubs. The suites also have Jacuzzis. The Garden Suite opens onto the pool, and the Home Suite opens onto a private terrace overlooking the garden. Seven of the bedrooms open onto a terrace with flowers and herbs, where guests can take their breakfast in summer.

Via Santa Maria di Constantinopoli 104, 80138 Napoli. ✆ **081-5571035.** Fax 081-5571051. www.costantinopoli104.it. 19 units. 220€ double; 250€ suite. Rates include buffet breakfast. AE, DC, MC, V. Parking 25€. Metro: Piazza Cavour. **Amenities:** Bar; airport transfers (35€); babysitting; heated pool; room service. *In room:* A/C, TV/DVD, CD player, hair dryer, minibar, Wi-Fi (free).

Grand Hotel Parker's ★★★   This is the finest hotel in town, surpassing the Vesuvio because of its more tranquil and scenic location on a hillside avenue. Its 1870 construction is evident in the neoclassical walls, fluted pilasters, and ornate ceilings. The hotel became part of World War II history when it was the Allied headquarters in the mid-'40s. The guest rooms are traditionally furnished; each is in a different style. Most guests seek out one of the front rooms whose narrow terraces open onto bay views. The delicious food at the hotel's rooftop restaurant, George's, competes with anything available by the bay.

Corso Vittorio Emanuele 135, 80121 Napoli. ✆ **081-7612474.** Fax 081-663527. www.grandhotelparkers.it. 83 units. 255€–360€ double; 450€–1,300€ suite. Rates include buffet breakfast. AE, DC, MC, V. Parking 25€. Bus: C24 or C27. **Amenities:** Restaurant; babysitting; room service; spa. *In room:* A/C, TV, hair dryer, minibar, Wi-Fi (free).

Grand Hotel Santa Lucia ★★   The Santa Lucia, whose neoclassical facade overlooks a sheltered marina, is better maintained than its nearby competitors. The interior has undergone extensive renovations and is decorated in Neapolitan style, with terrazzo floors. The guest rooms are large, containing quality beds with wrought-iron headboards and ceiling stenciling that lends a classical effect. The tiled bathrooms often contain party-size outdoor pools. The rooms in back are quieter but have no views. The balconied front rooms bring you lots of traffic noise but offer views of the Bay of Naples.

Via Partenope 46, 80121 Napoli. ✆ **081-7640666.** Fax 081-7648580. www.santalucia.it. 96 units. 295€–410€ double; 650€–1,200€ suite. Rates include buffet breakfast. AE, DC, MC, V. Parking 26€. Bus: 140 or C25. **Amenities:** Restaurant; bar; babysitting; room service. *In room:* A/C, TV, hair dryer, minibar, Wi-Fi (free).

Grande Hotel Vesuvio ★★   This deluxe and fabled hotel is one of the foremost choices along the Bay of Naples, especially if you get a room with a balcony overlooking Mount Vesuvius. The seafront landmark overlooking the Bay of Naples and Castel dell'Ovo has long been a refuge for heads of state and artistic luminaries (including Enrico Caruso, who died here in 1921). Built in 1882, the Vesuvio features a marble-and-stucco facade with curved balconies. The 1930s-style guest rooms have lofty ceilings, cove moldings, parquet floors, and large closets. Traditionalists should request second-floor rooms, which are decorated in a 1700s style. You'll also find a scattering of antiques throughout the echoing halls.

Via Partenope 45, 80121 Napoli. ℰ **081-7640044.** Fax 081-7644483. www.vesuvio.it. 181 units. 199€–420€ double; from 650€ suite. Rates include buffet breakfast. AE, DC, MC, V. Parking 24€. Bus: C25 or 140. **Amenities:** Restaurant; bar; babysitting; health club and spa; indoor heated pool; room service. *In room:* A/C, TV, hair dryer, minibar, Wi-Fi (free).

Hotel Britannique ★ ✦   Its bones are a bit creaky with age, but this remains a longtime Neapolitan favorite, especially for traditionalists. It's actually part of the same building as Parker's (see above), but without that hotel's grandness. Nonetheless, the Britannique remains charmingly old-fashioned. The service is old-fashioned, too, in the best sense. The view of the Bay of Naples and even Vesuvius is so compelling that many guests rave about the place. Tropical plants and flowers abound in the garden, but the lobby is a bit seedy. The guest rooms, from small to spacious, have some antiques, but mostly the look is functional.

Corso Vittorio Emanuele 133, 80121 Napoli. ℰ **081-7614145.** Fax 081-660457. www.hotel britannique.it. 86 units. 170€–190€ double; 220€ junior suite. Rates include buffet breakfast. AE, DC, MC, V. Parking 15€. Metro: Piazza Amedeo. Bus: C24 or C27. **Amenities:** Restaurant; bar; babysitting; room service; Wi-Fi (free, in lobby). *In room:* A/C, TV, hair dryer, minibar.

Hotel Excelsior ★   This is the third luxe choice for Naples, excelled only by Parker's and the Vesuvio. The Excelsior occupies a dramatic position on the waterfront, with views of Santa Lucia and Vesuvius from its dramatic roof garden terrace. After a long decline, the hotel has bounced back under Sheraton (which also owns the posh Vesuvio next door) and boasts elegant details such as Venetian chandeliers, Doric columns, wall-size murals, and bronze torchiers. Most of the spacious guest rooms are furnished in the Empire style, with heavy wood furniture, elegant fabrics, paneled walls, and brass trim.

Via Partenope 48, 80121 Napoli. ℰ **081-7640111.** Fax 081-7649743. www.excelsior.it. 121 units. 215€–360€ double; from 850€ suite. Rates include buffet breakfast. AE, DC, MC, V. Parking 23€. Bus: 140 or C25. **Amenities:** Restaurant; babysitting; concierge; room service. *In room:* A/C, TV, hair dryer, minibar, Wi-Fi (10€ per 24 hr.).

Hotel Miramare ★   Its roof garden alone is reason enough to stay here, opening as it does onto panoramas of the Gulf of Naples and Vesuvius. In a superb location, opposite Castel dell'Ovo, seemingly thrust out toward the harbor on a dockside boulevard, the Miramare was originally an aristocratic villa from 1914 but was transformed into a hotel in 1944 after serving for a short period as the American consulate. Its lobby evokes a little Caribbean hotel with a semitropical look. The guest rooms have been renovated and are pleasantly furnished, with soundproof windows and well-kept bathrooms.

Via Nazario Sauro 24, 80132 Napoli. ℰ **081-7647589.** Fax 081-7640775. www.hotelmiramare. com. 31 units. 145€–299€ double. Rates include buffet breakfast. AE, DC, MC, V. Parking 18€. Bus: 140 or CS. **Amenities:** Bar; babysitting; room service; Wi-Fi (free, in lobby). *In room:* A/C, TV, hair dryer, minibar.

Palazzo Alabardieri ★ ★ ⚑   Naples continues to open one luxury hotel after another in its once-decaying *palazzi*. Among the latest and greatest is this oasis of tranquillity in the city center. Lying off Piazza dei Martiri, Palazzo Alabardieri dates from 1870 and was built on the site of an antique cloister. Meticulously restored, the standard doubles and suites are elegantly furnished in a style that harmoniously blends the modern with the traditional. The marble bathrooms are the most elegant of any hotel in Naples, often with double-topped washbasins, steam-resistant mirrors, and a Jacuzzi.

Via Alabardieri 38, Chiaia 80121 Napoli. *℮* **081-415278.** Fax 081-401478. www.palazzoalabardieri. it. 33 units. 145€–275€ double; 260€–390€ junior suite. AE, DC, MC, V. Parking 30€. Metro: Piazza Amedeo. **Amenities:** Bar; babysitting; exercise room. *In room:* A/C, TV, hair dryer, minibar.

Palazzo Turchini ★   Behind the imposing Fontana di Nettuno, this boutique hotel is installed in an 18th-century building which has been restored and now receives guests from all over the world. There are many grace notes here, including the use of golden Calacatta marbles and a beautiful inner garden. Guest rooms have been modernized, some with a view over the domes of the city. From others you can look out at Vesuvius. The elegant design mixes traditional style with contemporary. Most of the rooms are a bit small, however. If you need more space ask for an "executive double."

Via Medina 21. 81032 Napoli. *℮* **081-5510606.** Fax 081-5521473. www.palazzoturchini.it. 27 units. 260€–300€ double; 340€ junior suite. Rates include buffet breakfast. AE, DC, MC, V. Parking 25€. Bus: R2. **Amenities:** Bar; babysitting; concierge; room service; W-Fi (free in lobby). *In room:* A/C, TV, hair dryer, minibar.

San Francesco al Monte ★★   Once a Franciscan monastery, this hotel is somewhat out of the way but worth the difficulty in getting here. From its perch above the city, you can enjoy the same jaw-dropping view of the Bay of Naples that the monks did in the 16th century. Skillfully restored and converted into a hotel, San Francesco boasts such features as a modern art collection, a pool surrounded by greenery, and a hanging garden where the monks raised vegetables. The spacious to midsize bedrooms are artfully decorated with delicate colors and classic furnishings; each comes with a bathtub or Jacuzzi. In the monastery's ancient wine cellar, today's La Cantina dei Barbanti features wrought-iron tables and Plexiglas chairs designed by Philippe Stark.

Corso Vittorio Emanuele 328, 80135 Napoli. *℮* **081-4239111.** Fax 081-2512485. www.hotel sanfrancesco.it. 44 units. 195€–340€ double. AE, DC, MC, V. Parking 28€. Metro: Uanvitelli. **Amenities:** Restaurant; bar; outdoor rooftop pool; room service. *In room:* A/C, TV, minibar.

MODERATE

Art Resort Galleria Umberto ★★ 📦   This boutique hotel lies within the landmark Galleria Umberto, making it unique in Naples. Rooms, each named after a different artist, are done in a classic romantic style, some with fabric-draped four-poster beds. Accommodations are decorated in tasteful and harmonious colors; the windows are soundproof, and each unit has a large wardrobe, along with luxurious bathrooms with hydroshowers or bathtubs. Rooms with balconies are reserved for smokers. Opera singers and musicians from the nearby opera house often stay here.

Galleria Umberto I, 83, 80132 Napoli. *℮*/fax **081-4976224.** www.artresortgalleriaumberto.it. 10 units. 130€–160€ double; 165€–180€ junior suite. AE, MC, V. Bus: R2 or R3. **Amenities:** Airport transfers (35€); babysitting; room service. *In room:* A/C, TV, hair dryer, minibar, Wi-Fi (free).

Chiaja Hotel de Charme ★ 📦   Once it was a notorious brothel where "most human desires" could be satisfied. Lying a 2-minute walk from the landmark Piazza Plebiscito, today it is a small boutique of charm and grace, one of the most elegant in the city. Naples's most famous pizzeria, Pizzeria Brandi, lies on the ground floor of the same building. The hotel occupies the second floor of the four-story Neapolitan palace and is owned by the descendants of the original owner, Marchese Nicola Lecaldano Sasso La Terza. Although the rooms are a bit small, they are nonetheless comfortable and furnished with a scattering of family heirlooms.

Via Chiaia 216, 80121 Napoli. ℂ **081-415555.** Fax 081-422344. www.hotelchiaia.it. 27 units. 145€–185€ double. AE, DC, MC, V. Parking 18€. Bus: R2 or R3. **Amenities:** Bar; Wi-Fi (free, in lobby). *In room:* A/C, TV, hair dryer, minibar.

Decumani Hotel de Charme ★   Here is a rare chance to stay in the palace of the last bishop of the Bourbon Kingdom of Naples. The residence has undergone massive renovation to turn it into a modern hotel. The chief architectural feature is a large, princely hall covered with mirrors and stuccoes from the 18th century. Bedrooms are beautifully furnished with antiques or reproductions, yet contain such modern features as soundproof windows. The location is in the heart of the historic center of Naples.

Via San Giovanni Maggiore Pignatelli 15, 80134 Napoli. ℂ/fax **081/5518188.** www.decumani. com. 24 units. 104€–150€ double; 154€–174€ triple. Rates include continental breakfast. AE, MC, V. Parking 25€. Metro: Montesanto. **Amenities:** Airport transfers (35€); bikes; concierge. *In room:* A/C, TV, hair dryer, minibar, Wi-Fi (free).

Hotel Paradiso ★ 👜   This Best Western hotel might be paradise, but only after you reach it. It's 6km (3¾ miles) from the central station, but one irate driver claimed that it takes about 3½ hours to get here. Once you arrive, however, your nerves will be soothed by the view, one of the most panoramic of any hotel in Italy. The Bay of Naples unfolds before you, and in the distance Vesuvius looms. The guest rooms range from medium to spacious, each with a well-kept bathroom. From the Paradiso, you can take taxis to the major attractions or use a funicular that takes you from a hillside site near the hotel to the center of Naples.

Via Catullo 11, 80122 Napoli. ℂ **800/528-1234** in the U.S., or 081-2475111. Fax 081-7613449. www. hotelparadisonapoli.it. 74 units. 79€–220€ double. Rates include buffet breakfast. AE, DC, MC, V. Parking 18€ nearby. Metro: Mergellina. **Amenities:** Restaurant; airport transfers (35€); baby-sitting; room service; outdoor tennis court (lit). *In room:* A/C, TV, hair dryer, minibar, Wi-Fi (free).

INEXPENSIVE

Albergo San Germano   Designed like an Italian version of a Chinese pagoda, this brick-and-concrete Best Western hotel is ideal for late-arriving motorists reluctant to negotiate the traffic of Naples. A terraced pool and garden are welcome respites after a day of sightseeing. The guest rooms are clean but simple. All are a bit small—as are the tiled bathrooms—but tidily maintained.

Via Beccadelli 41, 80125 Napoli. ℂ **081-5705422.** Fax 081-5701546. www.hotelsangermano napoli.it. 105 units (shower only). 89€–170€ double. Rates include continental breakfast. AE, DC, MC, V. Parking 12€. Bus: C5 or C6. From the autostrada, follow the signs to Tangenziale Napoli; exit 13km (8 miles) later at Agnano Terme. The hotel is on your right less than 1.6km (1 mile) from the toll booth. **Amenities:** Restaurant; bar; outdoor pool (summer only); room service. *In room:* A/C, TV, hair dryer, minibar, Wi-Fi (free).

Alloggio dei Vassalli ★ 👜   One of the most charming of Naples's upscale B&Bs, this winning choice lies on the second floor of the historic 18th-century Palazzo Donnalbina. In the heart of Naples, the B&B is imbued with some of its

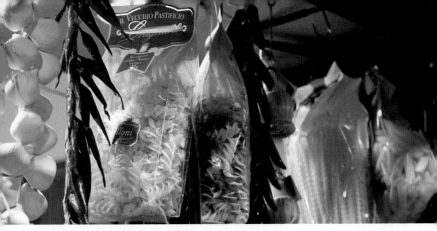

Bags of dried pasta hang in the doorway of a Naples shop.

original architectural details, including ceilings of antique wooden rafters and decorative stucco work. Bedrooms are spacious and bright, each tastefully and comfortably furnished.

Via Donnalbina 56, 80134 Napoli. ✆ **081-5515118.** Fax 081-4202752. www.bandbnapoli.it. 5 units. 65€–99€ double; 105€–125€ triple. Rates include breakfast. MC, V. Parking 22€. Metro: Montesanto. **Amenities:** Airport transfers (19€); room service; spa. *In room:* A/C, TV/DVD, Wi-Fi (free).

Belle Arti ★ 📋 One of the most distinguished B&Bs in Naples lies on the second floor of the historic 17th-century *palazzo* of Baroni Sgueglia della Marra. This authentic period residence has been turned into one of the most modern boutique hotels of Naples. The midsize bedrooms combine tradition with modern amenities and are furnished with designer pieces. The architectural charm of yesterday is reflected in antique doors, frescoes, and original stuccos. A bed can be added to make doubles accommodate three guests.

Via S. Maria di Costantinopoli 27, 80138 Napoli. ✆/fax **081-5571062.** www.belleartiresort.com. 7 units. 110€–160€ double or suite. Rates include continental breakfast. AE, DC, MC, V. Metro: Museo. Parking 15€–20€. *In room:* A/C, TV, hair dryer, minibar.

Il Convento ★ 🖊 An oasis of charm and tranquillity, this small hotel in the Quartieri Spagnoli has been converted from a 1600s convent. A few steps from the shop-flanked Via Toledo, Il Convento stands next to the Convent of S. Maria Francesca. The old architectural features have been retained, yet everything else is stylishly modern in the former nuns' cells. The most desirable units are the junior suites, which have private roof terraces. The Mediterranean decor in the bedrooms is relatively simple with dark wooden furnishings and traditional terracotta floors.

Via Speranzella 137A, 80132 Napoli. ✆ **081-403977.** Fax 081-400332. www.hotelilconvento.com. 14 units. 80€–180€ double; 110€–210€ junior suite. Rates include buffet breakfast. AE, DC, MC, V. Parking 21€. Bus: R2. **Amenities:** Bar; Internet (free, in lobby); room service. *In room:* A/C, TV, hair dryer, minibar.

Pinto Storey ★ 📋 This little discovery lies on the fourth and fifth floors of an 1878 Liberty-style building off Piazza Amedeo in the heart of the Chiaia district.

The welcome from the helpful staff is among the warmest in Naples. Rooms are spacious and furnished with a certain style, without being luxurious. Wooden and wrought-iron furnishings predominate, and the place is beautifully kept and atmospheric. A sumptuous breakfast is served in the bar. It's recommended that you reserve well in advance.

Via G. Martucci 72, Chiaia, 80121 Napoli. ✆ **081-681260.** Fax 081-667536. www.pintostorey.it. 16 units. 129€–160€ double; 165€ triple. Rates include continental breakfast. AE, MC, V. Parking nearby 25€. Bus: C24 or C27. **Amenities:** Bar; room service. *In room:* A/C, TV, hair dryer, minibar, Wi-Fi (3€ per hr.).

Weekend a Napoli ★ 🎁   It lies away from the major sights, but this restored family villa is one of the most inviting B&Bs in Naples. It's worth the short funicular ride to its hillside location. Both rooms and suites have a delightful elegance, opening onto views of the bay. You can ask for one of the classic rooms on the garden floor, each with its own separate entrance. The most luxurious way to stay here is to book the Pompeii Suite, with an indoor pool.

Via Alvino 157, Vomero, 80129 Napoli. ✆ **081-5781010.** www.weekendanapoli.com. 13 units. 156€ double; from 184€ junior suite; from 250€ suite. AE, DC, MC, V. Funicular to Montesanto. *In room:* A/C, TV, fridge, hair dryer, Wi-Fi (free).

Where to Dine

Naples is the home of pizza and spaghetti, and it's great fun to sample the authentic versions. However, if you like subtle cooking and have an aversion to olive oil or garlic, you won't fare as well.

Locals gather at **Al 53,** 53 Piazza Dante (✆ **081/549-9372;** www.ristorantealcinquantatre.com), for a pasta bake—that is a ring of pasta filed with peas in a tomato sauce and baked with béchamel sauce, mozzarella, and Parmesan. It's a real taste of Naples flavor. Another savory local treat is found at **Bellini,** 79 Via Santa Maria di Costantinpoli (✆ **081/45-97-74;** www.ilbellini ristorante.it), which specializes in *linguine al cartoccio*—mixed seafood and pasta served in paper.

For dessert, you might want to gather at **Scaturchio,** Piazza San Domenico Maggiore 19 (✆ **081-5517031;** www.scaturchio.it), which serves the best coffee in town along with amazing gelato. Other desserts include a rum-drenched *babà,* a warm ricotta-filled *sfogliatella,* and a layered *cassate.*

EXPENSIVE

Caruso Roof Garden Restaurant ★★ ITALIAN/NEAPOLITAN   We've never made a career out of recommending hotel dining rooms in Naples. But this gem on the ninth floor of this deluxe hotel is an exception. The panoramic view of the Bay of Naples alone merits a visit. The restaurant is dedicated to that great gourmet Enrico Caruso, Italy's greatest opera singer who made the Grande Hotel Vesuvio his home in Naples. We feel that the cuisine here would satisfy Caruso's passion for food. The ingredients are first-rate, and the chefs are supremely talented. Begin perhaps with their fettuccine dedicated to Caruso (made with fresh tomatoes and peppers). Another rich, classic pasta is served with fresh tomatoes, mussels, chopped garlic, and virgin olive oil. It achieves perfection in its simplicity. Try, if featured, a main dish order of a delectable white fish, *pezzogna,* which is found only in the cold outer waters of the Bay of Naples. Meats are high-quality cuts, and all the sumptuous desserts are homemade and enticing.

In the Grande Hotel Vesuvio, Via Partenope 45. (C) **081-7640044.** www.vesuvio.it. Reservations, and jackets for men, are required. Main courses 18€–28€. AE, DC, MC, V. Tues–Sun 1–3pm; 8:30–11pm. Bus: C25.

Coco Loco ★★★ MEDITERRANEAN   In the Chiaia district, this stylish restaurant with its innovative cuisine is all the rage among some of the most discerning and demanding palates in Naples. Off Via Filangieri, it lies a 10-minute walk from Palazzo Reale. Chef Diebgo Nuzzo is the darling of the media. That cuisine is light and precise, well flavored, and nicely balanced between regional products and seafood.

Appetizers are tangy delights, including thyme-flavored fresh lobster salad or an anchovy and zucchini pie. For your main, try one of the succulent pastas, including one with artichokes and baked ricotta. The chef prepares one of Naples's best risottos with seafood and pumpkin flowers. For something truly local, try scabbard fish stuffed with eggplant, black olives, and Provola cheese.

Piazzetta Rodino 31. (C) **081-415482.** Reservations required. Main courses 18€–30€. AE, MC, V. Mon–Sat 12:30–3pm and 8pm–midnight. Closed 3 weeks in Aug. Metro: Piazza Amedeo.

George's ★★ MEDITERRANEAN/INTERNATIONAL   Oscar Wilde claimed that the view over the Bay of Naples was one of the reasons to visit the city. That panoramic sweep is seen at its best on the top floor of Grand Hotel Parker's, in a previously recommended hotel. To be here having a drink as the sun sets over the Gulf is one of these memorable experiences that will be imbedded in your brain. Fortunately, the cuisine, based on the richest of the sea and the finest of regional produce, is sublime.

Many of the chef's dishes reflect the cookery of Naples in the 1800s, although all recipes have been lightened and adapted for the more modern palate. To take advantage of the best in any season, the menu is adjusted from month to month. But you can always count on the catch of the day, sometimes served with an elegant sprinkling of truffles. A medley of vegetables is often sautéed in virgin olive oil to accompany many meat dishes. Tender cutlets of lamb with eggplant is a specialty. Most of the wine available comes from the grapes of Campania.

Corso Vittorio Emanuele 135. (C) **081-7612474.** www.grandhotelparkers.it. Reservations required. Main courses 26€–35€. AE, DC, MC, V. Daily 12:30–2:30pm and 8–10:30pm. Bus: C24 or C27.

La Cantinella ★★ NEAPOLITAN/SEAFOOD   Cantinella serves grilled seafood at its finest. The restaurant is on a busy street skirting the bay in Santa Lucia; speakeasy-style doors open after you ring. You'll find a well-stocked antipasto table and—get this—a working phone on each table. The chefs have a deft way of handling the region's fresh produce and turn out both Neapolitan classics and more imaginative dishes. The menu includes four preparations of risotto (including one with champagne), many kinds of pasta (including *tagliolini* with lobster and clams), and most of the classic beef and veal dishes of Italy. One especially delightful specialty is pumpkin flowers stuffed with swordfish mousse on crispy vegetables with a cherry tomato sauce.

Via Cuma 42. (C) **081-7648684.** www.lacantinella.it. Reservations required. Fixed-price menus 50€–70€. AE, DC, MC, V. Daily noon–3pm and 7:30pm–midnight. Closed Aug 9–27 and Sun Apr–Nov. Bus: C25 or 140.

La Stanza del Gusto ★★★ 🍴 CREATIVE NEAPOLITAN "The Room of Taste" (its English name) reflects the imagination of Mario Avallone, its creative chef, who is a specialist in cheese and wine. His wine *carte* is the best in Naples, and even he even features a wine of the week for connoisseurs. Depending on what is good and fresh at the market, his menu changes daily and, of course, depends on seasonal adjustments. The chef takes justifiable pride in such dishes as octopus *timballo* with a potato cream sauce, or *millefoglie di melanzane* (eggplant pie) with smoked dried cod. For the gourmet palate, he whips up a homemade pasta with fresh sea urchins, although the breaded filet of grouper with fresh herbs will appeal to more conventional tastes.

Via Costantinopoli 100. ℂ **081-401578.** www.lastanzadelgusto.com. Reservations required. Main courses 8€–18€; fixed-price menus 35€–65€. AE, MC, V. Tues–Sat 10:30am–midnight. Closed 3 weeks in Aug. Metro: Museo.

MODERATE

Don Salvatore ★ NEAPOLITAN/SEAFOOD   This restaurant is on the Mergellina seafront, near the departure point of hydrofoils for Capri. Owner Vincenzo Esposito takes his wine as seriously as his food in this atmospheric restaurant, which was once a warehouse for boats. The menu is likely to include an array of fish and a marvelous assortment of fresh Neapolitan vegetables grown in the countryside. The fish comes right out of the Bay of Naples (which might or might not be a plus). Favorite seafood dishes include shrimp with lemon zest or baked filet of white fish with green olives. One of the most savory pasta dishes is homemade *chiaffoni* with clams, mussels, black olives, and cherry tomatoes. You can get a reasonably priced bottle from the wine cellar, said to be the finest in Campania.

Via Mergellina 4A. ℂ **081-681817.** www.donsalvatore.it. Reservations recommended. Main courses 10€–24€. AE, DC, MC, V. Thurs–Tues 12:30–4pm and 7:30pm–midnight. Metro: Mergellina.

Giuseppone a Mare ★★ NEAPOLITAN/SEAFOOD   At this restaurant, known for the best and freshest seafood in Campania, you can dine in Neapolitan sunshine on an open-air terrace with a bay view. Diners make their selections from a cart likely to include everything from crabs to eels. You might begin your dinner with some fritters (a batter whipped up with seaweed and fresh squash blossoms). Among the most enticing items are pasta cooked with pumpkin and swordfish, and baked fish under a potato crust. Much of the day's catch is deep-fried a golden brown. The *pièce de résistance* is an octopus casserole. If the oven's going, you can order a pizza. The restaurant stocks some fine southern Italian wines, especially from Ischia and Vesuvio.

Via Ferdinando Russo 13. ℂ **081-5756002.** www.giuseppone.com. Reservations required. Main courses 12€–22€. AE, DC, MC, V. Tues–Sat 12:30–3:30pm and 7:30–11pm; Sun 12:30–3pm. Closed Aug 16–31. Bus: C3 or 140.

Il Gallo Nero ★ NEAPOLITAN   Gian Paolo Quagliata maintains his hillside villa with its period furniture and accessories. In summer, the enthusiastic crowd is served on an elegant terrace. Many of the dishes are based on 100-year-old recipes, although a few are more recent inventions. You might enjoy the Neapolitan linguine with pesto, rigatoni with fresh vegetables, tagliatelle primavera, or macaroni with peas and artichokes. The fish dishes are usually well prepared—

grilled, broiled, or sautéed. The meat dishes include slightly more exotic creations, such as prosciutto with orange slices and veal cutlets with artichokes.

Via Torquato Tasso 466. © **081-643012.** www.ilgalloneronapoli.it. Reservations recommended. Main courses 13€–27€. AE, DC, MC, V. Tues–Sat 7pm–midnight; Sun 12:30–3pm. Closed Aug. Metro: Mergellina.

Mimi alla Ferrovia ★ 🎁 NEAPOLITAN   The neighborhood is a bit seedy, but this joint attracts celebrities and others seeking good food. Fellini used to swear that it served the best food in Naples; even Italian presidents have come to here to dine. Elegantly old-fashioned, it opened for business in 1943 in the war-torn city.

The chef adjusts the menu seasonally to take advantage of the best products on the market. Perfectly executed dishes include rigatoni with pumpkin flowers and fresh shrimp. The catch of the day is often baked with fresh vegetables, and the risotto with fresh lobster is also worthy of praise. Begin with a selection from the antipasti table, perhaps sweet peppers stuffed with mozzarella. Squid, often served in a light tomato sauce, is another specialty.

Via Alfonso d'Aragona 21. © **081-5538-525.** www.mimiallaferrovia.com. Reservations recommended. Main courses 7.50€–24€. AE, MC, V. Mon–Sat noon–3:30pm and 7:30–11:30pm. Closed 1 week in Aug.

Ristorante La Fazenda ★ NEAPOLITAN/SEAFOOD   It would be hard to find a more typically Neapolitan restaurant than this one. On a clear day, you can see Capri. The decor is rustic, loaded with agrarian touches and an assortment of Neapolitan families, lovers, and visitors who have made it one of their preferred places. In summer, the overflow from the dining room spills onto the terrace. Menu specialties include linguine with scampi, fresh grilled fish or grilled meat, sautéed clams, a mixed Italian grill, savory stews, and many chicken dishes, along with lobster with fresh grilled tomatoes. Look for "Mr. Nappo," allegedly "the largest pizza ever."

Via Marechiaro 58A. © **081-5757420.** Reservations required. Main courses 8€–18€. AE, DC, MC, V. Tues–Sat 1–3pm and 7pm–midnight; Sun 1–3pm; Mon 7pm–midnight. Bus: 140.

INEXPENSIVE

Da Michele ★ PIZZA   Opened in 1789, this pizzeria is locked in a struggle with Pizzeria Brandi to see which eatery serves the best pie in Naples. Aficionados disagree on which is best. A long line forms at the door every night, consisting of hungry diners eager to sample only two types of pizza.

The Margherita is made with tomatoes, mozzarella and basil, and the marinara is graced with tomato, fresh garlic and oregano. Get a number and then hang outside until your number is called. The location is between Piazza Garibaldi and Piazza Amore.

Via Sersale 1-3. © **081-15539204.** Reservations not accepted. Pizzas 6€–10€. No credit cards. Mon–Sat 10am–11pm. Bus: C55, C58, or R2.

Giovanni Scaturchio PASTRIES   This place has been satisfying and fattening locals since around 1900. Pastries include the entire selection of Neapolitan sweets, cakes, and candies, including brioches soaked in liqueur, *cassate* (pound cake) filled with layered ricotta, and cheesy ricotta pastries known as *sfogliatelle*. Another specialty is *ministeriale*, a chocolate cake filled with liqueur and chocolate cream.

Piazza San Domenico Maggiore 19. © **081-5516944.** www.scaturchio.it. Pastries start at 1.50€ if consumed standing up, or 2.50€ if enjoyed at a table. MC, V. Daily 7:20am–8:40pm. Closed 2–3 weeks in Aug.

La Sacrestia PASTA/SEAFOOD   The *trompe l'oeil* frescoes on the two-story interior and the name La Sacrestia vaguely suggest the ecclesiastical, but that's not the case at this patrician villa. Perched near the top of a seemingly endless labyrinth of streets winding up from the port (take a taxi or go by funicular), this bustling place is sometimes called "the greatest show in town." In summer, a terrace with its flowering arbor provides a view over the harbor lights. Meals emphasize well-prepared dishes with strong doses of Neapolitan drama. You might try what's said to be the most luxurious macaroni dish in Italy ("Prince of Naples"), made with truffles and mild cheeses. Less ornate selections are a full array of pastas and dishes composed of octopus, squid, and shellfish.

Via Orazio 116. © **081-664186.** www.lasacrestia.it. Reservations required. Main courses 9€–29€. AE, DC, MC, V. Daily 1–3pm and 8pm–1am. Closed Sun in July and 2 weeks in mid-Aug. Funicular: from Mergellina.

L'Ebbrezza di Noe ★ 🍴 ITALIAN/MEDITERRANEAN   In the prestigious Chiaia shopping district, this wine bar and restaurant is a showcase for the culinary wares of a talented chef, Luca di Leva. It is decorated in a rustic style evoking a farmhouse, with lots of wooden furniture. Careful attention is paid not only to the wine selection but to the market-fresh ingredients. The wine cellar stocks more than 1,200 varieties of wine. Much of the antipasti is made with fresh vegetables, and there is also a selection of rare cheeses from the country. On the blackboard is posted a daily changing list of specialties. Some of the best dishes include the chef's white lasagna with fresh vegetables and a white wine sauce, or else a savory cheese pie with porcini mushrooms. Inspired by Morocco, the couscous is another tasty delight, prepared with vegetables.

Via Vetriera a Chiaia 9. © **081-400104.** Reservations recommended. Main courses 7€–13€; fixed-price menu 35€. AE, V. Tues–Sun 7pm–midnight. Metro: Piazza Amedeo.

Masaniello ★ 📱 NEAPOLITAN   Located in a former stable, this hard-to-find restaurant is named for the celebrated leader of a people's uprising in 1647. It prints no menus, so the owner, Lina Iannelli, will tell you what's offered. Put yourself in his hands and be prepared for a bounteous feast. The food is cooked to order after elaborate consultations about the taste of each customer. The cuisine is exquisitely prepared and based on only the freshest of ingredients. The traditional dishes based on antique recipes include linguine with *lupini di mare* (Neapolitan clams) and pecorino cheese. The chef is also proud of his special pasta with potatoes; although it sounds like an unlikely combination, it's filled with flavor from the smoked Provola cheese and the fresh little tomatoes.

Via Donnalbina 28. © **081-5528863.** Reservations recommended. Main courses 6€–20€; fixed-price menu 8€. AE, DC, MC, V. Daily Dec–May Mon–Sat noon–3:30pm and 7pm–midnight. Bus: C57, R3, or R4.

Pizzeria Brandi ★ NEAPOLITAN/PIZZA   Naples is famous for pizza, and this is the place to go to sample the best. The most historic pizzeria in Italy, Brandi was opened by Pietro Colicchio in 1889. His successor, Raffaele Esposito, was requested to prepare a banquet for Margherita di Savoia, the queen of Italy.

So successful was the reception of the pizza made with tomato, basil, olive oil, and mozzarella (the colors of the newly united Italy's flag) that the queen accepted the honor of having the dish named after her. Today you can order the pizza that pleased a queen, as well as linguine with scampi, fettuccine "Regina d'Italia," and a full array of seafood dishes.

Salita Santa Anna di Palazzo 2 (Via Chiaia). © **081-416928.** www.brandi.it. Reservations recommended. Main courses 8€–20€; pizza from 6€. AE, MC, V. Daily 12:30–3pm and 7:30pm–midnight. Bus: R2 or R3.

Vini e Cucina ★ 🎁 NEAPOLITAN   The best ragout sauce in all Naples is said to be made at this *trattoria*, which has only 20 tables. You can get a satisfying meal, but we must warn you: It's almost impossible to get in. Get there early and expect to wait. The cooking is the best home-style version of Neapolitan cuisine we've been able to find in this city. The spaghetti, in that fabulous sauce, is served al dente.

Corso Vittorio Emanuele 762. © **081-660302.** Reservations recommended. Main courses 8€–15€. Daily noon–3:30pm and 7–11:30pm. Closed Aug 14–28. Metro: Mergellina.

Shopping

The shopping in Naples can't compare to that in Milan, Venice, Florence, and Rome. Nevertheless, there are some good buys for those willing to seek them out. The finest shopping area lies around **Piazza dei Martiri** and along such streets as **Via dei Mille, Via Calabritto,** and **Via Chiaia.** There's more commercial shopping between Piazza Trieste e Trento and Piazza Dante along **Via Toledo/ Via Roma.**

We never visit Naples without waiting in line to get into a tiny store, **Marinella,** Riviera di Chiaia 287 (© **081-2451182;** www.marinellanapoli.it), which enjoys worldwide fame. It's worth the wait. Inside you'll find a great collection of accessories for men, along with shirts and sweaters that you'll keep forever. Wherever you look, you encounter a feast of indigo or red ties or else scarves printed in England just for Marinella. Royalty, politicians, and international movie stars are also likely to be waiting in line with you.

Coral: A costly souvenir

Exquisite coral jewelry is abundant in Naples and much sought after by collectors, but ecologically minded shoppers may wish to steer clear. Because Mediterranean coral reefs are already so depleted, much of the coral crafted in Naples arrives from Thailand, the Philippines, and other Asian-Pacific nations, where there is little to no regulation of coral harvesting and reefs are disappearing at an alarming rate. The World Wildlife Fund is urging coral designers and manufacturers to pledge not to use red and pink coral, the most at-risk—and also the most precious—varieties, until the industry is more closely regulated. Though we cannot attest to the sustainability of their practices, the most venerable firm is the century-old **Basilio Liverino,** Via Montedoro 61 (© **081-8811225;** www.liverino.it). If you wish to appreciate coral artistry without making a purchase, you can visit their museum (call ahead), displaying the world's best collection of cameos and corals.

Modeled on Milan's galleria, the **Galleria Umberto I,** Via San Carlo (see below), was built as part of Naples's urban renewal scheme following an 1884 cholera epidemic. The massive glass- and iron-frame barrel vaults of its four wings and central dome soar some 60m (187 ft.) above the inlaid marble flooring (it had to be largely rebuilt after World War II bomb damage). It makes for a pleasant shopping stroll. You'll find a wide range of stores selling typical area products, from fashion to ceramics.

Naples After Dark

A **sunset walk through Santa Lucia** and along the waterfront is one of the lasting pleasures in Naples. You can stroll by the glass-enclosed **Galleria Umberto I,** off Via Roma across from the Teatro San Carlo. The 19th-century gallery is still standing today, although it's a little the worse for wear. It's a kind of social center for Naples, with lots of shopping and dining possibilities.

Naples's oldest cafe, dating from 1860, is the palatial **Gran Caffè Gambrinus,** Via Chiaia 1, near the Galleria Umberto I (℡ **081-417582**; www.caffe gambrinus.com). Along the vaulted ceiling of an inner room, Empire-style caryatids spread their togas in high relief above frescoes of mythological playmates. The cafe is known for its espresso and cappuccino, as well as pastries and cakes whose variety dazzles the eye. You can also order potato-and-rice croquettes and fried pizzas for a light lunch. Cappuccino goes for 3.50€ a table (coffee 3€ a table). The cafe is open daily 7am to 2am.

OPERA   The **Teatro San Carlo,** Via San Carlo 98, across from the Galleria Umberto (℡ **081-7972331**; www.teatrosancarlo.it), is one of the largest opera houses in Italy, with some of the best acoustics. In our view, the operas staged here are just as impressive as anything opening at Milan's more celebrated La Scala. Even Callas and Pavarotti had trod the boards at San Carlo. Built in only 6 months for King Charles's birthday in 1737, it was restored in a gilded neoclassical style. Grand-scale productions are presented on the main stage. October through May, the box office is open Monday to Saturday 10am to 7pm; and Sunday 10am to 3:30pm. Tickets cost 30€ to 250€.

BARS & CLUBS   On its nightclub/cabaret circuit, Naples offers more sucker joints than any other Mediterranean port. If you're starved for action, you'll find plenty of it—and you're likely to end up paying for it dearly.

Chez Moi, Via del Parco Margherita 13 (℡ **081-407526**; www.chez moi.it), is one of the city's best-managed nightclubs, refusing entrance to anyone who looks like a troublemaker. This is appreciated by the designers, government ministers, and socialites who enjoy the place. The crowd tends to be over 25. The place is open Wednesday to Sunday 10:30pm to 4 or 5am. Occasionally there's a cabaret act or a live pianist at the bar, but more frequently the music is disco. The cover is 18€.

Piazza Bellini thrives at night, especially at **Caffè Intramoenia,** Piazza Bellini 70 (℡ **081-2909720**; www.intramoenia.it), which opened shop in a former bookstore. Drinkers occupy outdoor tables here even in winter. Another popular gathering spot in the Chiaia district is **Enoteca Belledonne,** Vico Belledonne a Chiaia 18 (℡ **081-403162**; www.enoteca belledonne.com), the neighborhood's choice joint for an *aperitivo.* You'll be surrounded by genial people and glass-fronted cabinets filled with an array of wine bottles. Some of the best wines of Campania are available here by the glass.

Most gay nightlife is centered in the Posillipo neighborhood, where you'll find **Tongue,** Via Alessandro Manzoni 207 (⟨℗⟩ **081-7690800**). It has a mixed crowd, a large part of whom are gay, dancing to techno music. It is open only on weekends 9pm to 3am and charges a cover of 15€.

THE PHLEGREAN FIELDS & HERCULANEUM
The Phlegrean Fields ★★

One of the more bizarre attractions of southern Italy, the **Phlegrean Fields (Campi Flegrei)** form a backdrop for a day's exploring west of Naples and along its bay. The fiery fields contain the dormant volcano Solfatara, the cave of the Cumaean Sibyl, Virgil's gateway to the "Infernal Regions," the ruins of thermal baths and amphitheaters built by the Romans, deserted colonies left by the Greeks, and lots more.

The best center for exploring the area is **Pozzuoli,** reached by Metropolitana (subway) from Stazione Centrale in Naples. The fare is 1.10€. Once in Pozzuoli, you can catch one of the SEPSA buses at any bus stop and be in Baia in 20 minutes. You can also go to Cumae on one of these buses or to Solfatara or Lago d'Averno.

SOLFATARA ★★ About 12km (7½ miles) west of Naples, near Pozzuoli, is the ancient **Vulcano Solfatara,** Via Solfatara 161 (⟨℗⟩ **081-5262341;** www. solfatara.it). It hasn't erupted since the final year of the 12th century but has been threatening ever since. It gives off sulfurous gases and releases scalding vapors through cracks in the earth's surface. In fact, Solfatara's activity (or inactivity) has been observed for such a long time that the crater's name was once used by *Webster's* dictionary to define any "dormant volcano" emitting vapors.

You can visit the crater daily 8:30am to 7pm (until 4:30pm in winter) for 6€. From Naples, take bus no. 152 from Piazza Garibaldi or the Metropolitana from Stazione Centrale. Once you get off at the train station, you can board one of the city buses that go up the hill, or you can walk to the crater in about 20 minutes.

POZZUOLI ★ Just 2km (1¼ miles) from Solfatara, the port of Pozzuoli opens onto a gulf screened from the Bay of Naples by a promontory. The ruins of the **Anfiteatro Flavio ★★**, Via Nicola Terracciano 75 (⟨℗⟩ **081-5266007**), built in the last part of the 1st century, testify to past greatness. One of the finest surviving ancient arenas, it's particularly distinguished by its "wings," which, considering their age, are in good condition. The amphitheater is said to have entertained 40,000 spectators at the height of its glory. You can visit year-round Wednesday to Monday 9am to 1 hour before sunset. Admission is 4€. In another part of town, the **Tempio di Serapide ★** was really the Macellum (market square), and some of its ruined pillars still project upward. It was erected during the reign of the Flavian emperors. You can reach Pozzuoli by subway from Stazione Centrale in Naples.

TREADING LIGHTLY ON mount vesuvius

Stand at the bottom of the great market-place of Pompeii, and look up at the silent streets . . . over the broken houses with their inmost sanctuaries open to the day, away to Mount Vesuvius, bright and snowy in the peaceful distance; and lose all count of time, and heed of other things, in the strange and melancholy sensation of seeing the Destroyed and the Destroyer making this quiet picture in the sun.

—Charles Dickens, *Pictures from Italy*

A volcano that has struck terror in Campania, the towering, pitch-black **Mount Vesuvius** looms menacingly over the Bay of Naples. August 24, A.D. 79, is the infamous date when Vesuvius burst forth and buried Pompeii, Herculaneum, and Stabiae under ash and volcanic mud. Vesuvius has erupted periodically ever since (thousands were killed in 1631); the last major spouting of lava occurred in the last century (it blew off the ring of its crater in 1906). The last spectacular eruption was on March 31, 1944. The approach to Vesuvius is dramatic, with the terrain growing foreboding as you near the top. Along the way you'll see villas rising on its slopes, and vineyards—the grapes produce an amber-colored wine known as Lacrimae Christi (Tears of Christ); the citizens of ancient Pompeii enjoyed wine from here, as excavations have revealed. Closer to the summit, the soil becomes puce colored and an occasional wildflower appears.

It might sound like a dubious invitation (Vesuvius, after all, is an active volcano), but it's possible to visit the rim of the crater's mouth. As you look down into its smoldering core, you might recall that Spartacus, a century before the eruption that buried Pompeii, hid in the hollow of the crater, which was then covered with vines.

The **Parco Nazionale del Vesuvio** contains an **Observatory** (✆ 081-7777150; www.vesuviopark.it) at 608m (1,994 ft.) that is the oldest in the world, dating from 1841. Charging 8€ for admission, the park is open daily from 9am until sunset.

To reach Vesuvius from Naples, take the Circumvesuviana Railway or (summer only) bus service from Piazza Vittoria, which hooks up with bus connections at Pugliano. You get off the train at the Ercolano station, the 10th stop. The Vesuvio Express at the Ercolano stop leaves for the top of the crater in summer daily 9am to 6pm; in winter daily 9am to 3pm. The cost is 18€. For more information, call ✆ 081-7393666, or go to www.vesuvioexpress.it. Once at the top, you must be accompanied by a guide, which will cost 10€. Assorted willing tour guides are found in the bus parking lot; they are available from 9am to about 4pm.

BAIA ★★   In the days of imperial Rome, the emperors came here to frolic in the sun while enjoying the comforts of their luxurious villas and Roman baths. Emperor Claudius built a grand villa here for his first wife, Messalina, who spent her days and nights reveling in debauchery and plotting to have her husband replaced by her lover (for which she was beheaded). And it was here that Claudius was poisoned by his last wife, Agrippina, the controlling mother of Nero. Nero is said to have had Agrippina murdered at nearby Bacoli, with its Pool of Mirabilis—after she had survived his first attempt on her life, a collapsing boat meant to send her to a watery grave.

The Roman-era thermal baths at Baia.

Parts of Baia's illustrious past have been dug out, including both the Temple of Baiae and the thermal baths.

You can explore this archaeological district (☏ 081-8687592; www.ulixes. it) daily from 9am to 1 hour before sunset. Admission is 4€. Ferrovia Cumana trains depart from Stazione Centrale for the 15-minute trip from Naples.

LAGO D'AVERNO ★ About 16km (10 miles) west of Naples, a bit north of Baia, is a lake occupying an extinct volcanic crater. Known to the ancients as the **Gateway to Hades,** its vapors were said to produce illness and death. Lake Averno could well have been the source of the expression "still waters run deep." Facing the lake are the ruins of what has been known as the **Temple of Apollo** from the 1st century A.D. and what was once thought to be the Cave of the Cumaean Sibyl (see below). The Sibyl is said to have ferried Aeneas, son of Aphrodite, across the lake, where he traced a mysterious spring to its source, the River Styx. In the 1st century B.C., Agrippa turned it into a harbor for Roman ships by digging out a canal. Take the Napoli–Torre Gaveta bus from Baia to reach the site.

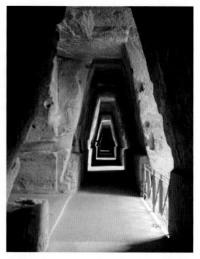

CUMA ★ Cuma was one of the first outposts of Greek colonization in what's now Italy. It's 19km (12 miles) west of Naples, and of interest chiefly because it's said to have contained the **Cave of the Cumaean Sibyl ★**. The cave, really a gallery, was dug by the Greeks in the 5th century B.C. and was a sacred spot to them. Beloved by Apollo, the Sibyl is said to have written

The Cave of the Cumaean Sibyl, just outside of Naples.

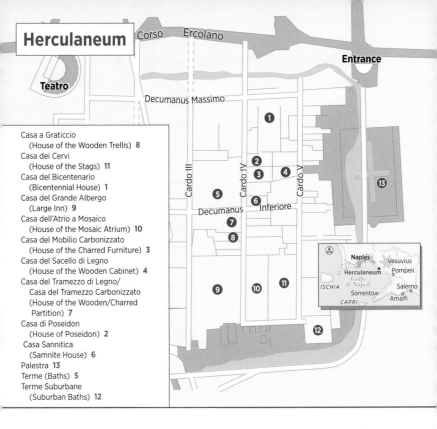

Herculaneum

Casa a Graticcio
  (House of the Wooden Trellis) **8**
Casa dei Cervi
  (House of the Stags) **11**
Casa del Bicentenario
  (Bicentennial House) **1**
Casa del Grande Albergo
  (Large Inn) **9**
Casa dell'Atrio a Mosaico
  (House of the Mosaic Atrium) **10**
Casa del Mobilio Carbonizzato
  (House of the Charred Furniture) **3**
Casa del Sacello di Legno
  (House of the Wooden Cabinet) **4**
Casa del Tramezzo di Legno/
  Casa del Tramezzo Carbonizzato
  (House of the Wooden/Charred
  Partition) **7**
Casa di Poseidon
  (House of Poseidon) **2**
Casa Sannitica
  (Samnite House) **6**
Palestra **13**
Terme (Baths) **5**
Terme Suburbane
  (Suburban Baths) **12**

the *Sibylline Oracles,* a group of books of prophecy. You may visit not only the caves but the ruins of temples dedicated to Jupiter and Apollo (later converted into Christian churches), daily 9am to 1 hour before sunset; admission is 4€ for adults (children 17 and under enter free). On Via Domitiana, to the east of Cuma, you'll pass the **Arco Felice,** an arch about 20m (64 ft.) high, built by Emperor Domitian in the 1st century A.D. Ferrovia Cumana trains run here, departing from Naples's Stazione Centrale.

Herculaneum ★★

The builders of Herculaneum (Ercolano) were still working to repair the damage caused by an A.D. 62 earthquake when Vesuvius erupted on that fateful August day in A.D. 79. Herculaneum, about one-fourth the size of Pompeii, didn't start to come to light again until 1709, when Prince Elbeuf launched the unfortunate fashion of tunneling through it for treasures, more intent on profiting from the sale of objets d'art than on uncovering a Roman town fossilized in time.

Subsequent excavations at the site, called the **Ufficio Scavi di Ercolano,** Corso Resina, Ercolano (𝄢 **081-7324311;** www.pompeiisites.org), have been slow and sporadic. In fact, Herculaneum, named after Hercules, is not completely dug out today. One of the obstacles has been that the town, which is much closer to Vesuvius than Pompeii, was as a result buried under a heavier lava flow than that which piled onto Pompeii. Of course, this formed a greater protection for the

buildings buried underneath—many of which were more elaborately constructed than those at Pompeii because Herculaneum was a seaside resort for patricians. The complication of having the slum of Resina resting over the yet-to-be-excavated district has further impeded progress and urban renewal.

Although all the streets and buildings of Herculaneum hold interest, some ruins merit more attention than others. The **baths** *(terme)* ★★★ are divided between those at the forum and the **Suburban Baths (Terme Suburbane)** ★ on the outskirts, near the more elegant villas. The municipal baths, which segregated the sexes, are larger, but the ones at the edge of town are more lavishly adorned. The **Palestra** was a kind of sports arena, where games were staged to satisfy the spectacle-hungry denizens. The plan for the typical town house was to erect it around an uncovered atrium. In some areas, Herculaneum possessed the forerunner of

The ruins at Herculaneum.

the modern apartment house. Important private homes to seek out are the **House of the Bicentenary (Casa del Bicentenario)** ★, the **House of the Wooden Cabinet (Casa a Graticcio)** ★★, the **House of the Wooden Partition (Casa del Tramezzo di Legno)** ★, and the **House of Poseidon (Casa di Poseidon)**, as well as the **Amphitheater (Anfiteatro),** containing the best-known mosaic discovered in the ruins.

The finest example of how the aristocracy lived is the **Casa dei Cervi,** named the **House of the Stags** because of the sculpture found inside. Guides are fond of showing the males on their tours a statue of a drunken Hercules urinating. Some of the best of the houses are locked and can be seen only by permission.

The ruins are open April to October daily 8:30am to 7:30pm (last admission at 6pm). Off-season hours are daily 8:30am to 5pm (last admission at 3:30pm). Admission is 11€. To reach the archaeological zone, take the regular train service from Naples on the Circumvesuviana Railway, a 20-minute ride that leaves about every half-hour from Corso Garibaldi 387, just south of the main train station (you can also catch Circumvesuviana trains underneath the main Stazione Centrale itself; follow the signs). This train will get you to Vesuvius (same stop), Pompeii, and Sorrento. Otherwise, it's a 7km (4⅓-mile) drive on the autostrada to Salerno (turn off at Ercolano). *Note:* A cumulative ticket for Herculaneum and Pompeii costs 20€, which is a good buy. You can purchase it at the Circumvesuviana Railway Station at Piazza Garibaldi in Naples.

POMPEII ★★★

24km (15 miles) S of Naples, 237km (147 miles) SE of Rome

When Vesuvius erupted in A.D. 79, Pliny the Younger thought the end of the world had come. The ruined city of Pompeii brings to light the life of 19 centuries ago and has sparked the imagination of the world.

Numerous myths have surrounded Pompeii, one of which is that a completely intact city was rediscovered. Actually, the Pompeians (that is, those who escaped) returned to their city when the ashes had cooled and removed some of the most precious treasures from the resort. But they left plenty behind to be uncovered at a later date and carted off to museums throughout Europe and America.

After a long medieval sleep, Pompeii was again brought to life in the late 16th century, quite by accident, by architect Domenico Fontana. However, it was in the mid–18th century that large-scale excavations were launched. Somebody once remarked that Pompeii's second tragedy was its rediscovery. It really should have been left to slumber for another century or two, when it might have been better excavated and maintained.

Essentials

GETTING THERE   The **Circumvesuviana Railway** (✆ **800-053939;** www. vesuviana.it) departs Naples every half-hour from Piazza Garibaldi. However, be sure you get on the train headed toward Sorrento and get off at Pompeii/Scavi (*scavi* means "archaeological excavation"). If you get on the Pompeii train, you'll end up in the town of Pompeii and have to transfer there to the other train to get to the ruins. A round-trip ticket costs 5€; trip time is 45 minutes each way. Circumvesuviana trains leave Sorrento several times a day for Pompeii, costing 2€ one-way. There's an entrance about 45m (150 ft.) from the rail station at the Villa dei Misteri. At the rail station in the town of Pompeii, **bus** connections take you to the entrance to the excavations.

To reach Pompeii by **car** from Naples, take the 22km (14-mile) drive on the autostrada toward Salerno. If you're coming from Sorrento, head east on SS. 145, where you can connect with A3 (marked NAPOLI). Then take the signposted turnoff for Pompeii.

VISITOR INFORMATION   The **tourist office** is at Via Sacra 1 (✆ **081-8507255;** www.pompeiturismo.it). It's open Monday to Friday 8am to 3:30pm (until 7pm Apr–Oct), and Saturday 8am to 2pm.

LOGISTICAL TIPS   After you pay for your entrance, you'll find a **bookstore,** where you can purchase guidebooks to the ruins (available in English and complete with detailed

Pompeii's Stabian Baths.

727

photos) that will help you understand what you're seeing. We highly recommend that you purchase one before you set out.

If you're here on a sunny day, wear sunscreen and bring along a bottle of water. There's almost no place in Pompeii to escape the sun's rays, and it can often be dusty.

Exploring the Ruins

Most people visit the **Ufficio Scavi di Pompeii,** Via Villa dei Misteri 1 (⟨℅⟩ **081-8610744;** www.pompeiisites.org), the best preserved 2,000-year-old ruins in Europe, on a day trip from Naples (allow at least 4 hr. for even a superficial look at the archaeological site).

The most elegant of the patrician villas is the **House of the Vettii (Casa dei Vettii)** ★★★, boasting a courtyard, statuary (such as a two-faced Janus), paintings, and a black-and-red Pompeian dining room known for its frescoes of delicate cupids. The house was occupied by two brothers named Vettii, both of whom were wealthy merchants. As you enter the vestibule, you'll see a painting of Priapus resting his gargantuan phallus on a pair of scales. The guard will reveal other erotic fertility drawings and statuary, although most such material has been removed to the Archaeological Museum in Naples. This house is the best example of a villa and garden that's been restored.

The second-most-important villa, the **House of the Mysteries (Villa dei Misteri)** ★★, near the Porto Ercolano, is outside the walls (go along Viale alla Villa dei Misteri). What makes the villa exceptional, aside from its architectural features, are its remarkable frescoes depicting scenes associated with the sect of Dionysus (Bacchus), one of the cults that flourished in Roman times. Note the Pompeian red in some of the backgrounds. The largest house, called the **House of the Faun (Casa del Fauno)** ★★ because of a bronze statue of a faun found there, takes up a city block and has four dining rooms and two spacious peristyle gardens. It sheltered the celebrated *Battle of Alexander the Great* mosaic that's now in the Museo Archeologico Nazionale in Naples.

In the center of town is the **Forum (Foro)** ★. Rather small, it was nonetheless the heart of Pompeian life, known to bakers, merchants, and the aristocrats

A view of the Pompeii's Forum, with its destroyer, Mount Vesuvius, in the background.

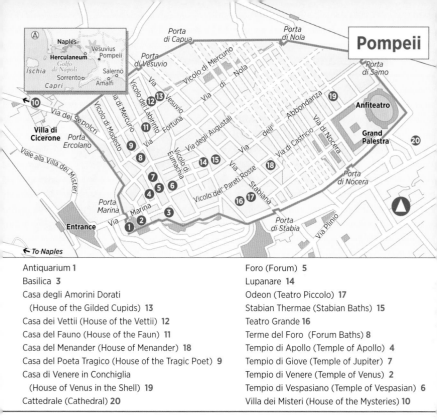

Pompeii

Antiquarium 1
Basilica 3
Casa degli Amorini Dorati
  (House of the Gilded Cupids) 13
Casa dei Vettii (House of the Vettii) 12
Casa del Fauno (House of the Faun) 11
Casa del Menander (House of Menander) 18
Casa del Poeta Tragico (House of the Tragic Poet) 9
Casa di Venere in Conchiglia
  (House of Venus in the Shell) 19
Cattedrale (Cathedral) 20

Foro (Forum) 5
Lupanare 14
Odeon (Teatro Piccolo) 17
Stabian Thermae (Stabian Baths) 15
Teatro Grande 16
Terme del Foro (Forum Baths) 8
Tempio di Apollo (Temple of Apollo) 4
Tempio di Giove (Temple of Jupiter) 7
Tempio di Venere (Temple of Venus) 2
Tempio di Vespasiano (Temple of Vespasian) 6
Villa dei Misteri (House of the Mysteries) 10

who lived in the villas. Parts of the Forum were severely damaged in an earth-quake 16 years before the eruption of Vesuvius and hadn't been repaired when the final destruction came. Three buildings surrounding the Forum are the **basilica** (the city's largest single structure), the **Temple of Apollo (Tempio di Apollo)** ★★, and the **Temple of Jupiter (Tempio di Giove)** ★★. The **Stabian Thermae (baths)** ★★★—where both men and women lounged between games of knucklebones (a game played with knucklebones or jacks, once used the way gamblers use dice)—are in good condition, among the finest to survive from antiquity. Here you'll see some skeletons. In the **brothel (Lupanare)** are some erotic paintings (tip the guide to see them).

Other buildings of interest include the **Great Theater (Teatro Grande)** ★, built in the 5th century B.C. During the Hellenistic period from 200 to 150 B.C., it was largely rebuilt, as it was again by the Romans in the 1st century A.D. This open-air theater could hold 5,000 spectators, many of them bloodthirsty as they screamed for death in the battles between wild animals and gladiators. The **House of the Gilded Cupids (Casa degli Amorini Dorati)** ★ was a flamboy-ant private home; its owner is unknown, although he probably lived during the reign of Nero. Obviously he had theatrical flair, attested to by the gilded and glass cupids known as *amorini*. Even though it's badly ruined, the house contains a peristyle with one wing raised almost like a stage. The **House of the Tragic Poet (Casa del Poeta Tragico)** ★ gets its name from a mosaic discovered here (later

A detail from Pompeii's Stabian Baths.

sent to Naples). It depicts a chained watchdog on the doorstep with this warning: CAVE CANEM ("Beware of the Dog").

An ancient **bathhouse** with erotic frescoes has been opened to the public for the first time, although the discovery was made back in the 1980s. The delay in opening was because of lack of funds for restoration. The 2,000-year-old thermal bathhouse was in remarkably good condition and was still adorned with elaborate mosaics, including an indoor waterfall. Controversy centers around eight frescoes in vivid green, reds, and golds. These frescoes depict graphic scenes of various sex acts, including the only known artistic representation of cunnilingus from the Roman era. Some scholars have suggested that they were meant to advertise sexual services available on the upper floor of the baths; other archaeologists maintain they were intended merely to amuse.

Entrances to the ruins are open April to October daily 8:30am to 7:30pm (last admission at 6pm), and November to March daily 8:30am to 5pm (last admission at 3:30pm), costing 11€ for adults but free for ages 17 and under.

Where to Stay

Accommodations in Pompeii appear to be for earnest archaeologists only, with the three below the only really suitable choices. Some hotels in Pompeii aren't considered safe because of robberies. Protect your valuables and your person, and don't wander the streets at night. Most visitors look at the excavations and then seek better accommodations at either Naples or Sorrento.

Hotel Villa dei Misteri   This 1930s motel is located 229m (751 ft.) from Scavi Station, about 2km (1¼ miles) south of the center of town. It features a little garden and a place to park your car. The family-style welcome might compensate for a certain lack of extras. The place could stand a face-lift, but many readers have expressed their fondness for it. The guest rooms are all bare-bones doubles, with reasonable comfort and well-kept bathrooms.

Via Villa dei Misteri 11, 80045 Pompei-Scavi. ✆ **081-8613593.** Fax 081-8622983. www.villadei misteri.it. 41 units. 84€ double; 112€ triple. Rates include buffet breakfast. DC, MC, V. From the Naples rail station Circumvesuviana, take the Sorrento train and get off at the Villa dei Misteri stop. Free parking. **Amenities:** Restaurant; bar; outdoor pool. *In room:* A/C (in some), hair dryer, minibar, no phone, Wi-Fi (free).

Maiuri   It's not located at the excavations, but this is one of the better recommendations in town. The accommodations are in up-to-date and soundproof rooms, most of which front a tranquil garden. The rooms are midsize and open in most cases onto small balconies. As an added convenience a shuttle bus runs to and from the airport at Naples, but a fee is charged.

Via Acquasala 20, 80045 Pompeii. ✆ **081-85622716.** Fax 081-8562716. www.maiuri.it. 30 units. 85€–105€ double; 95€–120€ triple. Rates include buffet breakfast. AE, MC, V. Free parking. **Amenities:** Restaurant; bar; babysitting; concierge; *In room:* A/C, TV, hair dryer, minibar, Wi-Fi (free).

Villa Laura   The Villa Laura is one of the best hotels in town, although the competition isn't exactly stiff. On a somewhat hidden street, it escapes a lot of the noise that plagues Pompeii hotels. The small guest rooms are comfortably but not spectacularly furnished. Try for one with a balcony.

Via della Salle 13, 80045 Pompeii. ✆ **081-8631024.** Fax 081-8504893. www.villalaurapompei. com. 25 units. 95€ double. Rates include continental breakfast. AE, DC, MC, V. Parking 5€. **Amenities:** Restaurant (only for groups); room service; Wi-Fi (free, in lobby). *In room:* A/C, TV, hair dryer, minibar.

Where to Dine

Il Principe ★★ CAMPANIAN/MEDITERRANEAN   This isn't just Pompeii's leading restaurant; it's one of the best in all of Campania. The decor incorporates the best decorative features of ancient Pompeii, including a scattering of frescoes and mosaics. You can dine in its beautiful interior or at a sidewalk table on the town's most important square, with views of the basilica. You might start with carpaccio or a salad of porcini mushrooms, and then follow with one of the pastas, such as ravioli with zucchini in a clam broth or *tagliolini* with scampi and lemon zest. Some of the dishes are based on recipes used in ancient Rome, notably *lagane* (a kind of pasta) *al garum,* an anchovy paste, or *cassata,* a goat cheese and dried fruit dessert. If you're fascinated by this culinary history, you can call ahead and make arrangements for your party to enjoy a 17-item menu of ancient Roman dishes.

Piazza Bartolo Longo. ✆ **081-8505566.** www.ilprincipe.com. Reservations required. Main courses 10€–20€. AE, DC, MC, V. Tues–Sat noon–3pm and 7:45–10:30pm; Sun noon–3pm.

Zi Caterina PIZZA/NEAPOLITAN   This choice is in the center of town near the basilica, with two spacious dining rooms. The antipasto table might tempt you with its seafood, but don't rule out the *pasta e fagioli* with mussels. The chef's special rigatoni with tomatoes and prosciutto is tempting, as is the array of fish and the live lobsters fresh from the tank.

Via Roma 20. ✆ **081-8507447.** www.zicaterinapompei.it. Reservations recommended. Main courses 8€–18€; fixed-price menus 18€–28€. AE, DC, MC, V. Daily 9am–11:30pm.

THE EMERALD ISLAND OF ISCHIA ★★

34km (21 miles) W of Naples

Dramatically situated in the Gulf of Gaeta, the island of Ischia is of volcanic origin. Its thermal spas claim cures for most anything that ails you—be it "gout, retarded sexual development, or chronic rheumatism," according to their brochure—which they've claimed as long as anyone can remember. Called the Emerald Island, Ischia is studded with pine groves and surrounded by sparkling waters that wash up on many sandy beaches. In Greek mythology, Ischia was the home of Typhoeus (Typhon), who created volcanoes and fathered the three-headed canine Cerberus, guardian of the gateway to Hades, and the Chimera and Sphinx. The island covers just over 47 sq. km (18 sq. miles), and its prominent feature is **Monte Epomeo,** a volcano that was a powerful force and source of worry for the Greek colonists who settled here in the 8th century B.C.

Today, the 789m (2,590-ft.) peak is dead, having last erupted in the 14th century, but it's still responsible for warming the island's thermal springs. Ischia slumbered for centuries after its early turbulence, although some discerning visitors discovered its charms. Ibsen, for example, lived in a villa near Casamicciola to find the solitude necessary to complete *Peer Gynt.* However, in the 1950s, Ischia was discovered by wealthy Italians trying to avoid the overrun resorts of Capri, who built a slew of first-class hotels.

The island is known for its sandy beaches, health spas (which utilize the hot springs for hydromassage and mud baths), and vineyards producing the red and

Taking the waters at Ischia.

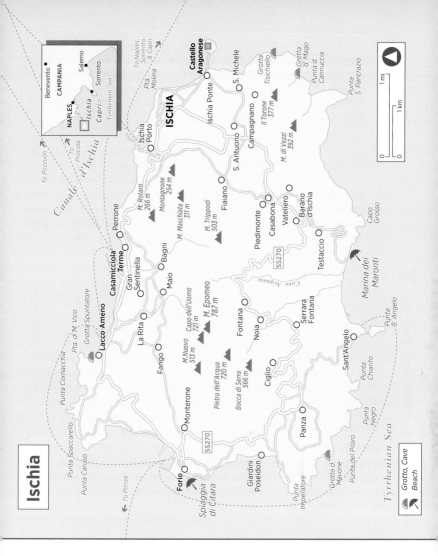

white Monte Epomeo, the red and white Ischia, and the white Biancolella. The largest community is at **Ischia Porto** on the eastern coast, a circular town seated in the crater of the extinct Monte Epomeo, which functions as the island's main port of call. The most lively town is **Forio** on the western coast, with its many bars along tree-lined streets. The other major communities are **Lacco Ameno** and **Casamicciola Terme,** on the north shore, and **Serrara Fontana** and **Barano d'Ischia,** inland and to the south.

Essentials

GETTING THERE The easiest way to get to the island is from Naples, where **hydrofoils** (passengers only) and **ferries** (passengers with their cars) make frequent runs throughout the year (three to seven times a day, depending on the season). The hydrofoil is the most convenient and most expensive option: The 40-minute ride costs 19€ per person each way. The ferry takes twice as long but costs only 11€ for foot passengers. On the ferry, a medium-size vehicle, with as many passengers as will fit inside, costs from 44€ to 57€ each way, depending on the size of the car. Hydrofoils depart from Naples's Mergellina Pier, near the Hotel Vesuvio; ferries leave from Molo Beverello, near Piazza Municipio. Two companies maintain both hydrofoils and ferries: **Caremar** (✆ **892-123;** www.caremar.it) and **Alilauro** (✆ **081-4972222;** www.alilauro.it). Caremar is somewhat more upscale, with better-maintained ships and a more cooperative staff.

VISITOR INFORMATION   In Porto d'Ischia, **Azienda Autonoma di Soggiorno e Turismo,** at Via Antonio Sogliuzzo 72 (✆ **081-5074211;** www.info ischiaprocida.it), is open Monday to Saturday 9am to 1:30pm and 3 to 7:30pm.

Ischia Porto

This harbor actually emerged from the crater of a long-dead volcano. Most of the population and the largest number of hotels are centered in Ischia Porto. The **Castello Aragónese ★★** (✆ **081-992834;** www.castelloaragonese.it) once guarded the harbor from raids. At the castle lived poet Vittoria Colonna, the confidante of Michelangelo, to whom he wrote celebrated letters.

References to a fortress on this isolated rock date from as early as 474 B.C. Today it's the symbol of Ischia. It's connected to the oldest part of town by the Ponte d'Ischia, a narrow bridge barely wide enough for a car. If you're driving, park on the "mainland" side of the bridge and cross on foot. The fortress is privately owned, and you pay 10€ to get inside. It's closed January and February but is open daily otherwise, 9:30am to 6pm.

WHERE TO STAY

Grand Hotel Excelsior ★★★   Ischia's best hotel was the private retreat of English nobleman James Nihn at the end of the 19th century; early in the 20th century, it was opened as a hotel by the counts of Micangeli. The decor never lets you forget that you're in the lap of luxury, while the lovely pool and private beach never let you forget that you're on the Mediterranean. The public spaces contain multitiered chandeliers, terra-cotta floors, Oriental carpets, and thickly padded furniture. In the guest rooms, curvaceous wrought-iron headboards rise above colorful bedspreads matched to the lampshades, curtains, and sheets. Each room has a private patio.

Via Emanuele Gianturco 19, 80077 Ischia Porto. ✆ **081-991522.** Fax 081-984100. www. excelsiorischia.it. 78 units. 180€–250€ per person double; 300€–400€ per person suite. Rates include breakfast and dinner. AE, DC, MC, V. Free valet parking. Closed Oct 18–Apr 23. **Amenities:** Restaurant w/outdoor terrace; bar; babysitting; exercise room; 2 pools (1 thermal indoor); room service; spa. *In room:* A/C, TV, hair dryer, minibar.

Grand Hotel Punta Molino Terme ★★   Standing amid cliffs and olive groves, this modern hotel combines comfort with excellent service and a full spa. The public areas feature a mix of contemporary with 17th- and 18th-century furnishings and stone, marble, or terra-cotta floors. The guest rooms are constantly updated and come in a variety of shapes and sizes; each is fitted with elegant fabrics and reproductions. Plants and fresh-cut flowers add life and color.

Lungomare Cristoforo Colombo 23, 80070 Ischia Porto. ✆ **081-991544.** Fax 081-991562. www. puntamolino.it. 90 units. 135€–255€ per person double; 350€–480€ per person suite. Rates include breakfast and dinner. AE, DC, MC, V. Free parking. Closed Oct 18–Apr 22. **Amenities:** Restaurant; babysitting; bikes; children's center; exercise room; 2 pools (1 heated indoor); room service; spa. *In room:* A/C, TV, hair dryer, minibar.

Hotel Continental Terme ★

The thermal springs at this sprawling complex are among the largest on the island. There are six thermal water pools (three covered), surrounded by the exotic greenery of 27,340 sq. m (294,285 sq. ft.) of gardens. The public spaces feature polished marble and terra-cotta floors, contemporary Italian seating, and wicker-and-glass tables, accented by cut flowers and plant life. The guest rooms are luxuriously furnished, set in a diverse collection of town-house villas scattered throughout the grounds.

Via M. Mazzella 74, 80077 Ischia Porto. ✆ **081-3336111.** Fax 081-3336276. www.continental terme.it. 244 units. 120€–350€ double; 230€–430€ suite. Rates include breakfast and dinner. AE, DC, MC, V. Free valet parking. Closed Nov–Mar. **Amenities:** Restaurant; 2 bars; babysitting; children's center; exercise room; 5 thermal pools (2 indoors); room service; spa; outdoor tennis court (lit); Wi-Fi (3€ per hr., in lobby). *In room:* A/C, TV, hair dryer, minibar.

Hotel Il Moresco ★

This hotel sits in a sun-dappled park whose pines and palmettos grow close to its arched loggias. From some angles, the Moorish-inspired exterior looks almost like a cubist fantasy. Inside, the straightforward design re-creates a modern oasis in the southern part of Spain, with matador-red tiles coupled with stark-white walls and Iberian furniture. Each well-furnished guest room has a terrace or a balcony and a tidy bathroom.

Via Emanuele Gianturco 16, 80077 Ischia Porto. ✆ **081-981355.** Fax 081-992338. www.ilmoresco. it. 70 units. 230€–460€ double; 560€–760€ suite. Rates include buffet breakfast. AE, DC, MC, V. Closed Oct 18–Apr 23. **Amenities:** Restaurant; 2 bars; exercise room; 3 pools (1 thermal pool outside, 1 thermal pool in a grotto, 1 covered thermal pool); room service; spa. *In room:* A/C, TV/DVD/CD player (in some), hair dryer, minibar.

Hotel La Villarosa ★★ 🏠

This is Ischia's finest *pensione,* set in a garden of gardenias and banana, eucalyptus, and fig trees. The dining room is in the informal country style, with terra-cotta tiles, lots of French windows, and antique chairs. What looks like a carriage house in the garden has been converted into an informal tavern with more antiques. The friendly staff maintains the personal atmosphere. The bright and airy guest rooms are well kept. Thermal treatments are available.

Via Giacinto Gigante 5, 80077 Ischia Porto. ✆ **081-991316.** Fax 081-992425. www.dicohotels.it. 37 units. 65€–110€ per person double. Rates include half board. AE, DC, MC, V. Closed Nov–Mar. **Amenities:** Bar; babysitting; thermal pool; room service; spa. *In room:* A/C, TV, hair dryer, minibar.

WHERE TO DINE

Ristorante Damiano ★ ISCHITANO/NEAPOLITAN   This charming restaurant, angled for the best sea views, is located about 1.6km (1 mile) southwest of the ferry terminal. Damiano Caputo infuses his cuisine with zest and very fresh ingredients. In the rustic setting—long communal tables and fresh flowers—you can select from an array of antipasti, homemade pasta, steamy bowls of minestrone, and some excellent veal and chicken dishes. Some especially savory specialties include fritters of arugula and shrimp; fresh mussels steamed in black pepper and garlic, or *vermicelli* pasta with seafood. Desserts include tiramisu and wonderful gelati.

Via delle Vigne 30. ☎ **081-983032.** Reservations recommended. Main courses 10€–22€. DC, MC, V. Daily 8pm–midnight. Closed Nov–Mar.

Lacco Ameno

Jutting up from the water, a rock named **Il Fungo (the Mushroom)** is the landmark natural sight of Lacco Ameno. It is the center of the good life and contains some of the best and most expensive hotels on the island. People come from all over the world either to relax on the beach and be served top-level food or to take the cure. The mineral-rich waters at Lacco Ameno have led to the development of a modern spa with extensive facilities for thermal cures, everything from underwater jet massages to mud baths.

WHERE TO STAY

Hotel La Reginella ★   Set in a lush garden typical of the island's accommodations, this hotel boasts a Mediterranean decor that combines printed tile floors with light woods and pastel or floral fabrics. Although aging, the guest rooms are still very comfortable, with wood furnishings and well-kept bathrooms.

Piazza Santa Restituta 1, 80076 Lacco Ameno d'Ischia. ☎ **081-994300.** Fax 081-980481. www. albergolareginella.it. 90 units (shower only). 100€–190€ per person double; 170€–280€ per person suite. Rates include breakfast and dinner. AE, DC, MC, V. Free parking. Closed Nov 1–Apr 16. **Amenities:** 2 restaurants; babysitting; 5 pools (4 outdoor/1 heated indoor); room service; spa; outdoor tennis court (lit). *In room:* A/C, TV, hair dryer, minibar.

Il Fungo, as seen from the beach at Lacco Ameno.

Hotel Regina Isabella ★★   This resort offers the finest accommodations and service in Lacco Ameno, plus a private beach. The refined setting successfully contrasts contemporary furnishings with rococo and less ornate antique styles. In the medium to spacious guest rooms, serene blues and greens are prevalent, and some printed tile floors are offset by earthy brown tiles and woodwork. Most have balconies.

Piazza Santa Restituta, 80076 Lacco Ameno d'Ischia. ℂ **081-994322.** Fax 081-900190. www. reginaisabella.it. 134 units. 250€–800€ double; 900€–2,900€ suite. Rates include breakfast and dinner. AE, DC, MC, V. Free parking. Closed Nov 8–Dec 27 and Jan 7–Mar 26. **Amenities:** 2 restaurants; 2 bars; babysitting; 4 pools (1 thermal covered); room service; spa; Wi-Fi (free, in lobby). *In room:* A/C, TV, hair dryer, minibar.

Hotel Terme di Augusto   This hotel, 46m (151 ft.) from the shore, provides excellent service in a setting less ostentatious than that of many competing resorts. It combines prominent arched ceilings, patterned tile floors, and floral drapery and upholstery to create light, airy spaces. The guest rooms are comfortable, with well-maintained bathrooms.

Viale Campo 128, 80076 Lacco Ameno d'Ischia. ℂ **081-994944.** Fax 081-980244. www.terme diaugusto.it. 119 units. 110€–165€ per person double; 165€–200€ junior suite. Rates include breakfast and dinner. AE, DC, MC, V. Free parking. Closed Nov 14–Dec 29 and Jan 6–23. **Amenities:** 2 restaurants; 3 bars; babysitting; exercise room; 4 pools (2 outdoor, 2 indoor); room service; spa; outdoor tennis court (lit); Wi-Fi (free, in lobby). *In room:* A/C, TV, hair dryer, minibar.

Hotel Terme San Montano ★★   This is an oasis of charm and grace, one of our favorite retreats on Ischia. The grounds spread out around the hotel in a luxuriant garden, leading to a private beach. Aged woods, leather, and brass are combined in the furnishings, and marine lamps shed light on almost every room. The headboards resemble a ship's helm, the windows are translated as portholes, and miniature ships and antiquated diving gear are decoratively scattered about. The guest rooms are well cared for and spacious. Rooms with sea views are the most requested.

Via Monte Vico, 80076 Lacco Ameno d'Ischia. ℂ **081-994033.** Fax 081-980242. www.san montano.com. 77 units. 140€–500€ double; 350€–600€ suite. Rates include buffet breakfast. AE, DC, MC, V. Free parking. Closed Nov–Apr. **Amenities:** Restaurant; 2 bars; babysitting; bikes; exercise room; 2 outdoor pools; room service; spa; outdoor tennis court (lit); limited watersports equipment. *In room:* A/C, TV, hair dryer, minibar (in some).

Forio

A short drive from Lacco Ameno, Forio stands on the west coast of Ischia, opening onto the sea near the Bay of Citara. Long a favorite with artists (filmmaker Luchino Visconti had a villa here), it's now developing a broader base of tourism. Locals produce some of the finest wines on the island. On the way from Lacco Ameno, stop at the **beach of San Francesco,** with its sanctuary. At sunset, many visitors head for a rocky spur on which sits the church of **Santa Maria del Soccorso.** The lucky ones get to witness the famous "green flash" over the Gulf of Gaeta. It appears on occasion immediately after the sun sets.

WHERE TO STAY

Grande Albergo Mezzatorre ★★   The best hotel in Forio, this complex is built around a 16th-century villa whose stone tower once guarded against invaders;

Santa Maria del Soccorso in Forio.

now it houses the least expensive of the doubles. The five postmodern buildings run a few hundred feet downhill to a waterfront bluff. A casual airiness prevails in the public spaces, which contrast soft lighting with terra-cotta floors. The decor in the guest rooms is contemporary, with wooden furniture, bright upholstered seating, and tiled bathrooms. Suites have a private garden and a whirlpool tub.

Via Mezzatorre 23, 80075 Forio d'Ischia. © **081-986111.** Fax 081-986015. www.mezzatorre.it. 59 units. 300€–720€ double; from 620€ suite. Rates include buffet breakfast. AE, DC, MC, V. Free parking. Closed Oct 24–Apr 21. **Amenities:** 2 restaurants; bar; babysitting; bikes; exercise room; saltwater heated pool; room service; thermal spa; 2 outdoor tennis courts (lit). *In room:* A/C, TV, hair dryer, minibar.

WHERE TO DINE

La Romantica NEAPOLITAN/ISCHIATANO   Near the dry-docked fishing vessels of Forio's old port, this is the most appealing nonhotel restaurant in town. It occupies a Neapolitan-style building that has welcomed everyone from Josephine Baker to Dr. Christian Barnard. Swordfish, grilled and served with lemon sauce or with herb-flavored green sauce, is delicious, as are several risotto and veal dishes. One of the homemade pasta specialties comes with squid, shrimp, and cherry tomatoes. Weather permitting, you might prefer a seat on the outdoor terrace.

Via Marina 46. © **081-997345.** Reservations recommended. Main courses 9€–20€. AE, MC, V. Daily noon–3pm and 7pm–midnight. Closed Wed Nov–Mar.

Sant'Angelo ★

The most charming settlement on Ischia, Sant'Angelo juts out on the southernmost tip. The fishing village is joined to the "mainland" of Ischia by a 91m-long (300-ft.) lava-and-sand isthmus. Driving into the town is virtually impossible. In summer you might have to park a long way off and walk. Its **beach** is among the best on the island.

The Emerald Island of Ischia

CAMPANIA

WHERE TO STAY

Park Hotel Miramare ★ This hotel is right on the sea, although it has no beach to speak of. There is, however, a concrete terrace with chairs and umbrellas, and a stairway that leads into the waters (clearing the rocky shores). Curved wrought-iron balconies, white wicker, and canopied iron bed frames are recurring decorative elements. Since 1923, the same family has welcomed guests to its old-fashioned accommodations (bathrooms have been recently renewed, however). The dining room features the seafood that the island is known for, and a snack bar offers an informal option. The hotel's health spa is a short walk away down a flower-lined path. Among its offerings are massage, 12 thermal pools, mud treatments, a sauna, and designated nudist areas.

Via Comandante Magdalena 29, 80070 Sant'Angelo d'Ischia. (✆) **081-999219.** Fax 081-999325. www.hotelmiramare.it. 50 units (shower only). 130€–207€ per person double; 325€ per person suite. Rates include buffet breakfast. Children 11 and under stay free in parent's room. AE, DC, MC, V. Parking nearby 12€. Closed Oct–Mar. **Amenities:** Restaurant; bar; babysitting; bikes; children's center; exercise room; 12 thermal pools (1 indoor); room service; spa; Wi-Fi (free, in lobby). *In room:* A/C, TV, hair dryer, minibar.

SORRENTO ★★

50km (31 miles) S of Naples, 256km (159 miles) SE of Rome, 50km (31 miles) W of Salerno

Strolling seaside in Sorrento.

Borrowing from Greek mythology, the Romans placed the legendary abode of the sirens (those wicked mermaids who lured seamen to their deaths with their songs) at Sorrento (Surrentum). Ulysses resisted their call by stuffing the ears of his crew with wax and having himself bound to the mast of his ship. Perched on high cliffs overlooking the bays of Naples and Salerno, Sorrento has been sending out its siren call for centuries, luring everybody from Homer to Lord and Lady Astor to busloads of international tourists who invade every summer.

The streets in summer tend to be as noisy as a carnival. And the traffic is horrendous (no traffic signals in such a bustling city!). The hotels on the "racing strip," **Corso Italia,** need to pass out earplug kits when they tuck you in for the night, although perhaps you'll have a hotel on a cliff side in Sorrento with a view of the sea (and paths and private elevators to take you down).

Essentials

GETTING THERE Sorrento is served by frequent express **trains** from Naples (trip time: 1 hr.). The high-speed train, called Ferrovia Circumvesuviana, leaves from one floor underground at Stazione Centrale (see "Essentials," earlier in this chapter).

By **car** from Naples, take the A3, then exit at Castellammare di Stabia and take S145.

VISITOR INFORMATION The **tourist office** is at Via de Maio 35 (✆ **081-8074033;** www.sorrentotourism.com), which winds down to the port where ships headed for Capri and Naples anchor. It's open year-round Monday to Saturday 8:30am to 6:30pm, and Sunday 8:30am to 6:30pm in summer.

Exploring the City

For such a famous resort, Sorrento's **beaches** are limited—most of them are just piers extending into the water. Chaise longues and umbrellas line these decks along the rock-strewn coastline. The best beach is **Punta del Capo,** reached by going along Corso Italia to Via del Capo.

If you'd like to go **hiking,** you can explore the green hills above Sorrento. Many of the trails are marked, and the tourist office will advise you.

From Sorrento, confident drivers can undertake the gorgeous but nerve-racking **Amalfi Drive.** If you want to leave the driving to someone else, you can take a blue SITA bus that runs between Sorrento and Salerno or Amalfi. In Sorrento, bus stations with timetables are outside the rail station and in the central piazza.

Although few visitors come to Sorrento to look at churches and monuments, there are some worth exploring. The **Chiesa di San Francesco,** Via San Francesco (✆ 081-8781269), dates from the 14th century. This **cloister** ★ is a pocket of beauty in overcrowded Sorrento, with delicate arches and a garden dotted with flowering vines. The cloister is open daily 9am to 6pm, and admission is free.

If time permits, visit the **Museo Correale di Terranova** ★, Via Correale (✆ 081-8781846), north of Piazza Tasso. A former palace, it has displays of ancient statues, antiques, and Italian art. Here's a chance to introduce yourself to *intarsia,* a technique of making objects with paper-thin pieces of patterned wood. Neapolitan bric-a-brac and other curiosities finish off the exhibits. After a visit to the museum, you can stroll through the gardens. From March to December, it's open Monday and Wednesday to Sunday 9am to 2pm. Admission is 6€ to the museum and gardens.

Sorrento has better **shopping** than anywhere else along the Amalfi Drive. The city's cobbled alleyways and flower-ringed piazzas encourage strolls, and the best ones for window-shopping are **Piazza Tasso** and **Via San Cesareo,** densely packed with shoppers on weekend afternoons.

Gargiulo & Jannuzzi ★★, Via Fuori Mura 1 (✆ 081-8781041; www.gargiulo-jannuzzi.it), is the region's best-known maker of marquetry furniture. Opened in 1863, the shop demonstrates the centuries-old technique in the

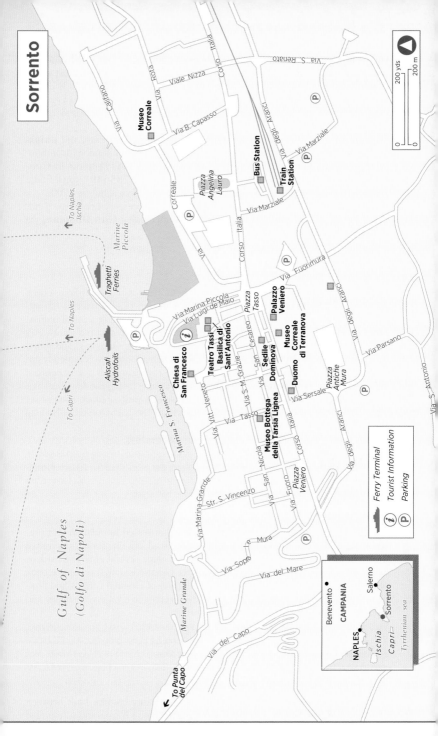

Sorrento

Museo Correale

Via B. Capasso

Via Rota

Viale Nizza

Via Califano

Corso Italia

Via S. Renato

Via degli Aranci

Via Marziale

Bus Station

Train Station

Piazza Angelina Lauro

Via Marziale

Correale

Via Fuorimura

Corso Italia

Marine Piccola

Gulf of Naples
(Golfo di Napoli)

To Naples, Ischia

To Naples

Traghetti Ferries

Aliscafi Hydrofoils

To Capri

Marina S. Francesco

Marine Grande

Via Marina Grande

Chiesa di San Francesco

Via Marina Piccola

Via Luigi de Maio

Teatro Tasso

Basilica di Sant'Antonio

Piazza Tasso

Palazzo Veniero

Via San Cesareo

Via S-M. Grazie

Sedile Dominova

Museo Correale di Terranova

Duomo

Via degli Aranci

Via Parsano

Via S-Antonio

Via Sersale

Piazza Antiche Mura

Via Tasso

Vitt. Veneto

Via San Nicola

Museo Bottega della Tarsia Lignea

Piazza Veniero

Str. S. Vincenzo

Via Fuoro

Corso Italia

Via del Mare

Mura

Via Sopra

Via Marina Grande

Via del Capo

Marine Grande

To Punta del Capo

Legend:
- Ferry Terminal
- *i* Tourist Information
- (P) Parking

0   200 yds
0   200 m

CAMPANIA

• Benevento

NAPLES

Salerno •

Ischia Capri • Sorrento

Tyrrhenian sea

741

basement, where an employee will combine multihued pieces of wood veneer to create patterns of arabesques and flowers. The sprawling showrooms feature an array of card tables, clocks, and partners' desks, each inlaid with patterns of elm wood, rosewood, bird's-eye maple, or mahogany. Upstairs is a collection of embroidered table linens, and the outlet has its own ceramic factory. The pottery can be shipped anywhere.

Embroidery and lace are two of the best bargains in Sorrento, and **Luigia Gargiulo,** Corso Italia 48 (📞 **081-8781081**), comes recommended for embroidered sheets and tablecloths; the shop also offers children's clothing. In **Cuomo's Lucky Store,** Piazza Antica Mura 2–7 (📞 **081-8785649**), you'll find a little bit of everything made in the area, including porcelain from the 1700s.

One of the most appealing assortments of cameos, meticulously hand-carved from seashells, is available at the reasonably priced **Ciro Bimonte,** Via Giuliani 62 (📞 **081-8071880**).

Where to Stay

VERY EXPENSIVE

Albergo Cocumella ★★   If you want a hotel filled with atmosphere, check into this longtime favorite, which first became a hotel in 1822. On a cliff-top garden overlooking the Bay of Naples, Cocumella was carved out of a Jesuit monastery from the 16th century. Its gardens stretch toward the sea with distant views of Mount Vesuvius in the background. Frescoed ceilings, antiques, and grand style greet you here. In spite of the age of the hotel, bedrooms are completely up-to-date, most of them decorated in a 16th-century style with the occasional antique. The most desirable ones open onto a terrace facing the bay. Summer concerts are presented in the on-site baroque chapel. Guests are taken on cruises aboard the hotel's own ship, *Vera,* which dates from 1880. The vessel sails along the Amalfi Coast to Capri.

Via Cocumella 7, 80065 Sant'Agnello, Sorrento. 📞 **081-8782933.** Fax 081-8783712. www. cocumella.com. 53 units. 220€–340€ double; 410€–930€ suite. Rates include buffet breakfast. AE, DC, MC, V. Closed Oct 18–Mar 31. Children 7 and under not permitted. Free parking. **Amenities:** 2 restaurants; bar; babysitting; exercise room; pool; room service; spa; outdoor tennis court (lit); Wi-Fi (free, in lobby). *In room:* A/C, TV, small fridge, hair dryer.

EXPENSIVE

Grand Hotel Ambasciatori ★   The heavily buttressed foundation that prevents this cliff-side hotel from plunging into the sea looks like something from a medieval monastery, and it was landscaped to include several rambling gardens along the precipice. A set of steps and a private elevator lead to the wooden deck of a bathing wharf. Inside, a substantial collection of Oriental carpets and armchairs provides plush comfort. The guest rooms come in a variety of shapes and sizes, each containing a compact tiled bathroom.

Via Califano 18, 80067 Sorrento. 📞 **081-8782025.** Fax 081-8071021. www.manniellohotels.com. 109 units. 129€–425€ double; 405€–585€ suite. Rates include buffet breakfast. AE, DC, MC, V. Parking 18€. **Amenities:** Restaurant; 3 bars; babysitting; bikes; concierge; heated whirlpool pool; room service; limited watersports equipment rental; Wi-Fi (6€ per hr., in lobby). *In room:* A/C, TV, hair dryer, minibar.

Grand Hotel Excelsior Vittoria ★★★   This luxury bastion, built between 1834 and 1882 on the edge of a cliff overlooking the Bay of Naples and surrounded by semitropical gardens with lemon and orange trees, combines 19th-century glamour with a modern flair. Oscar Wilde, Richard Wagner, and Lord Byron have long checked out but Vittoria remains the best hotel in Sorrento, and arguably the best in the south of Italy. The terrace theme predominates, especially on the water side. Three elevators will take you down to the harbor to sunbathe and swim. Inside, the atmosphere is old worldish, especially in the mellow dining room. The huge guest rooms boast their own drama, some with balconies opening onto the cliff-side drop; they have a wide mix of furnishings that includes many antique pieces.

Piazza Tasso 34, 80067 Sorrento. © **081-8777111.** Fax 081-8771206. www.exvitt.it. 105 units. 324€–650€ double; from 528€ suite. Rates include buffet breakfast. AE, DC, MC, V. Free parking. **Amenities:** 2 restaurants; bar; airport transfers (108€); babysitting; bikes; children's center; large pool; room service; spa. *In room:* A/C, TV, hair dryer, minibar, Wi-Fi (free).

Hotel Imperial Tramontano ★★   This pocket of posh in a semitropical garden is an excellent choice. It was the birthplace of Torquato Tasso, yet the 16th-century poet would hardly recognize the palatial villa today. The spacious guest rooms are well furnished, and some have balconies opening onto sea views. High ceilings and gilt-framed mirrors provide a traditional look. The drawing room is replete with English and Italian antiques. In the garden, you can walk down paths of oleander, hydrangea, acacia, coconut palms, and geraniums. An elevator takes guests down to the beach below the main hotel.

Via Vittorio Veneto 1, 80067 Sorrento. © **081-8782588.** Fax 081-8072344. www.hoteltramontano. it. 116 units. 180€–350€ double; from 335€ suite. Rates include buffet breakfast. AE, MC, V. Free parking. Closed Jan–Feb. **Amenities:** Restaurant; bar; babysitting; pool; room service. *In room:* A/C, TV, hair dryer, minibar.

MODERATE

Hotel Bristol ★   The Bristol was built pueblo style on a hillside at the edge of town; rooms open onto a view of Vesuvius and the Bay of Naples (all but 15 rooms that open onto a brick wall). The hotel lures with its contemporary decor and spaciousness and with well-appointed public and private rooms. The guest rooms are warm and inviting. Most have balconies overlooking the sea. In summer you can dine on the terrace.

Via Capo 22, 80067 Sorrento. © **081-8784522.** Fax 081-8071910. www.acampora.it. 150 units. 110€–270€ double; 230€–400€ suite. Rates include buffet breakfast. AE, DC, MC, V. Free parking. **Amenities:** 2 restaurants; bar; children's center; exercise room; pool; room service; sauna; Wi-Fi (free, in lobby). *In room:* A/C, TV, hair dryer, minibar.

Hotel Regina 🌶   Evenly spaced rows of balconies jut out over the Regina's well-tended garden. On its uppermost floor, a terrace boasts views of the Mediterranean extending as far as Naples and Vesuvius. The functional rooms have tile floors, private terraces, and well-kept bathrooms. A dozen open onto views from balconies and are the most requested. The hotel employs a helpful staff that provides road maps and offers hints about sightseeing.

Via Marina Grande 10, 80067 Sorrento. © **081-8782722.** Fax 081-8782721. www.hotelregina sorrento.it. 38 units (shower only). 80€–200€ double. Rates include buffet breakfast. AE, DC, MC, V. Parking 15€. Closed Nov–Apr. **Amenities:** Room service; Wi-Fi (5€ per hr., in lobby). *In room:* A/C, TV, hair dryer.

La Tonnarella ★   This is the most desirable of the host of inexpensive inns along Via Capo. There's a marvelous old-fashioned ambience here, with antiques gathered from all over southern Italy adorning the public areas. The panoramas, best seen at sunset from the terraces, are among the finest in Sorrento. Bedrooms range from midsize to spacious, furnished with new pieces and touches of the past. Neapolitan tiles are used widely, especially in the compact bathrooms. Although much of the plumbing remains old-fashioned, some rooms have jet showers or hydromassage tubs. Some of the accommodations open onto their own private terraces. An elevator takes you down to the rock-strewn beach.

Via Capo 31, 80067 Sorrento. ✆ **081-8781153.** Fax 081-8782169. www.latonnarella.it. 21 units (shower only). 112€–225€ double; 240€–400€ suite. Rates include buffet breakfast. AE, MC, V. Free parking. Bus: A. **Amenities:** Restaurant; bar; room service. *In room:* A/C, TV, hair dryer, Wi-Fi (free).

Villa di Sorrento   This is a pleasant villa in the center of town. Architecturally romantic, the Sorrento attracts travelers with its petite wrought-iron balconies, tall shutters, and vines climbing the facade. Some of the comfortably furnished guest rooms contain terraces. The tiled bathrooms are tiny.

Vialle Enrico Caruso 6, 80067 Sorrento. ✆ **081-8781068.** Fax 081-8785767. www.villadi sorrento.it. 21 units (shower only). 125€–160€ double; 180€–215€ triple. Rates include buffet breakfast. AE, DC, MC, V. Parking 20€ nearby. **Amenities:** Room service. *In room:* A/C, TV, hair dryer.

Where to Dine

EXPENSIVE

L'Antica Trattoria ★ CAMPANESE/INTERNATIONAL   Inside the weather-beaten walls of what was built 300 years ago as a stable, this 200-year-old restaurant, one of the best in Sorrento, is a favorite of locals. Although all its food is well prepared, the real highlight is its antipasti. For tempting appetizers, select such dishes as fresh-caught local prawns with green apple in aspic. The chef specializes in homemade ravioli—one with a smoked ricotta and pear served in a mild white cheese sauce and another with ricotta flavored with Sorrento lemon and orange zest and studded with seafood. For one of the signature dishes, sample filet of pezzogna (a local fish) baked in a salt crust and herb flavored or fried prawns with finely sliced zucchini served with a lemon-and-orange sauce.

Via P. R. Giuliani 33. ✆ **081-8071082.** www.lanticatrattoria.com. Reservations recommended. Main courses 15€–29€; fixed-priced menus 40€–80€. AE, MC, V. Daily noon–3pm and 7–11pm. Closed Jan 10–Feb 10.

INEXPENSIVE

La Favorita–O'Parrucchiano NEAPOLITAN/SORRENTINE   A former celebrity haunt, this is a good choice on the busiest street in town. In operation since 1868, it is like an old tavern, with an arched ceiling in the main dining room. On the terrace you can dine in a garden of trees, rubber plants, and statuary. Among the a la carte dishes, classic Italian fare is offered, including ravioli with eggplant and cherry tomatoes, cannelloni, and a mixed fish fry from the Bay of Naples. The chef will also prepare a pizza for you. Other menu items include grilled roulades of swordfish, ravioli with shrimp in clam sauce, *tronchetti* with artichokes, and filet of beef with arugula and cherry tomatoes.

Corso Italia 71. ✆ **081-8781321.** www.parrucchiano.com. Main courses 8.50€–15€. MC, V. Daily noon–3:30pm and 7–11:30pm. Closed Wed Nov 15–Mar 15.

Sorrento After Dark

At the **Taverna dell'Ottocento,** Via dell'Accademia 29 (℗ **081-8785970**), owner Tony Herculano dispenses flavorful home-style macaroni (pink-tinged, it combines tomatoes with ham, cream, and bacon) and good cheer. From 9pm to midnight, the music of a guitar and a piano duet enlivens a cozy bar lit with flickering candles. There's no cover charge, and the food is cheap. The joint is open Tuesday to Sunday 10:30am to 3pm and 6pm to midnight, and does lots of business throughout the day as a cafe and pub.

For a dose of Neapolitan-style folklore, head for the **Circolo dei Forestieri,** Via Luigi de Maio 35 (℗ **081-8773012**; www.terrazzadellesirene.com), a bar/cafe whose views extend out over a flowering terrace and the wide blue bay. Music from the live pianist is interrupted only for episodes of folkloric dancing and cheerful music from a troupe of players. This bar is open March to November.

The town's central square, **Piazza Tasso,** is the site of two worthwhile nightclubs. The one that presents folkloric music is **Fauno** (℗ **081-8781021**; www.faunonotte.it), where you can slug down a beer or two during the sporadic performances of *tarantella,* that traditional Italian music you've probably heard in numerous films, such as *The Godfather.* Brief but colorful, the live performances interrupt a program otherwise devoted to recorded dance (usually disco) music.

Sorrento is going pub crazy, with folks heading for **Chaplin's Pub,** Corso Italia 18 (℗ **081-8072551**; www.chaplinspub.com), which draws a lively, often boisterous crowd, some of whom keep drinking until the wee hours. Across the street, the **English Inn,** Corso Italia 56 (℗ **081-8074357**; www.englishinn.it), features recorded music and endless suds.

CAPRI ★★★

5km (3 miles) off the tip of the Sorrentine peninsula

The island of Capri (pronounced *Cap*-ry, not Ca-*pree*) is one of the loveliest resorts in Italy, a dramatic island soaring upward from the sea, with sweeping views, whitewashed homes and villas, lemon trees, narrow winding lanes, and flower-filled courtyards. It's completely overrun in summer (actually from Easter to the end of Oct), as throngs of international tourists and vacationing Italians arrive every day to soak up its romantic atmosphere and gorgeous scenery.

Touring the island is relatively simple. You dock at unremarkable **Marina Grande,** the port area. You can then take the funicular up the steep hill to the town of **Capri** above, where you'll find the major

The Faraglioni rocks off the coast of Capri.

hotels, restaurants, cafes, and shops. From Capri, a short bus ride will deliver you to **Anacapri,** also perched at the top of the island near Monte Solaro. The only other settlement you might want to visit is **Marina Piccola,** on the south side of the island, with the major beach. There are also beaches at **Punta Carnea** and **Bagni di Tiberio.**

Essentials

GETTING THERE You can get here from either Naples or Sorrento. From Naples's Molo Beverello dock (take a taxi from the train station), the **hydrofoil** takes just 45 minutes. The hydrofoil *(aliscafo)* leaves several times daily (some stop at Sorrento), and a one-way trip costs 20€. Regularly scheduled **ferry** *(traghetto)* service, departing from Porta di Massa, is cheaper but takes longer (about 1½ hr.). Fares are 16€ each way. For ferry schedules call ✆ **081-5513882;** for hydrofoils, phone ✆ **081-4285555.** There's no need to check all the dock offices for the best price.

From Sorrento, go to the dock right off Piazza Tasso, where you can board one of the **ferries** run by **Gescab** (✆ **081-8781430;** www.consorziolmp.it) or **Caremar** (✆ **892123;** www.caremar.it). Departures are four times per day from 7:45am to 7pm (the last ferry back leaves Capri at 6:15pm), costing 11€ one-way. It's much faster to take one of the **hydrofoils** operated by **Alilauro** (✆ **081-4972222;** www.alilauro.it), which depart every hour daily 7:20am to 6:30pm, take only 20 minutes, and cost 14€ one-way. Gescab also makes hydrofoil service to Capri (departures are 15 times per day, every half-hour 7:20am–6:20pm; 14€).

If you make reservations the day before with **Gescab** (✆ **089-811986**), you can take a hydrofoil or a ferry to Capri from Positano. Hydrofoils cost 17€ one-way, and a ferry ticket goes for 15€ one-way.

VISITOR INFORMATION Get in touch with the **Tourist Board,** Piazza Umberto I 19 (✆ **081-8370686;** www.capritourism.com), at Capri. From April to October, it's open Monday to Saturday 8:30am to 8:30pm, Sunday 8:30am to 2:30pm; November to March, hours are Monday to Saturday 9am to 1pm and 3:30 to 6:30pm.

GETTING AROUND There's no need for a car on tiny Capri. The island is serviced by funiculars, taxis, and buses. Capri's hotels are a long way from the docks, so we strongly recommend that you bring as little luggage as possible. If you need a porter, you'll find union headquarters in a building connected to the jetty at Marina Grande. Here you can cajole, coddle, coerce, or connive your way through the hiring process, where the only rule seems to be that there are no rules. But your porter will know where to find any hotel among the winding passageways and steep inclines of the island's arteries. Just bring a sense of humor. (Note that if you have reservations at one of the island's more upscale accommodations, your hotel might have its own porter on duty at the docks to help you with your luggage and get you settled.)

Marina Grande ★

The least attractive of the island's communities, Marina Grande is the port, bustling daily with the comings and goings of hundreds of visitors. It has a little sand-cum–pebble beach, on which you're likely to see American sailors (on shore leave from Naples) playing ball.

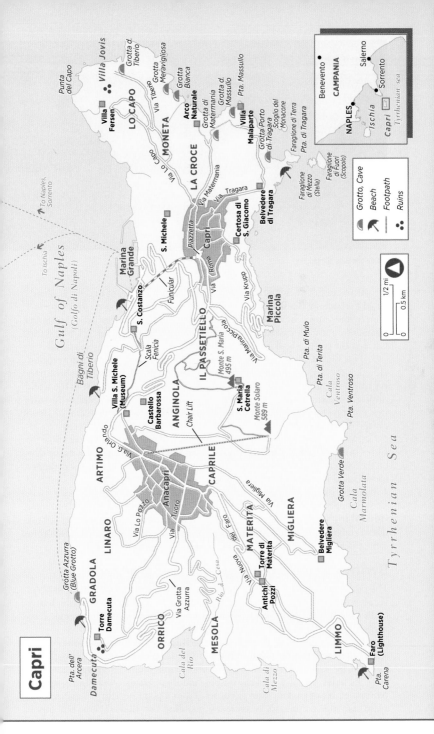

Capri

To Naples, Sorrento

To Ischia

Gulf of Naples
(Golfo di Napoli)

Tyrrhenian Sea

Grotto, Cave
Beach
Footpath
Ruins

0   1/2 mi
0   0.5 km

CAMPANIA
Benevento
Salerno
Sorrento
NAPLES
Ischia Capri Tyrrhenian sea

LO CAPO
Punta del Capo
Villa Jovis
Grotta d. Tiberio
Grotta d. Tiberio
Villa Fersen
Grotta Meravigliosa
Grotta Bianca
Via Tiberio

MONETA
Arco Naturale
Grotta di Matermania
Grotta d. Massullo
Pta. Massullo
Villa Malaparte
Grotta Porto di Tragara
Scoglio del Monacone
Faraglione di Terra
Pta. di Tragara

LA CROCE
Via Matermania
Via Tragara
Capri
Piazzetta
S. Michele
Certosa di S. Giacomo
Belvedere di Tragara
Faraglione di Mezzo (Stella)
Faraglione di Fuori (Scopolo)

Via Roma

Marina Grande
S. Costanzo
Funicular
Scala Fenicia
Bagni di Tiberio

Pta. dell' Arcera
Damecuta

Via Krupp
Marina Piccola
Pta. di Mulo

IL PASSETIELLO
Monte S. Maria 495 m
Via Marina Piccola
S. Maria Cetrella
Monte Solaro 589 m

Pta. di Terita
Cala Ventroso
Pta. Ventroso

ANGINOLA
Villa S. Michele (Museum)
Castello Barbarossa
Chair Lift

ARTIMO
Via G. Orlandi

LINARO
Via Lo Pozzo
Via Tuoro

Anacapri
CAPRILE

Via Migliera

GRADOLA
Grotta Azzurra (Blue Grotto)
Torre Damecuta

Via Grotta Azzurra
Rio d. Cesa

ORRICO
Cala del Rio

MESOLA
Cala di Mezzo

Via Nuova del Faro

MATERITA
Torre di Materita
Antichi Pozzi
Belvedere Migliera

MIGLIERA
Grotta Verde
Cala Marmolata

LIMMO
Faro (Lighthouse)
Pta. Carena

Tyrrhenian Sea

Inside the Blue Grotto.

If you're just spending the day on Capri, you might want to see the island's biggest attraction, the **Blue Grotto (Grotta Azzurra)** ★★, open daily 9am to 1 hour before sunset. In summer, boats leave frequently from the harbor at Marina Grande to transport passengers to the entrance of the grotto for 12€ round-trip. Once at the grotto, you'll pay 12€ for the small rowboat that takes you inside.

The Blue Grotto is one of the best-known natural sights of the region, although the way passengers are hustled in and out of it makes it a tourist trap. It's truly beautiful, however. Known to the ancients, it was later lost to the world until an artist stumbled on it in 1826. Inside the cavern, light refraction (the sun's rays entering from an opening under the water) achieves the dramatic Mediterranean cerulean color. The effect is stunning, as thousands testify yearly.

If you want, you can take a trip around the entire island, passing not only the Blue Grotto but the **Baths of Tiberius,** the **Palazzo al Mare** built in the days of the empire, the **Green Grotto** (less known), and the much-photographed rocks called the **Faraglioni.** Motorboats circle the island in about 1½ hours at 15€ per person.

Connecting Marina Grande with the town of Capri is a frequently running **funicular** charging 1.50€ one-way. However, the funicular, really a cog railway, doesn't operate off season (you'll take a bus from Marina Grande to Capri for the same price).

Swimming & Sunning

The coastline surrounding Capri is punctuated with jagged rocks that allow for very few sandy beaches. There are some spots for swimming, most of which have clubs called *stabilimenti balneari,* which you must pay to visit. Most people relax at their hotel pools and take in the gorgeous views from there.

For swimming, you might head for the **Bagni Nettuno,** Via Grotta Azzurra 46 (℗ **081-8371362**), a short distance from the Blue Grotto in Anacapri. Surrounded by scenic cliff sides, with an undeniable drama, it charges 22€. The price includes use of a cabana, towels, and deck chairs. Mid-March to mid-November, it's open daily 9am to sunset. From a point nearby, you can actually swim into the narrow, rocky entrance guarding the Blue Grotto, but this is advisable only after 5pm, when the boat services into the grotto have ended for the day, and only during relatively calm seas.

Another possibility for swimming is the **Bagni di Tiberio,** Via Palazzo a Mare (✆ **081-8370703**), a sandy beach a short walk from the ruins of an ancient Roman villa. To reach it, you have to board a motorboat departing from Marina Grande for the 15-minute ride to the site. Passage costs 18€ per person, unless you want to walk 30 minutes north from Marina Grande, through rocky landscapes with flowering plants and vineyards.

Closer to the island's south side is the **Marina Piccola,** a usually over-crowded stretch of sand extending between jagged lava rocks. You can rent a small motorboat here from the **Bagni le Sirene** (✆ **081-8370221**) for 100€ for 1 hour, 120€ for 2 hours, and 140€ for 3 hours.

The Town of Capri ★★★

The main town of Capri is the center of most of the hotels, restaurants, and elegant shops—and the milling throngs. The heart of the resort, **Piazza Umberto I,** is like a grand living room, lined with cafes.

One of the most popular walks from the main square is down Via Vittorio Emanuele, past the Quisisana hotel, to the **Giardini di Augusto,** the choice spot on Capri for views and relaxation. From this park's perch, you can see **I Faraglioni,** the rocks once inhabited by the "blue lizard." At the top of the park is a belvedere overlooking emerald waters and Marina Piccola. Nearby you can visit the **Certosa,** a Carthusian monastery erected in the 14th century to honor St. James. It's open Tuesday to Sunday 9am to 2pm and charges no admission.

Kayaking to the beach in Capri.

A statue amid the ruins of the Villa Jovis.

Back at Piazza Umberto I, head up Via Longano and then Via Tiberio, all the way to Monte Tiberio. Here you'll find the **Villa Jovis ★★**, the splendid ruin of the estate from which Tiberius ruled the empire from A.D. 27 to A.D. 37. Actually, the Jovis was one of a dozen villas that the depraved emperor erected on the island. Apparently, Tiberius had trouble sleeping, so he wandered from bed to bed, exploring his "nooks of lechery," a young girl one hour, a young boy the next. From the ruins there's a view of both the Bay of Salerno and the Bay of Naples, as well as of the island. You can visit the ruins of the imperial palace daily 9am to 1 hour before sunset for 3€. For information, call the tourist board at ✆ **081-8370686.**

WHERE TO STAY

This is a ritzy resort, with correspondingly high prices. If you're really watching your wallet, you might have to visit for the day and return to the mainland for the night. Don't even think of coming in summer without a reservation.

Very Expensive

Capri Palace Hotel & Spa   This luxurious retreat is an escape for hedonists. "We'll spoil you rotten," the manager assured us. Although modernized in every way, the hotel evokes the architecture of a Mediterranean palace from the 1700s. Cool creams and off whites are mere backdrops for the light that seems to bathe every corner. Modern furnishings and period furniture, along with touches of gilt, make this hotel a pocket of posh. Its views over the island and the bay are panoramic, and the entire property is enveloped in a well-manicured garden. The best accommodations open onto a terrace with heated private pools; other units front a garden. The on-site restaurant, Olivo, is Michelin-star rated.

Via Capodimonte 2B, 80071 Capri. ✆ **081-9780111.** Fax 081-8373191. www.capripalace.com. 85 units. 340€–1,250€ double; from 720€ junior suite; from 1,300€ suite. Rates include buffet breakfast. AE, DC, MC, V. Closed Oct 17–Mar 31. **Amenities:** 2 restaurants; 2 bars; babysitting; pool; room service; spa. *In room:* A/C, TV, hair dryer, minibar.

Grand Hotel Quisisana Capri ★★★   The island's grande dame since 1845, this is the favorite of a regular international crowd and a bastion of luxury. The sprawling buildings are painted a distinctive yellow and accented with vines and landscaping. Its guest rooms range from cozy singles to spacious suites—all opening onto wide arcades with a stunning view over the coast. They vary greatly in decor, with traditional and conservatively modern furnishings. All have a lovely, airy style, and all come with comfortable beds and tile or marble bathrooms. *Note:* Some rooms have a Jacuzzi.

Via Camerelle 2, 80073 Capri. ℂ **081-8370788.** Fax 081-8376080. www.quisi.com. 150 units. 320€–700€ double; from 660€ suite. Rates include buffet breakfast. AE, DC, MC, V. Closed Nov–Mar. **Amenities:** 2 restaurants; 3 bars; babysitting; exercise room; 2 heated pools (1 indoor, 1 outdoor); room service; spa; outdoor tennis court (lit). *In room:* A/C, TV, hair dryer, minibar.

Hotel Punta Tragara ★★   This former private villa, designed by Le Corbusier, stands above rocky cliffs at the southwest tip of the most desirable panorama on Capri. With big windows, substantial furniture, and all the modern comforts, each guest room opens onto a terrace or balcony that's brightened with flowers and vines, plus a sweeping view. Bathrooms are spacious. The hotel is isolated from many other island activities, which is either a drawback or a plus, depending on your point of view.

Via Tragara 57, 80073 Capri. ℂ **081-8370844.** Fax 081-8377790. www.hoteltragara.com. 45 units. 380€–820€ double; from 820€ suite. Rates include buffet breakfast. AE, DC, MC, V. Closed Oct 17–Apr 25. **Amenities:** Restaurant; bar; concierge; exercise room; 2 saltwater pools (1 heated w/hydromassage); room service; spa. *In room:* A/C, TV, hair dryer, minibar.

J. K. Place ★★★   Opened in 2007, this little boutique hotel above the cliffs over Marina Grande is the epitome of seaside chic. From the hotel, spectacular vistas unfold of the Bay of Naples and Vesuvius. The goal of the hotel was to "bring the sea into the hotel," and it succeeded admirably with this slightly nautical decor. The decor is avant-garde, the most stunning on island; and the midsize to spacious bedrooms are the most stylish—from the zebra-skin stools to the high-end Florentine furniture.

Via Provinciale Marina Grande 225, 80073 Capri. ℂ **081-8384001.** Fax 081-8370438. www.jk capri.com. 22 units. 700€–900€ double; 1,000€ junior suite; from 1,200€ suite. Rates include buffet breakfast. AE, DC, MC, V. Closed Oct 15-Apr 8. **Amenities:** Restaurant; bar; babysitting; concierge; exercise room; room service; heated pool; spa. *In room:* A/C, TV/DVD, CD player, hair dryer, minibar, Wi-Fi (free).

La Scalinatella (Little Steps) ★★   This delightful hotel is built like a private villa above terraces offering a panoramic view. It's an exclusive pair of 200-year-old houses, with a vaguely Moorish design, run by the Morgano family (which also owns the Quisisana). The ambience is one of unadulterated luxury; all units include a phone beside the bathtub, beds set into alcoves, elaborate wrought-iron accents ringing the inner stairwell and the ornate balconies, and a sweeping view over the gardens and pool. Half of the accommodations boast two bathrooms each, one with a whirlpool tub. The hotel shares the facilities of the Quisi Club Spa at the Grand Hotel Quisisana, a 5-minute walk away.

Via Tragara 8, 80073 Capri. ℂ **081-8370633.** Fax 081-8378291. www.scalinatella.com. 30 units. 300€–560€ double; 550€–1,200€ suite. Rates include breakfast. AE, MC, V. Closed Nov–Easter. **Amenities:** Restaurant; bar; babysitting; concierge; exercise room; Jacuzzi; pool; room service; sauna. *In room:* A/C, TV, hair dryer, minibar.

Expensive

Casa Morgano ★★ ✒   This Morgano family property loses out by a hair to La Scalinatella, its next-door neighbor, but with prices much cheaper, you might not notice the difference. Casa Morgano houses you in grand comfort in 20 of its rooms, which are spacious and deluxe; eight others are quite small. The best units are nos. 201 to 205 and 301 to 305. Most units contain good-size sitting areas along with terraces opening onto sea views. The bathrooms come with hydromassage bathtubs and showers.

Via Tragara 6, 80073 Capri. ✆ **081-8370158.** Fax 081-8370681. www.casamorgano.com. 28 units. 180€–490€ double; 450€–620€ junior suite. Rates include buffet breakfast. AE, DC, MC, V. Closed Nov–Mar. **Amenities:** Bar; babysitting; exercise room; heated pool; room service; outdoor tennis court (lit). *In room:* A/C, TV, hair dryer, minibar.

Hotel Luna ★ This first-class hotel stands on a cliff overlooking the sea and the rocks of Faraglioni. The guest rooms are a mix of contemporary Italian pieces and Victorian decor, most with recessed terraces overlooking the garden of flowers and semitropical plants. All are accompanied by tiled bathrooms.

Viale Matteotti 3, 80073 Capri. ✆ **081-8370433.** Fax 081-8377459. www.lunahotel.com. 54 units. 210€–480€ double; 380€–580€ suite. Rates include buffet breakfast. AE, MC, V. Closed Oct 24– Apr 20. **Amenities:** Restaurant; babysitting; Jacuzzi; pool; room service. *In room:* A/C, TV, hair dryer, minibar.

Villa Brunella ★ 🛏 A 10-minute walk from many of Capri's largest hotels, the Brunella was built in the late 1940s as a private villa. In 1963, it was transformed into a pleasant hotel by its present owner, Vincenzo Ruggiero, who named it after his hardworking wife. The hotel has been completely renovated and can hold its own with the other hotels in town. All the doubles have balconies or flowery terraces with sea views. The rooms come in various shapes and sizes, each with a small tiled bathroom.

Via Tragara 24, 80073 Capri. ✆ **081-8370122.** Fax 081-8370430. www.villabrunella.it. 20 units. 200€–360€ double; 360€–460€ suite. Rates include buffet breakfast. AE, DC, MC, V. Closed Nov–Mar. **Amenities:** Restaurant; bar; babysitting; heated pool; room service. *In room:* A/C, TV, hair dryer, minibar.

Moderate

Hotel La Vega This hotel began in the 1930s as the private home of the family that continues to run it today. It has a clear sea view and is nestled amid trees against a sunny hillside. The oversize guest rooms have decoratively tiled floors; each has a private balcony overlooking the water. Some beds have wrought-iron headboards. Below is a garden of flowering bushes, and on the lower edge is a free-form pool with a grassy border for sunbathing. Breakfast is served on your balcony or on a terrace surrounded by trees and potted flowers.

Via Occhio Marino 10, 80073 Capri. ✆ **081-8370481.** Fax 081-8370342. www.hotellavega.it. 24 units (some with shower only). 140€–320€ double; 320€–420€ suite. Rates include buffet breakfast. AE, DC, MC, V. Closed Nov–Easter. **Amenities:** Bar; babysitting; pool; room service. *In room:* A/C, TV, hair dryer, minibar.

Hotel Regina Cristina The white facade of the Regina Cristina rises four stories above one of the most imaginatively landscaped gardens on Capri. It was built in 1959 and has a sunny design of open spaces, sunken lounges, and cool tiles. Each guest room has its own balcony and is very restful. Their sizes range from small to medium, but each has a good mattress and a compact tiled bathroom. In general, the prices are high for what you get, but on Capri in July and August you're sometimes lucky to find a room at any price.

Via Serena 20, 80073 Capri. ☏ **081-8370744.** Fax 081-8370550. www.reginacristina.it. 55 units. 195€–450€ double. Rates include buffet breakfast. MC, V. **Amenities:** Restaurant; bar; Jacuzzi; pool; room service. *In room:* A/C, TV, hair dryer, minibar.

Villa Sarah ★ 🏠   The modern Sarah, though far removed from the day-trippers from Naples, is still very central. A steep walk from the main square, it seems part of another world, with its private garden and good views. One of the bargains of the island, it's often fully booked, so reserve ahead in summer. The sea is visible only from the upper floors. Most of the guest rooms are quite small, but some of them make up for this with pleasant terraces. Bathrooms are a bit small as well. Breakfast is sometimes served on the terrace.

Via Tiberio 3A, 80073 Capri. ☏ **081-8377817.** Fax 081-8377215. www.villasarah.it. 20 units. 145€–220€ double; 290€ triple. Rates include buffet breakfast. AE, MC, V. Closed Nov 1–Mar 19. **Amenities:** Bar; babysitting; pool. *In room:* A/C, TV, hair dryer, minibar.

Inexpensive

Villa Krupp 🐠   This is a longtime favorite known for its affordable prices. During the early 20th century, Russian revolutionaries Gorky and Lenin called this villa home. Surrounded by shady trees, it offers panoramic views of the sea and the Gardens of Augustus from its terraces. At this family run place, the front parlor is all glass with views of the seaside and semitropical plants set near Hong Kong chairs, intermixed with painted Venetian-style pieces. Rooms are comfortable and vary in size, with spacious bathrooms.

Via Matteotti 12, 80073 Capri. ☏ **081-8377473.** Fax 081-8376489. www.villakrupp.it. 12 units (shower only). 140€–180€ double. Rates include buffet breakfast. MC, V. Closed Nov–Mar. **Amenities:** Bar; room service. *In room:* A/C, hair dryer.

WHERE TO DINE

Expensive

Da Paolino ★★ CAPRESE/ITALIAN   Don't be surprised to spot a visiting celeb at this chic restaurant. The food is about the most authentic Caprese cuisine served on the island. Try everything from a Caprese salad to sautéed ravioli stuffed with fresh cacciotta cheese. The rigatoni pasta with sautéed pumpkin flowers is worthy of *Gourmet* magazine. Equally delectable is the penne with eggplant and fresh mozzarella. Just as enchanting as the food is the dining area placed in a lemon grove. The lemon motif pervades the restaurant, ranging from the waiters' vests to the plates placed before you.

Via Palazzo a Mare 11, Marina Grande. ☏ **081-8376102.** www.paolinocapri.com. Reservations required. Main courses 20€–48€. AE, DC, MC, V. Daily 8–11pm (Easter–May also lunch around noon–3pm). Closed Nov–Mar.

Vila Verde ★★ ITALIAN   The spacious dining room, the large cellar of expensive wines, the succulent pastas and seafood, and the finely honed cuisine have made Villa Verde the chic celebrity haunt of the island. Paparazzi in summer often hang out in front of the restaurant, searching for a star to photograph. On our last visit we spotted Anne Hathaway. Specialties include pizza covered with mozzarella, cherry tomatoes, and eggplant and the just caught catch of the day grilled and served with fresh vegetables. The best pasta dish is studded with seafood and chunks of zucchini. The dining room leads out onto a large covered terrace. The decor is classic, with wrought iron, terra-cotta floors, and beautifully set tables.

Vico Sella Orta 6. ✆ **081-8377024.** www.villaverde-capri.com. Main courses 10€–30€. AE, MC, V. Mar-Oct daily noon–3:30pm and 7–10pm. Closed Nov-Feb.

Moderate

Ai Faraglioni SEAFOOD/CONTINENTAL The food is secondary to the scene at this popular restaurant, where tables are set on the main street in nice weather. Stylish and appealing and occupying a stone-sided building at least 150 years old, it has a kitchen that turns out well-prepared European specialties, usually based on seafood from the surrounding waters. Examples are linguine with lobster, seafood crepes, rice Creole, fisherman's risotto, grilled or baked fish, and a wide assortment of meat dishes, such as *pappardelle* with rabbit. For dessert, try one of the regional pastries mixed with fresh fruit.

Via Camerelle 75. ✆ **081-8370320.** Reservations required. Main courses 13€–38€. AE, DC, MC, V. Daily noon–3pm and 7:30–11:30pm. Closed Nov-Mar.

Aurora ★ CAMPANIAN/SEAFOOD One of the island's most consistently reliable restaurants, this traditional Caprese favorite lies in the historic center of Capri. Run by the D'Alessio family, it is a celebrity favorite. The decor includes many elegant touches such as fine wooden furniture and terra-cotta floors. A fairly large restaurant, Aurora has a number of outside tables in summer. One of the oldest restaurants on island, Aurora is also a pizzeria. Light, harmonious flavors go into the creation of the regional dishes such as mixed raw vegetables with lobster as a starter, followed by such main courses as fresh fish baked in a potato crust. The most imaginative homemade pasta is *pacchero*, a Neapolitan pasta with pumpkin flowers and Parmesan shavings, and the chef's pizza specialty (*all'acqua*) is made with mozzarella and chili peppers.

Via Fuorlovado 18-22. ✆ **081-8370181.** www.auroracapri.com. Reservations required. Main courses 13€–22€. AE, MC, V. Daily noon–3:30pm and 7pm–midnight. Closed Nov-Feb.

Da Gemma CAPRESE/SEAFOOD Da Gemma is reached by passing through a vaulted tunnel beginning at Piazza Umberto I and winding through dark underground passages. The cuisine includes authentic versions of Caprese favorites, with an emphasis on fish, as well as more modern dishes such as pizzas. You might begin with a creamy version of mussel soup, followed by one of many kinds of grilled fish, as well as filets of veal or chicken prepared with lemon and garlic or with Marsala wine. A specialty is a *fritto alla Gemma,* a medley of fried foods that includes fried zucchini blossoms, potato croquettes, fried mozzarella, and a miniature pizza. During warm weather, the site expands from its cramped 14th-century core onto a covered open-air terrace with sweeping views of the Gulf of Naples. (To reach the terrace, you'll have to wander through the same labyrinth of covered passages and then cross the street.)

Via Madre Serafina 6. ✆ **081-8370461.** www.dagemma.it. Reservations recommended. Main courses 10€–28€. AE, DC, MC, V. Tues-Sun noon–3pm and 7:30pm–midnight. Closed late Nov-Feb.

Il Geranio NEAPOLITAN/CAMPANA One of the most scenically located restaurants, this place occupies a 1750 villa in a verdant park a short but soothing distance from the town center and a short walk from the Gardens of Augustus. Menu items include lots of pungent sauces and fresh seafood that's sometimes combined into pastas. One of the best examples of this is rigatoni in a shellfish sauce, or another pasta delight—a homemade local pasta with clams and zucchini. The chefs are known for making the island's best lobster thermidor.

In the Giardini Augusto, Via Matteotti 8. (C) **081-8370616.** www.geraniocapri.com. Reservations recommended. Main courses 13€–45€. AE, DC, MC, V. Daily 12:30–3pm and 7:30–11:30pm. Closed Nov–Mar.

La Capannina ★ CAMPANA/ITALIAN   This restaurant has drawn a host of glamorous people who come, paradoxically, for its lack of pretentiousness. The three dining rooms are decorated tavern style, although the main draw in summer is the inner courtyard, with ferns and hanging vines. At a table covered with a colored cloth, you can select from baby shrimp au gratin or *scaloppine Capannina*. Sicilian macaroni isn't always on the menu; if it is, order it. The most savory skillet of goodies is the *zuppa di pesce,* a soup made with fish from the bay. Some dishes were obviously inspired by the nouvelle cuisine school. Wine is from vineyards owned by the restaurant. Menu items include stuffed squids; *ravioli alla caprese* (filled with local cheese, marjoram, tomato, and basil); lasagna with eggplant; and *pezzogna* (a local fish) with potatoes. We heard complaints about the staff's rudeness, but that's Capannina's only drawback.

Via Le Botteghe 12B–14. (C) **081-8370732.** www.capannina-capri.com. Reservations required for dinner. Main courses 13€–34€. AE, DC, MC, V. Daily noon–3pm and 7:30pm–midnight. Closed Nov 4–Mar 15 and Wed in Mar and Oct.

La Pigna ✦ NEAPOLITAN   La Pigna serves the finest meals for the money on the island. Since the place opened in 1875, dining here has been like attending a garden party. The owner loves flowers almost as much as good food, and the

14

CAMPANIA   Capri

Cafe in Capri.

greenhouse ambience includes purple petunias, red geraniums, bougainvillea, and lemon trees. Much of the produce comes from the restaurant's gardens in Anacapri. Try the penne tossed in eggplant sauce, the chicken supreme with mushrooms, or the herb-stuffed rabbit. The dessert specialty is an almond-and-chocolate torte. Another specialty is the homemade liqueurs. The waiters are courteous and efficient, and the atmosphere is nostalgic, as guitarists stroll by singing sentimental Neapolitan ballads.

Via Lo Palazzo 30. (℗ **081-8370280.** Reservations recommended. Main courses 15€–28€. AE, DC, MC, V. Daily 11:30am–3pm.

Ristorante al Grottino SEAFOOD/NEAPOLITAN Founded in 1937, this was the retreat of the rich and famous during its 1950s heyday. To reach it, you walk down a narrow alley branching off from Piazza Umberto I. Bowing to the influence of the nearby Neapolitan cuisine, the chef offers four different dishes of fried mozzarella, all of which are highly recommended. Try a big plate of the mixed fish fry from the seas of the Campania. The *zuppa di cozze* (mussel soup) is a savory opener, as is the *ravioli alla caprese.* The linguine with scampi is truly wonderful.

Via Longano 27. (℗ **081-8370584.** www.ristorantealgrottino.net. Reservations required for dinner. Main courses 10€–25€. AE, MC, V. Daily noon–3pm and 7pm–midnight. Closed Nov–Mar and Tues in Oct.

SHOPPING

A little shop on Capri's luxury shopping street, **Carthusia-Profumi di Capri,** Via Camerelle 10 ((℗ **081-8370529;** www.carthusia.it), specializes in perfume made on the island from local herbs and flowers. Since 1948, this shop has attracted such clients as the late Elizabeth Taylor (before she started touting her own perfume). The scents are unique, and many women consider Carthusia perfumes collector's items.

Carthusia also has a **Perfume Laboratory,** Viale Matteotti 2D ((℗ **081-8370368**), which you can visit daily 9:30am to 6pm. There's another **Carthusia**

Bottles of limoncello for sale in Amalfi.

shop in Anacapri, at Via Capodimonte 26 ((℗ **081-8373668**), next to the Villa Axel Munthe. The shops are closed November to March, but the laboratory remains open year-round.

Capri is famed for its **limoncello,** a liqueur whose recipe was conceived several generations ago by members of the Canali family. It consists of lemon zest (not the juice or pith) mixed with alcohol, sugar, water, and herbs to produce a tart kind of "hyper-lemonade" with a mildly alcoholic lift. It's consumed alone as either an aperitif or a digestive, or it's mixed with vodka or sparkling wines for a lemony cocktail. In 1989, the Canalis formalized their family recipe, established modern distilleries on Capri and in nearby Sorrento, and hired professionals to promote the product as far away as the United States and Japan. Limoncello is sold at **Limoncello di Capri,** Via Roma 79 (☎ **081-8375561**) in Capri, or at Via Capodimonte 27 (☎ 081-8372927) in Anacapri, often in lovely bottles that make nice, affordable gifts.

Shoppers here also look for deals on sandals, cashmere, and jewelry, the town's big bargains. The cobblers at **Canfora,** Via Camerelle 3 (☎ **081-8370487;** www.canfora.com), make all the sandals found in their shop. If you don't find what you need, you can order custom-made footwear. The store also sells shoes made elsewhere. The great sandal maker of Capri is Antonio Viva, holding forth for nearly half a century at **L'Arte del Sandalo Caprese,** Via Orlando 75 in Anacapri (☎ **081-8373583;** www.sandalocaprese.it). In days of yore, Jackie O and Sophia Loren used to come here to purchase sandals. There are ready-made selections, but this cobbler will also design to order.

The eight talented jewelers at **La Perla Gioielli,** Piazza Umberto I 21 (☎ **081-8370641**), work exclusively with gold and gems and can design and create anything you want. Established in 1936 by a local matriarch, Mamma Olympia, this is the most elegant and prestigious jeweler on Capri, with rosters of famous star-quality fans from around Europe and the New World. It's also the local branch of Buccellati, the prestigious silversmith based in Rome. Ask for Angela, or any of her charming children, Giorgio, Giuseppe, or Claudio. Another little charmer we recently stumbled upon quite by accident is **Grazia Vozza Gioielli,** Via Fuorlovado 38 (☎ **081-8374010;** www.graziavozza.com), which sells freshwater pearls and a stunning collection of necklaces in peridot, jade, amber, and aquamarine.

CAPRI AFTER DARK

You'll find some fun nightclubs on the island, all of which you can enter without a cover. They cater to all ages and nationalities, but only between late April and September. Foremost among them is **Number Two,** Via Camerelle 1 (☎ **081-8377078;** www.numbertwocapri.com).

The presence of these high-tech dance clubs doesn't keep the crowds out of the dozens of cafes, bars, and taverns scattered throughout the narrow streets of Capri's historic center. Among the most appealing is **Taverna Guarracino,** Via Castello 7 (☎ **081-8370514;** www.oguarracino.com), a rustically decorated place done in a regional island style and a convivial joint at which to enjoy a beer or a glass of wine.

One of the major pastimes in Capri is cafe sitting at an outdoor table on Piazza Umberto I. Even some locals (this is a good sign) patronize **Bar Tiberio,** Piazza Umberto I (☎ **081-8370268**), open daily 6am to 2am (sometimes to 4am). Larger and a little more comfortable than some of its competitors, this cafe has tables inside and outside that overlook the busy life of the square.

Anacapri ★★★

Even farther up in the clouds than Capri is the town of Anacapri, which is more remote, secluded, and idyllic than the main resort. At one time, Anacapri and Capri were connected only by the Scala Fenicia, the Phoenician Stairs (which have been reconstructed a zillion times). Today, however, you can reach Anacapri on a daring bus ride more thrilling than any roller coaster. The fare is 2.80€ round-trip. One visitor remarked that all bus drivers to Anacapri "were either good or dead."

The Monte Solaro chairlift in Anacapri.

When you disembark at **Piazza della Vittoria,** you'll find a village of charming dimensions.

To continue your ascent to the top, hop aboard a chairlift (La Segiovia) to **Monte Solaro ★★**, the loftiest citadel on the island at 594m (1,950 ft.). The ride takes about 12 minutes and operates March to October daily 9:30am to sunset, and November to February 10:30am to 3pm. A round-trip costs 9€. At the top, the panorama of the Bay of Naples is spread before you.

Back in the village below, you can head out on Viale Axel Munthe from Piazza Monumento for a 5-minute walk to the **Villa San Michele ★**, Capodimonte 34 (*©* **081-8371401;** www.villasanmichele.eu). This was the home of Axel Munthe, the Swedish author *(The Story of San Michele),* physician, and friend of Gustav V, king of Sweden, who visited him several times on the island. The villa is as Munthe (who died in 1949) furnished it, in a harmonious and tasteful way. In the villa are several marbles, which Munthe purchased from the ruins of Tiberius's imperial villa, located right under the Villa San Michele. Walk through the gardens for another in a series of sweeping views of the island. You can visit the villa daily May to September 9am to 6pm, October and April 9am to 5pm, November to February 9am to 3:30pm, and March 9am to 4:30pm. Admission is 6€.

WHERE TO STAY
Very Expensive
Capri Palace ★★★   On the slopes of Monte Solaro, the contemporary, first-class Capri Palace sparkles. Its bold designer obviously loved wide-open spaces and vivid colors. The landscaped gardens with palm trees and plenty of bougainvillea have a large pool, which most guests use as their outdoor living room. Although it lacks the intimate charms of La Scalinatella in Capri (see earlier in this chapter), it's still a wonderful choice because of its setting. Each of the guest rooms is attractively and comfortably furnished, and from some on a clear day you can see smoking Vesuvius. Many beds (mostly twins) are canopied, and all of them feature quality linens. Children 9 years and under are not welcome from June to August. Each of the four special suites has a private pool and private garden.

Via Capodimonte 2, 80071 Anacapri. ✆ **081-9780111.** Fax 081-8373191. www.capri-palace.com. 79 units. 340€–1,250€ double; 720€–3,300€ suite. Rates include buffet breakfast. AE, DC, MC, V. Closed Oct 17–Mar 31. **Amenities:** 2 restaurants; bar; babysitting; heated pool; room service; spa. *In room:* A/C, TV, hair dryer, minibar.

Moderate

Hotel Bella Vista ✦ A 2-minute walk from the piazza, this is a modern retreat with a panoramic view and a distinct sense of a family-run regional inn. Lodged into a mountainside, the hotel is decorated with primary colors and has large living and dining rooms and terraces with sea views. The breakfast and lunch terrace has garden furniture and a rattan-roofed sun shelter. The guest rooms are pleasantly contemporary (a few have a bed mezzanine, a sitting area on the lower level, and a private entrance). The tiled bathrooms are compact.

Via Orlandi 10, 80071 Anacapri. ✆ **081-8371463.** Fax 081-8382719. www.bellavistacapri.com. 15 units. 130€–240€ double; 180€–260€ triple. Rates include buffet breakfast. AE, DC, MC, V. Closed Nov 1–Easter. **Amenities:** Restaurant; room service; 3 outdoor tennis courts (lit). *In room:* TV, fridge, hair dryer.

Hotel San Michele di Anacapri This well-appointed hotel offers spacious cliff-side gardens and unmarred views as well as enough shady or sunny nooks to please everybody. Guests linger in its private gardens, where the trees are softened by splashes of color from hydrangea and geraniums. The view includes the Bay of Naples and Vesuvius. The midsize bedrooms are tastefully and comfortably furnished.

Via Orlandi 1–3, 80071 Anacapri. ✆ **081-8371427.** Fax 081-8371420. www.sanmichele-capri.com. 60 units. 150€–230€ double; 250€–420€ suite. Rates include breakfast. AE, DC, MC, V. Closed Nov–Mar. **Amenities:** Restaurant; bar; babysitting; pool; room service. *In room:* A/C, TV, hair dryer.

Inexpensive

Il Girasole ✦ This series of four buildings with brick terraces opens onto views of the Bay of Naples. All the midsize to spacious bedrooms are handsomely decorated with padded headboards and tasteful modular furnishings. The accommodations open onto terraces draped with bougainvillea. The best units are the suites, Aurum and Raggio di Luna, which are decorated with reproduction antiques and painted motifs. Avoid room nos. 3 to 5 under the reception hall. The pool is a bit small, but otherwise this place is choice in every way.

Via Linciano 47, 80071 Anacapri. ✆ **081-8372351.** Fax 081-8373880. www.ilgirasole.com. 24 units. 78€–190€ double; 170€–230€ suite. MC, V. Closed late Oct to mid-Mar. **Amenities:** Bar; babysitting; pool; room service. *In room:* A/C, TV, hair dryer, minibar, Wi-Fi (5€ per 24 hr.).

Villa Eva ★ 🏠 This was the childhood home of its owner, Eva Balestrieri, who was born in no. 5. Her husband, Vincenzo Parlato, an artist and craftsman, is the on-site gardener, builder, painter, and decorator. He even made the furniture scattered throughout the property. Artists, regular people, and what the owners call "eccentric characters" return year after year to this homelike place. A series of small cottages have rooms. Each cottage comes with a private bathroom with shower, and all units are tastefully decorated and furnished, with patios overlooking the charming garden. The focal point of the grounds is a pool shaped like a piano.

Via La Fabbrica 8, 80071 Anacapri. ✆ **081-8371549.** Fax 081-8372040. www.villaeva.com. 15 units. 70€–140€ double; 110€–180€ triple; 150€–210€ quad. Rates include buffet breakfast. AE, MC, V. Closed Nov–Feb. **Amenities:** Bar; Internet (free, in lobby); pool. *In room:* No phone.

14

CAMPANIA

Capri

WHERE TO DINE

La Rondinella CAPRESE/PIZZA   Despite the competition from the more formal restaurants in some of Anacapri's hotels, this is the most appealing place, thanks to the likable staff, its garden view, and a location adjacent to the Santa Sophia church. The menu items are tried-and-true versions of classics, yet the chefs manage to produce everything in copious amounts and with lots of robust flavors. Look for shrimp with pumpkin flowers; a mixed grill of fresh seafood, braised radicchio, and artichokes; and filet of veal or chicken slathered with mozzarella, tomatoes, and fresh herbs. Emerging piping hot from their brick ovens, the pizzas here are the best on island. For dessert, you might try the sugary version of Sicilian tiramisu.

Via Orlandi 245. ✆ **081-8371223.** Reservations recommended. Main courses 8€–25€. AE, DC, MC, V. Daily noon–3pm and 7pm–midnight. Closed Oct–Apr.

Le Arcate ★ 🎁 CAMPANIAN/SEAFOOD   Nearly all restaurants on the island overflow with tourists, but this homey, rustic-looking place enjoys most of its business from savvy locals who gravitate to the outdoor tables in fair weather. Both a restaurant and a pizzeria, it lies only a few steps from Piazza Victoria, the center of Anacapri. At night many diners feast on one of the savory pizzas emerging from the large wood-burning oven. You'd be hard-pressed to find a better pasta dish on island than the ravioli filled with *caciottina* (a local cheese) and a savory tomato sauce. The most reliable main course is invariably the just-caught grilled fish of the day. For the best in regional fare, sample baby squid with potatoes and tomatoes. The chef's dessert specialty is torta Caprese, a typical island cake made with almonds and chocolate.

Viale de Tommaso 24. ✆ **081-8373588.** Reservations recommended. Main courses 9€–22€. AE, DC, V. July–Aug daily 11:30am–3pm and 7pm–midnight; Sept–June Tues–Sun 11:30am–3pm and 7pm–midnight.

Marina Piccola ★

It's a pleasant 20-minute walk from Capri down the hill to the little south-shore fishing village and beach of **Marina Piccola** (take a cab or a bus back up the

The winding walk from Capri to Marina Piccola.

steep hill to Capri). The village opens onto emerald-and-cerulean waters, with the Faraglioni rocks of the sirens jutting out at the far end of the bay. Treat yourself to lunch at **La Canzone del Mare,** Via Marina Piccola 93 (© **081-8370104;** www.lacanzonedelmare.com), daily noon to 4pm (closed Nov–Mar). Seafood and Neapolitan cuisines are served.

POSITANO ★★

56km (35 miles) SE of Naples, 16km (10 miles) E of Sorrento, 266km (165 miles) SE of Rome

A Moorish-style hillside village on the southern strip of the Amalfi Drive, Positano opens onto the Tyrrhenian Sea. Once, Positano was part of the powerful Republic of the Amalfis, a rival of Venice as a sea power in the 10th century. It's said that the town was "discovered" after World War II when Gen. Mark Clark stationed troops in nearby Salerno. Like many European resorts, it began as a sleepy fishing village that was visited by painters and writers (Paul Klee, Tennessee Williams) and then taken over by visitors in search of bohemia, until a full-scale tourism industry was born.

Today smart boutiques dot the village, and bikinis add vibrant colors to the gray beach, where you're likely to get pebbles in your sand castle. The village, you'll soon discover, is impossibly steep. Wear comfortable walking shoes.

If you make reservations the day before with **Gescab** (© **089-811986;** www.consorziolmp.it), you can take a hydrofoil or a ferry to Capri from Positano. Hydrofoils cost 17€ one-way, and a ferry ticket goes for 15€ one-way.

Essentials

GETTING THERE   SITA **buses** leave from Sorrento frequently throughout the day, more often in summer than winter, for the rather thrilling ride to Positano; a one-way fare is 1.40€. For information, call SITA at © **081-7527337.**

If you have a **car,** Positano lies along S145, which becomes S163 at the approach to the resort.

VISITOR INFORMATION   The **tourist office,** Via del Saracino 6 (© **089-875067;** www.azienda turismopositano.it), is open Monday to Friday 9am to 6pm, Sunday 9am to 1pm November to May, and Monday to Saturday 9am to 8pm June to October.

Positano.

Where to Stay

VERY EXPENSIVE

Hotel di San Pietro ★★★   This Relais & Châteaux property, with its gorgeous views, is the most luxurious retreat in the south of Italy. About 1.6km (1 mile) from Positano toward Amalfi, the San Pietro is signaled only by a miniature 17th-century chapel out on a high cliff. The hotel opened in 1970 and has been renovated virtually every winter since. An elevator takes you down to the cliff ledges to a private beach. The suitelike guest rooms are super-glamorous with state-of-the-art bathrooms, many with picture windows beside the bathtubs (there's even a huge sunken Roman bath in one suite). Antiques and art objects add to the effect. Room no. 8½ is named for longtime guest Federico Fellini. Bougainvillea from the terraces reaches into the ceilings of many living rooms.

Via Laurito 2, 84017 Positano. ✆ **089-875455.** Fax 089-811449. www.ilsanpietro.it. 62 units. 420€–650€ double; 600€–1,350€ suite. Rates include continental breakfast. AE, DC, MC, V. Free parking. Closed Nov 1–Mar 31. **Amenities:** Restaurant; bar; babysitting; concierge; exercise room; pool; room service; spa; outdoor tennis court (unlit). *In room:* A/C, TV, hair dryer, minibar.

Hotel Le Sirenuse ★★★   This is one of southern Italy's greatest resort hotels. It's been long celebrated as a retreat of the rich and famous. Despite stiff competition from San Pietro (see above), Le Sirenuse remains a gem, with stunning views. It's better than ever, after the addition of a high-tech fitness center and spa. This old villa a few minutes' walk up from the bay is owned by the Marchesi Sersale family; it was their home until 1951. The family selects all the furnishings, which include fine carved chests, 19th-century paintings and old prints, a spinet piano, upholstered pieces in bold colors, and a Victorian cabinet. The guest rooms, many with Jacuzzis in the luxurious bathrooms, are varied, and all have terraces overlooking the village. Children 6 and under aren't welcome from May to September.

Via Cristoforo Colombo 30, 84017 Positano. ✆ **089-875066.** Fax 089-811798. www.sirenuse.it. 63 units. 350€–1,210€ double; from 1,600€ suite. Rates include buffet breakfast. AE, DC, MC, V. Parking 40€. Closed Nov–Mar. **Amenities:** Restaurant (w/outdoor terrace dining in summer); 2 bars; babysitting; exercise room; heated pool; room service; spa. *In room:* A/C, TV/DVD, hair dryer, minibar.

EXPENSIVE

Albergo L'Ancora ★   This hillside villa-turned-hotel has the atmosphere of a private club. The hotel has made massive improvements, including installing an elevator, and is fresh and sunny. Each guest room is like a bird's nest on a cliff, with a private terrace. Well-chosen antiques, such as fine inlaid desks, are mixed with contemporary pieces. All have well-kept bathrooms. *Note:* The hotel has only two suites, each with Jacuzzi.

Via Colombo 36, 84017 Positano. ✆ **089-875318.** Fax 089-811784. 18 units. www.htlancora.it. 180€–232€ double; 360€–413€ suite. Rates include buffet breakfast. AE, DC, MC, V. Free parking. Closed Nov–Mar. **Amenities:** Saltwater pool; room service. *In room:* A/C, TV, hair dryer, minibar.

Albergo Miramare ★ 🏠   On a cliff in the town center, the Miramare is for those who like the personal touch that only a small inn can provide. Guests stay in one of two tastefully furnished buildings amid citrus trees and flamboyant bougainvillea. Your bed (with a firm mattress) will most likely rest under a vaulted ceiling, and the white walls will be thick. The bathrooms have a sense of whimsy, with pink porcelain clamshells as washbasins (the water rushes from a sea-green ceramic fish with coral-pink gills). Nine rooms have a glass wall in the bathroom, so you can enjoy a panoramic sea view while soaking in the tub. The conversation piece is room no. 210's glass bathtub (once an aquarium) on a flowery terrace. The beach is a 3-minute walk away down a series of stairs.

Via Trara Genoino 27, 84017 Positano. © **089-875002.** Fax 089-875219. www.miramare positano.it. 15 units. 185€–360€ double. Rates include buffet breakfast. AE, DC, MC, V. Parking 20€. Closed Nov–Mar. **Amenities:** Babysitting; room service. *In room:* A/C, TV, hair dryer, minibar.

Hotel Poseidon ★   This hotel was built in 1950 by the Aonzo family as their summer residence. In 1955, they enlarged it and turned it into a hotel; its terraced gardens and panoramic views lure new visitors every year. It's charming, discreet, and elegant, with antique furniture and objects. The Aonzo family still owns and operates the hotel, lending personal service, luxury, and style to each spacious guest room, without the high rates of San Pietro and Le Sirenuse.

Via Pasitea 148, 84017 Positano. © **089-811111.** Fax 089-875833. www.hotelposeidonpositano.it. 52 units. 240€–310€ double; 393€–632€ suite. Rates include buffet breakfast. AE, DC, MC, V. Parking 23€. Closed Oct 31–Apr 21. **Amenities:** Restaurant; bar; babysitting; exercise room; pool (covered and heated in winter); room service. *In room:* A/C, TV, hair dryer, minibar, Wi-Fi (free).

Hotel Villa Franca ★ 📷   At the top of Positano, about a 10-minute walk from the center, this hotel is a little gem. It offers brightly decorated guest rooms and beautifully tiled bathrooms. The top floor contains somewhat small rooms, but they open onto little balconies with the best views. The finest rooms are the three deluxe corner units; they're more spacious and also have great views of the coast. Ten rooms are in the less-inspired annex. The rooftop is the only spot in town with a 360-degree view of Positano.

Viale Pasitea 318, 84017 Positano. © **089-875655.** Fax 089-875735. www.villafrancahotel.it. 38 units. 180€–410€ double. Rates include buffet breakfast. AE, DC, MC, V. Parking 21€. Closed Nov–Mar. Bus: 318. **Amenities:** Restaurant; bar; babysitting; exercise room; pool; room service; sauna; Wi-Fi (free, in lobby). *In room:* A/C, TV, hair dryer, minibar.

Palazzo Murat ★   This delightful 18th-century nest offers quiet and serenity. It was once the retreat of Napoleon's brother-in-law, the king of Naples, who was notorious for confiscating statuary and church art from the former occupants—in this case, an order of Benedictine monks. The jasmine and bougainvillea in the garden are so profuse that they spill over their enclosing wall onto the arbors of the narrow street. The best (and most expensive) rooms are nos. 1 to 5 in the original 18th-century wing, which boasts high ceilings and antiques; the newer annex has smaller and less atmospheric rooms. Only the third-floor rooms have views of the sea.

Via dei Mulini 23, 84017 Positano. © **089-875177.** Fax 089-811419. www.palazzomurat.it. 30 units. 120€–475€ double. Rates include buffet breakfast. AE, DC, MC, V. Parking 20€ nearby. Closed Nov–Mar. **Amenities:** Restaurant; babysitting; room service; Wi-Fi (8€ per hr., in lobby). *In room:* A/C, TV, hair dryer, minibar.

MODERATE
Casa Albertina ★   This villa guesthouse, up a steep and winding road, offers a view of the coast from its perch. Guest rooms are gems, color-coordinated in

mauve or blue and furnished with well-selected pieces, such as gilt mirrors and fruitwood end tables. Each has wide French doors leading out to a private balcony, and a few have Jacuzzis. You can breakfast on the terra-cotta–tiled terrace.

Via Tavolozza 3, 84017 Positano. ✆ **089-875143.** Fax 089-811540. www.casaalbertina.com. 20 units. 120€–240€ double. Rates include continental breakfast. AE, MC, V. Parking 20€–25€ nearby. **Amenities:** Restaurant; bar; room service; Wi-Fi (in lobby, 10€ per 3 hr.). *In room:* A/C, TV, hair dryer, minibar.

Where to Dine

EXPENSIVE

Buca di Bacco ★★ CAMPANIA/ITALIAN   Right on the beach you'll find one of Positano's top restaurants, opened just days after the end of World War II. Guests often stop for a drink in the bar before heading up to the dining room on a big covered terrace facing the sea. On display are fresh fish, special salads, and fruit, such as luscious black figs and freshly peeled oranges soaked in caramel. An exciting opener is a fresh seafood salad; you might prefer the *zuppa di cozze* (mussels) in a tangy sauce. Other items not to miss are linguine with lobster and *grigliata del Golfo,* a unique mixed fish fry. The pasta dishes are homemade and the meats are well prepared with fresh ingredients. Finish with a limoncello, the lemon liqueur celebrated along the Amalfi Drive.

Via Rampa Teglia 8. ✆ **089-875699.** www.bucadibacco.it. Reservations required. Main courses 13€–38€. AE, DC, MC, V. Daily noon–3:30pm and 7–11:30pm. Closed Nov–Mar.

La Cambusa ★ AMALFITAN/SEAFOOD   Head here for local fish grilled to perfection. Local fishermen save the finest catch for owner Luigi Russo (you can see them bringing it in early in the morning). The food items are prepared with care, and the cooking is designed to bring out the natural flavor in the fish. You can make a lunch out of a bowl of the fish chowder. The catch of the day is often oven roasted and served with a white-wine sauce. Mediterranean king prawns are served fresh from the grill. A true fish lover might begin a meal with carpaccio of sea bass and fresh shrimp, and follow with boiled octopus with a lemon-and-olive-oil dressing. Little Neapolitan tomatoes are used for the sauces; they not only add extra flavor to the sauce but also enrich most of the fish dishes. For a special treat, ask for the zucchini soufflé flavored with basil and parmigiano.

Piazza Amerigo Vespucci 4. ✆ **089-875432.** www.lacambusapositano.com. Reservations recommended. Main courses 15€–30€. AE, DC, MC, V. Daily noon–4pm and 7pm–midnight.

La Sponda ★★ MEDITERRANEAN   This stylish restaurant occupies the third floor of a hotel of the same name. Waiters will tell you that its terrace is "just 80 steps above the level of the sea." Bougainvillea, geraniums, hibiscus, and lemon trees are artfully massed in the terrace corners, and during nice weather the inside dining room closes completely in favor of the alfresco experience. The menu items revolve around what's available at the seafood markets and include linguine le Sirenuse, with lobster, scampi, and crayfish; linguine with artichoke hearts and scampi that's been cooked *en papillote* (in parchment); fresh salads and antipasti; and a grilled medley of fish and shellfish prepared for two or more. Expect lots of Mediterranean herbs, mozzarella, and homemade pastries.

In the Hotel Le Sirenuse, Via Cristoforo Colombo 30. ✆ **089-875066.** www.lesirenuse.it. Reservations required. Main courses 25€–40€. AE, DC, MC, V. Daily 1–2:30pm and 8–10:30pm. Closed Nov–Feb.

MODERATE

Chez Black SEAFOOD   Chez Black occupies a desirable position near the beach, and in summer it's in the heart of the action. The interior seems like an expensive yacht with varnished ribbing, a glowing sheath of softwood and brass, and semaphore symbols. A stone-edged aquarium holds fresh lobsters, and the racks and racks of local wines give you a vast choice. Seafood is the specialty, as well as a wide selection of pizzas. Two succulent dishes are risotto with shrimp in a zucchini sauce and fried baby squid; you'll also find an array of veal, liver, chicken, and beef dishes. One of the most prized and sought-after dishes is the spicy *zuppa di pesce* (fish soup)—a meal in itself, brimming with succulent finned creatures. Regrettably, the unhelpful staff leaves a lot to be desired.

Via del Brigantino 19–21. ✆ **089-875036.** www.chezblack.it. Reservations required in summer. Main courses 14€–30€. AE, DC, MC, V. Daily 12:30–3pm and 7:30–11pm. Closed Jan 7–Feb 13.

INEXPENSIVE

Da Adolfo ★ 🏕️ SEAFOOD/AMALFITAN   Don't even think of coming here via car or taxi because you'd have to descend around 450 rugged stone steps from the highway above. The owner provides a 25-passenger motorboat to take you from Positano's main jetty across the water to the restaurant. (You'll recognize the boat by the large red fish on its side.) During the season when Da Adolfo is open, the boat departs daily every 30 minutes 10am to 1pm, and 4pm to whenever the last customer has left the beach, usually between 6:30 and 8pm or even later on Saturdays in July and August (these late-summer Sat evenings are the only time dinner is served). The shuttle service is free, as is the use of the sands, changing rooms, and freshwater showers maintained by the restaurant. The only things you'll pay for are whatever you eat and drink in the restaurant and the optional rental of a beach chair and an umbrella for 14€.

Da Adolfo seems like a beachfront restaurant in Greece, complete with pungent summery food, an utter lack of pretension, and sun and fun. Menu items focus on the fish, herbs, mozzarella, and zest of the Mediterranean. Especially appealing are the heaping bowls of mussel soup, slices of fresh mozzarella wrapped in lemon leaves, and spaghetti with squid and zucchini.

Via Laurito, Località Laurito. ✆ **089-875022.** www.daadolfo.com. Reservations recommended. Main courses 10€–22€. AE, DC, MC, V. Late May to Sept daily 10am–6pm; July–Aug Sat 8pm–midnight.

Shopping

The shop at the Hotel Le Sirenuse (see review above), **Emporio Le Sirenuse,** Via Cristoforo Colombo 103 (✆ **089-811468;** www.lesirenuse.it), has the town's toniest merchandise, everything from ballerina slippers from Porselli (who designs them for Milan's La Scala) to sexy one-piece bathing suits.

If you're in the market for brightly colored, intricately patterned regional pottery, visit **Umberto Carro,** Via Pasitea 98 (✆ **089-811596;** www.umberto carro.it), where the focus is on dishes, cookware, and ceramic tiles. For the best collection of ceramics from the Amalfi town of Vietri sul Mare, head for

L'Africana nightclub in Positano.

Ceramica Assunta, Via Cristoforo Colombo 97 (☏ **089-875008;** www.ceramica
ssunta.it), known for its colorful ceramics with fine artisanal decorations.

Positano After Dark

Music on the Rocks, Spiaggia Grande Via Grotte dell'Incanto 51 (☏ **089-
875874;** www.musicontherocks.it), is designed on two levels, one of which contains a quieter piano bar. It's owned by the same man who owns the chic Chez
Black (see above).

Similar in its choice of music, crowd, and setting is **L'Africana,** Via Torre a
Mare 2 (☏ **089-874042;** www.africanadisco-champagnebar.com), in the resort
of Praiano, about 7km (4½ miles) from Positano. Local fishermen come in during
the most frenzied peak of the dancing. At a sinkhole at the edge of the dance
floor, they lower their nets to pull up a catch of seafood for local restaurants. The
contrast of New Age music with old-world folklore is as riveting as it is bizarre.
Many chic guests from Positano arrive by boat. Both clubs open nightly at around
10pm June to August, but only Friday and Saturday in May and September, and
they're closed the rest of the year.

AMALFI ★★

61km (38 miles) SE of Naples, 18km (11 miles) E of Positano, 34km (21 miles) W of Salerno, 272km
(169 miles) SE of Rome

From the 9th to the 11th century, the seafaring Republic of Amalfi rivaled the
great maritime powers of Genoa and Venice. Its maritime code, the *Tavole Amalfitane,* was followed in the Mediterranean for centuries. But raids by Saracens
and a flood in the 14th century devastated the city. Amalfi's power and influence
weakened, until it rose again in modern times as the major resort on the Amalfi
Drive.

From its position at the slope of the steep Lattari hills, it overlooks the Bay
of Salerno. The approach to Amalfi is dramatic, whether you come from Positano
or from Salerno. Today Amalfi depends on tourist traffic, and the hotels and *pensioni* are located right in the milling throng of vacationers. The finest and most
highly rated accommodations are on the outskirts.

Essentials

GETTING THERE SITA **buses** run every 2 hours during the day from Sorrento, costing 2.50€ one-way. There are also SITA bus connections from Positano, costing 1.40€ one-way.

By **car** from Positano, continue east along the narrow hairpin turns of the Amalfi Drive (S163).

VISITOR INFORMATION The **tourist office,** at Via delle Repubbliche Marinare (✆ **089-871107;** www.amalfitouristoffice.it), is open Monday to Friday 8:30am to 1:30pm and 3 to 5pm, and Saturday 8:30am to 1:30pm. It closes early in the winter months.

Exploring the Town

Amalfi lays some claim to being a beach resort, and narrow public **beaches** flank the harbor. In addition, between rocky sections of the coast, many of the first-class and deluxe hotels have carved out small stretches of sand reserved for their guests. However, better and more expansive beaches are adjacent to the nearby villages of **Minori** and **Maiori,** a short drive along the coast. Those beaches are lined with a handful of cafes, souvenir kiosks, and restaurants that thrive mostly during the summer. You can reach the villages by buses leaving from Amalfi's Piazza Flavio Gioia at 30-minute intervals during the day. Expect to pay 1€ each way.

The **Duomo ★**, Piazza del Duomo (✆ **089-871059**), evokes Amalfi's rich past. It is named in honor of St. Andrew (Sant'Andrea), whose remains are said to be buried inside the crypt (see below). Reached by climbing steep steps, the cathedral is characterized by its black-and-white facade and mosaics. The one nave and two aisles are all richly baroque. The cathedral dates from the 11th century, although the present structure has been rebuilt. Its bronze doors were made in Constantinople, and its campanile (bell tower) is from the 13th century, erected partially in the Romanesque style. The Duomo is open, and admission is free.

You can also visit the **Cloister of Paradise (Chiostro del Paradiso) ★★**, to the left of the Duomo, originally a necropolis for members of the Amalfitan "establishment." This graveyard dates from the 1200s and contains broken columns and statues, as well as sarcophagi. The aura is definitely Moorish, with a whitewashed quadrangle of interlaced arches. One of the treasures is fragments of Cosmatesque work, brightly colored geometric mosaics that once formed parts of columns and altars, a specialty of this region. The arches create an evocative setting for concerts, both piano and vocal, held on Friday nights July to September. The cloister is open in March daily 9am to 5:30pm, April to September daily 9am to 9pm, and October to December daily 10am to 1pm, and charges 3€ adults, 1€ children. It is closed January and February. You reach the **crypt** from the

The Cloister of Paradise.

cloister. Here lie the remains of St. Andrew—that is, everything except his face. The pope donated his face to St. Andrew's in Patras, Greece, but the back half of his head remained here.

A minor attraction, good for that rainy day, is the **Civic Museum (Museo Civico),** Town Hall Piazza Municipio (☏ **089-8736200**), which displays original manuscripts of the *Tavole Amalfitane.* This was the maritime code that governed the entire Mediterranean until 1570. Some exhibits relate to Flavio Gioia, Amalfi's most famous merchant adventurer. Amalfitani claim that he invented the compass in the 12th century. "The sun, the moon, the stars and—Amalfi," locals used to say. What's left from the "attic" of their once-great power is preserved here. The museum is open Monday to Friday 8:30am to 1:30pm and 4:30 to 6:30pm. Admission is free.

For your most **scenic walk** in Amalfi, start at Piazza del Duomo and head up Via Genova. The classic stroll will take you to the **Valley of the Mills (Valle dei Mulini),** so called because of the paper mills along its rocky reaches (the seafaring republic is said to have acquainted Italy with the use of paper). You'll pass by fragrant gardens and scented citrus groves. If the subject interests you, you can learn more details about the industry at the **Museum of Paper (Museo della Carta),** Via delle Cartiere 24 (☏ **089-8304561;** www.museodellacarta. it), filled with antique presses and yellowing manuscripts from yesterday. It's open daily 10am to 6:30pm in summer and Tuesday to Saturday until 3:30pm from November to February. Admission is 4€. Guided tours are included.

Where to Stay

VERY EXPENSIVE

Hotel Santa Caterina ★★★   This mellow, traditional old choice still reigns supreme as the grande dame of Amalfi. Perched atop a cliff, Santa Caterina has an elevator that'll take you down to a private beach (or you can stroll down the paths past citrus groves and gardens). There you'll find a saltwater pool, a sun deck, a fitness center, a cafe/bar, and an open-air restaurant. Built in 1880, the structure was destroyed by a rock slide on Christmas Eve 1902, prompting a rebuilding on a "safer" site in 1904. You're housed in the main structure or in one of the small "villas" in the citrus groves. The guest rooms are furnished in good taste, with an eye toward comfort. Most have private balconies facing the sea. The furniture respects the tradition of the house, and in every room is an antique piece.

S.S. Amalfitana 9, 84011 Amalfi. ☏ **089-871012.** Fax 089-871351. www.hotelsantacaterina.it. 70 units. 290€–790€ double; 690€–2,300€ suite. Rates include buffet breakfast. Dinner 70€–84€.

AE, DC, MC, V. Parking 15€ in garage; free outside. **Amenities:** 2 restaurants (w/outdoor dining); bar; babysitting; exercise room; saltwater pool; spa. *In room:* A/C, TV, hair dryer, minibar.

EXPENSIVE

Hotel Belvedere ★   Below the coastal road outside Amalfi on the drive to Positano, the aptly named Belvedere has one of the best locations in the area. The house originated as a private villa in the 1860s and was transformed by its present owners into a hotel in 1962. The guest rooms have terraces overlooking the water. They range in shape and size, each with a tiled bathroom. The family owners see to it that guests are happy. There's a shuttle bus into Amalfi. An interior elevator will take you down to the pool and the path to the sea.

Via Smeraldo 19, Conca dei Marini, 84010 Amalfi. ✆ **089-831282.** Fax 089-831439. www.belvedere hotel.it. 35 units. 160€–250€ double; 280€–350€ suite. AE, DC, MC, V. Free parking. Closed Oct 25–Apr 20. **Amenities:** Restaurant; 2 bars; saltwater pool; room service. *In room:* A/C, TV, hair dryer, minibar.

Hotel Luna Convento ★★   The second-best hotel in Amalfi (only the Santa Caterina, above, is better) boasts a 13th-century cloister said to have been founded by St. Francis of Assisi. Most of the building, however, was rebuilt in 1975. The long corridors, where monks of old (and, later, Wagner and Ibsen) used to tread, are lined with sitting areas used by the very unmonastic guests seeking a tan. The guest rooms have sea views, terraces, and modern furnishings, although many are uninspired in decor. The gorgeous pool, scooped out of the rocks overlooking the sea, is itself worth a stay here, as is the private beach.

Via Pantaleone Comite 33, 84011 Amalfi. ✆ **089-871002.** Fax 089-871333. www.lunahotel.it. 43 units. 190€–340€ double; 380€–840€ suite; rates include buffet breakfast. AE, DC, MC, V. Valet parking 20€ in garage; free outside. **Amenities:** 2 restaurants; bar; saltwater pool; room service; Wi-Fi (free, in lobby). *In room:* A/C, TV, hair dryer, minibar.

MODERATE

Excelsior Grand Hotel   Three kilometers (2 miles) north of Amalfi at Pogerola, the Excelsior is a modern first-class hotel on a high mountain perch. Its structure is unconventional: an octagonal glass tower rising above the central lobby, with exposed mezzanine lounges and an open stairs. All its guest rooms are angled toward the view, so you get the first glimmer of dawn and the last rays of sunset. They're individually designed, with lots of space and good reproductions, as well as some antiques. Transportation to and from the private beach is provided by boat and bus for 10€. They also provide shuttle bus service to and from the town center.

Via Papa Leone X, 84011 Amalfi. ✆ **089-830015.** Fax 089-830085. www.excelsior-hotel.it. 97 units. 190€–240€ double; from 257€ suite. Rates include buffet breakfast. AE, DC, MC, V. Free parking. **Amenities:** 2 restaurants; bar; pool in natural grotto; room service; Wi-Fi (free, in lobby). *In room:* A/C, TV, hair dryer, minibar.

Hotel Miramalfi   On the western edge of Amalfi, the Miramalfi lies below the coastal road on its own beach. The guest rooms are wrapped around the curving contour of the coast and have unobstructed sea views. The stone swimming pier (used for sunbathing, diving, and boarding motorboats for water-skiing) is down a winding cliff-side path, past terraces of grapevines. Breakfast is served on one of the main terraces overlooking the sea, or your own balcony. Each room is well equipped, with built-in headboards and cool tile floors.

Via Quasimodo 3, 84011 Amalfi. ℂ **089-871588.** Fax 089-871287. www.miramalfi.it. 49 units. 200€–300€ double; 360€–500€ suite. Rates include buffet breakfast. Dinner 40€ extra per person. AE, DC, MC, V. Parking 15€. **Amenities:** Saltwater pool; room service. *In room:* A/C, TV, hair dryer, minibar.

Villa Lara   In the heart of the resort, this restored villa from the late 19th century lies close to the Duomo and the water. It is perched on a cliff with views of Amalfi and the coast. The antique villa is surrounded by lemon trees and flowering bougainvillea. The furnishings are antiques but are combined with functional amenities, including such luxuries as a hydromassage shower. There is a high level of taste throughout, and much of the old has been retained, including the majolica tiles and the vaulted ceilings. Breakfast is taken on a panoramic terrace and is seasonally adjusted to take advantage of the typical products of the Amalfi coast, such as fresh fruit or freshly squeezed orange juice.

Via delle Cartiere 3, 84001 Amalfi. ℂ **089-8736358.** Fax. 089-9830119. www.villalara.it. 7 units. 100€–195€ double; 175€–275€ suite. Rates include buffet breakfast. AE, DC, MC, V. Parking 18€. **Amenities:** Bar; babysitting; Internet (free, in lobby); room service. *In room:* A/C, TV, hair dryer, minibar.

INEXPENSIVE

Hotel Lidomare 🍴   One of the best bargains in Amalfi, this pleasant small hotel is a few steps from the sea in a 13th-century building. The high-ceilinged guest rooms are airy and contain a scattering of modern furniture mixed with Victorian-era antiques. The Camera family extends a warm welcome. Breakfast is the only meal served, but you can order it until 10am.

Largo Piccolomini 9, 84011 Amalfi. ℂ **089-871332.** Fax 089-871394. www.lidomare.it. 15 units (8 with shower only). 103€–145€ double. Rates include continental breakfast. AE, MC, V. Parking 18€. *In room:* A/C, TV, hair dryer, minibar, Wi-Fi (free).

Where to Dine

MODERATE

Da Gemma ★ SEAFOOD/AMALFITAN   Located near the cathedral, Da Gemma is one of Amalfi's best restaurants, with a strong emphasis on fresh seafood. It has been overseen by members of the Grimaldi family for many generations, a fact that caused a lot of fuss when Princess Caroline of Monaco (whose family name is also Grimaldi, but with a link that's very distant) came to dine. The kitchen sends out platefuls of savory pastas, grilled or sautéed fish, casseroles, and an enduring favorite—*zuppa di pesce,* a full meal in its own right and prepared only for two. The pasta specialty is *paccheri all'acquapazza,* made with shrimp and monkfish. For dessert, order the *crostata* (pie with jam), the best you're ever likely to have; it's made with pine nuts and homemade marmalades of lemon, orange, and tangerine.

Via Frà Gerardo Sasso 11. ℂ **089-871345.** www.trattoriadagemma.com. Reservations required. Main courses 16€–26€. AE, MC, V. Thurs–Tues 12:30–2:45pm and 7:45–10:30pm. Closed Jan 7–Feb 15.

La Caravella–Amalfi ★ AMALFITAN/CAMPANIA   The stone building containing this restaurant was a boatyard and marine warehouse during the 1400s.

Today, it's one of the most prominent restaurants in town, with a menu featuring authentic Italian specialties. The essentially regional repertoire contains some hearty choices, beginning with such starters as fresh anchovies filled with Provola cheese. The brawny flavors continue with such superb main courses as black *panzerottini* (a homemade pasta) made with ricotta and shellfish. Locals flock here to sample filet of fish au gratin with fennel, sun-dried tomatoes, mint, and Greco di Tufo wine.

Via Matteo Camera 12. © **089-871029.** www.ristorantelacaravella.it. Reservations required. Main courses 20€–30€; tasting menu 80€. AE, MC, V. Wed–Mon noon–2:30pm and 7–11pm. Closed Nov 5–Dec 5 and Jan 8–Feb 12.

Ristorante Luna Convento AMALFITAN/ITALIAN   If you're unable to reserve a table at dinner, try for lunch at this stylish place; there's likely to be less of a crowd, and the sunny view over the town and the sea will be clearer. The restaurant is half indoor/half outdoor and staffed by consummate professionals. The menu items are usually based on seafood and include fresh seafood salad, seafood pastas, baked slices of sea bass or monkfish with herbs and garlic, and *risotto alla pescatora* (fisherman's rice); other choices are chicken, veal, beef, and pork. The antipasti are particularly tantalizing.

If you can't get a reservation even for lunch, try the restaurant's sibling, the **Ristorante Torre Saracena,** a short walk away; any staff member will contact it for you. The prices, menu, and hours are more or less the same.

In the Hotel Luna Convento, Via Pantaleone Comite 33. © **089-871002.** Reservations recommended. Main courses 15€–28€. AE, DC, MC, V. Daily 12:30–2pm and 7:30–9:30pm.

Shopping

The coast has long been known for its **ceramics,** and the area at **Piazza del Duomo** is filled with hawkers peddling "regional" ware (which often means Asian). But the real thing is still made at nearby **Vietri sul Mare,** 13km (8 miles) west of Amalfi. The pottery made in Vietri is distinguished by its florid colors and sunny motifs. Vietri's best outlet is **Ceramica Solimene,** Via Madonna degli Angeli 7 (© **089-210243;** www.solimene.com), which has been producing quality terra-cotta ceramics for centuries. It's fabled for its production of lead-free surface tiles, dinner- and cookware, umbrella holders, and stylish lamps.

In Amalfi itself, look for **limoncello,** a sweet lemon liqueur that tastes best chilled. It's manufactured in town by the **La Valle dei Mulini** factories. You can drop by its headquarters

Ceramics for sale in the Piazza del Duomo in Amalfi.

on Salita Chiarito 9 to buy a bottle or two (call ℂ **089-873211** for information). A bottle of limoncello costs about 15€. At **Antichi Sapori d'Amalfi,** Sottoportico Ferrara (ℂ **089-872303;** www.antichisaporidamalfi.it), you get not only limoncello but a full array of local products, such as jams, honeys, lemon perfumes, and grappa.

At **La Grotta di Masaniello,** Largo Cesareo Console 7 (ℂ **089-871929**), owner Francesco Mangieri (call him Mao) makes sculptures from ancient pieces of marble or a stalactite or stalagmite from one of the nearby grottoes.

RAVELLO ★★★

275km (171 miles) SE of Rome, 66km (41 miles) SE of Naples, 29km (18 miles) W of Salerno

Ravello is one of the loveliest resorts along the Amalfi Drive. It has attracted artists, writers, and celebrities for years (Richard Wagner, Greta Garbo, André Gide, and even D. H. Lawrence, who wrote *Lady Chatterley's Lover* here). Ravello's reigning celebrity for many years was Gore Vidal, who once purchased a villa here as a writing retreat. William Styron set his novel *Set This House on Fire* here. Boccaccio dedicated part of the *Decameron* to Ravello, and John Huston used it as a location for his film *Beat the Devil,* with Bogie.

The sleepy village seems to hang 335m (1,100 ft.) up, between the Tyrrhenian Sea and some celestial orbit. You approach from Amalfi, 6km (3¾ miles) southwest, by a wickedly curving road cutting through the villa- and vine-draped hills that hem in the Valley of the Dragon.

Essentials

GETTING THERE **Buses** from Amalfi leave for Ravello from the terminal at the waterfront at Piazza Flavio Gioia (ℂ **089-871009** for schedules and information) almost every hour 7am to 10pm, costing 1.10€ one-way.

A view from Villa Cimbrone in Ravello.

If you have a **car** and are in Amalfi, take a circuitous mountain road north of the town (the road is signposted to Ravello).

VISITOR INFORMATION   The **tourist office,** Piazza Duomo 10 (𝄐 **089-857096;** www.ravellotime.it), is open daily 10am to 7pm (until 8pm in summer).

SPECIAL EVENTS   The hilltop town is known for its summer **Ravello Festival.** Internationally famed artists sometimes appear. The venues range from the Duomo to the gardens of Villa Rufolo. Tickets, which you can buy at the tourist office, start at 20€.

Seeing the Sights

Although most of your time will be spent sunbathing, relaxing, strolling, and taking in the view, Ravello has a few outstanding sightseeing attractions, too.

Duomo   It's unusual for such a small place to have a cathedral, but Ravello boasts one because it was once a major bishopric. The building dates from the 11th century, but its bronze doors are the work of Barisano da Trani and were crafted in 1179. Its **campanile** (bell tower) was erected in the 13th century. One of its major treasures is the pulpit of the Rufolo family, decorated with intricate mosaics and supported by spiral columns resting on the backs of half a dozen white marble lions. This is the work of Nicoló di Bartolomeo da Foggia in 1272. Another less intricate pulpit from 1130 features two large mosaics of Jonah being eaten and regurgitated by a dragonlike green whale. To the left of the altar is the **Chapel of San Pantaleone (Cappella di San Pantaleone),** the patron saint of Ravello to whom the cathedral is dedicated. His "unleakable" blood is preserved in a cracked vessel. The saint was beheaded at Nicomedia on July 27, A.D. 290. When Ravello holds a festival on that day every year, the saint's blood is said to liquefy. A museum of religious artifacts is also on-site.

Piazza Duomo. Duomo free admission; museum 2€. Duomo daily 9am–noon and 5:30–7pm. Museum Easter–Oct daily 9am–7pm; off season daily 9am–6pm.

Villa Cimbrone ★★   One of Ravello's most aristocratic-looking palaces is the Villa Cimbrone. A 10-minute walk uphill from the main square, it's accessible only via a signposted footpath punctuated with steps and stairs. Built in the 15th century, it was occupied by a wealthy and eccentric Englishman, Lord Grimthorpe, who renovated it to its present status. During his tenure, he entertained such luminaries as Henrik Ibsen, D. H. Lawrence, Virginia Woolf, Greta Garbo, and Tennessee Williams. Lord Grimthorpe died in London in 1917, but his heirs followed his orders and buried his remains near his replica of the Temple of Bacchus. When you reach the villa's entrance, ring the bell to summon the attendant. You'll be shown vaulted cloisters, evocative architecture, ruined chapels, and panoramic views over the Bay of Salerno. The view from some of the platforms in the garden is simply stunning.

You can also stay at the villa because it's now a hotel (see below).

Via Santa Chiara 26. 𝄐 **089-857459.** Admission 6€. Daily 9am–sunset.

Villa Rufolo ★★   The Villa Rufolo was named for the patrician family that founded it in the 11th century. Once the residence of kings and popes, such as Hadrian IV, it's now remembered chiefly for its connection with Richard Wagner. He composed an act of *Parsifal* here in a setting he dubbed the "Garden of

14

CAMPANIA

Ravello

Klingsor." He also lived and composed at Palazzo Sasso (see below). Boccaccio was so moved by the spot that he included it as background in one of his tales. The Moorish-influenced architecture evokes Granada's Alhambra, and the large tower was built in what's known as the "Norman-Sicilian" style. You can walk through the flower gardens leading to lookout points over the memorable coastline.

Piazza Duomo. ℭ **089-857657.** www.villa rufolo.it. Admission 5€. Daily 9am–6pm (until 8pm Apr–Sept).

Where to Stay

The **Ristorante Garden** (see "Where to Dine," below) also rents rooms.

VERY EXPENSIVE

Hotel Caruso ★★★ Greta Garbo and other luminaries once used this 11th-century property as a hideaway. Orient Express took it over and gave the whitewashed structure a complete overhaul to the tune of $40 million. It

The gardens at Villa Rufolo in Ravello.

stands atop a 351m (1,150-ft.) limestone cliff in a dazzling position overlooking the Gulf of Salerno. The infinity pool is the most dramatic along the coast, and the frescoes burst with color. Designer Federico Forquet brought renewed life and luxury to the deluxe bedrooms, adding such extras as bronze lamps and Neapolitan-style furnishings. The best and most expensive here is the Exclusive Suite, with a terrace, private pool, and garden.

Piazza San Giovanni del Toro 2, 84010 Ravello. ℭ **089-858801.** Fax 089-858806. www.hotel caruso.com. 54 units. 580€–950€ double; from 1,400€ suite. Rates include buffet breakfast. AE, DC, MC, V. Closed Nov–Mar. **Amenities:** Restaurant; bar; babysitting; concierge; exercise room; heated pool; room service. *In room:* A/C, TV/DVD, CD player, hair dryer, minibar, Wi-Fi (free).

Hotel Palumbo/Palumbo Residence ★★ This 12th-century palace is now a charming boutique hotel. It has been favored by the famous since composer Richard Wagner persuaded the Swiss owners, the Vuilleumiers, to take in paying guests. If you stay, you'll understand why Humphrey Bogart, Ingrid Bergman, Tennessee Williams, and John and Jacqueline Kennedy found it ideal. D. H. Lawrence even wrote part of *Lady Chatterley's Lover* while staying here. The hotel offers gracious living in its drawing rooms full of English and Italian antiques. Most of the snug but elegant guest rooms have their own terraces with glorious views. The original Hotel Palumbo contains the more glamorous accommodations; seven rooms are in the annex in the garden, but a few have sea views. The bathrooms are often a delight, with gigantic tubs and dual basins.

Via San Giovanni del Toro 16, 84010 Ravello. ℭ **089-857244.** Fax 089-858133. www.hotel palumbo.it. 21 units. 295€–395€ double; 595€–795€ suite. Rates include buffet breakfast. AE, DC,

MC, V. Parking 25€. **Amenities:** Open-air restaurant; bar; babysitting; Jacuzzi; room service; Wi-Fi (free, in lobby). *In room:* A/C, TV, hair dryer, minibar.

Hotel Rufolo ★ 🎁   This little gem of an inn is evocative of a Ravello of an earlier era. Enlarged and modernized, the hotel lies in the center between cloisters of pine trees of the Villa Rufolo, from which the hotel takes its name, and the road leading to the Villa Cimbrone. Mr. Schiavo and his family take good care of their guests. The view from the sun decks is superb—chairs are placed on a wide terrace. The attractive pool sits amid an elegantly landscaped garden, overlooking the sea. Some guest rooms are spacious and others are cramped; the suites have Jacuzzis.

Via San Francesco 1, 84010 Ravello. ✆ **089-857133.** Fax 089-857935. www.hotelrufolo.it. 30 units. 235€–350€ double; 400€–550€ suite. Rates include buffet breakfast. AE, DC, MC, V. Free parking. **Amenities:** Restaurant; bar; babysitting; exercise room; Jacuzzi; pool; room service; sauna; Wi-Fi (5€ per hr., in lobby). *In room:* A/C, TV, hair dryer, minibar.

Palazzo Sasso ★★★   At this opulent, idyllic retreat, you're coddled in luxury and comfort. Built in the 1100s for an aristocratic family, this palace began functioning as a hotel in 1880. Richard Wagner composed parts of *Parsifal* here, and Ingrid Bergman found a snug retreat with producer Roberto Rossellini in the days when their affair was causing a scandal. The hotel fell into ruin in 1978, but in 1997 it reopened thanks to a flood of money from Virgin Airlines top-dog Richard Branson. The Sasso is perched 305m (1,000 ft.) above the coast and evokes a Moorish pavilion. The guest rooms are luxurious, even if not overly large, and the views of the Mediterranean compensate for the lack of space. Ask for room no. 1, 201, 204, or 301, or the grand suite, no. 304, because they have the most all-encompassing views.

Via San Giovanni del Toro 28, 84010 Ravello. ✆ **089-818181.** Fax 089-858900. www.palazzo sasso.com. 44 units. 264€–650€ double; 680€–1,200€ junior suite; from 960€ suite. Rates include buffet breakfast. AE, DC, MC, V. Parking 34€. Closed Oct 16–Mar 31. **Amenities:** Restaurant; bar; babysitting; concierge; exercise room; 2 heated pools; room service; spa. *In room:* A/C, TV, hair dryer, minibar.

Villa Cimbrone ★★   You can't even drive up to its entrance because there's no road. But despite the inconvenience, few connoisseurs of art and literature would pass up the chance to stay in one of the most historically evocative villas in Ravello (see above). Amid gardens dotted with statuary, ancient ruins, and late-19th-century re-creations of Greek and Roman temples, it contains only a handful of rooms—high-ceilinged and gracefully furnished with antiques and fine fabrics. Most rooms enjoy views over the countryside. The best choices are nos. 10 and 11. The Garbo Suite is the most requested. If you arrive by car, park it in the municipal parking lot, a short walk downhill from Ravello's main square, and then call the hotel for a porter, who will haul your luggage up the winding paths to the villa.

Via Santa Chiara 26, 84010 Ravello. ✆ **089-857459.** Fax 089-857777. www.villacimbrone.it. 19 units. 330€–660€ double; from 760€ suite. Rates include buffet breakfast. AE, DC, MC, V. Closed Nov–Mar. From the main square of Ravello, walk uphill along a well-marked footpath for an arduous 10 min. **Amenities:** Restaurant; bar; babysitting; concierge; exercise room; pool; room service. *In room:* A/C, TV, hair dryer, minibar, Wi-Fi (4€ per hr.).

14

CAMPANIA | Ravello

MODERATE

Hotel Giordano e Villa Maria   The older but more obviously modernized of these two hotels is the Giordano, built in the late 1700s as a private manor house of the family that runs it today. In the 1970s, the owners bought the neighboring 19th-century Villa Maria, and the two operate as quasi-independent hotels with shared facilities. Accommodations in the Villa Maria are generally better than those in the Giordano and usually contain high ceilings and antiques and offer sea views. However, a few of the rooms at Villa Maria, rented to late arrivals when the other units are booked, are rather cramped, with less-than-adequate mattresses. The Giordano's rooms have garden views and reproductions of traditional furniture.

Via Trinità 14, Via Santa Chiara 2, 84010 Ravello. ⓒ **089-857255.** Fax 089-857071. www.giordano hotel.it. 32 units. Hotel Giordano 160€–245€ double. Villa Maria 195€–305€ double. AE, DC, MC, V. Free parking. **Amenities:** 2 restaurants; bar; pool; room service; Wi-Fi (5€ per hr., in lobby). *In room:* A/C, TV, hair dryer, minibar.

INEXPENSIVE

Hotel Toro 🎣   Just off the village square with its cathedral, this real bargain is a charming small villa that has been converted into a hotel. You enter the Toro through a garden. It has semimonastic architecture, boasting deeply set arches, long colonnades, and a tranquil character. The guest rooms are a bit plain but still offer reasonable comfort, each containing a small bathroom. The owner is especially proud of the Mediterranean meals he serves.

Via Roma 16, 84010 Ravello. ⓒ **089-857211.** Fax 089-858592. www.hoteltoro.it. 9 units (shower only). 118€ double with breakfast. Room with half board 88€ per person. DC, MC, V. Closed Nov 6–Mar. *In room:* Hair dryer, Wi-Fi (free).

Where to Dine

Most guests take meals at their hotels. But the following are worth a special trip.

Cumpa' Cosimo AMALFITAN   Here's where you're likely to find everyone from the electrician down the street to a movie star looking for the best home cooking in town. Pictures of Jackie O still decorate the walls, a reminder of a long-ago visit. The restaurant was opened in 1929 by a patriarch known affectionately as Cumpa' (Godfather) Cosimo and his wife, Cumma' (Godmother) Chiara. Today their daughter, Netta Bottone, runs the place, turning out well-flavored regional food in generous portions. Menu items include homemade versions of seven pastas, served with your choice of seven sauces. Any of these might be followed by a mixed grill of fish, giant prawns, roasted lamb seasoned with herbs, *zuppa di pesce, frittura di pesce* (fish fry), veal scaloppine, or beefsteak with garlic-and-wine sauce. Fresh local artichokes, asparagus, and mushrooms are among the vegetables available seasonally.

Via Roma 44–46. ⓒ **089-857156.** Reservations recommended. Main courses 11€–30€. AE, MC, V. Daily noon–3:30pm and 7pm–midnight.

Rossellinis ★★★ MEDITERRANEAN   In the previously recommended Palazzo Sasso, this deluxe restaurant reigns supreme in the area. Visitors along Amalfi Coast drive for miles just to sample the cuisine here. You dine like an aristocrat on stone floors under 12-foot ceilings. Under your feet is a vintage wine cellar.

Pino Lavarra, the chef, has mastered his art, with his sublime cuisine crafted from excellent raw materials. The food is inventive and the dishes are lightened for modern tastes. Specialties include deep-fried crab ravioli with zucchini and a creamed potato sauce or else filet of cod crusted with a covering of black olives, tomatoes, and anchovy sauce. Filet of lamb is served with a rose liqueur and white asparagus, or else you might succumb to scorpion fish with an anchovy sauce.

Via San Giovanni del Toro 28. ℂ **089/ 818181.** Reservations required. Main courses 27€–38€; 7-course degustation menu 120€. AE, MC, V. Daily 7–11pm. Closed Nov–Mar.

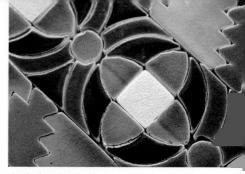

Mosaics for sale at Ceramu.

Ristorante Garden CAMPANIA   This pleasant restaurant's greatest claim to fame was in 1962, when Jacqueline Kennedy dined here with the owner of Fiat. Today some of that old glamour is still visible on the verdant terrace, which was designed to cantilever over the cliff below. The Mansi family offers well-prepared meals that might include one of four kinds of spaghetti, cheese crepes, an array of soups, a well-presented antipasto table, brochettes of grilled shrimp, a mixed fish fry, and sole prepared in several ways. The restaurant also rents 10 well-scrubbed **guest rooms,** each with its own phone, bathroom, and terrace with a view, for 130€ for a double, including breakfast.

Via Boccaccio 4, 84010 Ravello. ℂ **089-857226.** www.gardenravello.com. Main courses 13€– 23€. AE, DC, MC, V. Apr–Sept daily noon–3pm and 7:30–10pm; Nov–Mar Wed–Mon noon–3pm and 7:30–10pm.

Shopping

When Hillary Rodham Clinton came to visit and to call on former resident Gore Vidal, she also visited **Cammeo,** Piazza Duomo 9 (ℂ **089-857461**), where owner Giorgio Filocamo designed a coral brooch for her. He can make one for you, too, or sell you any number of readymade pieces. In the back of the shop, he has collected his most treasured pieces, all worthy of a museum.

Brothers Marco and Piero Cantarella are waiting for you at **Ceramu,** Via Roma 58 (ℂ **089-858181**), where they'll sell you mosaics in majolica, and garden tables with wrought-iron or mosaic-bordered mirrors with wood.

PAESTUM & ITS GLORIOUS GREEK TEMPLES ★★★

40km (25 miles) S of Salerno, 100km (62 miles) SE of Naples, 304km (188 miles) SE of Rome

The ancient city of Paestum (Poseidonia), founded by colonists from the Greek city of Sybaris, dates from 600 B.C. It was abandoned for centuries and fell to ruins. But the remnants of its past, excavated in the mid–18th century, are the finest heritage left from the Greek colonies that settled in Italy. The roses of Paestum, praised by the ancients, bloom two times yearly, splashing the landscape of the city with scarlet, a good foil for the salmon-colored temples that still stand in the archaeological garden.

Paestum is an easy day trip from anywhere in Campania, even Naples. You need an hour or two to explore the temples, and another hour for the museum. Break up the two sights with lunch at Nettuno (see below).

Essentials

GETTING THERE You must go to Salerno to get to Paestum via public transit. Take a southbound **train,** which departs Salerno with a stop at Paestum about every 2 hours. For schedules, call ℭ **892021** toll-free in Italy. A one-way fare is 6€, and the journey takes 30 minutes. The **bus** from Salerno leaves from Piazza Concordia (near the rail station) about every 30 minutes. Call ℭ **089-252228** for information. A one-way fare is 3€.

By **car,** from Salerno take S18 south.

VISITOR INFORMATION The **tourist office,** Via Magna Grecia 887 (ℭ **0828-811016;** www.infopaestum.it), in the archaeological zone, is open Monday to Saturday from 9am to 3pm (until 7pm July–Aug) and Sunday from 9am to 1pm.

Exploring the Temples

The **basilica** ★★★, a Doric temple from the 6th century B.C., is Italy's oldest temple from the ruins of the Hellenic world. The basilica is characterized by 9 Doric pillars in front and 18 on the sides (they're about 1.5m/5 ft. in diameter). The walls and ceiling long ago gave way to decay. Animals were sacrificed to the gods on the altar.

The **Temple of Neptune (Tempio di Nettuno)** ★★★ is the most impressive of the Greek ruins at Paestum. It and the Temple of Hephaestus ("Theseum") in Athens remain the best-preserved Greek temples in the world, both from around 450 to 420 B.C. Six columns in front are crowned by an entablature, and there are 14 columns on each side. The **Temple of Ceres (Tempio di Cerere)** ★★, from the 6th century B.C., has 34 columns still standing and a large altar for sacrifices to the gods.

The temple zone is open daily 9am to sunset.

You can visit the **National Archaeological Museum of Paestum (Museo Archeologico Nazionale di Paestum),** Via Magna Grecia 917 (ℭ **0828-811023**), across from the Ceres Temple. It displays the metopes removed from the treasury of the Temple of Hera (Juno) and some of southern Italy's finest tomb paintings from the 4th century B.C. The Diver's Tomb is an extraordinary example of painting from the first half of the 5th century B.C. The museum is open daily 9am to 7pm. (It's closed the first and third Mon of every month.) Admission is 6€, but there is also a cumulative ticket, which includes the museum and the archaeological area, for 7.50€.

New discoveries have revealed hundreds of Greek tombs, which have yielded many Greek paintings. Archaeologists have called the finds astonishing. In addition, other excavated tombs were found to contain clay figures in a strongly Impressionistic vein.

Where to Stay

Strand Hotel Schuhmann ★ If you'd like to stay at a beachside resort while you devote more time to Italy's archaeological past, try the Strand. Set in a pine grove removed from traffic noises, it has a large terrace with a view of the sea and a subtropical garden that overlooks the Gulf of Salerno and the Amalfi Coast to Capri. Its guest rooms are well furnished and maintained, each with a balcony or terrace. The bathrooms are neatly kept. Guests get use of the beach facilities and deck chairs.

Via Marittima, 84063 Paestum. ℂ **0828-851151.** Fax 0828-851183. www.hotelschuhmann.com. 53 units (tubs only). 130€–220€ double. Rates include breakfast and dinner. AE, DC, MC, V. Free parking. **Amenities:** Restaurant; babysitting; bikes; room service. *In room:* A/C, TV, hair dryer, minibar, Wi-Fi (free).

Where to Dine

Nettuno Ristorante SALERNITAN/SEAFOOD   Nettuno's only drawback is that throughout most of the year it's open only for lunch. At the edge of Paestum's ruins, it's built from the same beige-colored limestone blocks used by the ancient Romans. Its core consists of an ancient tower built in the 2nd century B.C. Seated in the dining room or garden ringed with vines, oleander, and pines, you can order *crespolini*, a crepe stuffed with mozzarella and raw Parma ham; succulent pastas; a wide selection of fish; and veal, chicken, and beef dishes. Specialties include *pezzogna* (a local fish) baked with potatoes and olives, or risotto with lobster. Some of the best of the tantalizing appetizers are shrimp with wild arugula and Parmesan or else fresh asparagus and shrimp salad.

Via Principe di Piemonte 2, Zona Archeologica. ℂ **0828-811028.** www.ristorantenettuno.com. Reservations recommended. Main courses 15€–25€. AE, DC, MC, V. Apr–Sept daily noon–3:30pm; Oct–Mar Tues–Sun noon–3:30pm. Closed in Nov and Jan 7–Feb 7.

THE PONTINE ISLANDS

Scattered in the Tyrrhenian Sea between Rome and Naples, the Pontine Islands form an archipelago that is one of the undiscovered gems of Italy, known mainly to the Italians themselves who flock here in July and August. Only two of the islands are inhabited, **Ventotene** of volcanic origin, and **Ponza,** the site of a small tourist industry with some hotels and restaurants. Instead of a visit to pricey, overcrowded Capri, many visitors come to Ponza in the summer.

Ponza itself is a half-moon-shaped island, long and narrow, with Monte La Guardia at 279m (915 ft.), its highest point. The island is about 8km (5 miles) long with a jagged, cove-studded coastline.

Essentials

GETTING THERE   If you're exploring Naples and want to extend your trip, **Snav** operates hydrofoils departing from the Mergellina dock (ℂ **0814-285555;** www.snav.it). Departures are one time a day from mid-June to August, the trip taking 3 hours and costing 58€. The Snav office in Ponza is at Via Banchina Nuova (ℂ **077-180743**) in the port area.

More regular departures are from the port of Formia, lying along the coast between Rome and Naples. Formia is 153km (95 miles) south of Rome but more easily reached from Naples 86km (53 miles) to the south.

Caremar, at Via Banchina Azzurra in Formia (ℂ **892123;** www.caremar.it), operates ferries year-round, making the trip to Ponza in 2 hours, 30 minutes, and costing 17€ per person one-way. The cost of transporting a standard car is 70€. Ferries leave Formia daily at 9am, 2:30 and 5:30pm. The Caremar office in Ponza is at Molo Musco (ℂ **892123**) at the port.

VISITOR INFORMATION   The **Ponza Tourist Office** is at Via Molo Musco 2 (ℂ **077-180031**) at the port, and it's open daily year-round from 9am to 1pm.

14

CAMPANIA | The Pontine Islands

Exploring Ponza

The largest of the Pontine Islands, crescent-shaped Ponza was called Tyrrhenia in ancient times. Ponza is said to have been connected to the mainland of Italy by a narrow strip of land, which long ago sunk into the sea. Recent archaeological investigations have suggested that Ponza was once a large city that gave way to the sea. For example, Roman temples were found on a harbor floor that had sunk and risen several times in the past 5,000 years.

Ponza was once viewed as a place of exile for political dissidents, a tradition that lasted from Roman times until the Mussolini era. Il Duce himself was imprisoned on the island for several weeks in 1943. Settlements on Ponza were abandoned during the Middle Ages because of frequent raids by Saracens and pirates. When the pirate menace was wiped out, a newer generation of settlers returned.

The island is famed for its Blue Grottoes, the creation of the Etruscans. Built by the Romans, a tunnel connects the port of Ponza with the best large sandy beach on the island. Lying on the west side, it's called **Chiaia di Luna.**

The most spectacular site on island is the **Pilatus Caves ★**, with their maze of tunnels linked to the sea and each other and dug into the rocky bank to the southeast of the port. **Cooperativa Barcaioli** (✆ **077-1809929;** www.barcaioliponza.it) offers year-round excursions to the caves, costing 15€ per person. The agency also features a circular tour of the island for 25€ per person. To contact the agency, go to Corso Pisacane (✆ **077-1809929**) in Ponza.

Exploring the Pilatus Caves on Ponza.

In summer the agency will also arrange tours of the other remote islands, including a visit to **Zannone** 11km (6½ miles) from the port of Ponza. This speck of an island is part of the **Circeo National Park.** The island is uninhabited (there are no tourist facilities). On the island you can see the ruins of a Benedictine convent dating from the 13th century, and you can follow well-marked paths along the upper ridge of the island to take in the scenic views. The cost of this tour is 25€ per person.

Except for the port of Ponza, the only other real village on island is **La Forna,** home of **Le Piscine Naturali ★**, a series of grottoes, enclosed pools of ocean water that have collected in lava rock basins. Take the bus from Ponza to Le Forna and walk down to the grottoes.

Where to Stay

Bellavista   It's not as grand as the Grand Hotel (see below), but Bellavista is the second-best and most acceptable choice on Ponza. In the center of town, the four-story building is located on a cliff overlooking the sea. Rooms are utterly simple, yet comfortable, the grace note being in the most desirable accommodations that open onto small balconies with views of the sea. There is also a regional restaurant on-site, serving a Mediterranean cuisine, which consists mostly of seafood.

Via Parata 1, Ponza 04027. © **077-180036.** Fax 077-180395. www.hotelbellavistaponza.it. 24 units. 140€–200€ double. Rates include buffet breakfast. AE, MC, V. **Amenities:** Restaurant; bar; room service. *In room:* A/C, TV, hair dryer, minibar.

Grand Hotel Santa Domitilla ★★   This is the best hotel in the entire archipelago. Lying 100m (328 ft.) from the beach, it brings a bit of style and a certain decorative flair to the island. In the heart of Ponza, the hotel is surrounded by beautiful gardens. The hotel offers a variety of rooms in different sizes and decor, and all of them are comfortable. Elegant suites have a Jacuzzi and a spacious outside terrace for sunbathing. Some of the accommodations feature twin bathrooms with steam showers. Units open onto a garden view or else a panorama of the sea. The hotel's amenities are the best on the island, including a seawater grotto where you can swim in a natural cove.

Via Panoramica 10, 04027 Ponza. © **077-1809951.** Fax 077-1809955. www.santadomitilla.com. 57 units. 180€–370€ double; 300€–600€ suite. Rates include buffet breakfast. AE, DC, MC, V. Closed Nov–Mar. **Amenities:** Restaurant; bar; babysitting; room service; 2 saltwater pools; Wi-Fi (free, in lobby). *In room:* A/C, TV, hair dryer, minibar.

Where to Dine

Acqua Pazza ★★★ SEAFOOD/MEDITERRANEAN   It comes as a complete surprise to find a Michelin-starred restaurant in this remote outpost. Patrizia Ronca and Gino Pesce have raised the culinary bar so high on island that no other chef comes anywhere near meeting their standards. Their elegant restaurant is found on the main square of Ponza, right at the port. Tables with white napery and crystal open onto a view of the town and water. Start with some of their delectable specialties, including a pie made with artichokes and squid. You can then proceed to the mussel stew or else vermicelli with swordfish roe and a lime flavoring. The *tagliolini* with butter, anchovies, and capers is sublime, as is the grilled white fish with aromatic herbs of the Mediterranean.

Piazza Carlo Pisacane 10. ✆ **077-180643.** www.acquapazza.com. Reservations required. Main courses 18€–35€; fixed-price menu 70€. AE, MC, V. Daily 8–11:30pm. Closed Nov–Feb.

Gennarino a Mare MEDITERRANEAN/SEAFOOD   In a small inn of the same name, this restaurant is a portside choice, a favorite of locals and visitors. The eatery stands on a wooden pile-work structure constructed on top of the water. The chefs essentially cook a Mediterranean cuisine with lots of fish, but they also serve some dishes based on old Ponza recipes. Start with one of their savory pasta dishes such as fettuccine alla Gennarino with shrimp and mussels or else *mezzemaniche,* a homemade pasta with shrimp, swordfish roe, and cherry tomatoes. The restaurant rents 12 very basic rooms, each with its own balcony overlooking the sea, costing 120€ to 170€ for a double.

Via Dante 64. ✆ **077-180071.** www.gennarinoamare.com. Reservations recommended. Main courses 15€–32€. AE, DC, MC, V. Daily 8–10:30pm. Closed mid-Oct to Easter.

Orestorante ★ MEDITERRANEAN/SEAFOOD   This is a three-level restaurant in the center of town, standing on a cliff overlooking the sea with an open-air view terrace. It's long been a favorite with visitors who like the regional seafood, based on the harvest of the day and the well-chosen Mediterranean dishes prepared from fresh ingredients whenever possible. "We don't specialize in delicacies here," a waiter told us, "but we do serve the food of the people." That cuisine might start with a platter *tri trito,* three kinds of fish—shrimp, tuna, and sea bream—or else an appetizer of marinated red snapper on potato ice cream. The most recommendable pasta is spaghetti with clams and wild fennel, followed by a main dish of filet of sea bream stuffed with mozzarella and escarole sautéed with sultana and black olives.

Via Dietro La Chiesa 4. ✆ **077-180338.** www.orestorante.it. Reservations recommended. Main courses 20€–35€. MC, V. Daily 8:15–11:30pm. Closed Oct–Easter.

APULIA

T

he district of Apulia encompasses the southeastern-most section of Italy, the heel of the boot. For many travelers, it's the gateway to Greece from the port of Brindisi. Apulia is little known but fascinating, embracing some of Italy's most poverty-stricken areas and some of its most interesting sections (such as the Trulli District).

The land is rich in archaeological discoveries, and some of its cities were shining sapphires in the crown of Magna Graecia (Greater Greece). The Ionian and Adriatic seas wash up on its shores, which have seen the arrival of diverse civilizations and of the armies seeking to conquer this access route to Rome. The Goths, Germanic hordes, Byzantines, Spanish, and French sought to possess it. Saracen pirates and Turks came to see what riches they might find.

Trulli's unique beehive homes.

Apulia offers the beauty of marine grottoes and caverns, as well as turquoise seas and sandy beaches. Forests of wind-twisted pines, huge old carob trees, junipers, sage, and rosemary grow near the sea; orchards, vineyards, grain fields, and vegetable gardens grow inland. Flocks of sheep and goats dot the landscape.

In recent years, Apulia has been caught in the eye of the "Albanian Hurricane." Political turmoil and economic upheaval have sent many thousands of Albanians to commandeer yachts, ferries, and tugboats and cross the narrow Strait of Otranto into this region.

The most luxurious and certainly the most comfortable way to visit this rugged district of Italy is to fly from Rome to either Bari or Brindisi in about an hour, where you can rent a car to tour the *trulli* (beehive-shaped houses) district for about 2 or 3 days. The best places to stay are **Hotel Il Melograno** (p. 797) and **Masseria San Domenico** (p. 798). After time here, take the 2-hour drive to Lecce for 2 days and know that you have experienced the best of Apulia.

PREVIOUS PAGE: Santa Maria di Siponto in Manfredonia.

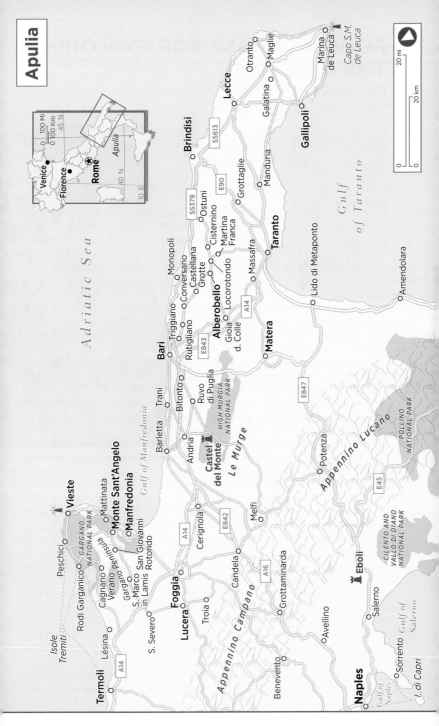

Apulia

Adriatic Sea

Gulf of Manfredonia

Gulf of Taranto

Isole Tremiti

Termoli

Rodi Garganico

Peschici

Vieste

Cagnano Verano

GARGANO NATIONAL PARK

Mattinata

Monte Sant'Angelo

Gargano peninsula

S. Marco in Lamis

San Giovanni Rotondo

Manfredonia

Lésina

S. Severo

Lucera

Foggia

Troia

Cerignola

Candela

A14

E842

A16

Melfi

Grottaminarda

Benevento

Avellino

Salerno

Sorrento

I. di Capri

Gulf of Naples

Naples

Gulf of Salerno

Eboli

Appennino Campano

CILENTO AND VALLO DI DIANO NATIONAL PARK

Appennino Lucano

Potenza

POLLINO NATIONAL PARK

E45

E847

Amendolara

Lido di Metaponto

Matera

Gioia d. Colle

Alberobello

Locorotondo

Castellana Grotte

Conversano

Monopoli

Triggiano

Rutigliano

Bari

Bitonto

Trani

Barletta

Andria

Ruvo di Puglia

Castel del Monte

Le Murge

HIGH MURGIA NATIONAL PARK

E843

A14

Massafra

Taranto

Manduria

Grottaglie

Cisternino

Martina Franca

Ostuni

SS379

E90

SS613

Brindisi

Lecce

Otranto

Galatina

Maglie

Gallipoli

Marina de Léuca

Capo S.M. de Léuca

20 mi

20 km

Venice

Florence

Rome

Apulia

0 100 Mi

0 100 Km

45 N

40 N

10 E

FOGGIA: A BASE FOR EXPLORING THE GARGANO

97km (60 miles) W of Bari, 174km (108 miles) NE of Naples, 362km (224 miles) SE of Rome

Foggia is the capital of Capitanata, Apulia's northernmost province. A history of tragedy, including a serious earthquake in 1731 and extensive bombing during World War II, has left Foggia with little in the way of attractions, although it's a good base for exploring nearby attractions such as Lucera and Troia. You can also use the city as a base for a day's drive around the Gargano Peninsula. Aside from the ancient cathedral, the city is pleasant but thoroughly modern, with parks and wide boulevards and a decent selection of hotels and restaurants. This is a good place to take care of business—rent a car, exchange money, mail postcards, or whatever—because it's relatively safe, easy to get around, and centrally located.

A detail from the Cattedrale di Santa Maria Icona Vetere.

The 12th-century **Cattedrale di Santa Maria Icona Vetere** (✆ 0881-773482) lies off Piazza del Lago. The province's largest cathedral, it was constructed in an unusual Norman and Apulian baroque style. Today, after extensive repairs and expansions, the Duomo is an eclectic mix of styles. The present **campanile (bell tower)** was built to replace the one destroyed in the 1731 quake. The crypt was built in the Romanesque style, and some of its "excavation" was compliments of Allied bombers in 1943. The cathedral is open daily from 8am to noon and 5 to 8pm; admission is free.

Essentials

GETTING THERE Foggia is at the crossroads of the Lecce-Bologna **rail** line and the Bari-Naples run, so it's easy to get here from just about anywhere in Italy. Trains from Naples, involving a change in Caserta, arrive four times daily; the trip lasts about 3 hours and costs 28€ one-way. Trains arrive from Bari every hour during the day, taking 1½ hours and costing 7.50€ one-way. There are also four trains daily from Rome, which take 4 hours and cost 44€. Trains arrive at Foggia's **Stazione Centrale** in the center of Piazza Vittorio Veneto (✆ 892021).

By **car,** take the A1 from Naples, then take the A16 and exit at the tollgate Candela-Foggia, and then take the S655 toward Foggia.

The **tourist office** is at Corso Giannone Pietro 1 (*✆ 0881-720984*), open Monday to Saturday from 9am to 1pm and 4 to 7pm.

Where to Stay

Hotel Mercure Cicolella ★ The Cicolella is the town's best hotel, lying 100m (328 ft.) from the train station. The 1920s building has been modernized, with glass and marble dominating. The guest rooms are large and pleasantly decorated, each with a small tiled bathroom. Some of the units open onto balconies.

Viale XXIV Maggio 60, 71100 Foggia. *✆* **0881-566111.** Fax 0881-778984. www.mercure.com. 102 units. 204€–259€ double; from 259€ suite. Rates include buffet breakfast. AE, DC, V. **Amenities:** Restaurant; bar; babysitting; concierge; room service. *In room:* A/C, TV, hair dryer, minibar, Wi-Fi (free).

White House Hotel This first-class hotel is in the heart of Foggia, a few steps from the train station, making it a good choice for convenience. Its housekeeping is the finest in town. The guest rooms are comfortably furnished, though lacking any particular style. They range from small to medium, with compact tiled bathrooms.

Via Sabotino 24, 71100 Foggia. *✆* **0881-721644.** Fax 0881-721646. www.whitehousehotel.it. 40 units. 105€–125€ double; 140€–150€ triple. Rates include buffet breakfast. AE, DC, MC, V. Parking 15€ nearby. **Amenities:** Bar; babysitting; bikes; Internet (free, in lobby); room service. *In room:* A/C, TV, hair dryer, minibar.

Where to Dine

Il Ventaglio ★★ ITALIAN This elegant restaurant is known for its inventive cuisine, among the finest in southern Italy. The chef, who adds a personal touch to everything, says she never makes the same dish twice. Some of her specialties are *fagottino di pesce* (fish) and *agnolotti ripieni* (pasta stuffed with chopped fish or seasonal vegetables). The *orecchiette* comes in clam sauce with the freshest seasonal vegetables. *Baccalà* (dried codfish) is served with a creamy sauce made of puréed beans and aromatic herbs. A rare specialty is lampacioni pie, a real delicacy to the people of Puglia, made with bitter wild onions that grow in uncultivated soils, taking 4 to 5 years to mature. Take the chance to sample some of the finest cheeses in the area, such as pecorino, scamorza, and manteca. Service, depending on when you arrive, might be sweet and charming or hysterically overworked.

Via Gaetano Postiglione 6E. *✆* **0881-661500.** www.ristoranteventaglio.it. Reservations recommended. Main courses 11€–18€. AE, DC, MC, V. Tues–Sat 1–2:45pm and 8:30–10:30pm; Sun 1–2:45pm. Closed Sat–Sun in summer. Closed Jan 1–7 and Aug 13–31.

La Nuova Mangiatoia ★ APULIAN/SEAFOOD Calling to mind a tavern from the Middle Ages, this local favorite is in a converted antique farmhouse, still containing its time-blackened wood-beamed ceilings and several arches. In fair weather, guests prefer a place in the big garden, sitting at tables made from wagon wheels and surrounding the original well. Some of the best of local recipes served here have been handed down from generation to generation. Among our favorite pastas is a platter of *orecchiette* with scampi and fresh arugula. Of course, nothing beats the freshly caught fish grilled to your specifications. Regulars request a local fish (gilthead) with almonds au gratin.

Via Virgilio 2. ☎ **0881-634457.** Reservations recommended, essential on Sat–Sun. Main courses 9€–25€; fixed-price lunch 25€. DC, MC, V. Wed–Mon 12:30–3pm and 7:30pm–midnight. Bus: 12 from train station (restaurant lies on the main road to Bari).

THE GARGANO PENINSULA ★★★

Called the Gargano, this mountainous wooded promontory is the "spur" of Italy. The best time to come is autumn, when you can enjoy the colors of the Umbra Forest (Foresta Umbra), featuring maples, ashes, cedars, and chestnuts. There's a timeless quality here. You'll find pristine salt lakes at Lesina and Varano, where you can enjoy swimming and watersports in the mild climate and calm waters. The coast is a series of cliffs, rocks, caves, islets, and beaches. Vegetable gardens grow inland on a landscape dotted with flocks of sheep and goats. In addition to nature's wild and varied landscape, the promontory is rich in historical interest, boasting monuments that are Byzantine, Romanesque, Norman, and medieval.

It'll take a leisurely 7 hours to drive around the Gargano, staying on S89. We consider this sometimes-difficult route among the most scenic drives in Italy. In ancient times, the peninsula was an island, until the sediment from a river eventually formed a "bridge" linking it to the mainland. Train service is limited to a private spur along the northwestern coast. Travelers who want to fully explore the area by bus or car will use Manfredonia as the gateway.

Apulia's Rugged Coastline Essentials

GETTING THERE We strongly advise readers to rent a car for exploring this difficult-to-access corner of rural southern Italy. But if you insist on public transport, get ready for confusion, long delays, and schedules that change frequently. Most of the rail traffic from other parts of Italy originates in Foggia and, to a

The Manfredonia Castello.

Apulia's rugged coastline.

lesser degree, San Severo. From either of those points, transport by bus or by rail continues to sites that include Manfredonia and Monte Sant'Angelo. For information about these lines, contact **Trenitalia** at ✆ **892021,** or for information about the smaller, local train lines that operate only within the Gargano Peninsula, contact **Ferrovie del Gargano** at ✆ **0881-725188.**

Alternatively, some sites within the Gargano Peninsula are best accessed by bus lines or by a combination of bus and train service. For information about buses and their connections to train lines throughout Gargano, contact **SITA** (✆ **0881-352011;** www.sitabus.it) or **ATAF** (✆ **800-424500;** www.ataf.net; many of their routes and schedules are interconnected and overlap). The routes include service, usually at intervals of between 60 and 90 minutes every day, between such major settlements as Foggia, Manfredonia, and Vieste. Less frequent connecting service is available to such hamlets as Mattinata, Monte Sant'Angelo, and Peschici.

If you have a **car,** you'll note that three roads dissect the peninsula and connect its major sights. S89 runs a 130km (81-mile) circuit around the coast. S528 cuts through the heart of the peninsula, starting 8km (5 miles) west of Peschici on the northern coast and running south through the Umbra Forest before ending at S272 just west of Monte Sant'Angelo. S272 slices east to west through the southern part of the region, from San Marco in Lamis in the west through San Giovanni Rotondo and over to Monte Sant'Angelo, ending on the coast near Punta Rossa.

VISITOR INFORMATION   The **Manfredonia tourist office** is at Piazza del Popolo 10 (✆ **0884-581998**), open Monday to Friday from 9am to 1pm. You can pick up a map and get advice about touring the district, including bus and train schedules if you're not driving (important because, in most towns, there are no actual bus stations). The **Vieste tourist office** is at Piazza Kennedy 13 (✆ **0884-708806**), open Monday, Wednesday, and Friday from 8:30am to 2pm, Tuesday and Thursday 4 to 7pm. It'll give you information about the many excursion possibilities, especially the excellent beaches along the southern shore.

Manfredonia

43km (27 miles) NE of Foggia, 119km (74 miles) NW of Bari, 217km (135 miles) NE of Naples

If you approach Gargano from the south, your first stop, perhaps at lunchtime, will be **Manfredonia,** a small port known for its castle. It was named for Manfred, illegitimate son of Frederick II. In the heyday of the Crusades, this was a bustling port, with knights and pilgrims leaving for the Levant. Much later, the town was noted in World War I documents as the place where the first blow of the conflict was launched—the Austrians bombed the rail station in 1915. Manfredonia is on a rail route from Foggia.

After arriving in town, turn right and go along Viale Aldo Moro to Piazza Marconi. Across the square, Corso Manfredi leads to the **Manfredonia Castello,** built for Manfred and later enlarged by the Angevins. Other bastions were constructed in 1607 by the Spanish, who feared an invasion from Turkey. Regrettably, their fortifications didn't do the job: The Turks arrived in 1620 and destroyed a lot of Manfredonia, leaving only some of its former walls standing. Today the castle is home to the **National Museum of Manfredonia** (**Museo Nazionale di Manfredonia;** Via Castello Svevo, ℂ **0884-587838**), open daily (except the first and fourth Mon of each month) from 8:30am to 7:30pm. It charges 2.50€ for admission. The archaeological remnants and finds include a collection of Stone Age objects from area villages. The most striking of these are the **Daunian steles,** stone slabs decorated like human torsos and topped with stone heads, the legacy of the Daunian civilization that settled in the region around the 9th century B.C.

Three kilometers (2 miles) outside town is **Santa Maria di Siponto,** a church in a setting of pine woods that once was the site of the ancient city of Siponto, abandoned after being ravaged by an earthquake and a plague. Dating from the 11th century, the church is in the Romanesque style, showing both Tuscan and Arabic influences.

WHERE TO STAY

Hotel Gargano ⚑   This is the largest and most appealing hotel in town, a government-rated four-star place that's incredibly bargain priced. The rooms have simple summery furnishings; each faces the sea from a private terrace or veranda.

Viale Beccarini 2, 71043 Manfredonia. ℂ **0884-587621.** Fax 0884-586021. www.hotelgargano. net. 46 units (shower only). 90€–150€ double. Rates include buffet breakfast. AE, MC, V. Parking 15€. **Amenities:** Restaurant; bar; saltwater pool; room service; Wi-Fi (free, in lobby). *In room:* A/C, TV, hair dryer.

WHERE TO DINE

Trattoria il Baracchio APULIAN/SEAFOOD   Occupying an early 1900s building close to Piazza Municipio, this is the most appealing restaurant in town, although it serves only lunch. The great selection of antipasti is mostly seafood and vegetarian. Pasta dishes include spaghetti and *orecchiette,* prepared in simple versions of tomatoes, pesto, and local cheese; with garlic, olive oil, and fresh broccoli; or more elaborately with seafood, especially octopus. Look for aromatic grilled baby lamb and the chef's special, *zuppetta ai frutti di mare,* the area's most savory shellfish soup.

Corso Roma 38. ℂ **0884-583874.** Reservations recommended. Main courses 8€–15€. MC, V. Fri–Wed 12:30–3pm.

Monte Sant'Angelo ★

60km (37 miles) NE of Foggia, 135km (84 miles) NW of Bari, 233km (144 miles) NE of Naples

The interior's principal town, Monte Sant'Angelo, 16km (10 miles) north of Manfredonia in the great Umbra Forest, is a good place to start your drive. From here you can venture into a landscape of limes, laurels, and towering yews populated with foxes and gazelles. Narrow passages, streets that are virtually stairways, and little houses washed a gleaming white characterize the town.

The site of Monte Sant'Angelo, standing on a spur, commands panoramic views of the surrounding terrain. Before you leave town, you might want to visit the **Sanctuary of San Michele (Santuario di San Michele),** Via Reale Basilica (© **0884-561150;** www.santuariosanmichele.it), built in the Romanesque-Gothic style. The campanile is octagonal, dating from the last years of the 13th century. The sanctuary commemorates the legend of St. Michael, who's said to have left his red cloak after he appeared to some shepherds in a grotto in 490. You can also visit the grotto; to enter from the church, go through some bronze doors, made in Constantinople in the 11th century. Crusaders stopped here to worship before going to the Holy Land. The sanctuary is open daily from 7:30am to 12:30pm and 2:30 to 5pm (7am–8pm in summer). It charges no admission; however, donations are appreciated.

Opposite the campanile is the **Tomb of Rotharis (Tomba di Rotari),** which is said to hold the bones of Rotharis, the king of the Lombards, although it's a baptistery dating from as early as the 12th century.

Continuing past the sanctuary, you'll find the semirestored ruins of the **Norman Swabian Aragónese Castle (Castello Normanno Aragónese Svevo),** Piazzale Ferri, with a second entrance on Piazza San Francesco 15 (© **0884-587838**). It's open daily from 8:30am to 7:30pm and charges 2.50€ admission. Its Torre dei Giganti was built in 837, although most of the castle dates from later in the Middle Ages. From its ramparts is one of the most sweeping views in the Gargano.

You can also visit the **Tancredi Museum (Museo Tancredi),** Piazza San Francesco d'Assisi (© **0884-562098**), exhibiting artifacts used by local farmers and vintners in their trades. It's open April to October Monday to Friday 9am to 1pm and 2:30 to 7pm; off-season hours are Monday to Friday 9am to 1pm and 2:30 to 6pm. Admission is 1.50€.

As you wander, look for local shops selling **wrought-iron goods,** which are among the finest in Italy. Ironwork has a long tradition here, with sons following in their fathers' footsteps. The locals also make wooden furniture and utensils. Most shops are located in an area called **Juno,** in the center of town.

WHERE TO STAY

Hotel Rotary & Hotel Santangelo   The 24-room Rotary and the 61-room Hotel Santangelo form a complex that provides one of the best and most affordable accommodations in the area, lying less than a kilometer (½ mile) from the center of town. The landscape is on an ancient terrain of olive groves and almond trees. Rooms are more modern and up-to-date in the Santangelo section, although all the accommodations are midsize with neat, well-kept bathrooms with tubs or showers. Because of the hotel's location at a relatively high altitude, ocean breezes keep the temperature comfortable.

Via per Pulsano Km 1, 71037 Monte Sant'Angelo. © **0884-565536.** Fax 0884-568427. www. hotelsantangelo.com. 85 units. 62€–73€ double. Rates include continental breakfast. AE, MC, V. Free parking. **Amenities:** Restaurant; bar; pool; room service. *In room:* TV, hair dryer.

15

APULIA

The Gargano Peninsula

WHERE TO DINE

Ristorante Medioevo 🎁 CONTADINA   The Medioevo's dining room takes its name from the weather-beaten but historic neighborhood surrounding it. The cuisine is firmly entrenched in recipes rehearsed by countless generations of *contadine* (peasant women), such as *zuppa di pane cotto* (a savory soup made of chicory and fava beans), homemade pasta (especially *orecchiette*) served with turnip greens, and a wide roster of meat or fish and roasted lamb from rocky meadows nearby. The kitchen is particularly proud of its *orecchiette Medioevo* (pasta with roasted lamb, braised arugula, and fresh tomatoes).

Via Castello 21. ✆ **0884-565356.** www.ristorantemedioevo.it. Reservations recommended. Main courses 7€–16€. AE, DC, MC, V. Daily noon–2:30pm and 8–10pm. Closed Nov 15–30 and Mon Oct–July.

ALBEROBELLO & THE TRULLI DISTRICT ★★

72km (45 miles) NW of Brindisi, 60km (37 miles) SE of Bari, 45km (28 miles) N of Taranto

The center of a triangle made up by Bari, Brindisi, and Taranto, the Valley of Itria has long been known for olive cultivation and the beehive-shaped houses dotting its landscape. These curious structures, called **trulli,** were built at least as early as the 13th century. Their whitewashed limestone walls and conical fieldstone roofs utilize the materials available in the area in such a way that mortar isn't needed to keep the pieces together. Theories abound as to why they aren't built with mortar, the most popular being that the *trulli,* considered substandard peasant dwellings, had to be easily dismantled in case of a royal visit.

The center of the Trulli District, and home to the greatest concentration of *trulli,* is Alberobello. Here the streets are lined with some 1,000 of the buildings. You might feel as if you've entered into a child's storybook as you walk amid the maze of cobbled streets curving through Italy's most fantastic village. The crowds of visitors will quickly relieve you of any such thoughts, however.

Many of the *trulli* have been converted into souvenir shops where you can buy everything from postcards to miniature models of the dwellings. Be careful, though: If you enter, you're expected to buy something—and the shop owners let you know it.

Essentials

GETTING THERE   FSE **trains** leave Bari every hour (every 2 hr. on Sun) heading to Alberobello. The trip takes about 1¾ hours and costs 4€. To find the *trulli,* follow Via Mazzini, which turns into Via Garibaldi, until you reach Piazza del Popolo. Turn left on Largo Martellotta, which will take you to the edge of the popular tourist area. If you have a **car,** head south of Bari on S100 and then east (signposted) on S172.

VISITOR INFORMATION   The **tourist office** in Alberobello is off the central square, Piazza del Popolo, at Piazza Ferdinando IV (✆ **080-4325171**). It's open Monday, Wednesday, and Thursday 8:30am to 1pm, Tuesday and Friday 9am to 1pm and 4 to 7:30pm.

Exploring the Town

The best-known of the *trulli* is the **trullo sovrano** (**sovereign trullo**) at Piazza Sacramento in Alberobello. The 15m (50-ft.) structure, the only true two-story *trulli,* was built during the 19th century as headquarters for a religious confraternity and Carbonari sect. To find it, head down Corso Vittorio Emanuele until you get to a church, and then take a right. The *trullo sovrano* is open daily from 10am to 1pm and 3 to 7pm, charging no admission.

On the outskirts of Alberobello, you can also visit the small town of **Castellana,** home to a series of caverns that have been carved out over the centuries by water streaming through the rocky soil. A wide stairway leads you down through a tunnel into a cavern called the **Grave.** From here, a series of paths winds through other

The *trullo sovrano* in Alberobello.

underground rooms filled with the strange shapes of stalagmites and stalactites. The culmination of the journey into the earth ends with the majestic **Grotta Bianca,** where alabaster concretions are the result of centuries of Mother Nature's work. You can visit the Grotte di Castellana only on guided tours,

Inside the Grotta Bianca, near Alberobello.

usually one per hour until early afternoon, at 15€; call ⓒ **080-4998211** (www. grottedicastellana.it) for a schedule. Be sure to bring a sweater; the average underground temperature is 15°C (59°F), even on hot summer days.

Most visitors like to buy the hand-painted clay figurines that abound in every souvenir shop. You can also find a good assortment of fabrics and rugs at reasonable prices. One of the most evocative souvenirs would be a miniature re-creation of the region's legendary *trulli*. Crafted in the same type of stone that was used by the ancient builders, they're small-scale duplicates of the originals, ranging in size from a simple rendering to a replica of an entire village.

Where to Stay

Most people visit the area on a daylong excursion; if you want to stay overnight, know that Alberobello's hotels are limited. You might be able to find individual renovated *trulli* that are rented to two to eight people for a relatively cheap rate. Call the tourist office for information. Otherwise, the accommodations here are usually more expensive than those in other nearby towns.

Hotel Dei Trulli ★ Almost a village unto itself, Dei Trulli offers the experience of living in one of the unique beehive-shaped *trulli*. Each mini-apartment might have one, two, or three cones, circular buildings wedged together in Siamese fashion. Most have a bedroom with a well-kept bathroom, a small sitting room with a fireplace, and a patio. The complex has the most attractively landscaped grounds.

Via Cadore 32, 70011 Alberobello. ⓒ **080-4323555.** Fax 080-4323560. www.hoteldeitrulli.it. 20 units (shower only). 130€–280€ double. Rates include buffet breakfast. AE, MC, V. Free parking. **Amenities:** Restaurant; babysitting; pool; room service. *In room:* A/C, TV, hair dryer, minibar, Wi-Fi (free).

Where to Dine

You can also dine at the superb restaurant in the **Hotel Il Melograno** (p. 797).

Il Poeta Contadino ★★ ITALIAN/APULIAN In the center of Alberobello, beneath the arched and vaulted stone ceilings of what was a barn in the 1700s, this is the region's most elegant restaurant. It's managed by Leonardo Marco and his Canadian-born wife, Carol, who serve sophisticated dishes based mostly on seafood. Their menu changes with the season but is likely to include such home-made pastas as black *tagliolini* with clams and a variety of seaweed; sea bass ravioli; or *orecchiette* with turnips, dried tomatoes, and walnuts. A signature dish, and most worthy, is the stuffed pheasant with black truffles. For dessert, few diners can resist the almond cake with a black-cherry sauce. The wine list is one of the region's most comprehensive and has won a *Wine Spectator* award.

Via Indipendenza 21. ⓒ **080-4321917.** www.ilpoetacontadino.it. Reservations recommended. Main courses 14€–32€. AE, DC, MC, V. Winter Tues–Sun 12:30–2:30pm and 7:30–10:30pm; summer daily 12:30–2:30pm and 7–11pm. Closed Mon Oct–June and Jan 7–22.

Trullo d'Oro ★ ITALIAN/APULIAN Housed in several linked *trulli,* this rustic restaurant is one of the town's best. The cuisine consists mainly of well-prepared local and regional dishes. Specialties are purée of fava beans and chicory leaves, roast lamb with *lampasciuni* (a wild onion), and the chef's special pasta, *orecchiette* with bitter greens or tomatoes, olive oil, garlic, and arugula.

Southern desserts, such as ricotta cooked with marmalade or chocolate soufflé, are also served.

Via Felippe Cavallotti 27. ✆ **080-4321820.** www.trullodoro.it. Reservations required Sat–Sun. Main courses 8€–20€. AE, DC, MC, V. Tues–Sun noon–3pm and 8–11:30pm. Closed Jan 8–23.

Side Trips from Alberobello

Frankly, unless you have a reason to stay over, we'd visit Alberobello just for the day, check out the *trulli,* and then move on to neighboring towns. Alberobello has a crowded tour bus scene and a lot of tacky souvenirs being hawked. The satellite towns of **Monopoli** and **Martina Franca** are far less discovered, within an easy commute, and full of charm.

Martina Franca

This town, with its Moorish flavor, is still part of the Trulli District. Its earliest settlers fled from the coastal cities to escape Saracen attacks in the 10th century and founded this town, which still retains its ancient squares. Ignore the high-rises around the city and concentrate on its core from the Middle Ages, which makes a trip here worthwhile.

From the train station walk up the Viale della Libertà to Corso Italia, which you follow to the town center. Our favorite square is the **Piazza Roma,** the center of which is the mammoth **Palazzo Ducale,** Piazza Roma 32, from 1688. Today it is the city hall. Sometimes you can go inside, at least in the morning. There are some classical 18th-century Arcadian murals, though it's no great loss if the building is closed. When it's open, there is no admission charge.

The **Martina Franca Tourist Office** is at Piazza Roma 37 (✆ **080-4805702;** www.martinafrancatour.it), open year-round Monday to Saturday 9am to 1pm. On Tuesday and Thursday it is also open 4 to 7pm.

From here take the narrowing **Via Vittorio Emanuele** to the heart of the old town and the **Piazza Plebiscito,** dominated by an 18th-century church, **Chiesa di San Martino** (✆ **080-4306536**). A bell tower still survives from a Romanesque church that once stood here. Admission is free; the church is open daily 8am to 12:30pm and 4:30 to 8pm.

The baroque-style balconies on Via Cavour in Martina Franca.

You can continue your tour to the adjoining **Piazza Immacolata,** where you can go left onto **Via Cavour ★★**. This street has a certain charm, filled as it is with baroque *palazzi* and balconies. From belvedere points in the town, you can take in a view of **Valle d'Intria,** with its *trulli*-dotted plains.

There is a rail link from Alberobello, with trains departing from Piazza Stazione in Alberobello and arriving in Martina Franca at Via della Stazione. The trip takes only 15 minutes, costing 1.30€ one-way. For more information and schedules, call ✆ **800-079090.**

WHERE TO STAY

Park Hotel San Michele ★   There is grand comfort here, but don't expect too much from the ill-mannered staff. As its name suggests, the hotel is in the park in the center of town. The structure was built on the site of an ancient vineyard. Handsomely renovated, the hotel offers midsize to spacious bedrooms with all of the modern amenities, such as tiled bathrooms with showers or water-massage bathtubs, thick carpeting, and vital air-conditioning. Its cuisine is some of the best in town; and on a summer day, there is no more inviting spot than its cool outdoor pool.

Viale Carella 9, 74015 Martina Franca. ✆ **080-4807053.** Fax 080-4808895. www.parkhotelsan michele.it. 85 units. 109€ double. Rates include continental breakfast. AE, DC, MC, V. Free parking. **Amenities:** Restaurant; bar; children's center; pool; room service. *In room:* A/C, TV, hair dryer, minibar, Wi-Fi (2€ per hr.).

Relais Villa San Martino ★★   Surpassing the Park Hotel in attentive service, refined living, and a tranquil location, this villa is now numero uno in town. At the entrance to Martina Franca, the government-rated five-star hotel offers luxuriously furnished doubles and five even more elegant suites. Since its debut, it remains one of the greatest hotels to open in the south and is a particular standout in this relatively poor region. There is a large garden with pool, and the public rooms are furnished with original Louis XVI furnishings. Ancient paintings, tasteful silks, and antiques embellish the bedrooms. Traditional recipes of a refined Mediterranean cuisine are served in the luxe restaurant.

Via Taranto 59, Sud: 2.8km, 794 74015 Martina Franca. ✆ **080-4805152.** Fax 080-4801026. www.relaisvillasanmartino.com. 21 units. 250€–380€ double; 350€–700€ suite. Rates include buffet breakfast. AE, DC, MC, V. Free parking. **Amenities:** Restaurant; bar; airport transfers 80€; babysitting; bikes; concierge; exercise room; Jacuzzi; pool; room service; sauna. *In room:* A/C, TV, hair dryer, Jacuzzi (in some), minibar, Wi-Fi (free).

WHERE TO DINE

Villaggio In ★ APULIAN   This town's finest restaurant is quite elegant and comes as a surprise in such a provincial outpost. The restaurant is housed in an old *palazzo* in the historic center of town. It has been winning friends among locals and attracting discerning palates from abroad for 20 years. There is a beautiful view from its terrace. The chefs specialize in grilled meats spiced with fresh herbs, and cooked to your specifications. You might begin with one of their succulent pastas, especially *orecchiette alle cime di rapa* (pasta served with fresh turnip tops). A classic eggplant-and-zucchini parmigiana is also served, but most diners order the grilled beef or grilled lamb before plunging into one of the variety of homemade desserts.

Via Arco Grassi 6. ✆ **080-4805911.** www.villaggioin.it. Reservations recommended. Main courses 10€–23€. AE, DC, MC, V. Tues–Sun 1–3pm and 8pm–midnight.

MONOPOLI

494km (307 miles) SE of Rome, 45km (28 miles) SE of Bari, 70km (44 miles) NW of Brindisi, 60km (37 miles) N of Taranto, 21km (13 miles) E of Alberobello

This small town, with a charming historic core, lies in the province of Bari opening onto the sea. Monopoli was originally populated by the ancient settlers known as the Egnazians. Their maritime tradition lives on in the city today. A flourishing seaside town, it was exposed to the raids and attacks of Turkish pirates in the early days because of its location.

After being under the control of the Venetians, the port later fell to the Spaniards. The town's Spanish conquerors fortified Monopoli, building defensive walls with seaward bastions and creating a castle, which still stands. Monopoli easily merits an afternoon of your time.

There is no vast array of attractions to see here: just the port, the sea, and the historic core. You can wander around at your leisure, exploring whatever narrow, steep street that catches your fancy. Specific sights to look for are the **Museo della Cattedrale,** Piazza Cathedrale 1 (🕿 **080-742253;** www.museo diocesanomonopoli.it), open Thursday to Saturday 6 to 9pm, Sunday 10:30am to 12:30pm and 4:30 to 9:30pm, charging an admission of 2€. Inside, you'll find an array of ecclesiastical art, the most notable of which is a Byzantine reliquary from the 10th century.

Another gem to seek out is the chapel of **Santa Maria Amalfitana,** Largo Plebiscito (🕿 **080-9303059**), open daily from 8am to 6pm; admission is free. It was built in the 12th century by rich merchants sailing here from the Amalfi Coast. The earlier church that stood here is now the crypt.

South of the port lie the ruins of the ancient city of **Egnazia** (🕿 **080-4827895;** www.egnazia.cchnet.it), which can be explored daily in summer from 8:30am to 7pm, or daily in winter 8:30am to 4:30pm, for an admission fee of 3€. A bus runs here from Villa Communale in Monopoli. During the 5th century B.C., Egnazia was a major Messapanic trading center and was fortified against pirates with 2km (1¼ miles) of defensive walls. The Greeks and later the Romans arrived to colonize the town. The Romans remained to build a forum, a colonnaded public hall, and an amphitheater.

It is said that Horace arrived one day, seeking out the town's then-famous altar (now long gone). Ancients believed the altar could ignite wood without a match.

The **Pro Loco,** the local tourist office, is at Via Vasco 2 (🕿 **328-3785237**), open June to September daily from 10am to 1pm and 6 to 9pm.

There is no train service from Alberobello to Monopoli. Lentini operates a bus departing three times a day from Alberobello at 6:30am, 3:30pm, and 7:30pm, the trip taking 1 hour and costing 3.50€. From Alberobello, buses depart from the Bar Royal at Via Cavour. For information about schedules, call the travel agent **Tourist Intercontinental,** Via Capitano Pirrelli 37 in Monopoli (🕿 **080-9306860**).

Where to Stay

Hotel Il Melograno ★★★ This is the only Relais & Châteaux property south of Naples. Occupying what was the centerpiece for a large farm and estate during the 16th century and enlarged with a discreet modern wing in the mid-1900s, it sits less than 1.6km (1 mile) from the port of Monopoli, surrounded by a grove of ancient olive trees. Camillo Guerra's polite staff spend long hours maintaining the important antiques and paintings in this charming inn. The guest rooms range from medium to spacious, each with a well-kept bathroom. The hotel will shuttle guests to a private beach facility nearby with a bar and buffet restaurant right on the Adriatic. Some rooms have an individual patio and Jacuzzi.

Contrada Torricella 345, 70043 Monopoli. ☏ **080-6909030.** Fax 080-747908. www.melograno. com. 37 units. 300€–470€ double; 590€–1,200€ suite. Rates include continental breakfast. AE, DC, MC, V. Free parking. From Alberobello, follow the signs to Monopoli and drive 18km (11 miles) east. Closed Dec–Mar. **Amenities:** Restaurant; 2 bars; babysitting; Jacuzzi; pool; room service; spa; 2 tennis courts (lit); Wi-Fi (free, in lobby). *In room:* A/C, TV, hair dryer, minibar.

Masseria San Domenico ★★★ This is the single finest and most refined hotel in Apulia, even better than Il Melograno. A government-rated five-star hotel and spa, it lies 500m (1,640 ft.) from the sea on the coast between Bari and Brindisi, a 20-minute drive south of Monopoli along Rte. S379. Set among mammoth, gnarled olive trees on this ancient coastal estate, it has been restored with a healthy respect for its past, but with the best modern amenities in the province. As a welcome relief in this hot, arid climate, an irregularly shaped pool is encircled by rocks and plants. You live like one of the Knights of Malta (except better) in a field of orchards spread across 60 hectares (148 acres). Rich fabrics, antique reproductions, and grand comfort greet you in the bedrooms with their luxurious bathrooms.

Strada Litoranea 379, 72010 Savelletri di Fasano (Brindisi). ☏ **080-4827769.** Fax 080-4827978. www.imasseria.com. 50 units. 300€–580€ double; from 600€ suite. Rates include buffet breakfast. AE, DC, MC, V. Free parking. Closed Jan 3–Mar 30. No children 11 and under. **Amenities:** Restaurant; bar; babysitting; bikes; exercise room; 18-hole golf course; saltwater pool; room service; sauna; spa; 2 outdoor tennis courts (lit). *In room:* A/C, TV, DVD player (in some), hair dryer, minibar, Wi-Fi (20€ per 24 hr.).

Vecchio Mulino ★ Although its charms are dwarfed by Il Melograno and Masseria San Domenico, this is the best and worthiest choice for overnighting in Monopoli. Built on the water, the hotel lies in an antique but fully restored coastal structure. Transfers to and from the train station or nearest airport at Bari are available on request. There is also a free shuttle service to the nearest beach, where umbrellas, lounge chairs, and deck chairs are provided. The bedrooms have a classic decor, with marble floors, comfortable and first-rate furnishings, and marble-tiled bathrooms. The hotel also offers such attractions as a solarium and a beautiful garden.

Viale Aldo Moro 192, 70043 Monopoli. ☏ **080-777133.** Fax 080-77654. www.vecchiomulino.it. 30 units. 134€–153€ double; 162€–179€ triple. AE, DC, MC, V. Parking 11€. **Amenities:** Restaurant; bar; babysitting; room service. *In room:* A/C, TV, fax, hair dryer, minibar.

Where to Dine

If you, like us, are a devotee of antipasti, the best offering of this delight is at the **Osteria Perricci,** Via Orazio Comes 1 (☏ **080-937-2208**). Though you may disagree, we've found that the best antipasto selection in all of Puglia is offered here in the form of salt-cod fritters, fresh anchovies, boiled octopus, raw cuttlefish, tomato bruschetta—you name it. Main dishes are served as well, but we've never been able to eat beyond the antipasti.

La Mia Terra ★ APULIAN/ITALIAN/INTERNATIONAL   Outside of the hotels, this restaurant serves the town's finest cuisine. The brothers Giorgio opened this restaurant in 1933, and it's been going strong ever since. It's located in *trulli,* the white-stone and clinically shaped homes of the region. The menu features an array of dishes made from market-fresh ingredients. We like to begin with a most satisfying dish, small gnocchi with pumpkin flowers, cured ham, saffron, and poppy seeds. The local pasta, *orecchiette,* is served with fresh turnip tops, or it comes in a black version when it's sautéed with arugula, cherry tomatoes, and anchovies. A purée of fava beans is delectable with fresh chicory, and you can also enjoy our favorite dish here—*mare e monti* with clams, cuttlefish, baby shrimp, and fresh mushrooms. The chef specializes in grilled meats such as beef and lamb and prepares these platters to perfection. In fair weather, it's possible to eat outside. **Note:** To reach this restaurant, take a cab from the train station in Monopoli.

Contrada Impalata 309. ✆ **080-6900969.** www.ristorantepizzerialamiaterra.com. Reservations recommended on weekends. Main courses 8€–20€. AE, DC, MC, V. Thurs–Tues 12:30–2:30pm and 7:30pm–midnight.

LECCE ★★

40km (25 miles) SE of Brindisi, 87km (54 miles) E of Taranto, 905km (561 miles) SE of Rome

Often called "the Florence of the South," Lecce lies in the heart of the Salento Peninsula, the "heel" of the Italian boot. The town was founded before the time of the ancient Greeks, but it's best known for the *barocco leccese* (Lecce baroque) architecture of many of its buildings. Dating from Lecce's heyday in the 16th, 17th, and 18th centuries, these structures are made mostly of fine-grained yellow limestone. Masons delighted in working with the golden material; their efforts turned the city into what one architectural critic called a "gigantic bowl of overripe fruit." Alas, recent restorations have taken away much of the color as workers have whitewashed the buildings.

For centuries, Lecce has been neglected by tourists. Perhaps it's for this reason that many of the baroque-style buildings have remained intact—progress hasn't overrun the city with modern development. Lecce's charm lies in these displays of the lighter baroque (although many buildings are now in dire need of repair).

Lecce's limestone buildings.

Essentials

GETTING THERE   Lecce is connected to Brindisi by hourly **train** service on the state-run FS line. For service from points east and south, you'll have to take the FSE line, which isn't known for its speed. Several trains coming from Gallipoli enter Lecce each day. The train station is about 2km (1¼ miles) from Piazza Sant'Oronzo, in the center of the old quarter. Call ✆ **892021** in Italy for schedules and information.

If you have a **car,** take Rte. S613 from Brindisi.

VISITOR INFORMATION   The **tourist office** is at Via Monte San Michele 20 (✆ **0832-314117;** www.pugliaturismo.com), open Monday, Wednesday, and Friday from 8am to 2pm, Tuesday and Thursday 3 to 6pm.

Exploring the Town

Piazza Sant'Oronzo is a good place to begin a stroll through Lecce. The 2nd-century-A.D. Roman column erected here, **Colonna Romana,** once stood near its mate in Brindisi; together they marked the end of the Appian Way. Lightning toppled this column in 1528; and the Brindisians left it lying on the ground until 1661, at which time the citizens of Lecce bought it and set up the pillar in their hometown. St. Oronzo, for whom the square is named, now stands atop it guarding the area. At the southern side of the piazza are the remains of a **Roman amphitheater.** Dating from the 1st century B.C., it accommodated 20,000 fans, who came to watch bloody fights between gladiators and wild beasts.

North of the piazza, Via Umberto I leads to the **Basilica di Santa Croce ★★** (✆ **0832-241957;** www.basilicasantacroce.eu). This ornate display of Leccese baroque architecture took almost 1½ centuries to complete. Architect Gabriele Riccardo began work in the mid–15th century; the final touches weren't added until 1680. The facade bears some similarity to the Spanish plateresque style and is peopled by guardian angels, grotesque demons, and a variety of flora and fauna. St. Benedict and St. Peter are also depicted. The top part of the facade (the flamboyant part) is the work of Antonio Zimbalo, who was called Zingarello (Gypsy). The interior is laid out in a Latin cross plan in a simple Renaissance style. The basilica is open daily from 9am to noon and 5 to 8pm. Admission is free.

Down Via Vittorio Emanuele, the **Duomo ★**, Piazza del Duomo (✆ **0832-308557**), stands in a closed square. The building, which has two facades, was reconstructed between 1659 and 1670 by Zingarello. To the left of the Duomo, the **campanile** towers 64m (210 ft.) above the piazza. The cathedral is open daily from 7am to noon and 4 to 7pm, and admission is free. On the opposite side of the cathedral is the **Bishop's Palace (Palazzo Vescovile),** where Lecce's archbishop still lives today. Also in the courtyard is a **seminary,** built between 1694 and 1709 by Giuseppe Cino, who was a student of Zimbalo. Its decorations have been compared to those of a wedding cake. A baroque well, extraordinarily detailed with garlands and clusters of flowers and fruit, stands in the courtyard.

The collection of bronze statuettes, Roman coins, and other artifacts at the **Provincial Museum (Museo Provinciale) ★**, Viale Gallipoli (✆ **0832-683503**), will keep your interest for a while. It's worth the time to stop by to have a look at the ornately decorated 13th-century gospel cover. Inlaid with enamel of blue, white, and gold, it's a rare treasure. There's also a small picture gallery. It's open Monday to Saturday 9am to 1:30pm and 2:30 to 7:30pm, Sunday 9am to 1:30pm. Admission is free.

For a selection of local crafts, including *cartapesta* (papier-mâché), ceramics, and terra-cotta, go to **Mostra dell'Artigianato,** Via Francesco Rubichi 21

(℡ **0832-246758;** www.mostrartigianato.le.it). And if you're interested in any of the wines and foodstuffs of the region, head for a food emporium that's been here as long as anyone can remember, **Enoteca,** Via Cesare Battisti 23 (℡ **0832-302832**). Usually they'll let you taste a glass of whatever wine you're interested in before you buy a bottle.

Where to Stay

Lecce's hotels don't offer the baroque architecture for which the town is famous. Most are modern structures built to accommodate visitors who care more about seeing the town and the surrounding area than spending time in their rooms.

Albergo Delle Palme 🍴 This is the best affordable hotel in town, and it's within easy walking distance of the major sights. The public rooms, with their overstuffed leather furniture and paneled walls, are warm and inviting. The guest rooms are comfortably decorated with painted iron beds and small sitting areas, and bathrooms are spacious.

Via di Leuca 90, 73100 Lecce. ℡/fax **0832-347171.** www.hoteldellepalmelecce.it. 96 units (some with shower only). 110€ double. Rates include buffet breakfast. AE, DC, MC, V. Free parking. **Amenities:** Restaurant; room service. *In room:* A/C, TV, hair dryer, minibar, Wi-Fi (free).

Hotel Cristal This metal-and-glass high-rise is a good choice for comfort at a reasonable price. The marble lobby/lounge area is severe but not sterile and offers a pleasant place to sit and enjoy a drink. The guest rooms vary in size and are decorated monochromatically in purples, pinks, or blues.

Via Marinosci 16, 73100 Lecce. ℡ **0832-372314.** Fax 0832-315109. www.hotelcristal.it. 64 units (shower only). 88€–122€ double; 160€ suite. Rates include buffet breakfast. AE, DC, MC, V. Parking 10€. **Amenities:** Bar; babysitting; concierge; room service. *In room:* A/C, TV, fridge, hair dryer, minibar, Wi-Fi (free).

Patria Palace Hotel ★★ Lecce's finest hotel is also its most luxurious. Once the *palazzo* of rich family landowners, it was turned into an inn in 1797. It stands proudly in the midst of the baroque monuments of this old city. Without being overly pretentious, the hotel is a bastion of elegance, comfort, and good taste. The bedrooms are beautifully furnished in a rich Liberty style. Each room comes with its own original decorative paintings. Master artisans were called in to preserve the original architectural features, which were not obliterated when modern comforts were added. The best rooms with the finest service are found on the VIP floor.

Piazzetta Riccardi 13, 73100 Lecce. ℡ **0832-245111.** Fax 0832-245002. www.patriapalacelecce.com. 67 units. 170€–290€ double; 205€–350€ junior suite. Rates include buffet breakfast. AE, DC, MC, V. Parking 15€. **Amenities:** Restaurant; bar; babysitting; bikes; concierge; room service. *In room:* A/C, TV, hair dryer, minibar, Wi-Fi (10€ per hr.).

Where to Dine

Be sure to sample some of the specialties of the Salento region, such as *rustico,* a tasty combination of mozzarella and tomato wrapped in a light pastry shell.

Osteria degli Spiriti APULIAN This is one of the most typical regional restaurants in the area, lying in the historic center opposite Giardini Pubblici, a public park. Dark wooden tables and chairs and a high-arched ceiling evoke its former role as a farmhouse. The kitchen staff has won a loyal following among locals attracted to the market-fresh cuisine and the skill in preparation. Many habitués begin with one of the homemade pasta dishes such as *orecchiette* with clams and chickpeas, or spelt wheat spaghetti with eggplant, cheese, and cherry tomatoes. A main dish specialty is a succulent roast lamb, and the vegetable specialty is a dish of puréed fava beans and chicory.

Via Cesare Battisti 4. ✆ **0832-246274.** www.osteriadeglispiriti.it. Reservations recommended. Main courses 8€–22€. AE, DC, MC, V. Tues–Sun 12:30–2:30pm; Mon–Sat 8–11pm. Closed last week of June.

Ristorante Villa G.C. della Monica ★ SOUTHERN ITALIAN/INTERNATIONAL   The charming Valente family runs this restaurant in one of Lecce's most stately villas, built of chiseled stone between 1550 and 1600. There are four dining rooms (one available only for private parties) and a flower-strewn terrace overlooking a historic neighborhood near Piazza Mazzini. The menu items are steeped in local culinary traditions and emphasize a regional tubular pasta called *strozzapreti* (a bit smaller than penne), served with lobster sauce. A well-crafted dish is the risotto with asparagus and clams, or else the gnocchi with pine nuts and a pistachio sauce. Other specialties are well-seasoned filet steak with black truffles, and fresh fish that is baked in a salt crust to seal in the moisture.

Via SS. Giacomo e Fillippo 40. ✆ **0832-458432.** www.villadellamonica.it. Reservations recommended. Main courses 10€–18€. AE, DC, MC, V. Wed–Mon 12:30pm–midnight. Closed Jan.

Trattoria Cucina Casareccia APULIAN   The owner and chef, Mrs. Anna Carmela, claims that she serves *cucina povera,* which translates as "cooking of the poor." Don't get the wrong idea. At her rustic family *trattoria,* you are served some of the most authentic ingredients of the region. Begin with one of our favorite dishes—purée of fava beans parboiled and mashed with a little olive oil and salt and served with sautéed chicory. We also are fond of her potato pie with mussels and her beef meatballs with a white-wine sauce. Only for aficionados do we suggest the filet of horse in a light spicy sauce.

Via Costadura 19. ✆ **0832-245178.** www.lezietrattoria.com. Reservations recommended. Main courses 8€–14€. MC, V. Tues–Sun 1–2:30pm and 7–10pm. Closed last week of Aug and 1st week of Sept.

Lecce After Dark

Because of the large student population at the University of Lecce, there's usually something going on to keep night owls entertained. After nightfall, folks head to the main piazza to join friends for a drink. **Piazzetta del Duca d'Atena** is an especially popular hangout. For a more active night, you might want to head to **Corto Maltese,** Via Giusti 23 (no phone). From Wednesday to Monday from 9pm to 2am, crowds gather to dance the night away.

TARANTO ★

71km (44 miles) W of Brindisi, 100km (62 miles) SE of Bari, 533km (330 miles) SE of Rome

Taranto, known to the ancient Greeks as Taras, is said to have been named for a son of Poseidon who rode into the harbor on a dolphin's back. A less fantastic theory, trumpeted by historians, is that a group of Spartans was sent here in 708 B.C. to found a colony. Taranto was once a major center of Magna Graecia and continued as an important port on the Ionian coast throughout the 4th century

B.C. A long period of rule under Archytas, a Pythagorean mathematician/philosopher, was the high point in the city's history. According to some, Plato himself came to Taranto during this time to muddle through the mysteries of life with the wise and virtuous ruler.

Ten years of war with the Romans in the 3rd century B.C. ended in defeat for Taranto. Although the city lost much of the power and prestige it had been known for, it did survive the Dark Ages to become an important port once more during the time of the Crusades.

Taranto lent its name to the tarantula, but don't be alarmed; the only spiders here are small, harmless brown ones. The dance known today as the tarantella also takes its name from this city. (Members of various dancing cults believed that individuals who had been bitten by spiders should dance wildly to rid their bodies of the poison; the inflicted person would sometimes dance for days.) In modern times, the tarantella is characterized by hopping and foot tapping, and it is one of the most popular folk dances of southern Italy.

Taranto is a modern industrial city that many visitors pass by. The once-prosperous old city has begun to crumble, and the economy of the town has hit a slump, in part because the naval forces stationed in Taranto have been scaled back. However, the new city, with its wide promenades and expensive shops, still draws crowds. Come here if only to taste some of Italy's best seafood. Taranto's location on a peninsula between two seas, the Mare Piccolo and Mare Grande, ensures that plenty of oysters, mussels, and other shellfish will wind up on your plate.

Essentials

GETTING THERE   Regular service from both Bari and Brindisi is provided by the FS and FSE **train** lines. Trains leave Bari about once an hour for Taranto; the trip takes 1½ to 2 hours and costs 6.80€. For 4€, you can take the hour-long ride from Brindisi; trains leave every 2 hours. The station is on the western outskirts of town; from there, you take a bus or taxi into the center. For information and schedules, call ℂ **892021.**

Three **bus** companies—FSE, SITA, and CTP—provide service to Taranto. From Bari, take the FSE bus, departing every 2 hours. The trip takes from 1 to 2 hours and costs 7€. Call ℂ **800-079090** for information and schedules.

If you have a **car,** take A14 here from Bari; E90 comes in from Brindisi, and S7 makes the trek west from Lecce.

VISITOR INFORMATION   The **tourist office** is at Corso Umberto I 113, near Piazza Garibaldi (ℂ **099-4532392**). It's open Monday to Friday from 9am to 1pm and 4:30 to 6:30pm, and Saturday from 9am to noon.

Exploring the City

For the best view of the city, walk along the waterfront promenade, the **Lungomare Vittorio Emanuele ★★**. The heart of the old town, the **Città Vecchia,** lies on an island, separating the Mare Piccolo from the Mare Grande. The modern city, the **Città Moderna,** lies to the north of the Lungomare Vittorio Emanuele.

Evidence of Taranto's former glory as an important city in Magna Graecia can be found at the **Archaeological Museum of Taranto (Museo Archeologico**

The Lungomare Vittorio Emanuele in Taranto.

di Taranto) ★★, Via Cavour 10 (✆ **099-4532112;** www.museotaranto.it). Displayed here is an assortment of artifacts documenting Pugliese civilization from the Stone Age to modern times. Most of the items are the result of archaeological digs in the area, especially the excavated necropolis. The museum boasts the world's largest collection of terra-cotta figures, along with a glittering array of Magna Grecian art, such as vases, gold ware, marble and bronze sculpture, and mosaics. The designs of many of these works would be considered sophisticated even by today's standards. Admission is 5€. The museum is open daily from 8:30am to 7:30pm.

If the ornate vases at the National Museum enchanted you, you might want to visit **Grottaglie,** a nearby small town that's the ceramics capital of southeast Italy. Modern styles are crafted here, but most shoppers prefer to purchase traditional pieces, such as the giant vases that originally held laundry or the glazed wine bottles that mimic those of the ancient Greeks. You can buy pieces for a standard 50% discount over what you'd pay anywhere else for Grottaglie pottery, which is sold all over Italy. The whole village looks like one great china shop. Plates and vases are stacked on the pavements and even on the rooftops. Just walk along, looking to see what interests you; then bargain, bargain, bargain.

Where to Stay

Hotel choices here are limited. In fact, inexpensive accommodations might be impossible to find. Many third- or fourth-class hotels, especially around the waterfront, are unsafe. Proceed with caution. Make reservations in advance—the good hotels, though expensive, fill up fast.

Grand Hotel Delfino ★   Built in the 1960s and radically renovated, this Mercure-chain hotel is the biggest government-rated four-star hotel in town. The Delfino stands on the waterfront, much like a beach club. The well-furnished guest rooms are modern and beachy, with tile floors, wooden furniture, and small balconies.

Viale Virgilio 66, 74100 Taranto. ✆ **099-7323232.** Fax 099-7304654. www.grandhoteldelfino.it. 198 units. 140€ double; from 250€ suite. Rates include buffet breakfast. AE, DC, MC, V. Free parking. **Amenities:** Restaurant; bar; babysitting; exercise room; pool; room service. *In room:* A/C, TV, hair dryer, minibar, Wi-Fi (5€ per 24 hr.).

Hotel Europa ★   Of the lackluster hotels in town, this restored 19th-century hotel is the best of the lot. Enjoying a panoramic perch over Mare Piccolo, it opens onto views of the Città Vecchia, the sea, the Castello Aragónese, and the bridge, Ponte Girevole. The entryway and public halls are somber yet have a refined elegance, and the bar is one of the town's best rendezvous points in the evening. The accommodations offer the guest a range of options—elegant mansard suites, small apartments, or singles. Each is furnished in a tasteful, contemporary mode; and the suites are especially delectable, as they open onto small balconies fronting the sea.

Via Roma 2, 74100 Taranto. ✆/fax **099-4525994.** www.hoteleuropaonline.it. 43 units. 135€ double; 190€ suite. Rates include buffet breakfast. AE, DC, MC, V. Free parking. **Amenities:** Restaurant; bar; babysitting; room service. *In room:* A/C, TV, hair dryer, minibar, Wi-Fi (2€ per hr.).

Where to Dine

Taranto is blessed with a bountiful supply of seafood; it's fresh from the water, delicious, and inexpensive. However, avoid anything raw—the locals might like some fish dishes this way, but you don't want to risk spending your vacation in the hospital.

Il Caffè ★ SEAFOOD/APULIAN   The best restaurant within the town seats 100 satisfied diners in its two dining rooms, and there is also a bustling pizzeria. The upstairs is elegantly decorated with high ceilings and Venetian stucco walls. Only the freshest of the locally caught seafood is used here, and most in-the-know diners prefer it grilled. Start, perhaps, with a savory bowl of fish soup. If you've never tried grilled cuttlefish, this is your opportunity. Homemade pasta dishes are a specialty, including fusilli au gratin with shrimp, calamari, capers, and mussels, or *tagliolini* with shrimp flambéed with brandy and baked.

Via d'Aquino 8. ✆ **099-4525097.** Main courses 7.50€–20€; pizzas 5€–11€; fixed-price menu (only in the summer) 20€. AE, MC, V. Oct–May Mon–Sat 7pm–midnight, Tues–Sun noon–3pm; June–Sept daily noon–3pm and 7pm–midnight.

L'Assassino ITALIAN/INTERNATIONAL   Described by its owners as "normal but nice," this restaurant is exactly that—nothing too fancy, but a pleasant place for a good, affordable meal. The dining area offers a panoramic view of the water and a wide range of Italian dishes. Of course, L'Assassino has a variety of fresh fish dishes, including *risotto ai frutti di mare* (rice with the "fruits of the sea"). Other specialties are *orecchiette* and spaghetti marinara. The proprietors, who've run the place for more than 30 years, are friendly and provide good service.

Lungomare Vittorio Emanuele III, 29. ✆ **099-4593447.** Reservations recommended. Main courses 8€–16€. AE, MC, V. Daily 12:30–3pm and 7:30–11:45pm.

Le Vecchie Cantine ★★ SEAFOOD/APULIAN   This restaurant is the best in the greater Taranto area, both in terms of food and cuisine, but it lies 8km (5 miles) south of center and, as such, is better for motorists. A restaurant/pizzeria, it lies in the village of Lama and is installed in an old farmhouse from the 18th century. We like to come here in summer just to dine in the lovely garden outdoors. The menu is adjusted seasonally to take advantage of the changing produce, as the chefs prefer the best of regional seafood and fruits and vegetables.

From these top-quality products, they fashion a cuisine full of flavor and freshness. One of our favorite dishes, though it may be an acquired taste, is *risotto ai ricci di mare* (risotto with fresh sea urchins). Another succulent offering is pumpkin gnocchi with truffles. The best main course for us is the fish cooked in a salt crust to preserve its juice. When the crust is broken, an aroma of the sea emerges.

Via Girasoli 23, Lama. ✆ **099-7772589.** Reservations recommended. Main courses 8€–19€. AE, DC, MC, V. Tues–Sun 8pm–midnight; Sun 1–3pm.

SICILY

Sicily is a land unto itself, proudly different from the rest of Italy in its customs and traditions. On the map, the toe of the Italian boot appears poised to kick Sicily away, as if it didn't belong to the rest of the country. The largest of the Mediterranean islands, it's separated from Italy by the 4km (2½-mile) Strait of Messina, a dangerously unstable earthquake zone that makes the eventual construction of a bridge doubtful.

Although the island's economy is moving closer to that of Europe and the rest of Italy, its culture is still very much its own. Its vague Arab flavor reminds us that Sicily broke away from the mainland of Africa, not Italy, millions of years ago. Its Greek heritage still lives. Although there are far too many cars in Palermo and parts of the island are polluted by industrialization, Sicily is still a different country than Italy. Life is slower, tradition is respected, the myths and legends of the past aren't forgotten.

Sicily has been inhabited since the Ice Age, and its history is full of natural and political disasters. It has been conquered and occupied over and over: by the Greeks in the 6th to 5th centuries B.C., then the Romans, the Vandals, the Arabs (who created a splendid civilization), the Normans, the Swabians, the fanatically religious House of Aragón, and the Bourbons. When Garibaldi landed at Marsala in 1860, he brought an illusion of freedom, soon dissipated by the patronage system of the Mafia. Besides the invaders, the centuries have brought a series of plagues, volcanic eruptions, earthquakes, and economic hardships to threaten the interwoven culture of Sicily.

This land has a deep archaeological heritage and is full of sensual sights and experiences: vineyards and citrus groves, horses with plumes and bells pulling painted

carts, blooming almond and cherry trees in February, Greek temples, ancient theaters, complex city architecture, and aromatic Marsala wine. In summer the *sirocco* winds whirling out of the Libyan deserts dry the fertile fields, crisping the harvest into a sun-blasted palette of browns. Beaches are plentiful, but most are rocky, crowded, or dirty. The best are at Mondello, outside Palermo, and around Taormina in the east.

If you want to see most of Sicily's highlights, plan on spending at least 5 to 7 days and moving a few times.

Mount Etna blows off some steam.
PREVIOUS PAGE: **The Hercules Temple in the Valley of the Temples.**

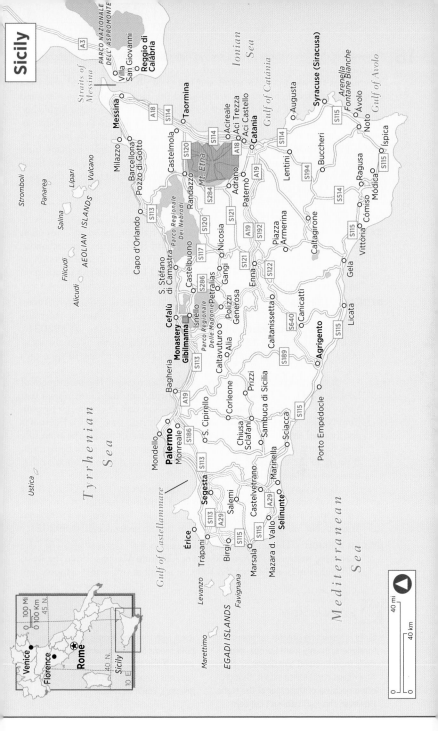

Sicily

Strombi

Panarea

Lipari Lipari

Salina

Filicudi

AEOLIAN ISLANDS

Alicudi

Marettimo

Levanzo

Favignana

EGADI ISLANDS

Ustica

Tyrrhenian Sea

Gulf of Castellammare

Mondello
Palermo
Monreale
S186
S113
Segesta
S113
A29
Érice
Trápani
Salemi
S115
Birgi
Castelvetrano
A29
Marsala
S115
Mazara d. Vallo
Marinella
Selinunte
S115
Sciacca
Porto Empédocle
S115

S. Cipirello
Corleone
Chiusa
Sclafani
Prizzi
Sambuca di Sicilia

Bagheria
A19
S113
Cefalù
Monastery
Gibilmanna
Isnello
Alia
Caltavuturo
Parco Regionale Delle Madonie
Polizzi
Generosa
S286
Petralias
Gangi

Capo d'Orlando
S113
S. Stéfano di Camastra
Castelbuono
S117
Parco Regionale Dei Nebrodi
S120
Nicosia

Milazzo
Barcellona
Pozzo di Gotto
Castelmola
S120
Randazzo
S284
Adrano
Paternò
A19

Messina
S114
A18
Taormina
S114
Castelmola
S120
Acireale
Aci Trezza
A18 Aci Castello
Catania
S114

Straits of Messina
Villa
San Giovanni
Reggio di Calábria
A3
PARCO NAZIONALE DELL' ASPROMONTE

Ionian Sea

Gulf of Catánia
Augusta
S115
Syracuse (Siracusa)
Arenella
Fontane Bianche
Ávola
Noto
S115 Íspica
Gulf of Ávolo

Lentini
S194
Buccheri
Caltagirone
S514
Ragusa
Módica
Cómiso
Vittória
S115
S115

Piazza
Armerina
A19 S192
Enna
S121
S122
Caltanissetta
Canicattì
S640
Gela
Licata
S115

Agrigento
S189

Nicosia
S121
Gangi

Mediterranean Sea

Sicily

Venice
Florence
Rome
0 100 Mi
0 100 Km
45° N.
40° N.
10° E
Sicily

40 mi
40 km

809

Remember that everything is very spread out (Sicily is the largest island in the Mediterranean, 178km/110 miles north to south and 282km/175 miles wide). Taormina is the most popular resort and is a great place to relax and play for a couple of days; from here you can visit Mount Etna. However, the town is isolated in the east, so it's not a good base for seeing the island's other major highlights. The quickest and most efficient way to see most of Sicily is to fly into Palermo, rent a car, and travel east to Taormina; then return your car and fly back to the mainland from Catania. (Conversely, you can fly into Catania, perhaps from Rome, and end your itinerary in Palermo, returning the car there before flying back to Rome.) You could easily spend a week or more getting to know this fascinating island, one of the most intriguing destinations in Italy.

Getting to Sicily

BY PLANE   Flights into Palermo from mainland Italy are the most convenient and the fastest links. Palermo's airport, **Punta Raisi,** is the island's largest, with the greatest number of flights. It's 31km (19 miles) west of Palermo on the A29 highway. You can call ✆ **091-7020111** in Palermo for information on domestic flights or international connections.

BY TRAIN   Palermo has good rail links with the rest of Sicily and to Italy. After a 3-hour ride from Messina on the northeast coast, you arrive at Palermo's main terminal, **Stazione Centrale,** at Piazza Giulio Cesare (✆ **892021**), lying on the eastern side of town and linked to the center by a network of buses or taxis. The ticket office here is open daily from 5:30am to 9pm, with luggage storage available.

It's possible to book trains from major Italian cities. The most frequent bookings are from Rome, an 11-hour trip with four trains arriving per day. Visitors in Naples most often take the ferry. You can, of course, go by train from Naples. There are about three trains daily (trip time: 9 hr.). Palermo is also hooked up conveniently to other major cities in Sicily. The train ride from Catania in the east takes 3½ hours, and there are frequent departures. If you're in the west at Trapani, it's a 2½-hour train ride to Palermo, with 6 trains arriving daily.

If you have opted for the rail haul from Rome, you'll pay 52€ to 84€ for a one-way ticket, depending on the train. On-island train tickets are cheap: 12€ from Catania, 12€ from Messina, 8€ from Agrigento, and 10€ from Trapani. For rail information for Sicily or Italy in general, call ✆ **892021.**

BY CAR & FERRY   Three autostrade link Palermo with the rest of Sicily. The most used route is A19 from Catania or A20 from Messina. From the west, A29 comes in from Mazara del Vallo. In addition, two main highways link

---

Safety in Sicily

Sicily is attracting greater numbers of foreigners, mainly from Europe, especially from England and Germany. Many Americans continue to skip it, though, often because of their fear of the Mafia. However, the Mafia doesn't concern itself with tourists. It does exist, but its hold seems to have lessened over the years. If you take the usual safety precautions (keep alert and don't flash jewelry), you'll be fine.

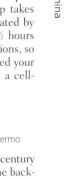

Palermo: S113 from Trapani in the west or Messina in the east, and S121 from Catania and Enna in the east. Palermo is cut off from mainland Sicily. To reach it by car, you'll have to cross the Strait of Messina by ferries operated by FS, the state railway authority.

Once the ferry has landed at Messina, you still must face a drive of 233km (145 miles) to Palermo. If you're planning to drive down from Naples or Rome, as many visitors do, prepare yourself for a long ride: 721km (448 miles) south from Naples or 934km (580 miles) south from Rome.

BY SEA From Naples, the most convenient service over to Palermo is provided by **SNAV** (𝄐 **081-4285555;** www.snav.it). The ferry trip takes 10½ hours and costs 50€ to 78€ per person. A rival ferry is operated by **Tirrenia Lines** (𝄐 **892123;** www.tirrenia.it), which takes 10½ hours and costs 50€ to 94€. Schedules vary depending on weather conditions, so always call on the day of departure even if you've already confirmed your reservation the day before. To call Tirrenia from abroad or from a cellphone, dial 𝄐 **02-26302803.**

TAORMINA ★★★

53km (33 miles) N of Catania, 53km (33 miles) S of Messina, 250km (155 miles) E of Palermo

Taormina was just too good to remain unspoiled. Dating from the 4th century B.C., it hugs the edge of a cliff overlooking the Ionian Sea. Looming in the background is Mount Etna, an active volcano. Noted for its mild climate, Italy's most beautiful town seems to have no other reason to exist than for the thousands upon thousands of visitors who flock here for shopping, dining, barhopping, and enjoying the nearby beaches.

International tourists pack the main street, Corso Umberto I, from April to October. After that, Taormina quiets down considerably. In spite of the hordes that descend in summer, Taormina is still charming, with much of its medieval character intact. It's filled with intimate piazzas and *palazzi* dating from the 15th to the 19th centuries. You'll find a restaurant for every day of the week, and countless stores sell everything from antiques to cheap souvenirs and trinkets.

You can always escape the throngs during the day by seeking out adventures, perhaps climbing Mount Etna, walking to the Castelmola, or making a day trip to Syracuse (all described later this chapter). In summer you can hang

Taormina, below looming Mount Etna.

Taormina's stunning Teatro Greco.

out at the beaches below the town (although Taormina itself isn't on a beach). At night you can enjoy jazz and disco or just spend some time in a local tavern or restaurant.

A lot of people contributed to putting Taormina on the map. First inhabited by a tribe known as the Siculi, it has known many conquerors, among them Greeks, Carthaginians, Romans, Saracens, French, and Spanish. Its first tourist is said to have been Goethe, who arrived in 1787 and recorded his impressions in his *Journey to Italy*. Other Germans followed, including a red-haired Prussian, Otto Geleng. Arriving at 20 in Taormina, he recorded its beauties in his painted landscapes, which were exhibited in Paris. They caused much excitement—people had to find out for themselves whether Taormina was really that beautiful.

Another German, Wilhelm von Gloeden, arrived in 1878 to photograph not only the town but also nude boys crowned with laurel wreaths. His pictures sent European high society to Taormina. Von Gloeden's photos, some of which are still printed in official tourist literature, form one of the most enduring legends of Taormina. Souvenir shops still sell his pictures, which, though considered scandalous in their day, seem tame—even innocent—by today's standards.

Essentials

GETTING THERE   You can make **rail** connections on the Messina line south. It's possible to board a train in Rome for the 8-hour trip to Messina, where you make connections on to Taormina. Call ✆ **892021** for schedules. There are 19 trains a day from both Messina and Catania; trips from either town take 1 to 1½ hours and cost 4€ one-way. The Sicilian Gothic train station for Taormina/Giardini–Naxos is 1.6km (1 mile) from the heart of the resort, below the town. Buses run uphill from the station daily from 9am to 9pm, every 15 to 45 minutes (schedules vary throughout the year); a one-way ticket costs 2€. You can also take a taxi for 15€ and up.

In addition, you can take the train as far as Messina and then hop a Taormina-bound **bus.** There are nine a day, taking 1½ hours and costing 6.50€ one-way. More details are available by calling **Interbus** at ✆ **0942-625301.**

By **car** from Messina, head south along A18. From Catania, continue north along A18. If you're arriving by car, the main parking lot is **Lumbi Parking,** Contrada Lumbi, which is signposted off the Taormina Nord Autostrada junction. There is another garage at **Mazzarò Parking** along

Taormina

ACCOMMODATIONS

Capotaormina Atahotel **21**
Grand Hotel Mazzaró Sea
Palace **20**
Grand Hotel San Pietro **19**
Grand Hotel Timeo **16**
Hotel Isabella **10**
Hotel La Campanella **12**
Hotel Villa Diodoro **17**
Palazzo San Domenico **3**
Romantik Hotel Villa Ducale **1**
Villa Belvedere **18**
Villa Fiorita **15**
Villa Paradiso **7**
Villa Schuler **8**
Villa Taormina **2**

DINING

Al Settimo Cielo del
Paradiso **9**
Bella Blu **14**
Granduca **4**
La Giara **6**
Maffei's **5**
Ristorante La Griglia **11**
Tirami Su **13**

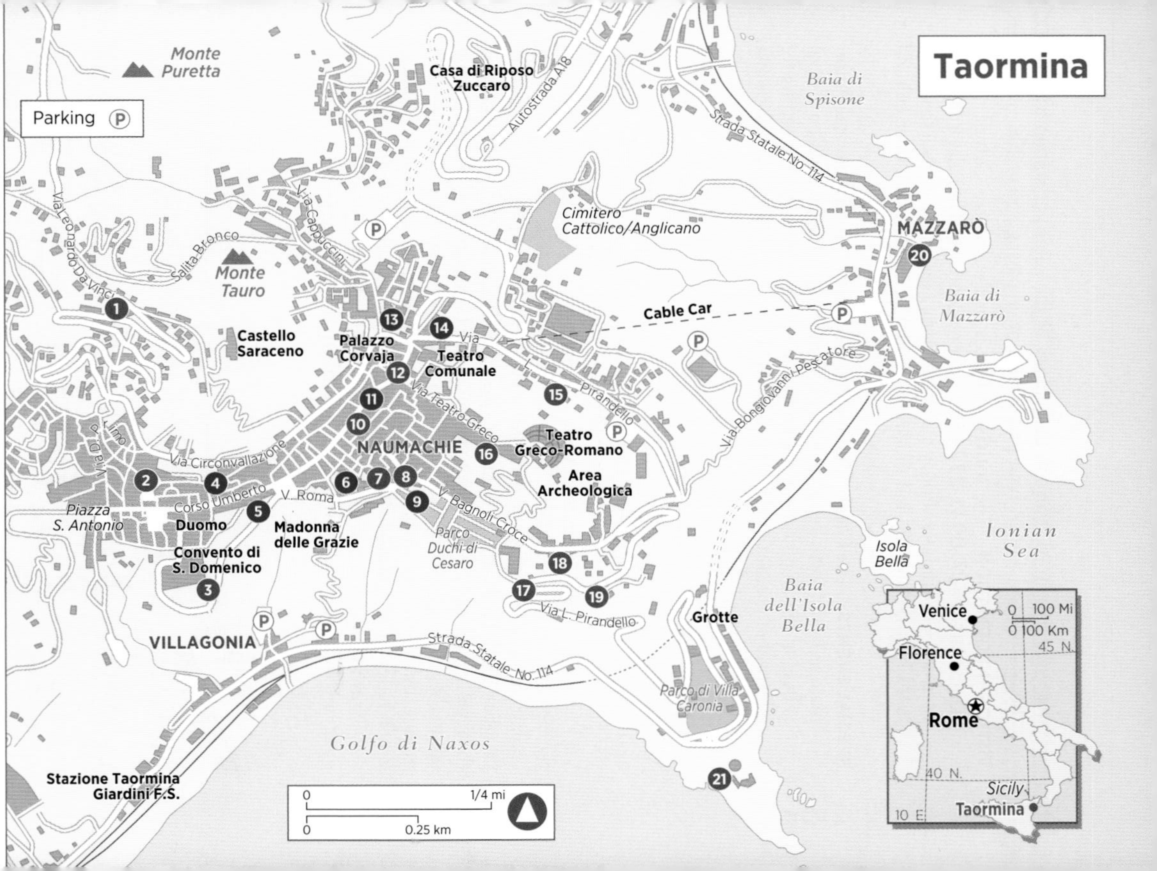

Parking **P**

Monte Puretta

Casa di Riposo Zuccaro

Autostrada A18

Via Cappuccini

Castello Saraceno

Monte Tauro

Salita Branco

Via Leonardo da Vinci

Via Pirello

Piazza S. Antonio

Duomo

Convento di S. Domenico

VILLAGONIA

Via Circonvallazione

Corso Umberto

V. Roma

Madonna delle Grazie

Palazzo Corvaja

Via Teatro Greco

Teatro Comunale

NAUMACHIE

Via Bagnoli Croce

Parco Duchi di Cesaro

Teatro Greco-Romano

Area Archeologica

Via Pirandello

Cimitero Cattolico/Anglicano

Cable Car

Via Dionisio Primo

MAZZARÓ

Baia di Spisone

Baia di Mazzaró

Baia di Mazzaró

Strada Statale No.114

Ionian Sea

Venice

Florence

Rome

Sicily

Taormina

100 Mi
100 Km

45 Km

40 N.

10 E

Isola Bella

Baia dell'Isola Bella

Grotte

Parco di Villa Carona

Golfo di Naxos

Strada Statale No.114

Stazione Taormina Giardini F.S.

1/4 mi
0.25 km

N

Via Nazionale in Mazzarò, in the vicinity of the cable-car station lying off the coastal road. For 24-hour parking, count on paying 15€ to 20€.

VISITOR INFORMATION   The **tourist office** is in the Palazzo Corvaja, Piazza Santa Caterina (✆ **0942-23243**); it's open Monday to Thursday 8:30am to 2pm and 4 to 7pm, and Friday 8:30am to 2pm. Here you can get a free map, hotel listings, bus and rail timetables, and a schedule of summer cultural events staged at the Greek Amphitheater.

SPECIAL EVENTS   The Greek Amphitheater (see below) offers theatrical performances from July to September. Each summer, an international film festival is held in the amphitheater. Churches and other venues are the setting for a festival of classical music from May to September. Check with the tourist office for exact dates.

Exploring Taormina

Many visitors to Taormina come for the beach, although the sands aren't exactly at the resort. To reach the best and most popular beach, **Lido Mazzarò ★★**, you have to go south of town via a cable car (✆ **0942-23605**) that leaves from Via Pirandello every 15 minutes. A one-way ticket costs 2€. This beach is one of the best equipped in Sicily, with bars, restaurants, and hotels. You can rent beach chairs, umbrellas, and watersports equipment at various kiosks from April to October. To the right of Lido Mazzarò, past the Capo Sant'Andrea headland, is the region's prettiest cove, where twin crescents of beach sweep from a sand spit out to the minuscule **Isola Bella** islet. You can walk here from the cable car in a minute, but it's more fun to paddle a boat from Mazzarò around Capo Sant'Andrea, which hides a few grottoes with excellent light effects on the seaward side.

North of Mazzarò are the long, wide beaches of **Spisone** and **Letojanni,** more developed but less crowded than **Giardini,** the large, built-up resort beach

Taormina's Duomo.

MEET MIGHTY mount etna

Warning: Always get the latest report from the tourist office before setting out for a trip to Mount Etna. Adventurers have been killed by a surprise "belch" (volcanic explosion). Mount Etna remains one of the world's most active volcanoes, with sporadic gas, steam, and ash emissions from its summit.

Looming menacingly over the coast of eastern Sicily, **Mount Etna ★★★** is the highest and largest active volcano in Europe—and we do mean active. The peak changes in size over the years but is currently in the neighborhood of 3,292m (10,800 ft.). Etna has been active in modern times (in 1928, the little village of Mascali was buried under its lava), and the eruptions in 1971, 1992, 2001, and 2003 rekindled Sicilians' fears.

Etna has figured in history and in Greek mythology. Empedocles, the 5th-century-B.C. Greek philosopher, is said to have jumped into its crater as a sign that he was being delivered directly to Mount Olympus to take his seat among the gods. It was under Etna that Zeus crushed the multiheaded, viper-riddled dragon Typhoeus, thereby securing domination over Olympus. Hephaestus, the god of fire and blacksmiths, made his headquarters in Etna, aided by the single-eyed Cyclops.

The Greeks warned that when Typhoeus tried to break out of his prison, lava erupted and earthquakes cracked the land. That must mean that the monster nearly escaped on March 11, 1669, one of the most violent eruptions ever—it destroyed Catania, about 27km (17 miles) away.

You can drive here. Etna lies 31km (19 miles) north of Catania and 60km (37 miles) south of Messina. One of the easiest approaches is via E45 south from Messina or Taormina to Acireale. From here, you can approach by following the

signs west going via the little towns of Aci Sant'Antonio and Viagrande, continuing west until you reach the Nicolosi. Allow about 45 minutes from Acireale to Nicolosi. At Nicolosi, you can book one of the official guides from **Funivia del Etna** (*© 095-911158*; www.funiviaetna.com). From Nicolosi, the road winds its way up to Rifugio Sapienza, the starting point for all expeditions to the crater.

In the faux alpine hamlet of Piano Provenzana you can purchase tickets for bus excursions to the top of Mount Etna. The 2-hour round-trip costs 52€ for adults or 28€ for ages 11 and younger. Departures are whenever business merits, but in summer, buses leave usually every hour.

From Rifugio Sapienza, it's also possible to hike up to the **Torre del Filosofo (Philosopher's Tower)**, at 2,920m (9,580 ft.). The trip here and back takes about 5 hours. At the tower you'll have a panoramic sweep of Etna, with its peaks and craters hissing with steam. This is a difficult hike and not for the faint of heart. The climb is along ashy, pebbly terrain, and once you reach the tower, you have another risky 2-hour hike to the craters. Because the craters can erupt unexpectedly, all guided tours to the craters have been suspended—if you insist on going all the way, you'll have to do it alone. On the return from the Philosopher's Tower to Rifugio Sapienza, you'll pass Valle de Bove, the original crater of Etna.

south of Isola Bella. A local bus leaves Taormina for Mazzarò, Spisone, and Letojanni, and another heads down the coast to Giardini.

The **Teatro Greco (Greek Amphitheater) ★★★**, Via del Teatro Greco (*© 0942-23220*), is Taormina's most visited monument, offering a view of rare

Hiking around Mount Etna.

beauty of the seacoast and Mount Etna. In the Hellenistic period, the Greeks hewed the theater out of the rocky slope of Mount Tauro; the Romans remodeled and modified it greatly. What remains today dates from the 2nd century A.D. The conquering Arabs, who seemed intent on devastating the town, slashed away at it in the 10th century. That leaves us with a rather sparse and dusty ruin, less evocative than the Greek theater in Catania. On the premises is a small museum containing artifacts from the classical and early Christian periods. Today, the Greek Amphitheater is the site of the annual Taormina film festival. It's open from April to September daily from 9am to 7pm, and from October to March daily from 9am to 4pm. Admission is 8€ for adults, 4€ for those 18 to 25, and free for seniors 66 and over and children 17 and under. The ruins lie on the upper reaches of Taormina, near the Grand Hotel Timeo.

Behind the tourist office, on the other side of Piazza Vittorio Emanuele, is the **Roman Odeon,** a small theater partly covered by the church of Santa Caterina next door. The Romans constructed this theater around A.D. 21. Much smaller than the Greek theater and with similar architecture, it was discovered in 1892 by a blacksmith digging in the area. A peristyle (colonnade) was also discovered here, perhaps all that was left of a Greek temple dedicated to Aphrodite.

Chiesa Santa Caterina, Piazza Santa Caterina, off Corso Umberto I (© 0942-23123), was consecrated to St. Catherine of Alexandria (exact consecration date unknown); it may have been built in the mid–17th century. It sits on a piazza that abuts the highest point of the town's main street, Corso Umberto I. Within its severely dignified exterior are baroque detailing and a trussed wood-beamed ceiling.

Farther along the main drag, **Corso Umberto I ★,** you'll arrive at Piazza del Duomo and the **Duomo,** or cathedral, of Taormina. Built around 1400 on the ruins of a church from the Middle Ages, this fortress cathedral has a Latin cross plan and a trio of aisles. The nave is held up by half a dozen monolithic columns in pink marble; a fish-scale decoration graces their capitals in honor of the island's maritime tradition. The cathedral is open daily 9am to 8pm.

A local sightseeing oddity here is **Villa Comunale,** sometimes called **Parco Duca di Cesarò ★★,** Via Bagnoli Croce, off Corso Umberto I. One of the most beautiful little parks in all of Sicily, the gardens were the creation of Lady Florence Trevelyan in the late 19th century. This Scottish lady was "invited" to leave Britain after a well-publicized romance with the future king, Edward VII, son of Victoria. She built various amusements in the gardens, including a fanciful stone-and-brick pavilion that might have been conceived as a teahouse. The gardens are open daily 8:30am to 7pm (6pm in winter); admission is free.

Another flower-filled garden in Taormina is the **Giardino Pubblico (Public Garden),** Via Bagnoli Croce. It overlooks the sea, making it a choice spot for views. You can order drinks at a bar in the park. The garden is open from dawn until dusk.

It's worth a trip to the nearby village of **Castelmola ★**, 3km (2 miles) northwest of Taormina. This is one of the most beautiful places in eastern Sicily, with a panoramic view of Mount Etna on clear days. You might also visit the ruined *castello* (castle) on the summit of **Mount Tauro** (390m/1,280 ft.), about 3km (2 miles) northwest of Taormina along the Castelmola road. Hikers can follow a footpath here. Ruins of a former acropolis are visible, but most people come simply for the views.

FARTHER AFIELD TO THE ALCANTARA GORGES

To see some beautiful rapids and waterfalls, head outside of town to the **Gole dell'Alcantara ★** (⌀ **0942-985010;** www.parcoalcantara.it), a series of gorges. The waters are extremely cold—uncharacteristic for Sicily, but quite refreshing in August. It's usually possible to walk up the river from May to September (when the water level is low), though you must inquire about current conditions before you do so. From the parking lot, take an elevator partway into the scenic abyss and then continue on foot. You're likely to get wet, so bring your bathing suit. If you don't have appropriate shoes, you can rent rubber boots at the entrance. Allow at least an hour for this trip. From October to April, only

A gorge at Gole dell'Alcantara.

the entrance is accessible, but the view is always stunning. It costs 4€ to enter the gorge, which is open daily from 7am to 7:30pm. By car, head up SS.185 some 17km (11 miles) from Taormina. Or take **Interbus** (⌀ **0942-625301**) for the 1-hour trip departing from Taormina at 9:15, 11:45am, 1:15, and 4:45pm. Buses from Gole dell'Alcantara return to Taormina at 9:25am, 12:35, 2:35, and 3:45pm. The round-trip fare is 6€. You can also go by taxi from Taormina. To get to the Gole dell'Alcantara from Taormina, call **Servizio Taxi Taormina** at ⌀ **346-5810872,** or go to www.taxirobertomirabile.com. The taxi fare from Taormina to the Grotte dell'Alcantara is around 40€.

Shopping

Shopping is easy in Taormina—just find **Corso Umberto I** and go. The trendy shops here sell everything upscale, from lacy linens and fashionable clothing to antique furniture and jewelry. If you're a little more adventurous, you'll want to veer off the Corso and search out the little shops on the side streets.

One of the best outlets for ceramics, in terms of both quality and design, is **Giuseppa di Blasi,** Corso Umberto I 103 (✆ **0942-24671**), which specializes in the highly valued "white pottery" from Caltagirone.

Mixing the new and the old, **Carlo Panarello,** Corso Umberto I 122 (✆ **0942-23910**), offers Sicilian ceramics (from pots to tables) and also deals in eclectic antique furnishings, paintings, and engravings.

Gioielleria Giuseppe Stroscio, Corso Umberto I 169 (✆ **0942-24865**), features antique gold jewelry from 1500 to the early 1900s.

Where to Stay

The hotels in Taormina are the best in Sicily—in fact, they're the finest in Italy south of Amalfi. All price ranges are available, with accommodations ranging from army cots to sumptuous suites.

If you're coming primarily to hit the beach, at least in July and August, you may want to stay at **Mazzarò,** 5km (3 miles) from the center, and trek up the hill for shopping, nightlife, and dining. Mazzarò is the major beach and has some fine hotels (see the Grand Hotel Mazzarò Sea Palace, p. 822). Buses connecting Mazzarò and Taormina leave every 30 minutes daily from 8am to 9pm; the fare is 2€. Otherwise, we recommend that you stay in Taormina—it has far more charm than anything down by the sea.

In summer, the curse of Taormina hotels is the noise, not only of traffic but also of visitors who turn the town into an all-night party. If you're a light sleeper and you've chosen a hotel along Corso Umberto, ask for a room in the rear—you'll be trading a view for a good night's sleep.

If you're driving to a hotel at the top of Taormina, call ahead to see what arrangements can be made for your car. Ask for exact driving directions as well as instructions on where to park—the narrow, winding, one-way streets can be bewildering once you get here.

VERY EXPENSIVE

Grand Hotel San Pietro ★★★   The resort's latest government-related five-star hotel is the only one to compete successfully with Palazzo San Domenico. Surrounded by the best hotel gardens on the eastern coast, it offers a huge terrace and pool, situated to evoke the bow of a ship. The interiors are bright and vast, everything graceful, including a wood-paneled library. Guest rooms are elegantly furnished, often in olive green, silver, gold, or apricot pink. They are rated classic and superior, or else junior and executive suites. The location of this Mediterranean-style building, rising six floors, is set on a hillside overlooking the sea, some 800m (2,625 ft.) from the center.

Via Pirandello 50, 98039 Taormina. ✆ **0942-620711.** Fax 0942-620770. www.gaishotels.com. Free parking. 63 units. 196€–408€ double; 336€–980€ suite. Rates include buffet breakfast. AE, DC, MC, V. Free parking. **Amenities:** 2 restaurants; bar; babysitting; exercise room; Internet (free, in lobby); pool; room service. *In room:* A/C, TV, hair dryer, minibar, Wi-Fi (free).

Grand Hotel Timeo ★★   Hidden in a tranquil private park just below the Greek Amphitheater, the Timeo opened in 1873 but was completely renovated in 2010. It evokes a 19th-century neoclassical villa that manages to be baronial at the same time. It lacks the manorial dignity of the Palazzo San Domenico and has none of its ecclesiastical overlays. You get the feeling instead that the Timeo was built purely for pleasure, and it carries the aura of a sophisticated and private villa. Guests are treated to a winning combination of old-world elegance and contemporary conveniences. All rooms are spacious and well outfitted, with balconies. The hotel has a private beach; the staff will arrange tee times at nearby golf courses.

Via Teatro Greco 59, 98039 Taormina. 🕐 **0942-6270200.** Fax 0942-6270606. www.grand hoteltimeo.com. 87 units. 390€–700€ double; from 750€ suite. Rates include buffet breakfast. AE, DC, MC, V. Free parking. **Amenities:** Restaurant; piano bar; babysitting; exercise room; heated pool; room service; spa. *In room:* A/C, TV/DVD, hair dryer, minibar, Wi-Fi (free).

Palazzo San Domenico ★★★   This is one of the greatest hotels of Italy. Set in the heart of the resort's oldest neighborhood, it originated in the 14th century as a semifortified Dominican monastery. Today, after generations of meticulous upgrades, it's surrounded by walled-in terraced gardens lit at night. What you'll find inside are massive and dignified areas (reception rooms, hideaway chapels, paneled salons) outfitted with museum-quality antiques, a genuinely impressive patina, and a physical setting that no one would ever dare modernize. The result is old-fashioned in the most appealing sense of the word. Guest rooms are located in either the old monastery part of the hotel, where furnishings are severely dignified and very comfortable, or in the somewhat more opulent wings added in 1897, which evoke the Gilded Age and its aesthetics a bit more richly.

Piazza San Domenico 5, 98039 Taormina. 🕐 **0942-613111.** Fax 0942-625506. http://san domenicopalace.hotelsinsicily.it. 105 units. 189€–621€ double; from 455€ suite. Rates include buffet breakfast. AE, DC, MC, V. Free parking. **Amenities:** 4 restaurants; piano bar; babysitting; concierge; exercise room; heated pool; room service. *In room:* A/C, TV, hair dryer, minibar.

EXPENSIVE

Hotel Villa Diodoro ★   This is one of Taormina's better hotels, with tasteful design through and through. There are sunny spots where you can swim, sunbathe, and enjoy the view of mountains, trees, and flowers. The vistas of Mount Etna, the Ionian Sea, and the eastern coastline of Sicily are reason enough to stay here. Guest rooms are elegant and comfortable, with parquet floors, balconies, and compact bathrooms with tub/shower combinations. From June to October, a shuttle bus runs to the beach at nearby Lido Caparena.

Via Bagnoli Croce 75, 98039 Taormina. 🕐 **0942-23312.** Fax 0942-23391. www.gaishotels.com. 99 units. 99€–326€ double. Rates include buffet breakfast. AE, DC, MC, V. Free parking. **Amenities:** Babysitting; bikes; exercise room; pool; room service. *In room:* A/C, TV, hair dryer, minibar, Wi-Fi (5€ per hr.).

Villa Paradiso ★ 🎁   This charming boutique hotel originated in 1921 when the grandfather of the present owner bought a villa originally built in 1892. Set within a warren of narrow streets adjacent to the town's most beautiful public gardens, the Paradiso contains tastefully furnished public rooms outfitted with antiques and fine art. Each of the cozy, individually decorated guest rooms has a balcony, conservative furnishings, and a tiled bathroom. Between June and October, the hotel offers free shuttle service and free entrance to the Paradise Beach Club, about 6km (4 miles) to the east, in the seaside resort of Letojanni.

Via Roma 2, 98039 Taormina. ✆ **0942-23921.** Fax 0942-625800. www.hotelvillaparadisotaormina. com. 35 units. 120€–200€ double; 160€–220€ junior suite. AE, DC, MC, V. Parking 15€. **Amenities:** Restaurant; bar; room service; Wi-Fi (8€ per hr., in lobby). *In room:* A/C, TV, hair dryer.

Villa Taormina ★★ 🏨   In the heart of Taormina, this antique residence, restored in 2008, is imbued with more Sicilian character than any similar establishment in town. On a narrow street, the residence stands above the Duomo piazza. You get a combination of elegance, charm, and comfort in what might be called a glorified B&B. Filled with antiques and objets d'art, the villa is like the private home of some grand don. Each spacious bedroom is individually decorated with hand-chosen fabrics, warm colors, Oriental rugs, and traditional Sicilian furniture. Baroque, neoclassical, and imperial styles are blended harmoniously. In other words, it's a class act. Breakfast is served on a sun-filled terrace, opening onto views of Mount Etna in the distance.

Via T. Fazzello 39, 98039 Taormina. ✆ **0942-620072.** Fax 0942-623003. www.hotelvilla taormina.com. 8 units. 200€–300€ double; 290€–370€ suite. Rates include buffet breakfast. AE, DC, MC, V. Parking nearby 15€. Closed Nov–Feb. **Amenities:** Bar; babysitting; Jacuzzi; room service; Wi-Fi (free, in lobby). *In room:* A/C, TV, hair dryer, minibar.

MODERATE

Hotel Isabella ★   Only one other hotel, the Victoria, enjoys a location directly on the main street of Taormina; the Isabella is the better of the two. Small-scale and chic in a way that only a boutique hotel can be, it welcomes visitors with a lobby that might remind you of a living room with a peaches-and-cream color scheme. Its pleasing decor evokes a sun-flooded English country house. Guest rooms are not particularly large, though cozy and plush. Some have views over the all-pedestrian hubbub of the town's main street. On the rooftop is a solarium.

Corso Umberto I 58, 98039 Taormina. ✆ **0942-23153.** Fax 0942-23155. www.hotel-isabella.it. 32 units. 96€–196€ double. Rates include buffet breakfast. AE, DC, MC, V. **Amenities:** Restaurant; bar; babysitting; bikes; free access to beach club w/watersports rentals. *In room:* A/C, TV, hair dryer, minibar.

Hotel Villa Ducale ★★   This restored old villa sits on a hillside, a 10-minute walk up from the center, in the quiet hamlet of Madonna della Rocca (midway btw. the heart of the resort and high-altitude Castelmola). It boasts magnificent views of the Mediterranean, the town, and Mount Etna. Each guest room has a veranda, terra-cotta floors, wrought-iron bed, and a compact bathroom with tub/shower combination. The service is warm and helpful. Breakfast is usually served on an outdoor terrace with a gorgeous view.

Via Leonardo da Vinci 60, 98039 Taormina. ✆ **0942-28153.** Fax 0942-28710. www.villaducale. com. 15 units. 99€–319€ double; 179€–480€ suite. Rates include buffet breakfast. AE, MC, V. Parking 10€. Closed Jan 18–Mar 4. **Amenities:** Jacuzzi; room service. *In room:* A/C, TV, hair dryer, minibar, Wi-Fi (free).

Villa Belvedere   With a friendly reception, professional maintenance, and old-fashioned style, this hotel near the Public Garden offers the same view enjoyed by guests at more expensive hotels nearby. Head to the cliff-side terrace in the rear to enjoy the vista of the Ionian Sea, the cypress-studded hillside, and smoldering Mount Etna. The small to midsize guest rooms feature functional furniture with a touch of class. Most units have slivers of balconies from which to enjoy views over the neighboring Public Garden to the sea; top-floor rooms have small terraces. The hotel is located near the cable car and the steps down to the beach.

Via Bagnoli Croce 79, 98039 Taormina. ✆ **0942-23791.** Fax 0942-625830. www.villabelvedere. it. 47 units. 95€–236€ double; 200€–400€ suite. Rates include continental breakfast. MC, V. Parking 10€. Closed late Nov to mid-Dec and mid-Jan to mid-Feb. **Amenities:** 2 bars; babysitting; pool; room service; Wi-Fi (4€ per hr.). *In room:* A/C, TV, hair dryer.

Villa Schuler ★ 🌢 Filled with the fragrance of jasmine, this hotel offers style and comfort at a good price. Family owned and run, it sits high above the Ionian Sea, with views of Mount Etna and the Bay of Naxos. It's only a 2-minute stroll from Corso Umberto I and about a 15-minute walk from the cable car to the beach below. Guest rooms are comfortably furnished, with bathrooms with tub/shower combinations; many have a small balcony or terrace. Breakfast can be served in your room or taken on a lovely terrace with a panoramic sea view. The most luxurious way to stay here is to book the garden villa suite with its own private access. It's spacious and beautifully furnished, with two bathrooms (one with a Jacuzzi). The villa comes with a kitchenette, patio, private garden, and veranda, and costs from 258€ per day for two, including breakfast.

Piazzetta Bastione, Via Roma, 98039 Taormina. ✆ **0942-23481.** Fax 0942-23522. www.villa schuler.com. 26 units, most with shower only. 138€–196€ double; 196€–212€ junior suite. Rates include continental breakfast. AE, MC, V. Parking 15€ in garage; free outside. Closed Nov 21–Mar 4. **Amenities:** Bar; babysitting; bikes; room service. *In room:* A/C, TV, hair dryer, Wi-Fi (free).

INEXPENSIVE

Hotel La Campanella This hotel is rich in plants, paintings, and hospitality. It sits at the top of a seemingly endless flight of stairs, which begin at a sharp curve of the main road leading into town. You'll climb past terra-cotta pots and the dangling tendrils of a terraced garden, eventually arriving at the house. The owners maintain clean, simple, homey guest rooms.

Via Circonvallazione 3, 98039 Taormina. ✆ **0942-23381.** Fax 0942-625248. lacampanella@tao. it. 12 units. 90€ double. Rates include continental breakfast. No credit cards. *In room:* Hair dryer.

Villa Fiorita ★ 🌢 This small inn stretches toward the Teatro Greco from its position beside the road leading to the top of this cliff-hugging town. Its imaginative decor includes a handful of ceramic stoves, which the owner delights in collecting. A well-maintained garden lies alongside an ancient but empty Greek tomb whose stone walls have been classified a national treasure. The guest rooms are arranged in a steplike labyrinth of corridors and stairwells, some of which bend to correspond to the rocky slope on which the hotel was built. Each unit contains antique furniture and a shower-only bathroom; most have private terraces.

Via Luigi Pirandello 39, 98039 Taormina. ✆ **0942-24122.** Fax 0942-625967. www.villafiorita hotel.com. 26 units. 125€ double; 165€ suite. Rates include continental breakfast. AE, MC, V. Parking 12€. **Amenities:** Outdoor pool; room service. *In room:* A/C, TV, hair dryer.

WHERE TO STAY NEARBY

If you visit Taormina in summer, you might prefer to stay at **Mazzarò,** about 5km (3 miles) away. This is the major beach and has some fine hotels. To get to

Mazzarò from the center of Taormina, you can take a cable car leaving from Pirandello daily every 15 minutes. A one-way ticket costs 2€.

Atahotel Capotaormina ★★★ This barren cape was transformed in the 1960s with the addition of the most avant-garde architectural statement in or around Taormina—an oasis of comfort and poshness within a spectacularly inhospitable natural setting. Surrounded by the Ionian Sea on three sides, and with a layout that resembles an irregular pentagon, the hotel contains five floors with wide sun terraces. Elevators take you through 46m (150 ft.) of solid rock to the beach and to a large, free-form pool far below the level of the hotel, directly adjacent to the sea. Guest rooms are handsome and well proportioned, each with a private terrace.

Via Nazionale 105, 98039 Taormina. ✆ **0942-572111.** Fax 0942-625467. www.atahotels.it. 202 units. 170€–500€ double; 460€–1,100€ suite. AE, DC, MC, V. Parking 15€. Closed Oct 16–Mar 25. **Amenities:** 3 restaurants; 3 bars; babysitting; exercise room; seawater Jacuzzi; saltwater pool; room service; sauna; watersports rentals. *In room:* A/C, TV, hair dryer, minibar, Wi-Fi (9€ per hr.).

Grand Hotel Mazzarò Sea Palace ★★★ The leading hotel in Mazzarò opens onto the most beautiful bay in Sicily and has its own private beach. Completed in 1962, this government-rated five-star deluxe hotel has been renovated frequently since. From the coastal highway, you won't be able to see very much of this spectacular lodging—only a rooftop and masses of bougainvillea. You'll register on the top floor, then ride an elevator down to sea level for access to a stylish, airy set of marble-sheathed public rooms. The hotel is very elegant, genuinely charming, and well staffed. Big windows let in cascades of light and offer views of the coast. Guest rooms are well furnished, filled with wicker and veneer pieces along with original art and wood or tile floors; most have panoramic views.

Via Nazionale 147, 98030 Mazzarò. ✆ **0942-612111.** Fax 0942-626237. www.mazzaroseapalace. it. 88 units. 190€–475€ double; 510€–960€ suite. AE, DC, MC, V. Parking nearby 35€. Closed Nov 15–Mar 15. **Amenities:** Restaurant; bar; babysitting; bikes; concierge; exercise room; pool; room service. *In room:* A/C, TV, hair dryer, minibar, Wi-Fi (free).

Where to Dine

EXPENSIVE

La Giara ★★ SICILIAN/ITALIAN Glossy, airy, and reminiscent of Rome during the heyday of Gina Lollobrigida, La Giara evokes a warmed-over *la dolce vita*. The restaurant is almost excessively formal and has remained predictably stable since its founding in 1953. Views sweep from the veranda's outdoor tables over the bay of Taormina. The Art Deco ambience is also inviting, with marble floors and columns shaped from stone quarried in the fields outside Syracuse. The pastas are meals in themselves; unusual specialties include a sea bass roll stuffed with bread crumbs, cherry tomatoes, capers, and mussels, and served in a potato sauce, or else potatoes and mushroom dumplings in a sea urchin sauce. The fresh fish of the day is grilled to perfection, and meats are cooked equally well.

Vico la Floresta 1. ✆ **0942-23360.** www.lagiara-taormina.com. Reservations required. Main courses 19€–28€. AE, DC, MC, V. Apr–July and Sept–Oct Tues–Sun 8:15–11pm; Nov–Mar Fri–Sat 8:15–11pm; Aug daily 8:15–11pm.

MODERATE

Maffei's ★ 🎏 SICILIAN/SEAFOOD   Maffei's is very small, with only 10 tables, but it serves the best fish in Taormina. Every day the chef selects the freshest fish at the market, and you simply tell him how you'd like it prepared. We often choose the house specialty, swordfish *alla Messinese,* braised with tomato sauce, black olives, and capers. The *fritto misto* (a mixed fry with calamari, shrimp, swordfish, and sea bream) is made superbly light by good-quality olive oil.

Via San Domenico de Guzman 1. 🕐 **0942-24055.** Reservations required. Main courses 12€–18€. AE, DC, MC, V. Daily noon–3pm and 7pm–midnight. Closed early Jan to mid-Feb.

Ristorante La Griglia ★ SICILIAN   One of the city's newer restaurants seems much older, thanks to its country-elegant location within the thick stone walls of what was a private *palazzo* in the 1600s. Our favorite seats are those against the most distant back wall, where windows overlook one of Taormina's oldest streets, a ravinelike alley known as Via Naumachia, whose walled edges were built by the ancient Romans. Start with one of the best selections of antipasti in town or with a classic island pasta dish—we enjoyed one prepared with swordfish and baby eggplant. The chef will be happy to prepare grilled fresh vegetables for vegetarians. The wine list is wonderful.

Corso Umberto I 54. 🕐 **0942-23980.** www.ristorantelagrigliataormina.com. Reservations recommended for dinner during midsummer. Main courses 10€–20€. AE, DC, MC, V. Wed–Mon noon–3:30pm and 7–11pm.

INEXPENSIVE

Al Settimo Cielo del Paradiso ★ 🍴 SICILIAN   It's far from being the most popular restaurant in Taormina, but in some ways it's our undisputed budget favorite, thanks to sense of chic and its high-altitude view that seems to sweep over half of Sicily. To reach it, take an elevator from the lobby of the also-recommended hotel, **Villa Paradiso** (p. 819), and then dine on a rooftop where Orson Welles and John D. Rockefeller IV once ate. Dishes are likely to include well-crafted versions of *pennette* or risotto with salmon, succulent salads of grilled prawns with a limoncello sauce, and roulades of grilled swordfish layered with vegetables and herbs. **Note:** You must enter the restaurant between 8 and 9pm, as it has the shortest opening times of any place along the coast.

In the Hotel Villa Paradiso, Via Roma 2. 🕐 **0942-23922.** Reservations recommended. Main courses 10€–27€; fixed-price menu 25€. AE, DC, MC, V. Daily 8–9pm. Closed mid-Nov to mid-Mar.

Bella Blu ★ SICILIAN/INTERNATIONAL   This chic international spot is a restaurant and pizzeria, as well as a piano bar and disco. In addition to offering fine cuisine, Bella Blu is one of the most entertaining places to be in Taormina after dark. Located a 150m (492-ft.) walk from the center, it has a rich, luxurious aura. Its menus and fine food are based on the freshest of local ingredients. The chef specializes in barbecued and grilled meats flavored with fresh herbs, as well as fresh fish. A Sicilian favorite includes homemade pasta with fresh sardines in a savory tomato sauce with wild fennel and pine nuts.

Via Luigi Pirandello 28. 🕐 **0942-24239.** www.bellablutaormina.com. Reservations required June–Aug. Main courses 8€–16€. AE, DC, MC, V. Daily noon–3pm and 7–11pm.

Granduca ★ 🍴 ITALIAN/SICILIAN   This is the most atmospheric choice in town, entered through an antiques store; it also serves an excellent, carefully executed cuisine. In fair weather, request a table in the beautiful gardens. Our favorite pasta here is *spaghetti alla Norma* (with tomato sauce, eggplant, and ricotta). If you want something truly Sicilian, ask for pasta with sardines. The best meat dish is the grilled roulades. At night, various pizzas are baked to perfection in a wood-fired oven.

Corso Umberto I 172. 📞 **0942-24983.** www.granduca-taormina.com. Reservations recommended. Main courses 12€–25€. AE, DC, MC, V. Daily 12:30–3pm and 7:30pm–midnight.

Tirami Su ★ 🍴 SICILIAN   This is one of the most frequently praised inexpensive restaurants in Taormina, drawing appreciative comments from both residents and visitors. It's small and basic looking, set beside a busy, narrow commercial street. You'll enjoy dishes that may include beef with mushrooms and cream sauce, swordfish roulades, and spaghetti with seafood.

Via Costantino Patricio 1. 📞 **0942-24803.** Reservations recommended. Pizzas 7€–12€; main courses 12€–19€. AE, DC, MC, V. Wed–Mon 12:30–3pm and 7:30pm–midnight.

Taormina After Dark

Begin your evening at the **Caffè Wunderbar,** Piazza IX Aprile 7, Corso Umberto I (📞 **0942-625302;** www.wunderbar.it), a popular spot that was once a favorite watering hole of Tennessee Williams. Beneath a vine-covered arbor, the outdoor section is perched as close to the edge of the cliff as safety allows. We prefer one of the Victorian armchairs beneath chandeliers in the elegant interior. There's a well-stocked bar, as well as a piano bar. It's open daily 9am to 2:30am (closed Tues Nov–Feb).

The entire town is geared to having fun, and you'll find many bars and clubs. **Bella Blu,** Via Luigi Pirandello 28 (📞 **0942-24239;** www.bellablutaormina. com), caters to a high-energy European crowd.

Morgana Bar, Scesa Morgana 4 (📞 **0942-620056**), is named after the seductive fairy (Morgan la Fée) of Camelot days, who lured valiant knights to their doom. It is an ultrahip, cutting-edge bar that's tucked into one of the narrow alleyways running downhill from the Corso Umberto I. Centered around a semicircular bar top, it flows out onto a candlelit terrace.

En Route to Syracuse: A Stop at Catania ★

Catania is a suitable base if you're planning a jaunt up Mount Etna. It lies 52km (32 miles) south of Taormina and 60km (37 miles) north of Syracuse. Largely industrial (with sulfur factories), the important port opens onto the Ionian Sea. Its history is fraught with natural disasters. In 1693, an earthquake virtually leveled the city, and Etna has rained lava on it on many occasions.

Somehow Catania has learned to live with Etna, but the volcano's presence is felt everywhere. For example, in certain parts of the city you'll find hardened remains of lava flows, all a sickly purple color. Grottoes in weird shapes, almost fantasy-like, line the shores, and boulderlike islands rise from the water.

Catania's present look, earning for it the title of the "baroque city," stems from just after the 1693 earthquake. The Camastra duke, with several architects and artists, decided to rebuild the city in the baroque style. This reconstruction took the whole 18th century. The most famous artists involved were Alonzo Di Benedetto, Antonino and Francesco Battaglia, Giovanni Vaccarini, and Stefano

Ittar. Fragments of solidified black lava were used (first by the Romans and then until the end of the 19th c.) in the construction of walls. This lava, and the way it was positioned into the masonry, gave added strength to the walls.

Splitting the city is **Via Etnea** ★, flanked with 18th-century *palazzi.* The locals are fond of strolling through the **Bellini Garden (Giardini Bellini),** named to honor Vicenzo Bellini, the young (dead at 32) composer of operas such as *Norma* and *La Sonnambula,* who was born in Catania in 1801.

Built in the late 11th century, Catania's **Duomo** ★, Piazza del Duomo (✆ **095-320044**), honors St. Agatha, the city's patroness. It was rebuilt after the 1693 earthquake, and its most outstanding feature is the curving baroque facade, a Vaccarini masterpiece. The chapel to the right as you enter contains the sarcophagus of Costanza, wife of Frederick III of Aragón, who died in 1363. The southern chapel honors St. Agatha. An elaborate Spanish doorway leads into the reliquary and treasury. Note also the carved choir stalls, illustrating scenes from the life of St. Agatha. Admission is free, and the cathedral is open daily 7am to noon and 4:30 to 7pm.

Most rushed visitors today pass through only on their way to or from Catania's airport, Sicily's busiest airport. Flights on Alitalia, including those from Rome, arrive at **Aeroporto Fontanarossa** (✆ **095-7239111;** www.aeroporto. catania.it), 5km (3 miles) south of the city center. From here, you can take the Alibus (or a taxi) into the Catania train station, where you'll find 22 trains per day for Taormina, costing 4€ one-way.

WHERE TO STAY

Albergo Savona   This solid, well-located hotel lies a 2-minute walk from the Duomo. Converted into a hotel about a century ago, it has three floors of quiet

The Duomo in Catania.

soundproof bedrooms with high ceilings, severely dignified yet comfortable furniture, and shower-only bathrooms. Guest rooms are accessed via a grandiose flight of marble-capped stairs flanked with elaborate wrought-iron railings. Although some have views of the cathedral, room numbers 102 and 104 are the best, with views over a medieval-looking courtyard. One of the best aspects of this place is the plush paneled bar, complete with soaring ceiling vaults, deep armchairs, and plenty of dignified style. It doubles as a breakfast room. As for some members of the staff, they need to go back and take Manners 101 again.

Via Vittorio Emanuele 210, 95124 Catania. ℂ/fax **095-326982.** www.hotelsavona.it. 30 units. 95€ double. AE, DC, MC, V. Bus: 401, 429, 432, or 457. **Amenities:** Bar; room service; Wi-Fi (free in lobby). *In room:* A/C, TV, hair dryer, minibar.

Excelsior Grand Hotel ★★   No other hotel in Sicily so gracefully manifests the flowing sense of *la dolce vita* modernism as Catania's leading establishment. It brought postwar tourism to Catania with a stately and monumental facade, built in 1954, that's almost a mirror image of the Palazzo di Giustiza (Municipal Courthouse), which lies immediately across Piazza Verga, the most impressive square in Catania. A radical renovation retained the best aspects of this hotel's retro, Sputnik-era design and added zillions of new grace notes.

Expect a modern-style lobby in perfect taste, with a resident pianist, deep and comfortable settees, and the kind of bar you might find on Rome's Via Veneto. Half of the bedrooms overlook Piazza Verga and faraway Mount Etna, and all units are soundproof. These standard double rooms are called deluxe rooms, and each comes with a loggia-style balcony. The remainder ("superior rooms") are just as large, plush, and comfortable, but they face the back of the hotel and in most cases lack balconies.

Piazza Verga, 95129 Catania. ℂ **095-7476111.** Fax 095-7476747. www.amthotels.it. 176 units. 240€–270€ double; 350€–450€ suite. Rates include breakfast buffet. AE, DC, MC, V. Bus: 443, 457, 721, or 722. **Amenities:** Restaurant; bar; babysitting; bike rentals; concierge; exercise room; room service; sauna. In room: A/C, TV, hair dryer, minibar, Wi-Fi (5€ per hr.).

Hotel Mediterraneo ★   Well designed and unpretentious, with three stars from the local tourist authorities, this is one of Catania's most modern hotels and features a tactful, hardworking staff. In 2002, after a well-planned reconfiguration by celebrity architect Romeo Francesco, the place was reincarnated as a member of the Best Western hotel chain. The blue-floored lobby includes dramatic murals inspired by the great masterpieces of the Italian renaissance. Guest rooms are predictably angular and simple, with big windows and well maintained bathrooms.

Via Dottor Consoli 27, 95124 Catania. ℂ **800/528-1234** in the U.S., or 095-325330. Fax 095-715818. www.hotelmediterraneoct.com. 63 units. 79€–165€ double. Rates include buffet breakfast. AE, DC, MC, V. Parking 10€–18€. Bus: 431. **Amenities:** Bar; exercise room; room service. *In room:* A/C, TV, hair dryer, minibar, Wi-Fi (free).

Villa Paradiso dell'Etna ★★   If you need to stay near the Fontanarossa airport, you might want to spend the night here, 11km (7 miles) from Catania. This elegant hotel lies on the slopes of Mount Etna, between the towns of San Giovanni La Punta and Viagrande. Surrounded by gardens, the hotel was opened in 1927 and has been restored to its former glory. Its original furnishings are still here, and the atmosphere of the past lives on splendidly. Guest rooms are beautifully and comfortably furnished with antiques and old prints; all have views of Etna. Most bathrooms have tubs; the rest have showers, and the suites have hydromassage tubs. The villa also has a wine cellar, a panoramic roof garden, and a disco on summer Sundays.

Via per Viagrande 37, 95030 San Giovanni La Punta. © **095-7512409.** Fax 095-7413861. www.paradisoetna.it. 34 units. 150€–290€ double; 250€–450€ suite. Rates include buffet breakfast. AE, DC, MC, V. From Catania, follow the Catania-Messina motorway in the direction of Etna and San Gregorio. The hotel is signposted at the yellow signs leading to Le Zagare shopping center. Free parking. **Amenities:** Restaurant; piano bar; exercise room; pool; room service; sauna; Wi-Fi (free, in lobby). *In room:* A/C, TV, hair dryer, minibar.

WHERE TO DINE

Il Canile SICILIAN/CONTINENTAL   Elegant and traditional, this restaurant in the Villa del Bosco hotel is very appealing. You can dine in a richly frescoed interior room or take a seat on a terrace without a hint of Sicilian traffic. Menu items include a *risottini* of porcini mushrooms from the slopes of Mount Etna. We sampled our finest seafood pasta in Catania here and went on to devour a succulent sea bream under an oven-crisp potato crust. The restaurant's name, which translates as "The Kennel," is taken from the pair of 18th-century stone dogs that stand near its entrance.

In the Villa del Bosco, Via del Bosco 62. © **095-7335100.** www.ristoranteilcanile.com. Reservations recommended. Main courses 16€–22€. AE, DC, MC, V. Daily 1–2:30pm and 8–11pm. Bus: 129, 314, or 421.

La Siciliana SICILIAN   Decorated in a classic and rustic style, this restaurant was established in 1968 and is today managed by two sons of the original owner. Located in north Catania, it's set in a 19th-century villa that's furnished in provincial island style. In winter, diners sit in one of the four cozy rooms; in summer, tables overflow onto a garden terrace. The cuisine is both innovative and respectful of tradition. You can enjoy carpaccio of fresh swordfish, grilled stuffed calamari, and risotto with squid ink and fresh ricotta. For dessert, typical favorites are always on the menu.

Viale Marco Polo 52A. © **095-376400.** Reservations required. Main courses 11€–25€. AE, DC, MC, V. Tues–Sat 12:30–3pm and 8–11pm; Sun 12:30–3pm. Closed July 1–15.

Trattoria La Paglia ★ 🍴 SICILIAN   If you like your food ethnic and your atmosphere hale and hearty, you can enjoy the most authentic Catanian dining experience at the site of the lively fish market. If you don't prefer the day's offerings, one of the staff might step out to the market and buy a fish you like, cooking it to your specifications. Start with *la triaca pasta,* an excellent pasta in fresh bean sauce, or *sarda al beccafico* (sardines fried in bread crumbs with pecorino cheese). We're also fond of the spaghetti whipped with sea urchins in an extra-virgin olive oil with fresh garlic. One local dish that's highly favored is *tonno con cipollata* (broiled tuna with onions and a dash of vinegar). Most of the dishes are based on the sea, and the atmosphere is very rustic.

Via Pardo 23. © **095-346838.** Reservations required Fri–Sat. Main courses 8€–16€. MC, V. Mon–Sat 12:30–2:30pm and 8–11pm. Bus: 457.

CATANIA AFTER DARK

Lapis (www.lapisnet.it) is a monthly bulletin issued by the tourist office and available at hotels and bars throughout Catania. It lists special concerts and festivals, movies, and nightclubs.

Music lovers should head for the **Teatro Massimo ★**, sometimes called Teatro Bellini in honor of the hometown composer. It's at Piazza Teatro Massimo, Via Perrotta Giuseppe 12 (© **095-7306111;** www.teatromassimobellini.it; bus: 429). Some of Italy's best operas and concerts are presented here, with tickets costing from 16€ to 70€. Nothing is grander than hearing Bellini's *Norma* or *La Sonnambula* on its home turf. The opera and ballet seasons extend from mid-January to right before Christmas, and the concert season runs from mid-October to late May. The box office is open Tuesday to Friday 9:30am to 12:30pm, Monday and Saturday 9:30am to 12:30pm and 5 to 7pm.

Pubs and dance clubs rule the night. One such option is **Royal Pub Ceres,** Via San Giuseppe al Duomo 17–21 (© **095-7152294**), on a block northwest of the Duomo. This woodsy-looking English pub comes complete with a carved Victorian-style bar and a crowd of good-looking people under 35. Its reputation for beers on tap is unequaled in Catania. The venue sometimes spills onto the narrow street outside. The place rocks daily from 7am (for that early libation) to 2am. Take bus no. 448, 449, 457, 722, or 733.

SYRACUSE ★★★ & ORTYGIA ISLAND ★★★

56km (35 miles) SE of Catania

Of all the Greek cities of antiquity that flourished on the coast of Sicily, Syracuse (Siracusa) was the most important, a formidable competitor of Athens. In its

heyday, it dared take on Carthage and even Rome. At one time, its wealth and size were unmatched by any other city in Europe.

Colonists from Corinth founded Syracuse on the Ionian Sea in about 735 B.C. Much of its history was linked to despots, beginning in 485 B.C. with Gelon, the tyrant of Gela, who subdued the Carthaginians at Himera. Syracuse came under attack from Athens in 415 B.C., but the main Athenian fleet was destroyed and the soldiers on the mainland were captured. They were herded into the Latomia di Cappuccini at Piazza Cappuccini, a stone quarry. The "jail," from which there was no escape, was particularly horrid: The defeated soldiers weren't given food and were packed together like cattle and allowed to slowly die.

Syracuse's waterfront.

Dionysius I was one of the greatest despots, reigning over the city during its height of influence as a sea power, in the 4th century B.C. But in A.D. 212, the city fell to the Romans under Marcellus, who sacked its riches and art. In that attack, Syracuse lost its most famous son, the Greek physicist/mathematician Archimedes, who was slain in his study by a Roman soldier.

Although the ruins of Syracuse will be one of the highlights of your trip to Sicily, the city itself has been in a millennia-long decline. Today it's a blend of often unattractive modern development (with supermarkets and high-rises sprouting along speedways) and the ruins of its former glory, a splendor that led Livy to proclaim it "the most beautiful and noble of Greek cities."

A lot of what you'll want to see is on the island of Ortygia, which is filled with not only ancient ruins but also small crafts shops and dozens of boutiques. From the mainland, Corso Umberto leads to the Ponte Nuova, which leads to the island. Parking is a serious problem on Ortygia, so if you're driving, park in one of the garages near the bridge and then walk over and explore the island on foot. Allow at least 2 hours to explore, plus another hour to shop along the narrow streets. You'll also want to sit for half an hour or so on Piazza del Duomo, off Via Cavour. This is one of the most elegant squares in Sicily.

The ancient sights are a good half-hour's walk back inland from Ortygia, past a fairly forgettable shopping strip, so you might want to take a cab (they're easily found at all the sights). If you don't see a cab, you can call ✆ **0931-69722,** and one will be sent for you. You'll find buses on Ortygia at Piazza Pancali/Largo XXV Luglio. The harborfront is lined with a collection of 18th- and 19th-century town houses.

Syracuse is a cauldron in summer. You can do as the locals do and head for the sea. The finest **beach** is about 19km (12 miles) away at **Fontane Bianche;** bus nos. 21 and 22 leave from the Syracuse post office, Piazza delle Poste 15. If you're driving, Fontane Bianche lies to the south of the city (it's signposted); take SS115 to reach it. The same buses will take you to **Lido Arenella,** only 8km (5 miles) away but not as good.

🖉 Read Before You Go . . .

Before your trip, you might want to read Mary Renault's novel *The Mask of Apollo,* set in Syracuse in the 5th century B.C. As one critic put it, "It brings the stones to life."

Essentials

GETTING THERE From other major cities in Sicily, Syracuse can be reached by **train,** although many visitors find the bus (see below) faster. By train, Syracuse is 1½ hours from Catania, 2 hours from Taormina, and 5 hours from Palermo. Usually you must transfer in Catania. For information, call ✆ **892021.** Trains arrive in Syracuse at the station on Via Francesco Crispi, centrally located between the Archaeological Park and Ortygia. The nearest airport is at Catania.

From Catania, 18 Interbus **buses** per day make the 1¼-hour trip to Syracuse. The one-way fare is 7€. Call ✆ **0931-66710** in Syracuse, or 095-7461333 in Catania, for schedules.

By **car** from Taormina, travel south along A18 and then on E45, past Catania. Allow at least 1½ hours.

VISITOR INFORMATION   The **tourist office** is in the historic center at Via Vincenzo Mirabella 27 (☎ **0931-464657**), open Monday to Friday 8:15am to 2pm and 2:30 to 5:30pm, Saturday 8:15am to 2pm.

SPECIAL EVENTS   Some of the most memorable cultural events in Sicily are staged in May and June, when actors from the Instituto Nazionale del Dramma Antico present **classical plays** by Aeschylus, Euripides, and their contemporaries. The setting is the ancient Teatro Greco (Greek Theater) in the Archaeological Park. Tickets cost 30€ to 62€. For information, contact **INDA,** Corso Matteotti 29, 96100 Siracusa (☎ **0931-487200;** www.inda fondazione.org).

Exploring the Ancient Sights

Catacomba di San Giovanni (Catacombs of St. John) ★★   Evoking the more famous Christian burial grounds along Rome's Appian Way, the Catacombs of St. John contain some 20,000 ancient tombs, honeycombed tunnels of empty coffins that were long looted of their "burial riches" by plundering grave robbers.

In Roman times, Christians were not allowed to bury their dead within the city limits, so they went outside the boundaries of Syracuse to create burial chambers in what had been used by the Greeks as underground aqueducts. The early Christians recycled these into chapels. Some faded frescoes and symbols etched into stone slabs can still be seen. Syracuse has other subterranean burial grounds, but the Catacombs of St. John are the only ones open to the public.

You enter the "world of the dead" from the **Chiesa di San Giovanni,** now a ruin. St. Paul is said to have preached on this spot, so the early Christians venerated it as holy ground. Now overgrown, the interior of the church was abandoned in the 17th century. In its heyday, it was the cathedral of Syracuse.

The church's roots date from the 6th century, when a basilica stood here, but it was eventually destroyed by the Saracens. The Normans reconstructed it in the 12th century, but in 1693 an earthquake destroyed it. A baroque church was then built, but was left in ruins by the earthquake of 1908. All that remains are roofless Norman walls and about half of the former apse. A beautiful rose window is still visible on the facade of the Norman church.

Underneath the church is the **Cripta di San Marciano (Crypt of St. Marcian),** constructed on the spot where the martyr is alleged to have been beaten to death. His Greek-cross chamber is found 5m (16 ft.) below the ground.

Warning: Make sure that you exit well before closing. Two readers who entered the catacombs after 5pm were accidentally locked in.

Piazza San Giovanni, at end of Viale San Giovanni. No phone. Admission 5€ adults, free for children 15 and under. Tues–Sun 9:30am–1pm and 2:30–5:30pm. Closed Feb.

Paolo Orsi Regional Archaeological Museum (Museo Archeologico Regionale Paolo Orsi) ★★★   One of the most important archaeological museums in southern Italy surveys the Greek, Roman, and early Christian epochs. Crafted from glass, steel, and Plexiglas, and designed as an ultramodern showcase for the objects unearthed from digs throughout Sicily, this is the kind of museum that reinvigorates an appreciation for archaeology. Its stunning modernity is in direct contrast to the sometimes startling portrait busts and vases unearthed from around the island. Laid out like a hexagon, the museum is set in a garden dotted with ancient sarcophagi.

Section A takes us back before the dawn of recorded history. We're always fascinated by the skeletons of prehistoric animals found here, including dwarf elephants. Many artifacts illustrate life in Paleolithic and Neolithic times. Look for the stunning red-burnished **Vase of Pantalica ★**.

Section B is devoted to Greek colonization. The celebrated **Landolina Venus ★★** is here, without a head but alluring nonetheless. After all these centuries, the anatomy of this timeless Venus is still in perfect shape. A Roman copy of an original by Praxiteles, the statue was found in Syracuse in 1804. When he visited the town in 1885, Guy de Maupassant fell in love with this Venus and left a vivid description of her. Although it's not the equal of the Landolina Venus, the singular limestone block of a **Mother-Goddess ★** suckling twins dates from the 6th century B.C. and was recovered from a necropolis.

Section C brings the subcolonies and Hellenistic centers of eastern Sicily alive once more. It's a hodgepodge of artifacts and fragments, including votive terra cottas, sarcophagi, and vases from Gela. Interspersed among some rather dull artifacts are stunning creations such as an enthroned male figure from the 6th century B.C., a horse and rider from the same era, a terra-cotta goddess from the late 6th century B.C., and a miniature 6th-century-B.C. altar with a relief depicting a lion attacking a bull. You can also seek out three rare wooden statues from the 7th century B.C. (found near Agrigento).

In the gardens of the Villa Landolina in Akradina, Viale Teocrito 66. ✆ **0931-464022.** Admission 8€. Tues–Sat 9am–7pm; Sun 9am–1pm.

Parco Archeologico della Neapolis ★★★   Syracuse's Archaeological Park contains the town's most important attractions, all on the mainland at the western edge of town, immediately north of Stazione Centrale. The entrance to the park is down Via Augusto.

On the Temenite Hill, the **Teatro Greco (Greek Theater) ★★★**, Viale Teocrito, was one of the great theaters of the classical period. Hewn from rock during the reign of Hieron I in the 5th century B.C., the ancient seats have been largely eaten away by time; but you can still stand on the remnants of the stone stage where plays by Euripides were mounted. Today, the Italian Institute of Ancient Drama presents classical plays by Euripides, Aeschylus, and Sophocles. In other words, the show hasn't changed much in 2,000 years.

Outside the entrance to the Greek Theater is the most famous of the ancient quarries,

Latomia del Paradiso (Paradise Quarry) at Parco Archeologico della Neapolis.

Latomia del Paradiso (Paradise Quarry) ★★, one of four or five from which stones were hauled to erect the great monuments of Syracuse in its glory days. Upon seeing the cave in the wall, Caravaggio is reputed to have dubbed it the "Ear of Dionysius" because of its unusual shape. But what an ear: It's nearly 60m (200 ft.) long. You can enter the inner chamber of the grotto, where the tearing of paper sounds like a gunshot. Although it's dismissed by some scholars as fanciful, the story goes that the despot Dionysius used to force prisoners into the "ear" at night, where he was able to hear every word they said. Nearby is the **Grotta dei Cordari,** where rope makers plied their craft.

An evocative site lies on the path down into the Roman amphitheater. The **Ara di Ierone,** or Altar of Heron, was once used by the Greeks for sacrifices involving hundreds of animals at once. A few pillars still stand, along with the mammoth stone base of this 3rd-century-B.C. monument. The longest altar ever built, it measured 196×23m (643×75 ft.).

The **Anfiteatro Romano (Roman Amphitheater)** ★ was created at the time of Augustus. It ranks among the top five amphitheaters left by the Romans in Italy. Like the Greek Theater, part of it was carved from rock. Unlike the Greek Theater with its classical plays, the Roman Amphitheater tended toward gutsier fare. Gladiators faced each other with tridents and daggers, and slaves were whipped into the center of a battle to the death between wild beasts. Either way, the victim lost: If his opponent, man or beast, didn't do him in, the crowd would often scream for the ringmaster to slit his throat. The amphitheater is near the entrance to the park, but you can also view it in its entirety from a belvedere on the road.

Via Del Teatro (off the intersection of Corso Gelone and Viale Teocrito). ✆ **0931-66206.** Admission 6€. Apr–Oct daily 9am–5pm; Nov–Mar daily 9am–3pm.

EXPLORING ORTYGIA ISLAND ★★★

Ortygia, inhabited for many thousands of years, is also called the Città Vecchia (old city). It contains the town's Duomo, many rows of houses spanning 500

Ortygia's Duomo.

Baroque details in the Piazza del Duomo in Ortygia.

years of building styles, most of the city's medieval and baroque monuments, and some of the most charming vistas in Sicily. In Greek mythology, it's said to have been ruled by Calypso, daughter of Atlas, the sea nymph who detained Ulysses (Odysseus) for 7 years. The island, reached by crossing the Ponte Nuova, is about 1.6km (1 mile) long and half as wide.

Heading out the Foro Italico, you'll come to the **Fonte Arethusa ★**, also famous in mythology. The river god Alpheius, son of Oceanus, is said to have fallen in love with the sea nymph Arethusa. The nymph turned into this spring or fountain, but Alpheius became a river and "mingled" with his love. According to legend, the spring ran red when bulls were sacrificed at Olympus.

At Piazza del Duomo is the **Duomo ★**, which was built over the ruins of the Temple of Minerva and employs the same Doric columns; 26 of the originals are still in place. The temple was erected after Gelon the Tyrant defeated the Carthaginians at Himera in the 5th century B.C. The Christians converted it into a basilica in the 7th century A.D. In 1693, an earthquake caused the facade to collapse, and in the 18th century the cathedral was rebuilt in the baroque style by Andrea Palma. It's open daily 8am to noon and 4 to 7pm. Admission is free.

The irregular **Piazza del Duomo ★** is especially majestic when the facade of the cathedral is dramatically caught by the setting sun or when flood-lit at night. Acclaimed as one of the most beautiful squares in Italy, it's filled with other fine baroque buildings. They include the striking **Palazzo Beneventano del Bosco,** with its lovely courtyard. Opposite it is the **Palazzo del Senato,** with an inner courtyard displaying a senator's carriage from the 1700s. At the far end of the square stands **Santa Lucia,** although it hardly competes with the Duomo.

The other important landmark square is **Piazza Archimede,** with its baroque fountain festooned with dancing jets of water and sea nymphs. This square lies directly northeast of Piazza del Duomo, forming the monumental heart of Ortygia. It, not the cathedral square, is the main square of the old city. On this piazza, Gothic windows grace the 15th-century **Palazzo Lanzo.** As you wander around Ortygia, you'll find that Piazza Archimede is a great place from which to orient yourself. Wander the narrow streets wherever your feet will take you. When you get lost, you can always ask for directions back to Piazza Archimede.

Where to Stay

The best place to stay in the Syracuse area is on Ortygia. The island has far more character and charm than "mainland" Syracuse. On the downside, both these hotels might be full, especially during summer. Just in case, we've included some backup choices.

EXPENSIVE

Algilà Ortigia Charme Hotel ★ 💼 In a stately old building in the historic heart of Ortygia, this hotel opens onto panoramic views of the ancient Ortygia Sea. The latest restoration in 2010 has preserved its antique architecture while installing the latest amenities. Each of the rooms is furnished differently with antiques, four-poster beds, and elegant decoration, and each contains a colorfully tiled bathroom. Rooms open onto a blissful inner courtyard. Both a Mediterranean and an international cuisine are served in the hotel restaurant, with a special menu for vegetarians.

Via Vittorio Veneto 93, 96100 Siracusa. ✆ **0931-465186.** Fax 0931/463889. www.algila.it. 30 units. 149€–550€ double; 199€–450€ junior suite. AE, MC, V. **Amenities:** Restaurant; room service; Wi-Fi (free, in lobby). *In room:* A/C, TV, hair dryer.

Grand Hotel ★★★ Originally built in 1905, this is the best hotel in Syracuse, with a very appealing mix of modernity and old-world charm. It's set directly on the waterfront, near Ortygia's main access bridge to the Italian "mainland," in a stately four-story building that contains lots of inlaid marble and polished Belle Epoque hardwoods. The vaulted cellar has a bar with comfortable sofas and a collection of remnants—some museum quality—unearthed from this site during long-ago excavations. Guest rooms are contemporary and comfortable, with color schemes of beige and champagne. In some of the suites, duplex setups include interior staircases of polished steel. The bus station is only 100m (328 ft.) away.

Viale Mazzini 12, 96100 Siracusa. ✆ **0931-464600.** Fax 0931-464611. www.grandhotelsr.it. 58 units. 240€–250€ double; from 300€ suite. Rates include buffet breakfast. AE, DC, MC, V. Free parking. **Amenities:** Restaurant; 2 bars; babysitting; concierge. *In room:* A/C, TV, hair dryer, minibar, Wi-Fi (free).

Grand Hotel Villa Politi ★ For decades after its inauguration in 1862, the Grand Hotel Villa Politi was one of the three most elegant and sought-after hotels in Sicily. Today, it's a lot less prestigious, evoking, at least from the outside, either a hospital or a battered public school. The hotel is located in a residential neighborhood that's connected by roaring boulevards to the Archaeological Park, a 10-minute drive away. It's situated above what was used thousands of years ago as a rock quarry, the historic Latomie dei Cappuccini. The result is bizarre, even surreal, incorporating a dry, dusty garden with a deep chasm almost at the hotel's foundation. Most of the rooms reflect somewhat dowdy taste of lace curtains, high ceilings, comfy beds, and a definite sense of the south Italian bourgeoisie.

Via M. Politi 2, 96100 Siracusa. ✆ **0931-412121.** Fax 0931-36061. www.villapoliti.com. 100 units. 110€–240€ double; 360€ suite. Rates include buffet breakfast. AE, DC, MC, V. Free parking. Bus: 1 or 4. **Amenities:** 2 restaurants; bar; bikes; pool; room service; Wi-Fi (free, in lobby). *In room:* A/C, TV, hair dryer, minibar.

MODERATE

Albergo Domus Mariae ★ 🛏 This small-scale hotel originated in 1995 when a Catholic elementary school was transformed into a decent, well-managed lodging. It's owned by an order of Ursuline nuns, and although the desk staff and porters are likely to be laypersons, its manager is a hardworking, habit-clothed member of the order. This is the only hotel in Syracuse with its own chapel and a genuinely contemplative reading room. There's also a rooftop terrace for sunbathing. Rooms are fairly priced, with modern furniture and a no-nonsense approach to decor. Each has a tiled bathroom with shower. There are no attempts to foist religious education on guests; for most purposes, this is a conventional hotel, without any evangelistic mission.

Via Vittorio Veneto 76, 96100 Siracusa. ✆ **0931-24854.** Fax 0931-24858. www.domusmariae1.
it. 17 units. 140€–160€ double. Rates include continental breakfast. AE, MC, V. Free parking.
Amenities: Bar; room service. *In room:* A/C, TV, hair dryer, minibar.

INEXPENSIVE

B&B Artemide This converted old *palazzo* lies right in the historic center of Ortygia. It's the best bed-and-breakfast in the area, drawing young people, often backpackers, from all over the world. Furnishings are bare-bones yet comfortable, and the price is right. Only three of its units have private bathrooms, the others sharing a well-scrubbed hallway bathroom that's generally adequate for its purpose.

Via Maestranza 111, 96100 Siracusa. ✆ **338-3739050.** www.bedandbreakfastsicily.com. 6 units.
50€–80€ double. Rates include buffet breakfast. No credit cards. *In room:* No phone.

Gran Bretagna ★ No one knows the exact age of this once-decaying three-story *palazzo,* located between two restaurant-flanked side streets lying at the north end of the old city in the heart of Ortygia, but it has been restored with sensitivity. During a wholesale renovation, workers uncovered parts of the city's 16th-century fortifications which can be viewed through glass floor panels. In the courtyard you can also view some of the ancient wall. Bedrooms are well furnished and exceedingly spacious, with antique reproductions and in some cases frescoed ceilings. Some accommodations are suitable for three or four guests.

Via Savoia 21, 96100 Siracusa. ✆/fax **0931-68765.** www.hotelgranbretagna.it. 17 units. 100€–
125€ double; 135€–145€ triple. Rates include continental breakfast. AE, DC, MC, V. Free parking.
Amenities: Bar; bikes; room service. *In room:* A/C, TV, hair dryer, minibar.

Hotel Como ★ 😊 🍸 This small hotel, not far from the historic core, is one of the city's best bargains. It's located in the square at the train station and is convenient for those arriving on trains from Catania. It's little more than a utilitarian lodging, but many of the rooms are quite spacious and comfortably furnished. Each comes with a small, shower-only bathroom. Since some of the units are triples, this is a favorite with families, often from other parts of Sicily. Plus, its low-slung design and sense of style set the place apart from a typically tacky train-station hotel.

Piazza Stazione 13, 96100 Siracusa. ✆ **0931-464055.** Fax 0931-464056. www.hotelcomo
siracusa.com. 20 units. 70€–100€ double; 90€–120€ triple; 150€ suite. Rates include buffet
breakfast. AE, DC, MC, V. **Amenities:** Bar. *In room:* A/C, TV, hair dryer, minibar, Wi-Fi (free).

Hotel Gutkowski Modern, unpretentious, and with a distinct sense of being alive to the creative arts scene of Syracuse, this small hotel opened in 1999 in a waterfront town house on Ortygia. Don't expect any particular luxury, as everything here is utilitarian and a bit less comfortable than rooms at the nearby Albergo Domus Mariae (see above). It nonetheless has a welcoming atmosphere. The only meal offered is breakfast, which is served in a spartan-looking room next to the reception desk.

Lungomare Vittorini 26, 96100 Siracusa. ☎ **0931-465861.** Fax 0931-480505. www.guthotel.it. 25 units. 110€ double; 130€ triple. Rates include buffet breakfast. AE, MC, V. Free parking. **Amenities:** Bikes; Internet (free, in lobby). *In room:* A/C, TV, minibar.

L'Approdo delle Sirene 🕯   One of the town's best B&Bs is in an old *palazzo* by a canal; it's been restored and handsomely converted to receive guests. It offers excellent Sicilian hospitality with a panoramic terrace in a setting of jasmine and bougainvillea overlooking the sea. While the decor is simple, there's a kind of elegance to the comfortably furnished midsize bedrooms.

Riva Garibaldi 15, 96100 Siracusa. ☎ **0931-24857.** Fax 0931-483765. www.apprododellesirene. com. 8 units. 70€–99€ double; 90€–130€ triple. Rates include buffet breakfast. AE, DC, MC, V. Parking 18€. **Amenities:** Bikes; room service. *In room:* A/C, TV, hair dryer, minibar, Wi-Fi (free).

Where to Dine

Don Camillo ★ SEAFOOD/SICILIAN   This is one of the city's finest dining rooms, built near the historic center on the foundation of a 15th-century monastery that collapsed during an earthquake in 1693. The classy joint is full of atmosphere, with vaulted ceilings and potted plants. The cuisine is among the most creative in town, featuring lighter versions of time-tested Sicilian recipes. If you're a devotee of sea urchins (and not everyone is), the delectable morsels are particularly fresh tasting here. All kinds of fish are served, and the catch of the day can be prepared almost any way you like it. More than 450 different wines are available.

Via Maestranza 96. ☎ **0931-67133.** www.ristorantedoncamillosiracusa.it. Reservations recommended. Main courses 10€–14€. AE, DC, MC, V. Mon–Sat 12:30–2:30pm and 7:30–10:30pm. Closed Nov.

Minosse di Visetti ★ 🍴 SICILIAN   This well-run restaurant is more formal and a lot more sedate than many of its competitors on Ortygia Island. The chef wins praise for his fresh mussels with cherry tomatoes. The spaghetti with clams is marked by intense, refined flavors, and the fish soup is one of the best in town.

In the Hotel Roma, Via Roma 66. ☎ **0931-465626.** www.hotelromasiracusa.it. Main courses 10€–18€. MC, V. Daily noon–3pm and 7–11pm. Take any minibus leaving Piazza delle Poste and get off at Via Mirabella.

Syracuse After Dark

Much of the nightlife in summer takes place in satellite villages, particularly along the coast. Unless specifically stated, hours can be irregular; check before heading to one of the hot spots, especially those out of town.

In Syracuse itself, you can visit **La Nottola,** Via Gargallo 61 (☎ **0931-60009;** www.lanottolaricevimenti.it), on a small street near Via Maestanza. This stylish jazz club/piano bar/disco attracts a well-dressed younger crowd.

Syracuse has a number of other worthy bars and cafes, including **Bar Bonomo,** Corso Gelone 48 (☎ **0931-67845**), which is more of a bar/bakery. Its gelato is some of the best in town. The spacious **Bar del Ponte,** Piazza Pancali (© **0931-64312**), is near Syracuse's most famous fountain and serves all kinds of drinks, snacks, and excellent gelato. Tables overflow onto the square in fair weather.

A Side Trip to Baroque Noto ★★

From Syracuse, head southwest on A18 for 31km (19 miles) to reach Noto, which is set amid olive groves and almond trees on a plateau overlooking the Asinaro Valley. Noto dates from the 9th century and knew a Greek, Roman, Byzantine, Arab, Norman, Aragónese, and even Spanish culture before the 1962 earthquake destroyed it. Many Sicilian artists and artisans have worked to rebuild the town into a baroque gem with uniform buildings of soft limestone. Constructed somewhat like a stage set, curvaceous and curvilinear accents and potbellied wrought-iron balconies adorn the facades.

To get your bearings, stop at the **tourist office** at Via Gioberti 13 (© **0931-836503**), to pick up a map and some tips about exploring the town on foot. The office is open from May to September daily from 9am to 1pm and 3:30 to 6:30pm, and from October to March Monday through Friday from 8am to 2pm and 3:30 to 6:30pm.

Mercifully, traffic has been diverted away from Noto's heart, to protect the fragile buildings on which restoration began in 1987—and not a moment too soon. Your best approach is through the monumental **Royal Gate (Porta Reale),** crowned by three symbols—a dog, a swan, and a tower, representing the town's former allegiance to the Bourbon monarchy. From here, take **Corso Vittorio Emanuele,** going through the **old patricians' quarter.** The rich-looking, honey-colored buildings along this street are some of the most captivating on the island. This street will take you to the three most important piazzas.

You arrive first at **Piazza Immacolata,** dominated by the baroque facade of **San Francesco all'Immacolata** (© **0931-573192**), which still contains artworks rescued from a Franciscan church in the old town. Notable works include a painted wooden *Madonna and Child* (1564) believed to be the work of Antonio Monachello. The church is open daily 8:30am to noon and 4 to 7:30pm; admission is free. Immediately to the left stands the **St. Salvador Monastery (Monastero del Santissimo Salvatore),** characterized by an elegant tower, its windows adorned with wrought-iron balconies. When it reopens, it will contain a minor collection of religious art and artifacts.

The next square is **Piazza Municipio ★**, the most majestic of the trio. It's dominated by the **Palazzo Ducezio** (© **0931-98611**). The graceful town hall with curvilinear elements is enclosed by a classical portico, the work of architect Vincenzo Sinatra (no relation to Ol' Blue Eyes). The upper section of this palace was added as late as the 1950s. Its most beautiful room is the Louis XI–style Hall of Representation (Salone di Rappresentanza), decorated with gold and stucco. On the vault is a Mazza fresco representing the mythological figure of Ducezio founding Neas (the ancient name of Noto).

On one side of the square, a broad flight of steps leads to the **Duomo,** flanked by two horseshoe-shape hedges. The cathedral was inspired by models of Borromini's churches in Rome and completed in 1776. In 1996, the dome collapsed, destroying a large section of the nave. The cathedral reopened after an 11-year, $53-million restoration. Over the years, restoration employed 83,000

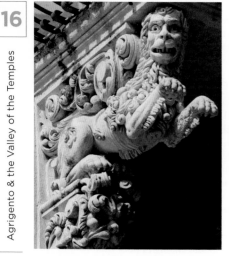
A detail from one of Palazzo Villadorata's balconies in Noto.

workers at various times. Many of them were trained in traditional building techniques and had to use stone from nearby quarries. The cathedral was rebuilt exactly as it was in its heyday, using whenever possible the original material. On the far side of the cathedral is the **Palazzo Villadorata,** graced with a classic facade. Its six **extravagant balconies ★★** are supported by sculpted buttresses of horses, griffins, and grotesque bald and bearded figures with chubby-cheeked cherubs at their bellies. The *palazzo* is divided into 90 rooms; the most beautiful are the Yellow Hall (Salone Giallo), the Green Hall (Salone Verde), and the Red Hall (Salone Rosso), with their frescoed domes from the 18th century. The charming Feasts Hall (Salone delle Feste) is dominated by a fresco representing mythological scenes. In one of its aisles, the *palazzo* contains a *pinacoteca* (picture gallery) with antique manuscripts, rare books, and portraits of noble families.

The final square is **Piazza XVI Maggio,** dominated by the convex facade of its **Chiesa di San Domenico ★**, with two tiers of columns separated by a high cornice. The interior is filled with polychrome marble altars and is open daily 8am to noon and 2 to 5pm. Directly in front of the church is a public garden, the **Villetta d'Ercole,** named for its 18th-century fountain honoring Hercules.

Right off Corso Vittorio Emanuele is one of Noto's most fascinating streets, **Via Nicolaci ★**, lined with magnificent baroque buildings.

Noto in summer also is known for some fine **beaches** nearby; the best are 6km (3¾ miles) away at **Noto Marina.** You can catch a bus at the Giardini Pubblici in Noto. The one-way fare is 3.50€.

AGRIGENTO ★★★ & THE VALLEY OF THE TEMPLES ★★★

129km (80 miles) S of Palermo, 175km (109 miles) SE of Trapani, 217km (135 miles) W of Syracuse

Agrigento's amazing Valley of the Temples is one of the most memorable and evocative sights of the ancient world. Greek colonists from Gela (Caltanissetta) called this area Akragas when they established a beachhead in the 6th century B.C. In time, the settlement grew to become one of the most prosperous cities in Magna Graecia. A great deal of that growth is attributed to the despot Phalaris, who ruled from 571 to 555 B.C. and is said to have roasted his victims inside a brass bull. He eventually met the same fate.

Empedocles (ca. 490–430 B.C.), the Greek philosopher and politician (also considered by some the founder of medicine in Italy), was the most famous son of Akragas. He formulated the theory that matter consists of four elements (earth, fire, water, and air), modified by the agent's love and strife. In modern times the town produced playwright Luigi Pirandello (1867–1936), who won the Nobel prize for literature in 1934.

Like nearby Selinunte, the city was attacked by war-waging Carthaginians, beginning in 406 B.C. In the 3rd century B.C., the city changed hands between the Carthaginians and the Romans until it finally succumbed to Roman domination by 210 B.C. It was then known as Agrigentium.

The modern part of Agrigento occupies a hill, and the narrow casbahlike streets show the influence of the conquering Saracens. Heavy Allied bombing during World War II necessitated much rebuilding. The result is, for the most part, uninspired and not helped by all the cement factories in the area. But below the town stretch the long reaches of the Valley of the Temples (Valle dei Templi), where you'll see some of the greatest Greek ruins in the world.

Visit Agrigento for its past, not for the modern incarnation. However, once you've been awed by the ruined temples, you can visit the *centro storico* (town center) with its tourist boutiques hawking postcards and T-shirts, and enjoy people-watching at a cafe along Via Atenea. When it gets too hot (as it so often does), flee to a beach at nearby San Leone.

Essentials

GETTING THERE The main rail station, **Stazione Centrale,** Piazza Marconi (© **892021**), is downhill from Piazzale Aldo Moro and Piazza Vittorio Emanuele. The train trip from Palermo takes 2 hours and costs 8€ one-way; there are 12 trains daily. From Syracuse, you must first take one of four daily trains to Catania; the 6-hour trip costs 20€ one-way. Three trains a day make the trip from Ragusa to Agrigento, at a cost of 12€ one-way. This is an extremely awkward connection, as you have to change trains at Gela and then at Canicattì. Depending on the train, the trip can last from 5 to 9 hours.

Cuffaro (© **0922-403150;** www.cuffaro.info) runs nine buses per day from Palermo; the trip takes 2 hours and costs 9€ one-way.

By **car** from Syracuse, take S115 through Gela. From Palermo, cut southeast along S121, which becomes S189 before it finally reaches Agrigento and the Mediterranean. Allow about 2½ hours for this jaunt.

VISITOR INFORMATION The **tourist office,** Piazzale Aldo Moro 7 (© **0922-20454**), is open Sunday through Friday 8am to 1pm and 3 to 8pm, Saturday 8am to 1pm. Another tourist office is at Via Empedocle 73 (© **0922-20391**), open Monday to Friday 8am to 2:30pm and Wednesday 3:30 to 7pm.

Wandering Among the Ruins

Many writers are fond of suggesting that the Greek ruins in the **Valley of the Temples (Valle dei Templi)** be viewed at dawn or sunset, when their mysterious aura is indeed heightened. Regrettably, you can't get very close at those times. Instead, search them out under the cobalt-blue Sicilian sky. The backdrop is idyllic, especially in spring, when the striking almond trees blossom.

Ticket booths are found at the west and east entrances (© **0922-26191;** www.consorzioarcadia.it); they're 10€ for adults and free for those 17 and under.

The Temple of Concord.

Hours are daily from 8:30am to 7pm. Board a bus or climb into your car to investigate. Riding out the Strada Panoramica, you'll first approach (on your left) the **Temple of Juno (Tempio di Giunone)** ★★, erected sometime in the mid–5th century B.C. Many of its Doric columns have been restored. As you climb the blocks, note the remains of a cistern as well as a sacrificial altar in front. The temple affords good views of the entire valley.

The **Temple of Concord (Tempio della Concordia)** ★★★, which you'll come to next, ranks with the Temple of Hephaestos in Athens as the best-preserved Greek temple in the world. With 13 columns on its side, 6 in front, and 6 in back, the temple was built in the peripheral hexastyle. You'll see the clearest example in Sicily of an inner temple. In the late 6th century A.D., the pagan structure was transformed into a Christian church, which might have saved it for posterity, although today it's been stripped down to its classical purity.

The **Temple of Hercules (Tempio di Ercole)** ★★ is the oldest, dating from the 6th century B.C. Badly ruined (only eight pillars are standing), it once ranked in size with the Temple of Zeus. At one time the temple sheltered a celebrated statue of Hercules. The infamous Gaius Verres, the Roman magistrate who became an especially bad governor of Sicily, attempted to steal the image as part of his temple-looting tear across the island. Astonishingly, you can still see black sears from fires set by long-ago Carthaginian invaders.

The **Temple of Jove/Zeus (Tempio di Giove)** ★ was the largest in the valley, similar in some respects to the Temple of Apollo at Selinunte, until it was ruined by an earthquake. It even impressed Goethe. In front of the structure was a large altar. The giant on the ground was one of several *telamones* (male caryatids) used to support the largest Greek temple in the world.

The so-called **Temple of Castor and Pollux (Tempio di Dioscuri),** with four Doric columns intact, is composed of fragments from different buildings. At various times it has been designated as a temple honoring Castor and Pollux, the twin sons of Leda and deities of seafarers; Demeter (Ceres), the goddess of marriage and of the fertile earth; and Persephone, the daughter of Zeus and the symbol of spring. **Note:** On some maps, this is called Tempio di Castore e Polluce. The temples can usually be visited daily from 8:30am until 1 hour before sunset. City bus nos. 1, 2, and 3 run to the valley from the train station in Agrigento.

More Attractions

A combination ticket for admission to the Museo Regionale Archeologico and the Valley of the Temples costs 10€. The **Museo Regionale Archeologico (Regional Archaeological Museum)** ★, near San Nicola, on Contrada San Nicola at the outskirts of town on the way to the Valle dei Templi (𝒞 **0922-401565**), is open daily 9am to 7pm. Admission is 8€, free for children 17 and under. Its most important exhibit is a head of one of the *telamones* from the Tempio di Giove. The collection of Greek vases is also impressive. Many of the artifacts on display were dug up when Agrigento was excavated. Take bus no. 1, 2, or 3.

Casa di Pirandello (Pirandello's House), Contrada Caos, Frazione Caos (𝒞 **0922-511826**), is the former home of the 1934 Nobel Prize winner, known for his plays *Six Characters in Search of an Author* and *Enrico IV*. Although Agrigentans back then might not have liked his portrayal of Italy, all is forgiven now, and Pirandello is the local boy who made good. In fact, the Teatro Luigi Pirandello at Piazza Municipio bears his name. His *casa natale* is now a museum devoted to memorabilia pertaining to the playwright's life. His tomb lies under his favorite pine tree, a few hundred yards from the house and grounds, which are open daily from 9am to 1pm and 2 to 7pm. Admission is 4€. The birthplace lies outside of town in the village of Caos (catch bus no. 1 from Piazza Marconi), just west of the temple zone.

The Temple of Hercules.

Where to Stay

Colleverde Park Hotel ★★

Sheathed in a layer of ocher-colored stucco, this is one of our favorite hotels in Agrigento, partly for its verdant garden, partly for its helpful staff, and partly for its location convenient to both the ancient and the medieval monuments of Agrigento. It has the finest hotel garden in town, a labyrinth of vine-covered arbors, terra-cotta terraces, and enormous sheets of white canvas stretched overhead as protection from the glaring sun. The hotel's eminently tasteful glass-sided restaurant is the site of many local wedding receptions. The decor throughout is discreetly elegant, providing refuge from the hysteria that sometimes permeates Agrigento, particularly its roaring traffic.

Guest rooms have tiled bathrooms (all with tub/shower combinations), lots of exposed wood, charming artwork, and big windows that in some cases reveal views of the temples of Concordia and Juno.

Via Panoramica dei Templi, 92100 Agrigento. ℂ **0922-29555.** Fax 0922-29012. www.colleverde hotel.it. 48 units. 135€–190€ double; 160€–210€ junior suite. Rates include continental breakfast. AE, DC, MC, V. Free parking. Bus: 1, 2, or 3. **Amenities:** Restaurant; bar. *In room:* A/C, TV, hair dryer, minibar, Wi-Fi (6€ per hr.).

Foresteria Baglio della Luna ★★ 📖 In 1995, one of the most historic medieval sites in Agrigento was meticulously restored by a local antiques dealer. The first impression you'll get is of a squarish medieval tower, ringed by a protective wall, in a well-landscaped compound that rises above a sun-blasted setting west of Agrigento. Originating in the 1200s as a watchtower, then rebuilt in the 1500s by Emperor Charles V, it eventually evolved into an aristocratic manor house. You'll enter a cobble-covered courtyard, off of which lie the stylishly decorated guest rooms. Each evokes a romantic lodging in an upscale home, and many have antique headboards, flowered upholsteries, and marble-clad bathrooms. Hotel Villa Athena (see below) may have a closer view of the temples, but this place far surpasses it in charm and hospitality.

Contrada Maddalusa (SS640), Valle dei Templi, 92100 Agrigento. ℂ **0922-511061.** Fax 0922-598802. www.bagliodellaluna.com. 24 units. 200€–280€ double; 300€–501€ suite. Half board (breakfast and dinner) 50€ extra per person. AE, DC, MC, V. Free parking. Bus: 1 or 3. **Amenities:** 2 restaurants; bar; babysitting; bikes; Jacuzzi; room service. *In room:* A/C, TV, hair dryer, minibar, Wi-Fi (free).

Hotel Villa Athena ★ 🖐 This 18th-century villa rises from the landscape in the Valley of the Temples, less than 3km (1¾ miles) from town. It's worn and overpriced, but its location at the archaeological site is so dramatic that we like to stay here anyway, if only to see the ruins lit up at night from our room. Guest rooms are comfortable, with little style. Ask for a room with a view of the temple, preferably one with a balcony. The perfect choice would be no. 205, which frames a panorama of the Temple of Concord. Frankly, this could be a great hotel with a major overhaul. The staff is known for being the unfriendliest in Agrigento, yet the setting is so compelling that there are those of us who can overlook the drawbacks. At any rate, it remains the most popular and most famous hotel in Agrigento; be sure to reserve at least a month in advance.

Via Passeggiata Archeologica 33, 92100 Agrigento. ℂ **0922-596288.** Fax 0922-402180. www. hotelvillaathena.it. 40 units. 190€–330€ double; 290€–390€ junior suite; from 400€ suite. Rates include continental breakfast. AE, DC, MC, V. Free parking. Bus: 2. **Amenities:** Restaurant; 2 bars; concierge; pool; room service. *In room:* A/C, TV/DVD, CD player, minibar, Wi-Fi (free).

Where to Dine

Restaurant at the Hotel Villa Athena ★ CONTINENTAL The formally dressed staff here tends to be brusque, despite a long tradition of welcoming visitors from far away. But the site can be so magical, at least for first-timers to Agrigento, that a midsummer dinner on the terrace can be a memorable experience unaffected by food, staff, weather, or circumstances. If you opt for lunch here, it will be served in a crescent-shaped stone-and-stucco building whose curtains are usually closed against the noon glare. But it's at dinner that the true magic emerges. Views sweep from the torch-lit terrace to the nearby Temple of

Concordia (which literally looms before you) in ways unmatched by any other establishment in Agrigento. Begin, perhaps, with a duet of smoked salmon and swordfish or else a fish shellfish salad. We're fond of the sea bass flavored with saffron. The special risotto is made with pumpkin flowers, lobster, zucchini, and vodka. A "fantasy" of ice creams and sherbets is served to end the repast.

Via Passeggiata Archeologica 33. © **0922-596288.** www.hotelvillaathena.it. Reservations required. Main courses 18€–24€. DC, MC, V. Daily 12:30–2:30pm and 7:30–9:30pm (until 10pm June–Sept). Bus: 2.

Trattoria dei Templi ★ SICILIAN   This charming, discreet, and extremely well-managed restaurant sits at the bottom of the hill between medieval Agrigento and the Valley of the Temples. Inside, you'll find brick-trimmed ceiling vaults, a polite crowd of diners from virtually everywhere in Europe, and excellent food that's served on hand-painted china. Menu items, served with efficiency by a staff of young, well-trained waiters, include *cavatelli valle dei Templi tipo Norma* (pasta with eggplant and cheese); *panzerotti della casa* (big ravioli stuffed with white fish and served with a seafood sauce); and local fish with herbs, white wine, lemon juice, capers, olives, and orange zest.

Via Panoramica dei Templi 15. © **0922-403110.** www.trattoriadeitempli.com. Reservations recommended. Main courses 9€–22€. AE, DC, MC, V. July–Aug Mon–Sat 12:30–3pm and 7:30–11pm; Sept–June Sun–Thurs 12:30–3pm and 7:30–11pm. Bus: 1, 2, or 3.

LAMPEDUSA

240km (149 miles) S of Argigento

After visiting the ancient glories of Agrigento, you can drive only 7km (4¼ miles) southwest to the Porto Empedocle. Take the ferry to the African island of Lampedusa, which is owned by Sicily, for an offbeat adventure.

Little more than dry rocks, the remote and barren Isole Pelagie have at long last been discovered by visitors, mostly Italians from the mainland, who flock here in July and August. The main island is **Lampedusa,** which is the name of both the largest island and its chief town. It lies farther from the mainland of Sicily than Malta. Upon arrival, you'll think you've arrived in Tunisia or even Libya, which is not surprising. The islands belong to Sicily but are really islands of an archipelago of the African continent (and in recent years, Lampedusa has become a major route for Africans immigrating illegally to Europe). Lampedusa's flora and fauna are similar to those of North Africa nearby, and it's an arid island with a constant water shortage because of irregular rainfall.

If you go by ferry (see below), you'll stop first at **Linosa,** the northernmost of the islands and the tip of a submerged, ancient volcano. The ferry continues to Lampedusa, its final stop. Lampedusa lies 50km (31 miles) south of Linosa and is shaped like a giant raft inclined to one side.

Essentials

GETTING THERE   The quickest way is to fly from Palermo to Lampedusa year-round on **Meridiana** (© **892928;** www.meridiana.it). The trip takes only 1 hour. The small airport lies on the southeastern side of town. Always book your hotel in advance, and chances are a courtesy bus will be arranged for you at the airport.

Most arrivals are from Porto Empedocle on a **Siremar** ferry, operating year-round and making the trip from Porto Empedocle to Lampedusa in 8 hours, 15 minutes. Ferries from Porto Empedocle leave daily at midnight, returning the following morning at 10:15am. The trip costs 39€ to 80€ one-way, and cars are transported for 157€ to 192€. The Sirremar office in Porto Empedocle is at Via Molo 13 (℡ **0922-636683;** www.siremar.it); in Lampedusa, the office is on Longomare L. Rizzo (℡ **0922-970003**). Ferries arrive at the harbor in Lampedusa, Porto Vecchio, a 10-minute walk into town. Taxis await arrivals, or you can take a minibus into town in summer.

If you wish, you can rent a motor scooter at **Autonoleggio d'Agostino,** Via Bixio 1 (℡ **0922-970755;** www.autonoleggiodag.com), and circle the island in a day. A motor scooter costs 15€ per day. You can rent a bike at **Prometeomare** on Via S. Pellico 12 (℡ **0922-971607;** www.autonoleggio dag.com). Bikes cost about 10€ a day.

Exploring the Island

"We have the sun, we have the Mediterranean Sea," claims the island's director of tourism. "What more could you want?" That about says it.

The best beach on this 11km (6¾-mile) island is **Isola dei Conigli** or Rabbit Island, lying 7km (4¼ miles) south of town. It's right off the shore, and you can swim over to it except when the tide is out and then you can walk over. In addition to good sandy beaches, there is a small nature reserve here where the endangered Caretta turtle lays her eggs between July and August. A small bus in town runs to the departure point for Rabbit Island every hour during the day. There are no facilities on Rabbit Island, so take what provisions you need.

In summer, you can go down to the quay side in Lampedusa and negotiate a boat tour around the island with one of the local fishermen. Count on paying 20€ per person for the half-day trip. Double the price for a full-day jaunt, with lunch included. There is little of interest in the interior.

The beach at Isola dei Conigli, just offshore from Lampedusa.

Where to Stay

Cavalluccio Marino 🦐   This is one of the best bargains in town, although it's a simple place furnished very basically yet comfortably. Opened in 1980, it lies only 100m (328 ft.) from the sea and about 500m (1,640 ft.) from the center of town. Two of its units contain verandas and some of the others have balconies with a view. The food is good and hearty, mainly fresh fish dishes.

Contrada Cala Croce 3, 92010 Lampedusa. ℂ **0922-970053.** Fax 0922-970672. www.hotel cavallucciomarino.com. 10 units. 85€–130€ per person double. Rates include half board. AE, DC, MC, V. Free parking. Closed Nov–May 15. **Amenities:** Restaurant; bar; room service. *In room:* A/C, TV, hair dryer.

Cupola Bianca ★   At 1km (½ mile) from the center of town, this modern hotel—decorated in a Mediterranean Arabesque style—is the best in the archipelago. On a headland studded with olive and palm trees, it rises from the earth like an oasis in Morocco. Bedrooms are spacious for the most part, ranging from standard to superior. The most expensive are in a North African–like structure called Dammusi, with extensive verandas. Furnishings are in rattan. The place has great style in this remote part of the world.

Contrada Madonna, 92010 Lampedusa. ℂ **0922-971274.** Fax 0922-973885. www.hotelcupola bianca.it. 23 units. 140€–230€ double; 270€–385€ suite. Rates include half board. AE, MC, V. Free parking. Closed Nov–May. **Amenities:** Restaurant; bar; airport transfers (free); pool; room service. *In room:* A/C, TV, hair dryer.

Martello   This hotel might have been transported from the center of Tangier. It lies on a spit of land dividing Cala Guitgia from Cala Salina, a small marina, at a point 80m (263 ft.) from the beach. Guests gather in the small garden to enjoy drinks and night breezes. Most of the rooms are spacious with a sea view from a private balcony. All are comfortably furnished in a standard motel style.

Contrada Guitgia, 92010 Lampedusa. ℂ **0922-970025.** Fax 0922-971696. www.hotelmartello. it. 25 units. 40€ per person. Rates include buffet breakfast. AE, MC, V. Free parking. Closed mid-Nov to mid-Mar. **Amenities:** Restaurant; bar. *In room:* A/C, TV, hair dryer.

Where to Dine

In your search for a bar or restaurant, walk along **Via Roma** in the center of town at night. All the kitchens here serve fresh fish or couscous from North Africa.

Gemelli MEDITERRANEAN/SICILIAN   While competition may not be very steep, Gemelli earns its status as the best restaurant in town with hearty cuisine that's a favorite with islanders. The local spaghetti appears with a fresh sardine sauce, and the chef even makes a must-try Spanish paella. We are especially fond of the *seppie ripiene* or stuffed cuttlefish, and also couscous made with grouper. The Sicilian fish soup is also the best in town.

Via Cala Pisana 2. ℂ **0922-970699.** Reservations recommended July–Aug. Main courses 12€–30€. AE, DC, MC, V. Daily 7:30–11:30pm. Closed Nov–Mar.

SELINUNTE ★★

122km (76 miles) SW of Palermo, 113km (70 miles) W of Agrigento, 89km (55 miles) SE of Trapani

Guy de Maupassant called the splendid jumble of ruins at Selinunte "an immense heap of fallen columns, now aligned and placed side by side on the ground like dead soldiers, now having fallen in a chaotic manner." Regardless of what shape they're in, the only reason to visit Selinunte is for its ruins, not for the unappealing modern towns (Mazara del Vallo and Castelvetrano) that have grown up around it.

One of the superb colonies of ancient Greece, Selinunte traces its history from the 7th century B.C., when immigrants from Megara Hyblaea (Syracuse) set out to build a new colony. They succeeded, erecting a city of power and prestige adorned with many temples. But that was calling attention to a good thing. Much of Selinunte's history involves seemingly endless conflicts with the Elymi people of Segesta (see "Segesta," later in this chapter). Siding with Selinunte's rival, Hannibal virtually leveled the city in 409 B.C. The city never recovered its former glory and ultimately fell into decay.

Getting There

From Palermo, Trapani, or Marsala, you can make rail connections to Castelvetrano on the southern coast of Sicily, 23km (14 miles) from the ruins. Once at Castelvetrano, you board a bus for the final push to Selinunte. Rail fares are reasonable; a one-way ticket from Palermo to Castelvetrano, for example, costs only 9€ each way, the trip taking 2½ hours.

Lumia buses (© **0922-20414;** www.autolineelumia.it) run to Castelvetrano from Agrigento. Schedules vary; call for information. Buses arrive in Castelvetrano in front of the rail depot. From here you must go the rest of the way by a bus operated by **Autoservizi Salemi** (© **0923-981120;** www.autoservizisalemi.it); the one-way fare for the 20-minute trip is 1.50€.

The ruins at Selinunte.

Selinunte is on the southern coast of Sicily and is best explored by **car** because public transportation is awkward. From Agrigento, take S115 northwest into Castelvetrano; then follow the signposted secondary road marked SELINUNTE, which leads south to the sea. Allow at least 2 hours to drive here from either Palermo or Agrigento.

Exploring the Archaeological Garden

Selinunte's temples lie in scattered ruins, the honey-colored stone littering the ground as if an earthquake had struck (as one did in ancient times). Some sections and fragments of temples still stand, with great columns pointing to the sky. From 9am to 1 hour before sunset daily, you can walk through the monument zone. Some of it has been partially excavated and reconstructed. Admission is 6€ for adults, free for children 17 and under.

The temples, in varying states of preservation, are designated by letters. They're dedicated to such mythological figures as Apollo and Hera (Juno); most date from the 6th and 5th centuries B.C. Near the entrance, the Doric **Temple E** contains fragments of an inner temple. Standing on its ruins before the sun goes down, you can look across the water that washes up on the shores of Africa, from which the Carthaginian fleet emerged to destroy the city. **Temple G,** in scattered ruins north of Temple E, was one of the largest erected in Sicily and was also built in the Doric style. The ruins of the less impressive **Temple F** lie between temples E and G. Not much remains of Temple F, and little is known about it.

After viewing temples E, F, and G, all near the parking lot at the entrance, you can get in your car and drive along the Strada dei Templi west to the Acropoli (or walk there in about 20 min.). The site of the western temples was the **Acropoli,** which was enclosed within defensive walls and built from the 6th century to the 5th century B.C.

The most impressive site here is **Temple C.** In 1925, 14 of the 17 columns of Temple C were reerected. This is the earliest surviving temple of ancient Selinus, built in the 6th century B.C. and probably dedicated to Hercules or Apollo. The pediment, ornamented with a clay Gorgon's head, lies broken on the ground. Temple C towers over the other ruins and gives you a better impression of what all the temples might have looked like at one time.

Also here is **Temple A,** which, like the others, remains in scattered ruins. The streets of the Acropoli were laid out along classical lines, with a trio of principal arteries bisected at right angles by a grid of less important streets. The Acropoli was the site of the most important public and religious buildings, and it was also the residence of the town's aristocrats. If you look down below, you can see the site of the town's harbor, now overgrown. After all this earthquake damage, you can only imagine the full glory of this place in its golden era.

Where to Stay

The site of the ruins contains no hotels, restaurants, or watering holes of note. Most visitors come to visit the temples on a day trip while they're based elsewhere. But there are a handful of accommodations in the seafront village of Marinella, about 1.6km (1 mile) east of Selinunte. To reach Marinella, you'll travel along a narrow country road.

Hotel Alceste This concrete structure is about a 15-minute walk from the ruins. Guest rooms have small tiled bathrooms with tub/shower combos. Most visitors, however, stop only for a visit to the plant-filled courtyard, where in summer there's musical entertainment, dancing, cabaret, and theater. In July and August, the hotel hosts what may be the highest percentage of academics of any accommodations in Sicily; they come from universities throughout the world. The somewhat shy and very kind owner, Orazio Torrente, is charming, as is his family. The airy, bustling restaurant is open daily for lunch and dinner, and is sometimes filled with busloads of visitors from as far away as Milan. Main courses cost from 8€ to 15€.

Via Alceste 21, 91022 Marinella di Selinunte. ✆ **0924-46184.** Fax 0924-46143. www.hotel alceste.it. 30 units. 50€–90€ double. Rates include continental breakfast. AE, DC, MC, V. **Amenities:** Restaurant; bar; bikes; room service. *In room:* A/C, TV, hair dryer.

Where to Dine

Hotel Alceste, above, is also a good choice for dining.

Ristorante Pierrot ★ ✂ SICILIAN Ristorante Pierrot, the best place in the area for regional food, boasts a terrace opening onto the Mediterranean. With a seafront table and a rustic decor, you can enjoy fresh produce from the market and fish caught that same day. Tired travelers visiting the ruins refresh themselves with invigorating cuisine prepared by skilled cooks. Since you're so close to North Africa, fish couscous regularly appears on the menu. *Orecchiette* (a homemade pasta) is served with succulent scampi. Another homemade pasta, and one we like even better, is *spaccatelle con melenzane e pesca spada* (homemade pasta sautéed with swordfish, eggplant, and tomato sauce). Nearly everyone orders one of the seafood pasta dishes, such as one with sea urchins, mussels, and shrimp. But you can also order your catch of the day grilled or sautéed to your specifications.

Via Marco Polo 108, Marinella. ✆ **0924-46205.** www.ristorantepierrotselinunte.it. Reservations recommended. Main courses 6€–18€; fixed-price menus 15€–30€. AE, DC, MC, V. Daily 10am–3pm and 7pm–midnight.

PALERMO ★★★

233km (145 miles) W of Messina, 721km (447 miles) S of Naples, 934km (579 miles) S of Rome

As you arrive in Palermo, you start spotting blond, blue-eyed bambini all over the place. Don't be surprised. If fair-haired children don't fit your concept of what a Sicilian should look like, remember that the Normans landed here in 1060 and launched a campaign to wrest control of the island from the Arabs. Today you can see elements of both cultures, notably in Palermo's architecture—a unique style, Norman-Arabic.

The city is Sicily's largest port, its capital, and a jumble of contradictions. Whole neighborhoods remain bombed out and not yet rebuilt from World War II, yet Palermo boasts some of the greatest sights and museums in Sicily. Unemployment, poverty, traffic, crime, and crowding are rampant, and city services just don't run as they should. But amid the decay, you'll find gloriously stuccoed oratories, glittering 12th-century mosaics, art museums, baroque palaces, and busy fish markets bursting with life and color. Palermo is not the most welcoming of towns, and parts of the city can be downright dangerous; but there's a lot of

Palermo

Villa Malfitano

Piazza Lolli

Piazza S. Oliva

Piazza di Giustizia

Piazza Castelnuovo

Piazza Sturzo

Borgo Vecchio

Piazza Florio

NEW CITY

Teatro Massimo

Piazza Verdi

Piazza San Domenico

La Cala

Duomo

OLD CENTER

Vucciria Market

Piazza Indipendenza

Piazza Bellini

San Francesco d'Assisi

Piazza Marina

Ballarò Market

Piazza Magione

LA KALSA

Santa Teresa

Piazza G. Cesare

Stazione Centrale

Venice
Florence
Rome
Palermo
Sicily

0   100 Mi
0   100 Km

fascinating culture and history to discover if you're the adventurous sort. Thankfully, restoration efforts are underway. More than $60 million has been spent to restore buildings, clean up facades, and repair streets. The picture is mixed, but it's slowly brightening.

Essentials

GETTING THERE   If you **fly** from Rome or Naples, you'll land at **Falcone e Borsellino airport** (© 091-7020111; www.gesap.it), 31km (19 miles) west of Palermo. You can catch a local airport **bus** from the airport to Piazza Giulio Cesare (central train station); the fare is 6€. For the same trip, a **taxi** is likely to charge at least 35€—and more, if the driver thinks he can get away with it. It's also possible to rent a **car** at the airport (all the major firms are represented) and drive into Palermo. Allow 20 to 30 minutes—longer, if traffic is bad—to get to the center of town from the airport.

For information about traveling by **train,** see "Getting to Sicily," at the beginning of the chapter. After a 3½-hour ride from Messina across the north coast, you arrive at Palermo's station at **Piazza Giulio Cesare** (© 892021), on the east side of town, linked to the center by buses and taxis.

If you prefer bus travel, we'd suggest it for shorter hauls on the island itself. There are convenient links to major cities by **SAIS,** Via Balsamo 16 (© 091-6166028; www.saisautolinee.it). From Messina, it takes 3¼ hours and from Catania 2½ hours to reach Palermo overland. **Segesta,** Via Balsamo 26 (© 091-6169039; www.segesta.it) also has bus links to Trapani in the west (trip time to Palermo: 2 hr.). **Cuffaro,** Via Balsamo 13 (© 091-6161510; www.cuffaro.info), runs between Palermo and the city of Agrigento in 2½ hours.

Palermo's Duomo.

The bus stations in Palermo along Via Balsamo are adjacent to the rail station. After you arrive by **car** from mainland Italy at Messina, head west on A20, which becomes S113, then A20 again, and finally A19 before its final approach to Palermo.

VISITOR INFORMATION   There are tourist offices at strategic points, including the Palermo airport (© **091-591698;** www.palermotourism.com) and the main train station (© **091-6165914**). The principal office is the **Azienda Autonoma Turismo,** Piazza Castelnuovo 34 (© **091-6058351**), open Monday to Friday 8:30am to 2pm and 3 to 6pm. When you stop in, ask for a good city map.

SAFETY   Be especially alert. Palermo is home to some of the most skilled pickpockets on the continent. Don't flaunt expensive jewelry, cameras, or wads of bills. Women who carry handbags are especially vulnerable to purse snatchers on Vespas. It's best to park your car in a garage rather than on the street; wherever you leave it, don't leave valuables inside. Police squads operate mobile centers throughout the town to help combat street crime.

GETTING AROUND   A ride on a municipal bus costs 1.30€. For information, call **AMAT,** Via Borrelli 16 (© **848-800817;** www.amat.pa.it). Most passengers buy their tickets at tobacco shops (*tabacchi*) before boarding.

A tourist bus called *City Sightseeing* (www.palermo.city-sightseeing.it) begins and ends its circuit at the landmark Teatro Politeama (via the Emerico Amari side). It stops at many of the major monuments of Palermo, including the Duomo and the Royal Palace. Departures are at 9:30am daily; tickets are sold on board, and there are no advance reservations. The cost is 20€ for adults, 10€ ages 14 and under. For more information call © **091-589429.**

Palermo also has a **metropolitana** subway system, but it's not well developed. It's often faster to take a bus. The system will get you to the Capella Palatina, but it's mostly for use to the nontouristy residential suburbs.

If you can afford it, consider renting a taxi for the day to explore Palermo attractions. A taxi sightseeing of Palermo costs 70€ to 150€. For further information on taxi sightseeing call © **091-513311.** Most drivers speak only a few words of English, but somehow they manage. You can request an English-speaking driver; perhaps one will be available.

SPECIAL EVENTS   July brings a month of performances to the **Teatro di Verdura Villa Castelnuovo,** an open-air seaside theater that hosts classical music, jazz, and ballet performances. For information or tickets, contact the **Teatro Politeama Garibaldi.**

Exploring the Old Town

The "four corners" of the city, the **Quattro Canti di Città ★**, is in the heart of the old town, at the junction of Corso Vittorio Emanuele and Via Maqueda. The ruling Spanish of the 17th century influenced the design of this grandiose baroque square, replete with fountains and statues. From here you can walk to **Piazza Bellini ★**, the most attractive square, although it's likely to be under scaffolding for a long time during a renovation project.

Opening onto this square is **Santa Maria dell'Ammiraglio (Chiesa della La Martorana),** which was erected in 1143 (see below). Also fronting the square is **San Cataldo** (1160), in the Arab-Byzantine style. Here, too, is the late-16th-century **Santa Caterina,** attached to a vast Dominican monastery constructed in 1310. The church contains interesting 18th-century multicolored marble ornamentation.

Adjoining the square is **Piazza Pretoria,** dominated by a fountain designed in Florence in 1554 for a villa but acquired by Palermo about 20 years later. A short walk will take you to **Piazza di Cattedrale** and the Duomo.

Catacombs of the Capuchins (Catacombe dei Cappuccini) ★★ If you've got a secret yearning to join mummified cadavers, and your tastes lean to the bizarre, you should spend at least an hour at these catacombs under the Capuchins Monastery.

Some 350 years ago, it was discovered that the catacombs contained a mysterious preservative that helped mummify the dead. As a result, Sicilians from nobles to maids—at least 8,000 in all—demanded to be buried here. The oldest corpses date from the late 16th century. The last corpse to be buried here was that of 2-year-old Rosalia Lombaro, who died in 1920. She still appears so lifelike that locals have dubbed her "Sleeping Beauty." Giuseppe Tommasi, prince of Lampedusa and author of one of the best-known works of Sicilian literature, *The Leopard,* was buried here in 1957. His body was not embalmed, but buried in the cemetery next to the catacombs instead.

Visitors can wander through the catacombs' dank corridors among the mummified bodies. Some faces are contorted as if posing for Edvard Munch's *The Scream.* Although many corpses are still remarkably preserved, time and gravity have been cruel to others. Some are downright creepy, with body parts such as jaws or hands missing.

Capuchins Monastery, Piazza Cappuccini 1. ✆ **091-212117.** Admission 3€. Daily 9am–noon and 3–5pm (until 7pm in summer). Closed holidays.

Chiesa della Martorana/San Cataldo ★★ These two Norman churches stand side by side. If you have time for only one, make it La Martorana, as it is the most celebrated church in Palermo remaining from the Middle Ages. Visit it if only to see its series of spectacular **mosaics** ★★.

Named for Eloisa Martorana, who founded a nearby Benedictine convent in 1194, this church is dedicated not to her, but to Santa Maria dell'Ammiraglio (St. Mary of the Admiral). History was made here as well: It was in this church that Sicily's noblemen convened to offer the crown to Peter of Aragón.

Today's baroque facade regrettably conceals a Norman front. You enter through a beautiful combined portico and bell tower with a trio of ancient columns and double arch openings. The bell tower is original, dating from the 12th century. Once you go inside, you'll know that your time spent seeking out this church was worthwhile. The stunning mosaics were ordered in

Interior of San Cataldo.

1143 by George of Antioch, the admiral of King Roger and a man of Greek descent. He loved mosaics, especially when they conformed, as these did, to the Byzantine iconography of his homeland. It's believed that the craftsmen who designed these mosaics also did the same for the Cappella Palatina. The mosaics are laid out on and around the columns that hold up the principal cupola. They're at their most beautiful in the morning light when the church opens.

Dominating the dome is a rendition of Christ, surrounded by a bevy of angels with the Madonna and the Apostles pictured off to the sides. Even with the passage of centuries the colors remain vibrantly golden, with streaks of spring green, ivory, azure blue, and what one art critic called "grape-red."

On a visit to La Martorana, you can obtain a key from the custodian sitting at a tiny table to your right as you enter the chapel. This key allows entry into the tiny **Chiesa di San Cataldo** next door. Also of Norman origin, it was founded by Maio of Bari, chancellor to William I. But because he died in 1160, the interior was never completed. The church is famous for its Saracenic red golf-ball domes. Sicilians liken these bulbous domes to a eunuch's hat.

Piazza Bellini 2, adjacent to Piazza Pretoria. ⓒ **091-6161692.** Free admission. La Martorana: Mon–Sat 9:30am–1pm and 3:30–6:30pm; Sun 8:30am–1pm. San Cataldo: Tues–Fri 9am–5pm; Sat–Sun 9am–1pm. Bus: 101 or 102.

Chiesa di Santa Cita/Oratorio del Rosario di Santa Cita ★★★ The

Oratory of the Rosary of St. Cita is a far greater artistic treasure than the church of St. Cita, on which Allied bombs rained in 1943. Only a glimmer of its former self, the church still contains a lovely **marble chancel arch ★** by Antonello Gagini. Look for it in the presbytery. From 1517 to 1527, Gagini created other sculptures in the church, but they were damaged in the bombing. In the second chapel left of the choir is a **sarcophagus of Antonio Scirotta,** also the creation of Gagini. To the right of the presbytery is the lovely **Cappella del Rosario ★**, with its polychrome marquetry and intricate lacelike stuccowork. The sculpted reliefs here are by Gioacchino Vitaliano.

On the left side of the church, and entered through the church, is the **oratory,** the real reason to visit. This was the crowning achievement of the leading baroque decorator of his day, Giacomo Serpotta, who worked on it between 1686 and 1718. His cherubs and angels romp with abandon, delightfully climbing onto the window frames or spreading garlands of flowers in their path. They can also be seen sleeping, eating, and simply hugging their knees deep in thought.

The oratory is a virtual gallery of art containing everything from scenes of the flagellation to Jesus in the garden at Gethsemane. The *Battle of Lepanto* bas-relief is meant to symbolize the horrors of war, while other panels depict such scenes as *The Mystery of the Rosary.* At the high altar is Carlo Maratta's *Virgin of the Rosary* (1690). Allegorical figures protect eight windows along the side walls.

Via Valverde 3. ⓒ **091-332779.** Admission: Church free (donation appreciated); entrance to oratory 3€. Mon–Sat 9am–1pm. Bus: 107.

Galleria Regionale della Sicilia (Regional Gallery) ★★★ This is the

greatest gallery of regional art in Sicily and one the finest art galleries in all of Italy. It's housed in the **Palazzo Abatellis ★**, itself an architectural treasure, a Catalan-Gothic structure with a Renaissance overlay designed by Matteo Carnelivari in 1490. Carnelivari constructed the building for Francesco Abatellis, the

Chiesa di Santa Cita.

praetor of Palermo. After World War II bombings, the architect Carlo Scarpa restored the *palazzo* in 1954.

The superb collection shows the evolution of the arts in Sicily from the 13th to the 18th centuries. Sculpture predominates on the main floor. Beyond room 2, the former chapel contains the gallery's most celebrated work, the **Triumph of Death ★★★**, dating from 1449 and of uncertain attribution (though it's sometimes credited to Pisanello). In all its gory magnificence, it portrays a horseback-riding skeleton (representing Death, of course) trampling his victims. The painter depicted himself in the fresco, seen with a pupil praying in vain for release from the horrors of Death. The modernity of this extraordinary work, including the details of the nose of the horse and the men and women in the full flush of their youth, is truly amazing, especially for its time.

The second masterpiece of the gallery lies at the end of the corridor exhibiting Arabic ceramics in room 4: the white-marble, slanted-eyed bust of **Eleonora di Aragona ★★**, by Francesco Laurana, who created it in the 15th century. This was Laurana's masterpiece.

The second-floor galleries are filled mainly with paintings from the Sicilian school, including a spectacular **Annunciation ★★**, the creation of Antonello da Messina, in room 11.

In the salon of Flemish paintings rests the celebrated **Triptych of Malvagna ★★**, the creation of Mabuse, whose real name was Jean Gossaert. His 1510 work depicts a Madonna and Bambino surrounded by singing angels with musical instruments.

Via Alloro 4, Palazzo Abatellis. ℭ **091-6230011.** Admission 6€ adults, 3€ children. Tues–Sun 9am–1:30pm and 2:30–6:30pm. Bus: 103, 105, or 139.

Il Duomo ★★   If too many cooks in the kitchen can spoil the broth, then too many architects turned Palermo's cathedral into a hodgepodge of styles. It is still a striking building, however, and well worth an hour or more of your time. Regrettably, the various styles—Greek-Roman, Norman, Arabic, Islamic—were not blended successfully with the overriding baroque overlay.

In 1184, during the Norman reign, the archbishop of Palermo, Gualtiero Offamiglio, launched the cathedral on the site of a Muslim mosque, which had been built over an early Christian basilica. Offamiglio was green with envy at the supremacy of the cathedral of Monreale. As the Palermo Duomo took shape, it became an architectural battleground for what was known as "the Battle of the Two Cathedrals."

Today, the facade is closed between two soaring towers with double lancet windows. The middle portal, dating from the 15th century, is enhanced by a double lancet with the Aragónese coat of arms. The four impressive campaniles (bell towers) date from the 14th century, the south and north porches from the 15th and 16th centuries.

But if anyone could be called the culprit for the cathedral's playground of styles, it is the Neapolitan architect Ferdinando Fuga. In 1771 and 1809, he gave both the exterior and the interior of the Duomo the sweeping neoclassical style popular in his day. In retrospect, he should have left well enough alone. The only section that the restorers didn't touch was the **apses** ★, which still retain their impressive geometric decoration.

The Duomo is also a pantheon of royalty. As you enter, the first chapel on the right contains six of the edifice's most impressive tombs, including that of Roger II, the first king of Sicily, who died in 1154. He was crowned in the Duomo in 1130. His daughter Constance, who died in 1198, is buried here along with her husband, Henry VI, who died the year before. Henry VI was emperor of Germany and the son of Frederick Barbarossa. Their son, another emperor of Germany and king of Sicily, Frederick II, was also buried here in 1250, as was his wife, Constance of Aragón, who died in 1222. The last royal burial here, of Peter II, king of Sicily, was in 1342.

Accessed from the south transept, the **Tesoro,** or treasury, is a repository of rich vestments, silverware, chalices, holy vessels, altar cloths, and ivory engravings of Sicilian art of the 17th century. An oddity here is the bejeweled caplike **crown of Constance of Aragón** ★, designed by local craftsmen in the 12th century and removed from her head when the tomb was opened in the 18th century. Other precious objects removed from the royal tombs are also on display here.

Piazza di Cattedrale, Corso Vittorio Emanuele. © **091-334373.** www.cattedrale.palermo.it. Duomo free (donation appreciated); crypt and treasury 2€. Mar–Oct Mon–Sat 9am–5:30pm, Sun 7:30am–1:30pm and 4–7pm; Nov–Feb Mon–Sat 9am–1:30pm, Sun 7:30am–1:30pm and 4–7pm. Bus: 101, 104, 105, 107, or 139.

Museo Archeologico Regionale ★★★   This is one of the grandest archaeological museums in Italy, stuffed with artifacts from prehistoric times to the Roman era. Spread over several buildings, the oldest from the 13th century, the museum's collection includes major Sicilian finds from the Phoenician, Punic, Greek, Roman, and Saracen periods, with several noteworthy treasures from Egypt. Even though some of the exhibitions appear shabby and the museum is definitely not state of the art, its treasures are worth wading through the dust to see.

You'll pass through small **cloisters** ★ on the ground floor, centered on a lovely hexagonal 16th-century fountain bearing a statue of Triton. In room 3 is some rare Phoenician art, including a pair of **sarcophagi** that date from the 5th century B.C.

In room 4 is the *Pietra di Palermo,* a black diorite slab known as the Rosetta Stone of Sicily. Dating from 2700 B.C., and discovered in Egypt in the 19th century, it was intended for the British Museum. Somehow, because of red tape, it got left behind in Palermo. It contains carved hieroglyphics detailing information about the pharaohs, including the delivery of 40 shiploads of cedar to Snefru.

The most important treasures of the museum, in room 13, are the **metopes of Selinunte** ★★. These finds were unearthed at the temples of Selinunte, once one of the major cities of Magna Graecia (Greek colonies along the coast of southern Italy). The Selinunte sculptures are remarkable for their beauty, casting a light on the brilliance of Siceliot sculpture in general. Displayed are three magnificent metopes from Temple C, a quartet of splendid metopes from Temple E, and, in the center, a 5th-century bronze statue, **Ephebe of Selinunte** ★. These decorative friezes cover the period from the 6th century B.C. to the 5th century B.C., depicting such scenes as Perseus slaying Medusa, the rape of Europa by Zeus, and Actaeon being transformed into a stag.

Etruscan antiquities grace rooms 14 to 17. Discoveries at the Tuscan town of Chisu, such as the unearthing of funereal *cippi* (stones), shed more light on these mysterious people. The **Oinochoe Vase,** from the 6th century B.C., is one of the most detailed artifacts of Etruscan blackened earthenware (called *bucchero*).

Other exhibit halls on the ground floor display underwater archaeology, with the most complete collection of **ancient anchors,** mostly Punic and Roman, in the world.

Finds from Greek and Roman sites in western Sicily are to be seen on the second floor in rooms 2 and 12. Here are more artifacts from Selinunte and other ancient Sicilian sites such as Marsala, Segesta, Imera, and Randazzo. These include **funereal aedicules** (openings framed by two columns, an entablature, and usually a pediment), **oil lamps,** and **votive terra cottas.**

In room 7 is a remarkable and rare series of large Roman bronzes, including the most impressive, a supremely realistic **bronze ram** ★★, a Hellenistic work from Syracuse. It's certainly worth the climb up the steps. Another notable work here is *Hercules Killing the Stag* ★, discovered at Pompeii, a Roman copy of a Greek original from the 3rd century B.C. In room 8, the most remarkable sculpture is *Satyr Filling a Drinking Cup* ★, a Roman copy of a Praxitelean original.

On the third floor is a prehistoric collection along with Greek ceramics, plus Roman mosaics and frescoes. The highlight of the collection is panels illustrating *Orpheus with Wild Animals* ★, from the 3rd century A.D.

Piazza Olivella 24. ✆ **091-6116805.** Admission 4€ adults, 3€ children. Tues–Sat 8:30am–2pm and 2:30–6:30pm; Sun–Mon 8:30am–1:30pm. Bus: 101, 102, 103, 104, or 107.

Oratorio del Rosario di San Domenico ★★★   Located near the colorful open-air market, Mercato della Vucciria, the Oratory of the Rosary of St. Dominic was founded in the closing years of the 16th century by the Society of the Holy Rosary. Two of its most outstanding members were the sculptor Giacomo

Serpotta and the painter Pietro Novelli, both of whom left a legacy of their artistic genius in this oratory.

In allure, this oratory is the equal of the Oratorio di San Lorenzo, which also displays Serpotta's artistic flavor. The sculptor excelled in the use of marble and polychrome, but it was in stucco that he earned his greatest fame. From 1714 to 1717, he decorated this second oratory with his delightfully expressive cherubs *(putti),* who are locked forever in a playground of happy antics.

Themes throughout the oratory are wide ranging, depicting everything from "Allegories of the Virtues" to the "Apocalypse of St. John." Particularly graphic is a depiction of a writhing "Devil Falling from Heaven." At the high altar is a masterpiece by Anthony van Dyck, *Madonna of the Rosary* (1628). Pietro Novelli frescoed the ceiling with the *Coronation of the Virgin.*

Via dei Bambinai. ℂ **091-332779.** Free admission. Mon 3–6pm; Tues–Fri 9am–1pm and 3–5:30pm; Sat 9am–1pm. Bus: 107.

Palazzo dei Normanni ★★ & Cappella Palatina ★★★ This is Palermo's greatest attraction and Sicily's finest treasure-trove. Allow 1½ hours and visit this site if you have to skip all the rest. The history goes back to the days of the Arab emirs and their harems around the 9th century, but they in time abandoned the site. Discovered by the conquering Normans, the palace was restored and turned into a sumptuous residence. Today it is the seat of Sicily's semiautonomous regional government. If you enter from Piazza Indipendenza you'll be directed to the splendid Cappella Palatina, representing the apex of the Arabo-Norman collective genius and built from 1130 to 1140 by Roger II when it was adorned with extraordinary Byzantine mosaics. You'd have to travel to Istanbul or Ravenna to encounter mosaics such as this. The whole cycle constitutes the largest cycle of Islamic paintings to survive to the present day.

At the entrance to the nave is a royal throne encrusted in mosaics. Note the towering **Paschal Candelabrum ★** carved with figures, wild animals, and acanthus leaves, a masterpiece from the 12th century. Covering the central nave is a honeycomb stalactite wooden *muqarnas* **ceiling ★★**, a masterpiece and the creation of Arab artisans brought in from North Africa. They depicted scenes from daily life, including animal hunts and dances.

Expect tight security as you wander around the **Royal Apartments ★★** above, because this is still a seat of government. On some days you may not gain entrance at all. When visits are possible, you enter Salone d'Ercole from 1560, the chamber of the Sicilian Parliament. The most intriguing room of

The interior of Palermo's Cappella Palatina.

MEN OF dishonor

In Sicily, they don't call it the Mafia (from the Arabic *mu'afah,* or "protection"). They call it Cosa Nostra, literally "our thing," but, more accurately, "this thing we have." Its origins are debated, but the world's most famed criminal organization seemed to grow out of the convergence of local agricultural overseers working for absentee Bourbon landowners—hired thugs, from the peasant workers' point of view.

Members of the Sicilian Mafia (or "Men of Honor," as they like to be called) traditionally operated as a network of regional bosses who controlled individual towns by setting up puppet regimes of thoroughly corrupt officials. It was a sort of devil's bargain with the national Christian Democrat Party, which controlled Italy's government from World War II until 1993 and, despite its law-and-order rhetoric, tacitly left Cosa Nostra alone as long as the bosses got out the party vote.

The Cosa Nostra trafficked in illegal goods, of course, but until the 1960s and 1970s, its income was derived mainly from low-level protection rackets, funneling state money into its own pockets, and ensuring that public contracts were granted to fellow *mafiosi* (all reasons why Sicily has experienced grotesque unchecked industrialization and modern growth at the expense of its heritage and the good of its communities). But the younger generation of Mafia under-bosses got into the highly lucrative heroin and cocaine trades in the 1970s, transforming the Sicilian Mafia into a world player on the international drug trafficking circuit—and raking in the dough. This ignited a clandestine Mafia war that, throughout the late 1970s and 1980s, generated headlines of bloody Mafia hits. The new generation was wiping out the old and turning the balance of power in their favor.

This situation gave rise to the first Mafia turncoats, disgruntled ex-bosses and rank-and-file stoolies who told their stories, first to police prefect Gen. Carlo Alberto Dalla Chiesa (assassinated 1982) and later to crusading magistrates Giovanni Falcone (slaughtered May 23, 1992) and Paolo Borsellino (murdered July 19, 1992), who staged the "maxitrials" of *mafiosi* that sent hundreds to jail. The magistrates' 1992 murders, especially, garnered public attention to the dishonorable methods that defined the new Mafia and, perhaps for the first time, began to stir true shame.

On a broad and culturally important scale, it is these young *mafiosi,* without a moral center or check on their powers, who have driven many Sicilians to at least secretly break the unwritten code of *omertà,* which translates as "homage" but means "silence," when faced with harboring or even tolerating a man of honor. The Mafia still exists in Palermo, the small towns south of it, and the provincial capitals of Catania, Trapani, and Agrigento. Throughout the rest of Sicily, its power has been slipping. The heroin trade is a far cry from construction schemes and protection money, and the Mafia is swiftly outliving its usefulness and its welcome.

the apartments is the Sala di Ruggero II, where King Roger himself slumbered. The room is decorated with 12th-century mosaics like the chapel just visited.

Piazza del Parlamento. ✆ **091-626833.** www.ars.sicilia.it. Admission 8.50€, free for children 17 and under. Mon–Sat 8:15am–5:45pm; Sun 8:30am–12:30pm. Bus: 104, 105, 108, 109, 110, 118, 304, or 309.

San Giovanni degli Eremiti ★★   This is one of the most famous of all the Arab-Norman monuments still standing in Palermo. It is certainly the most romantic building remaining from the heyday of Norman Palermo. Since 1132, this church with its series of five red domes has remained one of the most characteristic landmarks on the Palermo skyline. It is located on the western edge of the Albergheria district.

With an atmosphere appropriate for the recluse it honors, St. John of the Hermits (now deconsecrated), this is one of the most idyllic spots in Palermo. A medieval veil hangs heavily in the gardens, with their citrus blossoms and flowers, especially on a hot summer day as you wander around the cloister.

A single nave divides the simple interior into two bays, surmounted by a dome. A small cupola tops the presbytery. The right-hand apse is covered by one of the red domes. Surrounding the left-hand apse is a bell tower with pointed windows; it, too, is crowned by one of the church's red domes.

The small late Norman **cloister** ★, with a Moorish cistern in the center, was part of the original Benedictine monastery that once stood here. It has little round arches supported by fine paired columns.

Via dei Benedettini 3. ✆ **091-6515019.** Admission 6€ adults; 3€ students, seniors, and children. Tues–Sat 9am–1pm and 3–7pm; Sun 9am–6:30pm. Bus: 109 or 318.

Villa Malfitano ★★   One of Palermo's great villa palaces, built in the Liberty style, sits within a spectacular **garden** ★★. The villa was constructed in 1886 by Joseph Whitaker, grandson of the famous English gentleman and wine merchant Ingham, who moved to Sicily in 1806 and made a fortune producing Marsala wine. Whitaker had trees shipped to Palermo from all over the world to plant around his villa. These included such rare species as Dragon's Blood, an enormous banyan tree and the only one found in Europe. Local high society flocked here for lavish parties, and even British royalty visited. In World War II, Gen. George Patton temporarily stayed here as he planned the invasion of southern Italy. The villa today is lavishly furnished with antiques and artifacts from all over the world. The **Sala d'Estate (Summer Room)** is particularly stunning, with *trompe l'oeil* frescoes covering the walls and ceiling.

Via Dante 167. ✆ **091-6816133.** Admission 6€. Mon–Sat 9am–1pm. Bus: 103, 106, 108, 122, 134, 164, or 824.

EXPLORING LA KALSA ★★

Although it's a bit dangerous at night, crumbling La Kalsa is the most interesting neighborhood in Palermo (it's relatively safe during the day, although you should keep your wits about you). In the southwestern sector of the old city, it was built by the Arabs as a walled seaside residence for their chief ministers. It's bounded by the port and Via Garibaldi and Via Paternostro to the east and west, and by Corso Vittorio Emanuele and Via Lincoln to the north and south; one of its main thoroughfares is **Via Butero.** Much of the Arabs' work was destroyed when the Spanish viceroys took over, adding their own architectural interpretations.

One of the neighborhood's most dramatic churches (though not necessarily the oldest) is the fancifully baroque **Santa Teresa,** Piazza della Kalsa (✆ **091-6171658**). This church is open only for services, although you can admire it from the outside. If it should happen to be open at the time of your visit, you can see an interior designed by Giacomo Amato (1643–1732). He is known for introducing Roman High Baroque to Palermo, of which Santa Teresa is the most classic example. If it's open, you can visit the luminous interior to see impressive stuccoes of Giuseppe and Procopio Serpotta.

Another of the old town's most intriguing antique churches lies only a 5-minute walk northwest of Santa Teresa: the 13th-century **San Francesco d'Assisi** (✆ **091-6162819**). To reach it, begin at the Quattro Canti di Città and walk eastward along **Corso Vittorio Emanuele,** which locals usually refer to simply as "Il Corso." Cross over bustling Via Roma, and then turn right onto Via Paternostro until you reach the church on Piazza San Francesco d'Assisi. Visit the church, if for no other reason than to see its magnificent Cappella Mastratonio (Chapel of Mastrantonio), carved in 1468. Don't count on the church being open, however.

From Piazza San Francesco d'Assisi, follow Via Merlo to the **Palazzo Mirto** ★★, Via Merlo 2 (✆ **091-6164751**), to see how nobility lived in the days when this was an upmarket neighborhood. The palace, a splendid example of a princely residence of the early 20th century, contains its original 18th- and 19th-century furnishings. It's open Monday to Saturday 9am to 7pm, and Sunday 9am to 1pm. Admission is 3€.

Via Merlo leads into the landmark **Piazza Marina,** one of the most evocative parts of Palermo. The port of La Cala was here, but it silted up in the 1100s. Reminiscent of the deep American South, a garden is found at the **Villa Garibaldi** in the center of the square. The square is dominated by the **Palazzo Chiaramonte** on the southeast corner, dating from the early 14th century. Renaissance churches occupy the other three corners of this historic square.

Where to Stay

The hotel selection is generally not great in Palermo. Choose carefully.

VERY EXPENSIVE

Grand Hotel Federico II ★★   One of Palermo's best hotels rises six floors in the center of town. It was created after a massive restoration of an old *palazzo* once owned by the aristocratic Granatelli family. The location is on a quiet residential street, although it lies close to Ruggero Settimo Avenue, a fashionable shopping and business district. The well-furnished bedrooms are for the most part midsize, each decorated in an elegant way with marble and ceramics. The furnishings are refined with old paintings and period pieces. All the bedrooms are soundproof. The first-class Caesar Restaurant was installed on the fifth floor in a former princely apartment, and on the terrace is a roof garden created for alfresco dining in summer.

Via Principe di Granatelli 60, 90139 Palermo. ✆ **091-7495052.** Fax 091-6092500. www.grand hotelfedericoii.it. 60 units. 350€ double; 450€ suite. Rates include buffet breakfast. AE, DC, MC, V. Parking nearby 18€. Bus: 101 or 102. **Amenities:** Restaurant; bar; airport transfers (50€); babysitting; room service. *In room:* A/C, TV, hair dryer, minibar, Wi-Fi (free).

Villa Igiea Grand Hotel ★★★   The best hotel in town, Villa Igiea, built at the turn of the 20th century, is a remarkable example of Sicilian Art Nouveau. Managed by Hilton, it is in better shape and more comfortable than the also highly rated Grand Hotel et des Palmes, Palermo's other historic property. Once the private villa of the Fiorio family, whose claim to fame was coming up with the notion of putting tuna fish into a tin can, the villa hosts the moneyed elite of Sicily when they're in town for business or pleasure.

Located in the suburb of Acquasanta, 2.4km (1½ miles) north of the center and reached after you pass through a shabby district, the villa is surrounded by a park overlooking the sea. The old architecture has been preserved, including ceilings with stone vaults joining in an arch. Guest rooms contain valuable furnishings such as comfortable wrought-iron beds.

Salita Belmonte 43, Acquasanta, 90142 Palermo. ✆ **091-6312111.** Fax 091-547654. www.hilton. com. 124 units. 180€–437€ double; 435€–747€ suite. Rates include continental breakfast. AE, DC, MC, V. Free parking. Bus: 139. **Amenities:** Restaurant; bar; airport transfers (95€); babysitting; concierge; saltwater pool; room service; tennis court (lit). *In room:* A/C, TV, hair dryer, minibar, Wi-Fi (8€ per hr.).

EXPENSIVE

Astoria Palace Hotel ★   Chances are good that if a CEO or even a president is bunking down in Palermo, he or she will be sheltered at this government-rated four-star selection. For sheer comfort and convenience, and not for those seeking accommodations dripping with atmosphere, we consider Astoria Palace the number-two hotel in town. Don't let the word "palace" fool you, however. The name comes from the fact that it's a behemoth, not some classic antique. It is the biggest hotel in town and the setting for many large conventions. The rooms have modern, elegant furnishings, but not all are spacious; some are rather boxlike with just a small window. Naturally, the best units are those on the top floor where the view is less obstructed.

Via Monte Pellegrino 62, 90142 Palermo. ✆ **091-6281111.** Fax 091-6372178. www.ghshotels.it. 320 units. 189€ double; 255€ triple; 289€ suite. Rates include American buffet breakfast. AE, DC, MC, V. Free parking. Bus: 139 or 721. **Amenities:** 2 restaurants; bar; babysitting; exercise room; Jacuzzi; room service; Wi-Fi (free, in lobby). *In room:* A/C, TV, hair dryer, minibar.

Centrale Palace ★★   For atmosphere and comfort, we'd still give the edge to Villa Igiea or the Astoria Palace—but Centrale Palace is a close runner-up. No other lodging lies as close to the Duomo, the Quattro Canti, and the monumental medieval heart of Palermo. The core of the hotel is a 17th-century private home, although guest rooms occupy adjacent buildings that are newer. The original *palazzo* was converted into a hotel in 1892 during Palermo's Belle Epoque golden age. Some period or Empire antiques are placed about to take the curse off the *moderno.* But many furnishings, especially those in the guest rooms, have more function than flair. Doubles are generally midsize to spacious; the quietest rooms are on the side streets, and double-glazing on the front windows blocks street noise.

Corso Vittorio Emanuele 327 (at Via Maqueda), 99134 Palermo. ✆ **091-336666.** Fax 091-334881. www.angalahotels.it. 104 units. 200€–289€ double; 260€–339€ junior suite; 290€–850€ suite. Rates include buffet breakfast. AE, DC, MC, V. Parking 18€. Bus: 103, 104, or 105. **Amenities:** 2 restaurants; bar; babysitting; exercise room; room service; sauna; Wi-Fi (free, in lobby). *In room:* A/C, TV, hair dryer, minibar.

Principe di Villafranca ★★★ 📖   This charming 1998 property is the finest boutique-style hotel in Palermo. Stylish, intimate, and evocative of an elegant, unfussy private home, it occupies two floors of what was originally built as a low-rise apartment house. Its Sicilian theme includes enough antiques and architectural finesse to make you think the place is a lot older than it really is. Grace notes include Oriental rugs, marble floors, vaulted ceilings, and a baronial fireplace. The hotel and some of its neighbors were built within what was once one of Palermo's most beautiful gardens, the Ferriato. Guest rooms are midsize to spacious, with tile, granite, and travertine bathrooms.

Via G. Turrisi Colonna 4, 90141 Palermo. ℂ **091-6118523.** Fax 091-588705. www.principedivilla franca.it. 34 units. 230€ double; 280€ suite. Rates include buffet breakfast. AE, DC, MC, V. Free parking. Bus: 101 or 102. **Amenities:** Restaurant; bar; babysitting; exercise room; room service. *In room:* A/C, TV, hair dryer, minibar, Wi-Fi (4€ per hr.).

MODERATE

Excelsior Hilton ★   Even though it was completely restored in 2005, this nostalgic favorite still exudes much of the aura of the 19th century. It was built for the National Exhibition of 1891, when it was called Hotel de la Paix. Much of the Art Nouveau style of that elegant era remains, at least in the public rooms with their atmosphere of Palermitan Belle Epoque. The location is in a quiet neighborhood at the northern end of Via Libertà. Bedrooms range from midsize to large and have been completely modernized, with a well-equipped private bathroom. Many rooms open on a view of the hotel garden. The formal restaurant, where the staff is elegantly uniformed, serves first-rate Sicilian and international dishes.

Via Marchese Ugo 3, 90141 Palermo. ℂ **091-7909001.** Fax 091-342139. www.excelsiorpalermo.it. 117 units. 230€–270€ double; 385€ junior suite. Rates include buffet breakfast. AE, DC, MC, V. Parking 20€. Bus: 101, 104, 107, 108, or 806. **Amenities:** Restaurant; bar; babysitting; concierge; exercise room; room service. *In room:* A/C, TV, minibar, Wi-Fi (5€ per hr.).

San Paolo Palace ★   Built in 1990, this modern 14-story hotel offers serious competition to the Astoria Palace (see above). Like the Astoria, San Paolo calls itself a "palace" hotel, which is hardly evocative of what it is: a large, sprawling, though welcoming high-rise. Overlooking the sea, between Capo Zafferano and Mount Pellegrino, the hotel is not without its charms, among them a roof-garden restaurant with a spectacular view. The government gives San Paolo three stars instead of the four reserved for the Astoria, which means its rooms are slightly cheaper, yet you get basically the same deal. Guest rooms open onto the most famous gulf in Sicily and are extremely comfortable, though not particularly stylish. There's a wide choice of different bed arrangements, from king-size to cozy "matrimonial."

Via Messina Marine 91, 90123 Palermo. ℂ **091-6211112.** Fax 091-6215300. www.sanpaolopalace. it. 290 units. 190€ double; 250€ suite. AE, DC, MC, V. Free parking. Bus: 221, 224, 225, 250, or 824. **Amenities:** 2 restaurants; bar; babysitting; exercise room; rooftop pool (seasonal); room service. *In room:* A/C, TV, hair dryer, minibar, Wi-Fi (15€ per 24 hr.).

Ucciardhome ★ 🎁   One of the better boutique hotels of Palermo, this is an unexpected find. Rated four stars by the government, the hotel is known for its personal service by one of the city's most helpful hotel staffs. Ucciardhome has special features such as an exclusive wine bar that is both elegant and *intime*. The staff can make arrangements for you to visit a nearby gym, Turkish bath, or salon. Room service will also provide special lunches and dinners. Honeymooners form part of the clientele. Each of the spacious bedrooms is furnished with acute attention to detail, including minimalist designer furniture, precious materials, and dark wood, which is prominently featured in the hotel. Much use is made of ivory-white marble floors, and each of the bedrooms comes with soundproofing, big windows, terraces, or balconies.

Via Enrico Albanese 34–35, 90139 Palermo. ✆ **091-348426.** Fax 091-7303738. www.hotelucciard home.com. 16 units. 94€–179€ double; 159€–229€ junior suite; 179€–279€ suite. Rates include continental breakfast. AE, DC, MC, V. Bus: 101. Free parking. **Amenities:** Wine bar; babysitting; room service. *In room:* A/C, TV, CD player, hair dryer, minibar, Wi-Fi (free).

Villa D'Amato ★ 🍴 This little discovery, a completely renovated antique Sicilian villa opening onto the seafront, lies a 15-minute drive from the center. As a hotel, it is outclassed by Principe di Villafranca and Massimo Plaza Hotel, but it is not without its (considerable) charms. Set on its own parklike grounds, it is especially good for motorists who don't want to battle traffic in the heart of Palermo. We like it mainly for its gardens, a Mediterranean oasis. As you relax here, watching the plants grow, you'll be in Palermo but it won't feel like it. The guest rooms are completely comfortable, decorated in a sort of Italian Liberty style, yet they come off as plain; small to midsize, each comes with a tiled bathroom with shower.

Via Messina Marine 178–180, 90123 Palermo. ✆ **091-6212767.** Fax 091-6213057. www.hotelvilla damato.it. 37 units. 59€–79€ double; 99€ junior suite. Rates include buffet breakfast. AE, DC, MC, V. Free parking. Bus: 221, 224, 225, 250, or 824. **Amenities:** Restaurant; bar; babysitting; room service. *In room:* A/C, TV, minibar.

INEXPENSIVE

Hotel Joli Not to be confused with the Jolly chain, this is an inexpensive hotel on the third floor of a building on the beautiful old Piazza Florio. At the historic center of Palermo, it lies near the pricey Grand Hotel et des Palmes, a few blocks away from Piazza Castelnuovo. Of course, it's hardly comparable to des Palmes, which you might want to visit for a drink or a sumptuous meal. But if you're looking to save money and you don't demand elegance, this hotel offers small to midsize guest rooms; they're a bit boxy and furnished simply though comfortably. The best units come with small terraces overlooking the square.

Via Michele Amari 11, 90139 Palermo. ✆/fax **091-6111765.** www.hoteljoli.com. 30 units. 59€–108€ double; 120€–148€ junior suite. Rates include buffet breakfast. AE, DC, MC, V. Bus: 103, 106, or 108. Parking 12€. **Amenities:** Bar; babysitting; bikes; room service. *In room:* A/C, TV, hair dryer, Wi-Fi (free).

Hotel Moderno ★ 🍴 One of the city's best cost-conscious options lies on the third and fourth floors of a stately looking building that's among the grandest in its busy and highly congested neighborhood. Don't expect the same kind of grandeur inside that you see on the building's neoclassical exterior: You'll take a cramped elevator to the third-floor reception area, then proceed to a clean but very simple guest room. Each comes with a tiled, shower-only bathroom; lots of artwork; and sparse direct sunlight. In view of the oppressive heat outside, and in light of the reasonable prices, few of this hotel's repeat visitors seem to mind.

Via Roma 276 (at Via Napoli), 90133 Palermo. ✆/fax **091-588683.** www.hotelmodernopa.com. 38 units. 80€ double. AE, DC, MC, V. Bus: 101, 102, 103, or 107. Parking 15€. **Amenities:** Bar. *In room:* A/C, TV.

Hotel Orientale ★ 🍴 The former royal residence of Prince Alessandro Filangieri II, this 18th-century palace has been converted into a boutique hotel. Many of the original features were left intact, including a grand marble staircase, original hand-painted frescoes, and a courtyard. The location is in the historic center of the old city, near many famous landmarks, including the Teatro Massimo (p. 828). You can walk here from the central train station. We prefer room no. 7, because it is large and grandly comfortable, more like a ballroom than a bedroom. It was constructed over an archway through which traffic can reach the market streets behind the hotel. Antiques are mixed with 1950s-era furnishings.

Via Maqueda 26, 90134 Palermo. ✆ **091-616-5727.** Fax 091-616-1193. www.albergoorientale.191. it. 24 units. 60€–70€ double. AE, MC, V. Bus: 101, 102, 103, 104, 107, 122, or 225. *In room:* A/C, TV.

ON THE OUTSKIRTS

Letizia ★ 📷 A once-dreary *pensione* has been reincarnated as a boutique hotel of charm, grace, and elegance. Surrounded by decaying 18th-century *palazzo* from the golden age of Palermo, the hotel rises only two floors on the edge of Kalsa district, a half-block from the main drag, Corso Vittorio Emanuele. The public rooms are gracefully decorated with antiques and Persian carpets. The small to midsize bedrooms contain similar furnishings and are immaculately kept.

Via Bottai 30, 90133 Palermo. ✆ **091-589110.** Fax 091-6122848. www.hotelletizia.com. 13 units. 60€–130€ double; 134€–160€ suite. Rates include buffet breakfast. AE, MC, V. Parking 12€. Bus: 107. **Amenities:** Bar; airport transfers (50€); babysitting; concierge; room service; Wi-Fi (2.50€ per hr., in lobby). *In room:* A/C, TV, hair dryer, minibar.

Where to Dine

EXPENSIVE

Bellotero ★ SICILIAN   This is one of the most traditional of all Sicilian restaurants, lying in the Palermo new town, attracting mainly locals to its authentic cuisine. The 10-table restaurant draws mainly Palermo foodies, who feast on such dishes as fresh fish and shellfish, beginning with a seafood appetizer of calamari, mussels, and shrimp. Many diners start their meal with a lobster-studded pasta, and you can order such fare as spaghetti with sea bass or sea urchins with lemon zest, perhaps lamb with oven-roasted pistachios. The menu also features Sicilian rabbit and even serves filet of horse, which sounds revolting to many diners, although it is a traditional Sicilian dish with a long-standing reputation among gourmets. For dessert, we recommend the pistachio ice cream.

Via Giorgio Castriota 31. ✆ **091-582-158.** www.bellotero.altervista.org. Reservations required. Main courses 11€–24€. AE, MC, V. Tues–Sun 1–3pm and 8–10:30pm. Closed Aug 1–20. Bus: 101 or 107.

Graziano ★★★ SICILIAN   The restaurant of Adriano and Franscesco Graziano is one of the best in Sicily. It's well worth the 45-minute drive from the center of Palermo to reach this elegant country house, where you'll dine in ultimate comfort and be attended to by the region's best-trained waitstaff.

The cuisine is meticulously crafted and backed up by a well-chosen wine *carte* of regional, national, and international selections. The chef, Nino, takes superb ingredients to the limits of their innate possibilities, with a minimum of artifice and frills. The dishes of the day might include a sausage of fresh tuna flavored with mint, or perhaps a spicy *tagliolini* (long pasta) with pesto. Freshly caught fish is a delight, cooked in a salt crust to seal in its juices and served on a platter of grilled vegetables. Fava-bean purée *(macco)* might be a staple dish of the poor, but in the hands of Nino it becomes something of wonder, especially when it's paired with scampi, ricotta, peppercorns, and fried basil.

SS121, Località Bolognetta, Villafrati. ☎ **091-8724870.** www.grazianoadrianocatering.it. Reservations required. Main courses 10€–16€. AE, DC, MC, V. Tues–Sun 1–2:30pm and 8–10:30pm. Closed 2 weeks in July. From Palermo, take the autostrada east toward Catania; exit at AGRIGENTO-VILLABATE S.S. 121. Continue 17km (11 miles). The restaurant is on the right side of SS121.

Il Ristorantino ★★★ SICILIAN/MEDITERRANEAN   This restaurant is justifiably celebrated for its finely honed cuisine. The chef presides over an establishment that's not only elegant, but is one of the most stunningly modern in the city. The menu is creative, although old-time favorites are also included. He won our hearts with mackerel with caper sauce and a winning soup of zucchini and fresh seafood. Try the lobster *tortellini* with cherry tomatoes or the well-crafted swordfish au gratin. Desserts are luscious, so save some room. The restaurant lies in the suburbs north of the center and is best reached by taxi.

Piazzale Alcide De Gasperi 19. ☎ **091-512861.** Reservations required. Main courses 12€–22€. AE, DC, MC, V. Tues–Sun 12:30–3:30pm and 8:30pm–midnight. Closed 2 weeks in Aug and Jan 1–7.

La Scuderia ★★ INTERNATIONAL/ITALIAN   La Scuderia is near the top of our list. Dedicated professionals run this restaurant surrounded by trees at the foot of Monte Pellegrino, 5km (3 miles) north of the city center near the stadium at La Favorita. The talented chefs change the menu according to what looks good at the market; the ingredients are of top quality. The imaginative cuisine includes a mixed grill of fresh vegetables with a healthy dose of a Sicilian cheese called *caciocavallo involtini* (roulade) of eggplant or veal; risotto with seafood; and *strettini* (homemade pasta) sautéed with mussels, tuna roe, fresh thyme, and lemon. A curiosity and a worthy dish as well is the filet of tuna with melon (yes, melon), mint, and toasted pine nuts. Everything is beautifully presented and served with typical Sicilian courtesy.

Viale del Fante 9. ☎ **091-520323.** Reservations recommended. Main courses 12€–21€. AE, DC, MC, V. Mon–Sat 12:30–3pm and 8:30pm–midnight. Closed 2 weeks in Aug. Bus: 107 or 603.

MODERATE

Capricci di Sicilia 🍴 SICILIAN   Great care goes into the traditional Palermo cuisine here; to go really local, order *polpette* (fish balls of fresh sardines). The spaghetti with sea urchins is succulent, and the swordfish roulade is always dependable. Another good pasta dish is *casereccie Mediterranee* (homemade pasta sautéed with swordfish, tomatoes, almonds, and fresh mint). This is one of the best places to sample *cassata Siciliana* (ice cream with dried fruit), Sicily's fabled dessert. In warm weather, meals are served in a small garden. The central location is close to Piazza Politeama.

Via Instituto Pignatelli 6 (off Piazza Sturzo). ☎ **091-327777.** www.capriccidisicilia.it. Reservations recommended. Main courses 10€–16€. AE, DC, MC, V. Sept–July Tues–Sun 12:30–3pm and 8pm–midnight. Bus: 806 or 833.

Le Delizie di Cagliostro ★ 🍴 SICILIAN/INTERNATIONAL   The restaurant that bears his name celebrates the dubious achievements of Sicily's most successful (and, ultimately, tragic) swindler, Giuseppe Balsamo (alias Count Cagliostro; 1743–95). His mystical mumbo jumbo and sleight of hand looted the purses and pride of commoners and aristocrats alike (including Marie Antoinette), earning him a respected place in the pantheon of noteworthy Sicilian rogues.

Set on a busy boulevard in a commercial neighborhood, the restaurant boasts vaulted 18th-century ceilings covered with *trompe l'oeil* frescoes. Once you get past the overweening presence of the ghost of the count, you can sit back and enjoy the cuisine. Market-fresh ingredients go into dishes such as risotto with shrimp, cream, and curry; mushroom-stuffed crepes; and that Palermo favorite, pasta with fresh sardines. The platter of grilled vegetables, their flavors enhanced with olive oil and balsamic vinegar, is succulent.

Corso Vittorio Emanuele 150. (C) **091-332818.** www.ledeliziedicagliostro.it. Reservations recommended. Main courses 7€–15€. AE, DC, MC, V. Daily noon–2pm and 7pm–midnight. Bus: 101, 102, or 105.

Lo Scudiero ★★ SICILIAN   Set directly across the busy street from the Teatro Politeama Garibaldi (site of the Galleria d'Arte Moderno) is this cozy restaurant and brasserie (its name translates as "the Shield Bearer"). Do not confuse it with the grander and more expensive restaurant with a roughly similar name out in the suburbs near the soccer stadium. Honest, straightforward, and unpretentious, it's favored by locals, many of whom work or live in the nearby Via Libertà neighborhood. Fine raw materials and skilled hands in the kitchen produce such tempting dishes as grilled swordfish flavored with garlic and a touch of mint. The fish served here is really fresh, as the owner buys it every day at the market. This place gets our vote for some of Palermo's best roulades, grilled veal rolls with a stuffing of ground salami and herbs. Vegetarians can opt for the medley of grilled vegetables with balsamic vinegar and olive oil.

Via Turati 7. (C) **091-581628.** Reservations recommended. Main courses 8€–18€. AE, DC, MC, V. Mon–Sat 12:30–3pm and 7:30–11pm. Closed Aug 10–20. Bus: 101 or 107.

INEXPENSIVE

Antica Focacceria San Francesco ★★ ☺ FOCACCIE/SICILIAN   All visitors need to make at least one stop at this local favorite, a tradition since 1834, in the Palazzo Reale/Monte di Pietà district. Nearly every kid in Palermo has feasted on its stuffed focaccia sandwiches and other inexpensive eats. High ceilings and marble floors evoke the era in which the eatery was born; the food has changed little since. You can still get *panino con la milza* (real hair-on-your-chest fare: a bread roll stuffed with slices of boiled spleen and melted cheese). The *panelle* (deep-fried chickpea fritters) are marvelous, as are the *arancini di riso* (rice balls stuffed with tomatoes and peas or mozzarella). Try the specialty, *focaccia farcita* (flat pizza baked with various fillings).

Via A. Paternostro 58. (C) **091-320264.** www.afsf.it. Sandwiches 3€–5€; pastas 7€–12€. AE, DC, MC, V. Apr–Sept daily 11am–11pm; Oct–Mar Wed–Mon 11am–11pm. Bus: 103, 105, or 225.

Antica Focacceria San Francesco.

Antico Caffè Spinnato ★★ PASTRIES/SNACKS   Established in 1860, this is the most opulent cafe in its neighborhood. Set on a quiet, pedestrian-only street, it's the focal point for residents of the surrounding Via Libertà district, thanks to its lavish displays of sandwiches, pastries, and ice creams. Buy coffee at the bar and be tempted by the elaborate cannoli and almond cakes. If you're hungry, sit at a tiny table—either indoors or out—for one of the succulent *piatti del giorno*. (These include fresh salads, grills, and succulent pastas such as spaghetti with sea urchins.) In the evenings, the focus shifts from coffee to cocktails, and from pastries to platters. Live music entertains the nighttime crowd.

Via Principe di Belmonte 115. ✆ **091-583231.** www.spinnato.it. Pastries 1.50€–3€; platters 3€–12€. AE, DC, MC, V. Daily 7am–1am. Bus: 101, 104, 107, or 806.

Casa del Brodo ★ SICILIAN   For more than a century, this Palermitan institution in the Palazzo Reale/Monte di Pietà neighborhood has handsomely fed some of the island's most discerning palates, such as the late Count Giuseppe Tasca of Almerita, once Sicily's premier vintner. In its two intimate, plainly decorated rooms, it attracts an equal number of locals and visitors, its atmosphere unchanged over the years.

With a name like "House of Broth," you could well imagine that broth is its specialty. And in truth, there is no kettle of broth finer in all of Sicily than that served here. But Casa del Brodo has many other dishes, too, including *macco di fave* (meatballs and tripe), a recipe that seems long forgotten in the kitchens of most Sicilians today. The one specialty we always order is *carni bollite* (boiled meats). Trust us: It may not sound enticing, but it is a tantalizing assortment of tender, herb-flavored meats, especially good when preceded by a savory risotto with fresh asparagus.

Corso Vittorio Emanuele 175. ✆ **091-321655.** www.casadelbrodo.it. Reservations recommended. Main courses 6€–16€; fixed-price menus 18€–20€. DC, MC, V. Wed–Mon 12:30–3pm and 7:30–11pm (closed Sun June–Sept). Bus: 103, 104, 105, 118, or 225.

Shopping

For a touch of local color, join Palermoans for a visit to the **Vucciria,** their main market for meat and fresh vegetables, off Via Roma in the rear of San Domenico—this is one of Europe's great casbahlike markets. You'll find mountains of food, from fish to meat and vegetables. The array of wild fennel, long-stemmed artichokes, and blood oranges, as well as giant octopus and squid, will astound you.

Palermo also has a number of other street markets for the adventurous shopper, including the **Capo market,** which has a long line of vendors hawking clothing in stall after stall that winds along Via Vandiera and Via San Agostino in the heart of the city. The food stalls are found mainly at Via Porta Carini and Via Beatri Paolo lying off Via Volturno. Antiques vendors with many unusual buys lie along the **Piazza Peranni,** off Corso Vittorio Emanuele.

De Simone, Via Gaetano Daita 13B (✆ **091-6119867;** www.lafabbric adellaceramica.it), a family-run business, has been producing quality majolica stoneware since the 1920s. It also offers some of the most tasteful ceramics and some of the finest tiles in Palermo.

Fiorentino, Via Roma 315 (✆ **091-6047111;** www.fiorentinospa.it), has been a Palermo tradition since 1890. This jeweler offers traditional and contemporary designs. The jewelry is exquisite, but there's also a vast array of gift items, silverware, and watches.

Shoppers at Vucciria, Palermo's main market.

Frette, Via Ruggero Settimo 12 (*©* **091-585166;** www.frette.com), is a company whose linens are highly prized by people who demand the best. They have been royal purveyors of linen to everyone from some of the finest hotels in the world to the former royal families of Italy. The shop offers sheets, tablecloths, towels, bedspreads, pajamas, nightgowns, curtains, and tapestries, among other items.

I Peccatucci di Mamma Andrea, Via Principe di Scordia 67 (*©* **091-334835;** www.mammaandrea.it), contains one of the most diverse collections of Sicilian jams, honey, liqueurs, and candies in Palermo, each artfully wrapped into the kind of gift item that would delight recipients back home. Elegant glass bottles contain liqueurs distilled from herbs or fruits you might never have thought suitable, including basil, clementines, cinnamon, almonds, myrtle, fennel, laurel leaves, figs, and rose petals. Jams and honey showcase the agrarian bounty and aromas of Sicily.

Palermo After Dark

For such a large city, Palermo has a dearth of nightlife. In the hot summer months, the people of the town can be seen parading along the waterfront of Mondello Lido (see below) to cool off. Although they are improving a bit, many Palermo areas with bars and taverns, such as the Kalsa or Albergheria, are not safe for walking around at night.

The liveliest squares at night, and relatively safe because lots of people are there, are Piazza Castelnuovo and Piazza Verdi. Another "safe zone" is a pedestrian strip flanked by bars and cafes, many with sidewalk tables, along Via Principe di Belmonte, lying between Via Roma and Via Ruggero Settimo. Some of these bars have live pianists in summer. If you like the sound of things, drop in for a glass of wine or a beer or two.

If you're interested in the arts and cultural venues, go by the tourist office (see "Essentials," earlier in this section) and pick up a copy of *Agenda,* which lists cafes or other venues offering live music in summer.

THE ARTS   Palermo is a cultural center of some note, with an opera and ballet season running from November to July. The principal venue for cultural presentations is the restored **Teatro Massimo ★★**, Piazza G. Verdi (℡ **091-6053111;** www.teatromassimo.it), across from the Museo Archeologico. It boasts the third largest indoor stage in Europe. Francis Ford Coppola shot the climactic opera scene here for *The Godfather: Part III.* The theater was built between 1875 and 1897 in a neoclassical style and reopened after a restoration in 1997 to celebrate its 100th birthday. During the **Festival di Verdura** from late June to mid-August, many special presentations, most often with international performers, are presented here. Ticket prices range from 10€ to 125€. The box office is open Tuesday to Sunday 10am to 3pm. **Note:** The Teatro Massimo can be visited Tuesday through Sunday from 10am to 3pm. Visits cost 5€. Guided tours in English are given Tuesday through Saturday from 10am to 3pm (bus: 101, 102, 103, 104, 107, 122, or 225).

If you have only 1 night for theater in Palermo, make it the Teatro Massimo. However, **Politeama Garibaldi,** Piazza Ruggero Settimo (℡ **091-6053315**), is also grandiose, and it, too, presents a wide season of operatic and orchestral performances. Again, the tourist office will have full details on what is being performed at the time of your visit (bus: 101, 102, 103, or 124).

CAFES   We like to start off an evening by heading to the century-old **Caffè Mazzara,** Via Generale Maglicco 15 (℡ **091-321443**), to sample wonderful ice cream, sip rich coffee, or try heady Sicilian wine. You'll run into us hanging out at the espresso bar and pastry shop on the street level. The cafe is open daily from 7:30am to 11pm (bus: 101, 102, or 103).

DANCE CLUBS   Palermo's most popular dance clubs lie in the city's commercial center, although one good one is in north Palermo. The city's main club is **Candelai,** Via Candelai 65 (℡ **091-327151;** www.candelai.it). Mainstream rock blasts throughout the night in this crowded complex of gyrating 20-year-olds. The club is open Friday through Sunday from 8pm, with no set closing time. There is no cover.

PUBS   **Villa Niscemi,** Piazza Niscemi 55 (℡ **091-6880820**), has a rustic bar, plus overflowing sidewalk tables in summer. The pub also has musical instruments; if you're the master of one (or even if you're not), you can play an instrument and entertain the patrons. Live music is featured on Fridays. A crowd of mostly 25- to 45-year-olds patronizes the joint, open daily from 7pm to 3am (closed Mon in July–Aug; bus: 614, 615, 645, or 837).

GAY & LESBIAN   Gay and lesbian bars in conservative Palermo are scarce; most gay encounters occur on the streets, in cafes, and around squares. However, gays and lesbians from 18 to 70 converge at **Exit,** Piazza San Francesco di Paola 39–40 (℡ **348-4005251;** www.exitdrinks.com). Exit is open Saturday to Thursday 10pm to 3am. Live rock or pop is often presented. In summer, tables are placed outside fronting the beautiful square (bus: 108, 118, 122, or 124).

SIDE TRIPS FROM PALERMO
Monreale

The town of Monreale is 10km (6¼ miles) from Palermo, up Monte Caputo and on the edge of the Conca d'Oro plain. In Palermo, take bus no. 389 from Piazza Indipendenza, which drops you off at Monreale's Piazza Vittorio Emanuele 40 minutes later, depending on traffic. During the day, three buses per hour leave for Monreale, costing 1.30€ one-way.

The Normans under William II founded a Benedictine monastery at Monreale in the 1170s. Eventually a great cathedral was built near the monastery's ruins. Like the Alhambra in Granada, Spain, the **Chiostro del Duomo di Monreale ★★**, Piazza Guglielmo il Buono (*℘* **091-6404413;** www.cattedraledimonreale.it), has a relatively drab facade, giving little indication of the riches inside. The interior is virtually covered with shimmering mosaics illustrating scenes from the Bible. The artwork provides a distinctly original interpretation of the old, rigid Byzantine form of decoration. The mosaics have an Eastern look despite the Western-style robed Christ reigning over his kingdom. The ceiling is ornate, even gaudy. On the north and west facades are two bronze doors depicting biblical stories in relief. The cloisters are also of interest. Built in 1166, they consist of twin mosaic columns, and every other pair bears an original design (the lava inlay was hauled from Mount Etna). Admission to the cathedral is free; if you visit the cloisters, there's a charge of 6€, free for children 17 and under.

The cathedral is open daily 8am to 6pm. From May to September, the cloister is open daily 9am to 6:30pm; off-season hours are Monday to Saturday from 9am to 6:30pm, Sunday from 9am to 1pm.

You can also visit the **treasury** (2.05€) and the **terraces** (1.60€). The treasury and terraces are open May to September daily 8am to 6pm, and October to April daily 8am to 12:30pm and 3:30 to 6pm. The terraces are actually the rooftop of the church, from which you'll be rewarded with a view of the cloisters.

Before or after your visit to Monreale, drop in at **Bar Italia,** Piazza Vittorio Emanuele (*℘* **091-6402421**), near the Duomo. The plain cookies are wonderfully flavorful and fresh; if you go early in the morning, order one of the freshly baked croissants and a cup of cappuccino, Monreale's best.

WHERE TO DINE

Taverna del Pavone ★ SICILIAN/ ITALIAN The most highly recommended restaurant in Monreale faces a

Detail from the mosaics at Chiostro del Duomo di Monreale.

small cobblestone square, about a block uphill from the cathedral. Inside, you're likely to find a friendly greeting, an artfully rustic environment that's akin to an upscale tavern, and tasty Sicilian food. We delighted in the zucchini flowers braised in a sweet-and-sour sauce; a delightful *pennette* with fava-bean sauce; and the house-made *maccheroni,* which was loaded with country cheese and absolutely delicious. For dessert, the most soothing choice might be *semifreddo*—whipped cream folded into ice cream, given extra flavor with baked almonds.

Vicolo Pensato 18. 𝄐 **091-6406209.** www.tavernadelpavone.eu. Reservations recommended. Main courses 9€–18€. AE, DC, MC, V. Tues–Sun noon–3:30pm and 7:30–11:30pm.

Mondello Lido

When the summer sun burns hot, and when old men on the square seek a place in the shade and bambini tire of their toys, it's beach weather. For Palermo residents, that means **Mondello,** 12km (7½ miles) east. Before this beachfront town started attracting the wealthy of Palermo, it was a fishing village (and still is), and you can see rainbow-colored fishing boats bobbing in the harbor. A good sandy beach stretches for about 2.4km (1½ miles), and it's filled to capacity on a July or August day. Some women traveling alone find Mondello more inviting and less intimidating than Palermo. From Piazza Politeama in Palermo, bus no. 806 runs to Mondello daily and throughout the year.

Cefalù ★★

Another good day-trip destination lies 81km (50 miles) east from Palermo, where the fishing village of **Cefalù** is tucked onto every inch of a spit of land underneath an awesome crag called the Rocca. The village is known for its Romanesque cathedral, an outstanding achievement of Arab-Norman architecture (see below). Its beaches, its medley of architectural styles, and its narrow streets were captured in the Oscar-winning film *Cinema Paradiso.* You can tour the town in half a day and spend the rest of the time enjoying life on the beach, especially in summer.

From Palermo, three dozen **trains** make the 1-hour trip daily, costing 5€ one-way. For information and schedules in Palermo, call 𝄐 **892021. SAIS,** Via Balsamo 16 (𝄐 **091-6166028;** www.saisautolinee.it), runs **buses** between Palermo and Cefalù, costing from 7.50€ one-way for the 1½-hour trip. If you're **driving,** follow S113 east from Palermo to Cefalù. Driving time is about 1½ hours. You'll have to park at the top of the Rocca and then join lines of visitors walking up and down the narrow, steep streets near the water. You'll pass a lot of forgettable shops. In the past few years, it seems that half of the denizens of Cefalù have become trinket peddlers and souvenir hawkers.

You'll find the **tourist office** at Corso Ruggero 77 (𝄐 **0921-421050**), open Monday to Saturday 8am to 7:30pm, and Sunday 9am to 1pm (closed Sun in winter).

Make a beeline to Cefalù's Duomo first thing in the morning so that you can avoid the tour bus hordes. Resembling a military fortress, the **Duomo ★★**, Piazza del Duomo, off Corso Ruggero (𝄐 **0921-922021**), was built by Roger II to fulfill a vow he'd made when faced with a possible shipwreck. Construction began in 1131, and in time two square towers rose, curiously placed between the sea and a rocky promontory. The architectural line of the cathedral boasts a severe elegance that has earned it a position in many art history books. The

Cefalù's beach.

interior, which took a century to complete, overwhelms you with 16 Byzantine and Roman columns supporting towering capitals. The horseshoe arches are one of the island's best examples of the Saracen influence on Norman architecture. The celebrated **mosaic ★** of Christ the Pantocrator, one of only three on Sicily, in the dome of the cathedral apse is alone worth the trip. The nearby mosaic of the Virgin with angels and the Apostles is a well-preserved work from 1148. In the transept is a statue of the Madonna. Roger's plan to have a tomb placed in the Duomo was derailed by the authorities at Palermo's cathedral, where he rests today. Admission is free, and the church is open daily 8am to noon and 3:30 to 7pm. In the off season, it is open daily 8am to noon and 3:30 to 6pm.

Before leaving town, try to visit the **Museo Mandralisca ★**, Via Mandralisca 13 (© **0921-421547;** www.museomandralisca.it), opposite the cathedral. It has an outstanding art collection, including the 1470 portrait of an unknown by Antonello da Messina. Some art critics have journeyed all the way from Rome just to stare at this handsome work, and it's often featured on Sicilian tourist brochures. Admission is 5€. Opening hours are June, July, and September daily 9am to 7pm, August daily 9am to 11pm, October to May daily 9am to 1pm and 3 to 7pm.

WHERE TO DINE

Kentia ★★ ITALIAN   This restaurant manages to evoke a bit more glamour, and a lot more style, than some of its nearby competitors. It's a cool hideaway from the oppressive sun, thanks in part to tiled floors, high masonry vaulting, and an understated elegance. A dozen homemade pasta dishes are prepared daily, and you'd have to walk to Messina to find swordfish and wild fennel as good as that grilled here. We generally stick to the *pesce del giorno* (catch of the day), which can be grilled to your specifications. The chefs also prepare a daily vegetarian fixed-price menu as well as one devoted entirely to fish. We've sampled both and recommend them heartily.

Via N. Botta 15. ℰ **0921-423801.** Reservations recommended. Main courses 7€–16€; fixed-price vegetarian menu 22€, fish menu 30€. AE, DC, MC, V. June–Sept daily noon–3pm and 7:30–11pm; Oct–May Wed–Mon noon–3pm and 7:30–11pm.

Segesta ★★

There's only one reason to come to Segesta: to see a single amazing temple in a lonely field. For some visitors, that's reason enough because it's one of the best-preserved ancient temples in all Italy. It takes about an hour to get here from Palermo, and it makes a good brief stop en route to **Erice** (see below).

Segesta was the ancient city of the Elymi, a people of mysterious origin who are linked by some to the Trojans. As the major city in western Sicily, it was brought into a series of conflicts with the rival power nearby, Selinus (Selinunte). From the 6th to 5th centuries B.C., there were near-constant hostilities. The Athenians came from the east to aid the Segestans in 415 B.C., but the expedition ended in disaster, eventually forcing the city to turn to Hannibal of Carthage.

Twice in the 4th century B.C., Segesta was besieged and conquered, once by Dionysius, again by Agathocles (a brutal victor who tortured, mutilated, or made slaves of most of the citizenry). Segesta, in time, turned on its old but dubious ally, Carthage. Like all Greek cities of Sicily, it ultimately fell to the Romans.

The main sight in Segesta is its remarkable **Doric temple ★★★** from the 5th century B.C. Although never completed, it's in an excellent state of preservation. (The entablature still remains.) The temple was far enough away from the ancient town to escape being leveled during the "scorched earth" days of the Vandals and Arabs. From its position on a hill, the Doric temple commands a majestic setting. Although you can scale the hill on foot, you're likely to encounter boys trying to hustle you for a donkey ride. (We advise against it—some of these poor animals have saddle sores and seem to be in pain when ridden.)

The site is open daily from 9am to 7pm (closes at 4pm off season); admission costs 9€ for adults and free for children 17 and under. The ticket office closes an hour before the temple park closes.

After visiting the temple, you can take a bus to the large **Teatro ★** at the top of Mount Barbaro at 431m (1,414 ft.). The one-way fare costs 2€, and buses depart at the rate of two per hour during the day. The theater was constructed in a semicircle with a diameter of 63m (207 ft.). It was hewn right out of the side of the mountain, its stage area facing to the north. In olden days, the theater could hold as many as 4,000 spectators, and the site is still used for the staging of both modern and classical plays presented from mid-July to early August every other year. Dating from the 3rd century B.C., the theater was constructed during the Hellenistic period.

There are approximately four **trains** per day between Palermo and Segesta, and buses leave almost hourly. The station is about a 1km (½-mile) walk to the ancient site. Special bus service is usually offered in conjunction with the evening plays. For information, contact the tourist office in Palermo. By **car,** drive 57km (35 miles) west from Palermo along A29, then take the A29 (toward Trapani); after 7km (4⅓ miles) take the Segesta exit and follow the signs to the archaeological site. From Selinunte, head to Castlevetrano to connect to A29

A traditionally dressed street musician and his horse in Erice.

heading north. After about 20km (12 miles), follow the A29 toward Trapani; after 7km, take the Segesta exit and follow the signs to the archaeological site.

Erice ★★

Established some 3,000 years ago, Erice is an enchanting medieval city. From its thrilling mountaintop setting, two sheer cliffs drop 755m (2,478 ft.) to open up vistas across the plains of Trapani and down the west coast of Sicily. On a clear day, you can see Cape Bon in Tunisia, but this Sicilian aerie is often shrouded in a mist that only adds to the mystique (or, in winter, the misery; temperatures can plummet below Sicilian norms and snow and hail are not uncommon).

Erice is a lovely place to spend an afternoon wandering the medieval streets, with their baroque balconies and flowering vines, and drinking in the vistas. The southwest corner of town contains the Villa Balio gardens, originally laid out in the 19th century. Beyond the gardens, a path winds along the cliff edge up to Erice's highest point, the **Castello di Venere ★**, today little more than crumbling Norman-era walls surrounding the sacred site where a temple to Venus once stood. Piercing the walls are several windows and doorways with spectacular views across the countryside.

Erice is noted for its pastries. Stop off at **Pasticceria Grammatico,** Via Vittorio Emanuele 14, near Piazza Umberto (© **0923-869390;** www.maria grammatico.it), to sample sugary almond treats flavored with lemon or other citrus juices.

Erice craftspeople are as famous for their rugs as they are for their ceramics. **Ceramica Ericina,** Via Vittorio Emanuele 7 (© **0923-869140**), offers the best selection of multicolored Erice carpets. These rugs are highly valued and hand-woven in colors of red, yellow, and blue.

Rail passengers arrive at the station at Trapani, which is 14km (8½ miles) to the southeast. AST buses (© **840-000323;** www.aziendasicilianatrasporti.it) depart from Piazza Montalto in Trapani at the rate of seven per day, heading for

Erice. Service is daily year-round from 6:40am to 5:30pm in winter (8pm in summer), the trip lasting 50 minutes and costing 2.50€ one-way. If you're driving, follow the A29 southwest from Palermo or Segesta to the first Trapani exit, then continue along the switchback road up the mountain.

THE AEOLIAN ISLANDS ★★★

Lipari: 30km (19 miles) N of Milazzo; Stromboli: 81km (50 miles) N of Milazzo; Vulcano: 20km (12 miles) N of Milazzo

The Aeolian Islands (Isole Eolie o Lipari) have been inhabited for more than 3,000 years, in spite of volcanic activity that even now causes the earth to issue forth sulfuric belches, streams of molten lava, and hissing clouds of steam. Ancient Greek sailors believed that these seven windswept islands were the home of Aeolus, god of the winds. He supposedly lived in a cave on Vulcano, keeping the winds of the world in a bag to be opened only with great caution.

Lipari (36 sq. km/14 sq. miles) is the largest and most developed island; **Stromboli** (13 sq. km/5 sq. miles) is the most distant and volcanically active; and **Vulcano** (21 sq. km/8 sq. miles) is the closest island to the Sicilian mainland, with its brooding, potentially volatile cone and therapeutic mud baths. The other islands (**Salina, Filicudi, Alicudi,** and **Panarea**) offer only bare-bones facilities and are visited mainly by day-trippers.

Despite the volcanoes, the area attracts tourists (mainly Germans and Italians) with crystalline waters that have great snorkeling, scuba, and spearfishing, and beaches composed of hot black sand and rocky outcroppings jutting into the Tyrrhenian Sea. The volcanoes offer the thrill of peering into a bubbling crater.

The view from Salina.

Essentials

GETTING THERE Ferries and hydrofoils service all of the Aeolian Islands from the port of Milazzo, on the northeastern coast of Sicily 32km (20 miles) west of Messina. Both **Società Siremar,** Via Dei Mille (© **090-9283242;** www.siremar.it), and **Ustica Lines,** Via Rizzo (© **090-9287821;** www.usticalines.it), operate ferry and hydrofoil routes.

The Milazzo-Vulcano-Lipari-Salina ferry lines leave Milazzo twice daily at 7am and 9am. It takes 1½ hours to reach Vulcano; a one-way ticket costs 11€. Lipari is 2 hours from Milazzo; a one-way ticket costs 12€. To reach Stromboli, take the Milazzo-Panarea-Stromboli ferry line, departing Milazzo at 7am

Tuesday to Saturday, and at 2:30pm Monday, Wednesday, Thursday, Saturday, and Sunday. The Stromboli trip takes 5 hours and costs 23€ one-way.

For a faster option, take the Milazzo-Vulcano-Lipari-Salina hydrofoil line, which reaches Vulcano in 30 minutes; a one-way ticket costs 17€. It takes 1 hour to reach Lipari and costs 18€ one-way. Siremar makes the trip 6 to 12 times daily from 7:05am to 6:10pm, while Ustica Lines makes six runs daily from 6:20am to 7:10pm. To reach Stromboli, use the Milazzo-Panarea-Stromboli hydrofoil line, which takes 2½ hours and costs 23€ one-way. *Warning:* Always check the schedules, as they are subject to change at any time, depending on weather conditions and other factors.

For more information on ferry and hydrofoil connections, call ☎ **0923-873813,** or 892-123 within Italy only.

If you're driving from Messina in the east, take S113 west to Palermo until you come to the turnoff for the port at Milazzo.

VISITOR INFORMATION   The **tourist office** in Lipari is at Via Vittorio Emanuele 202 (☎ **090-9880095**). In July and August, it is open Monday to Friday 8:30am to 1:30pm and 4:30 to 7:30pm, Saturday 8am to 2pm. From September to June, hours are Monday to Friday 8:30am to 1:30pm and 4:30 to 7:30pm. There's no information center in Stromboli or Vulcano.

Lipari ★

Homer called it "a floating island, a wall of bronze and splendid smooth sheer cliffs." The offspring of seven volcanic eruptions, Lipari is the largest of the Aeolians. Lipari is also the name of the island's only real town. It's the administrative headquarters of the Aeolian Islands (except autonomous Salina). The town sits on a plateau of red volcanic rock on the southeastern shore framed by two beaches, Marina Lunga, which functions as the harbor, and Marina Corta.

Its dominant feature is a 16th-century **Spanish castle.** Within its walls lies a 17th-century cathedral featuring a 16th-century Madonna and an 18th-century silver statue of San Bartolomeo. There's also an **archaeological park** where stratified clues about continuous civilizations dating from 1700 B.C. have been uncovered.

Excellent artifacts from the Stone and Bronze ages, as well as relics from Greek and Roman acropolises that once stood here, are housed next door in the former bishop's palace, now the **Museo Archeologico Eoliano ★★**, Via del Castello (☎ **090-9880174**), one of Sicily's major archaeological museums. It houses one of the world's finest Neolithic collections. The oldest discoveries date from 4200 B.C. Lustrous red ceramics, known as the "Diana style," come from the last Neolithic period, 3000 to 2500 B.C. Other exhibits are reconstructed necropolises from the Middle Bronze Age and a 6th-century-A.D. depiction of Greek warships. Some 1,200 pieces of painted terra cotta from the 4th and 3rd centuries B.C., including stone theatrical masks, are on exhibit. The museum also houses the only Late Bronze Age (8th-c.-B.C.) necropolis found in Sicily. It's open daily 9am to 1:30pm and 3 to 6pm. Admission is 6€.

The most popular **beaches** are at **Canneto,** about a 20-minute walk north of Lipari on the eastern coast, and, just north of it, **Spiaggia Bianca** (named for the white sand, an oddity among the region's black sands). To reach the beach from Canneto, take the waterfront road, climb the stairs of Via Marina Garibaldi, and then veer right down a narrow cobbled path for about 300m (984 ft.).

Acquacalda (Hot Water) is the island's northernmost city, but it's not noted for beaches (the black sand is rocky and unpleasant for walking or lying on). The town also is known for its obsidian and pumice quarries. West of Acquacalda at Quattropani, you can make a steep climb to the **Duomo,** where the point of interest isn't the cathedral but the panoramic view from the church grounds. On the west coast, 4km (2½ miles) from Lipari, the island's other great view is available by making another steep climb to the **Quattrocchi Belvedere.**

Twenty-nine kilometers (18 miles) of road circle the island, connecting all its villages and attractions. Buses run by Lipari's **Autobus Urso Guglielmo,** Via Cappuccini 9 (✆ **090-9811262;** www.ursobus.com), make 10 circuits of the island per day. Tickets costing 2€ are purchased onboard from the driver. Along the way you'll pass the highlights of Lipari's scenery. It's also possible to summon one of the independently operated taxis, most of which are found at Marina Corta.

WHERE TO STAY

Hotel Carasco   This hotel enjoys the most dramatic location in Lipari, with its own private stretch of rocks opening onto the water and panoramic views from a bougainvillea-draped pool. The Carasco consists of two buildings that sit on a lonely bluff by the sea. The cool interior, with its terra-cotta floors and dark-wood furniture, contrasts with the bright heat of the outdoors. Each comfortable, well-furnished guest room comes with a ceiling fan, rustic artifacts, and a bathroom with shower or tub; ask for a room with a private balcony. Grace notes include an afternoon tea service and piano music in the lounge after dinner.

Porto delle Genti, 98055 Lipari. ✆ **090-9811605.** Fax 090-9811828. www.carasco.it. 89 units. 50€–200€ per person. Rates include continental breakfast. MC, V. Closed Nov 2–Apr 2. **Amenities:** Restaurant; bar; babysitting; saltwater pool; room service; Wi-Fi (2.50€ per hr., in lobby). *In room:* A/C, hair dryer, minibar.

Villa Meligunis ★★   This first-class hotel is as good as it gets in the Aeolian Islands. Less than 45m (148 ft.) from the ferry docks, the appealingly contemporary villa rose from a cluster of 17th-century fishermen's cottages at Marina Corta. It oozes stylish charm, from its lovely fountain to its dramatic rooftop terrace to its wrought-iron bedsteads used by fashion photographers as backdrops. Guest rooms are comfortably furnished with summery pieces and well-maintained bathrooms with either tub or shower.

Via Marte 7, 98055 Lipari. ✆ **090-9812426.** Fax 090-9880149. www.villameligunis.it. 32 units. 160€–325€ double; 225€–395€ suite. Rates include continental breakfast. AE, DC, MC, V. Free parking. Closed Nov 7–Dec 25. **Amenities:** Restaurant; 2 bars; babysitting; saltwater pool; room service. *In room:* A/C, TV, hair dryer, minibar, Wi-Fi (8€ per hr.).

WHERE TO DINE

E Pulera ★★ SICILIAN/AEOLIAN   Owned by the same family that runs the Filippino (see below), this restaurant emphasizes its Aeolian origins. Artifacts and maps of the islands fashioned from ceramic tiles are scattered about. Some tables occupy a terrace with a view of a flowering lawn. Specialties include a delightful version of fishermen's soup, swordfish ragout, and risotto with squid in its own ink. We had one of the most delightful pasta dishes we've ever tasted in the Aeolian Islands: fettuccine with yellow pumpkin, shrimp, and wild fennel.

Via Diana. ✆ **090-9811158.** www.pulera.it. Reservations recommended. Main courses 12€–20€. DC, MC, V. Daily 8pm–midnight. Closed Oct–May 15.

Filippino ★★ SICILIAN/AEOLIAN   It's a pleasant surprise to find such a fine restaurant in such a remote location. Filippino has thrived in the heart of town, near the town hall, since 1910. You'll dine in one of two large rooms or on a terrace ringed with flowering shrubs and potted plants. Menu items are based on old-fashioned Sicilian recipes and prepared with flair. The chef's signature pasta dish is "Aeolian orchids," a curly pasta topped with tomatoes, pine nuts, capers, garlic, basil, mint, and pecorino cheese. We especially enjoyed the swordfish with basil and the eggplant *caponata.*

Piazza Mazzini. ✆ **090-9811002.** www.filippino.it. Reservations required July–Aug. Main courses 8€–17€. AE, DC, MC, V. Daily noon–2:30pm and 7:30–10:30pm. Closed Mon, Nov 10–Dec 26.

La Nassa ★ 🍴 SICILIAN/AEOLIAN   At this enchanting restaurant, the delectable cuisine of Donna Teresa matches the friendly enthusiasm of her son Bartolo, who has thousands of interesting stories to tell. The food is the most genuine on the island, prepared with respect for both old traditions and modern tastes. After the *sette perle* (seven pearl) appetizer, a combination of fresh fish, sweet shrimp, and spices, you can try your choice of fish cooked to your specifications. Local favorites include *sarago, cernia,* and *dentice,* as delicate in texture as their names are untranslatable. For dessert, try cookies with Malvasia wine.

Via G. Franza 41. ✆ **090-9811319.** www.lanassa.it. Reservations recommended. Main courses 9€–21€. AE, MC, V. Apr–June Fri–Wed 8:30am–3pm and 6pm–midnight; July–Oct daily 8:30am–3pm and 6pm–midnight. Closed Nov–Easter.

Stromboli ★★★

The most distant island in the archipelago, Stromboli achieved notoriety and became a household word in the U.S. in 1950 with the release of a Roberto Rossellini cinéma vérité film starring Ingrid Bergman. The American public was far more interested in the "illicit" affair between Bergman and Rossellini than in the film. Although the affair was tame by today's standards, it temporarily ended Bergman's American film career, and she was denounced on the Senate floor. Movie fans today are more likely to remember Stromboli from the film of the Jules Verne novel *Journey to the Center of the Earth,* starring James Mason.

The entire surface of Stromboli is the cone of a sluggish but active volcano. Puffs of smoke can be seen during the day. At night on the **Slope of Fire (Sciara del Fuoco)** ★★, lava glows red-hot on its way down to meet the sea with a loud hiss and a cloud of steam—a memorable vision that might leave you feeling a little too vulnerable.

In fact, the island can serve as a fantasyland for those who have volcanomania. The main attraction is a steep, difficult climb to the lip of the 915m (3,000-ft.) **Gran Cratere** ★★★. The view of bubbling pools of ooze (which glow with heat at night) is accompanied by rising clouds of steam and a sulfuric stench. The journey is a 3-hour hike best taken in early morning or late afternoon to avoid the worst of the brutal sunshine—and even then it requires plenty of sunscreen and water and a good pair of shoes. The law states that you can climb the slope only with a guide. The island's authorized guide company is **Guide**

The Slope of Fire in Stromboli.

Alpine Autorizzate (© 090-986263; www.stromboliguide.it), which charges 35€ per person to scale the volcano. Guides lead groups on a 3-hour trip up the mountain, leaving at 5pm and returning at 11pm. The trip down takes only 2 hours, but you're allowed an hour at the rim.

In spite of the volcano and its sloped terrain, there are two settlements. **Ginostra** is on the southwestern shore, little more than a cluster of summer homes with only 15 year-round residents. **Stromboli** is on the northeastern shore, a conglomeration of the villages of Ficogrande, San Vincenzo, and Piscita, where the only in-town attraction is the black-sand beach.

WHERE TO STAY

La Locanda del Barbablu ★ 🎁 This is a quirky choice, a charming little isolated Aeolian inn with only a few rooms, standing against turn-of-the-20th-century breakfronts. Rooms are small but comfortably furnished, often with four-poster beds encrusted with cherubs and mother-of-pearl inlay. A wide terrace opens onto dramatic views of the volcano and the sea. All units have well-maintained bathrooms with tub/shower combinations. The restaurant is worth a visit even if you're not a guest.

Via Vittorio Emanuele 17–19, 98050 Stromboli. © **090-986118.** Fax 090-986323. www.barbablu. it. 6 units. 140€–220€ double. AE, DC, MC, V. Closed Nov 1–Apr 9.

La Sirenetta Park Hotel ★★ These are the island's finest accommodations, a well-maintained, government-rated four-star hotel. It's the best equipped, with a scenic terrace, a nightclub, and a restaurant serving the best cuisine of any hotel here. It also has an idyllic location on the Ficogrande Beach in front of Strombolicchio, the towering rock that rises out of the waters at San Vincenzo. Guest rooms are attractively furnished, with tiled floors and an airy feel. All come with private bathrooms—half with showers, half with tubs. The hotel is justly proud of having the island's best pool as well, complete with hydromassage. Facilities include a fitness center and a dive center that also offers water-skiing, sailing, and windsurfing.

Via Marina 33, 98050 Ficogrande (Stromboli). ✆ **090-986025.** Fax 090-986124. www.la sirenetta.it. 60 units. 130€–310€ double; 85€–190€ per person double with half board. Rates include continental breakfast. AE, DC, MC, V. Closed Nov–Mar. **Amenities:** Restaurant; 2 bars; exercise room; Internet (free, in lobby); saltwater pool; room service; tennis court; limited water-sports equipment. *In room:* A/C, TV, hair dryer, minibar.

WHERE TO DINE

As the sun sets and the volcano lights the sky, everybody heads for the island's most popular bar, **Bar Ingrid,** at Via Michele Bianchi 1 (✆ **090-986385**).

Il Canneto AEOLIAN   This typical island restaurant was constructed in the old style, with white walls and dark tables. It's nothing fancy, but it's one of the more reliable joints in town. The specialty is always fish caught in local waters. A delectable pasta dish is the macaroni with minced swordfish or white fish cooked in a light tomato sauce with fresh herbs. Swordfish roulades are also prepared with a certain flair here.

Via Roma 64. ✆ **090-986014.** Reservations recommended. Main courses 10€–19€. AE, MC, V. Daily 7–11pm. Closed Oct–Mar.

Punta Lena ★★ AEOLIAN   The island's best cuisine is served at this old Aeolian house tastefully converted into a 17-seat restaurant, with a terrace opening onto the sea. The restaurant lies on the beach, a 10-minute walk from the center of town. There is a genuine effort here to cook with fresh products whenever possible. Stick to whatever the fishermen have brought in that day. The *gnocchi alla Saracena,* with white fish, capers, olives, and tomatoes, is also excellent. The restaurant stocks the island's widest selection of wines.

Via Marina Garibaldi 8 (Località Ficogrande). ✆ **090-986204.** Reservations recommended. Main courses 10€–18€. AE, DC, MC, V. Daily noon–2:30pm and 7–11pm. Closed Nov–Mar.

Vulcano ★★★

The island closest to the mainland, the ancient Thermessa, figured heavily in the mythologies of the region. The still-active **Vulcano della Fossa** was thought to be not only the home of Vulcan, but also the gateway to Hades. Thucydides, Siculus, and Aristotle each recorded eruptions. Three dormant craters also exist on the island, but a climb to the rim of the active **Gran Cratere (Big Crater)** ★★★ draws the most attention. It hasn't erupted since 1890, but one look inside the sulfur-belching hole makes you understand how it could've inspired the hellish legends surrounding it. The 418m (1,372-ft.) peak is an easier climb than the one on Stromboli, taking just about an hour—though it's just as hot, and the same precautions prevail. Avoid midday, load up on sunscreen and water, and wear good hiking shoes.

Here the risks of mounting a volcano aren't addressed by legislation, so you can make the climb without a guide. Breathing the sulfuric air at the summit has its risks, though, because the steam is tainted with numerous toxins. To get to the peak from Porto Levante, the main port, follow Via Piano away from the sea for about 200m (656 ft.) until you see the first of the CRATERE signs, and then follow the marked trail.

Laghetto di Fanghi, famous free mud baths that reputedly cure every known ailment, are along Via Provinciale a short way from the port. Be warned that the mud discolors everything from cloth to jewelry, which is one explanation

Hiking the Gran Cratere on Vulcano.

for the prevalent nudity. Expect to encounter muddy pools brimming with naked, package-tour Germans. Within sight, the *acquacalda* features hot-water jets that act as a natural Jacuzzi. Either can scald you if you step or sit on the vents that release the heat, so take care if you decide to enter.

The island offers one of the few smooth beaches in the entire chain, the **Spiaggia Sabbie Nere (Black Sands Beach),** with dark sand so hot in the midday sun that thongs or wading shoes are suggested if you plan to while away your day along the shore. You can find the beach by following signs posted along Via Ponente.

A knowledge of street names is worthless, really, because there are no signs. Not to worry—the locals who gather at the dock are friendly and experienced at giving directions to tongue-tied foreign visitors, especially because all they ever have to point out are the paths to the crater, the mud baths, and the beach. You'll need to spend little time in the village center itself. This is a drab 1970s eyesore filled with souvenir shops and fast-food snack bars.

WHERE TO STAY

Hotel Eolian ★ 🐾 This hotel opens onto Ponente Bay. In typical Aeolian style, the main building is surrounded by stucco bungalows and set in a lush garden studded with palms. None of the bungalows have a view of the water—that's reserved for the restaurant and bar—but most guests spend their days beside the sea anyway. Guest rooms are midsize and furnished in a minimalist style; each has a tiled bathroom with shower. Walk down from the terrace of the bar to reach the beach, where you can indulge in various watersports or rent a small boat to explore the more remote parts of the coastline. The thermal sulfurous pool is said to aid poor circulation.

Via Porto Levante, 98050 Vulcano. 🕿 **090-9852151.** Fax 090-9852153. www.eolianhotel.com. 88 units. 70€–97€ per person double. Rates include continental breakfast. 83€–117€ per person with half board. AE, DC, MC, V. Closed Oct–Apr. **Amenities:** Restaurant; bar; babysitting; 2 salt-water pools; tennis court (lit). *In room:* A/C, TV, hair dryer, minibar.

Les Sables Noirs ★★   Les Sables Noirs is the most elegant place to stay on Vulcano, offering a surprising level of luxury and excellent service in this remote outpost. Its rooms overlook a black-sand beach and front a panoramic sweep of the Bay of Ponente. The stucco and bamboo touches evoke a Caribbean resort. Accommodations are spacious, comfortably furnished, and decorated in typical Mediterranean style; many units open onto a wide balcony. All have tiled bathrooms, about half with showers and the rest with tubs. There's a solarium as well. Another reason to stay here is the restaurant, which serves impressive regional specialties and opens onto a broad terrace in front of the beach.

Via Porto di Ponente, 98050 Vulcano. © **090-9850.** Fax 090-9852454. www.framonhotels. com. 48 units. 240€–320€ double; 280€–380€ suite. AE, DC, MC, V. Closed Oct–Mar. **Amenities:** Restaurant; 2 bars; babysitting; saltwater pool. *In room:* A/C, TV, hair dryer, minibar.

WHERE TO DINE

Vincenzino ◢ SICILIAN/AEOLIAN   This is the most appealing of the *trattorie* near the ferry port. Known for its hefty portions and affordable prices, it serves clients in a rustic setting. You might begin your meal with spaghetti with crayfish, capers, and a tomato sauce. We're fond of the *risotto alla pescatora,* with crayfish, mussels, and other seafood. Another good choice is the house-style macaroni with ricotta, eggplant, tomatoes, and herbs. From October to March, the menu is limited to a simple array of platters from the bar.

Via Porto di Levante. © **090-9852016.** www.ristorantevincenzino.com. Reservations recommended. Main courses 8€–14€; fixed-price menu 23€. AE, DC, MC, V. Daily noon–3pm and 7–10pm.

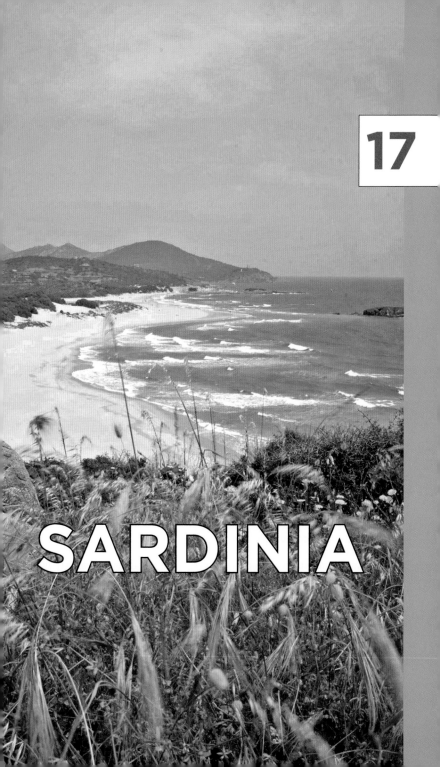

17

SARDINIA

After Sicily, Sardinia is the largest island in the Mediterranean. Although it seems far removed from the rest of Italy, it lies only 187km (116 miles) to the west of the mainland. It's much more closely linked to Corsica in France, a similar island lying only 16km (10 miles) to the north of Sardinia.

Its native language, Sardo, isn't automatically understood by speakers of Italian. Rather, Sardo is the Romance language closest to oral Latin, with heavy doses of the languages of the island's many conquerors (Arabic, Portuguese, Catalán, and Spanish) thrown in.

Sardinia is 206km (162 miles) north to south, and it is overgrown in many parts with a thick network of bushes *(maquis)* that make penetration extremely difficult. Dotted with hundreds of caves and grottoes, Sardinia earns its livelihood from the sea, from shepherding, and from the agricultural products that can be coaxed out of the island's hot and stony soil. The thick covering of forest that was the island's pride was burned to power northern Italy's industrial revolution in the 18th and 19th centuries, part of a pattern of abuse and exploitation that Sardinia has endured since prehistory.

Certain pockets of dazzling poshness have been carved out of Sardinia's northeast corner, most notably the Costa Smeralda. Here, the yachtsmen of Europe savor the island's tricky breezes and treacherous currents, sailing on the waters by day and reveling in sybaritic splendor by night. In that small congregation of upscale hotels, jewelry and fashionable nudity are the order of the day. Elsewhere parts of Sardinia slumber in the values and beliefs of another day, clinging tenaciously to ancient customs.

Many northern Europeans flock to Sardinia in summer, viewing it as an off-the-beaten track adventure. Rings of beaches surround the coast, but if you venture inland you will still find abundant wildlife, flora, and hundreds of seemingly unexplored grottoes. Much of the island is still so pristine that Clint Eastwood–style "spaghetti Westerns" were once filmed here. Aggressively out of sync with mainland Italy, the Sards begin their calendar on September 1; and each month has a name unrelated to any of those of Roman origin generally in use throughout western Europe.

Rural Sards still follow country rituals, and they still profess a quasi-belief in magic. Native dances are still danced to a strangely droning music, and prizes are awarded at weddings for spontaneous versification. Despite the encroachment of modern Italy upon the island, many islanders still cling to their traditional way of life.

PREVIOUS PAGE: **A view of the sea from a Sardinian beach.**

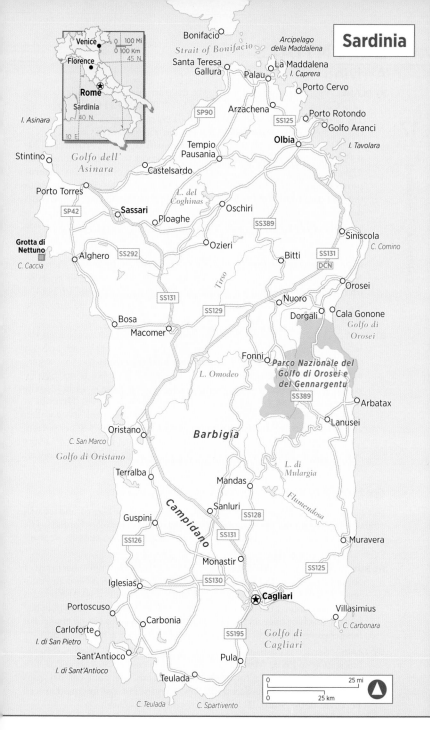

Sardinia

Bonifacio

Strait of Bonifacio

Arcipelago della Maddalena

Santa Teresa Gallura

La Maddalena

I. Caprera

Palau

Porto Cervo

Arzachena

SP90

Porto Rotondo

SS125

Golfo Aranci

Olbia

I. Tavolara

Tempio Pausania

I. Asinara

Stintino

Golfo dell' Asinara

Castelsardo

Porto Torres

L. del Coghinas

Oschiri

Sassari

SP42

Ploaghe

SS389

Siniscola

C. Comino

Grotta di Nettuno

Ozieri

Alghero

SS292

Bitti

SS131 DCN

C. Caccia

Orosei

SS131

Tirso

Nuoro

Bosa

SS129

Dorgali

Cala Gonone

Macomer

Golfo di Orosei

Fonni

Parco Nazionale del Golfo di Orosei e del Gennargentu

L. Omodeo

SS389

Arbatax

Lanusei

Oristano

C. San Marco

Barbagia

Golfo di Oristano

L. di Mulargia

Terralba

Mandas

Flumendosa

Guspini

Sanluri

SS128

SS126

SS131

Muravera

Campidano

Monastir

SS125

Iglesias

SS130

Portoscuso

Cagliari

Villasimius

Carloforte

Carbonia

C. Carbonara

I. di San Pietro

SS195

Golfo di Cagliari

Sant'Antioco

I. di Sant'Antioco

Pula

Teulada

C. Teulada

C. Spartivento

0   25 mi

0   25 km

Inset map

0   100 Mi
0   100 Km

45 N.

Venice

Florence

Rome

40 N.

Sardinia

10 E

I. Asinara

ESSENTIALS
Arriving

BY PLANE   Flight is the fast way to go. The main arrival point is outside the capital of Cagliari at Aeroporto-Cagliari-Elmas (℄ **070-211211;** www.sogaer.it). The airport lies 6km (4 miles) west of the center of Cagliari. Buses run from the airport to Piazza Matteotti in front of the train station in Cagliari.

The city of Alghero is serviced by **Aeroporto Alghero-Fertilia** (℄ **079-935282;** www.aeroportodialghero.it). The airport is 13km (8 miles) from Alghero and linked by a bus to the main station in the center of town. **Aeroporto Costa Smeralda** (℄ **0789-563444;** www.geasar.com) serves both the Emerald Coast and the town of Olbia, to which it is linked by bus. Taxis run the 4km (2½ miles) distance to the heart of the Costa Smeralda.

Meridiana (℄ **892928** for bookings in Italy, or 0789-52682 outside Italy; www.meridiana.it) offers the most flights. It has direct flights from most major Italian cities, including Milan, Rome, and Bologna, to the Olbia Costa Smeralda airport. Other flights connect Milan, Rome, Florence, Naples, Palermo, Turin, and Verona to Cagliari. Flights are also available from Paris to Olbia. **Alitalia** (℄ **800/223-5730** in the U.S., 08714/241424 in London, or 06-2222 in Italy) flies from Rome's Fiumicino Airport to Cagliari several times daily in 40 minutes.

BY BOAT   The major car-ferry route to Sardinia is from Civitavecchia on the Italian mainland, which is 80km (50 miles) north of Rome. Vessels arrive at Olbia on the eastern coast of Sardinia, providing access to the chic resorts of Costa Esmeralda and Porto Rotondo. The crossing takes 7 hours. Service is also available from Civitavecchia to Cagliari (trip time is 14 hr.). Many lines operate these car ferries, the most reliable of which is **Tirrenia** at Stazione Marittima in Civitavecchia. In July and August, book space well in advance. A one-way trip from Civitavecchia to Olbia costs 50€ per person. The lines also run ferries from Naples to Cagliari that take about 17 hours and cost 70€ per person. To call Tirrenia, dial ℄ **892123** in Italy, or 02-26302803 outside Italy.

Getting Around Sardinia

You can take your car by ferry from the Italian mainland (see above), and we recommend that you do so if you want to leave your resort and explore Sardinia. The main roads are in fairly good condition, but facilities such as gas stations are inadequate in the east.

BY BUS   **ARST** (℄ **800-865042;** www.arst.sardegna.it) links the major towns of Sardinia, including Cagliari and Alghero. The main station is Stazione Autolinee, Piazza Matteotti in Cagliari, which has schedules of all ARST buses serving the island. Standard fares can be purchased in advance and punched into the machine once on the bus. The Stazione Autolinee has no phone. For bus schedules of all ARST buses, call ARST at the phone number above.

BY TRAIN   Service is inadequate, the main station being in Cagliari next to the bus station on Piazza Matteotti. There are good connections between Olbia (if you're at the Costa Smeralda) and Cagliari; one train per day runs between Olbia and Cagliari and takes 4 hours. For rail information, call **Ferrovie dello Stato** (℄ **892021;** www.trenitalia.com).

CAGLIARI ★

268km (166 miles) S of Olbia

The capital of Sardinia, Cagliari, lies on the southern tier of the island, surrounded by sea and hills. Known to the Phoenicians and Romans, today it appears modern except for a dilapidated medieval quarter that occupies a long, narrow hill running north to south.

For the best overall view, head for a large terrace on the south side of the hill, **Passeggiata Umberto I ★★**. From here you can see the harbor, the lagoon, and the lower city.

In spite of ugly contemporary buildings on the outskirts, the old town, or **Castello ★★**, is much as D. H. Lawrence saw it in 1921, filled with *palazzi* from the 1300s and 1400s and some decaying churches of various styles. Lawrence described it as piling up "lofty and almost miniature. It makes me think of Jerusalem: without trees, without cover, rising rather bare and proud, remote as if back in history, like a town in a monkish, illuminated missal."

After exploring the old town, you can stroll along the broad avenues of the waterfront for a different prospective. The waterfront is enveloped by salt flats where hundreds of pink flamingos feed.

You can head east for the beach of **Il Poetto,** which stretches for some 9.6km (6 miles) from Margine Rosso (Red Bluff) to Sella del Diavolo (the Devil's Saddle). A bus marked Il Poetto leaves from Piazza Matteotti in Cagliari, taking you to the beaches in just 20 minutes for 1€ one-way.

Essentials

VISITOR INFORMATION   The **tourist office** is at Piazza Matteotti (✆ **070-669255**) across from the main bus station. The English-speaking staff is available Monday to Saturday 9am to 1pm and 5 to 8pm, with winter hours varying.

Exploring the City

Anfiteatro Romano ★   This is the greatest remaining Roman monument in Sardinia, dating from the 2nd century A.D. The amphitheater has a well-preserved arena that is riddled with underground passages; you can even see a pit for beasts shipped over from North Africa to battle gladiators. The impressive cellars were carved out of rock, and the amphitheater is the largest historical ruin in Sardinia.

Via Regina Margherita 43. ✆ **070-652956.** www.anfiteatroromano.it. Tickets 4.50€. Box office Apr–Oct Tues–Sat 9:30am–1:30pm, Sun 9:30am–1:30pm and 3:30–5:30pm; Nov–Mar Tues–Sat 9:30am–1:30pm, Sun 10am–1pm.

Basilica S. Di S. Saturnino   Built in the style of a Greek cross, this church traces its history back to the 5th century. The church has had a disastrous history and was partly dismantled in 1669, later to be bombed by the Allies in 1943. No one knows just how many restorations it has undergone. It finally reopened in 1996, at which time numerous tombs dating from the Roman and Byzantine ages went on display. The location is just off Via Dante on the eastern side of the city.

Piazza Di S. Cosimo. ✆ **070-659869.** Free admission. Mon–Sat 9am–1pm.

Cattedrale ★   Constructed in the 13th century in the Pisan style, the cathedral, a combination of Romanesque and Gothic architecture, contains major artworks. Chief among these are splendid **pulpits ★★** by Maestro Guglielmo

Cagliari's promenade.

(these were once owned by Il Duomo at Pisa). The carved panels magnificently illustrate the life of Christ. A door leads down to the Santuario, with its impressive 18th-century baroque tomb of Martin II of Aragón. There are tombs here of the princes of the House of Savoy, plus nearly 300 Christian martyr graves.

Piazza Palazzo, off Via Martini. ℰ **070-663837.** www.duomodicagliari.it. Free admission. Mon-Sat 7:30am–8pm; Sun 8am–1pm and 4:30–8:30pm.

Museo Archaeologico Nazionale ★   Near the Torre di San Pancrazio, this is a museum of treasures that dates from the days of the Phoenicians, with artifacts from both the Punic and the Roman eras. In addition to a wide display of arms and antique pottery, there is a stunning collection of **small bronzes ★★★** that date from the earliest days of the island's settlements. These artifacts are from the mysterious Nuraghic people, who lived in stone dwellings unique to Sardinia, from about 1300 to 1200 B.C.

Cittadella dei Musei, Piazza Arsenale. ℰ **070-684000.** Admission 4€, free for 17 and under. Tues–Sun 9am–8pm. Bus: 8.

Nora ★★   The most intriguing excursion from Cagliari is the drive to the town of Pula. Nora, just south of Pula, is the island's oldest city, founded by the Phoenicians before falling to the Carthaginians and later the Romans. On a narrow peninsula at Cape Pula, Nora lies 28km (18 miles) southwest of Cagliari. Ruins include a Roman theater of the republican era (in fairly good condition), the Temple of Tanit, and outlines of Roman roads. You'll also see the 11th-century church of Sant'Efisio and a watchtower from the 16th century.

Lies 3km (2 miles) south of Pula (Nora is signposted). ℰ **070-9209138.** Admission 5.50€. June–Aug daily 9am–8pm; Sept–May daily 9am–5:30pm. ARST buses leave Cagliari from Piazza Matteotti every hour for the 30-min. trip to Pula.

Torre di San Pancrazio   Dating from 1305, this defensive tower remains from the Pisan walls constructed to protect Caligari. It lies just outside the archaeological museum (see above) at the border of the historic Castello district. Climb the steps for a **panoramic view** ★★ of the city and its bay—the same view watchmen saw while looking for enemies approaching from the sea.

Piazza Indipendenza. ⓒ **070-6776400.** Admission 4€. Apr–Oct daily 9am–1pm and 3:30–7:30pm; Nov–Mar Mon and Wed–Sun 9am–4:30pm.

Shopping

If you want to go shopping, especially for regional crafts, stroll along the palm-lined **Via Roma** bordering the port and **Largo Carlo Felice.** Head inland toward the old town.

Your best single shopping bet is **ISOLA** ★, Via Bacaredda 176 (ⓒ **070-492756;** www.isola-cagliari.com), a government-run exhibition of the finest arts and crafts on the island. Some of the artisan work is for exhibition only, but the majority of the stock is for sale.

Where to Stay

If it's summer, many visitors prefer to anchor at one of the coastal resorts. One such option is the Santa Margherita di Pula, lying on the Gulf of Angels some 36km (22 miles) south of Cagliari. From here, you can visit the capital city on an easy day trip for shopping and sights. Pine woods skirt this pristine coast, and the sandy beaches and cliffs extend for 8km (5 miles).

VERY EXPENSIVE

Is Morus Relais ★★ Set in a natural park that slopes to the sea and the beaches, this Mediterranean-style, two-floor hotel is a golden oldie from 1960 that has stayed abreast of the times. More affordable is one of the rooms in the

The shopping arcade along Via Roma in Cagliari.

main building—most with balconies—or else you can live more grandly in one of the newer villas with patios and private gardens. Inside, there is elegance and grand comfort in both the public and the private bedrooms.

Sulla Strada Statale, 09010 Pula. ☎ **070-921-171.** Fax 070-921-596. www.ismorus.it. 85 units. 109€–305€ per person double. Rates include half board. AE, DC, MC, V. Free parking. **Amenities:** Restaurant; bar; babysitting; bikes; 2 outdoor freshwater pools; room service; Wi-Fi (5€ per hr., in lobby). *In room:* A/C, TV, hair dryer, minibar.

EXPENSIVE

Caesar's Hotel ★   This small, warmly decorated hotel has bedrooms that range from small to midsize and are furnished with modern, motel-style pieces with good comfort, especially those units with a bathtub with private Jacuzzi. The location is in a residential area 1.5km (1 mile) from the center.

Via Darwin 2-4 (per Viale Armando Diaz), 09126 Cagliari. ☎ **070-340750.** Fax 070-340755. www.caesarshotel.it. 48 units. 99€–200€ double; 139€–260€ junior suite. Rates include buffet breakfast. AE, DC, MC, V. Free parking. Bus: P or 5. **Amenities:** 2 restaurants; bar; babysitting; bikes; exercise room; room service. *In room:* A/C, TV, hair dryer, minibar, Wi-Fi (free).

Regina Margherita ★   In the center of the city, this hotel from the '80s opens onto water views. A postmillennium overhaul added modern tech to both the public and the private rooms, which are midsize, comfortable, and inviting without being particularly distinguished. The location is halfway between the Terraza Umberto and the port.

Viale Regina Margherita 44, 09124 Cagliari. ☎ **070-670342.** Fax 070-668325. www.hotelregina margherita.com. 99 units. 190€–210€ double; from 250€ suite. Rates include buffet breakfast. AE, DC, MC, V. Free parking. **Amenities:** Restaurant (for groups only); bar; babysitting; room service; Wi-Fi (free, in lobby). *In room:* A/C, TV, hair dryer, minibar.

T Hotel ★★   Our preferred choice within Cagliari itself is this oddly named hotel lying 1km (½ mile) north of the center and rising 14 stories in a high-rise steel-and-glass tube. The soothing colors, the innovative shapes, the natural materials, and the water-and-light effects invite you to linger. The stunningly contemporary bedrooms are havens of comfort; colors are bold—fiery red, vibrant orange, forest green, and sea blue.

Via dei Giudicati (per Via Dante), 09131 Cagliari. ☎ **070-47400.** Fax 070-474016. www.thotel.it. 207 units. 109€–189€ double; from 199€ junior suite; from 249€ suite. Rates include buffet breakfast. AE, DC, MC, V. Free parking. Bus: M. **Amenities:** 2 restaurants; bar; bikes; exercise room; 2 pools (1 heated indoor); spa. *In room:* A/C, TV, hair dryer, minibar, Wi-Fi (free).

Where to Dine

Antica Hostaria ★ SARDINIAN/ITALIAN   Part of the fun of dining at this harborside restaurant is the waterfront walk you navigate to reach it. The interior is elegant, the service correct, and your meal inspired by a host of seafood delicacies harvested in local waters. In addition to the fresh fish, the menu also offers a choice of game and meat dishes, everything backed up by a good wine list. We like our fish sautéed with fresh zucchini in a Spumante wine sauce. You might begin with thinly sliced gilthead with olive sauce or else a savory selection of Sardinian sausages. For a local specialty, try *malloreddus alla campidanese* (Sardinian homemade pasta with sausage, fresh tomatoes, pecorino cheese, and saffron). Another tasty pasta is a hard wheat version in clam broth.

Via Cavour 60. ✆ **070-665870.** www.anticahostaria.it. Reservations recommended. Main courses 8€–23€; fixed-price lunch 35€. AE, DC, MC, V. Mon–Sat 12:45–3pm and 8–11pm. Closed Dec 23–Jan 7.

Antico Caffè SARDINIAN/ITALIAN   Since 1838 this has been a local favorite. It's especially popular with students, many of whom come here just for the delicious crepes and ice-cream sundaes. But robust, hearty, and affordable food is also served. Dishes rarely disappoint here, including *tagliolini* with swordfish, cherry tomatoes, and arugula, or the tuna cooked in sesame crust with crispy onions.

Piazza Costituzione 10. ✆ **070-658206.** www.anticocaffe.it. Reservations not needed. Main courses 10€–17€. AE, DC, MC, V. Wed–Mon 7am–3am.

Dal Corsaro ★★ SARDINIAN/SEAFOOD   The best restaurant in town is classically elegant, lying in the historic center. The quality of the produce and the preparation are first-rate, and some of the finest of regional wines emerge from the cellar. The Deidda family has been in charge since 1967, and they are ambassadors of Sardinian regional cuisine, using only the freshest ingredients. They excel in their fresh fish dishes, including filet of red tuna with an onion fondant, black olives, and tomatoes. We also savor their gnocchi made with potatoes and cannellini beans, with added flavors from shrimp and saffron. You might also try roast spigola fish with mussels and lentils or else onion ravioli with pecorino and herbs.

Viale Regina Margherita 28. ✆ **070-664318.** www.dalcorsaro.com. Reservations required. Main courses 12€–25€; 4-course fixed-price menu 45€, 7-course 65€, 9-course 75€. AE, MC, V. Mon–Sat 1–3:30pm and 8–11pm. Closed Jan 1–15.

ALGHERO★

229km (142 miles) NW of Cagliari, 137km (85 miles) W of Olbia

On the northwest coast, this former Aragónese and Catalan fishing port is Sardinia's most beautiful town. Because of its heavy Catalan influence, it is called "Little Barcelona," though the comparison isn't quite apt. It is built on a rocky ledge above the sea, and in summer flowers and palm trees grow in profusion.

Former occupiers, the Aragónese (and later the Catalans) built ramparts and towers that today characterize the old town, or **Città Vecchia ★**. You can wander for 2 hours or so through the narrow, winding streets with their decaying palaces and churches. Many old town inhabitants still speak Catalán instead of Italian.

An excellent beach extends 5km (3 miles) to the north of Alghero, and the major attraction of the area is not in Alghero itself but in the environs at the **Grotta di Nettuno** (see below).

Essentials

VISITOR INFORMATION   The local tourist office is at Piazza Porta Terra (✆ **079-979054**), open year-round Monday to Saturday 8am to 8pm, Sunday 10am to 3pm.

Exploring the Old Town

Cattedrale di Santa Maria   An impressive example of Gothic and Catalan architecture, the Duomo took a long time to complete, from 1552 to 1730. It ended up a mixture of styles, with the nave and two aisles in the late Renaissance style and even a 20th-century narthex added to the bastardized facade. The bell tower and apse are in the original 16th-century style. There are also fine examples of marble furnishings dating from the 1700s.

Piazza Duomo. 🕿 **079-979222.** Free admission. Daily 9am–6pm.

Chiesa di San Francesco Dating from 1360 but rebuilt in the late 16th century, the Church of St. Francis contains much of its original Catalan and Gothic design, particularly over the high altar, in the presbytery chapels, and in the Sacramento Chapel. The campanile (bell tower) is from the early 1500s.

Via Carlo Alberto. 🕿 **079-979258.** Free admission. Daily 9:30am–noon and 5–8pm.

Museo Diocesano d'Arte Sacra Near the cathedral, this museum of sacred art is housed in a church founded in 1568. The museum shelters the Duomo's liturgical treasures and the sacred artifacts of the other town churches as well. The museum's collections are divided into sections devoted to silverware, paintings, wooden sculptures, and bronzes, among other art. In the silverware section is a reliquary of the True Cross, a Catalan work of an unknown silversmith in 1500. There is a particularly beautiful wood sculpture of the Madonna dei Naviganti, the work of an unknown Catalan carver from the 1400s.

Religious artifacts at the Museo Diocesano d'Arte Sacra in Alghero.

Piazza Duomo 1. 🕿 **079-9733041.** www.algheromuseo.it. Admission 2.50€ adults, 1.50€ children 10–18. Apr–June Thurs–Tues 10am–1pm and 5–8pm; July–Aug Thurs–Tues 10am–1pm and 6–10pm; Sept–Oct Thurs–Tues 10am–1pm and 5–9pm; Dec Thurs–Tues 4–7pm. Closed Nov and Jan–Mar.

Sights Outside Alghero

Grotta di Nettuno ★★★ One of the greatest natural attractions of Sardinia is Neptune's Cave. Its stairway of 654 steps leading down its cliff face is called the Escala del Cabirol, or "Stairway of Goats." This spectacular cavern is filled with small lakes, a forest of stalactite columns, and concretions in the form of "organ pipes." A public bus marked Nettuno runs here from Alghero, costing 4.50€ round-trip. You take a boat from Bastione della Maddalena in Alghero from mid-March to May and in October three times daily at 9 and 10am, and 3pm; from June to September daily trips are every hour from 9am to 5pm. The boat tour of the caves takes 2½ hours, costing 14€ per person.

Capo Caccia, 27km (17 miles) west of Alghero. 🕿 **079-946540.** Admission 12€ adults, 6€ children 3–12. Oct daily 10am–5pm; Nov–Mar daily 9am–4pm; Apr–Sept daily 9am–7pm.

Nuraghe Palmavera ★ These caves are the best place on the island to see prehistoric stone-built *nuraghe*, some 50 individual dwellings crowded close together. A central tower surrounds these huts, forming a limestone complex from 1500 B.C. Built with huge blocks of stone, the truncated cone tower is in the shape of a beehive and opens onto a panorama of the countryside. The remains of a "palace" founded in the 14th century B.C. can also be seen. The Nuragic civilization produced the most advanced and monumental architecture of this early period in the western Mediterranean.

SS. 127 bis (on the road linking Alghero-Fertilia to Capo Caccia at Km 45, 12km/7½ miles northwest of Alghero). ✆ **079-980040.** Admission 5€. Apr–Oct daily 9am–7pm; Nov–Mar daily 9:30am–4pm.

Where to Stay

El Faro ★ 🎁   This golden oldie is in the vicinity of **Grotta di Nettuno** (see above) at Porto Conte, the ancient Portus Nympharum or "port of the nymphs." The resort hotel, much improved since its opening in the 1950s, is enveloped by a nature park and a marine reserve opening onto a private beach. Naturally, the most desirable rooms are those fronting a panoramic sweep of the bay from the hotel's position 4km (2½ miles) north of Alghero. Bedrooms come in a wide range of sizes, but all of the units are furnished with a sophisticated, tasteful modern styling. Many guests can sun on their own private terrace.

Località Porto Conte, 07041 Alghero. ✆ **079-942010.** Fax 079-942030. www.elfarohotel.it. 92 units. 250€–580€ double; from 500€ suite. Rates include continental breakfast. AE, DC, MC, V. Closed Oct 17–Easter. **Amenities:** Restaurant; bar; bikes; exercise room; 2 pools; room service; tennis court (lit); Wi-Fi (free, in lobby). *In room:* A/C, TV, minibar.

Carlos V ★   This sea resort hotel on the waterfront lies only 200m (656 ft.) from the center of town. Surrounded by well-landscaped gardens and terraces, it's been around since 1971 but was completely renovated in 2006. If possible, try for a room with a view and avoid the units in the rear. Bedrooms are midsize to spacious, and tastefully and comfortably furnished with modern pieces that never quite transcend a good modern hotel.

Lungomare Fa Valencia 24, 07041 Alghero. ✆ **079-9720600.** Fax 079-980298. www.hotel carlosv.it. 179 units. 210€–610€ double. Rates include buffet breakfast. AE, DC, MC, V. Free parking. Tram: AP from train station. Closed Nov–Mar. **Amenities:** Restaurant; bar; babysitting; saltwater pool; room service; tennis court (lit). *In room:* A/C, TV, hair dryer, minibar.

San Francesco ✦   In the heart of the historic district, this hotel was converted from a former convent attached to the Church of San Francisco. The rooms are grouped around a cloister from the 1300s and are small yet comfortable, with simple wood furniture and tiled bathrooms. The cloister has 22 of its Roman sandstone columns still intact. Rooms lack TVs but there is a public room for television viewing. Furnishings are mostly reproductions of antiques.

Via Machin 2, 07041 Alghero. ✆/fax **079-980330.** www.sanfrancescohotel.com. 82€–101€ double; 110€–135€ triple. Rates include continental breakfast. AE, DC, MC, V. **Amenities:** Room service. *In room:* A/C, hair dryer.

Villa Las Tronas ★★★   This is the most romantic and elegant hotel in northeastern Sardinia, a place where Italian royalty used to spend their summer vacations. Built in the 1800s, the villa remained in private hands until the war in 1940. It is erected on a private promontory virtually surrounded by the sea, but only a short walk from Alghero. Piers and terraces attract sun worshipers. Much of the aristocratic atmosphere remains, including marble floors, tall ceilings, crystal chandeliers, and antiques. Bedrooms are elegantly styled with traditional pieces, and the hotel has the best facilities in Alghero.

Lungomare Valencia 1, 07041 Alghero. © **079-981818.** Fax 079-981044. www.hotelvillalas tronas.com. 25 units. 235€–490€ double; 485€–700€ suite. AE, DC, MC, V. Free parking. **Amenities:** Restaurant; bar; babysitting; bikes; concierge; exercise room; 2 saltwater pools (1 heated indoor); room service; spa. *In room:* A/C, TV, CD player, hair dryer, minibar, Wi-Fi (free).

Where to Dine

Al Tuguri SEAFOOD/SARDINIAN/CATALAN   This three-level restaurant in the old town, the domain of chef/owner Benito Carbonella, offers the most authentic recipes in town. It's housed in a building whose history dates from the 15th century. Grilled fish from the Alghero coast appears nightly, depending on the day's catch. The pasta delight is *taglierini* with artichokes or mussels and peas. The sautéed calamari stuffed with fresh vegetables is sublime, as is the octopus in a garlic-and-vinegar sauce. Desserts are homemade daily.

Via Maiorca 113. © **079-976772.** www.altuguri.it. Reservations recommended. Main courses 12€–35€; fixed-price menus 35€–45€. MC, V. Mon–Sat 12:30–3pm and 7–10:30pm. Closed Dec 20–Feb.

Andreini ★★ SARDINIAN   The town's finest and most elegant restaurant lies in the old part of town near the harbor area. At well-appointed tables, you'll enjoy fine service and regional ingredients crafted into intensely flavored dishes. You might start with *tagliolini* in pecorino cheese flavored with sage and the local "caviar" or roe. Or you can opt for a filet of tuna resting under a dried-fruit crust and served with balsamic-flavored onions. Some specialties include tuna cooked very rare with an oyster sauce; lamb marinated with yogurt, mint, radicchio, and peppers; and straccetti, a homemade pasta with red mullet and wild asparagus. The homemade desserts are superb, especially puff pastry filled with figs and served with cardamom ice cream.

Via Arduino 45. © **079-982098.** www.ristoranteandreini.it. Reservations recommended. Main courses 15€–35€; 7-course menu 65€. AE, DC, MC, V. Tues–Sun 12:30–3pm and 7–11pm.

Il Pavone SARDINIAN   Opening in 1979, this waterfront restaurant enjoys a steady clientele, mostly of locals who like its regional cuisine. Lying in a central position, within walking distance of most of the attractions, the restaurant has a rustic decor of antique furnishings and even old radios and lamps, graced with paintings and drawings. Dishes are prepared according to savory, time-tested recipes, which are served with island-produced wines. Start, perhaps, with steamed octopus with pesto or salt codfish with leeks and chickpeas. For a main course, you might dig into one of the homemade pastas, including an especially tasty *tagliatelle* with fresh shrimp, chickpeas, and cherry tomatoes. The fish is "just caught" and is prepared in a variety of methods, including cooked with fresh basil and tomatoes.

Piazza Sullis 3-4. © **079-979584.** Reservations recommended. Main courses 16€–19€; set price menus 50€–60€. DC, MC, V. Daily noon–3pm and 7–10:30pm.

Alghero After Dark

The classiest, most historic, and elegant gathering place at night is **Caffè Costantino** ★★ in the center of town near the harbor at Piazza Civica 30 (© **079-976154**), open daily from 6am to midnight. In the evening, the cafe draws a fun-loving young crowd to its ground-floor precincts in the 16th-century, Gothic-style Palazzo d'Albis.

An evening at Caffè Costantino in Alghero.

Young people gather at night at **Poco Loco,** Via Gramsci 8 (*©* **079-983604;** www.pocolocoalghero.it), a cybercafe, a bowling lane, and a pizza parlor. Poco Loco is open daily in summer from 7:30pm to 3am; winter hours are Friday and Saturday 7:30 to 11pm.

DORGALI ★

212km (132 miles) NE of Cagliari, 116km (72 miles) S of Olbia

Most visitors to Sardinia confine their sightseeing to the coastline. But for those who want to see more of local life and are intrigued by island handicrafts, a dip into the interior is a rewarding jaunt.

Dorgali is our preferred choice for the quintessential Sardinian town. While you could reach it in a day's drive from the resorts along Costa Smeralda (see below), your visit would be rushed. We recommend an overnight stopover to give you a chance to go shopping and to explore the natural wonders outside the town, including Nuragi ruins.

These ruins of a prehistoric civilization found in this dolomite landscape have long fascinated archaeologists. The Nuragic people had a flourishing civilization here between 5000 and 1800 B.C. We know little about them, except for the 7,000 megalithic towers and ruins they left behind.

Save some time for Dorgali itself, at least to go on shopping expeditions for such crafts as leatherwork and filigree. Some patterns are based on prehistoric Nuragic art. The town is also known for its regional wine and folkloric costumes. Located on the slopes of Monte Bardia, Dorgali was a Saracen colony. Many Sardinians living here still make their living from agriculture.

Essentials

VISITOR INFORMATION The **Dorgali Tourist Office** is at Via Lamarmora 108 (*©* **0784-96243**), open May to September Monday to Friday 9am to 1pm and 4 to 8pm, and October to April Monday to Friday 9am to 1pm and 3:30 to 7pm.

Natural Wonders in the Environs

Except for shopping, the best sights lie outside Dorgali in a parklike countryside full of caves and prehistoric ruins. Some tours depart from Cala Gonone (see "Where to Stay," below), site of most of the hotels.

The most popular and rewarding trip from Cala Gonone is to the **Grotto del Bue Marino ★★**, "cave of the sea oxen," which once was the last refuge of the Mediterranean monk seal, survivor of the Ice Age. The grotto stretches for 4.8km (3 miles). The caves, reached only by boat in summer, can be visited every hour daily from 9am to 5pm. A 2-hour tour costs 20€ per person. For information call the tourist office (see above).

Another popular tour is to the **Gorropu Canyon Gorge** ★, with its 400m (1,312-ft.) canyons and walls, the tallest and widest such canyon in Europe. The vistas from the gorge's limestone boulders, with plenty of wildflowers and pink oleander, are some of the most panoramic in the area. Costing 35€, including lunch, jeep tours depart from the office of the **Cooperative Ghivine** at Via Lamarmora 69E in Dorghali (© **0784-96721;** www.ghivine.com). Two-hour tours depart daily 9am to 4pm.

Tiscali ★ is a prehistoric Nuraghi village found in a cave lying on top of a mountain. The early settlers chose this remote setting to avoid invaders. Visit Tiscali only if you have extra time; for the best of Nuraghi ruins, take the tour to Serra Orrios Village (see below). The Cooperative Ghivine (see above) also offers tours to Tiscali, costing 35€ with lunch. Entrance to the hidden village is an extra 5€ for adults or 2.50€ for children 15 and under. The 2-hour tour departs daily May to October 9am to 7pm (last tour at 5pm off season).

The largest Nuraghi settlement is **Serra Orrios Village** ★★, lying 10km (6¼ miles) from Dorgali and reached only by car. Take S129; it's signposted. The site includes the ruins of 70 prehistoric huts and two small megaron (a great hall, with an open two-columned porch) temples. Entrance to the village costs 5€ for adults and 2.50€ for children 15 and under. Guided visits are conducted on the hour daily 9am to 1pm and 3 to 5pm.

Finally, **Ispinigoli Cave** ★, reached along SS.125 (it's signposted from Dorghali), boasts the longest stalagmite-stalactite column in Europe and the second longest on earth, measuring 38m (125 ft.) high. You take 280 steps down into the cave, taking in the stunning array of stalactites and stalagmites. The entrance is 7€ for adults or 3.50€ for kids 15 and under. Guided visits are conducted hourly and daily from 9am to noon and 3 to 5pm, with later tours June to August if demand warrants. **Consorzio Atlantika** does not have a phone number. To contact Consorzio Atlantika, go to www.atlantika.it.

Shopping

The main reason visitors flock to the center of Dorgali is to shop for Sardinian handicrafts. Wander the small streets in the heart of the old town, where skilled artisans still ply a trade most often learned from their ancestors. The main shopping street is **Via Lamarmora,** off of which branch several tiny streets where weavers weave, potters throw, and ceramic artists fire their ovens. The "flick knife" is a steel blade with a goat-horn handle sought by

The Gorropu Canyon Gorge, near Dorgali.

connoisseurs, as are leather objects, jewelry, and ceramics. The best selection of ceramics is found at **Ceramica Loddo,** Via Lamarmora 110 (✆ **0784-96327**), and an elegant array of *tappeti* (cotton and wool weaving) is sold at **Il Tapetto di Serafina Senette,** Piazza Giorgio Asproni 22 (✆ **0784-95202**), a mother-and-daughter operation. Most stores are open Monday to Saturday 9:30am to 1pm and 4 to 8pm.

Where to Stay

The best hotels lie not within the town itself but at the resort of Cala Gonore, lying 9km (5½ miles) east of the center of Dorgali. There are 10 splendid sandy beaches in this area, some of which can be reached by boat, others by foot from either of the hotels recommended below.

L'Oasi ★   This is the best-rated hotel in the area, lying near the departure point for boat trips to the underwater caves and grottoes. The small hotel overlooks the Gulf of Orosei and is surrounded by gorgeous natural scenery. The hotel has mid-size bedrooms that are comfortably furnished with motel-standard furnishings, with the grace note being the private balconies opening onto the sea. The hotel operates a restaurant for guests only, costing 18€ for a fixed-price menu.

Via Garca Lorca 13, Cala Gonone, 08020 Dorgali. ✆ **0784-93111.** Fax 078-493444. www.loasi hotel.it. 30 units. 98€–160€ double. Rates include half board. MC, V. Free parking. Closed Oct 20–Easter. **Amenities:** Restaurant; bar. *In room:* A/C, TV, hair dryer.

Miramare ★   From their position in the flowering garden, guests can admire the vista of crashing waves in the bay. This airy and sunny hotel rises over the sea, sitting on a rocky, sun-drenched perch. A wide assortment of celebrity guests have been drawn to this hotel over the years, everybody from Dizzy Gillespie to director Lina Wertmüller, along with famous athletes and underwater divers. Rooms are tastefully furnished and generally spacious, especially those with a terrace providing a view of the Gulf of Orosei.

Piazza Giardini 12, Cala Gonone, 08020 Dorgali. ✆ **078-493140.** Fax 078-493469. www.htl miramare.it. 35 units. 30€–78€ per person double. Rates include continental breakfast. AE, DC, MC, V. Free parking. Closed Nov–Mar. **Amenities:** Restaurant; bar. *In room:* A/C, TV.

Where to Dine

Most visitors eat at one of the hotels, since the independent restaurants are not one of the reasons to visit Dorgli.

Codula ✦ SARDINIAN   This restaurant in the Il Querceto Hotel is about the best in town (you can also rent rooms here). Lying in a natural park studded with oak trees, it is a tranquil spot for both dining and living. The regional menu changes with the seasons, including such delights as porcini mushrooms or wild asparagus harvested in the countryside. The chef's delightful specialty is *guillirgiones* (a local ravioli filled with regional cheese and potatoes). The other specialty is *bouchès,* which is a Sardinian gnocchi filled with ricotta, cheese, and fresh vegetables. The attractive, traditionally furnished bedrooms range in price from 69€ to 150€ in a double, including breakfast.

Via Lamarmora 4, Dorghali. ✆ **0784-96509.** www.ilquerceto.com. Reservations recommended. Main courses 9€–12€; fixed-price menu 22€. AE, MC, V. Thurs–Tues 12:30–2:30pm; daily 8–10pm.

COSTA SMERALDA ★★★

Yacht owners nod to each other at the harbor at Porto Cervo, and the white sands along the "Emerald Coast" in northeast Sardinia attract some of the richest and best-looking bodies in Europe in July and August.

The beaches along this coast are a luxurious vacation haven launched in 1961 by the late Aga Khan, the spiritual leader at the time of 15 million Ismaili Muslims. Khan spearheaded the development that today is filled with luxury villas, deluxe hotels, and marinas. Prices are higher than any other beach resorts in Europe, so be duly warned. You have a choice of destinations, all previewed below.

The coast stretches for some 55km (35 miles), featuring 80 bays with pinkish-white swimming beaches. Some of the most idyllic bays are remote and reached only by boat. Most hotels can arrange day trips to the alluring archipelago of **La Maddalena ★★**, with its 27 islands, including seven large ones. The government has turned this island cluster into a national park because of its unique wildlife and vegetation.

You can also visit the islands independently from the port of Palau, which lies directly north of Arzachena (see below). For ferry tickets, head out the main road of Palau, Via Nazionale, where you'll find the ticket office of **Saremar Ferries** (© **892-123;** www.saremar.it). During the busy summer season, three ferries per hour depart for the 15-minute trip to La Maddalena. The cost is 10€ to 12€ round-trip, depending on the season.

VISITOR INFORMATION   The main tourist office is in Olbia, at Via Alessandro Nanni 39 (© **0789-21453**). It's open Monday to Friday 8am to 2pm and 3 to 6pm, and Saturday 8am to 1pm.

The coast at La Maddalena on Costa Smerelda.

Olbia

Most visitors to Costa Smeralda arrive at this port city, the closest to the mainland of Italy. The town is rather industrial and not the most idyllic along the coast, although only a short distance away are pockets of posh. Think of Olbia as a refueling stop. It is also far more affordable than some of the luxurious resorts below. The best beach is **Le Salone** between Punta delle Saline and the bottom of Capo Ceraso. Follow the S125 5km (3 miles) south from Olbia; the beach is signposted. Olbia lies 30km (19 miles) south of Porto Cervo.

WHERE TO STAY

Martini ★   This modern, four-story hotel overlooking the harbor is the best place to stay in Olbia. It lies slightly north of the center on the shore of a lagoon. Count on a taxi ride from the center or else a 20-minute walk. The midsize bedrooms concentrate more on function and comfort than style, though they are sleekly modern. All units have a private terrace facing the sea or a park.

Via D'Annunzio 22, 07026 Olbia. ℂ **078-926066.** Fax 078-926418. www.hotelmartiniolbia.com. 70 units. 130€–150€ double; 150€–185€ triple. Rates include buffet breakfast. AE, DC, MC, V. Free parking. **Amenities:** Bar; babysitting; exercise room; spa. *In room:* A/C, TV, hair dryer, minibar, Wi-Fi (4€ per hr.).

WHERE TO DINE

Barbagia SARDINIAN/ITALIAN   This is a regional tavern decorated with island handicrafts that attracts mainly locals, though more and more visitors patronize it as well. In the harbor area, the chefs are known for their good and affordable food served at reasonable prices unless you go in for the more expensive shellfish. Start perhaps with a bowl of mussels gratinée. Some of the regional dishes come from ingredients from the interior, including roast wild boar in a sweet-and-sour sauce. Wild boar also appears in a sauce served with homemade pasta. From the coast comes the day's catch—perhaps grilled lobster or jumbo shrimp, also from the grill. At night the pizza ovens are heated up. Desserts are homemade fresh daily.

Via Galvani 94. ℂ **0789-51640.** www.ristorantebarbagia.it. Reservations recommended in summer. Main courses 7€–25€; 3 fixed-price menus 17€–32€. MC, V. Mon–Sat 12:20–2pm and 7–10pm.

Porto Rotondo

At a point 18km (11 miles) north of Olbia is a small vacation village that is more family oriented than the posher neighboring village of Porto Cervo, center of most of the coast's nightclubs. Nonetheless, Porto Rotondo is the summer home of Prime Minister Silvio Berlusconi, who has an extravagant house on one of the cliffs overlooking the sea.

The best beaches here are **Spiaggia dei Sassi,** with a fine sandy bottom and gray pebbles, and **Marinella,** between Olbia and Golfo Aranci. This area has snow-white sands with shallow waters and a gently sloping beach, one of the better choices in the area for families with small children.

Hotel Sporting ★   This long-established favorite sits on a promontory outside Olbia, fronting the open sea on one side and a marina and the village of Porto Rotondo on the other. It is one of the most sophisticated enclaves along the coast without the super chicdom of Porto Cervo. Each of the spacious bedrooms opens onto a private terrace and a ribbon of beach. Wicker chairs and dark wooden beams give a rustic overtone, though the amenities are luxurious.

Via Clelia Donà dale Rose, Porto Rotondo, 07020 Olbia. ⓒ **078-934005.** Fax 0789-34383. www.sportingportorotondo.it. 27 units. 220€–577€ per person double; from 440€ per person junior suite; from 770€ per person suite. Rates include buffet breakfast. AE, DC, MC, V. Closed Oct to late Apr. **Amenities:** Restaurant; bar; bikes; airport transfers (50€); babysitting; bikes; concierge; saltwater pool; room service. *In room:* A/C, TV, hair dryer, minibar.

Porto Cervo ★★

With its large parks, elegant boutiques, and nightlife, this is the nerve center of the Costa Smeralda, lying 30km (19 miles) north of Olbia. Porto Rotondo is a 20-minute drive to its south. A natural port here is filled with multihued houses surrounded by hills.

On the southeastern side, its Porto Vecchio, or old port, dates only from the 1960s. For the best beach, follow Via Granu toward the sea to **Cala Crano,** with its white sandy bottom surrounded by rocks set against a backdrop of hills. Another good beach is **Portisco** in the western part of the Golfo di Cugnana, a beach of white sand with rocky outcrops. It's reached from the coastal road leading from Porto Cero to Golfo Aranci.

Cervo ★★ Not quite the charmer that Cala di Volpe (below) is, this deluxe hotel is also built like an idealized Sardinian village. Life here is lush, pampered, and chic. The midsize to spacious bedrooms are built in a hacienda style, opening onto flower gardens, vine-covered vista arbors, and sunny patios. Most of the units contain a private terrace and are often decorated in painted wood pieces. A country-house atmosphere prevails.

Piazzetta Cervo, 07020 Porto Cervo. ⓒ **0789-931111.** Fax 0789-931613. www.starwoodhotels.com. 106 units. 305€–1,300€ double. AE, DC, MC, V. Free parking. **Amenities:** 4 restaurants; 3 bars; babysitting; exercise room; 3 pools (1 heated indoor); room service; sauna. *In room:* A/C, fax, hair dryer, minibar, Wi-Fi (free).

Gianni Pedrinelli ★ 🏠 SARDINIAN/ITALIAN This regional tavern is the best independent restaurant in the area, lying 2km (1¼ miles) outside Porto Cervo. Here is an opportunity to taste perfectly partnered food and regional wine. The chefs showcase the best of regional ingredients in specialties such as homemade Sardinian gnocchi with sausages, and oven-roasted suckling pig with myrtle sauce. Local favorites include the Catalan lobster salad and salt-crusted sea bass.

Località Piccolo Pevero, Porto Cervo. ⓒ **0789-92436.** www.giannipedrinelli.it. Reservations required June–Sept. Main

The white-sand beach at Porto Cervo.

courses 28€–40€. AE, DC, MC, V. Closed Oct–Feb. Mar–May daily 12:30–2pm and 7:30–10:30pm; June and Sept daily 7:30–10:30pm; July–Aug daily 12:30–2pm and 7:30pm–midnight.

Baja Sardinia

In the Gulf of Arczachena, Baja Sardinia lies 30km (19 miles) north of Olbia and directly to the northwest of Porto Cervo. Although still very expensive, hotels here are more affordable than at Porto Cervo and other posh spots. Most buildings here—hotels, private villas, bars, and restaurants—are grouped around a small square close to the beach.

The little resort faces the archipelago of La Maddalena, lying 4km (2½ miles) to the west of Porto Cervo. The best beach is **Cala Battistoni,** with its fine white sand set against a backdrop of rocky outcroppings. This beach lies right in front of the village of Baja Sardinia, which is 32km (20 miles) north of the port of Olbia.

Club Hotel ★★   The best hotel in the area also has the most style, seemingly emerging from the rocks and the sea in harmony with its landscaped surroundings. The hotel complex fronts the public beach at Baja Sardinia; only a 3-minute walk takes you to the hotel's private beach. Flowering terraces open toward the sea. The bedrooms are attractively furnished in a sleek modern style, and each opens onto a private balcony or terrace.

Club Hotel at Baia Sardinia, 07021 Arzachena. 🕐 **078-999006.** Fax 078-999286. www.club hotelbajasardinia.it. 114 units. 275€–460€ double; 380€–500€ junior suite. Rates include half board. AE, MC, V. Free parking. Closed Oct–Easter. **Amenities:** 3 restaurants; 2 bars; bikes; Internet (free, in lobby); tennis court (lit); room service. *In room:* A/C, TV, hair dryer, minibar.

La Bisaccia   Built in a rustic Sardinian style, this retreat enjoys a scenic position overlooking the bay. Its main structure—and the most desirable place to stay—offers well-furnished, midsize bedrooms overlooking La Maddalena archipelago. Private balconies open onto panoramic views. Handling the overflow is a *residenza* with comfortable, though smaller, bedrooms. The most attractive feature of the hotel is its position, only 30m (98 ft.) from its own private beach.

Via Baja Sardinia, 07021 Baja Sardinia. 🕐 **0789-990002.** Fax 0789-99162. www.hotellabisaccia. it. 109 units. 300€–320€ double; 345€–510€ junior suite. AE, DC, MC, V. Closed mid-Oct to mid-May. Free parking. **Amenities:** Restaurant; bar; babysitting; bikes; saltwater pool; room service. *In room:* A/C, TV, hair dryer, minibar.

Mon Repos Hermitage ★   This 1970s hotel is fine in every way. Built in a typical Mediterranean style, it lies in a well-landscaped, shady garden overlooking the Bay of Baja Sardinia. A footpath leads down 90m (295 ft.) to a good sandy beach. All the rooms are well furnished and comfortable here, but those rated superior live up to their label, as they are more spacious and open onto private balconies fronting the bay.

Via Baja Sardinia, 07021 Baja Sardinia. 🕐 **0789-99011.** Fax 0789-99050. www.hotelmon repos.it. 60 units. 50€–125€ per person double. Rates include continental breakfast. AE, DC, MC, V. Free parking. Closed Oct–Apr. **Amenities:** Restaurant; bar; bikes; exercise room; pool; room service; limited watersports equipment. *In room:* A/C, TV, hair dryer, minibar.

Cala di Volpe ★★★

This wonderful beach and small resort is actually a satellite of Porto Cervo to its immediate north. The location is 25km (16 miles) north of Olbia and 17km (11 miles) east of Arzachena. The region is visited mainly for its Cala di Volpe resort, arguably the grandest in all of Sardinia (see below). The beach here is equipped with the most luxurious services in Sardinia and lies in a sheltered bay crowned by shrub scented with juniper and "strawberry" trees. We consider this beach the most beautiful along the Emerald Coast.

Cala di Volpe ★★★   The late novelist Irwin Shaw once called this sprawling resort "for the spoiled darlings of our age"—and so it is. It remains our favorite resort along the coast. On a low sandbar, it looks like a Moorish-African village, a bit kitsch but stunning—in fact, its French architect called it an "operetta setting," and the deluxe citadel is filled with surrealist touches. Overlooking a scenic bay, it is one of the most beautiful places to stay in all of Europe, its private balconies opening onto the scenic bay. Bedrooms are spacious and luxurious with traditional and elegant furnishings.

Cala di Volpe, 07020 Porto Cervo. ℰ **0789-976111.** Fax 0789-976617. www.caladivolpe.com. 125 units. 545€–2,950€ double; 2,040€–4,300€ suite. Rates include buffet breakfast. AE, DC, MC, V. Free parking. Closed mid-Oct to mid-Mar. **Amenities:** 2 restaurants; 3 bars; babysitting; bikes; concierge; exercise room; saltwater pool; room service; sauna; 3 tennis courts (lit); extensive watersports rentals; Wi-Fi (free, in lobby). *In room:* A/C, TV/DVD, minibar.

Nibaru 🗡   Those who can't afford the lethal prices of Cala di Volpe will find a viable alternative at this low-slung, 1970s-style Mediterranean hotel. Arches surround its pool, and the traditional Sardinian dry stone wells blend into the landscaped setting. From the garden you can smell the scent of oleander and rosemary. The hotel is set in a grove of trees within sight of the sea. Rooms come in a combination of styles and sizes, some large enough to house three guests comfortably. Furnishings are comfortably first class and replaced on an as-needed basis. There are two good beaches nearby, Petra Manna and Capriccioli, lying 900m (2,953 ft.) from the hotel.

Località Cala di Volpe, 07020 Cala di Volpe. ℰ **0789-96038.** Fax 0789-96474. www.hotel nibaru.it. 50 units. 100€–180€ double. Rates include buffet breakfast. AE, DC, MC, V. Free parking. Closed mid-Oct to May. **Amenities:** Bar; bikes; exercise room; pool; room service; sauna; Wi-Fi (free, in lobby). *In room:* A/C, TV, hair dryer, minibar.

La Arzachena

Near the island of La Maddalena, the town of Arzachena lies 25km (16 miles) north of Olbia. Opening onto 80km (50 miles) of coastline, Arzachena was the launching pad for the international consortium that created the Costa Smeralda resorts in 1962. Most visitors use Arzachena as a jumping-off point for its satellite resorts of Porto Cervo, Cala di Volpe, and Baia Sardinia.

Tenuta Pilastru ★ 🛏   This undiscovered choice is tucked away in a scenic location 5km (3 miles) to the east of town along the Strada Arzachena-Bassacutena. A stay here is like living in the countryside, and you can see cattle grazing from your window. The main house, the Almond Tree, is the site of the lobby

The Cala di Volpe resort, near Porto Cervo.

and reception with some of the smaller guest rooms. The more desirable rooms are in small chalets spread across the landscaped grounds. The best beaches lie about a 15km (9⅓-mile) drive away.

Località Pilastru, 07021 Arzachena. ✆ **0789-982936.** Fax 0789-82684. www.tenutapilastru.it. 32 units. 36€–86€ per person double. Rates include continental breakfast. Free parking. **Amenities:** Restaurant; bar; outdoor pool; room service. *In room:* A/C, TV, minibar.

Lu Stazzu ★ 🎁 SARDINIAN   In a setting of olive and juniper trees, this rustic restaurant lies 2km (1¼ miles) from Arzachena on the road to Porto Cervo. It makes a good countryside visit for guests staying at either town. Go here for an authentic taste of Sardinia. The roast meats, including grilled lamb, are prepared in a little Sardinian house called a *stazzu.* Guests dine at simple rustic furnishings in the main dining room or out on the terrace. The chef has earned his fame for spit-roasted suckling pig, one of the best of all regional dishes. You might begin with an order of ravioli stuffed with regional cheese and topped with a savory tomato sauce. Another regional is grilled wild boar sausage. Many patrons come here to feast on *malloreddos,* which is gnocchi with homemade sausage and a spicy tomato sauce.

Strada Provinciale Arzachena-Portocervo. ✆ **0789-82711.** www.lustazzu.com. Reservations recommended. Main courses 8€–18€. AE, DC, MC, V. Daily noon–2:30pm and 7–10pm (until 11:30pm July–Aug). Closed Oct–Easter.

18

PLANNING YOUR TRIP TO ITALY

T his chapter is devoted to the where, when, and how of your trip—the advance planning required to get it together and take it on the road. Because you might not know exactly where in Italy you want to go or what surrounds the major city you want to see, we'll start off with a quick rundown of the various regions.

For additional help in planning your trip and for more on-the-ground resources in Italy, please turn to "Fast Facts," later in this chapter.

WHEN TO GO

The best months for traveling in Italy are from **April to June** and **late September to October**—temperatures are usually mild and the crowds aren't quite so intense. Starting in mid-June, the summer rush really picks up, and from **July to mid-September** the country teems with visitors. **August** is the worst month: Not only does it get uncomfortably hot, muggy, and crowded, but the entire country goes on vacation, at least from August 15 to the end of the month—and many Italians take off the entire month. Many hotels, restaurants, and shops are closed (except at the spas, beaches, and islands, where 70% of the Italians head). From **late October to Easter,** most attractions go on shorter winter hours or are closed for renovation. Many hotels and restaurants take a month or two off between **November and February,** spa and beach destinations become padlocked ghost towns, and it can get much colder than you'd expect (it might even snow).

Weather

It's warm all over Italy in summer; it can be very hot in the south, especially inland. The high temperatures (measured in Italy in degrees Celsius) begin in Rome in May, often lasting until sometime in October. Winters in the north of Italy are cold, with rain and snow, but in the south the weather is warm all year, averaging 10°C (50°F) in winter.

For the most part, it's quite dry in Italy, so high temperatures don't seem as bad because the humidity is lower. In Rome, Naples, and the south, temperatures can stay in the 30s (90s Fahrenheit) for days, but nights are most often comfortably cooler.

PREVIOUS PAGE: **A priest in Lucca, Tuscany.**

Italy's Average Daily Temperature & Monthly Rainfall

ROME

	JAN	FEB	MAR	APR	MAY	JUNE	JULY	AUG	SEPT	OCT	NOV	DEC
TEMP. (°F)	49	52	57	62	72	82	87	86	73	65	56	47
TEMP. (°C)	9	11	14	17	22	28	31	30	23	20	13	8
RAINFALL (IN.)	2.3	1.5	2.9	3.0	2.8	2.9	1.5	1.9	2.8	2.6	3.0	2.1

FLORENCE

	JAN	FEB	MAR	APR	MAY	JUNE	JULY	AUG	SEPT	OCT	NOV	DEC
TEMP. (°F)	45	47	50	60	67	76	77	70	64	63	55	46
TEMP. (°C)	7	8	9	16	19	24	25	21	18	17	13	8
RAINFALL (IN.)	3	3.3	3.7	2.7	2.2	1.4	1.4	2.7	3.2	4.9	3.8	2.9

NAPLES

	JAN	FEB	MAR	APR	MAY	JUNE	JULY	AUG	SEPT	OCT	NOV	DEC
TEMP. (°F)	50	54	58	63	70	78	83	85	75	66	60	52
TEMP. (°C)	9	12	14	17	21	26	28	29	24	19	16	11
RAINFALL (IN.)	4.7	4	3	3.8	2.4	.8	.8	2.6	3.5	5.8	5.1	3.7

Italy Calendar of Events

For an exhaustive list of events beyond those listed here, check http://events.frommers.com, where you'll find a searchable, up-to-the-minute roster of what's happening in cities all over the world. For major events for which tickets should be procured well before arriving, contact **Keith Prowse** (© **800/669-8687** in the U.S.; www.keithprowse.com), one of the world's largest independent ticket agencies and packagers; or go to **Culturalitaly.com** (see "Before You Leave Home: Tickets & Seats in Advance," below).

JANUARY

Epiphany celebrations, nationwide. All cities, towns, and villages in Italy stage Roman Catholic Epiphany observances, which celebrate the visit of the Magi to the infant Jesus. One of the most festive celebrations is the Epiphany Fair at Rome's Piazza Navona. January 6.

Festa di Sant'Agnese, Sant'Agnese Fuori le Mura, Rome. In this ancient ceremony, two lambs are blessed and shorn; their wool is used later for palliums (Roman Catholic vestments). Mid-January.

Foire de Saint Ours, Aosta, Valle d'Aosta. Observing a tradition that has existed for 10 centuries, artisans from the mountain valleys display their wares—often made of wood, lace, wool, or wrought iron—created during the long winter. Late January.

FEBRUARY

Carnevale, Piazza Navona, Rome. This festival marks the last day of the children's market and lasts until dawn of the following day. Dates vary. The week before Ash Wednesday.

Almond Blossom Festival, Agrigento, Sicily. This folk festival includes song, dance, costumes, and fireworks (© **0922-401352;** www.mandorloinfiore.net). First half of February.

Carnevale, Venice. At this riotous time, theatrical presentations and masked balls take place throughout Venice and on the islands in the lagoon. The balls are by invitation only (except the Doge's Ball), but the street events and fireworks are open to everyone. Contact the **Venice Tourist Office,** APT Venezia, Castello 5050, 30122 Venezia (© **041-5298711;**

www.turismo.venezia.it). The week before Ash Wednesday, the beginning of Lent.

MARCH

Festival della Canzone Italiana (Festival of Italian Popular Song; www.sanremo. rai.it), San Remo, the Marches. At this 5-day festival, major artists perform the latest Italian song releases. Early March.

Festa di San Giuseppe, the Trionfale Quarter, north of the Vatican, Rome. The heavily decorated statue of the saint is brought out at a fair with food stalls, concerts, and sporting events. Usually March 19.

APRIL

Holy Week observances, nationwide. Processions and age-old ceremonies—some from pagan days, some from the Middle Ages—are staged. The most notable procession is led by the pope, passing the Colosseum and the Roman Forum up to Palatine Hill; a torch-lit parade caps the observance. Sicily's observances are also noteworthy. Beginning 4 days before Easter Sunday; sometimes at the end of March but often in April.

Easter Sunday (Pasqua), Piazza di San Pietro, Rome. In an event broadcast around the world, the pope gives his blessing from the balcony of St. Peter's.

Scoppio del Carro (Explosion of the Cart; www.duomofirenze.it), Florence. At this ancient observance, a cart laden with flowers and fireworks is drawn by three white oxen to the Duomo, where at the noon Mass a mechanical dove detonates it from the altar. Easter Sunday.

Festa della Primavera (www.festadella primavera.com), Rome. The Spanish Steps are decked out with banks of azaleas and other flowers; later, orchestral and choral concerts are presented in Trinità dei Monti. Dates vary.

MAY

Maggio Musicale Fiorentino (Musical May Florentine), Florence. Italy's oldest and most prestigious music festival emphasizes music from the 14th to the 20th centuries, but also presents ballet and opera. Some concerts and ballets are presented free in Piazza della Signoria; ticketed events are held at the Teatro Comunale, Corso Italia 16, or the Teatro della Pergola, Via della Pergola 18. For schedules, tickets, and prices, contact the **Maggio Musicale Fiorentino/Teatro Comunale,** Corso Italia 16, 50123 Firenze (✆ **055-2779350;** www.maggiofiorentino. com). Late April to end of June.

Concorso Ippico Internazionale (International Horse Show), Piazza di Siena in the Villa Borghese, Rome (www.piazzadisiena.com). Late May.

Corso dei Ceri (Race of the Candles), Gubbio, Umbria. In this centuries-old ceremony celebrating the feast day of St. Ubaldo, the town's patron saint, 1,000-pound 9m (30-ft.) wooden "candles" *(ceri)* are raced through the streets of this perfectly preserved medieval hill town (✆ **075-9220693**). May 15.

JUNE

San Ranieri, Pisa, Tuscany. The town honors its patron saint with candlelit parades, followed the next day by eight-rower teams competing in 16th-century costumes. For more information, call ✆ **050-42291.** June 16 and 17.

Festival di Ravenna, Ravenna, Emilia-Romagna. This summer festival of international renown draws world-class classical performers. A wide range of performances are staged, including operas, ballets, theater, symphonic music concerts, solo and chamber pieces, oratorios, and sacred music. Tickets and reservations are needed for the most popular events. For details, call ✆ **0544-249211** (fax 0544/36303; www.ravennafestival. org). Mid-June to July.

Calcio in Costume (Ancient Football Match in Costume), Florence. This is a revival of a raucous 16th-century football match, pitting four teams in medieval costumes against one another. There are four matches, usually culminating around June 24, the feast day of San Giovanni. For info, call ✆ **055-23320,** or go to www.aboutflorence.com.

Gioco del Ponte, Pisa, Tuscany. Teams in Renaissance costumes take part in a much-contested tug-of-war on the Ponte di Mezzo, which spans the Arno River. Last Sunday in June.

Festa di San Pietro, St. Peter's Basilica, Rome. This most significant Roman religious festival is observed with solemn rites. June 29.

Son et Lumière, Rome. The Roman Forum and Tivoli areas are dramatically lighted at night. Early June to end of September.

La Biennale di Venezia (International Exposition of Modern Art), Venice. One of the most famous art events in Europe takes place during alternate odd-numbered years. Call ✆ **041-5218711.** June to October.

La Giostra del Saraceno (Joust of the Saracen), Arezzo, Tuscany. A colorful procession in full historical regalia precedes the tilting contest of the 13th century, with knights in armor in the town's main piazza. For information, call ✆ **0578/267238** (www.giostradel saracino.it). Mid-June.

Festival Puccini, near Lucca, Tuscany. Puccini operas are performed in this Tuscan lakeside town's open-air theater, near the celebrated composer's former summertime villa. Call ✆ **0584-350567,** or go to www.puccinifestival.it. Mid-June to mid-September.

JULY

Shakespearean Festival, Verona, the Veneto. Ballet, drama, and jazz performances are included in this festival of the Bard, with a few performances in English. For tickets call ✆ **899-111178** or go to www.geticket.it (www.verona. world-guides.com/verona_events). Throughout July.

Il Palio, Piazza del Campo, Siena, Tuscany. Palio fever grips this Tuscan hill town for a wild and exciting horse race from the Middle Ages. Pageantry, costumes, and the celebrations of the victorious *contrada* (sort of a neighborhood social club) mark the spectacle. It's a "no rules" event: Even a horse without a rider can win the race. For details, contact the **Azienda di Promozione Turistica,** Piazza del Campo 56, 53100 Siena (✆ **0577-280551;** www.terresiena.it). Early July to mid-August.

Arena di Verona (Arena Outdoor Opera Season), Verona, the Veneto. Culture buffs flock to the 20,000-seat Roman amphitheater, one of the world's best preserved. Call ✆ **045-8005151,** or go to www.arena.it. Early July to late August.

Festa di Noantri, Rome. Trastevere, the most colorful quarter, becomes a gigantic outdoor restaurant, with tables lining the streets, and merrymakers and musicians providing the entertainment. After reaching the quarter, find the first empty table and try to get a waiter—but keep a close eye on your valuables. For details, contact the **Azienda di Promozione Turistica,** Via Parigi 11, 00185 Roma (✆ **06-488991**). Mid-July.

Umbria Jazz, Perugia, Umbria. The Umbrian region hosts the country's (and one of Europe's) top jazz festivals, featuring world-class artists. Call ✆ **075-5732432,** or go to www. umbriajazz.com. Mid-July.

Festa del Redentore (Feast of the Redeemer; www.italyheaven.co.uk), Venice. This festival marks the lifting of the plague in July 1578, with fireworks, pilgrimages, and boating. Third Saturday and Sunday in July.

Festival Internazionale di Musica Antica, Urbino, the Marches. At this cultural extravaganza, international performers converge on Raphael's birthplace. It's the most important

Renaissance and baroque music festival in Italy. For details, contact the **Azienda di Promozione Turistica,** Piazza del Rinascimento 1, 61029 Urbino (☎ **0722-2613**). Mid-July.

AUGUST

Rossini Opera Festival, Pesaro, the Marches. The world's top bel canto specialists perform Rossini's operas and choral works at this popular festival. Call ☎ **0721-3800201,** or go to www.rossini operafestival.it. Throughout August.

Venice International Film Festival, Venice. Ranking after Cannes, this festival brings together stars, directors, producers, and filmmakers from all over the world. Films are shown between 9am and 3am in various areas of the Palazzo del Cinema on the Lido. Although many of the seats are reserved for international jury members, the public can attend whenever they want, if there are available seats. For information, contact the **Venice Film Festival,** c/o the La Biennale office, Ca' Giustinian, San Marco 1364A, 30124 Venezia. Call ☎ **041-521-8711** for details on how to acquire tickets, or check out www.labiennale.org. Late August to early September.

SEPTEMBER

Regata Storica (www.veniceonline.it/events/regatastorica.asp), the Grand Canal, Venice. Here's a maritime spectacular. Many gondolas participate in the canal procession, although gondolas don't race in the regatta itself. First Sunday in September.

Partita a Scacchi con Personaggi Viventi (Living Chess Game; www.marosticascacchi.it), Marostica, Veneto. This chess game is played in the town square by living chess pieces in period costumes. The second Saturday/Sunday of September during even-numbered years.

Fiera Del Tartufo Bianco D'Alba, Alba, Piedmont. This festival honors the expensive truffle in Alba, Italy's truffle capital, with contests, truffle-hound competitions, and tastings of this ugly but very expensive and delectable fungus. For details, contact the **Ufficio Turistico,** Piazza Risorgimento 2, 12051 Alba (☎ **0173/35833;** www.langheroero.it). Late September to mid-November.

DECEMBER

La Scala Opera Season, Teatro alla Scala, Milan. At the most famous opera house of them all, the season opens on December 7, the feast day of Milan's patron St. Ambrogio, and runs into July, and September to mid-November. Even though opening-night tickets are close to impossible to get, it's worth a try; call ☎ **02/860-775** (www.teatroallascala.org) for information and reservations.

Christmas Blessing of the Pope, Piazza di San Pietro, Rome. Delivered at noon from the balcony of St. Peter's Basilica, the pope's words are broadcast around the world. December 25.

ENTRY REQUIREMENTS

Passports

For information on how to get a **passport,** see "Embassies & Consulates" in "Fast Facts," later in this chapter. The websites listed provide downloadable passport applications as well as the current fees for processing applications. For an up-to-date country-by-country listing of passport requirements, go to the "Foreign Entry Requirement" Web page of the U.S. State Department at **www.travel.state.gov**.

All **children traveling abroad** must have their own passport. To prevent international child abduction, E.U. governments may require documentary evidence of relationship and permission for the child's travel from the parent or legal guardian not present. For up-to-date details on entry requirements for children, visit the **U.S. State Department** website: http://travel.state.gov/travel/travel_1744.html.

It is advised to always have at least one or two consecutive blank pages in your passport to allow space for visas and stamps that need to appear together. It is also important to note when your passport expires. Many countries require your passport to have at least 6 months left before its expiration in order to allow you into the destination.

Visas

U.S., Canadian, U.K., Irish, Australian, and New Zealand citizens with a valid passport don't need a **visa** to enter Italy if they don't expect to stay more than 90 days and don't expect to work there. For information on obtaining a visa, please visit the Ministry of Foreign Affairs website (www.esteri.it).

Customs

WHAT YOU CAN BRING INTO ITALY

Foreign visitors can bring along most items for personal use duty-free, including fishing tackle, a pair of skis, two tennis rackets, a baby carriage, two hand cameras with 10 rolls of film or a digital camera, computer, CD player with 10 CDs, tape recorder, binoculars, personal jewelry, portable radio set (subject to a small license fee), and 400 cigarettes and a quantity of cigars or pipe tobacco not exceeding 500 grams (1.1 lb.). There are strict limits on importing alcoholic beverages. However, for alcohol bought with tax included in the price, limits are much more liberal than in other countries of the European Union.

WHAT YOU CAN TAKE HOME FROM ITALY

Rules governing what you can bring back duty-free vary from country to country and are subject to change, but they're generally posted on the Web. Anyone caught buying counterfeit products can be fined up to 10,000€, and anyone caught selling counterfeit products could face criminal charges.

For information on what you're allowed to bring home, contact one of the following agencies:

U.S. Citizens: U.S. Customs & Border Protection (CBP), 1300 Pennsylvania Ave., NW, Washington, DC 20229 (✆ **877/287-8667;** www.cbp.gov).

Canadian Citizens: Canada Border Services Agency, Ottawa, Ontario, K1A 0L8 (✆ **800/461-9999** in Canada, or 204/983-3500; www.cbsa-asfc.gc.ca).

PLANNING YOUR TRIP TO ITALY | Entry Requirements

U.K. Citizens: HM Customs & Excise, Crownhill Court, Tailyour Road, Plymouth, PL6 5BZ (✆ **0845/010-9000;** from outside the U.K., 020/8929-0152; www.hmce.gov.uk).

Australian Citizens: Australian Customs Service, Customs House, 5 Constitution Ave., Canberra City, ACT 2601 (✆ **1300/363-263;** from outside Australia, 612/6275-6666; www.customs.gov.au).

New Zealand Citizens: New Zealand Customs, The Customhouse, 17–21 Whitmore St., Box 2218, Wellington, 6140 (✆ **04/473-6099** or 0800/428-786; www.customs.govt.nz).

Medical Requirements

No special vaccinations or inoculations are required for entry into Italy.

GETTING THERE & AROUND
Getting to Italy
BY PLANE

High season on most airlines' routes to Rome is usually from June to the beginning of September. This is the most expensive and crowded time to travel. **Shoulder season** is from April to May, early September to October, and December 15 to December 24. **Low season** is from November 1 to December 14 and December 25 to March 31.

FROM NORTH AMERICA **Flying time** to Rome from New York, Newark, and Boston is 8 hours; from Chicago, 10 hours; and from Los Angeles, 12½ hours. Flying time to Milan from New York, Newark, and Boston is 8 hours; from Chicago, 9¼ hours; and from Los Angeles, 11½ hours.

American Airlines (✆ **800/433-7300;** www.aa.com) offers daily nonstop flights to Rome from Chicago's O'Hare, with flights from all parts of American Airlines' vast network making connections into Chicago. **Delta/KLM/Air France** (✆ **800/221-1212;** www.delta.com) flies from New York's JFK to Milan and Rome; separate flights depart every evening for both destinations. **US Airways/AmericaWest** (✆ **800/622-1015;** www.usairways.com) offers one flight daily to Rome out of Philadelphia (you can connect through Philly from most major U.S. cities). And **Continental** (✆ **800/231-0856;** www.continental.com) flies several times a week to Rome and Milan from its hub in Newark.

Air Canada (✆ **888/247-2262;** www.aircanada.com) flies daily from Toronto to Rome. Two of the flights are nonstop; the others may touch down en route in Montreal, depending on the schedule.

British Airways (✆ **800/AIRWAYS** [245-9297]; www.britishairways.com), **Virgin Atlantic Airways** (✆ **800/821-5438;** www.virgin-atlantic.com), **Air France/KLM/Delta** (✆ **800/237-2747;** www.airfrance.com), and **Lufthansa** (✆ **800/645-3880;** www.lufthansa-usa.com) offer some attractive deals for anyone interested in combining a trip to Italy with a stopover in, say, Britain, Paris, Amsterdam, or Germany.

Alitalia (✆ **800/223-5730;** www.alitalia.com) is the Italian national airline, with nonstop flights to Rome from many North American cities, including New York (JFK), Newark, Boston, Chicago, Miami, Washington, and Toronto. Nonstop flights into Milan are from New York and Newark. From Milan or Rome, Alitalia can easily book connecting domestic flights if your final destination is elsewhere in Italy. Alitalia participates in the frequent-flier programs of other airlines, including Continental and US Airways.

Incidentally, the name Alitalia has been retained even though the carrier declared bankruptcy in 2008 and was taken over by Compagnia Aerea Italiana (CAI), a group of private investors. The owners have merged Alitalia assets with those of Air One. CAI also owns Air One, Italy's largest private airline.

FROM THE UNITED KINGDOM   Operated by the European Travel Network, **www.discountairfares.com** is a great online source for regular and discounted airfares to destinations around the world. You can also use this site to compare rates and book accommodations, car rentals, and tours. Click on "Special Offers" for the latest package deals.

British newspapers are always full of classified ads touting slashed fares to Italy. One good source is *Time Out.* London's *Evening Standard* has a daily travel section, and the Sunday editions of almost any newspaper will run many ads. Although competition is fierce, one well-recommended company that consolidates bulk ticket purchases and then passes the savings on to its consumers is **Trailfinders** (✆ **0845/058-5858;** www.trailfinders.com). It offers access to tickets on such carriers as SAS, British Airways, and KLM.

Both **British Airways** (✆ **0870/850-9850** in the U.K.; www.british airways.co.uk) and **Alitalia** (✆ **0871/424-1424;** www.alitalia.it) have frequent flights from London's Heathrow to Rome, Milan, Venice, Pisa (the gateway to Florence), and Naples. Flying time from London to these cities is from 2 to 3 hours. British Airways also has one direct flight a day from Manchester to Rome.

BY CAR

If you're already on the Continent, particularly in a neighboring country such as France or Austria, you may want to drive to Italy. However, you should make arrangements in advance with your car-rental company.

It's also possible to drive from London to Rome, a distance of 1,810km (1,125 miles), via Calais/Boulogne/Dunkirk, or 1,747km (1,085 miles) via Oostende/Zeebrugge, not counting channel crossings by Hovercraft, ferry, or the Chunnel. Milan is some 644km (400 miles) closer to Britain than is Rome. If you cross over from England and arrive at one of the continental ports, you still face a 24-hour drive. Most drivers budget 3 days for the journey.

Most of the roads from western Europe leading into Italy are toll-free, with some notable exceptions. If you use the Swiss superhighway network, you'll have to buy a special tax sticker at the frontier. You'll also pay to go through the St. Gotthard Tunnel into Italy. Crossings from France can be through the Mont Blanc Tunnel, for which you'll pay, or you can leave the French Riviera at Menton and drive directly into Italy along the Italian Riviera toward San Remo.

If you don't want to drive such distances, ask a travel agent to book you on a Motorail arrangement where the train carries your car. This service is good only to Milan—no car or sleeper expresses run the 644km (400 miles) south to Rome.

BY TRAIN

If you plan to travel heavily on the European rails, you'll do well to secure the latest copy of the *Thomas Cook European Timetable of Railroads.* It's available online at www.thomascookpublishing.com.

Electric trains have made travel between France and Italy faster and more comfortable than ever. **France's TGVs** travel at speeds of up to 320kmph (199 mph) and have cut travel time between Paris and Turin from 7 to 5½ hours and between Paris and Milan from 7½ to 6¾ hours. **Italy's ETRs** travel at speeds of up to 280kmph (174 mph) and currently run between Milan and Lyon (5 hr.), with a stop in Turin.

Europe-Wide Rail Passes

Many travelers to Europe take advantage of one of the greatest travel bargains, the **Eurail Global Pass,** which allows you unlimited travel in 18 Eurail-affiliated countries. You can travel on any of the days within the validity period, which is available for 15 days, 21 days, 1 month, 2 months, 3 months, and some other possibilities as well.

The advantages are tempting: There are no tickets; simply show the pass to the ticket collector, then settle back to enjoy the scenery. Seat reservations are required on some trains. Many trains have couchettes (sleeping cars), for which an extra fee is charged. Obviously, the 2- or 3-month traveler gets the greatest economic advantages. To obtain full advantage of a 15-day or 1-month pass, you'd have to spend a great deal of time on the train.

Eurailpass holders are entitled to considerable reductions on certain buses and ferries as well. You'll get a 20% reduction on second-class accommodations from certain companies operating ferries between Naples and Palermo or for crossings to Sardinia and Malta.

Prices for first-class adult travel are $1,135 for 15 days, $949 for 21 days, $1,179 for 1 month, $1,665 for 2 months, and $2,049 for 3 months. Children 4 to 11 pay half fare; those 3 and under travel for free.

A **Eurail Global Pass Saver,** also valid for first-class travel in 18 countries, offers a special deal for two or more people traveling together. This pass costs $965 for 15 days, $805 for 21 days, $999 for 1 month, $1,409 for 2 months, and $1,749 for 3 months.

A **Eurail Global Youth Pass** for those 12 to 25 allows second-class travel in 18 countries. This pass costs $739 for 15 days, $615 for 21 days, $765 for 1 month, $1,079 for 2 months, and $1,335 for 3 months.

The **Eurail Select Pass** offers unlimited travel on the national rail networks of any three, four, or five bordering countries out of the 22 Eurail nations linked by train or ship. Two or more passengers can travel together for big discounts, getting 5, 6, 8, 10, or 15 days of rail travel within any 2-month period on the national rail networks of any three, four, or five adjoining Eurail countries linked by train or ship. A sample fare: For 10 days in 2 months you pay $509 for three countries. **Eurail Select Pass Youth** for travelers under 26 allows second-class travel within the same guidelines as Eurail Select Pass, with fees starting at $328. **Eurail Select Pass Saver** offers discounts for two or more people traveling together, first-class travel within the same guidelines as Eurail Select Pass, with fees starting at $428.

In **North America,** you can buy these passes from travel agents or rail agents in major cities such as New York, Montreal, and Los Angeles. Eurailpasses are also available through **Rail Europe** (✆ **800/622-8600** in the U.S., or 800/361-7245 in Canada; www.raileurope.com). No matter what everyone tells you, you can buy Eurailpasses in Europe as well as in America (at the major train stations), but they're more expensive. Rail Europe can give you information on the rail/drive versions of the passes.

For details on the rail passes available in the **United Kingdom,** stop in at or contact the **National Rail Enquiries,** Victoria Station, London SW1V 1JZ (📞 **020/7278-5240;** www.nationalrail.co.uk). The staff can help you find the best option for the trip you're planning. Some of the most popular are the **Inter-Rail** and **Under 26** passes, entitling you to unlimited second-class travel in 26 European countries.

Italy Train Pass

This pass may be a good deal in that it grants unlimited travel on the national rail network of Italy (3 days of unlimited travel within a 2-month period). Travel days may be used either consecutively or nonconsecutively. The pass sells for $258 per person in first class or $210 in second class. Children 4 to 11 pay $129 or $105, respectively.

Getting Around

BY PLANE

Italy's domestic air network on **Alitalia** (📞 **800/223-5730** in the U.S., or 0871/424-1424 in the U.K.; www.alitalia.com) is one of the largest and most complete in Europe. Some 18 airports are serviced regularly from Rome, and most flights take less than an hour. Fares vary, but some discounts are available.

BY CAR

U.S. and Canadian drivers don't need an international driver's license to drive a rented car in Italy. However, if driving a private car, they need such a license.

You can apply for an International Driver's License at any **American Auto-mobile Association (AAA)** branch. You must be at least 18 and have two 2-by-2-inch photos and a photocopy of your U.S. driver's license with your AAA application form. The actual fee for the license can vary, depending on where it's issued. To find the AAA office nearest you, check the local phone directory or contact **AAA's national headquarters** (📞 **877/288-4546;** www.aaany.com). Remember that an International Driver's License is valid only if physically accompanied by your original driver's license and only if signed on the back. In Canada, you can get the address of the **Canadian Automobile Association** closest to you by calling 📞 **800/267-8713** (www.caa.ca).

The **Automobile Club d'Italia (ACI),** Via Marsala 8, 00185 Roma (📞 **06-49981;** www.aci.it), is open Monday through Friday from 8am to 2pm.

RENTALS   Many of the loveliest parts of Italy lie away from the main cities, far away from the train stations. For that, and for sheer convenience and free-dom, renting a car is usually the best way to explore the country. But you have to be a pretty aggressive and alert driver who won't be fazed by super-high speeds on the *autostrade* (national express highways) or by narrow streets in the cities and towns. Italian drivers have truly earned their reputa-tion as bad but daring.

However, the legalities and contractual obligations of renting a car in Italy (where accident and theft rates are very high) are a little complicated. To rent a car here, a driver must have nerves of steel, a sense of humor, a valid driver's license, and a valid passport and (in most cases) be over 25. Insurance on all vehicles is compulsory, though any reputable rental firm will arrange it in advance before you're even given the keys.

Travel Times Between the Major Cities

CITIES	DISTANCE	AIR TRAVEL TIME	TRAIN TRAVEL TIME	DRIVING TIME
Florence to Milan	298km/185 miles	55 min.	2 hr., 10 min.	3½ hr.
Florence to Venice	281km/174 miles	2 hr., 5 min.	4 hr.	3¼ hr.
Milan to Venice	267km/166 miles	50 min.	3½ hr.	3 hr., 10 min.
Rome to Florence	277km/172 miles	1 hr., 10 min.	2½ hr.	3 hr., 20 min.
Rome to Milan	572km/355 miles	1 hr., 5 min.	3½ hr.	6½ hr.
Rome to Naples	219km/136 miles	1 hr., 21 min.	2½ hr.	2½ hr.
Rome to Venice	528km/327 miles	1 hr., 5 min.	5¼ hr.	6 hr.
Rome to Genoa	501km/311 miles	1 hr.	6 hr.	5¾ hr.
Rome to Torino	669km/415 miles	1 hr., 5 min.	9–11 hr.	7¾ hr.

The three major rental companies in Italy are **Avis** (☎ **800/331-1084;** www.avis.com), **Budget** (☎ **800/472-3325;** www.budget.com), and **Hertz** (☎ **800/654-3001;** www.hertz.com). **Auto Europe** (☎ **888/223-5555;** www.autoeurope.com) is a U.S.-based company specializing in European car rentals.

In some cases, discounts are offered to members of the American Automobile Association (AAA) or AARP.

GASOLINE Gasoline, or petrol (known as *benzina*), is very expensive in Italy. Be prepared for sticker shock every time you fill up even a medium-size car with *super benzina,* which has the octane rating appropriate for most of the cars you'll be able to rent. Gas stations on the autostrade are open 24 hours, but on regular roads gas stations are rarely open on Sunday; also, many close from noon to 3pm for lunch, and most shut down after 7pm. Make sure the pump registers zero before an attendant starts filling your tank. A popular scam, particularly in the south, is to fill your tank before resetting the meter, so you pay not only your bill but also the charges run up by the preceding motorist.

Warning: About 75% of cars in Italy are diesel powered. Check carefully before filling your tank to see if gasoline or diesel fuel is required. Be careful not to put gasoline into a diesel tank. Even a liter of gasoline added to the tank of a modern diesel car can cause irreversible damage to the pump and other components. If you realize you've made a mistake, don't start the vehicle, as severe damage to the vehicle may result and you'll be liable for the repair costs. Service stations in Italy serve both gasoline and diesel.

DRIVING RULES Driving is on the right; passing is on the left. Violators of the highway code are fined; serious violations might also be punished by imprisonment. In cities and towns, the speed limit is 50kmph (31 mph). For all cars and motor vehicles on main roads and local roads, the limit is 90kmph (56 mph). For the autostrade, the limit is 130kmph (81 mph). Use the left lane only for passing. If a driver zooms up behind you on the autostrade with his or her lights on, that's your sign to get out of the way! Use of seat belts is compulsory.

BREAKDOWNS & ASSISTANCE In case of car breakdown or for any tourist information, foreign motorists can call ☎ **803-116** (24-hr. nationwide telephone service). For road information, itineraries, and travel assistance, call ☎ **06-514971.**

BY TRAIN

Trains provide a medium-priced means of transport, even if you don't buy the Eurailpass or one of the special Italian Railway tickets (see above). As a rule of thumb, second-class travel usually costs about two-thirds the price of an equivalent first-class trip. The relatively new **InterCity trains** (IC on train schedules) are modern, air-conditioned trains that make limited stops; compared to the slower direct or regional trains, the supplement can be steep, but a second-class IC ticket will provide a first-class experience.

A couchette (a private fold-down bed in a communal cabin) requires a supplement above the price of first-class travel. Children 4 to 11 receive a discount of 50% off the adult fare, and children 3 and under travel free with their parents. Seniors and travelers under age 26 can also purchase discount cards. Seat reservations are highly recommended during peak season and on weekends or holidays; they must be booked in advance.

Trenitalia Pass for Italy covers 3 to 10 days of travel within 2 months. The price for 3 days is 182€ first class, 148€ second class. Additional days are 21€ to 23€ first class, 16€ to 18€ second class.

Discounts and bonuses include ferries to Sicily; they do not include international Artesia, France-Italy Night, and Elipsos trains, but they do offer passholder fares on those trains.

You can buy these passes from any travel agent or by calling ☏ **800/848-7245.** You can also call ☏ 800/4-EURAIL (438-7245) or 800/EUROSTAR (387-6782).

BY BUS

Italy has an extensive and intricate bus network, covering all regions. However, because rail travel is inexpensive, the bus isn't the preferred method of travel. Besides, drivers seem to go on strike every 2 weeks.

One of the leading bus operators is **SITA,** Viale dei Cadorna 105, Florence (☏ **055/478-2870;** www.sitabus.it). SITA buses serve most parts of the country, especially the central belt, including Tuscany, but not the far frontiers. Among the largest of the other companies, with special emphasis in the north and central tiers, is **Autostradale,** Autostazione Garibaldi, Milan (☏ **02-637901;** www.autostradale.it). **Lazzi,** Via Mercadante 2, Florence (☏ **055-363041;** www.lazzi.it), goes through Tuscany, including Siena, and much of central Italy.

Where these nationwide services leave off, **local bus companies** operate in most regions, particularly in the hill sections and the Alpine regions where rail travel isn't possible. For information, see "Getting There" in the city, town, and village sections.

MONEY & COSTS

THE VALUE OF THE EURO VS. OTHER POPULAR CURRENCIES

Euro	US$	Can$	UK£	Aus$	NZ$
1	$1.30	C$1.34	84p	A$1.34	NZ$1.77

Frommer's lists exact prices in the local currency. The currency conversions quoted above were correct at press time. However, rates fluctuate, so before departing consult a currency exchange website such as **www.oanda.com/convert/classic** to check up-to-the-minute rates.

WHAT THINGS COST IN ITALY	EURO
Taxi from the airport to downtown Rome	45
Double room, moderate	155
Double room, inexpensive	85
Three-course dinner for one without wine, moderate	65
Glass of wine	5–8
Bottle of Coca-Cola	2.50
Cup of coffee	1
1 liter of premium gas	1.40
Admission to most museums	3–10
Admission to most national parks	5

ATMs

These days, traveler's checks seem less necessary because most Italian cities and towns have 24-hour ATMs, allowing you to withdraw small amounts of cash as needed.

Credit Cards

More and more places in Italy are moving from cards with magnetic strips to the newer "chip and PIN" system. With this newer type of credit card, you must enter a four-digit PIN (personal identification number) on a keypad as part of the transaction. In fact, as a means of reducing credit card fraud, a limited number of establishments in Italy might not accept your credit card unless it adheres to these standards.

In the changeover in technology, some retailers have falsely concluded that they can no longer accept swipe cards, or can't accept signature cards that don't require a PIN. At least as of press time for this edition, both the new and old cards are accepted in most shops, hotels, and restaurants.

Beware of hidden credit card fees while traveling. Check with your credit or debit card issuer to see what fees, if any, will be charged for overseas transactions. Recent reform legislation in the U.S., for example, has curbed some exploitative lending practices. But many banks have responded by increasing fees in other areas, including fees for customers who use credit and debit cards while out of the country—even if those charges were made in U.S. dollars. Fees can amount to 3% or more of the purchase price. Check with your bank before departing to avoid any surprise charges on your statement.

STAYING HEALTHY

In general, Italy is viewed as a "safe" destination, although problems, of course, can and do occur anywhere. You don't need to get shots; most foodstuff is safe and the water in cities and towns is potable. If you're concerned, order bottled water. It is easy to get a prescription filled in towns and cities, and nearly all places throughout Italy contain English-speaking doctors at hospitals with well-trained medical staffs.

If You Get Sick

Any foreign consulate can provide a list of area doctors who speak English. If you get sick, consider asking your hotel concierge to recommend a local doctor—even his or her own.

U.K. nationals will need a **European Health Insurance Card (EHIC)** to receive free or reduced-costs health benefits during a visit to a European Economic Area (EEA) country (E.U. countries plus Iceland, Liechtenstein, and Norway) or Switzerland. The European Health Insurance Card replaces the E111 form, which is no longer valid. For advice, ask at your local post office or see www.dh.gov.uk/travellers.

We list **hospitals** and **emergency numbers** under "Fast Facts" in individual city chapters. For emergencies requiring an ambulance or immediate attention, call ✆ **113.**

If you suffer from a chronic illness, consult your doctor before your departure. Pack **prescription medications** in your carry-on luggage, and carry them in their original containers, with pharmacy labels—otherwise they won't make it through airport security. Carry the generic name of prescription medicines, in case a local pharmacist is unfamiliar with the brand name.

We list additional **emergency numbers** in "Fast Facts," p. 929.

CRIME & SAFETY

The most common menace, especially in large cities, particularly Rome and Naples, is the plague of pickpockets and roving gangs of Gypsy children who surround you, distract you in all the confusion, and steal your purse or wallet. Never leave valuables in a car, and never travel with your car unlocked. A U.S. State Department travel advisory warns that every car (whether parked, stopped at a traffic light, or even moving) can be a potential target for armed robbery. In these uncertain times, it is always prudent to check the U.S. State Department's travel advisories at **http://travel.state.gov**.

SPECIALIZED TRAVEL RESOURCES

In addition to the destination-specific resources listed below, please visit Frommers.com for other specialized travel resources.

LGBT Travelers

Since 1861, Italy has had liberal legislation regarding homosexuality, but that doesn't mean it has been looked on favorably in a Catholic country. Homosexuality is much more accepted in the north than in the south, especially in Sicily, although Taormina has long been a gay mecca. However, all major towns and cities have an active gay life, especially Florence, Rome, and Milan, which considers itself the "gay capital" of Italy, and Bologna, which is the headquarters of **Arcigay** (✆ **051-649-3055;** www.arcigay.it), the country's leading gay organization. Capri is the gay resort of Italy, rivaled only by the gay beaches of Venice.

The **International Gay and Lesbian Travel Association (IGLTA;** ✆ **800/448-8550** or 954/630-1637; www.iglta.org) is the trade association for the gay and lesbian travel industry, and offers an online gay- and lesbian-friendly travel directory.

Many agencies offer tours and travel itineraries specifically for gay and lesbian travelers. **Above and Beyond Tours** (✆ **800/397-2681;** www.above beyondtours.com) are gay Australia tour specialists. San Francisco–based **Now, Voyager** (✆ **800/255-6951;** www.nowvoyager.com) offers worldwide trips and cruises, and **Olivia Cruises & Resorts** (✆ **800/631-6277;** www.olivia.com) offers lesbian cruises and resort vacations.

Gay.com Travel (✆ **212/242-8100** or 415/834-6500; www.gay.com) is an excellent source for travel.

The website **Gaytravel** (✆ **800/GAY-TRAVEL** [429-8728]; www.gaytravel. com) offers trip-planning information and ideas; gay-friendly tours, cruises, destinations, and hotel listings; and general advice for gay travel all over the world.

Also look for the *Spartacus International Gay Guide,* 36th edition (Bruno Gmünder Verlag; www.spartacusworld.com/gayguide), or the *Damron* guides (www.damron.com), with separate, annual gay and lesbian books.

Travelers with Disabilities

Laws in Italy require rail stations, airports, hotels, and most restaurants to follow a strict set of regulations about **wheelchair accessibility** to restrooms, ticket counters, and the like. Even museums and other attractions have conformed to the regulations. Always call ahead to check on the accessibility in hotels, restaurants, and sights.

With overcrowded streets, more than 400 bridges, and difficult-to-board *vaporetti* (water buses), Venice has never been accused of being too user-friendly for those with disabilities. The Venice tourist office distributes a free map called *Veneziapertutti (Venice for All),* illustrating what parts of the city are accessible and listing accessible churches, monuments, gardens, public offices, hotels, and restrooms. According to various announcements, Venice will pay even more attention to this issue in the future, possibly adding retractable ramps operated by magnetic cards.

Family Travel

Most Italian hoteliers will let children 12 and under stay in a room with a parent for free—with a little negotiation at the reception desk. Italians love bambini but don't offer a lot of special amenities for them. For example, a kids' menu in a restaurant is a rarity. You can, however, order a half portion (*mezza porzione*) for your little one. At attractions, inquire if a *sconto bambino* (kids' discount) is available. For European Union kids under 18, admission is free to state-run museums.

The friendliest hotels in Italy are the more than 20 **Starwoods** (✆ **888/625-5144;** www.starwoodhotels.com).

Recommended family travel websites include **Family Travel Forum** (www. familytravelforum.com), a comprehensive site that offers customized trip planning; **Family Travel Network** (www.familytravelnetwork.com), an online magazine providing travel tips; and **TravelWithYourKids.com** (www.travelwithyourkids. com), a comprehensive site written by parents for parents. For a list of more family friendly travel resources, turn to the experts at frommers.com.

Other great Frommer's guides for your trip include *Frommer's Northern Italy with Your Family* and *Frommer's Tuscany & Umbria with Your Family.*

To locate accommodations, restaurants, and attractions that are particularly kid-friendly, look for the "Kids" icon throughout this guide.

Senior Travel

Mention the fact that you're a senior when you first make your travel reservations. Some major airlines and many Italian hotels offer discounts for seniors.

Members of **AARP,** 601 E St. NW, Washington, DC 20049 (🕿 **888/687-2277;** www.aarp.org), get discounts on hotels, airfares, and car rentals. AARP offers members a wide range of benefits, including *AARP The Magazine* and a monthly newsletter. Anyone over 50 can join.

Many reliable agencies and organizations target the 50-plus market. **Road Scholar** (🕿 **800/454-5768;** www.roadscholar.com) arranges worldwide study programs for those age 55 and over.

Check out the quarterly magazine *Travel 50 & Beyond* (www.travel50and beyond.com) and the bestselling paperback ***Unbelievably Good Deals and Great Adventures That You Absolutely Can't Get Unless You're Over 50 2002–2010,*** 17th edition (McGraw-Hill), by Joann Rattner Heilman.

European Walking Tours (🕿 **800/231-8448** or 217/398-0058; www. walkingtours.com) sponsors walking tours for the mature traveler in Italy. The founder, Jacqueline Tofte Hess, is a native of the Swiss Alps, and has charted special routes across Alpine meadows, remote valleys, and over mountain passes or alongside serene lakes. The search is for wildflowers, birds, and mountain animals, with lessons in local architecture, traditions, and history thrown in as well.

For more than 2 decades, **Vantage Deluxe World Travel** (🕿 **800/322-6677;** www.vantagetravel.com) has taken thousands of mature travelers on extraordinary travel adventures in various European countries, including Italy. Travel is on river cruises and fully escorted land tours. Groups are deliberately kept small.

RESPONSIBLE TOURISM

Italy not only protects its national and historical monuments, but it also preserves its landscapes with nearly two dozen national parks and dozens of regional parks and nature reserves. In all, nearly 5% of the landmass is under government protection.

These parks encompass lakes, forests, mountains, and even the sea. One of the greatest parks to visit in Italy is **Parco Nazionale d'Abruzzo** (www.parco abruzzo.it). This park contains the highest peaks in the Apennines and is the home of the brown bear and the chamois (hoofed, goatlike animals with horns).

Another park of spectacular beauty is **Parco Nazionale delle Cinque Terre** (www.parconazionale5terre.it), a seaside setting riddled with olive groves, vineyards, rainbow-hued houses, and fishing villages, five in all.

If you plan to tour the national parks, a good source of information is **Feder-parchi,** the Italian Federation of Parks and Nature Reserves, an association dating from 1989. Its headquarters is at Via Cristoforo Colombo 163, 00147 Roma (🕿 **06-51604940;** www.parks.it). The organization issues a magazine, *Parchi,* documenting information about the parks, including the latest developments,

RESOURCES FOR responsible TRAVEL

If you'd like to travel green in Italy and stay at environmentally sensitive hotels, seek out the recommendations from **It's a Green Green World** (www.itsagreengreenworld. com). Its site previews green hotels across Italy, from an ancient family wine production factory converted to receive guests in Sicily to an Umbrian inn opening onto a panoramic view of Lake Trasimeno.

In addition to the site listed above, the following websites provide valuable wide-ranging information on sustainable travel.

- **Responsible Travel** (www.responsible travel.com) is a great source of sustainable travel ideas; the site is run by a spokesperson for ethical tourism in the travel industry. **Sustainable Travel International** (www.sustainable travelinternational.org) promotes ethical tourism practices, and manages an extensive directory of sustainable properties and tour operators around the world.

- **Carbonfund** (www.carbonfund.org), **TerraPass** (www.terrapass.org), and **Cool Climate** (http://coolclimate. berkeley.edu) provide info on "carbon offsetting," or offsetting the greenhouse gas emitted during flights.

- **Greenhotels** (www.greenhotels.com) recommends green-rated member hotels around the world that fulfill the company's stringent environmental requirements. **Environmentally Friendly Hotels** (www.environmentally friendlyhotels.com) offers more green accommodations ratings.

- **Volunteer International** (www. volunteerinternational.org) has a list of questions to help you determine the intentions and the nature of a volunteer program. For general info on volunteer travel, visit **www. volunteerabroad.org** and **www. idealist.org**.

various events taking place, as well as an eco-section on the preservation of the parks and other environmental concerns.

Lega Italiana Protezione Uccelli (LIPU) is the Italian League for Bird Protection, a charitable organization founded in 1965 and devoted to the protection of the country's wildlife, especially birds. Volunteers work to conserve bird habitats and even nurse injured birds back to health. Contact LIPU at Via Trento 49, 43100 Parma (✆ **05-21273043;** www.lipu.it).

Travelers can make a difference in conserving Italy's natural habitats by learning about environmentally responsible tourism before they go. For information on the subject, contact one of the following organizations: **Conservation International,** 2011 Crystal Dr., Ste. 500, Arlington, VA 22202 (✆ **800/ 429-5660** or 703/341-2400; www.conservation.org); the **International Ecotourism Society,** 1333 H St. NW, Ste. 300E, Washington, DC 20005 (✆ **202/506-5033;** www.ecotourism.org), or the **United Nations Environment Programme (UNEP),** 39 Quai André Citroën, Paris 75739 in France (✆ **33-1-44-37-14-50;** www.unep.fr). If you have time to contact only one of these organizations, make it the International Ecotourism Society, as it is the world's oldest and largest ecotourism organization. An admirable organization for the ecotourist is **Leave No Trace Center for Outdoor Ethics,** P.O. Box 997, Boulder, CO 80306 (http://lnt.org). It has drawn up a code for outdoor travelers who want to protect the wilderness for future generations. The whole aim is to reduce one's impact on the environment. The rules make sense, including one to bag trash and carry it out when you go, or else use cookstoves instead of campfires.

SPECIAL-INTEREST & ESCORTED TRIPS

Special-Interest Trips

For special-interest travel, a good overview of what's out there is available from **Specialty Travel** (www.specialtytravel.com), which issues a biannual magazine devoted to adventure and special-interest tours. Contact information is provided for some 400 tour operators, including those operating in Italy. Everything is covered, from details on art classes in Florence to how to explore the mysteries of Sicily. Contact them at P.O. Box 458, San Anselmo, CA 94979 (✆ **888/624-4030**).

Tennis fans set their calendars by the events that transpire every year at the Italian Open, which is held in mid-May at the Foro Italica in Rome, near Mussolini's Olympic site. A California-based company, **Advantage Tennis Tours,** 33 White Sail Dr., Ste. 100, Laguna Niguel, CA 92677 (✆ **800/341-8687** or 949/661-7331; fax 949/489-2837; www.advantagetennistours.com), conducts tours to the Open that include 6 nights' accommodations in a deluxe Roman hotel, Center Court seats at three sessions of the tournament, city tours of ancient Rome, a farewell dinner, the organizational and communications skill of a tour hostess, and the opportunity to play tennis.

Some of the best outdoor vacations in Italy, ranging from walking trips to self-guided biking trips in Sardinia, are offered by **ResponsibleTravel.com,** Pavilion House, 5 Ole Steine, Brighton, BN1 1EJ in England (✆ **44-127-360-0030;** www.responsibletravel.com). One trip, for example, offers a stay in the Marches at a 185-acre farm, a short haul to the UNESCO-protected town of Urbino.

Many vacationers prefer to travel *agriturismo* style. It's not only inexpensive but is a people-to-people way of seeing Italy. Local families take in paying guests, feeding them well (often from their own produce), everything paired with homemade wine. These farmhouses are often remotely located, granting tranquillity. To check on these farm holidays in the Italian countryside, visit **Associazione Nationale per l'Agriturismo** at www.agriturist.it. Bookings can be made by phoning ✆ **39-0564-417418;** the website is www.byfarmholidays.com.

Readers in the past have heaped praise on the well-organized jaunts of **Go Ahead Tours,** 1 Education St., Cambridge, MA 02141 (✆ **800/590-1170;** www.goaheadtours.com). They especially cater to those with academic or professional backgrounds, people interested in experiencing other cultures. The group's vast repertoire takes in tours (often 9 or 10 days) that cover everything from "A Taste of Tuscany & Umbria" to "Walking the Amalfi Coast."

Academic Trips & Language Classes

Tuscans are said to speak "the most perfect" Italian in the country, so why not enroll in the best center if you want to learn Italian? Not only that, but you get to live in Florence. Studies are sponsored by **Centro Fiorenza,** V.S. Spirito 14,

50125 Florence (© **055-2398274;** www.centrofiorenza.com). Those interested in the fine arts might enroll at the **Studio Arts Center International** at Palazzo dei Cartelloni, Via San'Antonio 11, 50123 Florence (© **977/257-7225,** 212/248-7225, or 055-289948 in Italy; www.saci-florence.org). Its programs specialize in art and art history, along with various other Italian studies. Affiliated with Bowling Green State University, the center admits only students who are 18 and over.

Some groups in Italy are dedicated to the restoring of the country's rich cultural past. Offering 1-week programs in archaeological field work, **Archeo Venezia,** Cannaregio 1376A 30121 Venezia (© **041-710515;** www.archeove.com), is one of the best of these cultural heritage groups. Its weeklong programs cost from 150€ to 400€, including room and board.

Adventure & Wellness Trips

For the nature lover, camping is a good alternative in Italy, as there are some 1,700 campgrounds scattered throughout the country. The better ones, rated four stars by the government, feature a grocery market, swimming pool, even a bar. The simpler ones, beginning at only 10€ per person, get only one star. For those without tents, some of these groups offer bungalows for the night. Campsites and tourist villages are previewed in a guide, *EasyCamping* (www.easycamping.it).

For a century and a half, **Club Alpino Italiano** (© **02-2057231;** www.cai.it) has been the best source for all things associated with biking in Italy, from the north to the "boot." You can rent a bike by the week or longer at outlets in most Italian towns or cities. The club promotes mountaineering, hiking, and caving initiatives throughout Italy, and it is a font of information. The outfit is also a good source for information on *trekking,* which is Italian for hiking or walking.

For biking across Italy, some of the best tours in general are sponsored by **Ciclismo Classico** (© **800/866-7314** or 781/646-3377; www.ciclismo classico.com) in the U.S. The season for this operator, in business since 1988, is April to November. Cycling tours of Tuscany and Umbria are to be expected, but Classico also specializes in lesser known regions, including Puglia.

For travelers who want to experience and explore the homeland of Michelangelo and Leonardo da Vinci, **VBT Bicycling Vacations** (© **800/245-3868;** www.vbt.com) offers 8-day vacations through Tuscany, Sicily, and Puglia. Accommodations are included in the overall package deal.

The best mountain adventure tours are offered by **Mountain Travel-Sobek,** 1266 66 St., Emeryville, CA 94608 (© **888/831-7526** or 510/594-6000; www.mtsobek.com). The best hiking tours of Italy are a feature of **Above the Clouds Trekking,** P.O. Box 388, Hinesburg, VT 05461 (© **800/233-4499** or 802/482-4848; fax 802/482-5011; www.abovecloudss.com).

Since 1995, **Classic Journeys** has earned a devoted following—many repeat visitors—for its cultural walking adventures throughout Italy. Some of their best tours take in the spectacular island of Sardinia, or Tuscany through the back door. They often go to the lesser known parts of Italy, including Puglia, the "heel" of Italy's boot. Their tours are likely to include a picnic at an 11th-century abbey or a visit to Etruscan ruins, and, most definitely, walks through the countryside. For more information, call © **800/200-3887** or 858/454-5004; www. classicjourneys.com in the U.S., or write Classic Journeys, 7855 Ivanhoe Ave., Ste. 220, La Jolla, CA 92037.

The best trekking through the national parks is organized by **La Boscaglia Walking Tours** (℡ 0039-051-6264169; www.boscaglia.it). A guide from this outfit will accompany you along the most hidden and evocative routes. Two types of walks are featured, including "Wildlife Walks," which bring you in touch with the inhabitants of the parks. You sleep in tents or mountain huts, eat in typical *trattorie,* or cook your own organic-vegetarian meals with the group. The other is "Wayfarers Walks," where you follow centuries-old footpaths made by hunters, shepherds, and pilgrims. To participate in this program, you need to pay a membership fee of 20€.

Food & Wine Trips

Born in Tuscany, Giuliano Bugialli is the most popular Italian cooking teacher in the U.S. His first book, *The Fine Art of Italian Cooking,* published in 1977, is today a classic. He conducts weeklong classes in summer, with lodging in Florence and classes conducted in a kitchen in the Chianti Region directly south of that city. Each week includes about 35 recipes and dozens of wines to be tasted. For more data, contact **Foods of Italy, Inc.,** 105 S. 12th St., Apt. 205, the White Bldg., Philadelphia, PA 19107 (℡ **215/922-2086;** www. bugialli.com).

Hailed as the best cooking school in Italy, **Apicius Cooking School of Florence,** Via Guelfa 85, 50129 Florence (℡ **055-2658135;** www.tuscan cooking.com), caters to both professionals and nonprofessionals in their food and wine studies. The cooking courses are taught in English, but Italian-language classes are also available. Programs featured by this school include room and board.

Epiculinary was founded by Lorenza de Medici, author of *Tuscany: The Beautiful Cookbook,* at the 12th-century abbey and wine estate of Badia a Coltibuono in the Chianti region. Today her youngest son, Guido Stucchi Prinetti, conducts cooking courses from March to December. They range from 1 day, 3 days, or 7 days. The rather high prices include room and board in a late medieval abbey complex. For more information, call ℡ **888/380-9010** in the U.S. (www.epiculinary.com).

Many wine connoisseurs view **Cellar Tours** (℡ **310/928-7559;** www. cellartours.com) as offering the best wine tours of Italy. They take in such destinations as Florence and Tuscany, Rome and Umbria, Sicily and its islands, and Naples and the Amalfi Coast. Cellar Tours can also arrange deluxe culinary tours—for example, in Umbria you go on a private truffle hunt, visit wine estates, taste Sagrantino wines, and dine at a Michelin-starred eatery.

The above courses are a bit pricey. A more economical way to learn some of the secrets of the Italian kitchen is to book with **Divina Cucina.** Your host is Judy Witts Francini, author of *Secrets of My Tuscan Kitchen!* Prices start at 125€ per person, and classes begin at 11am with a shopping expedition to Florence's Central Market. By 4pm, a gourmet meal of a lifetime is composed. Three-day to 1-week tours of the Chianti food and wine district are also offered. For more information, call ℡ **055-292-578** (www.divinacucina.com).

Vacations are getting shorter, and if you're forced to absorb Italy in a nutshell, check out **Viva Holidays Tours & Travels** (http://vivaholidaystour. com). In just 7 days, Viva can whisk you through Rome to Florence and on to Venice, with a final stopover in Milan. Travel agents can hook you up with Viva's travel packages.

Volunteer & Working Trips

Ecovolunteer, CTS-Centro Turistico Studentesco e Giovanile, Department Ambiente, Via Albalonga 3, 00183 Roma (☎ **06-64960327**; www.ecovolunteer. org), is devoted to protecting nature and its inhabitants, especially some of the most fascinating animals on the planet. Its programs include a large number of wildlife conservation projects—perhaps tracking dolphins and other marine animals while sailing on a research boat in the Bay of Naples. One-week programs, costing around 850€, are sponsored annually from June to October.

Società Cooperative Greenwood, Via Pozzillo 21, 87045 Dipignano (☎ **0984/445526**; www.scgreenwood.it), is a volunteer operation that conducts research jaunts through the National Park of Calabria in the south of Italy. Devoted to ecotourism and ecological studies, the Greenwood Cooperation Society has full and adventure-filled programs such as tracking wolves and engaging in other outdoor activities. For 350€, camping, food, and supplies are included.

Escorted General-Interest Tours

The biggest operator of escorted tours is **Perillo Tours** (☎ **800/431-1515**; www.perillotours.com), family operated for three generations. Perillo's tours cost much less than if you arranged the same trip yourself. Accommodations are in first-class hotels, and guides tend to be well qualified and well informed.

Trafalgar Tours (☎ **866/544-4434**; www.trafalgartours.com) is one of Europe's largest tour operators, offering affordable guided tours with lodgings in unpretentious hotels. Check with your travel agent for more information on these tours (Trafalgar takes calls only from agents).

A competitor is **Insight Vacations** (☎ **800/582-8380**; www.insight vacations.com), which books superior first-class, fully escorted motorcoach tours lasting from 1 week to a 36-day grand tour.

Abercrombie & Kent (☎ **800/554-7016** in the U.S.; www.abercrombie kent.com) offers a variety of luxurious premium packages. Your overnight stays will be in meticulously restored castles and exquisite Italian villas, most of which are government-rated four- and five-star accommodations. Several trips are offered, including tours of the Lake Garda region and the southern territory of Calabria.

The oldest travel agency in Britain, **Cox & Kings** (☎ **020/7873-5000**; www.coxandkings.co.uk), specializes in organized tours through the country's gardens and sites of historical or aesthetic interest, opera tours, pilgrimage-style visits to sites of religious interest, and food- and wine-tasting tours. The staff is noted for its focus on tours of ecological and environmental interest.

STAYING CONNECTED
Mobile Phones

The three letters that define much of the world's wireless capabilities are **GSM** (Global System for Mobile Communications), a big, seamless network that makes for easy cross-border cellphone use throughout Europe. If your cellphone is on a GSM system and you have a world-capable multiband phone, just call your wireless operator and ask for international roaming to be activated on your account. Per-minute charges are high, so check with your provider.

For many, **renting** a phone is a good idea. While you can rent a phone from any number of overseas sites, including kiosks at airports and at car-rental agencies, we suggest renting the phone before you leave home. North Americans can rent one before leaving home from **InTouch USA** (✆ **800/872-7626;** www.intouchglobal.com) or **RoadPost** (✆ **888/290-1616** or 905/272-5665; www.roadpost.com). InTouch will also, for free, advise you on whether your existing phone will work overseas.

Buying a phone can be economically attractive, as many nations have cheap prepaid phone systems. Once you arrive at your destination, stop by a local cellphone shop and get the cheapest package; you'll probably pay less than $100 for a phone and a starter calling card. Local calls may be as low as 10¢ per minute, and in many countries incoming calls are free.

Internet & E-Mail

WITHOUT YOUR OWN COMPUTER

To find cybercafes in your destination, check **www.cybercaptive.com** and **www.cybercafe.com**.

Most major airports have **Internet kiosks** that provide basic Web access for a per-minute fee that's usually higher than cybercafe prices.

WITH YOUR OWN COMPUTER

More and more hotels, resorts, airports, cafes, and retailers are going **Wi-Fi** (wireless fidelity), becoming "hot spots" that offer free high-speed Wi-Fi access or charge a small fee for usage. To find public Wi-Fi hot spots at your destination, go to **www.jiwire.com**.

For dial-up access, most business-class hotels throughout Europe offer dataports for laptop modems.

Wherever you go, bring a **connection kit** of the right power and phone adapters, a spare phone cord, and a spare Ethernet network cable—or find out whether your hotel supplies them.

Newspapers & Magazines

In major cities, it's possible to find the *International Herald Tribune* or *USA Today,* as well as other English-language newspapers and magazines, including *Time* and *Newsweek,* at hotels and news kiosks.

Telephones

To call Italy from the United States, dial the **international prefix, 011;** then Italy's **country code, 39;** and then the city code (for example, **06** for Rome and **055** for Florence), which is now built into every number. Then dial the actual **phone number.**

A **local phone call** in Italy costs around .10€. **Public phones** accept coins, precharged phone cards *(scheda* or *carta telefonica),* or both. You can buy a *carta telefonica* at any *tabacchi* (tobacconists; look for a white T on a blue or black background) in increments of 5€, 10€, and 20€. To make a call, pick up the receiver and insert .10€ or your card (break off the corner first). Most phones have a digital display to tell you how much money you inserted (or how much is left). Dial the number, and don't forget to take the card with you.

To **call from one city code to another,** dial the city code, complete with initial 0, and then dial the number. (Numbers in Italy range from four to eight digits. Even when you're calling within the same city, you must dial that city's area code—including the zero. A Roman calling another Rome number must dial 06 before the local number.)

To **dial direct internationally,** dial **00** and then the country code, the area code, and the number. **Country codes** are as follows: the United States and Canada, 1; the United Kingdom, 44; Ireland, 353; Australia, 61; New Zealand, 64. Make international calls from a public phone, if possible, because hotels charge inflated rates for direct dial—but bring plenty of *monete* (change). A reduced rate is applied from 11pm to 8am on Monday through Saturday and all day Sunday. Direct-dial calls from the United States to Italy are much cheaper, so arrange for whomever to call you at your hotel.

Italy has recently introduced a series of **international phone cards** (*scheda telefonica internazionale*) for calling overseas. They come in increments of 50, 100, 200, and 400 *unità* (units), and they're available at *tabacchi* and bars. Each *unità* is worth .15€ of phone time; it costs 5 *unità* (.75€) per minute to call within Europe or to the United States or Canada, and 12 *unità* (1.55€) per minute to call Australia or New Zealand. You don't insert this card into the phone; merely dial ℂ **1740** and then *2 (star 2) for instructions in English, when prompted.

To call the free **national telephone information** (in Italian) in Italy, dial ℂ **12. International information** is available at ℂ **176** but costs .60€ a shot.

To make **collect or calling-card calls,** drop in .10€ or insert your card and dial one of the numbers here; an American operator will come on to assist you (because Italy has yet to discover the joys of the touch-tone phone). The following calling-card numbers work all over Italy: **AT&T** ℂ 172-1011, **MCI** ℂ 172-1022, and **Sprint** ℂ 172-1877. To make collect calls to a country besides the United States, dial ℂ **170** (.50€), and practice your Italian counting in order to relay the number to the Italian operator. Tell him or her that you want it *a carico del destinatario* (charged to the destination, or collect).

Because you can't count on all Italian phones having touch-tone service, you might not be able to access your voice mail or answering machine from Italy.

TIPS ON ACCOMMODATIONS

If you're looking to rent a villa or an apartment, one of the best agencies to call is **Rent Villas** (ℂ 800/726-6702; www.rentvillas.com). It's the representative for the Cuendet properties, some of the best in Italy, and its agents are very helpful in tracking down the perfect place to suit your needs. **Insider's Italy** (ℂ/fax 914/470-1612; www.insidersitaly.com) is a small, upscale outfit run by a personable agent who's familiar with all her properties and Italy in general.

For some of the top properties, call the **Parker Company, Ltd.** (ℂ 800/280-2811 or 781/596-8282; fax 781/596-3125; www.theparkercompany.com). This agency rents apartments, villas, restored farmhouses, and even castles, throughout Italy in almost every region from the Veneto in the northeast to remote Sicily in the southwest. In the U.K., contact **Cottages to Castles** (ℂ 1622/775-217; www.cottagestocastles.com); in the U.S., the agent to contact is **Italy My Dream**

The Government Star System

Accommodations in Italy are rated by regional council and awarded one to five stars, depending basically on the amenities offered. In general, the more amenities and stars a hotel has, the more expensive it will be.

(☎ **866/687-7700;** www.italy mydream.com). One of the most reasonably priced agencies is **Villas and Apartments Abroad, Ltd.** (☎ **212/213-6435;** fax 212/213-8252; www.ideal-villas. com). **Vacanze in Italia** (☎ **413/ 528-6610;** fax 413/528-6222; www.homeabroad.com) handles hundreds of rather upscale rentals.

A popular but very pricey agency is **Villas International** (☎ **800/221-2260** or 415/499-9490; www.villasintl.com).

If you want to stay in a historic *palazzo*, contact **Abitare la Storia,** Villa Dal Pozzo D'Annone, St. Le Del Sempione 5, 28832 Belgirate-Lago Maggiore (☎ **0322-772156;** fax 0332-292678; www.abitarelastoria.it).

For apartment, farmhouse, or cottage stays of 2 weeks or more, **Untours** (☎ **888/868-6871;** www.untours.com) provides exceptional lodgings for a reasonable price, which includes air/ground transportation, cooking facilities, and on-call support from a local resident. Best of all: Untours—named the "Most Generous Company in America" by Newman's Own—donates most profits to provide low-interest loans to underprivileged entrepreneurs around the world (see website for details).

Also try **www.venere.com** (☎ **877/214-4288** or 091/971-9981) for everything from Roman hotels and suites to Tuscan farmhouses and B&Bs.

TIPS ON DINING

For a quick bite, go to a **bar.** Although bars in Italy do serve alcohol, they function mainly as cafes. Prices have a split personality: *Al banco* is standing at the bar, while *a tavola* means sitting at a table where you'll be waited on and charged two to four times as much. In bars, you can find panino sandwiches on various kinds of rolls and *tramezzini* (giant triangles of white-bread sandwiches with the crusts cut off). These both run around 3€, but panini are traditionally put in a tiny press to flatten and toast them so the crust is crispy and the filling is hot and gooey; microwave ovens have unfortunately invaded and are everywhere, turning panini into something resembling a soggy hot tissue.

Pizza a taglio or *pizza rustica* indicates a place where you can order pizza by the slice—though Florence is infamous for serving some of Italy's worst pizza this way. Florentines fare somewhat better at *pizzerie,* casual sit-down restaurants that cook large, round pizzas with very thin crusts in wood-burning ovens. A full-fledged restaurant will go by the name **osteria, trattoria,** or **ristorante.** Once upon a time, these terms meant something—*osterie* were basic places where you could get a plate of spaghetti and a glass of wine; *trattorie* were casual places serving full meals of filling peasant fare; and *ristoranti* were fancier places, with waiters in bow ties, printed menus, wine lists, and hefty prices. Nowadays, fancy restaurants often go by the name of *trattoria* to cash in on the associated charm factor; trendy spots use *osteria* to show they're hip; and simple, inexpensive places sometimes tack on *ristorante* to ennoble themselves.

The *pane e coperto* (**bread and cover**) is a 1€ to 3€ cover charge that you must pay at most restaurants for the mere privilege of sitting at the table.

Most Italians eat a leisurely full meal—appetizer and first and second courses—at lunch and dinner and expect you to do the same, or at least a first and second course. To request the bill, ask *"Il conto, per favore"* (Eel *con*-toh, pore fah-*vohr*-ay). A tip of 15% is usually included in the bill these days, but if you're unsure, ask *"È incluso il servizio?"* (Ay een-*cloo*-soh eel sair-*vee*-tsoh?).

You'll find at many restaurants, especially larger ones and in cities, a ***menu tùristico*** (**tourist's menu**)*,* sometimes called ***menu del giorno*** (**menu of the day**)**.** This set-price menu usually covers all meal incidentals—including table wine, cover charge, and 15% service charge—along with a first course *(primo)* and second course *(secondo),* but it almost always offers an abbreviated selection of pretty bland dishes: spaghetti in tomato sauce, for example, with slices of pork. Sometimes a better choice is a ***menu a prezzo fisso*** (**fixed-price menu**). It usually doesn't include wine but sometimes covers the service and often offers a wider selection of better dishes, occasionally house specialties and local foods. Ordering a la carte, however, offers you the best chance for a memorable meal. Even better, forego the menu entirely and put yourself in the capable hands of your waiter.

The **enoteca** (wine bar) is a popular marriage of a wine bar and an *osteria,* where you can sit and order from a host of local and regional wines by the glass while snacking on finger foods (and usually a number of simple first-course possibilities) that reflect the region's fare. Relaxed and full of ambience and good wine, these are great spots for light and inexpensive lunches—perfect to educate your palate and recharge your batteries.

[FastFACTS] ITALY

ATMs   The easiest and best way to get cash away from home—the **Cirrus** (© 800/ 424-7787; www.mastercard.com) and **PLUS** (www.visa.com) networks—span the globe. Be sure you know your personal identification number (PIN) and your daily withdrawal limit before you depart. *Note:* Banks that are members of the **Global ATM Alliance** charge no transaction fees for cash withdrawals at other Alliance member ATMs; these include Bank of America, Scotiabank (Canada, Caribbean, and Mexico), Barclays (U.K. and parts of Africa), and Deutsche Bank (Germany, Poland, Spain, and Italy), and BNP Paribus (France).

Business Hours   Regular business hours are generally Monday through Friday from 9am (sometimes 9:30am) to 1pm and 3:30 (sometimes 4) to 7 or 7:30pm. In July and August, **offices** might not open in the afternoon until 4:30 or 5pm. **Banks** are open Monday through Friday from 8:30am to 1 or 1:30pm, and 2 or 2:30 to 4pm, and are closed all day Saturday, Sunday, and national holidays. The *riposo* (midafternoon closing) is often observed in Rome, Naples, and most southern cities; however, in Milan and other northern and central cities, the custom has been abolished by some merchants. Most shops are closed on Sunday, except for certain tourist-oriented stores that are now permitted to remain open on Sunday during the high season. If you're in Italy in summer and the heat is intense, we suggest that you, too, learn the custom of the *riposo.*

Cellphones (Mobile Phones)   See "Staying Connected," p. 925.

Currency   The **euro** became the official currency of Italy and 11 other participating countries on January 1, 1999. At the time of this writing, US$1 was worth approximately .71€. Inversely stated, 1€ was worth approximately US$1.40.

Drinking Laws   Italy has some of the most liberal drinking laws in Europe. In theory at least, those under the age of 16 are not to be served alcoholic drinks in public places. Unlike draconian England, Italy imposes no legal closing times for bars. Beer, wine, and liquor are sold almost anywhere—especially at cafes, which are found practically on any street corner throughout the cities of Italy.

Driving Rules   Drive on the right; pass on the left. Use your seat belts! Careless or reckless drivers face fines; serious violators could land themselves in prison! For more information, see "Getting There & Around," p. 911.

Drugstores   At every drugstore *(farmacia),* there's a list of those that are open at night and on Sunday.

Electricity   Electricity in Italy is 220 volts AC at 50 cycles per second. It's recommended that any visitor carrying electrical appliances obtain a transformer. Most laptops and cellphone chargers are dual voltage, operating at either 110 volts or 220 volts. That means that only an adapter is required. Plugs have prongs that are round, not flat; therefore, an adapter plug is also needed.

Wherever you go, bring a **connection kit** of the right power and phone adapters, a spare phone cord, and a spare Ethernet network cable—or find out whether your hotel supplies them to guests.

Embassies & Consulates   In case of an emergency, embassies have a 24-hour referral service.

The **U.S. Embassy** is in Rome at Via Vittorio Veneto 121 (📞 **06-46-741;** fax 06-46-74-2244; www.italy.usembassy.gov). **U.S. consulates** are in Florence, at Lungarno Amerigo Vespucci 38 (📞 **055-266-951;** fax 055-215-550); in Milan, at Via Principe Amedeo 2–10 (📞 **02-29-03-51;** fax 02-2903-5273); in Naples, on Piazza della Repubblica 1 (📞 **081-583-8111;** fax 081-761-1804); in Genoa, at Via Dante 2 (📞 **010-58-44-92;** fax 010-55-33-033); and in Palermo (Sicily), at Via Vaccarini 1 (📞 **091-305-857;** fax 091-625-6026). For consulate hours, see individual city listings.

The **Canadian Consulate** and passport service is in Rome at Via Zara 30 (📞 **06-854443937;** www.canada.it). The **Canadian Embassy** in Rome is at Via Salaria 243 (📞 **06-854441;** fax 06-854443919). The **Canadian Consulate** in Naples is at Via Carducci 29 (📞 **081-401338;** fax 081-410210).

The **British Embassy** is in Rome at Via XX Settembre 80 (📞 **06-422-00001;** fax 06-42202334; www.ukinitaly.fco.gov.uk). The **British Consulate** in Florence is at Lungarno Corsini 2 (📞 **055-284-133;** fax 055-219-112). The **Consulate General** in Naples is at Via Dei Mille 40 (📞 **081-4238-911;** fax 081-422-434). In Milan, contact the office at Via San Paolo 7 (📞 **02-723-001;** fax 02-86465081). There is also a Consulate General in Palermo on Via Cavour 117 (📞 091/326-412; fax 091/380-4901).

The **Australian Embassy** is in Rome at Via Antonio Bosio 5 (📞 **06-852-721;** fax 06-852-723-00; www.italy.embassy.gov.au). The **Australian Consulate** in Milan is at Via Borgogna 2 (📞 **02-77-67-41**).

The **New Zealand Embassy** is in Rome at Via Clitunno 44 (📞 **06-8537501;** fax 06-440-2984). The **Irish Embassy** in Rome is at Piazza di Campitelli 3 (📞 **06-697-9121;** fax 06-697-91231).

Emergencies Dial ✆ **113** for the police, ✆ **118** for an ambulance, and ✆ **115** in case of fire. In case of a car breakdown, dial ✆ **803-116** at the nearest telephone box; the nearest Automobile Club of Italy (ACI) will be notified to come to your aid.

Etiquette & Customs Some churches may require that you wear **appropriate attire:** Men need to wear long pants, and women must have their knees and shoulders covered in order to enter.

Gasoline (Petrol) See "Getting There & Around," p. 911.

Holidays See "Italy Calendar of Events," p. 906.

Hospitals Please see "Doctors" and "Hospitals" under "Fast Facts" in individual city chapters. For emergencies requiring an ambulance, call ✆ **118.**

Insurance For travel overseas, most U.S. health plans (including Medicare and Medicaid) do not provide coverage, and the ones that do often require you to pay for services upfront and reimburse you only after you return home.

As a safety net, you may want to buy travel medical insurance, particularly if you're traveling to a remote or high-risk area where emergency evacuation might be necessary. If you require additional medical insurance, try **MEDEX Assistance** (✆ **800/732-5309;** www.medexassist.com) or **Travel Assistance International** (✆ **800/821-2828;** www.travelassistance.com; for general information on services, call the company's **Europ Assistance Services, Inc.,** at ✆ **800/777-8710;** www.europ-assistance.com).

Canadians should check with their provincial health plan offices or call **Health Canada** (✆ **866/225-0709;** www.hc-sc.gc.ca) to find out the extent of their coverage and what documentation and receipts they must take home in case they are treated overseas.

Travelers from the U.K. should carry their **European Health Insurance Card (EHIC),** which replaced the E111 form as proof of entitlement to free/reduced cost medical treatment abroad (✆ **0845/605-0707;** www.ehic.org.uk). Note, however, that the EHIC covers only "necessary medical treatment," and for repatriation costs, lost money, baggage, or cancellation, travel insurance from a reputable company should always be sought; one such firm is Travel Insurance Web (www.travelinsuranceweb.com).

Travel Insurance: The cost of travel insurance varies widely, depending on the destination, the cost and length of your trip, your age and health, and the type of trip you're taking, but expect to pay between 5% and 8% of the cost of the vacation itself. You can get estimates from various providers through **InsureMyTrip.com.** Enter your trip cost and dates, your age, and other information for prices from more than a dozen companies.

U.K. citizens and their families who make more than one trip abroad per year may find an annual travel insurance policy works out cheaper. Check **www.moneysuper market.com,** which compares prices across a wide range of providers for single- and multitrip policies.

Most big travel agents offer their own insurance and will probably try to sell you their package when you book a holiday. Think before you sign. **Britain's Consumers' Association** recommends that you insist on seeing the policy and reading the fine print before buying travel insurance. The **Association of British Insurers** (✆ **020/7600-3333;** www.abi.org.uk) gives advice by phone and publishes *Holiday Insurance,* a free guide to policy provisions and prices. You might also shop around for better deals: Try **Columbus Direct** (✆ **0870/033-9988;** www.columbusdirect.net).

Trip Cancellation Insurance: Trip-cancellation insurance will help retrieve your money if you have to back out of a trip or depart early, or if your travel supplier goes bankrupt. Trip cancellation traditionally covers such events as sickness, natural disasters, and State Department advisories. The latest news in trip-cancellation insurance is the availability of **"any-reason"** cancellation coverage—which costs more but covers cancellations made for any reason. You won't get back 100% of your prepaid trip cost, but you'll be refunded a substantial portion. **TravelSafe** (✆ **888/885-7233;** www.travelsafe.com) offers this type of coverage. Expedia also offers any-reason cancellation coverage for its air-hotel packages. For details, contact one of the following recommended insurers: **Access America** (✆ 800/284-8300; www.accessamerica.com), **Travel Guard International** (✆ 800/826-4919; www.travelguard.com), **Travel Insured International** (✆ 800/243-3174; www.travelinsured.com), and **Travelex Insurance Services** (✆ 800/228-9792; www.travelex-insurance.com).

Internet Access   See "Staying Connected," p. 925.

Language   Italian, of course, is the language of the land, but English is generally understood at most attractions, such as museums, and at most hotels and restaurants that cater to visitors. Even if few staff members at a restaurant, for example, speak English, one person almost always does and can be summoned. As you travel in remote towns and villages, especially in the south, a *Berlitz Italian Phrase Book* is a handy accompaniment.

Legal Aid   The consulate of your country is the place to turn for legal aid, although offices can't interfere in the Italian legal process. They can, however, inform you of your rights and provide a list of attorneys. You'll have to pay for the attorney out of your pocket—there's no free legal assistance. If you're arrested for a drug offense, about all the consulate will do is notify a lawyer about your case and perhaps inform your family.

Liquor Laws   Wine with meals has been a normal part of family life for hundreds of years in Italy. Children are exposed to wine at an early age, and consumption of alcohol isn't anything out of the ordinary. In Italy the legal drinking age is 16. Alcohol is sold day and night throughout the year because there's almost no restriction on the sale of wine or liquor in Italy.

Lost & Found   Alert your credit card companies the minute you discover your wallet has been lost or stolen and file a report at the nearest police precinct. Your credit card company or insurer may require a police report number or record of the loss. Most credit card companies have an emergency toll-free number to call if your card is lost or stolen; they may be able to wire you a cash advance immediately or deliver an emergency credit card in a day or two. If you have lost your card, use the following numbers: **Visa,** ✆ 800/819-014; **MasterCard,** ✆ 800/870-866; **Amex,** ✆ 06-7290-0347.

If you need emergency cash over the weekend when all banks and American Express offices are closed, you can have money wired to you via **Western Union** (✆ **800/325-6000;** www.westernunion.com).

Mail   Mail delivery in Italy is notoriously bad. Your family and friends back home might receive your postcards in 1 week, or it might take 2 weeks (or longer). Postcards, aerogrammes, and letters weighing up to 20 grams sent to the United States and Canada cost .85€; to the United Kingdom and Ireland, .65€; and to Australia and New Zealand, 1€. You can buy stamps at all post offices and at *tabacchi* (tobacco) stores.

Maps   Most local tourist offices will provide fairly detailed maps of their city or town plans. These are particularly helpful in that all of the major sightseeing attractions are usually marked. Since most of these attractions are in the historic core of a town or city, the highlights can usually be covered on foot, except in such spread-out cities as Rome, where you'll need to rely on public transportation to get around.

The **Automobile Club d'Italia** (www.aci.it) issues a free map, available at state tourist offices, if you're planning a motor tour of Italy.

For general touring, you can also check out the following websites: www.mapquest.com, www.maporama.com, and www.michelin.com.

Measurements   See www.onlineconversion.com for details on converting metric measurements to nonmetric equivalents.

Newspapers & Magazines   See "Staying Connected," p. 925.

Passports   Allow plenty of time before your trip to apply for a passport; processing normally takes 3 weeks but can take longer during busy periods (especially spring). And keep in mind that if you need a passport in a hurry, you'll pay a higher processing fee.

For Residents of Australia: You can pick up an application from your local post office or any branch of Passports Australia, but you must schedule an interview at the passport office to present your application materials. Call the **Australian Passport Information Service** at ☎ **131-232,** or visit the government website at www.passports.gov.au.

For Residents of Canada: Passport applications are available at most main post offices throughout Canada or from the central **Passport Office,** Department of Foreign Affairs and International Trade, Gatineau, QC K1A 0G3 (☎ **800/567-6868;** www.ppt.gc.ca).

For Residents of Ireland: You can apply for a 10-year passport at the **Passport Office,** Setanta Centre, Molesworth Street, Dublin 2 (☎ **01/671-1633;** www.dfa.ie). You can also apply at 1A South Mall, Cork (☎ **021/484-4700**), or at most main post offices.

For Residents of New Zealand: You can pick up a passport application at any New Zealand Passports Office or download it from their website. Contact the **Passports Office** at ☎ **0800/225-050** in New Zealand, or 04/474-8100, or log on to www.passports.govt.nz.

For Residents of the United Kingdom: To pick up an application for a standard 10-year passport (5-year passport for children 15 and under), visit your nearest passport office, major post office, or travel agency; or contact the **United Kingdom Passport Service** at ☎ **0300/222-0000** or search its website at www.ukpa.gov.uk.

For Residents of the United States: Whether you're applying in person or by mail, you can download passport applications from the U.S. State Department website at **http://travel.state.gov.** To find your regional passport office, either check the U.S. State Department website or call the **National Passport Information Center** toll-free number (☎ **877/487-2778**) for automated information.

For Children: To obtain a passport, the child **must** be present, in person, with both parents at the place of issuance; *or* a notarized statement from the parents is required. Any questions parents or guardians might have can be answered by calling the **National Passport Information Center** at ☎ **877/487-2778** Monday to Friday 8am to 8pm Eastern Standard Time.

If your passport is lost or stolen, go to your consulate as soon as possible for a replacement. See "Embassies & Consulates," above.

Police   Dial ☎ **113** for police emergency assistance in Italy.

Restrooms   Bars, nightclubs, restaurants, cafes, gas stations, and all hotels have facilities. Public toilets are found near many of the major sights. Usually they're designated as wc (water closet) or donne (women) and uomini (men). The most confusing designation is signori (gentlemen) and signore (ladies), so watch that final *i* and *e!* Many public toilets charge a small fee or employ an attendant who expects a tip. It's a good idea to carry some tissues in your pocket or purse—they often come in handy.

Smoking   In 2005, Italy launched one of Europe's toughest laws against smoking in public places, including bars and restaurants. All restaurants and bars come under the ruling except those with ventilated smoking rooms. Otherwise, smokers can retreat to the outdoors or private homes. Smokers face fines from 29€ to 290€ if caught lighting up. Only 10% of Italian restaurants currently have separate smoking areas.

Taxes   As a member of the European Union, Italy imposes a value-added tax (called IVA in Italy) on most goods and services. The tax that most affects visitors is the one imposed on hotel rates, which is 10%.

Non-E.U. (European Union) citizens are entitled to a refund of the IVA if they spend more than 155€ at any one store, before tax. To claim your refund, request an invoice from the cashier at the store and take it to the Customs office *(dogana)* at the airport to have it stamped before you leave. ***Note:*** If you're going to another E.U. country before flying home, have it stamped at the airport Customs office of the last E.U. country you'll be in (for example, if you're flying home via Britain, have your Italian invoices stamped in London). Once back home, mail the stamped invoice (keep a photocopy for your records) back to the original vendor within 90 days of the purchase. The vendor will, sooner or later, send you a refund of the tax that you paid at the time of your original purchase. Reputable stores view this as a matter of ordinary paperwork and are businesslike about it. Less-honorable stores might lose your dossier. It pays to deal with established vendors on large purchases. You can also request that the refund be credited to the credit card with which you made the purchase; this is usually a faster procedure.

Many shops are now part of the "Tax Free Shopping" network (look for the sticker in the window). Stores participating in this network issue a check along with your invoice at the time of purchase. After you have the invoice stamped at Customs, you can redeem the check for cash directly at the Tax Free for Tourists booth in the airport (in Rome, it's past Customs; in Milan's airports, the booth is inside the duty-free shop), or mail it back in the envelope provided within 60 days.

Telephones   See "Staying Connected," p. 925.

Time   In terms of standard time zones, Italy is 6 hours ahead of Eastern Standard Time (EST) in the United States. Daylight saving time goes into effect in Italy each year from the end of March to the end of October.

Tipping   This custom is practiced with flair in Italy—many people depend on tips for their livelihoods.

In **hotels,** the service charge of 15% to 19% is already added to a bill. In addition, it's customary to tip the chambermaid .50€ per day, the doorman (for calling a cab) 1€, and the bellhop or porter 1.50€ to 1.95€ for carrying your bags to your room. A concierge expects about 15% of his or her bill, as well as tips for extra services performed, which could include help with long-distance calls. In expensive hotels, these euro amounts are often doubled.

In **restaurants and cafes,** 15% is usually added to your bill to cover most charges. If you're not sure whether this has been done, ask, *"È incluso il servizio?"* (Ay een-*cloo*-soh eel sair-*vee*-tsoh?). An additional tip isn't expected, but it's nice to leave the equivalent of an extra couple of dollars if you've been pleased with the service. Check-room attendants expect 1€, and washroom attendants should get the same. Restaurants are required by law to give customers official receipts.

Taxi drivers expect at least 15% of the fare.

Visitor Information   For information before you go, contact the **Italian Government Tourist Board** (www.enit.it and www.italiantourism.com).

In the United States   630 Fifth Ave., Ste. 1565, New York, NY 10111 (📞 **212/245-5618;** fax 212/586-9249); 500 N. Michigan Ave., Ste. 2240, Chicago, IL 60611 (📞 **312/644-0996;** fax 312/644-3019); and 12400 Wilshire Blvd., Ste. 550, Los Angeles, CA 90025 (📞 **310/820-1898;** fax 310/820-6357).

In Canada   110 Yonge St, Ste. 503, Toronto, ON M5C 1T4 (📞 **416/925-4882;** fax 416/925-4799).

In the United Kingdom   1 Princes St., London W1B 2AY (📞 **020/7408-1254;** www.italiantouristboard.co.uk).

You can also write directly (in English or Italian) to the provincial or local tourist boards of the areas you plan to visit. Provincial tourist boards **(Ente Provinciale per il Turismo)** operate in the principal towns of the provinces. Local tourist boards **(Azienda Autonoma di Soggiorno e Turismo)** operate in all places of tourist interest; you can get a list from the Italian Government Tourist Board.

Another helpful website is www.initaly.com.

Wi-Fi   See "Staying Connected," p. 925.

MOLTO ITALIANO

19

BASICS

USEFUL ENGLISH-ITALIAN PHRASES

English	Italian	Pronunciation
Thank you	Grazie	*graht*-tzee-yey
You're welcome	Prego	*prey*-go
Please	Per favore	*pehr* fah-*vohr*-eh
Yes	Si	see
No	No	noh
Good morning or Good day	Buongiorno	bwohn-*djor*-noh
Good evening	Buona sera	*bwohn*-ah *say*-rah
Good night	Buona notte	*bwohn*-ah *noht*-tay
It's a pleasure to meet you.	Piacere di conoscerla.	pyah-*cheh*-reh dee koh-nohshehr-lah
My name is _____.	Mi chiamo _____.	mee *kyah*-moh
And yours?	E lei?	eh lay
Do you speak English?	Parla inglese?	*pahr*-lah een-*gleh*-seh
How are you?	Come sta?	*koh*-may *stah*
Very well	Molto bene	*mohl*-toh *behn*-ney
Goodbye	Arrivederci	ahr-ree-vah-*dehr*-chee
Excuse me (to get attention)	Scusi	*skoo*-zee

GETTING AROUND

English	Italian	Pronunciation
Excuse me (to get past someone)	Permesso	**pehr-*mehs*-soh**
Where is . . . ?	Dovè . . . ?	**doh-vey**
the station	la stazione	**lah stat-tzee-*oh*-neh**
a hotel	un albergo	**oon ahl-*behr*-goh**
a restaurant	un ristorante	**oon reest-ohr-*ahnt*-eh**
the bathroom	il bagno	**eel *bahn*-nyoh**
I am looking for . . .	Cerco . . .	***chehr*-koh**
a porter	un facchino	**oon fahk-*kee*-noh**
the check-in counter	il check-in	**eel check-in**
the ticket counter	la biglietteria	**lah beel-lyeht-teh-*ree*-ah**
arrivals	l'area arrivi	***lah*-reh-ah ahr-*ree*-vee**
departures	l'area partenze	***lah*-reh-ah pahr-*tehn*-tseh**
gate number	l'uscita numero	**loo-*shee*-tah noo-meh-roh**
the waiting area	l'area d'attesa	***lah*-reh-ah daht-*teh*-zah**
the men's restroom	la toilette uomini	**lah twa-*leht* woh-mee-nee**
the women's restroom	la toilette donne	**lah twa-*leht dohn*-neh**
the police station	la stazione di polizia	**lah stah-*tsyoh*-neh dee poh-lee-*tsee*-ah**
a security guard	una guardia di sicurezza	***ooh*-nah *gwahr*-dyah dee see-koo-*ret*-sah**
the smoking area	l'area fumatori	***lah*-reh-ah foo-mah-*toh*-ree**
the information booth	l'ufficio informazioni	**loof-*fee*-choh een-*fohr*-mah-*tsyoh*-nee**
a public telephone	un telefono pubblico	**oon teh-*leh*-foh-noh *poob*-blee-koh**
an ATM/cashpoint	un bancomat	**oon *bahn*-koh-maht**
baggage claim	il ritiro bagagli	**eel ree-*tee*-roh bah-*gahl*-lyee**
a luggage cart	un carrello portabagagli	**oon kahr-*rehl*-loh pohr-tah-bah-*gahl*-lyee**

English	Italian	Pronunciation
a currency exchange	un cambiavalute	**oon kahm-byah-vah-loo-teh**
a cafe	un caffè	**oon kahf-feh**
a restaurant	un ristorante	**oon ree-stoh-rahn-teh**
a bar	un bar	**oon bar**
a bookstore	una libreria	**oo-nah lee-breh-ree-ah**
a duty-free shop	un duty-free	**oon duty-free**
To the left	A sinistra	**ah see-nees-tra**
To the right	A destra	**ah dehy-stra**
Straight ahead	Avanti (*or* sempre diritto)	**ahv-vahn-tee (sehm-pray dee-reet-toh)**

DINING

English	Italian	Pronunciation
Breakfast	Prima colazione	**pree-mah coh-laht-tzee-ohn-ay**
Lunch	Pranzo	**prahn-zoh**
Dinner	Cena	**chay-nah**
How much is it?	Quanto costa?	**kwan-toh coh-sta**
The check, please	Il conto, per favore	**eel kon-toh pehr fah-vohr-eh**

A MATTER OF TIME

English	Italian	Pronunciation
When?	Quando?	**kwan-doh**
Yesterday	Ieri	**ee-yehr-ree**
Today	Oggi	**oh-jee**
Tomorrow	Domani	**doh-mah-nee**
What time is it?	Che ore sono?	**kay or-ay soh-noh**
It's one o'clock.	È l'una.	**eh loo-nah**
It's two o'clock.	Sono le due.	**soh-noh leh doo-eh**
It's two-thirty.	Sono le due e mezzo.	**soh-noh leh doo-eh eh mehd-dzoh**
It's noon.	È mezzogiorno.	**eh mehd-dzoh-johr-noh**
It's midnight.	È mezzanotte.	**eh mehd-dzah-noht-teh**
It's early.	È presto.	**eh prehs-toh**

English	Italian	Pronunciation
It's late.	È tardi.	*eh tahr*-dee
in the morning	al mattino	ahl maht-*tee*-noh
in the afternoon	al pomeriggio	ahl poh-meh-*reed*-joh
at night	di notte	dee *noht*-the

DAYS OF THE WEEK

English	Italian	Pronunciation
Monday	Lunedì	loo-nay-*dee*
Tuesday	Martedì	mart-ay-*dee*
Wednesday	Mercoledì	mehr-cohl-ay-*dee*
Thursday	Giovedì	joh-vay-*dee*
Friday	Venerdì	ven-nehr-*dee*
Saturday	Sabato	*sah*-bah-toh
Sunday	Domenica	doh-*mehn*-nee-kah

MONTHS & SEASONS

English	Italian	Pronunciation
January	gennaio	jehn-*nah*-yoh
February	febbraio	fehb-*brah*-yoh
March	marzo	*mahr*-tso
April	aprile	ah-*pree*-leh
May	maggio	*mahd*-joh
June	giugno	*jewn*-nyo
July	luglio	*lool*-lyo
August	agosto	ah-*gohs*-toh
September	settembre	seht-*tehm*-breh
October	ottobre	oht-*toh*-breh
November	novembre	noh-*vehm*-breh
December	dicembre	dee-*chehm*-breh
spring	la primavera	lah pree-mah-*veh*-rah
summer	l'estate	lehs-*tah*-teh
autumn	l'autunno	low-*toon*-noh
winter	l'inverno	leen-*vehr*-noh

NUMBERS

English	Italian	Pronunciation
one	uno	*oo*-noh
two	due	*doo*-ay
three	tre	tray
four	quattro	*kwah*-troh
five	cinque	*cheen*-kway
six	sei	say
seven	sette	*set*-tay
eight	otto	*oh*-toh
nine	nove	*noh*-vay
ten	dieci	dee-*ay*-chee
eleven	undici	*oon*-dee-chee
twenty	venti	*vehn*-tee
twenty-one	ventuno	vehn-*toon*-oh
twenty-two	venti due	*vehn*-tee *doo*-ay
thirty	trenta	*trayn*-tah
forty	quaranta	kwah-*rahn*-tah
fifty	cinquanta	cheen-*kwan*-tah
sixty	sessanta	sehs-*sahn*-tah
seventy	settanta	seht-*tahn*-tah
eighty	ottanta	oht-*tahn*-tah
ninety	novanta	noh-*vahnt*-tah
one hundred	cento	*chen*-toh
one thousand	mille	*mee*-lay
five thousand	cinque milla	*cheen*-kway *mee*-lah
ten thousand	dieci milla	dee-ay-chee mee-lah

ARCHITECTURAL TERMS

Ambone   A pulpit, either serpentine or simple in form, erected in an Italian church.

Apse   The half-rounded extension behind the main altar of a church; Christian tradition dictates that it be placed at the eastern end of an Italian church, the side closest to Jerusalem.

Atrium   A courtyard, open to the sky, in an ancient Roman house; the term also applies to the courtyard nearest the entrance of an early Christian church.

Baldacchino (also ciborium)   A columned stone canopy, usually placed above the altar of a church; spelled in English *baldachin* or *baldaquin*.

Baptistery   A separate building or a separate area in a church where the rite of baptism is held.

Basilica   Any rectangular public building, usually divided into three aisles by rows of columns. In ancient Rome, this architectural form was frequently used for places of public assembly and law courts; later, Roman Christians adapted the form for many of their early churches.

Caldarium   The steam room of a Roman bath.

Campanile   A bell tower, often detached, of a church.

Capital   The top of a column, often carved and usually categorized into one of three orders: Doric, Ionic, or Corinthian.

Castrum   A carefully planned Roman military camp, whose rectangular form, straight streets, and systems of fortified gates became standardized throughout the empire; modern cities that began as Roman camps and still more or less maintain their original forms include Chester (England), Barcelona (Spain), and such Italian cities as Lucca, Aosta, Como, Brescia, Florence, and Ancona.

Cavea   The curved row of seats in a classical theater; the most prevalent shape was that of a semicircle.

Cella   The sanctuary, or most sacred interior section, of a Roman pagan temple.

Chancel   Section of a church containing the altar.

Cornice   The decorative flange defining the uppermost part of a classical or neoclassical facade.

Cortile   Courtyard or cloisters ringed with a gallery of arches or lintels set atop columns.

Crypt   A church's main burial place, usually below the choir.

Cupola   A dome.

Duomo   Cathedral.

Forum   The main square and principal gathering place of any Roman town, usually adorned with the city's most important temples and civic buildings.

Grotesques   Carved and painted faces, deliberately ugly, used by everyone from the Etruscans to the architects of the Renaissance; they're especially amusing when set into fountains.

Hypogeum   Subterranean burial chambers, usually of pre-Christian origins.

Loggia   Roofed balcony or gallery.

Lozenge   An elongated four-sided figure that, along with stripes, was one of the distinctive signs of the architecture of Pisa.

Narthex   The anteroom, or enclosed porch, of a Christian church.

Nave   The largest and longest section of a church, usually devoted to sheltering or seating worshipers and often divided by aisles.

Palazzo   A palace or other important building.

Piano Nobile   The main floor of a *palazzo* (sometimes the second floor).

Pietra Dura   Richly ornate assemblage of semiprecious stones mounted on a flat decorative surface, perfected during the 1600s in Florence.

Pieve   A parish church.

Portico   A porch, usually crafted from wood or stone.

Pulvin   A four-sided stone that serves as a substitute for the capital of a column, often decoratively carved, sometimes into biblical scenes.

Putti   Plaster cherubs whose chubby forms often decorate the interiors of baroque chapels and churches.

Stucco   Colored plaster composed of sand, powdered marble, water, and lime, either molded into statuary or applied in a thin concretelike layer to the exterior of a building.

Telamone   Structural column carved into a standing male form; female versions are called *caryatids*.

Thermae   Roman baths.

Transenna   Stone (usually marble) screen separating the altar area from the rest of an early Christian church.

Travertine   The stone from which ancient and Renaissance Rome was built, it's known for its hardness, light coloring, and tendency to be pitted or flecked with black.

Tympanum   The half-rounded space above the portal of a church, whose semicircular space usually showcases a sculpture.

ITALIAN MENU TERMS

Abbacchio   Roast haunch or shoulder of lamb baked and served in a casserole and sometimes flavored with anchovies.

Agnolotti   A crescent-shaped pasta shell stuffed with a mix of chopped meat, spices, vegetables, and cheese; when prepared in rectangular versions, the same combination of ingredients is identified as ravioli.

Amaretti   Crunchy, sweet almond-flavored macaroons.

Anguilla alla veneziana   Eel cooked in a sauce made from tuna and lemon.

Antipasti   Succulent tidbits served at the beginning of a meal (before the pasta), whose ingredients might include slices of cured meats, seafood (especially shellfish), and cooked and seasoned vegetables.

Aragosta   Lobster.

Arrosto   Roasted meat.

Baccalà   Dried and salted codfish.

Bagna cauda   Hot and well-seasoned sauce, heavily flavored with anchovies, designed for dipping raw vegetables; literally translated as "hot bath."

Bistecca alla fiorentina   Florentine-style steaks, coated before grilling with olive oil, pepper, lemon juice, salt, and parsley.

Bocconcini   Veal layered with ham and cheese, and then fried.

Bollito misto   Assorted boiled meats served on a single platter.

Braciola   Pork chop.

Bresaola   Air-dried spiced beef.

Bruschetta   Toasted bread, heavily slathered with olive oil and garlic and often topped with tomatoes.

Bucatini   Coarsely textured hollow spaghetti.

Busecca alla Milanese   Tripe (beef stomach) flavored with herbs and vegetables.

Cacciucco ali livornese   Seafood stew.

Calzone   Pizza dough rolled with the chef's choice of sausage, tomatoes, cheese, and so on, and then baked into a kind of savory turnover.

Cannelloni   Tubular dough stuffed with meat, cheese, or vegetables, and then baked in a creamy white sauce.

Cappellacci alla ferrarese   Pasta stuffed with pumpkin.

Cappelletti   Small ravioli ("little hats") stuffed with meat or cheese.

Carciofi   Artichokes.

Carpaccio   Thin slices of raw cured beef, sometimes in a piquant sauce.

Cassatta alla siciliana   A richly caloric dessert that combines layers of sponge cake, sweetened ricotta cheese, and candied fruit, bound together with chocolate butter-cream icing.

Cervello al burro nero   Brains in black-butter sauce.

Cima alla genovese   Baked filet of veal rolled into a tube-shaped package containing eggs, mushrooms, and sausage.

Coppa   Cured morsels of pork filet encased in sausage skins, served in slices.

Costoletta alla milanese   Veal cutlet dredged in bread crumbs, fried, and sometimes flavored with cheese.

Cozze   Mussels.

Fagioli   White beans.

Fave   Fava beans.

Fegato alla veneziana   Thinly sliced calves' liver fried with salt, pepper, and onions.

Dos & Don'ts

Italians measure foodstuffs by the kilogram or smaller 100g unit (ettogrammo, abbreviated to etto, equivalent to just under 4 oz.). Pizzerie al taglio (pizza slice shops) generally run on this system, but hand gestures can suffice. A good server poises the knife, then asks for approval before cutting. Più *(pyoo)* is "more," meno *(meh*-noh), "less." Basta *(bahs*-tah) means "enough." To express "half" of something, say mezzo *(mehd*-zoh).

Focaccia   Ideally, concocted from potato-based dough left to rise slowly for several hours and then garnished with tomato sauce, garlic, basil, salt, and pepper and drizzled with olive oil; similar to a deep-dish pizza most popular in the deep south, especially Bari.

Fontina   Rich cow's-milk cheese.

Frittata   Italian omelet.

Fritto misto   A deep-fried medley of whatever small fish, shellfish, and squid are available in the marketplace that day.

Fusilli   Spiral-shaped pasta.

Gelato (produzione propria)   Ice cream (homemade).

Gnocchi   Dumplings usually made from potatoes *(gnocchi alla patate)* or from semo-lina *(gnocchi alla romana),* often stuffed with combinations of cheese, spinach, veg-etables, or whatever combinations strike the chef's fancy.

Gorgonzola   One of the most famous blue-veined cheeses of Europe—strong, creamy, and aromatic.

Granità   Flavored ice, usually with lemon or coffee.

Insalata di frutti di mare   Seafood salad (usually including shrimp and squid) garnished with pickles, lemon, olives, and spices.

Involtini   Thinly sliced beef, veal, or pork, rolled, stuffed, and fried.

Minestrone   A rich and savory vegetable soup usually sprinkled with grated parmi-giano and studded with noodles.

Mortadella   Mild pork sausage, fashioned into large cylinders and served sliced; the original lunchmeat bologna (because its most famous center of production is Bologna).

Mozzarella   A nonfermented cheese, made from the fresh milk of a buffalo (or, if unavailable, from a cow), boiled, and then kneaded into a rounded ball, served fresh.

Mozzarella con pomodori (also caprese)   Fresh tomatoes with fresh mozzarella, basil, pepper, and olive oil.

Nervetti   A northern Italian antipasto made from chewy pieces of calves' foot or shin.

Osso buco   Beef or veal knuckle slowly braised until the cartilage is tender and then served with a highly flavored sauce.

Pancetta   Herb-flavored pork belly, rolled into a cylinder and sliced—the Italian bacon.

Panettone   Sweet yellow-colored bread baked in the form of a brioche.

Panna   Heavy cream.

Pansotti   Pasta stuffed with greens, herbs, and cheeses, usually served with a walnut sauce.

Pappardelle alle lepre   Pasta with rabbit sauce.

Parmigiano   Parmesan, a hard and salty yellow cheese usually grated over pastas and soups but also eaten alone; also known as *granna.* The best is Parmigiano-Reggiano.

Peperoni   Green, yellow, or red sweet peppers (not to be confused with pepperoni).

Pesci al cartoccio   Fish baked in a parchment envelope with onions, parsley, and herbs.

Pesto   A flavorful green sauce made from basil leaves, cheese, garlic, marjoram, and (if available) pine nuts.

Piccata al Marsala   Thin escalope of veal braised in a pungent sauce flavored with Marsala wine.

Piselli al prosciutto   Peas with strips of ham.

Pizza   Specific varieties include *capricciosa* (its ingredients can vary widely, depending on the chef's culinary vision and the ingredients at hand), *margherita* (with tomato sauce, cheese, fresh basil, and memories of the first queen of Italy, Marguerite di Savoia, in whose honor it was first made by a Neapolitan chef), *napoletana* (with ham, capers, tomatoes, oregano, cheese, and the distinctive taste of anchovies), *quattro stagione* (translated as "four seasons" because of the array of fresh vegetables in it; it also contains ham and bacon), and *siciliana* (with black olives, capers, and cheese).

Pizzaiola   A process in which something (usually a beefsteak) is covered in a tomato-and-oregano sauce.

Polenta   Thick porridge or mush made from cornmeal flour.

Polenta de uccelli   Assorted small birds roasted on a spit and served with polenta.

Polenta e coniglio   Rabbit stew served with polenta.

Polla alla cacciatore   Chicken with tomatoes and mushrooms cooked in wine.

Pollo all diavola   Highly spiced grilled chicken.

Ragù   Meat sauce.

Ricotta   A soft bland cheese made from cow's or sheep's milk.

Risotto   Italian rice.

Risotto alla milanese   Rice with saffron and wine.

Salsa verde   "Green sauce," made from capers, anchovies, lemon juice and/or vinegar, and parsley.

Saltimbocca   Veal scallop layered with prosciutto and sage; its name literally translates as "jump in your mouth," a reference to its tart and savory flavor.

Salvia   Sage.

Scaloppina alla Valdostana   Escalope of veal stuffed with cheese and ham.

Scaloppine   Thin slices of veal coated in flour and sautéed in butter.

Semifreddo   A frozen dessert; usually ice cream with sponge cake.

Seppia   Cuttlefish (a kind of squid); its black ink is used for flavoring in certain sauces for pasta and also in risotto dishes.

Sogliola   Sole.

Spaghetti   A long, round, thin pasta, variously served: *alla bolognese* (with ground meat, mushrooms, peppers, and so on), *alla carbonara* (with bacon, black pepper, and eggs), *al pomodoro* (with tomato sauce), *al sugo/ragù* (with meat sauce), and *alle vongole* (with clam sauce).

Spiedini   Pieces of meat grilled on a skewer over an open flame.

Strangolaprete   Small nuggets of pasta, usually served with sauce; the name is literally translated as "priest-choker."

Stufato   Beef braised in white wine with vegetables.

Tagliatelle   Flat egg noodles.

Tonno   Tuna.

Tortelli   Pasta dumplings stuffed with ricotta and greens.

Tortellini   Rings of dough stuffed with minced and seasoned meat, and served either in soups or as a full-fledged pasta covered with sauce.

Trenette   Thin noodles served with pesto sauce and potatoes.

Trippe alla fiorentina   Beef tripe (stomach).

Vermicelli   Very thin spaghetti.

Vitello tonnato   Cold sliced veal covered with tuna sauce.

Zabaglione/zabaione   Egg yolks whipped into the consistency of a custard, flavored with Marsala, and served warm as a dessert.

Zampone   Pigs' feet stuffed with spicy seasoned port, boiled and sliced.

Zuccotto   A liqueur-soaked sponge cake, molded into a dome and layered with chocolate, nuts, and whipped cream.

Zuppa inglese   Sponge cake soaked in custard.

19

Italian Menu Terms

MOLTO ITALIANO

Index

Photo Credits

© Riccardo De Luca; p. 382: © Riccardo De Luca; p. 387: © Riccardo De Luca; p. 388: © Riccardo De Luca; p. 390: © Riccardo De Luca; p. 391: © Riccardo De Luca; p. 398: © Sando Di Fatta; p. 300: © Sandro Di Fatta; p. 404: © De Agostini / SuperStock; p. 405: © Riccardo De Luca; p. 407: © Sandro Di Fatta; p. 410: © Riccardo De Luca; p. 411: © Riccardo De Luca; p. 413: © Riccardo De Luca; p. 417: © Riccardo De Luca; p. 419: © Riccardo De Luca; p. 422: © Riccardo De Luca; p. 425: © Cristina Fumi; p. 427: © Krys Bailey / Alamy; p. 429: © Riccardo De Luca; p. 432: © Riccardo De Luca; p. 435: © Riccardo De Luca; p. 441: © Riccardo De Luca; p. 462: © Riccardo De Luca; p. 470: © Riccardo De Luca; p. 472: © Riccardo De Luca; p. 473: © Riccardo De Luca; p. 477: © Riccardo De Luca; p. 480: © Riccardo De Luca; p. 481: © Sergio Pitamitz / Robert Harding Picture Library Ltd / Alamy; p. 482: © Giraudon / The Bridgeman Art Library; p. 483: © Cameraphoto Arte Venezia / The Bridgeman Art Library; p. 484: © Riccardo De Luca; p. 485: © Riccardo De Luca; p. 486: © Riccardo De Luca; p. 487: © Riccardo De Luca; p. 488: © Sandro Di Fatta; p. 489: © Lonely Planet / SuperStock; p. 490: © Riccardo De Luca; p. 491 left: © Walter Rawlings / Robert Harding Picture Library Ltd; p. 491 right: © Riccardo De Luca; p. 492: © Riccardo De Luca; p. 493: © Riccardo De Luca; p. 495: © Riccardo De Luca; p. 496: © Riccardo De Luca; p. 498: © Riccardo De Luca; p. 500: © Riccardo De Luca; p. 501: © Riccardo De Luca; p. 502: © Riccardo De Luca; p. 504: © Arco Images GmbH / Alamy; p. 507: © Sandro Di Fatta; p. 510: © Gavin Hellier / Robert Harding Picture Library / AGE Fotostock; p. 512: © Melba / AGE Fotostock; p. 514: © Melba / AGE Fotostock; p. 518 left: © The Bridgeman Art Library; p. 518 right: © Riccardo De Luca; p. 522: © Riccardo De Luca; p. 523: Courtesy Settimane Musicali al Teatro Olympico; p. 524: © Riccardo De Luca; p. 530: © Riccardo De Luca; p. 531: © Cristina Fumi; p. 532: © Cristina Fumi; p. 537: © Guido Alberto Rossi / TIPS Images / AGE Fotostock; p. 540: © Riccardo De Luca; p. 542: © Riccardo De Luca; p. 543: © Gaetano Barone / Corbis Cusp / Alamy; p. 547: © Riccardo De Luca; p. 548: © Riccardo De Luca; p. 552: © Riccardo De Luca; p. 553: © G Roli / De Agostini Editore / AGE Fotostock; p. 555: © Ian Dagnall / Alamy; p. 559: © Alex Genovese / Alamy; p. 560: © Alberto Campanile / Cubolmages / Alamy; p. 563: © Cristina Fumi; p. 566: Courtesy Pucci; p. 583: © Riccardo De Luca; p. 584: © The Bridgeman Art Library; p. 585: © Riccardo De Luca; p. 586: © The Bridgeman Art Library; p. 590: © Riccardo De Luca; p. 592: © Riccardo De Luca; p. 594: © Allen Brown / dbimages / Alamy; p. 598: © Riccardo De Luca; p. 602: © Marka / SuperStock; p. 612: © Sandro Di Fatta; p. 614: © Cristina Fumi; p. 616: © Cristina Fumi; p. 620: © Cristina Fumi; p. 624: © Cristina Fumi; p. 628 top: © Cristina Fumi; p. 628 bottom: © Cristina Fumi; p. 629: © Cristina Fumi; p. 633: © P Deliss / Godong / Corbis; p. 634: © Riccardo De Luca; p. 636: © Michael Jenner / Alamy; p. 637: © Riccardo De Luca; p. 645: © Cristina Fumi; p. 649: © Cristina Fumi; p. 652: © Cristina Fumi; p. 654: © Ken Welsh / AGE Fotostock; p. 656: © Riccardo De Luca; p. 658: © Riccardo De Luca; p. 662: © Riccardo De Luca; p. 665: © Riccardo De Luca; p. 666: © Sandro Di Fatta; p. 672: © Sandro Di Fatta; p. 673: © Sandro Di Fatta; p. 674: © Sandro Di Fatta; p. 677: © Riccardo De Luca; p. 678: © Riccardo De Luca; p. 682: © Riccardo De Luca; p. 685: © Riccardo De Luca; p. 686: © Riccardo De Luca; p. 688: © Riccardo De Luca; p. 692: © Riccardo De Luca; p. 693: © Raffaele Capasso; p. 694: © Raffaele Capasso; p. 697: © Raffaele Capasso; p. 702 top: © Raffaele Capasso; p. 702 bottom: © Raffaele Capasso; p. 703: © Raffaele Capasso; p. 705 top: © Raffaele Capasso; p. 705 bottom: © Raffaele Capasso; p. 708: © Raffaele Capasso; p. 709: © Riccardo De Luca; p. 714: © Riccardo De Luca; p. 724 top: © Raffaele Capasso; p. 724 bottom: © Maurizio Grimaldi / Marka / AGE Fotostock; p. 726: © Riccardo De Luca; p. 727: © Riccardo De Luca; p. 728: © Riccardo De Luca; p. 730: © Riccardo De Luca; p. 732: © Raffaele Capasso; p. 736: © Riccardo De Luca; p. 738: © Riccardo De Luca; p. 739: © Raffaele Capasso; p. 745: © Raffaele Capasso; p. 748: © Raffaele Capasso; p. 749: © Raffaele Capasso; p. 750: © Raffaele Capasso; p. 755: © Raffaele Capasso; p. 756: © Raffaele Capasso; p. 758: © Raffaele Capasso; p. 760: © Raffaele Capasso; p. 761: © Raffaele Capasso; p. 766: © Raffaele Capasso; p. 76: © Raffaele Capasso; p. 771: © Raffaele Capasso; p. 772: © Raffaele Capasso; p. 774: © Raffaele Capasso; p. 777: © Raffaele Capasso; p. 780: © donato r / Alamy; p. 783: © Riccardo De Luca; p. 784: © Riccardo De Luca; p. 786: © Riccardo De Luca; p. 788: © Riccardo De Luca; p. 789: © Riccardo De Luca; p. 793 top: © Riccardo De Luca; p. 793 bottom: © Ghigo Roli / Cubolmages / Photolibrary; p. 795: © Riccardo De Luca; p. 799: © Riccardo De Luca; p. 804: © Riccardo De Luca; p. 807: © Jessica Hauf; p. 808: © Juan Carlos Muñoz / AGE Fotostock; p. 811: © Giuseppe Piazza; p. 812: © Giuseppe Piazza; p. 814: © Jessica Hauf; p. 816: © Giuseppe Piazza; p. 817: © Jessica Hauf; p. 825: © Jessica Hauf; p. 828: © Giuseppe Piazza; p. 831: © Giuseppe Piazza; p. 832: © Jessica Hauf; p. 833: © Giuseppe Piazza; p. 838: © Giuseppe Piazza; p. 840: © Jessica Hauf; p. 841: © Jessica Hauf; p. 844: © Gianni Muratore / Alamy;